The Ultimate Yellowstone
Park & Surrounding Area
Atlas and Travel Encyclopedia

by
Michael Dougherty
Heidi Pfeil Dougherty
Kristen Hill
and
Lauri Olsen

Ultimate Press

Bozeman, Montana

an *Ultimate*® Guide Book

ISBN: 1-888550-16-3

Ultimate **Press**
an imprint of Champions Publishing, Inc.

301 Evergreen, Suite 201D
Bozeman, Montana 59715
406-585-0237

www.ultimateyellowstonepark.com
www.ultimatemontana.com
www.ultimatewyoming.com
www.ultimateidaho.com
www.ultimateglacierpark.com

Ultimate Press Staff

Michael Dougherty—Publisher
Heidi Dougherty—Co-Publisher
Elizabeth Dougherty—Maps & Graphics
Hiller W. Higman—Layout & Typesetting
Patricia DeWitt—Sales

Cover Photo Credits

Front Cover:
Lower Falls, NPS Photo by Bryan Harry

Back Cover:
Visitors watching Riverside Geyser, NPS photo by J. Schmidt
Grizzly bear, NPS photo by John Good
Visitors watching Old Faithful eruption, NPS photo by Jim Peaco
Moose, NPS photo by John Brandow

Printed in Canada

Attention schools, organizations and non-profit groups:
Quantity discounts are available on bulk purchases of this book for fund raising.

CONTENTS

ACKNOWLEDGMENT

We offer a sincere thank you to all of the sponsors who, without their financial support, this book would not have been possible. Throughout the book, you'll see their names in bold or in advertisements. Stop in and see them when you're in their area. They would like to hear from you.

DISCLAIMER

This guide focuses on recreational activities including traveling to some sites that are off the more frequently traveled roads. As all such activities contain elements of risk, the publisher, authors, affiliated individuals and companies included in this guide disclaim any responsibility for any injury, harm, or illness that may occur to anyone through, or by use of, the information in this book. Although the authors and publisher have made every effort to ensure that the information was correct at the time of going to press, the authors and publisher do not assume and hereby disclaim any liability to any party for any loss or damage to person or property caused by errors, omissions, or any potential travel disruption due to labor or financial difficulty, whether such errors or omissions result from negligence, accident, or any other cause.

Throughout this book, public domain documents of government agencies (National Park Service, USDA Forest Service, Bureau of Land Management, and Montana State Wildlife, Fish and Parks) were reprinted. Also, brochures published by local area chambers of commerce and from the various attractions were reprinted in part or in their entirety. Permissions were obtained where required.

INTRODUCTION

Yellowstone River and Hayden Valley. NPS Photo.

AMERICA'S CROWN JEWEL

The Greater Yellowstone area is a tapestry woven of three of our largest states: Montana, Wyoming and Idaho. Seven national forests introduce color and richness. At the heart of the pattern lies Yellowstone National Park. Edging the park on its northeast boundary are the Beartooth Mountains, their jagged peaks topping 10,000 feet. On the western boundary, the Madison, Centennial and Lionhead Mountains bring majesty to the tapestry. On the eastern border, the Absarokas lend a toughness to the weave. The Teton Range and the lower Absarokas on the southern border finish the pattern.

The sheen of the tapestry is supplied by 17 rivers that flow through the region, including the Gallatin, Madison, Snake, Yellowstone, Clarks Fork, Henry's Fork and the Salt. Through these river lands thread the valleys and roadways that allow visitors to wrap themselves warmly, comfortably in the beauty of the region.

Culturally and politically distinct groups provide the texture of this region. Mormon homesteaders settled in the Idaho valley towns and worked the land. Scottish coal miners entered the United States through British Columbia to man the mines in Montana and Idaho. Basque shepherds tended flocks in Wyoming. English nobility used the area for its hunts. At the same time, ranchers, loggers and trappers settled in the mountainous areas. European artisans came to ply their crafts in the emerging western towns, and built communities boasting generations of families.

The climate was sometimes harsh; the peoples' resolve was harder. That sturdy work ethic pervades the region today. Like a sturdy denim, the people of the area are hardworking, comfortable and resilient. Whether taming nature's elements or engaging in any number of new industries that cater to tourists, the folks of the Yellowstone area wear their responsibilities with pride and dignity.

Outdoor recreation is one of the area's leading draws. The beauty of the jagged Tetons, the tranquility of Jenny Lake and the impressive presence of Obsidian Cliff beckon artists and hikers, photographers and philosophers. A stroll along the Firehole River renews the spirit. The Grand Canyon of the Yellowstone, Old Faithful, thickly carpeted forests and snow-blanketed peaks offer visitors a diversity of landscapes coupled with an ease of access. Natural wonders abound. Salmon and trout dance in the crystalline waters. Bear, bison, elk, wolves, mountain sheep and goats, and deer herds inhabit the region. Birds from eagle to hummingbirds enjoy alpine meadows painted with fields of lupine. Aspen groves shimmer in the golden morning sunshine. More than 1,100 plant species flourish in the deserts, hills and mountains.

Natural beauty is just one aspect of the Greater Yellowstone Ecosystem. Another is the scientific preserve that provides crucial information on subjects from animal behavior to geological and other scientific discoveries. Studies on grizzly bears and elk herds have provided data on habitat needs and mating patterns. Unique microbes from area hot pools have been used in gene splicing and laundry detergent formulation. Paleontologists are drawn to fossil banks throughout the region. Meteorological studies are conducted in the region where temperatures sometimes fluctuate 70 degrees within eight hours!

It is a dichotomous land of art galleries and antelope herds, hotpots and hairpin turns, of rodeos and river floats. It boasts of operas and outhouses, princely estates and poker machines, of buckskin and bling. You can gaze at a grizzly, hike among the huckleberries, or just sit back and spin your spurs. In all aspects, the Greater Yellowstone Region is truly the Best of the West.

REGIONAL CLIMATE

While somewhat similar in climate, the three states of the Greater Yellowstone Eco-system have unique weather situations too. Visitors are encouraged to bring warm clothing all seasons of the year, as snow is a possibility even in July in Montana. The running joke about this region is that it has nine months of winter and three months of bad snowmobiling.

Recorded temperatures in this area have ranged from 122 degrees in July 1937, to –70 degrees in January 1954. Mountain prairies are

Ascent of Electric Peak. NPS Photo by RG Johnsson.

Line of snowmobiles passing bison on West Entrance road. NPS Photo by Jim Peaco.

arid and windy; mountainous areas of the region receive deep snowfalls that stay through May. Area lakes may be frozen from December at least through March.

In most areas of the region, wintertime has characteristic rapid and frequent changes between mild and cold spells. Usually there are less than 10 cold waves during a winter. The majority of cold waves move southward on the east side of the Divide. Many of the cold waves are not accompanied by enough snow to cause severe conditions, except in high mountain areas. In January, the coldest month generally, minimum temperatures usually range from 5 to 10 degrees F. During warming spells in the winter, nighttime

Lower Falls. NPS Photo by Miller.

temperatures frequently remain above freezing. Chinooks, warm down-slope winds, are common along the eastern slopes. Humidity averages range from 20 to 30 percent. Snowfalls may start in September and frequently go through late May. Falls of 10 to 15 inches in a single storm occur but are infrequent outside the mountains.

May and June are traditionally the wettest months for most of the region. Average rainfall is 15 inches. July and August are usually the warmest months of the year, with a pleasant "Indian summer", characterized by warm days and cool evenings, in September and October. In autumn, the area's tamaracks and aspen turn gold, providing a stunning contrast to the mountain evergreens.

Winter brings a new set of challenges the Yellowstone. Numerous valleys in the region provide ideal pockets for the collection of cold air drainage at night. Protecting mountain ranges prevent the wind from stirring the air, and the colder heavier air settles into the valleys, often sending readings well below zero. It is common to have temperatures in the valleys considerably lower than on the nearby mountainside. There can be quite a variation between readings in the lower part of the valley and those higher up. January, the coldest month, has occasional mild periods when maximum readings will reach the 50s; however, winters are usually long and cold. Road conditions in the winter vary by region, with mountain passes usually receiving first priority from highway department snowplows. Black ice, which occurs when thawed snow is re-frozen by dropping temperatures, or by fog, can be especially treacherous since it is nearly undetectable in advance.

Beware of high river waters in the spring due to melting snow. Before venturing out on a river adventure, contact knowledgeable local businesses or state recreation officials for the latest water conditions.

Summer is a glorious time in the Greater Yellowstone Region, with cloudless blue skies, bright sunshine and extended hours of daylight. Visitors sometimes forget that the higher altitude and lack of pollutants in the air increase the affects of the sun's rays. Sunscreen is of special necessity in this part of the country! River bottomlands tend to be a little breezy, as are western prairies.

Sunglasses or other eye protection are a precaution whether you're boating or digging for dinosaur bones.

When night falls, so does the temperature, even in summertime. Jackets and gloves are important parts of an after-dark Fourth of July celebration when you're in Yellowstone country. Loose, natural fabrics that can be layered help transition from sun-drenched days to cool mountain evenings.

WIDE OPEN SPACES

The wide open spaces of this region present circumstances you may not have faced in other parts of the country. This 'freedom of the West' carries its own set of responsibilities and courtesies.

Roads

Gravel roads are everywhere throughout the region. Be prepared to slow down for riders on horseback. While many horses are accustomed to cars, some spook if you drive too near. Much of the area is open range, which means livestock may be grazing on the road. Wildlife frequently cross roads too, especially at dawn or at dusk.

Gumbo is a hazard of driving (and even walking) in this region. The first warning of gumbo roads may be posted signs that say 'Impassable When Wet'. Heed those signs! A dusty rural road can be turned into a quagmire of gloppy, sticky, unshakeable gunk of gumbo by just a small amount of moisture. Tow trucks won't chance recovering a stranded vehicle in gumbo, and pedestrians find it will stick to shoes until walking is nearly impossible.

Blowing snow or dirt and wind can pose driving hazards in the region, as can fallen rock in mountain passes.

Rattlesnakes

Rattlesnake bites can be fatal if not properly treated. These snakes usually retreat unless threatened.

Bears, Moose and Other Large Animals

The Yellowstone Region is home to white-tailed and large-eared mule deer, mountain elk, bighorn sheep, mountain goats, mountain lions and several species of bears. Many of the country's threatened and endangered species, including the gray wolf, whooping crane, white sturgeon and bald eagle, call the area home.

Feeding or harassment of wildlife is prohibited and is dangerous. Bears, bison and moose move far more quickly than their size would indicate. Check with local rangers for bear updates and guidelines before heading into bear country.

Never hike alone, and make noise along the trail to warn bears of your presence. If you camp, don't sleep near strong smells or food. Cook meals and hang all food from branches at least 100 yards from your tent. Also be alert for mountain lions, which are rarely spotted but are violent predators when provoked. Moose, especially with offspring, have been known to charge if individuals get too close or the animal feels threatened.

'No Trespassing' Signs

The Greater Yellowstone Region boasts millions of acres of public land. This natural outdoor playground is brimming with campgrounds, trails and backcountry roads that invite discovery. Many of these pristine, wide-open spaces are under the active management of the U. S. Forest Service, the

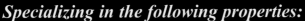

Swan Lake Flats. NPS Photo by J. Schmidt.

Bureau of Land Management and other federal and state agencies.

Intermingled with the region's stunning and well-maintained public land, however, are occasional plots of private land. While some private landowners are more than willing to share their piece of this marvelous state with others, some are not. 'No Trespassing' signs should be taken seriously. In all instances, exercise common courtesy and always receive permission from the property owner before entering or wandering across these privately maintained open spaces.

In some instances, public land access may be restricted. Federal and state agencies will occasionally close public roads to protect animal mating environments or preserve fragile forests or rangeland ecosystems. All recreational users are asked to respect such closures and should at all times practice "leave no trace" outdoor ethics. Detailed information and maps regarding public land access are available from regional land and forest managers.

HOW TO USE THIS BOOK

We've divided this region into nine sections. Each section has a common personality and at least one major city or town. We felt doing so makes it much easier to flow through the book. The material in each section is loosely ordered along the highway routes through the section and organized by locator numbers. Locator Numbers

These are the numbers o the map in white on a black circle ❶. All information relating to the area on the map marked by that number is presented together in the section. The sections of the book are ordered from southeast to northwest. The numbers in each section are ordered in roughly the same direction. This allows you to follow the routes mile by mile and quickly find information along your path relating to your location on the path. In a nutshell, find the number on the map, then find that number heading in the section and listed under that number is everything there is to see or do at that location on the map.

Category Classification
Each item listed is classified under one of eight categories. The classification key is the shaded letter immediately preceding the item listed. This makes it very simple to find the type of information you're looking for immediately. If you're hungry, look for any items preceded by an F. Looking for something to do? Look for a T or V. Want to buy something to take home with you? Look for an S. Here is a key for the categories:

H Historic Marker
We have taken the text from hundreds of historical markers throughout the region and reprinted them here. They're fun reading, and in total provide an excellent background on the history and growth of the region. We have entered them where they are located. Sometimes this is a different location than the actual item to which they refer. Even though we've presented the text of these markers here, take the time to stop at every one you can. They are only labels for the actual site or event and the experience is only complete if you are able to view the area surrounding them.

D Lewis & Clark and the Corps of Discovery in Montana
Under this heading, you will find notes from the Lewis & Clark journals as well as other related information relevant to this remarkable journey of exploration.

T Attraction
This category includes just about anything worth stopping for. It might be a museum, a ghost town, a park, or just some quirky thing on the side of the road that makes traveling through this state so interesting. Whatever it is, we've tried to provide enough information to let you decide whether you want to plan a stop or not.

V Adventure
This would be just about anything you would get out of your car and do. A whitewater raft trip, horseback ride, etc.

A Auto
These are anything related to the automobile, generally repair places.

F Food
We didn't discriminate. If there is prepared food available, we list it. We've listed everything ranging from the finest restaurants in the region (and there are lots of them), to fast food and hot dog stands. Bottom line: if they'll fix it for you, they're listed here. While we don't rate any of the establishments, we highly encourage you to try the mom and pop eateries and the locally owned fine dining spots. Dayton Duncan, in his excellent book Out West: American Journey Along the Lewis and Clark Trail (1987, Penguin Books) gave the best advice we've heard:

"Franchises are not for the traveler bent on discovery. Forsaking franchises, like forsaking interstates, means that you're wiling to chance the ups and downs, the starts and the stops of gastronomy as well s motoring. It means sometimes finishing a supper so good that you order the piece of pie you hadn't realized you wanted and you're sure you don't need—and spending the night in town just so you can have breakfast in the same place."

In this region, you're pretty safe. Just consider the logic. Most of these towns are so small that any place not putting up good grub isn't going to last long anyway. Accountability. While much of

Visitors watching Riverside Geyser. NPS Photo by J Schmidt.

American has forgotten that concept, it is still a harsh and unforgiving rule in the Yellowstone area.

As for fine dining, we'd put scores of our best against the best anywhere outside of the Yellowstone region. Some of the most talented culinary artists in the world have settled here for the lifestyle and share their talents with us.

L Lodging

If they'll put a roof over your head and a mattress under your back, they're listed here. Again, we don't discriminate. Truth is, it's hard to find a bad motel in this area. Surviving here as a business is tough, and if you don't put up a good product, you don't last long.

C Camping

These are private campgrounds that wished to be included in the main portion of each section. Otherwise, all private campgrounds are listed in the back of each section.

S Shopping

Do we need to explain this one? Obviously, we don't list every place in the region where you can buy something. Only those who wanted to be in here are included. And yes, they paid for the opportunity. It would be impractical to list every place in the region you can buy something. And you probably wouldn't want to wade through all of them to get to the ones that count. So we left it up to the merchants to decide whether or not they might have something of interest to you, and to choose whether or not to include themselves in this book.

M Miscellaneous Services

This would be just about anything that doesn't fall into one of the other categories above.

Maps

We've included a map for just about anything you would need a map for. At the beginning of each section is a detailed map of the section. We've also included a map of any town too big to see every part of town while standing on Main Street. We've also included a number of maps of special locations. On each of the section maps, we've marked where campgrounds, fishing sites, and Lewis & Clark points of interest are.

Rainy evening in the Upper Geyser Basin. NPS Photo by J Schmidt.

Campgrounds

Public campgrounds are marked on the map with a number. At the end of each section is a chart listing each campground along with pertinent information about that site. The listings are numbered and the numbers match those on the map. We only listed campgrounds that are maintained in some manner by a state or federal agency. There are countless primitive campgrounds in the region that are not maintained and have no facilities. You'll find almost all of the region's public campgrounds to be uncrowded. It's not unusual, even at the peak of tourist season, to be the only campers at a site. Most of them charge a small fee to cover the cost of maintaining them.

Private campgrounds are included in a chart at the back of each section and organized by town.

Forest Service Cabins – Montana and Idaho

One of the best-kept secrets in Idaho and Montana is the availability of cabins and lookout stations that the U. S. Forest Service makes available to the public at a nominal fee. At the end of each section, a list of available cabins along with detailed information on each has been provided. Following is some general information about reserving and using the cabins.

Making Reservations

The recreational cabins in the National Forests of Idaho and Montana are available for use on a first-come, first-served basis, but reservations are required. Reservations may be made in person, by mail, or by phone by contacting the specific ranger district listed. Reservations for some cabins may also be made through the national Recreation Reservation Service at 1-877-444-6777.

Facilities

The cabins available through the rental program are rustic and primitive. Most cabins are located in remote areas, generally accessible via narrow, winding, dirt or gravel roads. With the exception of a few cabins, there are no modern conveniences or the safeguards of modern society – no telephones, traffic jams, neighbors, and no emergency services.

When making reservations, inquire about

what is or is not furnished with the cabin or lookout. The facilities are generally equipped with the bare basics, including a table, chairs, wood stove, and bunks (some with mattresses, some without). Bedding is not furnished. Cooking utensils are available at some cabins, but not all. Electricity and piped-in water are generally not available. It may be necessary to bring in safe drinking water or be prepared to chemically treat or boil water for consumption. At some cabins, you will need to find and cut your own firewood. Expect to use outdoor privies.

Fishing Sites

We've listed hundreds of fishing sites in the region and marked and numbered them on the maps. Throughout the book you'll find charts giving information on regional fisheries. There are thousands of places to wet a line in this area. We have listed the major fisheries and only those that are relatively easy to access.

Scenic Drives

There are thousands of miles of roads available within the Region's national forests and grasslands. Some roads are high standard paved routes and others are low-standard "Jeep" trails. Seasonable closures to protect resources, such as calving elk or water quality, may affect the use of certain roads. Information about motorized access and road restrictions for each national forest is shown on the forest visitor map.

We have tried to offer some scenic or interesting side trips wherever possible. Some take you on back-roads, others just take you a different way. Some are day trips, some are longer. We feel the book itself offers one long scenic trip, but if you want to get off the path, these offer some chances. Heed the warnings about gumbo and other back-road hazards mentioned earlier in this book.

Camping & Picnicking

Visitors can camp and picnic almost anywhere on the national forests and grasslands. For those seeking more convenience, hundreds of developed sites usually contain a parking spur, table, fireplace, and toilets. Water is also provided in some areas. Some sites are accessible to the handicapped

Bicycling past Castle Geyser. NPS Photo by Jim Peaco

Hikers on Mt Washburn trail. NPS Photo by Ed Austin/Herb Jones - Kodak

or disabled. Showers, laundry facilities, electrical hookups, and hot water are not provided.

Campgrounds requiring a fee for use are signed and limitations on length of stay, if any, are posted. Horses and the shooting of firearms in developed campsites are prohibited. For the more venturesome, there are numerous isolated road-side and backcountry picnic and campsites. These sites do not contain improvements like toilet, table, or fireplaces. No matter where you are camping or picnicking, help keep the area clean.

Hikes

We have offered you a number of hikes at the end of most sections. There are a few section of the region that don't offer too many hiking options. We didn't provide a lot of detail about the hikes. We simply pointed them out and tell you how to get there.

Information Please

Here we give you phone numbers for just about anything we missed earlier in the section that might be of interest to you.

Dining and Lodging Quick Reference Guides

These charts allow you to take a quick scan of all of the dining and lodging facilities in a manner that allows you to find information quickly and make quick comparisons. The map locator numbers are listed with each entry to help you find their location and possibly additional information about them in the front of the section.

Notes

We've allowed you ample room throughout the book to make notes about your trip or to record additional information about your trip. This is a good place to store reservation confirmation numbers or schedule information.

We've made every effort to make this book a tool for you to get the most from your visit to the Yellowstone region. If you already live here, we hope it awakens you to the endless things there are to do and see in this magnificent chunk of America!

And finally...

This is a book that was not as much written as it was compiled and edited. We used articles and information provided by other sources whenever possible. To research and know about every resource and feature in the region intimately would take us years. If it was already researched and written (and written well) we used it when we could do so. We have credited every source as accurately as possible. It is our goal to provide you, the reader, the maximum amount of information possible to make your exploration of the region enjoyable, while providing all the resources you need in one book. Hopefully we accomplished that goal. We would certainly like to hear from you if there is anything we've overlooked.

Happy Trails!

BOOK SECTION GUIDE

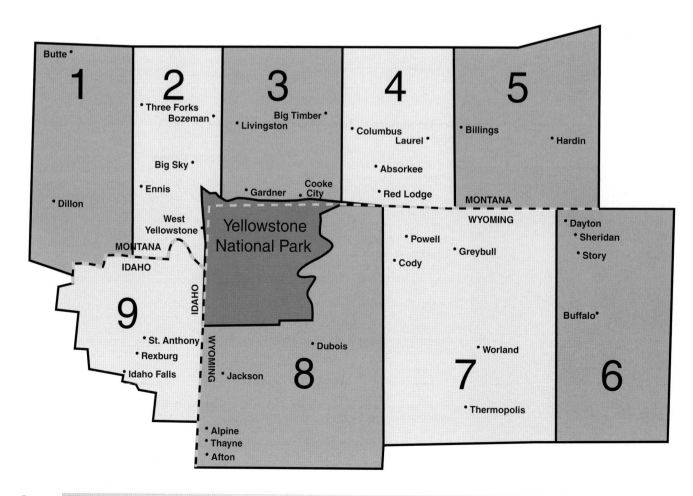

YELLOWSTONE

THE FIRST NATIONAL PARK

Great Fountain Geyser (Rick Huntchinson behind the tree on left). NPS Photo by William S Keller

AMERICA'S FIRST NATIONAL PARK

Welcome to Yellowstone National Park! Renowned throughout the world for its natural wonders, inspiring scenery, and mysterious wild nature, America's first national park is nothing less than extraordinary. Mud pots roil and boil like witch's brew, geysers spew their pent-up fury, waterfalls crash over precipitous ledges, and some of America's rarest and wildest species delegate Yellowstone as their home. It is no wonder, then, that this land of intrigue and oddity has long captured the attention of explorers, scientists, photographers, and tourists from every continent. More than three million visitors are drawn to the park's magnetic natural personality every year with some faithfully embarking on annual pilgrimages to the acclaimed national treasure.

Including the rugged Continental Divide in its massive 3,472 square miles, Yellowstone covers more area than the states of Rhode Island and Delaware combined. Its 2.2 million wild acres are predominantly cradled within Wyoming's northwestern corner, but the overwhelming land mass extends its mysterious fingers for a slight grasp of south-central Montana and northeastern Idaho.

Recognized as the continental U.S.' second largest national park, Yellowstone's voluminous size allows for great topographical variation. Contained within the Greater Yellowstone Ecosystem, Yellowstone National Park is unique in boasting the world's largest intact temperate ecosystem. Over 10,000 geysers and hot springs have earned Yellowstone the right to claim more geothermal phenomena than the rest of the world combined. Despite the familiar pictures touting such wonders, Yellowstone is more than hot pools and steaming fountains. Mountains blanketed with aspen and fir intermingle with arid plateaus, wildflower fields, and fossilized forests. Unbeknownst to most visitors, park elevations range from as low as 5,314 feet near the north entrance's sagebrush flats to 11,358 feet at the snowcapped Eagle Peak. Perhaps most interestingly, the park rests on a magma layer buried just one to three miles below the surface while the rest of the Earth lies more than six miles above the first traces of magma.

Yellowstone's captivating natural appeal is enhanced with an amazing display of wildlife. North America's largest species, the bison, wanders idly across the park's terrain and roads while the continent's fastest species, the pronghorn antelope, speeds purposefully into the horizon. The prehistoric looking moose shares Yellowstone's mountains and meadows with deer, wolves, elk, bighorn sheep, mountain lions, grizzly bears, and black bears. Soaring above in the breathtakingly crisp azure skies, peregrine falcons, bald eagles, osprey, and whooping cranes scour the fish-laden rivers below for their next meal. Although these and Yellowstone's other wild inhabitants are regularly glimpsed near the park's major attractions and highways, most actually shy away from public view. Many of Yellowstone's animals maintain habitats in the 98% of parkland humans rarely touch.

With the Earth's powerful geological forces constantly churning, Yellowstone National Park is a testimony to evolution. Those who tour Yellowstone today will find the park quite different than twenty years before, and the cycle of change will continue underneath the feet of curious visitors. Whether individual travel plans call for a brief tour of all the park's major attractions or an in-depth look at just one corner of Yellowstone, America's first national park will undoubtedly leave a lasting impression beckoning future exploration. Happy trails as you discover one of America's most beautiful and mysterious places!

THE HISTORY BEHIND YELLOWSTONE

Long before herds of tourists and automobiles crisscrossed Yellowstone's rare landscape, the unique features comprising the region lured in the West's early inhabitants, explorers, pioneers, and entrepreneurs. Their stories helped fashion Yellowstone into what it is today and initiated the birth of America's National Park System.

Native Americans

As early as 10,000 years ago, ancient inhabitants dwelled in northwest Wyoming. These small bands of nomadic hunters wandered the countryside, hunting the massive herds of bison and gathering seeds and berries. During their seasonal travels, these predecessors of today's Native American tribes stumbled upon Yellowstone and its abundant wildlife. Archaeologists have discovered domestic utensils, stone tools, and arrowheads indicating that these ancient peoples were the first humans to discover Yellowstone and its many wonders.

As the region's climate warmed and horses were introduced to American Indian tribes in the 1600s, Native American visits to Yellowstone became more frequent. The Absaroka (Crow) and Blackfeet tribes settled in the territory surrounding Yellowstone and occasionally dispatched hunting parties into Yellowstone's vast terrain. Possessing no horses and maintaining an isolated nature, the Shoshone-Bannock Indians are the only Native American tribe to have inhabited Yellowstone year-round. Called Sheepeaters, these peaceful Indians relied on the park's abundant bighorn sheep population for subsistence. Evidence of these Indians' area travels and presence is apparent to this day on the Bannock Trail gouged into the land near Tower Junction.

Golden Gate. NPS Photo by JW Stockert.

Visitors photographing Minerva Terrace at Mammoth Hot Springs. NPS Photo by William S Keller.

Fur Trappers, Mountain Men, and Miners

As visions of westward expansion consumed American, Canadian, and European politicians in the late eighteenth and early nineteenth centuries, it was inevitable that the remote life of the Shoshone-Bannock tribe in Yellowstone would be disturbed. French Canadians first arrived in the area in the late 1700s in search of prized beaver pelts. Following one of the Missouri River's largest tributaries, the Yellowstone River, these explorers and fur trappers named the area "Roche Jaune," meaning Yellow Rock. Their journals indicate that yellow rock cradled the river; however, no mention is ever made regarding Yellowstone's thermal features.

When Lewis and Clark made their famous westward journey to the Pacific Ocean and then back to Missouri between 1804 and 1806, their travel plans bypassed the park's northern boundary by just fifty-six miles. Noting the area's unique features and possessing an innate inquisitiveness, John Colter left the Corp of Discovery on its return journey and headed to the Yellowstone Region. Although Colter was in search of beaver, what he discovered was far more

important than a string of glossy pelts. During his employment at a Yellowstone River trading post between 1807 and 1808, Colter revealed Yellowstone's curiosities to the civilized world for the first time. His journals detailed unbelievable tales of bubbling mud pots, steaming geysers, mountain waterfalls, incredible canyons, and an endless beaver population. When Colter returned to Missouri, few believed his tales, chalking them up to a fanciful imagination. After all, Lewis and Clark had never mentioned hot springs. Why would Colter encounter anything different than the famous Corp of Discovery? Some, however, took Colter's recounting seriously and headed to "Colter's Hell" and the Yellowstone Region for themselves.

Among the few who believed Colter's tales were several of the American West's most famous mountain men. Jedediah Smith, Jim Bridger, and Daniel Potts frequented the area between the 1820s and 1840s, lending further credibility to Colter's detailed regional account. Tales of the mountain men's adventures eventually reached the East and sparked a renewed intrigue in the area. When Montana gold was discovered in 1862, the curious stories about Yellowstone and dreams of striking it rich finally spurred many to undertake their own exploration. Although hopeful miners scoured every square mile of the park, their search for gold was fruitless. Their adventures, however, produced the evidence and maps needed to finally launch exploration parties to the area.

Private Parties Explore Yellowstone

In 1869, a group of adventurers made preparations for the first official exploration of Yellowstone. Although the lack of a military escort warded off a few potential explorers who feared Indian attacks, three brave men weathered the situation and fearlessly pursued the thirty-six day expedition. David Folsom, Charles W. Cook, and William Peterson entered the park, encountered no hostile Indians, and returned to civilization armed with tales of a landscape unlike any other. When Folsom created an area map with surveyor Walter DeLacy and wrote an article for the Western Monthly magazine, national interest surged.

One year later, General Henry D. Washburn led his own party to the area with the accompaniment of military scout Lieutenant Gustavus C. Doane. Politician and park system promoter Nathaniel Langford also joined the influential men on what would be a life-changing journey. After their exploration, the men adamantly lobbied Congress for the establishment of Yellowstone as a national park. Langford garnered support for the cause with a series of lectures and articles appearing in Scribner's Monthly while Doane produced a detailed Yellowstone report for Congress' benefit. It would take one year, however, for Congress to respond to the increasing societal call for preservation.

The Official Birth of Yellowstone

Under great pressure from Yellowstone's private party explorers, Northern Pacific Railroad officials (who saw Yellowstone as a prosperous business venture), and the general public, the U.S. Congress finally gathered funds to send out its own scientific team of explorers. Territorial director of the U.S. Geological Survey Ferdinand V. Hayden was appointed in 1871 to lead photographer William H. Jackson, artist Thomas Moran, and a team of explorers to the area. Their return to Washington later that year confirmed every Yellowstone account dating back to Colter's first journal reports. Hayden immediately joined the ranks of Washburn, Doane, and Langford in lobbying Congress to preserve Yellowstone from the West's feverish homesteaders. Finally, in an unprecedented act, Congress passed the Yellowstone Park bill with little issue and turned the matter over to President Ulysses S. Grant. Grant wholeheartedly endorsed the legislation, and Yellowstone National Park was born on March 1, 1872.

Known as the Yellowstone Park Act, the bill reads: "Be it enacted by the Senate and House of Representatives of the United States of America in Congress assembled, That the tract of land in the Territories of Montana and Wyoming lying near the headwaters of the Yellowstone River...is hereby reserved and withdrawn from settlement, occupancy, or sale under the laws of the United States, and dedicated and set apart as a public park or pleasuring ground for the benefit and enjoyment of the people..."

Learning How to Manage Yellowstone and its Visitors

Although Congress and President Grant possessed the best intentions for Yellowstone when the Yellowstone Park Act was enacted in 1872, little thought was given to the actual management of the large tract of land. Most government officials assumed that the Department of the Interior would be able to manage the park with ease, despite receiving no budget and possessing no instruction about how to preserve a wilderness area. On the contrary, the west's frontier spirit wreaked havoc on Yellowstone during its early years, and the Department of the Interior was unprepared for the ensuing years of park abuse.

Accustomed to American homesteading policies that allowed pioneers to stake a claim and virtually destroy their land if the urge arose, Yellowstone's first tourists had anything but preservation on their minds. Greedy poachers slaughtered Yellowstone's precious elk, deer, and bison, sawing off valuable antlers and ivory teeth while leaving the carcasses to rot under the scorching blue skies. Tourists wealthy enough to travel to Yellowstone in its early years arrived with shovels and axes, ripping apart geysers for

Visitor viewing elk bull. NPS Photo by Leslie Quinn.

ancient pieces of geyserite and travertine while hauling away huge chunks of petrified trees. Other visitors chose to experiment with the power of Yellowstone's geysers. Logs, clothing, rocks, and a myriad of other natural items and personal belongings were shoved down the geysers in twisted delight of watching the articles spew heavenwards. As tourists skinny-dipped in the park's hot springs, laundry concessionaires dumped soap into the colorful pools and streams to create a profitable cleaning business.

Despite such travesties, little was done to stop the visitors' destructive behavior between 1872 and 1877. Congress had appointed Nathaniel Langford to an unpaid park superintendent position when the Yellowstone Park Act was passed. During his employment, however, Langford only visited the park three times and compiled just one report regarding the park's status. Officials in Washington, D.C. had little idea of the chaos plaguing the park, and almost no thought had been extended to building a road system that would generate profitable tourist dollars. When Philetus W. Norris assumed the park superintendent position in 1877, the pioneering scientist lobbied Congress and finally received a miniscule amount of funding. Funds were used to create the Norris Road, campaign against poachers and vandals, and excavate and ship valuable geological items to the Smithsonian. Although Norris himself maintained a preservation attitude, he found it difficult to foster the same appreciation in Yellowstone's visitors. Upon Norris' abandonment of the superintendent position, three other civilians with damaging management philosophies filled the position between 1882 and 1886. Greed and apathy allowed illegal concessionaires to operate throughout the park, and the arrival of the Northern Pacific Railroad at the park's North Entrance brought more tourists hungry to hack away at Yellowstone's most valuable resources. By 1886, the situation had become so grim that Congress withdrew funding for the park. The U.S. Military was now the park's only hope for survival.

Restoring Order to Yellowstone
Utilizing the Civil Sundry Appropriations Bill passed in 1884, the U.S. Secretary of the Interior

Hayden Valley & the Yellowstone River. NPS Photo by R Robinson.

requested military assistance from the Secretary of War in a final attempt to save the park from ruthless scavengers. The request was immediately honored, and in August 1886, the U.S. Calvary arrived in Yellowstone with a plan to restore park order.

After setting up a network of nineteen outposts at the park's most popular attractions, the soldiers began daily patrols against vandalism. The Army also adopted a wildlife protection policy in regards to Yellowstone's spectacular animals. Poachers were chased and caught with the aid of informants and mysterious telegraph codes, and the Lacey Act of 1894 designated any infraction of park law a federal offense. As a result, the threat of guaranteed prison time and extensive fines scared away many would-be poachers and vandals, and a wildlife refuge was established. By the late 1890s, sixteen snowshoe cabins had been added to extend military patrols year-round. With a force of 450 soldiers, Fort Yellowstone was

established at Mammoth Hot Springs, and Congress appropriated funding to maintain military presence through 1918.

In addition to cracking down on those bent on destroying the park, the Calvary also rallied the support of the Corps of Engineers to wipe away the park's primitive trails and create a user-friendly road system. Many of the routes constructed at the turn of the century remain in use today, and the Army was directly responsible for building the foundations of an enduring park tourist industry.

When the National Park Service, which was created in 1916, took control of park operations in 1918, many of the soldiers remained and became park rangers. A ranger-naturalist program aimed at educating rangers and informing tourists about Yellowstone's features was enacted, and rangers oversaw a variety of activities in the now restored park. Although Yellowstone possessed well under 100 rangers when the Park Service took over, the rangers diligently fulfilled their multiple job duties. They patrolled highways on motorcycles and backcountry areas on foot or horseback, tackled forest fires, dealt with problem bears that threatened visitor safety, dispensed first aid, and eventually checked cars at entrance gates. Under the management of Horace Albright from 1919 to 1929, Yellowstone finally saw its natural beauty restored, the last of the park's violators wiped out, and annual visitation numbers that jumped from 62,000 to 260,000. Yellowstone was on its way to becoming a family vacation destination, and the automobile was key in establishing that reputation.

The Arrival of Automobile Touring
When the first car made its way through Yellowstone's gates in 1902, park officials immediately evicted the automobile. Not only were cars viewed as polluting contraptions unfit for travel on Yellowstone's roads, but they were also seen as a nemesis to the railroad, stagecoach, and concessionaire owners who had aligned themselves with park superintendents and held great stakes in the Yellowstone tourist industry. With automobiles firmly prohibited, the park was a destination for the rich and the adventurous who were dependent upon trains, stagecoach drivers,

Horse pack train in Pelican Valley. NPS Photo by Jim Peaco.

Visitors viewing Cistern Spring emptying after May 2, 2000 Steamboat eruption. NPS Photo by Tom Cawley.

and primitive camping and "hotel" concessionaires to make their Yellowstone vacations successful. These greedy business owners were less than thrilled about the automobile's arrival, and until 1915, they enjoyed the right to charge overpriced rates to visitors willing to pay as much money as necessary to see Yellowstone's wonders.

The life of these concessionaires dramatically changed in 1915 when the Secretary of the Interior finally agreed to allow automobiles inside the park's boundaries. For the first time in its history, Yellowstone National Park became a truly national place. No longer relegated a destination for the affluent, the park assumed a commoner attitude allowing anyone with a vehicle to glimpse the park in all its magnificent glory. At the same time, the automobile provided visitors the freedom to set their own schedule without waiting upon the itinerary of a stagecoach or horse tour operator.

While the rest of the world reveled in the Secretary of Interior's decision, park concessionaires and railroad officials were furious. They balked at the announcement, crying out that automobiles would destroy their businesses and actually lessen the number of visitors. The order, however, was not to be reversed, and concessionaires were soon slapped with stringent guidelines. Only one tour bus company was allowed to operate in the park, along with one hotel concessionaire and one photographer. Other concessionaries and lunch stations were simply forced to shut up shop as park services geared themselves towards independent automobile travelers.

The Secretary of Interior's plan worked much to the chagrin of previous park concessionaries. Automobile travel significantly enhanced park visitation, and order was finally given to Yellowstone Park's concessionaire business. Despite experiencing growing pains where the Depression, wartime woes, and a decaying road, campground, and restroom system threatened the park's livelihood, Yellowstone has persevered for more than 125 years. It continues to garner a strong foothold as one of America's most beloved national parks.

YELLOWSTONE PARK TODAY

Considered a United Nations Biosphere Reserve and a World Heritage Site, Yellowstone Park has weathered its fair share of problems and continually faces an array of politically charged issues. Evidence of the disastrous 1988 fires that charred over half of the park is slowly fading away under new growth, but the National Park Service policy of not interfering with the laws of nature has now created new problems. The park's wildlife population, fiercely protected within the park's boundaries, has been allowed to overpopulate a few park areas. Elk, deer, and bison compete with one another for shrinking grazing lands, while the 1995 reintroduction of wolves has further complicated the park's wildlife habitation and food competition issue.

The increasing numbers of visitors also threatens Yellowstone's unique ecosystem. Emissions from snowmobiles choke the atmosphere with noise and exhaust that disturbs Yellowstone's wildlife and fragile flora. During summer, the park's narrow roads burgeon with traffic jams,

and little government funding is provided to repair and update Yellowstone's strained highway system.

Despite these heated issues, visitors continue to flock to Yellowstone. In an attempt to remedy a few of its current problems and effectively manage Yellowstone's precious land without much-needed federal aid, the National Park Service has opted to raise entrance fees. Most of these fees are then used to improve the general infrastructure of the popular park. As time goes by and increasingly more visitors make Yellowstone their year-round destination of choice, the National Park Service will no doubt face tough decisions in maintaining and preserving Yellowstone for the enjoyment of future generations. As a park visitor, you can help their cause by respecting the park's wonders and treating Yellowstone with the dignity it deserves.

GENERAL VISITOR INFORMATION

Since Yellowstone National Park welcomes over three million pilgrims each year, it is essential that visitors plan ahead to create a truly memorable experience. The following is a basic set of facts every visitor should know prior to his/her Yellowstone tour.

Important Contact Information

- Yellowstone National Park (307-344-7381; www.nps.gov/yell): Basic park information, maps, and road conditions

- Xanterra Parks and Resorts (307-344-7311; www.travelyellowstone.com): Information regarding Yellowstone lodging, boating, bus/snowcoach tours and reservations, horseback riding, campground information, group camping data, and future campsite reservations

- Same-Day Campground Reservations: (307) 344-7901

- Yellowstone Association (307-344-2293; www.YellowstoneAssociation.org): Information related to the park's educational programs, visitor centers, information stations, and museums

- Medical Emergencies: 911

- Mammoth Medical Clinic: (307) 344-7965

- Lake Medical Clinic: (307) 242-7241

- Old Faithful Medical Clinic: (307) 545-7325

Fly fishing. NPS Photo by Bob Greenburg.

Basic Park Facts

- Yellowstone National Park encompasses 2.2 million acres, spanning over 3,472 square miles in Wyoming, Montana, and Idaho.

- While most of Yellowstone's highway system lies at 7,500 to 8,000 feet (2,275-2,427 meters) above sea level, the rest of the park's elevation runs the gamut. The lowest elevation, 5,314 feet (1,608 meters), is at the park's north entrance in Gardiner, Montana; the highest elevation, 11,358 feet (3,640 meters), rests on the eastern boundary at Eagle Peak.

- Yellowstone's speed limit is 45 miles per hour (73 kilometers per hour) and is strictly enforced. In some areas, speed limits may be lower, and drivers should at all times be ready for reduced speed limits in construction areas.

- Yellowstone National Park boasts over 10,000 known thermal features, and researchers suspect that many others remain waiting discovery. Of these thermal wonders, more than 300 geysers sputter and spew.

- Circling near the park's major scenic attractions, the Grand Loop Road includes the 70-mile (113 kilometers) Upper Loop and the 96-mile (155 kilometer) Lower Loop. Highlights include the Yellowstone Grand Canyon and Old Faithful Geyser. Some attractions do require visitors to park and take a short walk.

- Short on time? Explore just one area of the park. Most people believe that it requires at least three full days to fully see and appreciate all the park's major features.

Park Entrances

- North Entrance: Located just south of Gardiner, Montana on U.S. Highway 89, Yellowstone National Park's North Entrance is marked with the grandeur of the Roosevelt Arch. An avid conservationist, President Theodore Roosevelt dedicated the fifty-foot tall basalt tower structure in 1903. The elevation at the North Entrance is 5,314 feet (1,608 meters), and the entrance is open all year with no facilities available.

- Northeast Entrance: Connecting Cooke City, Montana and Mammoth Hot Springs, the park's Northeast Entrance is open year-round. The entrance is located at 7,365 feet (2,245 meters) above sea level and features a year-round ranger station.

- East Entrance: Situated at an elevation of 6,951 feet (2,119 meters), Yellowstone's East Entrance is located 52 miles west of Cody, Wyoming on U.S. Highway 14/16/20. The scenic entrance is open from May through the first week in November with facilities including a museum, visitor center, campground, public showers, laundry, general store, service station, auto repair services, a winter warming hut, vending machines, and snowmobile fuel.

- South Entrance: Yellowstone National Park's South Entrance is situated on U.S. Highway 89/191/287 and parallels the Snake River north of neighboring Grand Teton National Park. Nestled at an elevation of 6,886 feet (2,099 meters), the entrance is generally open from mid-May through the first week of November. Facilities include a visitor center, ranger station, campgrounds, boat ramps, post office, general store, auto repair and towing services, food, lodging, laundry, public showers, and an amphitheater.

Gardner's Hole. NPS Photo by J. Schmidt.

- West Entrance: The park's West Entrance is located on the fringes of West Yellowstone, Montana and boasts a scenic elevation of 6,667 feet. The West Entrance is generally open to automobiles from the end of April through the first week in November. During winter months, the West Entrance is a popular launching area for snowmobiles and snowcoach tours.

Entrance Fees & Recreational Permits

In order to maintain the park system without further taxing the general population, the National Park Service charges moderate entrance fees and also collects fees for special recreation permits, including fishing and boating. Eighty-percent of park entrance fees at Yellowstone National Park stay within the park, while the remaining twenty-percent are contributed to a general National Park Service fund that maintains parks where no fees are charged. If you are planning on leaving and re-entering the park within seven days from the date of your first visit, be sure to keep your admission receipt as proof of payment. Visitors should also note that advance reservations are not necessary for park entrance.

- For private, vehicles, the entrance fee is $20. The fee provides visitors with a seven-day pass to both Yellowstone and Grand Teton National Parks.

- Motorcyclists and snowmobile operators are each charged a $15 entrance fee for a seven-day admission to both Yellowstone and Grand Teton. All motorcyclists and snowmobilers must possess a valid driver's license.

- Anyone over age sixteen who enters the park on foot, bicycle, skis, or snowshoes can expect to pay $10 for a seven-day pass.

- For those planning on visiting Yellowstone or Grand Teton National Park several times throughout the year, a $40 Annual Area Pass may be purchased. The permit is valid 365 days from the date of purchase.

- For National Park lovers, the $50 National Parks Pass guarantees admission to any national park. The pass is valid one year from the date of purchase.

- Permanently disabled or blind individuals may qualify for the Golden Access Passport with medical proof of their condition. The permit grants qualified individuals and any accompanying passengers free access to all national parks. The pass also entitles individuals to a fifty-percent discount on campground and other park fees.

- The Golden Age Passport is a lifetime passport for senior citizens over age sixty-two. A one-time $10 fee is charged, and qualified individuals receive free access to all national parks. The permit also provides a fifty-percent discount on campground and other park fees.

- Priced at $65, the Golden Eagle Passport allows the permit holder and all accompanying passengers access to all National Parks and nearly every national monument and federal preserve within the U.S. The permit is valid one year from the date of purchase.

- Backcountry User Permits are available free of charge, but all those on foot, horseback, or boat must acquire a permit. Overnight backcountry stays also require a special permit. Permits are available during summer up to forty-eight hours in advance from the following ranger stations: Bridge Bay, South Entrance, Bechler, Canyon, Grant Village, Mammoth, Old Faithful, Lake, West Entrance, and Tower.

- Boating permits are required for any watercraft occupying Yellowstone's scenic park waters. Motorized boaters may select from a $20 annual permit or a $10 seven-day pass. Non-motorized craft are charged a $10 annual permit or a $5 seven-day pass. Boating permits are available at the following ranger stations: South Entrance, Bridge Bay, Grant Village, and Lake. Water users should note that Yellowstone's rivers and streams are closed to all watercraft. The only exception is the Lewis River stretching between Lewis and Shoshone Lakes where non-motorized boats are allowed.

- Yellowstone's fishing season runs from Memorial Day weekend through the first Sunday in November. Exceptions include Yellowstone Lake, which opens on June 1; Yellowstone Lake tributaries, which are accessible on July 15; and selected portions of the Yellowstone River and

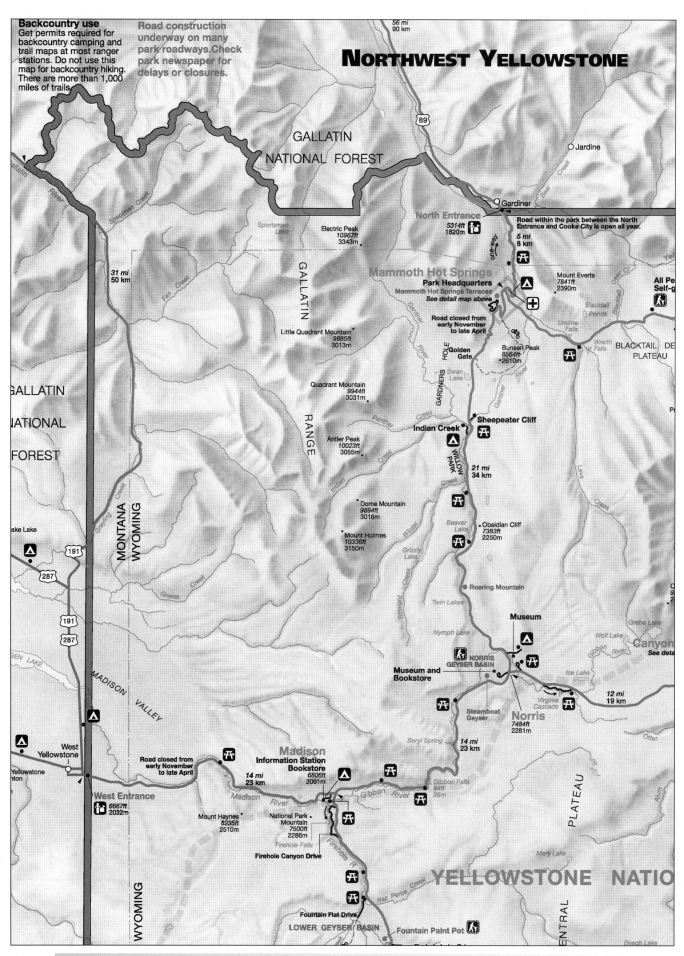

Backcountry use
Get permits required for backcountry camping and trail maps at most ranger stations. Do not use this map for backcountry hiking. There are more than 1,000 miles of trails.

Road construction underway on many park roadways.Check park newspaper for delays or closures.

GALLATIN

NATIONAL FOREST

56 mi
90 km

89

○ Jardine

○ Gardiner

North Entrance

Road within the park between the North Entrance and Cooke City is open all year.

5314ft
1620m

5 mi
8 km

Electric Peak
10967ft
3343m

Sportsman
Lake

31 mi
50 km

Mammoth Hot Springs
Park Headquarters
Mammoth Hot Springs Terraces
See detail map above

Mount Everts
7841ft
2390m

All Pe
Self-g

Little Quadrant Mountain
9885ft
3013m

Road closed from early November to late April

Blacktail
Ponds

GALLATIN

Golden Gate

Bunsen Peak
8564ft
•2610m

Wraith
Falls

Undine
Falls

BLACKTAIL DE
PLATEAU

Quadrant Mountain
9944ft
3031m

RANGE

Panther

Creek

GARDNERS   HOLE

Swan
Lake

Gardiner

River

Sheepeater Cliff

Antler Peak
10023ft
3055m

Indian Creek

WILLOW   PARK

21 mi
34 km

Lava

Creek

Dome Mountain
9894ft
3016m

Winter

Creek

Beaver
Lake

Obsidian Cliff
7383ft
2250m

Mount Holmes
10336ft
3150m

Grizzly
Lake

Indian

Creek

● Roaring Mountain

Straight   Creek

Twin Lakes

Museum

Grebe Lake

Canyon
See deta

Nymph Lake

Wolf Lake

ake Lake

191

287

GEN LAKE

MADISON

VALLEY

Gneiss

Creek

Grayling   Creek

MONTANA
WYOMING

191

287

NORRIS
GEYSER BASIN

Ice Lake

Gibbon   River

Museum and
Bookstore

Steamboat
Geyser

Norris
7484ft
2281m

Virginia
Cascade

12 mi
19 km

Otter

Beryl Spring

14 mi
23 km

West
Yellowstone

West
Yellowstone
nton

Road closed from early November to late April

Madison
Information Station
Bookstore
6806ft
2091m

14 mi
23 km

West Entrance
6667ft
2032m

Madison   River

Gibbon   River

Gibbon Falls
84ft
26m

Mount Haynes
8235ft
2510m

National Park
Mountain
7500ft
2286m

Firehole Falls

Firehole   R.

Firehole Canyon Drive

YELLOWSTONE   NATIO

Mary Lake

CENTRAL

PLATEAU

Alum

Fountain Flat Drive

LOWER GEYSER BASIN

Nez Perce   Creek

Fountain Paint Pot

Beach Lake

Yellowstone

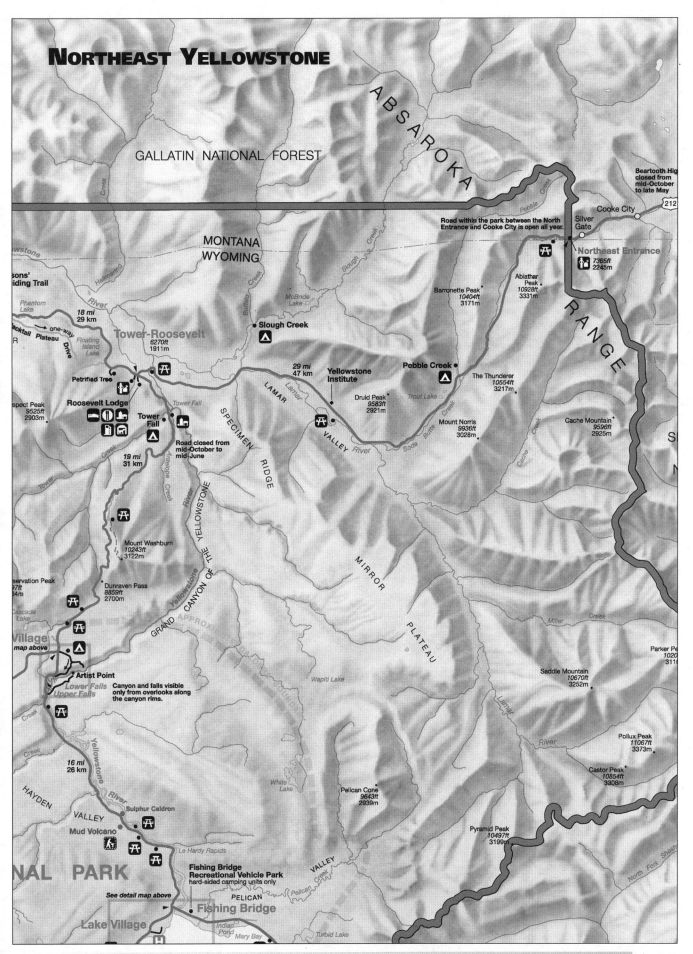

NORTHEAST YELLOWSTONE

GALLATIN NATIONAL FOREST

ABSAROKA RANGE

MONTANA
WYOMING

Beartooth Hig
closed from
mid-October
to late May

212

Cooke City

Silver
Gate

Road within the park between the North
Entrance and Cooke City is open all year.

Northeast Entrance
7365ft
2245m

Barronette Peak
10404ft
3171m

Abiathar
Peak
10928ft
3331m

sons'
iding Trail

Phantom
Lake

18 mi
29 km

one-way

acktail
Plateau
Drive

Floating
Island
Lake

Tower-Roosevelt
6270ft
1911m

Slough Creek

McBride
Lake

29 mi
47 km

Yellowstone
Institute

Pebble Creek

The Thunderer
10554ft
3217m

Petrified Tree

ospect Peak
9525ft
2903m

Roosevelt Lodge

Tower
Fall

Tower Fall

LAMAR

Lamar

Druid Peak
9583ft
2921m

Trout Lake

Mount Norris
9936ft
3028m

Cache Mountain
9596ft
2925m

19 mi
31 km

Road closed from
mid-October to
mid-June

SPECIMEN RIDGE

VALLEY

River

Soda

Butte

Cache

Creek

Mount Washburn
10243ft
3122m

servation Peak
97ft
34m

Dunraven Pass
8859ft
2700m

MIRROR

PLATEAU

Miller

Creek

Parker Pe
1020
311

Cascade
Lake

Village

map above

Artist Point

Lower Falls
Upper Falls

Canyon and falls visible
only from overlooks along
the canyon rims.

Wapiti Lake

Saddle Mountain
10670ft
3252m

GRAND

APPROXI

CANYON OF THE YELLOWSTONE

Lamar

River

Pollux Peak
11067ft
3373m

Creek

16 mi
26 km

HAYDEN

VALLEY

Yellowstone

River

Sulphur Caldron

Mud Volcano

White
Lake

Pelican Cone
9643ft
2939m

Castor Peak
10854ft
3308m

Le Hardy Rapids

NAL PARK

Fishing Bridge
Recreational Vehicle Park
hard-sided camping units only

VALLEY

Pelican

Pyramid Peak
10497ft
3199m

North Fork Shosh

See detail map above

Fishing Bridge

PELICAN

Lake Village

Indian
Pond

Mary Bay

Turbid Lake

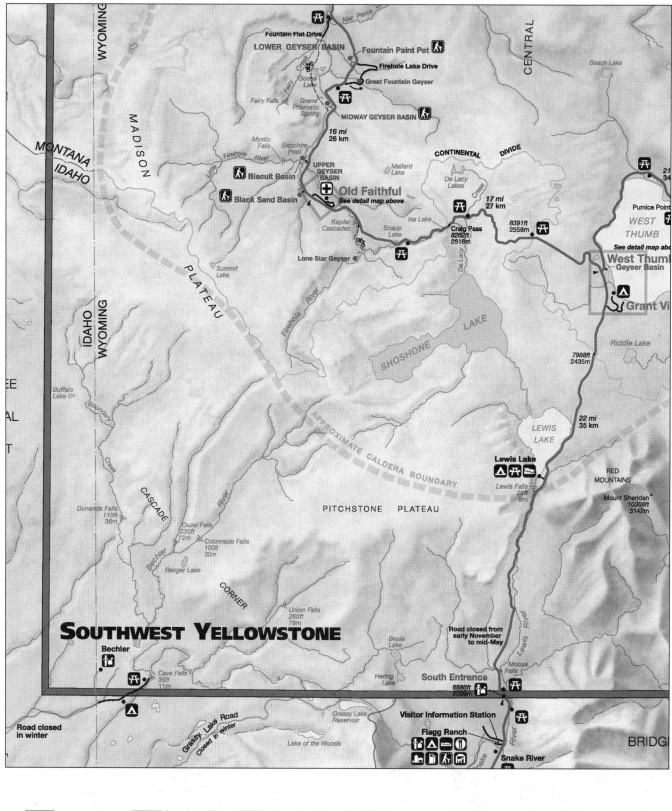

Fountain Flat Drive
LOWER GEYSER BASIN
Fountain Paint Pot
Firehole Lake Drive
Great Fountain Geyser

Naz Perce
CENTRAL
Beach Lake

Goose Lake
Fairy Falls
Fairy
Grand Prismatic Spring
MIDWAY GEYSER BASIN

16 mi
26 km

CONTINENTAL   DIVIDE

Mystic Falls
Little Firehole River
Sapphire Pool
UPPER GEYSER BASIN
Old Faithful
See detail map above

Mallard Lake
De Lacy Lakes

WYOMING
MONTANA
IDAHO

MADISON

Biscuit Basin
Black Sand Basin

Kepler Cascades
Scaup Lake
Isa Lake
Craig Pass
8262ft
2518m

8391ft
2558m

17 mi
27 km

21
34

Pumice Point
WEST THUMB

See detail map abo
West Thumb
Geyser Basin

Grant Vi

Lone Star Geyser

Firehole River

IDAHO
WYOMING

PLATEAU

De Lacy Creek

SHOSHONE LAKE

7988ft
2435m

Riddle Lake

Summit Lake

APPROXIMATE CALDERA BOUNDARY

LEWIS LAKE

22 mi
35 km

Buffalo Lake

Boundary

PITCHSTONE   PLATEAU

RED MOUNTAINS

Lewis Lake

Lewis Falls
29ft
9m

Mount Sheridan
10308ft
3142m

CASCADE

Dunanda Falls
110ft
36m

Ouzel Falls
235ft
72m

Colonnade Falls
100ft
30m

Bechler River

Ranger Lake

CORNER

Union Falls
260ft
79m

Beula Lake

Road closed from
early November
to mid-May

Lewis River

SOUTHWEST YELLOWSTONE

Bechler

Herring Lake

South Entrance

Moose Falls

6886ft
2099m

Cave Falls
35ft
11m

Grassy Lake Reservoir

Visitor Information Station

Flagg Ranch

BRIDG

Road closed
in winter

Grassy Lake Road
Closed in winter

Lake of the Woods

Snake River

Snake River

Gravel or dirt road	Approximate caldera boundary	Day-use bicycling/hiking trail (ask for more information)	Boating allowed
8 mi / 5 km Distance indicator	Geothermal feature		5 mph zone
One-way road	Continental Divide	Parking lot	Hand-propelled craft only

Boating
Boating permits are required for all watercraft. Inquire at ranger stations. Areas closed to watercraft include all rivers except Lewis River between Lewis and Shoshone lakes.

Fishing
A Yellowstone National Park fishing permit is required. State permits are not valid in the park and state regulations do not apply.

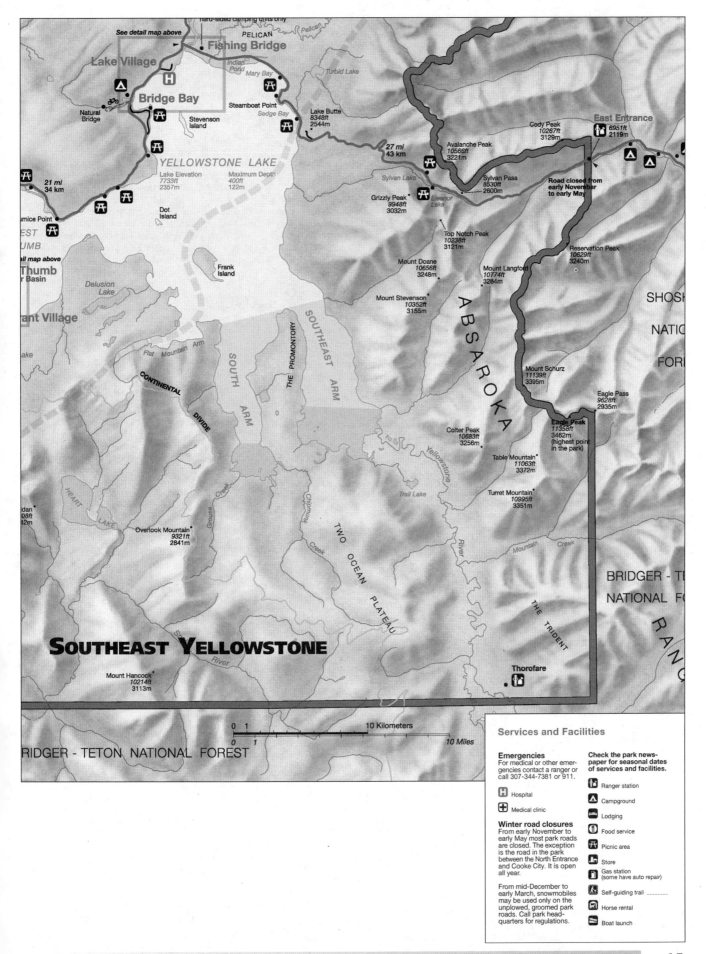

SOUTHEAST YELLOWSTONE

See detail map above

PELICAN

Fishing Bridge

Lake Village

Bridge Bay

Natural Bridge

Steamboat Point

Stevenson Island

YELLOWSTONE LAKE
Lake Elevation 7733ft 2357m
Maximum Depth 400ft 122m

Dot Island

Frank Island

Delusion Lake

THUMB

Thumb Basin

ant Village

Mary Bay

Sedge Bay

Lake Butte 8348ft 2544m

27 mi 43 km

Avalanche Peak 10566ft 3221m

Sylvan Lake

Grizzly Peak 9948ft 3032m

Eleanor Lake

Top Notch Peak 10238ft 3121m

Mount Doane 10656ft 3248m

Mount Stevenson 10352ft 3155m

Cody Peak 10267ft 3129m

Sylvan Pass 8530ft 2600m

Road closed from early November to early May

Reservation Peak 10629ft 3240m

East Entrance 6951ft 2119m

Mount Langford 10774ft 3284m

ABSAROKA

SHOSH

NATIO

FOR

Mount Schurz 11139ft 3395m

Eagle Pass 9628ft 2935m

Eagle Peak 11355ft 3462m (highest point in the park)

CONTINENTAL DIVIDE

SOUTH ARM

THE PROMONTORY

SOUTHEAST ARM

Flat Mountain Arm

HEART LAKE

Overlook Mountain 9321ft 2841m

Grouse Creek

Chipmunk Creek

TWO OCEAN PLATEAU

Colter Peak 10683ft 3256m

Table Mountain 11063ft 3372m

Trail Lake

Turret Mountain 10995ft 3351m

Yellowstone

River

Mountain Creek

BRIDGER - T
NATIONAL F

THE TRIDENT

RANG

Mount Hancock 10214ft 3113m

Thorofare

21 mi 34 km

ice Point

RIDGER - TETON NATIONAL FOREST

0 1 10 Kilometers
0 1 10 Miles

Yellowstone

Services and Facilities

Emergencies
For medical or other emergencies contact a ranger or call 307-344-7381 or 911.

Check the park newspaper for seasonal dates of services and facilities.

H Hospital

Medical clinic

Winter road closures
From early November to early May most park roads are closed. The exception is the road in the park between the North Entrance and Cooke City. It is open all year.

From mid-December to early March, snowmobiles may be used only on the unplowed, groomed park roads. Call park headquarters for regulations.

Ranger station

Campground

Lodging

Food service

Picnic area

Store

Gas station (some have auto repair)

Self-guiding trail

Horse rental

Boat launch

its tributary streams, which open July 15. All anglers must acquire a permit. For youth and adults over age sixteen, a $35 seasonal permit is available as well as a $20 seven-day pass and a $15 three-day permit. Youth ages twelve to fifteen must carry a permit, but there is no charge, while children under age twelve can fish without a permit when a paying adult accompanies them.

Traveling Seasons & Operating Hours

Spring, Summer, and Fall: With its dominant visitor season running from mid-April to early November, Yellowstone National Park opens its roads on different dates each year depending on how quickly road crews can clear the snow-covered highways. Once the highways open for the season, the roads are passable twenty-four hours a day, seven days a week, except in cases of road construction or weather-related incidents. Projected park opening and closing dates can be accessed on-line at www.nps.gov/yell/planvisit/orientation/travel/road open.htm.

Although the park's weather is certainly at its most ideal climate, summer in Yellowstone National Park also ushers in the highest number of visitors. Summer tourists should expect larger crowds at major attractions, slower traffic, and higher priced lodging and gas in Yellowstone's gateway communities.

For those who want a less crowded experience, spring and fall in Yellowstone is ideal. Prior to Memorial Day and after Labor Day, wildlife outnumbers cars and RVs. Spring wildflowers bloom in a rainbow palette while autumn's changing colors paint a picture perfect backdrop for some of the year's finest angling. Economically, spring and fall also reward visitors with lower gas prices and more lodging options at reduced rates.

Winter: Although the majority of cars, trucks, and RVs scamper away for the winter, Yellowstone is still alive with activity. Yellowstone's winter season operates from mid-December through mid-March, and snowmobilers congregate to explore Yellowstone's mysterious landscape shrouded in a veil of ice and snow. While the North and Northeast Entrances are open year-round to vehicles (four-wheel drive is highly recommended!), the rest of the park's roads and entrances are open only to snowmobiles, snowcoaches, and those on skis and snowshoes.

Lodging within Yellowstone Park

From rustic to elegant, Yellowstone National Park offers visitors a variety of in-park lodging options. In addition to reduced driving time and more convenient access to ranger-led park programs, visitors who stay inside the park are rewarded with breathtaking sunsets and bountiful wildlife viewing opportunities. Although some of the park's lodges have added television to their lounge offerings, most maintain an old-fashioned appeal with few modern technologies. For those who require air conditioning, telephones, modems, TV, and gaming systems, make reservations at a hotel in one of the gateway towns neighboring Yellowstone. However, those who can do without such posh amenities are granted a one-of-a-kind Yellowstone experience.

Under the operation of Xanterra Parks and Resorts, Yellowstone's lodging options are generally open for the primary tourist season from late spring through late October. During the winter

season of mid-December through mid-March, Mammoth Hot Springs and the Old Faithful Snow Lodge are the only facilities that remain open to accommodate snowmobilers and other winter enthusiasts. Please note that all accommodations are non-smoking, and wheelchair accessible units are limited due to the historic nature of most Yellowstone lodging. Accommodations book quickly, and those interested in staying at the park are encouraged to make reservations at least six months to one year in advance. Call Xanterra Parks and Resorts at (307) 344-7311 or log onto the web at www.travelyellowstone.com for additional information.

Mammoth Hot Springs Hotel and Cabins
Situated just five miles from Yellowstone's North Entrance, the Mammoth Hot Springs Hotel and Cabins offers 224 units ranging from standard rooms and suites to private cabins. Due to the hotel's close proximity to the park's entrance, rooms are often available even during the busiest season. Guests are treated to quaint dormer windows, well-maintained wood floors, an inviting lounge and Map Room accented with huge windows, and comfortable room accommodations. Suites are a bit more luxurious with private sitting rooms and sleeping areas. The cottage-style cabins, which occasionally feature decks and private hot tubs, are arranged near the hotel's standard rooms amid a large grassy area home to grazing elk. A formal dining room and fast-food restaurant are also available onsite, and medical facilities, a grocery store, gas station, and horse stables are located nearby. Please note that many of the standard rooms and cabins share a bathroom with private showers.

Open year-round, the hotel's standard room rates range from $50 to $85 depending on the season with suites priced around $245. The cabins, which generally sleep up to four, range from approximately $55 to $90 nightly. All major credit cards are accepted.

Canyon Lodge and Cabins
Combining old and new, the Canyon Lodge and Cabins are situated just one-half mile from the renowned Grand Canyon of the Yellowstone and offer Yellowstone's most centrally located lodging option. Western-inspired lodge rooms are available in the three-story Cascade Lodge completed in 1992 and the four-story Dunraven Lodge that opened in 1998. All rooms feature private baths, and a full-service restaurant, deli shop, gift store, reception desk, and horseback rides are available onsite. Handicap-accessible rooms are available on the first floor of each lodge. Capturing the 1950s and 1960s era, Western Cabins, Frontier Cabins, Pioneer Cabins, and Economy Cabins offer simple motel accommodations with private baths.

The Canyon Lodge and Cabins are generally open from early June through mid-September with 609 available units. Prices for lodge rooms slightly exceed $100, while cabin prices range from approximately $50 to $100. All major credit cards are accepted.

Roosevelt Lodge Cabins
Named after Yellowstone enthusiast Theodore Roosevelt the Roosevelt Lodge Cabins are situated twenty-three miles from the North Entrance and twenty-nine miles from the Northeast Entrance in the beautiful Lamar Valley. Guests are greeted with a quiet, uncrowded atmosphere and family dining reminiscent of the Old West. Rustic cabins combine with the lodge's front porch rockers to transport guests back to simpler times, and Old West dinner cookouts, horseback rides, and stagecoach trips infuse a cowboy flavor into every stay.

Eighty cabins are available, sixty-two of which

are Roughrider Cabins. Each of these sparsely furnished cabins feature a woodburning stove, firewood, and nearby communal showers and bathrooms. Frontier Cabins offer a bit more privacy with their own bathroom and shower facilities. Cabins are generally available from early June through early September with prices ranging from approximately $40 to $80. All major credit cards are accepted.

Lake Lodge Cabins
Priding itself on offering a family-friendly atmosphere, Lake Lodge Cabins are tucked on Lake Yellowstone's shoreline amid glistening mountain peaks. Boasting a large lobby, Lake Lodge welcomes visitors with two fireplaces, a gift store, lounge, and reasonably priced cafeteria-style dining. 186 cabins await in two different styles. While the Western Cabins provide more modern furnishings in a motel style setting, the smaller Frontier Cabins retain much of their simple 1920s charm. All cabins feature private bathrooms with showers, toilets, and sinks. In addition to lake recreation, the area is lined with self-guided nature trails.

Lake Lodge Cabins are generally open from early June through late September. Prices average $50 to $100. All major credit cards are accepted.

Lake Yellowstone Hotel and Cabins
Constructed on the north side of Lake Yellowstone in 1891 and restored in 1990 to its 1920s grandeur, the Lake Yellowstone Hotel and Cabins are proudly listed on the National Register of Historic Places. Featuring an elegant Victorian atmosphere accented with porticos, ionic columns, and dormer windows, the Lake Yellowstone Hotel offers some of Yellowstone's most spacious and comfortable rooms. Guests are treated to amazing lake views, a large sunroom, a casual dining room offering an extensive menu, and a lobby that encourages visitors to relax to the strains of a classical pianist or string quartet. With three and four-story wings, the hotel provides a posh Presidential Suite and several premium rooms with a 1920s ambience. Adjacent to the hotel, a two-story annex offers modern furnishings. All rooms include private full baths.

The hotel also offers economically priced Frontier Cabins. Although these cabins were built during the 1920s, they were completely renovated in 2003 and 2004 to include simple, yet comfortable accommodations.

Equipped with 297 total units, the Lake Yellowstone Hotel and Cabins are open from late May through early October. General pricing averages $80 per cabin, $95 to $150 for premium and annex hotel rooms, and approximately $375 nightly for the Presidential Suite. All major credit cards are accepted.

Grant Village
Completed in 1984 and named after President Ulysses S. Grant, Grant Village is situated on Lake Yellowstone's southwestern shore and provides the most convenient access to neighboring Grand Teton National Park. The village complex offers six two-story chalets featuring comfortably appointed single and double rooms. The most expensive rooms provide stunning views of the lake and are worth the extra cost. Also located onsite are two restaurants, a lounge, gift shop, gas station, convenience store, and guest laundry facilities.

Grant Village's 300 rooms are available from late May through early October. Prices range from approximately $80 to $95. All major credit cards are accepted.

Old Faithful Lodge Cabins

Featuring a one-story 1920s main lodge showcasing impressively large logs and stone pillars, Old Faithful Lodge Cabins offers stunning views of the famous Old Faithful geyser while providing an economical lodging option. Budget Cabins are sparsely furnished with beds and sinks and require guests to use communal showers and bathrooms. Just slightly more expensive and much more private, Frontier Cabins feature basic motel accommodations along with individual bathrooms. In addition to lodging, the area is home to a large lobby, a massive cafeteria, bakery, several snack shops, a large gift store, and an old gym that intermittently offers movies and dances.

Old Faithful Lodge Cabins provides 122 cabins (40 of which are Budget Cabins) that are generally open from early May through early October. Prices range from just over $30 to approximately $60. All major credit cards are accepted.

Old Faithful Snow Lodge and Cabins

Renowned as one of Yellowstone's finest full-service hotels, the Old Faithful Snow Lodge was completed in 1999 as a replacement for the old dormitory-style Snow Lodge demolished in 1998. The hotel features exterior log posts, cedar shingled rooflines, and heavy timber construction that accents the interior's western furnishings and fixtures. Spacious lodge rooms are adorned in tastefully appointed wildlife and Yellowstone Park themes and include private bathrooms. Recognized with Travel and Leisure's "Inn of the Month" distinction and the Cody Award for Western Design, the Old Faithful Snow Lodge also features the Bear Den Gift Store, a spacious dining room, the convenient Geyser Grill, and an inviting lounge complete with a two-sided fireplace.

At the lower end of the price scale, the onsite Western Cabins and Frontier Cabins are motel-style units comfortably furnished to include private bathrooms.

Old Faithful Snow Lodge and Cabins boasts 134 units with prices starting at just over $100 per cabin and approximately $125 for a lodge room. Lodge rooms and cabins are available year-round with summer reservations available from early May through late October. All major credit cards are accepted.

Old Faithful Inn

A National Historic Landmark featuring a rustic yet grand style, the Old Faithful Inn is located near the famous Old Faithful Geyser and is one of the park's most requested lodging facilities. Originally completed in 1904 under the design of Robert Reamer, the inn's seven stories feature a log and wood shingle exterior all contained under an impressively steep roofline. Although the hotel retains the original immense lobby and magnificent fireplace, the East and West Wings were added in the 1920s to accommodate more visitors. Most rooms have recently been remodeled, and an array of lodging options is available in a broad price range.

Suites include a well-appointed sitting room, refrigerator, two queen beds, and a private bathroom. The extra large semi-suites feature a sitting area, two queen beds, and private bathroom. Premium rooms are tastefully appointed with two double beds and a private bath, while high-range rooms were remodeled in 1998 to include modern furnishings and a small private bath. Mid-range rooms are simple but comfortable with a small bathroom. On the lower end of the price range, basic rooms feature a charming atmosphere and small sink with private showers located down the hall in a shared bathroom.

In addition to its lodging, the Old Faithful Inn is renowned for its interpretive tours, full-service restaurant, deli, and large gift shop.

The Old Faithful Inn provides 359 rooms generally from early May through mid-October. Visitors should note, however, that summer reservations are limited during the 2005 and 2006 summer season due to a large-scale renovation project. Room rates range from as low as $52 to more than $325 nightly. All major credit cards are accepted, and advance reservations are a must!

Camping in Yellowstone

In addition to standard hotel and cabin lodging, Yellowstone National Park provides visitors the chance to glimpse starry nights, wake up to the sound of chirping birds, and inhale the perfume of pine wafting through the air. Of the twelve campgrounds situated throughout the park, seven are first-come, first-served sites under the management of the National Park Service. These campgrounds include Indian Creek, Lewis Lake, Norris, Mammoth, Pebble Creek, Tower Fall, and Slough Creek. The remaining five campgrounds at Bridge Bay, Madison, Canyon, Fishing Bridge RV Park, and Grant Village are operated under Xanterra Parks and Resorts (Yellowstone's primary concessionaire) and may be reserved by calling (307) 344-7311 or visiting www.travelyellowstone.com. Campsites fill early, so plan to make reservations or arrive early at your destination campground.

While camping in Yellowstone, visitors are asked to follow a few simple rules. Camping in pullouts, parking areas, and picnic grounds is not permitted, and campers may only stay a total of fourteen days between June 15 and September 15. Respect your fellow campers; obey the 8 PM to 8 AM quiet hours (10 PM to 7 AM at Fishing Bridge RV Park) that prohibit loud music and generators. Checkout time is 10 AM for all park campgrounds. For those traveling in groups, group camping is available at the Grant, Madison, and Bridge Bay Campgrounds. Depending on the group's size, nightly fees range from $40-$70. Advance reservations for group camping are required.

The following provides an overview of each campground and the available amenities.

Bridge Bay: Open from late May through early September, Bridge Bay offers 430 total sites with no RV hookups. Amenities include a dump station, flush toilets, drinking water, fire pits, grills, and public phones. Reservations are accepted, and the nightly fee is $17.

Canyon: Open from June through September, Canyon provides 272 sites with no RV hookups. Amenities include a dump station, flush toilets, drinking water, showers, fire pits, grills, laundry facilities, and public phones. Reservations are accepted, and the nightly fee is $17.

Fishing Bridge: Open from late May through Labor Day Weekend, Fishing Bridge RV Park offers 341 total sites, and numerous RV hookups are available. Other amenities include a dump station, flush toilets, drinking water, showers, fire pits, grills, laundry facilities, and public phones. Reservations are accepted, and the nightly fee is $31.

Grant Village: Open from late May through September, Grant Village provides 425 sites with no RV hookups. Amenities include a dump station, flush toilets, drinking water, showers, fire pits, grills, laundry facilities, and public phones. Reservations are accepted, and the nightly fee is $17.

Indian Creek: Open from June through September, Indian Creek provides 75 sites with no RV hookups. Amenities include vault toilets, drinking water, fire pits, and grills. The nightly fee is $12.

Lewis Lake: Open from mid-June until November, Lewis Lake provides 85 sites with no RV hookups. Amenities include vault toilets, drinking water, fire pits, and grills. The nightly fee is $12.

Madison: Open from late May until November, Madison offers 280 sites with no RV hookups. Amenities include a dump station, flush toilets, drinking water, fire pits, grills, and public phones. Reservations are accepted, and the nightly fee is $17.

Mammoth: Open year-round, the Mammoth Campground provides 85 sites with no available RV hookups. Amenities include flush toilets, drinking water, fire pits, grills, and public phones. The nightly fee is $14.

A bison herd grazes in a meadow.

Norris: Open from mid-May through September, Norris offers 116 sites with no RV hookups. Amenities include flush toilets, drinking water, fire pits, grills, and public phones. The nightly fee is $14.

Pebble Creek: Open from mid-June through September, Pebble Creek offers 36 sites with no RV hookups. Amenities include vault toilets, drinking water, fire pits, and grills. The nightly fee is $12.

Slough Creek: Open from late May until November, Slough Creek provides 29 sites with no RV hookups. Amenities include vault toilets, drinking water, fire pits, and grills. The nightly fee is $12.

Tower Fall: Open from mid-May through late September, Tower Fall Campground offers 32 sites with no RV hookups. Amenities include vault toilets, drinking water, fire pits, and grills. The nightly fee is $12.

Dining in Yellowstone

Yellowstone may resemble a wilderness wonderland, but appearances can be deceiving. Despite its breathtaking natural wonders, Yellowstone is also commercialized just enough to meet visitors' basic needs. In addition to offering an array of lodging options, Yellowstone's primary concessionaire, Xanterra Parks and Resorts, provides unique in-park dining options sure to satisfy every palate. From casual fine dining in Yellowstone's legendary hotel dining rooms to delis and old western cookouts, every corner of Yellowstone is outfitted with an eatery to satiate your appetite. Box lunches, ideal for packing along on adventurous outings, are also available upon request from some of Yellowstone's delis. Reservations are accepted at some hotel dining rooms and are occasionally required for dinner dining. Visitors should expect higher prices in park dining rooms than the more economical cafeterias and snack shops. For additional information about park dining or reservations, call Xanterra Parks and Resorts at (307) 344-7901.

Canyon Village Area Dining

Yellowstone's Canyon Village visitors are treated to three different dining options, all of which are child friendly. The Canyon Lodge Dining Room offers the most upscale option, serving a phe-

nomenal salad bar along with steak, fish, chicken, and pasta in a relaxed dinner atmosphere. The dining room also serves breakfast and lunch on a first-come, first-served basis. For those in a hurry or on a budget, the Canyon Lodge Cafeteria serves up breakfast, lunch, and dinner quickly and casually. Also onsite, the Canyon Lodge Deli provides fresh deli sandwiches and other goodies ideal for picnic outings and meals on the run.

Canyon Village's dining areas are open from early June through mid-September. Reservations are not accepted, and the dress code is casual for all Canyon Village eateries. All major credit cards are accepted.

Grant Village Dining Room

Overlooking Yellowstone Lake, the Grant Village Dining Room specializes in delivering quality, ambience, and delicious food for breakfast, lunch, and dinner. An extensive breakfast buffet, specialty lunch sandwiches, and dinner items ranging from Huckleberry Chicken to regional cuisine are crowd favorites.

The Grant Village Dining Room is open from late May through early October with a casual dress code. Breakfast and lunch are served on a first-come, first-served basis, but reservations are required for dinner. All major credit cards are accepted.

Lake Lodge Cabins Cafeteria

Situated on the shores of Yellowstone Lake, the Lake Lodge Cabins Cafeteria is an ideal family dining option in a casual setting. Traditional American fare is served daily for breakfast, lunch, and dinner.

Lake Lodge Cabins Cafeteria is open from mid-June through late September with a casual dress code. Reservations are not accepted, as all meals are first-come, first-served. All major credit cards are accepted.

Lake Hotel Dining Room and Deli

Combining scenery with exquisite food, Yellowstone's Lake Hotel Dining Room and Deli is recognized as the park's most upscale dining facility. Providing breakfast, lunch, and dinner daily with views of glimmering Yellowstone Lake, the dining room treats guests to such specialties as Wild Alaskan Salmon, Certified Angus Beef

Steaks, Scallops, and much more. Although breakfast and lunch are served on a first-come, first-served basis, reservations are required for dinner. On the lower end of the price range, the onsite Lake Hotel Deli serves soup, made-to-order sandwiches, snacks, desserts, and a variety of beverages.

The Lake Hotel Dining Room and Deli are open from mid-May through mid-October with a casual dress code. Reservations are required for dinner in the dining room, but all other meals require no advance arrangements. All major credit cards are accepted at both facilities.

Mammoth Hotel Dining Room and Terrace Grille

Overlooking Old Fort Yellowstone's parade grounds and former officers' quarters, the Mammoth Hotel Dining Room serves a wide array of cuisine for breakfast, lunch, and dinner. An extensive breakfast buffet combines with creative lunch sandwiches and fine dinner cuisine that includes fresh fish and house-smoked specialties. For typical restaurant fare with more economical prices, the Terrace Grille serves breakfast, lunch, and dinner, with menu items including breakfast sandwiches, soups, salads, fast food, and ice cream.

Both the Mammoth Hotel Dining Room and Terrace Grille are open year-round with a summer season operating from mid-May through mid-October. All meals are served on a first-come, first-served basis during summer, and reservations are not accepted at either establishment. However, reservations are recommended during winter. The dress code is casual, and all major credit cards are accepted.

Old Faithful Inn Dining Room and Bear Paw Snack Shop

The majesty of Yellowstone's most famous inn is carried through to its dining room. The Old Faithful Inn Dining Room's famous stone fireplace is accented with an impressive painting depicting Yellowstone's most recognized geyser basin. Amid this ambience, diners are treated to hearty ala carte breakfast items, a large breakfast buffet, a western lunch buffet, salads, sandwiches, and a dinner menu featuring prime rib, pasta, fish, chicken, and more. For those in a hurry, the

Campground	Sites	Dates	Fee	Elev (ft)	Toilet	Showers/ Laundry Nearby	Dump Station	Generators Permitted (8 AM-8 PM)
Bridge Bay*	430	5/26-9/17	$15.00**	700	Flush		X	X
Canyon*	272	6/2-9/10	15.00**	8,000	Flush	X	X	X
Grant Village*	425	6/21-10/1	15.00**	7,800	Flush	X	X	X
Madison*	280	5/5-10/22	15.00**	6,800	Flush		X	X
Mammoth	85	All Year	12.00	6,200	Flush			X
Norris	116	5/19-9/25	12.00	7,500	Flush			X
Indian Creek	75	6/9-9/18	10.00	7,300	Vault			
Lewis Laki	85	6/23-11/5	10.00	7,800	Vault			
Pebble Creek	32	6/2-9/25	10.00	6,900	Vault			
Slough Creek	29	5/26-10/31	10.00	6,250	Vault			
Tower Fall	32	5/19-79/25	10.00'	6,600	Vault			
Fishing Bridge RV*	340	5/12-9/24	27.00"t	7,800	Flush	X	Sewer	X

*Reserve through Yellowstone National Park Lodges; call 307-344-7311 or TDD 307-344-5305.
**Plus sales tax
† 1-4 people
Dates are approximate and may change because of weather or resource management concerns.
Bridge Bay, Canyon, Grant Village, and Madison campgrounds all contain accessible sites.

Bear Paw Snack Shop is ideal, serving sandwiches, salads, and ice cream.

The Old Faithful Inn Dining Room, as well as the Bear Paw Snack Shop, are open mid-May through mid-October with a casual dress code. Although the dining room's breakfast and lunch are served on a first-come, first-served basis, dinner reservations are required. All major credits cards are accepted. Visitors should note that all Old Faithful Inn facilities offer limited summer service in 2005 and 2006 due to extensive remodeling.

Old Faithful Lodge Cafeteria and Bake Shop
Offering amazing views of the world-famous Old Faithful Geyser, the Old Faithful Lodge Cafeteria provides affordable, casual dining. A variety of hot entrees, sandwiches, salads, and pastas are served. For those craving something sweet, the Bake Shop specializes in freshly baked cinnamon rolls, muffins, cookies, and pretzels.

Both the Old Faithful Lodge Cafeteria and Bake Shop are open from early May through early October with a casual dress code. Reservations are not accepted, as all meals are served on a first-come, first-served basis.

Old Faithful Snow Lodge – Obsidian Dining Room and Geyser Grill

Opened in 1999, the Old Faithful Snow Lodge showcases a western ambiance in both the Obsidian Dining Room and the Geyser Grill. Maintaining a quieter atmosphere than other park dining rooms, the Obsidian Dining Room serves breakfast, lunch, and dinner with such specialties as Seafood Cioppino and Braised Lamb Shanks. The Geyser Grill is a less formal option for breakfast, lunch, and dinner with menu selections including breakfast sandwiches, deli items, and burgers.

The Obsidian Dining Room is open mid-May through mid-October for the summer season. Reservations are not accepted for any meal during the summer season but are recommended for dinner during winter season. The Geyser Grill is open mid-April through early November for the summer season. All meals are served on a first-come, first-served basis. Both establishments feature a casual dress code, and all major credit cards are accepted.

Roosevelt Lodge Dining Room and Western Cookouts

In an effort to maintain its reputable cowboy atmosphere, the Roosevelt Lodge Dining Room offers a more laid-back ambience and menu in comparison to the park's other dining options. Family-style breakfast, lunch, and dinner is served with menu items including such traditional western fare as baby-back ribs, fried chicken, and the famous Roosevelt Baked Beans.

For a unique western experience, make reservations at Roosevelt's Old West Dinner Cookouts. Guests enjoy a horseback or chuckwagon ride to the dinner site where everyone is treated to steak, potato salad, cornbread, coleslaw, Roosevelt Baked Beans, apple crisp, and cowboy coffee. Western entertainment accompanies the memorable dinner.

The Roosevelt Lodge Dining Room and Western Cookouts operate from mid-June through early September with a casual dress code. Although reservations are not accepted for the dining room, advance arrangements are recommended for the Western Cookouts. All major credit cards are accepted.

Rules and Regulations You Need to Know

Bicycling: Yellowstone is a popular destination for road bicyclists, and bicycling is allowed on maintained public roads, in parking areas, and on designated off-pavement bike routes. Bicyclists should note, however, that most of the park's highways are winding, narrow, and possess little to no shoulder. Bicycling is strictly prohibited on the park's boardwalks and backcountry trails.

Bicyclists should always be alert for vehicles and wear helmets along with highly visible clothing. Many motorists, especially large RVs with limited visibility, do not notice bicyclists on the road. Bicyclists should note that park drivers occasionally pass on blind corners or in oncoming traffic, which creates an additional hazard for riders. Additional information about biking in Yellowstone is available at park visitor centers.

Camping: In order to accommodate the growing number of visitors each year, individuals are only allowed to camp a total of fourteen days between June 15th and September 15th and no more than thirty total days in any given year. To protect wildlife and campers, food, garbage, cooking utensils, and toiletries must be stored in a locked vehicle or in a solid, airtight container. Backcountry users must contain these items (when not in use) in a bear bag at least ten feet above ground and five feet away from any trees.

Climbing: Amid Yellowstone's geysers and thermal features are several areas comprised of crumbling loose rock. For this reason, rock climbing is prohibited in Yellowstone's Grand Canyon, and rangers highly discourage climbing in all other park regions.

Falling Trees: While creating a charred black landscape, the 1988 fires also formed a new hazard for park visitors. Known as snags, thousands of dead trees were left precariously perched on Yellowstone's hills, ready to tumble without a moment's notice. Although many of these snags have already collapsed, a few dead trees remain standing. Visitors should always be alert for snags, particularly on roadways, backcountry trails, and in picnic areas and campgrounds. The park does not guarantee your safety and is not responsible for any negative incidents involving snags. Use your own best judgment.

Firearms: Although visitors may transport unloaded firearms through Yellowstone with a special permit when the weapons are cased and kept out of sight, loaded and operable firearms are not permitted (including state-permitted concealed weapons). Any ammunition for unloaded firearms must also be stored away from the weapons.

Littering: Visitors are reminded to be respectful of others and follow "Leave No Trace" ethics. If you bring something into the park, be sure to pack it out. Littering is not only unsightly, but it is also strictly prohibited. Throwing coins or any other object into mud pots, geysers, and thermal pools is also subject to a stiff fine.

Motorcycles and ATVs: All motorcycles, motorbikes, and power scooters must be licensed, and operators must possess a valid driver's license. These vehicles are required to stay on park highways at all times, and backcountry ATV and motorcycle use is prohibited.

Natural Souvenirs: Be a respectful park visitor, and leave as little impact on Yellowstone's landscape as possible. It is against the law to remove or destruct any park feature. Refrain from picking any flowers, removing even the smallest rock, or pocketing any part of Yellowstone. The park is not for personal possession; it is a national treasure that law requires all to share.

Picnic Areas: Yellowstone's picnic areas are designated for just that – picnicking. Overnight camping is prohibited in these areas. Most of the park's picnic grounds feature pit toilets, but visitors should plan ahead as none offer drinking water. Fires are only allowed in the fire pits found at the following picnic areas: Grant Village, Snake River, Cascade, Norris Meadows, Bridge Bay, Yellowstone River, Nez Perce, Spring Creek, and Old Faithful's east parking lot. At all other picnic grounds, fires are forbidden, but portable camp stoves are allowed.

Pets: If possible, leave your pets at home. For obvious reasons, pets in Yellowstone must be leashed and are forbidden in the backcountry, on park trails, on boardwalks, and in thermal regions. All pets, regardless of size, must be kept at least 100 feet from roads and parking areas, and it is against the law to leave any pet unattended or tied to a park object.

Smoking: Smoking is strictly forbidden in all of Yellowstone National Park's public areas, visitor centers, and ranger stations. In addition, smoking is not allowed in thermal areas. Ashes from cigarette butts could potentially ignite sulfur deposits, resulting in dangerous and even lethal gasses. For the safety of yourself and other visitors, refrain!

Snowmobiles: Snowmobiles must be registered in accordance with state law, and all snowmobile operators must possess a valid driver's license. Noise from snowmobile exhaust systems must register under 78 decibels in order to gain entry to the park. Snowmobiles must also stay on designated roads and follow all posted speed limits. The maximum speed limit is 45 miles per hour (72 kilometers per hour).

Swimming/Soaking: Although some of Yellowstone's springs may look inviting, appearances are deceiving; most of the park's hot springs can cause second and third degree burns - even death. For the safety of all visitors, swimming, soaking, or simply dipping your feet in thermal attractions is forbidden. The only exception is the "Boiling River" near Mammoth. Here, runoff from Yellowstone's springs provides a naturally warm soaking spot that is open year-round from 5 AM to 6 PM.

Visitors are also discouraged from swimming in Yellowstone Lake. The lake often possesses hazardously cold water temperatures, and unpredictable area weather can create dangerous conditions. If you have any questions about swimming or soaking in Yellowstone, contact a park ranger.

Traffic: Although Yellowstone features more than 350 miles of highway (564 kilometers), most roads are routinely jam-packed full of summer traffic. Drivers are urged to use caution at all times as many of the roads are narrow or steep with some featuring sharp drop-offs. Slow-moving vehicles or drivers interested in looking at Yellowstone's wildlife and scenery must use the park pullouts so as not to interrupt traffic flow.

Drivers are also reminded to watch for wildlife, bicyclists, and motorcyclists. Drive defensively, wear seat belts, and always obey the posted speed limits. Speeding tickets in the park are notoriously hefty, and rangers continuously patrol the roads.

THE GRIZZLY BEAR

NPS Photo

The Yellowstone ecosystem provides vital habitat for grizzlies in its two national parks (Yellowstone and Grand Teton), six national forests, state lands, and private lands. Some bears live either totally inside or outside of Yellowstone National Park; others may use portions of various different agency holdings.

Because grizzly bears range widely and are usually solitary, they are difficult to count. Biologists estimate their population within the Yellowstone ecosystem to be 280-610 bears.

The Yellowstone ecosystem is unique among areas inhabited by grizzly bears in North America because of the foods it provides. Here, grizzly bears depend more on animals, ranging from ants and moths to elk and bison. Bears here and elsewhere also eat large amounts of plants, but Yellowstone lacks the lush vegetation and berries found in northern Montana.

When Yellowstone grizzly bears emerge from hibernation in March and April, there is still a lot of snow and very little vegetation in most of the park. The bears move to the low country where elk and other ungulates (hoofed mammals) spent the winter. There, the bears feed on carcasses of ungulates that died during the winter. (Never approach a carcass-a bear may be nearby and it will often defend its food source.) Bears are not the only animal that depends on winter-killed ungulates for survival. Wolves, coyotes, wolverines, badgers, foxes, eagles, ravens, magpies, and carrion beetles also feed on the carcasses.

Grizzly bears prey on elk calves in the spring, usually from mid-May through early July. After early July, most elk calves can outrun bears. Some bears will feed on spawning cutthroat trout in the Yellowstone Lake area during the early summer. Bears also dig for small rodents (primarily pocket gophers), ants, roots, and tubers. Later in the summer, grizzly bears feed on army cutworm moths and whitebark pine nuts at high elevations. Despite their small size, these foods are important, high-protein foods for grizzly bears, especially as autumn approaches.

The restoration of wolves to the park appears to be providing bears more opportunities to obtain meat. During the years since the 1995 release of wolves into the park, bears have been observed successfully taking wolf-killed ungulates away from wolf packs. Will this new opportunity increase the grizzly bear population in Yellowstone? No one knows.

Wildlife: For many park tourists, Yellowstone's wildlife is unlike anything they have ever seen. As tempting as it is to approach the animals for a perfect picture, park law mandates that no individual may approach a bear within 100 yards and must keep a distance of at least 25 yards from other park wildlife. Feeding wildlife and making artificial animal calls are also prohibited. While viewing wildlife, keep in mind that if your presence causes an animal to stir, you are most likely too close. Always maintain a safe distance for your protection and that of the animals!

Visitor Information Stations, Museums, Research Centers, and Backcountry Stations

Throughout Yellowstone, sightseers will find an array of visitor centers, museums, research facilities, and backcountry offices. All visitors are encouraged to stop by these facilities, ask questions, and learn more about the nation's first national park.

Albright Visitor Center and Museum (Mammoth): Constructed by the U.S. Cavalry in the early 1900s as part of Fort Yellowstone, the Albright Visitor Center and Museum represents Yellowstone's largest information center. Formerly housing bachelor officers' quarters, the Albright Visitor Center now houses regional history and general park information. Visitors will find exhibits and displays regarding Native Americans, mountain men, exploration parties, the presence of the U.S. Cavalry, and the establishment of the National Park Service. A wildlife display on the second floor is complemented with the Moran Gallery and Jackson Gallery. These galleries showcase reproductions of painter Thomas Moran and original 1871 park photographs from William Henry Jackson.

The center also includes a theater where rangers show the films The Challenge of Yellowstone and Thomas "Yellowstone" Moran every half hour during the summer. Films are also presented upon request during winter. The visitor center is open 365 days a year with extended summer hours running through September. The Division of Resource Management and Visitor Protection also utilizes the Albright Center each summer to maintain a backcountry office. This office provides backcountry visitor permits for boating, fishing, and camping. Call (307) 344-2263.

Old Faithful Visitor Center (Old Faithful): Nestled just 200 yards from Old Faithful Geyser between the Old Faithful Inn and the Old Faithful Lodge, the Old Faithful Visitor Center provides general visitor information, a bookstore, and geyser eruption projections. The center features captivating views of Old Faithful and also offers multiple daily showings of the short film Yellowstone Revealed in a 100-seat auditorium. During summer and winter seasons, rangers lead educational evening programs, and a large selection of Yellowstone merchandise and souvenirs is available. The center is also home to a backcountry office, medical clinic, ranger station, and a district library. The center is open daily with extended summer hours. Call (307) 545-2750.

Grant Village Visitor Center (Grant Village south of West Thumb): The Grant Village Visitor Center draws its name from President Ulysses S. Grant, who signed Yellowstone National Park into existence in 1872. Established during the 1970s on the shore of Yellowstone Lake's West Thumb, the

visitor center houses general park information, a bookstore, and a unique exhibit that explores the role of fire in shaping Yellowstone's landscape. The center is open daily 9 AM to 6 PM from the park's spring/summer opening through early October. Call (307) 242-2650 for additional information.

Grant Village Backcountry Office (Grant Village Area): Located approximately 0.75 miles from Grant Village Junction on the Grant Village Road, this backcountry office is occasionally staffed during the spring and fall to provide visitors with backcountry permits. The office is only open when the Grant Village Visitor Center is closed.

West Thumb Information Station (West Thumb): Located inside a historic cabin, the West Thumb Information Station serves as summer visitor headquarters for ranger-led park walks and discussions. In winter, the log cabin is transformed into a warming hut where winter recreationists can browse through history exhibits. A variety of park merchandise is also available for purchase onsite. The station is open daily from 9 AM to 5 PM.

Canyon Visitor Center (Canyon Village): Situated just 1/8 mile southeast of Canyon Junction, the Canyon Visitor Center opened in 1957 to provide general park information and a bookstore. Once home to extensive Yellowstone geology displays, the center's current primary exhibit pertains to the region's bison. In June 2004, the visitor center was partially demolished for the reconstruction of a new facility slated to open in Spring 2006. A temporary center is located nearby, and plans are currently being made to incorporate a permanent geology display in the new center. The center is open 9 AM to 5 PM daily from the park's spring/summer opening through early October. Call (307) 242-2550 for additional information.

In addition, the Canyon Visitor Center hosts a ranger station and backcountry office under the direction of the Division of Resource Management and Visitor Protection. The office distributes first-aid assistance, backcountry permits, and float-tube permits.

Norris Geyser Basin Museum (Norris Junction): A National Historic Landmark dating back to 1929, the Norris Geyser Basin Museum features a staffed information desk, bookstore, and several exhibits on Yellowstone's geothermal wonders. Visitors are also treated to the museum's impressive stone and log architectural accents, a design that inspired numerous park buildings across America. The museum is open 9 AM to 5 PM daily from the park's spring/summer opening through early October. Call (307) 344-2812 for additional information.

Museum of the National Park Ranger (Norris): Constructed in 1908 as an outpost for patrolling soldiers, the Museum of the National Park Ranger is situated near the Norris Campground entrance. Although the structure has been rebuilt, it still features several of the original building materials and the original floorplan. Inside, visitors are treated to exhibits and a video tracing the history of the National Park Service and the life and duties of park rangers. Retired National Park Service employees voluntarily staff the museum and are happy to field visitor questions. The museum is open 9 AM to 5 PM daily from the park's opening through late September.

Fishing Bridge Museum and Visitor Center (East Entrance Road): The Fishing Bridge Museum and Visitor Center is situated on the East Entrance

Yellowstone

Road just one mile off the Grand Loop Road. A National Historic Landmark dating back to 1931, the Fishing Bridge Museum provides exhibits on Yellowstone's birds and wildlife, general park information, and a bookstore. The center is open 9 AM to 6 PM daily from the park's spring/summer opening through early October. Call (307) 242-2450 for additional information.

Lake and Bridge Bay Backcountry Offices (Lake and Bridge Bay): Under the operation of the Division of Resource Management and Visitor Protection, the Lake and Bridge Bay Ranger Stations distribute general park information, backcountry permits, and boating permits.

Madison Information Station (Madison Junction): The Madison Information Station, located near the Madison Picnic Area, was constructed in 1929 and is now a National Historic Landmark. Previously a museum, site of the Arts Yellowstone program, and intermittently abandoned, the Madison Information Station attained its current role in 1995. The station provides general park information and a bookstore. The site also reportedly rests near the campfire circle of the legendary Washburn-Langford-Doane exploration party. The station is open 9 AM to 5 PM daily from the park's spring/summer opening through early October.

Tower Ranger Station (Tower Junction): Constructed in 1923 and modeled after the 1907 Tower Soldier Station, the Tower Ranger Station is under the operation of the Division of Resource Management and Visitor Protection. The station distributes backcountry and fishing permits.

Lamar Ranger Station (Buffalo Ranch): Built at the dawn of the twentieth century, the Lamar Ranger Station is listed on the National Register of Historic Places. Primarily serving as the home base for the presiding Lamar Valley Ranger, the station also provides emergency visitor services when needed.

Northeast Entrance Ranger Station (Northeast Entrance Road): This National Historic Landmark was built in 1934 and is now under the direction of the Division of Resource Management and Visitor Protection. The station issues backcountry permits.

Yellowstone Heritage and Research Center: Recently opened, the Yellowstone Heritage and Research Center contains a museum, archives, and library that trace and preserve the history of America's first national park. Featuring over 200,000 items, the museum includes artifacts with exhibits related to natural science, geology, archaeology, paleontology, ethnology, biology, park flora and fauna, and fossils. The museum also features a historic park vehicle collection, historic park hotel furnishings, original Thomas Moran artwork, and over 80,000 historic park photos.

Affiliated with the National Archives, the center's archives date back to the park's U.S. Army administration and include more than 1,400 linear feet of records. The archives also house historic film clips, oral tapes, and park-related audio and videotapes.

The center's research library boasts a rare book collection, numerous manuscripts, and more than 10,000 volumes of information pertaining to park history.

The Yellowstone Heritage and Research Center is open by appointment Tuesday through Friday from 8 AM to 5 PM. All holdings must remain onsite to protect and maintain the park's prized collection.

HIKING AND CAMPING IN BEAR COUNTRY

Although the risk of an encounter with a bear is low, there are no guarantees of your safety. Minimize your risks by following the guidelines below.

A Fed Bear is a Dead Bear

Do not leave packs containing food unattended, even for a few minutes. Allowing a bear to obtain human food even once often results in the bear becoming aggressive about obtaining such food in the future. Aggressive bears present a threat to human safety and eventually may be destroyed or removed from the park.

While Hiking

Make bears aware of your presence on trails by making loud noises, shouting, or singing. This lessens the chance of sudden encounters, which are the cause of most bear-caused human injuries in the park. Hike in groups and use caution where vision is obstructed. Do not hike after dark. Avoid carcasses; bears often defend this source of food.

If You Encounter a Bear

Do not run. Bears can run 30 mph (48 kph), or 44 feet/second (13 m/second), which is faster than Olympic sprinters. Running may elicit an attack from an otherwise nonaggressive bear. If the bear is unaware of you, keep out of sight and detour behind and downwind of the bear. If the bear is aware of you and nearby, but has not acted aggressively, slowly back away.

Tree climbing to avoid bears is popular advice, but not very practical in many circumstances. All black bears, all grizzly cubs, and some adult grizzlies can climb trees. Plus, running to a tree may provoke an otherwise uncertain bear to chase you.

If A Bear Charges or Approaches You

Do not run. Some bears will bluff their way out of a threatening situation by charging, then veering off or stopping abruptly at the last second. Bear experts generally recommend standing still until the bear stops and then slowly backing away. If you are attacked, lie on the ground completely flat. Spread your legs and clasp your hands over the back of your neck. Another alternative is to play dead: drop to the ground, lift your legs up to your chest, and clasp your hands over the back of your neck.

When Camping

Never camp in an area that has obvious evidence of bear activity such as digging, tracks, scat, or where animal carcasses are present.

Odors attract bears. Avoid carrying or cooking odorous foods or other products. Keep a clean camp; do not cook or store food in your tent. All food, garbage, or other odorous items used for preparing or cooking food must be secured from bears. Hang all such items at least 10 feet (3 m) above the ground and at least 4 feet (1.2 m) out from tree trunks. Treat all odorous products such as soap, deodorant, or toiletries in the same manner as food.

Sleep a minimum of 100 yards (91m) from where you hang, cook, and eat your food. Keep your sleeping gear clean and free of food odor. Don't sleep in the same clothes worn while cooking and eating; hang those clothes in plastic bags.

Trip Checklist

In order to ensure the most successful and enjoyable trip to Yellowstone, visitors should plan ahead and take into account the following travel suggestions.

- Plan your trip and the features you want to see in accordance with the park's opening and closing road schedule. Most roads are accessible to vehicles as early as May 1, but some do open later. Check with the Park Service prior to setting your trip dates.

- Be prepared for road construction, and avoid stressing about unexpected delays. Yellowstone's website (www.nps.gov/yell/) provides links to the latest road construction reports for travelers' convenience.

- Worried about the weather or road conditions? An informational hotline provides current weather and road reports for Yellowstone's major regions. Call (307) 344-7381 for additional information.

- Familiarize yourself with the park's regulations and fees prior to your arrival. This will help you realistically budget your Yellowstone vacation expenses and ensure that you do not unknowingly violate park laws.

- Lodging has the ability to make or break your trip, so plan accordingly. Since the park receives over three million visitors each year, reserve your lodging as early as possible.

- If your travels involve camping within the park or near Yellowstone's boundaries, arrive as early as possible on the night of your stay in order to secure a site. After claiming your spot for the night, then continue your day's sightseeing.

- Yellowstone's weather can be unpredictable in all seasons. All visitors are encouraged to pack and wear clothes that can easily be layered. Even during the summer, cold temperatures are inevitable, so make sure to bring a jacket. Also, due to the area's high elevations and thinner atmosphere, pack and use sunscreen to avoid unpleasant burns.

- Be prepared for emergencies at all times, especially when hiking Yellowstone's trails. All visitors are urged to pack along extra food, clothing, a first-aid kit, water, and matches.

- Last but not least, remember your camera. Yellowstone is brimming with photo opportunities you will definitely want to capture!

The Seasons of Yellowstone: Weather & Climate

Summer's radiant sunlit skies suddenly cloud with expressions of thunderstorm fury. Light breezes rage into gale force winds. Pelting sleet takes early autumn visitors by surprise. In a nutshell, unpredictability is the name of the weather game in Yellowstone and the surrounding region. Although frequently changing weather conditions can certainly interfere with previously arranged travel plans, visitors who are armed with knowledge about Yellowstone's seasons should be able to enjoy the region's climate with little hassle.

Spring

The arrival of spring may signal warm weather in many parts of America, but in Yellowstone, be prepared for snow. Cold temperatures and snowstorms can remain frequent guests into April and May, and late spring snowstorms have often dumped more than a foot of snow in just 24 hours during these months. Although actual temperatures can vary drastically from regional norms, average daytime temperatures reach 40 to 50 degrees Fahrenheit (5-15 C) in early spring with readings gradually rising into the 60s and 70s (15-25 C). During the evenings, expect lows anywhere from the single digits to just above freezing.

As a result of these widely divergent temperature readings, spring visitors should be ready for all types of weather. Always pack along a warm jacket, rain gear, sturdy walking shoes, and a layered clothing system. It never hurts to bring along a warm hat and gloves in case of an unexpected snow flurry.

Summer

Summer undeniably provides the park's most comfortable temperatures with nearly non-existent humidity. Since Yellowstone never truly experiences extreme heat, summer visitors are treated to July daytime highs typically in the mid 70s (25 C) with lower elevations sometimes hitting the mid 80s (30 C). Despite the pleasant daytime readings, summer evenings are cool. Depending on the elevation of your destination, nighttime temperatures average between 30 and 40 degrees Fahrenheit (0-10 C) but may drop into the low 20s (-5 C). As with many western regions, summer afternoon thunderstorms are common. In the event of lightning, move away from water and beaches, lone trees, and exposed ridges.

During the summer, visitors are encouraged to wear sturdy walking shoes, slather on the sunscreen, dress in a layered garment system, and bring along a light jacket, waterproof shell, and an umbrella.

Autumn

Autumn weather in Yellowstone can be just as pleasant as summer during its early arrival. During mid-autumn, visitors can expect daytime average temperatures of 40 to 60 degrees Fahrenheit (5-20 C) with overnight lows in the teens and single digits. As the season progresses, snowstorms occur more frequently and increase in intensity as winter draws near. Sudden storms during late autumn are almost assured, so those visiting the park or Yellowstone's backcountry should pack extra clothing.

Like spring visitors, autumn travelers need to be prepared all weather patterns. Wear layered clothing and sturdy walking shoes, and always pack along a warm jacket, rain gear, hat, and gloves.

Winter

Winter is by far Yellowstone's longest and coldest season, but prepared visitors should still be able to enjoy the park's beauty with careful planning. Daytime temperatures often remain in the single digits, but on occasion, may climb to 20 degrees Fahrenheit (-5 C). Frigid nighttime readings dip well below zero. The coldest temperature ever recorded was –66 degrees Fahrenheit (-54 C) on February 9, 1933 near the park's West Entrance. At the other extreme, however, winter occasionally takes a break with the presence of warm Chinook winds that force the temperatures into the 40s and 50s. Average snowfall throughout the park is a moderate 150 inches (380 centimeters), while higher elevations often receive annual dumps in excess of 400 inches (5 to 10 meters).

As a result of its famous fluffy powder, Yellowstone's wintry landscape attracts hundreds of touring snowmobiles, snowcoaches, skiers, and snowshoe enthusiasts. Winter visitors should plan accordingly with weather forecasts and wind chill predictions. Wear a layered garment system that includes fleece underwear, vests, heavy shirts and coats, gloves, warm socks that wick away moisture, and heavy-duty boots. Always carry extra clothing, and recognize that even the proper gear may not be enough to protect you in a severe winter storm.

Yellowstone's Roads

Yellowstone's road system loops more than 350 miles through the park as it carries visitors to every major Yellowstone attraction. Although traffic jams and construction create less than ideal driving conditions, they are a perennial occurrence that all summer drivers must be ready to face. Patience is key in driving on Yellowstone's roads, so maintain your cool to ensure your safety and that of other visitors. For the latest in construction related road closures, visit Yellowstone on the web at www.nps.gov/yell/planvisit/orientation/travel/roadclos.htm.

Driving Yellowstone: Private Vehicles and Commercial Tours

Although private tours were historically the only means of traversing Yellowstone's unique terrain, today's visitors enjoy the luxury and convenience of creating their own touring schedule while using their personal vehicles. Most of Yellowstone's visitors opt to use their private automobiles, motorcycles, or bicycles to tour the park's major attractions. A few, however, prefer to let someone else drive.

Although no free public transportation is available in the park, those too nervous to drive Yellowstone's winding roads may take advantage of the Xanterra Parks and Resorts bus tours. Operating during the summer season only, these tours allow patrons to choose from a Lower Loop Tour, Upper Loop Tour, or the Grand Loop Tour. The Lower Loop tour departs daily in the southern portion of the park while the Upper Loop Tour departs from Canyon Lodge, Lake Hotel, and Fishing Bridge RV Park on an explorative journey of northern park regions. The Grand Loop Tour, which travels to all the park's major attractions in a single day, starts and ends its tours at both the Mammoth Hot Springs Hotel and in Gardiner, Montana. During the winter, Xanterra Parks and Resorts welcomes snow lovers to experience snowcoach tours departing from various points throughout the park. Those interested in a tour should make advance reservations.

In addition to the park-sponsored tours, several regional commercial businesses offer summer scenic tours, winter snowcoach tours, and snowmobile excursions. Other businesses provide winter bus transportation on the road linking Mammoth Hot Springs and Cooke City.

General Seasonal Road Opening and Closing Dates

The following is a general listing of Yellowstone's seasonal road conditions and openings, barring road construction or unexpected weather events. For additional information, visit Yellowstone's website at www.nps.gov/yell/planvisit/orientation/travel/roads.htm.

Spring: Road crews usually begin plowing Yellowstone's highways in early March. Although late spring storms may cause temporary road closures or delay a particular road's opening, most park routes generally open around the same time each year. In mid-April, the Mammoth to Norris, Norris to Madison, and West Yellowstone to Old Faithful routes open, while the South and East Entrances typically open in early May. Other park roads or regional routes leading to the park, such as the Beartooth Highway between Cooke City and Red Lodge, Montana, generally open on or before Memorial Day Weekend.

Summer: All park roads are typically open throughout the summer season. The only exceptions include roads closed for necessary construction or those routes temporarily barred due to accidents, rockslides, or mudslides.

Autumn: Although most routes are open, autumn ushers in the final wave of road construction. Routes closed due to road construction are often more frequent during autumn than summer, as crews sometimes wait to begin and finish work after the busy summer tourist season has ended. Autumn visitors may also encounter roads requiring snow tires/chains and closed routes due to early snowstorms. Depending on the year's climate and predicted weather patterns, major park routes close to vehicle travel in late October or early November. The only exception is the year-round route connecting Gardiner and Cooke City, Montana.

Winter: Tourists interested in visiting Yellowstone during the winter are either relegated to the vehicle route linking Cooke City and Gardiner, Montana or to snowcoach and snowmobile tours traveling on designated routes throughout the park. The winter season for snowcoach and snowmobile travel generally runs from mid-December to mid-March, and roads are specifically groomed for these vehicles. Off-road/trail travel is strictly prohibited.

Respecting Yellowstone with Wilderness Ethics

Trash. Trampled flowers. Eroded trails. Polluted lakes. Such images certainly stir up negative feelings, and few would appreciate finding such conditions amid Yellowstone's abundant wonders. However, the acts of just a few careless individuals could create these and worse conditions for the nation's first national park. In an effort to keep wildlife safe and preserve the park for the enjoyment of future generations, Yellowstone visitors are urged to follow wilderness ethics at all times.

What are wilderness ethics? Very simply, they are a set of guidelines designed to instill appreciation of America's wildest and most pristine places. Do your part to respect Yellowstone, and keep in mind the following principles on your next park visit.

The Rule of Positive Impact

When the concept of "Positive Impact" was first introduced, it simply asked visitors to leave only footprints during their travels and take nothing away from the site but pictures. Today, the "Leave No Trace" concept takes into account a growing number of wilderness and national park users, asking visitors to actually leave their destination in better condition than they found it. If you find litter in Yellowstone, pick it up to enhance the area's beauty for the next visitor. You'll feel good that you did, and those following in your footsteps will appreciate your effort.

Avoid Feeding Wildlife

No matter how you look at it, feeding Yellowstone's wildlife is hazardous to both humans and wildlife. While some of Yellowstone's mammals and birds have been habituated to beg for food, feeding the animals only perpetuates the harmful situation. Human food does not possess the nutrients upon which wild animals are dependent, and the animals then become subject to malnourishment, disease, and eventually death. Animals who become dependent upon human food also lose their innate hunting abilities, making winter survival nearly impossible.

Animals, however, are not the only ones adversely affected by feeding the wildlife. Humans that do feed Yellowstone's mammals and small rodents are more susceptible to animal bites and disease. Rabies can be potentially lethal if not treated, and rodents (such as squirrels and chipmunks) have been found with fleas carrying the bubonic plague. Although instances of humans contracting the plague are rare, they have occurred. Think twice about wildlife feedings!

Respect Yellowstone's Bears with Proper Food Storage
Although most people maintain a healthy respect for bears, this wilderness ethic goes far beyond fearing bears and their powerful abilities. To truly respect Yellowstone's bears, visitors must think about the bear's protection. A bear that successfully raids a campsite and enjoys a feast of human food sets off a negative chain of events. Bears are smart, and they will quickly link food with humans and campgrounds. Bears will then frequent campsites, creating unfortunate encounters with humans. If the behavior persists, rangers have no choice but to move the bear to a new habitat. In the event that a food-conditioned bear injures a visitor, rangers must then destroy the animal.

Respect the natural cycle of life, and avoid bear encounters with proper food storage etiquette. In maintained campsites, place food, toiletries, and garbage in your car trunk. In the backcountry, utilize backcountry storage boxes, or hang your food and garbage at least ten feet off the ground. Respect bears' amazing sense of smell, and never store food or toiletries in or near your tent.

Follow the Trail

As tempting as it may be to veer off the trail into the wilds of Yellowstone with nothing but a compass, this situation wreaks havoc on the landscape and is dangerous to your health. The park maintains established trails for a reason, and those who refuse to follow the trail compromise other area users' enjoyment. Protect Yellowstone's beauty, and stay on the trail at all times. Never shortcut a trail, especially on switchbacks. Shortcutting switchbacks disturbs area vegetation and eventually leads to erosion and hillside scarring. Those who abandon the trail are also more likely to suffer injury or get lost in the backcountry. Follow the trail!

Avoid Picking Wildflowers

A rug of wildflowers carpets Yellowstone's landscape with color and beauty every May through September. This mosaic of natural jewels often tempts visitors to pick a few blossoms, even though the flowers quickly whither when removed from their natural environment. What few people realize, however, is that these wildflowers play an integral role in sustaining a fragile ecosystem. At Yellowstone's high elevations, wildflowers possess just a brief moment in time to set their seeds. If the plants are removed prior to scattering their seeds, the natural process is disturbed. Annuals may not reproduce, and this in turn limits animals' food supply. Refrain from disrupting nature's cycle, and allow others to experience the beauty of Yellowstone's wildflowers.

Don't Pick or Eat the Vegetation

As with park wildflowers, refrain from picking other plant species in the park and surrounding region. Numerous varieties of poisonous plants and berries grow in Yellowstone, so it is unwise to eat any of the park's vegetation. In an emergency scenario, pick and eat only plants and berries you can positively identify with no hesitation.

Protect Yellowstone's Water

Water is one of the earth's most precious resources, and Yellowstone's lakes, rivers, and streams deserve the utmost care from their users. Whether you are in the backcountry or at a heavily visited site, protect Yellowstone's water by camping, disposing of waste, and washing dishes a minimum of 100 feet away from the shoreline. Never use soap (even those labeled biodegradable) in or near Yellowstone's water. Picnickers are urged to limit the spread of resource damage around lakeshores and rivers; picnic at previously used sites instead of opting for pristine sites. If possible, picnic on a boulder rather than on vegetated land.

Observe Park Rules

Park rules in Yellowstone are inherently designed to correspond with wilderness ethics. Refrain from violating park law, (such as removing rocks or breaking off tree limbs), and as a result, you will be following the basic tenets of wilderness ethics.

Refrain From Building

For those disposed to building with Mother Nature's materials, refrain from constructing creations in Yellowstone. Do not build rock cairns, assemble fire rings, or pile brush for a softer sleeping area. Although your intentions may be innocent, these structures grace the landscape long after your departure and affect how future visitors view the site. As always, leave no trace of your visit.

Maintain a Lead Free Environment

For over a decade, Yellowstone has followed a lead-free fishing policy. As of 1994, anglers are no longer allowed to use lead-weighted ribbon, leaded split-shot sinkers, or any other tackle equipment containing lead. Yellowstone's wildlife, particularly swans, loons, and shorebirds, are susceptible to lead poisoning. Protect Yellowstone's creatures with a lead-free fishing experience.

Refrain from Backcountry Bicycling
As in other wilderness areas across the country, bicycles are viewed as non-primitive modes of transportation. Refrain from impacting the fragile backcountry with your bike, and remain on designated routes and public roads where biking is permitted.

Cooking Stoves Versus Fires

Although small campfires are occasionally permitted in Yellowstone's backcountry in pre-established fire rings, park rangers wholeheartedly endorse the wilderness principle of lighting cook stoves, not fires. Unlike clean-burning cook stoves, fires scar the land, present a hazard during drought conditions, tarnish the sky with smoke, and pollute rivers, streams, and lakes. Maintain Yellowstone's health and vibrant ecosystem, and refrain from lighting campfires.

Visitor Precautions

Daily life involves following a basic set of precautions to ensure longevity, but a visit to Yellowstone comes with its own set of safety rules. Always be aware of the dangers described below, and know what to do in hazardous situations. It could mean the difference between a memorable vacation and one you would rather forget!

Wildlife

One of Yellowstone's greatest attractions is its diverse wildlife. However, wildlife is inherently unpredictable, and all species are capable of causing serious harm to visitors. Buffalo may appear to possess a relaxed, slow-moving nature, but they are actually very aggressive. Every year, tourists approach bison too closely, and as a result, severe injuries occur. Other large animals, such as elk, moose, deer, and bears, also pose a threat to your safety, and animals with their young in tow can be especially hostile. Never approach wildlife, and remember that park regulations prohibit advancing within 100 yards of bears and 25 yards of all other wildlife. For the safety of everyone, take wildlife photos from the protection of your vehicle.

Rattlesnakes

Park visitors rarely spot rattlesnakes, but the poisonous snake does reside in Yellowstone's northwestern corner near Gardiner, Montana. Reaching up to four feet long with a rattle on their tail, rattlesnakes bear brown skin with dark splotches. Most rattlesnakes will retreat unless threatened, but a bite can be fatal to humans if not treated quickly and properly. Visitors should be especially careful near rocky areas, as snakes frequently sun themselves on rocky ledges. If you hear a rattle, stop and slowly move in the opposite direction of the sound. If you are bitten, immobilize the area, and immediately seek medical attention. All rattlesnake sightings should be reported to the nearest ranger station.

Other snakes in the park include the rubber boa, the valley garter, and the wandering garter. All of these snakes, which generally never exceed three feet long, are the most likely snakes to be seen in Yellowstone. They are all harmless.

Ticks

Ticks and tick-borne illnesses are rarely reported in Yellowstone, but visitors should still be aware of ticks, the diseases they carry, and protection methods. Ticks carry and transmit Lyme disease, which can create severe problems when the disease is advanced. To protect yourself from ticks, spray an insect repellent containing DEET directly onto your clothes. Wear light-colored clothes so as to easily spot ticks, and frequently check for ticks on your clothing, skin, and scalp. Remember that ticks' primary habitats are grassy areas situated at 4,000 to 6,500 feet above sea level. Although ticks are most commonly found between March and mid-July, a few do linger into fall. Practice precaution in all seasons.

Thermal Pools and Geysers

Every year, a few reports stream in about careless or foolhardy Yellowstone tourists tragically burned in the park's thermal pools. Do not join the ranks of these headlines! Yellowstone's thermal pools and streams are extremely hot and are generally acidic or alkaline. The park's thermal features also often contain microscopic organisms capable of causing infections or even death.

To avoid an untimely fate, always stay on the park's boardwalks and trails. Never attempt to step on the ground surrounding these pools as the crust is generally thin and may break, plunging you into a pool of boiling water. Due to the park's high elevations, frost is a common occurrence year-round. Use extreme caution during frosty conditions as the wooden boardwalks become slippery.

Sun Exposure and Illness

Due to the park's high elevations, Yellowstone visitors are more susceptible to high levels of ultraviolet rays, which may in turn lead to heat-related illnesses. Visitors should take every precaution to avoid over-exposure to the sun, no matter the season, and should be careful on summit hikes and near water bodies where rays are especially intense. Protect your eyes with sunglasses, and wear sunscreen and hats at all times. Those pursuing highly active activities, such as hiking, paddling, or bicycling, should use caution to avoid dehydration, heat exhaustion, and heat stroke. Stop for regular water breaks, and carry salted snacks and liquids to help replace electrolytes lost through perspiration.

Hypothermia

Hypothermia, the lowering of the body's core temperature to a degree causing illness or death, is most frequently associated with winter weather. However, hypothermia can strike even when temperatures are well above freezing, and users of Yellowstone's backcountry are prime hypothermic candidates. Wind chill is a critical cause of hypothermia, and those with small bodies (especially children) are more susceptible to the condition.

Mild hypothermia symptoms include shivering, apathy, coordination loss, and general complaints of coldness. In severe cases, hypothermia creates slurred speech, irrepressible shivering, mental difficulties, and a body temperature low enough to trigger permanent damage or death. Children, who may not express their physical ailments as concretely as adults, may suddenly become cranky or fatigued. Adults should immediately check for other signs of hypothermia in such cases.

To protect against hypothermia, Yellowstone visitors and backcountry users should carry extra clothing, including socks, gloves, and hats that prevent heat loss from the body's extremities. Even when the weather appears warm and sunny, pack extra clothing; Yellowstone's weather can change on a moment's notice. For the best results, dress in layers, and always put on rain gear before it starts raining or snowing. If possible, avoid hiking in wet conditions altogether, and avoid prolonged exposure to wind. Visitors using Yellowstone's backcountry should also pack along plenty of warm liquids and high-carbohydrate/high-sugar foods that the body can easily process into heat.

If you suspect someone near you is experiencing the initial symptoms of hypothermia, immediately do everything possible to keep the person warm. Replace any wet clothes with dry ones, add more layers, and encourage the individual to drink warm liquids. In extreme cases, build a contained fire to provide additional heat to the victim. To warm suspected hypothermic children, hug the child close to your body, and cover yourselves with a blanket or sleeping bag.

High-Altitude Sickness

Commonly referred to as "Mountain Sickness," high-altitude sickness is an unpredictable illness that strikes young and old, fit and unfit. Since most park road elevations range from 5,300 to 8,860 feet (1,615-2,700 meters), Yellowstone visitors accustomed to sea level con-

WOLVES

As of August 2000, about 115-120 wolves inhabit the Yellowstone ecosystem. Approximately eighty-three known wolf mortalities have occurred in the ecosystem since wolf restoration began six years ago. There are about fourteen packs or groups in the ecosystem, most of which inhabit territories within the Yellowstone National Park or Grand Teton National Park. There are currently about eleven breeding pairs in the ecosystem.

Northern Rocky Mountain wolves, a subspecies of the gray wolf (Canis lupus), were native to Yellowstone when the park was established in 1872. Predator control was practiced here in the late 1800s and early 1900s. Between 1914 and 1926, at least 136 wolves were killed in the park; by the 1940s, wolf packs were rarely reported. By the 1970s, scientists found no evidence of a wolf population in Yellowstone; wolves persisted in the lower 48 states only in northern Minnesota and on Isle Royale in Michigan. An occasional wolf likely wandered into the Yellowstone area; however, no verifiable evidence of a breeding pair of wolves existed through the mid 1990s. In the early 1980s, wolves began to reestablish themselves near Glacier National Park in northern Montana; an estimated 75 wolves inhabited Montana in 1996. At the same time, wolf reports were increasing in central and north-central Idaho, and wolves were occasionally reported in the state of Washington. The wolf is listed as "endangered" throughout its historic range in the lower 48 states except in Minnesota, where it is "threatened."

National Park Service (NPS) policy calls for restoring native species when: a) sufficient habitat exists to support a self-perpetuating population, b) management can prevent serious threats to outside interests, c) the restored subspecies most nearly resembles the extirpated subspecies, and d) extirpation resulted from human activities.

The U.S. Fish & Wildlife Service 1987 Northern Rocky Mountain Wolf Recovery Plan proposed reintroduction of an "experimental population" of wolves into Yellowstone. In a report to Congress, scientists from the University of Wyoming predicted reductions of elk (15%-25%), bison (5%-15%), moose, and mule deer could result from wolf restoration in Yellowstone. A separate panel of 15 experts predicted decreases in moose (10%-15%) and mule deer (20%-30%). Minor effects were predicted for grizzly bears and mountain lions. Coyotes probably would decline and red foxes probably would increase.

In October 1991, Congress provided funds to the U.S Fish & Wildlife Service (USFWS) to prepare, in consultation with the NPS and the U.S. Forest Service, an Environmental Impact Statement (EIS) on restoring wolves to Yellowstone and central Idaho. After several years and a near-record number of public comments, the Secretary of Interior signed the Record of Decision on the Final Environmental Impact Statement (FEIS) for reintroduction of gray wolves to both areas. Staff from Yellowstone, the USFWS, and participating states prepared to implement wolf restoration. The USFWS prepared special regulations outlining how wolves would be managed as a

nonessential experimental population under section 10(j) of the Endangered Species Act. These regulations took effect in November 1994. As outlined in the Record of Decision, the states and tribes would implement and lead wolf management outside the boundaries of national parks and wildlife refuges, within federal guidelines. The states of Idaho, Wyoming, and Montana have begun preparation of wolf management plans.

Park staff assisted with planning for a soft release of wolves in Yellowstone. This technique has been used to restore red wolves in the southeastern United States and swift fox in the Great Plains and involves holding animals temporarily in areas of suitable habitat. Penning of the animals is intended to discourage immediate long-distance dispersal. In contrast, a hard release allows animals to disperse immediately wherever they choose, and has been used in Idaho where there is limited access to the central Idaho wilderness.

In the autumn of 1995 at three sites in the Lamar Valley, park staff completed site planning, and archaeological and sensitive plant surveys. Approximately 1 acre was enclosed at each site with 9-gauge chain link fence in 10' x 10' panels. These enclosures could be dismantled and reconstructed at other sites if necessary. The fences had a 2' overhang and a 4' skirt at the bottom to discourage climbing over or digging under the enclosure. Each pen had a small holding area attached, to allow a wolf to be separated from the group for medical treatment. Inside each pen were several plywood security boxes to provide shelter. For the 1996 release, one pen was relocated to Blacktail Plateau and another was constructed in the Firehole Valley in central Yellowstone. Subsequently pens have been relocated from Lamar to other areas in the park interior to facilitate releases into other geographic areas or the park or special circumstances that require the temporary penning of wolves.

USFWS and Canadian wildlife biologists captured wolves in Canada and released them in both recovery areas in 1995 and 1996. As planned, wolves of dispersal age (1-2 years old) were released in Idaho, while Yellowstone released pups of the year (7+ months old), together with one or more of the alpha pair (breeding adults). Young pups weigh about 75 lbs. and are less likely to have established a home range. The goal was to have 5-7 wolves from one social group together in each release pen.

Each wolf was radio-collared when captured in Canada. For about 8-10 weeks while temporarily penned, the wolves experienced minimal human contact. Approximately once each week, they were fed roadkills. They were guarded by rangers and other volunteers who minimized the amount of visual contact between wolves and humans. The pen sites and surrounding areas were closed and marked to prevent unauthorized entry. Biologists used radio-telemetry to check on the welfare of wolves.

Although concern was expressed about the wolves becoming habituated to humans or to the captive conditions, the temporary holding period was not long in the life of a wolf. In Alaska and Canada, wolves are seldom known to develop the habituated behaviors seen more commonly in grizzly bears. Wolves, while social

The wolf is the subject of more stories, myths, and legends than any other creature that exists today.
NPS Photo

duced multiple litters which, while documented in the literature, is still unusual. Alpha male wolves generally do not breed with their own offspring, possibly to prevent inbreeding. However, as wolves were matched up during temporary periods of penning and as pack members shifted or were killed and replaced by other dispersing wolves, the occasional result has been packs in which one or both of the alpha pair were not the parents of subordinate pack members. Consequently, the alpha males probably had less incentive to breed with only one female, especially since food was abundant and the packs were still in the early stages of establishing their territories. Lone wolves continued to roam widely, but most of the wolves remained primarily within the boundaries of Yellowstone National Park

An estimated 20,000 park visitors have observed wolves since their return in 1995. The program's visibility has resulted in opportunities to educate audiences about predator-prey relationships, endangered species restoration, and the importance of maintaining intact ecosystems. The program has also generated numerous partnerships with private groups and individuals who generously donated their time and money—critical in an era of reduced budgets and staff downsizing.

For both Idaho and Yellowstone, wolf population recovery is defined as having about 100 wolves, or approximately 10 breeding pairs, established in each area for 3 successive years. The goal to restore wolves and begin delisting them by approximately 2002 appears within reach. The return of the only species known to be missing from the world's first national park for the past half-century has been a milestone in ecological restoration. It has not only restored the wildlife complement of greater Yellowstone; it has been a symbolic victory for conservationists who patiently and persistently reversed the once-dominant attitude against predators to one of acceptance. We believe that Aldo Leopold would be proud that so many humans have come to respect even these "killer creatures" with whom we share the Earth.

among their own kind, typically avoid human contact. They are highly efficient predators with well-developed predatory instincts. Their social structure and pack behavior minimizes their need to scavenge food or garbage available from human sources. Compared to bears, whose diet is predominantly vegetarian, wolves have less specific habitat requirements. The wolves' primary need is for prey, which is most likely to be elk, deer, and other ungulates in these recovery areas.

In 1995, fourteen wolves were released into Yellowstone National Park. In 1996, seventeen more wolves were brought from Canada and released. After release, several thousand visitors were lucky to view wolves chasing and killing elk or interacting with bears during spring. A park ranger and a group of visitors watched a most exciting encounter between two packs which

likely resulted in one young wolf's death. This was not the first fatal encounter between wolves, although human-caused mortalities still outnumber inter-pack strife as a cause of wolf deaths.

Yellowstone's first fourteen wolves bore two litters totalling nine pups. In 1996, four packs produced fourteen pups. After the wolves' release in 1996, plans to transplant additional wolves were terminated due to reduced funding and due to the wolves' unexpected early reproductive success.

In early 1997, ten young wolves, orphaned when their parents were involved in livestock depredation on the Rocky Mountain Front in northwestern Montana, were released into the park. In the spring of the wolf restoration project's third year, nine packs of wolves produced 13 litters of 64 pups. Three of the packs pro-

ditions are particularly susceptible. Caused by decreased oxygen levels in the air, high-altitude sickness results in headaches, muscle weakness and dull pain, nausea/vomiting, fatigue, appetite loss, rapid heartbeat, and shortness of breath.

To reduce the likelihood of experiencing high-altitude sickness, Yellowstone visitors should begin their park visits at the lowest altitude possible, slowly acclimating to higher elevations. If you or someone you know experiences the symptoms of high-altitude sickness, move to lower ground as quickly as possible, eat only light meals, drink plenty of water and other non-caffeinated/non-alcoholic beverages, and provide your body with plenty of rest.

As an added precaution, the National Park Service recommends that anyone with a history of cardiac or respiratory problems contact their physician prior to arriving in Yellowstone.

Lightning
Although Yellowstone is noted for its blue skies, the park also occasionally packs along fierce summer afternoon thunderstorms with deadly lightning. Thunderstorms often arrive with little warning, and visitors should seek shelter immediately. If you are caught in a thunderstorm, do not

use large boulders, trees, or other exposed large natural items for shelter; these objects are more likely to be struck by lightning due to their size. Never seek shelter in a tent as the metal rods attract electricity. To reduce the risk of electrical shock, stay away from water. Although you should never lie flat on the ground during a thunderstorm, you should crouch down as low as possible.

Drinking Water
As in other American wilderness areas, it is never safe to assume that Yellowstone's water is safe for drinking. If your plans call for backcountry travel in Yellowstone, carry along safe drinking water and the knowledge and materials to secure additional safe water on your trek. Giardia (a parasite) is known to inhabit Yellowstone's waters, and boiling water for three to six minutes is regarded as the most effective manner to treat infected water. Filtration and chemical tablet treatments are also popular purification methods. Visitors should note that all water, whether it is used for cooking or brushing teeth, must be filtered. To reduce the likelihood of further contaminating water and spreading disease to other Yellowstone users, human waste should be buried at least 200 feet away from water and trails.

Snow, Ice, Rivers, and Waterfalls
Yellowstone visitors, especially backcountry users, are challenged with a variety of terrain and travel conditions. Although summer may signal warm weather in most American regions, Yellowstone's high country occasionally still reports snow and ice well into late July. Backcountry hikers should use extreme caution while traversing across snow and ice, and river/stream crossings also require extra care. River currents are often stronger than they appear, and children should be closely safeguarded in such situations. Waterfalls, both at major tourist destinations and in Yellowstone's wilds, deserve special treatment. Rocky ledges and precipitous drop-offs often accompany the beauty of Yellowstone's waterfalls and create potentially hazardous situations. Stay safely behind guardrails, and always closely supervise children to avoid tragic accidents.

Carry a First-Aid Kit
Whether you are driving the Grand Loop Tour of Yellowstone's major attractions or undertaking a remote adventure in the park's backcountry, always pack along a comprehensive first-aid kit. Pre-assembled kits are available from outdoor retailers and even in some grocery and convenience stores. Visitors can also opt to create their

own kit. The following are indispensable supplies necessary in composing a homemade kit: first-aid instruction book; adhesive bandages, adhesive tape, gauze pads, butterfly bandages for lacerations, elastic bandages for sprains, and triangle bandages for slings; antibiotic ointment; pain reliever; moleskin for blisters; antiseptic swabs; alcohol cleansing pads; small scissors and tweezers for removing wood slivers and ticks; and an emergency space blanket.

Avoid These Situations

As a final reminder, make your stay as enjoyable as possible, and follow all park regulations. Avoid breaking the following park regulations and common-sense guidelines: speeding, off-road vehicle or bicycle travel, camping violations, improper food storage, unleashed pets, littering, spotlighting animals, boating and fishing violations, removal of both natural and historical objects, and approaching, feeding, or pestering wildlife. The above violations have the potential to destroy an otherwise memorable trip. Ensure that your visits with park rangers are enjoyable, and follow the rules!

PRESERVING YELLOWSTONE ON FILM

Point. Zoom. Click. Basic camera functions are synonymous with Yellowstone and tourist season, and few people would dream of leaving this American treasure without some record of their visit preserved on film. The introduction of digital cameras has further heightened the Yellowstone photo craze, allowing visitors to make sure they capture just the right shot. Think photographing Yellowstone is just a recent obsession? Think again. The tradition of preserving Yellowstone on film dates back to the nineteenth century.

The First Camera in Yellowstone

Sponsored by Congress and directed to verify early regional reports, Ferdinand Vandiveer Hayden led a group of cartographers, scientists, and explorers to Yellowstone in 1871. To ensure that Congress believed the fantastic tales of boiling mud pots, spouting geysers, and breathtaking scenery, Hayden hired notable photographer, William Henry Jackson, to accompany the group and record the magnificent sites.

Jackson took his assignment seriously, lugging along a 6.5 by 8.5 inch camera and an 8 by 10 inch camera to complete his work. He utilized pack mules to carry heavy loads of glass plates, photo developing chemicals, and an array of tripods that were necessary in steadying the cameras and their slow five to fifteen second shutter speeds. As most individuals would guess, taking a picture in the late nineteenth century required much more than the point, zoom, and click mentality of today's amateur photographers. Once Jackson located his subject, he covered a piece of glass the same size as the camera with a light-sensitive emulsion coating. Jackson then took his picture, exposing the emulsion layer. Since the photograph would be ruined if the emulsion coating dried, Jackson was forced to develop his photos on a print-by-print basis. Unlike today's split-second process, Jackson's photography method averaged forty-five minutes for a single shot!

Despite the grueling task of capturing Yellowstone's many wonders, Jackson's work was instrumental in convincing Congress to designate Yellowstone a National Park. His photographs were circulated across the US as the first published pictures of Yellowstone, and they helped him establish a flourishing career as a landscape photographer.

Following Jackson's Lead

The work of William Henry Jackson inspired a new generation of photographers to capture Yellowstone on film. Frank J. Haynes was one of these photographers, and his works played an essential role in showcasing Yellowstone's natural wonders to individuals across the globe.

Initially employed by the Northern Pacific Railroad in 1875 to record the train route leading from Minnesota to the Pacific Coast, Haynes abandoned his position and landed in Yellowstone in 1881. Yellowstone's beauty stunned Haynes, and he set out to capture pictures of all that the area offered. Just three years later, his passion for photography earned him the first official photographer position for Yellowstone National Park.

As the official photographer, Haynes immediately set to work documenting Yellowstone's natural features and the changes the park underwent as more tourists arrived for a first-hand glimpse. Among Haynes' many photos are Yellowstone's natural landscapes, thermal features, stagecoaches, park roads and bridges, Yellowstone Lake steamships, hotels, lodges, campgrounds, and train stations in the gateway towns of West Yellowstone and Gardiner. His photo credits also include the first pictures of Yellowstone during winter, which he attained as a member of the 1887 Schwatka Expedition.

Haynes, however, did much more than simply take pictures. In 1897, Haynes developed his first professional photo finishing lab and print shop near Old Faithful Geyser. In 1900, he produced his first set of picture postcards. The hand-tinted postcards and stereocards were wildly popular with park visitors, as were the black and white reproductions of Haynes' park photos. Within no time, the Northern Pacific Railroad, US government, and transcontinental railroad promoters were distributing Haynes' work across the country. As a result, Haynes was directly responsible for introducing thousands to Yellowstone and played a significant role in driving tourists to the region. By the time he retired in 1916, Haynes' postcards, pictorial souvenirs, and photo prints had become the most widely distributed works of any American West photographer.

Upon Frank Haynes' 1916 retirement, his son Jack E. Haynes took over the family business. Jack further bolstered the family photographic reputation. In 1930, he garnered exclusive rights to sell Yellowstone photos within the park. Soon, Jack became "Mr. Yellowstone," carrying on the family reputation for fine photos with numerous "Haynes Photo Shops" operating throughout the park. Together with his father, Jack revolutionized the way the world saw Yellowstone and documented the gradual changes in Yellowstone's natural landscape.

Capturing Your Own Photos

Although most Yellowstone visitors are anything but professional photographers, it is still possible to capture all of Yellowstone's noteworthy sites with high-quality images. Occasionally during the summer season, professional photographers are stationed throughout Yellowstone to provide tourists with free hands-on instruction. The programs, which last approximately two hours, are offered several times each day to accommodate visitor schedules. For those unable to attend a free session or during seasons where the opportunity is not available, the following tips will ensure that visitors preserve their Yellowstone memories with the finest pictures possible.

Mastering the Basics

- Lighting is to photography as geysers are to Yellowstone; they simply go hand in hand. Photos can easily be ruined without proper lighting, so always pay attention to your scene's lighting. When the sun is shining brightly or your subject includes a bright background, use your camera's flash to balance the photo's light.

- If possible, refrain from taking pictures during the brightest part of the day. Yellowstone photos captured during early morning, late afternoon, and early evening frequently show the highest quality; animals are more prevalent during these times, lighter crowds create less congested backgrounds, and people are not forced to squint against Yellowstone's bright sunny skies.

- Never assume that photos are only worth taking on sunny days. Oftentimes, colors are actually more vivid on cloudy days. Pictures are for all seasons and should thus be taken in all kinds of weather.

- When metering your pictures either manually or automatically, be aware that inaccurate readings can arise from bright backgrounds (like thermal basins) and reflective surfaces such as snow.

Home Video Tips

- If your trip's videographer does not possess a steady hand, consider filming at a lower magnification or utilizing a tripod and image stabilizer.

- Many Yellowstone home videos are nothing more than zoomed-in clips of the park's famous wildlife. Refrain from making such video errors, and include the environment surrounding the wildlife. Your viewers back home will appreciate it.

Filming or Taking Pictures in Thermal Areas

- Geyser spray and mist from other thermal features can be damaging to cameras and video recorders. Immediately remove any overspray from your camera; otherwise, it may leave a permanent deposit.

- The best pictures of Yellowstone's thermal features are generally captured during early morning, and polarizing filters may help photographers capture the colorful brilliance of thermal sites.

- To capture the true size of Yellowstone's geysers, include park boardwalks and people for easy size comparisons.

Understanding the Effects of Cold Weather

- Cold weather is especially hard on cameras, and care should be taken to keep cameras, batteries, and film as warm as possible. When not in use, store your camera inside your jacket, and try to avoid sudden temperature changes that can affect your camera's performance.

- Protect your lens and viewfinder from fog, spray, rain, and snow.

- Keep in mind that cold weather is hard on batteries; to make sure your camera has enough life to capture all your cold weather Yellowstone memories, start with new batteries, and pack along extras.

Yellowstone's Wildlife

Yellowstone's unparalleled beauty and natural wonders combine with the continental U.S.' largest population of free-roaming wildlife to create a wonderland destination. As one of the world's most important wildlife habitats, Yellowstone is home to every major vertebrate wildlife species known to have roamed the earth since the Ice Age. 90,000 elk share the park with 4,000 bison (the continental U.S.' largest free-roaming herd), hundreds of endangered grizzlies, seventy smaller mammal species, 290 bird species, three varieties of wild cats, and dozens of other notable creatures that captivate tourists from far and wide. Although it is tempting to approach this abundant wildlife for a closer look, park visitors should remember that Yellowstone's critters are just as wild as the landscape they inhabit. Yellowstone is not a zoo; it is a sanctuary for one of America's most diverse wildlife populations and should be treated with the utmost respect for visitor and animal safety.

Bighorn Sheep

Once an important food source for Shoshone "Sheepeater" Indians, bighorn sheep (Ovis Canadensis) are synonymous with Yellowstone's rocky crags in the Washburn, Gallatin, and Absaroka Mountain Ranges. Drawing their name from the distinctive curved horns mounted to their heads, bighorn sheep in the park today are nearly identical to the bighorn sheep that roamed the region more than 10,000 years ago. Although bighorn sheep populations have significantly dwindled since the Ice Age, the animal's characteristically stocky body, white rumps, and brown-gray coats can still occasionally be found dotting Yellowstone's most rugged terrain. Researchers believe that Yellowstone's annual bighorn sheep population averages between 150 and 225, a relatively sparse number compared to the thousands that roamed the Rocky Mountain region prior to the 1900s.

Since the demise of hunting in the park, bighorn sheep have been free to roam Yellowstone's landscape with little trepidation. These members of the cattle family live in herds year-round where the rams (males) engage in a fierce competition for mating rights every November and December. Although the rams fiercely butt one another in the head with horns weighing up to forty pounds, calcium deposits known as ossicones protect the animals from brain damage. Winners of these ferocious battles then earn the right to mate with the herd's spiky-horned ewes, each of which will deliver one to two lambs during May or June.

In addition to their unusual horns, bighorn sheep also possess unique hooves. Hard and durable on the outside, the sheep's hooves feature a spongy underside allowing them to grip rocks and leap effortlessly from one crag to another. While not busy wandering across Yellowstone's steep terrain, the park's bighorn sheep graze on grass and brush, drink in the refreshing waters of Yellowstone's rivers, and stock up on minerals at natural salt licks. The ewes have a keen sense of lurking danger from mountain lions, eagles, and coyotes and are responsible for leading the rest of the herd to safety atop peaks inaccessible to their predators. Despite an innate sense of balance and comfort with climbing steep terrain, bighorn sheep do occasionally fall off cliffs to their deaths.

Many of Yellowstone's bighorn sheep shy away from public view, but a few have become accustomed to the traffic lining the Grand Loop Road. On Dunraven Pass, bighorn sheep frequently cause traffic jams as tourists snap photos and wait for the herd to clear the road. On such occasions, visitors are once again reminded not to feed the animals as it jeopardizes their innate food gathering ability.

Bison

Wild bison have continuously inhabited Yellowstone National Park since prehistoric days and easily rule as one of the park's most popular wildlife attractions. Retaining an ancient look, bison average six feet tall at the shoulder, sport curved horns, and occasionally carry up to 2,000 pounds of pure strength under their shaggy brown coats. Distinguished as North America's largest land mammal, bison bulls (males) weigh in at a hefty 1,800 pounds while the female cows average 1,000 pounds. Despite such massive proportions, bison's legs are unusually thin and delicate, and the creatures are amazingly agile.

Distinguished from males by their slender horns and thinner beards, bison cows mate with their vegetarian grazing counterparts every mid-July to mid-August. The cows give birth to a single calf each May and ensure the longevity of the herd. However, other factors also affect the bison's lifespan.

At the dawn of the nineteenth century, bison numbers in the park were as low as fifty in comparison to today's average population of 2,000 to 2,500. Policies were immediately enacted to prevent the extinction of the distinguished animal, and twenty-one bison were transplanted from private ranches to Yellowstone and the Lamar Valley Buffalo Ranch. Within no time, the wild and domestic bison had intermingled, bison hunting and poaching was outlawed, and population numbers were allowed to increase to an all-time high of 3,500 in 1996. At the same time that record bison numbers were recorded, more than half the bison were reported as carriers of the brucellosis virus (a virus that causes cattle to miscarry and can prevent ranchers from shipping livestock out of state). With much discussion, it was determined that ranchers, state officials, and federal agents could defy natural law and shoot any bison that wandered outside the park's boundaries in an effort to contain the spread of brucellosis. Along with this policy, annual winterkill and wolf predation has lowered bison populations to their relatively stable current level. Those bison that escape all of the above factors may live as long as forty years, but most average a lifespan of twelve to fifteen years.

Although bison may appear docile as they graze along the Firehole River and in the Hayden and Lamar Valleys, these creatures are anything but gentle. As wild animals, bison are highly unpredictable, are easily agitated, can move at speeds up to thirty miles per hour, and have been known to gore or even kill individuals who

Grazing Bison

approach too closely. Maintain your distance, and watch these magnificent animals from the safety of your vehicle!

Bobcats

The bobcat (Felix rufus) is one of Yellowstone's most elusive and least studied inhabitants. Due to the bobcat's solitary nature and nocturnal activity, no research has yet been conducted to determine the park's population numbers, and just fifty reported sightings have made their way to park officials since the 1940s.

With females averaging twenty pounds and males weighing in from sixteen to thirty pounds, bobcats are small creatures featuring yellow-brown or red-brown fur streaked with black splotches. Bobcat's paws rarely exceed 2 1/4 inches long, and visitors are lucky if they glimpse bobcat tracks. Despite their elusive nature that forces them to steer clear of Yellowstone's numerous visitors, bobcats are fairly well-suited to Yellowstone's terrain. The park's stands of trees and rocky ledges provide the bobcat with its ideal shelter, and bobcats' favorite prey of mice, rabbits, hares, deer, and birds populate Yellowstone in abundance. The only negative Yellowstone conditions affecting the bobcat are Yellowstone's deep snows and frequent harsh winter weather. As a result, most of the park's bobcats are suspected to inhabit Yellowstone's drier northern corridors.

Any visitor who does encounter a bobcat or spots bobcat tracks is encouraged to contact a park ranger immediately. Every observation counts in gleaning additional information about this mysterious Yellowstone inhabitant!

Coyotes

A member of the dog family, coyotes (Canis latrans) are among the most commonly spotted wildlife in Yellowstone. Approximately sixty-five packs wander across the park's landscape, housing a total of nearly 450 coyotes within their ranks. Although coyotes are often spotted in these packs, the animals are also well-suited to solitary travel.

Standing less than two feet tall with grayish-tan fur and averaging thirty to forty pounds, Yellowstone's coyotes are among America's largest with a wide selection of prey at their disposal. Generally feasting on small mammals, coyotes are capable of killing larger prey with the combined effort of an entire pack. Their long, pointed noses and perky ears distinguish them from their gray wolf relative, and they enjoy relatively short lives. Most coyotes live an average of only six years; however, longer lives can be expected if the coyote sticks with a pack and has no unfortunate encounters with its primary predator, the mountain lion.

Deer

Found across America, mule deer (often shortened to just "deer") thrive in great numbers in Yellowstone's ecosystem. Researchers believe that over 120,000 deer inhabit the greater Yellowstone ecosystem with at least 2,500 residing within the park's boundaries. The deer's black-tipped tails starkly contrast with their white rump, and huge bobbing ears similar to those of mule earned the deer its common name. The species' amazing sense of hearing allows the animal to survive in habitats filled with larger, stronger animals searching for prey. Inhabiting Yellowstone's forests and meadows, mule deer depend upon tree bark, shrubs, grasses, and leafy herbs for survival. Bucks (males) fight for mating rights each autumn, and mature does sustain the deer population, giving birth to twin fawns each summer.

Elk

Boasting a summer elk population over 30,000 and a winter population ranging between 15,000 and 22,000, Yellowstone is home to more elk than any other place in the world. Scientifically known as Cervus elaphus and recognized in the Shawnee language as "Wapiti," elk have foraged upon Yellowstone's shrubs, plentiful grass, pine needles, and aspen bark for over 1,000 years. Bulls (adult males) average 700 to 900 pounds, while cows (adult females) typically weigh 500 pounds.

As with other park species, the arrival of autumn signals the beginning of annual rut (mating) season. Bull elk, which begin growing antlers as yearlings, use their racks to assert dominance over other elk in the herd and garner a harem of over twenty cows during the September to mid-October mating season. Those bulls with the biggest antlers and loudest bugle frequently have the most success with the ladies, and park visitors arriving in the fall are privy to the unique, high-pitched sound of the elk's melodic mating cry. By November, mating season has ended, and the elk move to Yellowstone's lower, northern elevations where winters are marked with warmer temperatures and less snowfall than other park regions. By late May and early June, the elk disperse themselves throughout the park for summer season, and the cows give birth to the year's offspring. Most newborn elk calves weigh twenty-five to forty pounds at birth and begin walking within one hour of their arrival.

Marked with a distinct light beige rump, elk feature dark, heavy manes with reddish-brown coats. Racks weighing up to thirty pounds and featuring six to eight points on each side distinguish the stately bulls from their female counterparts. Yellowstone's elk travel in seven to eight different herds and are one of the most visible park animals. Despite their apparent ease in the public eye, visitors are reminded to provide elk with plenty of space. Take pictures from a distance, and never come between a cow and its calf.

Grizzly and Black Bears

Yellowstone tales of bear road jams, park visitors feeding bears, and tourists lining bleachers to watch as bears struggled over dumpster food flooded America between 1930 and 1970. Visitors across the world flocked to Yellowstone, desperately searching for their own bear tale; most achieved what they came for since the park's bears were so habituated to the presence of humans and human food. However, these legendary tales came with a price. During this era of abundant bear sightings, an average of forty-six people were annually injured in tussles with cantankerous bears. The National Park Service knew it had to intervene if the park were to continue as a safe family vacation destination.

And intervene it did. During the early 1970s, the National Park Service enforced a "no bear feeding" rule and closed the park's open garbage dumps. Despite visitor disappointment, the bears gradually retreated away from public view and learned to rely upon natural food sources. Today, bears are still sighted within the park's grassy areas, including Hayden Valley and Mount Washburn, and occasionally around the park's geysers and rivers. However, today's risk of a close encounter with a bear is relatively low.

Featuring a unique ecosystem that provides bears with both vegetation and animals as abundant food sources, Yellowstone is home to approximately 400 grizzlies and over 550 black bears (although researchers admit this is just a speculation due to the difficulty in tracking the solitary creatures). Although both species of bears rely on a similar diet of grass, tree bark, berries, insects, fish, carrion, and newborn mammals, the two animals do possess distinct differences.

Adult black bears measure just three feet high at their shoulder, with male boars averaging 200 to 300 pounds and female sows a much smaller 140 to 160 pounds. Although the bears possess only fair eyesight, they are renowned for their excellent olfactory capabilities. Featuring rounded ears, black bears possess short, curved claws and fur ranging from black to brown to blonde. Boars solitarily roam a territory of 6 to 124 square miles, while black bear sows maintain a habitat of 2 to 40 square miles.

Known as the black bear's ferocious cousin, Yellowstone's grizzlies average 3.5 to 4.5 feet tall from the ground to the distinctive hump rising between their shoulders. When standing, however, the grizzly becomes a massive giant stretching up to 8 feet tall! Males weigh a mighty 400 to 600 pounds while their female counterparts measure in at a hefty 250 to 350 pounds. Featuring flat, dish-like faces and curved claws frequently as long as a human adult's fingers, grizzly bears are known for their light brown fur tipped in striking silver. Like black bears, grizzlies possess an extraordinary sense of smell, using their tubular snouts to pick up the scent of territorial intruders or fresh prey. However, grizzlies are much more dangerous than black bears, and unfortunate encounters can occur when the bear's need for isolation is disturbed. Researchers suggest that the average male grizzly requires 813 square miles of its own space, while the female grizzly restricts her roaming patterns to just 200 square miles.

Despite such differences, black bears and grizzlies maintain the same winter hibernation pattern. Both species hide out in caves or snug dens of brush with sows waking just long enough to give birth to the two or three cubs bred during the June and July mating season. Black bear mothers allow their cubs to spend one additional winter with them, while grizzly cubs remain with their mothers for two full winters before being chased off to allow the sow to mate once again. Most wild bears average a life expectancy of fifteen to twenty years, but those in captivity may live longer depending on how well they are treated.

Yellowstone visitors are encouraged to review bear precautions prior to visiting the park. Know the difference between a black bear and grizzly, and do everything in your power to protect yourself and the bear's safety.

Moose

A member of the deer family, moose (Alces alces shirast Nelson) are often called "awkward," "homely," "prehistoric," and "strange" along with a host of other slurs. Nonetheless, these unusual creatures persevere with an array of unique bodi-

ly oddities. Boasting a naturally grumpy temperament, moose feature cloven webbed feet that make them both water and land lovers, large flapping ears that detect the presence of danger, long legs that enable them to travel up to thirty miles per hour, and a six to ten inch fleshy combination of skin and hair hanging from their throats that helps them efficiently shed water.

Although such curious creatures captivate all those lucky enough to see them, the chocolate-colored moose maintains a nearly solitary life and demands plenty of personal space. Male and female moose only congregate together during the September to November mating season, with bulls spending just one week with each cow before finding their next target of affection. Cows generally give birth to one calf each May or June, with newborns weighing in at a hefty thirty-five pounds. Visitors should be especially careful around cows with young. Female moose are notoriously protective of their babies, and despite an absence of antlers, are ferocious fighters who use their sharp hooves to kick and destroy predators. Female moose can weigh up to 800 pounds and are not as docile as they appear.

Males, who bear no interest in rearing their young, are distinguished with large antlers. Featuring palm-shaped antlers with finger-like extensions extending the rack to a total span of up to five feet, bull moose average 900 pounds but can weigh as much as 1,300 pounds. Both males and females live an average eighteen to twenty years if they are able to escape the predators of starvation, disease, wolves, and grizzly bears.

During their life, Yellowstone's moose spend most of their time in marshes, alder thickets, and near streams. They thrive on woody plants, with most of their diet dependent upon willows, sub-alpine fir, lodgepole pine, and buffaloberry. Each winter season, moose migrate to either the park's lower elevations near the west and south entrances or to higher, more solitary terrain above 8,500 feet.

Mountain Lions

Like bobcats, mountain lions (Felis concolor) maintain a secretive profile within Yellowstone. Although the cougar population numbered in the hundreds during the early 1900s, controlled hunts between 1904 and 1925 decimated the population. Today, twenty to thirty-five mountain lions reportedly inhabit the park, but sightings are rare.

As the largest member of the cat family occupying Yellowstone, male mountain lions average 140 to 160 pounds with females following closely behind at 100 pounds. Stalking their prey, the notoriously mean cats feast upon elk and deer. Occasionally, the species is known to prey upon porcupines as a dietary supplement. When winter food becomes scarce, most of Yellowstone's mountain lions migrate to lower elevations. Those lions that are dominant over other lions in the fight for food tend to inhabit the park's northern mountains where year-round prey is available.

Although reports of mountain lion attacks against humans have been increasingly documented in the American West during the last decade, no reported encounters have occurred within Yellowstone.

Pronghorn Antelope

Once as numerous as the park's bison, the pronghorn antelope bounds effortlessly across Yellowstone's landscape and is most frequently seen grazing near the park's north entrance. The only animal to feature forked horns, the pronghorn is actually not an antelope at all. Due to the descriptions of Lewis and Clark who likened the pronghorn to the Antilope of South Africa, the pronghorn was soon inaccurately being called an antelope. In reality, the animal belongs to its own class of species that has occupied and evolved on the North American continent for more than twenty million years.

Featuring black stripes, tan bodies with white bellies and rumps, black horns, and protruding eyes, the pronghorn outwits its predators with speed. Large windpipes, giant lungs, an oversized heart, and an extraordinary volume of blood enable the pronghorn to speed away at forty-five

to fifty miles per hour. The animals' petite body size, with males weighing a maximum of 125 pounds and females a slight 100 pounds, further heightens their speed.

Often traveling in herds, the pronghorns mate in the fall, band together in male/female herds for the winter, and then separate into same-sex herds each spring. Offspring, weighing a maximum of nine pounds at birth, are born in late May or early June. Although these fawns are needed to ensure the eventual survival of the species, they also pose an inherent risk to the herd. Young pronghorns are not capable of moving as quickly as the adults, and they often become an easy target for larger predators.

Researchers currently believe that this camera-shy species only numbers a mere 250 within Yellowstone's boundaries.

Wolves

In a historically noteworthy and controversial move, Canadian gray wolves (Canis lupus) were reintroduced to Yellowstone National Park in 1995 after a park absence of more than sixty years. Great care was taken to keep the wolves in established packs so as to ensure longevity of the new park species.

After temporarily being radio-collared and kept in securely guarded pens that limited human contact, the wolves were released into the wilds of Yellowstone to fend for themselves. Armed with extraordinary predatory skills and a social bond tying wolf packs together, the wolves adjusted to their new surroundings remarkably well. As the only Yellowstone species to live in families, the wolves survive in packs that include an alpha male, alpha female, their offspring, and a few subordinate wolves. Each wolf is crucial in maintaining the pack's survival. The wolves work together to hunt down elk, deer, and antelope, using unique facial expressions, urination scent-marking, and body language to indicate their feelings to one another. The distinctive wolf howl is used to draw pack members back together again as well as warn off lurking wolves from different packs.

Reproducing much quicker than scientists predicted, Yellowstone's wolves made a quick recovery. Approximately 100 wolves now populate the park, and the states neighboring Yellowstone's boundaries are in the process of developing wolf management plans to ensure the interests of the wolf as well as the ranchers and animals they threaten. Park visitors may occasionally glimpse wolves in the Lamar Valley, although most tend to avoid human contact. Since the wolves' 1996 reintroduction, more than 20,000 sightings have been reported.

Watching Yellowstone's Wildlife

With so many different animal species populating Yellowstone, it is virtually impossible for a park visitor to conclude their trip without at least a single sighting of one of Yellowstone's famous wild inhabitants. Wildlife habits and personality, weather patterns, mating seasons, and time of day greatly affect the potential for viewing Yellowstone's wildlife. Visitors who opt to enter Yellowstone in the early morning or late evening hours have the greatest potential to see a range of park wildlife during typical feeding hours. However, sightings are possible throughout the day. For specific viewing locations, contact a park ranger, check out the park's visitor center information, or simply take your chances at sighting some of Yellowstone's magnificent creatures roaming near the park's highways.

Location Suggestions for Wildlife Viewing

Beaver: Although certainly not gathering as much attention as many park animals, beavers are quite common near Yellowstone's streams, ponds, and rivers. Watch for them during the early morning and evening, especially near Harlequin Lake and Willow Park.

Bighorn Sheep: Bighorn sheep are most commonly sighted in the park's northern regions. They are frequently spotted around Gardiner, the Gardner River, Calcite Springs, Tower Fall, and Mount Washburn.

Black Bears: Black bears prefer to keep a low profile away from humans, so sightings are infrequent. Occasionally, bears are spotted in or near forests. Most reported sightings have occurred along the highways around Mammoth, Tower, the Northeast Entrance, Madison, Old Faithful, and the Canyon regions. Black bear sightings have also been documented on Yellowstone's backcountry trails.

Elk: Elk can be found throughout the entirety of Yellowstone's 2.2 million acres, but a large herd congregates around Mammoth Hot Springs nearly year-round. Elk can also be spotted on Mount Washburn's north slope and in the Lamar and Hayden Valleys.

Grizzly Bears: Open meadows provide some of the best possible viewing sites for grizzly bears. Preferring to hunt during dusk and dawn, grizzlies are most often spotted at these times of day in the Hayden and Lamar Valleys. Occasionally, sightings have occurred around the Tower, Canyon Lake, and Fishing Bridge Areas with many documented reports of grizzly bear presence in the backcountry.

Moose: These prehistoric-looking creatures make an appearance near marshy areas and willow-lined streams. They are especially prevalent around Mammoth, Norris, Lake, and the Northeast Entrance.

Mountain Lions: Mountain lion sightings are rare, so if you catch a glimpse, consider yourself lucky. Sporadic sightings have been reported in the late evening hours around Cooke City and the Northeast Entrance.

Mule Deer: Mule deer are prevalent throughout the park, especially in forests lining the park's highways. Most sightings occur during morning and evening hours, but drivers should watch for deer on the roads at all times of day.

Pronghorn: These speedy creatures prefer grassy habitats, so watch for them around Mammoth and on the road leading to the park's Northeast Entrance.

Wolves: Wolves, when sighted, most often appear in packs during dawn and dusk. The species appear to be most active and easily spotted along Soda Butte Creek and the open areas lining the Lamar River.

Maintain Your Distance

As wild, untamed animals, Yellowstone's wildlife needs plenty of undisturbed space, and park visitors are reminded that they are guests in these animals' homes. Respect the wild nature of these creatures, and wisely watch from a distance. By engaging in this behavior, park visitors are not only rewarded with a more natural look at the animals' activities, but they also ensure a greater level of safety for the wildlife and other nearby onlookers.

Wildlife watchers who choose not to follow these principles greatly jeopardize themselves and the animals they are viewing. An animal that becomes aware of an onlooker's presence experiences a rapid rise in heart rate, may move to a less desirable feeding location just to escape its watchers, and can become habituated to humans. These factors deplete animals' valuable energy supplies, create a nourishment deficit, and can potentially make animals unafraid of would-be poachers.

At the same time these disrespectful wildlife watchers are inherently harming the animals, they are also putting themselves at risk. Wildlife is unpredictable, and those animals that feel their territory has been encroached upon may fight back. Several park visitors are injured every year when they approach animals too closely, and encounters with some wildlife have resulted in visitors' deaths. Always maintain your distance, and keep in mind the following tips to help you become a wise wildlife watcher while minimizing your impact.

- Park law mandates that visitors must stay at least 100 yards (91 meters) away from bears and at least 25 yards away from all other large wildlife, including wolves, coyotes, moose, deer, elk, bison, and bighorn sheep.

- Never stop in the middle of the road to view wildlife. Always pull off to the road's shoulder or a pullout, and always shut off your engine so as not to disturb the wildlife.

- Refrain from shouting or exclaiming in excitement. Instead, talk quietly among yourselves, and stay in your car if possible. Vehicles often make the most appropriate photo blinds.

- Never distract animals or try to grab their attention for a photo opportunity. Instead, use a telephoto lens to capture animals in their natural state and environment.

- Never bait animals with food handouts. Not only is human food harmful to wildlife, but it also habituates wildlife to humans. This can eventually lead to negative encounters between park visitors and wildlife. Refrain from engaging in this illegal behavior; park rangers watch visitors closely and are not afraid to ticket violators.

YELLOWSTONE HIGHLIGHTS

For those who are short on time but still want the vivid memory of spewing geysers and scenic overlooks, the following are recommended sites for capturing the most Yellowstone has to offer to the drive-by tourist.

Geysers, Mud Pots, and Hot Springs: Home to more geothermal phenomena than anywhere else in the world, Yellowstone boasts geysers, mud pots, and hot springs throughout the entirety of its terrain. These thermal wonders come in every color of the rainbow, with some bursting hundreds of feet into the air as others fizzle and pop close to the Earth's surface. A constant reminder of Yellowstone's volcanic history, these features are often associated with Old Faithful and Mammoth Hot Springs. However, other thermal features include the West Thumb Geyer Basin, Mud Volcano, Midway Geyser Basin, Fountain Paint Pot, and the Norris Geyser Basin. Popular opinion declares Echinus Geyser in the Norris Geyser Basin one of the best thermal displays for its lively variety of activity. The Riverside Geyser near the Firehole River is also popular, shooting seventy-five foot tall arches of water across the river.

Grand Canyon: The Grand Canyon of Yellowstone

is one of the most famous park areas, with spectacular waterfalls and scenery around every roadside bend. Visitors to the Grand Canyon and surrounding Canyon Village will find the Upper and Lower Falls of the Yellowstone River, Tower Falls, Calcite Springs, and several scenic overlooks on the North and South Rim roads.

Mountain Vistas: Yellowstone's landscape is dotted with peaks, and famous mountain ranges surround the park's borders. The best mountain vistas are found on the road leading from Tower Junction to Canyon Village. Passing over the park's highest road at Dunraven Pass (8,600 feet), drivers on this highway are rewarded with views of the Teton Range to the south, the Yellowstone Caldera, and the Absaroka Mountains.

Natural Water Features: In addition to hosting boiling and roiling hot water features, Yellowstone is home to several famous rivers, streams, and lakes. Wildlife swarm to river banks in search of a fresh fish feast, and Yellowstone Lake is one of North America's great wonders. Measuring twenty miles long, fourteen miles wide, and more than 300 feet deep in most places, Yellowstone Lake is the continent's largest high-altitude body of water. Underneath the lake, a caldera formed from an ancient sunken lake is gradually filling with hot magma and tipping the lake in a northerly direction. Experts warn that a new volcanic blast is due sometime within the next 100,000 years. In the meantime, the lake is a popular destination for wildlife viewing, fishing, kayaking, and canoeing.

Wildlife Viewing: Yellowstone's wildlife can be found throughout the park, but one of the best places to view animals is in the Lamar Valley. Located in the northern portion of the park between Mammoth Hot Springs and the Northeast Entrance, Lamar Valley is a prime viewing spot for prowling wolves and grazing bison and elk.

RECREATING IN YELLOWSTONE

Miles of RVs and bumper-to-bumper traffic each summer may make some Yellowstone visitors cringe, but for those who choose a route less traveled, the park is actually an isolated place rivaling some of America's most pristine wilderness areas. For recreationists who choose to explore the park by bike, boat, or with their own two feet, miles of undisturbed open spaces await that leave the majority of Yellowstone's visitors clinging to the comfort of the park's main roads. Year-round outdoor opportunities (some more popular than others) abound within the park, providing visitors with an unforgettable Yellowstone experience.

Summer Activities

The sky is the limit when it comes to summer outdoor adventures in Yellowstone. However, all recreationists must comply with park guidelines. Following is a brief description of some of Yellowstone's most popular summer activities.

Bicycling: Although bicycles are not available for rent in the park and are prohibited in the backcountry, bicycling is allowed on all public roads, designated bike routes, and in parking areas. Despite the park's narrow, windy roads where bicyclists are given little room to maneuver around Yellowstone's congested highways, hundreds of bicyclists take the opportunity to imbibe the open air each year.

To avoid any mishaps with those touring

Yellowstone by vehicle, bicyclists are encouraged to heed the following guidelines:

- Always wear highly visible clothing and helmets.

- Equip all bikes with reflective lighting.

- Pack along plenty of water; most park facilities are at least twenty to thirty miles apart.

- Watch for motorists on Yellowstone's many blind curves.

- Remember that bikes are subject to the same traffic laws as vehicles.

- Avoid riding during April, May, and June when high snowbanks make Yellowstone's roads even narrower than usual.

- Park boardwalks are only for pedestrian use.

For those bicyclists seeking to escape vehicle traffic, consider the following trails that are open to both hikers and bicyclists:

- Mount Washburn Trail: Climbing 1,400 feet, the challenging Mount Washburn Trail departs from the Old Chittenden Road.

- Bunsen Peak Road/Osprey Falls Trails: Combining both bicycling and hiking, these trails depart near Mammoth Hot Springs. Bicyclists travel six miles to Bunsen Peak and then choose between hiking to the top of the peak or down to Osprey Falls.

- Lone Star Geyser Trail: This easy ride departs from Kepler Cascade near Old Faithful. A user-friendly road rather than a traditional trail, the Lone Star Geyser Trail typically takes one hour to complete.

Boating: Boating Yellowstone's lakes and the river channel linking Lewis and Shoshone Lakes is becoming an increasingly popular way to experience the park. Permits are required for all vessels, including simple float tubes, and strict guidelines dictate which areas are open to motorized boats. Keep in mind the following guidelines for a safe, fun trip:

- Permits are only available to those applying in person.

- Both motorized and non-motorized permits are available at the Lake Ranger Station, Grant Village Visitor Center, Bridge Bay Ranger Station, Lewis Lake Campground, and the park's South Entrance.

- Non-motorized boat permits are available at the Mammoth, Canyon, and Old Faithful Visitor Centers, as well as at the Bechler Ranger Station and West and Northeast Entrances.

- Motorized permits are $20 annually or $10 for a seven-day pass; non-motorized permits cost $10 annually or $5 for a seven-day pass.

- All individuals must wear a personal flotation device at all times.

Although Yellowstone visitors are encouraged to bring their own boating gear, Xanterra Parks and Resorts does rent outboard motorboats and rowboats on a first-come, first-served basis. Rentals are available on Yellowstone Lake at the Bridge Bay Marina. In addition, Xanterra also offers guided fishing boat tours, and advance reservations are accepted. Call (307) 344-7311 for more information.

Camping: Less removed from the general park visitor population than some recreational activities, camping is nonetheless a popular choice for many Yellowstone sightseers. Both first come, first served and reservation campsites are available throughout the park. Group camping is also

FIRE: A NATURAL FORCE

Fire, climate, erosion, and a vast assortment of life forms ranging from microbes to insects to mammals, including humans, have all played roles in the creation of the vegetative landscape of Yellowstone. Vegetation here has adapted to fire and, in some cases, may be dependent on it.

Ecologists have known for many years that wildfire is essential to the evolution of a natural setting. Records kept in Yellowstone since 1931 show that lightning starts an average of 22 fires each year. Large-scale fires burn through the conifer forests of the Yellowstone plateau every 250 to 400 years and take place in the low-elevation grass-lands on average every 25 to 60 years. When fires are, suppressed the habitat gradually becomes less diverse. This, in turn, affects the variety of animals able to successfully inhabit a particular area.

In the first few decades after Yellowstone was established as the world's first national park in 1872, no effective fire fighting was done. Then, during the Army administration of Yellowstone (1886-1918), fire suppression occurred most frequently on the grass lands of the northern range. Throughout the rest of the park, which is largely covered by a lodgepole pine forest, reliable and consistent fire suppression began with the era of modern airborne fire-fighting techniques of the past 30 to 40 years.

In natural areas such as Yellowstone National Park, preserving a state of wildness is a primary goal of management. In 1972, Yellowstone was one of several national parks that initiated programs to allow some naturally caused fires to burn. By 1988, scientists had learned much about the occurrence and behavior of fire. Tens of thousands of lightning strikes simply fizzled out with no acreage burned. While 140 lightning strikes produced fires, most burned only a small area. Eighty percent of the lightning starts in this period went out by themselves.

THE HISTORIC FIRES OF 1988

The summer of 1988 was the driest on record in Yellowstone. Though substantial precipitation fell during April and May, practically no rain fell in June, July, or August—an event previously unrecorded in the park's 112-year written record of weather conditions. In early summer, about 20 lightning-caused fires had been allowed to burn, and eleven of these fires burned themselves out.

But fires that continued to burn into the extremely dry weeks of late June and July met dramatically changed conditions. By late July, moisture content of grasses and small branches had dropped as low as 2 or 3 percent, and downed trees measured at 7 percent (kiln-dried lumber is 12 percent). After July 15, no new natural fires were allowed to burn and after July 21, all fires were fought.

The extreme weather conditions and heavy, dry accumulations of "fuel" (vegetation of various types) presented even the most skilled professional fire fighters with conditions rarely observed. Typical firefighting techniques were frequently ineffective because fires spread long distances by "spotting," a phenomenon in which wind carries embers from the tops of 200-foot flames far across unburned forest to start spot fires well ahead of the main fire. Fires routinely jumped barriers that normally stopped them such as rivers, roads, and major topographic features such as the Grand Canyon of the Yellowstone River. Fires advanced rapidly, making frontal attacks dangerous and impossible.

By the last week of September, about 50 lightning-caused fires had occurred in the park, 8 of which were still burning. More than $120,000,000 had been spent on fire control efforts in the greater Yellowstone area, and most major park developments—and a few surrounding communities—had been evacuated at least once as fire approached within a few miles of them. At the operation's peak, 9,000 firefighters (including Army and Marine units), more than 100 fire engines, and dozens of helicopters participated in the complex effort to control the fires and protect developments. It was the largest such cooperative effort ever undertaken in the United States.

CHANGES SINCE 1988

Changes in both the natural landscape of Yellowstone and the management of naturally-caused fires have taken place since the historic fires of 1988. Scientists knew that the vegetative cover of Yellowstone was, in large part, the product of fires that had burned for millennia before the arrival of European humans. The growth of new plants and entire plant communities began immediately. In most places, plant growth is unusually lush because minerals and other nutrients are released by fire into the soil and because increased light stimulates growth in what was previously shaded forest floor.

These fires did not annihilate all life in their paths. Burning at a variety of temperatures, sometimes as ground fires, sometimes as crown fires (burning through treetops), fires killed many lodgepole pines and other trees but did not kill most other plants. Instead, they burned off the tops, leaving roots to regenerate. The fires created a mosaic of burns, partial burns, and unburned areas that provide new habitats for plants and animals.

Yellowstone National Park is one of the greatest living laboratories on the planet. Here, we can observe the effects of fire and other natural forces and processes, and learn from them. And what we learn is that change is constant in the natural world, flowing from the past into the present—continuing into the future to outcomes both predictable and mysterious,

FACTS ABOUT THE FIRES OF 1988

Why They Occurred

Conditions occurred that were never before seen in the history of Yellowstone: extended drought & high winds.

Statistics

- 9 fires caused by humans
- 42 fires caused by lightning
- 36% of the park burned (793,880 acres)
- Fires begun outside of the park burned more than half of the total acreage
- About 400 large mammals, primarily elk, perished
- $120 million spent fighting the fires
- 25,000 people employed in these efforts

Fighting the Fires

- Until July 21, naturally-caused fires allowed to burn.
- After that, all fires fought, regardless of their cause.
- Largest fire-fighting effort in the history of the U.S.
- Effort saved human life and property, but probably had little impact on the fires themselves.
- Rain and snow finally stopped the advance of the fires.

After the Fires

- Enormous public controversy occurred.
- Several high-level task forces formed to review NPS fire policies.
- Their recommendations reaffirmed the importance of natural fire in an ecosystem.
- They recommended additional guidelines be established to manage natural fire in Yellowstone.

---

offered in select campgrounds. For additional information regarding campgrounds, amenities, and fees, see the "Camping in Yellowstone" section under the General Visitor Information heading.

Day Hiking: For visitors who simply want to dip their feet in a true wilderness experience, day hiking is ideal. Boasting 1,100 miles of hiking trails, Yellowstone's wilderness caters to day hikers of all abilities. Trails are found in every portion of Yellowstone; look for directions to specific day hikes in the respective sections highlighting features near Mammoth Hot Springs, Norris, Old Faithful, Madison, Canyon Area, Lake Village, Tower-Roosevelt, West Thumb and Grant Village, Bridge Bay, and Fishing Bridge.

Although day hiking provides a pleasurable means of soaking in Yellowstone's beauty, hikers must be aware of dangers lurking in the wild, including wildlife encounters, cold water lakes, hidden thermal areas, changing weather, loose rock, and turbulent streams.

For the most enjoyable trip, day hikers should always begin their trips with a visit to the nearest ranger station. Park rangers are armed with the latest information regarding trail conditions, animal activity, and expected area weather. While hiking, visitors should carry along sunscreen, insect repellent, a raincoat and hat, a first aid kit, and plenty of water. For maximum safety, always hike with another person, and make sure somebody knows your intended route.

Day hiking in Yellowstone is free and does not require a backcountry permit.

Fishing: Although park visitors have enjoyed fishing in Yellowstone's lakes and rivers for over a century, the world of Yellowstone fishing is changing to protect the park's valuable aquatic life. Once placing no restrictions on anglers, Yellowstone's fishing program now operates to manage the park's water resources and restore native fish species while providing recreational fishing opportunities. As a result, stringent guidelines are now in place, and as of 2001, all fish except lake trout must be released.

As more and more fly-fishing enthusiasts and drift-boat anglers inundate Yellowstone Lake and the park's riverbanks, season opening and closing dates have been added, restrictions on bait use are now enforced, and non-lead tackle and fishing gear is mandated. The cost of fishing permits has also escalated since 2000, with permits for those age sixteen and older costing $35 per season, $20 for a seven-day pass, and $15 for a three-day permit. For now, youth ages twelve to fifteen receive their permits for free, and children under eleven are allowed to fish without a permit if accompanied by a paying adult.

For those not turned off by the park's increasingly strict guidelines, fishing in Yellowstone provides anglers with the opportunity to catch cutthroat, rainbow, brook, brown, and lake trout along with grayling and mountain whitefish. While law dictates that lake trout must be kept and removed from Yellowstone, all other Yellowstone fish species must be released back into the wild. Anglers should note that some areas are closed to fishing due to endangered or sensitive wildlife populations, and fishing enthusiasts should always be on the lookout for bears. Fish are one of bears' favorite foods, so bears frequently roam the riverbanks in search of a tasty meal.

To ensure the sustained livelihood of fish, anglers should employ the following tips for properly releasing fish and keeping the waters clean:

- Use barbless hooks to make the release technique easier.

- When handling fish and removing hooks, keep the fish in water as much as possible. Never let the fish flail to the point of exhaustion.

- Remove all hooks as gently as possible, being careful not to squeeze the fish or contaminate the fish's gills with germs from your fingers.

- If a fish is deeply hooked, do not attempt to remove the hook as it may severely injure the fish. In this case, it is better to leave the hook; most fish do survive even with hooks left in them.

- Release fish as close as possible to where they were retrieved, and always point the fish upstream.

- Never dump trash in the water, especially extra fishing line and plastic pop/beer holders. These items can seriously injure and even kill Yellowstone's precious fish.

Horseback Riding: Offering visitors the chance to escape the crowds for an hour or two, Xanterra Parks and Resorts offers guided horseback rides departing from Mammoth Hot Springs, Tower-Roosevelt, and Canyon. Rides generally book quickly, so advance reservations are recommended. For a longer trip, Xanterra also provides wagon rides leading to an evening western cookout site. Those interested should call (307) 344-7311 for additional information and reservations.

For those seeking a true wilderness experience, guided overnight and weekly horseback and llama treks to Yellowstone's backcountry are available. Call Yellowstone Park at (307) 344-

7381 for a complete list of outfitters licensed to guide in Yellowstone.

Backcountry Use and Regulations: Backpacking in Yellowstone provides a rewarding experience for hardcore wilderness lovers who delight in isolation and self-sufficiency. Whether you're staying just one night or an entire week, though, all backcountry users must acquire a permit and are encouraged to let others know their intended route. Backcountry equestrians and boaters must also obtain the same permit.

User permits are free of charge and available during summer up to forty-eight hours in advance from the following ranger stations: Bridge Bay, South Entrance, Bechler, Canyon, Grant Village, Mammoth, Old Faithful, Lake, West Entrance, and Tower.

While exploring Yellowstone's backcountry, remember that the park is a wild place full of wild animals and unexpected dangers. Use caution at all times, and watch for hidden thermal features, slippery or loose rocks, dangerous water crossings, and changing weather patterns. Remember: horses and other pack animals are not permitted in the backcountry until after July 1, campfires are permitted only in established fire pits, all items packed in must be packed out, water must be treated either by boiling or filtering, and users must stay on established trails.

Winter Activities

The majority of Yellowstone's main highways may be closed during winter, but that does not put a damper on the park's activity. Yellowstone's winter recreation is renowned, but visitors must use extra caution.

Since winter temperatures in Yellowstone can be severe, winter recreationists must dress in a layered clothing system. Wear long underwear, wool or synthetic pants, and wool or other insulated shirts. Thick wool socks, gloves, a hooded windproof parka, and a stocking cap are musts. Refrain from wearing jeans, cotton sweatshirts, cotton undershirts, and cotton socks, as they do not effectively wick moisture away from the body. Be sure to carry extra clothing as well as dark sunglasses and sunscreen. Even though temperatures may be below zero, the high altitude sunlight and reflection of pristine snow can cause serious sunburns.

Winter services are limited within the park's boundaries, but a few of Yellowstone's main regions do operate year-round. Lodging and food are available at the Old Faithful Snow Lodge and Mammoth Hot Springs Hotel, while fast food is served in the Canyon and Madison warming huts. Snowmobilers can locate fuel at Mammoth Hot Springs, Old Faithful, Fishing Bridge, and Canyon. Warming huts and restrooms are situated at the Canyon and Madison warming huts, Mammoth Hot Springs Campground, Mammoth Hot Springs Visitor Center, and the Old Faithful Visitor Center.

No matter the winter activity in which you engage, be alert for signs of hypothermia, and be prepared for all types of weather conditions. The following is a brief description of the most popular winter activities in Yellowstone.

Camping: Although camping is typically associated with summer, a few hardy souls do camp in Yellowstone each winter. The Mammoth Hot Springs campground is the only site available during winter season, and backcountry winter camping requires a permit. For additional infor-

mation regarding campgrounds, amenities, and fees, see the "Camping in Yellowstone" section under the General Visitor Information heading.

Cross Country Skiing/Snowshoeing: With most of its 2.2 million acres managed as wilderness, Yellowstone provides a winter wonderland for cross country skiers and snowshoe enthusiasts. Many of the park's trails are marked with orange metal tags fastened to nearby trees, and most trails have no set track. In order to accommodate these conditions, skiers should select touring or mountaineering boots and skis. All other skis are inappropriate for breaking Yellowstone's trails. Should you decide to ski on the park's unplowed roadways, stay to the right while watching out for snowmobiles.

While skiing or snowshoeing into Yellowstone's backcountry, visitors should learn as much as possible about winter survival and be prepared for changing weather patterns, avalanche danger, deep snow, and unfrozen streams hidden under blankets of fresh snow. Those who ski or snowshoe should also dress appropriately for Yellowstone's harsh winter weather. Wear a layered clothing system, a wind and waterproof parka, warm gloves, and a stocking cap. Be prepared with extra clothes, plenty of water, and a large supply of food.

When planning a winter cross-country ski or snowshoe trip, accommodate for shortened daylight hours, the experience and physical capabilities of those going on the trip, and expected temperature and weather patterns. Keep in mind that December and January trips are most difficult due to extreme temperatures and fairly continual snowfalls. Also be aware that proper snow conditions are only found between 7,000 and 10,000 feet.

Prior to embarking on a backcountry ski or snowshoe excursion, tell someone where you will be going, and always check in with the nearest park ranger. If you plan to stay overnight, you must acquire a backcountry permit.

Wilderness users are encouraged to supply their own skis and snowshoes, but a limited selection is available for rent at the Mammoth Hot Springs Hotel and Old Faithful Snow Lodge. Most rentals average $12-$15 per day. In addition to providing rentals, the above facilities also provide guided ski tours, ski lessons, and shuttles to various locations in the park.

Ice Skating: As one of Yellowstone's cheapest winter activities, ice skating at the Mammoth Hot Springs Skating Rink is a popular choice. For those who can stand the cold, the outdoor rink rents out affordable skates at both hourly and daily rates. During December, holiday music sounds from the rink's PA system, and occasionally, campfires are lit beside the rink's edge to help patrons warm their frosty hands and feet.

Snowcoach Tours: Not up for braving Yellowstone's weather on a snowmobile? Then consider taking a snowcoach tour. Snowcoach tours offer a more protected option for viewing Yellowstone's pristine mountain scenery with the added comfort of turning over the wheel to an experienced winter driver. Snowcoach tours depart from West Yellowstone, Mammoth Hot Springs, the Flagg Ranch near the South Entrance, and the Old Faithful Snow Lodge. For more information, contact Xanterra Parks and Resorts at (307) 344-7311 or Yellowstone National Park at (307) 344-7381. Advance reservations are highly recommended.

Snowmobiling: Snowmobiling is by far the most popular winter sport in Yellowstone, and thousands of speedy machines zip through the park each winter. Although controversy clouds the winter sport in a haze of heated debates and environmental concerns, snowmobilers still roar through the park every December through March.

As with other winter sports in the park, dressing and being prepared for winter weather is critical. Underneath snowmobile suits, dress in a layered garment system consisting of long underwear, wool or synthetic trousers, and wool or insulating shirts. Warm socks, gloves, stocking caps, and appropriate footwear are key.

For those not owning a snowmobile, rentals and guided tours are available from the Old Faithful Snow Lodge and the Mammoth Hot Springs Hotel, as well as in the neighboring towns of West Yellowstone and Gardiner. Lessons are also available at many places offering rentals, and all first-time users are encouraged to receive some basic instruction prior to riding in the park.

To maintain the Yellowstone snowmobiling tradition for years to come, all users should keep in mind the following regulations and safety tips.

- All snowmobile operators must possess a valid driver's license, and all machines must be registered within their home state.

- Snowmobiles must feature working lights and brakes, and exhaust and mufflers must be in excellent operating condition. Maximum noise from exhaust systems cannot exceed seventy-eight decibels at full acceleration with a fifty-foot distance. Currently, most stock exhaust systems are in accordance with this mandate, but aftermarket exhaust systems are often too loud. To avoid being denied park access, check the levels of your exhaust system prior to arrival.

- Snowmobiles are subject to the same guidelines as cars. Always use hand signals to stop or turn, drive on the right side of the road in single file, pass only when visibility is high, never exceed the maximum speed limit of forty-five miles per hour (seventy-two kilometers per hour), and obey all traffic signs.

- Always stay on designated routes and park roads. Off-road travel, including sidehilling and berm-riding, is strictly prohibited and punishable with a fine up to $5,000.

- Snowmobiling and alcohol do not mix, and those driving while intoxicated will be caught and charged. Any open alcoholic beverage container is also illegal, including the popular botabags.

- Since they are permanent park residents, Yellowstone's wildlife always have the right of way. Never approach, feed, or chase the wildlife. Winter alone is hard enough on animals without wildlife being forced to exert extra energy to quickly move off the road.

- If wildlife blocks the roadway, stop no less than twenty-five yards away, and wait for them to move. If the animal begins walking toward you, turn around if possible, and move to a different location. If you do not have time to turn around, step off your machine, and protect yourself by keeping the machine between you and the wildlife. In all cases, never attempt to pass animals if they appear agitated. In such scenarios, animals are likely to stampede, and your safety is at risk.

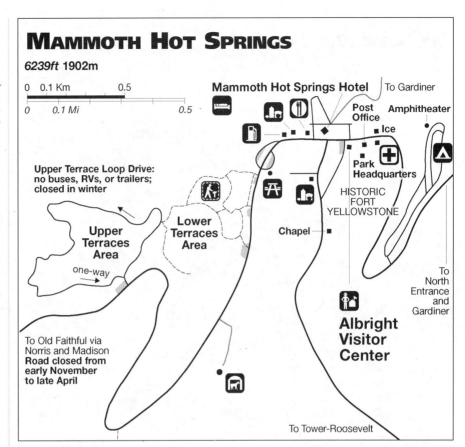

Yellowstone's Self-Guided Park Trails

Yellowstone is equipped with several self-guiding trails carrying visitors to many of the park's most famous attractions. Most self-guiding trails are easy, following wooden boardwalks or paved paths. On occasion, these trails do feature stairs, so take that into account prior to setting out on a trek. Maps, area information, and photos of the self-guided trail destinations are available at Yellowstone's numerous visitor centers.

Historic Fort Yellowstone: As the nation's oldest park, Yellowstone has many well-preserved buildings reflecting the presence of the U.S. Army during the park's early years. The Fort Yellowstone Historic Trail wanders around Mammoth Hot Springs' historical buildings, most of which were constructed between 1886 and 1918 as part of Fort Yellowstone. Today, the buildings are home to park headquarters.

Fountain Paint Pot: After leaving your vehicle in the large parking area 8 miles north of Old Faithful on the Madison Junction Road, get ready to explore some of Yellowstone's most impressive geysers. Extremely active mud-pots combine with colorful hot springs, geyser plumes, and hissing vents in the Earth's crust on the Fountain Paint Pot trail.

Grand Canyon of the Yellowstone: The trail along the rim of the Yellowstone Grand Canyon provides stunning overlooks of the Upper and Lower Falls. One of the park's most visited sites, the canyon features lookouts that are aptly named Artist Point, Grandview, and Inspiration.

Mammoth Hot Springs: Travertine terraces marked with colorful cascading hot springs are one of Yellowstone's most breathtaking sites. Boardwalks roam amid the Upper and Lower Terraces. Although driving is allowed through the Upper Terrace, visitors are strongly encouraged to take the self-guided trail for a close-up view of these Yellowstone wonders.

Mud Volcano Area: Mudpots and their distinctive sulphur smell are the featured attraction at Mud Volcano Area. Famous area mudpots include Sulpur Caldron, Dragon's Mouth, and Mud Volcano. The area is located 6 miles (9.6 kilometers) north of the Fishing Bridge Junction on the highway between Canyon and Lake.

Norris Geyser Basin: Researchers from across the world recognize this Yellowstone area as the park's hottest and most active geyser region. The trail winds past Steamboat (the world's tallest geyser that last erupted in May 2000) and hundreds of thermal features in Porcelain Basin.

Upper Geyser Basin: Recognized for holding the world's largest concentration of geysers in a single area, Upper Geyser Basin is home to Yellowstone's favorite – Old Faithful. The area also houses such geysers and hot springs as Castle, Morning Glory, Riverside, Grotto, Beehive, and hundreds more.

West Thumb Geyser Basin: Nestled in the shadow of jagged mountain peaks, the self-guiding path in West Thumb Geyser Basin is one of the park's most scenic trails. Runoff from the basin's boiling springs trickles into Yellowstone Lake, and the Fishing Cone Hot Spring is a crowd favorite.

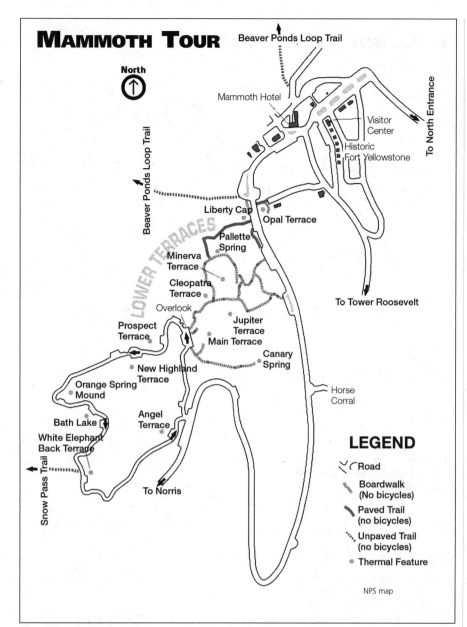

MAMMOTH TOUR

North ↑

Beaver Ponds Loop Trail

Mammoth Hotel

Visitor Center

Historic Fort Yellowstone

To North Entrance

Beaver Ponds Loop Trail

Liberty Cap

Opal Terrace

Pallette Spring

LOWER TERRACES

Minerva Terrace

Cleopatra Terrace

Overlook

Prospect Terrace

Jupiter Terrace

Main Terrace

To Tower Roosevelt

Canary Spring

New Highland Terrace

Orange Spring Mound

Horse Corral

Bath Lake

Angel Terrace

White Elephant Back Terrace

Snow Pass Trail

To Norris

LEGEND

〜 Road

Boardwalk (No bicycles)

Paved Trail (no bicycles)

Unpaved Trail (no bicycles)

• Thermal Feature

NPS map

DISCOVERING THE MAMMOTH AREA

Recognized for spectacular wildlife and mineral-rich, colorful hot springs, Mammoth Hot Springs is located five miles from the North Entrance.

Historical Attractions

Serving as park headquarters, Mammoth Hot Springs was one of Yellowstone's first commercialized sites. Prior to prohibition of soaking in Yellowstone's thermal features, many late nineteenth and early twentieth century visitors swarmed to Mammoth for its purported healing effects. The area is accessible year-round and is famous for its Native American history, military presence, and visits from well-respected U.S. Presidents.

Traces of Native Americans

Several Native American tribes settled in the region surrounding Yellowstone, and the Shoshone-Bannock (Sheepeater) Indians actually resided within the park. As a testimony to this Native American presence, archaeologists discov-

ered a Clovis point in 1959 near the old Gardiner post office. Researchers believe the point, dated more than 10,000 years old, belonged to an early ancestor of Rocky Mountain Native American tribes.

Traces of the Bannock Indian trail, ancient cooking pits, and the 1877 flight of the Nez Perce have also been noted in the region.

Obsidian Cliff

Skyrocketing almost 200 feet above Obsidian Creek, Obsidian Cliff is situated eleven miles from Mammoth Hot Springs on the road to Norris. This massive rock outcropping of obsidian is quite rare due to its size; most obsidian is found as very small rocks strewn amid other formations. This unique cliff was formed thousands of years ago during a volcanic eruption where the lava cooled so quickly that it escaped crystallization.

Named a National Historic Landmark in 1996, Obsidian Cliff is famous for providing Native Americans with obsidian to make tools and weapons. Arrowheads located as far away as Ohio have been traced back to the high quality character of Yellowstone's Obsidian Cliff.

Fort Yellowstone and the U.S. Calvary

After years of poor park management and visitor abuse, the U.S. Government intervened in Yellowstone's affairs, and the U.S. Calvary was called to the rescue. In 1886, the Army arrived in force and established a temporary tent camp. Five years later, the Army decided it would be a force in Yellowstone for years to come and erected the first permanent building. Construction began with clapboard buildings in 1891 and expanded to rows of red-roofed stone buildings in 1909. At the height of its use as a military post, Fort Yellowstone housed over 400 men and helped re-establish park control and dignity. When the National Park Service assumed park management duties in 1918, Fort Yellowstone was the logical headquarters for the growing park. To this day, historic Fort Yellowstone remains the heart of park management operations.

Roosevelt Arch

Currently serving as Yellowstone's major year-round entrance, the North Entrance at Gardiner also retains the historical distinction as Yellowstone's first major gateway. Although wealthy visitors originally lurched into the park with little fanfare on simplistic wagons, the 1903 arrival of the railroad in Gardiner called for a grander, more noticeable entrance.

Famous Yellowstone architect, Robert Reamer, designed a massive basalt stone archway to welcome tourist stagecoaches and eventually automobiles. The idea of hexagonal columns featuring regionally quarried rock impressed early twentieth century park officials so much that Yellowstone enthusiast President Theodore Roosevelt laid the arch's cornerstone. Roosevelt subsequently dedicated the structure in 1903.

Towering fifty feet over Yellowstone visitors arriving through the North Entrance, the Roosevelt Arch honors its most famous supporter and is inscribed with words from the 1872 Organic Act that granted Yellowstone its official park status. The inscription reads: "For the benefit and enjoyment of the people."

Additional Historic Sites in the Mammoth Area

• Designed by Hiram Chittenden of the U.S. Army Corps of Engineers, the Engineer's Office dates back to 1903.

• Famous for designing the Roosevelt Arch, Robert Reamer leant his talent to create the Prairie-style "Reamer House." The building dates to 1908.

• The Scottish Rite Chapel was constructed in 1913.

• Capitol Hill was once used as the headquarters blockhouse for former Park Superintendent Philetus W. Norris during Yellowstone's infancy.

• Dating back to the 1880s, Kite Hill Cemetery holds the remains of former Yellowstone park employees and settlers who lived near the park's boundaries.

• Linger in Gardiner before entering the park. The community is home to several historic bridges, railroad beds, and old highways that Yellowstone's first visitors utilized in reaching America's first national park.

Natural Attractions

Mammoth is loaded with Mother Nature's glory, from rivers to canyons and hot springs to mountains.

Bunsen Peak

Rising 8,564 magnificent feet, Bunsen Peak memorializes the life of famous German physicist,

Geothermal Features and How They Work

With half of the earth's geothermal features, Yellowstone holds the planet's most diverse and intact collection of geysers, hot springs, mudpots, and fumaroles. Its more than 300 geysers make up two thirds of all those found on earth. Combine this with more than 10,000 thermal features comprised of brilliantly colored hot springs, bubbling mudpots, and steaming fumaroles, and you have a place like no other. Geyserland, fairyland, wonderland—through the years, all have been used to describe the natural wonder and magic of this unique park that contains more geothermal features than any other place on earth.

Yellowstone's vast collection of thermal features provides a constant reminder of the park's recent volcanic past. Indeed, the caldera provides the setting that allows such features as Old Faithful to exist and to exist in such great concentrations.

Hot Springs and How They Work

In the high mountains surrounding the Yellowstone Plateau, water falls as snow or rain and slowly percolates through layers of porous rock, finding its way through cracks and fissures in the earth's crust created by the ring fracturing and collapse of the caldera. Sinking to a depth of nearly 10,000 feet, this cold water comes into contact with the hot rocks associated with the shallow magma chamber beneath the surface. As the water is heated, its temperatures rise well above the boiling point to become superheated. This superheated water, however, remains in a liquid state due to the great pressure and weight pushing down on it from overlying rock and water. The result is something akin to a giant pressure cooker, with water temperatures in excess of 400°F.

The highly energized water is less dense than the colder, heavier water sinking around it. This creates convection currents that allow the lighter, more buoyant, superheated water to begin its slow, arduous journey back toward the surface through rhyolitic lava flows, following the cracks, fissures, and weak areas of the earth's crust. Rhyolite is essential to geysers because it contains an abundance of silica, the mineral from which glass is made. As the hot water travels through this "natural plumbing system," the high temperatures dissolve some of the silica in the rhyolite, yielding a solution of silica within the water.

At the surface, these silica-laden waters form a rock called geyserite, or sinter, creating the massive geyser cones; the scalloped edges of hot springs; and the expansive, light- colored, barren landscape characteristic of geyser basins. While in solution underground, some of this silica deposits as geyserite on the walls of the plumbing system forming a pressure-tight seal, locking in the hot water and creating a system that can withstand the great pressure needed to produce a geyser.

With the rise of superheated water through this complex plumbing system, the immense pressure exerted over the water drops as it nears the surface. The heat energy, if released in a slow steady manner, gives rise to a hot spring, the most abundant and colorful thermal feature in the park. Hot springs with names like Morning Glory, Grand Prismatic, Abyss, Emerald, and Sapphire, glisten like jewels in a host of colors across the park's harsh volcanic plain.

Mudpots & How They Work

Where hot water is limited and hydrogen sulfide gas is present (emitting the "rotten egg" smell common to thermal areas), sulfuric acid is generated. The acid dissolves the surrounding rock into fine particles of silica and clay that mix with what little water there is to form the seething and bubbling mudpots. The sights, sounds, and smells of areas like Artist and Fountain paint pots and Mud Volcano make these curious features some of the most memorable in the park.

Fumeroles (Steam Vents) and How They Work

Fumaroles, or steam vents, are hot springs with a lot of heat, but so little water that it all boils away before reaching the surface. At places like Roaring Mountain, the result is a loud hissing vent of steam and gases.

Mammoth Hot Springs Terraces and How They Work

At Mammoth Hot Springs, a rarer kind of spring is born when the hot water ascends through the ancient limestone deposits of the area instead of the silica-rich lava flows of the hot springs common elsewhere in the park. The results are strikingly different and unique. They invoke a landscape that resembles a cave turned inside out, with its delicate features exposed for all to see. The flowing waters spill across the surface to sculpt magnificent travertine limestone terraces. As one early visitor described them, "No human architect ever designed such intricate fountains as these. The water trickles over the edges from one to another, blending them together with the effect of a frozen waterfall."

How They Work

As ground water seeps slowly downward and laterally, it comes in contact with hot gases charged with carbon dioxide rising from the magma chamber. Some carbon dioxide is readily dissolved in the hot water to form a weak carbonic acid solution. This hot, acidic solution dissolves great quantities of limestone as it works up through the rock layers to the surface hot springs. Once exposed to the open air, some of the carbon dioxide escapes from solution. As this happens, limestone can no longer remain in solution. A solid mineral reforms and is deposited as the travertine that forms the terraces.

Geysers and How They Work

Sprinkled amid the hot springs are the rarest fountains of all, the geysers. What makes them rare and distinguishes them from hot springs is that somewhere, usually near the surface in the plumbing system of a geyser, there are one or more constrictions. Expanding steam bubbles generated from the rising hot water build up behind these constrictions, ultimately squeezing through the narrow passageways and forcing the water above to overflow from the geyser. The release of water at the surface prompts a sudden decline in pressure of the hotter waters at great depth, triggering a violent chain reaction of tremendous steam explosions in which the volume of rising, now boiling, water expands 1,500 times or more. This expanding body of boiling superheated water bursts into the sky as one of Yellowstone's many famous geysers.

There are more geysers here than anywhere else on earth. Old Faithful, certainly the most famous geyser, is joined by numerous others big and small, named and unnamed. Though born of the same water and rock, what is enchanting is how differently they play in the sky. Riverside Geyser shoots at an angle across the Firehole River, often forming a rainbow in its mist. Castle erupts from a cone shaped like the ruins of some medieval fortress. Grand explodes in a series of powerful bursts, towering above the surrounding trees. Echinus spouts up and out to all sides like a fireworks display of water. And Steamboat, the largest in the world, pulsates like a massive steam engine in a rare, but remarkably memorable eruption, reaching heights of 300 to 400 feet.

Robert Wilhelm Bunsen. During the 1800s, Bunsen was at the forefront of pioneering geyser research, and many of his theories remain true to this day. Interestingly, the "Bunsen burner" made famous in high school chemistry classes across the world resembles a mini-geyser and also honors the physicist's brilliant career.

Although Bunsen Peak still shows scars from the disastrous 1880s and 1988 Yellowstone fires, the area still captures the interest of outdoor recreationists. Hikers, mountain bikers, and skiers frequently traverse the old Bunsen Peak Road for close-up views.

Gardner River Canyon

Winding its way from the park's north entrance at Gardiner to Mammoth Hot Springs, the Gardner River travels beside area visitors as they navigate their way through the scenic Gardner River Canyon. Layered thick with cottonwood trees, Douglas fir, Rocky Mountain juniper, and willows, the canyon twists its way past old mudslides and rugged sandstone walls. As brilliant as the scenery is, the canyon is most noted for its spectacular wildlife. The canyon is home to a large herd of bighorn sheep, eagles, osprey, and kingfishers, most of which are visible throughout the year. Keep your eyes peeled for the impressive bighorn sheep on the canyon's steep sandstone ledges.

Mammoth Hot Springs

The famous springs in the Mammoth region are renowned throughout the park and actually provided the district with its name. Travertine wonders formed from the combination of rising hot water and limestone are sprinkled throughout the area's Upper and Lower Terraces. White mineral deposits characterize much of the area, along with a soft palette of colors situated amidst rising steam from thermal vents. Although the springs occasionally appear to cease activity, visitors should remember that every Yellowstone thermal feature is continually in flux. Water volume changes daily, and thus, an apparently inactive spring is likely just inactive for a short period of time.

Mt. Everts

Comprised of uniquely layered sandstone and shale deposited 70 to 140 million years ago, Mt. Everts draws its name from 1870 Washburn Expedition explorer, Truman Everts. In a freak mishap, Everts became separated from his fellow expedition members and spent thirty-seven days in the wilds of Yellowstone. Possessing no food and clothed inappropriately for the elements, Everts suffered severe hallucinations and was just hours away from death when he was rescued. Although Everts never made it to the mountain that bears his name, officials decided to name the mountain in honor of his courage and perseverance.

Today, Mt. Everts features a solid lava rock peak dated ninety million years younger than the softer sediments forming the mountain's base. Interestingly, Everts' tale of the Yellowstone backcountry remains one of the most historically popular survival stories. Yellowstone archivist Lee Whittlesey edited Everts' tale into the book Lost in the Yellowstone. The book continues to be a bestseller, and Everts' harsh wilderness experience transformed him into an American celebrity.

The Boiling River and 45th Parallel

The Boiling River and 45th Parallel are two Mammoth areas that tourists frequently overlook in their hurry to reach Yellowstone's more famous hot springs and geysers. However, these two features are unique in their own right and worth further exploration.

The imaginary line known scientifically as the 45th Parallel marks locations lying halfway between the North Pole and the Equator. The same line that passes through Minneapolis-St. Paul and the Japanese Islands also makes its presence known near the Montana/Wyoming border within Yellowstone's boundaries. A small sign on the road's edge alerts travelers to this natural highlight.

Nearby, the Boiling River is a regional favorite and one of the only park areas where soaking in the naturally warm water is allowed. In this area, a large hot spring enters the icy cold Gardner River to create an ideal swimming hole. The area requires swimmers to take a half-mile hike up a gentle footpath to the river's edge. Open midsummer through winter, the free area is maintained under the Boiling River Trail Project. Swimsuits are required at all times, and alcoholic beverages and glass containers are not allowed. Large clouds of steam and a parking area on the road's east side mark the must-see Boiling River.

Geological Highlights

Mammoth Hot Springs is geologically noted for its abundant thermal activity that continues to shape and recreate the region's interesting landscape.

Liberty Cap

Nestled at the base of the Lower Terrace Interpretive Trail, Liberty Cap rises thirty-seven feet against Mammoth's travertine terraces. Members of the 1871 Hayden Expedition named the dome-shaped hot spring cone after the hats that Colonial Patriots donned in the French Revolution.

Mammoth Hot Springs

Surfacing at a nearly consistent 170 degrees Fahrenheit, the thermal waters surrounding Mammoth Hot Springs date back thousands of years to the Pinedale Glaciation period. Glacial till and gravel cloaks Terrace Mountain and the Gardner River bed while pockets of ice carved the small valleys and streams now cradling Phantom Lake and Floating Island Lake.

Light-colored limestone known as travertine extends from Mammoth's popular upper formations to the Boiling River near the park's North Entrance. Sink holes dot the area, and evidence of volcanic forces and underground thermal activity is associated with a fault line paralleling the Mammoth Hot Springs/Norris highway.

Opal Spring Terrace

Nestled across from Liberty Cap at the base of Capitol Hill (a short glacially carved formation), Opal Spring Terrace sat dormant for several years

before surprising tourists and park researchers with a sudden 1926 awakening. Since then, Opal Spring has consistently deposited one foot of limestone per year.

Although such travertine terraces are beautiful, Opal Spring's deposits threaten to destroy historical sites in the Mammoth area. In 1947, park officials were forced to remove a tennis court nestled on the historic Fort Yellowstone grounds. Today, the oozing deposits are leaching their way towards a historic 1908 Prairie Style home designed by prominent park architect, Robert Reamer. Torn between protecting the home and the spring's natural expansion, the Park Service erected an earthen wall around the Reamer home and frequently utilizes sandbags for increased protection.

Palette Spring

Showcasing a patchwork splash of browns, greens, and oranges, Palette Spring owes it vibrant coloring to various heat-tolerant bacteria. The spring begins on a flat and subsequently flows down a steep hillside.

A Tour of Mammoth's Most Popular Sites

Mammoth's popular visitor sites are dependent upon the area's volcanic history, steaming hot water, and a system of small fissures running throughout the entire region. Approximately

600,000 years ago, Yellowstone experienced a catastrophic volcanic explosion that left behind a molten magma chamber. This chamber serves as the key ingredient in supplying the area with the hot water needed to form the region's renowned terraces.

As rain and snow trickle down from Yellowstone's slopes, cold ground water seeps deep underneath the park's surface through a series of small cracks. The molten magma chamber then heats the water, forcing it back above the surface in over fifty hot springs lining the Mammoth area. During this cycle, the water joins forces with carbon dioxide gasses to form an acidic solution. As the water/acid solution journeys to the surface, it dissolves and picks up underground limestone deposits. Upon reaching the oxygenated surface, the carbon dioxide gasses escape, leaving the liquefied limestone to harden into travertine terraces.

Each of the following springs and terraces, all of which undergo continual reshaping, owe their formation in part to the above geological processes.

Cleopatra Terrace

The name "Cleopatra Springs" has referred to at least three different springs in the Mammoth area since Yellowstone's founding. Due to dormant periods in the springs' activity, confusion still exists as to which terrace truly is Cleopatra.

Minerva Terrace

Marked with a palette of bright colors and intriguing travertine deposits, Minerva Terrace is by far one of Mammoth's most beloved visitor destinations. Although records of Minerva Spring indicate that the natural wonder was inactive for several years during the early 1900s, the spring has remained active since 1951. In fact, Minerva Spring was once so prolific that it occasionally deposited masses of travertine that buried the park's boardwalks. In an effort to keep the feature open to the public, the National Park Service elevated the boardwalk surrounding the terrace and made it an easily moveable structure in light of Minerva Spring's temperamental nature.

Jupiter Terrace

Prone to long periods of great activity followed by inactivity, Jupiter Terrace has sat idle since 1992. While active during the 1980s, Jupiter Terrace was so fruitful that its deposits often showered over park boardwalks in incredible displays of color and unique formations. Researchers speculate that Jupiter Terrace will someday be active again.

Main Terrace

Lying in the shadow of Mt. Everts, Mammoth's Main Terrace provides an ideal representation of the Earth's powerful forces at work. The landscape surrounding the Main Terrace is in a constant state of change as new springs boil to the surface and older ones become inactive. In addition to its stunning scenery, the Main Terrace offers visitors clear views of historic Fort Yellowstone resting in the distance.

Overlook

The Overlook provides visitors with stunning views of the Main Terrace framed with a mountainous backdrop.

Canary Spring

Featuring a cream-colored base, Canary Spring draws its name from the bright yellow deposits spotting the formation. The spring owes its color to sulfur dependent bacteria and is recognized as one of the most distinctive Yellowstone terraces.

Prospect Terrace

Located on the Upper Terrace Loop Drive, Prospect Terrace was originally named the "Eleventh Terrace" in 1872 by Dr. Peale. Arnold Hague, however, changed the name to "Prospect Terrace" in the late 1880s while leading a U.S. Geological Survey. Although the exact reason behind the terrace's new name is unknown, many speculate the terrace was renamed simply because it offers a wonderful vantage point of the surrounding landscape and distant mountains.

New Highland Terrace

Although relatively inactive since the 1950s, the New Highland Terrace holds keys to the history of hot spring activity in Yellowstone. Located on the Upper Terrace Loop Drive, New Highland Terrace features the twisted remains of dead trees swallowed up in travertine deposits.

Orange Spring Mound

Featuring a distinctive large mounded shape, Orange Spring Mound formed over the course of thousands of years with a combination of sluggish water movement and small mineral deposits. The spring, located on the Upper Terrace Loop Drive, is characterized with unique streaks of color created from the presence of algae and microscopic bacteria.

Bath Lake

Named in the 1880s, Bath Lake was once a popular bathing site for Fort Yellowstone soldiers. Although bathing and swimming in the park's thermal features has long since been outlawed, the thermal feature retains its original name. Depending on the year and water levels, Bath Lake may actually be just as empty as it is full. Bath Lake experiences dramatic changes in thermal activity, most of which dates back to the destruction of fragile formations during the lake's early use a

White Elephant Back Terrace

Resembling an elephant's vertebral column, White Elephant Back Terrace showcases a long mounded ridge unlike most of Yellowstone's thermal features. Water flow through a large fissure in the earth's crust created the very old terrace.

Angel Terrace

Recognized for its brilliant white formations intermingled with colorful bacteria left behind during major thermal activity, Angel Terrace is highly unpredictable. Once dry and brittle, Angel Terrace is now showing new signs of awakening thermal activity.

Day Hiking the Mammoth Hot Springs Area

Day hiking in Yellowstone provides an ideal opportunity for people of all ages to get out and experience the park's many wonders away from the crowds. Thousands of miles of trails await, and wildlife sightings are nearly always guaranteed. Those planning a day trip into Yellowstone's wilderness are encouraged to stop by a ranger station or visitor's center for trail maps and the latest information regarding weather, animal activity, and trail closures. The following trails are available in the Mammoth Hot Springs Area.

Beaver Ponds Loop Trail

Distance: 5-mile (8 km) loop
Climb: moderate
Difficulty: moderate
Location: Locate the Clematis Gulch Trailhead

Steam rises off of the terraces at Mammoth.

between the Judge's historic stone house and Liberty Cap near the Lower Terraces.

Rising 350 feet amid stands of Douglas fir, the Beaver Ponds Loop Trail winds next to a creek in the Clematis Gulch and through open aspen meadows before arriving at an assortment of beaver lodges and dams. The hike is noted for offering spectacular views and wildlife sightings of moose, deer, elk, and pronghorn antelope.

Blacktail Deer Creek-Yellowstone River Trail

Distance: 25 miles (42 km) roundtrip
Climb: gentle
Difficulty: moderate (due to length)
Location: Locate the Blacktail Trailhead 7 miles east of Mammoth on the Mammoth-Tower Road.

During the first 12.5-miles of this hike near the Yellowstone River, users descend 1,100 feet amid Douglas fir trees and rolling hills. After crossing the Yellowstone River on a steel suspension bridge, hikers continue down to Knowles Falls and the trail's halfway mark in Gardiner. Hikers must then follow the same trail 12.5 miles back to the trailhead.

Bunsen Peak Trail

Distance: 10 miles (16.1 km) roundtrip
Climb: gentle
Difficulty: moderate
Location: The trailhead is located 5 miles south of Mammoth at the entrance to the Old Bunsen Peak Road.

Providing sweeping vistas of the Yellowstone River Valley, Gallatin Mountain Range, Blacktail Plateau, and Swan Lake Flats, the Bunsen Peak Trail gradually climbs 1,300 feet to Bunsen Peak's summit. Hikers can descend back to the trailhead along the same trail or take an optional hike to nearby Osprey Falls (see hike description below).

Lava Creek Trail

Distance: 7 miles (11.3 km) roundtrip
Climb: gentle
Difficulty: moderate
Location: The trailhead is located near the Lava Creek Picnic Area Bridge on the Mammoth-Tower Road.

Descending gradually beside Lava Creek, the Lava Creek Trail passes Undine Falls on its journey to

the Gardner River and a pullout area directly north of the Mammoth Hot Springs Campground. Hikers can either have a shuttle vehicle waiting at this destination or return to the trailhead via the same route.

Osprey Falls Trail

Distance: 8 miles (12.9 km) roundtrip
Climb: steep
Difficulty: difficult
Location: The trailhead is located on the Old Bunsen Peak Road 5 miles south of Mammoth.

Passing through grassland and burnt forest while following the Sheepeater Canyon Rim, the Osprey Falls Trail begins switchbacking down to Sheepeater Canyon's floor after 2.5 miles. At the base of the canyon, hikers are greeted with stunning views of the canyon's 500-foot walls and the 150-foot tall Osprey Falls.

Rescue Creek Trail

Distance: 16 miles (12.9 km) roundtrip
Climb: moderate
Difficulty: moderate
Location: Rescue Creek Trail departs 7 miles east of Mammoth at the Blacktail Trailhead on the Mammoth-Tower Road.

After hiking 0.75 miles on the Blacktail Deer Creek Trail, hikers veer off onto the Rescue Creek Trail. Gradually winding its way through open wildflower and aspen meadows, the trail then drops 1,400 feet to the Gardner River and continues to the park's North Entrance. Hikers may either return to the trailhead on the same trail or arrange a shuttle from the North Entrance Station.

Sepulcher Mountain Trail

Distance: 11-mile (17.7 km) loop
Climb: steep
Difficulty: strenuous
Location: Locate the Sepulcher Mountain Trail at the Clematis Gulch Trailhead between the Judge's Stone House and Liberty Cap.

Upon following the Beaver Ponds Trail to its junction with the Sepulcher Mountain Trail, hikers then climb 3,400 feet to the 9,652-foot peak of Sepulcher Mountain. Upon reaching the summit, the trail descends on the mountain's opposite side past Snow Pass Trail Junction to the Howard

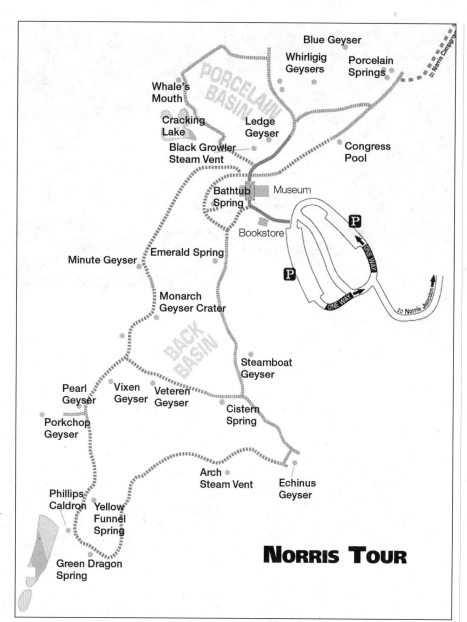

NORRIS TOUR

(Map labels:) Blue Geyser · Whirligig Geysers · Porcelain Springs · PORCELAIN BASIN · Whale's Mouth · Cracking Lake · Ledge Geyser · Black Growler Steam Vent · Congress Pool · Bathtub Spring · Museum · Bookstore · to Norris Canyon · ONE WAY · to Norris Junction · Minute Geyser · Emerald Spring · Monarch Geyser Crater · BACK BASIN · Steamboat Geyser · Pearl Geyser · Vixen Geyser · Veteren Geyser · Cistern Spring · Porkchop Geyser · Arch Steam Vent · Echinus Geyser · Phillips Caldron · Yellow Funnel Spring · Green Dragon Spring

---

Eaton Trail. The Howard Eaton Trail carries hikers west to the trailhead. The scenic trail offers outstanding views while hiking through pine trees and open meadows.

Wraith Falls
Distance: 1 mile (1 km) roundtrip
Climb: level
Difficulty: easy
Location: The trailhead is located on the Mammoth-Tower Road at a pullout 0.25 miles east of the Lava Creek Picnic Area.

Located on Lupine Creek, Wraith Falls awaits hikers on this short trip appropriate for park visitors of all ages and skill levels. The trail passes through Douglas fir stands and open sagebrush plains.

DISCOVERING THE NORRIS AREA

Situated twenty-eight miles from Yellowstone's West Entrance, the Norris Area honors the memory of early park superintendent, Philetus W. Norris. The region is renowned as Yellowstone's most changeable thermal area, and researchers believe geysers have been active in the area for over 115,000 years!

Historical Attractions

Yellowstone's Norris Area has been the subject of extensive research and occupation. From hosting the region's ancient inhabitants to Fort Yellowstone soldiers and park rangers, Norris has been a hotbed of activity for thousands of years.

Archaeological Findings
After conducting digs at the Norris and Madison campgrounds, the Midwest Archaeological Center concluded that ancient inhabitants utilized the Norris area campsites as early as 10,000 years ago. Ancient campfire residue, bone fragments, and obsidian flakes have been discovered throughout the region. Many of these archaeological findings were unearthed along the Solfatara Trail that links Obsidian Cliff to the present-day Norris Campground.

Norris Geyser Basin Museum
Featuring beautiful stone and log architecture, the single-story Norris Geyser Basin Museum was constructed between 1929 and 1930 as one of Yellowstone's first museums. The facility houses exhibits related to the Norris Area's geothermal phenomena, and ranger-led programs are offered several times each day during the summer season.

Norris Soldier Station/Museum of the National Park Ranger
Nestled on the Gibbon River's north bank, the Norris Soldier Station was originally built in 1886 to house Calvary soldiers on ski and horseback patrol duty. After a fire destroyed the station in 1897, a new structure was built that was subsequently remodeled in 1908. In 1916, the National Park Service assumed control of the station, modifying it into a ranger station and private residence. The station, one of the park's longest occupied, remained in use until the 1959 Hebgen Lake earthquake created significant structural damage. Once the building was restored in 1991, it became home to the Museum of the National Park Ranger. The history of park rangers is presented along with a few Yellowstone artifacts.

Natural Attractions

The Norris Area may best be known for its geysers, but the region also boasts waterfalls, thermal pools, mountains, rivers, and forests.

Gibbon River
Reliant upon both cold and hot springs for its sustained flow, the Gibbon River winds its way from Wolf Lake through the Norris region to its junction with the Firehole River. The river is heavily populated with grayling, rainbow trout, brook trout, and brown trout, and fly-fishing is allowed below Gibbon Falls.

Norris-Canyon Pine Swath
In 1984, a fierce windstorm blew its way through Yellowstone, and the Norris Area was heavily hit. During the course of its fury, the storm blew down a twenty-two square mile patch of native lodgepole pine. The swath subsequently burned during the 1988 North Fork fire and became the site of a worldwide news report that stated, "Tonight, this is all that's left of Yellowstone." Visitors can learn more about the storm and fire in a nearby roadside marker.

Norris Geyser Basin
Providing a constant testimony to Yellowstone's amazing underground composition, the Norris Geyser Basin is the park's oldest, hottest, and most active thermal area. Researchers have recorded temperatures as hot as 459 degrees Fahrenheit (237 degrees Celsius) underground while surface temperatures are a consistent 199 degrees Fahrenheit (93 degrees Celsius).

Due to the presence of such hot water, Norris Geyser Basin is home to the park's most active geysers, including Steamboat Geyser and Echinus Geyser. The area is extremely acidic, and rare acid geysers are distributed throughout the region. The region's highly active nature also ensures that thermal features transform daily as the result of water pressure changes and frequent seismic activity.

In addition to spectacular geysers, the Norris Geyser Basin features wooded and barren basin areas, including Porcelain Basin, Back Basin, and One Hundred Springs Plain. Travel is strictly restricted to maintained boardwalk trails, as many of the basin areas are hollow and dangerous.

Roaring Mountain
Located four miles north of Norris on the east side of the Grand Loop Road, Roaring Mountain is a bare plot of land dotted with numerous steam vents called fumaroles. Although several of these vents are still present today, records suggest that the acidic thermal area possessed hundreds of additional fumaroles during the late 1800s and

early 1900s. The thermal area received its name from a characteristic rumbling that was once so loud, it could be heard more than four miles away. Today, the mountain's roar has diminished as the number of fumaroles has decreased.

Virginia Cascades
The Gibbon River plunges sixty feet to form the Virginia Cascades. Visitors can locate the waterfall after a three-mile hike or bicycle ride on the well-marked old Norris Road. The scenic waterfall is sheltered away from the crowds and is well worth the side trip.

Geological Highlights

Featuring three major fault lines and evidence of ancient glacial sculpting, the Norris Area is rich with geological wonders.

Norris-Mammoth Corridor Fault and Hebgen Lake Fault
Extending north from Norris, the Norris-Mammoth Corridor Fault runs through Mammoth on its journey to Gardiner, Montana. This fault intersects with the Hebgen Lake Fault at a 600,000 year old ring fracture created from the Yellowstone Caldera. The Hebgen Lake Fault, best known for triggering a 7.4 magnitude earthquake in 1959, runs from Norris past the park's West Entrance in West Yellowstone, Montana. Together, these two faults are largely responsible for the Norris Geyser Basin's dynamic activity.

Madison Fault
The Madison Fault owes its existence to the ancient Yellowstone Caldera eruption. After the massive volcano exploded, stream channels carved their way through the area's extensive lava flows. The Madison Fault rests within these eroded channels and encompasses the Virginia Cascades and Gibbon Falls.

Glacial Remains
In glaring contrast to the region's piping hot thermal features, glaciers also once occupied the Norris Area. As the glaciers sculpted valleys, raised mountains, and eventually began receding, the Norris Area's underground thermal features altered the glacial moraines left behind. Glacial ice melted rapidly, and the resulting massive piles of debris and rock were shaped anew with the area's steam and hot water.

A Tour of Norris' Most Popular Sites

Unforgettable odors, hissing steam vents, and a spectacular display of rainbow colors stimulate the senses on a tour of the Norris Area's most popular visitor sites. Packed with geothermal features around every corner, the Norris Area is home to a high concentration of geysers and thermal wonders that appear starkly different from one year to the next. Loop trails wind near most of the area's favorite features, and many trails are wheelchair accessible.

Porcelain Basin Terrace Overlook
Situated in the northern portion of the Norris Geyser Basin, Porcelain Basin is renowned for its wide variety of geysers. Featuring both active and inactive displays, Porcelain Basin is cloaked in a thin rock layer that pulses with the movement of underground pressure and steam. New geysers are born with little notice, and while some last for weeks, others last just minutes before dying out.

Porcelain Basin Hot Springs
Milky white mineral deposits of siliceous sinter provide Porcelain Basin Hot Springs with its logical name. After hot water carries the mineral to the surface, a thin white sheet spreads across the flat basin. This mineral layer (also known as geyserite) seals off existing hot springs and geysers, forcing the hot underground water to circulate to a weaker area where it is able to release pressure and blow through the white crust. The process is continually repeated, ensuring that Porcelain Basin is one of the most active regions within Yellowstone.

Congress Pool
Congress Pool is just one of many Norris features that experience dramatic disturbances to its "normal" thermal activity. While most visitors report that Congress Pool is a tranquil pool showcased in pale blue, others view the site as a boiling violet or muddy pool. Although such violent changes in Congress Pool's activity have yet to be fully explained, it has been noted that most shifts in thermal activity occur during late summer or early fall. Disturbances may last from just a few short hours to as long as a week before returning to "normal."

Black Growler Steam Vent
Located on the 0.75-mile Porcelain Basin boardwalk, the Black Growler Steam Vent is one of the basin's hottest features. Steam violently erupts from a fumarole (vent) at temperatures ranging from 199 to 280 degrees Fahrenheit.

Ledge Geyser
Equipped with enough thermal power to shoot out 125-foot tall water towers, Ledge Geyser is distinguished as the Norris Geyser Basin's second largest geyser. On most occasions, however, the geyser prefers to explode at an angle, spraying water over 220 feet away. Although Ledge Geyser historically erupted at fourteen-hour intervals, the geyser is just as famous for its periods of inactivity. Between 1979 and 1993, the geyser remained quiet. Then, in 1994 and 1995, the geyser suddenly awakened with eruption intervals of four to six days. Today, the geyser intermittently spews its thermal secrets.

Norris Geyser Basin's Bacteria and Colorful Water
Although most of Norris' thermal wonders feature extremely acidic water, unique bacteria thrive upon such harsh conditions and add spectacular coloring to geysers and basins. Microscopic Cyanidium algae cast a lime green presence while Cyanobacteria coats Porcelain Basin's runoff streams with rust-colored deposits.

In addition to providing natural coloring to Yellowstone's thermal features, these organisms have also played key roles in recent scientific research. DNA fingerprinting technology and innovations in AIDS/HIV research has depended upon these tiny Yellowstone inhabitants.

Crackling Lake
Formerly designated Spring 39 in Dr. Peale's Gibbon Geyser Basin, Crackling Lake was renamed in 1967. Ed Leigh proposed the new name after hearing popping sounds emitted from hot springs lining the lake's southern shore.

Whale's Mouth
Drawing its name from its distinctive fish mouth shape, Whale's Mouth Hot Spring was appropriately named by a park naturalist in 1967.

Whirligig Geysers
Possessing water that swirls in its crater every time it erupts, Whirligig Geyser was named after this unique characteristic. Nearby, the inactive Little Whirligig is speckled with iron oxide deposits and is noted as one of Porcelain Basin's most colorful geysers.

Blue Geyser
This geyser, originally known as Iris Spring as early as 1886, was accidentally renamed Blue Geyser in 1904 when an early area map was misread and redrawn. Although Blue Geyser once regularly erupted over sixty feet, the geyser has remained dormant since February 1997.

Emerald Spring
Located in Norris' Back Basin, Emerald Spring draws its unique color from sulfur deposits and refracted light. Lined with yellow sulfur that crystallizes at the Earth's surface, the twenty-seven-foot deep pool combines this brightly colored sulfur with reflected blue light to create an amazing green appearance.

Minute Geyser
Drawing its name from regular sixty-second eruptions that occurred during the park's early years, Minute Geyser is now a living testimony to the destructive nature of many of Yellowstone's nineteenth century tourists. The geyser, which once blew from a large west vent, is no longer capable of such eruptions because early park visitors carelessly clogged the vent with rocks. Smaller eruptions occur irregularly from the geyser's eastern vent. Although park officials have toyed with the idea of removing the rocks from the west vent, heavy equipment required to complete such a task would likely destroy the entire geyser.

Steamboat Geyser
Producing memorable eruptions since its first noted outburst in 1878, Steamboat Geyser is the world's tallest active geyser. When it first exploded, Steamboat hurled boiling mud and boulders into Wyoming's clear blue skies. Although the geyser calmed down for several years thereafter, a violent 1911 eruption was followed by over fifty years of dormancy. Eruptions occurred with great frequency during the 1960s with the most recent major outburst occurring on May 2, 2000. During its violent three to forty minute eruptions, Steamboat is capable of skyrocketing more than 300 feet (90 meters). The sound is reportedly so deafening that people shouting to one another in the area cannot make themselves heard! After a major eruption, steam then rolls from the geyser for hours upon end.

Full eruptions such as these are highly unpredictable, and minor eruptions are the norm. Most of Steamboat's activity is limited to irregular ten to forty-foot bursts of water and steam.

Cistern Spring
Joined underground with Steamboat Geyser, Cistern Spring is normally a crystal blue pool overflowing with water. In contrast to many Yellowstone geysers that build one-half to one-inch sinter deposits over the course of an entire century, Cistern Spring is quite productive and deposits up to one-half inch of gray sinter annually! Its topographical influence is far reaching. Lodgepole trees once dotted the landscape but have retreated and died with the continual flooding of Cistern Spring's silica rich water.

During major eruptions at nearby Steamboat, Cistern Spring's vast pool of water drains completely dry. Such occasions, however, are rare, so most visitors view Cistern Spring in its normal overflowing blue splendor.

Echinus Geyser

Boasting a 3.3 to 3.6 pH that is nearly as acidic as vinegar, Echinus Geyser is the world's largest acid-water geyser. Although the geyser once faithfully erupted at thirty-five to seventy-five minute intervals, Echinus has exhibited widely sporadic behavior since late 1998. Eruptions that once shot forty to sixty feet high and lasted anywhere from four minutes to 118 minutes are now infrequent. Researchers believe that a secondary water source once supplying the geyser's major eruptions mysteriously disappeared sometime during the mid 1990s. As with other geysers in the park, however, Echinus may once again become active in the future.

Green Dragon Spring

Characterized by a unique cavern shape, the sulfur-lined Green Dragon Hot Spring is noted for its boiling green water. Clouds of steam, however, frequently mask the spring's beauty. On warm summer afternoons, though, the steam will frequently clear for a few minutes and allow patient visitors a glimpse inside Green Dragon Spring.

Porkchop Geyser/Hot Spring

Historically a small geyser that occasionally boasted minor eruptions, Porkchop Geyser began changing its behavior in 1985 with regular eruptions. Four years later, Porkchop violently spewed rocks and water more than 216 feet away. Since this outburst, Porkchop Geyser has transformed itself into a calmly roiling hot spring.

Veteran Geyser

Poised as though its ready to erupt at any moment, Veteran Geyser captures the interest of faithful geyser watchers ready to wait for an unpredictable performance. The geyser, which reaches heights up to forty feet, erupts at intervals varying from twenty minutes to three hours.

Day Hiking the Norris Area

Day hiking in Yellowstone provides an ideal opportunity for people of all ages to get out and experience the park's many wonders away from the crowds. Thousands of miles of trails await, and wildlife sightings are nearly always guaranteed. Those planning a day trip into Yellowstone's wilderness are encouraged to stop by a ranger station or visitor's center for trail maps and the latest information regarding weather, animal activity, and trail closures. The following trails are available in the Norris Area, and all hikers are reminded to stay on the trail. The Norris Area is a highly active geothermal region, and surfaces may be weak. Again, stick to the trail!

Artist Paint Pots

Distance: 1 mile (1 km) roundtrip
Climb: moderate
Difficulty: moderate
Location: The trailhead is located 4.5 miles south of Norris on the Norris-Madsen Road.

The Artist Paint Pots trail takes hikers on a mod-erate stroll through an open meadow and lodge-pole pine forest on its short journey to two prolific mudpots. A short loop at the trail's end features some of the Norris Area's most colorful geysers and springs. The trail is appropriate for users of all ages and hiking abilities.

Cygnet Lakes Trail

Distance: 8 miles (14.4 km) roundtrip
Climb: level
Difficulty: easy
Location: The trailhead is located 5.5 miles west of the Canyon Junction at a pullout on the south side of Norris-Canyon Road.

A day-use only trail, the Cygnet Lakes Trail winds through partially burned lodgepole pine forests to the meadow-lined Cygnet Lakes. The lakes, which are small and boggy, are the trail's primary destination. The trail is not maintained after the lakes, so hikers seeking a longer trek must use the route at their own discretion.

Grizzly Lake Trail

Distance: 4 miles (6 km) roundtrip
Climb: moderate
Difficulty: moderate
Location: The trailhead is located on the Mammoth-Norris Road 1 mile south of Beaver Lake.

Meandering through lush meadows as well as remnants of lodgepole forests scorched in 1976 and 1988, the Grizzly Lake Trail takes hikers to a favorite angling destination. Heavily wooded, the narrow lake is home to a large population of brook trout. Grizzly Lake is difficult to access during late spring and early summer due to bogs and mosquitoes but is an ideal day hike during mid and late summer.

Ice Lake Trail

Distance: 0.6 miles (1 km) roundtrip
Climb: level
Difficulty: easy
Location: The trailhead is located on the Norris-Canyon Road 3.5 miles east of Norris.

Just slightly removed from the park's major crowds, Ice Lake is cradled within a lush pine forest. The small lake provides a beautiful destination in and of itself, but hikers may opt to continue onwards to Wolf Lake, Grebe Lake, and Cascade Lake.

Monument Geyser Basin

Distance: 2 miles (3 km) roundtrip
Climb: moderate to steep
Difficulty: moderate to difficult
Location: The trailhead is located 5 miles south of Norris Junction directly after the Gibbon River on the Norris-Madison Road.

After winding gradually along the Gibbon River, the Monument Geyser Basin Trail climbs 500 feet in less than 0.5 miles to the peak of Monument Geyser. The steep portion of the trail is lined with eroding rocks and geyserite deposits, but the geyser basin provides a fascinating look at several inactive thermal features. Although the area's mounds and cones have been dormant for many years, hikers are reminded to stay on the trail as the surface is still fragile.

Solfatara Creek

Distance: 13 miles (20 km) roundtrip
Climb: gradual
Difficulty: easy to moderate
Location: 0.75 miles south of the Beaver Lake Picnic Area at the beginning of Loop C in the Norris Campground

Twisting near Solfatara Creek, this trail gently

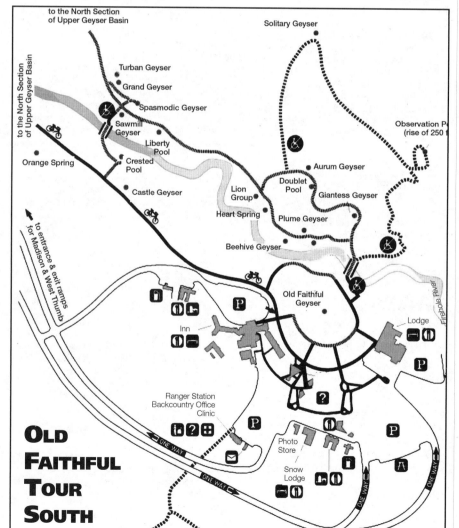

OLD FAITHFUL TOUR SOUTH

works its way up to Whiterock Springs and Lake of the Woods before passing Amphitheater Springs and Lemonade Creek. The above areas are noted for their colorful hot springs but are also subject to bear visits. Before embarking on the trail, be sure to stop by a ranger station for the latest animal activity reports.

Wolf Lake Cut-off Trail
Distance: 6 miles (10 km) roundtrip
Climb: moderate
Difficulty: moderate to difficult
Location: The trailhead is located 0.25 miles east of the Ice Lake Trailhead on the Canyon Norris Road. The trailhead is unmarked, but a large pull-out marks the access point.

The Wolf Lake Cut-off Trail wanders beside the Gibbon River, passes Little Gibbon Falls, enters an intermittently burned pine forest, and eventually ends at Wolf Lake. Hikers should note that the trail does require stream crossings, and fallen trees may block the trail at times. Trail users should be in good physical condition.

DISCOVERING THE OLD FAITHFUL AREA

Garnering more attention than any other park attraction, Old Faithful Geyser is synonymous with Yellowstone. Old Faithful, however, is much more than a time-conscious geyser. The term also applies to the surrounding area of geyser basins, waterfalls, rivers, and lakes. The area is located approximately thirty miles from the park's West Entrance in West Yellowstone, Montana and is home to the park's largest number of hydrothermal features.

Historical Attractions

Housing tales of Native Americans, outfitters, early entrepreneurs, and curious sightseers, the Old Faithful Area boasts a history as legendary as its natural oddities.

Howard Eaton Trail
Operating as an early park guide and outfitter, Howard Eaton provided horseback tours of the park on a trail that paralleled much of today's Grand Loop Road. Portions of the trail are still evident, and the route honors Eaton and his commitment to opening Yellowstone to the world. Although seldom used, the Howard Eaton Trail is maintained as a backcountry route leading to Lone Star Geyser.

Lower Hamilton Store
Dating back to 1897 and originally situated 700 feet southwest of Beehive Geyser, the Lower Hamilton Store was constructed as a photo studio for famous park photographer, Frank J. Haynes. Today, the Lower Hamilton Store rests near the crosswalk on Grand Loop Road and is recognized as the oldest Old Faithful Area building still in use. A wooden porch welcomes visitors to soak up the wonderful views of Geyser Hill.

Nez Perce Creek Exhibit
In a tragic flight from their Oregon homeland to an attempted Canadian border crossing, 700 Nez Perce found their way through Yellowstone during the 1877 Nez Perce War. Desperately attempting to flee 600 Army soldiers and outwit U.S. Army General O.O. Howard, the Nez Perce entered the newly established park on August 23, 1877. The men, women, and children wandered the park for two weeks, encountering all twenty-five tourists known to be visiting the park at the

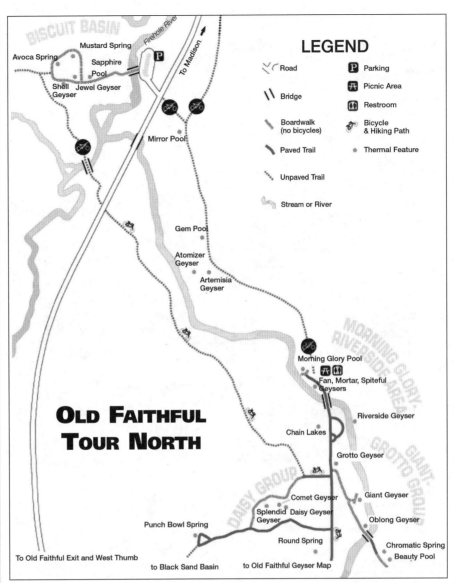

OLD FAITHFUL TOUR NORTH

time. Hostages were taken, and several of the tourists were injured or killed. As quickly as the Nez Perce arrived in Yellowstone, though, they soon departed on the last leg of their journey to Canada. A few of the Nez Perce did successfully cross the border, but over 350 tribal members surrendered just shy of reaching freedom.

Nez Perce Creek was named in honor of the legendary 1,700-mile journey of the Nez Perce people and their retaliation against encroaching American policies. The roadside exhibit relates the story of this incredible historic tale.

Old Faithful Historic District
The area surrounding Old Faithful Geyser has long catered to tourists with food, lodging, and various other amenities. With development dating back to the dawn of the twentieth century, the Old Faithful Area is home to an official Historic District dedicated to preserving the region's structural treasures.

Old Faithful Inn
Boasting 327 rooms and rumored to be the world's largest log structure, the Old Faithful Inn is a National Historic Landmark dating back to 1904. Famous park architect Robert Reamer designed the legendary inn with massive logs, a four-sided rhyolite lobby fireplace, and twisted lodgepole pine balcony railings. Although various

informational brochures and individual accounts report the ceiling height as sixty-five, seventy-nine, eighty-four, or ninety-two feet high, it is a known fact that the ceiling's log rafters cradled a

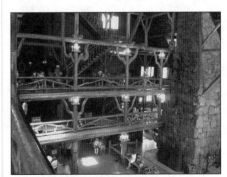
The lobby of the Old Faithful Inn.

platform where musicians played beautiful strains to entertain the park's first visitors and hotel guests. With new hotel wings added in 1915 and 1927, the inn expanded to accommodate growing numbers of guests and continues to receive extensive remodeling on a regular basis.

Today, guided tours are available that recount the inn's incredible construction process and his-

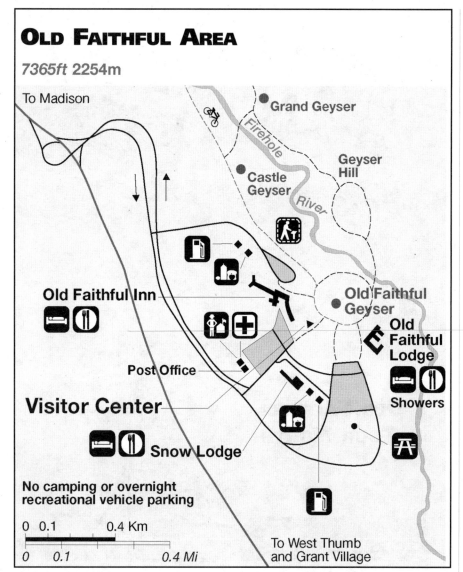

OLD FAITHFUL AREA

7365ft 2254m

To Madison

Grand Geyser

Firehole River

Castle Geyser

Geyser Hill

Old Faithful Inn

Old Faithful Geyser

Old Faithful Lodge

Post Office

Showers

Visitor Center

Snow Lodge

No camping or overnight recreational vehicle parking

0   0.1   0.4 Km

0   0.1   0.4 Mi

To West Thumb and Grant Village

---

tory as the park's most popular lodging destination. Rooms are still offered with an array of amenities, but advance reservations are required.

Old Faithful Lodge

Old Faithful Lodge offers a much different atmosphere than the grand Old Faithful Inn but dates back to the same era in park history. When Yellowstone first opened, tent camps were a popular means of hosting park visitors, and the Wylie Permanent Camping Company and Shaw & Powell Camping Company served as primary concessionaires. The tent camp system worked well, as hotels and lodges were initially absent from the park scene. However, when automobiles were allowed into the park, visitor numbers rapidly rose, and a new system for lodging tourists was needed. As permanent overnight lodging popped up around Yellowstone, the camping companies decided to eliminate some of their old camps. At the same time, the Yellowstone Park Camping Company was born, and work began on the rustic Old Faithful Lodge. Finally, after a construction period of ten years, the lodge was completed in 1928 in its present form and offered overnight lodging and laundry services to park guests.

Today, the Old Faithful Lodge still offers cabin-style accommodations to guests at affordable prices. The lodge also provides a coffee shop, gift store, and cafeteria. Advance reservations are recommended.

Natural Attractions

Geyser basins, steaming rivers, mudpots, and more await sightseers visiting the Old Faithful Area. Boasting the park's largest number of concentrated geysers, the area spews thousands of gallons of water from the surface every day in memorable displays of the Earth's dynamic power.

Craig Pass and Isa Lake

Located on the Grand Loop Road seven miles south of Old Faithful, Craig Pass rests at 8,262 feet on the Continental Divide. The pass cradles the geologically unique phenomenon of Isa Lake. Unlike most of Yellowstone's water features, Isa Lake contains both Atlantic and Pacific Ocean drainages. Flowing into the Firehole drainage, the lake's west side eventually dumps into the Atlantic. The eastern side, however, drains into the Snake River and flows to the Pacific Ocean. The lake's unusual feature is related to the Earth's powerful gyroscopic forces.

Firehole River

The beautiful thirty-five mile long Firehole River originates at Madison Lake on the Continental Divide's north side. Twisting its way through the Upper and Midway Geyser Basins, the river is world-renowned for brown, rainbow, and brook trout as well as the characteristic steam responsible for its unusual name. Noticing the steam ris-

ing in the distance and unable to identify its source, early trappers mistakenly interpreted the steam as smoke mounting from an unknown fire in a valley below them. Since the trappers referred to mountain valleys as "holes," the region became known as "Firehole." The regional term was then applied to the river upon its discovery.

Kepler Cascades

Stair-stepping down the Firehole River, Kepler Cascades drops 150 feet in a spectacular outpouring that is easily reached. The waterfall is situated just 2.5 miles south of the Old Faithful Geyser, and a pullout offers an overlook of one of the area's most easily accessed cataracts.

Lone Star Geyser Basin

Lone Star Geyser Basin is farther removed from Old Faithful's major attractions and requires visitors to take an easy five-mile roundtrip hike. The trail begins near Kepler Cascades just 2.5 miles south of the Old Faithful Geyser and carries visitors past small hot springs and scenic meadows on its journey to Lone Star Geyser. Resting in a twelve-foot cone, the geyser spews thirty to fifty foot columns of steaming water every three hours. Most eruptions last thirty minutes, and a logbook located near Lone Star records the geyser's latest witnessed eruption times and event descriptions.

Lower Geyser Basin

Lower Geyser Basin is understandably famous for its large area of hydrothermal activity. A boardwalk trail and the three-mile Firehole Lake Drive provide incredible views of the area's thermal features, including the renowned Great Fountain. The geyser is known for its 100 to 200 foot eruptions that send tiny droplets of water racing down the surrounding terraces. Although Great Fountain regularly erupts twice per day, the timing of its displays can be unpredictable. Park staff attempt to predict the next eruption time, but viewers should take into account that the predictions can be off by up to two hours.

Midway Geyser Basin

Situated along the Firehole River, Midway Geyser Basin may be one of the smallest basins in the Old Faithful Area, but it is home to two of the park's most historically impressive features. Excelsior Geyser, which now releases over 4,000 gallons of hot water every minute into the Firehole River, was once regarded as Yellowstone's most impressive geyser. Between 1882 and 1888, the geyser erupted every 20 to 120 minutes and blasted towers of water more than 300 feet skywards. Today, a 200 by 300 foot gaping crater marks the geyser's once impressive outlet. Researchers believe the geyser's sheer force and pressure destroyed its own underground water piping system, causing the geyser to now remain dormant.

Another noteworthy site in Midway Geyser Basin is the Grand Prismatic Spring. Featuring an abundance of beautiful water, Grand Prismatic is Yellowstone's largest hot spring and the world's third largest spring. The spring measures 121 feet deep with a diameter spanning 370 feet.

Shoshone Geyser Basin

Although it requires a seventeen-mile roundtrip hike to visit, the backcountry Shoshone Geyser Basin is often noted as one of Yellowstone's best thermal sites. Visitors cross the Continental Divide at Grants Pass and view Shoshone Lake along the way. Upon reaching the basin area, visitors are encouraged to use extreme caution. No boardwalks exist, and the remote thermal area is fragile.

To visit Shoshone Geyser Basin, depart from the DeLacy Creek Trailhead located nine miles south of Old Faithful.

Upper Geyser Basin

Boasting up to 300 geysers bunched together in just one square mile, the Upper Geyser Basin houses the largest number of Yellowstone's thermal features. In addition, the basin is home to nearly sixty percent of the world's geysers and includes some of Yellowstone's favorite visitor destinations. Old Faithful, Castle, Riverside, Grand, and Daisy Geysers are subject to regular predictions while smaller geysers and several hot springs round out the basin's amazing sites. Numerous walking trails and overlooks provide visitors with close-up views of the basin's thermal wonders.

Geological Highlights

Continually the subject of geological shaping, the Old Faithful Area exhibits signs of glacial activity, catastrophic volcanic eruptions, lava flows, erosion, and mountain building. Rhyolitic lava flows covering the hillsides around Old Faithful and the Upper Geyser Basin date back more than 600,000 years while glacial till deposits formed such notable features as Porcupine Hills and Fountain Flats.

The Firehole River drainage has been subjected to years of erosion, and small channels carved into the base of geyser basins are also the result of the Earth's amazing attritional power. At the opposite end of the geographical scale, mountain building is evident at Craig's Pass, an area that divides Yellowstone into both Pacific and Atlantic Ocean watersheds.

A Tour of the Old Faithful Area's Most Popular Sites

Prominent geysers, beautiful springs, and geyser basins combine to give the Old Faithful Area some of Yellowstone's most impressive scenery.

Sapphire Pool

Situated in Biscuit Basin three miles north of Old Faithful, Sapphire Pool once featured biscuit-shaped deposits around its base. However, in the 1959 Hebgen Lake Earthquake, the deposits were blown to pieces when Sapphire became a short-lived geyser. In addition to Sapphire Pool, the area features other colorful wonders like Mustard Spring, Jewel Geyser, and Shell Geyser.

Morning Glory Pool

Originally showcasing an uncanny resemblance to its flowering namesake, Morning Glory Pool was named in the 1880s. The pool has been a favorite visitor destination for years, but vandalism has started to take its toll. Coins, trash, rocks, and logs have thoughtlessly been thrown into the pool. As a result, natural vents are now blocked, water circulation has been affected, and the pool's natural coloring is now altered.

Fan and Mortar Geysers

Fan and Mortar Geysers are located so close to one another that an eruption in one geyser generally triggers a simultaneous spouting in the other. While Fan's outbursts reach up to 125 feet, Mortar's eruptions are much tamer at an average of forty to eighty feet. Both geysers average eruptions lasting forty-five minutes or longer, but predicting the event can be difficult. The timing between eruptions can vary from one day to several months.

Riverside Geyser

Touted as one of Yellowstone's most picturesque geysers, Riverside Geyser gracefully sprays a seventy-five foot arch of water over the Firehole River during its regular twenty-minute eruptions. As a result, rainbows dance off the water column under Yellowstone's brilliant sunlight. Eruptions generally occur every 5 1/2 to 6 1/2 hours.

Grotto Geyser

Grotto Geyser is one of the park's most unusually shaped geysers. Researchers believe geyserite deposits piled up over tree trunks and shaped the unique formation. Erupting at intervals of eight hours, the geyser spews water ten feet high for as little as one hour to more than ten hours!

Comet Geyser

Located near the Daisy and Splendid Geysers, Comet Geyser splashes on a nearly continuous basis. The geyser possesses the largest cone of its neighboring geysers, but Comet's eruptions are less remarkable and rarely tower more than six feet.

Splendid Geyser

Although Splendid Geyser's eruptions are infrequent and generally hard to predict, those who witness its wonder are in for a memorable treat. Splendid Geyser is noted as one of Yellowstone's tallest active geysers with eruptions over 200 feet tall.

Punch Bowl Spring

Punch Bowl Spring draws its name from a sinter deposit that has raised the thermal feature above the geyser basin floor. As a result of this elevation, the intermittently boiling spring features a punch bowl shape.

Daisy Geyser

Usually an easily predictable thermal feature, Daisy Geyser erupts approximately every ninety minutes. The angled eruptions generally last three to five minutes and shoot water over seventy-five feet away. The only disruption to this natural cycle is when nearby Splendid Geyser decides to erupt.

Giant Geyser

Dormant from 1955 to 1997, Giant Geyser has slowly awakened with crowd-pleasing eruptions lasting up to one hour. The geyser spurts water columns ranging in height from 180 to 250 feet. Since 1997, eruptions have continued to occur sporadically.

Beauty Pool

Colored bacteria frame Beauty Pool's spectacular blue water in a stunning rainbow palette. The pool's name accurately reflects its beautiful nature and appears to be connected underground to nearby Chromatic Spring.

Chromatic Spring

Linked to nearby Beauty Pool, Chromatic Spring is one of Yellowstone's most interesting thermal features. Periodically, energy levels below Chromatic Spring and Beauty Pool shift. As a result, one spring's water levels descend while the other spring elevates and overflows. These energy shifts occur at intervals ranging from one month to several years. For additional information about Chromatic Spring's and Beauty Pool's latest activity, contact a park ranger.

Grand Geyser

Grand Geyser erupts from a large pool every seven to fifteen hours and is recognized as the world's tallest predictable geyser. The geyser dis-

Old Faithful Geyser.

plays classic fountain behavior with its powerful bursts of water instead of a continuous spray. Most eruptions last no longer than twelve minutes and include one to four water bursts rising 200 feet.

Sawmill Geyser

Resembling a rotating circular blade, water in this thermal feature spins in its crater while erupting. As a result, Sawmill Geyser was given its appropriate name. A somewhat unpredictable geyser, Sawmill displays its power every one to three hours with eruptions lasting from nine minutes to four hours!

Crested Pool

Extending forty-two feet below Yellowstone's surface, Crested Pool is a thermal powerhouse. Water temperatures are impressively hot, ranging from a mere simmer to roiling boils raging eight to ten feet tall.

Castle Geyser

Possessing the largest cone of all other geysers in the Old Faithful Area, Castle Geyser is one of the park's oldest recorded geysers. Over the course of its long life, Castle's behavior has changed considerably. Currently, the geyser blows its top every ten to twelve hours with water columns reaching up to ninety feet high. Following the average twenty-minute eruption, Castle Geyser lets off a fury of steam for thirty to forty minutes.

The Lion Group

The Lion, Lioness, Big Cub, and Little Cub Geysers come together to form the Lion Group formation. Connected underground, the geysers typically unveil sudden bursts of steam and deep roaring noises prior to an eruption. Of the four, Lion Geyser features the largest cone and longest eruptions; most eruptions last one to seven minutes.

Heart Spring

Shaped like a human heart, the fifteen-foot deep Heart Spring measures 7 1/2 by 10 feet at the surface. Park Geologist George Marler christened the spring in 1959.

Beehive Geyser

Beehive Geyser features a narrow, nozzle-shaped cone capable of shooting water 130 to 190 feet. Eruptions generally last four to five minutes and occur twice daily.

Plume Geyser

Plume Geyser, created when a 1922 steam explosion opened its vent, is one of Yellowstone's newest geysers. The geyser shoots three to five bursts of water twenty-five feet high. Eruptions occur at twenty-minute intervals.

Giantess Geyser

Exploding underground steam announces the arrival of one of Giantess Geyser's rare, but violent, eruptions. With the earth quaking and shaking, Giantess Geyser bursts at heights of 100 to 200 feet. The fountain type geyser generally erupts just two to six times annually, but the eruptions are extended. Most are sustained for a continuous twelve to forty-three hours.

Doublet Pool

Doublet Pool's rich blue water, ornamental borders, and complex ledges make this thermal feature a favorite photography subject. Occasionally, collapsing gas bubbles underneath the pool's surface create noticeable vibrations that rattle below nearby visitors' feet.

Observation Point

Situated 250 feet above Old Faithful, Observation Point provides a sweeping overlook of Yellowstone's Upper Geyser Basin.

Solitary Geyser

Solitary Geyser originated as Solitary Spring during Yellowstone's early years. A docile spring when the park was established, Solitary provided naturally hot water to a nearby swimming pool. However, this artificial diversion of Solitary Geyser's hot water drastically changed the nature of the thermal feature. When the water level was lowered sufficiently, Solitary Spring built up enough pressure to erupt and become a geyser. Although the water level was restored to its original level in 1940, Solitary Geyser continues to erupt every four to eight minutes with most displays less than six feet tall.

Old Faithful Geyser

Although other park geysers are larger, taller, and more predictable, Old Faithful continues to reign as Yellowstone's worldwide favorite. The geyser's name dates back to the 1870 Washburn Expedition where party members noted the geyser's regular performances. And regular it is. Old Faithful erupts an average of twenty-one to twenty-three times daily with an average seventy-six minute interval between eruptions. While some eruptions reach just 106 feet, many spew up to 184 feet, and 3,700 to 8,400 gallons of boiling water is expelled in each one to five minute eruption. Although eruptions used to occur more frequently, visitor vandalism and seismic activity has altered the famous geyser's behavior. For the best views, plan on arriving at least fifteen minutes prior to the predicted eruption time.

Day Hiking the Old Faithful Area

Day hiking in Yellowstone provides an ideal opportunity for people of all ages to get out and experience the park's many wonders away from the crowds. Thousands of miles of trails await, and wildlife sightings are nearly always guaranteed. Those planning a day trip into Yellowstone's wilderness are encouraged to stop by a ranger station or visitor's center for trail maps and the latest information regarding weather, animal activity, and trail closures. The following trails are available in the Old Faithful Area, and all hikers are reminded to stay on the trail.

Black Sand and Biscuit Basin Trails

Distance: 0.5 miles (0.5 km) roundtrip each
Climb: level
Difficulty: easy
Location: Black Sand Trail is located 0.5 miles north of Old Faithful while Biscuit Basin Trail originates 2 miles north of the famous geyser.

Although the Black Sand Basin and Biscuit Basin receive little use in comparison to their famous Upper, Midway, and Lower Basin counterparts, the area is worth stepping away from the crowds. Boardwalks lead walkers to Sapphire Pool, Jewel Geyser, Sunset Lake, and Emerald Pool.

Fairy Falls Trail

Distance: 5 miles (5.5 km) roundtrip from the Steel Bridge Trailhead or 7 miles (8 km) from the second trailhead on Fountain Freight Road.
Climb: level
Difficulty: easy
Location: The Steel Bridge Trailhead is located 1 mile south of the Midway Geyser Basin in a parking area. The second trailhead, which requires a longer hike, begins 1 mile south of the Nez Perce Picnic Area at the Fountain Freight Road parking area.

Fairy Falls is a semi-popular backcountry destination for hikers. The scenic waterfall plunges an impressive 200 feet. Hikers should expect some company from other visitors but no large crowds.

Fountain Paint Pot Trail

Distance: 0.5-mile (0.5 km) loop
Climb: level
Difficulty: easy
Location: The trailhead originates 8 miles north of Old Faithful in a parking area.

Although the Fountain Paint Pot Basin may be less impressive than the tall columns of water spouting off in other park areas, the region is recognized as one of the park's most active. Strolling along a boardwalk, visitors are treated to all four types of Yellowstone thermal features, including fumaroles (steam vents), hot springs, mudpots, and geysers. Trail guides are available for this tour upon request.

Geyser Hill Loop Trail

Distance: 1.3-mile (1.2 km) loop
Climb: level
Difficulty: easy
Location: The trail follows the boardwalk in front of the Old Faithful Visitor Center.

This short trail, appropriate for people of all ages and abilities, travels past numerous geysers lining the Old Faithful Area. Highlights include the spectacular Beehive Geyser and frequent eruptions from the Anemone Geyser.

Lone Star Geyser Trail

Distance: 5 miles (8 km) roundtrip
Climb: gradual
Difficulty: easy
Location: The Lone Star Geyser Trail is located adjacent to the Kepler Cascades parking area 3.5 miles southeast of Old Faithful.

Winding beside the Firehole River through thick stands of lodgepole pine, this trail leads visitors to the Lone Star Geyser. The geyser erupts every three hours, and a logbook is onsite to record the latest eruption data. Except for the final approach to the geyser, bikes are allowed on this trail.

Mallard Lake Trail

Distance: 6.8 miles (5.3 km) roundtrip
Climb: moderate
Difficulty: moderate
Location: The Mallard Lake Trail originates near the Old Faithful Lodge cabins.

On its journey to scenic Mallard Lake, this trail climbs moderately through meadows and forests partially burned in the 1988 fires.

Midway Geyser Basin Trail

Distance: 0.5-mile (0.5 km) loop
Climb: level
Difficulty: easy
Location: The trail begins 6 miles north of Old Faithful at a parking area.

This boardwalk trail is appropriate for visitors of all ages and abilities. The short loop carries visitors past the Grand Prismatic Spring and Excelsior Geyser.

Mystic Falls Trail

Distance: 2.4 miles (4 km) roundtrip
Climb: moderate
Difficulty: moderate
Location: The Mystic Falls Trail is located on the

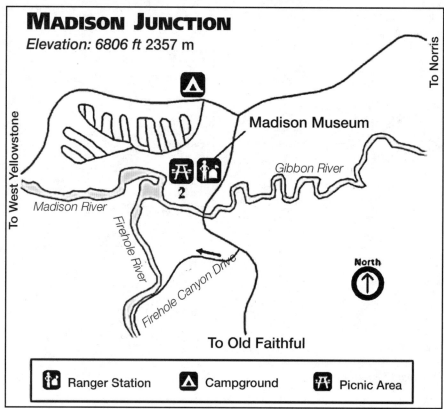

MADISON JUNCTION
Elevation: 6806 ft 2357 m

To Norris

To West Yellowstone

Madison Museum

Gibbon River

Madison River

Firehole River

Firehole Canyon Drive

North

To Old Faithful

Ranger Station | Campground | Picnic Area

Biscuit Basin Boardwalk 2 miles north of Old Faithful.

Following a series of switchbacks beside a creek, this scenic trail wanders through a lodgepole pine forest before leading visitors to a stunning overlook of the seventy-foot tall Mystic Falls.

Observation Point Loop Trail
Distance: 1.1-mile (1 km) roundtrip
Climb: moderate
Difficulty: moderate
Location: The trail begins behind the Old Faithful Geyser at the Firehole River footbridge.

Gaining 200 feet in the course of its short trek, the Observation Point Loop Trail provides a panoramic view of the Upper Geyser Basin.

DISCOVERING THE MADISON AREA

Situated slightly north of Old Faithful and a few short miles east of Yellowstone's West Entrance, the Madison Area encompasses a much smaller region than many of the other park areas. Featuring a similar geological history as Old Faithful, the Madison Area is best known for its smattering of natural wonders and scenic drives.

Natural Attractions

The Madison Area's natural attractions run the gamut from mineral terraces to waterfalls to mudpots.

Artist Paint Pots

Located just five miles south of the Norris Junction, Artist Paint Pots is a small area containing a variety of thermal features. Large mudpots, colorful hot springs, a few small geysers, and steam vents line the one-mile boardwalk looping through the area. The natural highlight also provides access to the Geyser Creek Thermal Area, Gibbon Hill Geyser Basin, and Sylvan Springs.

Firehole Canyon Drive and Firehole Falls

Affording spectacular views of the impressive Firehole Canyon and the forty-foot Firehole Falls, the scenic Firehole Canyon Drive departs from the Madison Junction. As the road twists beside the Firehole River, sightseers glimpse 800-foot thick lava flows resting in the shadow of National Park Mountain. This scenic drive through a narrow canyon eventually links back to the Grand Loop Road

Firehole River

Renowned worldwide as one of Yellowstone's most pristine rivers, the Firehole River steams its way south of Old Faithful before joining the Gibbon and Madison Rivers. Fly-fishing is allowed, and anglers are likely to find abundant populations of rainbow, brown, and brook trout.

Gibbon Falls

Gibbon Falls jumps off the remains of the Yellowstone Caldera rim in a stunning eighty-four foot display of beauty. Directly below the falls, a picnic area rests on an open flat.

Madison River

Originating east of the West Entrance at Yellowstone's Madison Junction, the Madison River is born from the Firehole and Gibbon Rivers. After winding through Yellowstone meadows, the Madison River drains into Montana on its journey to form the headwaters of the Missouri River. The Madison River is world-renowned as a blue-ribbon stream full of prized rainbow trout and mountain whitefish.

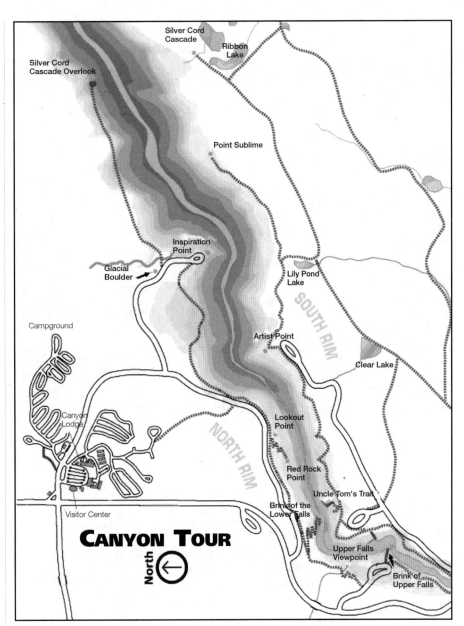

CANYON TOUR
North ←

Monument Geyser Basin

Monument Geyser Basin is nestled at the top of a short, but steep, trail. Although now dormant, the basin is home to several geyser cones testifying to the area's once active landscape.

National Park Mountain

Legend theorizes that Yellowstone National Park owes its existence to this mountain and the 1870 Washburn-Langford-Doane Expedition. After a day of scouting the region, the expedition party supposedly camped on this mountain and discussed the idea of turning Yellowstone into America's first national park. Although the story is nice and provides logical testimony to the mountain's name, no evidence exists to verify the tale. Regardless, the mountain is still impressive and is partially comprised of ancient lava flows that once covered the Madison Junction area in a sea of magma.

Terrace Springs

A short boardwalk tour gives visitors a close-up view of the Madison Area's most noted hot springs. Located directly north of Madison Junction, Terrace Springs is a small but impressive thermal region.

Day Hiking the Madison Area

Day hiking in Yellowstone provides an ideal opportunity for people of all ages to get out and experience the park's many wonders away from the crowds. Thousands of miles of trails await, and wildlife sightings are nearly always guaranteed. Those planning a day trip into Yellowstone's wilderness are encouraged to stop by a ranger station or visitor's center for trail maps and the latest information regarding weather, animal activity, and trail closures. The following trails are available in the Madison Area, and all hikers are reminded to stay on the trail.

Harlequin Lake Trail
Distance: 1 mile (1 km) roundtrip
Climb: gentle
Difficulty: easy
Location: The trailhead is located on the West Entrance Road 1.5 miles west of the Madison Campground.

Drawing its name from rare sightings of Harlequin ducks, the Harlequin Lake Trail is a quick and easy escape from Yellowstone's crowds. The trail gently wanders through stands of lodgepoles scorched in the 1988 fires and ends at

Harlequin Lake. Waterfowl sightings are common, and the trail is appropriate for people of all ages and hiking abilities.

Purple Mountain Trail
Distance: 6 miles (10 km) roundtrip
Climb: moderate to steep
Difficulty: moderate
Location: The trailhead is located on the Madison-Norris Road just 0.25 miles north of Madison Junction.

Featuring an elevation gain of 1,500 feet, the Purple Mountain Trail leads hikers to spectacular overlooks of the lower Gibbon Valley, Firehole Valley, and the Madison Junction area. The trail passes through a partially burned forest and does require a moderate level of fitness to complete.

Two Ribbons Trail
Distance: 1.5 miles (2 km) roundtrip
Climb: level
Difficulty: easy
Location: The unmarked trailhead is situated 5 miles east of the park's West Entrance near a large pullout area lined with roadside exhibits.

Visitors can learn more about the 1988 Yellowstone fires with this short boardwalk tour. The trail travels through a collage of burned trees and brush now dotted with traces of new green growth. Although no interpretive signs are found along the boardwalk, the trail's scenery clearly illustrates the cycle of fire, destruction, and renewal.

DISCOVERING THE CANYON VILLAGE AREA

Drawing its name from the amazing Grand Canyon of the Yellowstone and ancient canyons that once lined this region, the Canyon Village Area is located near Yellowstone's center. Visitors will find Canyon Village nestled thirty-eight miles from the North Entrance, forty-eight miles from the Northeast Entrance in Cooke City, forty-three miles from the East Entrance, and forty miles from the West Entrance.

Historical Attractions

Although a heavily visited park site, Canyon Village comes up short on historical attractions. Most of the buildings date back to the 1950s, and only the former sites of the region's famous hotel and historic lodge are considered cultural resources.

Canyon Hotel
Established during the park's early administration years, the Canyon Hotel was located approximately one mile south of Canyon Junction. Featuring a one square mile perimeter, the Canyon Hotel was one of the park's largest buildings. As new hotels and lodges were added around the park, however, the Canyon Hotel

received less use and was eventually demolished and burned in 1962. Today, the hotel's dump and cistern are the only remains. Historic photographs of the hotel can be found in the Canyon Village Visitor Center.

Canyon Lodge
Nestled amidst the meadows now home to Canyon Village's restrooms, the old Canyon Lodge was situated on the present site of Uncle Tom's outfitting service parking lot. Most traces of the lodge have disappeared, but on occasion, a few remains of the defunct lodge can be found.

Natural Attractions

Mother Nature's dynamic forces worked diligently to shape the dramatic landscape surrounding the Canyon Village Area. Visitors will find rugged mountains, gushing waterfalls, untamed rivers, and scenic valleys and canyons.

Grand Canyon of the Yellowstone
Carved at the same time volcanic forces unleashed their fury to create Yellowstone Lake, the Grand Canyon of the Yellowstone is one of the region's most impressive geologic features. Existing in its present state for just 10,000 to 14,000 years, the schism is 800 to 1,200 feet deep with widths ranging from 1,500 to 4,000 feet. Erosion is largely responsible for shaping the canyon into its current manifestation, and the canyon's steep rock walls display a kaleidoscope of yellows, reds, golds, and oranges. Unlike most American canyons, the Grand Canyon of the Yellowstone also features thermal vents linked to an old geyser basin.

An inspiration to Native Americans and early explorers, the Grand Canyon of the Yellowstone continues to amaze spectators from around the world.

Hayden Valley
Cloaked in a 4,000-foot-thick layer of ice just 10,000 years ago, the Hayden Valley is now an oasis of green meadows and forested riverbanks. The valley's lush habitat supports a wide variety of wildlife, and viewing opportunities abound. Grizzly bears and bison, which are especially prevalent here, share the valley with elk, coyotes, Canadian geese, American white pelicans, sandhill cranes, northern harriers, ducks, and bald eagles. Visitors should bring along binoculars to capture the best wildlife views.

Mt. Washburn
Casting a 10,243-foot shadow over the western side of the Grand Canyon of the Yellowstone, Mt. Washburn is the primary peak residing in the Washburn Mountain Range. The mountain formed thousands of years prior to the canyon it guards, and volcanic and erosive forces sculpted the mountain into its present form. Subalpine habitat, wildflower fields, and bighorn sheep line the mountain's easily accessible slopes. The mountain draws its name from 1870 Washburn-Langford-Doane Expedition leader, General Henry Dana Washburn.

Upper and Lower Falls of the Yellowstone
Releasing their mighty thunder and glory down the Grand Canyon of the Yellowstone, the Upper and Lower Falls of the Yellowstone formed when the Yellowstone River eroded soft rock underneath its powerful current. The resulting falls are now regarded as some of Yellowstone's finest.

The Upper Falls drops 109 feet into a tranquil pool and is viewable from the Brink of the Upper Falls Trail as well as Uncle Tom's Trail. Directly below the cataract, Lower Falls makes its impres-

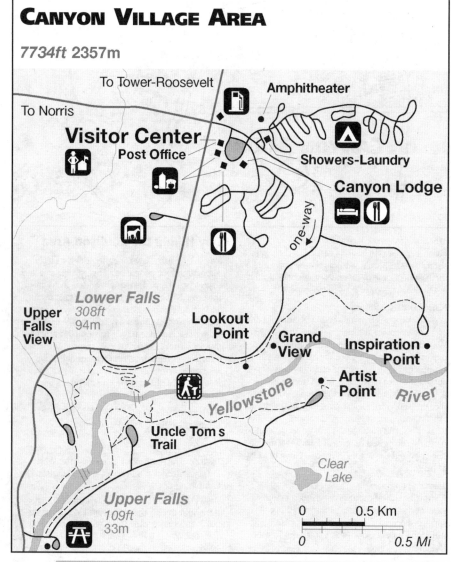

CANYON VILLAGE AREA

7734ft 2357m

To Tower-Roosevelt
To Norris
Amphitheater
Visitor Center
Post Office
Showers-Laundry
Canyon Lodge
one-way

Lower Falls
308ft
94m
Upper Falls View
Lookout Point
Grand View
Inspiration Point
Artist Point
Yellowstone *River*
Uncle Tom's Trail
Clear Lake
Upper Falls
109ft
33m

0   0.5 Km
0   0.5 Mi

sive 308 foot leap while releasing anywhere from 5,000 to 63,500 gallons of water per second. Lower Falls is twice as tall as Niagara and can be seen from the South Rim Trail, Brink of the Lower Falls Trail, Red Rock Point, Artist Point, and Lookout Point.

Although hiking and cross-country ski trails are abundant in the area, visitors are reminded that the Upper and Lower Falls reside in bear country. Use extreme caution, and never throw anything into the waterfalls or canyon below.

Yellowstone River
The Yellowstone River originates south of Yellowstone on the slopes of Yount Peak in Wyoming's Shoshone Mountain Range and is one of the longest undammed rivers in the lower forty-eight states. The river travels through some of Yellowstone's wildest country before continuing its 600-mile journey to the Missouri River in North Dakota. Popular with both anglers and bears, the Yellowstone River is inundated with cutthroat trout.

Geological Highlights

Several interesting features line the Canyon Village Area, but the most prominent attraction receiving geological attention is the Grand Canyon of the Yellowstone. Popular opinion theorized for several years that the canyon was the product of moving glaciers, but recent research concludes that glaciers played little role in the massive canyon's sculpting process. It appears that the classic elements of water and erosion are to blame for the magnificent gorge.

Glaciers Versus Rivers
After the Yellowstone Caldera erupted 600,000 years ago, the canyon area was sheathed in a blanket of lava flows. Ancient faulting in the area accelerated the erosion process of these flows, and glacial deposits excreted during the Ice Age were also swept away through erosion.

Major sculpting activity, however, did not occur until 14,000 to 18,000 years ago at the conclusion of the last Ice Age. Several glaciers situated at the outlet of Yellowstone Lake began to melt as temperatures started rising. The natural ice dam consequently broke, and a flood of water surged downstream in numerous flash flood occurrences. The constant release of water created a continual erosion force that cut out the classic V-shaped valley forming the canyon. Such shaping provides geological testimony to running water/river erosion. To this day, the Yellowstone River continues to carve the canyon with its natural erosion properties.

Thermal Features
Although researchers are unsure of its formation date, a geyser basin once filled the canyon area below the Lower Falls. Lava flows, underground hot spots, and fault lines created the extensive geyser basin. The basin spurred a few hot springs and geysers into existence, many of which are visible to this day. Geologists speculate that nearby Clear Lake is also a product of this early geyser basin.

Canyon Coloring
Thousands of years of hydrothermal activity has altered the canyon's natural mineral compounds, causing unique shades of red, yellow, gold, and orange to bleed down the canyon walls. The chemical alteration in the canyon walls dates back to the area's old geyser basin. Heat from the basin essentially baked the rock and created chemical changes in the canyon's iron deposits. As a result,

when the transformed rocks were exposed to air and water, they began to oxidize and rust. These rocks continue to oxidize and add new coloring on an annual basis.

A Tour of Canyon Village's Most Popular Sites

The Grand Canyon of the Yellowstone and the Upper and Lower Falls of the Yellowstone are obviously the main draw to Canyon Village. As a result, formations and observation points along the canyon rim and near the waterfalls attract large crowds of visitors every year.

Artist Point
Although it is rumored that famous painter, Thomas Moran, crafted his stunning portrait of the Upper and Lower Falls from this point, park officials disagree. Photographer Frank J. Haynes actually named the area in 1883 and used it in his 1890 park guidebook. Regardless, the point is inspiring, and artists and photographers from around the world flock here to create their own artistic version of the waterfalls.

Brink of the Lower Falls
Visitors can stand on the brink of the Lower Falls and watch just steps away as the cataract tumbles 308 feet into the Grand Canyon of the Yellowstone. A captivating sight, the Lower Falls have always intrigued park residents and visitors. Jim Bridger visited the site in 1851, and newspaper stories regarding the breathtaking waterfall began circulating as early as 1867.

Brink of the Upper Falls
The 1869 Folsom Party assigned the name "Upper Falls" to this cataract for the first time, and the famous waterfall has been known as such ever since. Dropping 109 feet, the waterfall invites visitors to take a close-up look at its descent from the Brink of the Upper Falls platform.

Glacial Boulder
During the Pinedale Glacier Period 80,000 years ago, this giant granite boulder rolled forty miles from its previous perch in the Beartooth Mountains to its present location. The boulder weighs approximately 500 tons and rests along the north rim of the Grand Canyon of the Yellowstone.

Inspiration Point
Inspiration Point is situated at 8,000 feet above sea level and provides a natural overlook of the Lower Falls and canyon below. The point is so inspirational, it spurred Nathanial P. Langford of the 1870 Washburn Expedition to write: "The place where I obtained the best and most terrible view of the canyon was a narrow projecting point situated two to three miles below the lower fall. Standing there or rather lying there for great safety, I thought how utterly impossible it would be to describe to another the sensations inspired by such a presence. As I took in the scene, I realized my own littleness, my helplessness, my dread exposure to destruction, my inability to cope with or even comprehend the mighty architecture of nature."

Lookout Point
Prior to 1880, this observation point was known as Mount Lookout, Prospect Point, Lookout Rock, and Point Lookout. Early Park Superintendent Philetus W. Norris gave the point its current name in 1880 after noting that the point frequently boasted numerous visitors. The point is still a favorite tourist destination offering outstanding views of the Grand Canyon of Yellowstone.

Point Sublime
Point Sublime offers another vantage point of the Lower Falls and surrounding canyon. The 1869

The Lower Falls of the Yellowstone.

Cook-Folsom Expedition supposedly inspired the point's naming, using such terms as beautiful, sublime, and grand to describe the sight they beheld from this point. Point Sublime was officially named during an early 1920s survey.

Red Rock Point
Displaying red coloring from iron oxide, Red Rock is situated below Lower Falls. Yellowstone Park photographer, Frank J. Haynes, christened the point in 1886.

Silver Cord Cascade
Plunging in a long series of multiple waterfalls, Silver Cord Cascade was first discovered in 1870. The Washburn Expedition Party dubbed the cascade Silverthread Fall, but the 1885 Hague Party gave the waterfall its present name. The waterfall is reportedly responsible for rumors of a hidden Yellowstone waterfall descending more than 1,000 feet. Although Silver Cord measures nowhere near 1,000 feet tall, its long cord of water is nonetheless impressive.

Upper Falls Viewpoint
Standing on the brink of the Upper Falls, visitors will feel the sheer power of the Yellowstone River as it tumbles 109 feet down the steep canyon walls. Waterfall mist and impressive thundering accompanies outstanding views at this vantage point.

View of the Lower Falls from Uncle Tom's Trail

Uncle Tom's Trail honors the life of early outfitter/guide, "Uncle" Tom Richardson. Uncle Tom capitalized on tourists' curiosity, leading them down ladders to the base of Lower Falls for a one-of-a-kind view. Today, Uncle Tom's Trail doesn't require ladders, but it does lead visitors down 300 stairs to the same magnificent vantage point.

Day Hiking the Canyon Village Area

Day hiking in Yellowstone provides an ideal opportunity for people of all ages to get out and experience the park's many wonders away from the crowds. Thousands of miles of trails await, and wildlife sightings are nearly always guaranteed. Those planning a day trip into Yellowstone's wilderness are encouraged to stop by a ranger station or visitor's center for trail maps and the latest information regarding weather, animal activity, and trail closures. The following trails are available in the Canyon Village Area, and all hikers are reminded to stay on the trail.

Cascade Lake Trail
Distance: 4.5 miles (7.2 km) roundtrip
Climb: level
Difficulty: easy
Location: The trailhead is located 1.5 miles north of Canyon Junction at the Cascade Lake Picnic Area.

This easy trail meanders through open meadows near babbling brooks. The trail is noted for its brilliant wildflower displays and abundant wildlife. Users should plan three hours for this day hike and note that the trail is generally muddy through July.

Grebe Lake Trail
Distance: 6 miles (9.7 km) roundtrip
Climb: gentle
Difficulty: moderately easy
Location: The trailhead is located on the Norris-Canyon Road 3.5 miles west of Canyon Junction.

This three to four hour hike gently ascends through meadows and forests on its journey to and from Grebe Lake. The trail connects to the Howard Eaton Trail at the lake.

Howard Eaton Trail
Distance: Depending on the destination, 6 to 24 miles roundtrip
Climb: gentle
Difficulty: moderately easy
Location: Located on the Norris-Canyon Road, the trail originates 0.5 miles (0.8 km) west of Canyon Junction.

Winding through meadows, marshland, and forests, the Howard Eaton Trail lets hikers choose a destination that meets their time frame. Requiring anywhere from two hours to an overnight stay, the Howard Eaton Trail leads to Cascade Lake, Grebe Lake, Wolf Lake, Ice Lake, and eventually the Norris Campground. The trail is noted for bear activity in the early season, so use extreme caution.

Mary Mountain Trail
Distance: 21 miles one-way
Climb: gentle
Difficulty: moderate
Location: The trailhead is located 4 miles south of Canyon Junction slightly north of the Alum Creek pullout.

The Mary Mountain Trail, which is often faint and difficult to follow due to trampled trail markers, winds through the Hayden Valley. As hikers gently ascend up and over Mary Mountain and Central Plateau, views of distant Yellowstone meadows are afforded. Bison sightings are prevalent along this trail.

North Rim Trail
Distance: 4 miles roundtrip
Climb: level
Difficulty: easy
Location: The trail originates at Inspiration Point near the Upper and Lower Falls.

Hikers on the North Rim Trail are privy to unbeatable views of the famous waterfalls in the Grand Canyon of the Yellowstone. The footpath is rarely crowded, and the vantages are more scenic than the region's major overlook points.

Observation Peak
Distance: 11 miles roundtrip

Climb: steep
Difficulty: strenuous
Location: The trailhead is located 1.5 miles north of Canyon Junction on the Tower-Canyon Road at the Cascade Lake Picnic Area.

After arriving at Cascade Lake, hikers take a 1,400-foot strenuous climb to a mountain summit. The peak provides stunning views of Yellowstone, and the trail is renowned for its lush scenery of open meadows and forests. Hikers should note that no water is available beyond Cascade Lake, and the trail is not recommended for those with breathing difficulties or heart conditions.

Seven Mile Hole Trail
Distance: 11 miles roundtrip
Climb: steep
Difficulty: strenuous
Location: The trail begins on Inspiration Point Road at the Glacial Boulder Trailhead

The Seven Mile Hole Trail rewards hikers with views of the canyon and Silver Cord Cascade as it drops 1,400 feet to Seven Mile Hole. The area features both dormant and active thermal features, so extreme caution should be used. Hikers are also urged to conserve their energy, as the 1,400-foot climb out of Seven Mile Hole is strenuous. The trail is not recommended for those with breathing difficulties or heart conditions.

South Rim Trail
Distance: 6.4 miles roundtrip
Climb: level
Difficulty: easy
Location: The trail originates directly beyond the South Rim Drive Bridge in a designated parking area.

Much like its North Rim counterpart, the South Rim Trail affords outstanding views of the Grand Canyon of the Yellowstone and its famous waterfall inhabitants. The trail is not generally crowded, and several picture-friendly vantage points are accessed.

Washburn Trail/Washburn Spur Trail
Distance: 11.5 miles one way
Climb: steep
Difficulty: strenuous
Location: The trail begins 4.5 miles north of Canyon Junction at the Dunraven Pass Trailhead.

Wildflower meadows, grazing bighorn sheep, and amazing views line the Washburn Trail. The steep trail climbs to vantages of the Absaroka Mountains, Gallatin Mountains, and Yellowstone Lake at the summit of Mount Washburn. The trail then descends to the mudpots and thermal features housed at Washburn Hot Springs before ending at Glacial Boulder on the Inspiration Point Road. Hikers must then backtrack to the starting trailhead. Due to the hike's length and elevation gain, the trail is not recommended for those with breathing difficulties or heart conditions.

DISCOVERING THE TOWER-ROOSEVELT AREA

Situated twenty-three miles from the North Entrance at Gardiner and twenty-nine miles from the Northeast Entrance at Cooke City, the Tower-Roosevelt Area highlights the power of geological forces with its diverse mix of steep canyons, raging rivers, barren plateaus, and lush forests. The area comprises the park's northeast corner and was a favorite haunt of President Teddy Roosevelt.

Historical Attractions

Showcasing Native American history, early park structures, and a quiet atmosphere uncommon along Yellowstone's corridors, the Tower-Roosevelt Area provides visitors with a glimpse into the park's early history as a major tourist attraction.

Bannock Trail
Extending from Idaho's Snake River Valley to the Midwest plains, the Bannock Trail provided Native Americans with annual access to prosperous buffalo hunts from 1840 to 1876. A significant portion of the trail twisted its way through the Tower-Roosevelt Area, and faint remnants of the historic trail can still be found. From Blacktail Plateau, the trail continued to the Bannock Ford crossing of the Yellowstone River, ascended the Lamar River, and forked at Soda Butte Creek. The best locations to view the trail are near the Blacktail Plateau and the Lamar River.

Lamar Buffalo Ranch
In an effort to preserve and increase Yellowstone's dwindling bison population, the Lamar Buffalo Ranch was created during the early 1900s. Twenty-one bison from privately owned area ranches were acquired as the foundation stock for a fifty-year breeding program marked by success. The bison population surged, and with no fear of bison becoming extinct in Yellowstone, the park closed the Buffalo Ranch in the 1950s.

During its hey-day, the Lamar Buffalo Ranch constructed elaborate irrigation ditches to create fertile hay pastures capable of feeding a growing herd. Fences were also erected throughout the ranch to contain the large animals and ensure breeding success. Some of these original fences and ditches are still visible, and two original residences, one bunkhouse, and the ranch's barn still stand as Nationally Registered Historic Places. Although all the old cabins were replaced in 1993 to make way for modern facilities, the ranch retains a historic flavor. Today, the ranch is home to Yellowstone Institute classes and environmental education programs offered during spring and fall. None of the buildings are open for touring, but visitors are welcome to drive by.

Northeast Entrance Ranger Station
The Northeast Entrance Ranger Station features the same log construction techniques utilized in parks across the nation during the early 1900s. The rustic structure dates back to 1934 and is now recognized as a National Historic Landmark.

Pleasant Valley
"Uncle John" Yancey's Pleasant Valley Hotel was constructed between 1884 and 1893 as one of Yellowstone's first lodging facilities. The hotel housed hopeful miners headed to nearby Cooke City as well as park guests. Although none of the original buildings currently remain, Xanterra Parks and Resorts uses the hotel building site as the scenic backdrop for its famous Old West cookouts.

Tower Ranger Station & Roosevelt National Historic District
The Roosevelt National Historic District encompasses several of the park's earliest buildings, including the 1920 Roosevelt Lodge, Roosevelt Cabins, and the Tower Ranger Station. The Tower Ranger Station is not listed on the National Register of Historic Places but still serves as an important testimony to the park's early history; it is an accurate reconstruction of the 1907 Tower Soldier Station.

Yellowstone

Tower Falls.

Natural Attractions

The desert plateaus, fertile valleys, and lush forests of the Tower-Roosevelt Area house an array of Mother Nature's finest offerings, including waterfalls, hot springs, and petrified trees.

Calcite Springs Overlook

The Calcite Springs Overlook provides visitors with insight into the volcanic forces that helped shape the Tower-Roosevelt Area. Sightseers can peer nearly 500 feet down to the thermally charged springs located on the downstream portion of Yellowstone's Grand Canyon. Rocks smattered with color from hydrothermally altered rhyolite draw attention to the steep basalt walls and craggy spires forming the famous canyon. The overlook reportedly inspired one of Thomas Moran's famous paintings that were presented to Congress in 1872 in hopes of designating Yellowstone a national park. Today, the overlook, gorge, and surrounding canyon walls are home to osprey, red-tailed hawks, and bighorn sheep.

Petrified Tree

The Petrified Tree Exhibit situated near the Lost Lake Trailhead is just one of the Tower-Roosevelt Area's many eerie reminders of Yellowstone's violent volcanic past. The ancient redwood is easily accessible to all visitors.

Petrified trees form when volcanic eruptions bury trees under piles of ash. Over time, dissolved silica travels through the trees and replaces their original structure with minerals. The trees are preserved down to their unique cell structures, and leaves and pinecones are even occasionally trapped in time.

Although the tree once stood out in the open, vandals thoughtlessly removed two other trees in the area. As a result, the remaining petrified tree has been fenced to preserve the natural attraction for generations to come.

Specimen Ridge

Recognized as home to the world's largest concentration of petrified trees, Specimen Ridge is located east of Tower Junction on the Northeast Entrance Road. The area is an estimated forty-five to fifty million years old. Scientists have found over twenty-seven different petrified forests in the area with tree species including walnut, hickory, maple, oak, dogwood, redwood, pine, and magnolia. Leaf impressions, pollen, and conifer needles have also been discovered and indicate that Yellowstone's climate was much different than today. Nature tours of the area are offered, and interested parties should contact a park visitor center for days and times.

Tower Fall

Tower Creek plunges 132 feet through eroded volcanic pinnacles. Visitors, artists, and photographers from around the world have noted the idyllic setting framing the waterfall, and the cataract maintains itself as Tower-Roosevelt Area's most prominent natural feature. Early Native Americans passed by the tumbling creek while traveling the Bannock Trail, and Thomas Moran's painting of the waterfall helped inspire Congress to designate Yellowstone as the nation's first park. An overlook offers views of the waterfall and surrounding canyon. Those who are physically fit may also opt to take a short hike down to the waterfall's base where Tower Creek tumbles into the Yellowstone River.

Yellowstone River and Tributaries

Flowing through Yellowstone to the heart of Montana's Paradise Valley, the Yellowstone River and its tributaries are one of Yellowstone's most noted and used water features. The natural attraction provides plenty of angling opportunities along with habitat for several fish and bird species.

Geological Highlights

Glacier activity, volcanoes, and erosion have all affected the Tower-Roosevelt Area's landscape. Mountains were thrust to the sky, and ancient forests were preserved in ash. Today, the geology of the area continues to change and provide new keys to Yellowstone's violent past.

Volcanic Activity

Eruptions pounded Yellowstone forty-five to fifty million years ago, and as a result, mountains in the Tower-Roosevelt Area began to form. Further volcanic activity strengthened the bases of these mountains and forced the peaks to reach even higher, creating the region's tallest peaks at Mt. Washburn and in the nearby Absaroka Mountain Range. At the same time, tons of volcanic ash rolled across the region's forests, blanketing them in debris and preserving their cellular structure to this day in petrified remains.

Glacial Events

Following Yellowstone's last major volcanic eruption, glaciers barged across the region, moving mountains of ash and unearthing the petrified trees of a once colorful and vibrant forest. In their wake, glaciers left behind boulders, moraines, and lakes. Two of these ancient lakes once filled the Hayden and Pelican Valleys. The remaining lakebeds are now thriving meadows supporting a range of wildlife. Glacial moraines are also evident to this day in the Lamar Valley, the Hellroaring and Slough Creek drainages, and on Blacktail Plateau.

Forces of Erosion

For millions of years, running water has served as the Tower-Roosevelt Area's primary erosion force. Gravity and water combined to create the area's astounding features, including Tower Fall and its surrounding rock pinnacles, the Black Canyon, and the highly reputed Grand Canyon of the Yellowstone.

Water has also helped expose large outcrops of schist and gneiss in the Tower-Roosevelt region. Dated more than two billion years old, the rocks are among Yellowstone's oldest features.

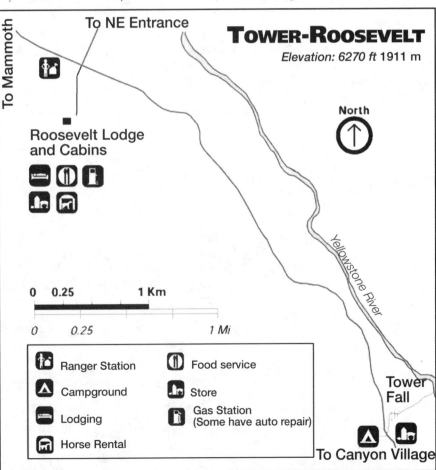

Although it may appear Yellowstone has reached the pinnacle of its natural beauty, erosion is still at work. The mighty power of running water continues to mold and craft new and existing Yellowstone features under visitors' watchful eyes.

Day Hiking the Tower-Roosevelt Area

Day hiking in Yellowstone provides an ideal opportunity for people of all ages to get out and experience the park's many wonders away from the crowds. Thousands of miles of trails await, and wildlife sightings are nearly always guaranteed. Those planning a day trip into Yellowstone's wilderness are encouraged to stop by a ranger station or visitor's center for trail maps and the latest information regarding weather, animal activity, and trail closures. The following trails are available in the Tower-Roosevelt Area, and all hikers are reminded to stay on the trail.

Garnet Hill and Hellroaring Trails

Distance: 4 miles (6.4 km) to 10 miles (16 km) depending on route taken
Climb: moderate
Difficulty: moderate
Location: Two trailheads provide access. One trailhead is located at Tower Junction while the second is situated 3.5 miles (5.6 km) west of Tower Junction.

Measuring 7.5 miles, the Garnet Hill Loop Trail begins near the service station at Tower Junction, follows an old stagecoach road, and meanders near Elk Creek on its journey around Garnet Hill. The trail loops back to the Northeast Entrance Road where hikers are required to take a short walk back to the parking lot trailhead.

Along the Garnet Hill Loop Trail, hikers will encounter a fork for the Hellroaring Trail. The trail leads to the Yellowstone River and Hellroaring Creek, both of which are popular angling destinations. The Hellroaring Trail is also accessible 3.5 miles west of Tower Junction where hikers gain stunning views while crossing the Yellowstone River Suspension Bridge. The Hellroaring Trail via Garnet Creek is a 10-mile roundtrip hike while the trek from Hellroaring Trailhead is 4 miles roundtrip.

Lost Lake Trail

Distance: 4 miles (6.4 km) roundtrip
Climb: moderate
Difficulty: moderate
Location: The Lost Lake Trail departs behind the Roosevelt Lodge

Climbing 300 feet to join the Roosevelt Horse Trail, the Lost Lake Trail provides glimpses of wildflowers, open meadows, sagebrush flats, waterfowl, and oftentimes black bears as it trav-

els to Lost Lake. Equestrians frequently use the trail, so hikers should step to the trail's downhill side when meeting a horse. Hikers are also reminded to remain still when a horse passes so as not to startle the animal.

Mt. Washburn Trail

Distance: 6 miles (9.6 km) roundtrip
Climb: moderate
Difficulty: moderate
Location: Two trailheads provide access to this trail. Access the trail 8.7 miles (13.9 km) south of Tower Junction at the Chittenden Road Parking Area or 13.6 miles (21.8 km) south of Tower Junction at the Dunraven Pass Parking Area.

The Mt. Washburn Trail is one of Yellowstone's most popular day hikes, and it is easy to understand why. Panoramic views and rare wildlife sightings combine for a memorable Yellowstone experience. Both trails switchback up to the summit, and hikers are reminded not to shortcut the trails. The alpine vegetation is fragile, and off-trail traffic can damage the ecosystem.

Slough Creek Trail

Distance: 10 miles (16 km) roundtrip
Climb: moderately steep at first, then level
Difficulty: moderately difficult at first, then easy
Location: The Slough Creek Trail departs near the vault toilet in the Slough Creek Campground vicinity.

Utilizing a historic wagon trail, the Slough Creek Trail switchbacks over Plateau and Elk Tongue Creeks on a scenic journey to meadow areas. The hike is difficult at first, but the trail does level out at the top of the switchbacks. Anglers frequent the area as do private wagons from a nearby ranch. Although wildlife is not the primary attraction in Slough Creek, bears are known to occasionally frequent the area. Hikers should use caution at all times.

Yellowstone River Picnic Area Trail

Distance: 3.7 miles (5.9 km) roundtrip
Climb: moderate
Difficulty: moderately difficult
Location: The trail is located 1.25 miles (2 km) northeast of Tower Junction at the Yellowstone Picnic Area.

Skirting the Yellowstone River's eastern rim, this trail provides outstanding vistas of Overhanging Cliff, the Narrows of Yellowstone, the historic Bannock Indian Trail, and towering basalt columns. Bighorn sheep frequent the area, and the river canyon is known for its steep dropoffs. The trail receives relatively little use, so hikers should expect dramatic scenery without the crowds.

DISCOVERING THE WEST THUMB AND GRANT VILLAGE AREAS

Recognized as home of the popular Yellowstone Lake, the West Thumb and Grant Village Areas encompass much more than just one of the world's largest natural freshwater jewels. The area is also renowned for mudpots, impressive geyser basins, rivers, and a cross-section of the Continental Divide. The region is situated approximately twenty-two miles from Yellowstone's South Entrance.

Historical Attractions

Although the historical attractions lining the West Thumb and Grant Village Areas are minimal, they

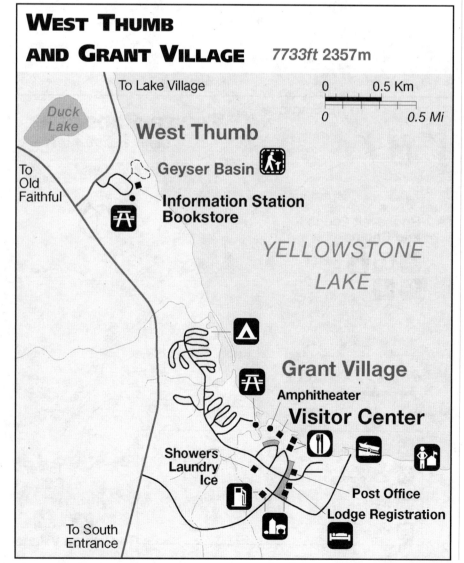

WEST THUMB AND GRANT VILLAGE *7733ft 2357m*

To Lake Village

Duck Lake

West Thumb
Geyser Basin

To Old Faithful

Information Station
Bookstore

YELLOWSTONE LAKE

0 — 0.5 Km
0 — 0.5 Mi

Grant Village
Amphitheater
Visitor Center

Showers
Laundry
Ice

Post Office
Lodge Registration

To South Entrance

are by no means insignificant. The sites explore Yellowstone's early inhabitants and the introduction of park rangers.

Archaeological Highlights
Archaeologists have discovered significant evidence suggesting that Native Americans frequented West Thumb's lakeshores. Traces of ancient camping, food gathering, and migration have all been found in the region.

West Thumb Information Station
The West Thumb Information Station dates back to 1925 and originally served as the West Thumb Ranger Station. The log structure provides an ideal example of historic architecture typical of Yellowstone's early buildings. The style was immediately idolized, and several other national parks across the country exhibit similar log buildings. The more modern and enclosed breezeway was added in 1966. Today, the station is open daily during summer season as an interesting visitor stop.

Natural Attractions

The West Thumb and Grant Village Areas are loaded with natural attractions guaranteed to spark intrigue in the Earth's amazing capabilities.

Abyss Pool
Located in the West Thumb Geyser Basin, Abyss Pool is aptly named after its incredible blue-green pool that seemingly has no floor. Visitors first knew the hot spring as "Tapering Spring," but Park Naturalist, C.M. Bauer renamed the pool in 1935. Featuring coral-like walls and water that reflects brilliantly in Yellowstone's intense sunlight, Abyss Pool is undoubtedly one of Yellowstone's most awe-inspiring hot springs.

Craig Pass
Craig Pass rests along the Continental Divide at an elevation of 8,262 feet just eight miles east of Old Faithful. Although most people realize the pass' importance as a dividing oceanic drainage line, few are unaware of Craig Pass' history and highway development.

Hired to construct a road leading through the heart of Yellowstone, Captain Hiram Chittenden found Craig Pass in 1891 while surveying for potential highway routes. Chittenden was responsible for naming the pass, but two different stories circulate regarding the name's meaning. The first story declares that Ida M. (Craig) Wilcox was the first visitor to utilize Chittenden's road when she crossed over the pass on September 10, 1891. Although Wilcox was married, Chittenden supposedly decided the pass should bear Ida's familial birth name since she crossed the pass singularly.

The second story is much more plausible. After Ida crossed over the pass, Chittenden decided to honor the entire Craig family. It turns out that Chittenden was a family acquaintance who thought quite highly of Ida's father, General James Craig, and her brother, Malin Craig, Sr.

Cutthroat Trout
Yellowstone Lake may contain North America's largest population of wild cutthroat trout, but the area's streams and rivers are by no means lacking a significant population. Cutthroat trout thrive in the cool waters of Big Thumb Creek and Little Thumb Creek, and the streams provide popular trout spawning habitat. Area visitors should note, however, that grizzly and black bears frequent the streams for its plentiful food during spawning season. Be extra vigilant about bears during this time, and heed all safety precautions!

DeLacy Creek
DeLacy Creek draws its name from Walter Washington DeLacy, a surveyor and engineer who passed through Yellowstone as one of its earliest explorers in 1863. While leading a prospecting expedition from Jackson, Wyoming to the Pitchstone Plateau, DeLacy and his fellow party members discovered a large lake. DeLacy named the lake after himself, and noted several strange features in the Yellowstone area. Although he created the first accurate Yellowstone map in 1865, DeLacy failed to earn due credit for his research since his findings remained unpublished until 1876.

In 1872, DeLacy faced further downsizing of his accomplishment when Frank Bradley decided DeLacy's map was horribly flawed. Bradley removed DeLacy's name from the park's second largest lake and bestowed it with its present title, "Shoshone Lake."

When Philetus W. Norris assumed the park superintendent position, he used his power and sympathy for DeLacy's situation to name the creek located above Shoshone Lake after the early explorer. Today, the area is known for its hiking trails and prime moose habitat.

Factory Hill
When Nathaniel Langford accompanied a Yellowstone discovery expedition in 1870, he commented on the numerous steam vents lining the base of the Red Mountain Range. Likening the rising steam to the hazy atmosphere of a New England factory village, Langford's description was published in a June 1871 edition of Scribner's. Hundreds of people across the country read Langford's depiction, and when the 1885 Hague expedition party visited Yellowstone, they renamed the mountain after Langford's famous simile.

Fishing Cone
Situated in the West Thumb Geyser Basin, Fishing Cone Hot Spring draws its name from an interesting event that wowed visitors beginning with the 1870 Washburn Expedition. When party member, Cornelius Hedge, caught a fish in Yellowstone Lake, the thrashing prize fell off the hook into a nearby boiling hot spring. The fish darted in search of an escape but quickly stopped moving as it was cooked alive. Fellow party members thought the boiled fish was an amazing feat, and the spring was initially named "Fish Pot."

When Philetus W. Norris assumed the park superintendent position in 1877, he turned "Fish Pot" into a major tourist attraction. Visitors decked out in chef's hats and aprons assembled around the hot spring anxiously seeking boiling fish demonstrations. The site was so popular that newspaper articles declared no Yellowstone Park tour was complete without a visit to "Fish Pot."

Over time, "Fish Pot" was changed to its present "Fishing Cone" title, and interest in the hot spring died out. Park officials capitalized on the loss of interest, declaring the boiling fish practice unhealthy and inhumane. Today, Fishing Cone draws attention for its unusual name and close proximity to Yellowstone Lake.

Heart Lake
Although Heart Lake does feature the shape of the popular romantic symbol, the lake's name was intended to reference the life of early hunter, Hart Hunney. An associate of famous mountain men, Hunney wandered through the area between 1840 and 1850 before dying in an 1852 battle with Crow Indians. Mountain men and other early explorers subsequently honored the lake after Hunney and his frequent visits to its beautiful shores.

However, the spelling of the lake's name was altered in 1871 when Captain John Barlow explored the park and assumed the name referenced the lake's shape. In his findings, Barlow inadvertently changed the spelling of the name to "Heart Lake" instead of its intended "Hart Lake." Although historian and park engineer Hiram Chittenden pleaded with the U.S. Geological Survey team in the 1890s to correct the spelling's name, his petition was denied. The lake's name still reflects this historical error.

Isa Lake
With its east side draining to the Pacific and the west side flowing into the Atlantic, Isa Lake is one of the world's only lakes that drains backwards into two oceans. U.S. Army Corps Engineer, Hiram Chittenden, reportedly discovered the lake at Craig Pass in 1891. The lake, however, remained nameless until 1893 when Northern Pacific Railroad officials honored Ohio resident, Isabel Jelke. To this day, researchers know little about Isabel's connection to Yellowstone, railroad officials, and Chittenden, and the reasoning behind the lake's naming remains a mystery.

Lewis River
A tributary of the Snake River that drains Shoshone and Lewis Lakes, the Lewis River was originally called Lake Fork after these characteristics. The scenic river flows through alpine habitat on its journey across the 500,000-year-old Pitchstone Plateau.

Lodgepole Pine Forests
Forests and fire are often viewed as incompatible forces of nature, but for lodgepole pine forests, fire is key to the sustenance of future trees. During the summer of 1988, a fierce fire unlike anything Yellowstone had ever experienced swept through the lodgepole forests lining the West Thumb and Grant Village Areas. Winds blew up to eighty miles per hour, and the fire defied natural law as it rolled across the Lewis River and continued its charring path of destruction.

News of the 1988 Yellowstone fires stunned the world, but scientists knew a fire of such magnitude was due to strike Yellowstone. After years of intense study, researchers discovered that a major fire strikes Yellowstone every 300 years and that the park's lodgepole pine forests have actually become dependent upon this cycle for sustenance. Many of the forests rely on fire's intense heat to open up stubborn pinecones and expose hundreds of seeds for the birth of new forests.

Despite horrific pictures that depicted the park as a burnt wasteland in 1988, the fire was necessary to ensure the healthy continuation of Yellowstone's forests. Today, numerous new lodgepole pine forests grace the West Thumb and Grant Village landscape.

Red Mountains
The Red Mountains draw their name from volcanic residue that gives a vibrant red tint to the small range. The mountains are completely contained within the park's boundaries and include twelve peaks.

Riddle Lake
Hayden Survey party member, Rudolph Hering, named this small lake in 1872. The name is reportedly the result of legendary fur-trapper stories describing a lake that drained into two oceans (now known as Isa Lake). Early expedition

party members believed Riddle Lake was that infamous body of water and boldly believed they had solved the mountain man riddle of "two-ocean water."

Shoshone Lake

Encompassing 8,050 surface acres and reaching a maximum depth of 205 feet, Shoshone Lake represents the park's second-largest lake. The large lake is also thought to be the largest backcountry lake in the continental U.S. Serving as the source for the Lewis River, the lake is situated southwest of West Thumb. The lake has long received visitors, with Jim Bridger arriving at its shores as early as 1833. Osborne Russell and James Gemmell were on Bridger's heels, and Gemmell referred to the lake as "Snake Lake" in 1846. The name was appropriate since the lake is included in the Snake River drainage.

In 1863, Walter DeLacy discovered the lake on a prospecting expedition. He promptly named the lake after himself, but the name refused to stick. Other explorers mistakenly decided the lake served as the Madison River's source, so the lake assumed the new "Madison Lake" title. In 1870, the lake's name changed again when the Washburn Expedition named the lake after their leader, General H.D. Washburn.

Shoshone Lake received its final name in 1872 when Frank Bradley and the Hayden Survey found DeLacy's area maps flawed; they subsequently decided the lake should reflect its location in the Snake River drainage. Believing "Snake Lake" carried a negative connotation, Bradley opted for the Native American translation of snake: Shoshone. Although controversy arose regarding the lake's new name, park officials deemed the title appropriate given the historic residence of Shoshone Indians in the surrounding region.

Today, Shoshone Lake is a prime fishing destination. The lake is home to brown trout, brook trout, and the Utah chub. The best time of year to fish Shoshone Lake is mid-June and early autumn. Permits are required, and motorboats are not allowed.

Shoshone Point

Shoshone Point designates the halfway mark between West Thumb and Old Faithful on the Grand Loop Road. When U.S. Army Corp Engineer Hiram Chittenden constructed the road in 1891, he named the point after the visible Shoshone Lake resting in the distance.

In the park's early days, stagecoaches frequented the route, and Shoshone Point was a popular stopping place. In 1914, Edward Trafton took advantage of that well-known fact when he robbed fifteen coaches and their eighty-two passengers of nearly $1,000 in cash and $130 worth of jewelry. He was later caught, charged with armed robbery, and sentenced to five years at the Leavenworth, Kansas federal prison.

Snake River

A major Columbia River tributary and America's fourth largest river, the Snake River begins at the Two Ocean Plateau on the Continental Divide just inside Yellowstone's boundaries. The river's name stems from the Shoshone (meaning Snake) Indians and was applied as early as 1812. Although the river subsequently received several name changes in the wake of early explorers' activity, the river's original name was destined to remain. On its journey to the Pacific Ocean, the Snake River winds forty-two miles through Yellowstone.

West Thumb Geyser Basin

Renowned for its scenic geysers situated beneath Yellowstone Lake's surface, on the lake's shoreline, and across the surrounding landscape, the West Thumb Geyser Basin instills intrigue with its multi-colored clay and spewing fountains. The West Thumb Geyser Basin is also recognized as the first Yellowstone area to be described in a publication.

Trapper Daniel T. Potts sent a letter to his brother in Philadelphia, Pennsylvania describing the unique features of what is now known as Potts Basin. His edited letter subsequently appeared in the September 27, 1827 issue of the Philadelphia Gazette.

Further reports of the area were not available until after the 1869 Folsom-Cook-Peterson Expedition. Later, stagecoaches escorted tourists eager to see the area's pale violet waters and deep springs. As the park became more modernized, traffic to West Thumb Geyser Basin increased, and a campground, cabins, cafeteria, gas station, and photo shop were added to capitalize on the growing number of visitors. Eventually, however, park officials noted that the increased traffic and area services were actually destroying what people had come to see. In the mid 1980s, the National Park Service removed all buildings and services from the West Thumb Geyser Basin in an effort to protect and preserve the beautiful area. Today, boardwalks in the basin protect the area's features and its visitors.

West Thumb – Yellowstone Lake

Resembling a large thumb, Yellowstone Lake's western bay was first reported with the arrival of the 1870 Washburn Expedition. The party members likened the lake to a human hand with large fingers and a thumb-shaped western bay. Although the Washburn Party subsequently referred to the area as "West Thumb," the 1878 Hayden Survey renamed the area "West Arm."

When Philetus W. Norris assumed the park superintendent position, he created a map in 1880 designating the area as "West Thumb." Park officials in the early 1900s later attempted to resurrect the "West Arm" title, but popular opinion refused to budge from the well-recognized "West Thumb" distinction.

Yellowstone Lake

Rivaling Old Faithful in terms of its natural appeal, Yellowstone Lake has attracted visitors long prior to the park's official establishment. Archaeological evidence of Native American campsites has been discovered on the lake's shoreline, and John Colter roamed the region on his 1806-1807 western discovery tour. Word of the scenic mountain lake spread like wildfire, and droves of mountain men, prospectors, and explorers flocked to the lake between 1820 and 1900 to gather their own research and sightings. Growing restless of simply exploring the lake's 110 miles of shoreline, explorers widened their horizons when the 1871 Hayden Survey set sail on the crystal clear waters. The successful sail of Anna inspired other explorers to take to the lake. Both government and privately funded expedition parties sponsored their own sails with boats reported on Yellowstone Lake in 1874, 1880, 1885, 1889, and 1905.

Through the insights of these historic explorers and the continued research of park/government employees, Yellowstone Lake is now recognized as the park's largest lake. Encompassing 136 square miles with an average depth of 140 feet and a maximum depth of 390 feet, Yellowstone Lake is also regarded as America's largest natural freshwater lake situated at an elevation above 7,000 feet.

The lake is peacefully placid most mornings, but its temper flares when prevailing winds stir up three to four-foot waves. Average water temperatures of just forty-one degrees Fahrenheit and a surface that remains frozen from early December through late May combine to make Yellowstone Lake one of the park's coldest attractions. Although the lake becomes thermally stratified each summer with different water layers featuring extremely divergent temperatures, the surface layer rarely peaks past sixty-six degrees Fahrenheit. As a result, park officials strongly discourage swimming and remind boaters of the very real danger of hypothermia. Even during summer, researchers estimate that survival in Yellowstone Lake's chilly waters is a mere twenty to thirty minutes.

Yellowstone Lake's cold temperatures may be unsuitable for water sports, but they are ideal for supporting North America's largest population of wild cutthroat trout. Anglers rush to the lake as soon as winter's one-inch to two-foot thick ice layer melts. Wildlife lovers in search of moose, grizzly bears, bald eagles, pelicans, osprey, and cormorants also populate the area.

One of Yellowstone Lake's most interesting features is its subsurface thermal activity that is becoming increasingly evident to park visitors. For several years, the park's thermal commotion has elevated and tilted the lake nearly one inch per year. Trees are now slowly being flooded on the lake's southern end as existing beaches on the northern shoreline expand. Although researchers predict that the Yellowstone Lake basin will eventually erupt in a cataclysmic explosion, visitors have little to fear at the moment. The lake's tilting behavior is moving at a geological snail's pace, ensuring that visitors will be able to enjoy Yellowstone Lake for several generations to come.

Geological Highlights

Ancient volcanic activity, blue-green thermal pools, and underwater thermal disturbances join together to provide a unique geological look into Yellowstone's West Thumb and Grant Village Areas.

West Thumb Geyser Basin

Regarded as the largest geyser area on Yellowstone Lake's shoreline, the West Thumb Geyser Basin features a heat source located just 10,000 feet below the surface. The nearly too-close-for-comfort heat source formed when an underground magma chamber cracked, spewing the magma towards the surface through tiny ring fractures.

West Thumb Thermal Features

Most of Yellowstone's thermal features are readily apparent to the naked eye on the park's surface. West Thumb, however, is unique in that many of the area's features are actually active underneath Yellowstone Lake's placid exterior. Researchers discovered numerous underwater geysers during the 1990s. Evidence of this activity is apparent as a slight bulge on the water's surface during summer and as melted holes in the lake's icy cloak during winter.

West Thumb Yellowstone Lake

A massive volcanic explosion approximately 150,000 years ago resulted in a large caldera (a collapsed volcano). When water filled the caldera and flowed over into the previously existent Yellowstone Lake, the West Thumb of Yellowstone Lake was born. The West Thumb crater is comparable in size to its famous caldera counterpart at Oregon's Crater Lake.

Day Hiking the West Thumb and Grant Village Areas

Day hiking in Yellowstone provides an ideal opportunity for people of all ages to get out and experience the park's many wonders away from the crowds. Thousands of miles of trails await, and wildlife sightings are nearly always guaranteed. Those planning a day trip into Yellowstone's wilderness are encouraged to stop by a ranger station or visitor's center for trail maps and the latest information regarding weather, animal activity, and trail closures. The following trails are available in the West Thumb and Grant Village Areas, and all hikers are reminded to stay on the trail.

Duck Lake Trail
Distance: 1 mile (1.6 km) roundtrip
Climb: moderate
Difficulty: moderate
Location: The trailhead is located across from the Lake Overlook Trailhead in the West Thumb Geyser Basin parking area.

Traces of the 1988 fires and the cycle of regrowth are evident along the Duck Lake Trail. After ascending a slight hill for a view of Yellowstone Lake, the trail descends to Duck Lake's shoreline.

Lewis River Channel/Shoshone Lake Loop Trail
Distance: 11-mile (17.5 km) loop
Climb: gentle
Difficulty: easy to moderate
Location: The trailhead is located directly north of Lewis Lake approximately 5 miles south of the Grant Village intersection.

Hikers wind through forested moose country as this trail journeys to the colorful Lewis River Channel. Continuing on to the scenic Shoshone Lake, the trail joins with the Dogshead Trail to make a complete loop. Trout are abundant in the Lewis River and Shoshone Lake, and eagles and osprey are frequently seen in the region.

Riddle Lake Trail
Distance: 5 miles (8 km) roundtrip
Climb: level
Difficulty: easy to moderate
Location: The trailhead is located near the Continental Divide sign approximately 3 miles south of the Grant Village intersection.

Located in popular bear habitat, Riddle Lake is a small but picturesque lake in Yellowstone's backcountry. The Riddle Lake Trail takes hikers across the Continental Divide through marshy meadows and lush forests. To increase hikers' safety, the trail does not open until July 15 when bear activity has decreased.

Shoshone Lake Trail (via DeLacy Creek)
Distance: 6 miles (10 km) roundtrip
Climb: level
Difficulty: easy
Location: The trailhead is located 8.8 miles west of the West Thumb Junction at DeLacy Creek.

Shoshone Lake is Yellowstone's largest backcountry lake, and this popular trail leads hikers to its shores. This easy hike skirts a forest before wandering through open meadows to the lake. Wildlife abound, so be sure to bring your camera, but follow all wildlife viewing safety tips.

West Thumb Geyser Basin Trail
Distance: 3/8-mile (1 km) roundtrip
Climb: level
Difficulty: easy
Location: The trailhead is located 0.25 miles east of the West Thumb Junction.

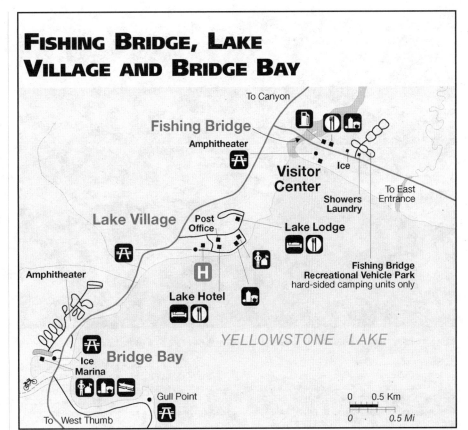

FISHING BRIDGE, LAKE VILLAGE AND BRIDGE BAY

The West Thumb Geyser Basin Trail meanders along a well-maintained boardwalk path. Users walk through a geyser basin filled with inactive lakeshore geysers and brightly colored hot pools.

Yellowstone Lake Overlook Trail
Distance: 2 miles (3 km) roundtrip
Climb: moderate
Difficulty: moderate
Location: The trailhead is located near the entrance to the West Thumb Geyser Basin parking area.

Yellowstone Lake rests in the shadow of the snowcapped Absaroka Mountains at the panoramic Yellowstone Lake Overlook. Although the trail is level at its start, hikers should be prepared for the 400-foot ascent up the hill leading to the overlook.

DISCOVERING THE LAKE, BRIDGE BAY, & FISHING BRIDGE AREAS

Vast green meadows, mudpots, steaming sulpher pools, natural rock bridges, rivers, and lakes can all be found in the Lake, Bridge Bay, and Fishing Bridge Areas. As one of Yellowstone's most diverse regions, the area receives plenty of attention during the major summer tourist season. The area is located approximately thirty miles from the East Entrance and just forty miles from the South Entrance.

Historical Attractions

Many of Yellowstone's historic landmarks are found in the Lake, Bridge Bay, and Fishing Bridge Areas. From lavish hotels to park ranger stations to stunning archaeological finds, this Yellowstone region is inundated with historical places and the stories of the people that frequented the area.

Fishing Bridge
At one time the only eastern entrance into Yellowstone National Park, Fishing Bridge was first constructed in 1902. The historic rough-sawn log bridge was incredibly popular, and anglers from far and wide were drawn to its prime location as a major cutthroat trout spawning area. Drawing its name from the nearly 50,000 anglers who annually flocked to the span, Fishing Bridge became so well-worn that park officials were forced to replace the original structure in 1937. This "new" bridge remains the primary route across the Yellowstone River to date, but fishing access was banned in the 1960s to preserve dwindling numbers of native fish. Today, the bridge serves as a popular fish and wildlife observatory destination.

Fishing Bridge Museum and Visitor Center
The Fishing Bridge Museum and Visitor Center dates back to 1931 and features native stone quarried from a nearby rock outcropping. The rustic structure, which inspired National Park architecture across the country, blends in with its surroundings to accurately reflect the beauty and simplicity of Mother Nature. The popular museum was designated a National Historic Landmark in 1987 and is recognized for its extensive wildlife displays.

Lake Lodge
When the admission of automobiles made Yellowstone a destination for the general public as well as the affluent, hordes of visitors streamed through the entrances. In response, Yellowstone was forced to accommodate this growing number of tourists with an array of lodging options in all price ranges. Previously, the Lake Hotel provided posh arrangements for Yellowstone's most elite visitors while tent camps serviced those who were not afraid of roughing the elements. Park officials knew, however, that many visitors would not feel comfortable in either of these lodging choices, so they created the Lake Lodge. Designed by park

Visitors on the boardwalk at LeHardy Rapids on the Yellowstone River. NPS photo

architect Robert Reamer, Lake Lodge was completed in 1926 and was an instant success. The lodge is now under the management of Xanterra Parks and Resorts, and rooms are still available. Advance room reservations at this historic lodge are recommended.

Lake Ranger Station
Showcasing a "trapper cabin" architectural style, the Lake Ranger Station was constructed in 1923 as one of Yellowstone's earliest park operations facilities. The station is famous for its impressive octagonal community room that provided early park visitors with Yellowstone information by day and lively fireplace discussions each evening.

Lake Village
Lake Village may provide tourists with all the modern amenities they want and need, but the little village situated on Yellowstone Lake's northwest shore is full of history. From rustic frontier cabins to the glorious Lake Yellowstone Hotel, the buildings comprising Lake Village are an important part of Yellowstone Park's early heritage.

Lake Yellowstone Hotel
Situated on the shores of Yellowstone Lake where mountain men and Native Americans congregated, the Lake Yellowstone Hotel was established in 1891 under the financial backing of the Northern Pacific Railroad. Originally a plain structure featuring a boxy shape, park architect Robert Reamer dreamed of something far grander in welcoming guests to the park's largest lake. In 1903, Reamer designed the ionic columns and false balconies while extending the roofline in three places. He later masterminded the addition of the hotel's famous dining room, sunroom, and portico that gave Lake Yellowstone Hotel the majestic image it proudly displays to this day.

Completely renovated and restored with a ten-year project that concluded in 1991, the hotel is now listed as a Nationally Registered Historic Place. Inside, visitors will find high ceilings, large windows offering incredible lake views, a blue-tiled fireplace, a grand staircase, and the gracious atmosphere of a fine 1920s hotel. Rooms are available, but advance reservations are highly recommended.

Native American Findings
The Mid-West Archaeological Center of the National Park Service recently conducted research along the East Entrance Road and were surprised to discover a cache of archaeological evidence. The findings indicated that Native Americans lived in or frequently traveled through the Lake Village Area nearly 9,600 years ago. Archaeologists located a bison harvest site, a cooking hearth, arrowheads, and mittens.

Natural Attractions

While Yellowstone Lake serves as the primary natural attraction in the Lake, Bridge Bay, and Fishing Bridge Areas, the area is also home to many other Yellowstone legends. Visitors will find bubbling mudpots, impressive springs with medieval names, scenic valleys, and more.

Hayden and Pelican Valleys
The large, open meadows characterizing Hayden and Pelican Valleys are the remains of ancient lakebeds. Respectively located six miles north and three miles east of Fishing Bridge, the Hayden and Pelican Valleys are covered with a variety of lush vegetation and sport one of America's finest wildlife habitats. Grizzly bears, bison, and elk all roam through the bountiful fields, and wildlife sightings are frequent. Visitors are reminded to follow all wildlife viewing safety tips.

LeHardy Rapids
LeHardy Rapids is a scenic waterfall situated three miles north of Fishing Bridge on the Yellowstone River. Drawing its name from 1873 Jones Expedition topographer Paul LeHardy, the cascade fills each spring with cutthroat trout journeying to Fishing Bridge for annual spawning. In 1984, park officials constructed a boardwalk to provide visitors with safe, close-up views. As a result, harlequin ducks that once inhabited the area have now disappeared. In an effort to once again attract this unique species, park officials periodically close the boardwalk during spring mating season. Visitors are asked to comply with the park service's closures and respect Yellowstone's wildlife.

Mud Volcano/Sulphur Caldron
Now comprising a large area rather than a single

feature, Yellowstone's Mud Volcano has long been known as one of the most marvelous, yet mysterious, places in the park. Park Superintendent Nathaniel Langford described the area in 1870, and frontier minister Edwin Stanley detested the area for its "villainous" properties.

Despite unsavory early descriptions that linked Mud Volcano to an evil uprising, the area features powerful springs and mudpots that intrigue researchers to this day. Historically, Mud Volcano was a single feature that announced its presence with loud rumblings and unsightly mud flinging. Now that the massive crater is quiet, other features in the area take precedence.

Dragon's Mouth Spring belches and steams as 180 degree Fahrenheit water splashes in its underground cave. Escaping steam and gasses cloak the surrounding landscape in a mysterious palette of orange and green. Nearby, Black Dragon's Caldron burst onto the scene in 1948 with a massive mud explosion that blew apart mature trees as if they were tiny matchsticks. The Black Dragon rumbles eerily throughout the day, and frequent earthquakes in the area continue to remold the activity of this popular backwoods creature.

Directly north of the Mud Volcano area, Sulphur Caldron's thrashing yellow waters feature a stable pH of just 1.3. The area, which is more than twice as acidic as battery acid, is one of the most acidic regions in Yellowstone, and visitors must exercise extreme caution. The springs are capable of disintegrating anything that falls into their lair.

Although the park service maintains a boardwalk that takes visitors to the brink of many of these strange features, some of the area's most dramatic mudpots and springs are located off the boardwalk. While visitors have illegally traveled across the fragile landscape for glimpses of these hot and extremely active sites, such activity is strictly forbidden. Those interested in visiting "Gumper" and other mudpots located behind Sour Lake in the Mud Volcano region are asked to contact a park ranger for a safely guided tour of such features.

Natural Bridge
A one-mile hike or bicycle ride departing directly south of the Bridge Bay Campground leads to a natural rhyolite bridge at the brink of Yellowstone's backcountry. Formed by erosion and spanning Bridge Creek, the natural feature rises fifty-one feet above the scenic stream. Although visitors may follow a trail to the top of the rock bridge, travel across the feature is strictly prohibited in an effort to preserve the bridge for future generations.

Yellowstone Lake
Nestled at an elevation of 7,733 feet and encompassing 136 square miles, Yellowstone Lake is recognized as North America's largest high elevation lake. The impressive lake served as a source of early explorer intrigue and continues to occupy the time of current researchers. Under the direction of Dr. Val Klump from the Center for Great Lakes Research and the University of Wisconsin, researchers utilized a submersible robot submarine to discover astonishing new evidence about Yellowstone Lake.

Scientists once believed that Yellowstone Lake's deepest point was 320 feet, but the submarine discovered an extensive canyon measuring 390 feet deep. Other significant findings proved that the lakebed of Yellowstone Lake is remarkably similar to the park's visible land features. Geysers, hot springs, and steam vents bubble with rage while impressive canyons, rock spires, and silica chimneys add diversity to the mix. Researchers now believe that Yellowstone Lake's underwater features are nearly identical to the thermal vents located on the Pacific Ocean's floor.

Yellowstone River
The Yellowstone River flows 671 miles on its course from Wyoming's Shoshone Mountains to its eventual merger with the Missouri River and the Atlantic Ocean. On its journey, the river flows through and departs Yellowstone Lake at Fishing Bridge, continues over LeHardy Rapids to Hayden Valley, tumbles over the Upper and Lower Falls in the Grand Canyon of the Yellowstone, meets the Lamar River at Tower Junction, and winds its way northeast through Montana.

The prized Yellowstone is one of America's last major undammed rivers and provides critical trout spawning habitat. As a result, grizzly bears often line the river and its tributaries, and anglers scour the riverbanks for the catch of the day. While visiting the Yellowstone River, visitors should be extra vigilant about bear safety and be aware of all current fishing regulations.

Geological Highlights
Earthquakes, glaciers, volcanic activity, unique water systems, and pockets of hydrogen sulfide gas have all played a role in the unique geological history comprising the Lake, Bridge Bay, and Fishing Bridge Areas.

Hayden Valley
Now a marsh covered with abundant plant life, the Hayden Valley was once hidden beneath the deep waters of Yellowstone Lake. When the water retreated, it left behind fine lake sediment deposits soon buried under glacial till from glacier activity dating back nearly 13,000 years. As a result of these ancient deposits, water is unable to penetrate through the ground layers of Hayden Valley, which results in the valley's marshy landscape.

Mud Volcano Region
A highly unique, eerily captivating site, the Mud Volcano Area's activity is easily explained through the Earth's natural geological processes. A unique water system where the ground water boils away faster than it settles leaves Mud Volcano nearly devoid of water. As a result, numerous steam vents form that allow hydrogen sulfide gas vapors to escape from deep within the Earth's surface. These vapors dissolve the area's rock into clay and also combine with water and bacteria to form highly acidic pools. When these sulphur pools, carbon dioxide, steam, and clay join together, visitors are treated to a spectacular display of bubbling mud-pots.

Since the area is highly acidic and soil temperatures average a consistent 200 degrees Fahrenheit, vegetation is unable to survive. "The Cooking Hillside" is a famous example of this characteristic, and shallow earthquakes further spread the range of these high temperatures, acid, and sulphuric gas by forming new fractures in the area's fragile crust.

Yellowstone Lake
Yellowstone is alive with volcanic activity, and researchers now look to Yellowstone Lake as proof of this conclusion. 600,000 years ago, major eruptions occurred at the volcanic vents of Mallard Lake Dome near Old Faithful and Sour Creek Dome near Fishing Bridge. As a result of these eruptions that measured 1,000 times the magnitude of the 1980 Mt. St. Helens explosion, Yellowstone Lake's 136-square mile lakebed formed.

Although no major explosion has since occurred, the Mallard Lake Dome and Sour Creek Dome remain active. Known as resurgent domes, these volcanic vents continue to rise and fall with each passing year. As a result of Sour Creek's activity, Yellowstone Lake is tilting right beneath researchers' eyes. The lake now angles towards the south, flooding forests in the southern arm and exposing new beaches on the lake's northern shoreline. Researchers believe it is only a matter of time before Yellowstone erupts again and clouds the continent in a sea of ash.

Day Hiking the Lake, Bridge Bay, and Fishing Bridge Areas

Day hiking in Yellowstone provides an ideal opportunity for people of all ages to get out and experience the park's many wonders away from the crowds. Thousands of miles of trails await, and wildlife sightings are nearly always guaranteed. Those planning a day trip into Yellowstone's wilderness are encouraged to stop by a ranger station or visitor's center for trail maps and the latest information regarding weather, animal activity, and trail closures. The following trails are available in the Lake, Bridge Bay, and Fishing Bridge Areas, and all hikers are reminded to stay on the trail.

Avalanche Peak Trail
Distance: 5 miles (8 km) roundtrip
Climb: steep
Difficulty: strenuous
Location: This trail begins on Eleanor Lake's west end across the road from a small creek.

Aptly named after its steep passage through an avalanche slide area to the scenic Avalanche Peak, this trail passes through forests and meadows before arriving at the base of Avalanche Peak. Majestic park vistas are available from the base of the peak, but adventurous hikers can opt to follow the rocky trail up to the peak's narrow ridgeline. An unmarked trail returns hikers to the meadow previously encountered where users then backtrack to the trailhead. This trail should never be attempted during the fall as grizzly bears abound. Also, hikers should be alert for approaching thunderstorms and use extreme caution while walking Avalanche Peak's ridgeline.

Elephant Back Mountain Trail
Distance: 3-mile (5 km) loop
Climb: moderate
Difficulty: moderate
Location: The trailhead is located 1 mile south of the Fishing Bridge Junction at a designated pull-out.

Elephant Back Mountain Trail is one of the most popular day hikes in the Lake, Bridge Bay, and Fishing Bridge Areas since it affords outstanding photo opportunities. After climbing a moderately steep trail through lodgepole pines, hikers arrive at the summit of Elephant Back Mountain for views of the Pelican Valley, Yellowstone Lake, and the Absaroka Mountains.

Howard Eaton Trail
Distance: 7 miles (11.3 km) roundtrip
Climb: level
Difficulty: easy
Location: The trail begins on the east side of Fishing Bridge at a parking lot.

The Howard Eaton Trail is a suitable trail for hikers of all abilities. The trail skirts the banks of the Yellowstone River before heading through forests, meadows, and sagebrush plains on a journey to LeHardy Rapids. The area frequently hosts grizzlies, so hikers are urged to contact the nearest ranger station for the latest information on area bear activity.

Natural Bridge Trail
Distance: 3 miles (5 km) roundtrip

Climb: level
Difficulty: easy
Location: The trailhead is located near the Bridge Bay Campground entrance at the Bridge Bay Marina parking lot.

Mother Nature's powerful erosion forces carved a spectacular fifty-one foot natural rhyolite bridge over Bridge Creek. The trail to the bridge is level, and an interpretive exhibit is available onsite. Those in fairly good physical condition may take a short hike up a switchback trail to the top of the bridge, but the bridge's span is closed to visitors in the name of preservation. Since bears feed in this area, this trail is closed late spring through early summer to protect both visitors and wildlife.

Pelican Creek Trail
Distance: 1-mile (1 km) loop
Climb: level
Difficulty: easy
ocation: The trailhead is located 1 mile east of the Fishing Bridge Visitor Center at Pelican Creek Bridge's west end.

The easy Pelican Creek Trail provides a short, but informative introduction to Yellowstone's many scenic treasures. The trail wanders through a variety of habitat and is a birdwatcher's paradise.

Pelican Valley Trail
Distance: 6 miles (10 km) roundtrip
Climb: gradual
Difficulty: moderate
Location: This hike begins on a dirt road across from Indian Pond 3 miles east of the Fishing Bridge Visitor Center.

Open only during daylight hours, this trail winds through Pelican Valley and some of America's prime grizzly bear habitat. Wildflower meadows, forests, and a valley loaded with wildlife all abound on this trail. While most hikers opt to turn around at the footbridge's 3-mile mark, an extended 16-mile loop is available for those hikers traveling in large groups. Pelican Valley is known for harboring grizzly bears, wolves, elk, bison, sandhill cranes, eagles, and trout, so use extreme caution when viewing this wildlife. Make noise to alert area bears of your presence, and always check in at a ranger station for the latest wildlife activity information. This trail is closed until after July 4th due to increased early summer bear activity.

Storm Point Trail
Distance: 2-mile (3 km) loop
Climb: level
Difficulty: easy
Location: This trail begins 3 miles east of the Fishing Bridge Visitor Center at a pullout near Indian Pond.

Beginning with overviews of Indian Pond and Yellowstone Lake, this trail meanders through lodgepole pine forests on its short journey to panoramic vistas at Storm Point. The rocky point is known for harboring a large population of yellow-bellied marmots, and bears also frequent the area. Hikers should check in at the nearest ranger station for the latest trail closures and bear activity information.

NOTES:

GRAND TETON NATIONAL PARK
YOUNGEST RANGE IN THE ROCKIES

Mt. Moran. NPS Photo.

GRAND TETON: AMERICA'S SANCTUARY FOR MOUNTAIN SPLENDOR

Encompassing 310,000 beautiful acres and connected to Yellowstone National Park with the 23,770-acre John D. Rockefeller, Jr. Memorial Parkway, Grand Teton National Park is a sanctuary for mountain splendor and outdoor recreation. The Rocky Mountains' youngest chiseled peaks stand guard over the 485-square-mile park as a diverse wildlife population plays in the shadow of towering forests. Alpine forget-me-nots, the park's official flower, raise their delicate heads to greet northwestern Wyoming's abundant sunshine while alpine lakes mirror the region's stunning landscape under signature blue skies. The ever-present Snake River ties this amazing wilderness scene together, creating a continually evolving space of unparalleled beauty.

Ranging in width from seven miles to a maximum twenty-six miles and running just forty-five miles from its northern boundary to the southern border, Grand Teton National Park covers significantly less terrain than its popular Yellowstone Park neighbor. By no means, however, does the park's comparably small size compromise its natural attractions and magnetic appeal. On the contrary, the small park crams every square inch full of scenic treasures, breathtaking vistas, and amazing topographical diversity. Elevations range from as low as 6,350 feet at the park's southern boundary to the staggering 13,770-foot pinnacle of the Grand Teton.

The park's elevation change, however, is just the beginning of the area's abundant natural wonders. More than a dozen glaciers rest in the Teton Mountains' craggy arms, and twelve of the majestic range's peaks soar above 12,000 feet. Possessing no foothills, the park's widely recognized mountains also cradle seven moraine lakes, 100-plus alpine lakes, seven species of coniferous trees, and over 900 different flowering plant species! Wildlife in all shapes and sizes graze the park's lush land and circle above the triumphant rock gardens, providing many visitors with their first glimpse of the Rocky Mountain West's wildest inhabitants.

These features are inarguably stunning in their own right, but the park's mesmerizing presence is further enhanced with its reputation as a renowned year-round outdoor playground.

Anglers and rafters flock to the blue-ribbon Snake River as boaters take on Jackson and Jenny Lakes, equestrians and backpackers explore the park's rugged backcountry, and rock climbers test their abilities on the Grand Teton. Bicycling, photography, camping, and wildlife viewing are also popular summer activities while winter ushers in months of cross country skiing, snowshoeing, and snowmobiling. With so much to offer, Grand Teton National Park hosts an average 2.3 million visitors every year!

Born of controversy and hard work, Grand Teton National Park embodies the American West's rugged nature and pioneering history. The park and its craggy peaks compel nature lovers into reverent silence, while its intensified focus on protecting the Greater Yellowstone Ecosystem wakens the support and cry of modern preservationists. As a result, today's visitors run the gamut from extreme conservationists to adventurous recreationists, industrious outfitters to drive-by tourists, all of whom Grand Teton National Park warmly welcomes. Whether your travel plans call for exploration of the park's towering peaks, a one-day tour of park highlights, or a laid back vacation, Grand Teton National Park promises visitors an unforgettable destination of unrivaled mountain splendor! Happy trails as you discover this Rocky Mountain legend!

THE HISTORY BEHIND GRAND TETON

The Grand Teton Mountains and Jackson Hole Valley have long provided an arena for habitation, discovery, and adventures. Prior to the attainment of its national park status, the region housed tales of Native Americans, mountain men, cowboys, outfitters, millionaires, conservationists, politicians, and greedy landowners. The tales of these legendary groups now intertwine to form Grand Teton National Park's story.

Native Americans

When North America's final Ice Age exhaled its last chilly breath 12,000 years ago, a wave of human occupation trickled into Jackson Hole. Ancient inhabitants hunted and raised crops in the park region as early as 10,000 B.C., basking in the grandeur of the area's mild summer climate before migrating to warmer regions each winter. Tribes of Blackfeet, Crow, Shoshone (Sheepeaters), and Gros Ventre Native Americans frequented the fertile

Grand Teton National Park	Jan	Feb	March	April	May	June	July	Aug	Sep	Oct	Nov	Dec
Average Max. Temperature (F)	26	32	38	48	60	70	80	78	68	56	38	28
Average Min. Temperature (F)	5	8	10	24	31	38	42	41	34	26	16	7
Extreme High (F)	55	60	64	75	85	98	95	96	93	84	65	58
Extreme Low (F)	-60	-63	-43	-28	0	18	24	18	7	-20	-36	-52
Days above 90°	0	0	0	0	0	0	1	1	0	0	0	0
Days below 32°	31	27	30	26	19	6	2	4	14	26	28	31
Average Total Precipitation (in.)	1.4	0.8	1.1	1.3	1.9	2.2	1.2	1.4	1.3	1.0	1.1	1.2
Maximum Precipitation (in.)	3.8	1.8	3.0	2.8	2.9	4.0	2.2	3.9	3.7	2.6	2.5	4.1
Maximum SnowFall (in.)	42	30	32	24	14	6	6	2	8	18	23	31
Days with measurable precipitation	14	12	12	10	10	10	7	8	8	9	10	13
Average No. Thunderstorms	0	0	0	1	5	11	14	12	2	0	0	0

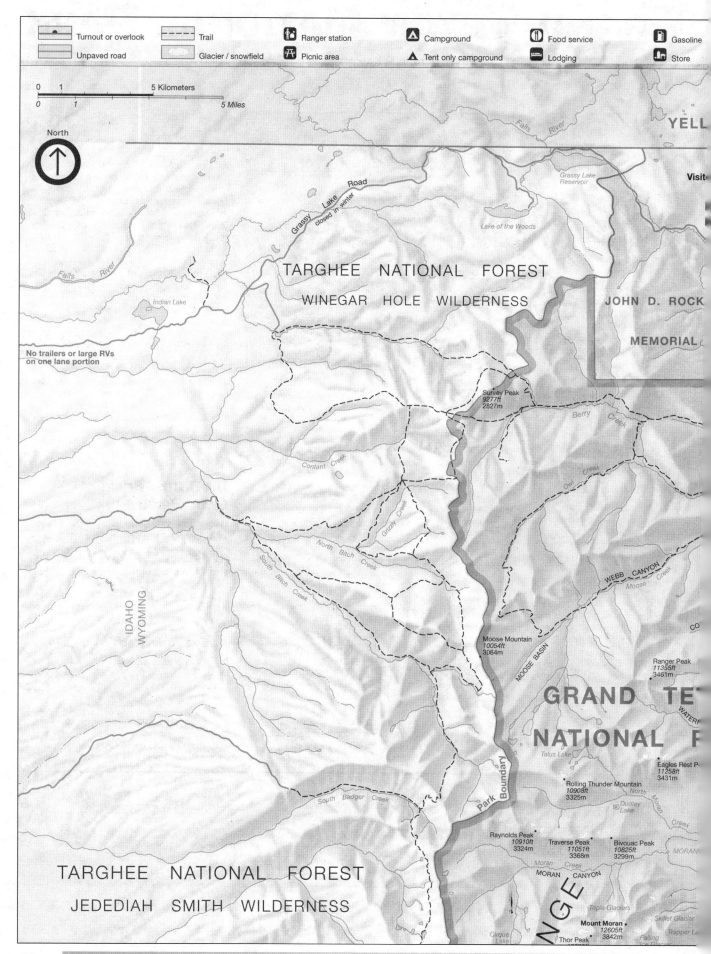

Legend

Turnout or overlook
Unpaved road
Trail
Glacier / snowfield
Ranger station
Picnic area
Campground
Tent only campground
Food service
Lodging
Gasoline
Store

5 Kilometers

5 Miles

North

No trailers or large RVs
on one lane portion

Falls River

Indian Lake

Grassy Lake Road
closed in winter

Grassy Lake
Reservoir

Lake of the Woods

YELL

Visit

TARGHEE NATIONAL FOREST

WINEGAR HOLE WILDERNESS

JOHN D. ROCK

MEMORIAL

Survey Peak
9277ft
2827m

Berry Creek

Contant Creek

Owl Creek

Grizzly Creek

North Bitch Creek

WEBB CANYON

Moose Creek

South Bitch Creek

IDAHO
WYOMING

Moose Mountain
10054ft
3064m

MOOSE BASIN

GRAND TE

NATIONAL F

Ranger Peak
11355ft
3461m

WATERF

Talus Lake

Eagles Rest P
11258ft
3431m

South Badger Creek

Park Boundary

Rolling Thunder Mountain
10908ft
3325m

North Moran Creek

Dudley Lake

Raynolds Peak
10910ft
3324m

Traverse Peak
11051ft
3368m

Bivouac Peak
10825ft
3299m

MORAN

Moran Creek

MORAN CANYON

TARGHEE NATIONAL FOREST

JEDEDIAH SMITH WILDERNESS

NGE

Triple Glaciers

Skillet Glacier

Mount Moran
12605ft
3842m

Thor Peak

Cirque
Lake

Falling
Ice Glacier

Trapper L

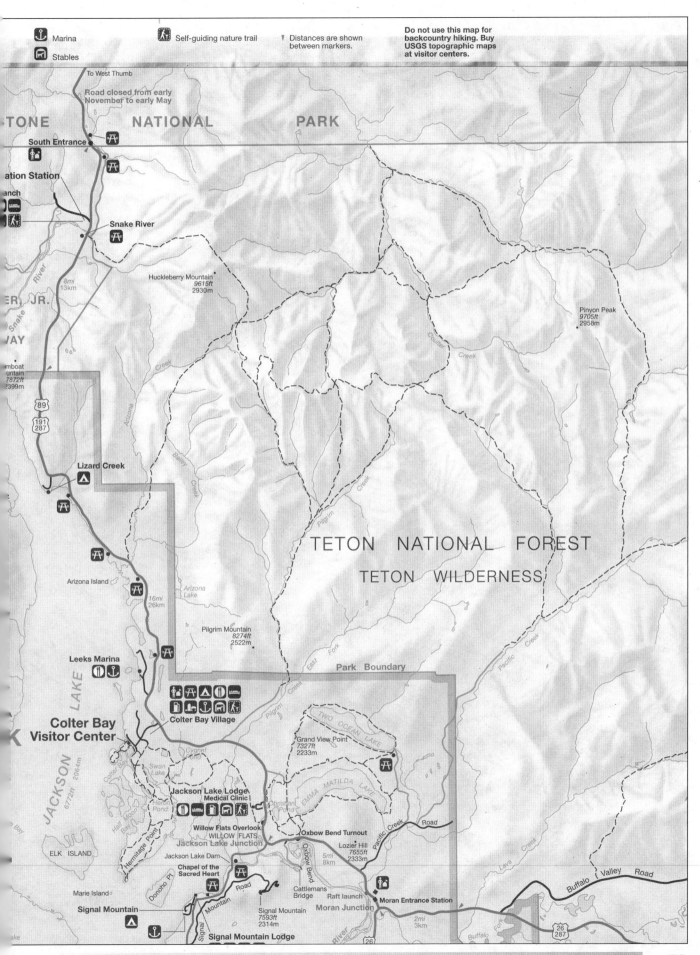

Marina

Stables

Self-guiding nature trail

Distances are shown between markers.

Do not use this map for backcountry hiking. Buy USGS topographic maps at visitor centers.

To West Thumb

Road closed from early November to early May

-STONE   NATIONAL   PARK

South Entrance

...ation Station

...anch

Snake River

8mi
13km

Huckleberry Mountain
9615ft
2930m

Pinyon Peak
9705ft
2958m

Coulter Creek

...ER JR.

...AY

Snake River

...mboat
...untain
...872ft
2399m

89
191
287

Arizona Creek

Lizard Creek

Bailey Creek

Arizona Island

16mi
26km

Arizona Lake

Pilgrim Creek

Pilgrim Mountain
8274ft
2522m

TETON   NATIONAL   FOREST

TETON   WILDERNESS

Leeks Marina

JACKSON   LAKE

Park   Boundary

East Fork

Pacific Creek

Colter Bay Village

Colter Bay
Visitor Center

Cygnet Pond

Swan Lake

Pilgrim

TWO OCEAN LAKE

Grand View Point
7327ft
2233m

EMMA MATILDA LAKE

Colter Bay

6772ft
2065m

Jackson Lake Lodge
Medical Clinic

Heron Pond

Popcorn Pond

Willow Flats Overlook
WILLOW FLATS
Jackson Lake Junction

Half Moon Bay

Hermitage Point

Pacific Creek Road

Oxbow Bend Turnout

Lozier Hill
7655ft
2333m

5mi
8km

ELK ISLAND

Jackson Lake Dam

Chapel of the
Sacred Heart

Marie Island

Donoho Pt.

Signal Mountain

Signal Mountain
Road

Cattlemans
Bridge

Raft launch

Moran Entrance Station

Moran Junction

Oxbow Bend

Buffalo Valley Road

Signal Mountain
7593ft
2314m

Signal Mountain Lodge

River

26

2mi
3km

Buffalo Fork

Lava Creek

26
287

Grand Teton National Park

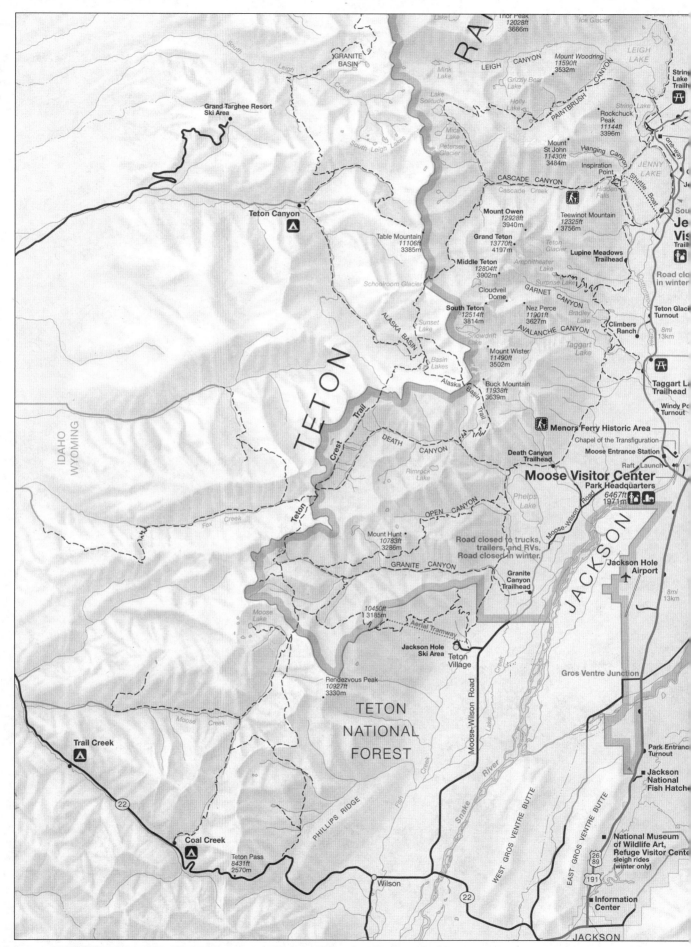

RAN

Thor Peak
12028ft
3666m

Ice Glacier

LEIGH
LAKE

IGRANITE
BASIN

LEIGH
CANYON

Mount Woodring
11590ft
3532m

Mink
Lake

Grizzly Bear
Lake

String
Lake
Trailh

South
Leigh

Creek

Grand Targhee Resort
Ski Area

Lake
Solitude

Holly
Lake

PAINTBRUSH
CANYON

String
Lake

Rockchuck
Peak
11144ft
3396m

one-way

South Leigh Lakes

Mica
Lake

Petersen
Glacier

Mount
St John
11430ft
3484m

Hanging Canyon

Inspiration
Point

JENNY
LAKE

Teton Canyon

CASCADE CANYON

Cascade Creek

Hidden
Falls

Shuttle Boat

Sou

Je
Vis
Trailh

Table Mountain
11106ft
3385m

Mount Owen
12928ft
3940m

Teewinot Mountain
12325ft
3756m

Grand Teton
13770ft
4197m

Teton
Glacier

Road clo
in winter

Lupine Meadows
Trailhead

Middle Teton
12804ft
3902m

Schoolroom Glacier

Cloudveil
Dome

Amphitheater
Lake

Surprise Lake

GARNET CANYON

Teton Glaci
Turnout

ALASKA BASIN

Sunset
Lake

South Teton
12514ft
3814m

Nez Perce
11901ft
3627m

Bradley
Lake

Climbers
Ranch

8mi
13km

Snowdrift
Lake

AVALANCHE CANYON

Taggart
Lake

Basin
Lakes

Mount Wister
11490ft
3502m

Alaska

Basin

Trail

Buck Mountain
11938ft
3639m

Taggart L
Trailhead

Windy P
Turnout

TETON

Crest

Trail

DEATH

CANYON

Menors Ferry Historic Area

Chapel of the Transfiguration

Teton

Rimrock
Lake

Death Canyon
Trailhead

Moose Entrance Station

Raft Launch

Fox

Creek

Trail

OPEN

CANYON

Phelps
Lake

Moose Visitor Center
Park Headquarters

6467ft
1971m

Mount Hunt
10783ft
3286m

Road closed to trucks,
trailers, and RVs.
Road closed in winter.

Jackson Hole
Airport

GRANITE CANYON

Granite
Canyon
Trailhead

JACKSON

IDAHO
WYOMING

10450ft
3185m

Aerial Tramway

8mi
13km

Moose
Lake

Jackson Hole
Ski Area

Teton
Village

Creek

Gros Ventre Junction

Rendezvous Peak
10927ft
3330m

Moose

Creek

TETON

NATIONAL

FOREST

Moose-Wilson Road

Lake

Snake

River

Park Entrance
Turnout

Trail Creek

Jackson
National
Fish Hatche

PHILLIPS RIDGE

Fish

Creek

WEST GROS VENTRE BUTTE

EAST GROS VENTRE BUTTE

National Museum
of Wildlife Art,
Refuge Visitor Cent
sleigh rides
(winter only)

22

Coal Creek

Teton Pass
8431ft
2570m

Wilson

22

26
89

191

Information
Center

JACKSON

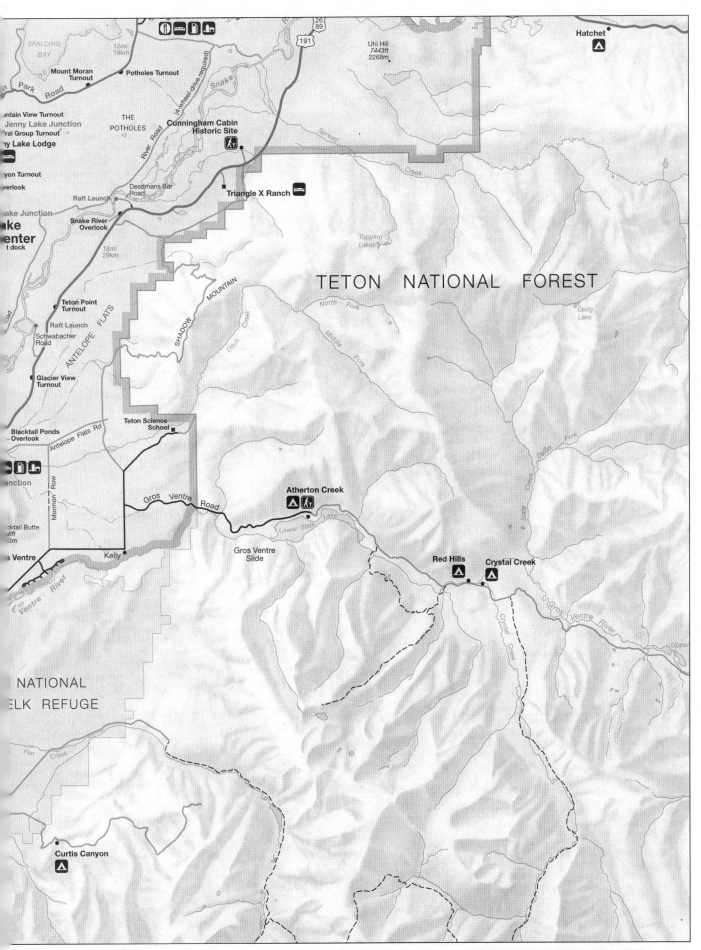

SPALDING BAY

Mount Moran Turnout

Potholes Turnout

12mi 19km

Park Road

THE POTHOLES

River Road

ntain View Turnout
Jenny Lake Junction
ral Group Turnout

ny Lake Lodge

yon Turnout
verlook

ake Junction

ke
enter

t dock

Raft Launch

Snake River Overlook

Deadmans Bar Road

Cunningham Cabin Historic Site

(4-wheel-drive required)

26 89

191

Snake

Spread

Creek

Uhl Hill 7443ft 2268m

Hatchet

Triangle X Ranch

Topping Lakes

18mi 29km

Teton Point Turnout

Raft Launch

Schwabacher Road

ANTELOPE FLATS

Glacier View Turnout

SHADOW MOUNTAIN

Ditch Creek

North Fork

Middle Fork

Leidy Lake

TETON   NATIONAL   FOREST

Blacktail Ponds Overlook

Teton Science School

Antelope Flats Rd

Mormon Row

unction

cktail Butte
8ft
3m

s Ventre

Gros Ventre Road

Kelly

Atherton Creek

Lower Slide Lake

Gros Ventre Slide

Slate Creek

Dallas Fork

Red Hills

Crystal Creek

NATIONAL

ELK REFUGE

Ventre River

s Ventre River

Gros Ventre   River

Crystal Creek

Upper

Flat Creek

Curtis Canyon

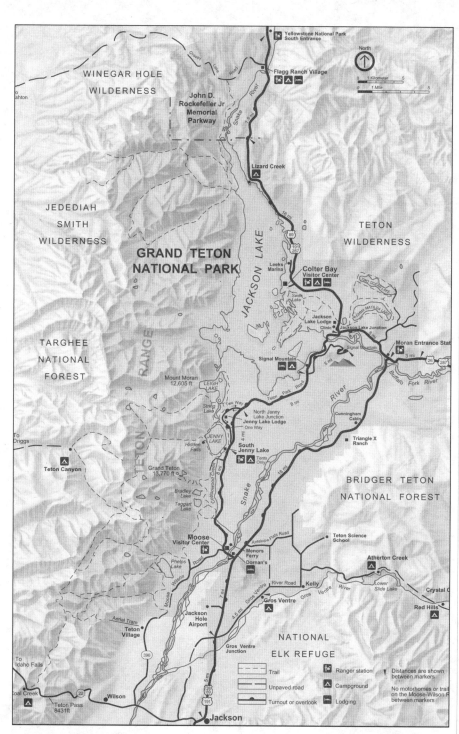

new, lucrative employment. The once bustling Teton Range sat ghostly silent, waiting for the next wave of industrious individuals to discover its lofty setting.

Hunters, Guides, Farmers, and Cowboys

When the beaver population and its surrounding mystique declined, the area's other wildlife claimed the spotlight. Rumors of prized elk, deer, bears, and bison permeated the country in the 1880s and 1890s, and rich hunters from across America flocked to Jackson Hole in hot pursuit of hides and horns. When these hunters arrived, early settlers were ready and willing to serve as area hunting guides. Ben Sheffield, who owned property near Jackson Lake in 1902, turned his ranching operation into a full-time expedition service. Sheffield's business flourished so well that his base of operations eventually bloomed into the community of Moran.

For those who had no desire to escort wealthy hunters through the wilds of the Teton Range, Jackson Hole also offered a fledgling agricultural industry. A short growing season and harsh winters prevented steady and profitable crop production, but homesteaders willing to work hard were able to eke out a living growing hay and raising cattle. Many business roots and ranches these diligent homesteaders planted remain a viable force in Jackson Hole to this day.

Other early homesteaders dreamed of the cowboy way. Turning their cattle property into dude ranches, these homesteaders capitalized on the area's beautiful mountains and brought tourist dollars from across the world to Jackson Hole. Respectively established in 1908 and 1912, the JY and the Bar BC Dude Ranches were highly successful and helped Jackson uphold its stake in Wyoming's "Cowboy State" motto.

Expanding Yellowstone: Controversy Awakens

As tourists began flooding the area in search of dude ranch vacations, homesteaders also decided to turn a buck off the land's beauty and wealthy visitors. Makeshift hotdog stands lined the highway, a dance hall polluted Jenny Lake's peaceful shores, and ruthless contractors erected buildings on fragile habitat with little regard to the wildlife that depended upon the land's pristine nature.

As such frivolous development became commonplace between 1910 and 1920, Yellowstone Park officials and supporters watched in dismay. Stephen Mather, National Park Service Director, and his assistant Horace Albright responded with urgent pleas to protect the area under an official Yellowstone Park expansion. Their policy called for extending Yellowstone's southern boundary to include the Tetons, Jackson Lake, and the headwaters of the Snake River. After presenting their proposal to the U.S. Secretary of the Interior and receiving government approval, Mather and Albright helped Wyoming's congressional delegates write a bill calling for Yellowstone's expansion. Although the House accepted the proposed bill in 1919 with only minor revisions, the measure died in the Senate at the hands of Idaho Senator John Nugent. Nugent adamantly opposed the bill, expressing grave concern that an extension of Yellowstone boundaries would jeopardize regional sheep grazing permits. Little did Nugent realize that his complaint would spark long-lasting controversy across the American West.

Soon, dude ranchers, cattlemen, and sheepherders in Wyoming and Idaho sided with Nugent

Jackson Hole Valley for centuries, and archaeologists have discovered significant traces of this early park activity. Researchers also speculate that the rugged Grand Tetons offered historically important routes to seasonal hunting grounds both inside and outside current park boundaries.

Explorers, Mountain Men, and Fur Trappers

By the time explorer John Colter arrived on the scene during the 1807-1808 winter, previously established Native American routes paved the way for his adventurous wanderings. Armed with Colter's extensive travel notes and spurred to the area with the international beaver pelt fashion craze, mountain men and fur trappers quickly followed Colter's footsteps. These entrepreneurs

began pouring into the region in the 1820s, and David E. Jackson and William Sublette became the famous proprietors of the Rocky Mountain Fur Company. Jackson was so highly regarded that the valley surrounding the Grand Tetons was soon referred to as "Jackson's Hole," while Jackson Lake at the base of the splendid mountains also drew its name from the legendary trapper. Although the 's' was later dropped from the title, Jackson Hole is still the term most commonly used to describe the region surrounding Grand Teton National Park.

Teton Country's beaver fever held on tight throughout the 1820s and 1830s. As the demand for beaver pelts declined, however, so did the demand for mountain men and fur trappers. When the beaver craze finally came to an end in the early 1840s, many of the outdoorsmen had already vacated Jackson Hole in hopes of finding

FACTS ABOUT THE PARK:

Teton Range

An active fault-block mountain front, 40 miles long (65 km), 7-9 miles wide (11-14.5 km).

Highest peak

Grand Teton, elevation 13,770 feet (4198 m). Twelve peaks over 12,000 ft (3658 m) in elevation.

Jackson Hole

Mountain valley, 55 miles long (89 km), 13 miles wide (21 km), average elevation 6,800 feet (2073 m). Lowest elevation at south park boundary, 6350 feet (1936 m).

Climate

Semi-arid mountain climate.
Extreme high: 93 degrees F (34 degrees C).
Extreme low: -46 degrees F (-43 degrees C).
Average snowfall: 191 inches (490 cm).
Avg. rainfall: 10 inches (26 cm).

Snake River

Headwaters of the Columbia River system, 1056 miles long. Approximately 50 miles lie within Grand Teton NP. Major tributaries: Pacific Creek, Buffalo Fork, and Gros Ventre River.

Lakes

Seven morainal lakes at the base of the Teton Range: Jackson, Leigh, String, Jenny, Bradley, Taggart, and Phelps. Jackson Lake: 25,540 acres (10,340 hectares) maximum depth 438 feet (134 m). Over 100 alpine and backcountry lakes.

Wildlife

17 species of carnivores (black and grizzly bears)
6 species of hoofed mammals
3 species of rabbits/hares
22 species of rodents
6 species of bats
4 species of reptiles (none poisonous)
5 species of amphibians
16 species of fishes
300+ species of birds
numerous invertebrates (no poisonous spiders)

Flora

7 species of coniferous trees
900+ species of flowering plants

---

and began lobbying against the proposed Yellowstone expansion. Local U.S. Forest Service personnel were next to join the campaign, opposing all National Park Service interference in Teton Country and the surrounding forestland. Jackson Hole businessmen despised the bill and any development of their beloved land. These individuals also knew that an extension of Yellowstone would decrease the number of grazing permits the Forest Service could distribute. Profits from these grazing permits provided crucial funding for local schools, and the businessmen had no intention of forking over any of their own money to compensate for such losses. With complaints running rampant, the proposed bill was put back on the shelf.

John D. Rockefeller, Jr. NPSPhoto.

Rockefeller Lends Support

Although enemies of the bill were temporarily satisfied, preservationists were less than happy with the outcome. John D. Rockefeller, Jr. was the most famous of these conservationists during the mid 1920s. He made it his mission to purchase all property surrounding the proposed park whose owners planned on carelessly developing the area. Forming the Snake River Land Company as a guise to his identity, Rockefeller dropped $1.4 million while purchasing over 35,000 acres of ranch-land at the base of the Teton Mountains. Rockefeller intended to donate the land to the American government and its citizens for designation as a park, but politicians would hear nothing of the plan. Rockefeller's land was doomed to take center stage in yet another heated debate.

Establishing a New Park

While Rockefeller channeled his energy and money into buying up precious land in Teton Country, National Park Service employees were revamping the original bill to extend Yellowstone's boundaries. The Coordinating Commission on National Parks and Forests convened in Wyoming in 1928 with the express purpose of swaying Jackson Hole residents into approving a new park that granted sheepherders, cattlemen, and dude ranchers plenty of land to sustain their businesses. The commission's proposal excluded all mention of Yellowstone, instead calling for a brand new park under its own name. This new park would encompass 96,000 acres, six glacial lakes, and the rugged Teton Mountains. Realizing that the craggy peaks were unsuitable for grazing purposes and most ranching activities, Jackson Hole locals finally acquiesced to the plan.

As a result, Wyoming Senator John Kendrick immediately proposed the establishment of Grand Teton National Park. When Congress passed Kendrick's bill, President Calvin Coolidge endorsed the bill. A mini version of today's Grand Teton National Park was finally born on February 26, 1929.

Rockefeller, FDR, and the Jackson Hole National Monument

When the Grand Teton area miraculously gained a thread of park status, Rockefeller assumed his land donation would finally be accepted. Rockefeller's donation, however, met with extreme criticism. Upon discovering that the Snake River Land Company was none other than Rockefeller's vested conservation interest, locals cried out in disgust.

Many of the individuals believed Rockefeller had duped his sellers, and such illegal tactics had to be addressed.

In 1933, a Senate Subcommittee reviewed the accusations and determined that neither Rockefeller nor the Snake River Land Company had committed any wrongdoing. The scene was now set for Rockefeller to donate his land, and Wyoming Senator Robert Carey proposed a bill in 1934 to expand the fledgling park's boundaries. Carey's bill and a subsequent 1935 proposal failed miserably. The National Park Service responded with a statement regarding the economic growth that national parks generally provide to their surrounding region and communities. Jackson Hole residents immediately bristled at the National Park Service, and the Jackson Hole Committee formed in opposition of any future park development in Teton Country. This committee aligned itself with Wyoming's Congress and House representatives while at the same time igniting outrage against the Park Service throughout Wyoming.

As Wyoming residents became increasingly opposed to the park in the late 1930s and early 1940s, Rockefeller was growing weary of the land situation he had now been dealing with for fifteen years. In a bold move to spur the U.S. government into action, Rockefeller threatened to sell his 35,000 prime Teton acres if America refused to accept his gift. Knowing that Rockefeller would follow through with his threat, President Franklin Delano Roosevelt circumvented any possible Congressional appeal and used his own presidential power to accept Rockefeller's land and create a new Teton Country monument. On March 15, 1943, Roosevelt formed the Jackson Hole National Monument with 212,000 acres located between Yellowstone and Jackson Hole. Slowly but surely, Grand Teton National Park was beginning to assume its present semblance, but the battle was far from over.

Backlash Against Grand Teton and its Monument Status

Roosevelt's personal decree immediately strengthened Jackson Hole's vehement resistance to the national park growing near them. Wyoming residents believed the monument was in direct violation of state rights, and Wyoming's Congressmen challenged the order's legality with a bill to abolish the monument. The bill passed in both the House and the Senate, but Roosevelt blocked the monument's abolishment with a pocket veto. Wyoming residents, however, could not easily be dissuaded.

Despite Roosevelt's veto against abolishing the monument, Wyoming residents made it clear they did not appreciate the monument's presence. Disgusted ranchers trampled across monument land with 500 grazing cattle in tow, and Wyoming filed a new suit against the National Park Service. The suit died when the federal court refused involvement, but regional animosity towards the monument continued. Local Jackson Hole business owners favoring the park were frequently boycotted or attacked, and new bills calling for abolishment were presented to Congress in 1945 and 1947. When both of these bills failed, though, a new attitude started sweeping over Jackson Hole. Local residents were weary of the constant political battles plaguing their once peaceful valley. At the same time, acceptance of tourism's benefits cautiously crept into the minds of once adamant park enemies. U.S. government officials became hopefully optimistic that the park battle was finally nearing its highly anticipated end.

WOLVES IN THE TETONS

In October of 1998, the howling of wolves could be heard in Grand Teton National Park for the first time in over fifty years. Two years after being reintroduced to Yellowstone, wolves began expanding their range south to encompass the sagebrush flats, forested hillsides, and river bottoms of Grand Teton National Park and the valley of Jackson Hole. Their return represents the restoration of an important part of this ecosystem.

Although their present distribution is limited to Canada, Alaska, and a few isolated areas in the northern United States, wolves once roamed the tundra, forests, and high plains of North America from coast to coast. By 1930, human activities, including extensive settlement, unregulated harvest, and organized predator control programs, had pushed the gray wolf to the brink of extinction in the United States. The last known wild wolf in the Yellowstone area was killed in the 1940s.

In 1987, the United States Fish and Wildlife Service recommended establishing three core wolf recovery areas in the Northern Rocky Mountain region: northwestern Montana, central Idaho, and Yellowstone. Biologists suggested allowing wolf populations to recover naturally in northwestern Montana while reintroducing wolves in central Idaho and Yellowstone.

In accordance with this plan, wolves captured in Canada were transported to the U.S. and released in central Idaho and Yellowstone National Park in 1995 and 1996.

Ecology

The gray wolf is a critical player in the Greater Yellowstone Ecosystem, which encompasses Yellowstone and Grand Teton National Parks and surrounding National Forests. Wolves are highly efficient and selective predators, preying on young, old, weak, and sick animals. By culling the herds of their prey species in this manner, wolves are important agents of natural selection, encouraging survivorship of those animals best suited to their environment—the fastest, strongest, and healthiest.

In the Greater Yellowstone Ecosystem, wolves usually prey on elk, although they will occasionally take moose, bison, pronghorn, bighorn sheep, and beavers. Wolf populations are naturally regulated by prey availability, which prevents decimation of prey species populations.

Although wolves do make surplus kills when convenient, the carcasses do not go to waste. They are either cached for later consumption or left for scavengers, including coyotes, ravens, magpies, golden and bald eagles, crows, bears, wolverines, fishers, mountain lions, and lynx.

Wolf Biology

The gray or timber wolf, Canis lupus, is the largest wild canid in existence, ranging from 60 to 175 pounds. Despite its common name the gray wolf may be white, silver/gray, or black in color. Wolves have been clocked at speeds in excess of thirty miles per hour and have been known to travel over a hundred miles in a day, although travels are more often ten or twenty miles per day. Wolves may live up to fifteen years in the wild.

Wolves are highly social animals, functioning primarily in packs. The social structure of the pack is based on a breeding pair comprised of an alpha male and female, followed by a hierarchy consisting of betas (second rank, males and/or females), subordinates, pups, and occasional omegas (outcasts, generally recipients of aggressive behavior from other pack members).

Because only the alpha pair breeds, subordinate wolves of reproductive age must disperse from their packs and form new associations in order to breed. Pack size is ultimately determined by hunting efficiency, which in turn depends on the size, type, and density of prey species available. Wolf packs average five to ten members.

Wolf packs defend home ranges of up to several hundred square miles. During the spring denning season, wolves are especially aggressive in defending core territories around their den sites. In the Greater Yellowstone Ecosystem, wolves generally breed in February and give birth in late April, after a gestation period of about 63 days. The alpha female usually remains at the den site with the pups, while the alpha male and other pack members bring food back to the den. When pups reach approximately two months of age, they are moved to an outdoor nursery referred to as a rendezvous site. By October, pups are usually traveling and hunting with the rest of their pack.

Eradication History

Wolves have long been the target of aggressive eradication efforts by humans. In 1630, the Colony of Massachusetts enacted the first bounty on wolves in what is now the United States. Wolves were effectively eliminated from the eastern United States by the end of the eighteenth century. With settlers' westward expansion, populations of predator and prey species were greatly reduced due to human development and unregulated harvest.

The decline in wild prey populations, especially bison, led many people to believe that wolves posed an unacceptable threat to domestic livestock. These beliefs fueled government-sanctioned, bounty-driven efforts to destroy the wolf in the west. From approximately 1850 through 1930, thousands of wolves were trapped, shot, and poisoned each year in the western U.S.

Government hunters destroyed the last known wolf in the Yellowstone area in the 1940s. By 1930, wolves were virtually absent from the contiguous U.S., except Minnesota and remote areas of northwestern Montana. Sizeable wolf populations remained in Canada and Alaska.

Recovery

1973 marked the passing of the federal Endangered Species Act (ESA), a pivotal event in the history of wildlife preservation. Under the ESA, the gray wolf is listed as endangered throughout the contiguous United States except Minnesota, where it is listed as threatened. The ESA defines an endangered species as one "in danger of extinction throughout all or a significant part of its range" and a threatened species as one "likely to become endangered" in the foreseeable future.

The Endangered Species Act requires the U.S. Fish and Wildlife Service (FWS) to create recovery plans for all listed species. In 1987, the FWS published a recovery plan for the gray wolf in the Northern Rockies, which recommended establishing three gray wolf populations, in northwestern Montana, central Idaho, and Yellowstone, respectively. Biologists predicted that wolves from Canada would naturally recolonize northwestern Montana. However, because central Idaho and Yellowstone were isolated from existing wolf populations, biologists determined that it was impractical to expect natural recolonization of these areas in the near future. Therefore, the Fish and Wildlife Service recommended reintroducing wolves into central Idaho and Yellowstone, while encouraging natural wolf recovery in northwestern Montana.

In 1995, wolves captured in Canada were transported to the U.S. and released in central Idaho and Yellowstone National Park. Because the central Idaho and Yellowstone area wolves are reintroduced populations, they are defined as "experimental" according to the Endangered Species Act. This designation allows more flexibility in managing these populations than is normally allowed for populations of endangered species.

Delisting/Reclassification of the Gray Wolf in the Northern Rocky Mountains

The minimum criteria for removal of the gray wolf from the endangered species list requires the establishment of ten breeding pairs, about 100 wolves, in each of three northern Rocky Mountain population areas (Yellowstone, central Idaho, and northwestern Montana) for three consecutive years. As a prerequisite for delisting from federal protection, the individual states within the recovery area must establish wolf management plans approved by the FWS. These state plans could allow for wolves to be managed in a manner similar to that in which individual states currently manage other large predators, such as bears and mountain lions.

Wildlife managers predicted that recovery goals for the northern Rocky Mountain region would be achieved by the year 2002 or 2003, and it seems that the restoration program is on track. In 1998, there were nine breeding pairs/packs in the Yellowstone area, ten in central Idaho, and seven in northwestern Montana.

Your Park Visit

As with all wildlife, it is smart to keep your distance from wolves in order to avoid disturbing the animals or endangering yourself. Many wild animals will attack people if provoked. However, according to wolf expert L. David Mech, there has never been a documented case of a healthy, wild wolf killing or seriously injuring a human in the Western Hemisphere.

There have been five documented cases of pets being killed by wolves in the Yellowstone area since the reintroduction, and rates of wolf attacks on pets have been similarly low in other areas inhabited by wolves. Grand Teton National Park regulations restrict pets to areas open to motorized vehicles, and require that pets be restrained on a leash at all times.

Welcoming Tourism and Grand Teton National Park

By 1949, the once violent roar against Rockefeller, Roosevelt, and the Jackson Hole National Monument had dulled to a mild chatter. Locals finally saw that pervasive development of the Grand Tetons might destroy the beautiful character of Jackson Hole, while a national park guaranteed that the area's natural resources would be sustained for years to come. The National Park Service's continual plug for tourism's benefits also began resounding with local residents and businessmen who were interested in expanding the region's economic base.

As a result, a local residential committee and Wyoming government officials gathered with a Senate Appropriation Committee in April 1949 to discuss the fate of the Teton Mountains. Within days, the committee members hammered out an agreement to eventually merge the original 1929 national park and a portion of the Jackson Hole National Monument. In doing so, a "new" 310,000-acre Grand Teton National Park would form for the enjoyment of all. Unlike most of America's national parks, however, the creation of Grand Teton National Park included compromises to appease locals and acquire their support.

The park's formation hinged on the following five principles, all of which still apply to Grand Teton National Park today: 1) cattlemen could maintain their existing grazing rights and area routes with assurance of these same rights in the future; 2) the National Park Service would be held accountable for any lost local tax revenue and would compensate the residents of Teton County for any negative impact that the park had on the region's tax structure; 3) with a Wyoming hunting permit, hunters and local guides would still be able to hunt elk within Grand Teton National Park's boundaries in an effort to curb growing elk populations; 4) all future U.S. Presidents were barred from creating a national monument in Wyoming without the prior consent of Wyoming's Congressional delegates and local residents; and 5) a portion of existing forest uses and access points were allowed to remain in effect.

Although true conservationists were displeased with the concessions involved in Grand Teton National Park's formation, they all agreed that any park establishment in beautiful Teton Country was better than none at all. After years of conflict and struggle, Grand Teton National Park was created in its present form with the pen stroke of President Harry S. Truman on September 14, 1950.

Forget-me-nots, the official park flower. National Park Service Photo.

The Park Today

As a result of the five concessions granted during the park's 1950s formation, Grand Teton is now a multiple use park that stuns many visitors and conservationists into outrage. Park visitors expecting a peaceful setting designed strictly for wildlife and resource preservation are increasingly disap-

List of Mammals

Insectivora (Insect-eaters)
c   Masked Shrew *Sorex cinereus*
c   Vagrant Shrew *Sorex vagrans*
r   Dwarf Shrew *Sorex nanus*
u   Northern Water Shrew *Sorex palustris*

Chiroptera (Bats)
c   Little Brown Bat *Myotis lucifugus*
u   Long-eared Myotis *Myotis evotis*
u   Long-legged Myotis *Myotis volans*
u   Silver-haired Myotis *Lasionycteris noctivagans*
r   Hoary Bat *Lasiuris cinereus*
u   Big Brown Bat *Eptisicus fuscus*

Lagomorpha (Rabbits and Hares)
c   Pika *Ochotona princeps*
c   Snowshoe Hare *Lepus americanus*
u   White-tailed Jackrabbit *Lepus townsendii*

Rodentia (Gnawing Mammals)
a   Least Chipmunk *Tamias minimus*
c   Yellow Pine Chipmunk *Eutamias amoenus*
u   Uinta Chipmunk *Tamias umbrinus*
c   Yellow-bellied Marmot *Marmota flaviventris*
a   Uinta Ground Squirrel *Spermophilus armatus*
c   Golden-mantled Ground Squirrel *Spermophilus lateralis*
a   Red Squirrel *Tamasciurus hudsonicus*
u   Northern Flying Squirrel *Glaucomys sabrinus*
u   Northern Pocket Gopher *Thomomys talpoides*
a   Beaver *Castor canadensis*
a   Deer Mouse *Peromyscus maniculatus*
u   Bushy-tailed Woodrat *Neotoma cinerea*

c   Southern Red-backed Vole *Clethrionomys gapperi*
c   Heather Vole *Phenacomys intermedius*
a   Meadow Vole *Microtus pennsylvanicus*
a   Montane Vole *Microtus montanus*
u   Long-tailed Vole *Microtus longicaudus*
c   Richardson Vole *Microtus richardsoni*
r   Sagebrush Vole *Lemmiscus curtatus*
c   Muskrat *Ondatra zibethicus*
c   Western Jumping Mouse *Zappus princeps*
c   Porcupine *Erethizon dorsatum*

Carnivora (Flesh-eaters)
Ursidae – Bear Family
c   Black Bear *Ursus americanus*
u   Grizzly Bear *Ursos arctos*

Canidae – Dog Family
a   Coyote *Canis latrans*
u   Gray Wolf *Canis lupus*
r   Red Fox *Vulpes vulpes*

Mustelidae – Weasel Family
c   Marten *Martes americana*
u   Short-tailed Weasel *Mustela erminea*
r   Least Weasel *Mustela nivalis*
c   Long-tailed Weasel *Mustela frenata*
u   Mink *Mustela vison*
r   Wolverine *Gulo gulo*
c   Badger *Taxidea taxus*
u   Striped Skunk *Mephitis mephitis*
c   River Otter *Lutra canadensis*

Felidae – Cat Family
r   Mountain Lion *Felis concolor*

r   Lynx *Felis lynx*
r   Bobcat *Felis rufus*
Procyonidae – Raccoon Family
r   Raccoon *Procyon lotor*

Artiodactyla (Even-toed Hooves)
Cervidae – Deer Family
a   Elk (wapiti) *Cervus elaphus*
c   Mule Deer *Odocoileus hemionus*
r   White-tailed Deer *Odocoileus virginianus*
a   Moose *Alces alces*

Antilocapridae – Pronghorn Family
c   Pronghorn *Antilocapra americana*

Bovidae – Cattle Family
c   Bison *Bison bison*
x   Mountain Goat *Oreamnos americanus*
u   Bighorn Sheep *Ovis canadensis*

Key to Symbols
a – Abundant – likely to be seen in appropriate habitat and season.
c – Common – frequently seen in appropriate habitat and season.
u – Uncommon – seen irregularly in appropriate habitat and season.
r – Rare – unexpected even in appropriate habitat and season.
x – Accidental – out of known range, or reported only once or twice.
? – Questionable – verification unavailable.

Abundance categories are based on the park and parkway wildlife database, research projects and observations by biologists and naturalists.

BIRD FINDING GUIDE

Grand Teton National Park and the John D. Rockefeller, Jr., Memorial Parkway encompass a range of habitats, from alpine meadows to sagebrush flats, from lodgepole pine forests to mountain streams. Birds use habitats that meet their needs for food, water, shelter and nest sites. Some birds frequent only one habitat type while others occupy a variety of habitats. This guide will acquaint you with some habitat types of the park and parkway as well as specific locations to look for birds. Use it in conjunction with the park map and the various bird identification books available at any of our vistor centers. Please report any sightings of birds listed as rare or accidental on the bird checklist.

Lodgepole Pine Forests

Lodgepole pine grows in dense forests covering much of the valley and the lower slopes of the mountains. Expect olivesided flycatchers, yellow-rumped warblers, ruby-crowned kinglets, mountain chickadees, white-crowned and chipping sparrows and dark-eyed juncos (especially in developed areas within lodgepole forests such as Colter Bay).

Aspens

Aspens occur chiefly in pure stands, often on hillsides. Many of the aspen stands in the park and parkway have rotting trunks that attract numerous woodpeckers. Sawwhet owls, house wrens, mountain and black-capped chickadees, tree swallows and violet-green swallows nest in old woodpecker cavities.

Sagebrush Flats

Sagebrush covers most of the valley called Jackson Hole. Despite the hot dry conditions existing where sagebrush grows, some species flourish. Look for sage grouse, vesper sparrows, Brewer's sparrows and sage thrashers.

Alpine

Above 10,000 feet, severe conditions limit vegetation to low-growing forms. Birds that nest above treeline migrate south or to lower elevations for winter. Watch for golden eagles, Clark's nutcrackers, rosy finches, white-crowned sparrows and water pipits.

Aquatic and Riparian

Numerous rivers, creeks, lakes and ponds provide habitats where Canada geese and other waterfowl nest and osprey and bald eagles hunt for fish. Common snipe, white-crowned and Lincoln sparrows, yellow and MacGillivray's warblers and common yellowthroats nest and forage in adjacent wet meadows. American dippers search for insects in fast-moving streams.

Bird-Watching Etiquette

Enjoy birds but be a responsible birder.

- Nesting birds of all species are easily disturbed. If an adult on a nest flies off at your approach or circles you or screams in alarm, you are too close to the nest. Unattended nestlings readily succumb to predation or exposure to heat, cold and wet weather.

- Good birding areas often attract other wildlife. Maintain a safe distance (300 feet) from large animals such as moose, bears and bison. Do not position yourself between a female and her offspring.

Cascade Canyon.

Glaciers gouged out Cascade Canyon thousands of years ago. Today Cascade Creek carries melted snow through conifer forests and meadows of wildflowers, while the Teton peaks tower above. American dippers frequent Cascade Creek near Hidden Falls. Western tanagers, rubycrowned kinglets and yellow-rumped warblers nest near the trail. Also look for golden eagles, Steller's jays, gray jays, golden-crowned kinglets, dark-eyed juncos and occasional Townsend's warblers. Secretive harlequin ducks sometimes nest along the creek.

Taggart Lake Trail

In 1985 a lightning-caused forest fire burned most of the trees on the glacial moraine surrounding Taggart Lake. Insects feeding on the decaying trees attract woodpeckers. Look for blackbacked and three-toed woodpeckers. Abundant insects also attract mountain bluebirds, tree swallows, olive-sided and dusky flycatchers, western wood-pewees and yellow-rumped warblers. Calliope hummingbirds frequently perch in willows near the base of the moraine.

Antelope Flats – Kelly Road.

Large hayfields attract raptors that search the fields for abundant small rodents. Look for American kestrels, prairie falcons, redtailed hawks, Swainson's hawks and northern harriers. Check fence posts for western meadowlarks, western and eastern kingbirds and mountain bluebirds. Scan irrigated pastures for long-billed curlews and savannah sparrows.

Menor's Ferry at Moose

Follow the self-guiding trail to homesteader cabins along the Snake River. Bird life abounds due to riparian habitat. Violet-green, tree, cliff and barn swallows scoop insects out of the air as western wood-pewees, dusky flycatchers and mountain bluebirds hawk for flying insects. Yellow warblers glean insects from cottonwood trees and willow and silverberry shrubs lining the Snake River. Calliope, broad-tailed and rufous hummingbirds seek nectar from wildflowers. Kingfishers, common mergansers, ospreys and bald eagles catch fish in the river.

Phelps Lake Overlook

The trail to the overlook traverses a lateral glacial moraine where mixed conifers and aspens grow. Because the trail follows a small creek, expect abundant birdlife. Look for western tanagers, MacGillivray's warblers, northern flickers, Lazuli buntings, ruby-crowned kinglets and greentailed towhees. Listen for the sweet songs of hermit and Swainson's thrushes. Calliope and broad-tailed hummingbirds feed on scarlet gilia below the overlook.

Grand View Point

Old growth Douglas firs support Williamson's sapsuckers, red-naped sapsuckers and other woodpeckers. Common songbirds include mountain chickadees, red-breasted nuthatches, dark-eyed juncos, western tanagers and

Townsend's solitaires. Blue grouse and ruffed grouse nest here. At the summit, look up for red-tailed hawks, white pelicans and other soaring birds.

Christian Pond

Several species of waterfowl nest here. Look for ruddy ducks, ring-necked ducks, American wigeon and American coots. Trumpeter swans occasionally nest on the pond. Because human presence interferes with the swans' nesting effort, remain on the trail on the west side of the pond, at least 300 feet from the edge of the pond, and obey all posted closures.

Willow Flats

Extensive willow thickets merge with wet grassy meadows. Small creeks and beaver ponds provide riparian and aquatic habitats. Look for cinnamon teal, greenwinged teal and American wigeon in ponds and creeks. Sandhill cranes, northern harriers, American bitterns, common snipes and soras nest here. Calliope hummingbirds feed on scarlet gilia growing near Jackson Lake Lodge. Red-naped sapsuckers and other woodpeckers abound. Frequently seen songbirds include willow flycatchers, cliff swallows, yellow warblers, MacGillivray's warblers, common yellowthroats, Wilson's warblers, fox sparrows, white-crowned sparrows, pine siskins and yellow-headed blackbirds. Lazuli buntings and greentailed towhees use the drier hillsides adjacent to Willow Flats.

Oxbow Bend

A slow-moving, cut-off meander of the Snake River, Oxbow Bend supports lush underwater plant growth and abundant fish, food for aquatic birds. Great blue herons and osprey nest here. White pelicans, double-crested cormorants, common mergansers and bald eagles fish in the shallow water. Because of Oxbow Bend's proximity to Willow Flats, the birdlife is quite similar.

Two Ocean Lake

Western grebes, trumpeter swans, common mergansers and occasional common loons summer on the lake. Western tanagers, pine grosbeaks, Cassin's finches and other songbirds abound in the open coniferous forests and aspen stands surrounding the lake.

Blacktail Ponds Overlook This overlook is just north of Moose Junction and is situated at the transition of three different plant communities: Sagebrush flats, the coniferous forest of Blacktail Butte, and the willow and cottonwood lined wetlands of the Snake River flood plane. Looking down on the wetlands from the overlook gives you a great vantage point to observe waterfowl such as American wigeons, bluewinged teal, mallards, and goldeneyes. Up to six species of swallows can also be seen at eye level as they skillfully fly through the air catching insects. Raptors such as bald eagles and osprey can be seen in the high cottonwoods. Strewn through out the willows, song sparrows and willow flycatchers among others can be seen and heard. An occasional greentailed towhee flutters through the sagebrush near the overlook and evening grosbeaks visit from the forest.

Bull Elk. NPS Photo.

pointed at the activities allowed within the mountain park's boundaries. Cattle graze on irrigated pastures just a short distance from sensitive wolf pack populations. Idaho potato farmers rely on the Jackson Lake Dam within the park for much-needed irrigation water. Outfitters exploit Grand Teton's peaks with private climbing tours. On top of it all, noise pollution from an adjacent airport clouds the park's natural aura with modern commercialism.

Many in Jackson Hole have become accustomed to these multiple uses in their local outdoor playground. Others, however, scoff at the allowances made that may eventually destroy the park's natural resources, wildlife, and innate beauty. Born out of controversy, Grand Teton National Park remains connected to its conflicted past with flare-ups between local commercial interests and die-hard advocates of ecosystem protection.

GENERAL VISITOR INFORMATION

Since Grand Teton National Park welcomes over two million annual visitors, it is crucial that visitors plan ahead to ensure a truly memorable experience. The following is a basic set of facts every visitor should know prior to his/her Grand Teton tour.

Important Contact Information

Grand Teton National Park (307-739-3300 or 307-739-3400; www.nps.gov/grte): Basic park information, maps, road conditions, and group campground reservations. Write them at PO Drawer 170, Moose, WY 83012-0170

Grand Teton Lodge Company (307-543-2811; www.gtlc.com): Information regarding some of Grand Teton's lodging and dining options, bus tours, and transportation to and from the park

Mountain Weather (307-733-2664; www.mountainweather.com): General Teton area forecast

Avalanche Activity (307-733-2664; 307-733-2759): These numbers respectively provide a recorded avalanche forecast and a current report of all observed avalanche activity

Jackson Hole Chamber of Commerce & Visitor Information Center (733-3316; www.jacksonholechamber.com): General recreational, lodging, and dining information for the Jackson Hole area

Snake River Flow Information: 1-800-658-5771

Medical Emergencies: 911

Grand Teton Medical Clinic (543-2514; 733-8002): General medical services at Jackson Lake Lodge; open daily from 10 AM to 6 PM

St. John's Hospital (733-3636): Complete medical services in Jackson

Grand Teton Commercial Services

The National Park Service does not make reservations with individual concessionaires operating throughout the park. The following companies are licensed to conduct commercial activities within the park. Visitors are asked to contact these companies directly for service information.

Colter Bay Village (307-543-2811; 543-3100; www.gtlc.com)
Colter Bay Village offers a myriad of services. In addition to dining and accommodations, the area offers:

Colter Bay Village General Store: This store provides general merchandise and gifts. It is open daily from late May through early October.

Colter Bay Highway Convenience Store: The convenience store offers general merchandise, including film, gifts, firewood, beer, soft drinks, and groceries.

Colter Bay Service Stations: Colter Bay offers two self-service stations – one on the highway and one inside the village area. The highway station offers regular fuel as well as diesel and is open from early May through late October. The village station offers regular fuel, RV accessories, and a dump station from late May through mid-September.

Laundry: Colter Bay Village's launderette is open daily from the end of May through early October.

Marina: Colter Bay Marina bustles with activity

from late May through early October. Visitors can take a narrated cruise, try guided lake fishing, and rent canoes and boats. The Marina Store provides Wyoming fishing licenses, fishing tackle, outdoor gear, film, snacks, and beer.

Public Showers: Colter Bay's public showers are available daily from the end of May through early October.

Dornans at Moose Village (307-733-2415; www.dornans.com)
Dornans is known for its Spur Ranch Cabins, restaurants, and the following amenities near Moose:

Gift Shop: The Dornan Gift Shop boasts handmade local items, crafts, gifts, and general area souvenirs. The store is open daily from mid-May through mid-September. Shorter winter hours are offered from late September through mid-May.

Grocery Store: This store offers general food supplies, an ATM, and firewood. The store is open daily during summer with extended evening hours; during winter, the store generally closes around 6 PM.

Fishing: Snake River Anglers provides Wyoming fishing licenses year-round, spin and fly-fishing equipment, and camping gear.

Mountaineering: Moosely Seconds is open daily during summer to provide mountaineering equipment and tips about climbing in Grand Teton.

Service Station: The Dornan Service Station is open year-round with extended summer hours.

Spirits: The Moose Bar Lounge provides good times and views year-round as well as a wine and packaged liquor store. During summer, the store usually remains open until 11 PM with winter hours shortened to 7 PM.

Sports Equipment Rentals: Adventure Sports is open early May through mid-October. The store rents bicycles, canoes, and kayaks while also offering repair services and sports accessories.

Flagg Ranch Resort (307-543-2861; 800-443-2311)

The Flagg Ranch Resort Area is open during summer from mid-May through mid-October. Winter hours operate from mid-December through mid-March. Between the summer and winter seasons, Flagg Ranch's hours vary considerably. Late autumn and early spring visitors should call ahead for more information. In addition to dining and lodging, Flagg Ranch offers:

Gift Shop: The Flagg Ranch Gift Shop stocks Native American jewelry, children's items, clothing, and general park souvenirs and gifts.

Grocery Store: This store supplies patrons with food essentials, packaged beer, ice, firewood, and general camping and fishing supplies.

Service Station: The Flagg Ranch Service Station provides both regular and diesel fuel.

Spirits: The Burnt Bear Saloon serves up a selection of drinks as well as packaged liquor and beer.

Snowmobiling/Snowcoach Tours: Daily snowcoach tours depart from Flagg Ranch mid-December through mid-March. These tours travel to Old Faithful with the accompaniment of a knowledgeable guide. Guided and self-guided snowmobiling is also available with treks starting at Flagg Ranch and traveling to Yellowstone.

Gros Ventre Slide In (Write to: PO Box 101, Kelly, WY 83011)

Flowering Times of Selected Flowers and Shrubs

White Flowers

	Valley	Canyons	Alpine
Huckleberry	Jun	Jul	
Mountain Ash		Jul	
Birchleaf Spirea	Jul	Jul	
Chokecherry	Jun		
Woodlandstar	Jun		
Richardson Geranium	Jun – Aug	Jun – Aug	
Thimbleberry		Jun – Jul	
Green Gentian	Jun – Jul	Jul – mid Aug	
Snowbrush Ceanothus	Jun – Jul		
Cowparsnip	late Jun – mid Aug	Jul – Aug	
Serviceberry	Jun		
American Bistort	Jun	Jul	Aug
Ladies-tresses	Aug – mid Sep	Aug – Sep	
White Bog-Orchid	late Jun – mid Aug	Jul – Aug	
Manyflowered Phlox	Jun – mid Jul	mid Jun – Jul	
Colorado Columbine		late Jun – Aug	
Marsh Marigold		Jun – mid Jul	Jun – Jul
Yampah	Jul – mid Aug	mid Jul – Aug	
Engelmann Aster		Jul – Aug	
Yarrow	Jul – early Aug	mid Jul – late Aug	Aug

Yellow Flowers

	Valley	Canyons	Alpine
Mules-ear Wyethia	mid Jun – Jul		
Hymenoxys			Jul – Aug
Sunflower	mid Jul – Aug		
Balsamroot	Jun – mid Jul		
Rabbitbrush	mid Aug – Sep		
Heartleaf Arnica	mid Jun – mid Jul	late Jun – late Jul	
Shrubby Cinquefoil	Jun – Sep		
Yellow Monkey-flower	Jun – mid Jul	mid Jun – mid Aug	
Lanceleaved Stonecrop	Jun – Aug		
Glacier Lily	Jun – Jul		Jul
Western Wallflower	Jun – Jul		
Subalpine Buttercup		Jul – Aug	
Deathcamas	Jun	mid Jun – early Aug	mid Jul – Aug
Oregongrape	May – Jun		
Sulfur Buckwheat	mid Jun – mid Aug		
Bracted Lousewort	late Jun – mid Jul	Jul	
Yellow Columbine	late Jun – Jul	Jul – late Aug	
Yellow Fritillary	mid May – mid Jun		
Butterweed Groundsel	late Jul – Sep		

Pink – Red Flowers

	Valley	Canyons	Alpine
Springbeauty	May	Jun – mid Jul	
Sticky Geranium	Jun – Aug		
Parry's Primrose		Jul – Aug	Aug
Prairiesmoke	Jun – early Jul		
Globemallow	Jul – mid Aug	mid Jul – Aug	
Steershead	late May – mid Jun	late Jun – mid Jul	
Subalpine Spirea		mid Jul – Aug	
Shooting Star	Jun	late Jun – late Aug	
Ladysthumb Knotweed	Aug		
Lewis Monkeyflower		late Jun – Aug	
Mountain Snowberry	Jun – Jul	Jul	
Spreading Dogbane	Jul – Aug		
Mountainheather		Jul – Aug	Aug – Sep
Fireweed	mid Jul – Aug		
Moss Campion			Jul – mid Aug
Calypso Orchid	Jun		
Elephanthead	late Jun – Jul	mid Jul – Aug	
Indian Paintbrush	Jun – Jul	Jul – Aug	mid Jul – early Sep
Striped Coralroot	Jun – Jul		
Skyrocket Gilia	mid Jun – Jul		

Blue – Purple Flowers

	Valley	Canyons	Alpine
Wild Blue Flax	July – Aug		
Rock Clematis	Jun	Jul	
Sky Pilot			July – Aug
Monkshood	late Jun – mid Jul	mid Jul – mid Aug	
Low Larkspur	mid May – Jun		
Mountain Bluebell		mid Jul – early Sep	
Fringed Gentian	late Jul – mid Aug	Aug – early Sep	
Harebell	mid Jun – early Sep		
Lupine	Jun – Jul		
Mountain Bog Gentian		late Jul – early Sep	
Silky Phacelia	late Jun – Jul	mid Jul – late Aug	late Jul – early Sep
Blue Camas	Jun		
Alpine Forget-me-not			Jul – early Aug

Situated near Kelly, Wyoming, the Gros Ventre Slide In carries snacks, crafts, ice, firewood, gifts, and American Indian items.

Leek's Marina (307-543-2494)

Leek's Marina is situated on Jackson Lake and features a gas dock and overnight buoys. The marina is open from late May through mid-September. A pizza restaurant is open daily from early June through early September and serves sandwiches, pizza, and beer.

Jackson Lake Lodge (307-543-2811; 307-543-3100)

In addition to its lodging and restaurants, the Jackson Lake Lodge offers an array of other amenities, including:

Gifts and Apparel: Jackson Lake Lodge's gift and apparel shops are open daily from mid-May through mid-October with a large selection of park souvenirs, western gifts, and clothing.

ATM Machine: Quick cash is always available at the ATM machine located near the Jackson Lake Lodge hotel registration area.

Newsstand: The Jackson Lake Lodge Newsstand is open daily from mid-May through mid-October. *Magazines, books, sundries, and cigars are available.*

Service Station: The self-service gas station provides regular fuel as well as diesel. The station is open daily from mid-May through mid-October.

Spirits: The Blue Heron Lounge and a package liquor store accommodate traveler's needs for spirits with a variety of drinks, wine, and beer. Both facilities are open from mid-May through mid-October.

The Snake River flows in the shadows of the Teton Range. NPS Photo.

Moose Village (307-733-3471)

Moose Village commercial services are limited to a general store and tackle shop. General merchandise as well as guided fly-fishing trips are available daily from late May through mid-September.

Signal Mountain (307-543-2831)

In addition to its wide selection of dining and lodging options, Signal Mountain provides the following services:

Gift Shop: The Signal Mountain Gift Shop specializes in Native American jewelry, mountain home furnishings and accessories, and general park gifts and souvenirs. The shop is open daily from early May through early October.

Teton Traditions: Teton Traditions serves Signal Mountain as a renowned source for outerwear, mountain-inspired clothing, and western/outdoor accessories. The store is open daily from early May through early October.

Marina: Signal Mountain Marina is situated on Jackson Lake and is open late May through mid-September. Visitors will find guided fishing trips, gas, docks, and a variety of boat rentals.

Service Station/Convenience Store: The self-service gas station and convenience store at Signal Mountain provides general traveler amenities. The facility is open daily from early May through early October. While the convenience store closes in winter, emergency gas is available to stranded motorists year-round.

MENOR'S FERRY

Menor's Ferry once belonged to William D. Menor who came to Jackson Hole in 1894, taking up a homestead beside the Snake River. Here he constructed a ferryboat that became a vital crossing for the early settlers of Jackson Hole Valley.

Jackson Hole was isolated by its surrounding mountains and had such a harsh climate that it was one of the last areas of the lower 48 states to be settled. Homesteaders came here, mainly from Idaho, beginning in the late 1880s. Most early settlement in the valley took place in the south, or on a few scattered areas with fertile soil on the east side of the Snake River. Menor was alone on the west side of the Snake for more than ten years.

Rivers are often important transportation corridors. However, the Snake River was a natural barrier that divided the valley. In dry months the river could be forded safely in several locations, but during periods of high water even the most reliable fords were impassable. After 1894, Menor's Ferry became the main crossing in the central part of Jackson Hole. Residents crossed on the ferry to hunt, gather berries and mushrooms, and cut timber at the foot of the mountains.

Bill Menor built the original ferryboat and cableworks. Today's ferry and cableworks are replicas. The ferry is a simple platform set on two pontoons. The cable system across the river keeps the ferry from going downstream, while allowing it to move sideways. By turning the pilot wheel, the rope attaching the boat to the cable is tightened and points the pontoons toward the opposite bank. The pressure of the current against the pontoons pushes the ferryboat across the river in the direction the pontoons point. This type of ferry existed in ancient times and was used elsewhere in the United States.

Menor charged 50¢ for a wagon and team and 25¢ for a rider and horse. Pedestrians rode free if a wagon was crossing. When the water was too low for the ferry, Menor suspended a platform from the cable and three to four passengers could ride a primitive cablecar across the river. In later years, Menor and his neighbors built a bridge for winter use, dismantling it each spring.

Menor sold out to Maude Noble in 1918. She doubled the fares, hoping to earn a living from the growing number of tourists in the valley. Noble charged $1 for automobiles with local license plates, or $2 for out-of-state plates. In 1927, a steel truss bridge was built just south of the ferry, making it obsolete. Maude Noble sold the property to the Snake River Land Company in 1929.

Bill Menor and his neighbors homesteaded here thinking of the local natural resources as commodities for survival, but many of them grew to treasure the beauty and uniqueness of Jackson Hole. In 35 short years, from Bill Menor's arrival until the establishment of the original park in 1929, this land passed from homestead to national treasure.

Spirits: Aspens Bar and Lounge serves a variety of drinks daily from 12 PM to 12 AM. The facility is open from early May through early October.

South Jenny Lake Area (307-733-2703)
Recognized for its mountaineering opportunities, the South Jenny Lake Area also provides a few other services:

General Store: The Jenny Lake Store carries film, gifts, groceries, t-shirts, camping accessories, hiking equipment, and outdoor clothing and supplies.

Boat Shuttles and Cruises: The Teton Boating Company provides park visitors with scenic tours of Jenny Lake. The company also offers fishing boat rentals and a shuttle service. Services are offered daily from early June until approximately mid-September, but water levels determine the exact closing date each year.

Teton Science School (307-733-4765; www.tetonscience.org; info@tetonscience.org)
The Teton Science School specializes in providing park visitors with an up-close understanding and perspective of the Greater Yellowstone Ecosystem. Naturalists lead one to four day field trips throughout Grand Teton from May through August.

Horseback Riding

Horseback riding is one of Grand Teton's most popular family outings, and three concessionaries provide equestrian activities:

Colter Bay Village Corral (307-543-2811)
The Colter Bay Village Corral provides standard trail rides of varying lengths and specialty breakfast and dinner rides. Limited wagon seats/rides are available. Weather permitting, rides are offered daily from early June through early September.

Flagg Ranch Resort (307-543-2861)
One-hour trail rides are a Flagg Ranch specialty. Rides are available daily from mid-June through early September.

Jackson Lake Lodge Corral (307-543-2811)·
Breakfast and dinner rides, standard trail rides of varying lengths, and limited wagon seats/rides are available at the Jackson Lake Lodge Corral. Weather permitting, rides are offered daily from late May through early October.

Mountaineering

The Teton Range is renowned worldwide for its challenging terrain and unrivaled beauty. As a result, mountaineering companies have lined up to help climbers of all abilities tackle these mountain heights.

Climber's Ranch (307-733-7271)
Courtesy of the American Alpine Club, climbers enjoy dormitory accommodations at the Climber's Ranch. The ranch also includes showers and a cooking area for just $10 per night. Sorry, no pets allowed.

Exum Mountain Guides and School of American Mountaineering (307-733-2297)
Accredited through the American Mountain Guides Association (AMGA), Exum Mountain Guides is located at Jenny Lake. The company provides year-round private guided ascents of every peak and route in the Grand Teton Range and works with individuals and groups. Basic and intermediate instruction is also offered on a daily basis at Hidden Falls, and Exum Mountain Guides is comfortable leading trips on rock, ice, and snow.

Jackson Hole Mountain Guides and Climbing School (307-733-4979)
Situated in downtown Jackson, Jackson Hole Mountain Guides is a member of the U.S. Mountain Guide Federation and is AMGA accredited. The company caters to both individuals and groups, providing year-round guided climbs of all peaks and routes in the Teton Range. The certified guides also provide daily education about climbing on rock, ice, and snow.

River and Lake Multi-Day Trips

One of the most scenic ways to enjoy Grand Teton National Park is on an extended river or lake trip with the Outdoor Adventure River Specialists (O.A.R.S.).

O.A.R.S. (800-346-6277; www.oars.com)
Offering trips across America since 1969, O.A.R.S. makes its presence known in Grand Teton with two-day scenic Snake River float trips and two-, three-, and five-day Jackson Lake sea kayaking excursions. Each trip includes hiking, fishing, and wilderness camping. Reservations are mandatory!

Snake River Floating and Fishing

The scenic Snake River meanders throughout Grand Teton and provides a myriad of recreation possibilities, including floating and fishing. The following companies are permitted to conduct activities on the Snake River during its journey through Grand Teton.

Barker-Ewing Float Trips (307-733-1800 or 800-365-1800; www.barkerewingscenic.com)
Specializing in ten-mile scenic trips, Barker-Ewing has provided float trips since 1963. The company also offers morning and evening wildlife trips and weekday dinner trips. Daily outings are offered early May through late September for most float trips, but dinner trips are only available mid-June through mid-August.

Flagg Ranch Float Trips (307-543-2861; www.flaggranch.com)
Flagg Ranch serves as the only provider for float trips north of Jackson Lake. Weather depending, both whitewater and scenic float trips depart daily from early June through Labor Day weekend.

Fort Jackson Float Trips (307-733-2583 or 800-735-8430)
Fort Jackson Float Trips boasts scenic sunrise floats, short three-hour trips, extended five-hour meal trips, and full and half-day guided fishing trips. All equipment and transportation is included in one affordable price.

Grand Teton Lodge Company (307-543-2811; www.gtlc.com)

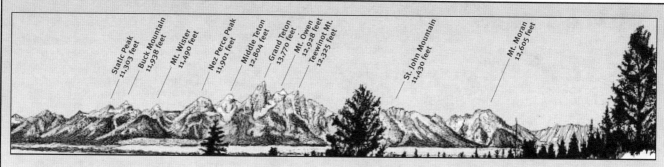

Static Peak 11,303 feet · Buck Mountain 11,938 feet · Mt. Wister 11,490 feet · Nez Perce Peak 11,901 feet · Middle Teton 12,804 feet · Grand Teton 13,770 feet · Mt. Owen 12,928 feet · Teewinot Mt. 12,325 feet · St. John Mountain 11,430 feet · Mt. Moran 12,605 feet

Peak Names

From the book Origins by Hayden and Nielsen.

Static Peak In the Teton Range north of Death Canyon. So named because it is so often hit by lightning.

Buck Mountain Named for George A. Buck, recorder for T.M. Bannon's 1898 mapping party. Bannon gave the name "Buck Station" to the triangulation station he and George Buck established on the summit in 1898.

Nez Perce Named for an Indian tribe whose well-known leader was Chief Joseph. Sometimes referred to as Howling Dog Mountain because of the resemblance when seen from the north.

The Grand Teton Highest mountain in the Teton Range. Named by French trappers. Upon viewing the Teton Range from the west, the trappers dubbed the South, Middle and Grand, Les Trois Tetons, meaning "the three breasts." Wilson Price Hunt called them "Pilot Knobs" in 1811 because he had used them for orientation while crossing Union Pass. In his Journal of a Trapper, Osborne Russel said that the Shoshone Indians named the peaks "Hoary Headed Fathers."

Mount Owen Neighboring peak of the Grand Teton to the northeast. Named for W.O. Owen, who climbed the Grand Teton in 1898 with Bishop Spalding, John Shive, and Frank Petersen.

Teewinot Mountain Towers above Cascade Canyon and Jenny Lake. Its name comes from the Shoshone word meaning "many pinnacles." Teewinot probably once applied to the entire Teton Range, rather than just this one peak. Fritiof Fryxell and Phil Smith named the peak when they successfully completed the first ascent of the mountain in 1929.

Mount Saint John Between Cascade and Indian Paintbrush canyons. Actually a series of peaks of nearly equal height. Named for Orestes St. John, geologist of Hayden's 1877 survey, whose monographs on the Teton and Wind River ranges are now classics. **MOUNT MORAN** Most prominent peak in the northern end of the Teton Range. Named by Ferdinand V. Hayden for the landscape artist Thomas Moran, who traveled with the 1872 Hayden expedition into Yellowstone and into Pierre's Hole on the western side of the Teton Range. He produced many sketches and watercolors from these travels.

Departing from Colter Bay Village and Jackson Lake Lodge, the Grand Teton Lodge Company float trips depart daily in both the morning and afternoon. The ten-mile scenic trips are available during summer season, and some trips feature a lunch or dinner stop on Deadman's Bar. Guided fishing trips are also available.

Heart Six Ranch Float Trips (307-543-2477; www.heartsix.com)
Sunrise wildlife trips and ten-mile scenic float trips are Heart Six Ranch's feature attractions. For ranch guests only, guided fishing trips are also available.

Jack Dennis Fishing Trips (307-733-3270; www.jackdennis.com)

National Park Float Trips (307-733-6445 or 307-733-5500)
National Park Float Trips captures the breathtaking nature of the Snake River and Grand Tetons on ten-mile wildlife trips. Tours depart several times daily during summer season, and large groups can be accommodated.

Signal Mountain Lodge (307-543-2831; www. signalmtnlodge.com)
Ten-mile scenic trips and guided fishing trips depart from Signal Mountain Lodge daily during summer season.

Solitude Float Trips (307-733-2871)
Solitude Float Trips provides guided fishing trips, five-mile scenic river tours, and ten-mile scenic trips.

Triangle X-Osprey Float Trips (307-733-5500 or 733-6445; www.trianglexranch.com)
Triangle X Ranch provides a variety of floating options, including five- and ten-mile scenic trips, wildlife trips, guided fishing, and breakfast, lunch, and dinner floats. Trips are available daily during the summer season.

Park Entrances

North Entrance: Visitors who exit Yellowstone's south entrance are welcomed to Grand Teton National Park with an eight-mile long John D. Rockefeller, Jr., Memorial Parkway. This stretch of scenic highway joins the two national treasures, and those visitors who enter Grand Teton from this direction have already paid the admission fee granting entrance to both parks. Grand Teton National Park information is located just south of Yellowstone's boundary at Flagg Ranch.

East Entrance: Grand Teton's East Entrance lies on U.S. Highways 26/287 west of Dubois, Wyoming. Visitors entering the park on this route cross over Togwotee Pass and proceed to the Moran Entrance Station. Travelers merely passing through the park en route to Jackson avoid paying a fee at this entrance station.

South Entrance: Located approximately twelve miles north of Jackson on U.S. Highways 26/89/191, the South Entrance at Moose serves as the park's official headquarters. A variety of amenities can be found in Moose Village along with general park information.

Fees and Permits

In order to maintain the park system without further taxing the general population, the National Park Service charges moderate entrance fees and also collects fees for special recreation permits, including fishing and boating. Those planning on leaving and re-entering the park within seven days from the date of their first visit should keep their admission receipt as proof of payment. Visitors should also note that advance reservations are unnecessary for park entrance.

Single Entry: Private, non-commercial vehicles may purchase a single entry pass for $20. The pass grants visitors seven-day access to both Grand Teton and Yellowstone National Parks.

Single Entry Motorcycle: Motorcycles may enter both Grand Teton and Yellowstone with a seven-day pass for just $15.

Single Entry Hiker/Bicyclist: A $10 seven-day permit grants hikers and bicyclists access to both Grand Teton and Yellowstone.

Commercial Tour Fee: This non-transferable pass provides commercial users a seven-day pass to Grand Teton and Yellowstone. The fee is based on vehicle passenger capacity. Vehicles carrying one to six people are charged $25 plus $10 per person. Those vehicles carrying seven to fifteen passengers are charged $125, while vehicles with loads of sixteen to twenty-five face a $200 fee. Vehicles with capacities over twenty-six are charged a standard $300.

Parks Specific Pass: For those planning on visiting Grand Teton or Yellowstone National Park several times throughout the year, a $40 Annual Area Pass may be purchased. The permit is non-transferable and is valid 365 days from the date of purchase.

National Park Pass: For National Park enthusiasts, the $50 non-transferable National Parks Pass guarantees admission to all National Park areas. The pass is valid one year from the date of purchase.

Golden Access Passport: Permanently disabled or blind individuals may qualify for the Golden Access Passport with medical proof of their condition. The permit grants qualified individuals and any accompanying passengers free access to all national parks. The pass also entitles individuals to a fifty-percent discount on campground and other park fees.

Golden Age Passport: The Golden Age Passport is a lifetime passport for senior citizens over age sixty-two. A one-time $10 fee is charged, and qualified individuals receive free access to all national parks. The permit also provides a fifty-percent discount on campground and other park fees.

Golden Eagle Passport: Priced at $65, the Golden Eagle Passport allows the permit holder and all accompanying passengers access to all National Parks and nearly every national monument and federal preserve within the U.S. The permit is valid one year from the date of purchase.

Winter Day Use: Valid for Grand Teton National Park only, the Winter Day Use permit costs $5 per day. The permit is offered mid-December through April 30 and is ideal for cross-country skiers and snowshoe enthusiasts.

Traveling Seasons and Operating Hours

Spring, Summer, and Fall: With its dominant visitor season running from early May to November 1, Grand Teton National Park opens its roads on different dates each year depending on how quickly road crews can clear the snow-covered highways. Once the highways open for the season, the roads are passable twenty-four hours a day, seven days a week, except in cases of road construction or weather-related incidents.

Although the park's weather is certainly at its most ideal climate, summer in Grand Teton also ushers in the highest number of visitors. Summer tourists should expect larger crowds at major attractions, slower traffic, and higher priced lodging and gas.

For those who want a less crowded experience, spring and fall in Grand Teton are ideal. Prior to Memorial Day and after Labor Day, wildlife outnumbers cars and RVs. Spring wildflowers bloom in a rainbow palette while autumn's changing colors paint a picture perfect backdrop for angling on the Snake River and mountain lakes. Economically, spring and fall also reward visitors with lower priced amenities and reduced lodging rates.

Winter: Although cars, trucks, and RVs scamper away for the winter, Grand Teton is still alive with activity. The park's winter season operates from mid-December through the end of April, and snowmobiles zoom between the park and its northerly Yellowstone neighbor. Snowshoe and cross-country skiing enthusiasts also flock to the pristinely frosted landscape. Although all park routes close to vehicles on November 1, the roads are available year-round for non-motorized use.

Grand Teton's Roads

Boasting 159 miles of paved roads, 62 miles of unpaved roads, and an additional 230 miles of trails, Grand Teton's road system takes visitors to every major park attraction and hidden backcountry wonder. Although traffic jams and construction create less than ideal driving conditions, they are a perennial occurrence that all summer drivers must be ready to face. Patience is key in driving on Grand Teton's roads, so maintain your cool to ensure your safety and that of other visitors. For the latest in construction related road closures, visit Grand Teton on the web at www.nps.gov/grte/trip/roadconstruct.htm. Road information may also be accessed by calling (307) 739-3614 or (307) 739-3682.

During all seasons, drivers are urged to exercise extreme caution as many park roads are narrow or steep. Slow-moving vehicles or drivers interested in looking at Grand Teton's abundant wildlife and mountain scenery must use park pull-

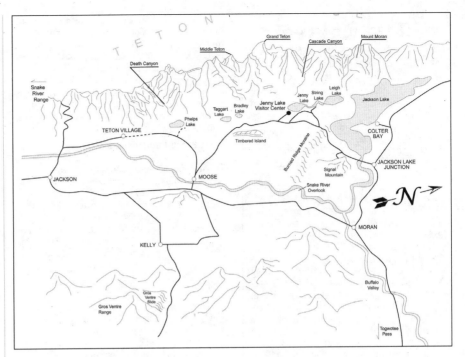

outs so as not to interrupt traffic flow. Drivers are also reminded to watch for wildlife, bicyclists, and motorcyclists. Drive defensively, wear seat belts, and always obey the posted speed limits. Speeding tickets in the park are notoriously hefty, and rangers continuously patrol the roads.

While most of Grand Teton's two-million plus visitors opt to use their private automobiles, motorcycles, or bicycles to tour the park's major attractions, a few prefer to let someone else drive. Although no free public transportation is available in the park, those too nervous to drive Grand Teton's mountain roads may take advantage of the Grand Teton Lodge Company's bus tours and charters. Transportation is available to and from Jackson, Yellowstone National Park, and all major Grand Teton National Park attractions. Transportation services are generally available from mid-May through early October. For more information, contact the Grand Teton Lodge Company at (307) 543-2811.

The Extremes of Grand Teton: Weather and Climate

Grand Teton National Park and Jackson Hole comprise a land of stark contrasts. While winter blankets the valley and jagged peaks with layers of thick white snow and bone-chilling temperatures, summer's bright sun warms the valley to an average 80 degrees Fahrenheit. During all seasons, visitors should be prepared for a variety of weather conditions, especially if travel plans call for outdoor recreation. In Grand Teton, every 1,000-foot gain in elevation results in an average temperature loss of four degrees Fahrenheit!

Spring
Grand Teton's short spring season runs between March and May and is marked with continually changing weather patterns. Mild days of abundant sun intermingle with periods of rain and snow. Daytime temperatures crawl to a peak of 49 degrees Fahrenheit while nighttime temperatures dip to a chilly average of 22 degrees Fahrenheit. Measurable precipitation falls on the area several times throughout the season, so visitors should plan accordingly; wear a layered garment system, and always pack along a waterproof jacket.

Summer
Summer graces Grand Teton's peaks and valleys every June through August. Warm days and mild nights are the norm with average daytime readings of 76 degrees Fahrenheit and evening temperatures in the low to mid 40s. Despite the warm temperatures, summer receives its fair share of moisture, and afternoon thunderstorms are common. As a precaution for these frequent thundershowers, visitors should heed the following lightning safety tips:

When a distant storm is approaching, seek shelter immediately; never wait for the storm to arrive before finding a safe place.

Water attracts lightning, so immediately vacate all lakes, streams, and rivers. Furthermore, never stand on the banks of any water body.

Never stand on tree roots, and never lie completely flat on the ground. The Earth's surface and trees are powerful electrical conductors.

Remove yourself from open areas, mountain peaks, and ridges. These natural features along with lone trees tend to attract lightning.

Autumn
September, October, and November mark Grand Teton's autumn season. Rain and occasional snow accent the peaks with whispers of winter, and daytime highs hover at an average 54 degrees Fahrenheit. Evening temperatures drop to a minimum of 25 degrees, so visitors should plan ahead and pack plenty of warm clothing and jackets to accommodate the differences between daytime and nighttime temperatures.

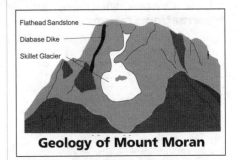

Geology of Mount Moran

THE COLTER STONE

The Colter Stone, discovered near Tetonia, Idaho in 1933, is a piece of rhyolite carved in the shape of a human head. It is engraved on one side with the name "John Colter", on the other side is the year "1808". If authentic, it represents the only solid proof of the route followed by trapper and explorer John Colter.

Colter explored the greater Yellowstone area during the winter of 1807-8, perhaps the first white man to do so. His route, however, is uncertain as no clear maps or records exist. Colter set out from a fur trapping fort in present-day southern Montana and headed south to near today's Cody, Wyoming. On his return he passed through what is now Yellowstone National Park. The middle section of his journey is a matter of conjecture. One theory indicates he traveled via Togowtee Pass. The other commonly held view traces Colter's route through Jackson Hole, over Teton Pass, and north along the west side of the Teton Range. No evidence exists to substantiate either route. The only available sources of information are vague accounts and maps derived from interviews with Colter after his return.

Thus, the significance of the Colter Stone becomes clear. The location of its discovery, the west side of the Teton Range, would prove that John Colter had traveled the Teton Pass route. But the Stone has not been fully authenticated, so the Colter Stone remains a fascinating piece of the puzzle yet to fit into the mystery of John Colter's pioneering sojourn through this region.

Winter

Heavy snows generally start falling on Grand Teton and Jackson Hole by November 1st with snowstorms occasionally lasting until mid-April. Clear sunny days promise frigid evenings, and temperatures range from a daily maximum of 29 degrees Fahrenheit to an average low of just 6 degrees. Blizzards are frequent, and travel is highly discouraged. Those participating in winter sports should dress in warm layers that wick away moisture. Gloves, hats, and windproof/waterproof outerwear are essential, and visitors are encouraged to always pack along extra clothing. Winter visitors should also be alert for signs of hypothermia, which include shivering, apathy, coordination loss, general complaints of coldness, slurred speech, mental difficulties, and a body temperature low enough to trigger permanent damage or death.

Visitor Centers, Museums, and Information Stations

Adding culture and history to Grand Teton's amazing scenery, visitor centers, museums, and informational ranger stations are scattered throughout the park. All visitors are encouraged to stop by these facilities, ask questions, and learn more about America's sanctuary for mountain splendor.

Colter Bay Visitor Center and Indian Arts Museum (307-739-3594)

The Colter Bay Visitor Center is situated beside Jackson Lake and provides a variety of intriguing displays along with general park information.

Numerous Native American artifacts are displayed in the David T. Vernon Collection, and museum tours, craft demonstrations, natural history hikes, nightly amphitheater discussions, and interpretive programs are offered throughout the summer season. Visitors will also find backcountry permits, an auditorium, telephones, restrooms, a staffed information desk, and a bookstore. The visitor center is generally open daily from early May through early October.

Flagg Ranch Information Station (307-543-2327)

Located just 2.5 miles south of Yellowstone's southern boundary, the Flagg Ranch Information Station provides books, park information, restrooms, and detailed information about John D. Rockefeller, Jr.'s contributions to Grand Teton National Park. The station is open daily from early June through early September. Visitors should note that the station is closed over the lunch hour.

Jenny Lake Ranger Station (307-739-3343)

The Jenny Lake Ranger Station is a must-see for backpackers. The station sells books and maps while providing extensive Grand Teton climbing and backpacking information. The station is open variable hours late May through late September. Visitors should call for the station's operating hours prior to arriving in the park.

Jenny Lake Visitor Center

The Jenny Lake Visitor Center is located at South Jenny Lake just eight miles north of Moose. The center features restrooms, telephones, a bookstore, area maps, and park activity schedules. In addition, the center is recognized for its fascinating geology information and exhibits. Jenny Lake Visitor Center is open daily early June through late September.

Moose Visitor Center (307-739-3399)

The Moose Visitor Center is located at the park's southern end near Moose Junction. The center offers a park introduction video, a relief model of Grand Teton, endangered species exhibits, a large bookstore, general park information, regional maps, park activity schedules, boat permits, backcountry camping permits, telephones, and restrooms. Moose Visitor Center is open daily year-round with extended summer hours from June through early September. The center is closed only on Christmas Day.

Dining in Grand Teton

Grand Teton's dining establishments specialize in combining tasty meals with one of America's finest mountain atmospheres. Since the park does not limit itself to just one concessionaire, visitors will find a wide array of entrees and prices to suit even the most discriminating tastes. From elegant fine dining to box lunches on the go, Grand Teton's dining options are available throughout the park. Reservations are necessary at some dining establishments or for specific meals, so heed these details in the restaurant descriptions below.

Flagg Ranch

Serving traditional American food off its home-style menu, Flagg Ranch is open daily year-round for breakfast, lunch, and dinner. A cozy ambience complements family-style selections that include chicken potpie, beef, fish, stews, and much more. Portion sizes are generous, and reservations are not required. A casual dress code accompanies the establishment, and all major credit cards are accepted.

Leek's Marina

Leek's Marina offers a fast-food alternative to the

dining rooms lining Grand Teton's northern corridor. Patrons are treated to pizza, sandwiches, and beer on a daily basis from early June through early September. Reservations are not required, dress is casual, and all major credit cards are accepted.

Colter Bay Village

Colter Bay Village is recognized for its assortment of dining options for breakfast, lunch, and dinner.

Chuckwagon Steak and Pasta House

The Chuckwagon wakes visitors up each morning with its extensive all-you-can-eat breakfast buffet. The lunch menu serves up all-you-can-eat salads, sandwiches, and soups, while dinner features a nightly special with standard entrees that include steak, pasta, trout, pork chops, chicken, and more. The restaurant is open daily late May through early October with a casual dress code that caters to families. Reservations are not required, and all major credit cards are accepted.

John Colter Café Court

The John Colter Café Court specializes in quick snacks and deli-style sandwiches, pizza, chicken, salads, and soups. Box lunches are also available for visitors to pick up and take on outdoor excursions. The café is open daily from June through early September with a casual ambience and dress code. Reservations are not required, and all major credit cards are accepted.

Meal Cruises

For those visitors wishing to add Grand Teton's outstanding scenery to their meal, Colter Bay Village offers scenic meal cruises. The breakfast and dinner cruises operate under the direction of the Grand Teton Lodge Company and travel from Jackson Lake to Elk Island. All major credit cards are accepted, and reservations are recommended. Contact Grand Teton Lodge Company at (307) 543-2811 for additional information. All major credit cards are accepted.

Jackson Lake Lodge

From fine dining to the casual atmosphere of a snack bar, Jackson Lake Lodge offers something for everyone under the direction of the Grand Teton Lodge Company.

Mural Room

Named after the Western murals lining eighty feet of its interior walls, the Mural Room serves as Jackson Lake Lodge's main dining room. Scenic Grand Teton views captured in panoramic picture windows combine with fine Rocky Mountain cuisine to create a memorable dining experience. From wild game and lasagna to Idaho trout, Caesar salad, and gourmet beef and chicken dishes, Jackson Lake Lodge caters to exquisite tastes with its breakfast, lunch, and dinner specialties. Catering services for group functions are also available. The restaurant operates mid-May through mid-October, and dinner reservations are highly recommended. For additional information and reservations, contact the Grand Teton Lodge Company at (307) 543-2811 ext. 1911. All major credit cards are accepted.

Pioneer Grill

Decorated in a 1950s atmosphere, the Pioneer Grill at Jackson Lake Lodge offers an old-fashioned soda fountain, snacks, and light lunch and dinner fare. Entrees are less expensive than Mural Room selections, take-out service is available, and the children's menu is a family favorite. The grill is open daily 6 AM to 10:30 PM mid-May through mid-October. All major credit cards are accepted.

Blue Heron Lounge

While the Blue Heron Lounge offers no "real" food

Photography is one of the most popular pastimes in the park. NPS Photo.

to speak of, it does provide snacks and a wide selection of cocktails and beer. Picture-perfect vistas and live entertainment highlight the lounge's offerings. The Blue Heron is open daily mid-May through mid-October. All major credit cards are accepted.

Pool Snack Bar

Jackson Lake Lodge's Pool Snack Bar offers standard snack bar fare with sandwiches, burgers, pizza, and salads provided for lunch and midday food cravings. Weather permitting, each evening ushers in a poolside western barbeque complete with all the trimmings. Patrons dine on hot dogs, hamburgers, barbeque chicken, and brisket while listening to the strains of live music. The Pool Snack Bar is open daily from early July through late August. All major credit cards are accepted.

Signal Mountain

Signal Mountain is recognized for its friendly service, no matter if it is provided in the more upscale dining room or the down-home café.

Aspens Dining Room

Fine evening dining featuring daily specials greets patrons at Signal Mountain's Aspens Dining Room. Entrees range from fresh trout to Chinese, Italian to traditional American beef dishes, and everything in between. A children's menu is available, and the casual atmosphere is ideal for families seeking a full meal for breakfast, lunch, or dinner. Reservations are not accepted, and meals are served daily mid-May through mid-October. All major credit cards are accepted.

Cottonwood Café

The Cottonwood Café is quickly becoming a dining staple for people with all taste preferences. The café's famous Nachos Supreme team up with burgers, scrumptious sandwiches, soups, and salads in a casual atmosphere. Patrons can overlook Jackson Lake from the main dining room, sit at the café's bar, or meander out to the deck. Margaritas are a house specialty, and the café does not accept reservations. Lunch and dinner are served daily mid-May to mid-September. All major credit cards are accepted.

Dornans at Moose

Dornans caters to families year-round with its selection of food and dining experiences.

Chuckwagon Restaurant

Dornans' Chuckwagon Restaurant has established itself as a favorite park tradition with annual summer chuckwagon meals served since 1948. All-you-can-eat items such as roast beef, Dutch-oven specialties, and barbeque ribs join with a fun atmosphere that families rush to experience. Patrons enjoy scenic views from the grassy lawn and picnic tables, while teepees guarantee a dry meal on rainy days. The restaurant is open daily for breakfast, lunch, and dinner from mid-June through early September. Reservations are recommended, and interested diners should call the Chuckwagon for more information at 733-2415. All major credit cards are accepted.

Moose Pizza and Pasta Company

The Moose Pizza and Pasta Company is open year-round for park visitor convenience, and the casual atmosphere always welcomes families. Patrons enjoy calzones, pasta, and gourmet pizza onsite, and take-out pizza is also available. The restaurant serves lunch and dinner daily, and reservations are unnecessary. All major credit cards are accepted.

Grizzly bear. Best to watch from a (long) distance. NPS Photo.

Jenny Lake Lodge

Cradled in a rustic log lodge, the Jenny Lake Lodge dining room embellishes its cozy atmosphere with white linen tablecloths and fresh flowers. While breakfast and lunch are always popular, dinner is the dining room's main attraction. With appetizers that include caviar and entrees featuring buffalo, antelope, ostrich, and other western specialties, the Jenny Lake Lodge is definitely not your normal park fare. An extensive award-winning wine list complements the fine cuisine. Guests are asked to dress up for dinner with men expected to wear jackets for the five-course meal. Reservations are required for breakfast and dinner, but lunch is served a la carte on a first-come, first-served basis. The dining room is open early June through mid-October. For additional information and reservations, contact the Grand Teton Lodge Company at (307) 733-4647.

Lodging in Grand Teton

Lodging in Grand Teton runs the gamut, and late spring, summer, and early fall visitors can select from such simple lodgings as canvas tent cabins to exquisite log cabin suites where pampering comes with a steep price. Like the park's dining options, Grand Teton's lodgings are under the direction of several different concessionaires. As a result, each hotel, cabin, and tent reflects the tastes and business preferences of its individual owner. Those planning on staying inside the park should note that telephones and televisions are kept to a minimum to encourage guests to tune into Grand Teton's magnificent natural beauty. If you cannot bear the thought of trading your favorite television show for some unrivaled mountain splendor, plan on reserving a room in nearby Jackson Hole or across the border in Idaho's Teton Valley. Lodgings book quickly, so advance reservations (at times up to a year) are absolutely necessary!

Flagg Ranch Resort (800-443-2311 or 307-543-2861; www.flaggranch.com)
Once home to a nearby historic military post, Flagg Ranch supposedly received its name from the traditional flag that waved a warm welcome to area visitors more than 100 years ago. Over time, the resort developed into a recreational haven where simple lodgings accompanied a quiet atmosphere tucked between the hubbub of Yellowstone and Grand Teton.

Today, this resort that is situated just two miles south of Yellowstone and five miles north of Grand Teton has revived itself into an all-season destination. Tourists traveling to both Yellowstone and Grand Teton designate Flagg Ranch as an ideal base camp for their park explorations. Three two-story motel units provide outstanding Snake River vistas with standard hotel amenities, minus telephones and televisions. In 1994, duplex and fourplex log cabins were added to the resort's offerings. All cabins feature vaulted ceilings, king-size beds, carpeting, baseboard heat, phones, coffeemakers, private bathrooms, and large sitting areas, while some also boast private decks and rockers perfect for enjoying one of Grand Teton's signature summer sunsets. While June through August guarantee rates in excess of $130 per night, off-season rates are generally much lower.

Both motel and cabin guests have access to the ranch's main lodge, which affords a coffee shop, pub, large screen TV, two-sided fireplace, gift shop, dining room, convenience store, and gas station. While staying at Flagg Ranch, guests also enjoy unlimited outdoor recreation possibilities, including horseback rides, hiking, fishing, Snake River floats, snowmobiling, and snowcoach tours traveling into Yellowstone. Flagg Ranch Resort is open mid-May through mid-October for its summer/autumn season with a winter season operating mid-December through mid-March. All major credit cards are accepted.

Colter Bay Village (800-628-9988 or 307-543-3100; www.gtlc.com/lodgeCBV.aspx)
Colter Bay Village bills itself as one of Grand Teton's most family-friendly and economical activity centers. In addition to two restaurants, a general store, gift shop, convenience store, RV park, gas station, laundry area, grocery store, and a full service marina, the village provides visitors with two lodging options.

166 rustic log cabins offer a cozy stay complete with old-fashioned furnishings, beamed ceilings, and area rugs that lend a homey feel to the place. Most cabins feature a private bathroom and shower, and some sleep up to six people. Although all the cabins have recently been refurbished, some actually date back to the area's first homesteaders! Prices range from just $38 for a one-room cabin with shared bath to $140 for two-room cabins with a private bath. Cabins are available late May through early October, and all major credit cards are accepted.

Those interested in stepping back in time and discovering park travel and lodging as it once was may wish to reserve one of Colter Bay's tent cabins. Featuring log walls, canvas roofs, and concrete floors, these tent cabins include wood burning stoves, two bunk beds (sleeping four total), a covered outdoor cooking area, grill, and picnic table. Guests may bring their own bedding or rent mattresses, sleeping bags, and blankets at the village. A shared restroom/shower facility is located nearby, and a communal lounge is available to all tent cabin guests. Tent cabins start just slightly below $40 per night for one to two people with a $5 charge per extra person. The economy of the tent cabins cannot be beat, and the simple accommodations keep the focus on enjoying Grand Teton's great outdoors. Tent cabins are available early June through early September, and all major credit cards are accepted.

Jackson Lake Lodge (800-628-9988 or 307-543-3100; www.gtlc.com/lodgeJac.aspx)
Overlooking Jackson Lake from its perch on a scenic bluff, the Jackson Lake Lodge specializes in comfortable accommodations and grand views of the park's famous peaks. The three-story main lodge boasts thirty-seven rooms while a smattering of nearby guest cottages contain 348 rooms. Most main lodge rooms include double beds, newly remodeled bathrooms, and electric heat while the cottages are nestled in the shade of pine trees. All guests enjoy access to the lodge's scrumptious dining options, gift shops, clothing stores, an outdoor heated pool, and outdoor recreation. While pool use is included in the price of lodging, all other services carry a separate fee. The resort is open late May through early October, and all major credit cards are accepted.

Signal Mountain (307-543-2831; www.signalmtnlodge.com)
Signal Mountain prides itself on a quiet atmosphere where guests select from three different lodging styles. One-room log cabins feature carpet, custom log furniture, electric heat, private bathrooms, covered porches, and occasionally a fireplace. Offering more amenities, motel rooms are contained in four-unit buildings and often include fireplaces. Some of these motel-style units also feature private beach access, a nice perk for those guests who simply want to soak up the sun on Jackson Lake's banks. The final option treats guests to newer lakefront apartments that are large enough to accommodate an entire family for extended area stays. Featuring decks that open onto Jackson Lake, the suite-style apartments include kitchenettes complete with refrigerators

---

and stoves, comfortable beds, private bathrooms, and foldout sofas perfect for accommodating large groups. All guests enjoy stunning Teton Mountain views.

Guests at any of Signal Mountain's lodgings will also find a gift and apparel shop, a convenience store, gas station, two restaurants, a lounge, marina, and guided outdoor activities. Signal Mountain offers rooms early May through mid-October with prices ranging from $85 to $200. All major credit cards are accepted.

Dornans Spur Ranch (307-733-2415 or 307-733-2522; www.dornans.com)
Although not a registered park concessionaire, Dornans Spur Ranch is located within the scenic confines of Grand Teton National Park. Cabins are situated on the Snake River bank in a wildflower meadow. Eight one-bedroom cabins and four two-bedroom cabins all feature fully equipped kitchens, living/dining rooms, queen beds, private bathrooms, and custom log furnishings.

In addition to amazing views, guests enjoy access to a grocery store, deli, wine shop, gift store, gas station, restaurant, lounge, fly-fishing, cross-country skiing, snowshoeing, and mountain bike and canoe rentals. The log cabins are available year-round with one-bedroom cabins starting at $125 during winter season and escalating to $185 in the summer. Two-bedroom cabins average $175 in winter and $230 during summer season. All major credit cards are accepted, and pets are not allowed.

Jenny Lake Lodge (800-628-9988 or 307-733-4647; www.gtlc.com/lodgeJen.aspx)
Nestled adjacent to Jenny and String Lakes amid a thick forest, Jenny Lake Lodge is the quintessential park destination for upscale lodging and class. As a result, the resort typically caters to wealthy and older patrons. Guests enjoy finely appointed accommodations in thirty-seven historic log cab-

---

ins featuring pillared porches perfect for enjoying a Grand Teton sunrise or sunset. Each cabin includes one queen, one king, or two double beds, handmade quilts, down comforters, wood floors, braided rugs, log furniture, beamed ceilings, and private bathrooms. The lodge has managed to establish itself as the only true resort setting within the park's boundaries, and guests receive the extra pampering that comes along with such a distinction.

In addition to luxurious accommodations, Jenny Lake Lodge includes horseback riding, mountain biking, and the lodge's award-winning breakfast and five-course dinner in the nightly rate. Tucked into the pines, this four-diamond property offers rooms early June through early October. Room rates start at $475 nightly for two guests in a one-room cabin and climb to $680 nightly for two persons in a log cabin suite. Each additional guest tacks on an extra nightly charge of $140. All major credit cards are accepted, and with a 60% return guest rate, accommodations book quickly. Reservations are often needed at least one year in advance.

Triangle X Ranch (307-733-2183; www.trianglex.com)
The Triangle X Ranch provides memorable dude ranch vacations within Grand Teton National Park near Moose, Wyoming. In addition to traditional wrangling and haying ranch activities, Triangle X provides horseback riding, river floating, fishing, western cookouts, square dancing, hiking, scenic tours, and wildlife viewing during its summer season. In winter, guests enjoy cross-country skiing, snowshoeing, snowmobiling, and sightseeing.

During the peak summer season of early June to late August, rates range from $1,270 to $1,800 per person per week. In the shoulder seasons, discounted rates range from $1,270 for two people per week to $1,380 for singles. The winter season of late December through late March provides economical rates of just $105 per person per night. All rates include lodging, dining, horseback riding, and all other provided ranch activities. No credit cards are accepted, so guests must pay with cash, personal check, or travelers' checks. A 35% deposit is required at the time of reservation, and guests should take into account that a 15% gratuity charge will be added along with 6% Wyoming sales tax on 40% of the invoice.

Snake River Lodge (800-445-4655; http://snakeriverlodge.rockresorts.com)
Nestled just outside Grand Teton's southwest entrance at the base of the spectacular Teton Mountains, the Snake River Lodge is one of the newest full-service resorts to hit the area. Although the resort is not officially located within the park, it has earned the endorsement of Grand Teton Lodge Company, a primary park concessionaire. The eighty-eight guest rooms and forty luxury residence suites were all renovated during spring and fall of 2001. Standard guest rooms feature western elegance and plush robes with an attention to detail. The two- and three-bedroom residence suites include gas fireplaces, spacious living areas, private bedrooms, kitchens, a spacious bath with jetted tub, and a utility closet complete with washer and dryer.

Guests also enjoy a full-service spa, an inviting lobby featuring handcrafted furniture and stone fireplaces, a cozy lounge, The GameFish Restaurant, a health club, indoor and outdoor heated pools, hot tubs, and a sauna. The lodge is open year-round with nightly rates starting at $119 during the off-season. Peak season rates, however, average $359 per night for two guests. Hotel/dining/spa packages are available with a minimum stay required, and all major credit cards are accepted. All rooms and suites book quickly, so advance reservations are a must.

American Alpine Club (307-733-7271; www.americanalpineclub.org)

The American Alpine Club is a worldwide tradition among mountain climbers of all skill levels, and the Grand Teton Climbers' Ranch is a proud affiliate. The accommodations are ideally suited to climbers, providing a small cabin with a private bath, bunk bed, and an outdoor covered cooking area. Guests must bring their own cookstoves and sleeping bags, but with prices at just $10 per night per person, the accommodations are more than reasonable. The Grand Teton Climbers Ranch also boasts a shower facility and a practice climbing wall. The ranch is open mid-June through late-September, and pets are not allowed. All major credit cards are accepted.

Camping in Grand Teton

In addition to standard hotel and cabin lodging, Grand Teton National Park offers visitors the opportunity to really experience nature at its best with an overnight camping adventure. Of the seven campgrounds situated within the park's boundaries and the John D. Rockefeller, Jr. Memorial Parkway, five are first-come, first-served sites under the management of the National Park Service. These campgrounds include Colter Bay, Gros Ventre, the tent-only Jenny Lake, Lizard Creek, and Signal Mountain. The remaining two campgrounds at Flagg Ranch and Colter Bay Trailer Village are concessionaire-operated, and these sites may respectively be reserved by calling (800) 443-2311 and (307) 543-2811. Campgrounds fill quickly, so plan to arrive early at your destination campsite or make reservations where they are accepted.

For those traveling in groups, group camping is available at the Colter Bay Campground and Gros Ventre Campground. Group camping is strictly limited to organized youth, education, or religious functions, and advance reservations are required. While Colter Bay offers eleven group sites, Gros Ventre boasts just five. Depending on the site, capacities range from ten to seventy-five people. Nightly fees at all group sites are based upon a $15.00 non-refundable reservation fee and a $3 per person charge. For group reservations, call (800) 628-9988 or (307) 543-3100. Interested parties may also write to: Campground Reservations, Grand Teton National Park, P.O. Drawer 170, Moose, WY 83012.

While camping in Grand Teton, visitors are asked to follow a few simple rules. Camping in pullouts, parking areas, and picnic grounds is not permitted, and adherence to campground quiet hours is appreciated. Campers are limited to a maximum fourteen-day stay, which is decreased to just seven-days at the popular Jenny Lake Campground. Visitors are also kindly reminded to follow all bear-safety precautions. Grand Teton National Park is in the middle of prime bear habitat, and bears are not afraid to roam through park campgrounds.

The following provides an overview of each campground and the available amenities.

Colter Bay: Open late May through late September, Colter Bay is a forested campground located just twenty-five miles north of Moose. The campground features 350 single sites, eleven group sites, and no RV hookups. This camp-

Tetons from Death Shelf. National Park Service Photo.

ground is generally full by noon due to its close proximity to Jackson Lake and numerous outdoor activities. Amenities include a dump station, toilets, showers, drinking water, fire pits, grills, and public phones with laundry facilities nearby. Reservations are not accepted for single sites, and the nightly fee is $12.

Colter Bay Trailer Village: Open mid-May through late September, Colter Bay Trailer Village features 112 RV sites with full sewer, electrical, and water hookups. Most sites are pull-through and all feature picnic tables perfect for enjoying Grand Teton's mild summer weather. Visitors should note that the village usually fills by noon. Amenities include a dump station, toilets, drinking water, fire pits, grills, a laundry facility, and public phones. Reservations are accepted, and the nightly fee is $42 from the end of May through early September. During the shoulder tourist seasons, the nightly fee drops to $27.

Flagg Ranch: Open the end of May through late September, Flagg Ranch is situated just five miles north of Grand Teton's boundaries in the John D. Rockefeller, Jr. Memorial Parkway. The forested campground features 100 RV sites and seventy-five tent sites, and RV hookups are available. Amenities include a dump station, toilets, showers, drinking water, fire pits, grills, a laundry facility, and public phones. Reservations are accepted with prices dependent upon the type of site reserved. RV and tent sites respectively run $45 nightly and $20 nightly for one to two adults with an additional $5 charge for every extra person.

Gros Ventre: Open early May through mid-October, Gros Ventre lies beside the Gros Ventre River eleven miles southeast of Moose. Featuring 360 sagebrush and cottonwood lined sites with five designated group areas, the campground generally keeps a few spots open at the end of the day. Although RV hookups are not available, other amenities include a dump station, toilets, drinking water, fire pits, grills, and public phones. Reservations are not accepted for single sites, and the nightly fee is $12.

Jenny Lake: Open mid-May through late September, Jenny Lake is situated eight miles north of Moose and is the park's most popular campground. The fifty-one tent-only sites are nestled amid pines and glacial boulders, each boast-

ing their own scenic value near the shores of Jenny Lake. Amenities include toilets, drinking water, fire pits, grills, and public phones. Reservations are not accepted, and the nightly fee is $12. Users should note that RVs are prohibited, and only one vehicle (less than fourteen feet) is allowed per site.

Lizard Creek: Open early June through early September, Lizard Creek is located thirty-two miles north of Moose near the park's northern boundary. The sixty-site campground partially rests in a fir forest while some sites overlook Jackson Lake. The campground generally fills by 2 PM, and although RVs are allowed, vehicles must not exceed thirty feet. Amenities include toilets, drinking water, fire pits, grills, and public phones. Reservations are not accepted, and the nightly fee is $12.

Signal Mountain: Open early May through mid-October, Signal Mountain Campground rests sixteen miles north of Jenny Lake. Varied topography categorizes this popular campground with a mix of lake views, mountain vistas, rolling hillsides, and dense forests. The eighty-one-site campground generally fills by 10 AM, and vehicle sizes are strictly limited to thirty feet. Amenities include a dump station, toilets, drinking water, fire pits, grills, and public phones. Reservations are not accepted, and the nightly fee is $12.

Regulations and Safety Tips You Need to Know

Grand Teton National Park is one of America's most beautiful places, and with that distinction comes major visitor responsibility. The park's future depends on the conscientious behavior of today's visitors, so maintain a healthy respect for Grand Teton at all times. The following regulations and safety tips will ensure the longevity of the park as well as the livelihood of park visitors.

Backcountry Use and Leave No Trace Ethics
Backcountry travel in Grand Teton comes with inherent risks, and numerous regulations/expectations exist to ensure the highest level of visitor safety. Still, hikers and all other backcountry users must assume responsibility for their personal safety and realize that rescue in an emergency situation is not necessarily a certainty.

Visitors' backcountry safety depends upon sev-

Cathedral Viewpoint. NPS Photo.

eral factors, including sound judgment, an attention to detail, proper physical condition, appropriate gear and clothing, and adequate preparation for all weather conditions and travel circumstances. It is highly recommended that backcountry users never hike alone. Backcountry permits are required for all overnight stays; these fees help manage the backcountry areas while and protect park resources for future generations.

During backcountry stays, visitors are kindly reminded to follow Leave No Trace ethics. These principles for respecting Grand Teton's backcountry are as follows:

Leave no trace of your travels, and pack out everything you pack in. This includes garbage, toilet paper, and all scraps of food. If you find litter left behind from previous backcountry users, pack it out as well.

Fire rings are not "natural" phenomena. If you construct a fire ring, make sure you disassemble it prior to leaving your campsite.

Backcountry permits require users to camp in designated sites or within a specific camping zone. A limited number of people are allowed to stay in camping zones; in these zones, campers should stay in previously used camping spots to minimize impact on the land. If a previously used site is not available, camp on bare ground at least 200 feet from water where resource damage will be minimal.

In places where no trail exists, hikers should walk beside one another instead of single file. Leave no trace principles mandate that it is better for a large amount of plants to be trampled just slightly than for a small amount of plants to be repeatedly trampled under a steady stream of footsteps.

Visitors are asked to refrain from picking park wildflowers and other vegetation that supports Grand Teton's unique ecosystem. Removing rocks and other natural/cultural objects is also strictly prohibited. Not only do these activities disrupt nature's cycle, but they also limit others from fully experiencing Grand Teton's beauty.

Many Grand Teton backcountry users seek out such remote areas for their characteristic silence and solitude. Keep in mind that loud voices and radios may disturb others' enjoyment of Grand Teton's scenery. Refrain from yelling, and avoid loudly playing portable music players.

In an effort to curb resource damage, park officials may occasionally close camping sites or reroute trails. Respect these closures, and use only non-restricted areas.

Getting lost in the backcountry is no one's idea of fun, but all backcountry users should be prepared if the situation arises. The first rule is to stay calm and stay put. Historically, those people who remain in one place have a greater chance of being found sooner. If possible, stay in a clearing where visibility is high and search and rescue teams are likely to see bright colored clothing. If a group member is injured, provide as much treatment as possible while staying with the injured party.

Bicycling

Grand Teton National Park and the John D. Rockefeller, Jr. Memorial Parkway welcome bicyclists with more than 100 miles of paved roadways. As a result, the park is a popular destination for road bicyclists. Bicyclists should note, however, that some roads have little to no shoulder, so extreme caution is urged.

Bicyclists should be alert for vehicles and wear helmets along with highly visible clothing. Bicyclists should always ride single file on the road's right side and obey all traffic signs. To avoid hazardous altercations with vehicles, bicyclists are reminded to communicate their actions to others through hand signals.

Since they are not a primitive mode of transportation under wilderness regulations, bicycles are prohibited on all trails within the park and parkway. Unpaved roads suitable for cars are open to bicyclists. Keep in mind, however, that unpaved roads are prone to dust (and thus low visibility!) during dry summer weather.

Boating

Grand Teton is known for its picture-perfect lakes, and as a result, boating is a popular activity. However, ensuring a memorable boating excursion involves responsibility and a commitment to safety. Prior to hitting the water, boaters are urged to check bulletin boards for water caution areas, low water postings, and Snake River flow rates. Lifejackets are required at all times, and boaters should pack along a waterproof container for extra clothes, a first aid kit, an extra paddle/oar, and a trash receptacle. For the utmost in safety, all inflatable boats should carry a patch kit, an air pump, and an emergency bucket for bailing water.

Camping

Camping is only allowed in designated National Park Service or concessionaire-operated campgrounds, and those camping in the backcountry must acquire a special permit. Overnight camping is strictly prohibited in Grand Teton's picnic grounds, parking lots, and roadside pull-outs. Campers must also follow stringent bear safety guidelines to ensure the safety of wildlife and all park guests. Food, garbage, cooking utensils, and toiletries must be stored in a locked vehicle or a solid, airtight container. Backcountry users must contain these items (when not in use) in a bear bag at least ten feet above ground and five feet away from any trees.

Climbing

Ascending Grand Teton's craggy peaks is a scenic thrill that lures climbers of all experience levels to the park year-round. The technical difficulty of many of the park's mountain summits, however, requires climbers to be skilled in a variety of equipment and terrain. Solo climbing is highly discouraged, and climbers should leave their intended route plan and return date with a family member or friend in case of emergency. Climbers should be prepared to face icy conditions even in mid-summer, so an ice ax, crampons, and mountaineering boots are essential in all seasons. Although permits are not required to climb any of Grand Teton's peaks, those planning on camping or bivouacking overnight must obtain a backcountry permit. Contact the climbing ranger at Jenny Lake Ranger Station for additional information about area climbs, route conditions, and the latest weather.

Fires

Human-caused fires are a primary concern in protecting Grand Teton National Park for the enjoyment of future generations. As a result, all park visitors must be vigilant about their use of fire. All cigarettes, cigars, and pipe tobacco must be stamped out and then properly disposed. Ashes from vehicle ashtrays should never be dumped on the ground, and fireworks are expressly prohibited on park property. Campers take on extra responsibility and must build campfires only in pre-established areas. Never leave a fire unattended, and always make sure that fires are completely extinguished before leaving your campsite. During especially dry years, special fire restrictions may be posted, all of which are strictly enforced.

Although small lakeshore campfires are permitted in metal fire grates at some Grand Teton backcountry sites, park rangers wholeheartedly endorse the wilderness principle of lighting cook stoves, not fires. Unlike clean-burning cook stoves, fires scar the land, present a hazard during drought conditions, tarnish the sky with smoke, and pollute rivers, streams, and lakes. Maintain

Grand Teton's health and vibrant ecosystem, and refrain from lighting campfires if at all possible.

High-Altitude Sickness

Commonly referred to as "Mountain Sickness," high-altitude sickness is an unpredictable illness that strikes young and old, fit and unfit. Since the park's elevations range from 6,400 feet on the valley floor to 13,770 feet at the summit of Grand Teton, park visitors accustomed to sea level conditions are particularly susceptible. Instigated by decreased oxygen levels in the air, high-altitude sickness results in headaches, muscle weakness and dull pain, nausea/vomiting, fatigue, appetite loss, rapid heartbeat, and shortness of breath.

Hiking

As tempting as it may be to veer off the trail into the wilds of Grand Teton with nothing but a compass, this situation wreaks havoc on the landscape and is dangerous to your health. The park maintains established trails for a reason, and those who refuse to follow the trail compromise other area users' enjoyment. Protect Grand Teton's beauty, and stay on the trail at all times. Never shortcut a trail, especially on switchbacks. Shortcutting switchbacks disturbs area vegetation and eventually leads to erosion and hillside scarring. Those who abandon the trail are also more likely to suffer injury or get lost in the backcountry. The only time a hiker should step off the trail is during an encounter with a horse. Horses always have the right of way, so hikers should step to the horse's downside while remaining quiet as the animal passes.

In addition to staying on the trail, hikers should pack along a map, drinking water, extra clothing, a water filtration system, and appropriate equipment for ensuring a safe and pleasurable stay in the wilds of Grand Teton. Make sure that someone knows your intended route and expected date of return, and follow all bear safety guidelines. Never leave backpacks, food, or toiletries unattended, and always make noise while hiking so as not to surprise a bear. In the case of a bear encounter, never run or drop your pack. Running only further provokes the bear's charge, and backpacks provide an extra ounce of protection against a potentially deadly attack. Prior to hiking, park visitors are encouraged to stop at the nearest visitor center for complete bear safety information and the region's latest bear activity reports.

Hypothermia

Hypothermia, the lowering of the body's core temperature to a degree causing illness or death, is most frequently associated with winter weather. However, hypothermia can strike even when temperatures are well above freezing, and Grand Teton backcountry users are prime hypothermic candidates. Wind chill is a critical cause of hypothermia, and those with small bodies (especially children) are more susceptible to the condition.

Mild hypothermia symptoms include shivering, apathy, coordination loss, and general complaints of coldness. In severe cases, hypothermia creates slurred speech, irrepressible shivering, mental difficulties, and a body temperature low enough to trigger permanent damage or death. Children, who may not express their physical ailments as concretely as adults, may suddenly become cranky or fatigued. Adults should immediately check for other signs of hypothermia in such cases.

To protect against hypothermia, Grand Teton visitors and backcountry users should carry extra clothing, including socks, gloves, and hats that prevent heat loss from the body's extremities. Even when the weather appears warm and sunny, pack extra clothing; Grand Teton's weather can change on a moment's notice. For the best results, dress in layers and always put on rain gear before it starts raining or snowing. If possible, refrain from hiking in wet conditions altogether, and avoid prolonged exposure to wind. Visitors using Grand Teton's backcountry should also pack along plenty of warm liquids and high-carbohydrate/high-sugar foods that the body can easily process into heat.

If you suspect someone near you is experiencing the initial symptoms of hypothermia, immediately do everything possible to keep the person warm. Replace any wet clothes with dry ones, add more layers, and encourage the individual to drink warm liquids. In extreme cases, build a contained fire to provide additional heat to the victim. To warm suspected hypothermic children, hug the child close to your body, and cover yourselves with a blanket or sleeping bag.

Littering

Littering is not only unsightly, but it is also strictly prohibited. Visitors are reminded to be respectful of others and follow "Leave No Trace" ethics. If you bring something into the park, be sure to pack it out.

Motorcycles and ATVs

All motorcycles, motorbikes, and power scooters must be licensed, and operators must possess a valid driver's license. These vehicles are required to stay on park highways at all times, and backcountry ATV and motorcycle use is strictly prohibited.

Pets

Out of respect to all visitors and deference to native wildlife, Grand Teton National Park maintains strict policies regarding pets in the park. Pets should never disrupt others' enjoyment of the park; therefore, pets must be caged, crated, or kept on a leash at all times. Pets may never be left unattended, tied to park objects, enter the backcountry, or enter buildings (with the exception of guide dogs). Pets must also be kept at least fifty feet from any road, and owners are responsible for cleaning up after their pets and disposing of all feces in a proper manner. Owners of pets who disturb the wildlife are subject to a fine, and unattended pets will be impounded at the owner's expense. If at all possible, leave your pets at home to avoid such situations.

Sun Exposure and Illness

Due to the park's high elevations, Grand Teton visitors are more susceptible to high levels of ultraviolet rays, which may in turn lead to heat-related illnesses. Visitors should take every precaution to avoid over-exposure to the sun, no matter the season, and should be careful on summit hikes and near water bodies where rays are especially intense. Protect your eyes with sunglasses, and wear sunscreen and hats at all times. Those pursuing highly active activities, such as hiking, paddling, or bicycling, should use caution to avoid dehydration, heat exhaustion, and heat stroke. Stop for regular water breaks, and carry salted snacks and liquids to help replace electrolytes lost through perspiration.

Water Warning

As in other American wilderness areas, it is never safe to assume that Grand Teton's water is safe for drinking. If your plans call for backcountry travel in Grand Teton, carry along safe drinking water and the knowledge and materials to secure additional safe water on your trek. Giardia, Campylobacter, and other harmful bacteria and parasites are known to inhabit Yellowstone's waters, and boiling water for three to six minutes is regarded as the most effective manner to treat infected water. Filtration and chemical tablet treatments are also popular purification methods. Visitors should note that all water, whether it is used for cooking or brushing teeth, must be filtered.

To reduce the likelihood of further contaminating water and spreading disease to other Grand Teton users, human waste should be buried at least 200 feet away from water and trails. In addition, visitors should never use soap (even those labeled biodegradable) in or near Grand Teton's numerous water bodies, and backcountry users should wash dishes a minimum of 100 feet away from the water's shoreline.

Wildlife

Wildlife safety and park regulations go hand in hand in Grand Teton. Park officials require visitors to maintain a viewing distance of at least 300 feet from all large animals for the safety of Grand Teton's wildlife and all park guests. Feeding, approaching, and chasing the park's wildlife is strictly prohibited, and those who disobey this mandate are subject to a stiff penalty. As another rule of precaution, visitors should never come between an adult animal and its young offspring.

Backcountry Use and Regulations

For those who take the time to explore Grand Teton's breathtaking backcountry, a vast land of pristine mountain wonder awaits. Unlike its Yellowstone neighbor, Grand Teton welcomes a significant amount of backcountry users each year with July and August hosting the most explorers. As a result, backcountry permits are at a premium. To ensure that you experience a memorable backcountry stay, heed the following suggestions and regulations.

Permits

All overnight backcountry trips require a permit, and permits are limited in an effort to maintain the park's natural resources. While one-third of the backcountry campsites may be reserved in advance, all other sites are filled at park permit offices on a first-come, first-served basis. Reserved permits must be claimed by 10 AM on the morning of your trip's starting date at the Moose Visitor Center, Colter Bay Visitor Center, or Jenny Lake Ranger Station. During winter, permits are only available at the Moose Visitor Center. For those who know they will be arriving in the park after 10 AM, special permit pick-up arrangements can be made.

All permits require a user signature that binds visitors to a code of backcountry ethics and regulations printed on the backside of each permit. Visitors must follow these rules at all times; those who do not may lose their permit and receive a hefty fine.

Reservations

Due to the park's popularity, reservations are highly recommended for all backcountry activities.

Mt. Moran. NPS Photo.

Reservation requests are processed in the order they are received from January 1 to May 15, so timeliness is critical. Reservations must include the visitor's name, address, telephone number, the number of people in the party, travel route and dates, preferred campsites, and alternate campsites. Reservations are accepted in person from 8 AM to 5 PM at the Moose Visitor Center or by faxing (307) 739-3438. Visitors may also mail their reservation request to Grand Teton National Park, Permits Office, P.O. Drawer 170, Moose, WY 83012. All reservations require a $15 non-refundable transaction fee, and visitors receive written confirmation of their reservation within two weeks of a request. Phone reservations are not available.

Group Size

Backcountry parties consisting of one to six people receive "individual" travel status, while summer parties of seven to twelve people are subject to a group designation. Groups must camp in designated campsites capable of hosting larger parties with limited resource damage. During winter, the group limit is raised to a maximum of twenty people.

Stay Limits

During the most popular use season between June 1 and September 15, visitors are limited to a maximum ten-night stay in the backcountry. In most areas, campers may only stay in a designated site or camping zone for two consecutive nights, with a three-night limit at Jackson Lake. During winter, campers may stay in any one spot for five consecutive nights.

Camping Zones and Regulations

Unless allocated to a designated camping site, all backcountry users must stay within an assigned camping zone based upon the travel plans indicated on the backcountry reservation request. Every zone is marked with signs as well as all group sites and improved campsites within each zone. Non-designated, unimproved campsites in each zone are not marked, but camping is allowed. Backcountry users are reminded to camp away from trails and other campers while maintaining a distance of at least 200 feet from all water. Since all group sites are assigned at the time of reservation requests, these sites are only available to groups assigned to them. Keep in mind that bears roam throughout all camp zones, so backcountry users must properly hang food or stow items in the airtight food storage boxes found at some sites.

The following is a description of major backcountry areas and camping zones in Grand Teton National Park.

Berry Creek, Webb Canyon, and canyons without trails: The Berry Creek, Webb Canyon, and surrounding canyons feature difficult hikes in prime grizzly bear habitat. Users of this area must be in excellent physical condition, feel comfortable in crossing rapid streams without bridges, and know how to use a map and compass. Backcountry users must also be confident in their self-evacuation skills in case of an emergency, and horse and llamas are only allowed at the Hechtman Stock Camp.

Death Canyon Zone: The Death Canyon Zone begins 4.5 miles from the Death Canyon Trailhead and extends 0.5 miles west of the unstaffed Death Canyon Patrol Cabin and 0.5 miles below Fox Creek Pass. The zone does include a group site situated approximately two miles west of the patrol cabin.

Death Canyon Shelf Zone: Home to a group site situated two miles north of Fox Creek Pass, the Death Canyon Shelf Zone runs from Fox Creek Pass to Mt. Meek Pass.

Holly Lake Designated Sites: Two designated, marked campsites rest along the Holly Lake Campsites trail. The trail begins at Holly Lake and departs from the main Holly Lake trail. Backcountry users will find a group site and stock site 0.25 miles below Holly Lake.

Lower Granite Canyon: Lower Granite Canyon extends near the Middle/North Fork trail junction and includes one group area nestled just south of the canyon trail. Users will locate the site 3.4 miles west of the Granite Canyon/Valley Trail junction.

Lower Paintbrush Canyon Zone: Beginning just below the first Paintbrush Creek crossing, the Lower Paintbrush Canyon Zone boundary ends near the Holly Lake Trail Junction. The zone includes one designated campsite situated one mile below Holly Lake.

Marion Lake Designated Sites: Marion Lake is home to three designated sites. All campers are asked to utilize tent pads that protect the area's natural resources.

Mt. Hunt Divide Zone: The Mt. Hunt Divide Zone runs directly south of Mt. Hunt Divide to the Granite Canyon Trail.

North Fork Cascade Zone: Encompassing the area from the North Fork's second bridge crossing to a stream crossing near Lake Solitude, the North Fork Cascade Zone features one group site. The site rests on a terraced landscape approximately 0.5 miles from the zone's lower boundary.

North Fork Granite Canyon Zone: The North Fork Granite Canyon Zone begins 0.25 miles north of the Middle/North Fork trail junction and continues to the North Fork Creek trail crossing.

Open Canyon Zone: Open Canyon Zone begins at the Open Canyon Creek trail crossing and extends slightly north of Mt. Hunt Divide.

South Fork Cascade Zone: This camping zone originates near the Cascade Canyon trail fork and extends slightly south of Hurricane Pass. One group site, located east of the trail, is available.

South-Middle Fork Zone: With its upper boundary marked at the ridge between the North and Middle Forks and a lower boundary resting slightly above the Middle/North Fork trail junction, the South-Middle Fork Zone contains one group site. The scenic spot rests in a grove of trees 1.4 miles south of Marion Lake near the Middle Fork Creek trail crossing.

Upper Paintbrush Canyon Zone: The Upper Paintbrush Canyon Zone starts near the Holly Lake Trail Junction and stretches towards the Paintbrush Divide on the canyon trail. Camping is regulated in the zone, so contact the Park Service for specific camping information prior to reserving a permit.

Lakeshore Sites

Backcountry lakeshore sites offer some of the most popular camping in the entire park. Receiving considerable use, these sites come with their own set of regulations.

Jackson Lake: Since bears are common in the area, provided bear boxes at each site must be used for food and toiletry storage. In addition, fires are only permitted in established metal fire grates, and pets are only allowed at Spalding Bay. All Jackson Lake campers should be alert for strong afternoon winds that create potentially hazardous waves on the lake.

Leigh Lake: At Leigh Lake, tents must be pitched on provided tent pads and food must be contained in the bear boxes located at each site. Fires are only allowed in established metal fire grates, and lake users should be aware that strong winds generate large waves.

Phelps Lake: Phelps Lake campers experience a few less restrictions, but regulations are nonetheless strictly enforced. Fires are prohibited, tents must be pitched on tent pads, and the bear boxes provided at each site must be used for proper food/toiletry storage.

Backcountry Conditions

Backcountry trails generally open in mid-June, but high country travelers should be prepared for snowy conditions throughout the entire summer season. Hurricane, Mt. Meek, and Fox Creek Passes along with Moose Basin, Paintbrush, and Static Peak Divides require the use of ice axes for safe travel. All trails in Grand Teton's backcountry begin at or above an elevation of 6,800 feet. Prior to entering the backcountry, visitors are encouraged to contact the nearest ranger station for the latest trail conditions.

Backcountry Regulations

In addition to requiring a permit, backcountry use in Grand Teton National Park comes with a special set of regulations to protect the area's natural resources. To ensure the longevity of the park's wilderness areas, users are asked to respect the following guidelines:

Fires, which are permitted only near lakeshores, must be contained within the park service's provided metal fire grates. All fires must be attended and extinguished.

If at all possible, use clean-burning gas cook stoves instead of lighting a fire.

The backcountry is closed to weapons, explosives, fireworks, pets, bicycles, motorized equipment, and all wheeled vehicles. The exclusion of such articles upholds the backcountry's commitment to allowing only primitive modes of transportation within its boundaries.

Campsite alterations, including rock fire rings, log benches, rock walls, and trenches, are strictly prohibited.

Remember that Grand Teton is bear country, and follow all bear safety guidelines. As a rule of thumb, always keep a safe distance from all wildlife and never feed the animals.

Pack out everything you pack in; never bury trash, attempt to burn aluminum foil, or leave any food scraps. Such behavior limits future visitors' enjoyment and also threatens the natural hunting abilities of area wildlife.

Grand Teton's water sources are precious. Do your part to keep the park's streams, lakes, and rivers clean, and never wash dishes or bathe in Grand Teton's water systems.

Horses, llamas, and mules are strictly relegated to pre-established stock camps and park service trails. Grazing is forbidden in the backcountry, so stock feed must be packed in and out.

Water

Backcountry users must treat all water sources, whether water is to be used for drinking, cooking, or brushing teeth. The safest treatment methods include boiling or filtering all water. Those who refuse to treat their water may potentially suffer severe intestinal disorders caused from giardia, campylobacter, and other harmful bacteria/organisms present in Grand Teton's water.

Sanitation

Adherence to proper backcountry sanitation is essential for the protection of Grand Teton's waterways. Human feces must be buried at least 200 feet away from all waterways in a six- to eight-inch hole. Visitors are also reminded to urinate in rocky areas (where animals cannot dig for

Mormon Row. NPS Photo.

the scent) at least 200 feet away from all water sources. All toilet paper, feminine hygiene products, and diapers must be packed out. For sanitation purposes, these items should be stored in sealed plastic bags.

Mountaineering

Although mountaineering permits are not required for climbing, those climbers planning an overnight trip or bivouac must obtain a backcountry permit. If in doubt whether your travel plans require a permit, contact the Jenny Lake Ranger Station at (307) 739-3343. During the summer, all technical climbing permits should be picked up at this station. In the winter, call (307) 739-3309 for more information.

Boating

All boats, regardless of make and model, must be registered with the park for an annual fee. Permits are available at the Moose Visitor Center and Colter Bay Visitor Center. Although camping is allowed on the shores of Jackson Lake and Leigh Lake, it is prohibited on the Snake River. Contact the park for a boating brochure outlining park guidelines.

Fishing

Fishing in any of Grand Teton's water bodies requires a Wyoming state fishing license. Licenses are available at Colter Bay, Moose Visitor Center, Flagg Ranch, and the Signal Mountain camp store. Angling restrictions do exist, and the park's fishing brochure outlines specific regulations for all park water systems.

Horses and Llamas

Stock may only travel on established backcountry trails, and some trails are open only to those on foot. Those traveling with stock are restricted to special campsites and must pack in their own stock feed. Grazing is not allowed, and those caught grazing their animals are subject to a hefty fine.

Trip Checklist

In order to ensure the most successful and enjoyable trip to Grand Teton National Park, visitors should take into account the following travel suggestions.

- Plan your trip and the features you want to see in accordance with the park's opening and closing road schedule. Most roads are accessible to vehicles as early as May 1 with many remaining open until November 1. Check with the Park Service prior to setting your trip dates.

- Be prepared for road construction, and avoid stressing about unexpected delays. Grand Teton's website (www.nps.gov/grte) provides links to the latest road construction reports for travelers' convenience.

- Worried about the weather or road conditions? An informational hotline provides current weather and road reports for Grand Teton's major regions. Call (307) 733-2664 for additional information.

- Familiarize yourself with the park's regulations and fees prior to your arrival. This will help you realistically budget your Grand Teton vacation expenses and ensure that you do not unknowingly violate park laws.

- Lodging has the ability to make or break your trip, so plan accordingly. Since the park receives over three million visitors each year, reserve your lodging as early as possible.

- If your travels involve camping within the park or near Grand Teton's boundaries, arrive as early as possible on the night of your stay in order to secure a site. After claiming your spot for the night, continue your day's sightseeing.

- Grand Teton's weather can be unpredictable in all seasons. All visitors are encouraged to pack and wear clothes that can easily be layered. Even during the summer, cold temperatures are inevitable, so make sure to bring a jacket. Also, due to the area's high elevations and thinner atmosphere, pack and use sunscreen to avoid unpleasant burns.

Jackson Lake

- Be prepared for emergencies at all times, especially when hiking Grand Teton's trails. All visitors are urged to pack along extra food, clothing, a first-aid kit, water, and matches.

- Last but not least, remember your camera. Grand Teton is brimming with photo opportunities you definitely want to capture!

UNDERSTANDING AND APPRECIATING GRAND TETON'S GEOLOGY

Jagged, snowcapped mountain peaks stand guard over the slithering Snake River as the verdant Jackson Hole Valley basks in the radiance of Wyoming's bright sunny skies. As dynamic as this setting may be, the processes that shaped the park's breathtaking landscape are even more phenomenal. Spanning billions of years, the geology of Grand Teton National Park has included everything from mountain building to volcanic spewing with significant changes still taking shape.

Rock Foundations

The Teton Range as it is seen today would not exist without the geological rock foundations that began surfacing more than 2.5 billion years ago. Over the course of millions of years, sand and volcanic remains were deposited into an ancient seabed and slowly transformed with heat and pressure into gneiss. This sediment banded together in dark and light layers is still evident in many of the park's stunning canyons.

As these bands of sediment filled in the ancient ocean, molten rock began oozing through cracks in the gneiss. When the magma cooled, it left behind blocks of granite ranging from just one inch to several hundred feet thick. Several of these blocks are still visible in the Jenny Lake and String Lake regions.

Shortly after the granite formations took hold, igneous diabase flowed from deep within the Earth's surface through the gneiss and granite. This 1.3 billion-year-old activity formed

nearly vertical spires of rock. Today, these dark-colored dikes are prominent features on the Middle Teton Peak and Mt. Moran.

The last stage of the Grand Tetons' rock foundation occurred between 600 and sixty-five million years ago when a tropical climate washed over the region. The era's shallow seas left behind sedimentary deposits as well as fossilized marine life and dinosaur bones. With these sediment and igneous layers in place, the stage was set for building Grand Teton National Park's signature mountain peaks.

Mountains Form

The Teton Range is an anomaly when it comes to the formation of the Rocky Mountain chain. Most geologists agree that the continuous chain of mountains extending from Canada to Mexico rose up from the Earth's crust between eighty and forty million years ago – with the solitary exception of the much younger Teton Range. Known as the youngest range in the Rockies, the Teton Mountains made their first appearance between six and nine million years ago.

In reaction to the earth's thinning crust and the subsequent creation of the Teton Fault Line, the solid block of rock situated on the west side of the fault jutted upwards to form the impressive Teton Mountains. The rock on the fault's eastern side subsequently fell to create the valley now known as Jackson Hole. Throughout the course of this rising and falling of sedimentary and igneous rocks, the Teton Fault Line has been accountable for over 30,000 feet of total vertical movement! Geologists have pinpointed such activity with the presence of Flathead Sandstone evident on both sides of the Teton Fault. While the famous sandstone is buried more than 24,000 feet below the Jackson Hole Valley, sandstone on the fault's western side caps Mt. Moran over 6,000 feet above the valley floor. Today, the sheer rock walls characterizing the famous Teton Range skyrocket more than a mile above the valley floor.

Volcanic Activity

In addition to the volcanic activity and magma flows that formed the igneous and sedimentary foundations of the Teton Range, volcanic activity surfaced again in the region approximately twenty million years ago. Ash from distant westerly and northerly volcanic explosions blew into the park, and one-mile thick deposits of white ash soon amassed on the valley floor. Between six million and 600,000 years ago, clouds of molten rock from Yellowstone explosions rained down on the Teton Mountains and added a new dimension to the range's character. Today, the range's northern end and Signal Mountain still show signs of this ancient volcanic activity.

Glacial Sculpting

When the regional climate cooled approximately 150,000 years ago, glaciers over 2,000 feet thick swept through the Jackson Hole Valley. These glaciers remained in the area nearly 50,000 years before melting with the arrival of a warmer temperature pattern. The warm climate, however, only lasted 40,000 years before another chilly Ice Age bore down upon the valley. A new wave of glaciers chiseled a path into the heart of today's current park between 60,000 and 20,000 years ago. In their wake, they sculpted the jagged points on the Teton Range and created the glacial Phelps, Jenny, Jackson, String, Taggart, Bradley, and Leigh Lakes. U-shaped valleys formed, rocks were smoothed, and cirque lakes established themselves in the depths of Grand Teton's backcountry.

Although the largest glaciers melted over 15,000 years ago, a few small glaciers actually remain in the Teton Range. Triple Glaciers, Skillet Glacier, and Falling Ice Glacier make their home on Mt. Moran, while Teton Glacier is cradled under Grand Teton's imposing stare. In Cascade Canyon, Schoolroom Glacier exhibits all the classic features of a glacier and is accessible with a ten-mile hike up the canyon's south fork. Moraines also provide evidence of the park's ancient glacial inhabitants, and Timbered Island and Burned Ridge offer stunning examples of a landscape built through geologic change.

GRAND TETON'S ABUNDANT NATURE: UNDERSTANDING AN ECOSYSTEM

It is hard to escape the popular notion that Grand Teton National Park and the Teton Range are one in the same. After all, famous photographers zoom in on the sharp-toothed peaks, outdoor enthusiasts across the world proclaim the range's mystique, and Jackson Hole residents revere the mountains as their personal treasure. Believe it or not, these captivating peaks are just the beginning of an amazingly diverse ecosystem. Over 1,000 species of vascular plants line every nook of Grand Teton National Park, and the dramatic elevation changes within the park allow for a dramatic ecosystem. Park visitors are not only treated to mountains, but also glaciers, forests, flood plains, wetlands, rivers, lakes, and much more. Together, these unique features join forces to create one of America's most beautiful national parks.

Flood Plains

Situated adjacent to a river and prone to flooding when water levels are high, flood plains play a significant role in the park's topography. The Snake

River flood plain is an example of this natural feature as it follows the river on a slithering course throughout the park's terrain. Wildlife depends on the flood plain's lush marshes and wetlands. As a result, wildlife viewing along the park's Snake River flood plain is exceptionally rewarding. Remember, though, always keep your distance for the safety of yourself and the animals.

Forests Grow

Grand Teton National Park is lined with forests displaying a diversity of hearty species adept at surviving the region's extreme seasonal temperature variation. While aspens, alders, willows, cottonwoods, lodgepole pine, douglas fir, and blue spruce line the valleys and rivers, subalpine fir, engelmann spruce, whitebark pine, and limber pine cling to life at elevations up to 10,000 feet. Most of the park's forests contain two to three different species of trees that create a unique habitat suitable to a specific set of wildlife residents. In addition, the park's forests supply the region with nutrients and carbon dioxide necessary for the ecosystem's survival.

Glacial Reminders

Migrating on thin sheets of water, glaciers have played a powerful role in the park's geological shaping for thousands of years. Ice fields as thick as 3,000 to 4,000 feet rumbled through the region eons ago, sculpting valleys and adding a new dimension to the mountain peaks visitors now see today. While most of these glaciers have long since melted and merged into the ocean, ancient remnants remain amid Grand Teton's awe-inspiring peaks. These glaciers feature v-shaped crevasses and carry rocks and other geological debris with them as they shift downwards at approximately thirty feet per year. Today, twelve mountain-carving glaciers and numerous snowfields remain as dramatic visual reminders of Grand Teton's dynamic geologic history.

Lakes

Mirroring the captivating reflection of snowcapped peaks and thick green forests, Grand Teton's lakes and ponds are a favorite park attraction. Swimming, boating, and fishing are all popular lake pastimes, and hiking and camping around the park's lakes have long been crowd pleasers. These lakes, however, possess much more than recreational value. Formed through ancient glacial sculpting, human activity, and natural sinkholes, the park's lakes and ponds afford critical habitat for park wildlife and vegetation. Cutthroat trout line the waterways, birds flock to the moist plant life, and moose and other mammals depend upon lakes and their surrounding environment for sustenance. As a result, wildlife viewing around the park's lakes and ponds offers a thrilling opportunity to see a range of animal life.

Mountain Grandeur

Mountains. Their image pierces postcards of Grand Teton National Park and blazes a lasting impression on the mind's eye. Undoubtedly, the park's magnificent mountains are the main visitor attraction, inspiring awe and spurring recreationists to reach new heights. Featuring more than twelve peaks that skyrocket to elevations exceeding 12,000 feet, Grand Teton National Park's mountains are distinguished as the youngest range in the entire Rocky Mountain chain. Today, these towering mountains formed through geological upheaval proudly straddle the Wyoming/Idaho

border, invoking reverence and creating picture-perfect memories.

Reminders of Yesterday: Fossils Unearthed

Grand Teton National Park is no doubt one of America's premier mountain destinations, but the landscape has not always been a craggy, forested masterpiece. In fact, oceans and a temperate climate once drenched the region with water and marine life now uncommon in the Rocky Mountain West. Scientists have discovered fish and plant life buried deep within the thick sediment layers forming Grand Teton National Park. These researchers have concluded that the relatively young mountainous landscape visible today was previously an ocean bottom 500 million years ago. Thousands of unearthed fossils provide supporting evidence for this theory, and new fossils are regularly discovered. If you are so lucky as to find a reminder of yesterday, please leave the fossil for the exploration and astonishment of future park visitors and scientists.

Moose. NPS Photo.

Watersheds

Grand Teton National Park is unique in possessing three distinct watersheds. Recognized as geological regions where water runs from a high point to a centrally located basin, watersheds direct precipitation flows across the world. The most widely noted North American watershed is the Continental Divide, which ushers water to the Pacific and Atlantic Oceans. Although by no means as large or impressive as the Continental Divide, Grand Teton National Park watersheds maintain an important role in the health of the Greater Yellowstone ecosystem. The Snake River Valley watershed is responsible for absorbing moisture that falls near the famous river. The most obvious watersheds are those existing on both sides of the Teton Range. While precipitation falling on the Wyoming side runs east to the Jackson Hole Valley, moisture on the Idaho side flows west into Teton Valley.

Wetlands

For those who think Grand Teton is simply composed of rocks, trees, and lakes, think again. While images of those natural curiosities certainly dominate the photo coverage of Grand Teton National Park, wetlands are by far one of the park's most abundant features. Wetlands, also known as marshes and swamps, form where land merges into water. Lilies, willows, tall grasses, and cattails thrive in the wetland environment, providing wildlife with important habitat and food. In addition, these marshy areas help control rising water levels during floods. Visitors to any of Grand Teton's wetland areas will likely see a myri-

ad of wildlife grazing on the nutrient-rich vegetation. Remember, keep an appropriate distance from these and all other park wildlife.

THE WILDLIFE OF GRAND TETON

Inhabiting the same ecosystem as Yellowstone, Grand Teton National Park houses several similar wildlife species as its northerly neighbor. Adept at surviving the park's dramatic elevations and seasonal temperature changes, these animals rely upon one another and the park's abundant vegetation for survival. Many also cross over the park's boundaries into the John D. Rockefeller, Jr. Memorial Parkway and Yellowstone in search of food and shelter.

Despite this annual influx and outgo of wildlife, park officials have determined that Grand Teton's wildlife is as varied as its spectacular topography. 300-plus species of birds, twenty-two species of rodents, seventeen carnivorous species, sixteen species of fish, six species of hoofed mammals, six bat species, five amphibious species, four species of non-poisonous reptiles, and three species of rabbits join with numerous invertebrates in populating every square inch of Grand Teton. As a result, birds soar in the park's crisp blue skies, fish dart in shadowy alpine lakes and twisting rivers, mammals graze the fertile land, and insects crawl amid the park's 900-plus species of flowering plants and shady trees. Although it may be tempting to approach this abundant wildlife for a closer look, park visitors should remember that Grand Teton's critters are just as wild as the landscape they inhabit. Grand Teton is not a zoo; it is a sanctuary for one of America's most diverse wildlife populations and should be treated with the utmost respect for visitor and animal safety.

Amphibians

Drawing their name from the Greek word meaning "double life," amphibians inhabit all of Grand Teton's rivers, streams, and lakes. These creatures, which breathe through gills when they are young and lungs after transforming into adults, play an extremely important role in the park's ecosystem. Since amphibians depend upon water in both of their life cycles, amphibians' health is often the first indicator of the park's water quality and environmental conditions. These species also help control insect populations and serve as valuable food for fish, birds, and otters.

Characterized by moist glandular skin and a cold-blooded nature, amphibians in Grand Teton include bullfrogs, boreal toads, boreal chorus frogs, northern leopard frogs, spotted frogs, and tiger salamanders. Taggart Lake, Schwabacher's Landing, and String Lake are all known to harbor amphibious populations, although visitors should be able to locate any one of these six species in the park's marshy areas.

Birds

From buzzing humming birds to the stately bald eagle, Grand Teton National Park is home to birds of all species and sizes. Owls hoot in the dark of night, songbirds whistle amid forest groves, ospreys dive for the catch of the day, and trumpeter swans float serenely on the park's lakes. All of these birds and hundreds more line the park's trees and waterways, adding tremendous depth to Grand Teton's animal life. As a result, bird watching in the park can be highly rewarding, and information about this activity is available from

View of the Grand from Black Tail Butte. NPS Photo.

National Park Service staff and park visitor centers.

All wildlife watchers are reminded that birds should never be harassed or distracted from their normal course of activity. In order to ensure this wildlife principle, never approach birds, and if possible, view from a distance with binoculars.

Fish

Living out of sight beneath the surface of Grand Teton's rivers, lakes, and streams, fish are an essential component of the Greater Yellowstone ecosystem's vitality. In addition to serving as a fundamental food source for mammals and birds, fish help control the delicate balance of plant life in the water and insect populations surrounding the park's water bodies. They also serve as a prime indicator of the ecosystem's health, responding negatively to water conditions that change with pollution and overfishing.

Although Grand Teton National Park is renowned worldwide for its blue-ribbon trout fishing, the park's rivers, streams, and lakes also harbor several other fish species in all shapes and sizes. Both warm-water and cold-water fish reside within the park's boundaries, and anglers are likely to catch at least one fish on any given outing. However, remember that fishing policies do exist within the park, and all rules are strictly enforced to ensure the ecosystem's healthiest possible future.

Mammals

Featuring an ability to adapt to nearly all environmental conditions, mammals have carved out a niche in every major habitat in Grand Teton National Park. From wetlands to sagebrush plateaus, mountains to forests, the park's sixty-one mammal species are present everywhere visitors turn and are the most common animals viewed in the park. Elk, deer, bison, and pronghorn antelope line the roadways while the more reclusive black bear, grizzly bear, mountain lion, and coyote roam the backcountry. On the smaller end of the size scale, badgers, chipmunks, pikas, marmots, beavers, and dozens of other creatures all call Grand Teton National Park home.

Characterized by the presence of hair and the nursing of their young, mammals have survived the test of time with their warm-blooded metabolism. Mammals are also different from other animals in that they prefer to raise and protect a small number of offspring instead of expending valuable energy in producing hundreds of offspring for whom they are unable to ensure survival. This unique twist on breeding has allowed mammals to reign supreme in the animal kingdom and successfully pass strong genes from one generation to the next. Grand Teton is an ideal example of this principle with its diverse mammal populations.

Reptiles

Relatively little research has been done to trace the presence and behavior of snakes in Grand Teton, but scientists do know for certain that three species of snakes and one species of lizard inhabit the beautiful mountain setting. Recognized by their dry, scaly skin and sleek slithering motion, snakes are able to bear their offspring live or in egg form. Although snake venom can be deadly, no poisonous snakes live within the confines of Grand Teton National Park.

The wandering garter snake is the most prevalent snake species in the park followed by the valley garter snake and the rubber boa. All three snakes reside in wet areas close to water bodies. In addition to snakes, the park is also home to the newly discovered northern sagebrush lizard. Inhabiting dry, sagebrush plains as its name suggests, this lizard was not identified in the park until 1992. Lizard sightings are infrequent, but the discovery gives rise to the idea that other reptiles may unknowingly be living within the park.

WATCHING GRAND TETON'S WILDLIFE: VIEWING TIPS AND SAFETY GUIDELINES

With so many different animal species populating Grand Teton National Park, it is virtually impossible for a park visitor to conclude their trip without at least a single sighting of a wild Grand Teton inhabitant. Wildlife habits and personality, weather patterns, mating seasons, and time of day greatly affect the potential for viewing park wildlife. Visitors who opt to enter the park in the early morning or late evening hours (typical feeding hours) possess the greatest potential for seeing a range of park wildlife. However, sightings are possible throughout the day. For additional information about specific viewing locations, contact a park ranger, check out the park's visitor centers, or simply take your chances at sighting some of Grand Teton's magnificent creatures roaming near the park's highways.

Where to Watch for Wildlife

Blacktail Ponds
Once home to beaver ponds, the now grassy Blacktail Ponds area is known for its abundant duck populations. Moose also graze on willows here during early morning and late evening. The site is located on Highway 26/89/191 0.5 miles north of Moose.

Cascade Canyon
Ground squirrels, pikas, yellow-bellied marmots, mule deer, and moose all reside west of Jenny Lake in Cascade Canyon. The shrubs and boulders lining the canyon provide perfect shelter for these species. Squirrels are especially prevalent at Inspiration Point. Although squirrels may be cute and small, visitors are reminded that these animals are wild and can carry disease. Refrain from feeding all wildlife!

Mormon Row
Located one mile north of Moose Junction east of Highway 26/89/191, Mormon Row features bison, pronghorn antelope, coyotes, Uinta ground squirrels, Northern harriers, and American kestrels. Birds such as sage grouse, sparrows, and sage thrashers also populate this region.

Oxbow Bend
Oxbow Bend provides a range of possible sightings. From moose grazing on willows and elk wandering through aspen groves to paddling beavers and soaring bald eagles, Oxbow Bend houses several wildlife species. Muskrats, white pelicans, otters, ospreys, trout, and suckers also inhabit this area located just one mile east of the Jackson Lake Junction.

Snake River
Winding south from Jackson Lake Dam to Moose, the Snake River and surrounding regions shelter large populations of elk, bison, beavers, and moose. The river is also a favorite destination for great blue herons, bald eagles, and ospreys that peruse the water for their daily fresh catch and nest near the riverbanks.

Timbered Island
Named Timbered Island after its heavily forested ridge, this area southeast of Jenny Lake contains large populations of elk. During dawn and dusk, elk and pronghorn antelope leave the shade and protection of Timbered Island to dine on the sagebrush flats surrounding the region.

Keep Your Distance

As wild, untamed animals, Grand Teton's wildlife needs plenty of undisturbed space, and park visitors are reminded that they are guests in these animals' homes. Respect these creatures' wild nature, and wisely watch from a distance. By engaging in this behavior, park visitors are not only rewarded with a more natural look at the animals' activities, but they also ensure a greater safety level for the wildlife and other nearby onlookers.

Wildlife watchers who disregard these principles greatly jeopardize themselves and the animals they are viewing. An animal that becomes aware of an onlooker's presence experiences a rapid rise in heart rate, may move to a less desirable feeding location just to escape its watchers, and can become habituated to humans. These factors deplete animals' valuable energy supplies, create a nourishment deficit, and can potentially make animals unafraid of would-be poachers.

At the same time these disrespectful wildlife watchers are inherently harming the animals, they are also putting themselves at risk. Wildlife is unpredictable, and those animals that feel their territory has been encroached upon may fight back. Several park visitors are injured every year when they approach animals too closely, and encounters with wildlife can be deadly. Always maintain your distance, and keep in mind the following tips to help you become a wise wildlife watcher while minimizing your impact.

- Park law mandates that visitors must stay at least 100 yards (91 meters) away from bears and at least 25 yards away from all other large wildlife, including wolves, coyotes, moose, deer, elk, bison, and bighorn sheep.

- Never stop in the middle of the road to view wildlife. Always pull off to the road's shoulder or a pullout, and always shut off your engine so as not to disturb the wildlife.

- Refrain from shouting or exclaiming in excitement. Instead, talk quietly among yourselves, and stay in your car if possible. Vehicles often make appropriate photo blinds.

- Never distract animals or try to grab their attention for a photo opportunity. Instead, use a telephoto lens to capture animals in their natural state and environment.

- Never bait animals with food handouts. Not only is human food harmful to wildlife, but it also habituates wildlife to humans. This can eventually lead to negative encounters between park visitors and wildlife. In addition, this type of behavior is against the law, and park rangers are not afraid to ticket violators.

Important Bear Safety Tips

Grand Teton National Park is prime grizzly bear and black bear habitat. Consequently, all visitors must follow bear safety tips to ensure the survival of park bears and sightseer safety. Those who discount bear safety guidelines are not only breaking both park regulations and federal law, but also threatening the existence of park bears. As a result of careless humans, numerous bears have become habituated to human food, and park rangers have unfortunately had to destroy several animals in the last few years. Do your part; enhance visitor safety and encourage bear survival with the following tips.

- Report all bear sightings to the nearest park ranger as soon as possible. Such data helps rangers inform other park visitors about regional bear activity.

- Keep a clean, bear-proof campsite at all times. Bears are active both day and night and will prowl for food left out in the open.

- All food, soap, toiletries, and garbage must be stored in bear-proof boxes, hung from a tree in a bear-proof container, or kept inside a locked vehicle with the windows rolled up. No odiferous items should ever be kept inside sleeping bags or tents.

- Coolers, stoves, dishes, thermoses, grills, and all other cooking utensils must be stored in the same manner as food.

- Never bury food scraps, used food containers, or fish and animal entrails. Bears have an amazing sense of smell and will dig for all buried odors.

- Always maintain a distance of at least 100 yards (ninety-one meters) from all bears, and never approach a black bear or grizzly bear. Both bears are dangerous and can be aggressive.

- Do not run if you encounter a bear in the park. If the bear is unaware of your presence, quietly and quickly move away. If the bear does notice you but is not acting aggressively, talk calmly and back away slowly. Never turn your back on a bear or run as such actions could incite an attack. If the bear acts aggressively and begins to charge, maintain your ground, avoid eye contact, and protect your head and neck at all times.

- Never try to dissuade an attack by throwing a backpack or food at the bear.

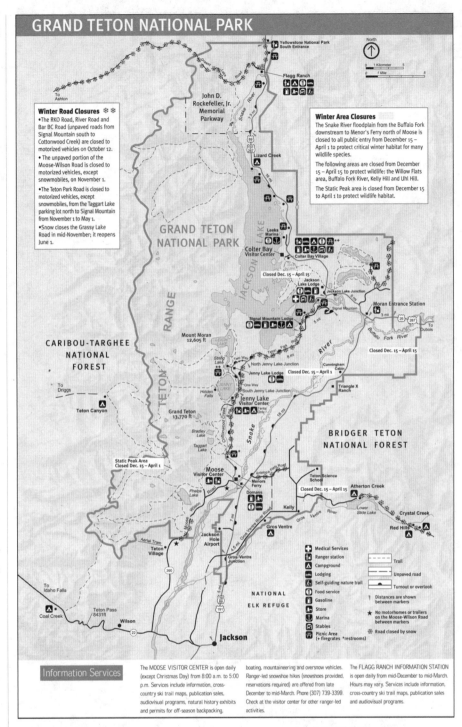

GRAND TETON NATIONAL PARK

- If you carry bear spray, make sure you know how to use it prior to a bear encounter. Bear sprays can ease an attack but only if the carrier uses the spray correctly.

RECREATING IN GRAND TETON NATIONAL PARK

Miles of RVs and bumper-to-bumper traffic each summer may make some Grand Teton visitors cringe, but for those who choose to travel off the beaten path, the park is actually an isolated place home to some of America's most pristine mountain wilderness. For recreationists who opt to explore the park via bike, boat, horse, skis, snowmobile, or with their own two feet, miles of undisturbed open spaces and phenomenal views await. Year-round outdoor activities abound within the park's boundaries, and those who take time to enjoy Grand Teton's natural attractions are rewarded with an unforgettable park experience.

Summer Activities

The sky is the limit when it comes to Grand Teton outdoor adventures. Whether your skills and interests call for mountain exhilaration, water exploration, or a land expedition, Grand Teton caters to everyone. Following is a brief description of the park's most popular summer activities. For more information, contact Grand Teton National Park at (307) 739-3300. Always remember to comply with all park guidelines.

Grand Teton National Park

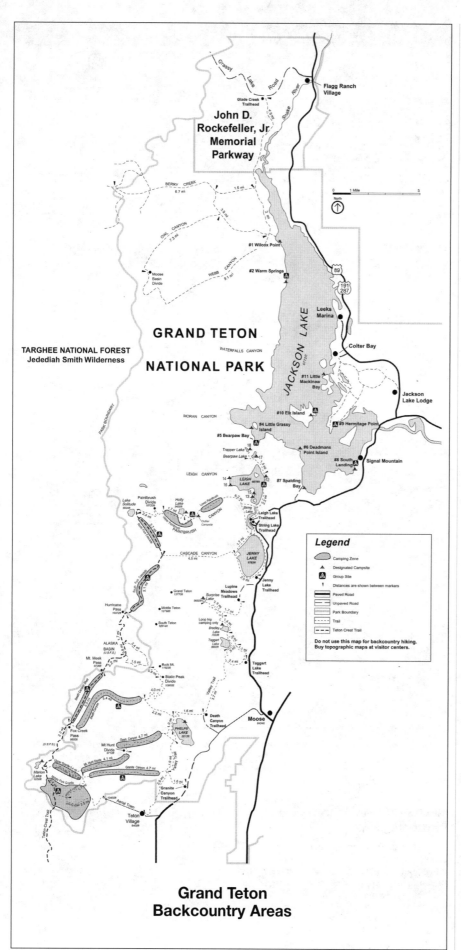

**Grand Teton
Backcountry Areas**

Backpacking/Backcountry Use

Possessing over 230 miles of scenic trails, Grand Teton National Park's backcountry draws hundreds of backpackers each year from across the world. While it may be tempting to take a spur of the moment trip to the park without making reservations, do not expect to access your top choice backcountry areas. Due to the backcountry's popularity, only a limited number of permits are granted each year, and camping reservations are required. Plan ahead, reserve a permit, and ensure that you see the areas you really want to see. For additional information and park guidelines, read the "Backcountry Use and Regulations" section found under the General Visitor Information heading, or contact the park directly.

The following backcountry routes offer some of the most popular backpacking trips in Grand Teton.

Cascade Canyon/Death Canyon: Traveling to Cascade Canyon and Death Canyon via the Static Peak Divide, visitors can access this trail at either the South Jenny Lake Trailhead or the Death Canyon Trailhead. The 24.8-mile trail requires two to three days to complete (one or two night stay).

Cascade Canyon/Paintbrush Canyon: This 19.2-mile loop trail is extremely popular during July and August, so users should plan accordingly. The trail begins at the String Lake Trailhead and requires two days to complete (one night stay).

Death Canyon/Cascade Canyon: Hikers access these canyons via the 29.5-mile Teton Crest Trail. Trailheads are available at the Death Canyon and String Lake parking areas, and hikers should plan three to four days to complete the trail (two to three night stay).

Death Canyon/Paintbrush Canyon: Following the Teton Crest Trail, this 36-mile hike is accessed at both the Death Canyon and String Lake parking areas. The hike requires four to five days to complete (three to four night stay).

Granite Canyon/Death Canyon: This 25.7-mile loop departs from the Granite Canyon parking area and follows the Valley Trail. The hike requires three days to complete (two night stay).

Granite Canyon/Open Canyon: Beginning at the Granite Canyon Trailhead, this 19.3-mile loop follows Valley Trail and requires two days to complete (one night stay).

Granite Canyon/Paintbrush Canyon: Following the Teton Crest Trail, this 37.9-mile hike can be accessed at the Granite Canyon Trailhead or the String Lake Trailhead. The hike takes five days to complete (four night stay).

Tram to Cascade Canyon: Accessible from both Teton Village and the South Jenny Lake Trailhead, this 28.5-mile hike follows the Teton Crest Trail. The hike takes three to four days to complete (two to three night stay), and a tram fee is charged.

Tram to Death Canyon: This 23.1-mile loop begins at Teton Village and follows the Valley Trail. The hike requires two to three days to complete (one to two night stay), and a tram fee is charged.

Tram to Granite Canyon: Following the Marion Lake trail, this 17.1-mile hike begins at Teton Village. The hike requires two days to complete (one night stay), and a tram fee is charged.

Bicycle Routes

GRAND TETON NATIONAL PARK

John D. Rockefeller, Jr. Memorial Parkway

Grassy Lake Road

Grassy Lake

Flagg Ranch Village

7.5 mi

16 mi

North

TETON RANGE

JACKSON LAKE

Colter Bay

Two Ocean Lake

Emma Matilda Lake

Two Ocean Lake Rd.

5 mi

Leigh Lake

String Lake

11 mi

3 mi

Jenny Lake

South Jenny Lake

Snake River Road

18 mi

Shadow Mountain Road

Bradley Lake

Taggart Lake

Teton Park Road

8 mi

Moose

Antelope Flats

Phelps Lake

Kelly

Gros Ventre River Road

Teton Village

8 mi

Paved road

Unpaved road

WARNING: Some roads in the park predate today's bicycling popularity. Most roads have a paved marked shoulder, providing limited space for safe bicycling. *Some roads have only a very narrow shoulder, or lack one altogether.* UsE EXTREME CAUTION.

Bicycling

Although Grand Teton possesses no formal bike paths and bicycling is strictly prohibited in the backcountry, biking is still one of the park's most popular activities. Nearly 100 miles of paved roads are available, and road pullouts provide impressive views of the park's crowning feature – the Teton Range. For those lacking their own equipment, bicycles are available for rent at Dornans'

Adventure Store in Moose and also at various sporting goods stores in nearby Jackson. Additional information about bicycling in the park may be obtained at the Colter Bay, Jenny Lake, or Moose Visitor Centers.

Bicyclists should note that many of the park's highways are narrow with little to no shoulder. To avoid any mishaps with those touring Grand Teton by vehicle, bicyclists should use extreme caution at all times and heed the following guidelines:

- Always wear highly visible clothing and helmets.
- Equip all bikes with reflective lighting.
- Remember that bikes are subject to the same traffic laws as vehicles.
- Riding bicycles abreast of one another on paved park roads is prohibited; all road bicyclists must ride single file on the highway's right side.
- Use hand signals to communicate your intentions to drivers and other bicyclists.
- Watch for motorists on Grand Teton's many blind curves.
- Avoid riding during April and May when high snowbanks make park highways even narrower than usual.
- Pack along plenty of water and snacks to maintain consistent energy levels.

For those bicyclists brave enough to tackle the narrow park highways, the following routes are often the most popular.

Teton Park Road: Winding from Moose through the park and into the John D. Rockefeller, Jr. Memorial Parkway, the Teton Park Road is a popular option for road bicyclists. The highway passes Jenny Lake and offers stunning views of the Teton Range's tallest peaks.

Antelope Flats/Kelly Area: Although no major highways run through this area, secondary paved routes are available here. The roads pass through sagebrush plateaus while offering unobstructed views of the Tetons.

Many Grand Teton bicyclists prefer to avoid the park's main highways and crowds. For these recreationists, the following mountain biking routes are highly recommended.

Grassy Lake Road: Originating slightly west of Flagg Ranch in the John D. Rockefeller, Jr. Memorial Parkway, Grassy Lake Road winds fifty-two miles to Ashton, Idaho. The route follows a historic Native American trail, and mountain bikers may choose to travel the trail in its entirety or just a portion.

River Road: This gravel trail is aptly named as it follows the Snake River's western bank from Signal Mountain to Cottonwood Creek. The fifteen-mile route is lined with wildlife, including bison, so maintain your distance from park animals to ensure your safety.

Two Ocean Lake Road: The three-mile Two Ocean Lake Road winds gently over rolling terrain from Pacific Creek Road to Two Ocean Lake. The dirt road is renowned for offering breathtaking park views.

Bird Watching

Boasting more than 300 species of birds, Grand Teton National Park provides a superb bird watching environment. While most bird watchers care greatly about the future of birds, some wildlife viewers are unaware of the general code of conduct governing this activity. Birds are easily disturbed, so maintain an appropriate distance, especially from nesting areas. If a bird squawks as you approach, you are likely too close to their nest and should back away. Areas home to abundant bird populations also frequently host other wildlife species. Remember to keep a minimum 300-foot distance from all large animals, and never come between a female and her young. For the best bird watching results and the safety of all concerned, use binoculars while viewing Grand Teton's intriguing bird species.

Day Hikes

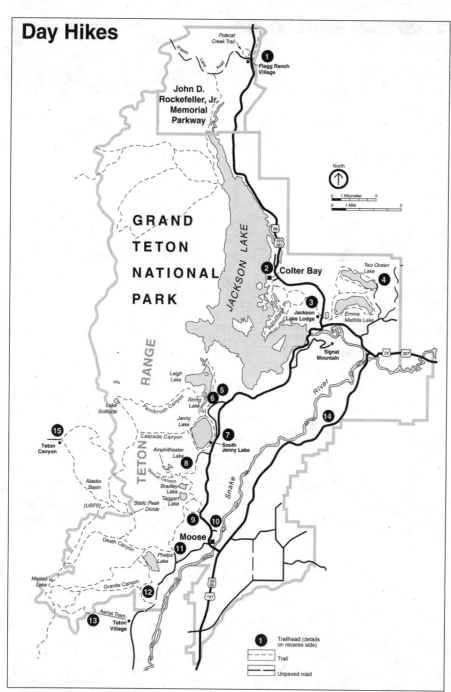

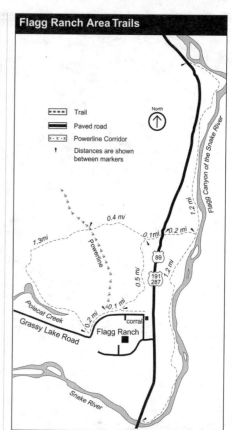

Flagg Ranch Area Trails

Trail

Paved road

Powerline Corridor

Distances are shown between markers

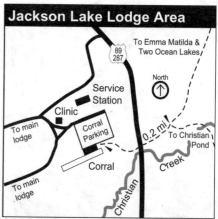

Jackson Lake Lodge Area

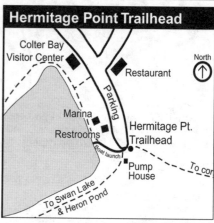

Hermitage Point Trailhead

Boating/Kayaking

Although mountains lay claim to most of the park's fame, water covers a large portion of Grand Teton National Park as well. Lakes, ponds, and the winding Snake River all provide plenty of opportunities for experiencing the park via water. From scenic cruises to sailboats, kayaks to motorboats, yachts to paddleboats, Grand Teton's waters are lined with all types of watercraft. While rental kayaks and canoes are available in Moose and nearby Jackson, visitors who bring their own personal watercraft into the park must register their boat and acquire a permit. Water recreationists are encouraged to contact the park prior to arrival for the latest boating regulations and fees.

Day Hiking and Recommended Routes

Overnight backpacking trips are by far more popular than day hiking Grand Teton, but day hikes provide a viable option for families with young children, those less physically fit, and individuals who simply do not want to take the time it requires to plan a successful backpacking trip in the park. Although these hikes do not necessitate overnight stays, visitors must still follow "Leave No Trace" ethics and be aware of bear safety regulations. The following are the most popular park day hikes with numbers corresponding to the accompanying map. Further information is available at the park's visitor centers and ranger stations.

Flagg Ranch Area

Flagg Canyon: Providing spectacular views of the

Snake River, this 5-mile roundtrip hike departs from the eastern side of the Polecat Creek Loop Trail. The easy trail climbs just forty feet and requires three to four hours to complete.

Polecat Creek Loop Trail: This easy 2.5-mile roundtrip trail traverses a marshy ridge and takes two hours to complete. Trail users should be alert for abundant area wildlife.

Colter Bay Area

Hermitage Point: The 8.8-mile roundtrip Hermitage Point Trail takes hikers through forests and meadows near streams and ponds. As a result, wildlife abounds on this easy trail requiring four hours to complete.

Heron Pond and Swan Lake: Requiring two hours to complete, this easy 3.0-mile roundtrip hike rises just forty feet in elevation before arriving at Heron Pond and Swan Lake. These water bodies harbor diverse bird species and wildlife.

Lakeshore Trail: This easy, level 2.0-mile roundtrip trail winds beside Colter Bay's northern and eastern shorelines. The trail also leads hikers to magnificent Teton Mountain views. The hike takes approximately one hour to complete.

Jackson Lake Lodge

Lunch Tree Hill: Possessing an appropriate name, this easy hike takes recreationists to a hilltop overlooking the Teton Mountains and Willow Flats. Interpretive signs highlight this 0.5-mile roundtrip hike that takes just thirty minutes to complete.

Two Ocean Lake Region

Emma Matilda Lake: Straddling the lakeshore, this

Backcountry travel is uncrowded and rewarding. NPS Photo.

9.1-mile roundtrip trail is noted for its stunning Teton vistas. The moderate hike climbs 440 feet and requires approximately five hours completion time.

Two Ocean Lake: Traveling through conifer forests, aspen groves, and lush meadows, this moderate 6.4-mile roundtrip trail requires approximately three hours to complete.

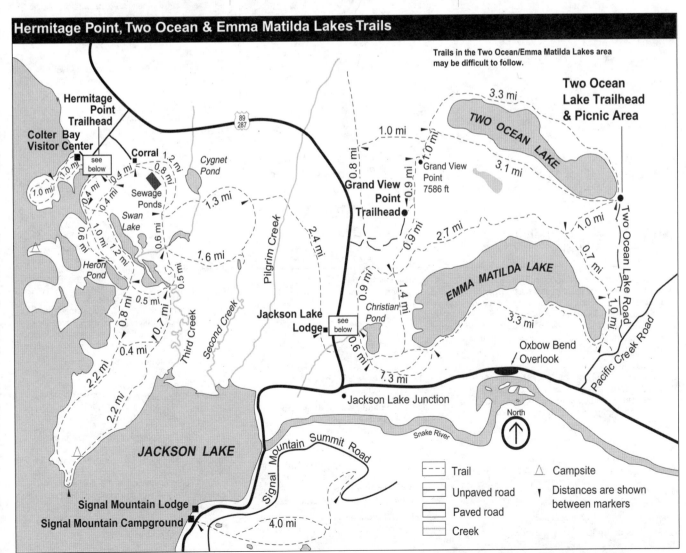

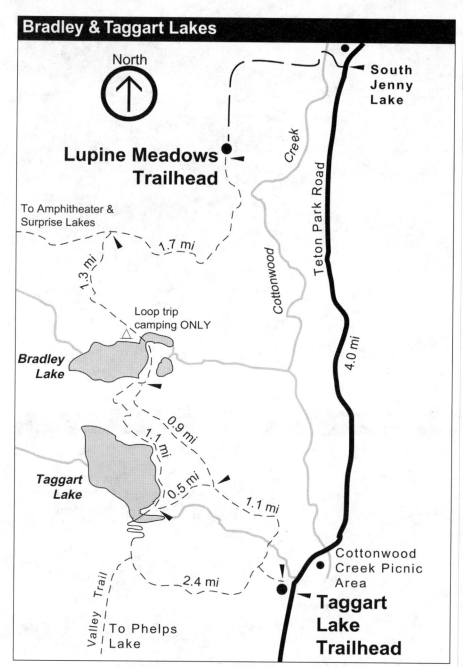

Bradley & Taggart Lakes

North

Lupine Meadows Trailhead

South Jenny Lake

To Amphitheater & Surprise Lakes

1.7 mi

1.3 mi

Loop trip camping ONLY

Bradley Lake

0.9 mi

1.1 mi

Taggart Lake

0.5 mi

1.1 mi

2.4 mi

Valley Trail

To Phelps Lake

Cottonwood Creek Picnic Area

Taggart Lake Trailhead

Cottonwood Creek

Teton Park Road

4.0 mi

roundtrip trail rises 150 feet and takes three hours to complete. Those who pay for a shuttle boat may access a 1.0-mile roundtrip version of this trail featuring the same elevation gain but an estimated completion time of just one hour.

Inspiration Point: From Hidden Falls, this trail climbs to an inspirational overlook of Jenny Lake. Gaining 417 feet and requiring four hours to complete, this trail measures in at 5.8-miles roundtrip. Those taking the fee shuttle boat take a 2.2-mile roundtrip hike to the same destination over the course of two hours.

Jenny Lake Loop: This easy, level trail features stunning Teton Mountain views over the course of a 6.6-mile roundtrip trail. Rising 100 feet, this hike takes approximately four hours to complete.

Lake Solitude: Featuring views of the Grand Teton and Mt. Owen on its path to Lake Solitude, this strenuous trail climbs 2,252 feet. Hikers can opt for a ten-hour, 18.4-mile roundtrip excursion or an eight-hour, 14.4-mile roundtrip trek via a paid shuttle boat.

South Fork of Cascade Canyon: This strenuous trail leads to views of Schoolroom Glacier on its 3,589-foot climb to Hurricane Pass. Hikers can opt for a twelve-hour, 23.2-mile roundtrip hike or an eleven-hour, 19.2-mile roundtrip trek via a paid shuttle boat.

Lupine Meadows
Amphitheater and Surprise Lakes: This strenuous hike to scenic alpine lakes gains 2,958 feet over the course of a 9.6-mile roundtrip trek. The strenuous trail requires approximately eight hours to complete. Please note that horses are prohibited on this route.

Garnet Canyon: Leading to Garnet Canyon's mouth, this 8.2-mile roundtrip hike climbs 2,160 feet. The strenuous hike takes seven hours to complete.

Taggart Lake Area
Bradley Lake: This moderate 4.0-mile roundtrip hike climbs 397 feet through a glacial moraine to Bradley Lake. The hike requires approximately three hours to complete.

Taggart Lake: Wandering through an area burned in 1985, this moderate 3.2-mile roundtrip trail features a 277-foot elevation change. The hike requires two hours to complete.

Taggart Lake and Beaver Creek: This 4.0-mile roundtrip hike winds through a 1985 burned area before ascending the glacial moraines cradling Taggart Lake. The moderate hike features a 277-foot elevation change and takes three hours to complete.

Chapel of the Transfiguration Area
Menor's Ferry: The 0.5-mile roundtrip Menor's Ferry Trail takes hikers to the Snake River banks and an original homestead. The easy hike climbs just ten feet and takes thirty minutes to complete.

Death Canyon and Surrounding Area
Death Canyon-Static Peak Trail Junction: Undertaking a strenuous course to Phelps Lake and into Death Canyon, this 7.6-mile roundtrip trail rises 1,061 feet. The difficult hike averages six hours to complete.

Phelps Lake Overlook: Two different trails provide two distinct overlook points of Phelps Lake. The moderate route gains 420 feet over the roundtrip course of 1.8 miles and takes two hours to complete. The more strenuous, 4.0-mile roundtrip route climbs 987 feet and averages four hours to complete.

Static Peak Divide: This incredibly strenuous 15.6-mile roundtrip trail passes through a whitebark

Two Ocean and Emma Matilda Lakes: This 12.9-mile roundtrip trail follows Two Ocean Lake's northern shoreline before climbing to Grand View Point and dropping to Emma Matilda Lake's southern shore. The trail then loops back to Two Ocean Lake. The moderately difficult trail rises 710 feet and requires approximately seven hours to complete.

Leigh Lake Area
Bearpaw Lake: Featuring views of nearby Mount Moran, this easy forested trail skirts Leigh Lake's shoreline. The 7.4-mile roundtrip hike gains just forty feet and requires four hours to complete.

Leigh Lake: This easy 2.0-mile roundtrip trail rises a mere forty feet and takes one hour to complete.

String Lake Region
Holly Lake: This strenuous trail features a 2,535-foot elevation change as it climbs through a wildflower-painted canyon. The 12.4-mile roundtrip trail takes eight hours to complete.

Paintbrush-Cascade Loop: The extremely strenuous 19.2-mile roundtrip Paintbrush-Cascade Loop trail

rises over Paintbrush Divide before dropping into Cascade Canyon. Featuring a 3,845-foot elevation gain, the trail takes fourteen hours to complete and generally requires hikers to use ice axes until early August.

String Lake: Under the shadow of Rockchuck Peak and Mt. St. John, this 3.3-mile roundtrip trail circles String Lake. The easy hike climbs approximately 120 feet and requires three hours to complete.

Cascade Canyon and Surrounding Area
Forks of Cascade Canyon: This moderately strenuous 13.0-mile roundtrip trail is extremely popular, leading hikers to views of Grand Teton, Mt. Owen, and Teewinot. The trail gains 1,057 feet and requires seven hours to complete. For those interested in paying for a shuttle boat, a shorter 9.0-mile roundtrip version of this trail rises just 105-feet and takes five hours to complete.

Hidden Falls: The Hidden Falls trail winds beside Jenny Lake's southern shore to a viewpoint of an impressive 200-foot-tall waterfall. The 5.0-mile

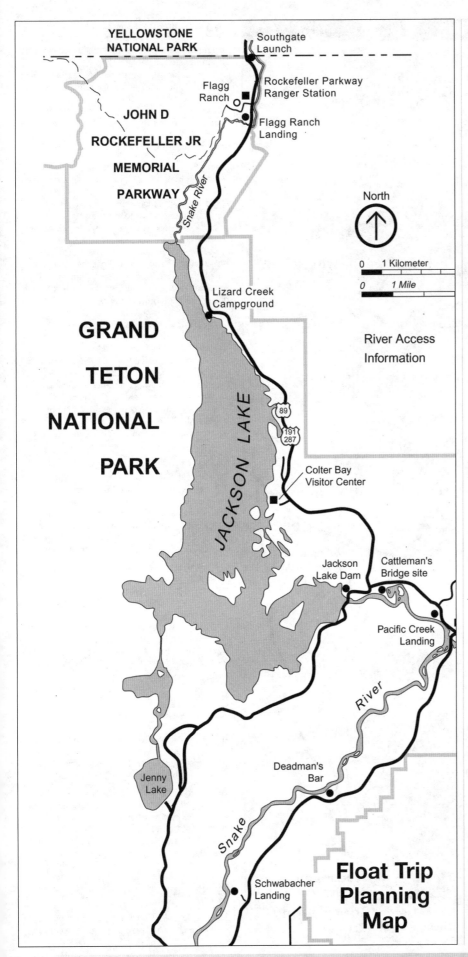

Float Trip Planning Map

GRAND TETON NATIONAL PARK

YELLOWSTONE NATIONAL PARK

Southgate Launch

JOHN D ROCKEFELLER JR MEMORIAL PARKWAY

Flagg Ranch

Rockefeller Parkway Ranger Station

Flagg Ranch Landing

Snake River

North

| 0 | 1 Kilometer |
| 0 | 1 Mile |

River Access Information

Lizard Creek Campground

JACKSON LAKE

89

191 287

Colter Bay Visitor Center

Jackson Lake Dam

Cattleman's Bridge site

Pacific Creek Landing

River

Jenny Lake

Deadman's Bar

Snake

Schwabacher Landing

pine forest as it steeply switchbacks up 4,020 feet. The trail provides panoramic views of the surrounding region and takes ten hours to complete. Hikers must also be comfortable using a variety of equipment, since ice axes are generally necessary until August.

Granite Canyon Area
Marion Lake: This strenuous 20.8-mile roundtrip hike climbs 2,880 feet to the subalpine meadows surrounding Marion Lake. The hike averages twelve hours to complete.

Tramway
These hikes require visitors to pay a small fee and ride a tram to the mountain summit. The following trails depart from the mountaintop and are accessible only after the majority of winter snow has melted.

Granite Canyon: Dropping 4,135 feet on this moderate downhill trail, hikers traverse through alpine meadows before arriving at Teton Village. The trail measures 12.4 miles and takes seven hours to complete.

Marion Lake: This moderately strenuous 11.8-mile roundtrip hike features a 1,206-foot elevation change. Hikers wind through alpine and subalpine flora before arriving at Marion Lake and returning to the tramway. The hike takes approximately seven hours to complete.

Cunningham Cabin Area
Cunningham Cabin: This easy 0.75-mile roundtrip hike features a mere twenty-foot elevation gain and leads to an early 1900s homestead. The hike takes just one hour to complete.

Teton Canyon Area
Targhee National Forest/Table Mountain: This strenuous trail follows Teton Creek on its 4,151-foot climb through Teton Canyon to the base of Table Mountain. The 11.0-mile roundtrip trail requires seven hours completion time, and those interested in ascending Table Mountain should be prepared to tackle a steep talus slope.

Fishing

Combining twenty-seven Snake River miles, numerous creeks, and the park's abundant lakes, Grand Teton is an angler's dream come true. Each of the park's water bodies is loaded with cutthroat trout, whitefish, and mackinaw, and prize catches more than fifty pounds have occasionally been reported. Average catches measure in between eighteen and twenty inches, and drift boats provide the most popular means of accessing the park's plentiful waters and fish.

The park does require all anglers to possess a valid Wyoming state fishing license, and anglers must obey all park fishing regulations. For those with little experience, professional guide services are available throughout the park and in nearby Jackson Hole.

Floating the Snake River

Lined with wildlife, including moose and soaring bald eagles, the twenty-seven-mile stretch of the Snake River passing through Grand Teton National Park offers an outstanding means of experiencing the area's abundant beauty. Although the river appears placid in most areas, logjams and numerous channels require floaters to be attentive at all times. Caution areas are frequently posted at park visitor centers and boat landings, so heed all warnings to ensure a safe float. Early spring runs are often the most dangerous due to increased snowmelt, high water depths, extremely cold water and air temperatures, and muddy water conditions that block floaters' abilities to

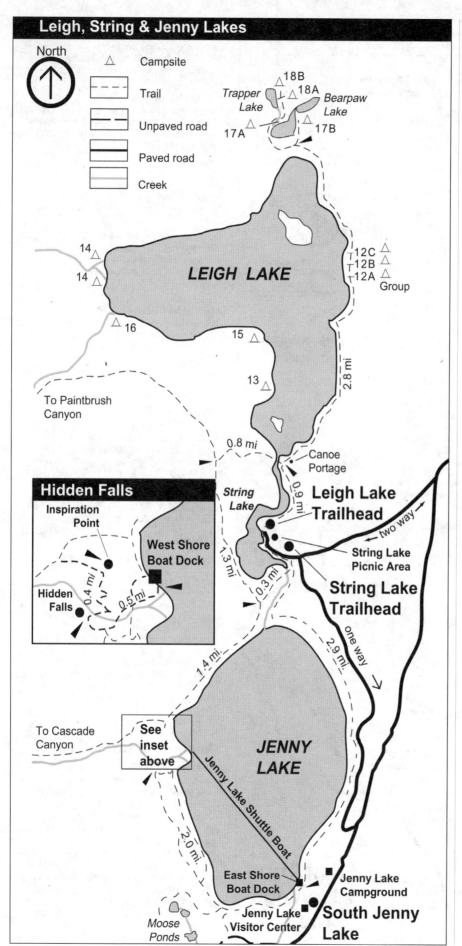

Leigh, String & Jenny Lakes

North

△ Campsite

---- Trail

Unpaved road

Paved road

Creek

Trapper Lake
Bearpaw Lake
18B
18A
17A
17B

14
14
16
15
13
12C
12B
12A
Group

LEIGH LAKE

2.8 mi

To Paintbrush Canyon

0.8 mi

Canoe Portage

String Lake

0.9 mi

Leigh Lake Trailhead

two way

String Lake Picnic Area

String Lake Trailhead

1.3 mi

0.3 mi

one way

2.9 mi

Hidden Falls

Inspiration Point

West Shore Boat Dock

0.4 mi

0.5 mi

Hidden Falls

1.4 mi

To Cascade Canyon

See inset above

JENNY LAKE

Jenny Lake Shuttle Boat

2.0 mi

East Shore Boat Dock

Jenny Lake Campground

Jenny Lake Visitor Center

Moose Ponds

South Jenny Lake

---

see river debris. Users should not, however, assume that late summer trips will be calm and peaceful. The Snake River maintains a consistently strong current.

The following river guidelines are aimed at helping floaters make the most of their Snake River experience. For those uncomfortable floating the river on their own, commercial rafting outfitters are available throughout the park and in nearby Jackson Hole with trip options ranging from scenic floats to raging whitewater.

River Etiquette and Regulations

Although hundreds of individuals float the Snake River every year, most still expect a peaceful experience where excessive noise from other floating parties ceases to exist. Ensure the pleasure of other floaters as well as wildlife's precious river habitat, and keep noise to a minimum. If you have any questions regarding this regulation, ask a ranger. Ranger patrol boats routinely frequent the Snake River and are equipped with two-way radios, first-aid supplies, and answers to visitor questions and concerns.

All boats must also carry a first-aid kit, trash/waste receptacle, a waterproof container filled with extra clothing, and an extra oar or paddle. Inflatable boats should include a patch kit, air pump, and a bucket for bailing water. In addition, individuals are reminded to pack along extra water and a water filtration system; river water is not safe to drink unless treated.

While swimming is not expressly prohibited, it is highly discouraged. The Snake River's surface is deceptively calm, and fast currents can easily sweep away inexperienced swimmers.

Beginner Level Trip Suggestions

Jackson Lake Dam to Cattleman's Bridge and Cattelman's Bridge to Pacific Creek: These two- and three-mile respective river stretches are known for their calm water, relatively little river debris, and scenic views. Due to faster currents around the Pacific Creek landing, floaters must dock approximately 100 yards upstream in shallower water.

Intermediate Level Trip Suggestions

Flagg Ranch to Lizard Creek Campground: Flowing ten miles total, this river section winds six miles from Flagg Ranch through the John D. Rockefeller, Jr. Memorial Parkway before entering Jackson Lake. While the last four miles of this trip are on Jackson Lake, floaters should not count on an easy finale. Strong afternoon winds can make paddling a challenge, and large waves have the potential to capsize small rafts and canoes. In addition to these challenges, the route can be difficult to navigate due to its braided channel characteristic.

Pacific Creek to Deadman's Bar: A significant river drop, increased current speed, and braided channels require floaters on this stretch to possess previous river rafting experience. This river stretch measures slightly over ten miles long, and floaters must feel comfortable in navigation.

Advanced Level Trip Suggestions

Deadman's Bar to Moose Landing: Featuring a series of complex river channels, raging currents, and steep river drops, this section of the legendary Snake accounts for more boating accidents than any other river course in Grand Teton National Park. Swift currents leave floaters with little time to maneuver, so individuals must be extremely confident in their boating skills on this ten-mile stretch.

Moose to South Park Boundary and Wilson: Since no takeout point is available at the park's southern

Phelps Lake

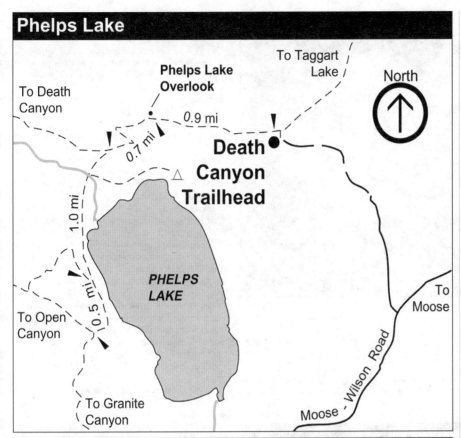

Phelps Lake Overlook

To Death Canyon

To Taggart Lake

North

0.9 mi

0.7 mi

Death Canyon Trailhead

1.0 mi

0.5 mi

PHELPS LAKE

To Open Canyon

To Moose

To Granite Canyon

Moose - Wilson Road

X-Country Ski Trails from Taggart Lake Parking Area

Jenny Lake

North

3.0 mi

2.8 mi

Cottonwood Creek

Snowmobiles and skiers share this trail

Bradley Lake

0.3 mi

0.7 mi

0.5 mi

1.1 mi

1.0 mi

1.2 mi

Taggart Lake

2.4 mi

Taggart Lake parking area

Taggart Lake Parking Area
Drive 4.5 mi. northwest of Moose Junction on the Teton Park Road to the Taggart Lake parking area at the end of the plowed road.

Jenny Lake Trail
Easy. Roundtrip: 7.6 mi., Elevation change: 100'. Follow the unplowed road 1/4-mile to Cottonwood Creek (be alert for snowmobiles), then ski north along the creek. The trail follows the west side of the creek and crosses several large meadows, then gently climbs a low ridge of glacial moraine and ends at an overlook of Jenny Lake. On clear days, the trail provides close views of the snow-draped peaks as it skirts the base of the Teton Range. The terrain is mostly level and is excellent for beginners. Skiing on Cottonwood Creek is not recommended. Return via the same trail. Another option is to follow the unplowed road (not flagged) to the east side of Jenny Lake (be alert for snowmobiles). To reach the flagged ski trail from the unplowed road, cross the bridge over Cottonwood Creek and head west along the edge of Jenny Lake.

Taggart Lake-Beaver Creek Loop
Difficult. Taggart Lake and return – roundtrip: 3.2 mi., elevation change: 277'. Taggart Lake/Beaver Creek Loop – roundtrip: 4 mi., elevation change: 397'. This loop through a forest that burned in 1985 has steep sections. From the parking area, ski directly toward the mountains. Turn north (right) and follow the trail as it climbs over the moraine (ridge of glacial debris). The trail forks in about one mile. The right fork climbs 0.7 mile for a view down to Taggart Lake. The left fork takes you directly to Taggart Lake nestled at the foot of the Tetons. If you return the way you came, you will encounter a steep, treelined section that is at times icy and treacherous, requiring downhill skiing ability. Another option from Taggart Lake is to turn south, cross the bridge over the lake outlet, and follow the trail that climbs the moraine. Then ski down the steep open slope and follow the trail to the east to return to the parking area.

X-Country Ski Trails from Moose-Wilson Road Area

Phelps Lake Overlook

0.9 mi

North

Death Canyon Trailhead

1.7 mi

PHELPS LAKE

To Moose

Moose - Wilson Road

Snowmobiles and skiers share this trail

2.0 mi

Teton Village

Moose-Wilson Road Area
The Moose-Wilson Road connects Moose and Teton Village, but plowing of the road ends one mile north of Teton Village. The trailhead for Phelps Lake is located 3.1 mi. south of Moose on the (west) right side of the Moose-Wilson Road and is accessible by vehicle only from Moose at the north end. The skiable section of the Moose-Wilson Road starts 6 mi. south of Moose and may also be reached by driving one mile north of Teton Village.

Phelps Lake Overlook
Moderate. Roundtrip: 5.2 mi., elevation change: 520'. The trail follows a narrow unplowed road through a forest of mixed conifers for the first 1.7 mi., making a

gradual ascent to the Death Canyon trailhead. Then the trail climbs westward through a lodgepole pine forest and over an open slope to reach the overlook of Phelps Lake framed by towering Douglas firs. Do not continue beyond the overlook because of high avalanche hazard. The return trip is all downhill. When the trail is well packed, skiing can be fast.

Moose-Wilson Road
Easy. Roundtrip: 4 mi., elevation change: 100'. Park at either end of this unplowed portion of road. The trail follows a winding unplowed road (be alert for snowmobiles) and is mostly flat but has enough changes in terrain and scenery to make it interesting. This trail through conifer and aspen forest is a good choice for beginners.

boundary, this river section flows twelve miles downstream from Moose to Wilson, Wyoming. Quick currents, braided river channels, significant route finding, and logjams all present hazardous difficulties to even the most experienced boaters.

Southgate to Flagg Ranch: Located one-half mile south of Yellowstone National Park's southern boundary, this river stretch flows three miles to Flagg Ranch. The steeply sloping river drops through a narrow passageway that fills each spring with large volumes of water, laterals, standing waves, and haystacks. During flows greater than 4,000 cfs, canoes are not recommended as rapids reach Class III and IV designation and can easily flip small vessels. Under 4,000 cfs, only highly experienced whitewater canoeists are recommended.

Horseback Riding

Stock use is restricted in several park areas, and grazing in the backcountry is never allowed. Nonetheless, horseback riding remains a popular means of getting off the main highway and catching a personalized look at the park's noteworthy scenery. Those owning stock are invited to bring their horses to Grand Teton as long as all park regulations and trail restrictions are followed. For those simply interested in a one or two hour scenic tour, trail rides are available from various vendors throughout the park and at nearby dude ranches in the Jackson Hole Valley.

Rock Climbing

The crowning peaks of Grand Teton National Park have long attracted thrill-seekers from around the world. Despite the mixed terrain that forces climbers to overcome year-round ice and snow, Grand Teton's peaks lure individuals with no experience to those at an expert level. For those with a limited skill base, park rangers recommend a few training courses at the local climbing school prior to summiting the peak. Always let someone know your route plan and intended return date, and acquire a free permit from the Jenny Lake Ranger Station if your climbing plans call for an overnight stay. Area guide services are available to assist those with no experience or climbers seeking to hone their existing skills.

Winter Activities

Grand Teton's roads generally close to vehicles and RVs on November 1, but by no means does park activity grind to a standstill. On the contrary, Grand Teton enjoys a surge of new activity as winter ushers in enthusiastic snowmobilers, snowshoers, and backcountry skiers. Although the park certainly does not see the massive influx of winter visitors to which Yellowstone is accustomed, Grand Teton attracts its fair share of snow-loving recreationists interested in seeing the park's quieter side.

Winter visitation, however, requires extra vigilance to safety. Since temperatures in Grand Teton can be bitterly cold, winter recreationists must dress in a layered clothing system. Wear long underwear, wool or synthetic pants, and wool or other insulated shirts. Thick wool socks, gloves, a hooded windproof parka, and a stocking cap are musts. Refrain from wearing jeans, cotton sweatshirts, cotton undershirts, and cotton socks, as they do not effectively wick moisture away from the body. Be sure to carry extra clothing as well as dark sunglasses and sunscreen. Even though temperatures may be below zero, the high altitude sunlight and reflection off pristine snow can cause

Grand Teton in winter. NPS Photo.

Cross-Country Skiing/Snowshoeing

The long winter months gracing Grand Teton National Park's serene landscape provide plenty of opportunity for snowshoers and cross-country skiers to explore the park's beautiful backcountry in peace and quiet. From steep downhill stretches to gently rolling plateaus to flat land, Grand Teton provides terrain for cross-country skiers and snowshoers of all abilities. For the less experienced or those simply interested in seeing the landscape at the hands of a park ranger, guided snowshoe hikes are available from the Moose Visitor Center December through March. Other area vendors licensed to lead park skiing and snowshoe tours include Jackson Hole Mountain Resort, The Hole Hiking Experience, Rendezvous Ski Tours, and NOLS/RMB.

While skiing or snowshoeing in Grand Teton's backcountry, visitors should know as much as possible about winter survival and be prepared for changing weather patterns, avalanche danger, deep snow, and unfrozen streams hidden under blankets of fresh snow. Those who ski or snowshoe should also dress appropriately for the park's harsh winter weather. Wear a layered clothing system, a wind and waterproof parka, warm gloves, and a stocking cap. Be prepared with extra clothes, plenty of water, and a large food supply.

When planning a winter cross-country ski or snowshoe trip, accommodate for shortened daylight hours, the experience and physical capabilities of trip participants, and expected temperature and weather patterns. Keep in mind that December and January trips are most difficult due to extremely cold temperatures and fairly continual snowfalls.

For additional information regarding park regulations, guided excursions, and winter safety precautions, contact Grand Teton National Park at (307) 739-3399.

Snowmobiling

Although not as popular in Grand Teton as in Yellowstone, snowmobiling still draws a loyal fan base to the park each winter. Controversy clouds the sport in Grand Teton as it does its northerly park neighbor, but snowmobilers still roar through the park on their quest to traverse the Continental Divide Snowmobile Trail (CDST).

The groomed CDST follows the plowed Outer Loop Road and connects Grand Teton with Yellowstone, Togwotee Pass, Lander, and Dubois. Featuring a short season dependent upon sufficient snow depth, the CDST averages just two months of operation. Snowmobilers may also access the unplowed portion of the Teton Park Road and any other designated unplowed routes, which are typically open from mid-December through mid-March. Snowmobiling on the frozen Jackson Lake, however, is discouraged due to unpredictable surface ice.

To maintain the presence of snowmobiles within Grand Teton, all users should bear in mind the following regulations and safety tips.

- All snowmobile operators must possess a valid driver's license, and all machines must be registered within their home state.

- Snowmobiles must feature working lights and brakes, and exhaust and mufflers must be in excellent operating condition to reduce park air pollution.

- Snowmobiles are subject to the same guidelines

---

serious sunburns.

Winter services are limited within the park's boundaries, and the Moose Visitor Center is sparsely staffed. As a result, make sure to pack along plenty of gas for snowmobiles, extra clothing, and food, and let somebody know your travel plans and expected return date. No matter the winter activity in which you engage, be alert for signs of hypothermia, and be prepared for all types of weather conditions. The following briefly describes popular winter activities in Grand Teton National Park.

X-Country Ski Trails from Colter Bay and Signal Mountain Areas

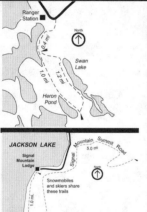

Colter Bay Area
Colter Bay is 10 mi. north of Moran Junction. Trailhead is located 300 ft. south of the Colter Bay Ranger Station. Park in front of the Ranger Station or near the trailhead on the spur road from the main highway.

Swan Lake-Heron Pond Loop
Easy. Roundtrip: 2.6 mi., elevation change: 40'. The trail first crosses an unplowed parking area, then passes the summer Hermitage Point Trailhead. Continue to the right of the trailhead sign and follow an old road for the first 0.4 mile. The trail then forks to either Swan Lake or Heron Pond. Ski 2.2 mi. in either direction on the gently sloping loop trail to return to this junction. Skiing on the ponds is not recommended. View the jagged Teton Range and Jackson Lake from the edge of Heron Pond. Beyond Heron Pond, unflagged trails lead to Hermitage Point; this loop adds 5.8 mi. (60' elevation) to the trip.

Signal Mountain Area
Signal Mountain is located 26 mi. north of Moose Junction (8 mi. west of Moran Junction). To reach the trailhead, follow Highways 26-89-191 north to Moran Junction, then 5.0 mi. west to Jackson Lake Junction and south 3.0 mi. on the Teton Park Road.

Signal Mountain Summit Road
Moderate. Roundtrip: 12 mi., elevation change: 700'. Park near Signal Mountain Lodge (closed in winter). Ski the unplowed road (be alert for snowmobiles) southward for approximately one mile until you reach the unplowed road that goes eastward (left) to the summit of Signal Mountain. The Signal Mountain Summit Road winds gradually uphill through conifer forests. The summit affords panoramic views of Jackson Hole and the Teton Range. The return trip is all downhill.

X-Country Ski Trails from Flagg Ranch Area

Flagg Ranch Area
Flagg Ranch is 26 mi. north of Moran Junction. The trailhead is located near the northwest corner of the Flagg Ranch parking area.

Polecat Creek Loop Trail
Easy. 2.5 mi., elevation change: 50'. Take the loop in either direction. The south side of the loop parallels the Grassy Lake road, which is open to snowmobiles. The west side of the loop follows a bench above Polecat Creek, kept open by thermal activity. The north and east sides of the loop traverse a dense conifer forest of lodgepole pines, sub-alpine firs and Engelmann spruce.

Flagg Canyon Trail North
Difficult. Roundtrip 4.0 mi., elevation change: 120'. Follow the east side of the Polecat Creek Loop Trail and travel north for 0.5 mi. Turn east (right) at the marked trail junction. The trail crosses the groomed snowmobile trail; use caution and watch for snowmobiles and snowcoaches. The flagged trail continues on the east side of the road and leads to the Flagg Canyon Trail, which follows the Snake River. Take the Flagg Canyon Trail north (left) to reach the South Gate of Yellowstone National Park. This section of trail contains a few short steep sections that can easily be avoided. **Use caution and avoid cornices where the trail follows the edge of the cliff above the Snake River.** Return via the same route or take the groomed snowmobile trail.

Flagg Canyon Trail South
Easy. Roundtrip 4.0 mi., elevation change: 40'. Reach the Flagg Canyon Trail as described for Flagg Canyon Trail north. At the junction with the Flagg Canyon Trail, turn south (right). The southern half of the Flagg Canyon Trail leads 1.2 mi. to end at the highway near the bridge over the Snake River. The trail follows rolling terrain and is suitable for beginners. Return via the same route.

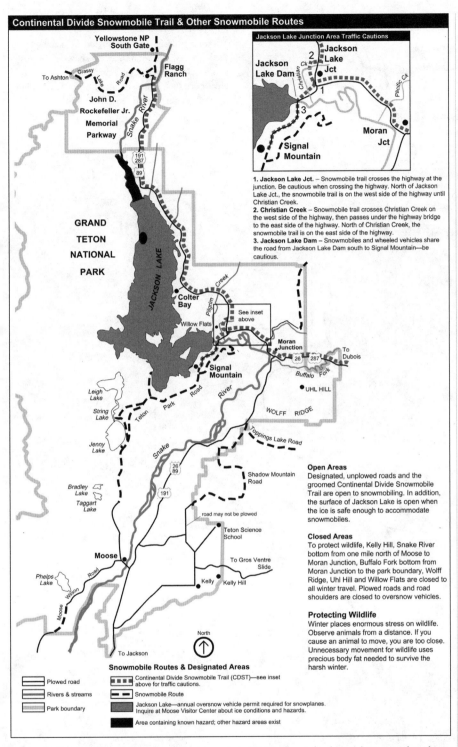

Continental Divide Snowmobile Trail & Other Snowmobile Routes

Jackson Lake Junction Area Traffic Cautions

1. **Jackson Lake Jct.** – Snowmobile trail crosses the highway at the junction. Be cautious when crossing the highway. North of Jackson Lake Jct., the snowmobile trail is on the west side of the highway until Christian Creek.

2. **Christian Creek** – Snowmobile trail crosses Christian Creek on the west side of the highway, then passes under the highway bridge to the east side of the highway. North of Christian Creek, the snowmobile trail is on the east side of the highway.

3. **Jackson Lake Dam** – Snowmobiles and wheeled vehicles share the road from Jackson Lake Dam south to Signal Mountain—be cautious.

Open Areas
Designated, unplowed roads and the groomed Continental Divide Snowmobile Trail are open to snowmobiling. In addition, the surface of Jackson Lake is open when the ice is safe enough to accommodate snowmobiles.

Closed Areas
To protect wildlife, Kelly Hill, Snake River bottom from one mile north of Moose to Moran Junction, Buffalo Fork bottom from Moran Junction to the park boundary, Wolff Ridge, Uhl Hill and Willow Flats are closed to all winter travel. Plowed roads and road shoulders are closed to oversnow vehicles.

Protecting Wildlife
Winter places enormous stress on wildlife. Observe animals from a distance. If you cause an animal to move, you are too close. Unnecessary movement for wildlife uses precious body fat needed to survive the harsh winter.

Snowmobile Routes & Designated Areas

- Plowed road
- Rivers & streams
- Park boundary
- Continental Divide Snowmobile Trail (CDST)—see inset above for traffic cautions.
- Snowmobile Route
- Jackson Lake—annual oversnow vehicle permit required for snowplanes. Inquire at Moose Visitor Center about ice conditions and hazards.
- Area containing known hazard; other hazard areas exist

Wolff Ridge, Uhl Hill, Kelly Hill, the Snake River bottom north of Moose to Moran Junction, and the Buffalo Fork River bottom from the park boundary to Moran Junction.

For additional information about snowmobiling Grand Teton, contact the Moose Visitor Center, the Flagg Ranch Information Station, or call (307) 739-3612. Information boards at the park's East Entrance, Signal Mountain, and Flagg Ranch's Snake River Bridge also provide valuable trail conditions, contact numbers, and weather data. To ensure a safe and memorable snowmobiling trip, plan ahead and be prepared for all weather possibilities.

Grand Teton's Junior Ranger/Young Naturalist Program. NPS Photo.

GRAND TETON FOR KIDS

Imagine the awe of seeing a beautiful mountain landscape for the first time. Glimmering peaks, shadowy forests, raging rivers, idyllic lakes, grazing wildlife. Now picture yourself glimpsing this setting through the absorbent eyes of a transfixed child. Grand Teton is no doubt a spectacular scene to adult visitors, but the park's wondrous beauty captivates children with an unexplainable attraction. Over the years, park rangers have noted this magnetic appeal and the curiosity of the park's youngest visitors. In response, the National Park Service has tailored some of its Grand Teton National Park offerings to the wide-eyed wonder of children.

Junior Ranger/Young Naturalist Program

Receiving an enthusiastic response from children across America, Grand Teton's Junior Ranger/Young Naturalist Program is one of the park's most popular activities. Utilizing "The Grand Adventure" activity guide, children watch wildlife, scour park terrain for animal tracks, refrain from feeding all animals, pick up litter and properly dispose of it in trash receptacles, and always model ranger-like behavior. After completing every activity in the guide and attending one Young Naturalist Program (ages 8-12) or two ranger-led programs, participants take their completed activity guide and a $1 donation to the Moose, Colter Bay, or Jenny Lake Visitor Center. There, eligible children take the Young Naturalist Pledge and receive a special patch signifying a lifelong dedication to protecting and preserving Grand Teton National Park.

In addition to this popular children's program, several summer ranger-led activities are geared towards young participants. Teewinot, the park's newspaper, provides a complete listing of these activities, including dates and times for scheduled

---

as cars. Always use hand signals to stop or turn, drive single file on the road's right side, pass only when visibility is high, and obey all traffic signs.

- Never stray from designated routes. Off-road travel, including sidehilling and berm-riding, is strictly prohibited and punishable with a hefty fine.

- Snowmobiling and alcohol do not mix, and those driving while intoxicated will be caught and charged. Any open alcoholic beverage container is also illegal, including the popular botabags.

- Since they are permanent park residents, Grand Teton's wildlife always have the right of way. Never approach, feed, or chase the wildlife.

Winter alone is hard enough on animals without wildlife being forced to exert energy to quickly move off the road.

- If wildlife blocks the roadway, stop no less than twenty-five yards away, and wait for them to move. If the animal begins walking toward you, turn around and move to a different location. If you do not have time to turn around, step off your machine; protect yourself by keeping the machine between you and the wildlife. In all cases, never attempt to pass animals if they appear agitated. In such scenarios, animals are likely to charge, and your safety is at risk.

- In an effort to protect wildlife, the following park areas are closed to snowmobiles: Willow Flats,

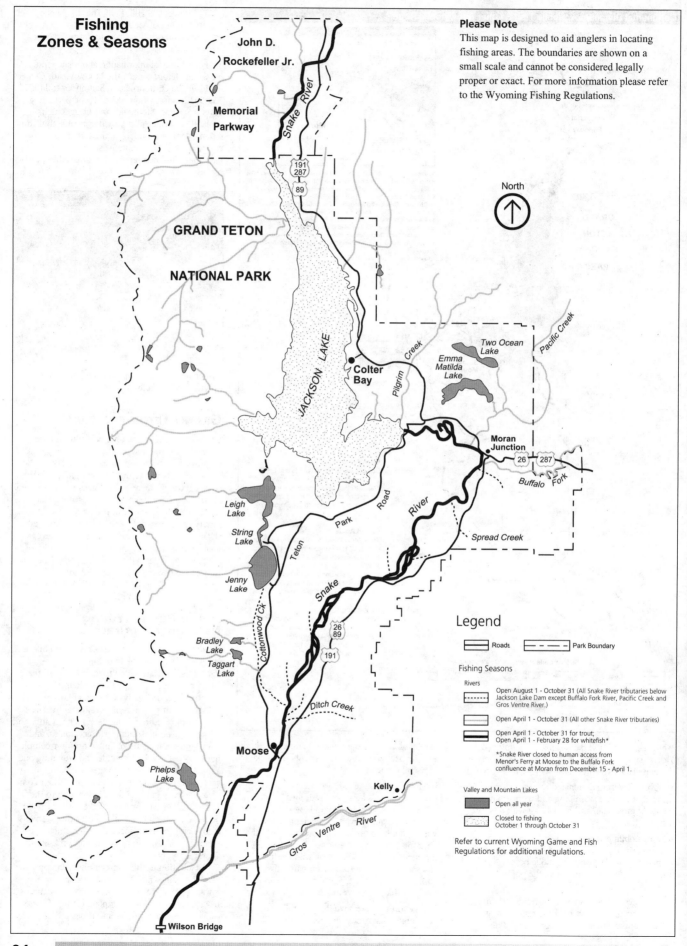

Fishing Zones & Seasons

John D.
Rockefeller Jr.

Memorial
Parkway

Snake River

191
287

89

GRAND TETON

NATIONAL PARK

JACKSON LAKE

Colter
Bay

Pilgrim Creek

Two Ocean
Lake

Emma
Matilda
Lake

Pacific Creek

Moran
Junction

26   287

Buffalo Fork

Leigh
Lake

String
Lake

Jenny
Lake

Park Road

River

Spread Creek

Teton

Snake

Cottonwood Ck

26
89

191

Bradley
Lake

Taggart
Lake

Ditch Creek

Moose

Phelps
Lake

Kelly

Gros Ventre River

Wilson Bridge

Please Note

This map is designed to aid anglers in locating fishing areas. The boundaries are shown on a small scale and cannot be considered legally proper or exact. For more information please refer to the Wyoming Fishing Regulations.

North

Legend

Roads

Park Boundary

Fishing Seasons

Rivers

Open August 1 - October 31 (All Snake River tributaries below Jackson Lake Dam except Buffalo Fork River, Pacific Creek and Gros Ventre River.)

Open April 1 - October 31 (All other Snake River tributaries)

Open April 1 - October 31 for trout;
Open April 1 - February 28 for whitefish*

*Snake River closed to human access from Menor's Ferry at Moose to the Buffalo Fork confluence at Moran from December 15 - April 1.

Valley and Mountain Lakes

Open all year

Closed to fishing
October 1 through October 31

Refer to current Wyoming Game and Fish Regulations for additional regulations.

events. The newspaper also features suggestions for family-related park activities of interest to both adults and children.

SCENIC DRIVES

While some people prefer exploring Grand Teton National Park with a solitary backcountry hike, most visitors cling to the comfort, convenience, and safety of their car. Luckily, those opting to spend most of their park visit in a vehicle are rewarded with a variety of scenic park drives capturing Grand Teton's beautiful mountains, forests, and wildlife inhabitants.

While traversing any scenic route, drivers should avoid stopping in the middle of the highway. Instead, use roadside pullouts for viewing wildlife and natural wonders. Drivers should also note that traffic generally moves at a snail's pace, so take advantage of the decreased speed to truly appreciate the scenery. At all times, watch for other vehicles, wildlife on the road, and bicyclists, and leave plenty of time to thoroughly enjoy the scenic driving experience. The following drives are the most popular within and near Grand Teton National Park's boundaries.

John D. Rockefeller, Jr. Memorial Parkway

Linking Yellowstone's southern boundary with the northern border of Grand Teton National Park, the 23,770-acre John D. Rockefeller, Jr. Memorial Parkway encompasses a scenic 6.8-mile drive. The highway is lined with thick forests, rising steam from nearby hot springs, and beautiful Teton Mountain views to the north. Flagg Ranch, the Teton Wilderness, Bridger-Teton National Forest, Huckleberry Mountain, and the Grassy Lake Reclamation Road are popular area attractions, and permit camping is available. The route is open year-round and takes ten minutes to drive when traffic is moving at a decent rate. To accommodate summer's congested highway scene, however, drivers should budget twenty minutes for this drive.

Teton Park Road

Also known as the Inner Loop Road, the thirty-seven-mile Teton Park Road extends from Moose to the park's northern boundary at the John D. Rockefeller, Jr. Memorial Parkway entrance. The route boasts captivating scenery as it continually cuts a path near the base of the Teton Mountain Range. Along the way, individuals may visit Menor's Ferry, Colter Bay Village, Taggert Lake, Jenny Lake, Leigh Lake, and Jackson Lake with easy hiking access to numerous alpine sites. Since stopping to enjoy the views and attractions is inevitable along this scenic drive, the time required to tour depends upon individual travel style and sightseeing preferences. On average, this drive with no stops consumes a minimum one hour, so plan accordingly. The route is open late May through late October depending on the weather. On this drive, visitors may view nearly every peak in the Teton Range. The following lists the individual peaks contained within the Rocky Mountain's youngest range along with the meaning behind each mountain's name.

Rendezvous Peak (10,450 feet): Situated just south of the park's southern entrance, this peak memorializes the region's early mountain men settlers and their traditional rendezvous activity.

Mount Hunt (10,783 feet): Named after Wilson Price Hunt who led an 1811 exploration party

across rugged Teton Pass, this mountain is located just inside the park's southern border.

Static Peak (11,303 feet): Rising parallel to the Moose Entrance Station, this peak and its dynamic name mirror a lightning rod's static-electricity property.

Buck Mountain (11,938 feet): George Buck served as recorder for the 1898 Thomas M. Bannon mapping party. This mountain, situated directly across from the Moose entrance, recognizes Buck's contributions to the exploratory group and the discovery of this region.

Mount Wister (11,490 feet): Tucked slightly behind Buck Mountain, this peak honors author Owen Wister, who spent some of his life living in the area. The early twentieth-century novelist wrote about Jackson Hole in his famous novel The Virginian.

South Teton (12,514 feet): The South Teton rises dramatically from the lush valley floor and is best viewed from Idaho's Teton Valley stretching between Ashton and Driggs.

Nez Perce (11,700 feet): This peak draws its name from the Native American tribe that once roamed this region. The term itself means "pierced nose" and reflects the traditional piercings worn by Nez Perce tribes. The lofty peak partially eclipses park views of South Teton.

Middle Teton (12,700 feet): Vertical black diabase ornaments this peak's eastern face, making it highly distinguishable from the rest of the range's towering pinnacles.

Grand Teton (13,770 feet): Reigning supreme over the range's other jagged marvels, the Grand Teton is Wyoming's second tallest peak and draws its name from French-Canadian fur trappers. While working for the Hudson Bay Company, these lonely trappers associated the peak and the Middle and South Teton with women's breasts (Trois Tetons). Although the name remains, present-day association centers upon mountain climbing. More than 2,000 climbers tackle the horn-shaped peak annually, and glaciers cover a portion of the summit year-round.

Mount Owen (12,928 feet): W.O. Owen, Bishop Spalding, and a few other area homesteaders successfully climbed Grand Teton in 1889. Since Grand Teton was already named, Mount Owen remembers their early feat. The peak rests just slightly behind Grand Teton.

Teewinot (12,325 feet): Meaning "many peaks" in the Shoshone Native American language, Teewinot generally blocks all highway views of Mount Owen.

Mount St. John (11,430 feet): This mountain is actually a sequence of several peaks all measuring approximately the same height. The name is taken from Orestes St. John, the 1877 Hayden Survey geologist who was one of the first to write about Wyoming's northern mountain ranges.

Rockchuck Peak (11,144 feet): Marmots commonly referred to as rockchucks or woodchucks inhabit this rocky skyscraper. As a result of their prolific presence, these creatures' mountain habitat bears their name.

Mount Woodring (11,590 feet): Serving as a Yellowstone National Park Ranger during the 1920s, Samuel Woodring later became Grand Teton National Park's first superintendent. The peak commemorates Woodring's role in the park's formative years.

Thor Peak (12,028 feet): Possessing an imposing

appearance, Thor Peak draws its name from the Scandinavian "God of Thunder." Neighbor Mount Moran overshadows Thor's visibility to highway drivers.

Mount Moran (12,605 feet): Thomas Moran, famous 1800s landscape artist who painted stunning portraits of Yellowstone's phenomena, lends his name to this radiant peak. Moran was influential in persuading government officials to establish Yellowstone National Park, which in turn paved the path for America's National Park Service and future park development.

Bivouac Peak (10,825 feet): Bivouac Peak conjures remembrances of an early park climbing adventure. Equipped with previous mountaineering experience, local residents Fritiof Fryxell and Gustav and Theodore Koven decided to scale this daunting peak's western summit. After miscalculating the time needed to complete their trek, the Kovens bivouacked for the night without food or bedding. Meanwhile, the Kovens' friend left them behind with little thought to their situation and headed to Jenny Lake. For his error in judgment, Fryxell christened the peak after his friends who rejoined him the next day.

Eagles Rest (11,258 feet): Although it may be presumed that eagles nest atop this lofty summit, the official reasoning behind this peak's name remains a mystery.

Doane Peak (11,354 feet): Doane Peak honors an 1870 Langford Expedition member who curiously explored and documented the marvels of what now encompasses Yellowstone National Park.

Ranger Peak (11,355 feet): The final peak in the famous Teton Mountains, Ranger Peak's name remains a mystery. Many speculate the peak rightly honors the service and dedication of America's past and present park rangers.

Jackson Lake Junction to Jackson, Wyoming

The thirty-four-mile route leading from Jackson Lake Junction to Jackson, Wyoming is commonly known as the Outer Loop Road and connects with the Inner Loop Road to make a complete park tour. Following U.S. Highway 26/89/191, the year-round route is an extension of the highway running through the John D. Rockefeller, Jr. Memorial Parkway. The scenic road winds beside the Snake River, providing lush valley scenery as the Teton Range rises majestically in the distance. In addition, the route is reputed for Oxbow Bend, the Gros Ventre slide area, Blacktail Butte, the historic Cunningham homestead, and numerous dude ranches. Outdoor enthusiasts along the route enjoy rafting, fishing, wildlife viewing, and camping while the Bridger-Teton National Forest and several mountain lakes are easily accessible. The highway eventually leads to the National Fish Hatchery, a National Elk Refuge, and all the entertainment and amenities of an old west town dressed up in its finest splendor to greet the tourists. (Yes, Jackson really was an old cow town before cleaning itself up for the crowds and skiers.) Depending on the number of stops drivers make, this popular route takes anywhere from thirty-five minutes to more than a day to complete.

Jenny Lake Scenic Drive

Hugging Jenny Lake's shores, this short drive offers unbeatable lake views framed inside a picture-perfect mountain backdrop. The tour begins at North Jenny Lake and proceeds southwest to

Sunset Lake on Teton Crest Trail. NPS Photo.

Cathedral Group Turnout views of the Grand Teton, Teewinot Peak, and Mt. Owen. From here, the two-way route travels to String Lake and Jenny Lake Lodge where it becomes a single-lane road. The relaxing lakeshore drive eventually ends near South Jenny Lake where the route rejoins the Teton Park Road (Inner Loop Road). The road is open May through October depending on the weather.

Signal Mountain Summit Road

Winding 800 feet to the top of Signal Mountain, this five-mile drive provides renowned valley vistas. The drive begins immediately south of Signal Mountain Lodge and Campground and follows a narrow road to an overlook of the Teton Range, Jackson Lake, and the Jackson Hole Valley. Since the road is winding and features limited summit parking, RVs and vehicles pulling trailers are prohibited. Depending on the weather, the route is open May through October.

Moran Junction to Dubois, Wyoming

This fifty-five mile drive crosses widely varied terrain on its short journey from Grand Teton National Park's Moran Junction to the western town of Dubois. Forested hillsides, mountain vistas, stratified rocks, sage-covered buttes, colorful sandstone, and historical markers await as the route twists its way up and over Togwotee (Toh-Gah-dee) Pass on U.S. Highway 287/26. Special attractions include the Wind River Range, Absaroka Mountains, the Shoshone National Forest, Bridger-Teton National Forest, the Teton and Washakie National Wilderness Areas, the National Bighorn Sheep Interpretive Center, and Tie Hack Memorial. In addition to camping, hiking, and fishing, convenient access is also available to Washakie Needles, the National Fish Hatchery, Turpin Meadow Recreation Area, Jackson Hole Ski Resort, Brooks Lake, and Brooks Lake Creek Falls. The

year-round route offers the best driving conditions during summer and early fall due to heavy winter snows and late spring storms. Drivers should budget at least one hour and fifteen minutes to complete this tour depending on the number of stops one intends to make.

Wilson, Wyoming to Moose, Wyoming

Following Wyoming Highway 390 and known locally as the Teton Village Road or Moose-Wilson Road, this sixteen-mile route is a picturesque country drive intended for the laid-back traveler. Lush hillsides, colorful wildflowers, babbling brooks, narrow wooden bridges, and natural roadside canopies of aspen, fir, and pine line the two-lane road. Featuring a mix of pavement and gravel, the route is also recognized for Sawmill Ponds, access to remote hiking areas, and willow marshes showcasing abundant populations of grazing moose. The road eventually ends near the park's southern entrance station at Moose. The paved portion of the road travels to Teton Village and is open year-round while the connecting gravel road leading to Moose is only open during summer. Those in a hurry should avoid this route, as the country drive takes at least forty-five minutes to complete.

TOURING GRAND TETON

Given Grand Teton National Park's relatively small size, touring the park in a single day is not impossible. A single-day visit treats individuals to a brief taste of the park's main attractions and mountain glory. For those with extra time, however, a longer park stay is highly encouraged. Multi-day trips allow plenty of time to savor the park's highlights, take a hike away from the crowds, tour visitor centers, discover the area's history and culture, and opt for a memorable recreational adventure. The following offers brief tour suggestions as well as an in-depth look at the park's major regions and visitor attractions.

Highlights for the Hurried Traveler

No matter where tourists travel in Grand Teton National Park or how many times they visit, the jagged mountain masterpiece lining the western horizon generally dominates every individual's focus. Although the peaks certainly paint a picture-worthy scene, Grand Teton offers several other highly memorable sites, including museums, lakes, scenic drives, hikes, and more. For those on a tight schedule, the National Park Service recommends the following activities. This tour begins in Colter Bay, south of the John D. Rockefeller, Jr. Memorial Parkway in the park's northern region. All stops may be visited within one day's time.

Colter Bay Visitor Center and Indian Arts Museum

The Indian Arts Museum at the Colter Bay Visitor Center captures the essence of nineteenth century Native American living. Visitors are privy to Native American art, wildlife films, park orientation programs, museum tours, natural history hikes, and summer evening amphitheater discussions.

Willow Flats

Located six miles south of Colter Bay with the mighty Tetons and Jackson Lake swirling together in one scenic backdrop, the marshy Willow Flats provides exceptional wildlife terrain. Birds, moose, and beaver densely populate this freshwater region, and wildlife sightings are frequent. Be sure to bring your camera!

Teton Park Road

A favorite among all national park scenic drives, Teton Park Road offers the quintessential view of the famous Teton Mountain Range. Also known as the Inner Loop Road, the route travels from Jackson Lake Junction to the Moose Visitor Center. The road provides endless scenery and access to several park highlights.

Jackson Lake Dam Overlook

Jackson Lake Dam is situated alongside Teton Park Road just one mile west of Jackson Lake Junction. Although the lake formed as a product of glacial activity, the manmade dam has now enlarged the lake into a full-fledged reservoir. The lake is a heavily trafficked boating and fishing destination, while the dam offers visitors a scenic vantage of Mount Moran.

Oxbow Bend

This twisting Snake River channel one mile east of Jackson Lake Junction is known for harboring wildlife and impressive views. Mount Moran gleams in the distance as deer, moose, and beaver live under the watchful eye of eagles and great blue herons.

Signal Mountain Summit Road

The five-mile Signal Mountain Summit Road climbs 800 feet to an impressive panoramic overlook of the Teton Mountains, Jackson Hole, and Jackson Lake. The winding, narrow road begins one mile south of the Signal Mountain Lodge and Campground.

South Jenny Lake

Cradled at the foot of the Teton Mountains, glacially sculpted South Jenny Lake is a mecca for sightseeing and recreation. In addition to a six-mile hiking trail that circles the lake's circumference, the area also provides shuttle boat tours transporting visitors to the lake's western shore. From here, visitors may hike to Cascade Canyon, Inspiration Point, and Hidden Falls. For the best scenery and least crowded trail conditions, plan to visit South Jenny Lake early in the morning or late in the afternoon.

Jenny Lake Scenic Drive
The Jenny Lake Scenic Drive begins at North Jenny Lake and continues to Cathedral Group Turnout where Grand Teton, Mount Owen, and Teewinot Peak radiate in their abundant natural beauty. The drive then parallels the lakeshore and eventually reconnects with Teton Park Road at South Jenny Lake.

Menor's Ferry and Chapel of the Transfiguration
Preserving the 1800s and 1900s homesteading history of Wyoming pioneers, Menor's Ferry is situated 0.5 miles north of Moose. A short trail leads visitors to Bill Menor's historic cabin, general store, and Snake River ferry. Although the original ferry has long since decayed into history, today's visitors may ride a replica ferry and imagine the lifestyle and hardships the region's early settlers endured.

In addition to Menor's Ferry, the Chapel of the Transfiguration is also located in this vicinity. The chapel hosts numerous summer weddings and showcases phenomenal Teton Mountain views.

Antelope Flats-Kelly Loop and the Gros Ventre Slide
The Antelope Flats-Kelly Loop takes visitors to the quaint town of Kelly as it passes historic ranches and hayfields. To access this area known for its grazing bison, bear east off U.S. Highway 26/89/191 five miles south of Moose Junction. The Gros Ventre Slide popularizes this region and can be found on a marked National Forest access road. The slide, which dammed the Gros Ventre River and created Lower Slide Lake, resulted when rain and a series of earthquakes shattered Sheep Mountain's northern end. The road eventually rejoins Highway 26/89/191.

Discovering Northern Grand Teton: Jackson Lake and Beyond
For most visitors, Grand Teton National Park's northern boundary offers the first glimpse into this mountainous wonderland. Yellowstone tourists hungry for additional sights and armed with a seven-day Yellowstone/Grand Teton park pass wind their way through the scenic John D. Rockefeller, Jr. Memorial Parkway, eager to see what wonders await in this Wyoming park. As expected, Grand Teton National Park lives up to its legendary reputation. Welcomed by Flagg Ranch Village, visitors are met with an array of amenities, activities, and numerous scenic sites in the park's northern region.

Jackson Lake and Jackson Lake Dam
Encompassing a huge crater left behind in the region's glacial sculpting process, the thirty-one square mile Jackson Lake has been dammed to substantially increase the lake's recreational and agricultural value. The massive seventeen-mile long lake dominates the park's northern landscape and provides valuable irrigation water to eastern Idaho farmers. As the highway skirts the lake's eastern shore, islands dot the deep blue waters, wildlife intermingles with recreationists, and summer boat rentals, scenic tours, and breakfast and dinner cruises offer a memorable means of experiencing the lake. Anglers also frequent the lake for exceptional year-round trout fishing. Although lake paddling receives considerable use on Jackson Lake, park rangers recommend that paddlers and floaters stay close to shore. Jackson Lake is lined with motorboats during summer, and sailboats, windsurfers, jet-skis, and water skiers populate the lake's surface, making it a fairly congested scene.

In addition to the lake, the dam itself deserves a visit. After the original log dam washed away in 1910, an earthen dam was built as a replacement. However, fears regarding the dam's stability forced park officials to create a sturdy concrete structure between 1914 and 1916. In 1989, the dam site was overhauled once again, ensuring that the dam was earthquake proof and heightening the lake's storage capacity to its current 425-foot depth. Today, the dam provides excellent views of the surrounding area, and interpretive signs overlooking the dam give insightful historical tidbits. A hidden treasure often overlooked, a small picnic area and boat launch awaits unsuspecting visitors near the dam's base.

Leeks Marina
Leeks Marina takes advantage of its ideal location on Jackson Lake's eastern shore. The area features several scenic pullouts perfect for a quick lakeside picnic, and a boat launching area and overnight buoys provide convenient access to the park's favorite recreational lake. In addition, Leeks Marina offers visitors a casual restaurant during summer where pizza appears to be the crowd's favorite fare.

Colter Bay Area
Named after the legendary John Colter, the area's presumed first white explorer, Colter Bay Recreation Area is brimming with all the resources and activities visitors need in one location. From lodging, dining, and camping on Jackson Lake's shores to boat rentals, convenience stores, gas, shopping, and fishing, Colter Bay offers enough activities to keep the whole family entertained for an entire week.

The Colter Bay Visitor's Center provides individuals with an introduction to the park's amenities and Colter Bay activities. Introductory slide programs, park wildlife videotapes, natural history hikes, ranger-led discussions, and summer evening amphitheater programs are designed to enhance visitors' park experiences. In addition to these offerings, the Colter Bay Indian Arts Museum offers Navajo and Plains Indians artifacts with items ranging from war clubs and dolls to historic photos and peace pipes.

Hermitage Point
Nestled near Colter Bay on Jackson Lake, Hermitage Point is a densely forested peninsula offering scenic lake views. The isolated point rests just 3.25 miles from Colter Bay, and the access trail passes through thick timber stands and wildflower meadows. The point and trail remain relatively uncrowded, even during the busy summer season, so peace and quiet abounds along with bears. Contact the nearest ranger station regarding bear activity prior to departing on this hike.

Jackson Lake Lodge
Situated near Jackson Lake's shoreline with easy hiking access to other nearby lakes, Jackson Lake Lodge affords a convenient visitor base camp in the park's northern region. Area wildlife sightings are frequent, and moose inhabit the brushy landscape surrounding the lodge. Restaurants in all styles and price ranges, accommodations, and shopping provide plenty of indoor discovery. For the more adventurous, the lodge hosts horseback riding tours and scenic float trips. Visitors may also opt for a lunch or dinner cookout as part of their river float, and guided angling trips are available by reservation.

Mount Moran
Framed in Jackson Lake Lodge's picture windows, Mount Moran dominates northern Grand Teton's skyline. The massive peak encompasses over fifteen acres with its flat summit and measures 600 feet by 1,600 feet. Climbers first began scaling the peak in 1919 when a road extending past Leigh Lake to the mountain's base provided easy access. When the road closed in 1953, climbing activity dramatically shifted away from Mount Moran to the Grand Teton. Today, the mountain memorializes famous Yellowstone Park artist Thomas Moran and is best known for harboring five active glaciers, some of which are visible from nearby Jackson's city limits.

Oxbow Bend
Bull elk bugle with the arrival of autumn's chilly morning breath. Prehistoric-looking moose feed on the verdant willow-lined riverbanks. Waterfowl float on the gentle river current. It is a natural wildlife scene unrivaled by most other park wildlife viewing regions, and best of all, sightings are easily accessible and frequent. Located near Jackson Lake Lodge, Oxbow Bend is a calm Snake River channel that shelters a verdant and diverse wildlife habitat. The famous channel also provides plenty of opportunity for canoeists to hit the water.

Emma Matilda Lake
Emma Matilda Lake is situated east of Jackson Lake Lodge as a popular day hike destination. The lake honors Emma Matilda Owen, the wife of famous Billy Owen who reached Grand Teton's summit in 1898. Owen was supposedly the first person to successfully scale the peak, although countless others had no doubt tried before him. The lake itself is an ideal setting for gleaning views of the Teton Mountains, Jackson Lake, and nearby Christian Pond. Dense forests surround the lake and the trail leading to it, so visitors should make plenty of noise so as not to surprise area bears.

Jackson Lake Junction
Jackson Lake Junction marks the point for determining the course of your remaining Grand Teton Park visit. Continuing west takes travelers down the Teton Park Road past the final stretches of Jackson Lake to scenic Jenny Lake. The eastern route leads to the Moran Entrance station. Here a southbound turn on U.S. Highway 26/89/191 leads visitors to unparalleled Snake River views on the short journey to Jackson Hole.

Teton Park Road
The Teton Park Road travels south from Jackson Lake Junction to the Moose Entrance Station. The route skirts the base of the Teton Mountain Range and offers unobstructed views of many of the range's peaks. Park guests will find numerous scenic pullouts and activities along the way.

Brinkerhoff House
Also known as the "Blue House," this once private home rests near the highway's western side. When the area became incorporated as part of Grand Teton National Park, the U.S. Government purchased the home in 1955 for $70,000. The house was then remodeled into a special VIP residence for park visitors of high-ranking status. Famous news reporter Walter Cronkite has stayed in "Old Blue" as well as former Presidents George Bush and Jimmy Carter.

Chapel of the Sacred Heart
Located less than one mile north of Signal Mountain Lodge, the Chapel of the Sacred Heart has served park visitors since 1935. The chapel works in coordination with Jackson's Our Lady of the Mountains Catholic Church, and services are provided once on Saturday and twice on Sunday every June through August. The quaint log

chapel, however, is open twenty-four hours a day, and park visitors are invited to stop by for quiet reflection time. While visiting, guests are encouraged to sign and flip through the guestbook, which includes signatures of individuals from nearly every country in the world.

Signal Mountain Lodge and Surrounding Area
Located just five miles south of Jackson Lake Junction on Teton Park Road, the Signal Mountain Area is another major developed tourist center in the park's northern region. The area's name stems from a nineteenth century incident when local entrepreneur Robert Ray Hamilton became lost on an 1890 hunting expedition. After waiting two weeks from Hamilton's expected return date, a search party began combing the area for any trace of the lost man. The party agreed that if Hamilton were found, a fire would be lit at the top of this mountain signaling the search's end. Although the search party hoped to find Hamilton alive, they tragically discovered him drowned. As planned, a fire was lit at the summit of the selected mountain, and Signal Mountain was born.

Today, log cabins, lakefront apartments, basic motel units, and camping offer a range of lodging choices for those wishing to make Signal Mountain their exploration base camp. Two dining options, gift and apparel shops, and a convenience store add to the amenities, and outdoor adventure is just moments away. Situated on Jackson Lake's southeastern shore, the Signal Mountain Area boasts a fully stocked marina eager to rent out canoes, pontoon boats, fishing boats, and deck cruisers to visitors who wish to tour the lake on their own. For those who prefer guidance in their recreational pursuits, Signal Mountain provides guided lake fishing, scenic cruises, and float trips.

Nearby, the winding scenic drive to Signal Mountain's summit takes visitors to a breathtaking vantage point of the geographical phenomena cradling Jackson in its signature "hole" or valley. The Tetons, Absarokas, Gros Ventres, and the Yellowstone Plateau rise majestically from the valley floor, all of which may be seen from this outstanding scenic vista. The drive is just a mere five miles long and begins one mile south of Signal Mountain Lodge.

Jackson Point Overlook
On the drive to the Signal Mountain vantage point (see above), visitors gain easy access to the notable and historical Jackson Point Overlook. Situated approximately two miles from the Signal Mountain Summit, a 100-yard paved path leads to the famed spot where 1872 Hayden Expedition photographer William Henry Jackson preserved the beauty of Jackson Lake and the Teton Mountains with a wet plate photograph. Jackson's photographs were instrumental in showing the world that the American West was not an uninhabitable wasteland but a place of splendid scenery.

Spalding Bay
Spalding Bay is known as one of Grand Teton National Park's favorite "hideaway" destinations for magnificent mountain and lake views. Its "hidden" status, however, does little to discourage the considerable use it actually receives each summer. An unmarked route is situated off Teton Park Road's western side two miles south of the Mount Moran scenic pullout. The unpaved path, passable by most cars and sport utility vehicles, takes visitors through meadows and forests to the crowd-pleasing Spalding Bay. The site, which takes its name from a Bishop Spalding who climbed Grand Teton in 1898, houses a small and primitive campground, restroom, and boat launch area.

Discovering Eastern Grand Teton: Moose Junction to Moran Junction

Following the Outer Loop Road, drivers are treated to wildlife sightings, historical sites, and famous Snake River and Grand Teton vistas. Although the route is most often viewed as a quick gateway to Jackson rather than a tourist destination, the Outer Loop Road is just as scenic as the Inner Loop Road and deserves just as much credit as a worthwhile means of exploring Grand Teton. The route offers easy access to many roadside and off-road attractions while treating visitors to several picture-worthy views.

Antelope Flats Road
Originating 1.2 miles north of Moose Junction, the Antelope Flats Road departs U.S Highway 26/89/191 for a quick jaunt into one of Grand Teton's most peaceful settings. Traveling through rolling pastures where bison, moose, and elk graze, the twenty-mile route heads south before looping back to the main highway via the Gros Ventre River Road. The fairly non-congested route is a popular bicycling destination.
Kelly

Nestled near the banks of the Gros Ventre River, the tiny town of Kelly is situated just inside Grand Teton National Park boundaries and is known for its eclectic personality. The community, which suffered significant damage during the 1925 Gros Ventre Slide, boasts several yurts and excellent year-round wildlife viewing.

Gros Ventre River Road
The Gros Ventre River Road is lined with interpretive signs revealing the story behind the Gros Ventre Slide. The road originates five miles north of Jackson off U.S. Highway 26/89/191 and connects with Antelope Flats Road to make a scenic loop tour. The road is aptly named after its winding course beside the Gros Ventre River.
Gros Ventre Slide and Lower Slide Lake

In 1925, fifty million cubic yards of rock crumbled 2,225 feet off Sheep Mountain's face into the Gros Ventre River. The massive pile of debris formed a natural dam across the river, holding back 65,000 acre-feet of water in the newly formed Lower Slide Lake. When much of the one-half mile wide dam collapsed in 1927, the resulting flood raged through the canyon walls, destroying several homes in Kelly and killing six people in its wake.

Today, scars from the tumbling landslide still cover Sheep Mountain's distinctive face as it rises south of the Gros Ventre River. A portion of Lower Slide Lake, which caters to boating enthusiasts, remains as testimony to Mother Nature's earth-shattering forces.

Teton Science School
The Teton Science School strives to protect and preserve the Greater Yellowstone Ecosystem through the hands-on natural world education of young and old. Serving students as young as eight to those nearly 100 years old, the non-profit Teton Science School annually welcomes over 5,000 students to its courses. The school, located outside Kelly with a new facility in Jackson, connects people to nature and fosters an appreciation for conservation ethics with a variety of educational classes taught by experts in the natural science field. Graduate programs, teacher workshops, children's programs, and adult and family programs have been part of this school's renowned offerings since its establishment in 1967.

The Teton Science School gears many of its programs to the limited timeframe of park visitors by offering one-day programs. From June through September, the facility provides numerous courses on a plethora of topics. Wildflower walks, astronomy tours of the park's crisp night skies, wildlife viewing via canoe expeditions, birding courses, tutorials on the many uses of plants, and dozens of other intriguing topics come together to ensure every individual will find at least one subject of interest. The school also offers longer residential programs for those seeking a more in-depth educational experience.

In addition to these affordably priced programs, the Teton Science School provides a Conservation Research Center as well as Wildlife Expeditions, a special year-round program focused on wildlife viewing and natural history interpretation. For additional information on any of these programs, contact the Teton Science School at (307) 733-4765.

Blacktail Ponds Overlook
Blacktail Ponds Overlook is located three miles north of Moose Junction on U.S. Highway 26/89/191. The marshy area boasts wonderful wildlife viewing with moose, elk, eagles, and osprey frequenting the ponds year-round. The site is also known for sheltering a significant beaver population, and visitors can glimpse the intricate handiwork of these hard-working creatures with several dams gracing the serene ponds.

Glacier View Turnout
Ancient glaciers helped carve the craggy mountain masterpiece comprising Grand Teton National Park's western boundary, and the Glacier View Turnout provides a breathtaking vista of this unparalleled scene. The turnout also offers views of a gaping gulch resting between the peaks that a 4,000-foot-thick glacier encompassed over 140,000 years ago. The turnout is located approximately five miles north of Moose Junction.

Lower Schwabacher Landing
Lower Schwabacher Landing is a popular picnic site providing easy boat access to the Snake River. The site is located on a dirt road, which may be accessed from U.S. Highway 26/89/191 approximately five miles north of Moose Junction. The landing receives relatively little use in comparison to other park areas, and moose, otters, bald eagles, and osprey are often sighted. In addition to boating and picnicking, Lower Schwabacher's Landing is a favorite haunt of avid anglers.

Snake River Overlook
Situated nine miles north of Moose Junction along U. S. Highway 26/89/191, the Snake River Overlook offers one of Grand Teton National Park's most famous portraits. During his expansive and legendary career, photographer Ansel Adams stood near this overlook to record the majestic Teton peaks standing proudly above the braided Snake River. His black and white shot became famous around the world, and today the Snake River Overlook is a favorite stopping point along the Outer Loop Road. In addition to the same image Adams captured, visitors are also privy to views of three rolling plateaus created during the glacial era. Although these hills are quiet today, the plateaus served as a favorite hunting ground to beaver trappers roaming the Rocky Mountains during the early 1800s.

Deadman's Bar Overlook
Deadman's Bar honors three miners who were tragically murdered and dumped here in 1886. The men's mining partner was suspected of the

crime, but after pleading self-defense, was freed on the basis of unsubstantial evidence linking him to the crime. Deadman's Bar Overlook provides a view of this scene from the Outer Loop Road, while a steep road departing from the highway traverses down to the bar and a Snake River landing popular with floaters.

Cunningham Cabin
Located slightly over five miles south of Moran Junction on U.S. Highway 26/89/191, the Cunningham Cabin represents one of the oldest remaining Jackson Hole homesteads. Pierce and Margaret Cunningham erected the cabin as part of their Bar Flying U Ranch in 1890. The ranch commemorates the pioneering lifestyle of the region's earliest settlers as well as the Old West's vigilante justice system.

In 1893, a pair of rustlers rented the cabin from the Cunninghams in what they believed was an unsuspecting winter hideout. However, when a local group of vigilante enforcers heard of the duo's presence, a posse formed to bring the rustlers to justice. On a cold winter evening, the posse surprised the rustlers with a legendary gun battle that left the rustlers dead. A historic marker pinpoints the approximate location of these rustlers' graves.

Bridger-Teton National Forest
Completely contained within Wyoming and easily accessed near the Cunningham Cabin off U.S. Highway 26/89/191, the 3.4-million acre Bridger-Teton National Forest is the largest national forest within the Greater Yellowstone Ecosystem. The forest is named after the Teton Mountain Range skyrocketing inside the forest's confines as well as Jim Bridger, the region's most famous 1800s mountain man. The forest encircles Jackson as it begins near Yellowstone's southern boundary, sweeps through Grand Teton, extends east to the Wind River Range, and heads southwest to the Utah border.

Bridger-Teton National Forest is lined with small alpine lakes and hiking trails, making it a popular scenic destination for anglers, backpackers, and campers. The forest also houses plenty of year-round recreation opportunities, including horseback riding, mountain biking, hunting, boating, cross-country skiing, downhill skiing, snowboarding, ice climbing, dog sledding, snowshoeing, and snowmobiling. Wildlife viewing is especially popular in this forest that borders the National Elk Refuge. Harboring six amphibious species, seventy-four mammal species, six species of reptiles, and twenty-five species of fish, the Bridger-Teton National Forest is home to abundant populations of grizzly bears, black bears, bison, elk, mule deer, bighorn sheep, moose, pronghorn antelope, coyotes, beavers, pikas, trumpeter swans, sandhill cranes, and bald eagles.

Bridger-Teton National Forest includes six ranger districts within its magnificent reaches, with each district providing its own list of available recreational activities. For additional information about recreating in the Bridger-Teton National Forest, contact the following district offices:

Jackson Ranger District: (307) 739-5400
Big Piney Ranger District: (307) 276-3375
Pinedale Ranger District: (307) 367-4326
Buffalo Ranger District in Moran: (307) 543-2386
Kemmerer Ranger District: (307) 877-4415
Greys River Ranger District in Afton: (307) 886-5300

Buffalo Fork Meadows
The Buffalo Fork River curls its way into Grand Teton National Park near the Moran Entrance

Albright view point. NPS Photo.

Station. During its journey, the river creates a marshy surrounding habitat before emptying into the mighty Snake River on a course towards the Pacific. The resulting lush valley, known as Buffalo Fork Meadows, features willow-clogged riverbanks. These willows lure dozens of grazing moose each spring and winter, and the Moran area is known for abundant moose sightings during these seasons. Visitors should note that the best wildlife viewing conditions are generally at dusk and dawn when animals are more apt to be feeding.

Discovering Southern Grand Teton: Jackson Lake Junction to Moose

For those who continue their southern journey through the park via the Teton Park Road (Inner Loop Road) or the Moose-Wilson Road, the routes maximize visitors' viewing potential of the magnificent Teton Mountains. Southern Grand Teton National Park exhibits similar attractions as the northern park region with abundant lakes, wildlife, visitor centers, and historic sites. Visitors should note that the Inner Loop Road is only open May through late October depending on weather, while travel on the Moose-Wilson Road is restricted in winter to the paved drive leading to Teton Village.

Leigh Lake
Measuring two miles long with depths up to 250 feet, Leigh Lake draws its name from legendary trapper, Beaver Dick Leigh, who spent a significant amount of time in the region now comprising Grand Teton National Park. Today, the lake is recognized for its beautiful green color, white sandy beaches, and water that is occasionally warm enough for a summer swim. The glacially formed lake is also popular for canoeing, and a trail around Leigh Lake's shoreline leading to two nearby cirque lakes is a favorite among day hikers.

String Lake
Connected to Jenny Lake with a small waterfall and to Leigh Lake with year-round water flow from mountain drainages, String Lake is the result of ancient glacial sculpting. String Lake averages just six feet deep and remains perfectly calm even on the windiest of park days. Consequently, String Lake is an ideal destination for canoeists of all ages and skill levels. Hiking trails surround the shallow

lake, and the String Lake Picnic Area is a favorite family destination easily accessed off the Teton Park Road via the Jenny Lake Scenic Drive.

Jenny Lake and Surrounding Area
Jenny Lake rests in a glacial moraine carved at the base of Mount Teewinot and honors the wife of legendary regional trapper, Beaver Dick Leigh. Jenny was a Shoshone woman who bore Leigh six children. Tragically, after kindly taking in a sick traveler, Jenny and all six youngsters died of smallpox during the 1876 Christmas season. Although he made a valiant effort, Leigh was unable to save his family and watched helplessly as they died in front of him.

Despite the tragic story behind its name, the 200-foot deep Jenny Lake is a serene place where crowds flock for beautiful Teton views and a variety of outdoor recreation. Boat shuttles, scenic cruises, and fishing boat rentals are an engrained part of Jenny Lake's culture. Hikers also head to the Jenny Lake region for convenient entry into the magnificent backcountry surrounding the lake. Hidden Falls and Inspiration Point are among the area's most popular day hikes, while anglers who stick to the lake may be lucky enough to catch a thirty or forty pound whopper!

Jenny Lake Lodge
Combining the atmosphere of a mountain lake resort with the cowboy feel of a dude ranch, Jenny Lake Lodge serves as the park's premier dining and lodging establishment. Rustic, yet refined, the lodge dates back to 1922 and Tony Grace's 160-acre homestead. The early homesteader quickly set to work improving upon his land, and six of his original cabins remain on the property. When the area became incorporated as part of Grand Teton National Park, Grace's sprawling homestead was transformed into one of the park's favorite lodge settings.

Today, those who can afford to pay fairly steep prices enjoy four-star treatment amid the park's resplendent beauty. Log cabins (each named after a park wildflower) feature log furniture, porches, exquisite bathrooms, guests' choice of king, queen, or double beds, and stunning views from every angle. The lodging rate also includes scrumptious six-course meals in the cozy dining room, horseback riding, and boating.

For those who cannot afford a full package

vacation at Jenny Lake Lodge, dinner reservations are available by advance request. The area also boasts plenty of opportunities for self-guided canoeing, horseback riding, fishing, mountain biking, hiking, and camping – without a stiff fee involved.

South Jenny Lake Area

Park visitors in need of food supplies and recreational equipment will find amenities to suit every need in the South Jenny Lake area. The area boasts a general store featuring outdoor gear, groceries, film, outdoor technical clothing, and gifts and souvenirs for individuals of all ages. The area also serves as a visitor center and the operation base for Jenny Lake boat shuttles and guided mountaineering expeditions on Grand Teton.

Cathedral Group Turnout

Inspiring some individuals to compare them to the spires of Gothic cathedrals, the Grand Teton, Mount Owen, and Teewinot Mountain come together in one frame to form the Cathedral Group. Nez Perce Peak and the Middle and South Tetons rise nearby, making the Cathedral Group one of the best places to capture the peaks on film. Visitors may access this viewpoint via the North Jenny Lake Scenic Loop. The area also boasts views of the Teton Fault running just a few hundred feet from the foot of the peaks.

Cascade Canyon

The Cascade Canyon pullout provides visitors with views of the Grand Teton and a glimpse into the park's alpine territory. The U-shaped Cascade Canyon serves as a popular gateway to Grand Teton National Park's backcountry, and the pullout includes an interpretive sign describing alpine vegetation and the importance of protecting the park's fragile ecosystem. Those wishing to explore the glacially carved gorge more deeply may follow any number of trails into the canyon's deep recesses. Individuals who do opt to hike into Cascade Canyon are reminded to stay on the trail at all times to avoid damaging the delicate alpine and subalpine vegetation. Keep in mind that bears inhabit this region, so all users should be familiar with bear safety guidelines. Contact the nearest ranger station or visitor center for reports on the area's latest bear activity.

Lupine Meadows

Running parallel to the highway and tucked up against Teewinot Mountain, Lupine Meadows fills with ravishing color each spring and summer. Thousands of lupine bloom into a lush carpet that encases the meadow in vibrant hews of lavender and blue. In addition to lupine, the meadow often also contains grazing herds of elk and deer. For outdoor and backcountry enthusiasts, Lupine Meadows serves as an important trailhead for Surprise and Amphitheater Lakes. The meadows may be viewed approximately six miles north of Moose on the Teton Park Road.

Teton Glacier Turnout

The Teton Glacier Turnout, situated approximately four miles north of Moose, affords Teton Park Road travelers the rare opportunity to see a still existent glacier. Cradled northeast of the mighty Grand Teton's base, Teton Glacier is a distant and much smaller relative of the glacial fields that helped sculpt the massive peaks and park valleys thousands of years ago. The glacier is just one of a dozen remaining within the park's boundaries today; however, global warming is taking its toll and threatens the future of these ancient inhabitants. Teton Glacier alone has melted away an astonishing 200 feet in thickness and 500 feet in length over the last 100 years. Today, the road turnout provides stunning views of this melting glacier along with an interpretive sign describing the

formation of glaciers and their critical role in sculpting the rugged peaks seen today.

Climbers' Ranch

Maintained and hosted by the donation-based American Alpine Club, the Climbers' Ranch welcomes climbers of all abilities to its simplistic and ideal base camp setting. Primitive cabins and campsites are available for one of the cheapest nightly fees around. In return for a bunk bed, private bath, and covered cooking area, guests are expected to bring their own mattress, sleeping bag, and cookstove. During their stay, guests may polish up their climbing skills on the ranch's small practice wall and access the latest weather reports, climbing conditions, and postings for available climbing partners. The ranch is located on a narrow road accessed approximately 3.5 miles north of Moose on the Teton Park Road. Phones are not available at the Climbers' Ranch, so guests should plan accordingly.

Cottonwood Creek

Located near a Teton Park Road turnoff just three miles north of Moose, Cottonwood Creek is a quaint picnic spot capturing the essence of Grand Teton National Park's peaceful and beautiful landscape. In addition to seasonal picnicking, the area opens to anglers from early August to late October. Although the weather may be less than ideal for picnicking in October, visitors should still plan on making a stop at Cottonwood Creek. Elk frequently roam through the area during their autumn rutting season, and visitors are often privy to exceptional views and sounds of bull elks wooing their potential mates.

Taggart Lake Area

Drawing its name from 1872 Hayden Survey party member W. Rush Taggart, the Taggart Lake region and trailhead pullout is situated approximately 2.4 miles north of Moose on the Teton Park Road. The area provides easy access to the backcountry Taggart and Bradley Lakes as well as a small picnic ground and rest area ideal for a midday snack or soaking up the park's astounding backdrop.

Directly beyond the trailhead pullout, another roadside stop features an interpretive sign describing the August 1985 Beaver Creek fire that burned several acres inside the park's boundaries. The sign also educates visitors on fire's key role in preserving and renewing a forest's healthy growth cycle. Much to the surprise of most individuals, fire actually replenishes soil nutrients faster than decaying plants. This in turn allows plant seeds to grow more quickly while drawing new wildlife to the area.

Windy Point

Windy Point is situated on Teton Park Road's eastern side just one mile north of Moose. The roadside pullout features interpretive signs describing the area's ecology and wildlife populations, and animals frequent the region in the early morning and late evening hours. Windy Point also provides an excellent vantage of Sleeping Indian Mountain rising on the eastern horizon. The mountain experienced a massive rockslide in 1925, which is still evident today as a red-colored scar streaking down the mountain's face.

Menor's Ferry

Preserving the history of Bill Menor and the region's pioneering lifestyle, Menor's Ferry is just a hop and a skip away from the Moose Entrance Station. Bill Menor arrived in the Jackson Hole Valley in 1894 and immediately set to work. On his Moose homestead, Menor built a home for his family, a general store, a blacksmith's shop, and a cable ferry across the Snake River. Menor's Ferry was instantly successful as it provided one of the easiest crossings over the normally braided and swift Snake River.

Charging $1.00 for a horse team or wagon, $0.50 for a horseback rider, and $0.35 for a packhorse, Menor turned his homestead into one of the region's most profitable businesses.

Menor eventually sold his ferry and acreage to Maude Noble in 1918. Although the ferry eventually fell to the withering hands of time, a replica ferry now transports visitors on a historic river crossing (when the weather permits). In addition, the site features the old Maude Noble cabin, a reconstructed general store that sells items reminiscent of the early twentieth century, and a building owned by the Rockefeller family featuring old forms of transportation used to settle and tour this scenic western region. Access to this free site is located off the main highway 0.2 miles north of Moose.

Chapel of the Transfiguration

Situated in a wildflower meadow with the Teton Range rising magnificently on the horizon, the rustic log Chapel of the Transfiguration is situated near the Menor's Ferry historical site north of Moose. The Episcopal chapel was established in 1925 on land donated by early settler Maude Noble. Church officials in Jackson hoped the creation of a chapel near Moose would provide the region's settlers with easier access to Sunday worship.

Complete with aspen pews, stained glass windows, and a picture window framing the mountains behind the altar, the Chapel of the Transfiguration met with widespread acceptance. Today, under the affiliation of Jackson's St. John's Episcopal Church, this chapel provides the Holy Eucharist and a prayer service each Sunday morning May through September. The chapel also provides a serene setting for funerals, weddings, and baptisms. All park tourists are welcome to visit.

Moose Visitor Center

Open year-round and serving as Grand Teton National Park headquarters, the Moose Visitor Center bustles with activity at the park's southern entrance. Visitors will find interpretive wildlife displays, an extensive bookstore, park maps, and backcountry permits. Rangers are also on hand to help visitors plan their backcountry tour, answer questions, and provide the latest bear activity reports.

Dornan's

Dornan's is a small but busy shopping, dining, and lodging complex situated slightly south of the Moose Visitor Center. Built on land owned by the family of an early homesteader, Dornan's caters to park visitors with its extensive variety of services. In addition to its famous Chuckwagon Restaurant and Moose Pizza and Pasta Company, visitors are privy to log cabins, a gift shop, gas station, post office, semi-gourmet grocery store, wine shop, lounge with occasional live music, fishing trips, and a well-equipped mountaineering store.

Sawmill Ponds

Located on the Moose-Wilson Road (Wyoming Highway 390) just south of the Moose Visitor Center, Sawmill Ponds is a scenic wildlife habitat surrounded by willows and wild grasses. The spring-fed ponds host moose and beavers year-round, while elk congregate on the surrounding grassy hillsides each spring and fall. Visitors' best opportunity for wildlife viewing arrives at dawn and dusk when animals engage in their typical feeding behavior. Viewers should also note the area's numerous beaver dams, which have dramatically changed the shape and size of these sequential ponds.

MONTANA

THE TREASURE STATE

Madison River north of West Yellowstone

THE TREASURE STATE

Montana—unrivaled splendor and awesome beauty! Over 147,000 square miles of mountains, prairies, farms, forests, rivers and streams await the traveler ready for spectacular scenery and adventure. Montana is a cornucopia of elaborate terrain; every geologic formation known on the planet can be found in Montana. Extraordinary? Yes, and so is Montana.

Although the name of Montana is derived from the Spanish word for mountain, only one third of the state is mountainous. Often described as if it were two states—an eastern prairie and a western mountain range—Montana provides a diverse range of scenery for the traveler. The northern part of Montana borders Canada, Wyoming flanks much of the south, the east borders North and South Dakota, and Idaho lines the west side with the Bitterroot Mountains.

Montana's share of the Rocky Mountains comprise two dozen distinct ranges. The elevations swing from 3,500 feet on valley floors to the peaks of the Beartooth Plateau near Yellowstone National Park that rise above 12,000 feet. The ranges that exist at higher elevations often create their own weather systems, inducing precipitation that supports dense coniferous forests of fir, pine, cedar, spruce, and larch. While snow can pile up hundreds of inches, measurable precipitation only ranges from 14 to 23 inches annually. Powder-white peaks are often still visible on the hottest days of summer.

The valleys that divide Montana's mountain ranges vary from narrow slots to broad floors up to 50 miles wide. The most unforgettable valleys—the Big Hole, Gallatin, Yellowstone, and Madison—are named after the rivers that drain them. Nearly one fourth of Montana, 22.5 million acres, is forested. Most of the forests occur west of the Continental Divide, where moist Pacific Coast air and mountainous areas provide favorable con-

ditions for the growth of approximately twenty-seven types of trees.

Eastern Montana, often deemed as monotonous, has a character of its own and is full of its own topographical surprises such as badlands, sandstone outcroppings, glacial lakes, ice caves and even an occasional pine forest or cluster of low mountains. The short grasses that grow in this region support a thriving livestock industry. Out of the wide, endless ranges of grass a legacy grew from the great trail drives that moved cattle and cowboys from Texas to Montana as early as the 1860s. While the prairie is not known for its trees, the savannahs of eastern Montana grow more than sagebrush. Willows take root in the river valleys while pine and cedars spot the hills. Cottonwoods, once prized for firewood and dugout canoes by many Native American tribes and early settlers, grow near river bottoms, while chokecherries and currants grow on lower ground.

Nowhere is the contrast between mountains and plains more striking than along the Rocky Mountain Front which some distinguish as the division of eastern and western Montana. The stretch of highway between Augusta and Browning is remarkable. To the west is a solid wall of peaks; to the east lie the unrelenting expanses of plains. Moods and colors are abundant in the tapestry of the wide open Montana sky as it changes daily, even hourly.

Two of the United States' most extraordinary national parks frame Montana. On the state's northern edge are the chiseled peaks of Glacier National Park, while along the southern Montana-Wyoming border lies the thermal wonder-world of Yellowstone National Park—the oldest national park in the world and largest in the United States. Fire and ice were the artists within Yellowstone, as it was created by a series of volcanic eruptions. These intense geothermal forces are still at work beneath the Earth's shallow crust making Yellowstone Park the largest hotspot on the globe.

HISTORY

The history of Montana is as remarkable and vast as are its open plains. Ghost towns stand as a reminder of towns once vibrant with life during the mining booms. Stand where General Custer stood; The Little Bighorn Battlefield Monument commemorates the battle of the same name and Custer's "Last Stand" against the Sioux and Cheyenne Indians. Native American culture is still thriving in Montana with seven different Indian reservations, as well as numerous commemorative state parks and historic sites. Two great rivers, the Missouri and the Yellowstone drain the eastern prairies where dinosaurs once roamed and where Crow, Cheyenne and Blackfeet tribes pursued the world's largest herd of American bison across the plains.

Tribes of early people first arrived in Montana from Asia about 10,000–15,000 years ago. Around 5,000 B.C., a desert climate in Asia caused game animals and the peoples who relied on them to migrate in search of more habitable conditions. The Shoshone entered Montana in about 1600, shortly after the Crow Indians settled along tributaries of the Yellowstone River. Over a century later, the Blackfeet came to Montana from the north and east in about 1730. Other tribes

MONTANA AT A GLANCE

Population (2000): 902,195

Entered union: November 8, 1889

Capital: Helena

Nickname: Treasure State

Motto: "Oro y Plata"(Gold and Silver)

Bird: Western Meadowlark

Flower: Bitterroot

Song: "Montana"

Stones: Sapphire and Agate

Tree: Ponderosa Pine

Animal: Grizzly Bear

Fish: Blackspotted Cutthroat Trout

Fossil: Maiasaura (Duck-billed Dinosaur)

Land area: 147,046 square miles

Size ranking: 4th

Geographic center: Fergus, 26 miles northeast of Lewistown

Length: 630 miles

Width: 280 miles

Highest point: 12,799 feet (Granite Peak)

Lowest point: 1,820 feet (Kootenai River)

Highest temperature: 117 deg. on July 5, 1937, at Medicine Lake

Lowest temperature: -70 deg. on Jan. 20, 1954, at Rogers Pass

Montana Introduction

COWBOY WAVE

Montana is largely rural, and like largely rural states, it is pretty friendly to most who care to be friendly back. When you're traveling the back roads, particularly the gravel roads, you'll encounter a variety of waves from passing pickups and motorists.

The most common is the one finger wave, accomplished by simply raising the first finger (not the middle finger as is common in urban areas) from the steering wheel. If the driver is otherwise occupied with his hands or if it is a fairly rough road, you may get a light head nod. Occasionally, you may get a two finger wave which often appears as a modified peace sign if the passerby is having a particularly good day. On rare occasions, you may get an all out wave.

The most important things is that whatever wave you get, be sure and wave back.

Running of the sheep at Reedpoint.

later found their way to Montana: Sioux, Cheyenne, Salish, and the Kootenai. Cree and Chippewa tribes entered Montana in the 1870s from Canada.

In the early 1800s, rivers provided the pathway into Montana for the first white explorers. Rivers and riverboats remained the only form of transportation linking Montana and the rest of the nation until the 1880s. Trappers and traders also used the rivers as thoroughfares, and forts were erected to support the lavish trapping and trading of beavers pelts. By 1840, prior to the cessation of this beaver trapping era due to the animal's near extinction, almost three dozen trading forts had been built. As the population of beavers drastically declined, trade continued in buffalo hides.

Mineral wealth, as well as the development of the railroad, fueled Montana's development in the late 1800s. People flocked to Montana searching for gold, creating instant towns in southwestern Montana. Bannack, Virginia City, and Nevada City all began as gold-rush towns. Other gold strikes and later discoveries of silver sparked similar rushes in Last Chance Gulch (now Helena), Confederate Gulch (Diamond City) and many other boom towns. The railroad arrived serendipituously to haul the mineral riches. The Union Pacific built a spur line north from Utah to Butte in 1881. The Northern Pacific spanned the length of Montana linking Portland and Chicago in 1883 and extending its rails across approximately 17 million acres. The Great Northern stretched its service along the Montana-Canada border, joining Minneapolis and Seattle in 1893. With access to the coastal markets, Montana opened wide its doors for development and immigration.

Towns emerged in river valleys and highways were built on their banks. Dams were built to harness water power and reservoirs soon spanned the state altering Montana's geography. Millions of gallons of water are dammed at Fort Peck Reservoir on the Missouri and in Lake Koocanusa on the Kootenai River. The Great Falls of the Missouri, which required Lewis and Clark twenty-two days to painstakingly portage in 1805, are now a series of hydroelectric dams. Further exploits of the Lewis and Clark expedition in Montana are thoroughly chronicled in actual journals they kept.

Montana became a territory in 1864 and gained its statehood in 1889. Although Montana

was, in many ways, detached from the rest of the country in its early years of statehood, the state was able to sustain itself by the diverse and rich resources within its borders. Today those same resources travel the world: cattle grown on Montana ranches may end up on the table of a Japanese restaurant, its coal fuels the cities of the Pacific Coast, its timber is used to erect homes across the country, and Montana's gold becomes circuitry in main frame computers and space craft.

Throughout these sections we have provided you enough history of the area to understand its origins. Much of this is provided through the text of historical markers throughout the state. They tell the story of Montana in a colorful way and do an excellent job of spotlighting the important milestones in Montana history. We have provided some background history on over 300 towns and cities in the state, if nothing more than the origin of the town's name. Quite often, the story of the town's name provides insight into its past.

12,000 MILES OF MONTANA

There are approximately 12,000 miles of roads in Montana. Many roads are originally routes blazed by the Native Indian tribes and migrating buffalo. The trails were the ones that made passing through mountain passes, around rivers, and other geographical obstacles. The first engineered road was a military supply route to the Northwest which was Mullan from Walla Walla to Fort Benton in 1862. This road linked Montana territory to a natural highway from the Pacific Ocean to the Atlantic Ocean.

Montana's interstate system was completed in 1988 and includes I-90, I-94, and I-15. There are a total of 1,200 Interstate miles in the state. Primary highways cover 5,450 miles in the state. Secondary roads which include county, state, and frontage roads cover a total of 4,760 miles and over a third of those roads are not paved.

LEWIS & CLARK

The Journey West

The Lewis & Clark Expedition left St. Louis in 1804, heading up the Missouri River to explore the unknown Western Territory, calling themselves the Corps of Discovery. The Corp was traveling upstream, moving up to 25 miles a day when the winds and weather permitted. They had already experienced many trials and tribulations throughout their travels through Nebraska, Iowa, South Dakota, North Dakota and into Montana.

When the Corps of Discovery was nearing the spot where the Missouri and the Yellowstone come together, they were forced to stop for several days due to high wind. The group knew they were close to the Yellowstone River, and on April 25 1805, Meriwether Lewis led a group by foot to the mouth of the Yellowstone to explore the territory that lay ahead. The small group spent the night on the riverbanks, and then headed back to meet the others, and the group completed the journey to the Yellowstone the next day.

This was the first time they reached the Yellowstone River, yet the group continued their journey up the Missouri, leaving the exploration of the Yellowstone for their return route. More miles were traveled through Montana by Lewis & Clark, than any other state. This is due to the fact that the group split up, Clark traveling through Bozeman Pass and following the Yellowstone River, while Lewis returned on the Missouri and explored the Marias River.

The Return Trip

On July 3, 1806, on their return, Lewis & Clark decided to split up the group, just south of today's city of Missoula. Clark's team, including Sacajawea and her baby Jean Baptiste, proceeded down the Yellowstone, past Pompey's Pillar, and spent the night of July 27 at Castle Rock by today's Forsyth. The next day they passed Rosebud Creek, spotted numerous herds of Elk, and spent the night of July 29, 1806 on an island just across from the Tongue River by Miles City. Clark observed the abundance of coal in the surrounding hills. On July 30, the group passed through a difficult stretch of river and went by Makoshika State Park. The night of July 31 was spent by present day Glendive where they reportedly experienced problems with mosquitoes, grizzly bears and spotted numerous bison. They traveled huge distances of up to 60 miles a day during this time, until they once again returned to the Missouri River on August 4, 1806, where they met up with Lewis and his party.

In each section of the book, you will find an account of the Corps of Discovery's travels through that particular area, mostly in their own words. The markers on the map correspond to the numbered excerpt from their journals in the *On The Trail of Lewis and Clark* sidebar in that section. For more information on the Montana portion of the Lewis & Clark Trail, see local chambers of commerce and look for signs pointing out the trail sites.

MONTANA'S NATIVE AMERICANS

The Native Americans of Montana were largely nomadic. Their history is characterized by movement with the seasons. They crossed the plains to follow the great herds of bison, then retreated when stronger tribes pushed them off the hunting grounds. As the white man moved in and warfare and disease decimated the tribes, there came the move to the reservations marking the end of an era and a permanent change in lifestyle for the tribes.

Archeological evidence reveals that Native Americans walked these plains and roamed these mountains more than 14,000 years ago. Artifacts link the Kootenai to these prehistoric tribes. The Kootenai made their home in the mountainous terrain west of the divide. They ventured east only to hunt buffalo. The Crow, Salish, and Pend d'Oreilles were probably the first of the "modern" tribes to join the Kootenai on these lands. The Salish and the Pend d'Oreilles were spread as far east as the Bighorn Mountains. During the 1700s, these tribes co-existed on the same hunting grounds. The Hellgate Treaty took their massive landholdings and confined them to the fertile grounds of the Flathead Reservation.

The Chippewa and Cree were latecomers to Montana. They came to the area after the reservation system was in existence. Today these tribes are intermixed and share the hybrid name, "Chippewa-Cree." They reside on the Rocky Boy's reservation.

Most of Montana's Indians arrived here after 1700. By the time they arrived, the white man's culture was already firmly established. The white man's influence on who would dominate the Montana territory was significant. Guns from the white frontiersman and horses from the Spaniards became deciding factors in a culture completely dependent on the bison.

In the 1880s, the bison-based economy began to crumble. White men were hunting the bison to near extinction, the U.S. and Canadian governments began to drive Indians from their lands, and the diseases brought by the whites all combined to diminish the population of the tribes and shatter their spirits. By the 1870s, large tracts of land were formally reserved for the Indians through various treaties and executive orders.

Today's Reservations

Today, reservations cover nine percent of the Montana land base. While not all is still owned by native people, all is governed by tribal or federal law. These reservations are not only important for the spiritual ties the Indians have to the land, but because they have become the Indians' last retreat and last chance to preserve the culture of the past.

Near Livingston.

Today, the people of Montana's reservations are working hard to create and sustain strong economic bases to perpetuate the culture for future generations.

Today, these reservations are reservoirs of Native American history. They are havens where the Indian culture can be experienced with a backdrop of sacred landscapes and at annual gatherings—where rituals are performed and traditional dress is worn as it has been for hundreds of years.

There are seven reservations in Montana occupied by eleven tribes. Each maintains a wealth of cultural institutions in their museums. Special events held frequently provide insight into their cultures. Historic sites are plentiful on all seven reservations. While Montana's Native Americans have struggled to adapt to the changing world and conflicting cultures around them, they have managed to maintain the rich culture and traditions of their past. This heritage is a major ingredient in the cultural flavor of Montana.

Visiting a Reservation

Each of the reservations have special social and cultural events and activities unique to the tribes occupying them. Many, like tribal powwows, rodeos, hand games, and shinny games are social events and usually open to the public. When visiting these events and the public places on the reservation, keep in mind that most of these are not held for the benefit of the public but as important parts of the tribe's culture. Thus it's incumbent on guests to show courtesy and respect when attending these activities.

Most of the cultural and religious ceremonies require a special invitation to attend. In some cases, visitors are not allowed at all. In some tribes, a host family will personally invite visitors and advise them of the protocol in attending. All of the tribes place great importance on their religion and traditions. Sacred sites must be respected and artifacts must not be removed. All reservations have places where mementos may be purchased.

A powwow is a social gathering featuring generations-old dancing and drumming, accompanied by traditional food and dress. Visitors should bring lawn chairs and blankets as seating space is limited at most of these functions. Guests may

join in the "Round Dance" where everyone dances in a circle, or by invitation of the emcee. They may also participate by invitation in a "Giveaway," which is a sharing of accomplishment or good fortune. But they should be constantly aware that the dance area is sacred.

All events and points of interest mentioned in this book are open to the public. To be sure about attendance at any other functions, contact the tribal office.

Flash photography is forbidden during contests. If you wish to take a picture of the dancers or singers, ask permission first.

Visitors should be aware that while on the reservation, tribal laws exist that do not exist off the reservation. Most tribes have their own laws regarding the environment and wildlife protection. For information concerning access and recreation, contact the tribal office.

ECONOMY

Montana, a rural state, claims agriculture, mining, and the timber industry to be its founding trades and are still among its most vital. Tourism continues to increase, drawing revenue to one of the nation's most beautiful states. Agriculture is strictly divided by Montanans between farms, which raise grain, and ranches, which raise livestock. Although many think of Montana as being comprised of huge ranches and roaming cattle, less than 10% of the population make their living from farming and ranching. Beef cattle production is the most common in Montana, with sheep providing a steady alternative. Spring and winter wheat are undoubtedly the most commonly harvested crops, with barley in close contention. Other popular crops, grown predominately in irrigation fields along the Yellowstone River, are corn, soybeans and sugar beets.

Though Montana was born of mining and prospecting camps, most of the gold, silver and copper have been depleted. However, the state remains rich in other mineral wealth such as sapphire, coal and oil. Although the timber industry is a lifestyle for some, early clear-cutting of forests and slow regrowth have limited the state's ability for competition in the world market. Christmas

Treeline in the Beartooth Mountains near Red Lodge.

tree farms spot the northwestern part of the state and log-home manufacturers have moved Montana into the forefront of home-kit producers in the world. More log homes are shipped to Japan than remain in Montana.

POPULATION

People come to Montana to get away from city life, not to find it. A little over 900,000 people live in this state, even though it is the fourth largest state area-wise in the U.S. trailing only Alaska, Texas and California. Montana's largest city, Billings, has less than 100,000 residents, translating to six persons per acre of the state's 145,556 square miles of land. The entire state of Montana has even been likened to a mid-size American city, each town representing a different neighborhood with a unique personality. Each city and town lends itself to a distinct purpose and all contribute to the diversity that is so harmonious with its terrain.

The contrasting values of independence and neighborliness define the character of a typical Montanan. People here still share stories at cozy roadside saloons as glassy-eyed, stuffed animal heads hover as if monitoring the conversations. And when calling anywhere within Montana you just have to remember one area code, 406, and the entire state is on mountain time.

ARTS AND CULTURE

Montana is brimming with art and literary talent, both past and present day. From pioneers who kept journals and sent letters back east to established novelists who make their home in Montana, the literary tradition is a great source of pride to Montanans. A state that can fill a 1,150 page bestselling anthology with its literature is impressive and bespeaks of a tradition worth noting. *The Last Best Place* chronicles the literary history of Montana, from Native American stories to modern cowboy poetry.

Art walks and displays are commonplace and rural cafes will often sell local arts and crafts, from homemade pottery to mountain scenes painted on old barn boards. One of the more famous artists is the Montana painter Charlie Russell who began sketching in bars and around campfires. His studio in Great Falls is now the Charles Russell Memorial Museum.

WILDLIFE

Both white-tailed and large-eared mule deer dot the countryside as you drive through the state. Montana is home to more than 150,000 Rocky Mountain elk, which can often be viewed from the roadside. Bighorn sheep, mountain goats and grizzly bears are more likely to be seen high in the slopes of the Rockies. Moose are common but typically avoid humans. Montana's vast wilderness areas serve as valuable homes for many of the country's threatened and endangered species including the gray wolf, whooping crane, white sturgeon, grizzly bear and bald eagle. Mountain lions are also residents of Montana and can show up in unlikely spots, such as the city parks of Missoula or the streets of Columbia Falls, though this is not common.

Magpies, loud, large black & white birds, seem to monopolize Montana's airways, but there are also many other less-aggressive birds. Some to look for in the eastern part of the state are grouse, bobolinks, horned lark, western meadowlark (Montana's state bird), goldfinches and sparrow hawks. In the mountainous western area of the state you may catch the thrill of a bald eagle gliding across the valley or perched on a branch in a tree near the highway. Other birds that frequent the west are owls, woodpeckers, chickadees, ospreys, western tanagers, jays and Rufous hummingbirds. However, these are only a few of the 294 species that have been documented as reliably occurring in Montana.

Over 2,500 species of wildflowers and non-flowering plants can be found in three different areas within Montana: above the timberline (6,000–7,000 feet elevations) in northwestern Montana, mountain forest beginning at 5,000-feet elevations, and those found in open terrain of desert, plains, valleys and foothills.

There are several colorful flowers that can be frequently seen while driving. One is the Shooting Star, which has a rosy purple flower banded with a red and yellow ring pointing downward; elk and deer relish this adornment for meals. Also common is the Wild Rose Scrub, which grows from three to eight feet tall and in the fall produce small red rose-hips (or berries) that make a pleasant tea rich in vitamin C.

The Indian Paintbrush usually has red blossoms that bloom from June to early August in dry to moist soils. The most common flora of Montana is the Wood Violet which comes in a variety of colors ranging from white to purple. It blooms in early spring in wet, wooded areas, usually on slopes and ledges of deciduous forests. The petals of this plant can be eaten in salads or made into jelly, jam or candy. Wildflower meadows of Glacier lilies, Alpine poppies, columbine, asters, arnica spread their colors in midsummer hillsides while Dogtooth violets and Mariposa lilies grow a little farther down the slopes.

A mainstay for the bears of Montana is the huckleberry bush. A grown bear can consume 80 to 90 pounds of food per day, 15% of this poundage may consist of huckleberries. Late July is a good time to hunt huckleberries. They require a good amount of moisture and grow best on a north slope at elevations of 3,500 to 7,000 feet.

Most of western Montana supports lush growth dominated by coniferous forests. This area is usually divided into two categories: lower montane and higher subalpine. Ponderosa pines dominate the lower slopes. A little higher, the Douglas fir takes over and above that are the lodgepole pines so common in Montana-made furniture. Western cedar, grand fir, white pine, aspen and birch are also prevalent.

WIDE OPEN SPACES

While traveling on the backroads, you will sometimes get a sense that nobody lives here. You can travel for miles without seeing any sign of civilization beyond the occasional small herds of cattle. Occupied houses are rare and outnumbered by abandoned homesteaders shacks and log cabins. Fences often disappear entirely and are replaced by the infrequent "Open Range" signs that warn you cattle may be having their mid-day siesta in the middle of the road.

None-the-less, most of this land is privately owned unless posted otherwise. Before abandoning your car and heading out across these open spaces, it's a good idea and common courtesy to find the property owner and get permission. If you see fenceposts or gates with bright orange blazes, then getting permission isn't an option. They mean "no trespassing" in no uncertain terms.

However, I've never been shot at for stopping the car, getting out and smelling the sage, listening to the sound of silence, or to the voice of the wind, or the gurgle of a stream, the howl of a coyote, or the unidentified song of a prairie bird. I've never been asked to move along when I've stopped to admire a sunset, or simply marvel at the splendor of the endless sky.

Most of those that have bought and paid for a piece of this marvelous state don't mind sharing it with those who come to visit. They simply ask that you respect it and leave no trace you were there.

THE ROADS

Gravel roads are the rule rather than the exception in this part of the state. While most of the paved roads are well maintained, they are often narrow and have little or no shoulder. While you may want to slow down on gravel roads, don't expect the locals to do so. The vast distances between towns necessitate speed for those who live here. Remember, until a couple of years ago, Montana didn't even have a posted speed limit. While speed limits are now in effect, it hasn't changed the driving habits of people here much at all.

Be prepared at any time to slow down for riders on horseback. Most horses are accustomed to cars, but can spook if you drive too near. Much of Montana is open range. Cattle may be grazing on the road. A head-on with a steer can be just as deadly as a head-on with another automobile.

And speaking of cattle, don't be surprised if you come upon a cattle drive. If you do, follow the instructions of the drovers. They will make every effort to clear a path to allow you through. Usually the cattle just part ways and make a path, but don't go on unless you're given instructions to.

Rural unpaved roads have cattle guards at frequent intervals. Good idea to slow down for these. Most often they're not level with the road and can wreak havoc on the suspension, possibly even disabling the car.

Beware of black ice! This is a virtually invisible layer of ice that forms on road surfaces after a fog. Be particularly careful of stretches of road that parallel rivers and creeks. The early morning fog rising from them can settle on the road freezing instantly. If you feel yourself sliding, tap your brakes gently. If you slam on the brakes, it's all but over. Gently steer into the direction of your skid (if your back end is going right—steer right.

Gumbo

We gave this subject its own headline. It is very important that you read it—and heed it.

While Montana isn't the only state that has gumbo, it certainly seems to have cornered the market. If you become a resident, it is one of the first things you develop a respect (a healthy respect) for. Grizzlys and rattlesnakes might be the hazards you're warned of, but gumbo is the one that will get you.

You'll find it mostly in the eastern half of the state. It lies in wait on what in dry weather appears to be an ordinary rock hard dirt road. Your first clue is the occasional sign that reads *Road Impassable When Wet.* This is a clear understatement. When these roads become even mildly wet, they turn into a monster that swallows all sizes of vehicles—and yes, even 4-wheel drive SUVs. Think you'll get a tow? Forget it. No tow truck operator with a higher IQ than dirt will venture onto it until it dries. If you walk on it, you will grow six inches taller and gain 25 pounds all on the bottom of your shoes. Of course, this is if it doesn't swallow you whole first like an unsuspecting native in a Tarzan movie who steps into quicksand.

Bottomline, heed the signs. If it looks like rain, head for the nearest paved road. When it comes to swallowing things whole, the Bermuda Triangle is an amateur compared to Montana Gumbo.

RIVERS

It is fascinating that Montana has within its borders portions of the three major river drainage systems of North America. From Triple Divide in

The Bighorn Canyon.

Glacier National Park, raindrops falling only a few feet apart can take widely differing routes to the seas. Depending on which side of the three-sided point of land on which they fall, the raindrops may flow east into the Missouri and Mississippi rivers, the Gulf of Mexico, and the Atlantic Ocean; west to the Columbia River and the Pacific, or north and east into the rivers that lead to the Hudson Bay.

Rivers and streams that feed upon mountain snow runoff thrive throughout western Montana. They sing to hundreds of fisherman every year and effortlessly carry kayaks, rafts and inner tubes to all who seek beauty and adventure.

RECREATION

In Montana, pristine nature is so prevalent that it is hard to go anywhere and not find beauty and recreation. The abiding treasures of this state are two national parks, a national recreation area, fifteen wilderness areas, ten national forests, eight national wildlife refuges, 370 miles of national wild and scenic river, and several national scenic trails. In addition, there are also forty-two state parks, seven state forests, and approximately 600 miles of prized, blue-ribbon trout streams.

Montana is well-known for its prized fly fishing trout streams. Though it's possible to fish year-round in lakes and rivers, late June through October are the most popular fishing months. The state has more than 300 fishing access areas. A fishing license is reasonably priced and much more affordable than the fine one receives if caught without one. Contact Montana Department of Fish, Wildlife, and Parks (444-2535) for up-to-date information regarding licenses, prices and seasons for both hunting and fishing.

Whitewater rivers send many dancing rafts and kayaks into thrills of summer fun. Relaxing or more invigorating river trips by guides or alone position one to take in some spectacular scenery. Don't forget to take a dip in one of the state's hot springs; indoor or outdoor, they are a real delight both in the winter and warmer seasons. Hot water gurgles up all over the state into a wide variety of resorts, from the most rustic to the chic—there's something for everyone's fancy.

The national forests and mountain ranges provide endless opportunities for hikes on foot or on horseback. Hunters flock to Montana in the fall for elk, antelope, pronghorn, pheasants, deer, and bear. In the winter, both downhill and cross country skiing are all-time favorites.

MONTANA'S NATIONAL FORESTS

The national forests and grasslands of Montana stretch from the prairies and badlands of far eastern Montana, to the rolling hills and isolated ponderosa pine woodlands of the middle part of the state, to the rugged mountain tops and steep timbered canyons in the west.

Recreation opportunities are as diverse as these lands. Everything from sightseeing to motorcycling; horseback riding to picnicking; hunting to snowshoeing; and crosscountry skiing to kayaking await the outdoor enthusiast.

You can get away and experience the solitude and challenges of wildlands. On the other hand, campgrounds and visitor centers provide opportunities to associate with other people and enjoy the convenience of facilities.

Take your pick of the special places available in Montana… enjoy our forests and grasslands.

Wilderness

"A wilderness, in contrast with those areas where man and his own works dominate the landscape, is hereby recognized as an area where the earth and community of life are untrammeled by man, where man himself is a visitor who does not remain." - From the Wilderness Act September 3, 1964

Wildernesses in Montana encompass more than 4 million acres of rugged and beautiful mountain landscapes. Here, in relative solitude, visitors find areas maintained in their natural and undeveloped state providing relief from the pressures of today's society.

Somewhere near Tosten.

Northern Region Wildernesses:

Absaroka Beartooth
Anaconda Pintler
Bob Marshall
Cabinet Mountains
Gates of the Mountains
Great Bear
Lee Metcalf
Mission Mountains
Rattlesnake
Scapegoat
Selway
Bitterroot
Welcome Creek

Wildlife & Fisheries

From elk herds roaming the forested mountains of western Montana to antelope racing across the eastern plains, the National Forests are home to a magnificent wildlife and fish resource. Chinook salmon, grizzly bears, northern grey wolves, bald eagles and over 600 other kinds of fish and wildlife thrive here.

There is no place like this vast unspoiled country where wildlife is so diverse and so easily found. It's a great place to watch or photograph animals, large and small. Bighorn sheep, songbirds, moose and prairie dogs are not limited to zoos and refuges. They live everywhere and are part of everyday life.

Some of the best hunting in North America is also found in the region. The state carefully regulates hunting to ensure wildlife populations and quality recreation for future generations.

More stream miles criss-cross this region than any other in the lower 48 states. Names of famous blue ribbon trout streams like the Big Horn, Big Hole and Madison roll off the lips of fishermen like priceless jewels. Hundreds of lakes and reservoirs provide exceptional fishing as well.

Want help finding the best place for photography, hunting or fishing? State licensed guides and outfitters know the country and have the gear to ensure an enjoyable trip even in rugged remote country.

Trails

Trails provide the primary access to most of the undeveloped wildlands and millions of acres of wilderness.

Over 15,000 miles of trails provide a variety of challenges and scenic vistas to hikers, backpackers, horseriders, and cyclists. Most trails are open for recreational use year long; however, in some areas, seasonal restrictions are imposed to protect resources.

Winter Activities

The national forests of Montana are a winter wonderland.

The 16 alpine ski areas provide slopes for every talent. Winter sports areas have been developed in cooperation with private industry and are operated under national forest special-use permits.

In addition to spectacular downhill runs, there is a vast and diverse landscape for crosscountry skiers and snowmobilers. Crosscountry skiers can follow over 600 miles of designated ski touring trails of varying difficulty across timbered slopes, open meadows, and ridgelines. Or experienced skiers, with appropriate precautions, can do some exploring on their own.

Snowmobilers can tour thousands of miles of designated snowmobile trails. In some areas, wildlife winter ranges are closed to snowmobiling.

There are many rustic cabins and lookouts available for rent, some accessible to only the skier or snowmobiler in winter. A directory is available.

The harsh conditions of winter can turn an outing into a tragedy. Knowledge of the area, weather, route, and the limitations of your body and equipment-plus a little common sense-can ensure safe and enjoyable outings.

Scenic Drives

There are thousands of miles of roads available within the Region's national forests and grasslands. Some roads are high standard paved routes and others are low-standard "jeep" trails. Seasonal closures to protect resources, such as calving elk or water quality, may affect the use of certain roads. Information about motorized access and road restrictions for each national forest is shown on the forest visitor map.

Scenic drives abound throughout Montana. A few of the more popular routes include the drive around Hungry Horse Reservoir on the Flathead National Forest; the scenic loop around Lake Koocanusa behind Libby Dam on the Kootenai National Forest; and the route around Georgetown Lake on the Beaverhead-Deerlodge National Forest. These roads take you through rugged, scenic country and provide access for fishing and boating as well as to camping and picnicking sites.

For other driving adventures, follow the trail of Lewis and Clark across the Bitterroot Mountains on the Lolo and Clearwater National Forests. Or follow 27 mile Pioneer Mountains National Forest Scenic Byway, along the Pioneer Mountain Range on the Beaverhead-Deerlodge National Forest. Or visit Porphyry Peak Lookout on King's Hill Pass on the Lewis and Clark National Forest. Travel the fabulous Beartooth Highway across 10,942 foot Beartooth Summit on the Custer, Shoshone, and Gallatin National Forests.

Whether you are seeking solitude or scenic splendor, a national forest road will take you there.

Camping & Picnicking

Visitors can camp and picnic almost anywhere on the national forests and grasslands. For those seeking more convenience, hundreds of developed sites usually contain a parking spur, table, fireplace, and toilets. Water is also provided in some areas. Some sites are accessible to the handicapped or disabled. Showers, laundry facilities, electrical hookups, and hot water are not provided.

Campgrounds requiring a fee for use are signed and limitations on length of stay, if any, are posted. Horses and the shooting of firearms in developed campsites are prohibited.

For the more venturesome, there are numerous isolated roadside and backcountry picnic and campsites. These sites do not contain improvements like toilet, table, or fireplaces.

No matter where you are camping or picnicking, help keep the area clean.

FOREST SERVICE CABINS

One of the best kept secrets in Montana is the availability of cabins and lookout stations that the U.S. Forest Service makes available to the public at a very nominal fee. At the end of each section we have provided a list of available cabins along with detailed information on each. Following is some general information on reserving and using the cabins.

Application For Permits

Permits for use of recreational cabins in the National Forests of the Northern Region are issued on a first-come, first-served basis. Permits may be obtained in person or by mail by contacting the Ranger District having administrative responsibility for the cabin of your choice. Advance reservations of a week or more may be required. Lengths of stay are limited to 14 days and in some cases less. Maps and information may be obtained by Forest Service District maintaining each cabin/lookout.

The daily rate for occupancy is listed. Checks or postal money orders should be made payable to USDA Forest Service.

Facilities

Cabins and lookouts available through the rental program are rustic and primitive in nature. Most of these cabins are guard stations or work centers

MONTANA MOVIES

Whether you've ever actually set foot in Montana or not, you've no doubt seen lots of it. If you haven't seen it in any of these movies, you've probably seen it in countless commercials and catalogues. It is a favorite backdrop for film makers. Montana State University has one of the top film schools in the country providing excellent support to film makers shooting in the state. Here is a list of movies filmed here.

2000: *The Flying Dutchman*, *The Slaughter Rule* (Great Falls) 1999: *Big Eden* (Glacier National Park)

1998: *The Hi-Line* (Livingston/Clyde Park)

1997: *Everything That Rises* (Livingston), *The Horse Whisperer* (Big Timber/ Livingston/ Bozeman), *Me and Will*, *The Patriot* (Ennis), *What Dreams May Come* (Glacier National Park)

1996: *Almost Heros*

1995: *Amanda* (Red Lodge), *Broken Arrow* (Lewistown), *The Real Thing*, *Under Siege 2: Dark Territory* (MIssoula)

1993: *Beethoven's 2nd* (Glacier National Park/Flathead), *Forrest Gump* (Glacier National Park/Blackfeet Reservation), *Holy Matrimony* (Great Falls), *Iron Will* (West Yellowstone), *The Last Ride* (Livingston/ Deer Lodge), *Montana Crossroads*, *Return to Lonesome Dove* (Virginia City/ Butte/Billings, *The River Wild* (Libby/ Flathead)

1992: *Ballad of Little Jo* (Red Lodge), *Josh and S.A.M* (Billings)

1991: *A River Runs Through It* (Bozeman/Livingston), *Diggstown* (Deer Lodge), *Far and Away* (Billings), *Keep the Change* (Livingston), *Season of Change* (Bitterroot Valley)

1990: *Common Ground* (Columbia Falls), *Son of the Morning Star* (Billings), *True Colors* (Big Sky)

1989: *Always* (Libby), *Bright Angel* (Billings), *Montana* (Bozeman/Gallatin Gateway), *A Thousand Pieces of Gold* (Nevada City)

1988: *Cold Feet* (Livingston), *Disorganized Crime* (Hamilton/Darby/Missoula)

1987: *Pow Wow Highway* (Hardin/North Cheyenne Reservation/Colstrip), *War Party* (Browning/Cut Bank/Choteau)

1986: *Amazing Grace and Chuck* (Bozeman/Livingston/Helena), *Stacking* (Billings), *Untouchables* (Cascade), *Amy Grant: Home for the Holidays* (Kalispell/ Glacier Park)

1985: *Runaway Train* (Butte/Anaconda)

1983: *The Stone Boy* (Great Falls) , *Triumphs of a Man Called Horse* (Cooke City/Red Lodge)

1982: *Firefox* (Glasgow/Cut Bank)

1980: *Continental Divide* (Glacier National Park), *Fast Walking* (Deer Lodge)

1979: *Heartland* (Harlowton), *Heaven's Gate* (Kalispell/Glacier National Park), *Legend of Walks Far Woman* (Billings/Red Lodge/Hardin), *South by Northwest* (Virginia City/Nevada City)

1978: *Rodeo Red & The Runaway* (Billings), *The Shining* (Glacier National Park)

1977: *Christmas Miracle in Caulfield USA* (Roundup), *Grey Eagle* (Helena), *The Other Side of Hell* (Warm Springs), *Telefon* (Great Falls)

1976: *Beartooth* (Red Lodge), *Damnation Alley* (Lakeside), *Pony Express Rider* (Virginia City/Nevada City)

1975: *Missouri Breaks* (Billings/Virginia City/Red Lodge), *Winds of Autumn* (Kalispell)

1974: *The Killer Inside Me* (Butte), *Potato Fritz* (Helena), *Rancho Deluxe* (Livingston)

1973: *Route 66* (Butte), *Thunderbolt and Lightfoot* (Malpaso/Livingston/Great Falls), *Winterhawk* (Kalispell)

1972: *Evel Knievel* (Butte)

1970: *Little Big Man* (Virginia City/Billings)

1958: *Dangerous Mission* (Glacier National Park)

1954: *Cattle Queen of Montana* (East Glacier)

1953: *Powder River*

1951: *Timberjack*, *Warpath* (Missoula)

1950: *Red Skies Over Montana* (Missoula)

1920: *Devil's Horse* (Hardin), *Where the Rivers Rise* (Columbia Falls)

---

located in remote areas that are occasionally used to house Forest Service employees. As the need for these cabins declines, they are being made available to the general public. With the exception of a few cabins, do not expect the modern conveniences that we all are so accustomed to enjoying.

It is suggested that an inquiry be made to the Ranger District that has administrative responsibility for the cabin as to what is and what is not furnished and disabled access information. Based on the information received, you can then plan your needs.

Cabins are generally equipped with the bare basics, including a table, chairs, wood stove and bunks (most with mattresses, some without). Bedding is not furnished. Cooking utensils are available at some cabins but not all of them. Electricity and piped-in water are generally NOT available. It may be necessary to bring safe drinking water or be prepared to chemically treat or boil drinking water. At some cabins, you will need to find and cut your own firewood. Expect to use outdoor toilets. Telephones are not available.

Before leaving, users are requested to: burn all combustible waste materials; make sure fires in stoves are out; pack out all garbage and empty bottles or cans; clean the cabin; leave a supply of firewood and return the key.

Potential Risks

Travel in the National Forests and use of rustic cabins and lookouts invokes a degree of risk. Recreationists must assume the responsibility to obtain knowledge and skills necessary to protect themselves and members of their party from injury and illness. Weather, snow conditions, personal physical skill and condition along with other factors can influence travel time and difficulty. Parents are strongly discouraged from bringing children under 12 years of age to Lookout Towers. Persons afraid of heights, or lacking physical strength, should also avoid climbing Lookout Towers. Prior to the trip, permit holders are advised to contact the local Ranger District for current conditions. *Reprinted from U.S. Forest Service brochure.*

MONTANA'S STATE PARK SYSTEM

Because of the exceptional recreational opportunities on Montana's federal lands, the diversity of opportunities available in the Montana State Park System is sometimes overlooked. This would be a mistake, as the true picture of Montana's natural, cultural, and recreational resources is not complete without the state parks.

Montana's State Park System was created in 1939, when the Montana Legislature created a State Parks Commission. Lewis and Clark Caverns became the state's first state park when the site was transferred to Montana from the federal government. Today, the network of sites has grown to forty-one, in addition to a number of affiliated sites.

State parks are found in every region of the state, offering a wide range of landscapes, natural features, history, and recreational opportunities. Some parks feature a diversity of visitor facilities such as showers, boat launch sites, and concessions, while others are much less developed.

State Park Information: For more detailed state park information, call the Montana Parks Division at 444-3750. Hearing impaired recreationists may call the TDD number at 444-1200.

Camping: Camping is offered at many state parks for a modest fee. Campsites are available on a first-come, first-served basis; there is no comprehensive, statewide reservation system. While services vary between individual parks, most sites have a picnic table, a fire ring or grill, and parking for one vehicle and RV.

Group Camping: Several state parks have sites set aside for group use. A special brochure is available with more detailed information on group camping opportunities at state parks and fishing access sites.

Rental Cabins: Rustic cabins are available for rent at Lewis and Clark Caverns State Park. Call 287-3541 for reservations.

Day Use Parks: Some Montana state parks are open for a range of day uses, but do not allow overnight stays.

Primitive Service Parks: A primitive parks system was established by the Montana Legislature in 1993. Primitive parks have a minimum of services available, with visitors expected to pack out their own trash.

Season: Some parks are open for day use and camping year-round, while others close at least some of their facilities during the winter. For the most current information, call the number listed for each park.

Fees: Day use fees are charged at many state parks. Purchase of an annual State Parks Passport allows free entry to all Montana State Parks. Camping fees vary according to the level of service provided.

Camping fees are charged per "camper unit" for a campsite. A "camper unit" is defined as a motorized vehicle, motor home, camping bus, pull-type camper, tent, or any other device designed for sleeping,

Montana Introduction

MONTANA LICENSE PLATE NUMBERS

Montana counties were originally numbered for license plates based on the size of the county. Since the original numbering, populations have shifted—sometimes dramatically. The numbering system, however, has remained the same.

1: Silver Bow (Butte)
2: Cascade (Great Falls)
3: Yellowstone (Billings)
4: Missoula (Missoula)
5: Lewis & Clark (Helena)
6: Gallatin (Bozeman)
7: Flathead (Kalispell)
8: Fergus (Lewistown)
9: Powder River (Broadus)
10: Carbon (Red Lodge)
11: Phillips (Malta)
12: Hill (Havre)
13: Ravalli (Hamilton)
14: Custer (Miles City)
15: Lake (Polson)
16: Dawson (Glendive)
17: Roosevelt (Wolf Point)
18: Beaverhead (Dillon)
19: Chouteau (Fort Benton)
20: Valley (Glasgow)
21: Toole (Shelby)
22: Big Horn (Hardin)
23: Musselshell (Roundup)
24: Blaine (Chinook)
25: Madison (Virginia City)
26: Pondera (Conrad)
27: Richland (Sidney)
28: Powell (Deer Lodge)
29: Rosebud (Forsyth)
30: Deer Lodge (Anaconda)
31: Teton (Choteau)
32: Stillwater (Columbus)
33: Treasure (Hysham)
34: Sheridan (Plentywood)
35: Sanders (Thompson Falls)
36: Judith Basin (Stanford)
37: Daniels (Scobey)
38: Glacier (Cut Bank)
39: Fallon (Baker)
40: Sweet Grass (Big Timber)
41: McCone (Circle)
42: Carter (Ekalaka)
43: Broadwater (Townsend)
44: Wheatland (Harlowton)
45: Prairie (Terry)
46: Granite (Philipsburg)
47: Meagher (White Sulphur Springs)
48: Liberty (Chester)
49: Park (Livingston)
50: Garfield (Jordan)
51: Jefferson (Boulder)
52: Wibaux (Wibaux)
53: Golden Valley (Ryegate)
54: Mineral (Superior)
55: Petroleum (Winnett)
56: Lincoln (Libby)

A self-registration system is in use at most state parks. Recreation use fees are also charged for designated group use facilities, guided tours, and other services. Fee information is available from the individual parks. Special floater fees are in effect on the Smith River.

Picnicking: Many state parks have developed facilities for picnicking, and some include special facilities for group use. Consult the data given with each state park description. *Reprinted from Montana Fish, Wildlife & Parks brochure.*

FISHING

Seasons

You can fish year round in Montana, but seasonal regulations do exist, and water conditions will affect your success. Generally, lakes and larger rivers can be fished all year, while smaller tributaries are closed in the winter and early spring to allow fish to spawn. Ice fishing is popular in the winter. The lakes are usually frozen from December through at least March. During the spring runoff when many freestone rivers are high and muddy, flyfishermen find luck in the smaller streams and spring creeks. The prime fishing season is from late June through October.

Licenses

A Montana fishing license is required for all anglers 15 years of age and older. You can purchase a license just about anywhere fishing tackle is sold or from any of the Montana Fish, Wildlife and Parks offices. Non-residents can purchase licenses in two-day increments or by the season. There are special requirements for youths under 15, residents 62 years of age or older, and for taking paddlefish. Contact Montana Fish, Wildlife and Parks for a fishing regulations brochure.

Fishing sites

We have marked over 250 fishing sites on our maps. Each section has a reference chart referring to the numbered sites on the maps. The charts include species available and facilities available. The charts are at the end of each section.

WEATHER

Montana is known for its unpredictable weather. The weather maintains as much variety as does the state's topography. The lowest temperature recorded in the lower 48 states was -70°F, recorded northwest of Helena. Hot summers are common; 117 degrees has been recorded in both Glendive and Medicine Lake, but the hottest day in Montana is not suffocating due to its low humidity which generally ranges between 20 and 30 percent. The real beauty of Montana's weather, is that it is very dry. Extremes of hot or cold never feel oppressive as a result.

May and June are the wettest months for most of the state. Average rainfall is 15 inches, which can vary from less than 10 inches on the plains and to more than 50 inches in the mountains. July and August are usually Montana's warmest, driest periods and serve as the busiest time for tourism and recreation. Often there is a pleasant Indian summer in September and October. Warm, bright days with cool nights make it an exhilarating time with fishing at its prime. During the fall, Montana's forests may not flaunt the vibrant colors of the eastern woodlands, but its tamaracks are bright yellow contrasting nicely against the evergreens, and the aspen groves turn a dazzling gold.

The infamous Montana winter rarely settles in

A Montana roller coaster.

for keeps. Even though snow can fall in July, roads can also be clear throughout November. Montana's cold spells and blasts of arctic air bring blizzards which often melt the following week from dry chinook winds blowing from the west. (Native Americans called these winds the "snow eaters.") Even when roads are clear, travelers must be careful as one could hit a patch of ice in a shaded, mountainous area although the road may be dry for miles. While temperatures can be extreme in Montana, the low humidity never causes the weather to be oppressively hot or cold.

PRECAUTIONS

Water Sports: Beware of high river waters in the spring due to melting snow; it is best to contact knowledgeable people in the area for information before venturing out on your own.

Animal Caution: Grizzly bears are found in both Glacier and Yellowstone National Parks and in smaller populations in the northern Rockies. Grizzlies are vicious when provoked, and it doesn't take much to rile them. Check with local rangers for bear updates and guidelines before heading into bear country. When hiking even on trails make noise to warn bears of your presence. If you camp, don't sleep near strong smells or food. Hang all food from branches 100 yards from tents. Also, watch for moose on or near hiking trails. Moose, especially those with offspring, are often known to charge if hikers get too close and the animal feels threatened.

Rattlesnake Warning: Rattlesnakes are common primarily in eastern parts of Montana. A bite from the snake can be fatal if not properly treated. These snakes are not aggressive and will usually retreat unless threatened. It is recommended that you wear strong and high top boots when hiking and be mindful of your step. Be especially careful near rocky areas; snakes often sun themselves on exposed rocks. If you hear a rattle, stop and slowly back away. If bitten, immobilize the area and seek medical care immediately.

Weather: Extremes are commonplace in Montana without a moment's notice. In high temperatures drink plenty of water; Montana is very dry which aides dehydration in warm weather. Even in warmer weather, nights can be cold so have extra clothes on hand. Sudden storms can blow in; be prepared with rain and wind gear. The windiest areas are Great Falls, Livingston, and Cut Bank. When driving, listen for wind warnings.

Winter weather is the greatest concern. While roads can be treacherous if snow covered, melting snow and ice can also leave small and invisible patches of ice on the road. Also, wildlife commonly descend from the mountains looking for food; be aware of deer or elk on the road particularly at dusk, sunset or at night when visibility is limited. If you travel by automobile during Montana's winter, have plenty of blankets or a sleeping bag, warm clothing, flashlight, and some food and water on hand.

Place	Zip
Absarokee	59001
Acton	59002
Alberton	59820
Alder	59710
Alzada	59311
Anaconda	59711
Angela	59312
Antelope	59211
Arlee	59821
Ashland	59003
Augusta	59410
Avon	59713
Babb	59411
Bainville	59212
Baker	59313
Ballantine,	59006
Basin	59631
Bearcreek	59007
Belfry	59008
Belgrade	59714
Belt	59412
Biddle	59314
Big Arm	59910
Bigfork	59911
Bighorn	59010
Big Sandy	59520
Big Sky	59716
Big Timber	59011
*Billings	59101
Birney	59012
Black Eagle	59414
Bloomfield	59315
Bonner	59823
Boulder	59632
Box Elder	59521
Boyd	59013
Boyes	59316
*Bozeman	59715
Brady	59416
Bridger	59014
Broadus	59317
Broadview	59015
Brockton	59213
Brockway	59214
Browning	59417
Brusett	59318
Buffalo	59418
Busby	59016
*Butte	59701
Bynum	59419
Cameron	59720
Canyon Creek	59633
Capitol	59319
Cardwell	59721
Carter	59420
Cascade	59421
Cat Creek	59087
Charlo	59824
Chester	59522
Chinook	59523
Choteau	59422
Circle	59215
Clancy	59634
Clinton	59825
Clyde Park	59018
Coffee Creek	59424
Cohagen	59322
Colstrip	59323
Columbia Falls	59912
Columbus	59019
Condon	59826
Conner	59827
Conrad	59425
Cooke City	59020
Coram	59913
Corvallis	59828
Corwin Springs	59030
Crane	59217
Creston	59902
Crow Agency	59022
Culbertson	59218
Custer	59024
Cut Bank	59427
Dagmar	59219
Danvers	59429
Darby	59829
Dayton	59914
De Borgia	59830
Decker	59025
Deer Lodge	59722
Dell	59724
Delphia	59073
Denton	59430
Dillon	59725
Divide	59727
Dixon	59831
Dodson	59524
Drummond	59832
Dupuyer	59432
Dutton	59433
Edgar	59026
E. Glacier Park	59434
East Helena	59635
Ekalaka	59324
Elliston	59728
Elmo	59915
Emigrant	59027
Enid	59220
Ennis	59729
Epsie	59317
Essex	59916
Ethridge	59435
Eureka	59917
*Evergreen	59901
Fairfield	59436
Fairview	59221
Fallon	59326
Ferdig	59437
Fishtail	59028
Flaxville	59222
Florence	59833
Floweree	59440
Forestgrove,	59441
Forsyth	59327
Fort Benton	59442
Fort Harrison	59636
Fortine	59918
Fort Peck	59223
Fort Shaw	59443
Fort Smith	59035
Four Buttes	59263
Frazer	59225
Frenchtown	59834
Froid	59226
Fromberg	59029
Galata	59444
Gallatin Gateway	59730
Gardiner	59030
Garneill	59445
Garrison	59731
Garryowen	59031
Geraldine	59446
Geyser	59447
Gildford	59525
Glasgow	59230
Glen	59732
Glendive	59330
Glentana	59240
Goldcreek	59733
Grantsdale,	59835
Grass Range	59032
*Great Falls	59401
Greenough	59836
Greycliff	59033
Hall	59837
Hamilton	59840
Hammond	59332
Hardin	59034
Harlem	59526
Harlowton	59036
Harrison	59735
Hathaway	59333
Haugan	59842
Havre	59501
Hays	59527
Heart Butte	59448
*Helena	59601
Helmville	59843
Heron	59844
Highwood	59450
Hilger	59451
Hingham	59528
Hinsdale	59241
Hobson	59452
Hogeland	59529
Homestead	59242
Hot Springs	59845
Hungry Horse	59919
Huntley	59037
Huson	59846
Hysham	59038
Ingomar	59039
Inverness	59530
Ismay	59336
Jackson	59736
Jeffers	59737
Jefferson City	59638
Joliet	59041
Joplin	59531
Jordan	59337
Judith Gap	59453
*Kalispell	59901
Kevin	59454
Kila	59920
Kinsey	59338
Kremlin	59532
Lake McDonald	59921
Lakeside	59922
Lambert	59243
Lame Deer	59043
Landusky	59533
Larslan	59244
Laurel	59044
Laurin	59738
Lavina	59046
Ledger	59456
Lewistown	59457
Libby	59923
Lima	59739
Lincoln	59639
Lindsay	59339
Livingston	59047
Lloyd	59535
Lodge Grass	59050
Lolo	59847
Loma	59460
Lonepine	59848
Loring	59537
Lothair	59461
Lustre	59225
Luther	59068
Malmstrom AFB	59402
Malta	59538
Manhattan	59741
Marion	59925
Martin City	59926
Martinsdale	59053
Marysville	59640
Maudlow	59714
Maxville,	59858
McAllister	59740
McCabe	59245
McLeod	59052
Medicine Lake	59247
Melrose	59743
Melstone	59054
Melville	59055
Mildred	59341
Miles City	59301
Mill Iron	59342
Milltown	59851
*Missoula	59801
Moccasin	59462
Moiese	59824
Molt	59057
Monarch	59463
Moore	59464
Mosby	59058
Musselshell	59059
Nashua	59248
Nelhart	59465
Niarada	59845
Norris	59745
Noxon	59853
Nye	59061
Oilmont	59466
Olive	59343
Olney	59927
Opheim	59250
Otter	59062
Outlook	59252
Ovando	59854
Pablo	59855
Paradise	59856
Park City	59063
Peerless	59253
Pendroy	59467
Perma	59857
Phillipsburg	59858
Pinesdale	59841
Plains	59859
Plentywood	59254
Plevna	59344
Polaris	59746
Polebridge	59928
Polson	59860
Pompeys Pillar	59064
Pony	59747
Poplar	59255
Powderville	59345
Power	59468
Pray	59065
Proctor	59929
Proctor	59914
Pryor	59066
Radersburg	59641
Ramsay	59748
Rapelje	59067
Ravalli	59863
Raymond	59256
Raynesford	59469
Red Lodge	59068
Redstone	59257
Reedpoint	59069
Regina	59539
Reserve	59258
Rexford	59930
Richey	59259
Richland	59260
Ringling	59642
Roberts	59070
Rock Springs	59346
Rollins	59931
Ronan	59864
Roscoe	59071
Rosebud	59347
Roundup	59072
Roy	59471
Rudyard	59540
Ryegate	59074
Saco	59261
St. Ignatius	59865
St. Labre	59004
Saint Marie	59231
Saint Marie	59230
St. Mary	59417
St. Regis	59866
St. Xavier	59075
Saltese	59867
Sand Coulee	59472
Sanders	59076
Sanders	59038
Sand Springs	59077
Santa Rita	59473
Savage	59262
Scobey	59263
Seeley Lake	59868
Shawmut	59078
Shelby	59474
Shepherd	59079
Sheridan	59749
Shonkin	59450
Sidney	59270
Silesia	59041
Silverbow	59750
Silver Gate	59081
Silver Star	59751
Simms	59477
Snider	59869
Somers	59932
Sonnette	59348
Springdale	59082
Stanford	59479
Stevensville	59870
Stockett	59480
Stryker	59933
Sula	59871
Sumatra	59083
Sunburst	59482
Sun River	59483
Superior	59872
Swan Lake	59911
Sweetgrass	59484
Teigen	59084
Terry	59349
Thompson Falls	59873
Three Forks	59752
Toston	59643
Townsend	59644
Trego	59934
Trident	59752
Trout Creek	59874
Troy	59935
Turner	59542
Twin Bridges	59754
Twodot	59085
Ulm	59485
Utica	59452
Valier	59486
Vandalia	59273
Vaughn	59487
Victor	59875
Vida	59274
Virginia City	59755
Volborg	59351
Wagner	59543
Walkerville	59701
Warm Springs	59756
West Glacier	59936
West Yellowstone	59758
Westby	59275
Whitefish	59937
Whitehall	59759
White Sulphur Sprngs	59645
Whitetail	59276
Whitewater	59544
Whitlash	59545
Wibaux	59353
Willard	59354
Willow Creek	59760
Wilsall	59086
Winifred	59489
Winnett	59087
Winston	59647
Wisdom	59761
Wise River	59762
Wolf Creek	59648
Wolf Point	59201
Worden	59088
Wyola	59089
Yellowtail	59035
Zortman	59546
Zurich	59547

*This zip code is for general delivery only. Contact your local post office for other zip codes.

MONTANA COUNTIES

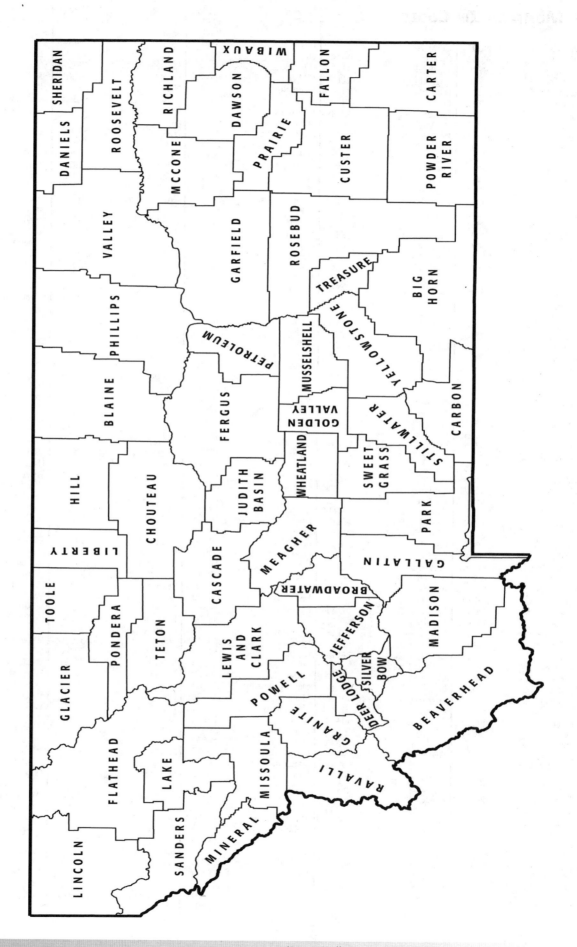

Montana Distances

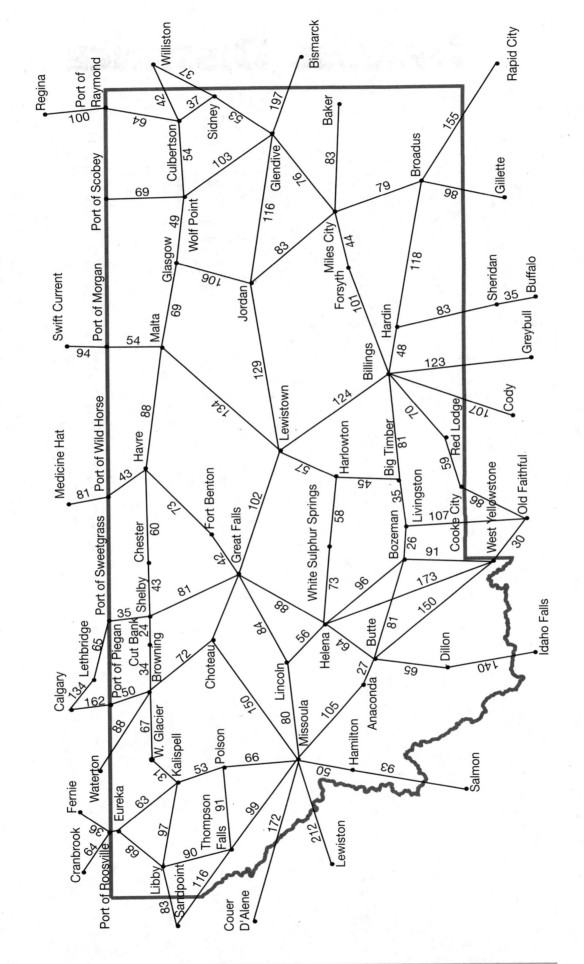

All Montana Area Codes are 406

Driving Distance

Anaconda to
- Baker 476
- Big Timber 170
- Billings 251
- Boulder 64
- Bozeman 109
- Broadus 419
- Browning 253
- Butte 27
- Chester 290
- Chinook 308
- Choteau 181
- Circle 459
- Columbus 210
- Conrad 223
- Cooke City 244
- Culbertson 548
- Cut Bank 270
- Deer Lodge 27
- Dillon 78
- E. Glacier Park 266
- Ekalaka 511
- Eureka 279
- Forsyth 351
- Fort Benton 216
- Gardiner 188
- Glasgow 445
- Glendive 473
- Grass Range Jct. 293
- Great Falls 172
- Hamilton 126
- Hardin 297
- Harlowtown 205
- Havre 287
- Helena 83
- Hysham 328
- Jordan 392
- Kalispell 213
- Laurel 235
- Lewistown 262
- Libby 295
- Livingston 135
- Malta 375
- Miles City 396
- Missoula 105
- Philipsburg 31
- Plentywood 590
- Polson 171
- Poplar 515
- Red Lodge 258
- Roundup 274
- Ryegate 235
- Scobey 549
- Shelby 248
- Sidney 523
- Stanford 232
- Superior 162
- Sweetgrass 282
- Terry 434
- Thompson Falls 205
- Three Forks 80
- Townsend 106
- Virginia City 99
- West Glacier 234
- W. Yellowstone 177
- Whitefish 227
- W Sulphur Springs 148
- Wibaux 499
- Winnett 316
- Wolf Point 494

Baker to
- Anaconda 476
- Big Timber 306
- Billings 225
- Boulder 450
- Bozeman 367
- Broadus 157
- Browning 525
- Butte 449
- Chester 440
- Chinook 359
- Choteau 453
- Circle 120
- Columbus 266
- Conrad 461
- Cooke City 351
- Culbertson 162
- Cut Bank 506
- Deer Lodge 482
- Dillon 479
- E. Glacier Park 538
- Ekalaka 35
- Eureka 670
- Forsyth 125
- Fort Benton 392
- Gardiner 394
- Glasgow 222
- Glendive 71
- Grass Range Jct. 262
- Great Falls 398
- Hamilton 591
- Hardin 200
- Harlowtown 295
- Havre 380
- Helena 426
- Hysham 154
- Jordan 165
- Kalispell 622
- Laurel 241
- Lewistown 293
- Libby 711
- Livingston 341
- Malta 292
- Miles City 81
- Missoula 541
- Philipsburg 507
- Plentywood 209
- Polson 607
- Poplar 185
- Red Lodge 285
- Roundup 226
- Ryegate 265
- Scobey 219
- Shelby 482
- Sidney 125
- Stanford 338
- Superior 598
- Sweetgrass 518
- Terry 110
- Thompson Falls 641
- Three Forks 397
- Townsend 394
- Virginia City 434
- West Glacier 593
- W. Yellowstone 443
- Whitefish 618
- W Sulphur Springs 352
- Wibaux 45
- Winnett 239
- Wolf Point 173

Big Timber to
- Anaconda 170
- Baker 306
- Billings 81
- Boulder 144
- Bozeman 61
- Broadus 249
- Browning 299
- Butte 143
- Chester 302
- Chinook 254
- Choteau 227
- Circle 298
- Columbus 40
- Conrad 235
- Cooke City 144
- Culbertson 390
- Cut Bank 382
- Deer Lodge 184
- Dillon 173
- E. Glacier Park 312
- Ekalaka 341
- Eureka 412
- Forsyth 181
- Fort Benton 177
- Gardiner 88
- Glasgow 304
- Glendive 303
- Grass Range Jct. 132
- Great Falls 172
- Hamilton 290
- Hardin 127
- Harlowtown 44
- Havre 252
- Helena 150
- Hysham 158
- Jordan 231
- Kalispell 346
- Laurel 65
- Lewistown 101
- Libby 435
- Livingston 35
- Malta 234
- Miles City 226
- Missoula 263
- Philipsburg 201
- Plentywood 437
- Polson 329
- Poplar 363
- Red Lodge 88
- Roundup 113
- Ryegate 74
- Scobey 397
- Shelby 260
- Sidney 353
- Stanford 112
- Superior 320
- Sweetgrass 294
- Terry 264
- Thompson Falls 363
- Three Forks 91
- Townsend 118
- Virginia City 128
- West Glacier 367
- W. Yellowstone 142
- Whitefish 360
- W Sulphur Springs 94
- Wibaux 329
- Winnett 155
- Wolf Point 351

Billings to
- Anaconda 251
- Baker 225
- Big Timber 81
- Boulder 225
- Bozeman 142
- Broadus 168
- Browning 346
- Butte 224
- Chester 310
- Chinook 229
- Choteau 274
- Circle 241
- Columbus 41
- Conrad 282
- Cooke City 126
- Culbertson 309
- Cut Bank 329
- Deer Lodge 265
- Dillon 254
- E. Glacier Park 359
- Ekalaka 260
- Eureka 486
- Forsyth 100
- Fort Benton 224
- Gardiner 169
- Glasgow 279
- Glendive 222
- Grass Range Jct. 97
- Great Falls 219
- Hamilton 371
- Hardin 46
- Harlowtown 93
- Havre 250
- Helena 224
- Hysham 77
- Jordan 174
- Kalispell 420
- Laurel 16
- Lewistown 128
- Libby 509
- Livingston 116
- Malta 209
- Miles City 145
- Missoula 339
- Philipsburg 282
- Plentywood 356
- Polson 405
- Poplar 306
- Red Lodge 60
- Roundup 53
- Ryegate 63
- Scobey 340
- Shelby 307
- Sidney 272
- Stanford 159
- Superior 396
- Sweetgrass 341
- Terry 183
- Thompson Falls 439
- Three Forks 172
- Townsend 192
- Virginia City 209
- West Glacier 414
- W. Yellowstone 218
- Whitefish 434
- W Sulphur Springs 150
- Wibaux 248
- Winnett 98
- Wolf Point 294

Boulder to
- Anaconda 64
- Baker 450
- Big Timber 144
- Billings 225
- Bozeman 83
- Broadus 393
- Browning 199
- Butte 37
- Chester 236
- Chinook 252
- Choteau 127
- Circle 412
- Columbus 184
- Conrad 169
- Cooke City 218
- Culbertson 492
- Cut Bank 216
- Deer Lodge 78
- Dillon 93
- E. Glacier Park 212
- Ekalaka 485
- Eureka 289
- Forsyth 325
- Fort Benton 160
- Gardiner 162
- Glasgow 389
- Glendive 447
- Grass Range Jct. 246
- Great Falls 116
- Hamilton 184
- Hardin 271
- Harlowtown 158
- Havre 231
- Helena 27
- Hysham 302
- Jordan 345
- Kalispell 223
- Laurel 209
- Lewistown 215
- Libby 312
- Livingston 109
- Malta 319
- Miles City 370
- Missoula 142
- Philipsburg 95
- Plentywood 534
- Polson 208
- Poplar 459
- Red Lodge 232
- Roundup 227
- Ryegate 188
- Scobey 493
- Shelby 194
- Sidney 487
- Stanford 176
- Superior 199
- Sweetgrass 228
- Terry 408
- Thompson Falls 242
- Three Forks 54
- Townsend 59
- Virginia City 93
- West Glacier 244
- W. Yellowstone 151
- Whitefish 237
- W Sulphur Springs 101
- Wibaux 473
- Winnett 269
- Wolf Point 438

Bozeman to
- Anaconda 109
- Baker 367
- Big Timber 61
- Billings 142
- Boulder 83
- Broadus 310
- Browning 267
- Butte 82
- Chester 304
- Chinook 313
- Choteau 195
- Circle 359
- Columbus 101
- Conrad 237
- Cooke City 135
- Culbertson 451
- Cut Bank 284
- Deer Lodge 123
- Dillon 112
- E. Glacier Park 280
- Ekalaka 402
- Eureka 357
- Forsyth 242
- Fort Benton 221
- Gardiner 79
- Glasgow 365
- Glendive 364
- Grass Range Jct. 193
- Great Falls 177
- Hamilton 229
- Hardin 188
- Harlowtown 105
- Havre 292
- Helena 95
- Hysham 219
- Jordan 292
- Kalispell 291
- Laurel 126
- Lewistown 162
- Libby 380
- Livingston 26
- Malta 295
- Miles City 287
- Missoula 202
- Philipsburg 140
- Plentywood 498
- Polson 268
- Poplar 424
- Red Lodge 149
- Roundup 174
- Ryegate 135
- Scobey 458
- Shelby 262
- Sidney 414
- Stanford 173
- Superior 259
- Sweetgrass 296
- Terry 325
- Thompson Falls 302
- Three Forks 30
- Townsend 63
- Virginia City 67
- West Glacier 312
- W. Yellowstone 91
- Whitefish 305
- W Sulphur Springs 80
- Wibaux 390
- Winnett 216
- Wolf Point 412

Broadus to
- Anaconda 419
- Baker 157
- Big Timber 249
- Billings 168
- Boulder 393
- Bozeman 310
- Browning 514
- Butte 392
- Chester 472
- Chinook 391
- Choteau 442
- Circle 195
- Columbus 209
- Conrad 450
- Cooke City 294
- Culbertson 241
- Cut Bank 497
- Deer Lodge 433
- Dillon 422
- E. Glacier Park 527
- Ekalaka 192
- Eureka 654
- Forsyth 122
- Fort Benton 389
- Gardiner 337
- Glasgow 276
- Glendive 154
- Grass Range Jct. 259
- Great Falls 387
- Hamilton 539
- Hardin 122
- Harlowtown 261
- Havre 412
- Helena 392
- Hysham 139
- Jordan 163
- Kalispell 588
- Laurel 184
- Lewistown 290
- Libby 677
- Livingston 284
- Malta 346
- Miles City 79
- Missoula 507
- Philipsburg 450
- Plentywood 288
- Polson 573
- Poplar 260
- Red Lodge 228
- Roundup 215
- Ryegate 231
- Scobey 294
- Shelby 475
- Sidney 204
- Stanford 327
- Superior 564
- Sweetgrass 509
- Terry 115
- Thompson Falls 607
- Three Forks 340
- Townsend 360
- Virginia City 377
- West Glacier 582
- W. Yellowstone 386
- Whitefish 602
- W Sulphur Springs 318
- Wibaux 180
- Winnett 237
- Wolf Point 248

Browning to
- Anaconda 253
- Baker 525
- Big Timber 299
- Billings 346
- Boulder 199
- Bozeman 267
- Broadus 514
- Butte 236
- Chester 100
- Chinook 181
- Choteau 72
- Circle 420
- Columbus 339
- Conrad 66
- Cooke City 402
- Culbertson 421
- Cut Bank 34
- Deer Lodge 226
- Dillon 292
- E. Glacier Park 13
- Ekalaka 560
- Eureka 145
- Forsyth 408
- Fort Benton 171
- Gardiner 346
- Glasgow 318
- Glendive 469
- Grass Range Jct. 263
- Great Falls 127
- Hamilton 254
- Hardin 392
- Harlowtown 255
- Havre 160
- Helena 172
- Hysham 423
- Jordan 362
- Kalispell 99
- Laurel 362
- Lewistown 232
- Libby 188
- Livingston 293
- Malta 248
- Miles City 444
- Missoula 204
- Philipsburg 263
- Plentywood 463
- Polson 138
- Poplar 388
- Red Lodge 387
- Roundup 307
- Ryegate 283
- Scobey 422
- Shelby 58
- Sidney 458
- Stanford 187
- Superior 224
- Sweetgrass 92
- Terry 483
- Thompson Falls 207
- Three Forks 238
- Townsend 204
- Virginia City 292
- West Glacier 68
- W. Yellowstone 347
- Whitefish 93
- W Sulphur Springs 224
- Wibaux 495
- Winnett 286
- Wolf Point 367

Butte to
- Anaconda 27
- Baker 449
- Big Timber 143
- Billings 224
- Boulder 37
- Bozeman 82
- Broadus 392
- Browning 236
- Chester 273
- Chinook 289
- Choteau 164
- Circle 432
- Columbus 183
- Conrad 206
- Cooke City 217
- Culbertson 529
- Cut Bank 253
- Deer Lodge 41
- Dillon 65
- E. Glacier Park 249
- Ekalaka 484
- Eureka 293
- Forsyth 324
- Fort Benton 197
- Gardiner 161
- Glasgow 426
- Glendive 446
- Grass Range Jct. 266
- Great Falls 153
- Hamilton 147
- Hardin 270
- Harlowtown 178
- Havre 268
- Helena 64
- Hysham 301
- Jordan 365
- Kalispell 227
- Laurel 208
- Lewistown 235
- Libby 310
- Livingston 108
- Malta 356
- Miles City 369
- Missoula 120
- Philipsburg 58
- Plentywood 571
- Polson 186
- Poplar 496
- Red Lodge 231
- Roundup 247
- Ryegate 208
- Scobey 530
- Shelby 231
- Sidney 496
- Stanford 213
- Superior 177
- Sweetgrass 265
- Terry 401
- Thompson Falls 220
- Three Forks 53
- Townsend 79
- Virginia City 72
- West Glacier 248
- W. Yellowstone 150
- Whitefish 241
- W Sulphur Springs 121
- Wibaux 472
- Winnett 289
- Wolf Point 475

Chester to
- Anaconda 290
- Baker 440
- Big Timber 302
- Billings 310
- Boulder 236
- Bozeman 304
- Broadus 472
- Browning 100
- Butte 273
- Chinook 81
- Choteau 117
- Circle 320
- Columbus 342
- Conrad 67
- Cooke City 409
- Culbertson 321
- Cut Bank 66
- Deer Lodge 263
- Dillon 329
- E. Glacier Park 113
- Ekalaka 475
- Eureka 245
- Forsyth 358
- Fort Benton 129
- Gardiner 353
- Glasgow 218
- Glendive 369
- Grass Range Jct. 213
- Great Falls 130
- Hamilton 319
- Hardin 350
- Harlowtown 258
- Havre 60
- Helena 209
- Hysham 381
- Jordan 312
- Kalispell 199
- Laurel 326
- Lewistown 228
- Libby 288
- Livingston 300
- Malta 148
- Miles City 394
- Missoula 269
- Philipsburg 300
- Plentywood 363
- Polson 238
- Poplar 288
- Red Lodge 370
- Roundup 257
- Ryegate 286
- Scobey 322
- Shelby 42
- Sidney 358
- Stanford 190
- Superior 324
- Sweetgrass 78
- Terry 400
- Thompson Falls 307
- Three Forks 275
- Townsend 241
- Virginia City 329
- West Glacier 168
- W. Yellowstone 384
- Whitefish 193
- W Sulphur Springs 227
- Wibaux 395
- Winnett 236
- Wolf Point 267

Chinook to
- Anaconda 308
- Baker 359
- Big Timber 254
- Billings 229
- Boulder 252
- Bozeman 313
- Broadus 391
- Browning 181
- Butte 289
- Chester 81
- Choteau 191
- Circle 239
- Columbus 270
- Conrad 148
- Cooke City 355
- Culbertson 240
- Cut Bank 147
- Deer Lodge 281
- Dillon 345
- E. Glacier Park 194
- Ekalaka 394
- Eureka 326
- Forsyth 277
- Fort Benton 96
- Gardiner 342
- Glasgow 137
- Glendive 288
- Grass Range Jct. 132
- Great Falls 136
- Hamilton 355
- Hardin 269
- Harlowtown 210
- Havre 21
- Helena 225
- Hysham 300
- Jordan 231
- Kalispell 280
- Laurel 245
- Lewistown 153
- Libby 369
- Livingston 289
- Malta 67
- Miles City 313
- Missoula 305
- Philipsburg 318
- Plentywood 282
- Polson 319
- Poplar 207
- Red Lodge 289
- Roundup 176
- Ryegate 215
- Scobey 241
- Shelby 123
- Sidney 277
- Stanford 161
- Superior 362
- Sweetgrass 159
- Terry 319
- Thompson Falls 388
- Three Forks 291
- Townsend 257
- Virginia City 345
- West Glacier 249
- W. Yellowstone 396
- Whitefish 274
- W Sulphur Springs 233
- Wibaux 314
- Winnett 155
- Wolf Point 186

Choteau to
- Anaconda 181
- Baker 453
- Big Timber 227
- Billings 274
- Boulder 127
- Bozeman 195
- Broadus 442
- Browning 72
- Butte 164
- Chester 117
- Chinook 191
- Circle 357
- Columbus 267
- Conrad 50
- Cooke City 330
- Culbertson 431
- Cut Bank 97
- Deer Lodge 154
- Dillon 220
- E. Glacier Park 85
- Ekalaka 488
- Eureka 217
- Forsyth 336
- Fort Benton 99
- Gardiner 274
- Glasgow 328
- Glendive 406
- Grass Range Jct. 191
- Great Falls 55
- Hamilton 210
- Hardin 320
- Harlowtown 183
- Havre 170
- Helena 100
- Hysham 351
- Jordan 290
- Kalispell 171
- Laurel 290
- Lewistown 160
- Libby 260
- Livingston 221
- Malta 258
- Miles City 372
- Missoula 160
- Philipsburg 191
- Plentywood 473
- Polson 210
- Poplar 398
- Red Lodge 315
- Roundup 235
- Ryegate 211
- Scobey 432
- Shelby 75
- Sidney 432
- Stanford 115
- Superior 217
- Sweetgrass 109
- Terry 411
- Thompson Falls 260
- Three Forks 166
- Townsend 132
- Virginia City 220
- West Glacier 140
- W. Yellowstone 275
- Whitefish 165
- W Sulphur Springs 152
- Wibaux 432
- Winnett 214
- Wolf Point 377

Circle to
- Anaconda 459
- Baker 120
- Big Timber 298
- Billings 241
- Boulder 412
- Bozeman 359
- Broadus 195
- Browning 420
- Butte 432
- Chester 320
- Chinook 239
- Choteau 357
- Columbus 282
- Conrad 365
- Cooke City 367
- Culbertson 98
- Cut Bank 386
- Deer Lodge 441
- Dillon 462
- E. Glacier Park 433
- Ekalaka 155
- Eureka 565
- Forsyth 163
- Fort Benton 296
- Gardiner 386
- Glasgow 102
- Glendive 49
- Grass Range Jct. 166
- Great Falls 302
- Hamilton 521
- Hardin 238
- Harlowtown 254
- Havre 260
- Helena 385
- Hysham 192
- Jordan 67
- Kalispell 519
- Laurel 257
- Lewistown 197
- Libby 608
- Livingston 333
- Malta 172
- Miles City 119
- Missoula 471
- Philipsburg 478
- Plentywood 140
- Polson 537
- Poplar 65
- Red Lodge 301
- Roundup 188
- Ryegate 227
- Scobey 99
- Shelby 362
- Sidney 75
- Stanford 242
- Superior 528
- Sweetgrass 398
- Terry 80
- Thompson Falls 571
- Three Forks 387
- Townsend 353
- Virginia City 426
- West Glacier 488
- W. Yellowstone 440
- Whitefish 513
- W Sulphur Springs 311
- Wibaux 75
- Winnett 143
- Wolf Point 53

Columbus to
- Anaconda 210
- Baker 266
- Big Timber 40
- Billings 41
- Boulder 184
- Bozeman 101
- Broadus 209
- Browning 339
- Butte 183
- Chester 342
- Chinook 270
- Choteau 267
- Circle 282
- Conrad 275
- Cooke City 114
- Culbertson 350
- Cut Bank 322
- Deer Lodge 224
- Dillon 213
- E. Glacier Park 352
- Ekalaka 301

Montana Introduction

Eureka 452
Forsyth 141
Fort Benton 217
Gardiner 128
Glasgow 320
Glendive 263
Grass Range Jct. 138
Great Falls 212
Hamilton 330
Hardin 87
Harlowtown 84
Havre 291
Helena 190
Hysham 118
Jordan 215
Kalispell 386
Laurel 25
Lewistown 141
Libby 475
Livingston 75
Malta 250
Miles City 186
Missoula 303
Philipsburg 241
Plentywood 397
Polson 369
Poplar 347
Red Lodge 48
Roundup 94
Ryegate 104
Scobey 381
Shelby 300
Sidney 313
Stanford 152
Superior 360
Sweetgrass 334
Terry 224
Thompson Falls 403
Three Forks 131
Townsend 158
Virginia City 168
West Glacier 407
W. Yellowstone 182
Whitefish 400
W Sulphur Springs 134
Wibaux 289
Winnett 139
Wolf Point 335

Conrad to
Anaconda 223
Baker 461
Big Timber 235
Billings 282
Boulder 169
Bozeman 237
Broadus 450
Browning 66
Butte 206
Chester 67
Chinook 148
Choteau 50
Circle 365
Columbus 275
Cooke City 342
Culbertson 388
Cut Bank 47
Deer Lodge 196
Dillon 262
E. Glacier Park 79
Ekalaka 496
Eureka 211
Forsyth 344
Fort Benton 107
Gardiner 286
Glasgow 285
Glendive 414
Grass Range Jct. 199
Great Falls 63
Hamilton 252
Hardin 328
Harlowtown 191
Havre 127
Helena 152
Hysham 359
Jordan 298
Kalispell 165
Laurel 298
Lewistown 168
Libby 254
Livingston 233
Malta 215
Miles City 380
Missoula 202
Philipsburg 233
Plentywood 430
Polson 204
Poplar 355
Red Lodge 323
Roundup 243
Ryegate 219
Scobey 389
Shelby 25
Sidney 425
Stanford 123
Superior 259
Sweetgrass 59
Terry 419
Thompson Falls 273
Three Forks 208
Townsend 174
Virginia City 262
West Glacier 134
W. Yellowstone 317
Whitefish 159
W Sulphur Springs 160
Wibaux 440
Winnett 222
Wolf Point 334

Cooke City to
Anaconda 244
Baker 351
Big Timber 144
Billings 126
Boulder 218
Bozeman 135
Broadus 294
Browning 402
Butte 217
Chester 409
Chinook 355
Choteau 330
Circle 367
Columbus 114
Conrad 342
Culbertson 435
Cut Bank 389
Deer Lodge 258
Dillon 233
E. Glacier Park 415
Ekalaka 386
Eureka 492
Forsyth 226
Fort Benton 321
Gardiner 56
Glasgow 405
Glendive 348
Grass Range Jct. 223
Great Falls 279
Hamilton 364
Hardin 172
Harlowtown 188
Havre 376
Helena 230
Hysham 203
Jordan 300
Kalispell 426
Laurel 110
Lewistown 245
Libby 515
Livingston 109
Malta 335
Miles City 271
Missoula 337
Philipsburg 275
Plentywood 482
Polson 403
Poplar 432
Red Lodge 66
Roundup 179
Ryegate 189
Scobey 466
Shelby 367
Sidney 398
Stanford 256
Superior 394
Sweetgrass 401
Terry 309
Thompson Falls 437
Three Forks 165
Townsend 198
Virginia City 176
West Glacier 447
W. Yellowstone 92
Whitefish 440
W Sulphur Springs 182
Wibaux 374
Winnett 224
Wolf Point 420

Culbertson to
Anaconda 548
Baker 162
Big Timber 390
Billings 309
Boulder 492
Bozeman 451
Broadus 241
Browning 421
Butte 529
Chester 321
Chinook 240
Choteau 431
Circle 98
Columbus 350
Conrad 388
Cooke City 435
Cut Bank 387
Deer Lodge 521
Dillon 561
E. Glacier Park 434
Ekalaka 197
Eureka 566
Forsyth 209
Fort Benton 336
Gardiner 478
Glasgow 103
Glendive 91
Grass Range Jct. 264
Great Falls 376
Hamilton 595
Hardin 284
Harlowtown 352
Havre 261
Helena 465
Hysham 238
Jordan 165
Kalispell 520
Laurel 325
Lewistown 295
Libby 609
Livingston 425
Malta 173
Miles City 165
Missoula 545
Philipsburg 558
Plentywood 47
Polson 559
Poplar 33
Red Lodge 369
Roundup 286
Ryegate 325
Scobey 88
Shelby 363
Sidney 37
Stanford 340
Superior 602
Sweetgrass 399
Terry 126
Thompson Falls 628
Three Forks 481
Townsend 451
Virginia City 518
West Glacier 489
W. Yellowstone 527
Whitefish 514
W Sulphur Springs 409
Wibaux 117
Winnett 241
Wolf Point 54

Cut Bank to
Anaconda 270
Baker 506
Big Timber 282
Billings 329
Boulder 216
Bozeman 284
Broadus 497
Browning 34
Butte 253
Chester 66
Chinook 147
Choteau 97
Circle 386
Columbus 322
Conrad 47
Cooke City 389
Culbertson 387
Deer Lodge 243
Dillon 309
E. Glacier Park 47
Ekalaka 541
Eureka 179
Forsyth 391
Fort Benton 154
Gardiner 333
Glasgow 284
Glendive 435
Grass Range Jct. 246
Great Falls 110
Hamilton 288
Hardin 375
Harlowtown 238
Havre 126
Helena 189
Hysham 406
Jordan 345
Kalispell 133
Laurel 345
Lewistown 215
Libby 222
Livingston 280
Malta 214
Miles City 427
Missoula 238
Philipsburg 280
Plentywood 429
Polson 172
Poplar 354
Red Lodge 370
Roundup 290
Ryegate 266
Scobey 388
Shelby 24
Sidney 424
Stanford 170
Superior 258
Sweetgrass 58
Terry 466
Thompson Falls 241
Three Forks 255
Townsend 221
Virginia City 309
West Glacier 102
W. Yellowstone 364
Whitefish 127
W Sulphur Springs 207
Wibaux 461
Winnett 269
Wolf Point 333

Deer Lodge to
Anaconda 27
Baker 482
Big Timber 184
Billings 265
Boulder 78
Bozeman 123
Broadus 433
Browning 226
Butte 41
Chester 263
Chinook 281
Choteau 154
Circle 441
Columbus 224
Conrad 196
Cooke City 258
Culbertson 521
Cut Bank 243
Dillon 92
E. Glacier Park 239
Ekalaka 517
Eureka 252
Forsyth 357
Fort Benton 189
Gardiner 202
Glasgow 418
Glendive 479
Grass Range Jct. 275
Great Falls 145
Hamilton 129
Hardin 311
Harlowtown 187
Havre 260
Helena 56
Hysham 342
Jordan 374
Kalispell 186
Laurel 249
Lewistown 244
Libby 269
Livingston 149
Malta 348
Miles City 402
Missoula 79
Philipsburg 57
Plentywood 563
Polson 145
Poplar 488
Red Lodge 272
Roundup 256
Ryegate 217
Scobey 522
Shelby 221
Sidney 516
Stanford 205
Superior 136
Sweetgrass 255
Terry 440
Thompson Falls 179
Three Forks 94
Townsend 88
Virginia City 113
West Glacier 207
W. Yellowstone 191
Whitefish 200
W Sulphur Springs 130
Wibaux 505
Winnett 298
Wolf Point 467

Dillon to
Anaconda 78
Baker 479
Big Timber 173
Billings 254
Boulder 93
Bozeman 112
Broadus 422
Browning 292
Butte 65
Chester 329
Chinook 345
Choteau 220
Circle 462
Columbus 213
Conrad 262
Cooke City 233
Culbertson 560
Cut Bank 309
Deer Lodge 92
E. Glacier Park 305
Ekalaka 514
Eureka 344
Forsyth 354
Fort Benton 253
Gardiner 191
Glasgow 468
Glendive 476
Grass Range Jct. 296
Great Falls 209
Hamilton 163
Hardin 300
Harlowtown 208
Havre 324
Helena 120
Hysham 331
Jordan 395
Kalispell 278
Laurel 238
Lewistown 265
Libby 361
Livingston 138
Malta 398
Miles City 399
Missoula 171
Philipsburg 109
Plentywood 602
Polson 237
Poplar 527
Red Lodge 261
Roundup 277
Ryegate 238
Scobey 561
Shelby 287
Sidney 526
Stanford 262
Superior 228
Sweetgrass 321
Terry 437
Thompson Falls 271
Three Forks 83
Townsend 209
Virginia City 57
West Glacier 299
W. Yellowstone 141
Whitefish 292
W Sulphur Springs 161
Wibaux 502
Winnett 319
Wolf Point 515

E. Glacier Park to
Anaconda 266
Baker 538
Big Timber 312
Billings 359
Boulder 212
Bozeman 280
Broadus 527
Browning 13
Butte 249
Chester 113
Chinook 194
Choteau 85
Circle 433
Columbus 352
Conrad 79
Cooke City 415
Culbertson 434
Cut Bank 47
Deer Lodge 239
Dillon 305
Ekalaka 573
Eureka 132
Forsyth 421
Fort Benton 184
Gardiner 359
Glasgow 331
Glendive 482
Grass Range Jct. 276
Great Falls 140
Hamilton 241
Hardin 405
Harlowtown 268
Havre 173
Helena 185
Hysham 436
Jordan 375
Kalispell 86
Laurel 375
Lewistown 245
Libby 175
Livingston 306
Malta 261
Miles City 475
Missoula 191
Philipsburg 265
Plentywood 476
Polson 125
Poplar 401
Red Lodge 400
Roundup 320
Ryegate 296
Scobey 435
Shelby 71
Sidney 471
Stanford 200
Superior 211
Sweetgrass 105
Terry 496
Thompson Falls 194
Three Forks 251
Townsend 217
Virginia City 305
West Glacier 55
W. Yellowstone 360
Whitefish 80
W Sulphur Springs 237
Wibaux 508
Winnett 299
Wolf Point 380

Ekalaka to
Anaconda 511
Baker 35
Big Timber 341
Billings 260
Boulder 485
Bozeman 402
Broadus 192
Browning 560
Butte 484
Chester 475
Chinook 394
Choteau 488
Circle 155
Columbus 301
Conrad 496
Cooke City 386
Culbertson 197
Cut Bank 541
Deer Lodge 517
Dillon 514
E. Glacier Park 573
Eureka 705
Forsyth 160
Fort Benton 427
Gardiner 429
Glasgow 257
Glendive 106
Grass Range Jct. 297
Great Falls 433
Hamilton 626
Hardin 235
Harlowtown 330
Havre 415
Helena 461
Hysham 189
Jordan 200
Kalispell 657
Laurel 276
Lewistown 328
Libby 746
Livingston 376
Malta 327
Miles City 116
Missoula 576
Philipsburg 542
Plentywood 244
Polson 642
Poplar 220
Red Lodge 320
Roundup 261
Ryegate 300
Scobey 254
Shelby 517
Sidney 160
Stanford 373
Superior 633
Sweetgrass 553
Terry 145
Thompson Falls 676
Three Forks 432
Townsend 429
Virginia City 469
West Glacier 628
W. Yellowstone 478
Whitefish 653
W Sulphur Springs 387
Wibaux 80
Winnett 274
Wolf Point 208

Eureka to
Anaconda 279
Baker 670
Big Timber 412
Billings 486
Boulder 289
Bozeman 357
Broadus 654
Browning 145
Butte 293
Chester 245
Chinook 326
Choteau 217
Circle 565
Columbus 452
Conrad 211
Cooke City 492
Culbertson 566
Cut Bank 179
Deer Lodge 252
Dillon 344
E. Glacier Park 132
Ekalaka 705
Forsyth 553
Fort Benton 316
Gardiner 436
Glasgow 463
Glendive 614
Grass Range Jct. 408
Great Falls 272
Hamilton 231
Hardin 532
Harlowtown 393
Havre 305
Helena 262
Hysham 563
Jordan 507
Kalispell 66
Laurel 477
Lewistown 377
Libby 68
Livingston 383
Malta 393
Miles City 589
Missoula 181
Philipsburg 255
Plentywood 608
Polson 115
Poplar 533
Red Lodge 500
Roundup 452
Ryegate 423
Scobey 567
Shelby 203
Sidney 603
Stanford 332
Superior 191
Sweetgrass 237
Terry 628
Thompson Falls 158
Three Forks 328
Townsend 294
Virginia City 365
West Glacier 77
W. Yellowstone 437
Whitefish 52
W Sulphur Springs 336
Wibaux 640
Winnett 431
Wolf Point 512

Forsyth to
Anaconda 351
Baker 125
Big Timber 181
Billings 100
Boulder 325
Bozeman 242
Broadus 122
Browning 408
Butte 324
Chester 358
Chinook 277
Choteau 336
Circle 163
Columbus 141
Conrad 344
Cooke City 226
Culbertson 204
Cut Bank 391
Deer Lodge 357
Dillon 354
E. Glacier Park 421
Ekalaka 160
Eureka 553
Fort Benton 275
Gardiner 269
Glasgow 242
Glendive 122
Grass Range Jct. 145
Great Falls 281
Hamilton 466
Hardin 75
Harlowtown 170
Havre 298
Helena 301
Hysham 29
Jordan 129
Kalispell 497
Laurel 116
Lewistown 176
Libby 586
Livingston 216
Malta 257
Miles City 45
Missoula 416
Philipsburg 382
Plentywood 256
Polson 482
Poplar 228
Red Lodge 160
Roundup 101
Ryegate 140
Scobey 262
Shelby 369
Sidney 172
Stanford 221
Superior 473
Sweetgrass 403
Terry 83
Thompson Falls 516
Three Forks 272
Townsend 269
Virginia City 309
West Glacier 476
W. Yellowstone 318
Whitefish 501
W Sulphur Springs 227
Wibaux 148
Winnett 146
Wolf Point 216

Fort Benton to
Anaconda 216
Baker 392
Big Timber 177
Billings 224
Boulder 160
Bozeman 221
Broadus 389
Browning 171
Butte 197
Chester 129
Chinook 96
Choteau 99
Circle 296
Columbus 217
Conrad 107
Cooke City 321
Culbertson 336
Cut Bank 154
Deer Lodge 189
Dillon 253
E. Glacier Park 184
Ekalaka 427
Eureka 316
Forsyth 275
Gardiner 265
Glasgow 233
Glendive 345
Grass Range Jct. 130
Great Falls 44
Hamilton 263
Hardin 267
Harlowtown 133
Havre 75
Helena 133
Hysham 298
Jordan 229
Kalispell 270
Laurel 240
Lewistown 99
Libby 359
Livingston 212
Malta 163
Miles City 311
Missoula 213
Philipsburg 226
Plentywood 378
Polson 279
Poplar 303
Red Lodge 265
Roundup 174
Ryegate 161
Scobey 337
Shelby 132
Sidney 371
Stanford 65
Superior 270
Sweetgrass 166
Terry 350
Thompson Falls 313
Three Forks 199
Townsend 165
Virginia City 253
West Glacier 239
W. Yellowstone 308
Whitefish 264
W Sulphur Springs 141
Wibaux 371
Winnett 153
Wolf Point 282

Gardiner to
Anaconda 188
Baker 394
Big Timber 88
Billings 169
Boulder 162
Bozeman 79
Broadus 337
Browning 346
Butte 161
Chester 353
Chinook 342
Choteau 274
Circle 386
Columbus 128
Conrad 286
Cooke City 56
Culbertson 478
Cut Bank 333
Deer Lodge 202
Dillon 191
E. Glacier Park 359
Ekalaka 429
Eureka 436
Forsyth 269
Fort Benton 265
Glasgow 392
Glendive 391
Grass Range Jct. 220
Great Falls 223
Hamilton 308
Hardin 215
Harlowtown 132
Havre 338
Helena 174
Hysham 246
Jordan 319
Kalispell 370
Laurel 153
Lewistown 189
Libby 459
Livingston 53
Malta 322
Miles City 314
Missoula 281
Philipsburg 219
Plentywood 525
Polson 347
Poplar 451
Red Lodge 122
Roundup 201
Ryegate 162
Scobey 485
Shelby 311
Sidney 441
Stanford 200
Superior 338
Sweetgrass 345
Terry 352
Thompson Falls 381
Three Forks 109
Townsend 142
Virginia City 138
West Glacier 391
W. Yellowstone 54
Whitefish 384
W Sulphur Springs 126
Wibaux 417
Winnett 243
Wolf Point 439

Glasgow to
Anaconda 445
Baker 222
Big Timber 304
Billings 279
Boulder 389
Bozeman 365
Broadus 276
Browning 318
Butte 426
Chester 218
Chinook 137
Choteau 328
Circle 102
Columbus 320
Conrad 285
Cooke City 405
Culbertson 103
Cut Bank 284
Deer Lodge 418
Dillon 468
E. Glacier Park 331
Ekalaka 257
Eureka 463
Forsyth 242
Fort Benton 233
Gardiner 392
Glendive 151
Grass Range Jct. 182
Great Falls 273
Hamilton 492
Hardin 317
Harlowtown 260
Havre 158
Helena 362
Hysham 271
Jordan 113
Kalispell 417
Laurel 295
Lewistown 203
Libby 506
Livingston 339
Malta 70
Miles City 197
Missoula 442
Philipsburg 455
Plentywood 145
Polson 456
Poplar 70
Red Lodge 339
Roundup 226
Ryegate 265
Scobey 104
Shelby 260
Sidney 140
Stanford 248
Superior 499
Sweetgrass 296
Terry 182
Thompson Falls 525
Three Forks 393
Townsend 359
Virginia City 432
West Glacier 386
W. Yellowstone 446
Whitefish 411
W Sulphur Springs 317
Wibaux 177
Winnett 189
Wolf Point 49

Glendive to
Anaconda 473
Baker 71
Big Timber 303
Billings 222
Boulder 447
Bozeman 364
Broadus 154
Browning 469
Butte 446
Chester 369
Chinook 288
Choteau 406
Circle 49
Columbus 263
Conrad 414
Cooke City 348
Culbertson 91
Cut Bank 435
Deer Lodge 479
Dillon 476
E. Glacier Park 482
Ekalaka 106
Eureka 614
Forsyth 122
Fort Benton 345
Gardiner 391
Glasgow 151
Grass Range Jct. 215
Great Falls 351
Hamilton 570
Hardin 197
Harlowtown 292
Havre 309
Helena 423
Hysham 151
Jordan 116
Kalispell 568
Laurel 238
Lewistown 246
Libby 657
Livingston 338
Malta 221
Miles City 78
Missoula 520
Philipsburg 504
Plentywood 138
Polson 586
Poplar 114
Red Lodge 282
Roundup 223
Ryegate 262
Scobey 148
Shelby 411
Sidney 54
Stanford 291
Superior 577
Sweetgrass 447
Terry 39
Thompson Falls 620
Three Forks 394
Townsend 391
Virginia City 431

All Montana Area Codes are 406

- West Glacier 537
- W. Yellowstone 440
- Whitefish 562
- W Sulphur Springs 349
- Wibaux 26
- Winnett 192
- Wolf Point 102

Grass Range Jct. to

- Anaconda 293
- Baker 262
- Big Timber 132
- Billings 97
- Boulder 246
- Bozeman 193
- Broadus 259
- Browning 263
- Butte 266
- Chester 213
- Chinook 132
- Choteau 191
- Circle 166
- Columbus 138
- Conrad 199
- Cooke City 223
- Culbertson 264
- Cut Bank 246
- Deer Lodge 275
- Dillon 296
- E. Glacier Park 276
- Ekalaka 297
- Eureka 408
- Forsyth 145
- Fort Benton 130
- Gardiner 220
- Glasgow 182
- Glendive 215
- Great Falls 136
- Hamilton 355
- Hardin 137
- Harlowtown 88
- Havre 153
- Helena 219
- Hysham 168
- Jordan 99
- Kalispell 362
- Laurel 113
- Lewistown 31
- Libby 451
- Livingston 167
- Malta 112
- Miles City 181
- Missoula 305
- Philipsburg 312
- Plentywood 306
- Polson 371
- Poplar 231
- Red Lodge 157
- Roundup 44
- Ryegate 83
- Scobey 265
- Shelby 224
- Sidney 241
- Stanford 76
- Superior 362
- Sweetgrass 258
- Terry 220
- Thompson Falls 405
- Three Forks 221
- Townsend 187
- Virginia City 260
- West Glacier 331
- W. Yellowstone 274
- Whitefish 356
- W Sulphur Springs 145
- Wibaux 241
- Winnett 23
- Wolf Point 219

Great Falls to

- Anaconda 172
- Baker 398
- Big Timber 172
- Billings 219
- Boulder 116
- Bozeman 177
- Broadus 387
- Browning 127
- Butte 153
- Chester 130
- Chinook 136
- Choteau 55
- Circle 302
- Columbus 212
- Conrad 63
- Cooke City 279
- Culbertson 376
- Cut Bank 110
- Deer Lodge 145
- Dillon 209
- E. Glacier Park 140
- Ekalaka 433
- Eureka 272
- Forsyth 281
- Fort Benton 44
- Gardiner 223
- Glasgow 273
- Glendive 351
- Grass Range Jct. 136
- Hamilton 219
- Hardin 265
- Harlowtown 128
- Havre 115
- Helena 89
- Hysham 296
- Jordan 235
- Kalispell 226
- Laurel 235
- Lewistown 105
- Libby 315
- Livingston 170
- Malta 203
- Miles City 317
- Missoula 169
- Philipsburg 182
- Plentywood 418
- Polson 235
- Poplar 343
- Red Lodge 260
- Roundup 180
- Ryegate 156
- Scobey 377
- Shelby 88
- Sidney 377
- Stanford 60
- Superior 226
- Sweetgrass 122
- Terry 356
- Thompson Falls 269
- Three Forks 155
- Townsend 121
- Virginia City 209
- West Glacier 195
- W. Yellowstone 264
- Whitefish 220
- W Sulphur Springs 97
- Wibaux 377
- Winnett 159
- Wolf Point 322

Hamilton to

- Anaconda 126
- Baker 591
- Big Timber 290
- Billings 371
- Boulder 184
- Bozeman 229
- Broadus 539
- Browning 254
- Butte 147
- Chester 319
- Chinook 355
- Choteau 210
- Circle 521
- Columbus 330
- Conrad 252
- Cooke City 364
- Culbertson 595
- Cut Bank 288
- Deer Lodge 129
- Dillon 163
- E. Glacier Park 241
- Ekalaka 626
- Eureka 231
- Forsyth 466
- Fort Benton 263
- Gardiner 308
- Glasgow 492
- Glendive 570
- Grass Range Jct. 335
- Great Falls 219
- Hardin 417
- Harlowtown 296
- Havre 334
- Helena 165
- Hysham 448
- Jordan 254
- Kalispell 165
- Laurel 355
- Lewistown 324
- Libby 240
- Livingston 255
- Malta 422
- Miles City 511
- Missoula 50
- Philipsburg 124
- Plentywood 637
- Polson 116
- Poplar 562
- Red Lodge 378
- Roundup 365
- Ryegate 326
- Scobey 596
- Shelby 277
- Sidney 596
- Stanford 279
- Superior 107
- Sweetgrass 311
- Terry 549
- Thompson Falls 150
- Three Forks 200
- Townsend 197
- Virginia City 219
- West Glacier 186
- W. Yellowstone 297
- Whitefish 179
- W Sulphur Springs 239
- Wibaux 596
- Winnett 378
- Wolf Point 541

Hardin to

- Anaconda 297
- Baker 200
- Big Timber 127
- Billings 46
- Boulder 271
- Bozeman 188
- Broadus 122
- Browning 392
- Butte 270
- Chester 350
- Chinook 269
- Choteau 320
- Circle 238
- Columbus 87
- Conrad 328
- Cooke City 172
- Culbertson 284
- Cut Bank 375
- Deer Lodge 311
- Dillon 300
- E. Glacier Park 405
- Ekalaka 235
- Eureka 532
- Forsyth 75
- Fort Benton 267
- Gardiner 215
- Glasgow 317
- Glendive 197
- Grass Range Jct. 137
- Great Falls 265
- Hamilton 417
- Harlowtown 139
- Havre 290
- Helena 270
- Hysham 52
- Jordan 204
- Kalispell 456
- Laurel 62
- Lewistown 168
- Libby 555
- Livingston 162
- Malta 249
- Miles City 120
- Missoula 385
- Philipsburg 328
- Plentywood 331
- Polson 451
- Poplar 303
- Red Lodge 106
- Roundup 93
- Ryegate 109
- Scobey 337
- Shelby 353
- Sidney 247
- Stanford 205
- Superior 442
- Sweetgrass 387
- Terry 158
- Thompson Falls 485
- Three Forks 218
- Townsend 238
- Virginia City 255
- West Glacier 460
- W. Yellowstone 264
- Whitefish 480
- W Sulphur Springs 196
- Wibaux 223
- Winnett 138
- Wolf Point 291

Harlowtown to

- Anaconda 205
- Baker 295
- Big Timber 44
- Billings 93
- Boulder 158
- Bozeman 105
- Broadus 261
- Browning 255
- Butte 178
- Chester 258
- Chinook 210
- Choteau 183
- Circle 254
- Columbus 84
- Conrad 191
- Cooke City 188
- Culbertson 352
- Cut Bank 238
- Deer Lodge 187
- Dillon 208
- E. Glacier Park 268
- Ekalaka 330
- Eureka 393
- Forsyth 170
- Fort Benton 133
- Gardiner 132
- Glasgow 260
- Glendive 292
- Grass Range Jct. 88
- Great Falls 128
- Hamilton 296
- Hardin 139
- Havre 208
- Helena 131
- Hysham 170
- Jordan 187
- Kalispell 327
- Laurel 109
- Lewistown 57
- Libby 416
- Livingston 79
- Malta 190
- Miles City 215
- Missoula 246
- Philipsburg 224
- Plentywood 394
- Polson 312
- Poplar 319
- Red Lodge 132
- Roundup 69
- Ryegate 30
- Scobey 353
- Shelby 216
- Sidney 329
- Stanford 68
- Superior 303
- Sweetgrass 250
- Terry 253
- Thompson Falls 346
- Three Forks 133
- Townsend 99
- Virginia City 172
- West Glacier 323
- W. Yellowstone 186
- Whitefish 341
- W Sulphur Springs 57
- Wibaux 318
- Winnett 111
- Wolf Point 307

Havre to

- Anaconda 287
- Baker 380
- Big Timber 252
- Billings 250
- Boulder 231
- Bozeman 292
- Broadus 412
- Browning 160
- Butte 268
- Chester 60
- Chinook 21
- Choteau 170
- Circle 260
- Columbus 291
- Conrad 127
- Cooke City 376
- Culbertson 261
- Cut Bank 126
- Deer Lodge 260
- Dillon 324
- E. Glacier Park 173
- Ekalaka 415
- Eureka 305
- Forsyth 298
- Fort Benton 75
- Gardiner 338
- Glasgow 158
- Glendive 309
- Grass Range Jct. 153
- Great Falls 115
- Hamilton 334
- Hardin 290
- Harlowtown 208
- Helena 204
- Hysham 321
- Jordan 252
- Kalispell 259
- Laurel 266
- Lewistown 174
- Libby 348
- Livingston 285
- Malta 88
- Miles City 334
- Missoula 284
- Philipsburg 297
- Plentywood 303
- Polson 298
- Poplar 228
- Red Lodge 310
- Roundup 197
- Ryegate 236
- Scobey 262
- Shelby 102
- Sidney 298
- Stanford 140
- Superior 341
- Sweetgrass 138
- Terry 340
- Thompson Falls 367
- Three Forks 270
- Townsend 236
- Virginia City 324
- West Glacier 228
- W. Yellowstone 379
- Whitefish 253
- W Sulphur Springs 212
- Wibaux 335
- Winnett 176
- Wolf Point 207

Helena to

- Anaconda 83
- Baker 426
- Big Timber 150
- Billings 224
- Boulder 27
- Bozeman 95
- Broadus 392
- Browning 172
- Butte 64
- Chester 209
- Chinook 225
- Choteau 100
- Circle 385
- Columbus 190
- Conrad 152
- Cooke City 230
- Culbertson 465
- Cut Bank 189
- Deer Lodge 56
- Dillon 120
- E. Glacier Park 185
- Ekalaka 461
- Eureka 262
- Forsyth 301
- Fort Benton 133
- Gardiner 174
- Glasgow 362
- Glendive 423
- Grass Range Jct. 219
- Great Falls 89
- Hamilton 165
- Hardin 270
- Harlowtown 131
- Havre 204
- Hysham 301
- Jordan 318
- Kalispell 196
- Laurel 215
- Lewistown 188
- Libby 285
- Livingston 121
- Malta 292
- Miles City 346
- Missoula 115
- Philipsburg 93
- Plentywood 507
- Polson 181
- Poplar 432
- Red Lodge 238
- Roundup 200
- Ryegate 161
- Scobey 466
- Shelby 167
- Sidney 460
- Stanford 149
- Superior 172
- Sweetgrass 201
- Terry 384
- Thompson Falls 215
- Three Forks 66
- Townsend 32
- Virginia City 120
- West Glacier 217
- W. Yellowstone 175
- Whitefish 210
- W Sulphur Springs 74
- Wibaux 449
- Winnett 242
- Wolf Point 411

Hysham to

- Anaconda 328
- Baker 154
- Big Timber 158
- Billings 77
- Boulder 302
- Bozeman 219
- Broadus 139
- Browning 423
- Butte 301
- Chester 381
- Chinook 300
- Choteau 351
- Circle 192
- Columbus 118
- Conrad 359
- Cooke City 203
- Culbertson 238
- Cut Bank 406
- Deer Lodge 342
- Dillon 331
- E. Glacier Park 436
- Ekalaka 189
- Eureka 563
- Forsyth 29
- Fort Benton 298
- Gardiner 246
- Glasgow 271
- Glendive 151
- Grass Range Jct. 168
- Great Falls 296
- Hamilton 448
- Hardin 52
- Harlowtown 170
- Havre 321
- Helena 301
- Jordan 158
- Kalispell 497
- Laurel 93
- Lewistown 199
- Libby 586
- Livingston 193
- Malta 280
- Miles City 74
- Missoula 416
- Philipsburg 359
- Plentywood 285
- Polson 482
- Poplar 257
- Red Lodge 137
- Roundup 124
- Ryegate 140
- Scobey 291
- Shelby 384
- Sidney 201
- Stanford 236
- Superior 473
- Sweetgrass 418
- Terry 112
- Thompson Falls 516
- Three Forks 249
- Townsend 269
- Virginia City 286
- West Glacier 491
- W. Yellowstone 295
- Whitefish 511
- W Sulphur Springs 277
- Wibaux 177
- Winnett 169
- Wolf Point 245

Jordan to

- Anaconda 392
- Baker 165
- Big Timber 231
- Billings 174
- Boulder 345
- Bozeman 292
- Broadus 163
- Browning 362
- Butte 365
- Chester 312
- Chinook 231
- Choteau 290
- Circle 67
- Columbus 215
- Conrad 298
- Cooke City 300
- Culbertson 165
- Cut Bank 345
- Deer Lodge 374
- Dillon 395
- E. Glacier Park 375
- Ekalaka 200
- Eureka 507
- Forsyth 129
- Fort Benton 229
- Gardiner 319
- Glasgow 113
- Glendive 116
- Grass Range Jct. 99
- Great Falls 235
- Hamilton 454
- Hardin 204
- Harlowtown 187
- Havre 252
- Helena 318
- Hysham 158
- Kalispell 461
- Laurel 190
- Lewistown 130
- Libby 550
- Livingston 266
- Malta 183
- Miles City 84
- Missoula 404
- Philipsburg 411
- Plentywood 207
- Polson 470
- Poplar 132
- Red Lodge 234
- Roundup 121
- Ryegate 160
- Scobey 166
- Shelby 323
- Sidney 142
- Stanford 175
- Superior 461
- Sweetgrass 357
- Terry 123
- Thompson Falls 504
- Three Forks 320
- Townsend 286
- Virginia City 359
- West Glacier 430
- W. Yellowstone 373
- Whitefish 455
- W Sulphur Springs 244
- Wibaux 142
- Winnett 76
- Wolf Point 120

Kalispell to

- Anaconda 213
- Baker 622
- Big Timber 346
- Billings 420
- Boulder 223
- Bozeman 291
- Broadus 588
- Browning 99
- Butte 227
- Chester 199
- Chinook 280
- Choteau 171
- Circle 519
- Columbus 386
- Conrad 165
- Cooke City 426
- Culbertson 520
- Cut Bank 133
- Deer Lodge 186
- Dillon 278
- E. Glacier Park 86
- Ekalaka 657
- Eureka 66
- Forsyth 497
- Fort Benton 270
- Gardiner 370
- Glasgow 417
- Glendive 568
- Grass Range Jct. 362
- Great Falls 226
- Hamilton 165
- Hardin 466
- Harlowtown 327
- Havre 259
- Helena 196
- Hysham 497
- Jordan 461
- Laurel 411
- Lewistown 331
- Libby 89
- Livingston 317
- Malta 347
- Miles City 542
- Missoula 115
- Philipsburg 189
- Plentywood 562
- Polson 49
- Poplar 487
- Red Lodge 434
- Roundup 396
- Ryegate 357
- Scobey 521
- Shelby 157
- Sidney 557
- Stanford 286
- Superior 125
- Sweetgrass 191
- Terry 580
- Thompson Falls 108
- Three Forks 262
- Townsend 228
- Virginia City 299
- West Glacier 31
- W. Yellowstone 371
- Whitefish 14
- W Sulphur Springs 270
- Wibaux 594
- Winnett 385
- Wolf Point 466

Laurel to

- Anaconda 235
- Baker 241
- Big Timber 65
- Billings 16
- Boulder 209
- Bozeman 126
- Broadus 184
- Browning 362
- Butte 208
- Chester 326
- Chinook 245
- Choteau 290
- Circle 257
- Columbus 25
- Conrad 298
- Cooke City 110
- Culbertson 325
- Cut Bank 345
- Deer Lodge 249
- Dillon 238
- E. Glacier Park 375
- Ekalaka 276
- Eureka 477
- Forsyth 116
- Fort Benton 240
- Gardiner 153
- Glasgow 295
- Glendive 238
- Grass Range Jct. 113
- Great Falls 235
- Hamilton 355
- Hardin 62
- Harlowtown 109
- Havre 266
- Helena 215
- Hysham 93
- Jordan 190
- Kalispell 411
- Lewistown 144
- Libby 500
- Livingston 100
- Malta 225
- Miles City 161
- Missoula 328
- Philipsburg 266
- Plentywood 372
- Polson 394
- Poplar 322
- Red Lodge 44
- Roundup 69
- Ryegate 79
- Scobey 356
- Shelby 323
- Sidney 288
- Stanford 175
- Superior 385
- Sweetgrass 357
- Terry 199
- Thompson Falls 428
- Three Forks 156
- Townsend 183
- Virginia City 193
- West Glacier 430
- W. Yellowstone 202
- Whitefish 425
- W Sulphur Springs 159
- Wibaux 264
- Winnett 114
- Wolf Point 310

Lewistown to

- Anaconda 262
- Baker 293
- Big Timber 101
- Billings 128
- Boulder 215
- Bozeman 162
- Broadus 290
- Browning 232
- Butte 235
- Chester 228
- Chinook 153
- Choteau 160
- Circle 197
- Columbus 141
- Conrad 168
- Cooke City 245
- Culbertson 295
- Cut Bank 215
- Deer Lodge 244
- Dillon 265
- E. Glacier Park 245
- Ekalaka 328
- Eureka 377
- Forsyth 176
- Fort Benton 99
- Gardiner 189
- Glasgow 203
- Glendive 246
- Grass Range Jct. 31
- Great Falls 105
- Hamilton 324
- Hardin 168
- Harlowtown 57
- Havre 174
- Helena 189
- Hysham 199
- Jordan 130
- Kalispell 331
- Laurel 144
- Libby 420
- Livingston 136
- Malta 133
- Miles City 212
- Missoula 274
- Philipsburg 281
- Plentywood 337
- Polson 340
- Poplar 262
- Red Lodge 188
- Roundup 75
- Ryegate 85
- Scobey 296
- Shelby 193
- Sidney 272
- Stanford 45
- Superior 331
- Sweetgrass 227
- Terry 251
- Thompson Falls 374
- Three Forks 190
- Townsend 156
- Virginia City 229
- West Glacier 300
- W. Yellowstone 243
- Whitefish 325
- W Sulphur Springs 114
- Wibaux 272
- Winnett 54
- Wolf Point 250

Libby to

- Anaconda 295
- Baker 711
- Big Timber 435
- Billings 509
- Boulder 312
- Bozeman 380
- Broadus 677
- Browning 188
- Butte 310
- Chester 288
- Chinook 369
- Choteau 260
- Circle 608
- Columbus 475
- Conrad 254
- Cooke City 515
- Culbertson 609
- Cut Bank 222
- Deer Lodge 269
- Dillon 361
- E. Glacier Park 175
- Ekalaka 746
- Eureka 68
- Forsyth 586
- Fort Benton 359
- Gardiner 459
- Glasgow 506
- Glendive 657
- Grass Range Jct. 451
- Great Falls 315
- Hamilton 240
- Hardin 555
- Harlowtown 416
- Havre 348
- Helena 285
- Hysham 586
- Jordan 550
- Kalispell 89
- Laurel 500
- Lewistown 420
- Livingston 406
- Malta 436
- Miles City 631
- Missoula 190
- Philipsburg 264
- Plentywood 651
- Polson 138
- Poplar 576
- Red Lodge 523
- Roundup 485
- Ryegate 446
- Scobey 610
- Shelby 246
- Sidney 646
- Stanford 375
- Superior 159
- Sweetgrass 280
- Terry 669
- Thompson Falls 90
- Three Forks 351
- Townsend 317
- Virginia City 382
- West Glacier 120
- W. Yellowstone 460
- Whitefish 103
- W Sulphur Springs 359
- Wibaux 683
- Winnett 474
- Wolf Point 555

Livingston to

- Anaconda 135
- Baker 341
- Big Timber 35
- Billings 116
- Boulder 109
- Bozeman 26
- Broadus 284
- Browning 293
- Butte 108
- Chester 300
- Chinook 289
- Choteau 221
- Circle 333
- Columbus 75
- Conrad 233
- Cooke City 109
- Culbertson 425
- Cut Bank 280
- Deer Lodge 149
- Dillon 138
- E. Glacier Park 306
- Ekalaka 376
- Eureka 383
- Forsyth 216
- Fort Benton 212
- Gardiner 53
- Glasgow 339
- Glendive 338
- Grass Range Jct. 167
- Great Falls 170
- Hamilton 255
- Hardin 162
- Harlowtown 79
- Havre 285
- Helena 121
- Hysham 193
- Jordan 266
- Kalispell 317
- Laurel 100
- Lewistown 136
- Libby 406
- Malta 269
- Miles City 261
- Missoula 228
- Philipsburg 166
- Plentywood 472
- Polson 294
- Poplar 398
- Red Lodge 123
- Roundup 148
- Ryegate 109
- Scobey 432
- Shelby 258
- Sidney 388
- Stanford 147
- Superior 285
- Sweetgrass 292
- Terry 299
- Thompson Falls 328
- Three Forks 56
- Townsend 89
- Virginia City 93
- West Glacier 338
- W. Yellowstone 107
- Whitefish 331
- W Sulphur Springs 73
- Wibaux 364
- Winnett 190
- Wolf Point 386

Malta to

- Anaconda 375
- Baker 292
- Big Timber 234
- Billings 209
- Boulder 319
- Bozeman 295
- Broadus 346
- Browning 248
- Butte 356
- Chester 148
- Chinook 67
- Choteau 258
- Circle 172
- Columbus 250
- Conrad 215
- Cooke City 335
- Culbertson 173
- Cut Bank 214
- Deer Lodge 348
- Dillon 398
- E. Glacier Park 261
- Ekalaka 327
- Eureka 393
- Forsyth 257
- Fort Benton 163
- Gardiner 322
- Glasgow 70
- Glendive 221
- Grass Range Jct. 112
- Great Falls 203
- Hamilton 422
- Hardin 249
- Harlowtown 190

Havre 88
Helena 292
Hysham 280
Jordan 183
Kalispell 347
Laurel 225
Lewistown 133
Libby 436
Livingston 269
Miles City 267
Missoula 372
Philipsburg 385
Plentywood 215
Polson 386
Poplar 140
Red Lodge 269
Roundup 156
Ryegate 195
Scobey 174
Shelby 190
Sidney 210
Stanford 178
Superior 429
Sweetgrass 226
Terry 252
Thompson Falls 455
Three Forks 323
Townsend 289
Virginia City 362
West Glacier 316
W. Yellowstone 376
Whitefish 340
W Sulphur Springs 247
Wibaux 247
Winnett 135
Wolf Point 119

Miles City to
Anaconda 396
Baker 81
Big Timber 226
Billings 145
Boulder 370
Bozeman 287
Broadus 79
Browning 444
Butte 369
Chester 394
Chinook 313
Choteau 372
Circle 119
Columbus 186
Conrad 380
Cooke City 271
Culbertson 165
Cut Bank 427
Deer Lodge 402
Dillon 399
E. Glacier Park 457
Ekalaka 116
Eureka 589
Forsyth 45
Fort Benton 311
Gardiner 314
Glasgow 197
Glendive 78
Grass Range Jct. 181
Great Falls 317
Hamilton 511
Hardin 180
Harlowtown 215
Havre 334
Helena 346
Hysham 74
Jordan 84
Kalispell 542
Laurel 161
Lewistown 212
Libby 631
Livingston 261
Malta 267
Missoula 461
Philipsburg 427
Plentywood 212
Polson 527
Poplar 184
Red Lodge 205
Roundup 146
Ryegate 185
Scobey 218
Shelby 405
Sidney 128
Stanford 257
Superior 518
Sweetgrass 439
Terry 39
Thompson Falls 561
Three Forks 317
Townsend 314
Virginia City 354
West Glacier 512
W. Yellowstone 363
Whitefish 537
W Sulphur Springs 272
Wibaux 104
Winnett 158
Wolf Point 172

Missoula to
Anaconda 105
Baker 541
Big Timber 263
Billings 339
Boulder 142
Bozeman 202
Broadus 507
Browning 204
Butte 120
Chester 269
Chinook 305
Choteau 160
Circle 471
Columbus 303
Conrad 202
Cooke City 337
Culbertson 545
Cut Bank 238
Deer Lodge 79
Dillon 171
E. Glacier Park 191
Ekalaka 576
Eureka 181
Forsyth 416
Fort Benton 213
Gardiner 281
Glasgow 442
Glendive 520
Grass Range Jct. 305
Great Falls 169
Hamilton 50
Hardin 385
Harlowtown 246
Havre 284
Helena 115
Hysham 416
Jordan 404
Kalispell 115
Laurel 326
Lewistown 274
Libby 190
Livingston 228
Malta 372
Miles City 461
Philipsburg 74
Plentywood 587
Polson 66
Poplar 512
Red Lodge 351
Roundup 315
Ryegate 276
Scobey 546
Shelby 227
Sidney 546
Stanford 229
Superior 57
Sweetgrass 261
Terry 499
Thompson Falls 100
Three Forks 173
Townsend 147
Virginia City 192
West Glacier 136
W. Yellowstone 270
Whitefish 129
W Sulphur Springs 189
Wibaux 546
Winnett 328
Wolf Point 491

Philipsburg to
Anaconda 31
Baker 507
Big Timber 201
Billings 282
Boulder 95
Bozeman 140
Broadus 450
Browning 263
Butte 58
Chester 300
Chinook 318
Choteau 191
Circle 478
Columbus 241
Conrad 233
Cooke City 275
Culbertson 558
Cut Bank 280
Deer Lodge 57
Dillon 109
E. Glacier Park 265
Ekalaka 542
Eureka 255
Forsyth 382
Fort Benton 226
Gardiner 219
Glasgow 455
Glendive 504
Grass Range Jct. 312
Great Falls 182
Hamilton 124
Hardin 328
Harlowtown 224
Havre 297
Helena 93
Hysham 369
Jordan 411
Kalispell 189
Laurel 266
Lewistown 281
Libby 264
Livingston 166
Malta 385
Miles City 427
Missoula 74
Plentywood 600
Polson 140
Poplar 525
Red Lodge 289
Roundup 293
Ryegate 254
Scobey 559
Shelby 258
Sidney 553
Stanford 242
Superior 131
Sweetgrass 292
Terry 465
Thompson Falls 174
Three Forks 111
Townsend 125
Virginia City 130
West Glacier 210
W. Yellowstone 208
Whitefish 203
W Sulphur Springs 167
Wibaux 530
Winnett 335
Wolf Point 504

Plentywood to
Anaconda 590
Baker 209
Big Timber 437
Billings 356
Boulder 534
Bozeman 498
Broadus 288
Browning 463
Butte 571
Chester 363
Chinook 282
Choteau 473
Circle 140
Columbus 397
Conrad 430
Cooke City 482
Culbertson 47
Cut Bank 429
Deer Lodge 563
Dillon 602
E. Glacier Park 476
Ekalaka 244
Eureka 608
Forsyth 256
Fort Benton 378
Gardiner 525
Glasgow 145
Glendive 138
Grass Range Jct. 306
Great Falls 418
Hamilton 637
Hardin 331
Harlowtown 394
Havre 303
Helena 507
Hysham 285
Jordan 207
Kalispell 562
Laurel 372
Lewistown 337
Libby 651
Livingston 472
Malta 215
Miles City 212
Missoula 587
Philipsburg 600
Polson 601
Poplar 80
Red Lodge 416
Roundup 328
Ryegate 367
Scobey 41
Shelby 405
Sidney 84
Stanford 282
Superior 644
Sweetgrass 441
Terry 173
Thompson Falls 670
Three Forks 527
Townsend 493
Virginia City 565
West Glacier 531
W. Yellowstone 574
Whitefish 556
W Sulphur Springs 451
Wibaux 164
Winnett 283
Wolf Point 96

Polson to
Anaconda 171
Baker 607
Big Timber 329
Billings 405
Boulder 208
Bozeman 268
Broadus 573
Browning 138
Butte 186
Chester 238
Chinook 319
Choteau 210
Circle 537
Columbus 369
Conrad 204
Cooke City 403
Culbertson 559
Cut Bank 172
Deer Lodge 145
Dillon 237
E. Glacier Park 125
Ekalaka 642
Eureka 115
Forsyth 482
Fort Benton 279
Gardiner 347
Glasgow 456
Glendive 586
Grass Range Jct. 371
Great Falls 235
Hamilton 116
Hardin 451
Harlowtown 312
Havre 298
Helena 181
Hysham 482
Jordan 470
Kalispell 49
Laurel 394
Lewistown 340
Libby 138
Livingston 294
Malta 386
Miles City 527
Missoula 66
Philipsburg 140
Plentywood 601
Poplar 526
Red Lodge 417
Roundup 381
Ryegate 342
Scobey 560
Shelby 196
Sidney 596
Stanford 295
Superior 97
Sweetgrass 230
Terry 565
Thompson Falls 91
Three Forks 239
Townsend 213
Virginia City 258
West Glacier 70
W. Yellowstone 336
Whitefish 63
W Sulphur Springs 255
Wibaux 612
Winnett 394
Wolf Point 505

Poplar to
Anaconda 515
Baker 185
Big Timber 363
Billings 306
Boulder 459
Bozeman 424
Broadus 260
Browning 388
Butte 496
Chester 288
Chinook 207
Choteau 398
Circle 65
Columbus 347
Conrad 355
Cooke City 432
Culbertson 33
Cut Bank 354
Deer Lodge 488
Dillon 527
E. Glacier Park 401
Ekalaka 220
Eureka 533
Forsyth 228
Fort Benton 303
Gardiner 451
Glasgow 70
Glendive 114
Grass Range Jct. 231
Great Falls 343
Hamilton 562
Hardin 303
Harlowtown 319
Havre 228
Helena 432
Hysham 257
Jordan 132
Kalispell 487
Laurel 322
Lewistown 262
Libby 576
Livingston 398
Malta 140
Miles City 184
Missoula 512
Philipsburg 525
Plentywood 80
Polson 526
Red Lodge 366
Roundup 253
Ryegate 292
Scobey 62
Shelby 330
Sidney 70
Stanford 307
Superior 569
Sweetgrass 366
Terry 145
Thompson Falls 595
Three Forks 452
Townsend 418
Virginia City 491
West Glacier 546
W. Yellowstone 505
Whitefish 481
W Sulphur Springs 376
Wibaux 140
Winnett 208
Wolf Point 21

Red Lodge to
Anaconda 258
Baker 285
Big Timber 88
Billings 60
Boulder 232
Bozeman 149
Broadus 228
Browning 387
Butte 231
Chester 370
Chinook 289
Choteau 315
Circle 301
Columbus 48
Conrad 323
Cooke City 66
Culbertson 369
Cut Bank 370
Deer Lodge 272
Dillon 261
E. Glacier Park 400
Ekalaka 320
Eureka 500
Forsyth 160
Fort Benton 265
Gardiner 122
Glasgow 339
Glendive 282
Grass Range Jct. 157
Great Falls 260
Hamilton 378
Hardin 106
Harlowtown 132
Havre 321
Helena 238
Hysham 137
Jordan 234
Kalispell 434
Laurel 44
Lewistown 188
Libby 525
Livingston 123
Malta 269
Miles City 205
Missoula 351
Philipsburg 289
Plentywood 416
Polson 417
Poplar 366
Roundup 113
Ryegate 123
Scobey 400
Shelby 348
Sidney 332
Stanford 200
Superior 408
Sweetgrass 382
Terry 243
Thompson Falls 451
Three Forks 179
Townsend 206
Virginia City 216
West Glacier 455
W. Yellowstone 158
Whitefish 448
W Sulphur Springs 182
Wibaux 308
Winnett 158
Wolf Point 354

Roundup to
Anaconda 274
Baker 226
Big Timber 113
Billings 53
Boulder 227
Bozeman 174
Broadus 215
Browning 307
Butte 247
Chester 257
Chinook 176
Choteau 235
Circle 188
Columbus 94
Conrad 243
Cooke City 179
Culbertson 286
Cut Bank 290
Deer Lodge 256
Dillon 277
E. Glacier Park 320
Ekalaka 261
Eureka 452
Forsyth 101
Fort Benton 174
Gardiner 201
Glasgow 226
Glendive 223
Grass Range Jct. 44
Great Falls 180
Hamilton 365
Hardin 93
Harlowtown 69
Havre 197
Helena 200
Hysham 124
Jordan 146
Kalispell 396
Laurel 69
Lewistown 75
Libby 485
Livingston 148
Malta 156
Miles City 146
Missoula 315
Philipsburg 293
Plentywood 328
Polson 381
Poplar 253
Red Lodge 113
Ryegate 39
Scobey 387
Shelby 268
Sidney 263
Stanford 120
Superior 372
Sweetgrass 302
Terry 184
Thompson Falls 415
Three Forks 202
Townsend 168
Virginia City 241
West Glacier 375
W. Yellowstone 255
Whitefish 400
W Sulphur Springs 126
Wibaux 249
Winnett 45
Wolf Point 241

Ryegate to
Anaconda 235
Baker 265
Big Timber 74
Billings 63
Boulder 188
Bozeman 135
Broadus 231
Browning 283
Butte 208
Chester 286
Chinook 215
Choteau 211
Circle 227
Columbus 104
Conrad 219
Cooke City 189
Culbertson 325
Cut Bank 266
Deer Lodge 217
Dillon 238
E. Glacier Park 296
Ekalaka 300
Eureka 423
Forsyth 140
Fort Benton 161
Gardiner 162
Glasgow 265
Glendive 262
Grass Range Jct. 83
Great Falls 156
Hamilton 326
Hardin 109
Harlowtown 30
Havre 236
Helena 161
Hysham 140
Jordan 160
Kalispell 357
Laurel 79
Lewistown 85
Libby 446
Livingston 109
Malta 195
Miles City 185
Missoula 276
Philipsburg 254
Plentywood 367
Polson 342
Poplar 292
Red Lodge 123
Roundup 39
Scobey 326
Shelby 244
Sidney 302
Stanford 96
Superior 333
Sweetgrass 278
Terry 223
Thompson Falls 376
Three Forks 163
Townsend 129
Virginia City 202
West Glacier 351
W. Yellowstone 216
Whitefish 371
W Sulphur Springs 87
Wibaux 288
Winnett 84
Wolf Point 280

Scobey to
Anaconda 549
Baker 219
Big Timber 397
Billings 340
Boulder 493
Bozeman 458
Broadus 294
Browning 422
Butte 530
Chester 322
Chinook 241
Choteau 432
Circle 99
Columbus 381
Conrad 389
Cooke City 466
Culbertson 88
Cut Bank 388
Deer Lodge 522
Dillon 561
E. Glacier Park 435
Ekalaka 254
Eureka 567
Forsyth 262
Fort Benton 337
Gardiner 485
Glasgow 104
Glendive 148
Grass Range Jct. 255
Great Falls 377
Hamilton 596
Hardin 337
Harlowtown 353
Havre 262
Helena 466
Hysham 291
Jordan 166
Kalispell 521
Laurel 356
Lewistown 296
Libby 610
Livingston 432
Malta 174
Miles City 218
Missoula 546
Philipsburg 559
Plentywood 41
Polson 560
Poplar 62
Red Lodge 400
Roundup 287
Ryegate 326
Shelby 364
Sidney 125
Stanford 341
Superior 603
Sweetgrass 400
Terry 179
Thompson Falls 629
Three Forks 486
Townsend 452
Virginia City 525
West Glacier 490
W. Yellowstone 539
Whitefish 515
W Sulphur Springs 410
Wibaux 174
Winnett 242
Wolf Point 55

Shelby to
Anaconda 248
Baker 482
Big Timber 260
Billings 307
Boulder 194
Bozeman 262
Broadus 475
Browning 58
Butte 231
Chester 42
Chinook 123
Choteau 75
Circle 362
Columbus 300
Conrad 25
Cooke City 367
Culbertson 363
Cut Bank 24
Deer Lodge 221
Dillon 287
E. Glacier Park 71
Ekalaka 517
Eureka 203
Forsyth 369
Fort Benton 132
Gardiner 311
Glasgow 260
Glendive 411
Grass Range Jct. 224
Great Falls 88
Hamilton 277
Hardin 353
Harlowtown 216
Havre 102
Helena 167
Hysham 384
Jordan 323
Kalispell 157
Laurel 323
Lewistown 193
Libby 246
Livingston 258
Malta 190
Miles City 405
Missoula 227
Philipsburg 258
Plentywood 405
Polson 196
Poplar 330
Red Lodge 348
Roundup 268
Ryegate 244
Scobey 364
Sidney 400
Stanford 148
Superior 282
Sweetgrass 36
Terry 442
Thompson Falls 265
Three Forks 233
Townsend 199
Virginia City 287
West Glacier 126
W. Yellowstone 342
Whitefish 151
W Sulphur Springs 185
Wibaux 437
Winnett 247
Wolf Point 309

Sidney to
Anaconda 523
Baker 125
Big Timber 353
Billings 272
Boulder 487
Bozeman 414
Broadus 204
Browning 458
Butte 296
Chester 358
Chinook 277
Choteau 432
Circle 75
Columbus 315
Conrad 425
Cooke City 398
Culbertson 37
Cut Bank 424
Deer Lodge 516
Dillon 526
E. Glacier Park 471
Ekalaka 160
Eureka 603
Forsyth 172
Fort Benton 371
Gardiner 441
Glasgow 140
Glendive 54
Grass Range Jct. 241
Great Falls 377
Hamilton 596
Hardin 247
Harlowtown 329
Havre 298
Helena 460
Hysham 201
Jordan 142
Kalispell 557
Laurel 288
Lewistown 272
Libby 646
Livingston 388
Malta 210
Miles City 128
Missoula 546
Philipsburg 553
Plentywood 84
Polson 596
Poplar 70
Red Lodge 332
Roundup 263
Ryegate 302
Scobey 125
Shelby 400
Stanford 317
Superior 603
Sweetgrass 436
Terry 89
Thompson Falls 646
Three Forks 444
Townsend 428
Virginia City 481
West Glacier 526
W. Yellowstone 490
Whitefish 551
W Sulphur Springs 386
Wibaux 80
Winnett 218
Wolf Point 91

Stanford to
Anaconda 232
Baker 338
Big Timber 112
Billings 159
Boulder 176
Bozeman 173
Broadus 327
Browning 187
Butte 213
Chester 190
Chinook 161
Choteau 115
Circle 242
Columbus 152
Conrad 123
Cooke City 256
Culbertson 340
Cut Bank 170
Deer Lodge 205
Dillon 260
E. Glacier Park 200
Ekalaka 373
Eureka 332
Forsyth 221
Fort Benton 65
Gardiner 200
Glasgow 248
Glendive 291
Grass Range Jct. 76
Great Falls 60
Hamilton 279
Hardin 205
Harlowtown 68
Havre 140
Helena 149
Hysham 236
Jordan 175
Kalispell 286
Laurel 175
Lewistown 45
Libby 375
Livingston 147
Malta 18
Miles City 257
Missoula 229
Philipsburg 242
Plentywood 282
Polson 295
Poplar 307
Red Lodge 200
Roundup 120
Ryegate 96
Scobey 341
Shelby 148
Sidney 317
Superior 286
Sweetgrass 182
Terry 296
Thompson Falls 329
Three Forks 187
Townsend 153
Virginia City 240
West Glacier 255
W. Yellowstone 254
Whitefish 280
W Sulphur Springs 111
Wibaux 317
Winnett 99
Wolf Point 295

Superior to
Anaconda 162
Baker 598
Big Timber 320
Billings 396
Boulder 199
Bozeman 259
Broadus 564
Browning 224
Butte 177
Chester 324
Chinook 362
Choteau 217
Circle 528
Columbus 360
Conrad 259
Cooke City 394
Culbertson 602
Cut Bank 258
Deer Lodge 136
Dillon 228
E. Glacier Park 211
Ekalaka 633
Eureka 191
Forsyth 473
Fort Benton 270
Gardiner 338
Glasgow 499
Glendive 577
Grass Range Jct. 362
Great Falls 226
Hamilton 107
Hardin 442
Harlowtown 303
Havre 341
Helena 172
Hysham 473
Jordan 461
Kalispell 125
Laurel 385
Lewistown 331
Libby 159
Livingston 285
Malta 429
Miles City 518
Missoula 57
Philipsburg 131
Plentywood 644
Polson 97
Poplar 569
Red Lodge 408
Roundup 372
Ryegate 333
Scobey 603
Shelby 282
Sidney 603
Stanford 286
Sweetgrass 316
Terry 556
Thompson Falls 69
Three Forks 230
Townsend 204
Virginia City 249
West Glacier 156
W. Yellowstone 327
Whitefish 139
W Sulphur Springs 246
Wibaux 603
Winnett 385
Wolf Point 548

Sweetgrass to
Anaconda 282
Baker 518
Big Timber 294

Montana Introduction

All Montana Area Codes are 406

Billings 341
Boulder 228
Bozeman 296
Broadus 509
Browning 92
Butte 265
Chester 78
Chinook 159
Choteau 109
Circle 398
Columbus 334
Conrad 59
Cooke City 401
Culbertson 399
Cut Bank 58
Deer Lodge 255
Dillon 321
E. Glacier Park 105
Ekalaka 553
Eureka 237
Forsyth 403
Fort Benton 166
Gardiner 345
Glasgow 296
Glendive 447
Grass Range Jct. 358
Great Falls 122
Hamilton 311
Hardin 287
Harlowtown 250
Havre 138
Helena 201
Hysham 418
Jordan 357
Kalispell 191
Laurel 357
Lewistown 227
Libby 280
Livingston 292
Malta 226
Miles City 439
Missoula 261
Philipsburg 292
Plentywood 441
Polson 230
Poplar 366
Red Lodge 382
Roundup 302
Ryegate 278
Scobey 400
Shelby 36
Sidney 436
Stanford 182
Superior 316
Terry 478
Thompson Falls 299
Three Forks 267
Townsend 233
Virginia City 321
West Glacier 160
W. Yellowstone 376
Whitefish 185
W Sulphur Springs 219
Wibaux 473
Winnett 281
Wolf Point 345

Terry to
Anaconda 434
Baker 110
Big Timber 264
Billings 183
Boulder 408
Bozeman 325
Broadus 115
Browning 483
Butte 407
Chester 400
Chinook 319
Choteau 411
Circle 80
Columbus 224
Conrad 419
Cooke City 309
Culbertson 126
Cut Bank 466
Deer Lodge 440
Dillon 437
E. Glacier Park 496
Ekalaka 145
Eureka 168
Forsyth 83
Fort Benton 350
Gardiner 352
Glasgow 182
Glendive 39
Grass Range Jct. 220
Great Falls 356
Hamilton 549
Hardin 148
Harlowtown 253
Havre 340
Helena 384
Hysham 112
Jordan 123
Kalispell 580
Laurel 199
Lewistown 251
Libby 669
Livingston 299
Malta 252
Miles City 39
Missoula 499
Philipsburg 465
Plentywood 173
Polson 565
Poplar 145
Red Lodge 243
Roundup 184
Ryegate 223
Scobey 179
Shelby 442
Sidney 89
Stanford 296
Superior 556
Sweetgrass 478
Thompson Falls 599
Three Forks 355
Townsend 352
Virginia City 392
West Glacier 551
W. Yellowstone 401
Whitefish 576
W Sulphur Springs 310
Wibaux 65
Winnett 197
Wolf Point 133

Thompson Falls to
Anaconda 205
Baker 461
Big Timber 363
Billings 439
Boulder 242
Bozeman 302
Broadus 607
Browning 207
Butte 220
Chester 307
Chinook 388
Choteau 260
Circle 571
Columbus 403
Conrad 273
Cooke City 437
Culbertson 628
Cut Bank 241
Deer Lodge 179
Dillon 271
E. Glacier Park 194
Ekalaka 676
Eureka 158
Forsyth 516
Fort Benton 313
Gardiner 381
Glasgow 525
Glendive 620
Grass Range Jct. 405
Great Falls 269
Hamilton 150
Hardin 485
Harlowtown 346
Havre 367
Helena 215
Hysham 516
Jordan 504
Kalispell 108
Laurel 428
Lewistown 374
Libby 90
Livingston 328
Malta 455
Miles City 561
Missoula 100
Philipsburg 174
Plentywood 670
Polson 91
Poplar 595
Red Lodge 451
Roundup 415
Ryegate 376
Scobey 629
Shelby 265
Sidney 646
Stanford 329
Superior 69
Sweetgrass 299
Terry 599
Three Forks 273
Townsend 247
Virginia City 292
West Glacier 139
W. Yellowstone 370
Whitefish 122
W Sulphur Springs 289
Wibaux 646
Winnett 428
Wolf Point 574

Three Forks to
Anaconda 80
Baker 397
Big Timber 91
Billings 172
Boulder 54
Bozeman 30
Broadus 340
Browning 238
Butte 53
Chester 275
Chinook 291
Choteau 166
Circle 387
Columbus 131
Conrad 208
Cooke City 165
Culbertson 481
Cut Bank 255
Deer Lodge 94
Dillon 83
E. Glacier Park 251
Ekalaka 432
Eureka 328
Forsyth 272
Fort Benton 199
Gardiner 109
Glasgow 393
Glendive 394
Grass Range Jct. 221
Great Falls 155
Hamilton 200
Hardin 218
Harlowtown 133
Havre 270
Helena 66
Hysham 249
Jordan 320
Kalispell 262
Laurel 156
Lewistown 190
Libby 351
Livingston 56
Malta 323
Miles City 317
Missoula 173
Philipsburg 111
Plentywood 527
Polson 239
Poplar 452
Red Lodge 179
Roundup 202
Ryegate 163
Scobey 486
Shelby 233
Sidney 444
Stanford 187
Superior 230
Sweetgrass 267
Terry 355
Thompson Falls 273
Townsend 34
Virginia City 61
West Glacier 283
W. Yellowstone 110
Whitefish 276
W Sulphur Springs 76
Wibaux 420
Winnett 244
Wolf Point 440

Townsend to
Anaconda 106
Baker 394
Big Timber 118
Billings 192
Boulder 59
Bozeman 63
Broadus 360
Browning 204
Butte 79
Chester 241
Chinook 257
Choteau 132
Circle 353
Columbus 158
Conrad 174
Cooke City 198
Culbertson 451
Cut Bank 221
Deer Lodge 88
Dillon 109
E. Glacier Park 217
Ekalaka 429
Eureka 294
Forsyth 269
Fort Benton 165
Gardiner 142
Glasgow 359
Glendive 391
Grass Range Jct. 187
Great Falls 121
Hamilton 197
Hardin 238
Harlowtown 99
Havre 236
Helena 32
Hysham 269
Jordan 286
Kalispell 228
Laurel 183
Lewistown 156
Libby 317
Livingston 89
Malta 289
Miles City 314
Missoula 147
Philipsburg 125
Plentywood 493
Polson 213
Poplar 418
Red Lodge 206
Roundup 168
Ryegate 129
Scobey 452
Shelby 199
Sidney 428
Stanford 153
Superior 204
Sweetgrass 233
Terry 352
Thompson Falls 247
Three Forks 34
Virginia City 89
West Glacier 249
W. Yellowstone 143
Whitefish 242
W Sulphur Springs 42
Wibaux 417
Winnett 210
Wolf Point 406

Virginia City to
Anaconda 99
Baker 434
Big Timber 128
Billings 209
Boulder 92
Bozeman 67
Broadus 377
Browning 292
Butte 72
Chester 329
Chinook 345
Choteau 220
Circle 426
Columbus 168
Conrad 262
Cooke City 176
Culbertson 518
Cut Bank 309
Deer Lodge 133
Dillon 57
E. Glacier Park 305
Ekalaka 469
Eureka 365
Forsyth 309
Fort Benton 253
Gardiner 138
Glasgow 432
Glendive 431
Grass Range Jct. 260
Great Falls 209
Hamilton 219
Hardin 255
Harlowtown 172
Havre 324
Helena 120
Hysham 286
Jordan 359
Kalispell 299
Laurel 193
Lewistown 229
Libby 382
Livingston 93
Malta 362
Miles City 354
Missoula 192
Philipsburg 130
Plentywood 565
Polson 258
Poplar 491
Red Lodge 216
Roundup 241
Ryegate 202
Scobey 525
Shelby 287
Sidney 481
Stanford 240
Superior 249
Sweetgrass 321
Terry 392
Thompson Falls 292
Three Forks 61
Townsend 89
West Glacier 320
W. Yellowstone 84
Whitefish 313
W Sulphur Springs 131
Wibaux 457
Winnett 283
Wolf Point 479

West Glacier to
Anaconda 234
Baker 593
Big Timber 367
Billings 414
Boulder 244
Bozeman 321
Broadus 582
Browning 68
Butte 248
Chester 168
Chinook 249
Choteau 140
Circle 488
Columbus 407
Conrad 134
Cooke City 447
Culbertson 489
Cut Bank 102
Deer Lodge 207
Dillon 299
E. Glacier Park 55
Ekalaka 628
Eureka 77
Forsyth 476
Fort Benton 239
Gardiner 391
Glasgow 386
Glendive 537
Grass Range Jct. 331
Great Falls 195
Hamilton 186
Hardin 460
Harlowtown 323
Havre 228
Helena 217
Hysham 491
Jordan 430
Kalispell 31
Laurel 430
Lewistown 300
Libby 120
Livingston 338
Malta 316
Miles City 512
Missoula 136
Philipsburg 210
Plentywood 531
Polson 70
Poplar 546
Red Lodge 455
Roundup 375
Ryegate 351
Scobey 490
Shelby 126
Sidney 526
Stanford 255
Superior 156
Sweetgrass 160
Terry 551
Thompson Falls 139
Three Forks 283
Townsend 249
Virginia City 320
W. Yellowstone 392
Whitefish 25
W Sulphur Springs 291
Wibaux 563
Winnett 354
Wolf Point 435

W. Yellowstone to
Anaconda 177
Baker 443
Big Timber 142
Billings 218
Boulder 151
Bozeman 91
Broadus 386
Browning 347
Butte 150
Chester 384
Chinook 396
Choteau 275
Circle 440
Columbus 182
Conrad 317
Cooke City 92
Culbertson 527
Cut Bank 364
Deer Lodge 191
Dillon 141
E. Glacier Park 360
Ekalaka 478
Eureka 437
Forsyth 318
Fort Benton 308
Gardiner 54
Glasgow 445
Glendive 440
Grass Range Jct. 274
Great Falls 264
Hamilton 297
Hardin 264
Harlowtown 186
Havre 379
Helena 175
Hysham 295
Jordan 373
Kalispell 371
Laurel 202
Lewistown 243
Libby 460
Livingston 107
Malta 376
Miles City 363
Missoula 270
Philipsburg 208
Plentywood 574
Polson 336
Poplar 505
Red Lodge 158
Roundup 255
Ryegate 216
Scobey 539
Shelby 342
Sidney 490
Stanford 254
Superior 327
Sweetgrass 376
Terry 401
Thompson Falls 370
Three Forks 110
Townsend 143
Virginia City 84
West Glacier 392
Whitefish 385
W Sulphur Springs 171
Wibaux 466
Winnett 297
Wolf Point 493

Whitefish to
Anaconda 227
Baker 628
Big Timber 360
Billings 434
Boulder 237
Bozeman 305
Broadus 602
Browning 93
Butte 241
Chester 193
Chinook 274
Choteau 165
Circle 513
Columbus 400
Conrad 159
Cooke City 440
Culbertson 514
Cut Bank 127
Deer Lodge 200
Dillon 292
E. Glacier Park 80
Ekalaka 653
Eureka 52
Forsyth 501
Fort Benton 264
Gardiner 384
Glasgow 411
Glendive 562
Grass Range Jct. 365
Great Falls 220
Hamilton 179
Hardin 480
Harlowtown 341
Havre 253
Helena 210
Hysham 511
Jordan 455
Kalispell 14
Laurel 454
Lewistown 325
Libby 103
Livingston 331
Malta 341
Miles City 537
Missoula 129
Philipsburg 203
Plentywood 556
Polson 63
Poplar 481
Red Lodge 448
Roundup 400
Ryegate 371
Scobey 515
Shelby 151
Sidney 551
Stanford 280
Superior 139
Sweetgrass 185
Terry 576
Thompson Falls 122
Three Forks 276
Townsend 242
Virginia City 313
West Glacier 25
W. Yellowstone 385
W Sulphur Springs 284
Wibaux 588
Winnett 379
Wolf Point 460

W Sulphur Springs to
Anaconda 148
Baker 352
Big Timber 94
Billings 150
Boulder 101
Bozeman 80
Broadus 318
Browning 224
Butte 121
Chester 227
Chinook 233
Choteau 152
Circle 311
Columbus 134
Conrad 160
Cooke City 182
Culbertson 409
Cut Bank 207
Deer Lodge 130
Dillon 151
E. Glacier Park 237
Ekalaka 387
Eureka 336
Forsyth 227
Fort Benton 141
Gardiner 126
Glasgow 317
Glendive 349
Grass Range Jct. 145
Great Falls 97
Hamilton 239
Hardin 196
Harlowtown 57
Havre 212
Helena 74
Hysham 227
Jordan 244
Kalispell 270
Laurel 159
Lewistown 114
Libby 359
Livingston 73
Malta 247
Miles City 272
Missoula 189
Philipsburg 167
Plentywood 451
Polson 255
Poplar 376
Red Lodge 182
Roundup 126
Ryegate 87
Scobey 410
Shelby 185
Sidney 386
Stanford 111
Superior 246
Sweetgrass 219
Terry 310
Thompson Falls 289
Three Forks 76
Townsend 42
Virginia City 131
West Glacier 291
W. Yellowstone 171
Whitefish 284
Wibaux 375
Winnett 168
Wolf Point 364

Wibaux to
Anaconda 499
Baker 45
Big Timber 329
Billings 248
Boulder 473
Bozeman 390
Broadus 180
Browning 495
Butte 472
Chester 395
Chinook 314
Choteau 432
Circle 75
Columbus 289
Conrad 440
Cooke City 374
Culbertson 117
Cut Bank 461
Deer Lodge 505
Dillon 502
E. Glacier Park 508
Ekalaka 80
Eureka 640
Forsyth 148
Fort Benton 371
Gardiner 417
Glasgow 177
Glendive 26
Grass Range Jct. 241
Great Falls 377
Hamilton 596
Hardin 233
Harlowtown 318
Havre 335
Helena 449
Hysham 177
Jordan 142
Kalispell 594
Laurel 264
Lewistown 272
Libby 683
Livingston 364
Malta 247
Miles City 104
Missoula 546
Philipsburg 530
Plentywood 164
Polson 612
Poplar 140
Red Lodge 308
Roundup 249
Ryegate 288
Scobey 174
Shelby 437
Sidney 80
Stanford 317
Superior 603
Sweetgrass 473
Terry 65
Thompson Falls 646
Three Forks 420
Townsend 417
Virginia City 457
West Glacier 563
W. Yellowstone 466
Whitefish 588
W Sulphur Springs 375
Winnett 218
Wolf Point 128

Winnett to
Anaconda 316
Baker 239
Big Timber 155
Billings 98
Boulder 269
Bozeman 216
Broadus 237
Browning 286
Butte 289
Chester 236
Chinook 155
Choteau 214
Circle 143
Columbus 139
Conrad 222
Cooke City 224
Culbertson 241
Cut Bank 269
Deer Lodge 298
Dillon 319
E. Glacier Park 299
Ekalaka 274
Eureka 431
Forsyth 146
Fort Benton 153
Gardiner 243
Glasgow 189
Glendive 192
Grass Range Jct. 23
Great Falls 159
Hamilton 378
Hardin 138
Harlowtown 111
Havre 176
Helena 242
Hysham 169
Jordan 76
Kalispell 385
Laurel 114
Lewistown 54
Libby 474
Livingston 190
Malta 135
Miles City 158
Missoula 328
Philipsburg 335
Plentywood 283
Polson 394
Poplar 208
Red Lodge 158
Roundup 45
Ryegate 84
Scobey 242
Shelby 247
Sidney 218
Stanford 99
Superior 385
Sweetgrass 281
Terry 197
Thompson Falls 428
Three Forks 244
Townsend 210
Virginia City 283
West Glacier 354
W. Yellowstone 297
Whitefish 379
W Sulphur Springs 168
Wibaux 218
Wolf Point 128

Wolf Point to
Anaconda 494
Baker 173
Big Timber 351
Billings 294
Boulder 438
Bozeman 412
Broadus 248
Browning 367
Butte 475
Chester 267
Chinook 186
Choteau 377
Circle 53
Columbus 335
Conrad 334
Cooke City 420
Culbertson 54
Cut Bank 333
Deer Lodge 467
Dillon 515
E. Glacier Park 380
Ekalaka 208
Eureka 512
Forsyth 216
Fort Benton 282
Gardiner 439
Glasgow 49
Glendive 102
Grass Range Jct. 219
Great Falls 322
Hamilton 541
Hardin 291
Harlowtown 307
Havre 207
Helena 411
Hysham 245
Jordan 120
Kalispell 466
Laurel 310
Lewistown 250
Libby 555
Livingston 386
Malta 119
Miles City 172
Missoula 491
Philipsburg 504
Plentywood 96
Polson 505
Poplar 21
Red Lodge 354
Roundup 241
Ryegate 280
Scobey 55
Shelby 309
Sidney 91
Stanford 295
Superior 548
Sweetgrass 345
Terry 133
Thompson Falls 574
Three Forks 440
Townsend 406
Virginia City 479
West Glacier 435
W. Yellowstone 493
Whitefish 460
W Sulphur Springs 364
Wibaux 128
Winnett 196

NOTES:

CITY/TOWN LOCATOR

Town/Population	Section
Absarokee	4
Acton	4
Alder	1
Alpine	4
Amsterdam	2
Ballantine	5
Bannack	1
Bearcreek, 83	4
Belfry	4
Belgrade, 5,728	2
Big Sky	2
Big Timber, 1,650	3
Billings, 89,847	5
Boyd	4
Bozeman, 27,509	2
Bridger, 745	4
Butte, 33,892	1
Cameron	2
Cardwell	1
Churchill	2
Clyde Park, 310	3
Columbus, 1,748	4
Cooke City	3
Corwin Springs	3
Crow Agency	5
Dean	4
Dell	1
Dewey	1
Dillon, 3,752	1
Divide	1
Edgar	4
Emigrant	3
Ennis, 840	2
Fishtail	4
Fort Smith	5
Fromberg, 486	4
Gallatin Gateway	2
Gardiner	3
Glen	1
Greycliff	3
Hardin, 3,384	5
Harrison	2
Huntley	5
Hysham, 330	5
Jardine	3
Jeffers	2
Joliet, 575	4
La Hood	1
Lakeview	2
Laurel, 6,255	4
Laurin	1
Lima, 242	1
Limestone	4
Livingston, 6,851	3
Lodge Grass, 510	5
Logan	2
Luther	4
Manhattan, 1,396	2
McAllister	2
McLeod	3
Melrose	1
Miner	3
Molt	4
Monida	1
Myers	5
Nevada City	1
Norris	2
Nye	4
Park City	4
Pine Creek	3
Pipestone	1
Pompeys Pillar	5
Pony	2
Pray	3
Pryor	5
Rapelje	4
Red Lodge, 2,177	4
Reedpoint	4
Roberts	4
Rocker	1
Rockvale	4
Roscoe	4
Rosebud	1
Saint Xavier	5
Sanders	5
Shepherd	5
Sheridan, 659	1
Silesia	4
Silver Gate	3
Silver Star	1
Springdale	3
Trident	2
Twin Bridges, 400	1
Virginia City, 130	1
Volborg	1
Walkerville, 714	1
Warren	4
Washoe	4
Waterloo	1
West Yellowstone, 1,177	2
Whitehall, 1,044	1
Willow Creek	2
Wilsall	3
Worden	5
Wyola	5

NOTES:

SECTION GUIDE

Libby

Whitefish

Kalispell

Polson

Cut Bank

Shelby

Great Falls

Missoula

Helena

Hamilton

Anaconda

Butte

Bozeman

Livingston

Dillon

1

2

3

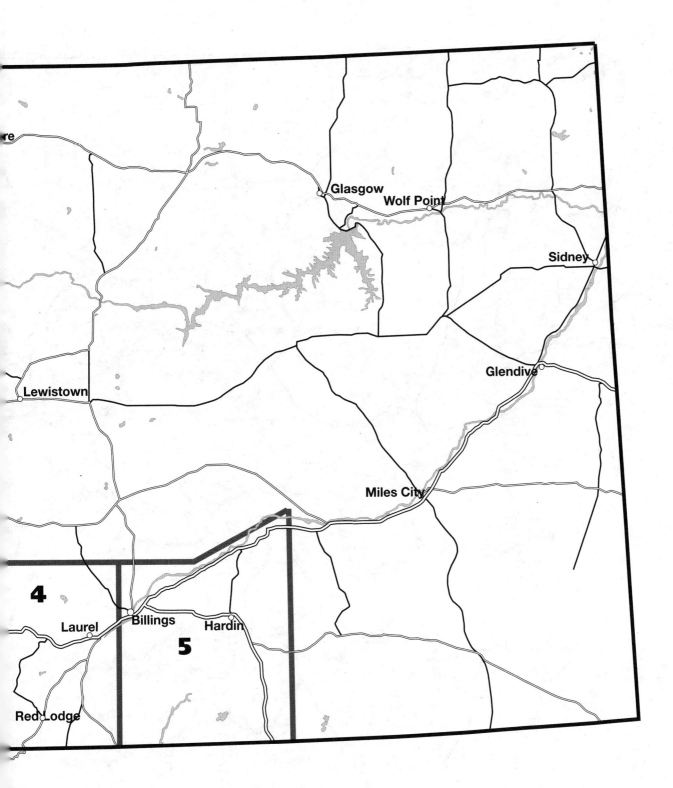

Glasgow

Wolf Point

Sidney

Glendive

Lewistown

Miles City

4

Laurel **Billings** **Hardin**

5

Red Lodge

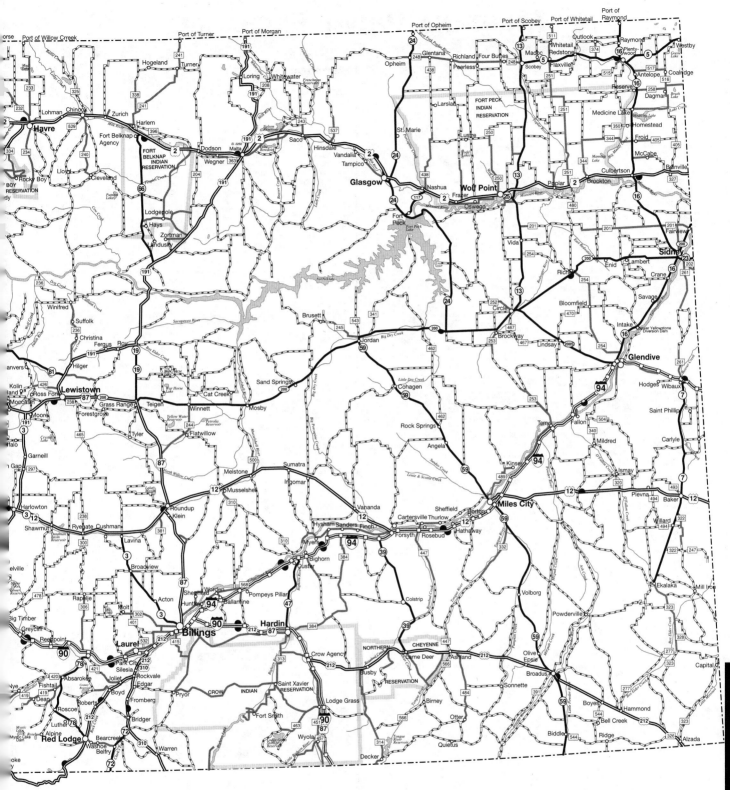

MONTANA PHONE EXCHANGES

Alphabetical

Name	No.	Name	No.	Name	No.	Name	No.
Absarokee	328	Denton	567	Jackson	834	Rock Springs	354
Alberton	722	Devon		Joliet	962	Ronan	676
Alberton S.	864	Dillon	683	Joplin	292	Rosebud	347
Alta	849	Divide	267	Jordan	557	Roundup	323
Alzada	828	Dixon	246	Jordan	977	Roy	464
Alzada S.	878	Dodson	383	Judith Gap	473	Rudyard	355
Amsterdam	282	Drummond	288	Kalispell	253	Ryegate	568
Anaconda	563	Dupuyer	472	Kalispell	257	Saco	527
Arlee	726	Dutton	476	Kalispell	752	Saint Ignatius	745
Ashland	784	E. Carlyle	688	Kalispell	755	Saint Mary	732
Augusta	562	E. Glacier Park	226	Kalispell	756	Saint Regis	649
Avon	492	Ekalaka	775	Kalispell	758	Savage	776
Babb	732	Ekalaka	975	Kevin-oilmont	337	Scobey	487
Bainville	769	Elmo	849	Kremlin	372	Scobey Rural	783
Baker	778	Ennis	682	Lakeside	844	Seeley Lake	677
Baker	978	Ethridge	339	Lambert	774	Shelby	434
Belfrey	664	Eureka	296	Lame Deer	477	Shepherd	373
Belgrade	388	Eureka Rural	889	Larslan	725	Sheridan	842
Belt	277	Fairfield	467	Laurel	628	Sidney	422
Big Fork	837	Fairview	742	Lavina	636	Sidney	433
Big Sandy	378	Fairview	747	Lewistown	538	Sidney	482
Big Sky	995	Fallon	486	Lewistown Cellular	366	Sidney	488
Big Timber	932	Finley Point	887	Libby	293	Sidney E.	481
Billings	245	Flaxville	474	Lima	276	Simpson	394
Billings	248	Flaxville Rural	779	Lincoln	362	Somers	857
Billings	252	Forsyth	356	Lindsay	584.	S. Wolf Point	525
Billings	254	Fort Benton	622	Livingston	222	Stanford	566
Billings	255	Fort Peck	526	Lodge Grass	639	Stevensville	777
Billings	256	Fortshaw	264	Lolo	273	Stockett	736
Billings	259	Fort Smith	666	Loma	739	Sunburst	937
Billings	657	Fortine	882	Malta	654	Superior	822
Billings	698	Frazer	695	Malta S.	658	Swan Lake	886
Billings	855	Frenchtown	626	Mammoth, Wy	344	Sweetgrass	335
Billings W.	652	Froid	766	Manhattan	284	Terry	635
Billings W.	655	Froid Rural E.	963	Marion	854	Terry	637
Billings W.	656	Fromberg	668	Martinsdale	572	Thompson- Falls	827
Billings W.	976	Gallatin Gateway	763	Mcgregor Lake	858	Three Forks	285
Billings Shepherd	373	Gardiner	848	Medicine Lake	789	Townsend	266
Birney	984	Geraldine	737	Melrose	835	Troy	295
Bloomfield	583	Geyser	735	Melstone	358	Turner	379
Boulder	225	Gildford	376	Melville	537	Twin Bridges	684
Box Elder	352	Glasgow	228	Miles City	232	Ulm	866
Bozeman	581	Glasgow	263	Miles City	233	Valier	287
Bozeman	585	Glasgow N.	367	Miles City	234	Valley Industrial Park	
Bozeman	586	Glendive	345	Miles City	853		524
Bozeman	587	Glendive	359	Miles City	874	Vaughn	965
Bozeman	994	Glendive	365	Miles City S.	421	Victor	642
Bozeman Cellular	580	Glendive	377	Milltown	258	Virginia City	843
Brady	753	Glendive Cellular	939	Missoula	240	Warm Spring	693
Bridger	662	Glentana	724	Missoula	243	W. Glacier	888
Broadus	436	Grant	681	Missoula	251	W. Glendive	687
Broadus N.	554.	Grass Range	428	Missoula	329	W. Sidney	798
Broadus S.	427	Great Falls	452	Missoula	523	W. Yellowstone	646
Broadview	667	Great Falls	453	Missoula	542	W.by	385
Brockton	786	Great Falls	454	Missoula	543	W.by E.	985
Browning	338	Great Falls	455	Missoula	544	White Sulphur Springs	
Busby	592	Great Falls	727	Missoula	549		547
Butte	490	Great Falls	731	Missoula	721	Whitefish	862
Butte	496	Great Falls	761	Missoula	728	Whitehall	287
Butte	723	Great Falls	771	Molt	669	Whitewater	674
Butte	782	Great Falls	788	Moore	374	Wibaux	795
Butte-south	494	Great Falls	791	Musselshell	947	Wibaux	796
Canyon Creek	368	Great Falls	799	Nashua	746	Wilsall	578
Canyon Ferry	475	Great Falls	833	Nashua N.	785	Winifred	462
Carlyle	588	Great Falls	966	Neihart	236	Winnett	429
Carter	734	Hamilton	363	N. Ryegate	575	Wisdom	689
Cascade	468	Hardin	665	Noxon	847	Wise River	832
Charlo	644	Hardin	679	Old Faithful, Wy	545	Wolf Creek	235
Chester	759	Harlem	353	Olney	881	Wolf Point	653
Chester S.	456	Harlowton	632	Opheim	762	Wolf Point N.	392
Chinook	357	Harrison	685	Opportunity	797	Worden	967
Choteau	466	Haugan	678	Outlook	895	Wyola	343
Circle	485	Havre	265	Ovando	793	Yellow Bay	982
Circle	974	Havre N.	398	Pablo	675		
Clancy	933	Havre S.	390	Park City	633		
Clark	645	Havre S.	395	Peerless	893		
Clinton	825	Hays	673	Pendroy	469		
Clyde Park	686	Heart Butte	338	Philipsburg	859		
Colstrip	748	Helena	439	Plains	826		
Columbia Falls	892	Helena	439	Plentywood	765		
Columbus	322	Helena	441	Plevna	772		
Condon	754	Helena	442	Plevna	971		
Conrad	278	Helena	443	Polson	883		
Conrad E.	627	Helena	444	Pompeys Pillar	875		
Cooke City	838	Helena	447	Poplar	768		
Corvallis	961	Helena	449	Poplar N.	448		
Crow Agency	638	Helena E.	227	Potomac	244		
Culbertson	787	Helena E.	458	Power	463		
Custer	856	Highwood	733	Pray	333		
Cutbank	873	Hingham	397	Rapelje	663		
Cut Bank N.	336	Hinsdale	364	Raynesford	738		
Dagmar	483	Hinsdale N.	648	Redlodge	425		
Darby	821	Hobson	423	Redlodge	446		
Decker	750	Hopp Illiad	386	Reedpoint	326		
Decker	757	Hot Springs	741	Reserve	286		
Deer Lodge	846	Hungry Horse	387	Richey	773		
		Huntley	348	Richey	979		
		Hysham	342	Roberts	445		

Numerical

No.	Name	No.	Name	No.	Name	No.	Name
222	Livingston	395	Havre South	635	Terry	785	Nashua North
225	Boulder	397	Hingham	636	Lavina	786	Brockton
226	East Glacier	398	Havre South	637	Terry	787	Culbertson
227	Helena East	421	Miles City South	638	Crow Agency	788	Great Falls
228	Glasgow	422	Sidney	639	Lodge Grass	789	Medicine Lake
232	Miles City	423	Hobson	642	Victor	791	Great Falls
233	Miles City	425	Red Lodge	644	Charlo	793	Ovando
234	Miles City	427	Broadus South	645	Clark	795	Wibaux
235	Wolf Creek	428	Grass Range	646	West Yellowstone	796	Wibaux
236	Neihart	429	Winnett	648	Hinsdale North	797	Opportunity
240	Missoula	431	Helena	649	Saint Regis	798	West Sidney
243	Missoula	432	Devon	652	Billings West	799	Great Falls
244	Potomac	433	Sidney	653	Wolf Point	821	Darby
245	Billings	434	Shelby	654	Malta	822	Superior
246	Dixon	436	Broadus	655	Billings West	825	Clinton
248	Billings	439	Helena	656	Billings West	826	Plains
251	Missoula	441	Helena	657	Billings	827	Thompson Falls
252	Billings	442	Helena	658	Malta South	828	Alzada
253	Kalispell	443	Helena	659	N Parkma, Wy	832	Wise River
254	Billings	444	Helena	662	Bridger	833	Great Falls
255	Billings	445	Roberts	663	Rapelje	834	Jackson
256	Billings	446	Redlodge	664	Belfry	835	Melrose
257	Kalispell	447	Helena	665	Hardin	837	Big Fork
258	Milltown	448	Poplar North	666	Fort Smith	838	Cooke City
259	Billings	449	Helena	667	Broadview	842	Sheridan
263	Glasgow	452	Great Falls	668	Fromberg	843	Virginia City
264	Fortshaw	453	Great Falls	669	Molt	844	Lakeside
265	Havre	454	Great Falls	673	Hays	844	E. Fairview
266	Townsend	455	Great Falls	674	Whitewater	846	Deer Lodge
267	Divide	456	Chester South	675	Pablo	847	Noxon
273	Lolo	458	Helena East	676	Ronan	848	Gardiner
276	Lima	462	Winifred	677	Seeley Lake	849	Elmo
277	Belt	463	Power	678	Haugan	853	Miles City
278	Conrad	464	Roy	679	Hardin	854	Marion
279	Valier	466	Choteau	681	Grant	855	Billings
282	Amsterdam	467	Fairfield	682	Ennis	856	Custer
284	Manhattan	468	Cascade	683	Dillon	857	Somers
285	Three Forks	469	Pendroy	684	Twin Bridges	858	Mcgregor Lake
286	Reserve	472	Dupuyer	685	Harrison	859	Philipsburg
287	Whitehall	473	Judith Gap	686	Clyde Park	862	Whitefish
288	Drummond	474	Flaxville	687	West Glendive	864	Alberton South
292	Joplin	475	Canyon Ferry	688	East Carlyle	866	Ulm
293	Libby	476	Dutton	689	Wisdom	873	Cut Bank
295	Troy	477	Lame Deer	693	Warm Springs	874	Miles City
296	Eureka	481	E Sidney, Nd	695	Frazer	875	Pompeys Pillar
322	Columbus	481	Sidney East	698	Billings	878	Alzada South
323	Roundup	482	Sidney	721	Missoula	881	Olney
326	Reedpoint	483	Dagmar	722	Alberton	882	Fortine
328	Absarokee	485	Circle	723	Butte	883	Polson
329	Missoula	486	Fallon	724	Glentana	886	Swan Lake
333	Pray	487	Scobey	725	Larslan	887	Finley Point
335	Sweetgrass	488	Sidney	726	Arlee	888	West Glacier
336	Cut Bank North	490	Butte	727	Great Falls	889	Eureka Rural
337	Kevin-oilmont	492	Avon	728	Missoula	892	Columbia Falls
338	Browning	494	Butte-south	731	Great Falls	893	Peerless
338	Heart Butte	496	Butte	732	Babb	895	Outlook
339	Ethridge	523	Missoula	733	Highwood	932	Big Timber
342	Hysham	524	Valley Industrial Park	734	Carter	933	Clancy
343	Wyola	525	South Wolf Park	735	Geyser	937	Sunburst
344	Mammoth,Wy	526	Fortpeck	736	Stockett	939	Glendive Cellular
345	Glendive	527	Saco	737	Geraldine	947	Musselshell
347	Rosebud	537	Melville	738	Raynesford	961	Corvallis
348	Huntley	538	Lewistown	739	Loma	962	Joliet
352	Box Elder	542	Missoula	741	Hot Springs	963	Froid Rural East
353	Harlem	543	Missoula	742	Fairview	965	Vaughn
354	Rock Springs	544	Missoula	745	Saint Ignatius	966	Great Falls
355	Rudyard	545	Old Fthfl, Wy	746	Nashua	967	Worden
356	Forsyth	547	White Sulfur Springs	747	Fairview	971	Plevna
357	Chinook	549	Missoula	748	Colstrip	974	Circle
358	Melstone	554	Broadus North	750	Decker	975	Ekalaka
359	Glendive	557	Jordan	752	Kalispell	976	Billings West
362	Lincoln	562	Augusta	753	Brady	977	Jordan
363	Hamilton	563	Anaconda	754	Condon	978	Baker
364	Hinsdale	566	Stanford	755	Kalispell	979	Richey
365	Glendive	567	Denton	756	Kalispell	982	Yellow Bay
366	Lewistown Cellular	568	Ryegate	757	Decker	984	Birney
367	Glasgow North	572	Martinsdale	758	Kalispell		
368	Canyon Creek	574	Silvertip, Wy	759	Chester		
372	Kremlin	575	North Ryegate	761	Great Falls		
373	Billings-shepherd	578	Wilsall	762	Opheim		
373	Shepherd	580	Bozeman Cellular	763	Gallatin Gateway		
374	Moore	581	Bozeman	765	Plentywood		
376	Gildford	583	Bloomfield	766	Froid		
377	Glendive	584	Lindsay	768	Poplar		
378	Big Sandy	585	Bozeman	769	Bainville		
379	Turner	586	Bozeman	771	Great Falls		
383	Dodson	587	Bozeman	772	Plevna		
385	Westby	588	Carlyle	773	Richey		
386	Hopp Illiad	592	Busby	774	Lambert		
387	Hungry Horse	622	Fortbenton	775	Ekalaka		
388	Belgrade	626	Frenchtown	776	Savage		
390	Havre South	627	Conrad East	777	Stevensville		
392	Wolf Point North	628	Laurel	778	Baker		
394	Simpson	632	Harlowton	779	Flaxville Rural		
		633	Park City	782	Butte		
				783	Scobey Rural		
				784	Ashland		

MONTANA GLOSSARY

Alkali - white powdery substance appearing on soil surface often around places that have been wet

Badlands - bleak, desolate, hostile-looking area

Basin - a bowl-shaped valley

Black ice - icy stretch of road or highway

Blizzard - a very heavy snowstorm with strong winds

Bull pine - common name for Ponderosa Pine

Borrow pit - a depression beside the road left after the dirt was removed to build the elevated roadway, out-of-staters call them "ditches"

Chains - actual chains attached to tires so you get better traction on snow and ice - required on many mountain passes

Chaps - ("shaps") leather leg protection for cowboys

Chinook - a warm winter wind in winter that melts snow and ice

Cooley - miniature valley

Creek - medium-sized flow of water, 10-20 feet wide, pronounced "crick"

Critter - usually refers to some form of livestock

Dog hair pine - very thick pine—trees, need to be thinned

Dogs - sometimes refers to coyotes

Down the road a piece - Not far - may be a quarter mile or twenty miles (distances seem different in Montana!)

Draw - same as a cooley, maybe bigger

Dryland Farm - Non-irrigated farm; watered only by rain/snow

Flood Irrigation - run ditch water across entire field

Foothills - gentle hills at base of mountains

Gelding - a male horse that has been castrated

Good handle - a good understanding or ability

Gulley - like a cooley, maybe smaller. but sharper, more vertical banks

Gulley washer - heavy rain storm

Heave - where water gets into crack in a road, freezes and expands. When it melts in spring, many depressions and wide cracks are left in the roadways

Heifer - a female bovine that hasn't yet had a calf

Hi-Line - Hwy. 2 running east to west along the northern part of the state from Bainville to Browning. The route of the Great Northern Railway.

Jack fence - x-crossed posts that sit on top the ground, used where it's too rocky to dig post holes

A little gun shy - a little jumpy/has had some bad experiences

Mare - a female horse

Missouri Breaks - canyons, ridges, draws, alongside the Missouri River

Outfit - usually refers to a vehicle, sometimes with horse trailer

Pair - means a cow and her calf

Pasty - a kind of meat pie made with a flour wrapper usually filled with diced beef, onion, turnip, potato and brown gravy. Started as a staple for miners lunch pails. The correct pronunciation is"pass' tee".

Plow - usually refers to snowplow - clears roads of snow - usually a pickup or truck

Plug-in - outlet at motel where you plug in engine heater of your vehicle so it won't freeze up overnight

Potbelly - semi-truck that hauls cattle

Pulling a big circle - taking a long trip

Range land - native grazing area

Rattler - a rattlesnake (beware - poisonous)

Ridge - abrupt change in elevation

Riding with a loose rein - relaxed, not heavily supervised

Rise - like a hill but maybe lower, can't see over it

River - a wide creek, maybe 30-40 feet across or more

Rode hard an' put away wet - really tired - could be animal or person who has worked hard

Row crop - type of farming, usually high-intensity crops planted in rows like potatoes, corn, sugar beets

Ruminate - think about something

Salt grass - grass that grows in highly alkaline soil

Sanded road - icy highways and roads are sanded to cut down skidding and sliding

Sheep fence - small mesh wire fence for securing sheep/goats

Short grass - doesn't require much moisture and is less than a foot tall

Snow fences - built to control drifting snow, usually seen along roadways to help keep roads clear

Snowblind - a winter condition where the snow is so bright from the sun it becomes difficult to see

Spring wheat - planted in the spring of the year

Spring - area where water comes up from deep inside earth

Stallion - a male horse that has not been castrated

Steer - a male bovine that has been castrated

Stock - short for 'livestock'

Stream - a small creek, a few feet wide

Strip farm - method of farming which rotates crops and controls wind erosion

Studs - tires with metal studs imbedded give better traction in snow and ice

Summer fallow - farming practice whereby ground is left bare of a crop every other year to conserve moisture and control weeds

Swather - machine that cuts hay

Top a the mornin' to ya - good morning/have a nice day

Valley - lowland surrounded by hills or mountains

Waddie: Cowboy

White Out - snowstorm so heavy that everything looks white, zero visibility, extremely dangerous to drive in

Wilderness Area - a Congressionally mandated area within Forest Service land that disallows roads, mining, logging and motorized vehicles

Winter wheat - variety of wheat planted in the autumn which germinates then continues growing in the Spring

Some place names you might like a little help with:

Absarokee: Ab-SOR-kee

Charlo: SHAR-low

Ekalaka: EEK-a-lack-a

Havre: Hav-er

Helena: HELL-en-ah

Hysham: HI-shum

Makoshika: ma-KOE-sheek-ah

Marias: Ma-RYE-us

Missoula: Ma-SOO-la

Rapelje: Ra-pell-jay

Ronan: ROE-nan

Winnett: WIN-ett

NOTES:

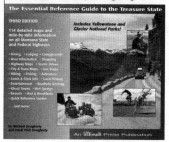

SECTION 1

BUTTE, DILLON AND VIRGINIA CITY AREA

Historic Virginia City

1. *Gas*

Cardwell

This town is the birthplace of Chet Huntley—famous TV newscaster and founder of Big Sky Resort. The town took its name from Edward Cardwell, a man with extensive property holdings in the area when the town was established. At one time, Cardwell was a station on the Northern Pacific Railroad. It saw a short boom time when the Mayflower Mine was in operation.

LaHood

This town started as a stopping point for travelers and freighters that traveled between Butte and the Madison River. The town is the namesake of Shadan LaHood, a Lebanese immigrant who came to Montana in 1902. From 1902 to 1919, he traveled between Butte, Dillon, Missoula and Madison County in a covered wagon canvassing for a dry goods firm. In 1909, he and his wife opened a general merchandise store at Jefferson Island. He built a park there that bears his name.

2. *Gas, Food, Lodging*

Whitehall

Old Whitehall was the name E. G. Brooke gave his large white ranch house in the mid-1800s. The house served as a stage stop for the stages running from Helena to Virginia City. The modern community of Whitehall was developed when the railroad ran a branch line from Garrison to Logan through the area. Today, the Golden Sunlight Mine on a nearby mountainside offers much of the economic fuel to the town.

Pipestone

The Indians of the area came to the nearby creek once a year to harvest clay from its shores. This clay was especially useful for making clay pipes. The springs were named Pipestone Springs, and thus the town drew its name as well. The first post office was opened in 1880, with Ollie Barnes as the postmaster. The post closed shortly thereafter, but reopened in 1887 with George Washington as postmaster. This second office closed in 1928.

H Father De Smet
I-90 Frontage Rd., Whitehall

The Lewis and Clark Expedition passed here, westward bound, August 2, 1805. Captain Lewis named the Boulder River "Fields Creek" for one of the party.

In August, 1840, Pierre Jean De Smet, S.J., a Catholic missionary of Belgian birth, camped near the mouth of the Boulder River with the Flathead Indians and celebrated the holy sacrifice of the Mass. Father De Smet left the Indians soon after to go to St. Louis. He returned the following year and established the original St. Mary's Mission in the Bitter Root Valley, hereditary home of the Flatheads.

Fearless and zealous, his many experiences during the pioneer days have been chronicled and form a most interesting chapter in the frontier annals of Montana.

H Lewis and Clark Expedition

On August 1, 1805, the Lewis and Clark Expedition camped at a point 200 yards west from this spot, on the south bank of the river facing the mouth of the creek which flows into the river from the north. Meriwether Lewis and three others, on a scouting expedition in the hope of finding Sacajawea's people, had crossed the mountains to the northeast of here and coming down the North Boulder Valley had reached here at 2:00 p.m. They found a herd of elk grazing in the park here and killed two of them. After taking time out for an elk steak lunch, they headed on upstream leaving the two elk on the bank of the river for the expeditions dinner.

Captain Clark with the expedition reached here late in the evening after a strenuous day spent in snaking the boats up the canyon rapids by means of a long rawhide tow line which had broken in the rapids immediately below here with near calamitous results. At sight of the two elk, the hungry men called it a day and pitched camp. Reuben and Jo Fields went on a short hunt up the creek and killed five deer in the willow brakes which caused the stream to be named Field's Creek, now known as North Boulder. A large brown bear was seen on the south side of the river; Clark shot a big horn sheep in the canyon and Lewis shot two antelope a short distance up stream. Near camp was seen the first Maximilan Jay known to science. The temperature at sunrise on August 2 was fifty degrees above zero.

D Mer. Lewis
August 2, 1805

"we say some very large beaver dams today. . .the brush. . .acquires a strength by the irregularity with which they are placed by the beaver that it would puzzle the engenuity of man to give them."

D Mer. Lewis
August 2, 1805

"After passing the river this morning Sergt. Gass lost my tommahawk in the thick brush and we were unable to find it, I regret the loss of this usefull implement, however accedents will happen in the best families"

T Golden Sunlight Mine
Whitehall, 287-2018

If you're driving on I-90 near Whitehall, you'll

Butte	Jan	Feb	March	April	May	June	July	Aug	Sep	Oct	Nov	Dec	Annual
Average Max. Temperature (F)	29.9	34.2	40.7	51.1	60.5	69.4	79.7	78.2	67.0	55.5	40.6	31.7	53.2
Average Min. Temperature (F)	7.3	10.7	17.6	27.1	34.8	41.9	47.0	45.3	36.9	28.5	18.1	9.9	27.1
Average Total Precipitation (in.)	0.62	0.53	0.81	1.07	1.90	2.27	1.28	1.14	1.11	0.80	0.63	0.60	12.77
Average Total SnowFall (in.)	8.5	7.3	10.2	6.9	3.7	0.5	0.0	0.1	1.1	3.7	6.5	8.4	56.8
Average Snow Depth (in.)	4	4	2	0	0	0	0	0	0	0	1	2	1

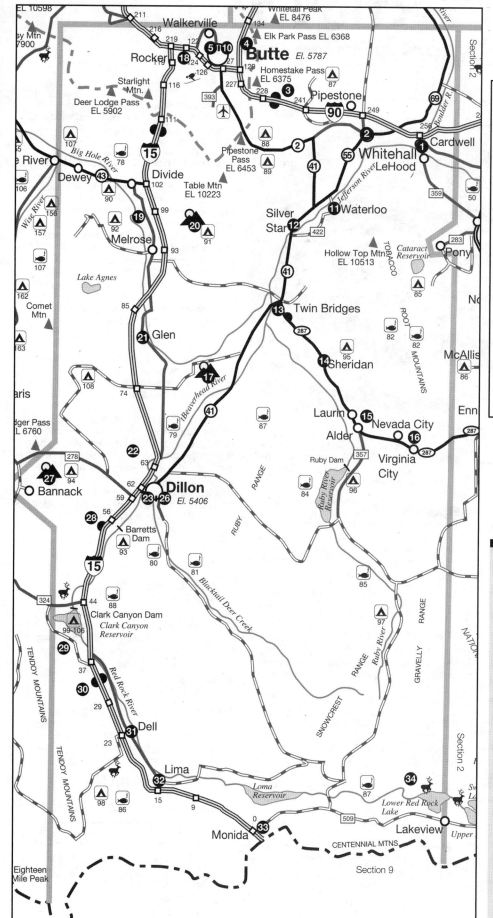

Legend

- ⓪⓪ Locator number (matches numeric listing in section)
- 🦌 Wildlife viewing
- ⛺ Campsite (number matches number in campsite chart)
- ⛰ State Park
- 🎣 Fishing Site (number matches number in fishing chart)
- ⛱ Rest stop
- ═══ Interstate
- ─── U.S. Highway
- ━━━ State Highway
- ─── County Road
- ‑‑‑‑ Gravel/unpaved road

It Happened in Montana

The first Montana legislative assembly convened at Bannack. The meeting was not held in a bastion of concrete, stone and marble; but rather in a cold log cabin with a dirt floor. They practiced the democratic principles of a country they were yet to be a part of as they huddled around a wood stove. The meeting was not without dissension. When Governor B. F. White called the meeting to order, he told the elected officials that they needed to recite the oath of allegiance to the United States. Most didn't hesitate to do so, but three vociferously disagreed. One, a man named Rogers, resigned rather than take the oath. Interestingly, Montanans have always been some of the most fiercely independent citizens of any state in the union. They are also the first to answer the call to defend our freedoms. They consistently send a higher percentage of their population to war than any other U. S. state.

All Montana Area Codes are 406

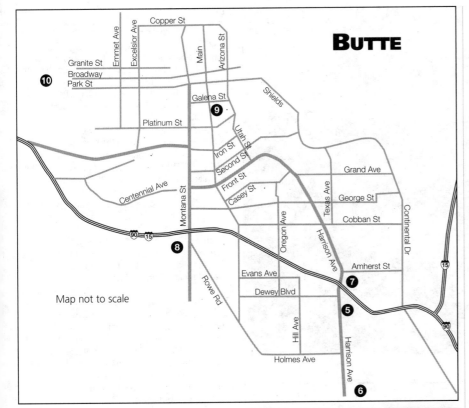

BUTTE

Map not to scale

vides detailed information on each mural and shows you where to find it. The publication is available at most of the area businesses and is free.

3.

H The Humbug Spires Primitive Area
I-15, south of Butte

Named for its unique granite peaks, this primitive area is part of a geologic system of large-scale volcanic intrusions known as the Boulder Batholith, which extends north beyond Helena and south into Idaho.

Humbug Spires, which can be seen to the southeast, is part of the Highland Mountains. In 1866, rich gold placers were discovered near the Spires. Most of the mining occurred on the east and south sides of the area and produced large amounts of silver, lead, copper, and gold. Total value of production between 1876 and 1947 is estimated to have been as much as $3 million. Although there currently (1999) is no mining in the Humbug Spires Primitive Area, prospecting is done on surrounding lands.

The Spires offer the finest high quality hard-rock climbing in Montana and are an excellent place to hike, ride horses, sightsee, fish, and hunt.

T Homestake Lake
I-90 Exit 233

This is a pleasant spot to picnic, swim and do a little fishing. From the exit go north for 1.5 miles to the right hand turn marked "Homestake Lake."

4.

H Meaderville
I-15, Butte

William Allison and G. O. Humphreys had the Butte hill, richest hill on earth, entirely to themselves when they located their first quartz claims there in 1864.

They discovered an abandoned prospect hole which had evidently been dug by unknown miners a number of years before. These mysterious prospectors had used elk horn tines for gads, and broken bits of these primitive tools were found around the shafts. Allison and Humphreys died, their property passed into other hands, and they never knew that they were the potential owners of untold wealth.

H Butte
I-15, Butte

The "greatest mining camp on earth" built on "the richest hill in the world." That hill, which has produced over two billion dollars worth of gold, silver, copper and zinc, is literally honeycombed with drifts, winzes and stopes that extend beneath the city. There are over 3,000 miles of workings, and shafts reach a depth of 4,000 feet.

This immediate country was opened as a placer district in 1864. Later Butte became a quartz mining camp and successively opened silver, copper and zinc deposits.

Butte has a most cosmopolitan population derived from the four corners of the world. She was a bold, unashamed, rootin, tootin', hell-roarin' camp in days gone by and still drinks her liquor straight.

notice the mountain to the north doesn't look quite right. In fact, it looks like it's been shaved off. This is the Golden Sunlight gold mine, and much of the smooth side of the mountain you see are mine tailings. From mid-June to mid-September, tours are offered daily at 10 a.m. If you would like to view an operational gold mine, this is the place. To get to the mine take the Cardwell Exit 256 and head north. The road curves around and parallels the interstate. Follow this road for almost 3 miles to Mine Road. Head north to the mine.

T Jefferson Valley Museum
303 S. Division in Whitehall

The bright red barn that houses this museum was built in 1914. In 1992, the owners donated the barn to use as a museum. As you would expect, the historical exhibits center on life in the Jefferson River Valley. The museum is open from Memorial Day through Labor Day. Admission is free.

T Cape Horn Taxidermy Museum
Whitehall

T Parrot Ghost Camp
Near Whitehall on the Jefferson River

A few building foundations are the only reminders that the town of Parrot, stood on the banks of the river back in the 1890s.

T The City of Murals
Throughout town of Whitehall

When you enter the small community of Whitehall, your attention is immediately drawn to a giant mural on the side of a building at the junction of the two main streets in the town. The 9' x 28' mural depicts Lewis and Clark's Corps of Discovery pulling boats upstream on the Jefferson River. An excerpt from Capt. Lewis' journal is in the lower corner. As you drive through the town, more of these murals pop into view. Currently there are ten gracing the sides of buildings in the

town--all depicting scenes from the journey of the Corps of Discovery. Two more are planned by summer of 2002. The Whitehall Chamber of Commerce organized the mural project in 1999 funded by over $17,000 in grants and local contributions. The first mural was painted by local residents Kit Mather and Michelle Tebay. The rest were done by many of the local residents who painted the base colors while Mather completed the detail. The wall space and even the paint and materials were donated by the building owners. All of the murals depict actual activities or events that took place in the Jefferson Valley when the Corps passed through the area in 1805 and 1806. Mather did extensive research of the Corps of Discovery journals prior to painting the murals. When you visit Whitehall you can pick up a publication printed by the local newspaper which pro-

The richest hill on earth.

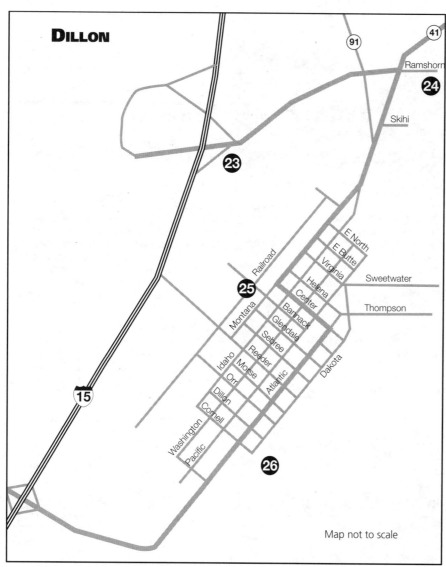

DILLON

41

91

Ramshorn

24

Skihi

23

E North

E Butte

Railroad

Virginia

Sweetwater

Helena

25

Center

Barnack

Thompson

Montana

Glendale

Selbree

Idaho

Reader

Molse

Orr

Atlantic

Dakota

Dillon

Cornell

Washington

Pacific

26

15

Map not to scale

All Montana Area Codes are 406

5. *Gas, Food, Lodging*

Butte

Butte's history is revealed in its skyline, the omnipresent black steel headframes, and the gaping hole in the earth known as Berkeley Pit. These are two of the more vivid reminders of a town that started as a mining camp and grew to a city of over 100,000 by 1917.

Before the gold rush of the 1860s brought prospectors and settlers to the area, Native Americans and fur traders frequented this semi-arid valley. When the placer ran out in 1867, the population of about 500 dwindled to around 240. It wasn't long though before the potential for mineral riches in the quartz deposits was recognized.

While the cost of smelting the complex copper-bearing ore was high, investors like William Andrews Clark and Andrew Jackson Davis began to develop Butte's mines and erect mills to extract the silver and gold. The riches in the hills made Davis Montana's first millionaire.

By 1876, Butte had become a prosperous silver camp with over 1,000 inhabitants. Marcus Daly arrived that year representing the Walker brothers, entrepreneurs from Salt Lake City. His mission was to inspect the Alice Mine for possible purchase by the brothers. Daly purchased the mine and successfully managed it for the Walkers. The town of Walkerville, which still overlooks the city of Butte, sprang up around the mine and other mines in the area.

In 1880, Daly sold his interest in the Walkers' properties and bought the Anaconda Mine. He did so with investment money from several San Francisco capitalists, including George Hearst, the father of media mogul William Randolph Hearst. Clark and Davis also attracted investors from Denver and points east. It wasn't long before capitalists from New York and Boston bought into the huge potential of the area. During the 1880s, copper mining came into the forefront and Butte became the world's greatest copper producer. The Union Pacific Railroad came to the area in 1881 allowing developers to build and equip smelters. The Butte smelters quickly became the best in the world at extracting the metal from the ore.

It wasn't long before Butte began to pay a price for the riches. The air filled with toxic sulfurous smoke. Daly responded by building a giant smelter in Anaconda, just 30 miles west of Butte. To this day, the giant smokestack remains a landmark. Shortly after Daly built the smelter, the Boston and Montana Co., with holdings only second to Daly's, built one in Great Falls. Trains carried the ore from Butte's mines to both smelters.

In 1899, Daly teamed up with Rockefeller's Standard Oil to create the giant Amalgamated Copper Mining Co., one of the largest trusts of the early Twentieth Century. By 1910, it had changed its name to the Anaconda Copper Mining Company swallowing several smaller mining companies along the way. The Company dominated Butte for the next 70 years. The battle between the Copper Kings Clark and Daly is a large chapter in Montana history. To stir the mix, another Copper King, F. Augustus Heinze, fought the dominance of Amalgamated, providing excitement to an already interesting chapter in Montana's legal history.

The mines brought whole families from every corner of the nation and around the world. They crowded into tiny houses and occupied apartment buildings called flats. The earlier skilled miners were Cornish, but the Irish soon followed, tempted by the prospects of steady pay. They came in droves and soon became the largest ethnic group. Suburbs of Butte, with names like Finntown, Meaderville, Dublin Gulch, Chinatown, Corktown, and Parrot Flat were soon filled with Italians, Croatians, Serbians, Finns, French Canadians, Lebanese, Scandinavians, Chinese, Mexicans, Germans, Austrians, and African-Americans.

Economic exploitation and the dangers of working in the mines led to the labor movement—an important part of Butte's heritage. The city soon had the tag of the "Gibraltar of Unionism." Butte's Miners Union, founded in 1878, became Local No. 1 of the Western Federation of Miners. At the 1906 International Workers of the World founding convention in Chicago, Butte's delegation was the largest.

In the late 1800s, the mining companies competed for scarce labor. This gave the unions leverage and many successes. But, as the Anaconda Company consolidated operations, the unions lost their leverage and their power. In the early 1900s, worker frustration and company opposition combined to form a violent atmosphere. The Miner's Union Hall was bombed in 1914, and in 1917 IWW organizer Frank Little was lynched. A fictional account of this incident is told in Dashiell Hammett's *Red Harvest*.

In 1917, the Speculator Mine fire killed 168 men—to this day the most lives lost in a hardrock mining disaster in American History. Despite the dangers, mining flourished. At an altitude of 5,775 feet above sea level, Butte claimed it was "a mile high and a mile deep." But like most mining camps, the riches extracted here—more than $22 billion by the 1980s—went to the speculators and investors far away from the mountains of Montana.

1955 saw the abandonment of labor intensive underground work when the Anaconda Company switched to more cost effective open-pit mining. The excavation of the Berkeley Pit and surrounding area, changed the face and the skyline of Butte. The population declined and the new method of mining wiped away hundreds of homes, flats, boarding houses, bars and corner groceries which once proliferated on Butte's East Side. Whole communities like Meaderville and McQueen vanished. Columbia Gardens was an elegant, old-fashioned amusement park with an elaborate dance pavilion nestled alongside the East Ridge. For generations it provided fun and amusement to Butte families. It too fell victim to the open pit mining. Anaconda Mining Company merged with Atlantic Richfield Co. (ARCO) in 1977. In 1985, ARCO's holdings were purchased by Montana billionaire Dennis Washington.

When you visit uptown Butte and it's older

Montana Trivia

The "richest hill on earth" has given up over twenty-one billion pounds of copper, ninety million ounces of silver, ninety million pounds of molybdenum, and three million ounces of gold. The veins of copper at Butte extended nearly a mile down. Over 70 percent of Montana's mineral wealth is concentrated in Silver Bow County.

sections, much of its history can be seen by looking up. By viewing the ornate architecture, fading signs on the sides of buildings, and the headframes surrounding the area, one can get a small sense of the grandeur this city once knew.

Walkerville

This small town, which now serves as a suburb to Butte, was once a mining town. It was first settled by prospectors from Cornwall, England, and was named for the Walker brothers of Salt Lake City, who owned and operated the nearby Alice Mine. The post office operated from 1878 to 1959, with Francis P. Carey presiding as first postmaster. Today, the remains of homes can still be seen amongst the ore dumps and mine tipples. A cemetery also exists, with one headstone reading, "In Memory of _____. Gone to Butte, U.S.A."

T Our Lady of the Rockies (Visitor Center)
3100 Harrison Ave., Butte. 494-2656

A statue weighing 51 tons, rising 90 feet high and requiring 6 years to construct is set atop the rugged Rocky Mountain ridge. This monument of Our Lady of the Rockies was built in the likeness of Mary, Mother of Jesus, but is intended to be a tribute to all women regardless of religion. Perched on the east ridge overlooking Butte, the statue is lit at night and can be seen glowing on Butte's skyline. A bus tour is available, and a possible gondola ride is under consideration.

T U.S. High Altitude Sports Center
Butte. 494-7570

When you first exit the Homestake Pass driving west into Butte, one of the first things you see is a large oval track. This track has been the training ground for several Olympic speedskating champions, including Bonnie Blair and Dan Jansen. The outdoor speed skating facility was completed in 1987, and has been the venue for several national and world speedskating competitions. In 1994, the Women's World Championship was held here. The World Cup Competition has been held here on six different occasions. What makes the Center unique is its altitude. At a 5,500 foot elevation, it is a premier training facility providing athletes from around the world a chance to build stamina through exercise programs tailored for varying competitions.

T Stodden Park and Community Pool
Corner of Holmes and Hills Ave., Butte. 494-3686

Stodden Park is Butte's main city park. There are tennis courts, a ball diamond, horseshoe pits, and large areas of shaded grassy areas for taking an afternoon nap while the kids play in the public swimming pool here.

6. *Gas*

T Silver Bow
15 miles south of Butte on Rte. 2

Also known as Highland City, many of the several hundred miners cabins that were built still exist near the graveyard. The city once had a fierce reputation for wild gun play and rich with gold during its boom years between 1865 and 1875. The site is accessible on a good Forest Service logging road.

7. *Gas, Food, Lodging*

8. *Attraction, Gas*

T Butte Chamber, Visitor & Transportation Center
1000 George St., I-90 Exit 126, Butte. 723-3177 or (800) 735-6814

This new visitor's center is more than just a good place to pick up literature on the area. Inside is a small museum that highlights the forming of the geology and early settlement of the area, the gold and silver era of Butte, the development of the richest hill on earth, the mining and smelting industry and the all-important transportation corridors.

Also inside the center is the George F. Grant

"GALLOWS" FRAMES

There is no skyline in the world like Buttes. Standing like sentries on the surrounding hillsides are stark black headframes of several mines no longer in use. The Orphan Girl headframe at the World Museum of Mining is visible from the interstate. Dominating the landscape are the Kelley, Steward, the Original, Belmont, Granite Mountain, Bell Diamond, Badger State, Travona, Lexington, Centerville's mighty Mountain Con and the Anselmo gallows frames.

To put it simply, headframes are like the tops of elevators, but not hidden in the inside of a tall building. The frames held the cables that lowered men, equipment, timbers, dynamite, ore cars and, in earlier days, the mules to pull the cars. Once the men and equipment were inside the mines, the frames hauled to the surface the copper ore which was then loaded on trains and shipped to the smelter in Anaconda.

At its peak, the Butte Hill was alive with the bright lights of the mine yards at night. The

sound of bells used as signals for the hoist operators, the shrill mine whistles signaling the shift changes, and the throaty "toots" of the trains as they hauled their ore loaded cars through town could be heard around the clock.

The Mother Lode Theatre

Fly Collection. Even if you don't know a thing about fly fishing, you'll marvel at these works of art. A legend in fly fishing circles, George's unique woven hackle monofilament bodied flies are artistic masterpieces and are prized by collectors. Learn more at www.butteinfo.org.

9. *Gas, Food, Lodging*

T Berkeley Pit
Mercury St., Butte. 723-3177

Think you've seen some big holes? Wait till you see this one. The pit was started in 1955 as a large truck-operated open-pit copper mine until mining ceased in 1982. By that time, nearly 1.5 billion tons of material had been removed including more than 290 million tons of copper ore.

Two communities and a large part of the one time populous East Side were consumed to create the pit. The homes, businesses and schools of the working-class towns of Meaderville and McQueen east of the pit site were purchased by the Anaconda Mining Company. Several deep shaft mines were also obliterated. The headframe of the Leonard was part of Meaderville's main street.

The pit is 7,000 feet long, 5,600 feet wide, and 1,600 feet deep. Groundwater seeping from the several thousand miles of interconnected tunnels that honeycomb the hills surrounding the pit has created a small lake in the pit. In April of 1996, pumping operations began to pump and treat 2.5 million gallons daily to prevent surface flows from entering the Pit. Today, copper is being recovered from the water in the pit for use in industry.

The Pit water is acidic from water contact with mineralized zones. Since it is a hazard to waterfowl, a number of devices are being used to keep the birds from landing on the water. Flares, shell crackers and electronic noise makers are some examples.

The Pit is just off of Continental Drive. An observation stand is open at the site from dawn to dusk late spring through early fall. There is no admission fee.

T Piccadilly Museum of Transportation
20 W. Broadway in uptown Butte. 723-3034

Butte's newest museum features oil company collectables, underground train (subway) memorabilia from the United States and Europe, a vintage replica 1920s service station complete with original gas pumps, license plates from around the world, and a small but interesting collection of motorized and non-motorized vehicles. Included in the collection is an exhibit of commercial advertising art and Coca Cola® and Pepsi® memorabilia. The museum is open June through September Tuesday through Sunday. Admission is free.

T Granite Mountain Memorial
In Butte head north on Main Street and turn right at the directional sign just beyond the St. Lawrence Church in Walkerville. 723-3177

168 men lost their lives in the tragic "Spec fire" disaster on June 8, 1917. This was the greatest loss of life in hardrock mining history. Interpretive plaques tell the story of this disaster and the turbulent times that surrounded this episode. From this point you can view an unforgettable panorama of the 10,000 ft. Highland Mountains and the scattered remnants of a once booming mining industry.

T The Mother Lode Theatre
316 W. Park St. in Uptown Butte. 723-3602

This beautiful building is located in Butte's historic district and is a showplace for the performing arts. Its proscenium theater seats 1,230 people.

T The Mai Wah Museum
17 W. Mercury, Butte. 723-3231

When the history of Butte's mining era is told, most of the focus is on the Irish. The Chinese played an important role as well. As the placer mining era declined, Chinese miners came to Butte to work the mines. As that work declined, they were relegated to work in laundries, domestic service and noodle parlors. The Mai Wah and Wah Chong Tai buildings are adjacent to China

Alley, a narrow thoroughfare which runs between Galena and Mercury Streets. In the building you'll see exhibits which interpret the history of Asians in Butte and the Rocky Mountain West.

The Mai Wah Society, was established for educational, charitable, and scientific purposes, including research and public education about the history, culture, and conditions of Asian people in the Rocky Mountain West. The Mai Wah Society is the caretaker for Montana's only authentic ceremonial parade dragon, a generous gift of the government of Taiwan to the people of Montana. Each summer an exhibit in the museum interprets aspects of the lives of Asian immigrants to the region. The museum is open June through August, Tuesday through Saturday from 11 a.m. to 3 p.m.

T The Dumas Brothel
45 E. Mercury, Butte. 723-6128

For more than 90 years, the Dumas operated continuously as a house of prostitution. The run from 1890 to 1982 gives it the dubious honor of being the longest-running house of ill repute in the United States. It is now the only remaining remnant of what was once a thriving red light district in Butte. When the building was threatened with demolition, Butte native Rudy Giecek purchased the building and began to restore it in 1990. Today, it is open as a museum depicting the history of this industry that was so vital to the miners of yesterday. The museum is open May through September from 9 a.m. to 5 p.m.

T St. Lawrence O'Toole Church
1308 N. Main in Butte

In 1897, miners and local families raised $25,000 in donations to build this church. A European artist painted 40 frescoes on the ceilings and a number of paintings in other parts of the church in 1907. The church is no longer used for services and is only open to visitors on Fridays and Saturdays from noon to 5 p.m.

T Arts Chateau
321 W. Broadway, Butte. 723-7600
www.artschateau.org

Charles Clark, the son of Copper King William A. Clark, built this mansion in 1898. It now serves the community as an arts center and museum.

When you first step into the entry way of this magnificent building, notice the beveled glass windows, ornate wrought iron, sandstone and vaulted brick ceiling. A free-standing spiral staircase inside is surrounded by 26 rooms adorned with exotic woods from around the world, several stained glass windows, hand-painted wallpaper by Marshall Field, and a redwood paneled 4th floor ballroom. Thousands of historic artifacts are on display in the museum including textiles, books, vintage clothing and accessories. The furniture collection here is on permanent loan from the

ON THE TRAIL OF LEWIS & CLARK

On July 31, the Expedition reached the third range of mountains which forms another close canyon. They were out of fresh meat. No game was killed on this day; indeed, no buffalo had been seen since entering the mountains. Lewis wrote: "When we have plenty of fresh meat I find it impossible to make the men take any care of it or use it with the least frugallity. Tho' I expect that necessity will probably teach them this art,"

On Aug. 1, Lewis, and three men, went ahead in search of Indians. Near his camp on the morning of Aug. 3, Clark discovered Indian tracks which he followed to an elevation where the Indians had apparently spied on his camp. But Clark found no Indians.

By now, the arduous task of pulling the eight heavily laden dugouts was taking its toll. At one place a tow line broke, at another they were dragging the vessels over rocks, Clark wrote: "The men were so much fatiegued today that they wished much that navigation was at an end that they might go by: land."

Lewis reached Big Hole River on Aug. 4, and after some investigation decided this was not the route the Expedition should follow. He left a note on a green willow for Clark, telling him not to go that way, but to wait there. By the time Clark's party arrived at the Big Hole River, a beaver had gnawed down the green willow upon which Lewis had left the note, and had taken off with it. Consequently, Clark's party began the difficult task of ascending the swift waters of that treacherous river. One boat turned over and two others filled with water before Lewis' party arrived and told them they would have to return to the Jefferson.

It had been 21 days since they left the Great Falls of the Missouri. The 33 travelers had used up enough provisions to warrant leaving one canoe on shore to be retrieved on the return journey.

Arts Chateau

University of Montana.

Inside the mansion are four fine art galleries featuring works by local, regional and national artists.

The Chateau is open all year. In the summer, hours are 10 a.m. to 5 p.m. Tuesday through Saturday and noon to 5 p.m. on Sunday. Winter

hours are Tuesday through Saturday 11 a.m. to 4 p.m. An admission fee is charged.

T Copper King Mansion
219 W. Granite St., Butte. 782-7580

The Copper King Mansion was built by William Clark, one of the world's richest men. The 34 room home was constructed from 1884-1888 at a cost of $260,000, a significant amount of money at the time. In 1971 it was designated as a National Historical Place, and in 1972 it became the first home in Montana to be designated a Montana Historic Site. It is now the only privately owned mansion in the state that is accessible to the public.

As you step inside, you will see the intricately carved wood of the entryway. The hall and staircase present the work of the finest craftsman of the times. Panels of birds and flowers carved in the golden oak staircase represented all the nations of the world when the home was built. Other lavish touches include embellishments of bronze, silver, and copper on the walls, nine original fireplaces, French beveled glass and Tiffany-style stained glass windows. The staircase landing surrounds a seven by thirteen foot window. Parquet floors, hand painted "fresco" ceilings, combed plaster designed walls and nine different kinds of wood contribute to the opulence of the manor. Anticipating the arrival of electricity, Clark had all of the chandeliers equipped for gas and electricity. The octagon shaped reception room, the massive dining room, the billiard room and library all reflect the lavish lifestyle of Mr. Clark.

In addition to the mansion itself, the current owners have numerous collections on display including dolls, toys, clocks, hats, demitasse cups and steins. The Mansion also operates as a bed

and breakfast, so if you plan ahead you can spend the night. The mansion is open daily May 1 through September 30th from 9 a.m. to 4 p.m. From October through April it is open by appointment only.

S Rediscoveries
83 E. Park in Butte. 723-2176 or (888) 723-2176.

Rediscoveries is a wonderful collection of extraordinary items from the past. Located in historic Uptown Butte for over fifteen years, this shop features antiques, vintage jewelry, accessories, and clothing. They also have wonderful antique dolls, linens, and home accessories. Discover a remarkable selection of antique fabrics for the decorator, collector, and quilting enthusiast. Rediscoveries has earned a wide and respected reputation for its collection of costume rentals, with a great selection of period and whimsical costumes. The shop is housed in one of Butte's exquisite historic buildings and has retained the original turn-of-the-century cast iron support columns and pressed tin ceiling architecture. Be sure and stop at Rediscoveries for a step back in time and discover a treasure or bring back a memory for yourself or someone special!

10.

T Mineral Museum
Montana Tech Campus, Butte. 496-4414

This is a rock hounds paradise. Butte's rich mining history is on display here through an impressive array of fine-quality mineral specimens from the underground mines.

Although it is impossible to permanently display the entire collection of 15,000 specimens, a large number are incorporated in the exhibits. At present, about 1,500 specimens are displayed in the Museum.

The Highland Centennial Gold Nugget, weighing 27,475 troy ounces, was recently donated to the Mineral Museum for permanent display. This very large nugget was found in September 1989 during placer mining in the Highland Mountains south of Butte. Also on display is a huge 400 pound quartz crystal.

A display of fluorescent minerals is exhibited in a separate room. Minerals in these cases are illuminated in both long and short wavelength ultraviolet light.

Two other cases deserve special mention. One is the exhibit of minerals from Butte, and the other is a display of some of the wide variety of minerals found in Montana.

The museum is open daily year round. Seasonal hours apply. There is no admission fee.

CHINESE PIONEERS

Chinese pioneers were one of the first distinctive ethnic groups to come to Montana during the late 19th century. During the 1870s ten percent of the state's residents were Chinese. These hardworking and often courageous immigrants worked in mining, railroad construction and numerous service industries.

Most of the Chinese immigrants who followed the lure of quick riches of "Gold Mountain" were young men who left villages and families. China was plagued with economic difficulties. Many Westerners were frightened by Chinese food, dress, customs, clannishness and religious beliefs. This resulted in name-calling, obstruction of their legal rights, anti-Chinese laws, and violence.

The Chinese immigrants sacrificed blood and dreams to help build the American West. The Mai Wah Society, an organization to preserve the Chinese cultural history of Butte, Montana, is researching the contributions that Chinese pioneers made to the settlement of the Montana area. The Chinese, who left behind their families and lives to travel east, also helped to build the foundation of our nation with their dreams and hopes for a better future.

Notable Chinese in the state are immortalized at the Mai Wah museum such as: Tommie Haw, who came on the first cattle drive into Beaverhead, came to Montana in 1850, adopted by a local rancher William Orr, and later raised cattle and sheep in the Dillon area; Dr. Rose Hum Lee, graduated from Butte High School in 1921. Her father came to the Butte area in the 1870s. He worked in ranching and mining, and had a laundry business. Dr. Lee later became the head of the sociology department at Roosevelt University, Chicago in 1956, according to the Mai Wah Society. Our nation was built on the dreams of all immigrants who came in search of a new beginning.

T World Museum of Mining
W. Park St., Butte. 723-7211

One of Butte's most popular attractions is nestled beneath the massive headframe of the once active Orphan Girl underground mine. Spread over 12 acres, this 1889 mining camp has displays both inside and outdoors and is appealing to the whole family.

This extensive Mining Museum and reconstructed 1899 Mining Camp are built on the original Orphan Girl Mine site and provide insights into the mining era that can only be captured here. The museum was built entirely with volunteer help

Montana Trivia

The six prospectors who dipped their pans in Alder Creek in 1863 were only looking for enough gold to pay for their tobacco. Over $10 million in gold was eventually taken out of history's richest placer gold discovery. In today's dollars that would equal $2.5 billion.

and donations. A replica of an actual mining camp, complete with cobblestone streets and boardwalks, shows the interiors of more than thirty businesses filled with antiques from the same era. The antiques can be viewed through the windows as the visitor strolls along the boardwalks of a time long ago past. Unique displays include a Chinese laundry, a sauerkraut factory, a funeral parlor, an ice house, a school, a general store, and of course, a saloon. On specific days, one can pan for gold; call ahead for days and times.

The Orphan Girl Express is a three car train

pulled by an underground trammer engine. You can take the 20 minute train ride around the grounds while the engineer points out historic features along the way.

At the Hardrock Mining Building early day mining life is depicted in the photo archives of over 6,000 photographs.

The museum is open April 1 through October 31 from 9 a.m. to 6 p.m. daily. To get there go up the hill to the Montana Tech campus and past the Marcus Daly statue. Just beyond th statue, you will see the sign pointing to the museum. An admission fee is charged.

T Anselmo Mine Yard
North Excelsior Street, Butte. 497-6275
or (800) 735-6814

This is the best surviving example of the surface support facilities that served Butte's underground copper mines. A guided tour reveals the colorful labor history of miners, pipefitters, carpenters, hoist operators and trainmen. Also on display is the B.A. & P. "Cow & Calf", a restored G.E. 1909 heavy haul electric locomotive & cars. The mine yard and surrounding Historic District was designated a National Historic Landmark in 1961. The Anselmo is open mid-June to mid-August Monday through Friday from 10 a.m. to 6 p.m.

M Montana Tech of The University of Montana
1300 West Park Street, Butte. 496-4178
or (800) 445-8324. www.mtech.edu

Originally the Montana School of Mines, founded in 1895, Montana Tech now offers programs with a focus on the technical sciences. Montana's Bureau of Mines and Geology, and the Division of Technology have expanded the school's offerings. The current enrollment is approximately 1,800 students.

11.

Waterloo
Settlers began coming to this area as early as 1864. A woolen mill was started here at one time, but failed. A pottery mill did survive for a while. The story goes the town got its name when a battle ensued over the location of the post office. The

A statue of Marcus Daly guards the entrance to Montana Tech.

settlers thought Waterloo was an appropriate name.

T Renova Hot Springs
Hwy 55, near Waterloo on the Jefferson River

Pools along the shoreline are accessible year-round and located on public land. Volunteers have built the rock pools to allow the water to mix with the seeps that are about 112 degrees F. Due to the changing levels of the river the soaking temperatures vary widely throughout the year. Midsummer and early fall are the most ideal times for soaking. The scenery on the river and view of the Tobacco Root Mountains are spectacular.

It Happened in Montana

January 2, 1865. For 185 rounds, Con Orem and Hugh O'Neill battled bare-knuckled to a draw in Virginia City. The fight was best described by Granville Stuart:

"...each man toed the mark and the battle begun and lasted three hours and five munutes, in which one hundred eighty-five rounds were fought. At this junction a sudden feeling seemed to animate the backers of both men. The referee was called on by both parties to stop the fight. (the men themselves were still game and ready to go.) This was accordingly done to the satisfaction of most people present. Bets were declared off and the ring money was divided evenly."

The prize purse was $1,000. As it was a draw, each man ended up receiving $425 and half of all the gold dust "pokes" thrown into the ring.

12.

Silver Star

Silver Star is the third oldest town in Montana and took its name from a nearby mining claim. It was at one time the only town between Helena and Virginia City and served as a supply point for silver miners in the area. Legend has it that Edward, Prince of Wales, and the son of Queen Victoria, spent three days at the Silver Star Hotel in 1878.

Now, with a population of about 40, you might think you could blink and miss the town as you drive through. You won't miss Lloyd Harkin's place though. Seven acres on Rte 41 are surrounded by a chain link fence that holds his enormous collection of mining equipment. He once had visions of creating a museum, later deciding that he didn't want to be tied down.

Today, as folks drive past they won't miss the seventy-eight-foot head frame that was used to lower cages of workers into a mine shaft or several twenty-one-foot wheels standing upright along the fence line. That's just part of it. The collection contains tons and tons of mining equipment from the 138 mines that Butte was once home to, and some from a few others. He managed to haul away just about everything imaginable from the mines, except the 4,000 miles of tunnel that still lie under the city of Butte.

The metallic assemblage contains everything from ore cars, pumps, railroad cars, pulleys, gas pumps, and some curious items not necessarily mining related. None of the items are a mystery to Lloyd. He was a miner in Butte for twenty-five years and knows the entire story behind each piece. He'll buy, sell, or trade for the right deal. You can get a pretty good idea of what just went into all those mines as you drive by. A few of the items were purchased by Walt Disney's set designers and used in movies. Lloyd's museum never materialized but a great deal of his collection has been donated to Butte's World Museum of Mining.

D William Clark
August 3, 1805

"in my walk I saw a fresh track which I took to be an Indian,…I think it probable that this Indian Spied our fires and Came to a Situation to view us from the top of a Small knob on the Lard. [left] Side."

13. *Gas, Food, Lodging*

Twin Bridges

This town was founded by two brothers, M.H. and John T. Lott. A year after it was established, the brothers built two bridges, one across the Big Hole River and one across the Beaverhead River. Assured that this would be the hub of the valley, they proceeded to build roads to and from the town. 130 years later their descendents still occupy the valley. The area today is a farming and ranching community. Alfalfa, grains and potatoes grow in the fields surrounded by the Tobacco Root, Highland, McCartney and Ruby Mountains. Near the Twin Bridges school, four Indian trails converged at a natural ford on the Beaverhead. Twin Bridges is now known as a quintessential Montana fly fishing town and home to R.L. Winston Rod, internationally known maker of custom fly rods.

The town sits at the conjuncture of four rivers: the Big Hole, Beaverhead, Ruby and Jefferson. When Lewis and Clark camped near hear in 1805, they decided to name the three rivers that formed the Jefferson River for the three "cardinal virtues" of their president and benefactor for whom they had just named the Jefferson River. Unfortunately, the names of Philosophy, Philanthropy, and Wisdom were a little hard for settlers that later came through and the rivers were renamed the Big Hole, Ruby, and Beaverhead.

H Jefferson Valley
North of Twin Bridges

The Lewis and Clark Expedition, westward bound, came up the Jefferson River in August, 1805. They were hoping to find the Shoshone Indians, Sacajawea's tribe, and trade for horses to use in crossing the mountains west of here. Just south of here the river forks, the east fork being the Ruby and the west fork the Beaverhead. They followed the latter and met the Shoshones near Armstead, which is now under the Clark Canyon Reservoir 20 miles south of Dillon.

On the return trip from the coast in 1806, Capt. Wm. Clark retraced their former route down this valley to Three Forks, and then crossed the Yellowstone. Capt. Lewis left Clark in the Bitter Root Valley, crossed the Divide via the Big Blackfoot River and thence to Great Falls. They met near the mouth of the Yellowstone, arriving within nine days of each other.

D Mer. Lewis
August 6, 1805

…we therefore determined that the middle fork was that which ought of right to bear the name we had given to the lower portion or River Jefferson, and called the bold rapid an[d] clear streem Wisdom, and the more mild and placid one which flows in from the S.E. Philanthrophy, in commemoration of two of those cardinal virtues, which have tso eminently marked that deservedly selibrated character through life.

T Rochester
10 miles northwest of Twin Bridges.

Rochester was once the major gold mining area in the region and at one time had a population of almost 5,000. Today all that remains is a few stone foundations and a fenced in cemetery, most of the town's buildings lost to vandalism. To get there drive west on Hwy. 41 out of Twin Bridges to just past where the road curves. Turn right on Melrose Twin Bridges County Road. Follow this road a little more than two miles until it crosses over Rochester Creek. A few yards on the other side of the creek is a road that follows the creek. Turn north here. The town is approximately seven miles down this road.

T Montana Children's Center
Twin Bridges, Twin Bridges Historical Association. 684-5701

The economy of Twin Bridges was waning after the decline of the mining boom at the end of the 1800s. That's when the Montana Children's Center was established to give the local economy a boost. Better known as the orphanage, the 223 acre complex on the Beaverhead River was home to over 6,000 children through it's 80 year history. Children were delivered to the orphanage for many reasons over the eighty-two years of it's duration.

The Children's Center was a self-sustaining community where residents were taught to be proficient in life skills. It had it's own hospital, swimming pool, dairy, livestock, and elementary school. The Center provided well for the children who lived there, teaching true work ethics and lifelong skills. The orphanage has been vacant since closing in 1975 and the buildings have fallen into disrepair, but remain an imposing part of the Twin Bridges landscape. The Twin Bridges Museum has preserved remnants and the history of the Children's Center.

14. *Gas, Food, Lodging*

Sheridan

Many of the miners who came to this area in the 1860s were Civil War veterans. The town was named for Gen. Phillip H. Sheridan, a Union cavalry leader.

L Moriah Motel
220 S. Main St., corner of Poppleton & Main, Sheridan. 842-5491. www.moriahmotel.com; moriah@sellit-montana.com

15. *Gas, Food, Lodging*

Alder

Once served as a shipping center during the early gold rush days, gold dredging operations at the turn of the century left large gravel mounds west of town. Near Alder Ponds lie piles of processed rock, called windrows, as well as the dredge ponds from the operation of one of the largest dredges to be used in 1911. Two of Harry Plummer's road agents were hanged near here in 1864. It's estimated over $100 million dollars in gold was extracted from

Twin Bridges	Jan	Feb	March	April	May	June	July	Aug	Sep	Oct	Nov	Dec	Annual
Average Max. Temperature (F)	34.2	40.1	47.3	57.0	67.0	75.2	84.0	82.3	72.2	60.5	44.1	35.3	58.3
Average Min. Temperature (F)	11.1	14.8	20.4	27.6	35.6	42.3	45.8	43.1	35.3	27.2	19.0	12.4	27.9
Average Total Precipitation (in.)	0.26	0.21	0.46	0.86	1.69	1.94	1.05	0.99	0.94	0.54	0.37	0.29	9.58
Average Total SnowFall (in.)	2.0	2.2	2.4	0.8	0.1	0.0	0.0	0.1	0.0	0.3	1.2	1.0	10.0
Average Snow Depth (in.)	0	0	0	0	0	0	0	0	0	0	0	0	0

this area. Even today, visitors can pan for gold at Alder Gulch River of Gold. A few buildings remain, along with a few residents.

Laurin

The town was a station on the Northern Pacific railroad between Sheridan and Alder. Originally know as Cicero, the name was changed to honor John Baptiste Laurin who ran a trading store nearby. John and his wife prospered by trading with the Indians and selling goods to the miners. He and his wife were in the mercantile and livestock business for almost forty years. While they had no children of their own, they raised fourteen who had been left to their care for one reason or another. They built a magnificent Catholic church of native stone and donated it to the community. The church still stands. Perhaps Laurin is best know for its "Hangman's Tree" where members of the Plummer Gang were dispatched at the end of a rope on January 4, 1864.

H Robbers' Roost
south of Sheridan

In 1863, Pete Daly built a road house on the stage route between Virginia City and Bannack to provide entertainment for, man and beast. The main floor was a shrine to Bacchus and Lady Luck. The second floor was dedicated to Terpsichore and bullet holes in the logs attest the fervor of ardent swains for fickle sirens. Occasionally a gent succumbed.

Pete's tavern became a hangout for unwholesome characters who held up stage coaches and robbed lone travellers. One of the road agents is alleged to have left a small fortune in gold cached in the vicinity.

In later years, time and neglect gave the building its present hapless look and it became known as Robbers' Roost. It is in the cottonwood grove just across the railroad tracks. Drive

Montana Trivia

The only Kentucky Derby winner to come from Montana came from the Bayer Ranch near Twin Bridges. Spokane won the 1886 Derby with six-to-one odds. The unusual wedding cake type barn of the Bayer Ranch can be seen from the highway to the east while driving south of Twin Bridges.

over and pay your respects but please don't dig up the premises trying to locate the cache.

H The Ruby Valley
Near Alder

The Ruby River was called the Passamari by the Indians and became known as the Stinking Water to the whites in the pioneer days. It joins the Beaverhead to form the Jefferson Fork of the Missouri.

Fur trappers, Indians, prospectors and road agents have ridden the trails through here in days gone by.

The large gravel piles to the west are the tailings resulting from gold dredging operations over about a twenty-year period beginning in 1899. The dredges are reported to have recovered between eight and nine million dollars in gold from the floor of the valley and the lower end of Alder Gulch.

FLC Chick's Motel & RV Park and Inback Steakhouse
MT Highway 287 in Alder. motel: 842-5366, restaurant: 842-7632

Chick's Motel & RV Park is home to the Inback Steakhouse in the heart of some Montana's most colorful historical areas and surrounded by great hunting and fishing. They are just ten miles from Virginia City and seven miles from the Ruby Dam on the way to West Yellowstone. The motel offers satellite TV, phones, refrigerators, microwaves, and a laundry room. The restaurant serves breakfast, lunch, and dinner seven days a week. Their famous prime rib is served Friday through Sunday evenings. Enjoy other specialties such as char-broiled steaks that are extra juicy and tender or 9-ounce hamburgers with home-cut fries. Breakfast is served until noon on weekends. This family operated restaurant offers great homemade soups and desserts along with friendly smiles. Order food to go or let them cater your party of 10 to 100!

16. *Food, Lodging*

Virginia City

Stories of colorful mining-era boomtowns in the American West are abundant. But, few are quite as colorful as the story of Virginia City. On May 26, 1863, six frustrated prospectors set up a camp on the banks of a small creek in the Tobacco Root Mountains. All they wanted was to find enough gold to buy tobacco when they returned to Bannack. Within hours, they had collected $12.30 in gold, and that there might be more here than a few days worth of tobacco. The area was named Alder Gulch for the bushes that grew along the creek.

The town of Virginia City was born, and within a year grew to 10,000 people. Within two years almost 30,000 people lived within 20 miles of the town. Within three years, Alder Gulch coughed up more than $30 million in gold, and to this day is the richest placer gold discovery in history yielding over $130 million in flakes, nuggets, and gold dust.

The stories that go with this town are just as rich. Henry Plummer, the criminal sheriff who plundered the area for years. The Montana Vigilante movement that finally hung the crooked sheriff and contributed numerous graves on the local Boot Hill. And, of course, the political intrigue and wrangling when the town served as Montana's Territorial Capital.

Probably the most unique thing about Virginia City is that most of it is still standing today—intact and preserved. Most of the buildings here have stood in the same spot for more than 130 years. The "downtown" of Virginia City is arguably one of the best collection of "boomtown" buildings still standing on their original sites. Ranks Mercantile, established in 1864, is Montana's oldest continuously operating general store.

Charles and Sue Bovey visited Virginia City in 1944 and immediately recognized its historic value. Their efforts to restore and preserve the town lasted for years until the Bovey estate sold the town to the State of Montana. Today, you can shop, dine, and sleep in a town so authentic you'll feel you've stepped back in time. Learn more about this rare historical treasure at www.viriginiacity.com and www.virginiacitychamber.com.

Nevada City

A celebrated ghost town, Nevada City recreates the mining era so authentically that it has been filmed in western movies such as *Little Big Man* and *Return to Lonesome Dove*. Buildings include five streets of shops, homes, a schoolhouse and Chinatown. The most popular exhibition is the Music Hall which contains one of the world's largest collections of mechanical music machines.

H Nevada City
Nevada City

A ghost town now, but once one of the hell roarin' mining camps that lined Alder Gulch in the 1860s. It was a trading point where gold dust and nuggets were the medium of exchange: where men were men and women were scarce. A stack of whites cost twenty, the sky was the limit and everyone was heeled. The first Vigilante execution took place here when George Ives, notorious road agent, was convicted of murder and hanged.

The gulch was once filled with romance, glamour, melodrama, comedy and tragedy. It's plumb peaceful now.

H Virginia City
Virginia City

All of Montana has the deepest pride and affection for Virginia City. No more colorful pioneer mining camp ever existed. Dramatic tales of the early days in this vicinity are legion.

Rich placer diggin's were discovered in Alder Gulch in the spring of 1863 and the stampede of gold-seekers and their parasites was on. Sluices soon lined the gulch and various "cities" blossomed forth as trading and amusement centers for freehanded miners. Virginia City, best known of these and the sole survivor, became the Capital of the Territory. Pioneers, who with their descendants were to mold the destinies of the state, were among its first citizens. If you like true stories more picturesque than fiction, Virginia City and Alder Gulch can furnish them in countless numbers.

H Adobetown
Northwest of Virginia City

Placer riches in Alder Gulch spawned many colorful communities. Among them, Adobetown flourished briefly as the center of mining activity in 1864. In that year alone, miners extracted over $350,000 in gold from nearby streams.

Taking its name from the numerous adobe shacks the miners constructed in the vicinity Adobetown assumed permanence in the fall of 1865 when Nicholas Carey and David O'Brien erected a large log store. The building's central location contributed to the growth of the settlement and the development of other businesses. Stages from Salt Lake City and later the Union Pacific Railroad at Corinne, Utah, made regular stops at the Adobetown store for passengers and mail.

The town received an official post office in 1875 with Carey as postmaster. He, and later his wife Mary, served as the community's only postmasters until her retirement and the subsequent close of the office in the fall of 1907.

Once in lively rivalry with Virginia City for social and political leadership of Alder Gulch, Adobetown's population and importance waned after 1865 as the placer gold gave out in the immediate area.

H Elling Bank
Virginia City

Bankers Nowland and Weary set up business in this brick-veneered building, one of the town's oldest stone structures, in 1864. Three well-proportioned gothic arches with elaborate tracery, removed during 1910 remodeling, originally graced its stone facade. In 1873, Henry Elling took over the banking business. His first fortune, made in merchandising, had disappeared along with his partner, but Elling quickly recouped his losses. The buying of gold dust proved a most profitable venture and Elling became an expert, able to determine the exact location of extraction from the texture and color of the dust. Under his shrewd direction, Elling's tiny bank became the first financial capital of Montana. The ornate vault, still intact, always carried large amounts of the dust. The Elling State Bank was organized in

Virginia City

1899 and Elling died a millionaire the following year. His family continued to operate the bank for another thirty years.

H Metropolitan Meat Market
Virginia City

George Gohn was one of the first to arrive at Alder Gulch in 1863 where he and Conrad Kohrs set up a meat market in a log cabin. Alkali dust sifted through the chinks and covered the meat prompting Gohn to experiment with various other locations until he settled on this site in 1880. When fire destroyed much of the block in 1888, only Gohn rebuilt. The present building, completed that year, long stood solitary on this section of Wallace Street. Decorative pilasters, brackets and imitation quarried stone highlight the cast iron storefront manufactured by George Mesker of Evansville, Indiana. Recent interior renovation included restoration of the tin ceiling. In the process, owners discovered a hidden treasure behind a plastered drywall: Gohn's elaborate oak meat cooler with beveled mirrors intact. This unusual example of 1880s state-of-the-art equipment stands sixteen feet high. Gohn advertised that his cooler was always well stocked with beef, veal, pork, game fowl and mutton and that his peddling wagons were "run regularly up and down the gulch."

H Pfouts and Russel (Rank's Drug-Old Masonic Temple)
Virginia City

Paris Pfouts, Vigilante president and Virginia City's first mayor, was instrumental in laying out the town. He and his partner, Samuel Russell, built a log store on this site in summer, 1863. Local hell-raiser Jack Slade was arrested here on March 10, 1864 and, in an execution controvesial even

amoung the Vigilantes, hanged on a corral gatepost behind the building. Pfouts and Russell constructed the present building in 1865. Lime was not yet available for mortar, so the stone walls were secured with adobe mud. A loyal Mason, Pfouts gave the second floor to the Masonic Lodge. There the Grand Lodge of Montana A.F. & A.M. was founded on January 24, 1866. W.W. Morris moved his drug store, established in the Hangman's Building in 1864, to this location circa 1877. C.W. Rank bought the business in 1889. He and his wife ran it until 1946. Now housing the oldest continuously-operated business in Montana, the building has been little altered since the 1860s.

ROCKHOUNDING

Radar Creek area near Toll Mountain southeast of Butte on Hwy. 2. Look here for smokey quartz crystals. At the Toll Mountain Campground look for limonite cubes. At the Boulder Batholith just east of Butte, look for quartz crystals.

Crystal Butte is about 8 miles west of Twin Bridges. This is a good place to find white quartz crystals.

Virginia City area. The gold rush may be over but you can still find placer deposits of gold in the tailings between Virginia City and Alder.

Sheridan area. Near Indian Creek west of town you can find white and honey-colored, banded masses of calcite.

Ruby Dam south of Alder is a good place to find calcite, garnets and opalite.

Virginia City	Jan	Feb	March	April	May	June	July	Aug	Sep	Oct	Nov	Dec	Annual
Average Max. Temperature (F)	33.2	37.7	43.0	52.6	62.2	71.0	80.6	79.5	69.1	57.8	42.1	34.6	55.3
Average Min. Temperature (F)	11.6	15.0	19.5	27.4	35.8	42.5	48.7	47.3	38.9	30.3	20.2	13.3	29.2
Average Total Precipitation (in.)	0.70	0.53	1.00	1.42	2.44	2.59	1.62	1.39	1.29	1.04	0.86	0.70	15.59
Average Total SnowFall (in.)	9.9	6.8	10.6	8.5	4.2	0.7	0.0	0.0	0.9	3.6	8.2	11.0	64.3
Average Snow Depth (in.)	4	4	2	0	0	0	0	0	0	0	1	3	1

T Virginia City Historical Museum
Virginia City

T Alder Gulch Short Line
Virginia City. 843-5377

The Short Line is a narrow gauge railroad that runs between Virginia City and Nevada City. The 1.25 mile trip is a favorite with kids. The train's engineer entertains you during the entire trip with narratives of the area's history. Early June to late-August. There is an admission charge.

T Alder Gulch River of Gold
Virginia City. 843-5402

Whether you just want to see how placer gold was mined during Virginia City's gold boom, or do a little gold panning yourself, you'll find this an enjoyable stop for every member of the family. An outdoor mining museum displays dredging equipment and other mining artifacts. You can pan for gold and garnets with a little professional help.

T The Brewery Follies
210 E. Cover in Virginia City. 843-5218 or (800) 829-2969, Ext. #3. www.breweryfollies.com

The Brewery Follies is a remarkable revue and an historical experience in a cabaret atmosphere. The always fun and captivating show takes place in Montana's first brewery, built in 1863 by German born brewmeister, H.S. Gilbert. A place where you can sit back and have a cold beverage, whether it is a Montana Microbrew or a soda pop. Enjoy lots of musical numbers, comedy sketches, and just plain silliness. The show is risqué, sometimes bawdy, and can involve social and political commentary, but it doesn't have violence or nudity, and they don't use "four letter words'. Kids are welcome if you don't mind exposing them to an environment where adults drink beer, laugh heartily, and may be called on to make fools of themselves. The show goes on from the end of May through Labor Day, 6 evenings a week with a Saturday Matinee, no show on Tuesdays. Reservations are highly recommended. Be sure and visit them on the web.

17.

Lakeview

George Shambrow served as postmaster when the settlement's first post office opened in 1897. Although the town sustained itself through the early 1900s, a decreasing population forced the postal service's closure in 1938. Today, Lakeview is a tiny village.

H Beaverhead Rock
Hwy 41, north of Dillon

On August 10, 1805, members of the Lewis and Clark expedition pushed their way up the Jefferson River's tributaries toward the Continental Divide and the Pacific Ocean beyond. Toward afternoon they sighted what Clark called a "remarkable Clift" to the west. Sacajawea (or, as Lewis spelled it: Sahcahgarweah), their Indian guide for this portion of the trip, said her tribe called the large promontory "Beaver's head."

Both Lewis and Clark agreed on the rock's likeness to the fur-bearing animal and recorded the name in their journals. They continued south only to encounter a heavy rain and hail storm. "the men defended themselves from the hail by means of the willow bushes but all the party got perfectly wet," Lewis said. They camped upstream from the Beaver's head, enjoyed freshly killed deer meat, then pushed on the next day.

Beaverhead Rock served as an important landmark not only for Lewis and Clark, but also for the trappers, miners, and traders who followed them into the vicinity. It is the namesake for the county in which it is now located, retaining the same appearance that inspired Sacajawea and her people to name it centuries ago.

D William Clark
August 5, 1805

"Men much fatigued from their excessive labours in hauling the Canoes over the rapids & very weak being in the water all day."

D William Clark
August 8, 1805

"the Indian woman recognized the point of a high plain to our right which she informed us was not very distant from the summer retreat of her nation on a river beyond the mountains which runs to the west. this hill she says her nation calls the beaver's head from a conceived remblance of it's figure to the head of the animal. . .I determined to proceed tomorrow. . .untill I find the Indians. . . "

T Beaverhead Rock State Park
14 miles south of Twin Bridges on MT 41. 834-3413

Sacajawea recognized this huge landmark, resembling the head of a swimming beaver, while traveling with Lewis and Clark in 1805, helping the party with their orientation. Day use only.

18. *Gas, Food, Lodging*

Rocker

This town has had its ups and downs. It first grew up around the Bluebird Mine, but faded when the mine closed in 1893. It was reborn when the Pacific Railroad chose Rocker as the division point

where ore cars were made up between Butte and Anaconda. The name came from a cradle-like machine called a rocker which was used to wash gold from gravel by early miners.

19.

Melrose

Just off of I15 south of Butte on the Big Hole River, is the town of Melrose. Some of the log cabins have survived the years and are still used as residences. Other original buildings that have been vacated are still standing from the days when this town was a supply depot for mining camps. There is also a motel, guest ranch, and Bed and Breakfast in the area and plenty of fishing.

Divide

Divide is named for the town's proximity to the Continental Divide. At one time the town was a station on the Union Pacific and was a distribution and stock shipping point for farms and ranches of the Big Hole Valley.

T Glendale
West of Melrose.

To reach this town, take Trapper Creek Road west out of Melrose for about 15 miles. This was the largest of several towns in the Bryant Mining District. The others, Lion City, Greenwood, Trapper City and Hecla have virtually vanished. At one time Glendale had a population of over 1,500 people, a school for 200 students, a Methodist church, commercial stores, and a water works system. The Hecla Mining Company was the main employer from 1881 to 1900. During it's short life, it mined ore that was valued at over $22 million. The most interesting remains are those of the old Coke ovens which provided over 100,000 bushels of charcoal a month for the smelter. The ovens and the smelter stack are still in evidence on the road north of town. When the Hecla Mine shut down in 1904, the residents quickly deserted the town.

Dewey

Rancher D.S Dewey is honored as this town's namesake after building the first cabin in the area during the late 1800s. Although the lumber industry initially attracted new settlers to the community, a quartz lode was later discovered. The subsequent mining boom drastically increased the town's population with peak activity occurring between 1877 and 1895. Today, Dewey is simply a mining ghost town whose location near the Big Hole River attracts area fisherman.

20.

T Humbug Spires Primitive Area
I-15 Exit 99

The gently rolling countryside here is starkly disrupted by nine 300 to 600-foot granite monoliths. No one knows how old these spires are. Estimates range from 70 million to 2 billion years old. They are part of the Boulder batholith that you see driving over Homestake Pass near Butte and are a remarkable piece of Montana geology.

21.

Glen

Located in a glen between the Big Hole and Beaverhead Rivers, Glen is surrounded by rocky hillsides and began in 1878 under the name "Willis Station." The town has seen several other name changes throughout its history, including

Willis, Reichele, and finally, its current designation as Glen. Once serving as a Union Pacific Railroad station, Glen has operated a post office since 1950 and rattlesnake hunts are a popular pastime for local residents.

H Browne's Bridge
North of Glen

Browne's Bridge was constructed as a toll bridge by Fred Burr and James Minesinger in late 1862 and early 1863. The bridge was located on the Bannack to Deer Lodge Road. Joseph Browne, a miner, bought the bridge in 1865. The territorial legislature granted him a charter to maintain the bridge and charge travelers for its use. Within a few years, Browne had acquired about 3,000 acres near the bridge and had developed nearby Browne's Lake for recreational purposes. A post office was located just west of the bridge from 1872 until the early 1880s. Even though most of Montana's counties assumed control of the state's toll facilities by 1892, Browne operated the bridge until his death in 1909. Beaverhead and Madison counties assumed joint ownership of the bridge in 1911.

In 1915 the counties petitioned the Montana State Highway Commission for a new bridge. The Commission designed the bridge in 1915; a Missoula company built it during the autumn and winter of that year. A riveted Warren through truss bridge, it was one of the first structures designed by the Commission's bridge department. In 1920 high water destroyed the old structure, which was located slightly upstream from this bridge.

Beaverhead County rehabilitated this bridge with funds provided by the Montana Department of Transportation.

22.

T Argenta
Hwy. 278, to Argenta Flats Road, west of Dillon

Argenta (formerly Montana) was the site of Montana's first silver-lead mine in Montana, The Legal Tender. It once had a population of over 1,500. Granville Stuart, in speaking of Argenta wrote, "The wealth of the Rothchilds is as nothing compared to the riches which lie concealed in the bowels of the Rattlesnake hills awaiting the coming of the enchanters with their wands (in the shape of greenbacks), to bring forth these treasures." In 1866, the St. Louis and Montana Mining Company funded and built the first smelter in the Montana Territory here. The only remnants of this town are mine shafts, slag heaps, some abandoned mine structures, and several private residences.

23. *Lodging*

Dillon

Dillon was born with the screech of a steam whistle. The Utah and Northern Railroad (present day Union Pacific) was forging north, toward Butte in 1880, as winter converged the railroad halted construction at Richard Deason's ranch. The location

Old train station adjacent to the Beaverhead County Museum in Dillon.

of the town was determined coincidentally when the rancher owning the land refused the railroad passage. Some enterprising businessmen travelling with the train bought the ranch to form a town site company. During the winter the railroad remained at the end of the track and when it moved north again in the spring, the town remained. Dillon was named after the president of the Union Pacific Railroad, Sidney Dillon.

With a population of about 4,000, Dillon is an agricultural community and the regional trade center for southwestern Montana. At one point it was the largest wool shipping point in Montana. It is also the county seat of Beaverhead County and boasts an "Entrance to Montana" Visitors Information Center located in the old Union Pacific Depot Building alongside the Chamber of Commerce. Western Montana College, built here in the early 1900s, has assisted Dillon's economic stability and development.

Nestled within the surrounding mountain ranges of the Beaverhead, the Tendoys, the Centennial Range and the Pioneer Mountains, Dillon enjoys a pocket of mild weather and a variety of geographical splendor.

24. *Gas, Food, Lodging*

T Clark's Lookout State Park
In Dillon on 490 at Montana 41 exit, .5 miles east, then .5 miles north on county road. 834-3413

This is the location of an observation site used by William Clark of the Lewis and Clark Expedition on August 13, 1805. This area has some great views. Undeveloped land makes it a great place for adventure and primitive camping.

25. *Gas, Food, Lodging*

T Beaverhead County Museum
15 S. Montana St. in downtown Dillon. 683-5027

The Beaverhead County Museum is a time machine reopening the past.

A tour of the museum will unfold the county's history… its inhabitants, wildlife, agriculture, mining and lifestyle. Included with Indian artifacts, early ranching relics and mining memorabilia, is a huge, mounted Alaskan brown bear towering over the exhibits.

Exhibits depict the manner in which Indians, early pioneers and the medical profession served as caretakers of land and man. A second room features the local mining industry, while another invites you into the domestic side of early life in Beaverhead County.

Outside, you can read 1,700 branded boards along the boardwalk, leading to an authentic homesteader's cabin and Dillon's first flush toilet. Mining equipment, a sheepherder's wagon, and an old Ford tractor are other interesting outdoor displays.

Continue south on the boardwalk to the 1909 Union Pacific Depot, now housing the Travel Montana Visitors' Center, the Beaverhead Chamber of Commerce, the Old Depot Theatre and a large diorama of Lewis and Clark.

Take a walk through time and enjoy your visit. Our friendly hosts and hostesses will be happy to answer your questions.

The museum is open year round. While no admission is charged there is a suggested donation. *Reprinted from Dillon Chamber of Commerce brochure.*

Dillon	Jan	Feb	March	April	May	June	July	Aug	Sep	Oct	Nov	Dec	Annual
Average Max. Temperature (F)	31.6	38.0	43.6	54.5	64.1	73.1	82.8	81.3	70.2	58.7	42.4	33.4	56.2
Average Min. Temperature (F)	9.8	14.8	19.5	28.1	36.4	43.7	48.8	47.6	39.0	30.7	20.0	12.4	29.2
Average Total Precipitation (in.)	0.27	0.24	0.53	0.89	1.73	1.85	1.03	0.99	0.96	0.55	0.38	0.26	9.68
Average Total SnowFall (in.)	4.9	3.8	7.6	6.5	2.6	0.1	0.0	0.0	1.3	2.9	4.2	4.1	38.0
Average Snow Depth (in.)	1	1	1	0	0	0	0	0	0	0	0	1	0

26. *Gas, Food, Lodging, Miscellaneous*

M Western Montana College of The University of Montana
710 S. Atlantic, Dillon. 683-7011
or (800) 962-6668. www.wmc.edu

Beginning in 1893 at Montana State Normal College, today Western Montana College has approximately 1,100 students. The school is known for it's liberal arts studies, especially in elementary and secondary education.

27.

T Bannack State Park
5 miles south of Dillon on I-15, then 21 miles west on Secondary 278, then 4 miles south on county road. 834-3413

Bannack was the site of the state's first big gold

It Happened in Montana

January 11, 1864. A band of Vigilantes hangs Dutch John Wagner in Bannack from the beam of a building. Not finished with their work for the day, they proceed to the cabin of a man they call Mexican Frank. Two of the vigilantes storm through the cabin door but are shot and manage to scramble to safety. The Chief Justice of the Idaho Territory, Sidney Edgarton, lends them a small howitzer and shells. The men fire three shells into the cabin collapsing the structure. The Vigilantes find the suspect trapped under a beam. They tie a clothesline around his neck and hoist him to a pole before firing more than a hundred shots into the strangling man. They then create a bonfire from the remains of the cabin and throw the corpse on the pyre. Unfortunately, Mexican Frank was not home that day. The unfortunate victim was a man named Joe Pizanthia. He was not on their list of suspected road agents. Rather than admit the screwup, the Vigilantes spread the rumor that Pizanthia was "one of the most dangerous men that ever infested our frontier."

---

strike in 1862 and the birthplace of Montana's government. Gold was discovered in Grasshopper Creek on July 28, 1862. This strike set off a massive gold rush that swelled Bannack's population to over 3,000 by 1863. The remnants of over 60 buildings show the extent of development reached during the town's zenith. When the gold ran out, the town died.

Montana's first territorial capital, was the site of many "firsts" in the state's history. Bannack had the first jail, hotel, chartered Masonic Lodge, hard rock mine, electric gold dredge, quartz stamp mill, and commercial sawmill. Bannack's two jails, built from hand-hewn logs, tell the story of the lawlessness that terrorized Grasshopper Gulch and the road to Virginia City. Road Agent's Rock, just a few miles from Bannack, was the lookout point for an organized gang of road agents, toughs, robbers, and murders. The infamous sheriff of Bannack, Henry Plummer, was secretly the leader of this gang called "The Innocents." The gang is said to have murdered over 102 men and robbed countless others during the eight months that Plummer served as sheriff. Many of their escapades were planned in Skinner's Saloon, which still stands in Bannack today. It could not last. Bannack's law-abiding citizens rose up and organized a vigilance group. In conjunction with a similar group in Virginia City, they quickly hunted down 28 of the "Innocents," including Henry Plummer, and hanged them on the gallows Plummer had just built.

"The Toughest Town in The West" soon grew quiet due to the reign of the vigilantes and a population of transient gold seekers that left to follow better gold strikes. However, gold mining activity continued for many years. The reputation of Bannack lives on today in Western history and fiction, forming the basis of many Western novels and movies. Many actors in the drama of early-day Bannack went on to play key roles in Montana history. The mines and placer diggings are quiet now, but the streets of Bannack still echo with the footsteps of those who seek the rich lode of Western history that Bannack hoards like the gold once hidden in its hills and creeks. Over 50 buildings remain at Bannack today, each one with a story to tell...from tumble-down, one-room bachelor cabins to the once-stately Hotel Meade. The diggin's are quiet now, but the streets still ring with the footsteps of those seeking the rich lode of Western history that Bannack hoards like the gold once hidden in its hills...a moment in time for modern-day visitors to discover and enjoy.

Walk the deserted streets of Bannack, and discover for yourself the way the West really was. Bannack is one of the best preserved of all of Montana's ghost towns. Bannack is unique...preserved rather than restored...protected rather than exploited. Reprinted from Bannack State Park brochure.

28. *Gas, Food*

H Bannack
I-15. MP 55

The Lewis and Clark Expedition, westward bound, passed here in August, 1805.

The old mining camp of Bannack is on Grasshopper Creek about twenty miles west of here. The first paying placer discovery in Montana was made in that vicinity by John

---

MONTANA'S VIGILANTES

The Vigilante movement began the winter of 1863 in Alder Gulch. While thousands came to the fields to mine gold others came with them who had other ideas for making money. Gamblers, dance-hall girls, and crooks flooded into the area with the miners. While every part of the west had its share of criminals, Alder Gulch had someone to organize them in the personage of Henry Plummer. A smooth, shrewd con man with a rap sheet going back 10 year, Plummer arrived in Bannack in the winter of '62-'63. By spring, he had conned everyone and was wearing the sheriff's badge. Now in control of the law, he began to organize the criminal elements into a cohesive unit that terrorized the thousands in the area.

After suffering through a year of Mr. Plummer's reign, the honest miners took matters into their own hands. A three day trial in Nevada City claimed its first "Road Agent," and George Ives was hanged, and the Montana Vigilantes were formed. During the next two months, the Vigilantes cleaned up the area. The nucleus of the Plummer gang were either hanged or banished and the consummate conman finished his reign at the end of a noose.

White, July 28, 1862, and Bannack became the first capital of Montana Territory. They should have built it on wheels. The following spring six prospectors discovered Alder Gulch and practically the entire population of Bannack stampeded to the new diggings where the new camp of Virginia City eventually became the capital until it was changed to Helena.

Henry Plummer, sheriff and secret chief of the road agents, was hanged at Bannack in 1864 by the Vigilantes. It tamed him down considerably.

D Mer. Lewis
August 11, 1805

"he suddonly turned his horse about, gave him the whip leaped the creek and disapeared in the willow brush in an instant. . .I now felt quite as much mortification and disappointment as I had preasure and expectation at the first sight of this indian."

D Mer. Lewis
August 17, 1805

"Capt. Clark arrived with the Interpreter Charbono and the Indian woman who proved to be the sister of the Chief Cameahwait, tge meeting of those people wsa really affecting. . .we had the satisfaction. . .to find ourselves. . .with a flattering propect of being able to abtain as many horses shortly as would enable us to prosicute our voyage by land should that by water be deemed unadvisable."

D William Clark
July 12, 1806

"this morning I was detained untill 7 A M making Paddles and drawing the nails of the Canoe to be left a this place and the one we had before left here."

29.

T Camp Fortunate Overlook and the Clark Canyon Recreation Area
I-15 S. of Dillon. 638-6472

Here Lewis and Clark expedition received horses from Sacajawea's brother, Chief Cameahwait, which were needed to cross the mountain ranges into the Columbia River drainage. The area is perfect for fishing, boating and camping. An interpretive memorial to Sacajawea is here. Clark Canyon Recreation Area has a man-made lake with great fishing for rainbow trout, or try the local favorite spot for water skiing.

T Big Sheep Creek
I-15 exit at Dell, 24 miles north of the Montana-Idaho border. Northern terminus is Montana Route 324 west of Clark Canyon Dam.

This isolated, spectacular mountain valley is a narrow canyon with a good dirt road that often provides exceptional opportunities to view bighorn sheep and other wildlife.

T Clark Canyon Reservoir
South of Dillon.

Clark Canyon Reservoir ranks as one of the finest places to catch large trout. Located 20 miles from Dillon it covers some six thousand acres and contains two major islands.

This great fishing haven didn't exist until 1964. Before this date, it was the location of the town named Armstead. The town was named after Harry Armstead, a local miner. It became the starting point of the Gilmore-Pacific Railroad, which began operation in 1910 only to meet financial failure in 1941. The post office was active until 1962. After that most of the buildings were moved, the dam was built, and the area was flooded in 1964.

The dam is under the control of the East Bench Irrigation District and supplies most of the irrigation water to Dillon. It has easy access from I-15, has a perimeter road around the reservoir, picnic areas and a marina.

Fishing brings many people to try their luck at Clark Canyon. A boat or floating device is the preferred way to fish. Rainbow and brown trout, along with ling are the main species in the lake. Some trout can get as big as 10 pounds, thus making this a great destination spot for anyone who likes to catch big fish. Water skiing and jet skiing can also be enjoyed here.

30.

H The Montana-Utah Road
I-15, Red Rocks

Interstate 15 is the latest in a series of roads that have traversed this area since prehistory. Although used for generations by Native Americans, the first recorded use of this route was by the Lewis and Clark Expedition on August 10, 1805. They named cliffs to the north of here after the scores of rattlesnakes they encountered on their trip upriver. With the discovery of gold at nearby Grasshopper Creek and Alder Gulch in the early 1860s, thousands of people came to southwest Montana to mine gold and to "mine the miners." The road originated in Corinne, Utah and traversed a series of high plateaus and narrow canyons on its way north to southwestern Montana, The road was the best route into the territory for the freighters who supplied the mining camps. Drawn by teams of mules or oxen, each wagon carried up to 12,000 pounds of freight. The trip from Utah typically took three weeks and a freighting outfit could usually make three or four round trips each year, Just south of here near Dell, the Montana-Utah Road branched into three separate trails that led to Bannack, Deer Lodge, Virginia City and Helena. This section of the road terminated at Helena. With the arrival of the Utah & Northern Railroad in 1880, the Montana-Utah Road became obsolete. In the 1920s, however, it again became an important travel corridor first as the Vigilante Trail/Great White Way, then as U.S. Highway 91 and, finally, as Interstate 15.

H Old Trail to the Gold Diggins'
I-15, Red Rocks

Along in the early 1840s the Americans were like they are now, seething to go somewhere. It got around that Oregon was quite a place. The Iowa people hadn't located California yet. A wagon train pulled out across the plains and made it to Oregon. Then everyone broke out into a rash to be going west.

They packed their prairie schooners with their household goods, gods, and garden tools. Outside of Indians, prairie fires, cholera, famine, cyclones, cloud bursts, quick sand, snow slides, and blizzards they had a tolerably blithe and gay trip.

When gold was found in Montana some of them forked off from the main highway and surged along this trail aiming to reach the rainbow's end. It was mostly one-way traffic but if they did meet a backtracking outfit there was plenty of room to turn out.

31. *Food*

Dell

This town took its name from the topography of the surrounding area. It was once a station on the Union Pacific and was a trading center for valley ranchers. Not much there today except for one of the quirkiest little cafes you'll find anywhere. The Calf-A and Yesterday's Museum appear at first glance to be an old brick building with a junk shed next door. Don't turn away, the diner serves over 30,000 meals a year to people from all over the world. The diner is housed in the old schoolhouse with high ceilings and bare pine floors. Memorabilia lines the walls, the menu is written on the old blackboard, and the salad is on the teachers desk. The museum next door isn't your run-of-the-mill gallery either. It is a warehouse of everything left behind when the mining and lumbering petered out. The original owner, Ken Berthelson, is now deceased. Before going he left a number of wildlife sculptures in an outdoor sculpture corral. No, these aren't the magnificent bronze sculptures that seem to dominate Montana. They are created from just about anything Ken could put his hands on. There are lots of fine cafes in Montana, but not too many that you'll take pictures of for the folks back home.

TF Yesterday's Cafe
I-90 Exit 23, Dell.

What do you do with an old school building in a virtual ghost town on an interstate exit? You could turn it into a cafe. That's what Ken Berthelson did. Actually, he only wanted the bell from the school, but got the whole building. The brick school building in the heart of "downtown" Dell was built in 1903 and stopped operating in 1963. Ken

ON THE TRAIL OF LEWIS & CLARK

The Beaver's Head
A few miles below the mouth of Ruby River, Sacagawea recognized a prominent point of land known to her people as the Beaver's Head. She informed the captains that they were not far from the summer retreat of her people, which, she said, was on a river beyond the mountains (Lcmhi River.)

On Aug. 9, Lewis, along with three men, again set out ahead of the main party in an attempt to find the Shoshones.

About 9 1/2 miles by water from the Beaver's Head, the main party reached an island which they named 3000-Mile Island—a reference to their distance up the Missouri River.

Fourth Range Of Mountains
Lewis's party, which was following an Indian road, passed through the fourth range of mountains on Aug. 10, and from the number of rattlesnakes about the cliffs called it "Rattlesnake Cliffs." The main party entered this canyon four days later and both Clark and Sacagawea were in danger of being struck by these serpents.

Lewis continued on the Indian road, and soon came to a fork at the head of the Jefferson River. He left a note here on a dry willow to inform Clark of his decision to follow the west fork. At about 15 miles from the forks, on Horse Prairie, Lewis finally saw a Shoshone on horseback—the first Indian the Expedition had seen in 1400 miles. The native, wary of the strangers, would not allow them to approach, and soon disap-peared into the mountains.

Fifth Range Of Mountains
Lewis fixed a small U.S. flag onto a pole as a symbol of peace, which was carried along as they followed the horse's tracks. They camped that night at the head of Horse Prairie. They were now about to enter the fifth range of mountains.

The following morning they came upon recently inhabited willow lodges, and a place where the Indians had been digging roots. They continued on until they reached what Lewis described as "the most distant fountain of the waters of the Mighty Missouri in surch of which we have spent so many toilsome days and wristless nights. Thus far I had accomplished one of those great objects on which my mind has been unalterably fixed for many years..." He then wrote that Private McNeal "exultingly stood with a foot on each side of the little rivulet and thanked his god that he had lived to bestride the mighty & heretofore deemed endless Missouri."

Reprinted from U.S. Forest Service pamphlet "Lewis and Clark in the Rocky Mountains"

BEAVERHEAD NATIONAL FOREST

Located in Southwest Montana, the Beaverhead-Deerlodge National Forest is the largest of the national forests in Montana. The forest offers breath-taking scenery for a wide variety of recreation pursuits. Whether it's wilderness trekking in the Anaconda-Pintler or Lee Metcalf wildernesses, driving the Gravelly Range Road or Pioneer Mountains Scenic Byway, or camping in one of the 50 small to medium-sized campgrounds in the forest, the Beaverhead-Deerlodge has it all. Winter enthusiasts find snowmobiling, cross-country skiing trails, as well as downhill skiing at Discovery, near Anaconda, and Maverick Mountain, near Dillon. Summertime affords chances to hike and drive primitive routes to high-mountain lakes or to drive more improved roads to places like Delmoe and Wade lakes. The Continental Divide National Scenic Trail and Nez Perce Historic Trail pass through the forest. Georgetown Lake offers winter and summer recreation near Philipsburg. At the ghost towns of Elkhorn and Coolidge, you can relive Montana's boom and bust past. Sheepshead Recreation Area, north of Butte, offers pleasant picnicking and lake fishing, accessible for the disabled. The Forest covers 3.32 million acres.

Directions:
The headquarters in Dillon is located on Interstate 15 just 63 miles north of the Utah border.

Beaverhead-Deerlodge National Forest
USDA Forest Service
420 Barrett Street
Dillon, MT 59725-3572
Phone: 406-683-3900
Email:Mailroom_R1_Beaverhead_Deerlodge
@fs.fed.us
Reprinted from www.recreation.gov

didn't just stop with starting a cafe. He gathered up a lot of the scraps from the fading community and started a museum next door. Today the diner serves more than 30,000 customers a year. The guestbook logs visits from all over the world. It's certainly worth a stop.

32. *Gas, Food, Lodging*

Lima
This hamlet sits close to the Idaho border on the Red Rock River. Like many towns in Montana, it has gone through several name changes. First Allerdice, then Spring Hill. The name that stuck was Lima, named after the Lima, Wisconsin hometown of settler Henry Thompson.

33.

Monida
Monida gets its name from its proximity to the Montana-Idaho border. Monida was once an important stop on the old Utah & Northern narrow-gauge railway which ran from Salt Lake City to Butte and Garrison. It was also a stage stop for the Monida-Yellowstone Park stagecoaches that met the trains.

Yesterday's Cafe

34.

H Sawtell's Ranch
Red Rock Lakes National Wildlife Refuge

In 1868, Gilman Sawtell started a dude ranch and Henry's Lake fishery that did much to develop this natural resort area.

Sawtell did everthing from supplying swans for New York's Central Park zoo to building a network of roads for tourist access to Yellowstone National Park. His commercial fishery served Montana mining markets. His pioneer Henry's Lake ranch was a major attraction here for a decade before rail service brought more settlers to this area.

H The Shambo Stagecoach Station
Red Rock Lakes National Wildlife Refuge

The historic Shambo waystation was once located on the opposite side of Shambo Pond. The station served as a livery and overnight stop for the M & Y stage line (Monida and Yellowstone) which acted as a link between the railhead at Monida, Montana and Yellowstone National Park The original outfit consisted of twelve 11-passenger and four 3-passenger Concord coaches with eighty horses and forty employees in 1898.

By 1915 the line brought In over forty percent of the more than twenty thousand people who entered Yellowstone National Park. In that year the "Red Line" was operating forty-five 11-passenger four-horse coaches; eight 11-passenger four-horse stages; thirteen 3-passenger two-horse surries; and sixty-one 5-passenger two-horse surries.

It was a big-time operation. The M & Y Line sold three different excursion trips from Monida through the park with either a return to Monida or to and exit from another gateway. It took one day to get from Monida to Dwell's, a ranch-hotel near the western boundary of the park—a distance of approximately 70 miles.

The Shambo family managed this station and were among the earliest settlers in the Centennial Valley. This pond and immediate area still carry their name.

T Red Rock Lakes National Wildlife Refuge
85 miles southeast of Dillon. 276-3536

The Red Rock Lakes National Wildlife Refuge is one of more than 500 National Wildlife Refuges across the United States. The Refuge was established in 1935 for the protection of trumpeter swans and other wildlife. Visitors to the Refuge will find a wildlife watcher's paradise. Trumpeter swans, bald, eagles, peregrine falcons, moose, elk, sandhill cranes, and a number of other species are

Montana Trivia

R.E. Mather and F.E. Boswell describe the fatal Virginia City shooting of Deputy Dillingham in "Gold Camp Desperadoes":

...a Virginia City miners' court met to settle a claim dispute. The courtroom was a conical tent of willows interlaced with brush, which stood on the creek bank at the foot of Wallace Street. Though the tent was barely large enough to hold judge, clerk, plaintiff, defendant, and attorneys, curious spectators followed the proceedings by peeping through gaps in the brush. As Charley Forbes (the former Ed Richardson) sat at Judge William Steele's elbow taking notes [he was clerk of the court], deputies Buck Stinson and Hayes Lyons burst through the doorway and whispered something in Charley's ear. They then hurried outside to confront Deputy D.H. Dillingham. Charley followed a few steps behind. An argument had arisen a few days earlier when Dillingham had stated that Stinson, Lyons, and Forbes intended to rob a miner. Now as the deputies faced off a few steps from the willow tent, Lyons cursed at Dillingham and then demanded, "Take back those lies." As hands moved toward revolver butts, Charley cried, "Don't shoot, don't shoot!" From that point on, events moved too rapidly for observers to determine exactly what happened, but in the end Dillingham lay dead with a shot in the thigh and a second in the chest. Deputy Jack Gallagher disarmed Stinson, Lyons, and Forbes and ordered them bound with logging chains and placed under guard in a cabin on Daylight Creek. But the memory of the Carson City shackles was still strong in Charley's mind, and when his turn to be chained came, he refused, declaring he would rather die first. Six guards drew on him, however, and he was forced to submit to the chains and padlock.

often seen. Much of the Refuge lies within a 32,350-acre wilderness area that provides additional protection and habitat. The Refuge has been designated as a National Natural Landmark, recognizing its significance as one of the best remaining examples of the geologic and biologic character of our Nation's landscape.

For centuries, the Centennial Valley has been rich in fish and wildlife resources. Indians favored the Valley as a summer hunting area. Mountain men, trappers, cowboys, and settlers all left their mark on this remote corner of Montana. It was in this Valley and in Yellowstone National Park, that the last remaining trumpeter swans in the continental United States found refuge from the plume hunters of the early 1900s.

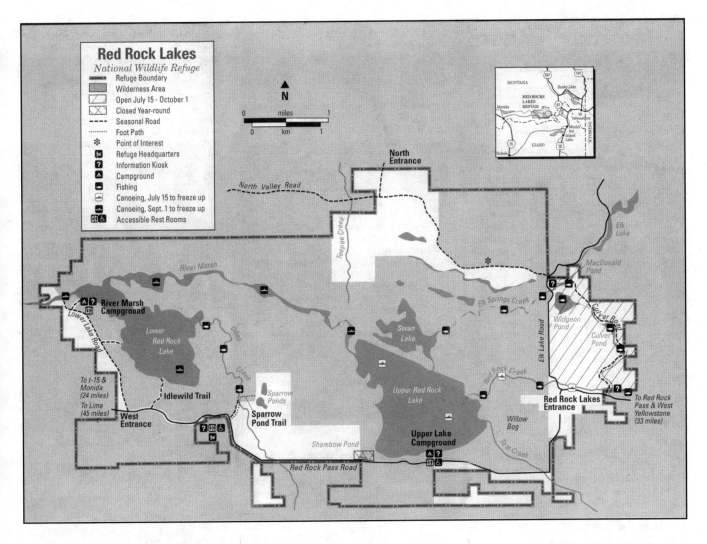

Red Rock Lakes
National Wildlife Refuge

- ▬ Refuge Boundary
- ▬ Wilderness Area
- ▭ Open July 15 - October 1
- ▨ Closed Year-round
- ---- Seasonal Road
- ········ Foot Path
- ✳ Point of Interest
- Refuge Headquarters
- ? Information Kiosk
- ⛺ Campground
- Fishing
- Canoeing, July 15 to freeze up
- Canoeing, Sept. 1 to freeze up
- Accessible Rest Rooms

Today, The Centennial Valley is known for its abundant wildlife, scenic beauty, primitive landscape, and secluded tranquility. The 45,000-acre Red Rock Lakes National Wildlife Refuge is an integral part of the Valley and helps to maintain a balance between human needs and the needs of wildlife.

SCENIC DRIVES

Highlands

The Highlands offer several opportunities for scenic drives accessing the Highland Lookout and Humbug Spires. One drive provides a scenic loop which winds through the Highlands and Burton Park and ends at the Feeley interchange on Interstate 15. From Butte take Montana Highway 2 south eight miles to Roosevelt Drive (Forest Service Road #84). Follow the road for 19 miles to Interstate 15. The drive provides scenic vistas of the Highland Mountains and meadows with opportunities to view moose, elk and deer throughout the drive. To return to Butte from the Feeley interchange, take I-15 north to Interstate 90 and continue east to Butte four miles. This drive will take approximately one and a half to two hours to complete and will accommodate two-wheel drive vehicles during the summer.

Delmoe Lake

From Whitehall, head west on Interstate 90 to the Pipestone exit just below Homestake Pass and continue north on Forest Service Road #222. The road will take you through sagebrush grasslands, into the timber, provide spectacular mountain vistas, and then return to Interstate 90 at Homestake pass 20 miles later. Approximately ten miles from Pipestone is Delmoe Lake campground and picnic area. Delmoe Lake has the same oblong rounded boulder landforms that you see along Homestake Pass. It also has fishing opportunities and a boat ramp (no docking facility). The drive will take you approximately one and half to two hours to complete and is maintained for two-wheel drive vehicles during the summer.

South Boulder, Tobacco Roots

This drive will take you up into a scenic canyon with high peaks, alpine meadows and lakes. From Whitehall, head east on Interstate 90 to the Cardwell exit where you will take Montana Highway 359 south approximately six miles to the South Boulder turnoff, heading southwest. The road turns into Forest Service Road #107 and continues for approximately 14 miles passing through the old mining town of Mammoth. The road will lead into the canyon through several dispersed recreation areas which are popular for picnicking. At the upper end of the canyon there are opportunities to park and take short hikes to several alpine lakes. The road can be rough. The first 13 miles can be traveled in a passenger car, but high clearance or 4-wheel drive is recommended beyond. The road is generally open from mid May to mid September depending on snow conditions. *Reprinted from U.S. Forest Service information handout.*

Red Rocks Lake Wildlife Refuge Tour

At one time, only a handful of the beautiful and graceful trumpeter swans remained in the Montana-Wyoming-Idaho area. To prevent their extinction in the area, Red Rock Lakes Wildlife Refuge in the Centennial Valley, was formed to offer the Trumpeters a refuge. Today, 400-500 swans call this area their home. Winter populations have been observed to reach as high as 1,500. Once you reach the refuge, the best place to observe the swans is in the open areas near Upper Red Rock Lake. April through September are the best viewing months. There are 18 other types of waterfowl at the refuge as well as moose, antelope, deer, and elk.

Depart from Dillon south on I-15. Clark Canyon Reservoir is 21 miles from Dillon. Great fishing and boating here (many public campgrounds and one marina.) Camp Fortunate Historical Point from Lewis and Clark journey.

Continue south on I-15 and drive 14 miles to Dell, Montana. From here you could elect to take the Sheep Creek/Medicine Lodge Backcountry Byway that ends back on Hwy 324—roads permitting. Also at Dell is the historic hotel that has been renovated and the old school house that is now a cafe.

From Dell, travel 9 miles south to Lima. Lima is a great little town with places to eat, sleep, camp, and a city park to picnic in.

From Lima continue on I-15 for 14 miles to Monida, Montana. Go through this tiny town, heading east on a gravel road. *Reprinted from Dillon Chamber of Commerce brochure.*

RED ROCK LAKES NATIONAL WILDLIFE REFUGE

A Quiet Retreat for Wildlife and People

Red Rock Lakes National Wildlife Refuge (NWR) was established in 1935 to protect the rare trumpeter swan. Today, this 45,000-acre Refuge continues to be one of the most important habitats in North America for these magnificent migratory birds. The Refuge lies in the eastern end of the Centennial Valley near the headwaters of the Missouri River. The Centennial Mountains border the Refuge on the south and east and catch the heavy snows of winter, providing a constant supply of water that replenishes the Refuge's 14,000 acres of lakes and marshes. The flat, marshy lands of the valley floor merge into the rolling foothills of the Gravelly Range to the north. This ideal habitat provides the solitude and isolation that are so essential to the trumpeter swan.

The Refuge includes a designated Wilderness Area and is also a registered National Natural Landmark. These special habitats are managed to retain as much of the wilderness character and landscape as possible. Likewise, public use is managed to provide visitors the rare opportunity to experience isolation and solitude.

Red Rock Lakes National Wildlife Refuge is one of more than 500 refuges in the National Wildlife Refuge System - a network of public lands set aside specifically for wildlife. The U.S. Fish and Wildlife Service manages these lands to conserve wildlife and habitat for people today and for generations to come.

Early Valley Visitors

The Centennial Valley was well known to the Bannock Indians as a favored travel route between the headwaters of the Big Hole River and Yellowstone country. Trapper Osborne Russell, in the mid-1800s, found many bison and signs of Blackfeet Indians in the valley. Settlement by the white man did not occur until 1876. With settlement, herds of livestock were driven into the valley, and homesteads sprang up at scattered locations.

In the early days, market hunting for waterfowl and big game brought some revenue to local residents, but most settlers concentrated on livestock and sporadic lumbering. The long winters, great distances to market, and small land parcels combined to make subsistence difficult. Few survived the depression of the 1930s. Visitors can still see some of the original homesteads on the Refuge today.

Return of the Trumpeters

The trumpeter swan once ranged over much of the interior of the United States, but their numbers decreased as they were shot for their plume feathers and as their habitat diminished. By the early 1900s, only a remnant population was left in the tri-state area of southwestern Montana, southeastern Idaho, and northwestern Wyoming, as well as in parts of Canada and Alaska. Less that 100 swans were in the tri-state area in 1935 when the Refuge was established. The Refuge provided protection and seclusion, and swan populations increased. Their slow, steady growth continued until the nesting population peaked in the early 1960s.

Current trumpeter swan summer populations for the tri-state area average about 400 birds. This population grows to more than 2,000 trumpeter swans during fall as migrating birds arrive from Canada. Most winter in the nearby Madison River Valley, at Ennis Lake, along the Henry's Fork River, and further south into Idaho. About 25 trumpeter swans winter in secluded sites on the Refuge.

During the winter, the birds are limited to the confines of the open water on the Refuge and elsewhere within the tri-state area. In earlier years, wildlife managers believed that naturally available foods were insufficient to maintain the growing population. As a result, grain was provided for the swans at MacDonald and Culver Ponds during the severe winters. Wintering swan numbers increased and became crowded enough on the small Refuge ponds to raise concern for the potential spread of diseases. In 1992, biologists throughout the traditional migration route of the swan agreed that the birds should be encouraged to migrate to areas with larger natural bodies of open water. Consequently, the feeding program was discontinued.

The U.S. Fish and Wildlife Service has intro-

duced swans from the Refuge to repopulate their former habitats in other areas. As a result, wild flocks of trumpeters are now reestablished in Oregon, Nevada, South Dakota, Nebraska, and Minnesota. Zoos and parks throughout the United States, Canada, and Europe exhibit trumpeter swans originating from Red Rock Lakes birds.

Wildlife Refuge Throughout the Seasons

The diverse habitats of the Refuge attract a variety of wildlife species throughout the year. Each spring, greater sandhill cranes nest in the Refuge meadows and marshes. These long-legged birds are most easily observed in the open areas near Upper Red Rock Lake from April through September. Their courtship display and dance take place in April and May. Great blue herons, willets, avocets, and long-billed curlews are other conspicuous waders and shorebirds that frequently nest on the Refuge.

The Refuge's lakes, marshes, and creeks provide attractive habitats for a multitude of ducks. Eighteen different kinds of waterfowl, including the Barrows goldeneye, raise their young here each year. In October and November, thousands of ducks and geese congregate on the Refuge before their southward migration. Tundra swans often make their appearance on the Refuge in November.

The timber-covered slopes and aspen stands on the south side of the Refuge prove attractive to blue and ruffed grouse and many different songbirds and raptors. Brewer's sparrows are among the more common sagebrush residents.

Moose are year-round residents, but most of the elk, deer, and pronghorn are forced to migrate out of Centennial Valley due to the severe winters. Refuge visitors will encounter other familiar mammals such as red fox, badger, striped skunk, and Richardson's ground squirrel.

Enjoy Your Visit

Feel free to enjoy recreational activities such as fishing, hunting, wildlife observation, photography, hiking, and camping at Red Rock Lakes NWR. The best time to visit the Refuge for most activities is from May through September.

Much of the Refuge can be seen from your car when the weather is good. To preserve the wilderness explorer spirit, there are no artificially-maintained back country hiking trails. Instead, nature provides many routes created by big game animals. You are welcome to cross-country hike throughout open areas of the Refuge, or follow big game routes and see the Refuge from the wildlife point of view.

Animals are best seen in the summer and fall during morning and evening hours. Visitors are encouraged to learn the habitats and behavior of specific animals, such as moose foraging in willow-covered streams, badgers digging holes in grasslands, and falcons swooping on concentrations of shorebirds. This is the key to successful wildlife viewing on the primitive, undeveloped landscape of the Refuge where artificial facilities have been minimized and wildlife is on the move.

Beginning in May, look for a myriad of wildflowers starting to appear on the Refuge. By July, the Refuge becomes a wildflower paradise. Shooting stars, buttercups, sticky geranium, and Indian paintbrush color the grasslands in hues of reds, pinks, blues, and yellows.

Staff is available at the Refuge headquarters during weekdays from 7:30 am to 4:00 pm to help you get oriented, answer questions, or provide more information.

Reprinted from U.S. Department of the Interior Fish and Wildlife Service pamphlet.

Glendale-Vipond Park Loop Tour
Take Interstate 15 north from Dillon 30 miles to Melrose exit.

Get off of I-15, turn left into Melrose. Do not take any turns but continue through Melrose, across the bridge over the Big Hole River. Head west on the gravel road approximately 7 miles where you will come to a fork in the road. Take the Canyon Creek Road on the right. Continue approximately 7 miles to the site of the town of Glendale. Just above the townsite, you will find the famous Charcoal Kilns, where coal was made for the silver extraction process. The kilns have been under restoration the past few years by the Forest Service.

In the summer/fall (when roads are dry) you can continue on past the town on the back country by-way through the scenic Vipond Park area that eventually comes out on Hwy 43 near the small town of Dewey. From here you can either return to Dillon by turning right and traveling back to I-15 or you can turn left and head west on Hwy 43 to Wise River and Wisdom.

Travel approximately 26 miles east to Lakeview and the Red Rock Lakes National Wildlife Refuge. Visit the Refuge Visitor Center. (This is an opportunity for great wildlife viewing and photography opportunities). Ask for road conditions and directions at the visitor center to return to Dillon via the scenic Blacktail Road. Elk Lake is also near this area. *Reprinted from Dillon Chamber of Commerce brochure.*

Yellowstone National Park via Virginia City
Leave Dillon on Hwy 41 and travel 28 miles to Twin Bridges. In Twin Bridges turn right on Hwy 287 heading southeast 30 miles to Nevada City and Virginia City. Stop and enjoy both of these towns reminiscent of frontier days in Montana… many displays, exhibits, museums, etc.

From Virginia City, continue on Hwy 287 to Ennis, another fun town to visit with several large sculptures on display along the main street.

From Ennis, go south on Hwy 287, 41 miles to junction on Hwy 87 and Hwy 287. Continue on Hwy 287 around Hebgen Lake. Take time to stop at the Earthquake Area Visitor Center. Continue the 22 miles to the junction of Hwy 287 and Hwy 191. Turn right and go 8 miles to West Yellowstone. Stop at the Visitor Center for information concerning the Park. *Reprinted from Dillon Chamber of Commerce brochure.*

HIKES

Whitehall Boulder Area
Lost Cabin Lake Trail #150 (National Recreation Trail) Tobacco Root Mountains

The Lost Cabin Lake Trail begins at the west end of Bismark Reservoir. The trail is five miles in length, is well maintained and is on an easy grade. A few sections are steep, but they can be traveled by young persons or older individuals who are in good physical condition. The peaks surrounding the lake reach elevations above 10,000 feet. Mountain goats can often be seen on the cliffs to the south and east of the lake. Depending on snow, the trail is usually open from July 1 to the middle of October. Snow drifts on the trail may be abundant during years of late thaws.

From Interstate 90 take the Cardwell exit seven miles east of Whitehall. Take Montana Highway 359 south for approximately five miles to the South Boulder Road #107. Travel south on Road #107 for approximately 15 miles to the trailhead at Bismark Reservoir. Passenger cars can drive this road, but the last two miles are best traveled by high clearance vehicles.

Louise Lake Trail #168 (National Recreation Trail)

Louise Lake Trail offers very scenic views. This is a new trail 3.5 miles in length and replaces a shorter steeper trail that was hard to maintain and partly located on private land. Louise Lake is a high alpine lake cradled among the 10,000-foot peaks that surround the lake. Mountain goats can often be spotted on the sheer rock faces. The trail is open from July 1 to the middle of October. Snowdrifts on the trail may be abundant during years of late thaws.

From Interstate 90, take Cardwell exit seven miles east of Whitehall. Take Montana Highway 359 south for approximately five miles to South Boulder Road #107. Travel south on Road #107 approximately 15 miles to the trailhead at Bismark Reservoir. This road can be driven by passenger cars, but the last two miles are best traveled by a high clearance vehicles.

Brownback Trail #156
Brownback Trail follows Brownback Gulch, a scenic narrow rocky canyon. The lower portion of the trail is mostly open country covered with grass, shrubs, and a few trees. It offers viewing of wildflowers, occasionally elk, deer, and a variety of other plants, animals, and birds. The trail is four miles long one way, and has an easy grade. The trail is open from mid May to mid November. This is a good trail to hike when the rest of the high country is still snowed in.

From Interstate 90, take the Cardwell exit seven miles east of Whitehall. Take Montana Highway 359 south for approximately five miles to South Boulder Road #107.

Travel south on Road #107 for four miles. Just past the Indiana University Geological Field station turn right on Forest road #5104 and travel one mile to the trailhead. There is parking for several cars and a horse unloading ramp. *Reprinted from U.S. Forest Service pamphlet*

"M" Trail
The "M" that looks down on Montana Tech was constructed in 1910 by students. Since its construction it has been fitted with lights so it can be seen at night. Unlike the "M"s in Missoula and Bozeman, you can actually drive up to the base of this landmark or hike to it from the college. It does provided some excellent views of the city. To get there take the Montana St. Exit on I-90 and head north to Park Ave. Go left to Excelsior St. and turn right. Follow Excelsior to Hornet and go left to the J.F. Kennedy Elementary School on Emmet and Hornet streets. Drive up the hill past the school for about .3 miles to a dirt road which turns to the left. Follow this to the turnaround just below the "M" and park.

Humbug Spires
is 26 miles south of Butte, Montana, along the western foot-hills of the Highland Mountains. It was designated a Primitive Area in 1972. About 8,800 acres of the 11,175-acre Humbug Spires Wilderness Study Area has been recommended for inclusion in the National Wilderness Preservation System.

Humbug Spires is characterized by rolling hills of Douglas fir and lodgepole pines accentuated by majestic granite spires. Lush meadows, dense forests and grassy flats are found throughout the area. Humbug offers many opportunities for primitive and unconfined recreation. The primary uses are hiking, stream fishing, rock climbing, backpacking, wildlife watching, nature photography, hunting, snowshoeing, cross country skiing and horseback riding.

To reach the area, take I-15 to the Moose Creek interchange and go east about 3 miles along the creek on an improved gravel road. Park at the trail head parking lot. To reach the hiking trail, cross the

foot bridge just downhill from rest room and the visitor information board. Humbug's main trail goes northeast from here along Moose Creek, passing through stands of Douglas fir trees more than 250 years old.

After about 1.5 miles, the trail forks. Take the right fork marked by white arrows. The trail continues for .3 miles up a small side drainage over a ridge, and then along the northeast fork of Moose Creek. From this drainage, numerous game trails leading in all directions are available to the adventurous hiker. These trails provide access to the rock spires located throughout the northern part of the area. To reach the "Wedge," one of the more prominent spires, continue 1.3 miles up the main trail along the intermittent creek. The Wedge is about a hundred yards uphill from an abandoned miner's cabin at the head of the drainage.

Given the diverse topography of the heavily timbered terrain, visitors hiking off the designated trail should have topographic maps, a compass, and drinking water. United States Geologic Survey 7-1/2 minute quadrangle maps cover the area and are available locally. You will need the Tucker Creek, Mount Humbug, Melrose and Wickiup quads for full coverage.

Offsite camping facilities are provided at BLM's Divide Bridge Campground, about 2 miles west of the Divide Interchange along Highway 43 on the west side of the Big Hole River. *Reprinted from BLM brochure.*

CROSS-COUNTRY SKI TRAILS

Beaverhead-Deerlodge National Forest

For more information contact District Ranger Dillon, MT 59725 (406) 683-3900

Elkhorn Hot Springs Ski Trails-37 mi. NW Dillon

233 km Most Difficult; no grooming
Trail begins at plowed parking lot near Elkhorn Hot Springs Resort Trail system consists of several loops with approximately 1000 ft of climb- Trail map available.

Birch Creek-21 mi. NW Dillon

5.0 km More Difficult; no grooming
Trail begins across Birch Creek bridge on the Birch Creek road about 1 mile west of the junction with the Willow Creek road. Trail map available.

INFORMATION PLEASE

All Montana area codes are 406

Road Information

Montana Road Condition Report
(800) 226-7623, (800) 335-7592 local 444-7696
Montana Highway Patrol   444-7696
Local Road Reports
  Butte   494-3666
  Statewide Weather Reports   453-2081

Tourism Information

Travel Montana (800) 847-4868 outside Montana
                             444-2654 in Montana
                          http://travel.mt.gov/.
Gold West Country 846-1943 or (800) 879-1159
                     www.goldwest.visitmt.com
Northern Rodeo Association   252-1122
Chambers of Commerce
Butte-Silver Bow   723-3177
Twin Bridges   684-5259
Virginia City   843-5555
Whitehall   287-2260

Airports

Butte   494-3771
Dell   444-2506
Twin Bridges   684-5574

Government Offices

State BLM Office   255-2885, 238-1540
Bureau of Land Management
  Billings Field Office   896-5013
  Butte Field Office   494-5059
Beaverhead/Deerlodge National Forest,
  Butte   522-2520
Helena National Forest   449-5201
Red Rock Lake Wildlife Refuge   276-3536
Montana Fish, Wildlife & Parks   994-4042
U.S. Bureau of Reclamation
  Dillon Field Office   683-6472
  Helena Field Office   475-3310

Hospitals

Highland View • Butte   782-2391
St. James Community Hospital • Butte 782-8361
Barrett Memorial Hospital • Dillon   683-2323
Ruby Valley Hospital • Sheridan   434-5536

Golf Courses

Beaverhead Golf Club • Dillon   683-9933
Red Rock Golf Course • Lima   276-3555
Highland View Golf Course • Butte   494-7900

Bed & Breakfasts

Bannock Pass Ranch • Dillon   681-3229

Bennett House Country Inn
  Virginia City   843-5220
The Centennial Inn • Dillon   683-4454
Copper King Mansion B&B • Butte   782-7580
Just An Experience • Virginia City   843-5402
Lynch's Lair B&B • Alder   842-5699
Gingerbread House • Virginia City   843-5471
Horse Prairie Inn • Dillon   681-3144
Healing Waters Lodge • Twin Bridges   684-5960
Iron Wheel Guest Ranch • Whitehall   494-2960
Montana Mountain Inn • Sheridan   842-7111
Ruby Valley Inn LLC • Virginia City   842-7111
Scott Inn Bed & Breakfast • Butte   723-7030
Stonehouse Inn • Virginia City   843-5504

Guest Ranches & Resorts

Hildreth Livestock Guest Ranch
  Dillon   681-3111
Fairmont Hot Springs Resort
  Fairmont   797-3241
Broken Arrow Lodge & Outfitters
  Alder   842-5437
Canyon Creek Guest Ranch • Melrose 276-3288
Centennial Guest Ranch • Ennis   682-7292
Crane Meadow Lodge • Twin Bridges   684-5773
Diamond J Ranch • Ennis   682-4867
Divide Wilderness Ranch • Lakeview 276-3300
Elk Lake Resort • Lima   276-3282
Great Waters Inn • Melrose   835-2024
Healing Waters Fly Fishing Lodge
  Twin Bridges   684-5960
Hidden Valley Guest Ranch • Dillon   683-2929
Madison Valley Ranch • Ennis   682-4514
Ruby Springs Lodge • Alder   842-5250
T Lazy B Ranch • Ennis   682-7288
Upper Canyon Ranch & Outfitting
  Alder   842-5884

Vacation Homes & Cabins

Arrow Cross Cabins • Dillon   835-2103
Back Country Angler • Dillon   683-3462
Beaverhead Rock Ranch Guest House
  Dillon   683-2126
Big Hole River Bunkhouse • Dillon   835-2501
Big Trout Ranch • Twin Bridges   684-5995
Centennial Outfitters • Lima   276-3463
CT Cabin Rentals • Dillon   683-2791
Goose Down Ranch • Dillon   683-6704
Hawke's Nest • Alder   842-5698
Jim McBee Outfitters • Dillon   276-3478
Rod & Rifle Inn • Sheridan   842-5960
Torrey Mountain Log Cabin Rental
  Dillon   683-4706

Forest Service Cabins

Beaverhead-Deerlodge National Forest
Hells Canyon Cabin

30 mi. SW of Whitehall, MT   287-3223
Capacity: 4   Nightly fee: $20   Available:
All year
Road to cabin not plowed. Access distance varies with snow conditions.

Black Butte Cabin

30 mi S of Ennis MT 20 mi NW on Standard Cr
Rd   682-4253
Capacity: 4   Nightly fee: $20   Available:
7/1 - 4/30
Depending on snow conditions, snowmobile travel may be necessary. Refer to Travel Plan Map regulations.

Canyon Creek Cabin

13 mi. W of Melrose, MT   832-3178
Capacity: 4   Nightly fee: $15   Available:
All year
Winter access varies with snow conditions, nor-

mally can drive to cabin with 4-wheel unit; otherwise, road may be blocked 6 miles from cabin.

Notch Cabin

41 mi S of Sheridan, MT   682-4253
Capacity: 3   Nightly fee: $20   Available:
7/2 - 12/1
Remote cabin. Access by road with 4-wheel drive vehicle. Access to Snowcrest Trail.

Antone Cabin

34 mi. SE of Dillon   682-4253
Capacity: 3   Nightly fee: $20   Available:
12/1-3/1
Depending on snow conditions, snowmobile travel of up to 6 miles may be required. Access is from Blacktail Road.

Vigilante

25 mi. S of Alder   682-4253
Capacity: 6   Nightly fee: $50   Available:
All year
Frame house w/2 bedrooms, living room, kitchen, electric lights. Water not available in fall & winter.

Fleecer

20 mi. SW of Butte   494-2147
Capacity: 6   Nightly fee: $40   Available:
11/1-5/1
Has electricity, heat, water. Winter access by snowmobile or skis.

High Rye

16 mi. SW of Butte   494-2147
Capacity: 4   Nightly fee: $20   Available:
5/15-12/1
High clearance vehicle access. Has three beds.

Car Rental

Avis Rent-A-Car   494-3131
Budget Rent-A-Car of Butte   494-7573
Enterprise Rent-A-Car   494-1900
Hertz Rent-A-Car   782-1054
U-Save Auto Rental   494-6001

Outfitters & Guides

F=Fishing H=Hunting R=River Guides
E=Horseback Rides G=General Guide Services
Four Rivers Fishing Company   GF 684-5651
Allman's Montana Adventure Trips G 843-5550
Al Wind's Trout Futures   F 684-5512
Atcheson Outfitting   H 782-2382
Back Country Angler   F 683-3462
Beaverhead Anglers   F 683-5565
Beavertail Outfitters   F 683-6232
Bloody Dick Outfitters   HFE 681-3163
Broken Arrow Lodge & Outfitters GE 842-5437
Cargill Outfitters   GHFE 494-2960
Centennial Outfitters   GHF 276-3463
Cougar Ridge Outfitters   HFE 2767-3288
Coyote Outfitters Inc   G 684-5769
Crane Meadow Lodge   GFH 684-5773
Curry Comb Outfitters   FH 276-3306
Dave Wellborn Outfitter   FH 681-3117
Diamond Hitch Outfitters   FHE 683-5494
Divide Wilderness Ranch   GHFW 276-3300
Eric Troth Fly Fishing Guide   F 683-9314
Experience Montana   FG 842-5134
Fish Montana/Bar Six Outfitters   F 683-4005
Five Rivers Lodge   F 683-5000
Flatline Outfitter & Guide Service GF 684-5639
Frontier Anglers   HF 683-5276
Garrett's Guide Service   F 683-5544
Great Divide Outfitters   GHFE 267-3346
Greg Lilly Fly Fishing Services GF 684-5960
Harmon's Fly Shop   F 842-5868
Horse Prairie Outfitters   HF 681-3173
Jim McBee Outfitters & Guides   HF 276-3478

Last Best Place Tours	G 681-3131	Tim Tollett's Frontier Anglers	GF 683-5276
Lone Tree Fly Goods	F 683-2090	Tom's Fishing & Bird Hunting Guide Service
M&M Outfitters	HF 683-4579		GF 723-4753
Montana High Country Tours	FG 683-4920	Watershed Fly Fishing Adventures F 683-6660
Montana Peaks Fly Fishing	F 683-3555	Uncle Bob's Fishing Supplies	GF 683-5565
Mossy Horn Outfitters	HFE 491-2236	Upper Canyon Ranch & Outfitting GE 842-5884
Southwest Montana Fishing Co.	F 842-5364	Watershed Fly Fishing Adventures GF 683-6660
Sundown Outfitters	GHEF 835-2751		

Cross-Country Ski Centers
Elkhorn Hot Springs
50 mi. NW of Dillon   586-9070

Snowmobile Rentals
All Seasons Adventures • Butte   723-4637

PRIVATE CAMPGROUNDS

Campsite Directions

	Season	Tent	RV	Water	Electric	Sewer	Dump	Shower	Laundry	Store
ALDER										
Alder/Virginia City KOA										
842-5677 or 842-5671 • (800) KOA-1898 • 9 mi. W of Virginia City on MT 287	All Year	18	32	•	•	•	•	•	•	•
BUTTE										
2 Bar Lazy H RV Park and Campground										
782-5464 or 782-1947 • I-90 Exit 122, .4 mi W	All Year		24	•	•	•	•	•	•	•
Butte KOA										
782-0663 or 782-8080 • (800) 562-8089 • I-90 Exit 126, 1 blk N, 1 blk E	4/15-10/31	20	100	•	•	•	•	•	•	•
Fairmont RV Park and Country Store										
797-3505 • 866-797-3505 • I-90 Exit 211, 2.5 mi SW	4/15-10/15	50	86	•	•	•	•	•	•	•
Pipestone Campground										
287-5224 • 888-287-5224 • I-90. 17 mi E of Butte. Pipestone Exit 241	4/1-10/15	20	55	•	•	•	•	•	•	•
DILLON										
Armstead Campground										
683-4199 • 20 mi S on I-15, Clark Canyon Exit 44	All Year	50	45	•	•	•	•	•	•	•
Countryside RV Park										
683-9860 or 660-8177 • 3 mi S of Dillon on I-15 Exit 59, Hwy 278	All Year	20	44	•	•	•	•	•	•	•
Dillon KOA										
Ph Fax 683-2749 • (800) KOA-2751 • 1-15 Exit 63 to MT St. R on Reeder to Park St	4/1-10/31	30	68	•	•	•	•	•	•	•
Skyline RV Park										
683-4692 or 683-5642 • 2.5 mi N of Dillon on Hwy 91 N	All Year	10	35	•	•	•	•	•	•	•
Southside RV Park										
683-2244 • 1-15 Exit 62, turn right on Poindexter St	3/1-12/1		40	•	•	•	•	•	•	•
VIRGINIA CITY										
Virginia City Campground and RV Park										
888-833-5493 • 843-5493 • 1/2 mi E end of town	5/31-9/6	15	15	•	•	•	•	•	•	•

NOTES:

BUTTE, DILLON, & VIRGINIA CITY AREA

PUBLIC CAMPGROUNDS

Campsite Directions

	Season	Camping	Trailers	Toilets	Water	Boat Launch	Fishing	Swimming	Trails	Stay Limit	Fee
87•Delmoe Lake FS Homestake Exit off I-90 E of Butte•10 mi. on Forest Rd. 222	5/26-9/17	25	32'	•	•	•	•	•		16	•
88•Toll Mountain FS 15 mi. W of Whitehall on MT 2•3 mi. N on Forest Rd. 240	5/25-9/15	5	22'	D					•	16	
89•Pigeon Creek FS 15 mi. W of Whitehall on MT 2•5 mi. S on Forest Rd. 668.	5/25-9/15	6		•			•		•	16	
90•Divide Bridge BLM 2.5 mi. W of Divide on MT 43	All Year	25	24'	D	•	A	•		B	14	
91•Humbug Spires BLM I-15 S of Divide•Moose Creek Exit•3 mi. NE on Moose Creek Rd.	All Year	•	24'	•					B	14	
92•Maidenrock FWP I-15 at Melrose•Milepost 93•6 mi. W & N on Cty. Rd.	All Year	30	•	•	•	B	•			7	
93•Barretts Park USBR 5 mi. S of Dillon on I-15	All Year	•	•	D	•	B	•			14	
94•Bannack FWP 5 mi. S of Dillon on I-15•21 mi. W on Rt. 278•4 mi. S on Cty. Rd.	All Year	20	•	D	•					7	•
95•Mill Creek FS 7 mi. E of Sheridan on Mill Creek Rd.	6/1-10/31	13	22'	•	•f					16	
96•Ruby Reservoir BLM S of Twin Bridges on MT 287 to Alder•S to E shore of Ruby River Reservoir	All Year	10	35'	•		C	•	•		14	
97•Cottonwood FS 36 mi. S of Alder•Follow Ruby Reservoir Rd. off MT 287	5/26-11/30	10f	•	•							
98•East Creek FS 8 mi. SW of Lima on Cty. Rd. 1791•1 mi. S on Forest Rd. 3929•1 mi. SE on Forest Rd. 3930	5/15-10/1	4	16'							16	
99•CLARK CANYON RESERVOIR USBR•Lonetree USBR Clark Canyon Reservoir•20 mi. S of Dillon on I-15	All Year	•	•	D	•	B	•			14	
100•CLARK CANYON RESERVOIR USBR•Hap Hawkins USBR Clark Canyon Reservoir•20 mi. S of Dillon on I-15	All Year	•	•	D	•					14	
101•CLARK CANYON RESERVOIR USBR•West Cameahwait USBR Clark Canyon Reservoir•20 mi. S of Dillon on I-15	All Year	•	•	d						14	
102•CLARK CANYON RESERVOIR USBR•Cameahwait USBR Clark Canyon Reservoir•20 mi. S of Dillon on I-15	All Year	•	•	D	0					14	
103•CLARK CANYON RESERVOIR USBR•Horse Prairie USBR Clark Canyon Reservoir•20 mi. S of Dillon on I-15	All Year	•	•	D		C				14	
104•CLARK CANYON RESERVOIR USBR•Lewis & Clark Clark Canyon Reservoir•20 mi. S of Dillon on I-15	All Year	•	•	D						14	
105•CLARK CANYON RESERVOIR USBR•Fishing Access USBR Clark Canyon Reservoir•20 mi. S of Dillon on I-15	All Year	•	•	D		C				14	
106•CLARK CANYON RESERVOIR USBR•Beaverhead USBR Clark Canyon Reservoir•20 mi. S of Dillon on I-15	All Year	•	•	D		C				14	
107•Beaver Dam FS 5 mi. W of Butte on I-90•12 mi. S on I-15•6 mi. W on Forest Rd. 96	5/25-9/15	15	50'	•	•		•		•	16	•
108•Dinner Station FS 12 mi. N of Dillon on I-15•12 mi. NW on Birch Creek Rd.	5/15-9/15	7	16'	D	•		•		•	16	

Agency
FS—U.S.D.A Forest Service
FWP—Montana Fish, Wildlife & Parks
NPS—National Park Service
BLM—U.S. Bureau of Land Management
USBR—U.S. Bureau of Reclamation
CE—Corps of Engineers

Camping
Camping is allowed at this site. Number indicates camping spaces available
H—Hard sided units only; no tents

Trailers
Trailer units allowed. Number indicates maximum length.

Toilets
Toilets on site. D—Disabled access

Water
Drinkable water on site

Fishing
Visitors may fish on site

Boat
Type of boat ramp on site:
A—Hand launch
B—4-wheel drive with trailer
C—2-wheel drive with trailer

Swimming
Designated swimming areas on site

Trails
Trails on site
B—Backpacking   N—Nature/Interpretive

Stay Limit
Maximum length of stay in days

Fee
Camping and/or day-use fee

Fishery

Fishery	Cold Water Species												Warm Water Species										Services					
	Brook Trout	Mt. Whitefish	Lake Whitefish	Golden Trout	Cutthroat Trout	Brown Trout	Rainbow Trout	Kokanee Salmon	Bull Trout	Lake Trout	Arctic Grayling	Burbot	Largemouth Bass	Smallmouth Bass	Walleye	Sauger	Northern Pike	Shovelnose Sturgeon	Channel Catfish	Yellow Perch	Crappie	Paddlefish	Vehicle Access	Campgrounds	Toilets	Docks	Boat Ramps	MotorRestrictions
78. Big Hole River	•	•				•	•																•	•	•		•	
79. Beaverhead River		•				•	•																•	•	•		•	
80. Poindexter Slough		•				•	•																					
81. Blacktail Deer Creek	•	•			•	•																	•					
82. Branham Lakes	•																						•					
83. Twin Lakes	•									•		•											•	•	•		•	•
84. Ruby River Reservoir		•				•	•																•	•	•		•	
85. Ruby River		•			•	•	•																•	•	•			
86. Big Sheep Creek		•				•	•																•					
87. Red Rock River		•				•	•																					
88. Clark Canyon Reservoir		•				•	•					•											•	•	•	•	•	

NOTES:

Dining Quick Reference

Price Range refers to the average cost of a meal per person: ($) $1-$6, ($$) $7-$11, ($$$) $12-up. Cocktails: "Yes" indicates full bar; Beer (B)/Wine (W), Service: Breakfast (B), Brunch (BR), Lunch (L), Dinner (D). Businesses in bold print will have additional information under the appropriate map locator number in the body of this section. [wi-fi] next to business name indicates free wireless internet is available to customers.

RESTAURANT	TYPE CUISINE	PRICE RANGE	CHILD MENU	COCKTAILS BEER WINE	SERVICE	CREDIT CARDS	MAP LOCATOR NUMBER
Crazy Bear Pizza [wi-fi]	Pizza	$	Yes	B/W	L/D	Major	2
A & W Family Restaurant	Fast Food	$	Yes		L/D	Major	2
Borden's Cafe	American	$	Yes	Yes	B/L/D		2
Subway	Fast Food	$	Yes		L/D		2
Two-Bit Saloon & Grill	Regional American	$	Yes	Yes	B/L/D	Major	2
4B's Restaurant	Family	$	Yes		B/L/D	V/M/D	5
Arby's	Fast Food	$	Yes		B/L/D		5
Asia Gardens	Asian	$$			L/D	Major	5
Burger King	Fast Food	$	Yes		B/L/D		5
Kentucky Fried Chicken/A&W	Fast Food	$	Yes		L/D		5
McDonald's	Fast Food	$	Yes		B/L/D		5
Perkins Family Restaurant	Family	$/$$	Yes		B/L/D	Major	5
Pizza Hut	Pizza	$/$$	Yes	B	L/D	V/M/D	5
Plaza Royale Casino & Restaurant	American	$$		Yes	B/L/D	Major	5
Subway	Fast Food	$	Yes		L/D		5
Taco Bell	Fast Food	$	Yes		L/D		5
Taco John's	Fast Food	$	Yes		L/D		5
Wendy's	Fast Food	$	Yes		L/D		5
Dairy Queen	Fast Food	$	Yes		L/D		6
Lamplighter Inn	American	$$$	Yes	Yes	D	Major	6
Lydia's	Steakhouse	$$/$$$	Yes	Yes	D	Major	6
Silver Bow Pizza Parlor	Pizza	$	Yes	Yes	L/D	V/M	6
Pork Chop John's	Fast Food	$	Yes		L/D		7
Arctic Circle	Fast Food	$	Yes		L/D		7
Copper City Restaurant	American	$		Yes	B/L/D		7
Domino's Pizza	Pizza	$			L/D		7
El Taco	Fast Food	$	Yes		L/D		7
Hardee's	Fast Food	$	Yes		B/L/D		7
It's Greek To Me	Greek	$			L/D		7
Joe's Pasty Shop	Pastys	$		B/W	L/D		7
Little Caesar's	Pizza	$			L/D		7
Papa John's Pizza	Pizza	$	Yes		L/D		7
Taco John's	Fast Food	$	Yes		L/D		7
The Derby	American	$/$$	Yes	Yes	L/D	V/M	7
VJ's Restaurant [wi-fi]	Fine Dining	$/$$	Yes	Yes	B/L/D	Major	7
Uptown Cafe	Eclectic	$-$$$		Yes	L/D	Major	9
Pork Chop John's	Fast Food	$	Yes		L/D		9
Acoma Restaurant & Lounge	Continental	$$/$$$	no	Yes	L/D	Majors	9
Spaghettini's	Italian	$/$$	Yes	W/B	L/D	V/M	9
Columbian Garden Espresso	Coffee House	$	Yes		B/L	Major	9
Northwest Noodle 'n Wrap	Asian	$	Yes		L/D	V/M	9
Bonanza Freeze	Fast Food	$	Yes		L/D		9
Dairy Queen	Fast Food	$	Yes		L/D		9
El Taco Dos	Fast Food	$	Yes		L/D		9
Gold Rush Casino [wi-fi]	Family	$/$$	Yes	Yes	B/L/D/SB	V/M/D	9
Joker's Wild Restaurant	Family	$	Yes	Yes	B/L/D	Major	9
La Cosina Mexican Restaurant	Mexican	$$	Yes	Yes	L/D	V/M	9
M&M Bar & Cafe	American	$		Yes	B/L/D		9
Ming's Chinese Restaurant	Chinese	$/$$			L/D	V/M	9
Rancho Los Arcos Mexican	Mexican	$	Yes		L/D	V/M	9
Subway	Fast Food	$	Yes		L/D		9
Blue Anchor Cafe	Family	$—$$$	Yes	Yes	B/L/D		13
The Old Hotel	Fine Dining	$$		B/W	D	V/M	13
The Weaver's Studio	Coffee House	$					13
Three Rivers Cenex	Fast Food	$		B	L/D	Major	13
Sheridan Bakery & Cafe	Homestyle	$			B/L	Major	14
Prospector Drive-in	Fast Food	$	Yes		L/D		14
Ruby Hotel Steakhouse	American	$/$$		Yes	L/D		14
Inback Steakhouse	Steakhouse	$$/$$$	Yes	Yes	B/L/D	Major	15
Star Bakery	Gourmet	$$/$$$			B/L/D		16
Banditos at the Wells Fargo	Southwestern	$$/$$$	Yes	Yes	L/D/BR	V/M	16

All Montana Area Codes are 406

Ultimate Yellowstone Park Atlas and Travel Encyclopedia

Dining Quick Reference-Continued

Price Range refers to the average cost of a meal per person: ($) $1-$6, ($$) $7-$11, ($$$) $12-up. Cocktails: "Yes" indicates full bar; Beer (B)/Wine (W), Service: Breakfast (B), Brunch (BR), Lunch (L), Dinner (D). Businesses in bold print will have additional information under the appropriate map locator number in the body of this section. [wi-fi] next to business name indicates free wireless internet is available to customers.

RESTAURANT	TYPE CUISINE	PRICE RANGE	CHILD MENU	COCKTAILS BEER WINE	SERVICE	CREDIT CARDS	MAP LOCATOR NUMBER
Bob's Place	Deli	$$	Yes		L/D	V/M	16
Lynch's Virginia City Cafe	Family	$/$$		Yes	B/L/D		16
Madison Dinner House	American	$/$$$	Yes		B/L/D	Major	16
Mexican Frank's Restaurant	Fast Food	$	Yes		L/D		16
Roadmaster Grill	American	$-$$$		B/W	B/L/D	Major	16
Arby's	Fast Food	$	Yes		B/L/D		18
Four B'S Restaurant	Family	$-$$	Yes		B/L/D	Major	18
Thad's Flying J Restaurant	Family	$	Yes		B/L/D	Major	18
Big Hole River Inn	Family	$$		Yes	B/L/D		19
Melrose Cafe	Family	$			L	V/M	19
Kentucky Fried Chicken	Fast Food	$	Yes		L/D		24
McDonald's	Fast Food	$	Yes		B/L/D		24
Pizza Hut	Pizza	$/$$	Yes	B	L/D	V/M/D	24
Subway	Fast Food	$	Yes		L/D		24
The Lion's Den	American	$$$	Yes	Yes	L/D	V/M/D	24
Best Western Paradise Inn	Family	$$		Yes	B/L/D	Major	24
Sweetwater Coffee [wi-fi]	Coffee House	$			B/L		25
Blacktail Station [wi-fi]	Steaks & Seafood	$$/$$$	Yes	Yes	L/D	Major	25
Klondike Cafe & Supper Club	Family	$$		Yes	B/L/D	V/M	25
Las Carmelitas	Mexican	$	Yes		L/D	V/M/D	25
Papa T'S	Family	$/$$	Yes	Yes	L/D	V/M	25
Stageline Pizza	Pizza	$/$$			L/D		25
Rookies	Family	$/$$		Yes	B/L/D		25
Western Wok	Chinese	$$	Yes	Yes	L/D	Major	25
Crosswinds Restaurant	Family	$/$$			B/L/D	V/M	26
Dairy Queen	Fast Food	$	Yes		L/D		26
Blondies Burgers	Fast Food	$			L/D		26
Taco John's	Fast Food	$	Yes		L/D		26
Yesterday's Café	Family	$/$$	Yes		B/L/D		31
Jan's Cafe 'n' Cabins	Family	$/$$	Yes		B/L/D	V/M	32

NOTES:

Motel Quick Reference

Price Range: ($) Under $40 ; ($$) $40-$60; ($$$) $60-$80, ($$$$) Over $80. Pets [check with the motel for specific policies] (P), Dining (D), Lounge (L), Disabled Access (DA), Full Breakfast (FB), Cont. Breakfast (CB), Indoor Pool (IP), Outdoor Pool (OP), Hot Tub (HT), Sauna (S), Refrigerator (R), Microwave (M) (Microwave and Refrigerator indicated only if in majority of rooms), Kitchenette (K). All Montana area codes are 406. [wi-fi] next to business name indicates free wireless internet is available to customers.

HOTEL	PHONE	NUMBER ROOMS	PRICE RANGE	BREAKFAST	POOL/ HOT TUB SAUNA	NON SMOKE ROOMS	OTHER AMENITIES	CREDIT CARDS	MAP LOCATOR NUMBER
Rice Motel	287-5497	10	$				P	Major	2
Whitehall Super 8	287-5588	33	$$		HT	Yes	P/DA	Major	2
Butte Super 8 Motel [wi-fi]	494-6000	104	$/$$	CB		Yes	P/DA	Major	5
Best Western Butte Plaza Inn [wi-fi]	494-3500	134	$$$/$$$$	FB	IP/HT/S	Yes	P/D/M/R/L/DA	Major	5
Hampton Inn [wi-fi]	494-2250	91	$$$	CB	IP/HT	Yes	DA	Major	5
Comfort Inn Of Butte [wi-fi]	494-8850	150	$$$	CB	HT	Yes	P/DA	Major	5
Motel 6	782-5678	66	$$			Yes	P	Major	5
Red Lion Hotel [wi-fi]	494-7800	131	$$$		HT/IP	Yes	R/L/P	Major	5
Ramada Copper King Inn [wi-fi]	494-6666	148	$$$		IP/HT/S	Yes	P/D/L/M/R/DA	Major	6
Skookum Motel & Restaurant	494-2153	25	$$			Yes	D/L/P	Major	6
Holiday Inn Express [wi-fi]	494-6999	83	$$-$$$	CB		Yes	M/R/DA	Major	7
Days Inn [wi-fi]	494-7000	74	$$-$$$	CB	HT	Yes	P/M/R/DA	Major	7
Capri Motel	723-4391	30	$$	CB	HT	Yes	DA	Major	9
Finlen Hotel & Motor Inn	723-5461	50	$/$$			Yes	M/F	Major	9
Eddy's Motel	723-4364	28	$$			Yes	D/L	Major	9
King's Motel	684-5639	12	$$			Yes	K/R	Major	13
Hemingways Lodging & Fly Shop	684-5648	6	$			Yes	P	Major	13
Moriah Motel	842-5491	12	$$			Yes	DA	Major	14
Mill Creek Inn	842-5442	6	$$			Yes	D/L/DA/P	Major	14
Chick's Motel & RV Park	842-5366	4	$$			Yes	DA/P	Major	15
Stonehouse Inn	843-5504	5	$$$	FB			FB		16
The Bennett House Country Inn	843-5220	5	$$$	FB	HT	Yes		Major	16
Nevada City Hotel & Cabins	843-5382	30	$$-$$$$			Yes	P/DA	V/M/D	16
Fairweather Inn	843-5377	15	$$			Yes		Major	16
Rocker Inn	723-5464	50	$$			Yes	P/L/M/F	Major	18
Sportsman Motel	835-2141	8	$$			Yes	P	Major	19
GuestHouse Inns & Suites [wi-fi]	683-3636	58	$$/$$$		IP/HT	Yes	K/P/M/R/DA	Major	23
Comfort Inn [wi-fi]	683-6831	48	$$	CB	IP	Yes		Major	23
Super 8 Dillon [wi-fi]	683-4288	48	$$			Yes	P/M/R/DA	Major	24
Best Western Paradise Inn [wi-fi]	683-4214	65	$$		IP/HT	Yes	P/D/L	Major	24
Sacajawea Motel	683-2381	15	$			Yes	K/P	V/M/D	24
Sundowner Motel	683-2375	32	$$			Yes	P/K	Major	25
Centennial Inn Bed & Breakfast	660-2304								25
Metlen Hotel Bar & Cafe	683-2335	32	$						25
Creston Motel [wi-fi]	683-2341	22	$$			Yes	P/DA	Major	26
Red Rock Inn	276-3501	7	$$$			Yes	R/L	Major	31
Mountain View Motel & RV	276-3535	18	$			Yes	K/P/M/R	Major	32

NOTES:

SECTION 2

GALLATIN RIVER AREA AND MADISON RIVER VALLEY

INCLUDING BOZEMAN, BIG SKY, ENNIS, THREE FORKS AND WEST YELLOWSTONE

Majestic Lone Mountain towers over the Big Sky area.

1. *Gas, Food, Lodging*

Bozeman

Bozeman is nestled in the midst of the pristine jewel of the Rockies, the Gallatin Valley. Located in the "Heart of Yellowstone Country" just 90 miles north of Yellowstone National Park, Bozeman is sophisticated, yet down to earth. It is happily isolated in the open and beautiful "Valley of the Flowers," as early Native Americans named it, yet remains almost entirely surrounded by the Rockies. The Bridger Mountains rise ruggedly on the east, the Tobacco Roots to the west, the Big Belts to the north and the Spanish Peaks and Gallatin Range to the south.

Bozeman was named after John Bozeman, who blazed a trail across Wyoming and in 1864 guided the first train of immigrants into the Gallatin Valley. When the first wagon train made its way through the canyon, frontiersman Jim Bridger was leading the way, thus the canyon, mountain range, and area trails now bear his name.

The area of Bozeman is brimming with adventure and an abundance of outdoor recreational possibilities, one of the most popular being fly fishing. The rivers, streams, and lakes in the region provide some of the finest fly fishing in the world with a backdrop of spectacular scenery. Over 2,000 miles of blue-ribbon trout streams weave through this sportsman's paradise, while golf courses, first-class tennis courts, indoor and outdoor pools and hot springs make Bozeman a city of diverse recreational opportunities. Just

minutes away is the Bridger Bowl ski area featuring 1,200 acres inside the Gallatin National Forest. Ski the well groomed slopes of 50 different runs.

The Yellowstone, Gallatin, and Madison rivers provide excellent rafting and kayaking for whitewater enthusiasts travelling to the Bozeman area, while the Gallatin National Forest is a wonderful place for nature or pleasure hikes.

Bozeman is an exceptional town offering many opportunities for recreational experiences, while retaining its flavor as a thriving arts and culture community. Here culture and entertainment are as abundant as the blue sky. Bozeman uniquely combines the classic Old West with the comforts and amenities of the new. Bozeman boasts art galleries, historic museums, symphony,and the state's only opera company. It is also home to the main campus of Montana State University, the Museum of the Rockies, and Compuseum.

H Gallatin Valley
Hwy 10, east of Bozeman

Captain Wm. Clark, of the Lewis and Clark Expedition, with a party of ten men, passed through this valley July 14, 1806, eastward bound, and guided by the Shoshone woman, Sacajawea. They camped that night at the toe of the mountains on the eastern edge of the valley. Captain Clark wrote in his journal: "I saw Elk, deer and Antelopes, and great deel of old signs of buffalow. their roads is in every direction…emence quantities of beaver on this Fork … and their dams very much impeed the navigation of it."

In the early 1860s John Bozeman, young adventurer, and Jim Bridger, grand old man of the mountains, guided rival wagon trains of emigrants and gold-seekers through here over the variously called Bonanza Trail, Bridger Cutoff, or Bozeman Road, from Fort Laramie, Wyo., to Virginia City, Mont. The trail crossed Indian country in direct violation of treaty and was a "cut off" used by impatient pioneers who considered the time saving worth the danger. Traffic was not congested.

L Bozeman's Western Heritage Inn
1200 E. Main St., Bozeman. 586-8534 or (800) 877-1094. www.westernheritageinn.com; info@westernheritageinn.com

Located near the center of Bozeman, Montana's renowned year-round playground, The Western Heritage Inn provides convenient access to Yellowstone, hiking, fishing, skiing, and more. For those who love shopping, the inn is a 10-minute walk from historic downtown and its many upscale stores and eateries. While you're not enjoying the area's abundant recreation and attractions, relax in comfort. The Western Heritage Inn provides non-smoking rooms featuring king and queen beds, movie channels, extended stay suites, family suites with full kitchens, bridal suites, deluxe continental breakfast, guest laundry, and free high-speed wireless DSL. The Inn's indoor whirlpool, therapeutic steam room, and Wolff

Bozeman	Jan	Feb	March	April	May	June	July	Aug	Sep	Oct	Nov	Dec	Annual
Average Max. Temperature (F)	31.3	35.3	42.2	53.6	63.1	71.5	81.0	80.2	69.1	57.4	42.0	33.6	55.0
Average Min. Temperature (F)	11.8	15.1	21.1	30.5	38.5	45.2	51.0	49.5	41.1	32.8	22.1	14.6	31.1
Average Total Precipitation (in.)	0.88	0.73	1.34	1.81	2.87	2.88	1.35	1.23	1.74	1.48	1.08	0.86	18.26
Average Total SnowFall (in.)	12.8	10.2	16.1	12.3	4.3	0.5	0.0	0.1	0.8	5.4	11.0	11.6	85.1
Average Snow Depth (in.)	5	5	3	1	0	0	0	0	0	0	2	3	2

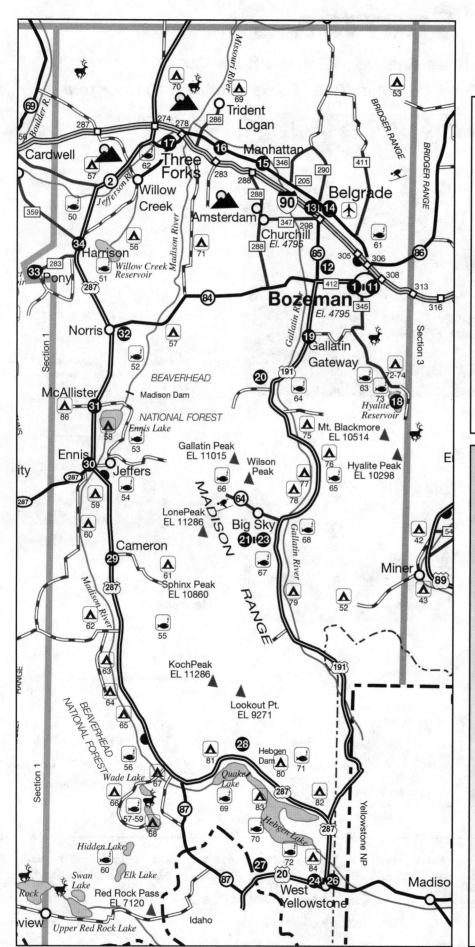

0 _____ Miles _____ 11 _____ 20
One inch = approximately 11 miles

Legend

00	Locator number (matches numeric listing in section)
	Wildlife viewing
00	Campsite (number matches number in campsite chart)
	State Park
00	Fishing Site (number match-es number in fishing chart)
	Rest stop
	Interstate
	U.S. Highway
	State Highway
	County Road
	Gravel/unpaved road

ON THE TRAIL OF LEWIS & CLARK

Clark's advance party had reached the Three Forks of the Missouri on July 25. They saw the prairie had recently been burned, and there were horse tracks which appeared to be only a few days old. Clark left a note for Lewis telling him he was going to continue on in search of the Shoshones; if he didn't find them he would return to the Three Forks.

The main party arrived at the Three Forks on July 27, making camp where Clark had left the note. Lewis ascended a prominent rock bluff to view the area which he believed "to be an essential point in the ge-ography of this western part of the Continent."

The officers named the east fork of the Three Forks in honor of Treasury Secretary, Albert Gallatin, the south fork in honor of Secretary of State James Madison, and the west fork in honor of President Jefferson.

On their westward journey the band camped near here for two days for rest and repairs and heard Sacajawea tell of her abduction by Hidatsa raiders five years earlier as her band of Shoshone camped at the same spot.

On the return trip Clark's party separated at the Three Forks. Sergeant John Ordway and nine men continued down the Missouri with the dugouts. Clark and the rest of the party headed east along Gallatin River on to explore the Yellowstone River. Clark crossed Clark's Pass (the current Bozeman Pass), and hit the Yellowstone near present-day Livingston.

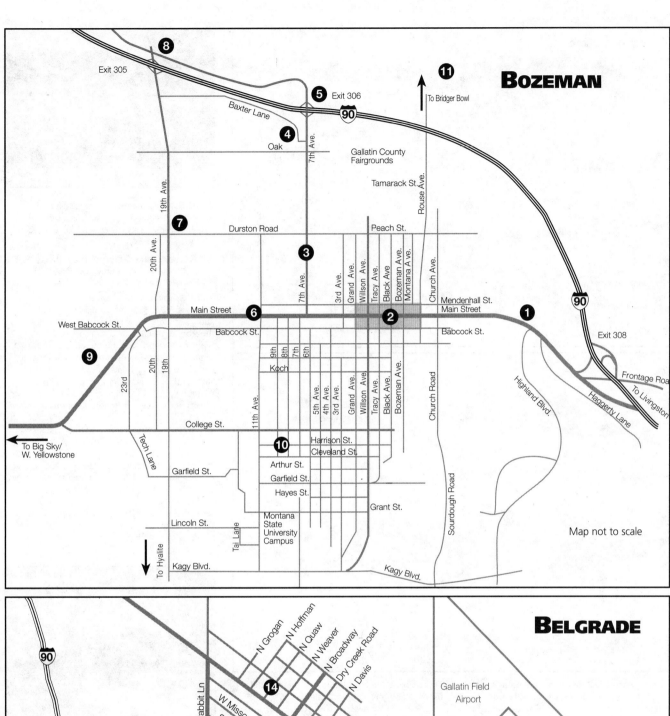

BOZEMAN

Exit 305

Baxter Lane

Oak

7th Ave.

Gallatin County Fairgrounds

Tamarack St.

Exit 306

To Bridger Bowl

90

19th Ave.

20th Ave.

Durston Road

Peach St.

7th Ave.

3rd Ave.

Grand Ave.

Wilson Ave.

Tracy Ave.

Black Ave.

Bozeman Ave.

Montana Ave.

Church Ave.

Rouse Ave.

Main Street

West Babcock St.

Babcock St.

Mendenhall St.
Main Street

Babcock St.

9th 8th 7th 6th

Koch

20th 19th

23rd

11th Ave.

5th Ave.

4th Ave.

3rd Ave.

Grand Ave.

Wilson Ave.

Tracy Ave.

Black Ave.

Bozeman Ave.

Church Road

Highland Blvd.

Haggerty Lane

Frontage Road

To Livingston

Exit 308

90

To Big Sky/
W. Yellowstone

College St.

Tech Lane

Harrison St.
Cleveland St.

Arthur St.

Garfield St.

Garfield St.

Hayes St.

Grant St.

Sourdough Road

Lincoln St.

Montana State University Campus

Tai Lane

Kagy Blvd.

Kagy Blvd.

To Hyalite

Map not to scale

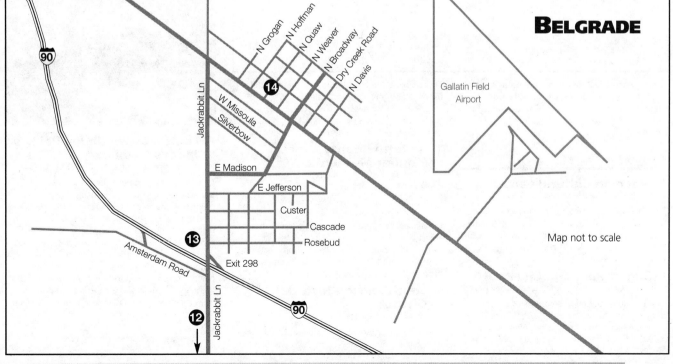

BELGRADE

90

Jackrabbit Ln

N Grogan

N Hoffman

N Quaw

N Weaver

N Broadway

Dry Creek Road

N Davis

Gallatin Field Airport

W Missoula

Silverbow

E Madison

E Jefferson

Custer

Cascade

Rosebud

Amsterdam Road

Exit 298

Jackrabbit Ln

Map not to scale

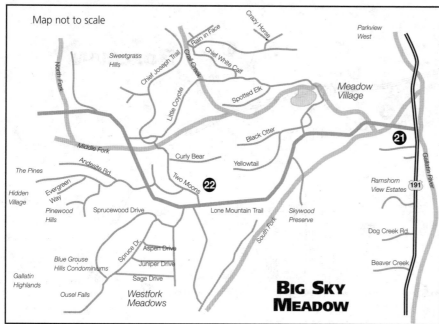

Map not to scale

Sweetgrass
Hills

North Fork

Chief Joseph Trail

Rain in Face

Crazy Horse

Chief White Calf

Coral Creek

Little Coyote

Spotted Elk

Parkview
West

Meadow
Village

Middle Fork

Andesite Rd.

Black Otter

Curly Bear

Yellowtail

21

The Pines

Evergreen
Way

Two Moons

22

Gallatin River

Hidden
Village

Pinewood
Hills

Sprucewood Drive

Lone Mountain Trail

Skywood
Preserve

Ramshorn
View Estates

191

Spruce Dr.

Aspen Drive

South Fork

Dog Creek Rd.

Blue Grouse
Hills Condominiums

Juniper Drive

Beaver Creek

Gallatin
Highlands

Sage Drive

Ousel Falls

Westfork
Meadows

BIG SKY MEADOW

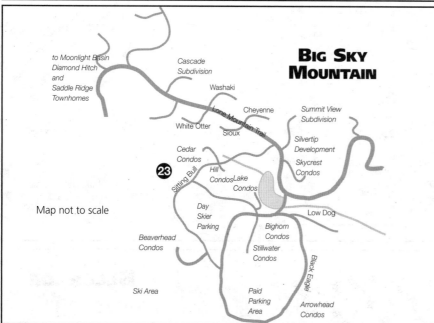

to Moonlight Basin
Diamond Hitch
and
Saddle Ridge
Townhomes

Cascade
Subdivision

BIG SKY MOUNTAIN

Washaki

Lone Mountain Trail

Cheyenne

Summit View
Subdivision

White Otter

Sioux

Silvertip
Development

Cedar
Condos

Skycrest
Condos

23

Sitting Bull

Hill
Condos

Lake
Condos

Day
Skier
Parking

Low Dog

Beaverhead
Condos

Bighorn
Condos

Stillwater
Condos

Black Eagle

Ski Area

Paid
Parking
Area

Arrowhead
Condos

Map not to scale

System tanning beds add to the inn's long list of amenities. Discover for yourself a place where comfort and the Rocky Mountains come together, and become one of the Western Heritage Inn's valued guests!

2. *Gas, Food, Lodging*

T Emerson Cultural Center
111 S. Grand Ave., Bozeman. 587-9797

The Emerson Cultural Center is home to many visual and performing arts as well as galleries that rotate exhibits of contemporary, Native American and local artists' work. Art related activities are sponsored through this community center.

T Bogert Park and City Pool
300 block of S. Church St. in Bozeman. 587-4724

If you want to cool off in an outdoor pool and enjoy a picnic in a nice shady park, this is a great place. On Saturday mornings beginning in July, the Farmer's Market fills the grounds. This is one of the largest and most popular farmer's markets in the state. Only items grown or made by the seller can be sold here, with lots of fresh flowers, fruits and vegetables, as well as baked goods and handmade crafts and clothing.

T Gallatin County Pioneer Museum
317 W. Main St. next to the courthouse in Bozeman. 582-3195

Located amidst the town of Bozeman is the Gallatin County Pioneer Museum which includes a former county jail, jailhouse isolation chambers, an actual gallows, a 12' x 14' hand-hewn log cabin, and various artifacts and exhibits that bring to life the county's colorful history. The museum is open year round and admission is free.

T South Willson Historic District
Willson St., Bozeman. 586-5421

The drive on Willson St. from the downtown area of Bozeman south takes you through a residential

district featuring houses that range from large mansions to small cottages, all preserved and maintained in the style they were originally constructed.

T American Computer Museum
2304 N. 7th Avenue in Bozeman. 582-1288.
www.compustory.com

The American Computer Museum offers insight into over 4,000 years of the history of computing and computers. View fascinating displays that tell the story of mechanical calculators, slide rules, typewriters, office machines, room-sized mainframe computers, an original Apollo Spacecraft Guidance Computer and astronaut items, the story of the personal computer, a working industrial robot, and the computer pioneer timeline. This is one of very few museums of this type in the world. You probably saw the American Computer Museum featured in the New Yorker Magazine, The New York Times, USA Today, and C-Span, to name a few. This fascinating and educational museum is an ideal family destination and no computer experience is required to enjoy. They are open seven days a week June through August. September through May they are open Tuesday through Saturday. Call ahead for hours. There is a modest admission charge. Visit them on the web for more information.

F Looie's Down Under, Rain, & Jadra's Sushi Bar
101 E. Main St., Bozeman. 522-8814.

Enjoy exquisite dining at the Looie's complex in the heart of Downtown Bozeman. There are two dining experiences to select from in this complex, which has housed the popular Looie's Down Under for eight years. Looie's Down Under serves a variety of choice steaks, seafood, and pasta. It is the perfect place for the Saturday and Sunday brunch buffet. Don't miss their Tuesday Crab Night! Looie's is open for lunch and dinner. Jadra's authentic sushi bar, Bozeman's original offers hand rolls, nigiri, and shahimi and is open for dinner. So many choices under one roof! Enjoy your favorite beer or wine at any of these fine restaurants. All are open seven days a week.

F Boodles
215 E. Main St., Bozeman. 587-2901.

Nestled in historic downtown Bozeman since 1997, Boodles is recognized as one of the Gallatin Valley's best fine dining establishments. Featuring a relaxed yet refined non-smoking atmosphere, Boodles warmly welcomes those celebrating in finery to individuals simply searching for a satisfying meal after a hard day's work. Guests are treated to hand cut steaks, fresh seafood, wild game, pasta, and nightly specials while receiving unsurpassed service from staff who delight in providing patrons with a memorable dining experience. Exquisite desserts, handcrafted cocktails featuring the freshest ingredients, and an extensive wine list showcasing over 225 bottled wines and 17 wines by the glass complement every meal. Boodle's full service bar is open Monday through Saturday from 3 pm to 2 am and dinner is served from 5:30 pm to 10 pm Reservations are suggested.

F Rocky Mountain Roasting Co.
777 E. Main St. & 111 E. Mendenhall, Bozeman. 585-0696 (Main St.) or 586-2428 (Mendenhall). www.rockymountainroasting.com; Hal@rockymountainroasting.com

Selecting, roasting, blending, and selling some of the world's best coffee, Rocky Mountain Roasting Company is a Bozeman staple. Opened in 1992, the company's legendary friendly service and unrivaled coffee selection soon outgrew its one Main Street location. Today, the company offers five locations in and around Bozeman/Belgrade and caters to every coffee preference with a range of beans selected from across the world. Upon arrival at the company, the organic-certified beans are fresh roasted daily into small batches. Wake up to the bold Jim Bridger Blend or slip into the dark Beartooth Blend. Can't visit in person? The company proudly roasts, hand packs, and ships their beans daily throughout the continental US for a flat fee of just $4.95. Experience great coffee with great service, and discover the "Roast of the Rockies."

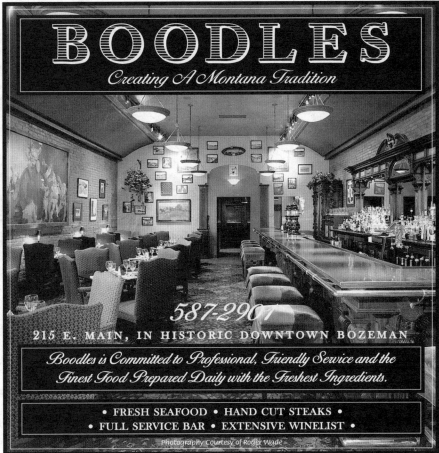

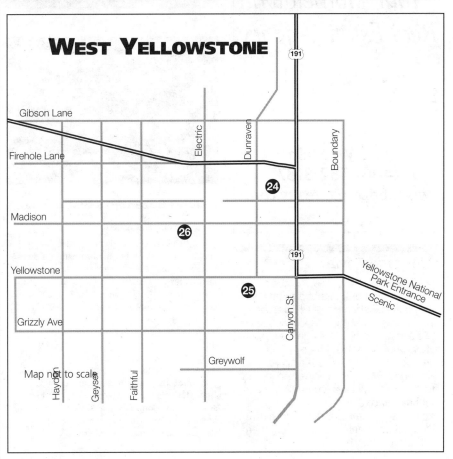

WEST YELLOWSTONE

Montana Trivia

In 1984, the Big Sky area was the scene of a Wild West drama that captured and held national attention. Kari Swenson, a world-class biathlete, was kidnapped by two self-professed mountain men. Soon after, Don Nichols and his son Dan shot and killed a would-be rescuer and wounded Swenson. They escaped and for five months were hunted by Sheriff Johnny France of Madison County, a former rodeo champion. A tip led him to their camp where he captured them without firing a shot.

F John Bozeman's Bistro
125 W. Main, Bozeman. 587-4100.
www.johnbozemansbistro.com

The Bistro has been renowned for legendary cooking since its 1984 establishment in downtown Bozeman. It's no secret that this is a local favorite for its warm inviting atmosphere and eclectic menu. Chef/Owner Tyler Hill loves to cook, and everyone who has dined at The Bistro knows it! It doesn't matter if you are hungry for a traditional meal or something refreshing and different, this is where you'll find it. Enjoy a menu that offers selections of fresh fish, steaks, pasta, and international cuisine. To accompany your meal, they offer an assortment of beers from Montana microbrews as well as an extensive wine list. John Bozeman's Bistro is open for lunch and dinner Tuesday through Saturday. Reservations are recommended.

F The Nova Cafe
312 E. Main Street, Bozeman. 587-3973.
ww.thenovacafe.com or email:
thenovacafe@yahoo.com

The Nova Café in the heart of downtown Bozeman serves breakfast and lunch with a delightful selection of homemade baked pastries, muffins, and scones. Enjoy a break from the ordinary with unique and delightful daily specials such as lemon blackberry ricotta pancakes, crab cake benedict, stuffed French toast, homemade quiches or a prosciutto and asparagus omelet. Try a regular menu items such as made from scratch pancakes, award-winning turkey hash, Cajun frittata, duck salad or a Reuben sandwich with all the freshest ingredients. Mouthwatering breakfast selections are served with fresh Rocky Mountain Roasting CO. coffee and a full espresso bar. The Nova Café also offers a children's menu and gluten-free-baked goods. A changing exhibit of the works of local artists is featured in the restaurant. They serve breakfast from 7-2 and lunch from 11-2 and are open daily.

MONTANA BALLET

In the late 70s and early 80s ballet wasn't taken very seriously in Montana. Ann Bates, Artistic Director of Montana Ballet, appealed to state legislators for a portion of the state coal-tax arts money to no avail. She finally persuaded Rep. Francis Bardanouve that it was unfair to ignore dance while supporting other arts. Lawmakers subsequently awarded her a $10,000 grant. She sent the venerable Bardanouve a tutu which he gamely wore on his head.

Today Montana Ballet is the only small dance company in the rural west with big company goals: 1) To educate the youth of the Gallatin Valley in dance at the professional level; 2) To present a season of international dance companies, world-known ballet stars, and local talent of amazingly high caliber; and 3) To offer a variety of outreach opportunities to schools as far as 100 miles away from Bozeman.

Comments about productions reflect astonishment that the Bozeman area could be the home to a ballet company equal to comparable companies in much larger communities.

The motivation for this excellence stems from the pride Montana Ballet staff and Board of Directors take in making art that surprises and delights. Visiting companies for each Fall's international performance have included *Woofa* from New Guinea, *Tangokinesis* from Buenos Aires, *Jose Greco* from Madrid, and the *Dance Masters of Bali*.

The full season of Montana Ballet Company's performances also includes the much-anticipated and usually sold-out holiday *Nutcracker* extravaganza presented the first weekend of every December, coinciding with Bozeman's Christmas Stroll. Another favorite of the community is the *New York Connection* production presented as part of the two-week New York Connection workshop offered each August in association with Montana State University's College of Arts and Architecture. Professional dance teachers offer classes in a variety of subjects and join the dancers in the two culminating productions performing works by Balanchine as well as classical repertoire.

More information about Montana Ballet Company and its affiliate, the privately-owned Montana Ballet School, is available at www.montanaballet.com.

MF Leaf & Bean
35 W. Main in Historic Downtown Bozeman. 587-1580 or (800) 485-5646

Established in 1977, The Leaf & Bean is Bozeman's original coffee house and bakery, and is as well known for its gourmet fare as for its cozy atmosphere and community spirit. "The Bean" offers a full menu of espresso drinks and teas, and a huge variety of bulk coffee including many organic, shade-grown and fair-trade beans. You'll also find exceptional sandwiches, salads, and pastries. Live entertainment is featured several nights a week, and includes local bands, touring performers, bluegrass and jazz jams, and open-mic events. The Leaf & Bean received attention from Travel and Leisure and Bon Appetit magazines in 2004 and 2005, and is consistently voted Bozeman's Best Coffee in an annual local poll. Both locations showcase unusual gifts and art from regional studies, and offer children's play areas and wireless internet service. Open early and late seven days a week.

S Montana Gift Corral
237 E. Main St., Bozeman. 585-8625 or (800) 242-5055. www.giftcorral.com; bert@mtgiftcorral.com

The Montana Gift Corral offers sensational products by talented and creative artists. They bring you the best of Montana. Many of the outstanding craftsmen represented live right here in the Gallatin Valley, sharing the friendly western lifestyle the area is known for. Enjoy a complimentary cup of coffee and convenient parking behind the store. The helpful staff at this special store invites you to visit the home of breathtaking scenery, rodeos, magnificent wildlife, world famous trout streams, ski resorts, and museums. They are also located at Gallatin Field Airport, or check out their full selection of items on the web!

S The Gem Gallery
402 E. Main St., Bozeman. 587-9339 or (800) 856-3709. www.gemgallery.com; gemgallery@aol.com

The Gem Gallery is an exquisite jewelry store specializing in making custom, handcrafted jewelry. It is known and recognized for its large and impressive collection of rare Yogo Sapphires. Found only in Montana, Yogo Sapphires are all natural and untreated sapphires. They are renowned for their

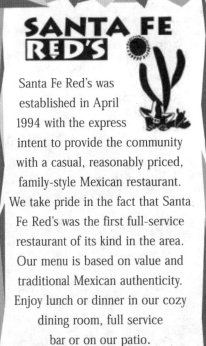

incredible cornflower blue color and are among the finest sapphires in the world. The Gem Gallery also offers fancy colored Montana Sapphires from different Montana mines that come in a rainbow of colors. Other featured precious gems at The Gem Gallery include exceptional-quality diamonds from Antwerp, Burmese rubies, and Tanzanites from Africa. Stop in and experience the vast selection offered alongside outstanding friendly service and quality provided by the award-winning goldsmiths comprising The Gem Gallery team.

S Absolutely Exquisite Furnishings & Gifts, Inc.
303 W. Mendenhall Street, Bozeman. 585-5447

Visit Absolutely Exquisite Furnishings and Gifts for an enchanting shopping experience in Downtown Bozeman on West Mendenhall Street. The store is located in a stunning 115 year-old Victorian home with plenty of convenient parking. Each delightful room presents a collection of exquisite gifts, furnishings, and accessories for any décor. Many of the featured items are exclusive works from local artists and craftsmen. You will enjoy discovering that hard to find gift or perfect accessory for your own home in one of the many themed rooms such as western, Victorian, rustic, cottage, kitchen, fantasy, Celtic. There are also garden and porch furnishings for entertaining or your own pleasure. Explore collections of jewelry, pottery, custom stained glass, and collectibles. Absolutely Exquisite Furnishings and Gifts is open Monday through Saturday.

M Bozeman Realty
612 W. Main St., Bozeman. 582-8187.
www.bozemanrealty.com; penny@bozemanrealty.com

Tired of being another face in the crowd in a long line of potential homebuyers and sellers?

It Happened in Montana

December 3, 1866. Nelson Story arrives in the Gallatin Valley (Bozeman area) with 3,000 longhorns. Not only did he fight his way through thousands of hostile Indians, but he also had to outwit the U.S. Army who wanted to turn back the expedition for its own safety. Story and his two dozen cowboys had to sneak the cattle past the Indians in the dark. Colonel Carrington offered to buy the cattle to provide beef for the soldiers at Fort Phil Kearney. Story declined. The cattle that he brought into the Gallatin Valley formed the nucleus for Montana's cattle industry.

Then discover the difference of Bozeman Realty. A small agency dedicated to traditional values of quality and honesty, Bozeman Realty is your one-stop source for Bozeman, Big Sky, and Belgrade real estate services and relocation information. While buyers receive access to free home buying reports, mortgage checklists, and glossaries of home buying terms, sellers receive a market analysis of their home along with helpful hints about obtaining the best price for their property. Integrity and personal service are always extended, and as local residents, the Bozeman Realty team has the answers to your Big Sky Country questions. Experience Bozeman Realty, and experience the difference of an agency committed to customers' best interests.

3. Gas, Food, Lodging

4. Gas, Food, Lodging

F Santa Fe Red's
1235 N. 7th Ave., Bozeman. 587-5838.

Santa Fe Red's has been providing Bozeman and the Gallatin Valley with a fun and festive, family-style Mexican Restaurant since 1994. They were voted "Best Mexican restaurant" in Bozeman's Tributary Magazine's Best of Bozeman 2005. Their menu is based on value and traditional Mexican authenticity using only the freshest ingredients and sauces made from scratch to provide a homemade taste. They offer specialty margaritas and have the most extensive selection of premium tequila anywhere in Montana. Enjoy lunch or dinner in your choice of the dining room, full service bar, sunroom or outside patio. A separate gaming room offers the newest and best keno and poker machines. So if you're local or just passing through, enjoy one of Bozeman's best and most popular hot spots, Santa Fe Red's

5. Gas, Food, Lodging

T East Gallatin Recreation Area
Griffith Drive, Bozeman

Known simply as "the Beach" by locals, the lake here has a 300 acre beach front which is a great spot for swimming, sun bathing, and picnicking. There are several shelters here maintained by the Sunrise Rotary Club and plenty of picnic tables. You can fish here for trout, perch, and sunfish. On any given day, you will see a number of windsurfers, kayakers, and canoeists practicing their skills.

T American Computer Museum
2304 N. 7th Ave., Ste. B, Bozeman. 582-1288. www.compustory.com.

Open since May 1990, american Computer Museum is the world's oldest information age history museum. Travel through thousands of years of computing history, and view the intriguing story behind mechanical calculators, slide rules, typewriters, office machines, and Apollo Spacecraft items. A room-sized mainframe computer is also displayed, along with an industrial robot, computer history, and thousands of other artifacts. The renowned museum has attracted visitors from around the world while earning recognition in the New Yorker Magazine, The New York Times, USA Today, C-Span, and other national publications. An ideal family destination, the fascinating museum requires no computer experience to enjoy. american Computer Museum is open daily June through August and Tuesday through Saturday from September through May with a modest admission charge. Call ahead for hours, and visit them on the web.

L Super 8 Motel of Bozeman
800 Wheat Dr., Bozeman. 586-1521 or (800) 800-8000. www.super8bozeman.com

The Super 8 in Bozeman is conveniently located just off I-90 on the north side of Exit 306. You'll enjoy many amenities sure to provide a restful and pleasant stay. Your room includes queen beds, free local calls, cable TV, and interior corridors with electronic door locks. Nonsmoking and handicap accessible rooms are available. The desk is staffed 24 hours a day with fax and copy services. The Super 8 motto says it all, "Start your day off right…spend the night with us." Start your morning with their complimentary continental breakfast. Children 12 and under stay free. ample parking for vehicles large and small include outside outlets. The Super 8 is conveniently located for your trips to Montana State University, Bridger Bowl Ski Area, and all area attractions.

T Bozeman Recreation Center
1211 W. Main St. next to High School. 587-4724

This is the only indoor 50 meter 8-lane swimming pool in the state. The pool is open year round with generous open swim hours. The kids will love the two waterslides in the pool. There is a hot tub and some exercise equipment available.

M Christine Delaney Bozeman 2000 Inc. - Absaroka Realty
1516 W. Main St., Bozeman. 581-7542.
www.AbsarokaRealty.com; Bozeman2000@aol.com

Christine Delaney, a Colorado native now living in her dream community, is a Realtor with Bozeman's Absaroka Realty. In Denver she owned a retail magic store and came to Yellowstone every autumn to recharge her batteries. The opportunity to relocate presented itself and she couldn't be happier. Customer Service has always been her passion, whether it's magic or real estate. She knows what it's like to rush into town, find a dream home, and struggle to coordinate everything long distance. Moving is a stressful time and Christine has been there and done that. She is there to dot the i's and cross the t's for her clients. Christine is an expert at putting the FUN back in the fundamentals of real estate. Visit Absaroka Realty's web site for more information or give her a call.

M Connie Garrett and Todd Saunders, Realtors®
Bozeman and Livingston. 585-5414 or (866) 647-5268. Connie's cell: 539-9255 or Todd's cell: 223-6193. www.BozemanMontanaProperties.com

Connie Garrett and Todd Saunders are the professionals many out of state brokers choose. As members of the local, state, and national REALTORS® associations and participating members of the Southwest Montana MLS, they offer the widest range of services to their clients. Their combined experience and expertise provide clients with a proactive professional real estate team. Connie specializes in first-time home-buyers and real estate

investors. Todd specializes in all aspects of relocating to Bozeman and re-selling and purchasing homes. Both Connie and Todd work with numerous buyers of vacation and second homes in Gallatin and Park Counties. As active volunteers and participants in local clubs and events, they are an excellent source for integrating your lifestyle into your new community. Visit their website to search for properties, plan your trip to southwest Montana, or learn about the surrounding communities.

F Leaf & Bean
1500 N. 19th Avenue at Bridger Peaks Town Center in Bozeman. 587-2132 or (800) 485-5646

Established downtown in 1977, The Leaf & Bean is Bozeman's original coffee house and bakery, and is

Leaf & Bean

as well known for its gourmet fare as for its cozy atmosphere and community spirit. "The Bean"

Continued on page 161

Section 2

GALLATIN RIVER AREA AND MADISON RIVER VALLEY
INCLUDING BOZEMAN, BIG SKY, ENNIS, THREE FORKS AND WEST YELLOWSTONE

THE BOZEMAN CEMETERY

There are few plots of land n Montana that have as much history buried in them as the Bozeman Cemetery. The stories of the individuals buried here—their dreams, achievements, and failures—give us a rich picture of not only Bozeman's history, but also the history of the West. Here are the stories of a select few.

John Bozeman
b. 1835 in Georgia d. 1867

When gold was discovered in Colorado, John Bozeman left Georgia in 1860 and headed West, leaving a wife and three children behind. By 1862 Bozeman had traveled to the gold strike in Bannack in what was to become Montana Territory.

The 1860s were turbulent years in Montana's history. The successive gold strikes brought thousands of fortune seekers within weeks of each discovery. The rich mining camps were terrorized by thieves and murderers; vigilante committees were organized. Meanwhile, the steady stream of wagon trains through Indian hunting grounds convinced the Sioux and Cheyenne that they must fight to keep their land. Back in the States the Civil War raged, creating tensions between Montana's Northern and Southern emigrants as well as between Southerners who were Confederate Army veterans and those who had avoided military service. It was indeed, the Wild West.

The mining camps of Bannack and Alder Gulch (Virginia City) were dependent on potatoes and flour freighted in from Salt Lake City 400 miles away. The immensely fertile Gallatin Valley was only 60 miles from Virginia City, and it was here in 1863 that John Bozeman conceived the idea of starting a farming community that could supply the miners. Bozeman guided several wagon trains into the area on a trail that shortened the trip by almost two weeks. Over time, it became known as the Bozeman Trail, but after 1864 his energy went into fostering the growth of his town site.

John Bozeman did not fit the typical image of the frontiersman in fringed buckskins. Various contemporaries described him as over six-feet tall, strong, brave, handsome, kind, stalwart, and tireless, with "the looks and ways of a manly man." He was a Southern gentleman, a well dressed Beau Brummel, and no doubt a heart throb.

He was murdered in 1867, only three years after the establishment of the town of Bozeman. While on a trip with Tom Cover to solicit business for the town's flour mill, he was shot on the banks of the Yellowstone River. The accepted story has been that he was murdered by Blackfeet Indians, but inconsistencies in the information have over time resulted in a mystery that variously points the finger of blame at Tom Cover (an interesting individual who was himself murdered under mysterious circumstances years later) or at a jealous husband of one of the few women in town.

John Bozeman's death insured the survival of his town. Fear of Indian attacks led to the establishment in 1867 of Fort Ellis three miles east of the town which provided both protection and a ready market for Bozeman's farms and merchants. Bozeman's remains were returned to the town three years later. His friend, fellow Georgian William McKenzie, died in 1913 and is buried next to him.

Nelson Story
b. 1838 in Ohio d. 1926

Ellen Trent Story
b. 1844 in Kansas d. 1924

Nelson and Ellen met and married in Kansas before coming to Bannack and Alder Gulch in 1863. Nineteen-year-old Ellen baked pies and bread to sell to the miners while Nelson operated a store and mined a claim from which he took $40,000 in gold.

It was in Alder Gulch that Story's famous participation in frontier justice took place. Road agent (robber) George Ives had been charged with murder by an informal judge and jury. A crowd of several thousand spectators gathered as darkness fell. Ives stood on a packing box with a noose around his neck. A rescue party of his friends stood up with their guns, but "quick as thought" Story pulled the box (or kicked it, depending on whose version you hear) out from under Ives and he was hanged.

The Storys decided to settle in Bozeman and Ellen stayed there in 1866 while Nelson went down to Texas to drive his famous herd of 3,000 longhorns and a wagon train up to Montana. Not only did he fight his way through thousands of hostile Indians, but he also had to outwit the U.S. Army who wanted to turn back the expedition for its own safety. Story had to sneak 3,000 longhorns past the troops in the dark. These cattle that were driven into the Gallatin Valley formed the nucleus for Montana's cattle industry.

Ellen gave birth to seven children. Three sons and one daughter survived. Nelson's successes in cattle, a flour mill and other business ventures enabled them to build a 17 room mansion in the 1880s. This exquisite building was torn down in 1938. Marble columns from the mansion were salvaged to decorate the family plot.

The Ellen Theatre on Main Street was named for Mrs. Story. Nelson Story was instrumental in bringing Montana State College to Bozeman. Both lived long and productive lives and were major figures in building the Bozeman community.

James D. Chesnut
b. 1834 in Ohio d. 1886

The life of James Chesnut was full of adventure. At the age of 19 he left for the California gold fields by steamer, but the boat exploded, killing 100 people. James escaped with only a slight scald. In San Francisco, after doing well in several merchandising enterprises, the 19-year-old Chesnut joined up with the audacious military adventurer, William Walker.

The prevailing mood of the times was that American civilization had a right and duty to expand itself; the lines between idealism and piracy were blurred. To the Hispanic South there were people to be liberated and great fortunes to be made in silver, gold and cattle ranching. As part of Walker's illegal Independence Brigade, Chesnut was one of 300 mercenaries to invade and conquer without a shot, the small, sleepy, coastal towns of Western Mexico. Walker proclaimed himself President of the Republic of Lower California and led his ill-equipped army on a rugged march to "liberate" mineral-rich Sonora. The brutal landscape and lack of food took its toll in desertions and death. The group never reached Sonora. All that remained of Walker's army were 34 men who surrendered at the U.S. border and returned to San Francisco.

A year later, Chesnut chose not to accompany Walker on his next venture, the bloody and successful invasion of Nicaragua, where he made himself President. Instead, Chesnut exchanged all his valuables for $7,000 in gold, and booked passage on a steamer bound for New York. The launch that was taking him to the steamer sank, and while 38 people drowned, Chesnut swam back to shore, hired a diver, retrieved his gold and boarded the steamer in time for departure.

Later, during the Kansas border wars, Chesnut was arrested and jailed for high treason. When the Civil War began, he worked at the unique job of enlisting Indians and blacks for the Union Army. He enlisted a regiment of Delaware Indians and himself commanded a regiment of black troops, achieving the rank of Colonel.

In 1867, he came to Montana and discovered coal in the Rocky Canyon Trail Creek area. For 15 years he developed his coal mining enterprise, benefiting the growth of the community. Chesnut liked to say that the coal in his claim ran all the way down to China, thereby making the famous coal mines of England an infringement on his rights. Coal was welcomed since wood was becoming scarce and high priced. But stove grates were not suited to coal, and the Colonel had difficulty promoting his product. The small town of Chestnut was named for him, however the name was misspelled.

Chesnut owned extensive real estate, including the Chesnut Corner, an elegantly appointed saloon, complete with a reading room and a club room in back. This club room was Bozeman's nerve center, where its leading male citizens discussed public problems and their genial host encouraged new enterprises for the rapidly growing town. The large upstairs floor was a social center, and in summer the Fort Ellis band played from its balcony on Main street. Although Chesnut was the focus of several romantic stories, he never married.

"Lady" Mary Blackmore
b. in England d. 1872

The sad story of 'Lady' Mary Blackmore and her husband William is part of Bozeman's lore. In 1872 they came from England to visit Yellowstone, stopping in Bozeman on their way because Lady Mary had become suddenly ill. She died of peritonitis at General Lester Willson's home and was buried on five acres purchased by 'Lord' Blackmore and given to the town for use as a cemetery.

Further investigation reveals that 'Lord' Blackmore was in fact not a lord, although he did expect to be knighted. It was Emma Willson who started referring to them as 'Lord' and 'Lady.' William Blackmore was, however, an extraordinary man. He had become quite wealthy working as a middle man between English investors and promoters in the American West. He and Mary lived on an extensive estate where they entertained a dazzling array of guests including Oliver Wendell Holmes, Charlotte Bronte, Alfred Lord Tennyson, and "Mark Twain". The beautiful Mary was a London social leader and an intimate of Queen Victoria. William had made several trips to the U.S., and from all evidence he loved the West. He had provided generous financial assistance to photographer William Jackson, artist Thomas Moran, and explorer Dr. Ferdinand Hayden. He had a deep interest in anthropology and in offers a full menu of espresso drinks, teas and house-made pastries. The Leaf & Bean received attention from Travel and Leisure and Bon Appetit magazines in 2004 and 2005, and is consistently voted Bozeman's Best Coffee in an annual local poll. This satellite location was opened in 2001 and features a charming children's playroom, wireless internet service and plenty of parking. Stop by for a quick, healthy lunch or late-night snack, and browse art from local studios and unusual gifts. While in historic downtown Bozeman, visit the flagship store, where live entertainment is featured several nights a week and includes local bands, touring performers, bluegrass and jazz jams, and open-mic events. Open early and late seven days a week.

Native American life and customs. His fourth trip to the U.S. in 1872 was to check on investments in the Southwest, as well as to join Hayden on his expedition to The Yellowstone. Mary and a nephew accompanied him on this trip, and the couple agreed that if either should die on their travels they would be buried where they died. Dr. Hayden named Mt. Blackmore in Mary's honor. Looking south from the grave site the mountain's pyramid-shaped peak can be seen. Hayden also named a newly discovered mineral Blackmorite in William's honor. In 1878 Blackmore's American investments brought him to financial ruin. In the library of his estate he committed suicide by shooting himself in the head.

Henry T.P. Comstock
b. 1820 in Canada d. 1870

Henry Comstock, nicknamed "Old Pancake" was said to have enough badness in him for three men. Lazy and conniving, he was making a meager living in 1859 mining for gold in western Nevada. When two naive Irish immigrants made a strike, Old Pancake showed up, said that the land was his (it wasn't), and demanded partnerships for himself and a friend if he were to allow the Irishmen to continue digging.

The odd-looking gold that came from the claim was soon discovered to be mostly silver. Comstock was a loudmouth and talked about "his" discovery and "his" claim so much that it became known as the Comstock Lode. The four prospectors sold out to a developer, and Comstock received $11,000 for his share. As was typical of the times, none of the discoverers held onto an interest in the mine that was to become the single greatest mineral strike in history, producing 400 million dollars in precious metals. The developers who took over the claim became phenomenally wealthy; many of the great American fortunes were founded with revenues from the mines in the Comstock Lode. Comstock quickly spent his money. Drifting and demented, he ended up in Bozeman where he lived in a shack just off the east end of Main Street. Dead broke and lonely, he committed suicide by shooting himself.

Monroe "Beaver" Nelson
b. 1861 in Iowa d. 1932

Frank "Doc" Nelson
b. 1867 in Montana d. 1964

Beaver and Doc were two of the seven children of John and Lavine Nelson. The couple came to the Gallatin Valley in 1864, just in time for the arrival of their son Pike, one of the first white children born in the area. Monroe "Beaver" Nelson was a boy at the time, but grew up to become foreman of the Two Dot Willson Cattle Co. Kid Curry of Butch Cassidy's "Hole in the Wall Gang" and the Logan boys rode under Beaver, as did Charlie Russell, who proclaimed Nelson the most ideal cowboy he had ever known and used him as the subject for many of his paintings.

In 1879, while drinking with two other cowboys at the Headquarters Saloon on Main Street, Beaver was involved in one of Bozeman's biggest shoot-outs. One of the cowboys drinking with Beaver got into a fight with a local trouble maker, beat him up, and ran him out of the saloon. The trouble maker sneaked back in and shot him in the back. The dying cowboy, Beaver, and the other cowboy all spun around and fired at the trouble maker. The cowboy and the trouble maker both hit the floor dead.

In another incident Beaver and his younger brother Doc witnessed the famous Lewistown shootout in which Rattlesnake Jake and three others were killed. Elsewhere in Montana, Doc was also around when a cowboy got into a gunfight and accidentally shot the local schoolmarm. This made the boys in town so mad that they hanged the cowboy and shot his body full of lead. The schoolmarm survived.

Doc had been a little boy of three when his father took him to see some friends who had just returned from the Rosebud Expedition. One of the men had a bloody mass of fresh Sioux scalps hung on a wire which he whirled through the air at the petrified child. At age 11, Doc helped on a drive of 1,000 head of cattle. At 14 he met 16-year-old Charlie Russell on another cattle drive and for several years the two wrangled for big brother Beaver's cattle outfit. One morning, Doc and an ornery pony bucked right through the cook's fire and became the subject of C.M. Russell's popular painting "Bronc to Breakfast." This image is engraved on Doc's tombstone, and Doc is in the National Cowboy Hall of Fame.

Chester R. "Chet" Huntley
b. 1911 in Montana d. 1974

Chet Huntley was born in the Cardwell Railroad Depot where his father worked as a telegrapher. In 1929, he came to Montana State College to study entomology, later transferring to the University of Washington. After getting a start in radio broadcasting, he went to Los Angeles where he eventually worked for all three television networks—CBS, ABC and NBC. During the nationally televised political conventions of 1956, he was teamed with David Brinkley. The two became a popular news team which lasted until Huntley quit in 1970. The Huntley/Brinkley Report won every major TV news award, including 7 Emmy awards. When Chet Huntley resigned from NBC, he returned to Montana to develop Big Sky, Inc., of Montana, a resort and ski complex in Gallatin Canyon. He died a few years later from lung cancer.

Reprinted with permission from "Who's Who in the Bozeman Cemetery—A Guide to Historic Gravesites" The Bozarts Press. Copyright 1987 by Anne Garner.

M Venture West Realty
822 Stoneridge Dr., Ste. 2, Bozeman. 522-9378 or (866) 521-9378. www.venturewestrealty.com; wrinfo@venturewestrealty.com

Specializing in residential, commercial, and land listings, Venture West Realty holds customers as its top priority. From the moment clients walk through the front door into the cozy environment, the brokerage's concierge-type treatment envelops customers in an atmosphere of warm hearts and friendly service. The diverse backgrounds of the brokerage's Realtors® complements this welcoming atmosphere. Striving to possess a resident expert for every client need, Venture West Realty boasts experience in all real estate transactions. Whether you're selling your home, purchasing the home of your future, or selecting an investment or recreational property, you'll find quality service backed with superior marketing, networking, and responsiveness. At Venture West Realty, it's not about being number one in volume, but being number one for every customer. Find out what Venture West Realty can do for you!

M Richards Land Co.
1174 Stoneridge Dr., Bozeman, 556-5614, Frederick's cell: 539-1885 or Erica's cell: 539-2997. www.richardslandco.com, email fmr@richardslandco.com

Discerning buyers will appreciate the attention to detail and knowledge of ranch, recreational, and home properties Richards Land Company offers. The sister and brother team of Erica and Frederick Richards provides extensive experience with all aspects of your real estate investment. To them, real estate isn't a job—it's a way of life. Let them help you find that perfect property for recreation, a beautiful home site, or ranch from many unique parcels in the Gallatin Valley. They can also help you find the right builder to complete your dream. Visit their web site to find listings, information about conservation easements, and general information to help you learn more about the area. Their expertise will guide you through finding everything from that ideal property to the best financing options available.

AmericInn Lodge & Suites

pool, whirlpool, and sauna are also available along with a business center and meeting/hospitality room for meetings or parties. Onsite, the gift shop and convenience store feature Montana souvenirs and other western gifts. For a quiet night's sleep, excellent customer service, and easy access to the region's numerous attractions, stay with the friendly staff of americInn Lodge & Suites. Children 12 and under free when accompanied by an adult.

L Wingate Inn of Bozeman
2305 Catron St. in Bozeman. 582-4995 or
(800) 228-1000. www.wingatebozeman.com

The Wingate Inn is a great place to stay whether you are attending a business meeting, events at Montana State University, or enjoying the natural wonders of southwestern Montana. Amenities include conveniences such as free wireless and T-1 high speed Internet access, a top-flight fitness center, complimentary expanded continental breakfast, heated indoor pool, 24-hour business center with complimentary fax service, copier, computer and printer. Plentiful upscale meeting

space with all the necessary services is also available. Their rooms provide separate areas for work and sleep, 25" color TV, cordless and two line phones, and oversized desks, all with your personal comfort in mind. The Wingate Inn is convenient to all area attractions and recreation. The Wingate Inn, Bozeman offers small-town hospitality and big city amenities, including complimentary airport shuttle.

9. *Gas, Food*

T Bozeman Ponds
Next to the Gallatin Valley Mall on Huffine Lane in Bozeman.

This pond recently received a complete makeover by the Bozeman Breakfast Optimist Club turning three separate ponds into one large one. The area has picnic tables, a pavilion, rest rooms, and walking trails. Swimming is allowed but there are no lifeguards present. The pond is stocked with rainbow, brook, and brown trout and perch.

10. *Gas, Food*

T Museum of the Rockies
On the MSU campus at 600 W. Kagy Blvd., Bozeman. 994-2251. www.museumoftherockies.org

When you walk through the Museum of the Rockies, you travel through more than four billion years in time. Learn about history and prehistory of the northern Rockies region through exhibits ranging from paleontology and Native American artifacts to historic photography and antique vehicles. Start your walk through time with a look at the universe and Montana's Big Sky in the Taylor Planetarium. The Taylor Planetarium is one of 25

Montana Trivia

The Bozeman based Vigilante Theater Company once toured with an original musical revue called *FTV: The Fishing Channel*. It was based on a twenty-four-hour channel devoted to fishing.

8. *Gas, Food, Lodging*

L AmericInn Lodge & Suites
1121 Reeves Rd. W., Bozeman. 522-8686 or
(800) 634-3444. www.americinn.com
At the americInn Lodge & Suites of Bozeman just 90 miles from Yellowstone, friendly service couples with immaculately clean and beautifully appointed lodging. From standard guestrooms to whirlpool/fireplace suites, king business rooms, and two-room suites, everyone's lodging needs are met. All rooms include free high-speed Internet, coffeemakers, hairdryers, and irons/ironing boards. Guest laundry, enhanced continental breakfast, an exercise room, and a spacious indoor

SHAKESPEARE IN MONTANA

Montana Shakespeare in the Parks is a theatrical outreach program of Montana State University Bozeman. The Company's mission is to bring quality, live theatrical productions of Shakespeare and other classics communities in Montana and vicinity at a reasonable cost with an emphasis on small, underserved communities. Shakespeare in the Parks opened in the summer of 1973. Since that time the company of professional actors has traveled over 250,000 miles, over 44 plays, presenting over 1,800 performances mostly in Montana to a cumulative audience of over half a million.

Since it's inception Montana Shakespeare in the Parks has employed a company of professionals who combine their theatrical talents with a love and appreciation for Montana and the audience they serve. Because of the Company's desire to bring a quality performance to people who would not otherwise have access to theatre of any kind, many company members have found the tour to be a rejuvenating professional experience, reminding them of "why they went into theatre to begin with." This unique combination of invested performer and receptive audience coupled with outdoor performances which make the actor even more accessible to the audience, has evolved into a unique performance style for the Company.

Recognition of SIP's unique contribution to the cultural fabric of Montana has been both regional and national in scope. The performances continue to entertain audiences of all ages, usually free of charge, due to the financial support of generous sponsors throughout the state. For a complete performance schedule and additional information call the office on the campus of Montana State University at 994-3901 or visit them at www.montana.edu/shakespeare

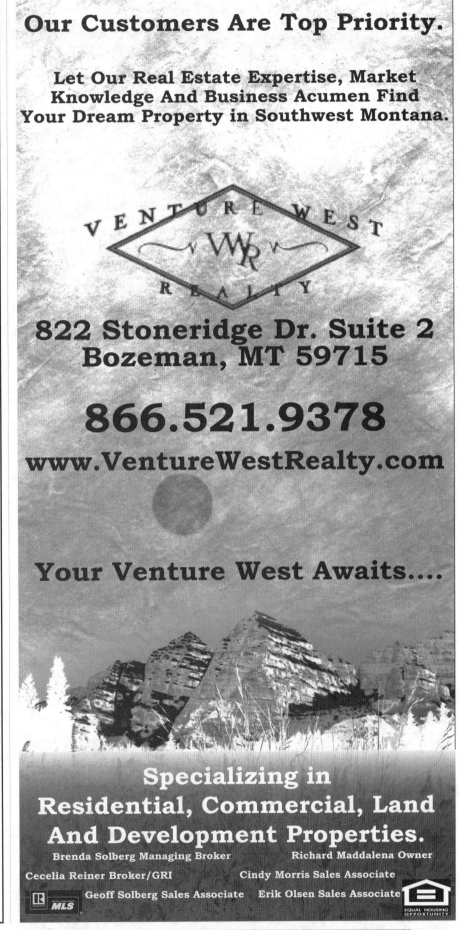

MUSEUM OF THE ROCKIES

Discover the world of dinosaurs, journey with Lewis and Clark, explore Native American cultures, visit the stars in a planetarium, and shop at the Museum Store. At the Museum of the Rockies there is something for everyone.

The Museum of the Rockies is home to one

"Big Mike," the first free-standing full-size bronze Tyrannosaurus rex in the world, welcomes you to the Museum of the Rockies. Cast from the actual bones of T. rex excavated in eastern Montana by Jack Horner and the museum's paleontology crew, the skeleton measures 38 feet in length, stands 12 feet tall and weighs 6,000 pounds.

of the largest dinosaur collections in the world and the largest dinosaur fossil collection in the United States. It is also home to renowned paleontologist Jack Horner who served as the model for the dinosaur researcher in the Jurassic Park movies.

When visitors arrive at the museum they are first greeted by a bronze cast from the actual bones of an intimidating Tyrannosaurus rex excavated in eastern Montana by the museum's paleontology crew, the skeleton measures 38 feet in length, stands 15 feet tall and weighs 6,000 pounds.

In order to display more of the fossil collection, the museum is opening the new Siebel Dinosaur Complex. The new hall will be Jack Horner's ultimate dinosaur exhibit and will feature 4500 fossils when complete. The first phase is already open and is called the Hall of Horns and Teeth. It features the upper Cretaceous dinosaurs of Montana including Tyrannosaurus rex, Torosaurus, Triceratops, Thescelosaurus and more. One of the highlights of the Hall of Horns and Teeth are the Torosaurus skulls which are the largest land animal skulls that have ever been found. Phase 2 of the Complex, the Media Center, will open in the summer of 2006, and phase 3, the Hall of Giants will open in 2007.

For fans of Lewis & Clark, during the summer there is an outdoor Lewis & Clark challenge course offering visitors the experience to climb aboard a keelboat, outrun a bear, and try to lift a cradleboard like Sacajawea carried. The challenge course also presents information about geography, botany, Native American culture, a military camp, and Corps tools. Costumed interpreters will be on the course daily.

Enduring Peoples: Native Cultures of the Northern Rockies and Plains traces the origins and development of Indians who have occu-

pied Montana and other parts of the region for more than 11,000 years. The reasons fur trappers and white settlers came west and the lifestyles they carved out for themselves are reflected in "Montana On the Move" in the Paugh History Hall. Historic artifacts, photographic wall murals and pieces form the Museum's extensive textile collection add to your understanding of Montana's past. Here you'll see evidence collected from the only Lewis and Clark campsite ever to be scientifically verified.

The Living History Farm on the museum grounds will be open during the summer months with daily activities, programs and livestock to illustrate life on a Montana homestead a century ago.

The Museum of the Rockies is also home to the world-class Taylor Planetarium. It is the only public planetarium in a three-state region and it has the capability to simulate flight through space and 3-dimensional effects. In addition to its main features which change quarterly, the planetarium offers live narrated tours of the night sky, laser shows and a children's show on Saturday mornings.

Your children will love the Martin Discovery Room, an interactive play area with dinosaur, pioneer and reading stations as well as an earthquake table. There is also a Museum Store that features jewelry and art by local artists, books, educational toys, and Montana-made gifts.

A constantly changing schedule for exhibits and planetarium shows mean there's always something new to see. From Memorial Day through Labor Day, the Museum is open from 8am to 8pm daily with planetarium shows throughout the day. During the rest of the year, the Museum is open from 9am to 5pm Monday through Saturday and Sunday afternoons from 12:30 to 5 pm. During the summer months, lunch is available at the T.rextaurant where the menu includes burgers and salads.

Museum admission is $8 for adults and $4 for children ages 5-18 with children under 5 free. Tickets for the Planetarium are $3 and laser show tickets are $5. A combination rate of $9.50 for adults and $6.50 for children gives a discount to visitors who see both the museum and the planetarium. For information on current exhibits and programs, call (406) 994-2251 or (406) 994-DINO or check the website at www.museumoftherockies.org. Hours and prices are subject to change.

The Museum is located on the Montana State University campus at 600 W. Kagy Boulevard. The most direct route is via the 19th Street exit from Interstate 90. Travel through Bozeman on 19th Street until you reach the stoplight at Kagy Boulevard, turn left and follow the street signs.

facilities in the world with a computer graphics system that can simulate flight through space. It is the only major public planetarium in the surrounding three-state region.

The museum is well known for its paleontology research. On display are several important finds including the skulls of Torosaurus, Tyrannosaurus Rex and Triceratops and an 80 million-year-old nest of dinosaur eggs. Working at Montana sites, the museum's curator of paleontology, Jack Horner, has discovered important information about dinosaur biology and in recent years has made discoveries of international significance. One of the most spectacular finds, a Tryannosaurus Rex, has been cast in bronze and the 38 foot long and 15 foot tall skeleton stands in front of the museum.

Montana's rich agricultural history is portrayed at the museum's living history farm where the daily life of early homesteaders is recreated for visitors.

The Museum of the Rockies is open daily from 8am–8pm (summer) and 9am–5 pm Monday through Saturday and 12:30–5pm Sundays (winter). An admission fee is charged to nonmembers. For more information call or visit the web site.

11. *Gas*

12. *Gas, Food*

F   Kountry Korner Cafe
81820 Gallatin Road at Four Corners, Bozeman.
586-2281 or (800) 905-2281

The Kountry Korner is a family-style café located at Four Corners just west of Bozeman. Look for the bear sitting on the roof! They are open for breakfast, lunch or dinner and offer daily home-cooked specials, with a wide selection of family favorites. Homemade pies and soups are made fresh daily. Locals love to eat here and are partial to the homemade chicken-fried steaks. You can enjoy a great meal anytime between 6 a.m. and 9 p.m. or have them pack a sack lunch to take on your outing. They are also known for a fantastic Sunday brunch buffet. A children's play area is available for the little ones and a large dining room is available for private parties and large groups. Off premises catering is available for private groups.

Montana Trivia

World famous paleontologist Jack Horner, who served as character model and technical advisor for the *Jurassic Park* series, struggled in school with dyslexia. He found his first dinosaur bone at the age of seven.

13. *Gas, Food, Lodging*

Belgrade

In 1882, Thomas B. Quaw, an entrepreneur, located land along the newly surveyed Northern Pacific Railway about ten miles from Bozeman. He found this property greatly to his liking, and thus, the community had its beginning. At that time, many European financiers invested money to complete the Northern Pacific Line. As a complimentary notice of appreciation to the Serbian investors, this blind siding was named Belgrade after the capital of Serbia.

From the turn of the century through the 1930s, Belgrade continued to expand, gaining businesses, professionals and the trappings of an established community. However, speculation in the community slowed, the depression took its toll, and Belgrade settled into the quiet farming community it was to remain for some time.

During the 1990s, Belgrade has experienced significant growth due largely to the boom environment of Gallatin County. While it is now somewhat of a bedroom community of Bozeman, it maintains its own character as a community. *Partially reprinted from Belgrade Chamber of Commerce brochure.*

F Country Kitchen
6269 Jackrabbit Lane and I-90, Exit 298 S. in Belgrade. 388-0808

Enjoy the Country Kitchen for family oriented dining in a smoke-free, homey, relaxing atmosphere, conveniently located at the Yellowstone Park-Belgrade I-90 exit. The menu provides a variety of home-style entrees, sandwiches, soups, salads, and their breakfast selections are served anytime, a welcome alternative to fast food for the traveler. Be sure to try their popular and pleasing skillet dishes. Country Kitchen signature pancakes keep people coming back time after time. Fresh and tasty selections will satisfy every appetite, including a "lighter side" and low carb menus at budget pleasing prices. Be sure and save room for dessert: cakes, pies, and their famous

Apple Dumpling. This kid friendly restaurant offers snacks, coloring, activity placemat menu, and Game Boys. Senior discounts are available. Breakfast, lunch, and dinner is served seven days a week from 7 am to 10 pm.

14. *Gas, Food*

15. *Gas, Food, Lodging*

Amsterdam/Churchill

As you would guess, this area was settled and named by Hollanders. The area is still largely occupied by families of Dutch descent who carry on many of the community oriented traditions of the old country, including dairy farming.

Manhattan

Manhattan, 20 miles northwest of Bozeman, is a small town which once had a profitable malting business until the time of prohibition. The stone malt house still stands and the town remains branded with a name given to it by investors who operated the Manhattan Malting Company. Originally called Moreland, a group from a landholding company in New York City renamed the town in 1891. Today it remains primarily an agricultural community.

T Manhattan Area Museum

A quaint museum located in downtown Manhattan gives visitors a taste of the railroad and rural roots of the area. Open during the summer months, Tuesday through Saturday, 10 a.m. to 4 p.m.

F Garden Café
107 S. Broadway, Manhattan. 284-3366.

Originally built as the Kid Johnson Theater in 1917, the Garden Café is owned by Ann Tappan and the Switzerland trained Nick Schmutz who has cooked in Europe, the Caribbean, and San Francisco. Renowned for its friendly atmosphere and home-style food featuring local fresh ingredients, the café offers burgers made from fresh ground beef, spaghetti, chicken fried steak, smothered pork chops, enchiladas, real ice cream shakes, homemade pies and cookies, and much

more! On Saturdays, enjoy amazing omelets and scrumptious biscuits and gravy. The Billings Gazette wrote "travelers from all over Montana stop by for their on-the-road meal." The café is open 6 am to 4 pm Monday-Saturday and provides wireless Internet access. Conference facilities are available after 4 pm, and live music is occasionally offered. Call for reservations.

16. *Food*

Logan

At one time this was a major railroad town and had a roundhouse. The train still goes through town, but doesn't have much need to stop. The railroad bought the right-of-way from Odelia Logan in 1885 and named the town for her. Today its main business is the legendary The Land of Magic Steakhouse. They hold Annual Branding Parties the first weekend in May and area ranchers leave their marks on the walls of the restaurant.

Trident

Named for the three forks of the Missouri River that meet near here. Today it is mostly a cement company town.

D William Clark
July 14, 1806 (along the East Gallatin River)

"I proceeded up this plain…and Crossed the main Chanel of the river,…and nooned it… the river is divided and on all the small Streams inoumerable quantities of beaver dams, tho' the river is yet navigable for Canoes."

T Madison Buffalo Jump State Park (Day use only)
23 miles west of Bozeman on I90 at Logan exit, than 7 miles south on Buffalo Jump Road. 994-4042.

As early as 2000 years ago and as recently as 200 years ago, the trampling of hoofs could be heard as Indians stampeded herds of buffalo off the cliffs to claim their meat and fur. Buffalo bone piles up to 60 inches deep and tepee rings on the plateau have left an unmistakable record of this form of buffalo hunting.

The story of the site is described in an outdoor display. Diagrams and descriptions point out the location of rock piles that formed drive lanes, the area below the cliff where Indian women butchered the bison, and a more settled site where Indians processed their trappings. Here you can experience the history and the breathtaking view of the Madison Valley and the Tobacco Root Mountains from the overlook.

17. *Gas, Food, Lodging*

Three Forks

Three Forks is situated near the convergence point of the three rivers of the Missouri River about 30 miles from Bozeman. The three forks making the confluence of the Missouri River are: the Jefferson River, the Gallatin River and the internationally-famous Madison River. The town lies at 4,081 feet and is protected by the Rocky Mountains leaving the eastern side mild in the winter with cool mountain breezes in the summer.

Historically, the three tributaries of the Missouri have brought people of various cultures together. The Indians came together at this point because it was a convergence for wildlife and a crossroads of hunting trails. Fur traders found these river junctions a useful trading location. Today the Headwaters Heritage Museum and Missouri Headwaters State Park preserve the history of this confluence of peoples and rivers.

The areas at the headwaters and of Three Forks has some of the most colorful early history in Montana. Three Forks was the crossroads of Indian trails. Just west of town, Sacajawea as a child was captured from her tribe, the Shoshones. She married a French-Canadian trapper, Toussaint Charbaneau, and together they guided the Lewis and Clark Expedition through the area in 1805.

The Corps of Discovery arrived at the headwaters of the Missouri River in July 1805. They camped for a week along the Jefferson River just above the headwaters, while Clark recovered from a fever. In 1806, Clark was guided by Sacajawea across the valley from the three forks to the pass leading directly into the Yellowstone River.

Three Forks is also the site of one of the bloodiest battles ever fought between the Blackfeet, the Flatheads and the Crow. John Colter took part in this fight on the side of the Flatheads and the Crows in 1808. Colter's allies, though fewer in number, won the battle. In April 1810, the Missouri Fur Company established Fort Three Forks, but because of constant Indian attacks, the fort was abandoned before it was completed. Kit Carson narrowly escaped from a Blackfeet brave whom he killed on the bluffs north of Three Forks. This fascinating history is displayed on plaques at the Headwaters State Park or from the Headwaters Heritage Museum in downtown Three Forks.

Only eighteen miles west of Three Forks is the Lewis and Clark Caverns State Park, a treasure you won't want to miss! This is Montana's first state park and has perhaps the most impressive limestone caves in northwestern United States. It is truly an underground fairyland of ancient stalactites and stalagmites created millions of years ago. There is a gradual sloping trail leading to the caverns entrance and once inside be prepared for over 600 steps leading through hands-and-knees crawl space, narrow rock slides and cathedral-size chambers. The cave's interior is a constant 50 degrees.

Willow Creek

The town was named for the creek that flows nearby, which in turn was named for the willows that line the banks of the creek.

H The Three Forks of the Missouri
Hwy 10, east of Three Forks

This region was alive with beaver, otter and game before the white man came. It was disputed hunting territory with the Indian tribes. Sacajawea, the Shoshone who guided portions of the Lewis and Clark Expedition, was captured near here when a child, during a battle between her people and the Minnetarees. Her memories of this country were invaluable to the explorers. The Expedition, westward bound, encamped near here for a few days in the latter part of July, 1805. The following year Captain Clark and party came back, July 13, 1806, on their way to explore the Yellowstone River.

In 1808, John Colter, discoverer of Yellowstone Park, and former member of the Lewis and Clark Expedition, was trapping on a stream in this vicinity when captured by a band of Blackfeet. His only companion was killed. Colter was stripped, given a head start, and ordered to run across the flat which was covered with prickly pear. The Indians were hot on his heels but Colter undoubtedly made an all-time record that day for sprints as well as distance events. He outran the Indians over a six-mile course and gained the cover of the timber along the Jefferson River. Once in the stream he dove and came up under a jam of driftwood. This hideout saved him from a lot of disappointed and mystified Indians. When night came he headed east, weaponless and outnuding the nudists. He traveled in this condition for seven days to Fort Lisa, his headquarters, at the mouth of the Big Horn River.

In 1810, the Missouri Fur Co. built a fur trading post close by but due to the hostility of the Blackfeet Indians were forced to abandon it that fall.

D Sgt. Ordway
July 13, 1806 (at the Three Forks)

"Capt. Clark & party leaves us hear to cross over to the River Roshjone. So we parted I and 9 more proceeded on down the river with the canoes verry well."

D William Clark
July 13, 1806

"The indian woman who has been of great Service to me as a pilot through this Country recommends a gap in the mountain more South which I shall cross."

T Parker Homestead State Park (Day use only)
8 miles west of Three Forks on Montana 2. 994-4042.

This is probably the smallest park in the system and officially lists visitation as zero. In fact, if you weren't looking for it, you would just pass right on by. There is no sign marking the site, and no interpretative displays explaining its history. It is simply a sod-roofed log cabin tucked under a few

FORT THREE FORKS

In the spring of 1810, Manuel Lisa sent Andrew and Pierre Menard with a party of about 30 men and John Colter as a guide to the Three Forks area to build a trading post. The resulting fort, Fort Three Forks, was one of the first trading posts between the Missouri and the Pacific Coast. The fort was built as a base for trapping beaver over the entire area of the Missouri river and its branches above the Great Falls.

Life was always interesting at the Fort. Eight of the party were killed by raiding Blackfeet Indians. When they weren't harassed by Indians, critters like rattlesnakes and grizzlies kept them on their toes. The business of beaver trapping was so hazardous that the fort was abandoned in 1811.

Nothing is left of the fort today. Time and the meandering river has destroyed most of the ground the fort stood on. A modern motel with the fort's name stands near the original site. However, an anonymous surveyor has given us a description of the fort: "A double stockade of logs set three feet deep, enclosing an area of 300 sq. feet situated upon the tongue of land about a half a mile wide, between the Jefferson and Madison Rivers, about two miles above the confluence, upon the south bank of the channel of the former stream, now called the Jefferson Slough. The store and warehouse were built on each side of the gates, and on the other side next to the interior of the fort, two buildings were connected by a gate, the space between buildings and stockade filled in with pickets, making a large strong room without any covering overhead. In each store, about five feet from the ground, was a hole 18 inches square, with a strong shutter fastening inside, opening into the enclosed space between the gates.

When the Indians wanted to trade, the inner gate was closed; a man would stand at the outer gate until a number of Indians had passed in and then lock the outer gate. He would then climb through the trading hole into the store. The Indians would pass whatever each one had to trade through the hole into the store and the trader would throw out of the hole whatever the Indians wanted to the value of the article received."

COLTER'S RUN

Excerpted from "John Bradbury's Travels in the Interior of America, 1809-1811" in Thwaites, Reuben G., (ed.) Early Western Travels, 1784-1846, Vol. V, Arthur H. Clark Co., Cleveland, 1904.

The year was 1806. The Lewis and Clark Expedition was heading down the Missouri on its way back to civilization. The group met two trappers—Dickson and Hancock—who were on their way west to the rich beaver country. The two persuaded one member of the Expedition, 35-year-old John Colter, to accompany them.

The three spent the winter of 1806-1807 trapping by the Yellowstone River. Following a quarrel with his partners, Colter left in the spring and once again made his way down the Missouri. At its junction with the Platte River, he met a large party of trappers, the newly-formed Missouri Fur Company headed by Manuel Lisa. The company included several veterans of the Lewis and Clark Expedition: George Drouillard, John Potts and Peter Wiser. The group intended to establish a trading post on the Yellowstone at the mouth of the Bighorn and felt that Colter's previous experience in the area would be invaluable. Colter was easily persuaded to fall in with his old companions and headed up the Missouri again.

Arriving at the Bighorn in October 1807, the trappers built their post. They sent Colter into the surrounding country to contact local bands of Indians, tell them about the post and invite them in to trade. This seemingly simple mission turned out to be the first of John Colter's amazing travels through the Rocky Mountains.

Yellowstone Geysers Discovered

Struggling through heavy snows and frigid temperatures of a Montana winter, Colter's journey took him to the smoking geyser basins in the vicinity of present-day Cody, Wyoming (which later became known as Colter's Hell) through the Wind River Mountains to the Tetons, then up past Yellowstone Lake and possibly through the Lamar Valley near what is now Cooke City. John Colter was thus the first white person to see the wonders of Yellowstone Park, but his accounts of the geological oddities sounded so farfetched that he was the butt of many a mountain man's jokes for years afterward.

Passing the summer at the Bighorn, Colter traveled west in the fall of 1808 toward the Missouri Headwaters with a band of Crow and Flathead Indians. One day's journey from the Three Forks, Blackfeet attacked the party. Wounded in the leg, Colter managed to survive, but the Blackfeet noted his presence with the Crow. This set the pattern of Blackfeet hostility toward whites in the Headwaters area, an antagonism which lasted for sixty years.

Colter at the Headwaters

This encounter with the Blackfeet didn't discourage the trapper from returning to the Headwaters. In later years, John Colter told of his adventure to John Bradbury, whose account is reprinted below:

"This man came to St. Louis in May, 1810, in a small canoe, from the head waters of the Missouri, a distance of three thousand miles, which he traversed in thirty days. I saw him on his arrival, and received from him an account of his adventures after he had separated from Lewis and Clark's party: one of these, from its singularity, I shall relate."

"Soon after he separated from Dixon, and trapped in company with a hunter named Potts…They were examing their traps early one morning, in a creek about six miles from that branch of the Missouri called Jefferson's Fork, and were ascending in a canoe, when they suddenly heard a great noise, resembling the trampling of animals… Colter immediately pronounced it to be occasioned by Indians… In a few minutes afterwards their doubts were removed, by a party of Indians making their appearance on both sides of the creek, to the amount of five or six hundred, who beckoned them to come ashore. As retreat was now impossible, Colter turned the head of the canoe to the shore; and at the moment of its touching, an Indian seized the rifle belonging to Potts; but Colter… immediately retook it, and handed it to Potts, who remained in the canoe, and on receiving it pushed off into the river. He had scarcely quitted the shore when an arrow was shot at him, and he cried out, "Colter, I am wounded." Colter remonstrated with him on the folly of attempting to escape, and urged him to come ashore. Instead of complying, he instantly levelled his rifle at an Indian, and shot him dead on the spot… He was instantly pierced with arrows so numerous, that, to use the language of Colter, "he was made of riddle of." They now seized Colter, stripped him entirely naked, and began to consult on the manner in which he should be put to death. They were first inclined to set him up as a mark to shoot at, but the chief interfered, and seizing him by the shoulder, asked him if he could run fast?"

Colter's Run

[Colter] knew that he had now to run for his life, with the dreadful odds of five or six hundred against him, and those armed Indians; therefore cunningly replied that he was a very bad runner, although he was considered by the hunters as remarkably swift. The chief… led Colter out on the prairie three or four hundred yards, and released him, bidding him to save himself if he could. At that instant the horrid war whoop sounded in the ears of poor Colter, who, urged with the hope of preserving life, ran with a speed at which he was himself surprised. He proceeded toward the Jefferson, having to traverse a plain six miles in breadth, abounding with the prickly pear, on which he was every instant treading with his naked feet. He ran nearly half way across the plain before he ventured to look over his shoulder, when he perceived that the Indians were very much scattered, and that he had gained ground to a considerable distance from the main body; but one Indian, who carried a spear, was much before all the rest, and not more than a hundred yards from him. He had now arrived within a mile of the river, when he distinctly heard the appalling sound of footsteps behind him, and every instant expected to feel the spear of his pursuer. Again he turned his head, and saw the savage not twenty yards from him. Determined if possible to avoid the expected blow, he suddenly stopped, turned round, and spread out his arms. The Indian, surprised by the suddenness of the action, also attempted to stop, but exhausted with running, he fell whilst endeavoring to throw his spear, which stuck in the ground, and broke in his hand. Colter instantly snatched up the pointed part, with which he pinned him to the earth, and then continued his flight. The foremost of the Indians, on arriving at the place, stopped till others came up to join them, when they set up a hideous yell. Every moment of this time was improved by Colter, who, although fainting and exhausted, succeeded in gaining the skirting of the cottonwood trees, on the borders of the fork, through which he ran, and plunged into the river."

Escape

Fortunately for him, a little below this place there was an island, against the upper point of which a raft of drift timber had lodged. He dived under the raft, and after several efforts, got his head above water amongst the trunks of trees, covered over with smaller wood to the depth of several feet. Scarcely had he secured himself, when the Indians arrived on the river, screeching and yelling, as Colter expressed it, "like so many devils." … In horrible suspense he remained until night, when hearing no more of the Indians, he dived from under the raft, and swam silently down the river to a considerable distance, when he landed, and traveled by night. Although happy in having escaped from the Indians, his situation was still dreadful: he was completely naked, under a burning sun; the soles of his feet were entirely filled with the thorns of the prickly pear; he was hungry, and had no means of killing game, although he saw abundance around him, and was at least seven days journey from Lisa's Fort, on the Bighorn branch of the Yellowstone River. These were circumstances under which almost any man would have despaired. He arrived at the fort in seven days, having subsisted on a root much esteemed by the Indians of the Missouri, now known by naturalists as *psoralca esculenta*."

GALLATIN CITY

In the 1860s, gold was discovered in Colorado, Idaho and Montana, and a flood of emigrants poured into the Northern Rockies. Mining camps with names like Bannack, Virginia City and Last Chance Gulch sprang up in western Montana.

Fortunes were not only made with pick and shovel; often larger ones were made by those who could supply and feed the hungry miners. One group of enterprising Missourians realized that existing freight routes into Bannack and Virginia City from Utah were long, arduous and uncertain. An easier route lay to the northwest-the Missouri River. By 1860, steamboats were beginning regular service to Fort Benton; if their service could be extended up to the Three Forks of the Missouri, it would then take only two or three days of easy overland travel to reach the gold camps.

City at the Headwaters

In 1862, the Missourians organized the Gallatin Town Company and received permission to navigate to the Three Forks. By January 1863, a town named Gallatin City had been laid out on the north bank of the combined Madison-Jefferson rivers, opposite the mouth of the Gallatin. The town was a speculative venture; the founders hoped it would become the commercial capital of the region. Their expectations never materialized, however, and the town was gradually deserted. Some of the cabins were moved to established farms on the south bank of the river, where a small community-also called Gallatin City-was incorporated February 2, 1865.

This second Gallatin City experienced brief prosperity. Its ferry became a busy link from the booming gold towns of Virginia City and Bannack to Last Chance Gulch (Helena). Food and wheat from Gallatin City farmers was much less expensive and more readily available for the gold camps than the supplies which had to be shipped in from "the States." At its height in the early 1870s, Gallatin City would boast of a grist mill, several stores, a hotel, a fairground and even a racetrack.

But the good days were fleeting ones. The ferry provided unreliable passage across the river; by 1871 several bridges had been constructed at more convenient points up the river. The neighboring town of Bozeman attracted more and more settlers and by the late 1879's perceptive Gallatin City merchants were disposing of their properties. The final blow was dealt by the railroad which came in 1883, bypassing Gallatin City by two miles.

Excerpted from the Headwaters Herald, Montana Fish, Wildlife & Parks.

large cottonwoods on 1.67 acres. The state brochure lists it as "This sod-roofed log cabin is representative of the frontier homes of pioneers who settled Montana." It was built by Nelson and Rosie Parker and is a good example of log homesteads built in the late 1800s and early 1900s.

The state originally had plans to repair the cabin, erect signs, and create a parking area. Those plans were abandoned long ago. The state tried unsuccessfully to give it to the county. It is still a state park costing the state literally nothing. There is no caretaker and the state collects no fees from the property. It is a fascinating place and offers a glimpse of life for settlers at the turn of the century.

T Missouri Headwaters State Park
Just off I-90 east of Three Forks. 994-4042

If you love to see moving waters, this is the place. The park embraces the wild rivers of the Gallatin, Jefferson, and Madison that converge near Three Forks and flow into the Missouri River. Missouri Headwaters was a geographical focal point important to early Native Americans, trappers, traders, and settlers. The now obliterated site of the Three Forks Post, built in 1810 by a group of trappers, is believed to be near here. Sacajawea lived near here as a teenager before she was kidnapped by a band of Hidatsa Indians and taken to North Dakota where she later met the Lewis and Clark Expedition. John Colter visited this area several times, and it was from here that he made his historic run over cactus, rocks and sagebrush after being stripped naked by a band of Blackfeet. It is now a wonderful place for outdoor activities such as hiking, fishing, camping and wildlife viewing.

T Luzenac America Talc Mine
2150 Bench Road, Three Forks. 285-5300

The second largest talc mine in the world is located between Three Forks and Willow Creek. Call for tour information.

T Headwaters Heritage Museum
Cedar & Main St., Three Forks. 285-4778

Housed in what was originally one of the first banks in Three Forks, the museum portrays the history of Three Forks through various displays and artifacts, including a turn-of-the-century village on the second floor. In 1925, the building suffered considerable damage from an earthquake but was restored to its original design.

The museum contains thousands of artifacts and memorabilia depicting the local history, such as a small anvil, all that remains of a trading post established here in 1810. The largest fish ever caught in the state of Montana—a 29 1/2 pound brown trout caught at Wade Lake in 1966 by a resident of Three Forks—is on display.

Nostalgic scenes from the past include a dental office, kitchen, laundry nook, schoolroom, blacksmith shop, beauty salon and millinery shop. The military room holds remembrances of our local veterans. Three Forks began as a railroad community, and the Milwaukee Railroad station agent's office holds an interesting assortment of memorabilia of those bygone days. Another excellent exhibit is 701 different types of barbed wire.

A log cabin from Gallatin City, built in the 1860s of cottonwood logs, can be seen in the picnic area directly behind the museum. The interior is furnished with the necessities of pioneer life, and prickly pear cactus grow and bloom on its rooftop.

The museum is open from May through September Monday through Saturday from 9 a.m. to 5 p.m. and Sunday from 1-5 p.m. Admission is free, but donations are appreciated. *Reprinted from museum brochure.*

T Lewis & Clark Caverns State Park
19 miles west of Three Forks on Montana 2. 287-3541

Located in the rugged Jefferson River Canyon, Lewis and Clark Caverns features one of the most highly decorated limestone caverns in the Northwest. Naturally air conditioned, these spectacular caves are lined with stalactites, stalagmites, columns, and helictites. The Caverns—which are part of Montana's first and best known state park—are electrically lighted and safe to visit. Guided cave tours are offered at Lewis and Clark Caverns State Park, including special candle light tours in December. To avoid peak use periods, call the park for suggested visitation and tour times.

Lewis and Clark Caverns are the largest limestone caves in Montana and have fascinated children as well as adults for many years. The labyrinth of these underground caves leads you through narrow passages among stalactites and stalagmites which glitter and drip. Truly a limestone fairyland decorated by nature, these colorful and intriguing formations make for a worthwhile two-hour tour. Also within the park are breathtaking views of the Tobacco Root Mountains and the Jefferson River valley.

L The Broken Spur Motel
124 W. Elm, Hwy 2 W., Three Forks. 285-3237. Reservations only (888) 354-3048. www.brokenspurmotel.com

The Broken Spur Motel is a western motel with old-fashioned hospitality conveniently located in historic Three Forks. Featuring deluxe rooms at reasonable rates, the Broken Spur's guestrooms include queen size beds, nonsmoking rooms, cable TV, phones, kitchenettes, special suites for families or meetings, and handicapped accessible accommodations. Enjoy complimentary continental breakfast with fresh coffee, tea, hot chocolate, juice, and homemade cinnamon rolls, muffins, and toast served in the spacious lobby. Stay connected during your visit with the high-speed wireless Internet and telephone in the motel's TV area, and don't miss the onsite gift shop featuring Montana-made gifts and souvenirs. The Broken Spur is close to many activities and sites in the area, and they welcome you to stay with them year-round!

Montana Trivia
Many of the scenes for the Robert Redford production *A River Runs Through It* were filmed in the Gallatin Canyon on the Gallatin River. The actual story was supposed to take place on the Blackfoot river

THREE RIVERS

Captain Lewis, July 28th, 1805:
Both Capt. C. and myself corrisponded in opinon with respect to the impropriety of calling either of these streams the Missouri and accordingly agreed to name them after the President of the United States and the Secretaries of the Treasury and state having previously named one river in honour of the Secretaries of War and Navy. In pursuance of this resolution we called the S.W. fork, that which we meant to ascend, Jefferson's River in honor of that illustrious personage Thomas Jefferson. *[the author of our enterprise.}* the Middle fork we called Madison's River in honor of James Madison, and the S.E. Fork we called Gallitin's River in honor of Albert Gallitin [Gallatin]. the two first are 90 yards wide and the last is 70 yards, all of them run with great velocity and th[r]ow out large bodies of water. Gallitin's River is reather more rapid than either of the others, is not quite as deep but from all appearances may be navigated to a consider-able distance. Capt. C. who came down Madison's river yesterday and has also seen Jefferson's some distance thinks Madison's reather the most rapid, but it is not as much so by any means as Gallitin's. the beds of all these streams are formed of smooth pebble and gravel, and their waters perfectly transparent; in short they are three noble streams…

S Willow Creek Gallery
101 Main St., Willow Creek. 285-3885.
www.willowcreekgallery.blogspot.com

The Willow Creek Gallery, a fine arts store, has been located in the same historic Willow Creek building since 1987. Owners and artists Don and Maren Kast welcome you to stop in and browse the collection of artwork, pottery, sculpture, metal work, jewelry, and woodwork offered. They exclusively feature original work by local and southwest Montana artists. Designer ladies' hats created by Maren are also featured. On the fourth Friday of each month during the summer, Willow Creek offers art walks. Additionally, Don was a fishing outfitter for 40 years and invites you to stop in and chat to enjoy free and valuable local fishing information. Willow Creek Gallery is located next door to the Willow Creek Café and Saloon, one of Montana's best restaurants.

18.
T Hyalite Canyon Recreation Area
17 miles south of Bozeman on S. 19th St.
587-6920

This is the most used recreation area in the state, and for good reason. A beautiful mountain lake sits at the end of a beautiful drive up the canyon of Hyalite Creek. The dam was constructed in the late 1940s, and the reservoir provides water for the community of Bozeman. Surrounding the lake are several campsites, picnic areas, and hiking trails. Fishing is good here and there is a boat launch with parking.

19. *Gas, Food, Lodging*

Gallatin Gateway
Named for its proximity to the entrance of the Gallatin Canyon. The town was originally named Salesville for the Sales brothers who were storekeepers and ran a sawmill in the area in the late 1860s.

20.
T Flying D Ranch: Bison Viewing Area
Just south of Gallatin Gateway.

This is the private property of media mogul Ted Turner. One of the first things he did when he bought the ranch was to remove all of the fences on the 130,000 acres to allow his bison herd (as many as 5,000) to roam as freely as they did in times past. Fortunately for visitors, there is a Forest Service road that traverses his property. The hundreds of "Turner Enterprises" signs along the road are a clear reminder that you are on private property if you leave the road. The road terminates at a trailhead and National Forest Access area.

While following the road, it is highly likely that you will see at least a few of the bison. On a good day, you may see hundreds if not thousands of them on the hillsides. This is probably the closest you will ever come to seeing a herd close to the size of herds that once roamed these areas. If you want to take pictures, do so from your car window. DO NOT get out of your car if bison are anywhere nearby. The can accelerate from standing still to 50 mph in seconds. They will charge suddenly and be on top of you before you can take your finger off the shutter. Almost every year, a tourist gets gored by a bison somewhere in the state because they got too close.

To find the ranch take Hwy. 191 into the Gallatin Canyon just south of Gallatin Gateway. Immediately after you enter the Canyon, watch for Spanish Creek Road veering off to the right of the paved road. As soon as you pass through the gate just a few yards ahead, you are on Turner property.

21. *Gas, Food, Lodging*

Big Sky
In 1902, Frank Crail first set foot in the Big Sky area. While hunting elk in the shadow of Lone Peak he fell in love with the beauty of the surroundings. He purchased the land from the original homesteaders and established the first cattle ranch in the area. Today, the original Crail Ranch house still stands in the meadow area by the golf course.

Following his lead, others moved into the area. Cattle ranching was soon superceded by dude ranches. Most of these, The 320 Ranch, Elk Horn Ranch, Lone Mountain Ranch, Covered Wagon Ranch and the Nine Quarter Circle Ranch are still in full operation today. This was the beginning of the Big Sky tourist trade.

Native Montanan Chet Huntley had a dream for the area as well. In 1969, Huntley and a group of investors including Conoco, Burlington Northern, Montana Power, Chrysler Corporation and Northwest Orient Airlines purchased the Crail Ranch land. In 1973, his dream of creating a year round resort community began to materialize with the official opening of Big Sky Ski & Summer Resort. In 1976, the Boyne Corporation acquired the property and began steps to develop and improve the area. Today it is a bustling year round resort community.

The drive to Big Sky through the Gallatin Canyon is arguably the most beautiful drive in the state, and the area surrounding the resort is arguably some of the most beautiful and dramatic mountain scenery found anywhere in the country. From atop the singular and majestic Lone Peak the view is one of endless mountain peaks. To the immediate north are the dramatic Spanish Peaks and the Spanish Peaks Wilderness area. Just 18 miles to the south is the boundary of Yellowstone National Park. Over 3 million acres of pristine land surrounding Big Sky is set aside as wilderness area. Big Sky sits in the middle of the greater Yellowstone ecosystem, which has some of the cleanest air and water quality in the world. It's not unusual to see moose, mountain goats, elk, big horn sheep, eagles, bear, deer or coyotes wandering around. The nearby Gallatin river is one of the best blue-ribbon trout streams in the world and was the site where "A River Runs Through It" was filmed.

Big Sky	Jan	Feb	March	April	May	June	July	Aug	Sep	Oct	Nov	Dec	Annual
Average Max. Temperature (F)	31.1	35.1	43.0	51.3	61.8	69.6	77.7	78.4	68.9	55.7	38.0	29.5	53.4
Average Min. Temperature (F)	7.4	7.3	15.3	22.7	29.6	35.7	40.0	38.3	31.8	23.2	13.3	6.1	22.6
Average Total Precipitation (in.)	1.41	1.18	1.16	1.34	2.75	2.60	1.66	1.51	1.54	1.43	1.33	1.31	19.22
Average Total SnowFall (in.)	31.8	21.2	19.6	7.1	4.9	0.9	0.2	0.0	0.2	4.7	16.9	31.7	139.5
Average Snow Depth (in.)	22	28	26	5	0	0	0	0	0	0	2	15	8

T Soldier's Chapel
Just south of entrance to Big Sky

This structure was built in 1955 as a World War II memorial. The inscription on the plaque in front of this beautiful little chapel reads: "In tribute to those immortal soldiers of the 163rd infantry who with courage and devotion died in pain, defending their country and the cause of freedom for all men. The 163rd Infantry, 41st Division, of Montana.

L Elkhorn Ranch
33133 Gallatin Rd., Gallatin Gateway. 995-4291. www.elkhornranchmt.com

Welcome to the Elkhorn Ranch, one of the few remaining traditional dude ranches where a natural outdoor experience is every activity's focus. Nestled just one mile from Yellowstone National Park amid millions of acres of beautiful mountain scenery and wildlife, the ranch offers log cabin lodging complete with modern facilities. Home-cooked meals are served in the log dining room or on trail-side cook-outs. Discover Rocky Mountain wilderness on trail rides accompanied by experienced wranglers, or fish on some of the finest blue ribbon streams. In the evening, get ready for cookouts, square dancing, bonfires, and sing-a-longs. Children of all ages are welcome; the ranch is also available for small conferences during June and September.

L Nine Quarter Circle Ranch
5000 Taylor Fork Rd., Gallatin Gateway. 995-4276. www.ninequartercircle.com; nineqtrcircle@mcn.net

Tucked in a beautiful valley where the only sounds at night are cascading waters, the Nine Quarter Circle Ranch boasts over fifty years of

Kelsey family dude ranching. Providing a perfect family vacation atmosphere, Kim and Kelly Kelsey invite you to explore a new world of fun and adventure with daily horseback riding, all day rides, overnight pack trips, and fly-fishing on the "Blue Ribbon" Gallatin River. Ranch guests are treated to home-cooked, family style dinners, comfortable log cabin accommodations, and a relaxed atmosphere that invites individuals of all ages to explore the magnificent Rocky Mountain country surrounding them. Other amenities and activities include child supervision, squaredancing, Gym Khana, hayrides, movies, sing-a-longs, a private trout pond, and fly-fishing instruction. Rough it in comfort, and experience one of the West's best remaining traditional dude ranches!

L The Covered Wagon Ranch
34035 Gallatin Rd., Gallatin Gateway. 995-4237 or (800) 995-4237,www.coveredwagonranch.com; info@coveredwagonranch.com

Operating since 1925, the family-oriented Covered Wagon Ranch offers refined vintage charm amid breathtaking scenery. Ten historic log cabins feature wood burning stoves, private bathrooms, log furniture, and porches. In the rustic main lodge, enjoy home-cooked, hearty western meals served family-style. Read a book in the quiet library, cozy up to the fireplace, soak in the outdoor hot tub, or explore the well-equipped rec hall. Looking for adventure? The Covered Wagon Ranch is located just three miles north of Yellowstone with easy access to fly-fishing, wildlife viewing, rafting, hiking, snowmobiling, snowshoeing, downhill and cross-country skiing, and more. Horseback rides are a ranch specialty, with rides tailored to guests' desires and skills. Experience the Covered Wagon Ranch's year-round tradition of excellence with a dude ranch vacation, or stop by for dinner during winter when the restaurant welcomes the general public

FL 320 Guest Ranch
205 Buffalo Horn Creek Rd., Gallatin Gateway. 995-4283 or (800) 243-0320. www.320ranch.com; info@320ranch.com

A truly western experience and vacation of a lifetime awaits you at the 320 Guest Ranch. Relax along the banks of the Gallatin River and cast your line into the stream or ride to an area mountain lake complete with float tube and fins. In the summer, experience trail rides to 10,000-foot mountain peaks, whitewater rafting, hiking, mountain biking, riverside barbecues, and abundant wildlife. For winter, ski, snowmobile, or snowshoe in deep powder. Choose from deluxe duplex cabins, 2 bedroom riverside cabins with fireplace and kitchenettes, or 3 bedroom/2bath log homes with fireplace, jetted tubs, and full-size kitchens. Stay as long as you like. The 320

320 Guest Ranch

family will help arrange your vacation and can also host your wedding, family reunion, or company retreat. Located only minutes from Yellowstone National Park

22. *Food, Lodging*

V Grizzly Outfitters
11 Lone Peak Dr., St. 101, Big Sky Town Center, Big Sky. 995-2939 or (888) 807-9452. www.grizzlyoutfitters.com; shop@grizzlyoutfitters.com

Grizzly Outfitters is all about freedom to explore a diversity of outdoor challenges in whatever style you choose. They are conveniently located in the Town Center of Big Sky. Their goal is to furnish everyone with the information and equipment to tackle multi-sport adventures. Their staff of seasoned outdoor adventurers has the knowledge and experience to assist everyone from novice to expert. During the summer they specialize in mountain biking, camping, hiking, and climbing. In the winter season, they offer the latest equipment for all snow sports—snowshoeing, snowboarding, downhill, telemark, randonee, and cross country skiing. You'll find product lines such as Patagonia, Black Diamond, Marmot, Solstice, Mountain Hardware, Lowa, Garmont, Voile, K2, Osprey, Boeri, Camelbak, Kavu, Dale of Norway, Oakley, Smith, Maui Jim, and more.

Montana Trivia

The nation's longest river begins in this part of Montana. The Gallatin, Madison, and Jefferson Rivers meet near Three Forks as the headwaters of the Missouri River.

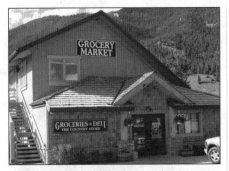

F Country Market & Deli
66 Market Place, Meadow Village Center, Big Sky.
995-4636. www.bigskygrocery.com;
antares@myfamily.com

Country Market & Deli, open 8 am-8 pm year-round, is Big Sky's only full-service grocery store. Offering delivery service and welcoming custom orders, the market prides itself on combining quality with reputable service. Select from carved-to-order meats, custom sliced gourmet deli meats, imported and domestic cheeses, and choice organic and natural foods, including fresh-picked fruits and vegetables. International coffee bean varieties and fresh-ground coffee accompany beers, microbrews, and the area's largest wine selection. In addition, pre-arrival fridge and cupboard stocking services are available. Stop by today to experience quality, service, and exceptional food!

F By Word of Mouth
2815 Aspen Dr., Ste. 3, Big Sky. 995-2992.
www.bigskycatering.com;
bwombigsky@montana.net

Welcome to delightful dining in a casual atmosphere at By Word of Mouth Restaurant and Catering. Scrumptious fare created by Chef/Owner, John Flach, varies from traditional to unique. Savor exquisite appetizers, salads, soups, and entrees featuring Montana organic products and Angus Beef. The Wine Spectator "Award of Excellence" Wine List and full bar complements any meal, and Tokyo Tuesdays and Friday Night Fish Fry are local favorites. For private events, the restaurant's catering services tailor menus to customer needs and range from intimate cocktail parties to outdoor Montana barbeques. Visit By Word of Mouth today for unbeatable service and food that is distinctly Montana! The restaurant is open seven days a week with open bar beginning at 4 pm, dinner served from 5-11 pm, and closings at midnight or later. Reservations are appreciated.

L Lone Mountain Ranch
750 Lone Mountain Ranch Rd., Big Sky. 995-4644
or (800) 514-4644. www.lmranch.com;
lmr@lmranch.com

Lone Mountain Ranch is a historic guest ranch located just 18 miles from Yellowstone Park. This

Lone Mountain Ranch

award winning resort specializes in family ranch and ski adventure vacations. Summer activities include horseback riding, hiking, guided trips into Yellowstone Park, an Outdoor Youth Adventures program, canoeing, kayaking, llama treks, campfire sing-a-longs, and much more. Winter offers 80 km of groomed cross-country ski trails, snowshoeing, downhill skiing at nearby Big Sky Ski Resort, Outdoor Youth Adventures and Yellowstone Park ski tours. Named the 2002 ORVIS Endorsed Fly Fishing Lodge of the Year, the Ranch offers guided trips year-round to the many nearby blue ribbon trout streams. Acclaimed cuisine, cozy log cabins, and on-site massage therapists provide guests with exceptional creature comforts after a day of fun and adventure.

L River Rock Lodge & Resort Property Management
3080 Pine Dr., Big Sky. 995-4455 or
(866) 995-4455. www.riverrocklodging.com and
www.rpmbigsky.com; info@riverrocklodging.com

Locally owned and operated, Resort Property Management offers superior guest service and exquisite Big Sky accommodations. The variety of lodging choices found within the special collection of vacation rental condominiums and homes ensures that Resort Property Management has the perfect place for you. Every property is fully furnished, and most provide indoor or outdoor hot tubs with some boasting swimming pools and saunas. The company also proudly offers the 29-room River Rock Lodge. This hidden gem anchors the northeast corner of Big Sky's West Fork Meadows and is within close proximity to year-round recreation, shopping, and dining. With an office and front desk that is staffed 24 hours a day, 7 days a week, Resort Property Management is your destination for fine lodging and the assistance you need in planning your next outdoor adventure!

M Montana Real Estate Co. of Big Sky
145 Center Ln., Unit E, Big Sky. 995-3322 or
(800) 369-4879. www.mtreco.com.

Located between Yellowstone and Bozeman, the Montana Real Estate Company of Big Sky showcases premier southwestern Montana properties and serves as the exclusive listing representative of Moonlight Basin Ranch. The brokerage's professionals offer more combined experience in premium Montana resort and recreation properties than anyone in Big Sky and pride themselves on covering territory from Ennis and West Yellowstone to Bozeman and Big Sky. Whether you're looking for investment property, ski-in/ski-out cabins, undeveloped ranch acreage, summer golf residences, Gallatin and Madison River fishing retreats, or a dream vacation home, Montana Real Estate Company of Big Sky provides Montana's best. The Realtors® guarantee to help you find your own piece of beautiful Rocky Mountain Country. Visit them today at their conveniently located offices in Meadow Village, Moonlight Lodge, and Madison Lodge on the Moonlight Basin slopes.

Connoisseurs of life.

Big Sky | Sotheby's
INTERNATIONAL REALTY

Big Sky Sotheby's International Realty
P.O. Box 160056   1927 Lone Mtn. Trail
Big Sky, MT 59716
t 866.995.2211   f 406.995.4511
bigskysothebysrealty.com

Each office is independently owned and operated.

L East West Resorts at Big Sky
1 Mountain Loop Rd., Big Sky. 995-7600 or
(866) 646-1688. www.eastwestbigsky.com;
bigskyres@eastwestresorts.com

Discover grand views and your own little piece of Big Sky with East West Resorts at Big Sky. Representing properties in Moonlight Basin, Mountain Village, and Meadow Village, East West Resorts features an extensive selection of lodging and accommodations to suit all preferences and needs. Whether you're looking for a premier ski-in/ski-out cabin, chalet, condominium, penthouse, or luxurious private home, East West Resorts and their professional staff will help you find the perfect accommodations for an unforgettable Big Sky vacation. All East West Resort guests also enjoy access to the Moonlight Basin spa and waterfall hot tub, housekeeping services, and exclusive concierge services covering everything from booking your dinner reservations to arranging private ski lessons. Be an East West Resorts' guest, and experience unrivaled accommodations, comfort, and customer satisfaction.

M Moonlight Spa
One Mountain Loop Rd., Big Sky. 995-7700.

Moonlight Spa is a year-round haven of rejuvenation, pampering, and serenity. Inspired by the surrounding natural beauty, Moonlight Spa offers numerous treatments, including Spanish Peaks Hot Stone Massage, Montana Wild Honeysuckle Salt Glow, River's Edge Detoxifying Ritual, and more. All signature treatments and custom-blended products incorporate ingredients indigenous to Moonlight Basin and Western Montana. Blurring the line between indoors and out, Moonlight Spa provides harmony and balance with tastefully incorporated natural elements, floor to ceiling windows in the intimate fitness area, and a unique indoor entrance to the outdoor heated pool. Guest experiences are built around the Ayurvedic principles of Earth, Water, Fire, Air, and Ether. With three massage therapy rooms, facial room, couple's room, vischy shower room, and a Relaxation Sanctuary, Moonlight Spa is Big Sky's only full-service luxury resort spa!

**M Big Sky Sotheby's
International Realty**
1927 Lone Mountain Trail, Big Sky. 995-2211 or
(866) 995-2211. www.bigskysothebysrealty.com;
info@bigskysothebysrealty.com

Big Sky is nestled between the Spanish Peaks and the Madison and Gallatin Ranges of southwest Montana. One of the biggest draws to Big Sky is the incomparable skiing, both downhill and cross-country. Fly-fishing, hiking, rafting, backpacking, mountain biking, horseback riding, and golfing are some of Big Sky's most popular warm weather activities. Big Sky Sotheby's International Realty is under the management of owners Cathy Gorman, Tim Cyr, Dave Cyr, and Anne Staudt. In addition to being rewarded with some of Big Sky's most exquisite listings, clients also receive the knowledge and expertise of professional Realtors® who truly understand the Big Sky real estate market. Whether you're thinking about relocating or simply want to own a piece of Montana vacation heaven, contact the friendly staff of Big Sky Sotheby's International Realty.

West Yellowstone

West Yellowstone is located at the West Gate to Yellowstone Park and offers four seasons of recreational opportunity. Although the town only has 900 year-round residents, well over one million people enter the park each year via this small town. Visitors across the globe come to take advantage of the endless possibilities for outdoor enjoyment, be it fishing the many blue-ribbon streams, or snowmobiling the nearly 1,000 miles of groomed trails accessible from hotel rooms, and cross country skiing. West Yellowstone is ideally located at the center of fun and recreation.

West Yellowstone may well be one of the finest meccas for fly fishing enthusiasts. Many scenes from the movie "A River Runs Through It" were filmed on the Gallatin River north of West Yellowstone. Professional guides and outfitters throughout the area offer advice and service to visiting fisher-folk, and are eager to help you make the most of your fishing excursion in Yellowstone Country.

With Yellowstone National Park at the front door, the hiking, biking, sightseeing, wildlife watching opportunities are endless, and the national forest lands which border West Yellowstone on the remaining three sides offer one breathtaking vista after another! Learn more at www.wyellowstone.com.

H The 1959 Earthquake
West Yellowstone

On August 17, 1959, at 11:37 P.M., this spectacularly scenic section of Montana became the focus of worldwide attention and made modern history. A heavy shock smashed the soft summer night, earth and rock buckled, lifted and dropped. In several mighty heaves Mother Earth reshaped her mountains in violent response to an agony of deep-seated tensions no longer bearable. A mountain moved, a new lake was formed, another lake was fantastically tilted, sections of highway were dropped into a lake, the earth's surface was ripped by miles of faults, and 28 persons were missing or dead. The area is now safe and much of it has been preserved and marked by the Forest Service for all to see. The Madison River Canyon Earthquake area, located a few miles northwest of here, is an awesome testimonial to Nature's might.

HF Timberline Café
135 Yellowstone Ave., 646-9349.
my.montana.net/timberlinecafe/

The Timberline Cafe, in operation since it was built in the early 1900's, offers a charming family atmosphere in a smoke-free environment. Homemade soups, entrees, pies, and pastries are prepared daily from fresh ingredients. They feature a full soup and salad bar. Check out the Idaho Spud with all the fixings. The menu offers the finest steak, chicken, buffalo steaks and burgers, classic burgers, gourmet entrees like fresh made lasagna, fabulous fresh breakfasts, cinnamon rolls and great snacks anytime. Their meat is fresh

because they grind it on site. Their menu will please even the most discriminating appetites any time of the day. They also offer vegetarian selections. Stop in, say hello to Tom, Dee, and the crew while enjoying a memorable meal while you are in West Yellowstone. Visit them on the web.

V SeeYellowstone.com
215 Yellowstone Ave. in West Yellowstone. 646-9310 or (800) 221-115. www.seeyellowstone.com or email: info@seeyellowstone.com

You are just one call away from a Yellowstone Country Adventure vacation of a lifetime! SeeYellowstone.com has been helping people plan their Yellowstone destination vacation for over twenty five years. They are a one-stop shop for all winter and summer Yellowstone, Glacier and Grand Teton Park area lodging, tours, activities, air, and ground transportation. SeeYellowstone.com specializes in individual and family vacations, group tours, and international travelers. Check out their discount airfares and custom value packages (combining lodging, tours,

and meals). Their Parade Rest Guest Ranch also provides all-inclusive cabin lodging and meals with horseback lessons and mountain trail riding. Winter snowmobile rentals and snowcoach tours are also available.

V Back Country Adventure Snowmobile & Snowcoach Tours
224 Electric, West Yellowstone. 646-9317 or (800) 924-7669. www.Backcountry-Adventures.com; Jerry@backcountry-adventures.com

Back Country Adventure Snowmobile and Snowcoach Tours is a great snowmobile headquarters while you enjoy your vacation in the Snowmobile Capital of the World. They offer a variety of the latest models from Polaris and Arctic Cat for rent in single and double machines. The highest quality equipment and maintenance helps insure a very safe, incredibly fun adventure. From sport to touring, they have a sled to meet your needs. Complete clothing package rentals, includ-

West Yellowstone	Jan	Feb	March	April	May	June	July	Aug	Sep	Oct	Nov	Dec	Annual
Average Max. Temperature (F)	24.2	30.8	38.0	47.6	59.3	68.5	79.2	77.2	66.4	52.5	34.5	25.3	50.3
Average Min. Temperature (F)	-0.2	2.5	8.7	19.7	28.7	35.3	39.6	37.2	29.4	22.1	10.3	1.8	19.6
Average Total Precipitation (in.)	2.14	1.72	1.72	1.53	2.05	2.37	1.50	1.37	1.48	1.54	1.95	2.20	21.56
Average Total SnowFall (in.)	32.9	26.6	23.3	10.7	3.3	0.6	0.0	0.1	1.1	7.3	22.9	31.8	160.4
Average Snow Depth (in.)	30	38	38	21	1	0	0	0	0	1	7	18	13

Section 2

GALLATIN RIVER AREA AND MADISON RIVER VALLEY
INCLUDING BOZEMAN, BIG SKY, ENNIS, THREE FORKS AND WEST YELLOWSTONE

EARTHQUAKE LAKE

A severe earthquake caused a massive landslide on August 17, 1959 at 11:37 p.m. Several faults in the Madison River area moved at the same time causing an earthquake that triggered a massive landslide.

The slide moved at 100 mph and happened in less than one minute. Over 80 million tons of rock crashed into the narrow canyon, burying an open meadow where some campers had stopped for the night.

The landslide completely blocked the Madison River and caused it to form Earthquake Lake. The force of the slide displaced both the air in the canyon and water of the Madison River. It created high velocity winds and a wall of water that swept through the area, just downstream from the slide, killing five people in its path.

Earthquake at Hebgen Lake

The Hebgen Lake Earthquake measured 7.5 on the Richter scale. At least three blocks of the earth's crust suddenly dropped as two faults moved simultaneously... the Red Canyon fault and the Hebgen Lake fault.

The north shore of Hebgen Lake dropped 19 feet and cabins fell into the water. Hebgen Lake sloshed back and forth. Huge waves called seiches crested over Hebgen Dam. This earth filled dam cracked in at least four places, but held. Three sections of Highway 287 fell into the lake. Hundreds of campers were trapped.

28 people lost their lives as a result of the earthquake. Their names appear on a bronze plaque on one of the massive dolomite boulders carried across the canyon by the slide. The dolomite boulder serves as a memorial.

Madison River Canyon Earthquake Area

This immense earthquake's impact shocked and chilled the world. Families gradually rebuilt their lives, structures and roads were reconstructed.

In 1960, a 38,000 acre area in the canyon was designated as the "Madison River Canyon Earthquake Area." This portion of the Gallatin National Forest is of great scientific and general interest.

As you travel through this area, the effects of the ever-changing earth can be seen all around you.

The Visitor Center is located on Highway 287, 17 miles west of Highway 191, and 25

Two people died at Cliff Lake Campground, 15 miles southwest of the Madison Canyon landslide, when a large boulder bounced over the picnic table and landed on their tent. Their three sons, sleeping a few feet away, were not injured. 1959 U.S. Forest Service photo.

miles to the town of West Yellowstone, Montana.

This facility is accessible to people with disabilities.

Open: Memorial Day - late September, 7 days a week, 8:30 - 6:00 p.m. Telephone: 646-7369 (V/TDD)

Map Guide

1. A Spillway was cut across the slide by the U.S. Army Corps of Engineers. On September 10, 1959 water passed through the 250 ft. wide and 14 ft. deep channel. On October 17, 1959 the channel was deepened another 50 ft.

2. Visitor Center and Slide - Come and view the slide from the observation room. Listen to the interpreter's story. Walk the trail to the Memorial Boulder and overlook.

3. Rock Creek Turnout - A Forest Service campground lies under 100 feet of water just off this point. Some campers escaped and others perished from the rising waters.

4. Earthquake Lake - The slide dammed the Madison River to form Earthquake Lake, which filled in three weeks and created a new body of water 190 ft. deep and 6 miles long.

5. Boat Launch - This portion of the old highway continues to serve the public. The old highway lies beneath the waters of Earthquake Lake.

6. Refuge Point - This ridge provided a place of protection during the night of August 17 for

many survivors of the earthquake. The next morning Forest Service smoke jumpers parachuted to this point and set up rescue operations. Later that day helicopters evacuated the survivors.

7. Ghost Village - These deserted cabins were displaced here from the waters of Earthquake Lake.

8. Cabin Creek Scarp - At this site a 21 foot fault scarp severed the old campground.

9. Hebgen Dam - The earth fill dam held, although it suffered damage from tremors and huge earthquake caused waves called seiches.

10. Building Destruction - A short walk will take you through this area. You can see the old resort cabins that are submerged in Hebgen Lake.

11. Road Destruction - One of the three places where the road collapsed into Hebgen Lake. Look along the old roadbed to see where the land shifted during the earthquake.

12. Red Canyon - You can view the fault scarp that extends 14 miles in this area. A fault scarp is a cliff created by movement along a fault.

13. Duck Creek Y - This is where the epicenter of the earthquake occurred.

Reprinted from U.S. Forest Service brochure.

The north shore of Hebgen Lake was submerged when the rock on which it rests dropped down adjacent to the new Hebgen fault scarp. The main residence at Hilgard Lodge dropped off its foundation into the lake and floated to this location. 1959 U.S. Forest Service photo.

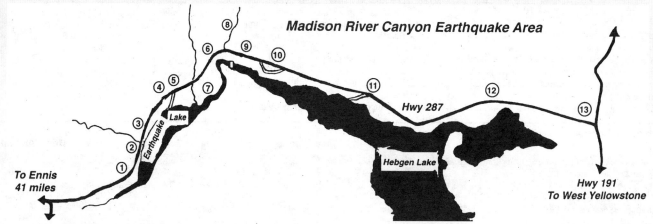

Madison River Canyon Earthquake Area

To Ennis 41 miles

Hwy 287

Earthquake Lake

Hebgen Lake

Hwy 191 To West Yellowstone

ing helmets, are also available, and a free tank of gas is included with each day's rental. Ask them about room/snowmobile packages and guided trips. They are licensed to guide in the Gallatin National Forest and Yellowstone National Park. All of their snowmobiles are also available for purchase.

F   Ernie's Bakery & Deli
406 Highway Ave., West Yellowstone. 646-9467.

Regarded as the Best Dog-Gone Deli in the West, Ernie's Deli & Bakery showcases tasty sandwiches and freshly baked sweet treats. For breakfast, sample scrumptious sticky buns, cinnamon rolls, and bagel sandwiches. Lunch fare includes hot and cold sandwiches made-to-order, homemade soups, chocolate chip cookies, and more. The food is so good that Travelocity selected Ernie's from more than 30,000 entries as a top U.S. insider spot for 2005! For those unable to stay and enjoy the deli's relaxed atmosphere and outdoor picnic tables, box lunches are available. Anglers, hunters, hikers, and travelers frequently call in pick-up orders, and beer and wine is also available to go. Popular

with locals and returning visitors from across the world, Ernie's Deli & Bakery invites you to stop by, say hi, and enjoy a great meal!

L   Parade Rest Ranch
7979 Grayling Creek Rd., West Yellowstone. 646-7217 or (800) 753-5934.
www.paraderestranch.com;
info@paraderestranch.com

Rejuvenate your spirit just minutes from Yellowstone at Parade Rest Ranch. Since the 1930s, the ranch's easy-going pace has coupled with recreational adventures ranging from blue-ribbon fly-fishing and horseback riding to mountain biking and hiking. Ranch guests can opt for hot western meals three times a day in the dining hall or pack a lunch for a day spent exploring Montana's outdoor wonders. In the evening, overnight guests retire to one of fifteen cozy log cabins boasting comfortable beds, modern bathrooms, porches, and sometimes a wood-burning stove. For those unable to spend a night, opt for a tantalizing taste of the West at Monday and Friday

night cookouts, or take a scenic trail ride. No matter your length of stay, Parade Rest Ranch welcomes you to experience Rocky Mountain beauty and friendship!

L   Ho Hum Motel
126 N. Canyon St., West Yellowstone. 646-7746 or (888) 331-7864.

The family-owned and operated Ho Hum Motel is located in the downtown area of West Yellowstone. Clean, comfortable, and economical accommodations are provided year-round with standard amenities. All rooms are equipped with queen beds, bathtubs and showers, large TVs, and electric heating. The Ho Hum Motel is centrally located to restaurants and shopping and next door to the West Park Mall with ten unique shops. They are just two blocks from the entrance to Yellowstone National Park and conveniently located to the area's wonderful attractions. Non-smoking rooms are available, and pets are allowed. There is plenty of parking for all sizes of vehicles, and winter plug-ins are available. The Ho Hum Motel can also help you arrange your snowmobile adventure!

25.   *Gas, Food, Lodging*

H   Madison Hotel
On Yellowstone Ave. in West Yellowstone

The Forest Service granted Jess Pierman a special-use permit to build a hotel and restaurant here in 1910. A large tent accommodated guests until the present hotel was under constrtiction in the fall of 1912. Doll Bartlett began cooking for Pierman in 1910, saving much of her weekly ten-dollar paycheck. Her husband Roxy drove the stage between Monida and West Yellowstone. By the time the hotel was under construction, the Bartletts had saved

It Happened in Montana

July 17, 2001, Bozeman hosted the world premiere of *Jurassic Park III*. The model for actor Sam Neills character is Bozeman's own Jack Horner, world famous paleontologist and curator of paleontology at the Museum of the Rockies in Bozeman. In one of the early scenes actress Laura Dern mentions she's using Horner as a source for her latest book. The next scene supposedly takes place at Fort Peck Lake in eastern Montana. In it, actor Neill is driving a Museum of the Rockies vehicle. Horner was the technical advisor for this movie as he was for the two previous Jurassic Park thrillers.

enough money to buy the business which they ran until Roxy died in the 1920s. Doll continued to run the hotel with her second husband, George Pickup. The two-story rectangular plan is of simple log construction with saddle-notched corner timbering and a prominent front dormer. The original six upstairs rooms, warmed by a cut stone fireplace in the downstairs lobby, catered to rail and stage travelers. Each room had a pitcher, a wash basin and a chamber pot. Water came from a well across the street. The hotel expanded adding fourteen rooms in 1921 and a bar and dance floor soon after, but there was no running water until the 1900s. In 1923, President Harding was a guest and antiquated registers show that such Hollywood greats as Wallace Beery and Gloria Swanson enjoyed the hospitality of the Madison Hotel. Log support

columns and beams, wood floors, light fixtures, the stone fireplace and many of the room furnishings are original. Although not the first hotel in West Yellowstone, the Madison is the only hotel that remains from this early period when tourism was in its infancy.

H Union Pacific Dining Hall
Yellowstone Ave. next to Museum of the Yellowstone

As tourism blossomed during the first decades of the twentieth century, the Union Pacific Railroad considered how to better accommodate travelers. Officials conceived the idea of building restaurants and pavilions architecturally similar to the monumental lodges being constructed in national parks. Acclaimed architect Gilbert Stanley Underwood, whose mastery of the Rustic style set the standard for national park architecture, designed this splendid dining lodge for the Union Pacific. Completed in 1926, it was an intermediate project built while Underwood was designing the world-renowned Ahwahnee Hotel at Yosemite National Park. The Rustic style of this lodge, its wood and welded tuff in grand harmony with the landscape, echoes that of the famed hotel. Featuring mammoth walk-in fireplaces, the multi-level interior is characteristic of Underwood's designs. As part of a national collection of Underwood's work, the lodge gains added significance as a rare surviving example of a railroad dining hall constructed to mimic park architecture.

T Yellowstone IMAX Theater
West entrance to Yellowstone Park, West Yellowstone. 646-4100 or (888) 854-5862

Grizzlies, geysers, and grandeur is what the centerpiece film, "Yellowstone", provides on a six story high screen with over 12,000 watts of digital surround sound. The IMAX experience will transport you to places you've only dreamed of. You are drawn into the film and become a player in the movie. Ten times the size of 35mm, the Imax experience is one of such detailed and crisp realism that it will become a memory of a lifetime. The theatre seats 354 and is open year round! IMAX movies all day and Hollywood blockbusters at night with new movies added often. Call for more information on shows and rates.

T Museum of the Yellowstone
124 Yellowstone Ave. in West Yellowstone. 646-1100. www.yellowstonehistoriccenter.org

Located in the 1909 Union Pacific Depot, this museum has historic exhibits featuring cowboys, mountain men, Native Americans, and Yellowstone Park. Come face to face with the wildlife of Yellowstone, including bison, elk and the legendary grizzly "Old Snaggletooth." Catch their fly-fishing exhibit that chronicles the history of the fly-fishing shops in West Yellowstone. Get derailed in the exhibit on the history of the Union Pacific railroad; complete with models of the train and the Northern and Union Pacific Depots. Transport yourself back to the fires of 1988. Experience the reality of man's struggle to save the famous Old Faithful Inn and the Town of West Yellowstone. Discover how the infernos rejuvenated the ecosystem of Yellowstone National Park and how the beauty still prevails. Shake, rattle, and roll with the quake that rocked the entire Yellowstone area. Can you build a structure to withstand an earthquake? Their earthquake table will give you the answer. Experience the Yellowstone of 1908-1960. With a train whistle, your trip to "Wonderland" begins. Put on your "duster" and take a magical tour through the finest souvenirs of yesteryear, including stagecoaches, memorabilia, and historic film footage. An admission is charged. The museum is open from July–August from 9 a.m. to 9 p.m. and September–October from 9 a.m. to 7 p.m.

T Grizzly and Wolf Discovery Center
201 S. Canyon St., West Yellowstone. 646-7001 or (800) 257-2570. www.grizzlydiscoverctr.org; info@grizzlydiscoveryctr.com

V Yellowstone Alpen Guides Co.
555 Yellowstone Ave., West Yellowstone. 646-9591 or (800) 858-3502. www.yellowstoneguides.com; scott@yellowstoneguides.com

Yellowstone memories last forever, and Yellowstone Alpen Guides is dedicated to helping you create those memories. Offering guided tours of Yellowstone National Park for 20 years, Alpen Guides specializes in providing close-up, intimate tours of this delicate ecosystem. Year-round tours are led by experienced naturalist guides and are customized to couples, families, and small groups in a relaxed atmosphere. Take a private guided tour during summer that may include wildlife viewing, a day hike to a backcountry geyser basin, or exploration of the famous sites. Winter snowcoach tours, which may include skiing and snowshoeing, operate daily to Old Faithful and the Grand Canyon of Yellowstone. Package tours are also available. Discover Yellowstone Alpen Guides, and discover the magic of Yellowstone on a trip of a lifetime!

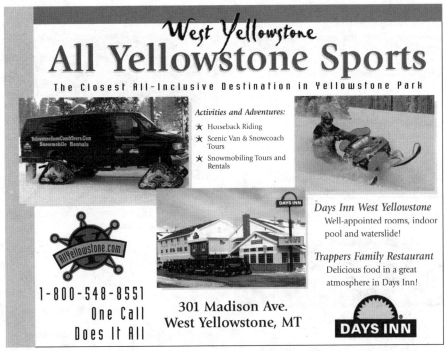

F Timberline Café
135 Yellowstone Ave., West Yellowstone. 646-9349. www.my.montana.net/timberlinecafe/ fivefoot21@montana.net

Western hospitality meets grandmother's home cooking at the Timberline Cafe. Operating since the early 1900s, the cafe offers a smoke-free family atmosphere with a menu satisfying all appetites. Homemade soups, entrees, pies, and pastries are prepared daily, and a 2005 issue of Montana Magazine recognized the cafe's "homespun apple pie" as one of the state's best. In addition to gourmet entrees like lasagna, specialty chicken dishes, fabulous fresh breakfasts, and cinnamon rolls, the Timberline Café's extensive menu offers registered Certified Angus Beef® with a fine selection of steaks, hamburgers, and buffalo. Vegetarian selections and a full soup and salad bar complete with the Idaho Spud complement the cafe's tasty fare. Stop in and say hello to Tom, Dee, and the crew while enjoying a memorable meal! Visit them on the web.

FL Three Bear Lodge & Restaurant
217 Yellowstone Ave. in West Yellowstone. 646-7353 or (800) 646-7353. www.threebearslodge.com

Three Bear Lodge has been a Yellowstone tradition for 30 years. Located just two blocks east of the West Gate entrance to Yellowstone you will find yourself within walking distance to every major attraction in West Yellowstone. Their restaurant is known as one of the best in town and is a local's favorite. As your vacation headquarters Three Bear Lodge can book activities for

both summer and winter activities, which include snowmobile, snow coach, and van tours, as well as horse back riding. Whether you're visiting Yellowstone for the first time or returning as a guest, Three Bear Lodge is an excellent choice for all of your vacation needs. Reservations are strongly encouraged in the summer and required in the winter.

L Kelly Inn
104 S. Canyon St., West Yellowstone. 646-4544 or (800) 259-4672. www.yellowstonekellyinn.com; westyellowstone@kellyinns.com

Stay at the Kelly Inn while visiting the breathtaking expanse of Yellowstone National Park. Enjoy their beautiful new three-story rustic log style property. The 78 large, comfortable guest rooms embody the charm and character of Yellowstone National Park. All rooms feature king or queen sized beds, cable TV, microwaves, and refrigerators, and specialty suites also contain a whirlpool, wet bar, and hairdryer. Other amenities include a large heated indoor pool, sauna, extra-large whirlpool, complimentary continental breakfast, internet access in the lobby, and wireless service throughout the hotel. There is also ample parking for all vehicle sizes and outdoor electric plug-ins. Kelly Inn is located at the entrance to the Park and within walking distance of restaurants and shopping. Open year-round. Visit them on the web.

S Bargain Depot Outlet Stores
Near the intersection of Canyon St. & Yellowstone Ave., West Yellowstone. 646-9047. www.wyellowstone.com/bargaindepot; rklein@mcn.net

The Bargain Depot Outlet Stores are proud of over 20 years of outstanding values and service, offering savings of 40% to 70% off retail prices on clothing for the entire family, including outerwear, travel gear, and Yellowstone Park t-shirts and sweatshirts. They are considered by many to be one of the truly outstanding bargain stores in the entire Northwest. Stop by and see them, and you will be pleasantly surprised to find out that there are indeed bargains in a tourist town! Find them on Main Street (22 Canyon) next to the Canyon Street Grill and across from the Visitors Center at 25 Yellowstone Avenue.

26. *Gas, Food, Lodging*

L ClubHouse Inn
105 S. Electric, West Yellowstone. 646-4892 or (800) 565-6803. www.yellowstoneclubhouseinn.com; westyellowstone@clubhouseinn.com

The West Yellowstone ClubHouse® Inn provides thoughtful amenities at moderate prices. Start each day with a complimentary expanded continental breakfast, including waffles, and enjoy friendly hospitality stemming from a genuine desire to make guests feel at home. Guests enjoy access to an indoor pool and Jacuzzi, fitness center, and coin laundry. Spacious rooms feature well-lit work desks, high-speed wireless Internet access, two phones, irons/ironing boards, hair dryers, and coffeemakers. All rooms also include refrigerators and microwaves. Adjacent to the IMAX Theater, Grizzly & Wolf Discovery Center, and the Museum of the Yellowstone, the ClubHouse® Inn is just a half block away from dining and shopping and two blocks from Yellowstone Park's west gate entrance. For an outstanding value and comfort around every corner, stay at any of the ClubHouse® locations nationwide.

L West Yellowstone Comfort Inn
638 Madison Ave., West Yellowstone. 646-4212 or (888) 264-2466. www.westyellowstonecomfortinn.com; wycomfortinn@aol.com

Located just minutes from Yellowstone National Park's west entrance, the West Yellowstone Comfort Inn offers true western hospitality year-round. Enjoy a large heated swimming pool and spa, high-speed internet, business room, complimentary deluxe continental breakfast, guest laundry, conference room, fax service, handicapped access, winter plug-ins, and more. Spacious, non-smoking rooms offer nice views and include satellite TV, direct dial phones, and full climate control. During your stay, experience western adventure at your doorstep with the area's blue ribbon trout streams, hunting, hiking, Nordic skiing, horseback riding, and snowmobiling. In addition, the hotel is pleased to arrange Yellowstone National Park sightseeing trips on heated snowcoach tours led by knowledgeable local guides. For comfort, convenience, and adventure, make reservations at the West Yellowstone Comfort Inn. Visit them on the web.

27. *Food, Lodging*

H Targhee Pass
Hwy 20, west of West Yellowstone

This pass across the Continental Divide takes its name from an early-day Bannack Chief. Free trappers and fur brigades of the Missouri River and Rocky Mountain Fur companies were familiar with the surrounding country in the early part of the last century.

Chief Joseph led his band of Nez Perce Indians through this pass in 1877 while making his famous 2,000-mile march from the central Idaho country in an effort to evade U.S. troops and find sanctuary in Canada. He was closely followed through the pass by the pursuing forces of General Howard. Joseph repulsed or outdistanced all the commands sent against him until finally forced to surrender to Col. Nelson A. Miles at the Battle of the Bear's Paw, when within a comparatively few miles of the Canadian line.

SHL Madison Hotel, Motel, Gift Shop, and Hostel
139 Yellowstone Ave., West Yellowstone. 646-7745 or (800) 838-7745. madisonhotel@direcway.com

Step back into "Old Yellowstone" ambiance at the Madison Hotel. Constructed in the early 1900s, this historical landmark quickly grew to include 28 rooms, a dance hall, and bar while hosting Presidents Harding and Hoover, Clark Gable, and Gloria Swanson. The historic hotel, featuring a lobby preserved with original furnishings, still offers clean and comfortable rooms May 25 to October 5. Visitors are welcome to tour unrented rooms before 6 pm. For those seeking a quaint place for the night, the West Yellowstone Hostel at the Madison Hotel is ideal. The hostel, housed within a cozy log hotel, provides public restrooms and showers, non-smoking rooms, and private rooms with or without bathrooms. The hostel's common rooms treat guests to a microwave, refrigerator, cable TV, Internet, and free coffee and hot chocolate. Located on-site with the same operating schedule as the hotel, the Madison Motel provides economical lodging with non-smoking, clean rooms that include showers and cable TV. Deluxe rooms feature queen beds, tubs, and air conditioning. Public phones are available, and the motel is within walking distance to restaurants and local activities. In 1959, the hotel's downstairs' rooms were replaced with what is now recognized as one of West Yellowstone's largest gift shops. The famous family-oriented Madison Gift Shop carries a unique selection of moderately priced souvenirs, gifts, collectible t-shirts, and more. On your next visit to Montana, discover Yellowstone the way it used to be with a fascinating stop or overnight stay at the Madison Hotel, Motel, Gift Shop, and West Yellowstone Hostel!

L Brook Trout Inn
1730 Targhee Pass Hwy., West Yellowstone. 646-4254. www.brooktroutinn.com; cabinets@wyellowstone.com

Experience Yellowstone Country with the homey atmosphere of Brook Trout Inn. Located on Yellowstone National Park's doorsteps just 7 minutes from the park's west entrance, the Brook Trout Inn offers comfortable facilities with abundant recreational opportunities. The spacious three-bedroom, two-bath home and a cozy one-

bedroom log cabin are each furnished with a fireplace, satellite TV, radio, microwave, dishwasher, full kitchen, cookware and utensils, linens, and a gas BBQ. In addition, the home includes a washer and dryer, and pets are allowed with permission. Guests of the inn are also privy to convenient outdoor adventure access, including Blue Ribbon fishing, snowmobiling, cross-country skiing, hiking, horseback riding, rafting, and more. On your next trip to Yellowstone Country, satisfy your lodging needs among nature's most beautiful resources, and enjoy the secluded hideaway of Brook Trout Inn.

28. *Food, Lodging*

T Earthquake Lake
See sidebar.

29. *Lodging*

Cameron
Cameron is the namesake of the Cameron family who were early pioneers in the area. In the settlement originally known as Bear Creek, Addison Cameron owned a building that contained the post office, a general store and a dance hall upstairs.

30. *Gas, Food, Lodging*

Ennis
Ennis is a bustling and picturesque western town in the heart of the Madison Valley, east of the Tobacco Root Mountains and 13 miles from historic Virginia City. Primarily a hunting and fishing center, Ennis' three blocks of downtown businesses boast Old West-style facades.

Ennis, like most of the towns in this area, was spawned from the discovery of gold in the area. Within months after gold was discovered at Alder Gulch, William Ennis homesteaded the site along the Madison that is now the town of Ennis. A Mr. Jeffers homesteaded the site across the river. Ranchers, farmers, and businesses soon flocked to the area. By the late 1880s there were three major stage lines servicing the community. The tall grass and favorable climate created an excellent environment to raise horses, cattle, and sheep. Chief White Cloud's tribe of Bannack Indians was friendly to the settlers and whites and Indians existed in harmony. Today this small town of 1,000 is known for its Black Angus and prize Herefords. Timber is harvested from the surrounding forests, and gold mining is making a comeback in the area. But nationally, Ennis is known as a staging area for some of the finest fly-fishing in the world on the blue ribbon Madison River. Another of Ennis' assets, The Ennis National Fish Hatchery, is located only twelve miles south of Ennis.

Nowhere is the love affair with livestock more apparent than in Ennis during Rodeo Weekend. This small town swells with excitement as people from all over come to celebrate one of Montana's most popular Fourth of July rodeos.

Jeffers
Jeffers, situated near the Madison River, is home to some of Montana's oldest ranches. The community draws its name from New York native, Myron D. Jeffers. As a young civil engineer and hopeful miner, Jeffers headed west in 1864 in search of gold. After abandoning this pursuit, Jeffers became interested in herding cattle from Texas. In 1871,

Jeffers made his break with more than 1,894 cattle and 37 head of horses. With this acquisition, Jeffers and his wife established the Yellow Barn Cattle Ranch, and in 1903, opened the area's first post office.

H Raynold's Pass
Hwy 287, south of Ennis

The low gap in the mountains on the sky line south of here is Raynold's Pass over the Continental Divide.

Jim Bridger, famous trapper and scout, guided an expedition of scientists through the pass in June of 1860. The party was led by Capt. W. F. Raynolds of the Corps of Engineers, U.S. Army. They came through from the south and camped that night on the Madison River near this point. Capt. Raynolds wrote "The pass is … so level that it is difficult to locate the exact point at which the waters divide. I named it Low Pass and deem it to be one of the most remarkable and important features of the topography of the Rocky Mountains."

Jim Bridger didn't savvy road maps or air route beacons but he sure knew his way around.

T Ennis National Fish Hatchery
12 miles SW of Ennis. 682-4845

This hatchery is different from most others. Most hatcheries produce fish of various sizes and then stock these fish in public lakes and streams, providing anglers with hours of fun, whereas the Ennis Hatchery is a broodstock hatchery. There are only three rainbow trout broodstock hatcheries in the Nationwide Federal Hatchery System. A broodstock hatchery raises fish to adult size, then takes eggs from those fish, incubating them and shipping them to production hatcheries. A visitor center is open seven days a week, year round.

T Wildlife Museum of the West
121 W. Main St., Ennis. 682-7141

L Fan Mountain Inn
204 N. Main St., Ennis. 682-5200 or (877) 682-5200. www.fanmountaininn.com; fanmtninn@3rivers.net

The Fan Mountain Inn offers small town country hospitality with clean, modern, spacious rooms and beautiful views of the Madison Mountains. The 27 units are complete with king or queen size beds, cable TV, air conditioning, and telephones. Adjoining units, handicap units, and nonsmoking units are also available. They are conveniently located with easy access to downtown Ennis for a variety of shopping and dining experiences. The Fan Mountain Inn is also within walking distance to the renowned Madison River where you can walk along the scenic banks or fish for blue-ribbon trout. Visit them on the web.

LS Rainbow Valley Lodge
4781 U.S. Hwy 287 N, Ennis. 682-4264 or (800) 452-8254. www.rainbowvalley.com

The Rainbow Valley Lodge is open year-round and hosted by Ed and Jeanne Williams, both well known in the world of fly fishing. Full service

Rainbow Valley Lodge

lodging offers 24 immaculate deluxe log cabin style units, fully equipped kitchens, private patios, phones, high speed internet, wireless, fax service, cable television, movies, heated pool, barbecue picnic area, horse corrals, winter plug ins, coin laundry, handicapped accessible, continental breakfast, guide and shuttle services. The breathtaking park-like setting offers and spectacular views of the Rocky Mountains, all in walking distance of the Madison River. Try spring creek fishing on O'Dell Creek behind the lodge. Guests have been returning year after year for over four decades. The shop offers fly rod rentals, fishing gear, gifts, along with pine needle baskets and fishing flies made by Jeanne, a nationally recognized artist

C Ennis RV Village
5034 Hwy 287 N., Ennis. 682-5272 or (866) 682-5272. www.ennisrv.com; ennisrvvillage@hotmail.com

Ennis RV Village is located in the Madison Valley with stunning mountain views, clear running streams flowing into the famed Madison River, and a one-of-a-kind community noted for its friendliness. Ennis RV Village features tent camping and 76 large pull-thru, full service sites with 50 amp electric, sewer, and water. The clean, convenient restrooms have never-ending hot showers that are heated from a geothermic source. Guests also enjoy over eight acres of private park with walking trails for visitors and pets, a large picnic area with BBQ pits and tables, a convenience store, and a club house that provides a place for families or groups to play cards, enjoy dinner together, or just sit and chat. Make Ennis RV

Village your base camp for exploring the area's many activities! Visit them on the web.

31. *Gas, Food, Lodging*

McAllister
The namesake of the McAllister family, local ranchers who settled the area in the late 1800s. In 1887, one of the first churches in Madison County was built here. The Methodist church still stands today.

H Madison Valley
On scenic view turnout just south of McAllister on Hwy. 287

Settlement of the Madison Valley followed on the heels of the Gold Rush to Alder Gulch in the mid 1860s. Homesteaders grazed their livestock in the lush meadows of the valley and surrounding mountains, raising beef and mutton to feed the miners.

Today, in addition to meat production, these ranches serve another important ecological role—maintaining open space and a place for wildlife to prosper.

Thousands of elk, mule deer, whitetail deer, antelope, and other smaller animals live, eat, and migrate through the valley. While public lands of the Beaverhead-Deerlodge National Forest provide protected habitat in the mountains surrounding the valley, ranch lands of the valley bottom provide essential food, security, and freedom of movement for many animals, particularly in winter.

One of the greatest threats to wildlife is the loss of this critical habitat to human encroachment. As ranches are subdivided, the open space and abundant food supply these area ranches provide are lost.

T Kobayashi Beach on Ennis Lake
McAllister. 683-2337

Ennis Lake is relatively shallow and acts like a giant solar collector. The waters in the lake can heat up to 85° (the temperature of a very warm swimming pool) in the summertime making it a great place to swim. Kobayashi Beach is a favorite locals hangout. Its sandy beach is managed by the BLM for Montana Power Company. It's easy to find and makes a great place to take a break from the traveling. At the tiny town of McAllister just north of Ennis, take the road heading east out of town for a little over 3 miles. After you pass through a housing area, you will see the signed beach.

32. *Gas, Food, Lodging*

Norris
As were many towns in this area, Norris was named for a rancher. The cattle from the rich pasturelands south of here were driven to Norris for shipment on the railroad. Cowboys, miners and travelers liked to partake of the nearby hot springs.

Ennis	Jan	Feb	March	April	May	June	July	Aug	Sep	Oct	Nov	Dec	Annual
Average Max. Temperature (F)	33.0	38.3	44.9	55.5	65.5	73.8	82.6	81.5	71.2	59.6	43.3	34.7	57.0
Average Min. Temperature (F)	14.3	17.8	22.1	29.2	36.6	43.2	47.7	46.0	38.5	31.5	23.4	16.8	30.6
Average Total Precipitation (in.)	0.39	0.39	0.72	1.12	2.04	2.32	1.27	1.22	1.17	0.89	0.56	0.42	12.50
Average Total SnowFall (in.)	6.0	4.5	6.0	3.4	1.2	0.1	0.0	0.0	0.3	2.0	4.8	5.2	33.5
Average Snow Depth (in.)	1	0	0	0	0	0	0	0	0	0	0	1	0

H Bozeman Trail
US Hwy 287, 5 miles south of Norris

In 1840, the Oregon Trail was the primary emigration route across the northern part of the United States. Two decades later, when gold was discovered west of here, a trail called the "Corrine Road" was used to bring supplies north from Salt Lake City to Bannack and Virginia City. John Bozeman, determined to shorten the time and distance to the gold strikes, scouted another route, departing from the Oregon Trail at the North Platte River. The Bozeman Trail, or Montana Cutoff, crossed here and can be seen on the opposite hillside.

This trail was used from 1863 to 1868. Sioux Indians frequently attacked the wagons and freight trains as they crossed the eastern leg of the trail. Consequently, Fort Reno, Fort Phil Kearney and Fort C. E. Smith were established to protect travelers but were also the target of Indian attacks.

T Beartrap Canyon
Hwy 84, between Ennis and Norris

This part of the Lee Metcalf Wilderness is popular for hiking, fishing and whitewater sports on the Madison River. The canyon is carved by the river cutting through 1,500 feet of granite rock.

T Norris Hot Springs
East of Norris on Hwy. 84. 685-3303

Near the Madison River this swimming hole has changed very little since the 1880s era open-air wooden pool and bath house were built. The water in the privately owned pool is about 105 degrees F. The hot springs has had a wild reputation over the years, primarily for the swimsuit-optional "buff nights" which were discontinued in the late 1990s in order to appeal to a wider base of clientele. The springs are open year round with an admission fee.

33. *Food, Lodging*

Pony

Pony is located 30 miles southwest of Three Forks on Hwy 287. This old mining town is perched on a steep incline deep in the Tobacco Root Mountains. Pony took its name from Tecumseh "Pony" Smith who mined here in 1868. The approach to Pony is so steep and so tight in the nook it occupies that one resident penned, "Pony, Pony, the beautiful little town where train backed in 'cause it couldn't turn around." Though it may seem like a ghost town, there are about 115 residents. Many of the historic buildings are standing and some are still in use. Pony is a pleasant blend of the past and the present. Nearby is the ghost Strawberry Camp that was named because a miner swinging his pick axe in a strawberry field discovered a vein that was rightly named the Strawberry. Several other ghost mines are above Pony. Pony is the nearest town to Potosi Hot Springs.

T Upper Potosi Hot Springs
West of Pony

Two primitive high-country hot springs pools on public land high in the Tobacco Root Mountains. The road to the nearby campground is unplowed during the winter. A little hiking and dodging cattle is about the only restriction to getting into the soaking pools. Water temperatures in the pools vary from 104 to 110 degrees F.

34. *Gas, Food*

Harrison

This ranch town in the Madison River valley was named for Henry C. Harrison who settled at Willow Creek in 1865. He was known for his Morgan horses and shorthorn cattle. He also operated a large steam dairy.

SCENIC DRIVES

Gallatin Canyon
This 85 mile drive is arguably one of the most beautiful and breathtaking drives in Montana, if not in the country. The drive parallels the Gallatin River and skirts the majestic Spanish Peaks where it ends at the northwest corner of Yellowstone National Park. The yellow cliffs rising from the river on much of the route are constant backdrops for the paintings of the world famous Gary Carter.

HIKES

Bozeman Area
Bozeman has a number of "urban" hikes within the city limits. Some of these trails turn into cross country ski trails in the winter.

Gallagator Trail
From Main St. on the east side of downtown take Church St. south. The trail starts on the right on Story Street just past Bogert Park. The trail follows what was once the Gallatin Valley Electric Railroad right-of-way. The trail goes 1.5 miles to the Museum of the Rockies. A half mile extension goes around the museum and continues south.

Peet's Hill and the Highland Ridge Trail
Peet's Hill provides great views of the city and the surrounding mountain ranges. The hill itself is the ultimate sledding hill for residents in the winter time. A short, but steep walk takes you to the ridge from the parking lot. The trail at the top of the ridge heads south to Kagy Blvd. for 2.3 miles and connects with some of the other trails. The parking lot is on the corner of S. Church Ave. and Story Street near Bogert Park.

Sourdough Trail
This hike on the south side of Bozeman follows a tree-lined creek from Goldenstein Lane to Kagy Blvd. There are plenty of access spots to the creek. The best place to access this trail is from the south end. Take 19th Ave. south from Main St. Drive on 19th for 3 miles to Goldenstein. Turn left (east) and drive until the road crosses Sourdough Creek. The trail starts here.

Painted Hills Trail
This trail on the outskirts of Bozeman is more rural than urban. It travels 1.25 miles up and down through a gully area. To find the trailhead take Church St. south of Main St. to Kagy Blvd. Turn left (east) on Kagy and go .7 mile to a small parking area on the right.

Triple Tree Trail
This is a longer wooded trail on the outskirts of Bozeman which takes you 6 miles towards the mountains. Take 19th Ave. south of Main St. to Kagy Blvd. Turn left (east) and drive to Sourdough Road. Turn right (south) and drive about 2 miles. The trailhead is on the left side of the road. There is a small parking lot here.

North of Bozeman
Traveling up Springhill Road along the base of the

Bridger Mountains you will find several trails leading into the mountains. Cruise the gravel roads to the east of Springhill Road and you will stumble on to several trailheads.

Sypes Canyon Trail
This trail winds up the west side of the Bridger Mountains through mostly wooded areas. There are several spots along the trail that offer scenic vistas of the Gallatin Valley. Take 19th Ave. north of Main St. until it crosses over the interstate. Immediately after that it terminates at Springhill Road. Turn right here and go about 1 mile to Sypes Canyon Road. Turn right (east) and follow the road to the end. There is a parking area and clearly marked trailhead.

South Cottonwood Trail 422
This trail follows the South Cottonwood Creek drainage and is a relatively easy hike. You can follow this for as far as you can handle hiking back. It is not a loop trail. Take 19th Ave. south of Main St. until it takes a sharp right. The next main road after the Hyalite Recreation area turnoff is Cottonwood Road. Turn left (south) here and go 2.1 miles to Cottonwood Canyon Road. Go left again for 2.2 miles to the signed trailhead.

Hyalite Recreation Area
Palisades Falls
This is one of the more popular destinations for locals. It really isn't as much of a hike as a short walk. But it is worth the trip to see the spectacular falls which plummet over a basalt cliff. Take S. 19th to Hyalite Canyon Road and go to Hyalite Reservoir. Cross the dam continuing around the far side of the lake. You will come to a fork in the road. Bear left and look for the parking lot just a short distance down the road. Because of snow, you probably won't want to attempt this trip until very late May or early June.

Mount Blackmore
Take S. 19th to Hyalite Canyon Road and go to Hyalite Reservoir. The trailhead for this pleasant hike starts at the parking lot of the Reservoir. It is a very well maintained trail and a moderate hike to a small mountain lake. From Blackmore Lake you can continue on up to the top of 10,514 ft. Mt. Blackmore, but the trail becomes more difficult. The lake alone is worth the hike, but the view from the top of Blackmore is incredible.

HIKING THE BRIDGER RIDGE

Take a Walk Through Time

"The old Lakota was wise. He knew that man's heart away from nature becomes hard: he knew that lack of respect for growing, living things soon led to lack of respect for humans, too. So he kept his youth close to its softening influence."

-Chief Luther Standing Bear, Oglala Sioux

Few places in Montana offer the adventurous and observant hiker a better opportunity to walk through time than do the Bridger Mountains. Pay close attention and you can experience the natural world much like the Native Americans and early explorers who traveled through these mountains in the past. Like them, you will discover that wildflowers still grow in profusion along the trails. Hawks and eagles still circle and soar overhead as they migrate home. Mountain goats, ground squirrels, pikas and marmots still skitter along the rocks and if you look closely, you'll discover that even the rocks themselves have a story to tell.

Stop, look, and listen as you walk along this spectacular ridge, and enjoy your walk through time.

Follow the Footsteps Of Early Explorers

Many of the early mountain tribes, including the Salish, the Pend d'Oreille, and the Kootenai, crossed Bridger Ridge to hunt buffalo in the Shields and Yellowstone valleys. Sacajawea, the Shoshone interpreter who traveled with Lewis and Clark, knew this area well. on their journey home, the two explorers separated. Lewis traveled a northern route while Clark headed south. When Clark entered the Gallatin Valley, two major routes across the mountains were visible to him. One was the Flathead Pass, north of here. The other was the Rocky Canyon, now known as the Bozeman Pass. On the advice of Sacajawea, Clark chose the Rocky Canyon route which brought him directly to the Yellowstone River near what is now Livingston, Montana. This route was also preferred by John Bozeman, and became part of the Bozeman Trail.

Jim Bridger preferred Sacajawea's other route. The Bridger Range was named in honor of Jim Bridger, the famous trail blazer who scouted a trail that passed through this mountain range.

Discover the Geological Past

The Bridger mountain range is the result of over 1.5 billion years of mountain building, a process which has included faulting, thrusting and folding. These so-called "tectonic" events are responsible for most of the mountain ranges in Western Montana. As recently as 10,000 years ago, large glaciers pushed their way through the area, carving the wide open valleys and cirque basins we see today.

But there's more to look for as you explore these ancient geological wonders. Sedimentary rocks such as the sandstone and limestone you see at the top of the Sacajawea Trail were once deposited at the bottom of ancient seas. These rocks have since been uplifted and folded to form many of the ridges along which the trail

follows. Look closely, and you will see signs of the sea, including bits of coral, shells, and other small aquatic animals and plants embedded in the rock.

Be Prepared for Weather

Because the Bridger Mountains trend north and south, weather often moves in from the west. So while the west side of the Bridgers receives more sun and wind (creating the thermals on which the raptors ride), it is cooler with more snow on the east side of the range. As you hike up the ridge, notice where the wind funnels the snow between Sacajawea and Hardscrabble Peaks above Fairy Lake. As the snow melts in the late spring and into the summer, you can still see bedrock scratched and smoothed by an ancient glacier which carved those open bowls and left behind stacks of tumbled rocks:

Watch for signs of how the wind and weather have created different growing environments as you proceed up the mountain. Above Fairy Lake, there is less soil and smaller, more dwarfed and twisted trees known as krummholz. Notice, too, how little, sheltered growing environments are created on the downward side of many of these wind-twisted trees. Here, only the hardiest alpine plants are able to survive in this harsh environment.

But pay close attention: these same wind-swept conditions can contribute to fast-moving changes of weather year-round. As you hike on the east side of the mountain, rain, hail, wind and lightning can move in suddenly from the west and put hikers at real risk. Always be prepared for a variety of conditions, and if the weather is questionable, plan your outing for earlier in the day.

Enjoy the Flowers

In the late spring and summer, the Bridger Mountains are awash with the bright colors of wildflowers. Depending on the time of year and where you are in the Bridgers, look for glacier lilies pushing through the lingering snow, followed by buttercups, alpine bluebells, columbine, and sandwort.

Even those knowledgeable in alpine wildflowers can have difficulty distinguishing one species from another, so bring along a field guide to identify each flower by name. Your world will be richer for knowing them. Please remember, though, that wildflowers are delicate and often struggle to survive, particularly in these higher elevations. Stay on the trails so you do not disturb them and their habitat.

Scan the Sky for Raptors

Bridger Ridge is one of the best places in the country to view migrating golden eagles. During

the peak migration period, early to mid-October, hikers might see more than 100 eagles in a day as well as up to sixteen other species of raptors, including hawks, ospreys, and falcons as they migrate home.

You know how skiers get to the top of the mountain, but did you know that raptors also catch a "lift" up to the ridge? The sun heats the ground and the warm air rises, drawing cooler air underneath. Raptors simply spread their wings and catch these rising "thermals," sometimes traveling thousands of feet into the air. They then glide for miles without even flapping their wings.

Although fall is the best time to view the largest number and variety of raptors along Bridger Ridge, look for these magnificent birds soaring overhead no matter what time of the year.

Look & Listen for Wildlife

If you're walking along the trail above Fairy Lake and hear a high-pitched call, it could be the sound of a pika warning of your arrival. These small mammals keep busy in the summer storing up "haystacks" of grasses upon which they feed all winter long.

You might encounter a number of other animals as they, too, forage for food. Watch for yellow bellied marmots, snowshoe hares, and weasels. You may even see a mountain goat or two, scrambling along the ridge. Moose and an occasional black bear have also been viewed along both the Bridger and Fairy Lake trails.

Remember, all of these animals are wild and should never be approached.

Listen too for the songs of birds in the forest and sub alpine meadows. You might hear the calls of pine siskins, whitecrowned sparrows, mountain bluebirds, American robins and rosy finches, to name a few. You may also hear the drumming of various woodpeckers as they communicate or search out insects in the trunks of trees. if you hear a strange call that you can't identify, it could very well be that of one of the jay species, which are noted for their ability to mimic a variety of sounds.

Have a Great Hike

The Bridger Bowl and Sacajawea trails will transport you through some of the most beautiful country in Montana. Stop, look, listen and enjoy the rich diversity of biology, geology, botany and history you encounter along the way. Like the earliest travelers who passed along this ridge before, explore it—and enjoy it.

Reprinted from National Forest Service brochure

Hyalite Peak (Grotto Falls) Trail

Follow the directions to Palisades Falls, but stay right at the fork. The road will terminate a couple of miles down at a large parking lot. The trailhead is here. This hike is 5.5 miles to a small lake sitting at the base of massive cliffs. Along the trail are 11 waterfalls, some visible from the trail, some only a few yards off the trail.

History Rock Trail 424

This is a short hike to a large rock where early pioneers carved their names and the dates they were there. It is a challenge finding the historical carvings in between the more recent carvings of local graffiti artists. It is still a nice short hike through a mostly wooded area. The trailhead and parking area are very clearly marked and are approximately 10 miles from the start of Hyalite Canyon Road.

Bridger Canyon Area

The "M"

No doubt one of the most traveled trails in the area. Sitting on the south flank of Mt. Baldy at the Bozeman end of the Bridger Range, the "M" is one of Bozeman's most visible landmarks. It's a short hike and their are two routes—the easy way, and the hard way. If you take the trail straight up, it is literally that. There are no real switchbacks and the climb is totally vertical. The other route switches back and forth up the mountain and is a more moderate hike. Once you reach the "M" you can continue on up Mt. Baldy for some incredible views of the valley and surrounding mountain ranges.

To get there take N. Rouse until it turns into Bridger Canyon Drives. You'll find the parking lot and trailhead just before entering the canyon.

Sacajawea Peak

This is a great hike at the end of a scenic drive. There are few residents here who haven't taken this trip at one time or another. The hike starts at the scenic little Fairy Lake and switches up the mountain to a saddle between Sacajawea Peak to the south, and Hardscrabble Peak to the north. Once you reach the saddle, the view of the Gallatin Valley is incredible. It's best to take this hike later in the summer as snow stays in the bowl beneath the saddle well into August. In fact, it seldom ever melts completely and you will have to traverse part of it just about anytime. To get there take Bridger Canyon Drive about 20 miles continuing past the Bridger Bowl Ski Area. You'll soon see the sign for the turnoff to Fairy Lake. Follow the road about 8 miles to the lake and campground. The trailhead starts just above the campground.

Bridger Bowl Trail

Take Bridger Canyon Drive northeast of Bozeman for approximately 15 miles to the Bridger Bowl Ski Area. Turn here and follow the road to the lodge. When you reach the lodge follow the road to the right and wind up the hill. You will reach a (usually) closed gate and a small parking area. The trail starts here and winds up to the ridge for approximately two miles. This is a moderate to difficult hike and follows some steep and sometimes difficult terrain. You will climb about 2,100 feet in elevation. At the top you will see the helicopter landing platform used by HawkWatch volunteers for viewing and observing raptors during the fall migration. You will also have an incredible view of at least six mountain ranges.

Gallatin Canyon

Golden Trout Lakes Trail 83

This is an easy to moderate 2.5 mile trail with a little climbing. The hike takes you to three picturesque alpine lakes. The first is the only one with fish. Take Hwy. 191 south into the Gallatin Canyon. Portal Creek Road is about 3 miles south of Moose Flats Campground. Turn left on Portal Creek Road and drive about 6 miles to the parking area and trailhead.

South Fork of Spanish Creek Trail

To find this trail take Hwy. 191 into the Gallatin Canyon just south of Gallatin Gateway. Immediately after you enter the Canyon, watch for Spanish Creek Road veering off to the right of the paved road. As soon as you pass through the gate just a few yards ahead, you are on media mogul Ted Turner's property. There's a good chance you will see anywhere from a few to possibly thousands of bison roaming the area. If any are nearby stay in your car. You are trespassing if you leave the road. The trailhead starts at the end of this road.

This is a very popular hike and you will more than likely pass others along the way. The full loop of this trail goes 26 miles. That is too long for a family hike, but hard core hikers may want to give it a go. The trail travels through sections of the Lee Metcalf Wilderness Area and provides some awesome scenery.

Swan Creek Trail 186

This is an easy 2-mile hike along the creek bottom. It's a good area to see wild roses, and at the right time of the year wild berries. The trail ultimately ends at Hyalite Peak. Take Hwy. 191 south of Bozeman into the Gallatin Canyon about 32 miles to the very visible Swan Creek Campground sign. Turn left (east) and go 1 mile to the campground road. Follow this to the end of the road.

Beehive Basin Trail 40

This hike takes you into the beautiful Beehive Basin where you can explore little Beehive Lake and an alpine meadow. You may very well spot moose or bighorn sheep up here on a good day. This hike is 8 miles round trip, but seems to be a family favorite. Take Hwy. 191 south of Bozeman into the Gallatin Canyon. When you come to the entrance to Big Sky, turn right (west) and drive up the mountain to the Mountain Village area. Instead of turning into the resort at the sign, continue straight on the road for 2.7 miles to the second trailhead parking lot. If you want a longer hike, start at the parking lot a mile back. The trailhead leaves from the left side of the road.

Porcupine Creek Trail 34

This is an easy 4.5 mile trail through a creek bottom and along low ridges. If you look closely, you may find some petrified wood in the creek and along the banks of Porcupine Creek. Take Hwy. 191 south of Bozeman into the Gallatin Canyon. Drive just past the entrance to Big Sky Resort and look for the Ophir school building on the right. Turn left just past this and cross the Gallatin River. The trailhead is a quarter mile past the river. This trail can be confusing because of the excessive horse usage and the numerous horse trails leading off the main path. Stay on the main trail.

Lava Lake

This 3-1/2 mile hike takes you to a beautiful mountain lake in the Spanish Peaks area of the Madison Range. The trail follows Cascade Creek through thick woods past a waterfall or two. You emerge from the woods at a small lake. This hike is best taken from mid to late summer. The lake can be covered in ice until at least mid-summer. To get there go south on Hwy. 191 from Bozeman into the Gallatin Canyon and watch for the Lava Lake parking area to your right.

Other areas

Bear Trap Canyon

This is an excellent early season hike through a magnificent canyon. The stretch of the Madison River that runs through here is a favorite of whitewater enthusiasts. The hike is along a fairly level trail along the Madison River. It is 7 miles long from end to end. To get there drive west of Bozeman to Four Corners. Continue straight on Hwy. 84 for about a half hour and watch for the signs to the Bear Trap Recreation Area. When you see the river you are close. Follow the 3 mile dirt road to the parking area and trail head. Keep your eyes open for rattlesnakes that frequent this area.

Cliff and Wade Lakes Interpretive Trail

These lakes are surrounded by tall cliffs created a billion years ago by a geologic shift. The cliffs are a natural nesting area for a variety of raptors including bald eagles, prairie falcons and ospreys. A signed interpretive trail connects the two lakes between Wade Lake Campground and the Hilltop Campground. It's a 1.4 mile round trip with a 400 foot elevation gain from Wade Lake to Hilltop. To get there take Hwy. 287 40 miles south of Ennis. Look for the turnoff on the right signed for the lakes. Go west here for about 6 miles. The trailhead is just before the Wade Lake Campground with parking at the trailhead. Start here as there is no parking at the Hilltop end.

CROSS-COUNTRY SKI TRAILS

Beaverhead-Deerlodge National Forest

For more information contact District Ranger. 5 Forest Service Road. Ennis, MT 59279 (406) 682-4253 or Wade Lake Resort (406) 682- 7560

Wade Lake Ski Trails-40 mi. S Ennis on Hwy. 287 to Wade Lake Access Road and 6 mi. to Resort
35 km; groomed
Several routes of set track provide skiers with touring of Cliff and Wade Lakes and scenic vistas of the area; food and lodging are available from the Resort. Trail map available.

Gallatin National Forest

For more information contact District Ranger, 3710 Fallen, Bozeman. MT 59715 (406) 522-2520

Brackett Creek/Fairy Lake Roads-20 mi. N Bozeman
24 km More Difficult; no grooming
Shared with snowmobiles.

New World Gulch-6 mi. S Bozeman
16 km Most Difficult; no grooming

Bozeman Creek—5 mi. S Bozeman
10 km More Difficult; intermittent grooming
Snowmobiles prohibited.

Moser Creek/Bozeman Creek–10 mi. S Bozeman
4.5 km Most Difficult; no grooming

Moser Creek/Face Draw Loop–11 mi. S Bozeman
5 km More Difficult; no grooming
Snowmobiles prohibited.

Hyalite Loop 15 miles S. Bozeman (Hyalite Reservoir)
24 km Most Difficult; no grooming;
Sections of loop trail are shared with snowmobiles

Wildhorse - Lick Creek 15 miles S. Bozeman
12.9 km More Difficult; no grooming.
Shared with snowmobiles

Bear Canyon 8 miles E. Bozeman
9.6 km More Difficult, no grooming.
Shared with snowmobiles

Spanish Creek 27 miles S. Bozeman
Starting point varies, depending on the condition of the Spanish Cr. rd. 5.6 km from the end of gravelled county road to Spanish Cr. parking area. From here there are many options for ski routes into the Lee Metcalf Wilderness. More/Most difficult, no grooming.
Spanish Creek recreation/rental cabin available for extended trips. Trips further up the canyon to the high country are recommended for strong and experienced ski parties only. Avalanche hazard areas are common.

Beehive Basin
5 km Most Difficult, no grooming.
Avalanche hazard areas are common. Ski route gose into Lee Metcalf Wilderness.

For more information on the following trails contact District Ranger, West Yellowstone, MT 59758 (406) 823-6961

Rendezvous Complex—West Yellowstone
16 km Easiest; daily grooming for classic/skate
U. S. Olympic Team official fall training camp in November; dogs • snowmobiles prohibited. Fees 12/1-3/31-$3.00 daily per person; $20 season pass; $40 family season pass.

Dead Dog Loop-West Yellowstone
5.5 km More Difficult; daily grooming for classic/skate
Access via Rendezvous system. Fees apply.

Windy Ridge-West Yellowstone
7 km More Difficult; intermittent grooming in November and December only for classic/skate   See above
Access via Rendezvous system. Fees apply.

INFORMATION PLEASE

All Montana area codes are 406

Road Information
Montana Road Condition Report
(800) 226-7623, (800) 335-7592 local 444-7696
Montana Highway Patrol   444-7696
Local Road Reports
Bozeman   586-1313
Statewide Weather Reports   453-2081

Tourism Information
Travel Montana (800) 847-4868 outside Montana
                444-2654 in Montana
                        www.visitmt.com
Yellowstone Country (800) 736-5276 or 646-4383
Gold West Country (800) 879-1159 or 846-1943
Northern Rodeo Association   252-1122
Chambers of Commerce
Belgrade   388-1616
Big Sky   995-3000
Bozeman   586-5421
Ennis   682-4388
Manhattan   284-6094
Three Forks   285-4556
West Yellowstone   646-7701

Airports
Bozeman   388-6632
Ennis   682-7431
West Yellowstone   444-2506

Government Offices
State BLM Office   255-2885, 238-1540
Bureau of Land Management
Billings Field Office   896-5013
Butte Field Office   494-5059
Gallatin National Forest,   522-2520

Beaverhead/Deerlodge National Forest
Butte   522-2520
Lee Metcalf National Wildlife Refuge 777-5552
Red Rock Lake Wildlife Refuge   276-3536
Montana Fish, Wildlife & Parks   994-4042
U.S. Bureau of Reclamation
Dillon Field Office   683-6472
Helena Field Office   475-3310

Hospitals
Bozeman Deaconess Hospital
    Bozeman   585-5000
Same Day Surgical Center •Bozeman   586-1956
Madison Valley Hospital • Ennis   682-4274

Golf Courses
Big Sky Resort • Big Sky   995-5780
Bridger Creek • Bozeman   586-2333
Cottonwood Hills • Bozeman   587-1118
Headwaters Public • Three Forks   285-3700
Madison Meadows • Ennis   682-7468

Bed & Breakfasts
Lehrkind Mansion Bed & Breakfast
    Bozeman   585-6932
West Yellowstone Hostel   646-7745
Artful Lodger B&B • Belgrade   587-2015
Aspen Grove B & B • Gallatin Gateway 763-5044
Bear Creek Angler Inn • Manhattan   282-9491
Bridger Inn • Bozeman   586-6666
Bridger Mountains Highland House   587-0904
Chokecherry Guest House • Bozeman   587-2657
Cottonwood Inn Bed & Breakfast   763-5452
Covered Wagon Ranch • Big Sky   995-4237
Fox Hollow B&B At Baxter Creek
    Bozeman   582-8440
Gooch Hill B&B • Bozeman   586-5113
Gallatin River Lodge • Bozeman   388-0148
Howlers Inn • Bozeman   586-0304
Lindley House Bed & Breakfast
    Bozeman   587-8403
Rachie's Crows Nest • Ennis   682-7371
Silver Forest Inn • Bozeman   586-1882
Voss Inn Bed & Breakfast • Bozeman   587-0982
Wild Rose B&B • Gallatin Gateway   763-4692

Guest Ranches & Resorts
320 Guest Ranch   995-4283
East West Resorts At Big Sky   995-2665
Lone Mountain Ranch   995-4644
Rainbow Ranch Lodge   995-4132
Covered Wagon Ranch   995-4237
Elkhorn Ranch   995-4291
Nine Quarter Circle Ranch   995-4276
Parade Rest Guest Ranch   646-7217
Covered Wagon Ranch   995-4237
River Rock Lodge & Resort   995-4455
B Bar Ranch   848-7729
Bar N Ranch   646-7121
Big EZ Lodge   995-7000
Big River Lodge   763-3033
Big Sky Resort   995-5000
Castle Rock Inn   763-4243
Cliff Lake Resort   682-4982
Centennial Guest Ranch   682-7292
Diamond J Ranch Main Ranch   682-4867
Elk Lake Resort   276-3282
Firehole Ranch   646-7294
Gallatin River Lodge   388-0148
International Backpackers Hostel   586-4659
Kirkwood Resort & Marina   646-7000
Lionshead Resort   646-9584
Moonlight Basin   993-6000
Mountain Meadows Guest Ranch   995-4997
Potosi Hot Springs Resort   685-3330
Twin Rivers Ranch   284-6485
Wade Lake Resort   682-7560

Yellowstone Holiday RV & Marina   646-4242

Vacation Homes & Cabins
East West Resorts • Big Sky   995-2665
Brook Trout Inn • West Yellowstone 646-0154
Bozeman Cottage Vacation Rentals
    Bozeman   580-3223
Intermountain Property Management
    Bozeman   586-1503
Madison River Cabins • Cameron   682-4890
Battle Ridge Ranch • Bozeman   686-4723
Bear Canyon Cabin • Bozeman   587-4749
Black Dog Ranch • Bozeman   686-4948
Bozeman Cottage • Bozeman   585-4402
Bozeman Vacation.com • Bozeman   580-1080
Canyon Cabins • Gallatin Gateway   763-4248
Canyon Pines Cottage • Bozeman   586-1741
Cinnamon Lodge • Big Sky   995-4253
Darham Vacation Rentals • Bozeman   586-0091
DJ Bar Guest House • Belgrade   388-7463
Faithful Street Inn • West Yellowstone 646-4329
Gallatin River Guest Cabin • Big Sky   995-2832
Gallatin River Hideaway • Bozeman   586-8446
Gallatin Riverhouse • Big Sky   995-2290
Hyalite Creek Guest House • Bozeman 585-3458
Laura's Lilac Cottage • Bozeman   586-4140
Madison River Lodge • Ennis   682-4915
Magpie Guest House • Bozeman   585-8223
McClain Guest House • Bozeman   587-3261
Middle Creek Lodging • Bozeman   522-5372
Moose Haven • West Yellowstone   646-9295
Mountain Home-Montana Vacation Rentals
    Bozeman   586-4589
Quarter Circle JK • West Yellowstone   646-4741
ResortQuest • Big Sky   995-4800
Sportsman's High Vacation Rental
    West Yellowstone   646-7865
Tamarack Guest House • Bozeman   585-2496
Twin Rivers Ranch • Manhattan   284-6485
Wagon Wheel RV Campground & Cabins
    West Yellowstone   646-7872
Wildflower Guest & Mountain Cabin
    Bozeman   586-6610
Yellowstone Townhouses
    West Yellowstone   646-9331
Yellowstone Village Condominiums
    West Yellowstone   646-7335

Forest Service Cabins
Beaverhead-Deerlodge National Forest
Bear Creek Bunkhouse
21 mi. S of Ennis, MT   682-4253
Capacity: Nightly fee: $20
Available: 12/1 - 4/30
On border of Lee Metcalf Wilderness; several trails available for cross-country skiing. $40/night for both bunkhouse & cabin.

Bear Creek Cabin
21 mi. S of Ennis, MT   682-4253
Capacity: 4   Nightly fee: $30
Available: 12/1 - 4/30
On border of Lee Metcalf Wilderness; several trails available for cross-country skiing.

Wall Creek Cabin
24 mi S of Ennis, MT   682-4253
Capacity: 4   Nightly fee: $20
Available: 5/16 - 12/1
Not available in winter.
West Fork Cabin
40 mi S of Ennis, MT   682-4253
Capacity: 3   Nightly fee: $30
Available: 7/2 - 3/31
Access by road in summer. Up to 30 mi. of snowmobile or ski travel required in winter.

Landon
50 mi. S of Ennis   682-4253

Capacity: 4   Nightly fee: $25
Available: 10/21-3/30
One room cabin w/propane stove & lights. High clearance or 4-wheel drive vehicle required. Winter access by snowmobile or skis

Gallatin National Forest

Basin Station Cabin
6.25 mi. W of West Yellowstone, MT.   646-7369
Capacity: 4   Nightly fee: $25
Available: All year
Accessible by cross-country skiing or snowmobile. Plowed within 3 miles of cabin. Road access in summer.

Beaver Creek Cabin
21 mi. NW of West Yellowstone, MT.   646-7369
Capacity: 4   Nightly fee: $25
Available: All year
Plowed within 3 miles of cabin. Accessible by cross-country skis or snowmobile in winter. Road access in summer.

Cabin Creek Cabin
22 mi. NW of West Yellowstone, MT.   646-7369
Capacity: 4   Nightly fee: $25
Available: All year
Access by horseback or hiking in summer and by snowmobile and cross-country skis in winter.

Fox Creek Cabin
14 mi. S of Bozeman, MT   587-6920
Capacity: 2   Nightly fee: $25
Available: 12 /1 - 10/15
Trail access from nearest road is 2.5 miles. Winter access distance varies with snow conditions.

Garnet Mountain (Lookout Cabin)
19 mi. SW of Bozeman, MT   587-6920
Capacity: 4   Nightly fee: $25
Available: 12/1 - 10/15
Trail access from nearest road is 3.5 miles in summer. 10 mile ski or snowmobile in winter.

Little Bear Cabin
14 mi. S of Gallatin Gateway, MT   587-6920
Capacity: 4   Nightly fee: $25
Available: All year
Approximately 10 miles to cabin via snowmobile or skis in winter. Can drive to cabin in summer.

Mystic Lake Cabin
8 mi. SE of Bozeman, MT (S of Mystic Lake)
587-6920
Capacity: 4   Nightly fee: $25
Available: 12/1 - 10/15
Two access routes - more difficult, 5.3 miles; or easier, 10 mile route. Area closed to motorized vehicles.

Spanish Creek Cabin
23 miles SW of Bozeman, MT   587-6920
Capacity: 4   Nightly fee: $25
Available: 12/1 - 4/30
Normally plowed within 3.5 miles of cabin.

Wapiti Cabin
19 mi. SW of Big Sky, MT.   646-7369
Capacity: 4   Nightly fee: $25
Available: 11/1 - 4/30
Plowed within 3 miles of cabin. Accessible by cross-country skis or snowmobile in winter. Road access in fall and spring.

Window Rock Cabin
15 mi. S of Bozeman, MT (S of Hyalite Reservoir)
587-6920
Capacity: 4   Nightly fee: $25
Available: Year around
Road access to cabin in summer. Winter access distance varies with snow conditions.

Windy Pass Cabin
28 mi. S of Bozeman, MT   587-6920
Capacity: 4   Nightly fee: $25   Available:

6/1 - 10/15
Trail access from road is 2.5 miles, 1300 foot elevation gain.

Yellow Mule Cabin
35 mi SW of Bozeman, MT. 14 mi W of US 191
587-6920
Capacity: 2   Nightly fee: $25   Available:
12/1 - 10/15
Not recommended for ski parties (14 mile trip); 8 mile hike during summer..

Car Rental

Avis-Rent-A-Car	388-6414
Budget Rent -A-Car	388-4091
Dollar Rent-A-Car	388-1323
Free Spirit Car Rental	388-2002
Rent A Wreck	388-4189
Thrifty Car rental	388-3484
Enterprise Rent-A-Car	586-8010
Hertz Rent-A-Car	388-6939
National Car Rental	388-6694
Practical Rent-A-Car	586-8373
Big Sky Car Rentals	646-9564
Budget Car & Truck Rental	646-7882

Outfitters & Guides
F=Fishing   H=Hunting   R=River Guides
E=Horseback Rides   G=General Guide Services

Nine Quart Circle Ranch	EF	995-4276
320 Guest Ranch	FRE	995-4283
Lone Mountain Ranch	GFER	995-4644
Grizzly Outfitters	G	995-2939
Backcountry Adv. Snowmobile	G	646-9317
SeeYellowstone.com	G	646-9320
Yellowstone Alpen Guides	G	646-9591
Campbell's Guided Fishing Trips	GF	587-0822
Riverside Motel & Outfitters	F	682-4241
Wild Trout Outfitters Fly Fishing Guide Service		
F		995-4895
Yellowstone Raft Company	R	995-4613
Arnaud Oufitting	H	763-4235
Arrick's Fishing Flies	G	646-7290
Beartooth Outfitting	F	682-7525
Big Sky Outfitters	HFRE	587-2508
The Bozeman Angler	F	587-9111
Bridger Outfitters	GFHER	388-4463
Buffalo Horn Outfitters	G	587-0448
C Francis & Co Sporting Agents	F	763-4042
Clark's Guide Service	FR	682-4679
Bar 88 Horses	HEF	682-4827
Bear Trap Express	R	682-4263
Bear Trap Outfitters	HEF	646-7312
Beardsley Outfitting & Guide	G	682-7292
Bleu Sky Pack Station Inc	G	685-3647
Blue Ribbon Flies	HR	646-7642
Bob Cleverly	FR	682-4371
Boojum Expeditions	G	587-0125
Broken Hart Ranch	EHF	763-4279
The Bozeman Angler	GF	587-9111
Bud Lilly's Trout Shop	F	646-7801
Buffalo Jump Outfitting	G	682-7900
B.W. Outfitters	HEF	284-6562
Canoe Rentals-shuttles & Fly Fishing Outfitter		
	GFR	285-3488
Cutthroat Services & Sales Inc	G	522-7723
Daniel E. Glines	FR	682-7247
Diamond "P" Ranch	E	646-7246
Diamond K Outfitters	E	995-4132
Diamond P Ranch	E	646-7246
Diamond R Stables	E	388-1760
Diamond Wing	HFREG	682-4867
Doud Gregory J	G	682-7336
Eaton Outfitters	ER	682-4514
East Slope Anglers	GF	995-4369
Firehole Ranch LLC	FE	646-7294
Flying D Ranch	H	763-4930
Flyfishing Montana Co.	F	585-9066
Flyfishing-Wild Trout Outfitters	GF	995-4895
Gallatin Riverguides	GHF	995-2290
Gallatin River Ranch Equestrian Center		
	E	284-3782

Gerald R. Clark	EFR	682-7474
Geyser Whitewater Expeditions	R	995-4989
Gone Clear Outfitters	F	388-0029
Greater Yellowstone Flyfishers	F	585-5321
Grossenbacher Guides	F	582-1760
Hawkridge Outfitters & Rods	F	585-9608
Headwaters Guide Service	FR	763-4761
Highlands to Islands Guide Service	HF	682-7677
Howard Outfitters	F	682-4834
Jake's Horses	GFEH	995-4630
Jack River Outfitters	F	682-4948
Jacklin's Outfitters For The World Of Fly Fishing		
	G	646-7336
Jim Danskin	F	646-9200
Kicking Ass Outfitters	G	682-4488
Kokopelli's Travels	EF	686-4475
Madison River Fishing Company	F	682-4293
Madison River Outfitters	GF	646-9644
Macgregor Fogelsong Flies	F	652-4252
Mcguire Dick	G	682-4370
McNeely Outfitting	HF	585-9896
Medicine Lake Outfitters	GF	388-4938
Montana Flycast Guide Service	GF	587-5923
Montana Horses	E	285-3541
Montana Troutfitters	GF	587-4707
Montana Whitewater Inc	ER	763-4465
Montana Rivers to Ridges	F	580-2328
Panda Sport Rentals	R	587-6280
Randy Brown's Madison Flyfisher	F	682-7481
The River's Edge	GF	586-5373
RJ Cain & Co. Outfitters	F	586-8524
Rod-n-Dog Outfitting & Guide Service		
	GF	682-7419
Running River Fly Guide	F	586-1758
Sphinx Mountain Outfitting	HREF	682-7336
Saunders Floating	F	682-7128
S & W Outfitters	H	995-2658
T Lazy B Ranch	HER	682-7288
The Tackle Shop Outfitters	HRF	682-4263
Thompson's ANgling Adventures	HF	682-7509
Wapati Basin Outfitters	H	388-4941
Wild Trout Outfitters	F	995-4895
Yellowstone Adventures	F	585-7494
Yellowstone LLamas	F	586-6872
Yellowstone Mountain Guides	HF	646-7230
Yellowstone Net	R	388-2100

Cross-Country Ski Centers
Bohart Ranch • Bozeman	586-9070
Lone Mountain Ranch • Big Sky	995-4644
Wade Lake Resort • 30 mi. W of West Y ellowstone	682-7560
Yellowstone Expediitons West Yellowstone	646-9333

Downhill Ski Areas
Big Sky Resort	995-5000
Bridger Bowl	586-2111
Moonlight Basin	993-6000

Snowmobile Rentals
Back Country Adventures Snowmobile Rentals
West Yellowstone	646-9317
Days Inn • West Yellowstone	646-7656
Bar T Z • Belgrade	388-7228
Team Bozeman Rentals • Bozeman	587-4671
Big Boys Toys • Bozeman	587-4747
Summit Motor Sports Inc • Bozeman	586-7147
Canyon Adventures •Gallatin Gateway	995-4450
Yellowstone Motor Sport Rentals & Snovan Tours West Yellowstone	646-7656
Alpine West Snowmobiles Of West Yellowstone West Yellowstone	646-7633
Big Western Pine Motel West Yellowstone	646-7622
Dude Motor Inn / Roundup Motel West Yellowstone	646-7301
Gray Wolf Inn & Suites West Yellowstone	646-0000
Hi Country Snowmobile Rental West Yellowstone	646-7541

High-mark Snowmobile Rentals	
West Yellowstone	646-7586
Old Faithful Snowmobile Rentals	
West Yellowstone	646-9695
Rendezvouz Snowmobile Rental	
West Yellowstone	646-9564
Roundup Motel • West Yellowstone	646-7301
Ski-doo Snowmobiles	
West Yellowstone	646-7735
Stage Coach Inn • West Yellowstone	646-7381
Targhee Snowmobiles	
West Yellowstone	646-7900
Targhee Snowmobiles Karl Cook	
West Yellowstone	646-7700
Three Bear Lodge Motor Lodge	
West Yellowstone	646-7353
Two-top Snowmobile Rental Inc	
West Yellowstone	646-7802
Westgate Station-snowmobile Rentals	
West Yellowstone	646-7651
Yellowstone Adventures	
West Yellowstone	646-7735
Yellowstone Arctic/Yamaha	
West Yellowstone	646-9636
Yellowstone Lodge • West Yellowstone	646-0020
Yellowstone Snowmobile	
West Yellowstone	646-7301

PRIVATE CAMPGROUNDS

Campsite Directions

Campsite / Directions	Season	Tent	RV	Water	Electric	Sewer	Dump	Shower	Laundry	Store
BOZEMAN										
Bear Canyon Campground 587-1575 • 800-438-1575 • 3 mi E Bozeman, I-90 Exit 313	5/1-10/15	30	80	•	•	•	•	•	•	•
Bozeman KOA 587-3030 • 800-KOA-3036 • 8 mi W on US 191, 8 mi S of Belgrade on MT 85	All Year	50	100	•	•	•	•	•	•	•
Sunrise Campground 587-4797 • (877) 437-2095 • I-90 Exit 309, left 1/4 mi	4/1-10/31	15	50	•	•	•		•	•	•
CAMERON										
Cameron Store & Cabins 682-7744 • Fax 682-7113 • 11 mi S of Ennis on US 287	5/15-11/30	6	12	•	•	•		•		•
Howlin' Mad Moon Resort 682-7935 • 40 mi S of Ennis on US 287, Milepost 11	All Year	20	22	•	•	•			•	•
West Fork Cabin Camp 682-4802 • Between Ennis & W Yellowstone on US 287	4/1-11/30	20	24	•	•	•			•	•
ENNIS										
Camper Corner RV 682-4514 • (877) 682-2267 • Fax 682-3203 • US 287 & MT 287	5/1-10/31	10	20	•	•	•			•	•
Ennis RV Village 682-5272 • (866) 682-5272 • Fax 682-5245 • 1 mi N of Ennis on US 287	4/15-11/15	14	41	•	•	•	•	•	•	•
Lake Shore Lodge 682-4424 • Fax 682-4551 • 8 mi N of Ennis. 2.5 mi E off US 287	5/1-10/1	3	12	•	•	•		•	•	•
MANHATTAN										
Manhattan RV Park 284-6930 • I-90 Exit 288, N 500 ft to Wooden Shoe Ln, W 1 blk	All Year		32	•	•	•		•	•	•
THREE FORKS										
Three Forks KOA Kampground 285-3611 • 800-KOA-9752 • I-90 Exit 274, 1 mi S on US 287	4/15-10/15	20	62	•	•	•	•	•	•	•
WEST YELLOWSTONE										
Campfire Lodge Resort, Inc. 646-7258 • 8 mi N on US 191, 14 mi W on US 287	5/20-9/10	4	17	•	•	•		•	•	•
Fort Jax RV Park 646-7729 • In W Yellowstone, corner of Madison Ave & Hayden St	5/1-11/1		19	•	•	•		•	•	
Hideaway RV Campground 646-9049 • Corner of Gibbon Ave & Electric St	5/1-10/15	2	14	•	•	•		•	•	
La Siesta RV Park 646-7536 or 640-1085 • In W Yellowstone at 510 Madison Ave	All Year		11	•	•	•		•	•	
Lionshead RV Resort 646-7662 • 7.5 mi from W Yellowstone on US 20 S	5/1-11/1	20	175	•	•	•		•	•	•
Madison Arm Resort and Marina 646-9328 • 3 mi N on US 191, 5 mi W on FS 291	5/15-10/1	22	52	•	•	•		•	•	•
Pony Express Motel & RV Park Ph/Fax 646-7644 • 1 block E of Jct US 191 & US 20	April-Nov.		16	•	•	•			•	
Rustic Wagon RV Campground & Cabins 646-7387 • 1 block N of US 20, on Gibbon Ave	4/15-11/1	9	38	•	•	•		•	•	•
Wagon Wheel RV Campground & Cabins 646-7872 • 408 Gibbon, 1 block N of US 20	5/15-9/30	8	38	•	•	•		•	•	
Yellowstone Cabins & RV Park 646-9350 • 504 US 20	5/1-9/30		9	•	•	•			•	
Yellowstone Grizzly RV Park 646-4466 • Fax 646-4335 • 210 S Electric St	5/1-10/20	18	152	•	•	•		•	•	•
Yellowstone Holiday RV Campground & Marina 646-4242 • 8 mi N on US 191, 5 mi W on US 287	5/28-9/15	10	27	•	•	•		•	•	•
Yellowstone Park KOA 646-7606 • 800-562-7591 • Fax 646-9767 • 6 mi W on US 20	5/22-10/1	116	188	•	•	•	•	•	•	•

Campsite Directions

Campsite / Directions	Season	Camping	Trailers	Toilets	Water	Boat Launch	Fishing	Swimming	Trails	Stay Limit	Fee
55•Lewis & Clark Caverns FWP• 19 mi. W of Three Forks on MT 2•Milepost 271	All Year	50	•	•	•		•		N	7	•
56•Harrison Lake FWP• 5 mi. E of Harrison on Cty. Rd.	All Year	25	•	•		B	•			7	•
57•Red Mountain BLM• 9 mi. NE of Norris on SR 289	All Year	8	35'	•	•	A	•		B	14	•
58•Valley Garden FWP US 287 1/4 mi. S of Ennis•Milepost 48•2 mi. N. on Cty. Rd	4/1-11/30	•	•	•		C	•			7	•
59•Ennis FWP• US 287 E of Ennis•Milepost 48	4/1-11/30	25	•	•	•	C	•			7	•
60•Varney Bridge FWP• 2 mi. W of Ennis on US 287•10 mi. S on Cty. Rd.	All Year	•	•	•		C	0			7	•
61•Bear Creek FS• 11 mi. S of Ennis on US 287•9 mi. E of Cameron Community Center	6/1-11/30	12	•	•	•				•	16	•
62•West Madison BLM• 18 mi. S of Ennis on US 287•3 mi. S on Cty. Rd.	All Year	22	35'	•	•		•			14	•
63•South Madison BLM• 26 mi. S of Ennis on US 287•1 mi. W	All Year	11	35'	•	•	C	•			14	•
64•West Fork FS• 24 mi. S of Cameron on US 287.1 mi. W on Forest Rd. 8381	6/1-9/15	7		•	•		•			16	•
65•Madison River FS• 24 mi. S of Cameron on US 287•1 mi. SW on Cty. Rd. 8381	6/1-9/30	10	22'	•	•		•			16	•
66•Wade Lake FS• 8 mi. N of West Yellowstone on US 191•27 mi. W on US 287•6 mi. SW on Forest Rd. 5721	6/1-9/30	30	24'	D	•	C	•	•	•	16	•
67•Hilltop FS• 8 mi. N of West Yellowstone on US 191•27 mi. W on US 287•6 mi. SW on Forest Rd. 5721	6/1-9/30	20	22'	•	•		•		•	16	•
68•Cliff Point FS• 8 mi. N of West Yellowstone on US 191•27 mi. W on US 287•6 mi. SW on Forest Rd. 5721	6/1-9/15	6	16'	•	•	C	•			16	•
69•Fairweather FWP• 1 mi. W of Logan on Rt. 205•3 mi. N on Logan-Trident Rd.•7 Mi. NE on Clarkston Rd.	All Year	10	16'				•			7	
70•Missouri Headwaters FWP• 3 mi. E of Three Forks on Rt. 205•3 mi. N on Hwy 286	All Year	20	•	•			•			7	•
71•Greycliff FWP• 23 mi. W of Bozeman on MT 84•6 mi. S on Madison River Rd.	All Year	30	•	•		C	•			7	•
72•Langhor FS• 11 mi. S of Bozeman on S 19th Ave. & Hyalite Canyon Rd. (Forest Rd. 62)	5/15-9/15	12	16'	D	•				•	16	•
73•Hood Creek FS 17 mi. S of Bozeman on S 19th Ave. & Hyalite Canyon Rd. (Forest Rd.62)	6/1-9/15	18	30'	D	•	C	•		•	16	•
74•Chisholm FS• 18 mi. S of Bozeman on S 19th Ave. & Hyalite Canyon Rd. (Forest Rd. 62)	5/15-9/15	10	40'	D	•		•			16	•
75•Spire Rock FS• 26 mi. S of Bozeman on US 191•2 mi. E on Forest Rd. 1321	5/15-9/15	17	30'	•						16	•
76•Greek Creek FS• 31 mi. S of Bozeman on US 191	5/15-9/15	14	40'	D	•	A	•		•	16	•
77•Swan Creek FS• 32 mi. S of Bozeman on US 191•1 mi. E on Forest Rd. 481	5/15-9/15	13	30'	•	•		•			16	•
78•Moose Flat FS• 32 mi. S of Bozeman on US 191	6/1-9/15	13	40'	D	•	A	•			16	•
79•Red Cliff FS• 48 mi. S of Bozeman on US 191	5/15-9/15	68	30'	•	•	A	•		•	16	•
80•Cabin Creek FS• 8 mi. N of West Yellowstone on US 191•14 mi. W on US 287	5/22-9/15	15	32'	D	•		•		•	16	•

Agency
FS—U.S.D.A Forest Service
FWP—Montana Fish, Wildlife & Parks
NPS—National Park Service
BLM—U.S. Bureau of Land Management
USBR—U.S. Bureau of Reclamation
CE—Corps of Engineers

Camping
Camping is allowed at this site. Number indicates camping spaces available
H—Hard sided units only; no tents

Trailers
Trailer units allowed. Number indicates maximum length.

Toilets
Toilets on site. D—Disabled access

Water
Drinkable water on site

Fishing
Visitors may fish on site

Boat
Type of boat ramp on site:
A—Hand launch
B—4-wheel drive with trailer
C—2-wheel drive with trailer

Swimming
Designated swimming areas on site

Trails
Trails on site
B—Backpacking   N—Nature/Interpretive

Stay Limit
Maximum length of stay in days

Fee
Camping and/or day-use fee

Campsite Directions

Directions	Season	Camping	Trailers	Toilets	Water	Boat Launch	Fishing	Swimming	Trails	Stay Limit	Fee
81•Beaver Creek FS• 8 mi. N of West Yellowstone on US 191•16 mi. W on US 287	6/15-9/15	64	32'	D	•	C	•			16	•
82•Rainbow Point FS• 5 mi. N of West Yellowstone on US 191•3 mi. W on Forest Rd. 610 •2 mi. N on Forest Rd. 6954	5/22-9/15	85-H	32'		•	C	•	•		16	•
83•Lonesomehurst FS• 8 mi. West of West Yellowstone on Hebgen Lake Rd.	5/22-9/15	26	32'	D	•	C	•	•		16	•
84•Bakers Hole FS• 3 mi. N of West Yellowstone on US 191	5/22-9/15	72-H	32'	D	•		•			16	•
85•Potosi FS• 3 mi. SE of Pony on Cty. Rd. 1601•5 mi. SW on Forest Rd. 1501	6/1-9/30	15	32'	•			•		•	16	
86•Branham Lakes FS• 6 mi. E of Sheridan on Cty. Rd. 1111•5 mi. E on Forest Rd. 1112•3 mi. N on Forest Rd. 1110	7/1-9/15	6	22'	•		C	•	•	•	16	

Fishery

Fishery	Brook Trout	Mt. Whitefish	Lake Whitefish	Golden Trout	Cutthroat Trout	Brown Trout	Rainbow Trout	Kokanee Salmon	Bull Trout	Lake Trout	Arctic Grayling	Burbot	Largemouth Bass	Smallmouth Bass	Walleye	Sauger	Northern Pike	Shovelnose Sturgeon	Channel Catfish	Yellow Perch	Crappie	Paddlefish	Vehicle Access	Campgrounds	Toilets	Docks	Boat Ramps	MotorRestrictions
50. Jefferson River		•				•	•																•	•	•		•	
51. Harrison Lake						•	•																•	•	•		•	
52. Madison River		•				•	•																•	•	•			•
53. Ennis Lake						•	•				•												•	•	•			
54. Odell Creek						•	•																•					
55. Madison alpine lakes					•		•																•	•	•			
56. West Fork Madison River					•	•	•																•	•	•			
57. Cliff Lake					•		•																•	•			•	
58. Wade Lake						•	•																•	•	•			
59. Hidden Lake							•																•					
60. Elk Lake					•					•	•												•	•	•	•		
61. East Gallatin River	•	•				•	•																•					
62. Three Forks ponds							•						•										•					
63. Hyalite Creek	•				•		•																•	•	•			
64. Squaw Creek	•						•																•	•				
65. Gallatin Mountains alpine lakes				•	•						•												•	•				
66. West Fork Gallatin River						•	•																•					
67. Taylor Fork					•	•	•																•	•				
68. Gallatin River	•	•				•	•																•					•
69. Quake Lake						•	•																•	•	•	•	•	
70. Hebgen Lake						•	•																•	•	•		•	
71. Grayling Creek					•																		•					
72. South Fork Madison River						•	•																•	•				

NOTES:

Section 2

GALLATIN RIVER AREA AND MADISON RIVER VALLEY
INCLUDING BOZEMAN, BIG SKY, ENNIS, THREE FORKS AND WEST YELLOWSTONE

Dining Quick Reference

Price Range refers to the average cost of a meal per person: ($) $1-$6, ($$) $7-$11, ($$$) $12-up. Cocktails: "Yes" indicates full bar; Beer (B)/Wine (W), Service: Breakfast (B), Brunch (BR), Lunch (L), Dinner (D). Businesses in bold print will have additional information under the appropriate map locator number in the body of this section. [wi-fi] next to business name indicates free wireless internet is available to customers.

RESTAURANT	TYPE CUISINE	PRICE RANGE	CHILD MENU	COCKTAILS BEER WINE	SERVICE	CREDIT CARDS	MAP LOCATOR NUMBER
Boodles	Creative	$$$		Yes	D	Major	2
John Bozeman's Bistro	Eclectic	$$/$$$	Yes	B/W	L/D/	Major	2
Looie's Down Under, Rain & Jadra's	American/European	$$$		B/W	BR/D	Major	2
Leaf & Bean [wi-fi]	Coffee House/Bakery	$			BR/D	V/MC	2
The Nova Cafe	Continental	$$/$$$	yes	B/W	B/L	V/MC	2
Rocky Mt. Roasting	Coffeehouse	$					2
Grandma's Ice Cream Café	American	$	Yes		L/D		2
Naked Noodle	Asian	$$					2
Pita Pit	Sandwich	$-$$			L		2
Soby's Mexican/American Restaurant	Mexican	$	Yes	B/W	L	V/M	2
Sweet Pea Café	Gourmet	$$			D	Major	2
Starkys	Sandwich	$$	Yes		L	Major	2
Dave's Sushi—Off Main	Sushi	$$			L/D	Major	2
Plonk Wine Bar	Tapas/Homemade	$$/$$$		B/W	L/D	Major	2
Montana Ale Works	Fine Dining/Pub Fare	$$/$$$		B/W	D	Major	2
MacKenzie River Pizza Co.	Pizza	$/$$		B/W	L/D	Major	2
Pickle Barrel	Deli	$			L/D		2
The Point After	American	$/$$		Yes	L/D	Major	2
Western Cafe	American	$			B/L/D		2
Burger Bob's	American	$$	Yes	Yes	L/D		2
Fiesta Mexicana	Mexican	$$			L/D	Major	2
Black Angus Steak House	Fine Dining	$$		Yes	B/L/D	V/M/A	2
Sunrise Cafe	Fresh Deli	$/$$			B/L		2
Cat Eye Cafe	Eclectic	$/$$	Yes	B/W	B/L/D	MC/V	2
Charlie's Deli & Coffee House [wi-fi]	Deli/Coffee House	$			L	MV	2
The Wok	Chinese	$$		B/W	L/D	Major	3
Ferraro's Restaurant and Lounge	Italian	$$/$$$		Yes	D	V/M/D	3
Brandi's Restaurant	American	$/$$	Yes	Yes	B/L/D	Major	3
Dairy Queen	Fast Food	$	Yes		L/D		3
Hipshots	American	$$			B/L/D	Major	3
Taco Bell	Fast Food	$	Yes		L/D		3
Taco John's	Fast Food	$	Yes		L/D		3
The Hippo [wi-fi]	Pizza	$/$$	Yes	B	L/D	V/M	3
Three Rivers	American	$$	Yes	Yes	B/L/D	Major	4
Best Western GranTree Inn [wi-fi]	American	$—$$$	Yes	Yes	B/L/D	Major	4
Applebee's Neighborhood Grill	Eclectic	$$/$$$	Yes	Yes	L/D	Major	4
Arby's	Fast Food	$	Yes		B/L/D		4
Santa Fe Reds	Mexican	$$/$$$	Yes	Yes	L/D	Major	5
Panda Buffet	Chinese	$$			L/D	Major	5
McDonald's	Fast Food	$	Yes		B/L/D		5
Rocky Mt. Roasting	Coffeehouse	$					6
Pork Chop John's	Fast Food	$	Yes		L/D		6
Community Food Co-op [wi-fi]	Natural Foods	$			L/D	V/D	6
Café Zydeco	Cajun	$/$$			B/L/D	Major	6
Cosmic Gourmet Pizza	Pizza	$$			L/D	V/M	6
Arby's [wi-fi]	Fast Food	$	Yes		B/L/D		6
Bagel Works	Coffee House/ Deli	$			B/L		6
Chinatown	Chinese	$			L/D	V/M	6
Hardee's	Fast Food	$	Yes		B/L/D		6
It's Greek To Me	Greek	$			L/D		6
La Parrilla	Wraps	$	Yes	B/W	L/D		6
McDonald's	Fast Food	$	Yes		B/L/D		6
Subway	Fast Food	$	Yes		L/D		6
Wendy's	Fast Food	$	Yes		L/D		6
Lewis & Clark Motel & Family Restaurant	Family	$/$$		B/W	B/L/D	Major	6
Leaf & Bean [wi-fi]	Coffee House	$			B/L/D	V/MC	7
Wheat Montana	Bakery/Deli	$	Yes		B/L	Major	7
Old Chicago	American	$$	Yes	All	L/D	Major	7
Taco Del Mar	Fast Food	$			L/D	V/MC	7
Johnny Carino's	Italian	$$/$$$	Yes	B/W	L/D	Major	7
Bennigans	Family	$$/$$$	Yes	Yes	L/D	Major	7

Dining Quick Reference-Continued

Price Range refers to the average cost of a meal per person: ($) $1-$6, ($$) $7-$11, ($$$) $12-up. Cocktails: "Yes" indicates full bar; Beer (B)/Wine (W), Service: Breakfast (B), Brunch (BR), Lunch (L), Dinner (D). Businesses in bold print will have additional information under the appropriate map locator number in the body of this section. *[wi-fi]* next to business name indicates free wireless internet is available to customers.

RESTAURANT	TYPE CUISINE	PRICE RANGE	CHILD MENU	COCKTAILS BEER WINE	SERVICE	CREDIT CARDS	MAP LOCATOR NUMBER
Mongolian Grill	Asian	$/$$			LD	V/M	7
A&W Root Beer/Kentucky Fried Chicken	Fast Food	$	Yes		L/D		7
19th Hole Grill	American	$		Yes	L/D	Major	8
Perkins Family Restaurant [wi-fi]	Family	$/$$	Yes		B/L/D	Major	9
The Bay Bar & Grill [wi-fi]	Steakhouse	$$/$$$	Yes	Yes	L/D	Major	9
Fuddrucker's	American	$-$$	Yes	Yes	L/D	Major	9
Casey's Corner	Fast Food	$			B/L/D	Major	9
Burger King	Fast Food	$	Yes		B/L/D		9
Domino's Pizza	Pizza	$			L/D		9
J B'S Restaurant	Family	$	Yes		B/L/D	V/M	9
Pizza Hut	Pizza	$/$$	Yes	B	L/D	V/M/D	9
Quizno's Classic Subs	Subs	$	Yes		L/D		9
Taco Time	Fast Food	$	Yes		L/D		9
Pickle Barrel	Deli	$			L/D		10
Casa Sanchez	Mexican	$$	Yes	B/W	L/D	Major	10
Colombo's Pizza & Pasta	Pizza	$		B/W	L/D		10
Hero's Subs	Deli	$			L/D		10
Spectators Sports Bar & Grill	American	$$		Yes	L/D	V/M	10
Stageline Pizza	Pizza	$/$$			L/D		10
Kountry Korner Cafe	Family	$/$$	Yes	B/W	B/L/D/BR	Major	12
Sandwich Company	Cajun	$/$$			B/L		12
B&H Restaurant	American	$$	Yes	Yes	B/L/D	Major	12
Country Kitchen [wi-fi]	Family	$-$$	Yes		B/L/D	Major	13
Corner Store Exxon/Grand Slam Grill	Fast Food	$			B/L/D	Major	13
Burger King	Fast Food	$	Yes		B/L/D		13
Dairy Queen	Fast Food	$	Yes		L/D		13
Hero's Subs	Deli	$			L/D		13
McDonald's	Fast Food	$	Yes		B/L/D		13
Pizza Hut	Pizza	$/$$	Yes	B	L/D	V/M/D	13
Rosa's Pizza	Pizza	$			L/D	V/M	13
Subway	Fast Food	$	Yes		L/D		13
Taco Time	Fast Food	$	Yes		L/D		13
Mama Mac's Bakery & Sandwich Shop	Family	$/$$	Yes		B/L/D		13
Duck-In Cafe	American	$	Yes		B/L	V/M	14
Overland Express	American	$$	Yes	All	B/L/D	Major	14
The Mint Bar & Cafe	Eclectic	$$$		Yes	L/D	Major	14
MacKenzie River Pizza Co.	Pizza	$/$$		B/W	L/D	Major	14
It's Greek to Me	Greek	$			L/D		14
Stageline Pizza	Pizza	$/$$			L/D		14
Sir Scott's Oasis	Steakhouse	$$$	Yes	Yes	D	Major	15
Garden Cafe [wi-fi]	Family	$/$$	Yes		B/L		15
Cafe on Broadway	Family	$/$$	Yes		B/L		15
Stageline Pizza	Pizza	$/$$			L/D		15
Land of Magic Dinner Club	Steaks & Seafood	$$		Yes	L/D	Major	16
Sacajawea Hotel	Fine Dining	$$/$$$	Yes	Yes	B/BR/L/D	Major	17
Wheat Montana Farms & Bakery	Deli	$			B/L		17
Willow Creek Cafe & Saloon	American	$$	Yes	Yes	L/D/BR	V/M	17
Custer's Last Root Beer Stand	Family	$	Yes		L/D		17
Stageline Pizza	Pizza	$/$$			L/D		17
Three Forks Cafe	Family	$/$$	Yes		B/L/D		17
Subway	Fast Food	$	Yes		L/D		17
Teasers	Steakhouse	$$		All	D	Major	17
MacKenzie River Pizza Co.	Pizza	$/$$		B/W	L/D	Major	18
Stacy's	American	$$	Yes	All	L/D	V/M	19
Gourmet Gas Station	Casual Gourmet	$/$$$	Yes	B/W	B/L/D	Major	19
Post Office Pizza	Pizza	$$			D		19
Castle Rock Inn	American	$$		Yes	B/L/D		19
Gallatin Gateway Inn [wi-fi]	Regional American	$$$	Yes	Yes	D	Major	19
320 Guest Ranch [wi-fi]	Steakhouse	$$/$$$	Yes	Yes	B/L/D	Major	21
The Covered Wagon Ranch	Family	$$$			D	V/M	21
Rainbow Ranch Lodge [wi-fi]	Continental	$$$	Yes	Yes	D	Major	21

Dining Quick Reference-Continued

Price Range refers to the average cost of a meal per person: ($) $1-$6, ($$) $7-$11, ($$$) $12-up. Cocktails: "Yes" indicates full bar; Beer (B)/Wine (W), Service: Breakfast (B), Brunch (BR), Lunch (L), Dinner (D). Businesses in bold print will have additional information under the appropriate map locator number in the body of this section. *[wi-fi]* next to business name indicates free wireless internet is available to customers.

RESTAURANT	TYPE CUISINE	PRICE RANGE	CHILD MENU	COCKTAILS BEER WINE	SERVICE	CREDIT CARDS	MAP LOCATOR NUMBER
Big Horn Cafe	Deli	$$		B/W	B/L	Major	21
Best Western Buck's T-4 Lodge *[wi-fi]*	Steaks/Wild Game	$$$	Yes	Yes	D	Major	21
Corral Steakhouse Cafe & Motel	Steakhouse	$$	Yes	Yes	B/L/D	Major	21
Canyon Conoco and Cafe	American	$/$$			B/L		21
Lone Mountain Ranch	Gourmet American	$$$	Yes	Yes	B/L/D/BR	V/M/D	22
Country Market & Deli	Deli	$		B/W	B/L/D	Major	22
By Word of Mouth	Montana Bistro	$$/$$$	Yes	Yes	D	Major	22
Lone Mountain Ranch	Gourmet	$$$	Yes	Yes	D	Major	22
The Cabin	Fine Dining	$$$		Yes	D	Major	22
Huckleberry Cafe	American	$$					22
Allgood's Bar & Grill	Barbeque	$/$$	Yes	Yes	B/L/D	Major	22
Blue Moon Bakery	Bakery/ Deli	$			B/L		22
Hungry Moose Market & Deli *[wi-fi]*	Deli	$	Yes		L/D	Major	22
Dante's Inferno	Regional	$$		Yes	L/D	Major	22
M R Hummers	Steaks/Seafood	$$/$$	yes	Yes	D	Major	23
Mountain Top Pizza	pizza	$$					23
Scissorbills Bar & Grill	American	$$		Yes	L/D	Major	23
Twin Panda	Chinese	$$		Yes	D	AX/V/MC	23
Ernie's Bakery & Deli	Deli	$		B/W	B/L		24
The Gusher Pizza Sandwich Shop	Pizza/Sandwiches	$/$$		B/W	L/D		24
Canyon Street Grill	American	$/$$			B/L/D		24
D&M Cafe	Mexican/American	$/$$			L/D		24
Dairy Queen	Fast Food	$	Yes		L/D		24
McDonald's	Fast Food	$	Yes		B/L/D		24
Mike's Cafe	American	$/$$			B/L/D		24
Pete's Rocky Mountain Pizza	Pizza & Pasta	$$			L/D		24
Silver Spur Cafe	Family	$/$$		B/W	B/L/D		24
Subway	Fast Food	$	Yes		L/D		24
Totem Cafe & Lounge	Steaks & Seafood	$$-$$$	Yes	Yes	D	V/M	24
Wolf Pack Microbrewery & Pub	Sandwiches	$$		B	L/D	Major	24
Timberline Cafe	American	$$			B/L/D	Major	25
Oregon Shortline Restaurant	Wild Game	$–$$$	Yes	Yes	B/L/D/BR	Major	25
Outpost Restaurant	American	$$			B/L/D		25
Three Bears Motel & Restaurant	Family	$/$$	Yes		B/D	Major	26
Rustler's Roost Restaurant	American	$$	Yes	Yes	B/L/D	Major	26
Ernie's Big Horn Deli	Deli	$					26
Firehole Grill	American	$-$$$		Yes	B/L/D	Major	26
Kentucky Fried Chicken	Fast Food	$	Yes		L/D		26
Montana Cafe	Family	$	Yes		B/L		26
Uncle Laurie's Riverside Cafe	Family	$	Yes		B/L		26
Bullwinkles Saloon & Eatery	American	$$	Yes	Yes	L/D	Major	26
Chinatown Restaurant	Chinese	$			L/D	V/M	26
Old Town Cafe	Family	$/$$	Yes		B/L/D	V/M	26
Running Bear Pancake House	American	$			B/L		26
Days Inn & Trappers Family Restaurant	Family	$/$$	Yes		B/L/D	Major	26
The Campobelo Lodge @ the Bar N Ranch	Steakhouse	$$		Yes	D	V/MC	27
Eino's Tavern	American	$		Yes	L/D		28
Sportsman's Lodge	Family	$/$$	Yes	Yes	B/L/D/BR	Major	30
Continental Divide	Gourmet	$$/$$$		Yes	L/D	Major	30
Dairy Queen	Fast Food	$	Yes		L/D		30
Ennis Cafe	Family	$/$$	Yes		B/L/D		30
Cafe 287	Family	$—$$$			B/L	V/M	30
Madison River Pizza	Pizza	$			L/D	V/M	30
Aunt Jenny's	Family	$/$$	Yes		B/L/D	Major	30
Scotty's Long Branch Supper	Steakhouse	$$/$$$		Yes	L/D	M/V	30
Silver Dollar Bar & Grill	American	$		Yes	B/L/D		30
Yesterday's Restaurant & Soda Fountain	Soda Fountain	$	Yes		B/L/SB	Major	30
Bear Claw Bar & Grill *[wi-fi]*	Steakhouse	$$/$$$		Yes	L/D	V/M	31
Norris Bar	American	$		Yes	L/D	V/M	32
Old Norris Schoolhouse Cafe	Mexican	$/$$	Yes	B/W	L/D	Major	32
Potosi Hot Springs Resort	Organic	$$$			B/L/D	MC/V	33
B & S Diner	American	$	Yes		B/L/D	Major	34

Motel Quick Reference

Price Range: ($) Under $40 ; ($$) $40-$60; ($$$) $60-$80, ($$$$) Over $80. Pets [check with the motel for specific policies] (P), Dining (D), Lounge (L), Disabled Access (DA), Full Breakfast (FB), Cont. Breakfast (CB), Indoor Pool (IP), Outdoor Pool (OP), Hot Tub (HT), Sauna (S), Refrigerator (R), Microwave (M) (Microwave and Refrigerator indicated only if in majority of rooms), Kitchenette (K). All Montana area codes are 406. [wi-fi] next to business name indicates free wireless internet is available to customers.

HOTEL	PHONE	NUMBER ROOMS	PRICE RANGE	BREAKFAST	POOL/ HOT TUB SAUNA	NON SMOKE ROOMS	OTHER AMENITIES	CREDIT CARDS	MAP LOCATOR NUMBER
Western Heritage Inn [wi-fi]	586-8534	38	$$/$$$$	CB	HT/S	Yes	K/P/M/R/DA	Major	1
Blue Sky Motel [wi-fi]	587-2311	27	$/$$	CB	HT		K/P/M/R	Major	1
Continental Motor Inn	587-9231	60	$/$$	CB	HT	Yes	K/P/M/DA	Major	1
Ranch House Motel	587-4278	16	$					Major	1
Montana Home-Montana Vacation Rentals	586-4589	30	$$$$		HT	Yes	K/P/M/R/DA	Major	2
Bozeman Cottage Vacation Rentals	580-3223		$$$/$$$$		HT	Yes	K/M/R	V/M	2
Best Western City Center [wi-fi]	587-3158	63	$$$$		IP/HT	Yes	D/DA	Major	2
Imperial Inn [wi-fi]	587-4481	37	$$			Yes	P	Major	2
Royal 7 Budget Inn	587-3103	47	$$	CB	HT	Yes	P/R	Major	3
Rainbow Motel	587-4201	43	$$		OP	Yes	P	Major	3
Bozeman Comfort Inn [wi-fi]	587-2322	87	$$$	CB	IP/HT/S	Yes	M/R/P/DA	Major	4
Hampton Inn [wi-fi]	522-8000	70	$$$$	CB	IP/HT	Yes	M/R/DA	Major	4
Bozeman Inn [wi-fi]	587-3176	49	$$$	CB	HT/S	Yes	P/D/M/R/L	Major	4
Days Inn [wi-fi]	587-5251	79	$$$$	CB/FB	HT	Yes	P/M/R/DA	Major	4
Holiday Inn [wi-fi]	587-4561	179	$$$$		IP/HT	Yes	K/P/D	Major	4
Best Western GranTree Inn [wi-fi]	587-5261	103	$$$$		IP/HT	Yes	D/DA	Major	4
Super 8 Motel Of Bozeman	586-1521	108	$$/$$$			Yes	P/M/R/DA	Major	5
TLC Inn [wi-fi]	587-2100	42	$$/$$$	CB	HT/S	Yes	P/DA	Major	5
Microtel Inn & Suites [wi-fi]	586-3797	61	$$		HT/IP	Yes	P/DA	Major	5
Ramada Limited [wi-fi]	585-2626	50	$$/$$$$	CB	IP/HT	Yes	K/P/M/R/DA	Major	5
Sleep Inn of Bozeman [wi-fi]	585-7888	56	$$$	CB	IP/HT	Yes	P/DA	Major	5
Fairfield Inn [wi-fi]	587-2222	57	$$$	CB	IP/HT	Yes	P/DA	Major	5
Lewis & Clark Motel & Family Restaurant [wi-fi]	586-3341	50	$$		IP/HT/S	Yes	D/L/DA	Major	6
Wingate Inn of Bozeman [wi-fi]	582-4995	86	$$$$	CB	IP/HT	Yes	K/M/R/DA	Major	8
Hilton Garden Inn	582-9900	123	$$$/$$$$	N	IP/HT	Y	DA/	Major	8
Holiday Inn Express [wi-fi]	388-0800	67	$$/$$$	CB	HT	Yes	P/M/R/DA	Major	12
Super 8 Motel Of Belgrade [wi-fi]	388-1493	72	$$	CB	IP/HT	Yes	P/DA	Major	12
Belgrade Inn & Suites [wi-fi]	388-2222	65	$$$$	CB	IP/HT	Yes	P/DA	Major	12
The Broken Spur Motel [wi-fi]	285-3237	24	$$	CB		Yes	K/P/M/R/DA	Major	17
Sacajawea Hotel	285-6515	31	$$$			Yes	P/D/L	Major	17
Fort Three Forks Motel & RV Park	285-3233	24	$$	CB	HT	Yes	P/M/R/DA	Major	17
Bud Lillie's Fly Fishing Retreat	586-5140	6	$$$			Yes	K/PB/M/R/DA	V/M	17
Lewis & Clark Sportsman's Lodge	285-3454	4	$$$				R/L	Major	17
Gallatin Gateway Inn [wi-fi]	763-4672	35	$$$$		OP/HT		D/L/DA	Major	19
Castle Rock Inn	763-4243	8	$$			Yes	R/L/P	Major	19
Elkhorn Ranch	995-4291								21
Nine Quarter Circle Ranch	995-4276	70							21
320 Guest Ranch [wi-fi]	995-4283	59	$$$$	CB	HT	Yes	P/D/DA/R/M/K	Major	21
The Covered Wagon Ranch	995-4237	10	$$$$	FB	HT	Yes	P		21
Rainbow Ranch Lodge	995-4132	21	$$$		HT	Yes	D/L/DA	Major	21
Comfort Inn Big Sky [wi-fi]	995-2333	62	$$$$	CB/FB	IP	Yes	K/P/M/R/DA	Major	21
Best Western Buck's T-4 Lodge [wi-fi]	995-4111	74	$$/$$$$		HT	Yes		Major	21
Corral Steakhouse Cafe & Motel	995-4249	8	$$		HT	Yes	R/L/P	Major	21
Cinnamon Lodge	995-4253	6	$$$			Yes	D/L/P/DA	Major	21
Lone Mountain Ranch	995-4644	30	$$$$	FB	HT	Yes	D/L/K	Major	22
River Rock Lodge	995-4455	29	$$$$	CB	HT	Yes	DA/R	Major	22
East West Resorts Big Sky [wi-fi]	995-4800	225+	$$		OP/HT	Yes	K/R/M	V/M/D	23
Mountain Meadows Guest Ranch	995-4997								23
Holiday Inn Express/Mountain Inn Hotel [wi-fi]	995-7858	90	$$$$	CB	IP/HT	Yes	L	Major	23
Big Sky Ski & Summer Resort Huntley [wi-fi]	995-5000	200+							23
Parade Rest Ranch	646-7217	15							24
Best Western Weston Inn [wi-fi]	646-7373	65	$/$$		OP/HT	Yes	P/D/DA	Major	24
Ho Hum Motel	646-7746	23	$$			Yes	K/P/DA	V/M	24
Kelly Inn [wi-fi]	646-4544	78	$$$$	CB	IP/HT/S	Yes	P/DA	Major	24
One Horse Motel	646-7677	19	$$/$$$		HT	Yes	M/R	Major	24
Brandin' Iron Inn & RV Park	646-9411	79	$$–$$$$	CB	HT	Yes	K/R/DA	Major	24
Best Western Desert Inn [wi-fi]	646-7376	76	$$-$$$$	CB	IP/HT	Yes	M/R/DA	Major	24
Best Western Executive Inn	646-7681	82	$$$		OP/HT	Yes	P/D/M/R	Major	24
Madison Hotel	646-7745	14	$/$$			Yes		Major	25
Holiday Inn Sunspree Resort [wi-fi]	646-7365	123	$$$$		IP/HT/S	Yes	M /D/L/DA	Major	25

Motel Quick Reference

Price Range: ($) Under $40 ; ($$) $40-$60; ($$$) $60-$80, ($$$$) Over $80. Pets [check with the motel for specific policies] (P), Dining (D), Lounge (L), Disabled Access (DA), Full Breakfast (FB), Cont. Breakfast (CB), Indoor Pool (IP), Outdoor Pool (OP), Hot Tub (HT), Sauna (S), Refrigerator (R), Microwave (M) (Microwave and Refrigerator indicated only if in majority of rooms), Kitchenette (K). All Montana area codes are 406. [wi-fi] next to business name indicates free wireless internet is available to customers.

HOTEL	PHONE	NUMBER ROOMS	PRICE RANGE	BREAKFAST	POOL/ HOT TUB SAUNA	NON SMOKE ROOMS	OTHER AMENITIES	CREDIT CARDS	MAP LOCATOR NUMBER
Gray Wolf & Suites	646-0000	102	$$$$	CB	IP/HT	Yes	P/DA	Major	25
Hibernation Station	646-4200	26	$$$$		HT	Yes	DA/P	Major	25
Yellowstone Lodge [wi-fi]	646-0020	77	$$$$	CB	IP/HT	Yes	P/DA	Major	25
Al's Westward Ho Motel	646-7331	34	$$			Yes	DA	Major	25
Traveler's Lodge	646-9561	46	$$	CB	IP/HT	Yes	P/D/DA	Major	25
Clubhouse Inn [wi-fi]	646-4892	77	$$$$	CB	IP/HT	Yes	DA	Major	26
West Yellowstone Comfort Inn	646-4241	78	$$$$	CB	IP/HT	Yes	M/R/DA	Major	26.
Days Inn & Trappers Family Restaurant [wi-fi]	646-7656	118	$$$$	CB	IP/HT	Yes	D/DA	Major	26
Three Bear Motel & Restaurant	646-7811	75	$$$		IP/HT	Yes	R/L	Major	26
Hadley's Motel & Gracy's Gifts	646-9534	15	$$			Yes	P/R/M/K	Major	26
Yellowstone Country Inn	646-7622	46	$$$		IP/HT	Yes	P/D/L	Major	26
Alpine Motel	646-7544	12	$$			Yes	K/P	Major	26
Sleepy Hollow Lodge	646-7707	13	$$$	CB			DA/P	Major	26
Rustic Wagon RV Campground & Cabins	646-7387								26
Crosswinds Best Western [wi-fi] ·	646-9557	72	$$/$$$$	CB	IP/HT	Yes	P/M/R/DA	Major	26
Evergreen Motel	646-7655	16	$$$			Yes	P	Major	26
Pine Shadows Motel	646-7541	14	$$			Yes	DA/P	Major	26
Pony Express Motel	646-7644	17	$$			Yes	P	Major	26
Yellowstone Cabins	646-9350	8	$$$	CB			DA/P	Major	26
Yellowstone Inn [wi-fi]	644-7633	10	$$/$$$$		S	Yes	K/P/M/R	Major	26
City Center Motel [wi-fi]	646-7337	25	$$$	CB	IP/HT	Yes	DA	Major	26
Dude Motor Inn	646-7301	30	$$			Yes	D/L	Major	26
Golden West Motel	646-7778	12	$$			Yes		Major	26
Pioneer Motel	646-9705	20	$$$			Yes	DA/P	Major	26
Stage Coach Inn [wi-fi]	646-7381	80	$$$$		HT	Yes	D/DA	Major	26
Westwood Lodge	646-7713	24	$$–$$$$			Yes	K/R	V/M	26
Madison Hotel	646-7745	139	$-$$$$			Yes		Major	27
Brook Trout Inn	646-4254								27
Crow's Nest Motel	646-7873	10	$$$$	CB	IP/HT	Yes	R/DA/P	Major	27
Super 8/Lionshead Resort [wi-fi]	646-9584	44	$$/$$$		HT/S	Yes		Major	27
Kirkwood Resort & Marina [wi-fi]	646-7200	9	$$$			Yes	DA	Major	28
Lakeview Cabins On Hebgen Lake	646-7257								28
Slide Inn	682-4804	9	$$				DA/K	V/M	29
Fan Mountain Inn [wi-fi]	682-5200	28	$$			Yes	P/M/R/DA	Major	30
Rainbow Valley Lodge [wi-fi]	682-4264	24	$$/$$$		OP	Yes	DA/R/M/K	Major	30
Riverside Motel	682-4240	12	$$			Yes	K/P	Major	30
El Western Resort	682-4217	29	$$$/$$$$			Yes	P/K	Major	30
Sportsman's Lodge	682-4242	29	$$/$$$	CB		Yes	P/D/L/DA	Major	30
Silvertip Lodge-Downtown Ennis	682-4384	9	$$			Yes	P/K	Major	30
Potosi Hot Springs Resort [wi-fi]	685-3330	4	$$$$		HT/OP	Yes	K		33

NOTES:

SECTION 3

LIVINGSTON, BIG TIMBER, GARDINER AND SURROUNDING AREA

The Yellowstone River in Paradise Valley.

INTRODUCTION

This section covers a unique landscape with an interesting past, including parts of Sweetgrass and Park County, and the area called Paradise Valley. The area consists of plains with rich soil and grasslands that are perfect for ranching and farming, surrounded by the Crazy and Absaroka Mountain Ranges in the background. Pioneers and settlers were drawn here in the 1800s for the wide open spaces, mining opportunities and railroad jobs. Park County was formed in 1887 and Sweetgrass County came about in 1896, from parts of Meagher, Yellowstone and Park Counties, and was named for the "creek of fragrant grasses." The Northern Pacific Railroad had a large impact on the population in this area and set up numerous job opportunities in Livingston. The railroad also carried an influx of people coming through to see the wonders of Yellowstone, the first National Park.

The Homestead Act, passed in 1862, gave 162 acres of land to every citizen over 21, or to the heads of the family who intended to become a citizen. This act, and the development of the railroad, brought many people out west to start a new life. Many Norwegians were drawn to Montana, attracted to the landscape that reminded them of their native homeland. Norwegians started their own communities in Sweetgrass County, Melville being the first, and introduced sheep to the area in 1881. Cattle ranching and sheep herding were popular among the settlers, and brought them prosperity in Sweetgrass County.

1.

Grey Cliff

Grey Cliff, named for the sandstone bluffs near the town, was established in 1882. The little town was located under the bluffs on the south side of Interstate 90 just east of the present site. There was a coal dock, water tank and a "Y" to turn the engines around on the railroad. A general store, saloon and boarding house with a few year-round residents made up the town. In 1890, the Northern Pacific Railroad moved Grey Cliff nearer to the tracks and the Yellowstone River. The first school was built in 1910. In 1949, the town was moved again to its present site. Between 1910 and 1924, Grey Cliff thrived. It boasted two general stores, a blacksmith shop, garage, livery barn, lumber yard, grain elevator, railroad depot, hotel, saloon, saddle shop, restaurant, post office, pool hall, dance hall and cigar factory. With the increase of motorized transportation, making it easier for the local people to get to the larger towns, the little town slowly became the close knit community it is today. Near Grey Cliff is the Pelican Fishing Access on the Yellowstone River. Across the Interstate is the Prairie Dog Town State Park. You can enjoy lunch while watching these little creatures in their natural habitat. *Reprinted from Sweetgrass Chamber information sheet.*

H The Thomas Party
East of Greycliff

In 1866, William Thomas, his son Charles, and a driver named Schultz left southern Illinois bound for the Gallatin Valley, Montana. Traveling by covered wagon, they joined a prairie schooner outfit at Fort Laramie, Wyoming, and started over the Bridger Trail. The train was escorted by troops detailed to build a fort (C. E Smith) on the Big Horn River.

From the site of this fort the Thomas party pushed on alone. A few days later they were killed at this spot by hostile Indians. Emigrants found the bodies and buried them in one grave.

The meager details which sifted back greatly impressed William Thomas's seven-year old nephew. Seventy-one years later (1937), this nephew closely followed the Bridger Trail by car and succeeded in locating the almost forgotten grave.

H Captain Wm. Clark

You are now following the historic trail of the Lewis and Clark Expedition. On his return from the Pacific in July 1806, Captain Clark camped for six days about forty miles downstream, near Park City. The Expedition had been looking for timber suitable for building canoes ever since striking the river near Livingston. They found a couple of large cottonwoods here that would serve. They fitted their axes with handles made from chokecherry and went to work making two canoes. When finished they laced them together with a deck of buffalo hides between. Seven men, Sacajawea and her child went curving down the river on this makeshift yacht, arriving at the mouth of the Yellowstone August 3rd. Captain Lewis split off north on the return trip and explored the Marias River and returned via the Missouri, joining them on August 12th.

H The Crazy Mountains
Called Awaxaawippiia by the Apsaalooka (Crow) Indians, the Crazy Mountains, which you can

Big Timber	Jan	Feb	March	April	May	June	July	Aug	Sep	Oct	Nov	Dec	Annual
Average Max. Temperature (F)	37.1	41.0	47.7	58.9	68.6	77.2	87.0	85.7	74.2	62.3	47.0	39.3	60.5
Average Min. Temperature (F)	16.3	18.8	23.0	31.7	39.8	47.4	52.8	51.0	42.4	34.6	25.6	19.4	33.6
Average Total Precipitation (in.)	0.61	0.49	0.97	1.51	2.66	2.53	1.27	1.14	1.42	1.26	0.78	0.56	15.22
Average Total SnowFall (in.)	8.6	6.5	8.7	4.4	0.9	0.0	0.0	0.0	0.5	3.4	6.7	6.6	46.3
Average Snow Depth (in.)	2	1	1	0	0	0	0	0	0	0	1	1	0

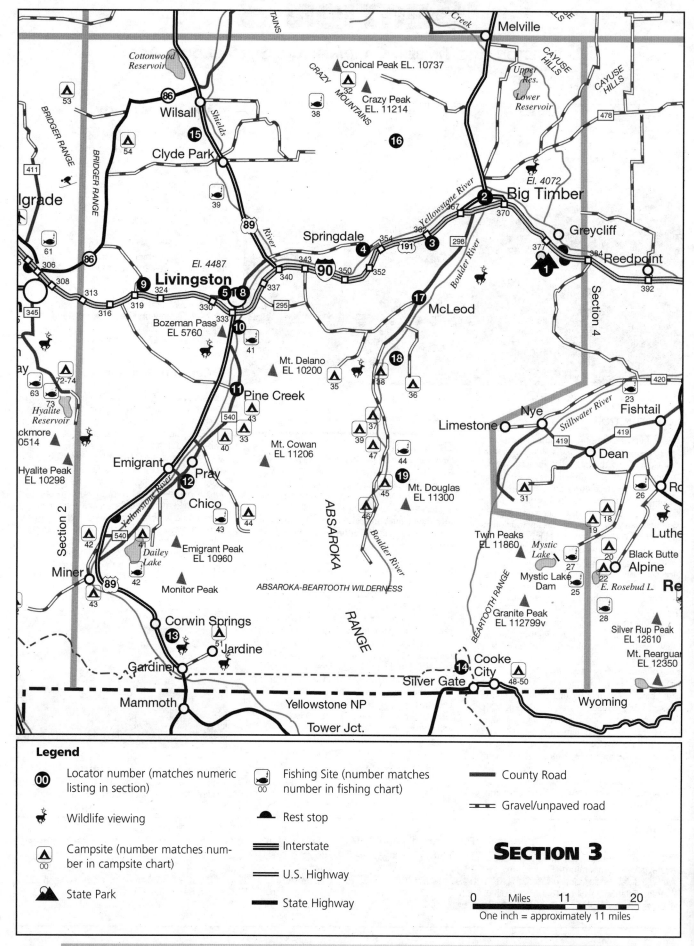

see to the northwest, are an igneous formation forged about 50 million years ago. For the Apsaalooka, they are the most sacred and revered mountains on the northern Great Plains. Awaxaawippiia was a place of refuge and protection. The Apsaalooka's enemies would not follow them into the mountains. Because of their great spiritual power, Awaxaawippiia continues to be an important vision quest site for the tribe. Famed Chief Plenty Coups had a vision there in 1857 in which, he said, the end of the plains Indian way-of-life was shown to him.

There are several stories about how the mountains got their current name. The most popular story goes that a woman traveling across the plains with a wagon train went insane. She escaped from the party and was found near these mountains. So they were called the Crazy Woman Mountains, a name which was eventually shortened. Perhaps the mountains were named, as others have claimed, because of their crazy appearance. The Crazy Mountains were an important landmark for Bozeman Trail emigrants in the Yellowstone Valley. This district was great cow and sheep country in the days of the open range, and there are still a number of large ranches in this vicinity, though now under fence.

D William Clark
July 15, 1806

"in the evening after usial delay of 3 hours to give the horses time to feed and rest and allowing our Selves time also to Cook and eate Dinner, I proceeded on down the river on an old bufalow road."

T Greycliff Prairie Dog Town State Park
9 miles east of Big Timber on I-90, at Greycliff exit. 247-2940

See Section 6.

2. *Gas, Food, Lodging*

Big Timber

Big Timber, 33 miles east of Livingston, is located near a geographical transition point. West of town, the Absaroka Range rises to lofty heights, while east stretch the vast Great Plains. The Crazy Mountains' jagged summits rise to the north of Big Timber towering more than 11,000 feet. Predominantly a livestock producing and recreational community, Big Timber is surrounded by the Gallatin National Forest.

Sweet Grass-land of livestock knee-deep in

This remarkable model of the town of Big Timber is on display at the Crazy Mountains Museum in Big Timber. It is precise in every detail.

good grass, sparkling clear water and air scented by sage and pine-became a county in 1895. The history of this 1,849 square mile area goes back many years before that to the Indian tribes who hunted the area. Crow, Cheyenne, Blackfoot, and raiding Sioux all claimed the area as hunting grounds.

Big Timber

William Clark came through the region in 1806 on his way back from the Pacific. "Rivers Across" in his journal refers to the spot on the Yellowstone just below Big Timber where, directly across from one another, the Boulder River and Big Timber Creek empty into the Yellowstone. Clark named Big Timber Creek for the unusually large cottonwood trees growing by its mouth.

The early 1880s brought the railroad to the

country. At its projected westward advancement for the winter of 1882, at the spot Clark named Rivers Across, a few enterprising individuals constructed the settlement of Dornix, meaning "large, smooth stones". Unfortunately, due to an open winter, the railroad didn't stop but went on to the foot of the Bozeman Hill. Having hurt Dornix, the railroad now gave it a purpose for existence. To build the roadbed, vast numbers of ties were cut in the mountains during the winter, then floated down the creeks during spring high water to points on the railroad. With its position, Dornix was the logical spot for docking ties coming down the Boulder.

Again the railroad interfered. Dornix was just below a hill; it was difficult for the trains to stop and then make a standing start at the hill. They preferred to run on up to the long flat above Dornix and then stop. In 1883, Dornix was moved lock, stock and barrel to its present site. Within several months of the move, nothing remained of Dornix. Several years after the move, the railroad again high-handedly affected the town when the officials in St. Paul renamed it Big Timber.

Parts are reprinted from Sweetgrass Chamber information sheet.

H The Bonanza or Bozeman Trail
Big Timber

In the early 1860s there wasn't a ranch in this country from Bismarck to Bozeman and from the Platte River to Canada. To whites it was land considered "fit only to raise Indians" and while some of them were hoping for a crop failure, the majority were indifferent. They didn't care how much the tribes fought amongst themselves. They were like the old-timer whose wife was battling a grizzly bear. He said he never had seen a fight where he took so little interest in the outcome.

Then the white man's greed asserted itself and he looked for a shortcut from the Oregon Trail at Laramie, Wyoming, to the gold diggin's of western Montana. The Bonanza or Bozeman Trail across Indian hunting grounds was the result. It forded the Yellowstone near here, coming from the southeast. It was a trail soaked with the blood of warriors, soldiers, and immigrants. Thousands of Sioux warriors, primarily under Red Cloud, bolstered by hundreds of Cheyennes and some Arapahos, fought the trail for six years and forced its closure by the Government in 1868.

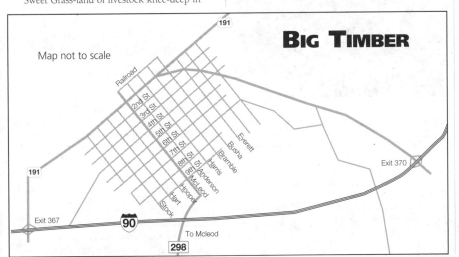

Map not to scale

BIG TIMBER

T Crazy Mountain Museum
Cemetery Road, Big Timber. 932-5126

Crazy Mountain Museum encompasses the historical background of Sweet Grass County and the surrounding areas. One of the more exceptional displays is a model replica of Big Timber in 1907. It includes 184 buildings which took 6 years to research and build. The model, a representation of miniature artistry and meticulous craftsmanship, is a historically accurate replica built on a scale of 1/16"=1' and depicts 12 1/2 square blocks of the town. 184 buildings—1,018 windows—406 doors—143 chimneys—152 power and telephone poles—135 people—22 vehicles—6 bicycles—35 horses—18 sheep—4 cows—20 chickens—8 dogs—4 cats—and 4 pigeons. The details are incredible. Look for clothes on a line, merchandise in windows, a hobo under a tree, axes in woodpiles, gardens, a blacksmith, wool sacks, coal bins, wheelbarrows, manure piles, milk cans, bars on jail and salon windows, a drunk, an apple tree, a red light on the porch of a female boarding house, a dog in a trash can, ladders, hitching posts, horse troughs, spokes on poles for linemen, a picture in front of the Auditorium, and a towel on a wall in back of the bathhouse, and more!

On the grounds of the museum is a unique structure known as a stabbur. The Stabbur was built as a memorial to the Norwegian pioneers who helped build Sweet Grass County. Buildings like these were a common site in Norway and often had flowers and small trees growing out of their sod roof. They were built as storehouses, and were often decorated with wood carvings. A farmer's wealth in Norway was measured by the

contents of his stabbur. It was his security and signature and was assurance of food for the long winters. The stabbur was usually two stories with the stairs leading to the lower locked door built a distance from the building— "greater than a rat could jump." The first level was where the grain and other foods were stored including the salted or dried fish, hams and mutton which hung from hooks in the ceiling. The second floor was for clothing, trunks, and other valuables.

M Sonny Todd Real Estate
301 W. 1st St., Big Timber. 932-6668 or (866) 932-1031. www.sonnytoddrealestate.com; info@sonnytoddrealestate.com

Sonny Todd Real Estate invites you to share the "Big Sky" experience with them. Staffed by native-born Montanans, the brokerage believes you will agree that Montana truly is one of the most beautiful, pristine, and uncrowded best last places. Lean back and take a deep breath of Montana air. Enjoy the state's immense grandeur, from wilder-

ness areas of snowcapped majestic mountains overlooking golden wheat fields to the Powder River cowboy country. Sonny Todd offers a full line of services with a marketing program covering Montana, Wyoming, Idaho, North Dakota, South Dakota, and the national and international communities. Listings include large recreational and working ranches, executive retreats, residential homes, and tracts of land from one to several hundred acres. When you decide to discover Montana, let the professionals at Sonny Todd Real Estate welcome you!

3.

H The Original Voges Bridge
Milepost 362, I-90

In late 1913, Sweet Grass County residents petitioned the County Commissioners to build a bridge across the Yellowstone River west of Big Timber. The petition was submitted to the commissioners by New York millionaire oil man and part-time Montana rancher, W. Dixon Ellis of the Briggs-Ellis Cattle Company. Dixon offered to donate $5,000 toward the construction of the bridge if the commissioners agreed to build it the following year. In April, 1914, the county contracted with the Security Bridge Company to construct a 2-span pin-connected Pratt through truss bridge at this site for $14,995. Designed by Sweet Grass County Surveyor J. B. Kleinhesselink and County Assessor D. J. Walvoord, the 378-foot long bridge included an experimental floor system that allowed use of the bridge by the new 20-ton tractors of the time. The Security Bridge

Company completed the structure in June, 1914 and it eventually became known as the Voges Bridge by area residents. Charles Voges owned a nearby sheep ranch and donated the land for the existing one-room school on the north bank of the river in 1920. When completed, the Voges Bridge provided access to the transportation systems on the south side of the river to the farmers and ranchers living north of the Yellowstone. The bridge was also the last pin-connected bridge built across the Yellowstone River.

4.
Springdale
This was a railroad station and a stopping place for travelers on their way to Hunter's Hot Springs. It took its name from the many springs that surround the area. The only thing left of Hunter's today is a fire hydrant sitting mysteriously in a field. This is near the spot where Capt. Lewis and his group lost their horses to Indian raiders. They were forced to travel down the Yellowstone in bull boats.

D William Clark
July 14, 1806

"I proceeded up this plain… and Crossed the main Chanel of the river. …and nooned it …the river is divided and on all the small Streams inoumerable quanities of beaver dams, tho' the river is yet navigable for Canoes."

D William Clark
July 15, 1806

"in the evening after usial delay of 3 hours to give the horses time to feed and rest and allowing our Selves time also to Cook and eate Dinner, I proceeded on down the river on an old bufalow road."

5. *Lodging*

Livingston
Located between the Gallatin and Crazy Mountain ranges and surrounded by the Absaroka-Beartooth Wilderness Area, the town of Livingston was established around the railroad in the 1880s. The Crow Indians occupied the land along the Yellowstone River for thousands of years before the white settlers moves in, and the Absaroka Mountains are named after the Crow. Lewis & Clark were among the first white men to travel through this area, and were followed by traders and trappers. As the Northern Pacific Railroad was making it's way through, they chose Livingston as their base camp, and set up a town that revolved around the railroad with repair shops and a thriving downtown.

It all started in 1882 with a man named Joseph McBride who was sent to find a location to open a store that would supply workers on the new railroad. He chose the site of present day Livingston, bypassing the settlement of Benson's Landing, a settlement that existed just a few miles down the Yellowstone. The store started out of tents, but it was not long until the down-

town began to develop. Originally named Clark City after William Clark, the name Livingston became widely accepted after the director of the Northern Pacific, Crawford Livingston.

The historic Main Street is a reminder of the past, with grand old buildings that have been restored and preserved. Many of the buildings date back to the turn of the century, and much local effort was put into their restoration, that gives the downtown area a real charm. Many of these old building were hotels for the tourists who came through Livingston on their way to Yellowstone National Park. Back in the day, tourists had to change trains in Livingston to get to Gardiner and many spent the night.

The Historic Depot Center was built by the Northern Pacific Railroad in 1902, was used until the 1970s, and still stands today as the Chamber of Commerce and a railroading museum. By 1882, Livingston was a thriving community, complete with 30 saloons, six general stores, two hotels, two restaurants and more. At one time, up to 2,200 men worked for the railroad and were based in Livingston. Calamity Jane spent a fair amount of time in Livingston, it is

said that she lived in a local hotel and even spent some time in the town's jailhouse.

Today, Livingston has much to offer the locals and tourists visiting Montana. Located on the Blue Ribbon Trout waters of the Yellowstone River, Livingston is a fly fishing community, with many outfitters and guides to accommodate the visitors. The city has over 13 art galleries to browse through, two playhouses, four museums, many unique downtown shops, and some great restaurants to choose from. Whitewater rafting is also popular on the Yellowstone River. The Livingston Roundup Rodeo is held every year from July 2–July 4 and draws competitors and visitors from all over the country.

D Sgt. Ordway
July 13, 1806

"Capt. Clark & party leaves us hear to cross over the River Roshjone. So we parted I and 9 more proceeded on down the river with the canoes verry well."

6. *Gas, Food, Lodging*

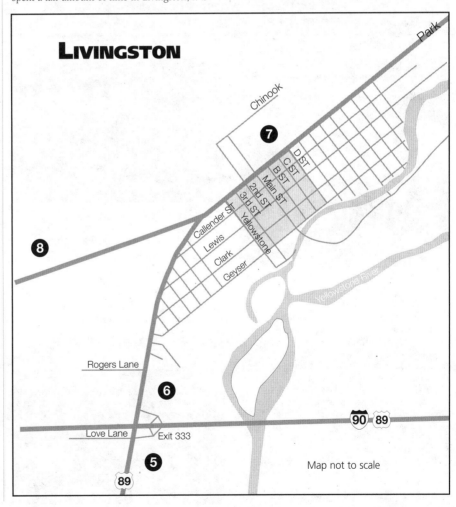

Livingston	Jan	Feb	March	April	May	June	July	Aug	Sep	Oct	Nov	Dec	Annual
Average Max. Temperature (F)	34.8	38.9	45.1	56.2	65.6	74.1	84.6	82.9	72.0	60.7	45.6	37.8	58.2
Average Min. Temperature (F)	16.2	18.9	23.1	31.3	38.8	46.0	51.7	50.3	42.7	35.7	26.3	20.3	33.5
Average Total Precipitation (in.)	0.63	0.51	0.93	1.30	2.51	2.16	1.28	1.15	1.49	1.20	0.82	0.56	14.55
Average Total SnowFall (in.)	10.7	5.2	10.8	4.2	0.2	0.0	0.0	0.0	0.2	2.7	5.0	5.0	44.2
Average Snow Depth (in.)	2	2	2	0	0	0	0	0	0	0	1	2	1

7. *Gas, Food, Lodging*

T Livingston Depot Center
200 W. Park St. in Livingston. 222-2300

Built by the Northern Pacific Railroad in 1902, the grand Italian style Passenger depot complex holds an art and cultural museum with records of railroading in the Pacific Northwest and Montana. There are exhibits of photographs describing one of America's most important industries. Hands-on displays for children, including a small train, make this a really fun stopover. Tours are also available through The Mountain Rockies Rail Tours. The museum is open May through September and there is a modest admission fee.

Montana Trivia

Alzada in the southeast corner of Montana is closer to the Texas panhandle, than it is to Yaak, Montana in the far northeast corner of the state. It is 800 miles, or 12 hours driving from Alzada to Yaak.

T Yellowstone Gateway Museum
118 W. Chinook in Livingston. 222-4184

Experience the pioneer days in this museum filled with interesting artifacts, railroad memorabilia, and archaeological finds. Located in a turn-of-the-century schoolhouse, the museum also offers displays of the early explorers, including a real-life stagecoach, a caboose from the 1890s, and a covered wagon. Open Memorial Day–Labor Day, 10 a.m.–5 p.m.

T Federation of Fly Fishers Fly Fishing Museum
215 E. Lewis in Livingston. 222-9369

This Fly Fishing Center is the only one of its kind in the nation. The center has live fish, explanations about fish habits and habitats, informative displays, a coldwater fish room with a tank of Yellowstone cutthroat trout and a warmwater fish room with an aquarium display of bass, sturgeon and others. Free fly-fishing classes are also available during the summer months.

F 2nd Street Bistro
123 N. 2nd St., Livingston, 222-9463, Email: 2ndstreetbistro@bridgeband.com, www.secondstreetbistro.com

The Second Street Bistro combines the techniques of classic French cooking with locally sourced Montana ingredients. Enjoy classic French bistro fare with a distinctly Mediterranean twist including wonderful appetizers, eclectic salads, local lamb and pork, and amazing desserts. The cocktails are handcrafted and they offer the largest wine list in the region with all bottles hand selected by a certified sommelier. The Second Street Bistro was recognized in 2005 as having the "Best Fine Dining", "Best Service", " Best Wine List", "Best Martini", and "Best Chef" in Livingston. Open daily at 11 am and closed Mondays. A wonderful brunch on Sunday morning, opening at 10 am. Dinner selections are served starting at 2 pm. Reservations are suggested. Catering is available for parties ranging in size from 4 to 400. Please call for current hours of operation.

L Country Motor Inn
814 E. Park St., Livingston. 222-1923. countrymotorinn@bresnan.net

Nestled just fifty miles from Yellowstone in the quiet east end of Livingston close to shopping and great restaurants, Country Motor Inn welcomes you to stay with them. Clean, comfortable rooms are standard with most featuring refrigerators and microwaves. Handicapped rooms are also available, and small pets are allowed. As an added bonus, guests can learn about the area from owners Susan and Allen Leens. The Leens are native Montanans who delight in helping guests discover all that the region offers. For those simply interested in relaxing onsite, the

Montana Trivia

The Absarokee (Crow) Indians are thought to be the the only Plains tribe that never made war against the white man.

Country Motor Inn features a lovely flower garden and lawn, and guests are encouraged to barbecue and picnic during the summer. On your next trip to the Rocky Mountain region, make Country Motor Inn your destination for an enjoyable stay and hometown service.

L Econo Lodge
111 Rogers Ln. I-90 at exit 333, Livingston.
222-0555 or (800) 4-CHOICE.
www.choicehotels.com

Situated near the Yellowstone River and framed by mountains, the Econo Lodge is located just off Interstate 90. The well-appointed rooms feature king or queen beds, cable TV with Starz and Disney, dataports, free local calls, and coffeemakers. Some rooms also include microwaves and refrigerators. Non-smoking and handicapped rooms are available, as well as guest laundry facilities, meeting rooms, fax/copy services, free continental breakfast, free wireless high-speed Internet in the lobby, and truck parking. AAA approved and pet friendly, the hotel adds relaxation to every stay with its heated indoor pool and hot

tub. Restaurants, shopping, museums, art galleries, and outdoor recreation are within walking distance, and Yellowstone National Park is a mere 56 miles south through Paradise Valley. For comfort and convenience in one location, stay with the friendly folks at Econo Lodge.

S The Cowboy Connection
110 S. Main in the Downtown Livingston.
222-0272. www.thecowboyconnection.com

The Cowboy Connection invites you to step back in time for a feel of the Old West! They've corralled a passel of Western Antiques and Cowboy collectables for you from the low end to the high-minded. There are spurs, chaps, saddles, Stetsons, old boots, holsters, cartridge belts, Native American textiles, jewelry, original Western art, bronzes, antique Colts and Winchesters, Bowie knives, pocket watches, photos, gambling, and advertising memorabilia are just some of the treasures you will find. Jerry and Vangie Lee's store is celebrating its 12th Anniversary. Mention this ad and receive 10% off any item. Appointments are welcome after store hours. Experience a unique atmos-

phere of Western Frontier Americana and discover the many antique and collectable items on display and for sale. Their web site doesn't get any shuteye-check it out anytime sunrise or sunset.

8. *Gas, Food*

9.

H Bozeman Pass
Milepost 321 on I-90

Sacajawea, the Shoshone woman who guided portions of the Lewis and Clark Expedition, led Captain Wm. Clark and his party of ten men over an old buffalo road through this pass on July 15, 1806. They were eastward bound and planned to explore the Yellowstone River to its mouth where they were to rejoin Captain Lewis and party who were returning via the Missouri River.

In the 1860s John M. Bozeman, an adventurous young Georgian, opened a trail from Fort Laramie, Wyoming, to Virginia City, Montana, across the hostile Indian country east of here. He brought his first party through in 1863 and the next year guided a large wagon train of emigrants and gold-seekers over this pass, racing with an outfit in charge of Jim Bridger. Bridger used a pass north of here. These pioneer speed demons made as much as fifteen to twenty miles a day—some days. The outfits reached Virginia City within a few hours of each other.

10. *Food, Lodging*

Section 3

PRAIRIE DOG TOWN

This 98-acre facility is operated by the Parks Division of Montana Fish, Wildlife & Parks to preserve the black-tailed prairie dog ecosystem for the public's educational and viewing enjoyment. Protection of this prairie dog town is due to the efforts of Edward Boehm of Livingston, Montana, who spearheaded the efforts to save it as the Interstate Highway was being built. Cooperative efforts by the Nature Conservancy and the Montana Department of Highways also helped preserve the park. Interpretive displays and picnic tables are provided. A day-use fee is charged at the park entrance to support ongoing maintenance. Restrooms are available about 1 mile east. Camping facilities are located at the KOA about 1/4 mile west.

Range

Five species of prairie dogs are native to North America. The black-tailed prairie dog (*Cynomys ludovicianus*), inhabits Greycliff Prairie Dog Town State Park and is the most common species. These ground dwelling squirrels live on the plains from southern Canada to northern Mexico. Large prairie dog towns, or colonies, are further divided into coteries. One coterie (the family territory) is usually comprised of one adult male, three to five adult females and their offspring.

It is typical for black-tailed prairie dogs to dig 15-40 burrow entrances per acre, many more than other species. Each burrow usually has two entrances which lead to a tunnel 4-7 feet deep and perhaps 15-25 feet long. Look for tunnel entrances marked by mounds of excavated soil compacted into a crater of dome shape. Often two feet high, these mounds serve as good lookouts and prevent running water from entering the tunnels. Burrowing aerates and mixes soil types, as well as incorporating organic matter to enhance soil formation.

Life Cycle

Black-tailed prairie dogs are usually sexually mature after their second winter and will breed in March each year. One to ten pups (average of 5) are born about 34 days after conception. The pups are born hairless and blind. They remain in the safety of their burrow for 48-49 days before emerging above ground. Prairie dogs are fully grown by October or November, averaging 1-3 pounds and 14-17 inches long. When late spring arrives, black-tailed prairie dogs may remain in the coterie in which they were born. If they cannot replace another member of the coterie who has left or died, the young prairie dog must leave. Young prairie dogs are most vulnerable during this time of dispersal. Watch for conflicts between males as the young attempt to join existing family territories or establish new coteries. If they survive their first two years of turmoil, prairie dogs may live five years or more.

Communication

Watch for a variety of postures or displays, such as lifting their heads or standing on their hind legs to scrutinize the terrain for signs of danger. Listen for at least 11 different calls used to communicate with each other. If a predator approaches, the prairie dog scampers to his burrow mound and sounds a series of short nasal yips to alert others. A jump-yip, or "whee-oo," call is given as an "all clear" message when danger has passed. Different calls and displays are used depending upon the relationship between caller and target (ie. resident vs. nonresident of the caller's coterie). Coterie members engage in a greeting ceremony by touching teeth, followed by elaborate grooming. This display seems to encourage harmony among the family and helps to identify intruding prairie dogs.

Activities

Black-tailed prairie dogs and Mexican prairie dogs do not hibernate as do the three white-tailed species. You should easily spot a few prairie dogs during daylight hours. They may retreat to their burrow seeking relief from the summer's midday heat or shelter from a winter storm. Prairie dogs can be seen eating green grasses, broad leafed, non-woody plants (forbs), and digging for roots and bulbs. Seeds and insects add variety to their diet. They are adept at removing the spines from prickly-pear cactus before eating the leaves.

Predators

Coyotes, foxes, and bobcats may be seen stalking along the outer perimeters of prairie dogtowns, or they may sit and wait at burrow entrances to make captures. Ferruginous hawks and golden eagles perch or soar near towns hunting prey. Look for enlarged burrow entrances, evidence of badgers who can dig deep into the burrows. Weasels have streamlined bodies allowing them to prowl through

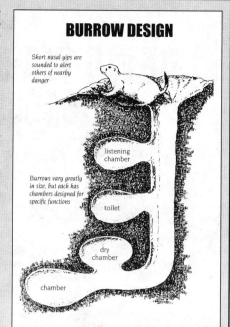

BURROW DESIGN

Short nasal yips are sounded to alert others of nearby danger

Burrows vary greatly in size, but each has chambers designed for specific functions

listening chamber

toilet

dry chamber

chamber

the tunnels. Keep an eye out for prairie rattlesnakes and bull snakes which occasionally use the tunnels for shelter and may dine on the young prairie dogs.

Can Prairie Dogs and Man Coexist

Black-tailed prairie dogs have long been viewed as a detriment to successful livestock production because they create dangerous holes and compete with livestock for grasses and forbs. In reality, prairie dogs have a variable effect on livestock production depending on habitat conditions and climate. In some areas, new plant growth is more nutritious and compensates for loss of forage volume.

Black-tailed prairie dogs have been reduced by 80-90% in various portions of their range. This reduction has had an impact on some species that use prairie dog towns. The most famous of these is the black-footed ferret which lives only in prairie dog towns and feeds almost exclusively (85-90%) on prairie dogs. The black-footed ferret is an endangered species, extinct in the wild except for one site in Wyoming. A recovery program is underway to restore this ferret to certain portions of its range. Over 101 vertebrate species inhabit the special ecosystem found near prairie dog towns, including the burrowing owl, golden eagle, ferruginous hawk, mountain plover, and swift fox.

Please Do Not Feed the Prairie Dogs

The digestive tracts of wild animals are specifically adapted to utilize their natural foods. Human foods, often with preservatives and chemicals, can compromise their ability to survive, especially during times of stress. Wild animals may ingest foil, plastic or paper wrappers which smell or taste like food. The results could be fatal.

Reprinted from Greycliff Prairie Dog Town State Park brochure. Montana Fish, Parks & Wildlife.

Downtown Livingston.

11. *Lodging*

Pine Creek

This tiny community located at the base of the Absaroka Mountains is a great place for flyfishing on the Yellowstone or hiking to Pine Creek Lake.

12. *Gas, Food, Lodging*

Emigrant

Tucked away in Paradise Valley, Emigrant is located halfway between Livingston and Gardiner on the Yellowstone River. Named after Emigrant Peak, the back drop of the town, the town prospered with the discovery of gold back in 1862. The locals used to soak in the natural hot springs at the base of Emigrant Peak.

Emigrant was named for Emigrant Peak, towering nearby at 10,960 feet. Gold was discovered in Emigrant Gulch in 1862 and the area also served as a spa for early trappers and prospectors who enjoyed the natural hot springs.

Miner

Located near the Yellowstone River, just outside Yellowstone National Park, Miner began as a mining settlement. The first post office operated from 1898 to 1920, with Maggie Morrison presiding as postmistress. The post later operated from 1921 to 1967.

Pray

Pray mainly exists today as a post office in Paradise Valley, along the beautiful Yellowstone River. The first post office was established in 1909, with Valentine Eggers presiding as postmaster.

H Emigrant Gulch
Milepost 28 on Hwy. 89 south of Emigrant

A party of emigrants who had traveled with a wagon train across the Plains via the Bozeman or Bonanza Trail arrived in this gulch August 28, 1864. Two days later three of these men explored the upper and more inaccessible portion of the gulch and struck good pay. A mining boom followed.

When cold weather froze the sluices the miners moved down to the valley, built cabins and "Yellowstone City" began its brief career. Provisions were scarce that winter. Flour sold for $28 per 96 lb. sack, while smoking tobacco was literally worth its weight in gold.

The strike was not a fabulous one, but snug stakes rewarded many of the pioneers for their energy and hardships.

H The Absaroka-Beartooth Wilderness
Milepost 24 on Hwy. 89, south of Emigrant

The Absaroka-Beartooth Wilderness, which lies to the east, contains the largest single expanse of land above 10,000 feet in elevation in the United States. The U.S. Forest Service set aside portions of the region as primitive areas in 1932, and Congress voted it a wilderness area in 1978. Visitors spent 392,000 collective days here in 1983, making it the fourth most visited wilderness in America.

Artifacts and pictographs indicate that people have hunted in these mountains for thousands of years, but it has always been country for people to visit, not live in. Reserved by treaty for the Crow in the early 1800s, the tribe shared with the less-rugged mountains on the west side of the wilderness (that you can see from here) their name for themselves, Absaroka (Absoarkey). The rugged mountains on the east side they named Beartooth, after one tooth-shaped peak. Gold discoveries in the 1860s attracted prospectors to Emigrant Gulch, and an 1880 treaty moved the reservation boundary eastward to allow previously clandestine mining claims to be developed.

The entire wilderness is a watershed for the Yellowstone, the longest undammed river left in the United States. It flows over 670 miles from its sources out of Yellowstone National Park and is the lifeblood of about one-third of Montana and much of northern Wyoming.

Montana Trivia

In his 1994 book, *Nothing But Blue Skies*, author Tom McGuane chronicles the happenings in the fictional town at Deadrock. He is taking a humorous jab at the town of Livingston ("living stone") where he resides.

T Old Chico
Old Chico Road, 5 miles south of Chico Hot Springs

Chico began as a mining camp when a group of miners moved up the gulch from Yellowstone City. Some of them took up farming. It wasn't a fun place to live for the early families there. The Crow Indians constantly attacked the settlement and stole their horses. During the winters, many of the families would take boats up the Yellowstone River for warmer parts of Montana. At one time, the town supported a hotel, meat market, blacksmith shop, store, schoolhouse, a post office, and sixty cabins. Mining operations ceased in 1933 and the town pretty much went away. A few people still live in this ghost town. Few buildings remain as reminders from busier days, but the scenery is spectacular.

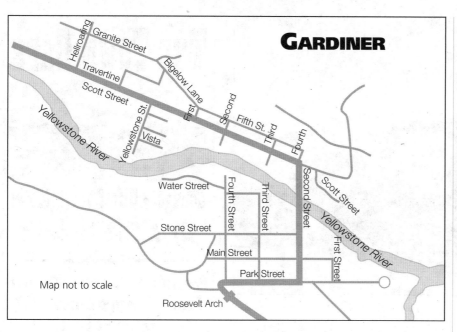

GARDINER

All Montana Area Codes are 406

Hellroaring
Granite Street
Travertine
Scott Street
Bigelow Lane
Yellowstone St.
Vista
First
Second
Fifth St.
Third
Fourth
Yellowstone River
Water Street
Fourth Street
Third Street
Second Street
Scott Street
Stone Street
Main Street
First Street
Park Street
Yellowstone River
Roosevelt Arch

Map not to scale

Section 3

13. *Gas, Food, Lodging*

Gardiner

The town of Gardiner began to prosper when Yellowstone National Park opened in 1872, and is the north entrance to this first National Park. Gardiner began serving tourists when the Northern Pacific Railroad brought them from Livingston to the small town called Cinnabar, where they would get on stagecoach to finish the journey to Gardiner. After many disputes, the railroad expanded the last few miles to Gardiner, making it the new gateway to the park. Roosevelt Arch was built in 1903, marking the entrance to the world's first National Park. Gardiner is a quaint town with lots of lodging, shopping and dining to accommodate the large volume of tourists. Sitting in between the Absaroka-Beartooth Wilderness and Yellowstone National Park, seasonal outdoor activities abound in Gardiner. Fishing, hunting, horseback riding, whitewater rafting and kayaking are all popular. Elk, deer, bighorn sheep, and an occasional bear will often be seen roaming on the various lawns throughout town.

Gardiner, the first gateway to Yellowstone, is located in southwest Montana, along the Yellowstone River. Gardiner was founded in 1880 at the North Entrance to the Yellowstone Park and became a center of activity for visitors to the region, as it served as the original and only year-round entrance to the park. Gardiner offers a fine selection of motels, restaurants, shops, art galleries, churches, a small airport and related visitor services. Campgrounds and trailer parks with hookups offer overnight services.

Sandwiched between the Absaroka-Beartooth Wilderness to the north and the world's most famous park to the south, seasonal outdoor activities abound in Gardiner. Spring, summer and fall offer fishing, hunting, pack trips, river-rafting and kayaking. During the winter, Yellowstone Country is magically transformed under a blanket of snow and cross-country skiing and snowmobiling are the activities of popular demand.

Viewing wild antelope on the hills and in the meadow across Park Street in Gardiner is a thrill that few towns can boast. Listen carefully and coyotes can be heard in the foothills. Bears will occasionally wander into town, while Elk roam freely throughout town.

Gardiner has survived a rough and tumble existence of gold rushes, the railroad and destructive fires. A tough little frontier town, it fed and sheltered miners, entertained the early soldiers who ran Yellowstone Park, and learned to host the pioneer visitor. Gardiner has matured, tempered and grown to meet the needs of today's visitor. It's a good place, rich in history, in the heart of some of the West's finest country.

Jardine

Jardine is an old western mining town that once supported a gold mine up until World War II. This town can only be reached by a gravel road that heads west from Gardiner. You can see the old bunkers and other remnants of the mine, and the town is a great place to take advantage of some hiking or biking opportunities.

Corwin Springs

Located near Yellowstone National Park's north entrance, Corwin Springs was named after Doctor Corwin who constructed and ran a hotel resort in the community.

T **Corwin Hot Springs**
Hwy 89, 6 miles north of Gardiner

Corwin Hot Springs runs off into the Yellowstone River and is located on Forest Service land. Nearby is La Duke Springs which is extremely dangerous for soaking. The springs are surrounded by the Royal Teton Ranch that until recently was owned by the Church Universal and Triumphant. The ruins of a bathhouse and elegant resort built in the early 1900s are nearby. A much safer place to soak on the Yellowstone River is 10 miles south, at Boiling River, inside the North entrance to Yellowstone Park at Gardiner.

T **Roosevelt Arch**
Gardiner. North Entrance to Yellowstone Park. 848-7971

This imposing stone archway on the edge of Gardiner is the North Entrance to Yellowstone Park and has marked the only year-round, drive-in entrance since 1903. In that year, it was dedicated by President Theodore Roosevelt before an estimated 5,000 spectators.

V **Yellowstone Raft Company**
406 Hwy. 89, Gardiner. 848-7777 or (800) 858-7781. www.yellowstoneraft.com; info@yellowstoneraft.com

The Yellowstone Raft Company pioneered white water rafting on the Yellowstone, Gallatin and Madison Rivers. Their professional guides, superior training, experience and commitment to white water excellence combine to give each family the best possible raft trip. The office is conveniently located on the main street of Gardiner, one block north of the bridge, and less than a mile from the north entrance of Yellowstone Park. The office meeting place provides changing rooms, restrooms, and a large inventory of rental wetsuits for all sizes. They run half or full day guided raft trips every day from Memorial Day to mid-September. Kayak instruction and trips designed for beginners are also offered. Rafting a wild Montana river will be the highlight of your family vacation in the Yellowstone Park area.

Gardiner													
	Jan	Feb	March	April	May	June	July	Aug	Sep	Oct	Nov	Dec	Annual
Average Max. Temperature (F)	33.0	38.3	46.1	55.9	66.6	76.3	85.9	84.5	73.8	60.9	42.7	34.0	58.2
Average Min. Temperature (F)	13.7	17.1	22.9	30.1	38.3	45.5	51.4	50.3	41.7	33.1	22.7	15.8	31.9
Average Total Precipitation (in.)	0.44	0.34	0.56	0.66	1.60	1.53	1.10	0.95	0.91	0.74	0.60	0.45	9.89
Average Total SnowFall (in.)	5.8	3.0	3.8	2.9	0.5	0.0	0.0	0.0	0.1	0.2	3.3	5.6	25.2
Average Snow Depth (in.)	2	1	0	0	0	0	0	0	0	0	0	1	0

FL Town Cafe, Motel, Lounge & Gift Shop
122 Park St., Gardiner. 848-7322.

A warm welcome greets you at The Town Café along with fine dining and family-style menus. The Café opens at 6 am for one of the heartiest breakfasts you'll ever eat. Lunch begins at 11:30 am with a family lunch and dinner menu served until 9 pm. Try the Town Loft upstairs for seafood and steaks while enjoying incredible Yellowstone Park views. The Loft is open 5:30 pm to 10 pm and features a 30+ item salad bar. A variety of Montana and Yellowstone souvenirs awaits at the Town Gift Shop, and the Casino Lounge is perfect for grabbing a late night drink while testing your luck at the Poker and Keno machines. There are 11 rooms available at the adjoining motel.

L Absaroka Lodge
310 Scott St. W., Hwy. 89. Gardiner. 848-7414 or reservations at (800) 755-7414. www.yellowstonemotel.com; ablodge@aol.com

This beautifully appointed lodge is located directly on the banks of the Yellowstone River. There are 41 rooms including eight suites. Each room has its own private balcony or deck overlooking the Yellowstone River. You can even see Yellowstone Park in the near distance. The suites also offer fully equipped kitchens. You'll find delightful gift shops along with the fishing and hunting shops and great eating establishments, all within walking distance. In the mornings and evenings, complimentary coffee and tea are served in the lobby. Enjoy sitting on the park benches in their front lawn or your own private balcony, and see great views including Yellowstone Park. They are open year-round, and their friendly office personnel can help you book adventures such as horseback riding, fishing, snowmobiling, and whitewater rafting. Visit their website for more information.

L Westernaire Motel
910 Scott St. W., U.S. Hwy. 89, Gardiner. 848-7397 or reservations only at (888) 273-0358.

C Rocky Mountain Campground
14 Jardine Rd., Gardiner. 848-7251 or (877) 534-6931. www.rockymountaincampground.com; info@rockymountaincampground.com

Nestled on a bluff overlooking the Yellowstone River, Rocky Mountain Campground is located off Interstate 90 through scenic Paradise Valley. Yellowstone's north entrance is just four blocks away, and Gardiner's shops and restaurants are within easy walking distance. 50-amp pull-thrus, full-hookups, grassy tent sites, cabins, wi-Fi Internet connections, cable TV, coin-operated laundry, and clean restrooms and showers guarantee comfortable stays. Check out the onsite Christmas shop and camp store, stock up on supplies and free maps, take a Yellowstone bus tour departing daily from the campground, play miniature golf, and watch from the sunset patio as color washes over the nearby mountains in a gorgeous display. Outdoor adventure waits with nearby horseback riding, river rafting, fishing, and hunting. With these amenities and more, Rocky Mountain Campground is your ideal Yellowstone exploration base camp!

The historic towns of Colter Pass, Cooke City, and Silver Gate are nestled in the heart of the Absaroka-Beartooth Mountains at the Northeast Entrance of Yellowstone National Park.
-Cooke City Chamber of Commerce

An Angler's Guide to Paradise Valley

by Mathew Long—Long Outfitting

As fishing has grown in popularity, so has the desire to fish in the northern gateway to Yellowstone Park, Paradise Valley. The majestic mountains seem to have an overpowering effect to draw anglers from around the globe to its abundance of blue ribbon trout fisheries. The valley, 50 miles in length, offers dozens of opportunities to fish for trout of various species and sizes, in a variety of waters from the mighty Yellowstone River to remote alpine lakes. A bit of exploration by an angler, or a day of fishing with one of the area's professional guides can make for a successful and pleasant outing. The following brief descriptions of some of the area's most popular fisheries are designed to lead you in the proper direction in relation to the type of water you desire to fish, the species and size of trout you would like to catch, and the amount of money you would like to spend.

The Yellowstone River

By far, the most popular of all the angling activities is a float trip down the Yellowstone river. This wild and scenic river provides anglers with over 60 miles of floatable, fishable water in Paradise Valley. Some of the sections throughout the valley support up to 1,000 fish per mile. Do not overlook the sections upstream in Yellowstone Park and downstream towards Big Timber, though. These areas hold excellent populations of larger trout. The types of water, as well as the speciation of the trout change rapidly throughout the rivers length.

Depending on the time of the year, trout will feed on various orders of insects. Spring and fall provide excellent mayfly and midge hatches, while the hot, dry summer days make for excellent terrestrial and caddis action.

Take a comfortable drift boat down the river, or use one of the public access areas to gain access for wade fishing. Remember that once you have legally gained access to the river, everything below the high-water mark is public property. The most effective way to fish this large river is to hire a guide and cover a lot of water in a drift boat. Look for the pods of trout in back eddies containing foam lines and on deeper shelves off of cut banks and current seams. Yellowstone River trout usually average between 10 and 18 inches.

The Spring Creeks

For the discriminating fly fisherman, the spring creeks are among the most famous in the world. Located in the northern end of Paradise Valley and minutes from Livingston, Montana, Armstrongs, Depuys, and Nelsons spring creeks are a convenient and popular destination. Gin clear water, prolific, complex hatches, and tricky currents all combine to make for a challenging, yet hopefully rewarding day. Breathtaking views of the lush weed beds, dimpling trout, and white-tailed deer combined with the backdrop of the Absaroka-Beartooth Wilderness to the east and the Gallatin Mountains to the west offer picturesque moments.

Catching trout here is anything but easy. Reading the feeding trout, matching the hatch, floating perfect drifts, and presenting accurate casts all can increase your odds of taking these selective trout. Brown, rainbow, and cutthroat trout can all be found in the privately-owned spring creeks.

All the streams are managed as fee fishing areas and have limited access to insure a quality experience for all of the anglers. Rod dates book early and it is wise to call in advance. Approximate cost per fisherman is $75.00 per day. Some local fly shops reserve extra rods for client's use, so don't be afraid to stop in and ask questions. Despite all the rumors about the damage done by the floods of 1996 and 1997, the creeks fish just as well now as before.

Private Lakes

Another option that fly fishermen often take advantage of, especially during the snow-melt run-off, are the numerous private lakes located in Paradise Valley. Fishing these still waters often produces large trout in the 14-25 inch range. Some of these lakes can be fished effectively from shore, while others are large enough to require the use of a drift boat or float tube. Some lakes require fishermen to be accompanied by a guide, while others just require a daily access rate.

Often times, fish can be caught on a variety of fly patterns from tiny midge to large leeches. The famous damsel hatch in mid-July is a wonderful time to fish dry flies. Just to give you an example of the quality of some of these fisheries, Merrell Lake, located in Tom Miner Basin, has been rated by Fly Fisherman Magazine as one of the top six privately owned lakes in North America. This is a pretty impressive status for a 90-acre trout lake in the heart of Paradise Valley.

Other local lakes can produce some great fishing for very large rainbow, cutthroat, and brown trout. Check with a Livingston fly shop on access and price information. Prices range from $50 per angler, while others are free when fishing with a guide.

Alpine Lakes and Small Tributaries

For the fisherman who likes to get away to a "less traveled to" location, many small tributaries to the Yellowstone River and the high-altitude lakes of the Absaroka and Gallatin ranges can provide solitude, serenity and excellent fishing. Many of the fish are small, but are eager to feed on flies and are certainly some of the feistier fish you will ever encounter.

A topographic map can help you locate some destinations including Mill Creek, Big Creek, Rock Creek, Tom Miner Creek, Bear Creek, Emerald Lake, Thompson Lake, Shelf Lake, and Ramshorn Lake. There are too many of these small streams and lakes to even begin to list them all. Take your hiking shoes and some bear spray, and check your fishing regulation book before going on your trek. Some of these lakes are in Yellowstone Park and some are located in forest service and wilderness areas.

It is easy to see how Paradise Valley has received its name. For anglers, it is truly an angling paradise. For non-anglers, it is a geological and wildlife paradise. Come see for yourself the impressive scenery and the awesome fishing south of Livingston. Fond memories and feeding trout await your arrival.

For more information on fishing Paradise Valley call:

Matthew Long
222-6775 or Email: longoutfit@ycsi.net
www.longoutfitting.com

Cooke City

Cooke City is located on the northeastern edge of the Yellowstone National Park boundary, and is accessed either by the Beartooth National Scenic Byway or by driving through the park.

Shoo-Fly, the original name of the mining town now known as Cooke City was changed by the miners in 1880 to honor Jay Cooke, Jr. Cooke, a Northern Pacific Railroad contractor and the son of an investor in the Northern Pacific Railroad, promised not only to promote the area's development, but also to help bring a railroad to the town. However, he got into financial difficulties, forfeited his bond, and his bonded mining claims reverted back to the original owners. by the 1870s, the town was booming. A few years later, Chief Joseph and the Nez Perce stormed through town and burnt down much of the gold mining facilities. Although they were reconstructed, due to it's hard to reach location, the boom did not last very long. Old cabins are left over from the mining days and the town reflects the past very well.

The town of Cooke City and the land around it were within the Crow Reservation until 1882, when the boundaries of the reservation were shifted eastward. Shortly after moving these boundaries, 1,450 mining claims were staked and recorded in the New World District. Most of these claims lapsed after a year. By 1883, Cooke City had grown to a community of about 135 log huts and tents.

John P. Allen was the first person to drive a four-horse team and loaded wagon to town. In 1883 he built the Allen Hotel, later renamed the Cosmopolitan. Eventually he opened three mines: the O-Hara, War Eagle and McKinley.

The town site was platted in 1883, had two hundred twenty seven voters, two smelters, two sawmills three general stores, two hotels, two livery stables and a meat market. However, because of the large number of irregularly shaped mining claims and the problems of organizing them, it took eight years to complete the surveying and platting.

Today, Cooke City has a year around population of approximately 90 people. The population expands to over three hundred when summer residents arrive The town has a rustic "old west" atmosphere, which can be traced to its mining roots. However, tourism is currently the main stay of the economy.

This is a tourist destination, with people pouring in from both sides, but with Cooke City's past, it is easy to see why. *Source: Cooke City Chamber of Commerce*

Silver Gate

The town of Silver Gate is located on land home steaded by Horace S. Double, for which he was granted a patent on May 2, 1897. In 1932, John L Taylor and J. J. White later founded the town of Silver Gate on part of the homestead. They intended to create a rustic, western town to serve the tourist trade and to provide building sites for summer recreationists. The year-round population includes only a few, but the summer population is well over a hundred. Covenants written for the original town site covered setbacks, signs, and building standards requiring log construction and rustic architecture. *Source: Cooke City Chamber of Commerce*

H Cooke City
Cooke City

In 1868 a party of prospectors came into this country by way of Soda Butte Creek. They found rich float but were set afoot by Indians. Caching their surplus supplies on the stream now called Cache Creek they made it back to the Yellowstone and reported their find. In the next few years many prospectors combed these mountains; the first real development began about 1880 with Jay Cooke's infusion of eastern capital.

Chief Joseph's band of fugitive Nez Perce Indians came through here in 1877. In 1883 there were 135 log cabins in the settlement, two general stores and thirteen saloons.

Cooke City had been waiting years for reasonable transportation connections to the outside world so that her promising ore deposits could be profitably mined. She's no blushing maiden, but this highway was the answer to her prayers.

VL Big Bear Lodge and Stillwater Outfitters
714 U.S. Hwy. 212, Cooke City. 838-2267 or (888) 341-2267. www.montanabigbearlodge.com and www.stillwateroutfitters.com; info@stillwateroutfitters.com

Nestled at the gateway to Yellowstone and the Absaroka Beartooth Wilderness, Big Bear Lodge and Stillwater Outfitters is your destination for year-round lodging and outdoor adventure. Clean, comfortable log cabins feature two double beds, private bathrooms, refrigerators, and coffeemakers. Two cabins include kitchens, and meal packages offering family-style home cooked meals are available. Guests also enjoy the lodge's recreational room complete with satellite TV, pool table, hot tub, and phones. During your stay, book a summer horseback wilderness pack trip with Stillwater Outfitters. Carrying the Montana Board of Outfitters permit, Stillwater Outfitters also specializes in big game hunts, fly-fishing, sightseeing, and photography. On your next visit to Yellowstone Country, experience spectacular views, endless recreation, and comfortable lodging in a peaceful Montana setting with the help of Big Bear Lodge and Stillwater Outfitters!

L Big Moose Resort
715 Hwy. 212, Cooke City. 838-2393. www.bigmooseresort.com; info@bigmooseresort.com

Located on the Beartooth Highway All-american Road seven miles from Yellowstone's Northeast Entrance, Big Moose Resort offers year-round western hospitality and clean, comfortable accommodations. The family owned and operated resort provides convenient access to outdoor recreation, Yellowstone sightseeing, and the Beartooth Mountains. The friendly owners delight in sharing their area knowledge while guests enjoy world-class fishing, snowmobiling, skiing, wildlife watching, mountain biking, hiking, hunting, and horseback riding. After a day of exploration, relax in the resort's hot tub and retreat to cozy cabins featuring queen beds, DirecTV, free wireless Internet, gas log fireplaces, BBQ grills, porches, and kitchenettes. Camping and RV spots with full hookups and a shower facility are also available. Competitive nightly rates and discounted multi-night stays are standard. Hang your hat and stay awhile in one of America's most beautiful settings!

Clyde Park

Originally named Sunnyside, Clyde Park was chosen because the post office was on a ranch that raised Clydesdale horses and the town resembled a park. This small town revolved around farming and ranching and with the help of the Northern Pacific Railroad, the trains still haul the harvest goods to larger towns.

Wilsall

This small community began when the Northern Pacific laid a spur line through the area. Wilsall is located in serene Shields Valley, with immaculate views of the Crazy Mountains to the East. The town's name was the culmination of Walter B. Jordan's son, Will, and his daughter-in-law, Sally. Jordan initially laid out the town. In 1910 when the first post office was established, Albert Culbertson acted as postmaster.

Cooke City	Jan	Feb	March	April	May	June	July	Aug	Sep	Oct	Nov	Dec	Annual
Average Max. Temperature (F)	24.1	30.5	37.1	44.5	54.7	64.7	73.8	72.4	62.2	48.9	32.0	23.8	47.4
Average Min. Temperature (F)	3.9	5.5	11.0	18.4	27.4	33.6	38.3	37.0	29.7	22.1	12.0	4.3	20.3
Average Total Precipitation (in.)	2.39	1.77	1.91	1.82	2.70	3.00	2.10	2.06	1.93	1.57	2.13	2.29	25.67
Average Total SnowFall (in.)	41.3	28.9	26.0	16.9	8.7	1.9	0.0	0.0	2.5	10.3	29.9	40.3	206.9
Average Snow Depth (in.)	29	36	37	28	6	0	0	0	0	1	8	20	14

H Shields River Valley
Wilsall

This river was named by Capt. Wm. Clark of the Lewis and Clark Expedition in honor of John Shields, a member of the party. Capt. Clark and his men, guided by Sacajawea, the Shoshone woman, camped at the mouth of the river July 15, 1806, while exploring the Yellowstone on their return trip from the coast.

Jim Bridger, famous trapper, trader and scout, guided emigrant wagon trains from Fort Laramie, Wyoming, to Virginia City, Montana, in the 1860s, crossing hostile Indian country via the Bonanza Trail. Bridger's route came up this valley from the Yellowstone, followed up Brackett Creek, crossed the divide west of here to strike Bridger Creek and thence down the latter to the Gallatin Valley.

16. *Food*

T Crazy Mountains
I-90 Exit 367, Big Timber

This island mountain range stands in stark contrast to the surrounding plains. Its rugged granite peaks are snow capped a good part of the year. The majestic peaks, alpine lakes, cascading streams and infinite views make this one of Montana's most magnificent alpine areas. The Robert Redford movie *Jeremiah Johnson* was based on the life of Liver Eatin' Johnson, who frequented these mountains.

The Crazy Mountains were formed by igneous rock and carved by glaciers. They have been inhabited by man for 11,500 years and now provide beauty and recreation to the people of Big Timber and her visitors. Indians, most recently the Shoshone and Crow, have camped in the canyons, drunk the clear water from the streams, and eaten of the vast herds of deer, antelope, and elk. Between 1860 and 1880 the Indians gave way to trappers, traders, and settlers.

The Crazies weren't named until the 1860s with fact blending with fiction about how they came by their title. In the first theory, Indians called them the "Mad Mountains" for their steepness, rugged beauty, and haunting winds that blow down the canyon. Geology plays a part in the second theory. The lava upthrusts are young in perspective of time and do not fit in with the neighboring rock formations, hence the name "Crazy". In the third, and most widely accepted, a woman-some say Indian and some say white-went mad on the prairie, possibly due to the death of her family, and took refuge in the mountains. Indian belief required the crazy people be left alone and so she was.

However the name came about, the fact remains, the Crazy Mountains are a beautiful backdrop for the surrounding area, and offer much in the way of recreation.

17. *Food, Lodging*

McLeod

In 1882, W.F. McLeod drove a herd of 125 cattle and 200 horses into the Boulder Valley from Oregon. He was recognized as the first permanent homesteader in the valley, with the little town named after him. The Boulder Valley residents conducted their first election in 1884. On June 11, 1886, the McLeod Post Office was established with the mail coming in on horseback from Big Timber. In the spring of 1887, the first school started with five children.

Settlers moved into the valley, including Thomas Hawley, who assisted in the discovery of the valuable mineral deposits farther up the river valley. Prospecting had started in 1869, so by the spring of 1887, the mining operations had attracted considerable attention. A pack trail was cut through the timber and the Independence Mining Company took the first stamp mill up the mountain in 1888. Independence Mine was running full blast in '92 and '93, boasting a population of 500 or more persons. One long street with a few cabins, four saloons and two general stores made up the town. All that remains of Independence and the other mining camps today are a few tumbled down log structures and the glory of this magnificent mountain valley. Hiking trails lead to hidden valleys and lakes where wildlife such as moose, bear, elk and the many small animals make their home.

The little town of McLeod has a school, post office, cabins, camping and the infamous Road Kill Cafe. Take a drive south to one of the most beautiful mountain valleys in Montana. Enjoy the peaceful surroundings of the valley, fish in the pristine waters of the Boulder River, and picnic at the Natural Bridge and Falls. *Reprinted from Sweetgrass Chamber information sheet.*

18.

T Natural Bridge
27 miles south of Big Timber on Hwy. 298.
932-5131

This is one of the more unusual waterfalls you will ever see. The Boulder River literally drops into a hole and exits out of the face of a 100 foot cliff. If you catch it at the right time during spring runoff (usually early to mid-June) the river rises above the hole and cascades over the bridge to the gorge below. The appearance is that of a mini-Niagara. The river and canyon below the falls is equally spectacular. The viewpoints for the falls are wheelchair accessible and much of the walk to and around the falls is paved. A parking area and points along the trail have interpretive signs explaining the geology of the falls.

19.

T Independence Ghost Town
Hwy 298, south of McLeod

It's a little challenging to get to the mine shafts, cabins, and brothel that still stand here. You might even see an occasional moose, elk, deer, or grizzly bear. Located at an altitude of about 10,000 feet, the view of the Absaroka-Beartooth Wilderness area is stunning from Independence. Plan on using 4WD or a good pair of hiking boots. Both wouldn't be a bad idea.

SCENIC DRIVES

Boulder River Valley

Big Timber marks the confluence of the Boulder and Yellowstone Rivers. The Boulder River Valley is a beautiful drive just south of Big Timber on Route 298. Occupied by the Crow Indians until 1882, the area was opened to settlers shortly after. The discovery of gold and silver drew many settlers to the area, and farming and ranching became the mainstay that is still popular today. Many settlers built guest ranches along the Boulder Valley to accommodate travellers, and a few still remain today.

On this beautiful drive, you will pass Natural Bridge State Park and travel through the Gallatin National Forest which lines much of the Boulder River. The historic ranger station built in 1905 sits along Route 298. Native American Caves can be seen from the road just west of the ranger station, and used to shelter the Crow. There are pictographs on the walls of one of the caves. As you head further down the Main Boulder, you can visit the ghost town Independence.

Paradise Valley

Paradise Valley has been carved by the Yellowstone River running through the land, separating the Gallatin Range to the west and the Absaroka Range to the east. Leading from Livingston to the Gardiner entrance to Yellowstone National Park, the valley offers spectacular landscape and great fly fishing and recreational activities. The Crow Indians inhabited this area along the river for many years before the white man settled here. Today celebrities such as Dennis Quaid, Peter Fonda and others call it home much of the year.

After striking gold in Emigrant Gulch in 1862, a few small mining towns sprouted up along the valley, including Old Chico and Yellowstone City. By the late 1800s, coal mines exceeded gold mines, and much was extracted from this area. Nowadays ranching is how the locals make a living in the area, among other things.

Wilsall													
	Jan	**Feb**	**March**	**April**	**May**	**June**	**July**	**Aug**	**Sep**	**Oct**	**Nov**	**Dec**	**Annual**
Average Max. Temperature (F)	32.4	36.1	40.1	52.3	62.7	72.4	82.3	81.2	69.2	61.1	43.5	35.9	55.8
Average Min. Temperature (F)	6.3	12.0	14.5	24.8	33.6	40.1	45.0	43.0	35.0	27.8	17.2	11.4	25.9
Average Total Precipitation (in.)	0.58	0.47	0.79	1.08	2.47	2.53	1.26	1.24	1.38	0.89	0.72	0.41	13.82
Average Total SnowFall (in.)	11.6	5.3	3.1	1.6	0.0	0.1	0.0	0.0	0.1	0.3	2.9	3.4	28.4
Average Snow Depth (in.)	4	5	3	0	0	0	0	0	0	0	1	1	1

HIKES

Pine Creek Lake
This isn't a hike for couch potatoes. It will take you into some gorgeous mountain scenery with a pristine alpine lake at the end. To get there, travel south of Livingston on Hwy. 89 to East River Road. Cross the Yellowstone and travel another nine miles. Turn left and follow the signs to the Pine Creek campground. The trailhead starts here and takes you immediately to a spectacular waterfall. From here it begins a steep ascent climbing 3,000 feet in 4 miles.

Blue Lake
This 5 mile hike can be a bit rugged, particularly the second half that takes a pretty steep ascent. The trails switch back frequently though and are not that strenuous. The trail starts into Big Timber Canyon as a jeep trail and gradually narrows to a hiking trail. Along the way you will pass Big Timber Falls, a beautiful cascading falls on Big Timber Creek. The source of this stream is your destination. About 2 miles along the trail, you will come to a clearly marked trailhead for Blue Lake. The trail immediately crosses the creek and begins switching back and forth up the mountain. The lake itself is a beautiful post card scene of an alpine lake. There are several excellent camp sites around the lake and a trail completely circles it. There is excellent fishing here. If you walk to the far side of the lake to the roaring sound you will see where the lake spills down the mountain side and the beginnings of Big Timber Creek.

East Fork Boulder River Trail 27
From Big Timber head south on McLeod Street (the main street) through the residential area of town until it takes a sharp right and turns into Hwy. 298. Follow this for 19 miles past McLeod to the East Boulder Road turnoff on your left (east). Follow this road for 6 miles on a bumpy gravel road past the Ricks Park Campground and Upsidedown Creek Trailhead to the Box Canyon Trailhead. The trailhead is well signed. This trail used to be an old wagon road. It is a 3.5 mile hike to a log bridge that is an excellent picnic area.

West Boulder Trail 41
This easy trail goes 16 miles to Mill Creek Pass if you go the whole way. The trail pretty much follows the river into the wilderness area. The lower part of the trail passes through some private property and you may share some of it with cattle grazing the area. From Big Timber head south on McLeod Street (the main street) through the residential area of town until it takes a sharp right and turns into Hwy. 298. Follow the highway for 16 miles to Hwy. 35 on your right (west). Drive 6.5 miles to a major fork in the road. Go left and follow this road for 8 miles till you see the sign marking the turn to the campground. To reach the trailhead, go straight past the campground for a few hundred feet. You will see the sign marking the trailhead.

CROSS-COUNTRY SKI TRAILS

Gallatin National Forest
For more information contact District Ranger, Gardiner, MT 59030 (406) 848-7375

Bannock Trail—Cooke City to Silver Gate
4.8 km
Easiest trail is on groomed snowmobile trail.

Republic Creek—Cooke City
3 km More Difficult; no grooming
Trail enters Wyoming and the North Absaroka Wilderness.

Woody Creek-Cooke City
2 km More Difficult, 1 km Most Difficult; no grooming
Steep climb through timber near Cooke City; trail breaks into open timber and meadows.

Bear Creek Trail System— Jardine
7 km Easiest, 7.5 km more difficult; intermittantly groomed
Easy climb through timber along Bear Creek Road. Climbs through timber along old logging road to a meadow on the ridge.

Tom Miner—Tom Miner Basin, 26 mi. W Gardiner
6.4 km Easiest; no grooming
Road plowed by County; stay on road—do not trespass on private land.

Sheep Creek-Cooke City
4 km Easiest; no grooming
Follow Miller Loop snowmobile trail for first mile.

Gallatin National Forest
For more information contact District Ranger, Livingston, MT 59047 (406) 222-1892

Suce Creek—8 mi. SE Livingston
2.0 miles Moderate; no grooming. Trail crosses private property, please stay on trail.
Suce Creek Forest Service road #201 is plowed to a private driveway in Section 20, T3S, R10E. Do Not block driveway. Parking capacity 3 cars. Please respect private property.

Trail Creek-15 mi. SW Livingston
1.9 miles Moderate; no grooming. Trailhead and trail crosses private lands, please stay on trail.
Trail begins at the Trail Creek Trailhead on Park County's Newman Creek Rd; parking capacity 10 cars; shared with snowmobiles. Depending upon snow and road conditions Park County's Newman Creek Rd may be impassable to wheeled vehicles. Parking then would be at the junction of Park County's Trail Creek and Newman Creek Roads; parking capacity 8 cars. This will add 1.2 mi. to the trail length. Please respect private property.

INFORMATION PLEASE

All Montana area codes are 406

Road Information
Montana Road Condition Report
(800) 226-7623, (800) 335-7592 local 444-7696
Montana Highway Patrol   444-7696
Local Road Reports
Bozeman   586-1313
Statewide Weather Reports   453-2081

Tourism Information
Travel Montana (800) 847-4868 outside Montana
                     444-2654 in Montana
                     http://travel.mt.gov/.
Yellowstone Country (800) 736-5276 or 646-4383
Northern Rodeo Association   252-1122

Chambers of Commerce
Big Timber   932-5131
Cooke City   838-2495
Gardiner   848-7971
Livingston   222-0850

Airports
Big Timber   932-4389
Gardiner   848-7794
Livingston   222-0520
Red Lodge   446-2537
Wilsall   222-0520

Government Offices
State BLM Office   255-2885, 238-1540
Bureau of Land Management
    Billings Field Office   896-5013
Custer National Forest, Beartooth Ranger District
                                 446-2103
Gallatin National Forest,   522-2520
Montana Fish, Wildlife & Parks   994-4042
U.S. Bureau of Reclamation   247-7295

Hospitals
Sweet Grass Community Hospital
    Big Timber   932-5449
Stillwater Community Hospital
    Columbus   322-5316
Livingston Memorial Hospital
    Livingston   222-3541

Golf Courses
Overland Golf Course   932-4297
Livingston Golf Club   222-1031

Bed & Breakfasts
Blue Winged Olive • Livingston   222-8646
Dome Mountain Ranch • Emigrant   333-4361
North Yellowstone B & B • Gardiner   848-7651
Pleasant Pheasant B & B • Livingston 333-4659
Yellowstone Basin Inn • Gardiner   848-7080
Buckin' Horse Bunkhouse•Big Timber   932-6537
Burnt Out Lodge • Big Timber   932-6601
Big Timber Inn B&B • Big Timber   932-4080
Cabin By The River • Corwin Springs 848-2223
Carriage House Inn • Big Timber   932-5339
Davis Creek B&B • Livingston   333-4768
Gibson Cassidy House • Clyde Park   686-4490
Headwaters B & B • Gardiner   848-7073
Java Inn B&B • Big Timber   932-6594
Johnstad's B & B & Log Guest House
    Emigrant   333-9003
Log Cabin Cafe And B & B•Silver Gate 838-2367
Medicine Bow Ranch • Big Timber   932-4463
O'Carroll's B&B on the Yellowsone
    Livingston   333-9099
Paradise Gateway B & B • Emigrant   333-4063
Querencia B & B • Emigrant   333-4500
Remember When B & B • Livingston   222-8367
Teneagles Lodge • Clyde Park   686-4285
The Elliott Guest House • Livingston 222-2055
The Grand • Big Timber   932-4459
The River Inn • Livingston   222-2429
Wickiup B&B • Emigrant   333-4428
Yellowstone Country B & B•Emigrant   333-4917
Yellowstone Riverview Lodge B & B
    Emigrant   848-2156
Yellowstone Suites B & B • Gardiner 848-7937

Guest Ranches & Resorts
Big Moose Resort • Cooke City   838-2393
Dome Mountain Ranch • Emigrant   333-4361
Chico Hot Springs • Pray   333-4933
B Bar Guest Ranch • Emigrant   848-7523
Hawley Mountain Guest Ranch
    Mc Leod   932-5791
High Country Motel • Cooke City   838-2272
High Country Outfitters Fly Fishing Lodge
    Pray   333-4763
Lazy K Bar Ranch • Big Timber   537-4404
Logans Guest Ranch • Clyde Park   686-4684
Luccuck Park Camp & Cabins
    Livingston   222-3025
Mcleod Resort • Mcleod   932-6167
Mountain Sky Guest Ranch • Emigrant 333-4911
Point Of Rocks Guest Ranch•Emigrant 848-7278
Range Riders Ranch • Big Timber   932-6538
Soda Butte Lodge • Cooke City   838-2251
Sweet Grass Ranch • Big Timber   537-4477

Ten Eagles Lodge• Clyde Park	686-4285
Triple R Corporation • Livingston	222-8363
Yellowstone Yurt Hostil • Cooke City	586-4659

Vacation Homes & Cabins

Dome Mountain Ranch • Emigrant	333-4361
Montana Guide Service • Gardiner	848-7265
Pine Creek Lodge • Livingston	222-3628
4M Ranch Log Guest House • Pray	333-4784
Above the Rest • Gardiner	848-7747
Absaroka Cabins • Livingston	222-6519
Bearclaw Service & Cabins	
Cooke City	838-2336
Big Timber Creek Vacation Cabin	
Big Timber	932-4790
Cabin on the Yellowstone • Livingston	222-1404
Cedar Bluffs • Livingston	222-0190
Crystal Spring Ranch • Big Timber	932-6238
CWC Ranch Houses • Big Timber	932-4359
Deep Creek Guest Cabin • Livingston	222-2380
Dupuy Spring Creek Villa	
Livingston	222-5432
Elliot Guest House • Livingston	222-2055
Eidelweiss Cabins • Cooke City	838-2332
Luccock Park Cabins • Pine Creek	333-3025
Emigrant Creek Cabin • Pray	333-4396
Island Guest House • Livingston	222-3788
Montana Getaway • Mcleod	932-6141
Mountain Retreat • Gardiner	848-7272
Paradise Valley Vacation Home	
Emigrant	848-7477
Patricia Blume Properties	
Livingston	222-3793
Shields River Home • Livingston	222-5264
Silver Gate Cabins • Silver Gate	838-2371
The Arch House • Gardiner	848-2205
The Centennial • Livingston	222-5456
The Holler • Reed Point	932-6532
The Pond Cabin • Pray	222-4499
The River House • Livingston	222-2658
The School House • Livingston	222-2527
The Trout House & Tipi • Pray	333-4763
White Pines Cabin • LIvingston	222-6765

Forest Service Cabins
Gallatin National Forest
Battle Ridge Cabin
20 mi. NE of Bozeman, MT   587-6920
Capacity: 4   Nightly fee: $25
Available: All year
Road access to cabin. Plowed within .25 miles of cabin.

Big Creek Cabin
35 mi. S of Livingston, MT on U.S. Highway 89, then 5 mi. W on Big Creek Road.   222-1892
Capacity: 10   Nightly fee: $25
Available: All year
Wood cook/heating stoves, lantern, no drinking water. Big Creek Rd access within 1/2 mi of cabin; walk or ski last 1/2 mi from Mountain Sky Guest Ranch.

Deer Creek Cabin
33 mi. S. of Big Timber, MT on I-90, ll mi. on W. Bridger Cr. Rd., 4 mi S & SE by trail on foot or horseback.   932-5155
Capacity: 4   Nightly fee: $20
Available: All year
Primitive road last 1/2 mile to trailhead. Not recommended for low clearance vehicles. Hikers need to ford Lower Deer Cr. numerous times. Corrals for horses, supplemental feed required. Wood heat cookstove. No power or drinking water.

Fourmile Cabin
42 mi. S of Big Timber, MT in Main Boulder Canyon   932-5155

Capacity: 5   Nightly fee: $30
Available: All year
Between 6/1 - 9/30 reservations taken no more than 2 weeks in advance. Access by snowmobiles, cross-country skis, or snowshoes in winter. Grazing of livestock is not allowed in either of administrative pastures. Power, electric stove and refrigerator.

Ibex Cabin
15 mi. E of Clyde Park, MT   222-1892
Capacity: 4   Nightly fee: $25
Available: All year
Wood heating stove, lantern, no drinking water. Plowed within 5 miles of cabin. Accessible by snowmobile or cross-country skis, in winter. High clearance vehicles in summer.

Kersey Lake Cabin
4 mi. E of Cooke City, MT on Kersey Lake 848-7375

Capacity: 10   Nightly fee: $30
Available: 6/15 - 9/15 & 12/15 - 03/15
Winter skis or snowmobiles from Cooke City. Summer hike l.5 mi. along Russell Creek Trail. Can also bike or use ATV along Kersey Lake Jeep Road. - foot access last 400 yds.

Mill Creek Guard Station
15 mi. Hwy. 89 S Livingston, MT 12 mi. E Mill Creek Road 486   222-1892
Capacity: 4   Nightly fee: $25
Available: All year
Wood stove for heat, electric stove, lights, lantern, no drinking water. Road is plowed to Snowbank Snowmobile Parking Area which is adjacent to Mill Creek area.

Porcupine Cabin
16 mi. NE of Wilsall, MT.   222-1892
Capacity: 8   Nightly fee: $25
Available: All year
Wood heating stove, lantern, no drinking water. Road access to cabin plowed within l.5 miles; accessible by snowmobile or cross-country skis in winter, high clearance vehicles in summer.

Round Lake Cabin
4.5 mi. N of Cooke City, MT   848-7375
Capacity: 4   Nightly fee: $20
Available: 6/15 - 9/15 Winter
Snowmobile or ski from Cooke City. Summer hike or 4x4 up Round Lake Road (primitive) from Fish Creek Rd.

Trail Creek Cabin
20 mi. SW of Livingston, MT (N end Gallatin Mtn. Range)   222-1892
Capacity: 4   Nightly fee: $25
Available: All year
Wood heat stove, lantern, no drinking water. Access via Goose Creek Rd. Summer the last 5 mi. restricted to vehicles 50 wide or less. Winter access varies with snow conditions.

West Boulder Cabin
30 mi. SW of Big Timber, MT on W Boulder River. Adjacent to FS campground.   932-5155
Capacity: 6   Nightly fee: $30
Available: All year
Between 6/1 - 9/30 reservations taken no more than 2 weeks in advance. 14 mi. on gravel road. Winter; ski, snowshoe or snowmobile short distance on county road. Power, electric stove, wood stove & refrigerator available. No drinking water.

West Bridger Station
27 mi. SE of Big Timber, MT on W. Bridger Road 932-5155

Capacity: 4   Nightly fee: $20
Available: All year
1/4 mile driveway to cabin; slick in wet weather. Winter access varies with snow conditions. Wood heat and cook stove. Pasture available for horses. No power or drinking water.

Car Rental
Bob Faw Chevrolet-Oldsmobile, Inc.	932-5465
Livingston Ford	222-7200
Rent A Wreck	222-0071
Yellowstone Country Motor	222-8600

Outfitters & Guides
F=Fishing H=Hunting R=River Guides
E=Horseback Rides G=General Guide Services

Yellowstone Raft Co	R	848-7777
Big Bear Lodge	F	838-2267
Dome Mountain Ranch Outfitters	G	333-4361
Montana Guide Service	FREHG	848-7265
Montana Whitewater	R	848-7398
Wild West Rafting	R	848-2252
Absaroka Beartooth Outfitters	HF	287-2280
Anchor Outfitting	H	537-4485
Anderson's Yellowstone Angler	GF	222-7130
Bear's Den Outfitters	G	222-0746
Bear Paw Outfitters	HFE	222-6642
Beartooth Plateau Outfitters	HFER	838-2328
Big Sky Flies & Guides	GF	333-4401
Big Sky Guides & Outfitters	GHRFE	578-2270
Big Sky Whitewater	R	848-2112
Big Timber Fly Fishing	RF	932-4368
Big Timber Guides	FREHG	932-4080
Black Mountain Outfitters	HFR	222-7455
Black Otter Guide Service	G	333-4362
Blue Rbbon Fishing Tours	F	222-7714
Brant Oswald Fly Fishing Services	F	222-8312
Castle Creek Outfitters & Guide	HEF	333-4763
Chan Welin's Big Timber Fly Fishing		
	GF	932-4368
Chimney Rock Outfitters	G	222-5753
Country Angler	F	222-7701
Covered Wagon Outfitters	HFRG	222-7274
Cudney Guide Service	RF	223-1190
Crazy Mountain Outfitter	GFHEF	686-4648
Dan Bailey's Fly Shop	F	222-2673
Dave Handl Fly Fishing Outfitter	FR	222-1404
Depuy's Spring Creek Reservations	F	222-0221
Double Creek - Running M	HFER	632-6121
Elk Creek Outfitters	HRE	578-2216
Elk Ridge Outfitters	GFHRE	578-2379
Fish Hawk Outfitting	F	222-0551
Flying Diamond Guide Service	GE	222-1748
Greater Yellowstone Flyfishers	F	838-2468
Hatch Finders Fly Shop	F	222-0989
Hawley Mountain Guides	HE	932-5791
Hell's A' Roarin Outfitters	HEF	848-7578
High Country Outfitters	ERG	333-4763
Horse Creek Outfitters	EFR	333-4977
Hubbard's Yellowstone Lodge	F	848-7755
James Marc Spring Creek Specialist	F	222-8646
John Greene's Fly Fishing	F	222-4562
J R Outfitters	H	932-4452
Johnson Edwin Outfitting	H	848-7265
Jumping Rainbow Ranch	F	222-5425
Lazy Heart Horse & Mule	GHFR	222-7536
Lone Creek Outfitters	HFRG	222-7155
Long Outfitting	GF	222-6775
Lost Creek Outfitters	H	222-1167
Lucky Day Outfitter	HFGRE	686-4402
Montana's Master Angler	HF	222-2273
North Fork Creek Outfitters	HFE	848-7859
Paradise Valley Planes & Reins	E	333-4788
Park's Fly Shop	F	848-7314
Paul Tunkis Flyfishing Guide	F	222-8480

Pine Mountain Outfitters	GH	848-7570
Rendevous Outfitters	G	848-7110
Rising Sun Outfitters	H	333-4624
Roy Senter	F	222-3775
Rubber Ducky River Services & Shuttles	R	222-3746
Silver Run Outfitting	GF	328-4694
Shiplet Ranch Outfitters	H	686-4696
63 Ranch	GHRFE	222-0570
Slip & Slide Ranch	GHREF	848-7648
Stevenson's Montana Wild	F	222-0341

Story Cattle Co. & Outfitting	GFHEF	333-4739
Sun Raven Guide Service	F	333-4454
Sweet Cast Angler	F	932-4469
Track Outfitter & Guide	HG	222-0406
Troutwest	HFR	222-8233
Wilderness Connection Inc	GHE	848-7287
Wilderness Pack Trips	RF	333-9046
Williams Guide Service	RF	222-1386
Wine Glass Mountain Trail Rides	E	222-5599
Yellowstone Flyfisher	F	222-7385
Yellowstone International Fly Fisherman's Lodge		

	F	222-7437
Bear Paw Outfitters	GE	222-5800
Parks' Fly Shop	GF	848-7314
Wildlife Outfitters	H	848-7675

Cross-Country Ski Centers
B Bar Guest Ranch • Basin   848-7523

Snowmobile Rentals
Cooke City Exxon & Polaris/Ski-doo
 Cooke City   838-2244
Soda Butte Lodge • Cooke City   838-2251

PRIVATE CAMPGROUNDS

Campsite Directions

Campground / Directions	Season	Tent	RV	Water	Electric	Sewer	Dump	Shower	Laundry	Store
BIG TIMBER										
Big Timber KOA Campground Ph/Fax 932-6569 • I-90 Exit 377, 9 mi E	5/15-9/2	25	50	•	•	•	•	•	•	•
Spring Creek Campground & Trout Ranch Ph/Fax 932-4387 • 2 mi S on Hwy 298	4/15-10/15	30	53	•	•	•	•	•	•	•
GARDINER										
Rocky Mountain Campground 848-7251 • (877) 534-6931 • 1 blk E of US 89, Jardine Rd, US 89	4/1-11/1	20	50	•	•	•	•	•	•	•
Yellowstone RV Park & Campground Ph/Fax 848-7496 • 1/4 mi N of Gardiner, US 89	5/1-10/31	10	46	•	•	•		•	•	•
LIVINGSTON										
Livingston Campground 222-1122 • I-90 Exit 333, 1 blk N on US 89, W off Rogers Ln	5/1-10/31	20	25	•	•	•		•	•	•
Osen's RV Park and Campground 222-0591 • 3 blocks S on US 89, right on Merrill Ln	All Year	14	30	•	•	•		•	•	•
Paradise Valley/Livingston KOA 222-0992 • (800) 562-2805 • 10 mi S on US 89, then 1 mi E	5/1-10/31	27	52	•	•	•		•	•	•
Rock Canyon RV Park 222-1096 • 3 mi S on US 89 5/1-10/31	10		28	•	•		•	•	•	•
Yellowstone's Edge RV Park 333-4036 • (800) 865-7322 • 18 mi S of Livingston on US 89	5/1-10/15	20	81	•	•	•		•	•	•
MCLEOD										
McLeod Resort Ph/Fax 932-6167 • 16 mi S of Big Timber on Hwy 298	5/1-10/31	5	10	•	•			•	•	

Fishery

	Cold Water Species												Warm Water Species										Services				
	Brook Trout	Mt. Whitefish	Lake Whitefish	Golden Trout	Cutthroat Trout	Brown Trout	Rainbow Trout	Kokanee Salmon	Bull Trout	Lake Trout	Arctic Grayling	Burbot	Largemouth Bass	Smallmouth Bass	Walleye	Sauger	Northern Pike	Shovelnose Sturgeon	Channel Catfish	Yellow Perch	Crappie	Paddlefish	Vehicle Access	Campgrounds	Toilets	Docks	Boat Ramps	MotorRestrictions
38. Crazy Mountains alpine lakes	•			•	•		•																					
39. Shields River		•			•	•	•																					
40. Hyalite Reservoir					•																		•	•	•			
41. Yellowstone River		•			•	•	•					•											•	•	•		•	•
42. Dailey Lake						•	•								•							•	•	•	•		•	•
43. Sixmile Creek					•	•																	•					
44. Boulder River	•	•			•	•																	•	•	•			

NOTES:

PUBLIC CAMPGROUNDS
Campsite Directions

Campsite Directions	Season	Camping	Trailers	Toilets	Water	Boat Launch	Fishing	Swimming	Trails	Stay Limit	Fee
32•Half Moon FS 11 mi. N of Big Timber on US 191<15 mi. W on Cty. Rd 25 (Big Timber Canyon Rd.)	All Year	8	22'	•	•		•		•	16	
33•Mallard's Rest FWP 13 mi. S of Livingston on US 89 to Milepost 42	All Year	20	•	•	•	B	•			7	•
34•Pine Creek FS 9 mi. S of Livingston on US 89•6 mi.E on Pine Creek Rd.	5/26-9/1526	26	22'	D	•		•		•	16	•
35•West Boulder FS 16 mi. S of Big Timber on Rt.298•6.5 mi. SW on Cty. Rd. 30•8 mi. SW on W Boulder Rd.	All Year	10	20'	•	•		•		•	16	
36•East Boulder FS 19 mi. S of Big Timber on Rt. 298•6 mi. E on E Boulder Rd.	All Year	2	16'	•			•			16	
37•Big Beaver FS 25 mi. SW of Big Timber on Rt. 298•8 mi. S on Cty. Rd. 212	All Year	5	32'	•			•			16	
38•Falls Creek FS 25 mi. SW of Big Timber on Rt. 298•5 mi. S on Cty. Rd. 212	All Year	8		•	•		•			16	
39•Aspen FS 25 mi. SW of Big Timber on Rt. 298•8.5 mi. S on Cty. Rd. 212	All Year	8	32'	D	•		•			16	
40•Loch Leven FWP 9 mi. S of Livingston on US 89 to Milepost 44•2 mi. E•4 mi. S on Rt. 540	All Year	30	•	•	•	C	•			7	•
41•Dailey Lake FWP 1 mi. E of Emigrant•4 mi. S on Rt. 540•6 mi. SE on Cty. Rd.	All Year	35	•	•	•	C	•			7	
42•Carbella BLM 20 mi. N of Gardiner on US 89•1 mil. W at Miner•Primitive	All Year	5	35'			B	•			14	
43•Yankee Jim Canyon FS 18 mi. N of Gardiner on US 89	All Year	12	48'	•						16	
44•Snow Bank FS 15 mi. S of Livingston on US 89•13 mi. SE on Mill Creek Rd. (Forest Rd. 486)	5/26-9/15	11	22'	•	•		•		•	16	•
45•Hells Canyon FS 25 mi. SW of Big Timber on Rt. 298•15.5 Mi. S on Cty Rd. 212	All Year	11	16'	•			•		•	16	
46•Hicks Park FS 25 mi. SW of Big Timber on Rt. 298•21 mi. S on Cty Rd. 212	All Year	16	32'	D	•		•		0	16	
47•Chippy Park FS 25 mi. SW of Big Timber on Rt. 298•9.5 mi. S on Cty Rd. 212	All Year	7	32'	D	•		•			16	
48•Soda Butte FS 1 mi. E of Cooke City on US 212	7/1-9/15	21	22'	•	•		•			16	•
49•Colter FS 2 mi. E of Cooke City on US 212	7/15-9/15	23	48'	•	•		•			16	•
50•Chief Joseph FS 4 mi. E of Cooke City on US 212	7/1-9/30	6	20'	•	•		•		•	16	•
51•Eagle Creek FS 2 mi. NE of Gardiner on Jardine Rd.	All Year	12	30'	D	•					16	
52•Tom Miner FS 20 mi. N of Gardiner on US 89•12 mi. SW on Tom Miner Rd. (Forest Rd. 63) •4 mi. SW on Forest Rd. 63	6/1-9/30	16	22'	•	•		•		•	16	•
53•Fairy Lake FS 22 mi. N of Bozeman on MT 86•5 mi. W on Fairy Lake Rd.	7/15-9/15	9		D	•		•	•	•	16	
54•Battle Ridge FS 22 mi. NE of Bozeman on MT 86	6/10-9/30	13	16'	D	•					16	

Agency
FS—U.S.D.A Forest Service
FWP—Montana Fish, Wildlife & Parks
NPS—National Park Service
BLM—U.S. Bureau of Land Management
USBR—U.S. Bureau of Reclamation
CE—Corps of Engineers

Camping
Camping is allowed at this site. Number indicates camping spaces available
H—Hard sided units only; no tents

Trailers
Trailer units allowed. Number indicates maximum length.

Toilets
Toilets on site. D—Disabled access

Water
Drinkable water on site

Fishing
Visitors may fish on site

Boat
Type of boat ramp on site:
A—Hand launch
B—4-wheel drive with trailer
C—2-wheel drive with trailer

Swimming
Designated swimming areas on site

Trails
Trails on site
B—Backpacking   N—Nature/Interpretive

Stay Limit
Maximum length of stay in days

Fee
Camping and/or day-use fee

NOTES:

Dining Quick Reference

Price Range refers to the average cost of a meal per person: ($) $1-$6, ($$) $7-$11, ($$$) $12-up. Cocktails: "Yes" indicates full bar; Beer (B)/Wine (W), Service: Breakfast (B), Brunch (BR), Lunch (L), Dinner (D). Businesses in bold print will have additional information under the appropriate map locator number in the body of this section.[wi-fi] next to business name indicates free wireless internet is available to customers.

RESTAURANT	TYPE CUISINE	PRICE RANGE	CHILD MENU	COCKTAILS BEER WINE	SERVICE	CREDIT CARDS	MAP LOCATOR NUMBER
Timber Bar	American	$$		Yes	L/D	V/M	2
City Club Lanes & Steakhouse	Steakhouse	$$/$$$	Yes	Yes	D	All Major	2
American Legion Post No. 19	American	$/$$		Yes	L/D		2
Frosty Freez	Family	$			B/L/D	No	2
Prospector Pizza Plus	Pizza	$		B/W	B/L/D	V/M/D	2
The Grand Hotel B&B [wi-fi]	Fine Dining	$$$		Yes	L/D	V/M/D	2
Country Skillet	Family	$/$$	Yes	B/W	B/L/D	Major	2
Buffalo Jump Steakhouse	Steakhouse	$$/$$$	Yes	Yes	D	Major	5
Hardee's	fast Food	$	Yes		B/L/D		5
McDonald's	Fast Food	$	Yes		B/L/D		5
Subway	Fast Food	$	Yes		L/D		5
Crazy Coyote Mexican Food	Mexican	$$	Yes		L/D		6
Dairy Queen	Fast Food	$	Yes		L/D		6
Domino's Pizza	Pizza	$			L/D		6
Mark's In & Out	Fast Food	$	Yes		L/D		6
Pizza Hut	Pizza	$/$$	Yes	B	L/D	V/M/D	6
The Homemade Cafe	Family	$	Yes		B/L		6
Paradise Inn	American	$$	Yes	Yes	B/L/D	Major	6
2nd Street Bistro	Classic Bistro	$$$	Yes	Yes	B/L/D	V/M/A	7
Montana's Rib & Chop House	Family	$$$	Yes	Yes	L/D	Major	7
Murray Lounge & Grill	American	$$		Yes	L/D/BR	Major	7
Coffee Crossing [wi-fi]	Coffee/Soup	$			B/L		7
Pinky's	Deli	$			B/L	Major	7
49er [wi-fi]	American	$$	Yes	Yes	B/L/D	Major	7
Chatham's Livingston Bar & Grille	Continental	$$$	Yes	Yes	D	Major	7
Pickle Barrel	Deli	$			L/D		7
Stockman	Steak			Yes	L/D		7
Taco John's	Fast Food	$	Yes		L/D		7
The Sport	American	$$	Yes	Yes	L/D	V/M/D	7
Dusty Boots Grill	American	$$	C	All	B/L/D	Major	7
Livery Stable	American	$$	C	All	B/L/D	Major	7
Road Kill Cafe	American	$$	Yes	Yes	L/D		8
Rosa's Pizza	Pizza	$			L/D	V/M	10
Pine Creek Cafe	Mexican/American	$$	Yes	B/W	B/L/D	Major	11
Four Winds Store	Deli	$			L/D	V/M	12
Chico Hot Springs [wi-fi]	Casual Gourmet	$$/$$$	Yes	Yes	B/L/D	Major	12
Livery Stable & Old Saloon	Steakhouse	$–$$$	Yes	Yes	B/L/D	V/M	12
Two Bit Saloon	Family	$$	Yes	Yes	B/L/D		13
Town Cafe	American	$$/$$$	Yes	Yes	B/L/D	Major	13
Antler Pub & Grill, Comfort Inn	Family	$$	Yes	B/W	B/D	Major	13
The Yellowstone Mine & Rusty Rail Lounge	Steaks & Seafood	$–$$$	Yes	Yes	B/D	Major	13
Outlaws Pizza and Casino	Pizza	$/$$		B/W	L/D	Major	13
Bear Country Restaurant	American	$$	Yes		B/L/D	V/M	13
Corral Drive Inn	Fast Food	$					13
Sawtooth Deli	Deli	$/$$	Yes	B/W	L		13
Beartooth Cafe	American	$$	Yes	B/W	L/D		14
Big Bear Lodge	American	$$/$$$	Yes	B/W	B/L/D	Major	14
Village Market Coffee House	Deli/ Coffee House	$			B/L		14
Soda Butte Lodge, Tavern, & Prospector Restaurant [wi-fi]	Regional	$$/$$$	Yes	Yes	B/L/D	Major	14
Clyde Park Tavern	American	$		Yes	B/L/D	V/M/D	15
Stageline Pizza	Pizza	$/$$			B/L/D		15
Wilsall Bar & Cafe	American	$$	Yes	Yes	B/L/D	V/M	15

NOTES:

Motel Quick Reference

Price Range: ($) Under $40 ; ($$) $40-$60; ($$$) $60-$80, ($$$$) Over $80. Pets [check with the motel for specific policies] (P), Dining (D), Lounge (L), Disabled Access (DA), Full Breakfast (FB), Cont. Breakfast (CB), Indoor Pool (IP), Outdoor Pool (OP), Hot Tub (HT), Sauna (S), Refrigerator (R), Microwave (M) (Microwave and Refrigerator indicated only if in majority of rooms), Kitchenette (K). All Montana area codes are 406. [wi-fi] next to business name indicates free wireless internet is available to customers.

HOTEL	PHONE	NUMBER ROOMS	PRICE RANGE	BREAKFAST	POOL/ HOT TUB SAUNA	NON SMOKE ROOMS	OTHER AMENITIES	CREDIT CARDS	MAP LOCATOR NUMBER
River Valley Inn [wi-fi]	932-4943	22	$$			Yes	DA/R	Major	2
Big Timber-Super 8 Motel [wi-fi]	932-8888	39	$$			Yes	P/D/R	Major	2
Lazy J Motel	932-5533	15	$				P	Major	2
Livingston Comfort Inn [wi-fi]	222-4400	49	$$$$	CB	IP/HT	Yes	M/R/DA	Major	5
Super 8 Motel [wi-fi]	222-7711	36	$$		HT	Yes	DA	Major	5
The River Inn	222-2429								5
Yellowstone Inn & Conference Center [wi-fi]	222-6110	99	$$/$$$		IP	Yes	K/P/D/DA	Major	6
Budget Host Parkway Motel	222-3840	28	$$		OP	Yes	K/P	Major	6
Del Mar Motel	222-3120								6
Econo Lodge [wi-fi]	222-0555	50	$$$$	CB	IP/HT	Yes	P/M/R/DA	Major	6
Livingston Inn Motel	222-3600	16	$$			Yes	P	V/M/A	6
Country Motor Inn	222-1923	24	$$/$$$			Yes	P/DA	Major	7
Murray Hotel [wi-fi]	222-1350	30	$$-$$$$		HT	Yes	K/P/D/R/L	Major	7
Rainbow Motel	222-3780	24	$$			Yes	P	Major	7
Guest House Motel	222-1460	40	$			Yes	P/L	Major	7
Pine Creek Cabins	222-3628	5	$$/$$$				P/D/L/R	Major	10
Dome Mountain Ranch	333-4361	12	$$$$	FB	HT/OP		P/D/R		12
Golden Ratio River Ranch	333-4455	6	$$$/$$$$			Yes	P	Major	12
Town Club Motel	848-7322	11	$/$$$	FB			P/D	V/M/D	13
Westernaire Motel	848-7397	10	$/$$$			Yes	P	Major	13
Absaroka Lodge	848-7414	44	$$/$$$$			Yes	K/P/DA	Major	13
Yellowstone Comfort Inn	848-7536	77	$$$/$$$$	CB	HT	Yes	P/D/L/DA	Major	13
Yellowstone Basin Inn	848-7080	13	$$/$$$$	CB	HT	Yes	K/M/R/DA	Major	13
Yellowstone Village Inn	848-7417	43	$$/$$$	CB	IP/S	Yes	K/M/R/DA	Major	13
Best Western Mammoth Hot Springs [wi-fi]	848-7311	85	$$/$$$$		IP/HT	Yes	K/P/D/M/R/DA	Major	13
Jim Bridger Court Cabins	848-7371	21	$/$$				P/D/L	Major	13
Super 8 Motel	848-7401	66	$$$	CB	IP		P/DA	Major	13
Hillcrest Cottages	848-7353	14	$$			Yes		Major	13
Travelodge	848-7520	40	$$$			Yes		Major	13
Big Bear Lodge	838-2267		$$$		HT		D	V/M	14
Elkhorn Lodge	838-2332	8	$			Yes	P/K	Major	14
Soda Butte Lodge [wi-fi]	838-2251	32	$$$		IP/HT	Yes	D/L/DA	Major	14
Alpine Motel	838-2262	27	$$$			Yes	K	Major	14
High Country Motel	838-2272	15	$$				P/K	Major	14
Grizzly Lodge	838-2219	17	$$		HT	Yes	DA/K/P	Major	14
Range Riders Lodge	838-2371	18	$				L/P		14

NOTES:

Section 3

SECTION 4

RED LODGE, LAUREL, COLUMBUS AND SURROUNDING AREA

Atop the Beartooth Plateau.

1. *Gas*

Laurel

Laurel has railroad tracks going through the center of town, that reflect the town's history as the railroad hub in the early 1900s. As the coal mining production grew in the Red Lodge area, the demand for transportation became greater and Laurel became a division point for different railroad companies. Because Laurel is only 16 miles from Billings, it has also become a suburb of the big city. Toward the end of her life, Calamity Jane was said to have resided about 9 miles from Laurel near the Canyon Creek Battleground. Laurel is said to have the largest fireworks show in the state on the 4th of July. The Mountain Man Rendezvous, is a yearly celebration, held towards the end of July. It recaptures the Lewis & Clark Expedition that charted the Yellowstone River.

Laurel is considered by many to be the "recreational hub of Montana." From this small town, Yellowstone National Park can be entered four different ways. It is straddled on both sides by a complex labyrinth of railroad tracks, the largest and busiest rail yard in Montana. The first post office opened its doors in 1886, and the city was incorporated in 1908. The "Laurel Leaf" refinery began operation in 1930 with the present-day name of CENEX.

Laurel is replete with history: On Lewis & Clark's return trip from the West Coast, they split up into two teams exploring the rivers. Clark's party camped near the junction of the Clarks Fork of the Yellowstone and the Yellowstone River which is near present day Laurel. Downtown you will find a statue in Fireman's Park commemorating the great Nez Perce leader, Chief Joseph.

Laurel is near many recreational areas. To the south there is the majestic Big Horn Canyon with the Yellowtail Reservoir, known for its sheer beauty and as an adventureland for boaters. Below the reservoir lies the Bighorn River, which carries with it some of the finest trout fishing. Northeast of Laurel is the nation's largest earth-filled dam at Fort Peck; to the west is the renowned Yellowstone River.

Also, observe Montana's largest free Fourth of July fireworks display in Laurel each year if in the area during this holiday.

D **William Clark**
July 24, 1806

" for me to mention or give an estimate of the differant Species of wild animals on this river. . .would be incredible. I shall therefore be silent on the Subject further."

2. *Gas, Food, Lodging*

3. *Gas, Food, Lodging*

T **Fireman's Park**
Laurel

4. *Gas, Food, Lodging*

Park City

Park City used to be a docking point for boats traveling on the Yellowstone River, and was called Young's Point. A group of settlers from Wisconsin settled here and planted many elm and maple trees on their land. When the railroad came through, the area was named Rimrock because of the dry sandstone landscape, but the settlers were aiming for more trees and green grass and chose the name Park City instead.

5.

H **Columbus**

The town of Columbus is located about 9 miles west of here. There is probably no town (or city) in Montana that had a more spectacular career, or more hectic embarrassment in finally "lighting" on an incorporated name than did the county seat of Stillwater. From 1875, when the Countryman stage station was known as Stillwater, until its incorporation in 1907, its name was changed every time the whims of a merchant moved his stock of merchandise, or a new business appeared. First it was "Eagle's Nest," about two miles west of town; then an Indian trading post was listed as "Sheep Dip," and it was not until the Northern Pacific built a station here in 1882 and named it Stillwater that the town's location attained permanence. Even this name didn't last long, however, as the N.P. had already listed a Stillwater, Minnesota, on their main line and the similarity of Minnesota and Montana led to misdirected shipments, so the name of Columbus replaced Stillwater on January 1, 1894.

There was just reason, perhaps, that this part of the Yellowstone was slow in getting settled. It was borderland on the north side of the Crow Reservation, and there were constant raids on the area by Sioux and Cheyenne war parties who would just as soon attack the white invaders. This ever-present danger didn't appeal to many prospective home-seekers, who hightailed it over to the Gallatin or other points farther west.

H **Park City**

The town of Park City is located about seven miles east of here. In 1882, a colony from Ripon, Wisconsin, making the trip in the prairie schooners, settled in this region. It was to be their future home, so they planted trees and made what improvements they could to ultimately beautify the little city. A section of land was donated to them, and things started off in

Laurel	Jan	Feb	March	April	May	June	July	Aug	Sep	Oct	Nov	Dec	Annual
Average Max. Temperature (F)	36.2	41.3	49.7	62.1	71.3	79.9	89.0	87.5	76.4	64.7	48.4	39.1	62.1
Average Min. Temperature (F)	11.9	15.4	22.7	32.5	41.3	49.2	54.7	52.0	42.7	33.6	23.2	15.4	32.9
Average Total Precipitation (in.)	0.56	0.44	0.76	1.34	2.24	2.35	1.02	0.92	1.27	1.18	0.63	0.50	13.21
Average Total SnowFall (in.)	6.8	4.4	5.2	2.3	0.1	0.0	0.0	0.0	0.2	0.8	1.7	5.1	26.5
Average Snow Depth (in.)	3	2	1	0	0	0	0	0	0	0	1	2	1

SECTION 4

Legend

00	Locator number (matches numeric listing in section)	Fishing Site (number matches number in fishing chart) 00	County Road
🦌	Wildlife viewing	Rest stop	Gravel/unpaved road
⛺ 00	Campsite (number matches number in campsite chart)	Interstate	
🏔	State Park	U.S. Highway	0 Miles 11 20
		State Highway	One inch = approximately 11 miles

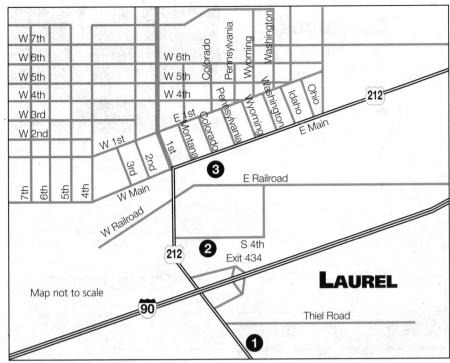

W 7th
W 6th
W 5th
W 4th
W 3rd
W 2nd

W 1st
3rd
2nd
1st

7th
6th
5th
4th

W Main

W Railroad

Colorado
Pennsylvania
Wyoming
Washington

W 6th
W 5th
W 4th

Pennsylvania
E Montana
Colorado
Wyoming
Washington
Idaho
Ohio

1st

E 1st

E Main

212

3

E Railroad

212

2   S 4th
Exit 434

LAUREL

90

Thiel Road

Map not to scale

1

BEARTOOTH MOUNTAINS

The Beartooth Mountains, part of the Rocky Mountains, are the result of about seventy million years of geological formations, leaving a spectacular mountain range that is full of geological wonders and leaves the sightseer awe struck. In 1931, local Red Lodge physician J.C.F Siegfriedt had a vision of a "high road" to connect Red Lodge to Cooke City, and draw tourists to this beautiful spot. After the local mines had closed, the area needed prosperity, and the Beartooth Highway was the key. With the help of O.H.P. Shelley, the owner of the Carbon County News, Siegfriedt convinced congress of the need for "approach highways" that lead tourists to National Parks. The building started in 1931, and after spending $2.5 million, the road opened in June of 1936.

Visitors can drive the Scenic 65-mile Beartooth Highway that connects Red Lodge to Cooke City and Yellowstone National Park. The highway consists of major switchbacks, as you climb to the elevation of 10,942 ft. At the top, on a clear day, you will experience amazing views of up to 75 miles in distance, with mountain lakes, glaciers, mountain ranges and field of wildflowers in the summer. Because of the elevation, snow often covers some fields through most of July, and you may even spot skiers throughout the summer months. The Beartooths are home to Granite Peak, the highest peak in Montana at 12,799 ft. In 1989, the Beartooth Highway received recognition as one of the most beautiful drives in America, and was made one of 52 other National Scenic Byways. The driving is slow going, due to the many switchbacks, and many necessary stops to soak in the awesome views.

---

a prosperous pleasant manner. The railroad soon came through and established a station. The bare, sandstone bluffs north of town inspired the officials to christen the place Rimrock, but not so with the persons who had planted sprigs and started a city of trees. Bravely they clung to the name Park City, and Rimrock finally disappeared with the list of unused titles. This was unfortunate inasmuch as the general manager of the N.P. resented this stubbornness on the part of the homesteaders, and in retaliation he changed the location of the proposed railroad yards and shops from this townsite to Laurel.

D William Clark
July 18, 1806

" I observed a Smoke rise to the S.S.E in the plains . . .this Smoke must be raisd, by the Crow Indians. . .as a Signal for us, or other bands."

T Buffalo Mirage Access

Buffalo Mirage Access: This is the spot where Lewis and Clark dug out two canoes to continue their exploration of the Yellowstone River.

6. Gas, Food, Lodging

Columbus

Columbus dates back to 1875 when a man by the name of Horace Countryman opened a trading post and stage station stop along the Yellowstone Trail a few miles west of present day Columbus. This area used to be part of the Crow Indian Reservation lands, and Countryman followed the Crow Agency from Mission Creek to Rosebud Creek. He opened his business just off the reservation. Countryman built the Log Hotel to accommodate visitors that were traveling between Miles City and Bozeman, and by 1882 this area became a major stop on the Northern Pacific Railroad. The railroad named this stop Stillwater Village. In 1894, the railroad renamed the town Columbus, due to shipping mixups with Stillwater, Minnesota.

Hagar & Co. opened a sandstone quarry in the mid 1890s, which supplied building materials

for a large portion of the Montana State Capitol Building in Helena. At this time there was a population of about 550, with many small businesses sprouting up. The main business was, and still is agriculture and ranching. Columbus is the Stillwater County seat. Located at the confluence of the Stillwater River and Yellowstone River, Columbus offers plenty of outdoor recreation with great trout fishing, whitewater rafting, hunting, hiking, horseback riding and much more.

D William Clark
July 17, 1806

I can See no timber Sufficient large for a Canoe which will Carry more than 3 men and Such a one would be too Small to answer my purpose"

D William Clark
July 16, 1806

"the emence Sworms of grass Hoppers have distroyed every Sprig of Grass for maney miles."

S River Bend Trading Co. & Montana Silversmiths Outlet
549 N. 9th St. #2, Columbus. 322-4753.
www.riverbendtrading.com

Established in 1997, River Bend Trading Co. & Montana Silversmiths Outlet is your source for american West items and Montana-crafted goods. Featuring a friendly staff, the store proudly carries the largest variety of Montana Silversmiths products under the Big Sky with selections ranging

from belt buckles and jewelry to watches and home décor. Customers will also find specialty gifts and clothing, including suede jackets with fringe, western style attire, Lawman jeans, and a wonderful assortment of western-inspired purses and accessories. On your next trip to Yellowstone and Montana, pop off scenic I-90, and visit the River Bend Trading Co. & Montana Silversmiths Outlet. For those unable to visit in person, be sure to check out the company website where orders are always secure and ship the same or next day (excluding custom orders).

It Happened in Montana

On February 27, 1943, an explosion ripped through the Smith Mine just south of Red Lodge. Seventy-four miners perished making it the worst mine disaster in Montana history. This disaster was the beginning of the end of the coal industry in Carbon County.

Section 4

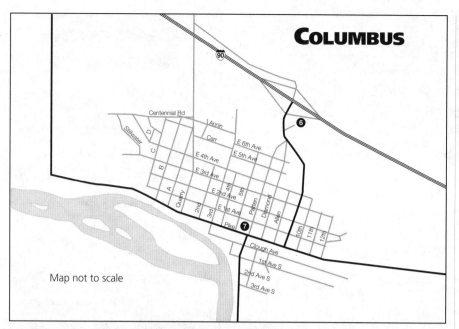

COLUMBUS

Map not to scale

M Parks Real Estate
608 E. Pike Ave., Columbus. 322-4115 or (800) 689-0889. www.parksrealestate.com; joyce@parksrealestate.com

Discover outdoor delights and Columbus properties with the professionals at Parks Real Estate. Occupying the same building since 1990 and boasting a staff always available to answer your questions, Parks Real Estate thrives on introducing clients to the beautiful "pocket oasis" of Columbus. From acreage to residential and commercial listings, the brokerage's properties are backed with the expertise of agents well-versed in real estate and the character of the area's land. Not only will agents show you Stillwater County property but also the greatest outdoor adventure destinations. Don't be foolhardy and buy area property without first contacting Parks Real Estate. Let them show you this beautiful land where the Stillwater meets the Yellowstone. They guarantee to provide you with all the information you need to confidently make your next real estate decision!

7. Gas, Food, Lodging

T Museum of the Beartooths
I-90 Exit 408 in Columbus. 322-4588

The Museum of the Beartooths is a great place to visit the history of the homestead era. The museum offers displays of farm equipment and machinery showing the rich agricultural history in the area and carries artifacts of the Rosebud River Crow Indians, Northern Pacific railroad memorabilia and World War II history. Open seasonally. Look for the red NP caboose at the corner of 5th and 5th North.

MH The New Atlas Bar
528 E. Pike Ave., Columbus. 322-9818 or 322-4033.

The New Atlas Bar originally opened in the late 1800s under the name, The Headquarters Bar. It is one of the oldest licensed bars in Montana. The unique western atmosphere is complete with over 50 mounted animals on display throughout the bar. You'll see a two-headed calf, an albino mule deer, spectacular eagles, and a friendly beaver just to name a few. There is also a large variety of antiques on display for your further enjoyment. It is a full service bar with air conditioning and keno on poker machines. Stop in on your way through town for a cold drink or your favorite cocktail in this cool and comfortable one-of-a-kind uniquely Montana bar. There is always something new along with the old at the New Atlas Bar.

S Montana Gem
637 N. 9th St., Columbus. 322-5977. www.montanagem.com; randy@montanagem.com

Discover quality craftsmanship while fulfilling your gemstone needs at Montana Gem. Boasting over twenty years of experience, owner Randy Gneiting is a skillful gemologist and faceter offering Montana Yogo Sapphires and other natural gemstones from across Montana and the world. Montana Gem's extensive inventory showcases gemstones in all colors and sizes and ranges from the common agate and garnet stones to the rare sugilite, meteorite, tourmaline, Baltic amber, and dinosaur bone. Gold-in-quartz jewelry, gold nugget items, and fine 14k gold and silver jewelry complement the precious gems in a broad range of prices. Gem sourcing, appraisals, custom designs, and jewelry repair are also available for customers' convenience and pleasure. Whether you're searching for a special gem, fine jewelry, or unique gifts, Montana Gem is your one-stop source for quality and beauty!

S Keyser Creek Smoked Meats and Made in Montana Gifts
637 N. 9th St., Columbus. 322-5666 or (888) 816-5666. www.keysercreek.com; stwpackingco@yahoo.com

Keyser Creek Smoked Meats was established in 1994 as a way to bring the enjoyment of their tasty family sausage and jerky recipes to the retail community. This family-owned business operated by fifth generation butchers offers products featuring pork and beef raised by local Montana ranchers. Their commitment to quality is experienced in every bite. Honored as the Grand Champion in the Montana and U.S. Cured Meat Championship, Keyser Creek's offerings include sausages, jerky, bacon, smoked pork lion, smoked turkeys, ham, and more. As a special treat, create or order a custom basket filled with Keyser Creek meats and other Montana Made items such as pasta, taffy, honey, mustard, and craft items. From gifts to food, this special store prides itself in showcasing the best of Montana and meeting customer needs for every occasion!

Columbus	Jan	Feb	March	April	May	June	July	Aug	Sep	Oct	Nov	Dec	Annual
Average Max. Temperature (F)	35.7	42.6	49.4	60.1	69.9	78.6	87.6	86.6	75.2	63.7	47.1	38.2	61.2
Average Min. Temperature (F)	9.3	15.2	21.6	30.3	39.6	47.2	52.3	50.2	41.1	31.6	20.9	12.7	31.0
Average Total Precipitation (in.)	0.62	0.50	0.90	1.76	2.66	2.21	1.10	0.93	1.28	1.11	0.61	0.53	14.22
Average Total SnowFall (in.)	7.2	5.4	6.0	3.1	0.8	0.0	0.0	0.0	0.4	2.0	3.7	6.8	35.3
Average Snow Depth (in.)	3	2	1	0	0	0	0	0	0	0	1	2	1

Reed Point

Reed Point is a town that has a genuine feeling of the wild west, and is one of the smallest communities along the Yellowstone River. It was a booming little town in the early part of the century with 54 operating businesses. Most of the surrounding area was homesteaded and after a three year drought and realization by the homesteaders that they needed more than the 320 acre allotment in order to make a living in this area, they picked up and moved on further west. The little town began its slow demise at that time.

Bellies to the bar for Italian Sodas at the Montana Hotel in Reed Point.

The focal point of this town is the Hotel Montana. Built in approximately 1909, this two story brick building was originally Walkers Store, a mercantile that sold anything from farm equipment (as evidenced by the original McCormick Deering-Walkers Store sign on the south wall of the restaurant) to fancy bloomers from New York. Upstairs was a doctor's office, a lawyer's office and living quarters of the Walkers. The downstairs was always a mercantile or general store and in later years a grocery store. The upstairs was turned into a boarding house for students and teachers and in later years into three separate apartments.

Guests at the Montana Hotel can "dress" for dinner in the period costumes found in each room.

It was purchased in 1994 by long time Reed Point residents Russ and Connie Schlievert. At the time, the downstairs had been a grocery store that was closed up three years prior to their purchase and the upstairs was full of tenants in the three apartments. After about a year of using the downstairs as a warehouse for antiques and running the apartments, Russ and Connie decided to use their great store of antiques and Russ's extensive collection of old west saloon items to create the building you see

today. The project, of course, cost three times their original estimate, and took approximately 18 months to complete.

But complete it they did, and opened it as the Hotel Montana in 1997. Everything used to create Hotel Montana is antique and original and was collected from many other old buildings, in Montana primarily, and put together here. Each item you see in the building has its own story to tell and little pieces of history attached.

The public is welcome to tour the upstairs rooms and stay the night in them if you are so moved (it is, after all, a hotel). The costumes hanging in the rooms are for the guests. Connie says a large number of the guests dress up in the costumes and come downstairs for dinner and maybe some pictures.

D William Clark
July 16, 1806

"two of the horses was So lame owing to their feet being worn quit Smooth and to the quick... I had Mockersons made of... Buffalow Skin... which Seams to releve them very much in passing over the Stoney plains."

9.

T Battle At Canyon Creek
Hwy. 532, 9 miles north of Laurel.

In 1877, just after The Battle at the Big Hole, the Nez Perce, led by Chief Joseph, started heading towards Yellowstone National Park in hopes of fleeing to Canada. On September 13, 1877, as they crossed the Yellowstone River just nine miles from Laurel, they Nez Perce were confronted by Colonel Sturgis and the new Seventh Cavalry, which led to the Battle at Canyon Creek. This battle took three of the cavalry men and wounded three Nez Perce. There is a small marker at the site.

10.

T Halfbreed National Wildlife Refuge

Halfbreed National Wildlife Refuge is another great spot to view birds and Pronghorn Sheep.

11.

Acton

Acton is a very small town that is supported by a sprawling ranching community, even though the population is said to be 10. The town originally served as a stop along the Great Northern Railroad.

Molt and Rapelje

Molt and Rapelje are both very small agricultural communities that are tucked away on the in the northern part of Stillwater County. The area is popular among hunters.

12.

T Hailstone National Wildlife Refuge

This is a great stop for Birdwatchers-with the large lake and prairie lands that attracts a large amount of waterfowl including white pelicans, mallards, teals, grebes and many more-especially during migration. There is a viewpoint on the hill, where you may also spot, pronghorn, eagles, owls and hawks.

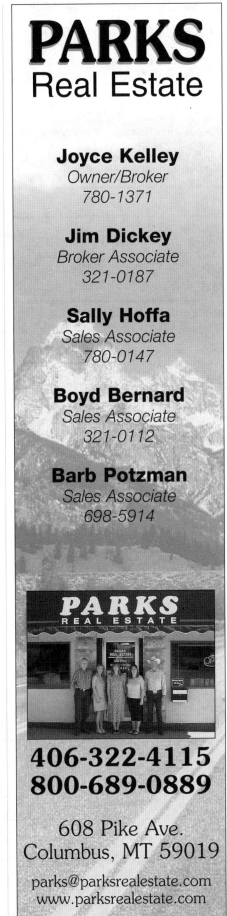

It Happened in Montana

On March 24, 1978, Congress establishes the Absarokee-Beartooth Wilderness area. This remote and rugged alpine wilderness comprises the largest single expanse of land above 10,000 feet in the lower 48 states. The entire area covers over a million acres and includes two national forests. 28 peaks over 12,000 feet tower over more than 950 lakes and nine major drainages.

13. *Food*

Silesia

Just south of Laurel, Silesia is a small town named after a local family that was from the German Province Silesia.

14. *Gas, Camping*

Rockvale

Once a main stop along the Northern Pacific Railroad. A few businesses get business from tourists and skiers going to and from Red Lodge. A few buildings remain along with a few residents.

Edgar

Named after gold prospector Henry Edgar, this community lies in the Clark Fork River's lower valley. When the town originated with land donated by a man named Thornton, the community was to be laid out with a strict moral code and no saloons allowed. Thornton's village remains to this day, although it is unknown if residents adhere to Thornton's early wishes.

15. *Food*

Fromberg

Fromberg is a Slavic name, that was given to the town by the large population of Slavics who moved here in the early 1900s and started farmlands. It was originally called Gebo after a man who started a coal mine in this town. The area was called "Poverty Flats" because of droughts that occurred, almost causing locals to starve. After the irrigation system was installed, the land prospered and still remains rich farming land.

T Clark Fork Valley Museum
101 E. River St. in Fromberg. 668-7650

16.

H The Pryor Mountains
At Bridger Rest Area on U.S. 310

The Pryor Mountains to the east cover roughly 300,000 acres. Once entirely Crow Indian territory, now only the north end of the range is on the Crow Reservation. The south end is in the Custer National Forest. The range is bound on the east by Bighorn Reservoir and on the south by the Pryor Mountain National Wild Horse Range. The mountains came by their name indirectly from Pryor Creek, which Captain William Clark named for Lewis and Clark Expedition member Sergeant Nathaniel Pryor.

The Pryors hold many intriguing features, including ice caves, sinks, and caverns, and archeological finds, such as Clovis Points indicating human occupation as long as 10,000 years ago. In the south end of the range, remains of log and frame houses and barns attest to the homesteads staked after passage of the Forest Homestead Act in 1906. Most of the settlers came from this area. Though they cultivated some crops, for many homesteading was a pretense for mountain grazing on adjacent forest and reservation ranges. One forest ranger observed that some claimants had applied for places where it would be impossible to winter over, though to hear them talk "one would think that Pryor Mountain contained the biggest part of the Banana Belt and that pineapples grew wild."

17. *Gas, Food, Lodging*

Bridger

The town of Bridger is named after explorer Jim Bridger, who was one of the first white men to travel through this area and into Yellowstone National Park. The town was originally called Georgetown, after the coal mine that was started up by a man named George Town. Mining became extremely popular in this area, and another small community developed, and was called Stringtown. In 1864, Jim Bridger came through the area, leading a wagon train to the mining areas in Virginia City. On his way through, he led the train across the Clark's Fork River-which they referred to as "Bridger's Crossing." Eventually the name of the whole town was changed to Bridger.

Warren

This small town began as a Burlington Northern railroad station. The tracks were mainly used to ship limestone from the Pryor Mountains to various sugar factories. The first post office was established in 1911, with George Town presiding as its first postmaster. The post closed in 1953. Since that time, residents have received their mail through Frannie, Wyoming, as Warren is located on the border of Wyoming and Montana.

H Jim Bridger, Mountain Man
Bridger

Jim Bridger arrived in Montana in 1822 as a member of a Rocky Mountain Fur Co. brigade.

For years he had no more permanent home than a poker chip. He roamed the entire Rocky Mountain region and often came through this part of the country. A keen observer, a natural geographer and with years of experience amongst the Indians, he became invaluable as a guide and scout for wagon trains and Federal troops following the opening of the Oregon Trail.

He shares honors with John Colter for first discoveries in the Yellowstone Park country. He was prone to elaborate a trifle for the benefit of pilgrims, and it was Jim who embroidered his story of the petrified forest by asserting that he had seen "a peetrified bird sitting in a peetrified tree, singing a peetrified song."

The Clarks Fork of the Yellowstone was named for Capt. Wm. Clark of the Lewis and Clark Expedition. Chief Joseph led his band of Nez Perce Indians down this river when he made his famous retreat in the summer of 1877.

18. *Gas, Food*

Belfry

Named after Dr. William Belfry, the town started out as the headquarters for the railroad. The Yellowstone Park Railroad Company started building a road that would connect Belfry to the park, but the project was never completed.

19.

Washoe

Washoe is on Hwy 308 between Belfry and Red Lodge. Washoe is most notable for the Smith Mine Disaster, which took the lives of 74 coal miners in 1943. In 1907, the town was the base of the Anaconda Copper Mining Company and Washoe Coal Mine. The Northern Pacific Railroad came through town, delivering hundreds of tons of coal to Anaconda on a daily basis. The formation of Montana Power Co. in 1912, cut back the need for coal operations. The unique coal mines of the area were beginning to decline by the late 1920s, following a period of strikes and labor disturbances.

Newer mines were established about the same time and remained busy until World War II. One being the Smith Mine that stayed busy until the disaster effectively ended coal mining in the area. Remnants of the mine still stand, but to truly understand the impact of such a disaster, visit the Bearcreek Cemetery. A handful of people, along with a few remnants of the mine, still live in Washoe which was once home to 3,000. Details of the Smith Mine and the ending disaster are available at the Peaks to Plains Museum in Red Lodge. Call them at 446-3667.

H Smith Mine Disaster
Washoe

Smoke pouring from the mine entrance about 10 o'clock the morning of February 27, 1943, was the first indication of trouble. "There's something wrong down here. I'm getting out"

Bridger	Jan	Feb	March	April	May	June	July	Aug	Sep	Oct	Nov	Dec	Annual
Average Max. Temperature (F)	34.3	40.0	48.6	59.8	69.9	78.9	88.0	86.7	75.3	62.8	46.6	36.8	60.6
Average Min. Temperature (F)	11.6	16.3	22.6	31.8	40.3	47.7	52.9	50.7	41.8	33.4	23.3	15.3	32.3
Average Total Precipitation (in.)	0.50	0.38	0.74	1.37	1.88	1.84	0.76	0.74	1.25	1.04	0.56	0.43	11.49
Average Total SnowFall (in.)	7.0	4.7	7.3	5.3	0.5	0.0	0.0	0.0	0.5	2.8	4.6	5.6	38.3
Average Snow Depth (in.)	2	1	1	0	0	0	0	0	0	0	1	1	1

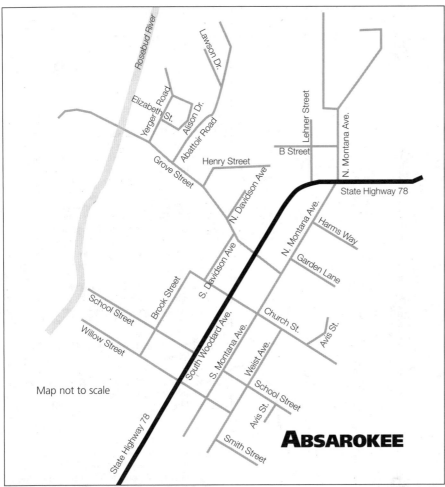

Map not to scale

ABSAROKEE

Many of the tombstones in the nearby cemetery mark the same tragic date in history.

the hoist operator called up. He and two nearby miners were the last men to leave the mine alive.

Rescue crews from as far away as Butte and Cascade County worked around the clock in six-hour shifts to clear debris and search for possible survivors. There were none. The night of March 4, workers reached the first bodies. More followed until the toll mounted to 74. Some died as a result of a violent explosion in No. 3 vein, the remainder fell victim to the deadly methane gasses released by the blast.

The tragedy at Smith Mine became Montana's worst coal mine disaster, sparking investigations at the state and national level. Montana Governor Sam C. Ford visited the scene, offered state assistance and pushed a thorough inquiry into the incident.

Today's marker of the Smith Mine Disaster follows a simpler one left by two of the miners trapped underground after the explosion, waiting for the poisonous gas they, knew would come.

"Walter & Johnny. Goodbye. Wives and daughters. We died an easy death. Love from us both. Be good."

H Bearcreek
Washoe

Platted in 1905 by George Lamport and Robert Leavens, Bearcreek was the center of an extensive underground coal mining district. At its height during World War I, Bearcreek boasted a population of nearly 2,000 people. The community was ethnically diverse and included Serbians, Scotsmen, Montenegrans, Germans, Italians and Americans. They were served by seven mercantiles, a bank, two hotels, two billiard halls, a brickyard, and numerous saloons. The town also boasted concrete sidewalks and an extensive water system. No church was ever built in Bearcreek. Foundations of many of the town's buildings, in addition to some structures themselves, consisted of sandstone quarried in the nearby hill. The local railway, the Montana Wyoming and Southern, carried coal from the mines through Bearcreek where it was distributed to communities across Montana.

The Lamport Hotel was once located on the foundation to the right of this marker. Built in 1907, it was described as "well furnished … the beds being especially soft and sleep producing. [The] meals are served with a desire to please the guests and no one leaves without a good impression and kindly feelings for the management." The hotel was razed about 1945.

In 1943, Montana's worst coal mining disaster at the nearby Smith mine took the lives of 74 men, many of whom lived in Bearcreek.The tragedy hastened the decline of the town. Many buildings in Bearcreek were moved to other communities or demolished, leaving haunting reminders of their presence along Main Street. The railroad tracks were removed in 1953 and the last mining operation closed in the 1970s. Today, Bearcreek is the smallest incorporated city in the state.

T Bear Creek & Pig Races
3 miles east of Red Lodge

A few people and abandoned mine buildings still remain after the Smith Mine disaster of 1943. During the past two decades it is better known for the state's only pig races. Every weekend from Memorial Day to Labor Day the town's population of 50 residents grows to 500 or more for the pig event. The races have been held since 1989 at Bearcreek Downs next to the Bear Creek Saloon where you can also get one heck of a steak dinner. This nonprofit fundraiser is perfectly legal and the four-legged racers, like all sports celebrities are pampered, live high on the hog. The winning pigs pays $25 on a $2 ticket that buys a spot on the sports pool-style board. The race has become a widely known event and has attracted media and people from all over the world. Bring the whole family and know that the little squealers are racing for a good cause—scholarships for Carbon County high school students.

20.   *Food, Lodging*

Red Lodge

The story varies on how Red Lodge got its name. One version has the Crow Indians applying red clay to their tipis, or the clay adhering to the tipis as they were pulled on travois behind the horses. Another version tells of a Crow leader named Red Bear whose tipi was painted red.

The first Europeans in the area were probably Spaniards. A Spanish expedition led by Cabezo de Vaca may have visited the area in 1535. It would be 200 years before Lewis & Clark came through the area along the Yellowstone River north of here. Shortly after that, a trickle of explorers turned into

Red Lodge	Jan	Feb	March	April	May	June	July	Aug	Sep	Oct	Nov	Dec	Annual
Average Max. Temperature (F)	32.8	35.3	40.9	51.1	60.5	69.4	78.2	77.1	66.4	55.5	42.3	35.1	53.7
Average Min. Temperature (F)	10.6	12.8	17.9	27.7	36.1	43.4	49.5	48.0	39.7	31.3	20.7	13.9	29.3
Average Total Precipitation (in.)	0.98	0.90	1.86	2.85	3.53	2.80	1.41	1.24	1.97	1.68	1.18	0.89	21.30
Average Total SnowFall (in.)	15.1	13.8	22.3	21.3	7.9	0.5	0.0	0.0	3.8	11.5	13.7	13.8	123.6
Average Snow Depth (in.)	7	7	6	3	0	0	0	0	0	1	3	5	3

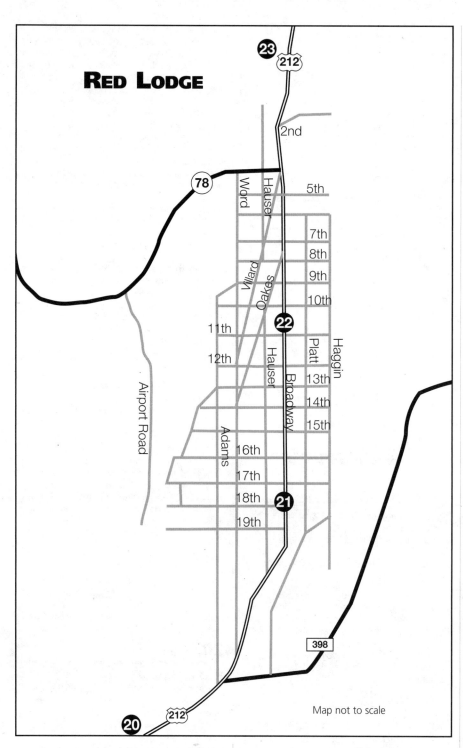

RED LODGE

Map not to scale

Johnson's cabin is preserved at the south end of town.

With the growth of the coal mines came a diversity of ethnic backgrounds. Finnish, Irish, Scottish, Slavic, Italian, and Scandinavian miners and their families settled here. When Red Lodge was made the seat of newly-formed Carbon County in 1896, the town boasted twenty saloons. In 1906, there were six churches, 14 fraternal orders, two newspapers, public schools, two telephone systems, three banks, an electric plant, three hotels and a population of 4,000. Before its decline, the population reached 6,000, almost triple today's population.

In the mid 20s, the depression forced mines to close. The town turned to manufacturing bootleg liquor, which was marketed as cough syrup and sold as far away as Chicago and San Francisco. In 1943, the Smith Mine disaster at Bear Creek killed 74 miners. This pretty much led to the end of coal mining in Carbon County. Today, the community is largely supported by agriculture and tourism.

H The Beartooth Highway

Although these mountains were criss-crossed by trails used by Native Americans since prehistory, it was not until the early 20th century that many sought a permanent route over the mountains to Cooke City and Yellowstone National Park.

Beginning in 1924, a group of Red Lodge businessmen, led by Dr. J. C. E. Siegfriedt and newspaper publisher O. H. P. Shelley, lobbied Montana's congressional delegation to construct a road between their community and Cooke City. Because of their efforts, President Herbert Hoover signed the Park Approach Act into law in 1931. The Act funded the construction of scenic routes to the country's national parks through federally-owned land. The Beartooth Highway was the only road constructed under the Act. Construction on the $2.5 million project began in 1932.

The Beartooth Highway is an excellent example of "Seat-of-Your-Pants" construction with many of the engineering decisions made in the field. Some 100 workers employed by five companies blasted their way up the side of the 11,000-foot plateau. The workmen gave names to many features of the road that are still used today, including Lunch Meadow, Mae West Curve and High Lonesome Ridge. The road officially opened on June 14, 1936. The spectacular Beartooth Highway is a testimonial to the vision of those who fought for its construction and a tribute to those who carved it over the mountains.

F Old Piney Dell

U.S. Hwy. 212, 5 miles south of Red Lodge at Rock Creek Resort. 446-1196 or (800) 667-1119. www.rockcreekresort.com; rcresort@wtp.net

Enjoy creek side dining in the relaxed and charming surroundings of this long time local

a flood. John Colter, one of the Lewis & Clark members, returned to explore this area along the Clarks Fork just east of Red Lodge. Jim Bridger trapped here, and a town nearby bears his name.

The Red Lodge area was, for a period, a part of the Crow reservation. But as often happened in the history of the West, discovery of minerals led

the government to change the deal. In this case it was the rich coal deposits discovered in 1886. At that time there were three Indians to every settler and four men for every woman. The Rocky Fork Coal Company opened the area's first mine in 1887 and shortly thereafter the Rocky Fork and Cooke City Railways came to the area. The area prospered as Red Lodge became the shipping point for the vast area to the south.

Red Lodge has had its share of colorful characters. In addition to John Colter and Jim Bridger, Buffalo Bill Cody used the railway to supply his Cody enterprises. Calamity Jane frequented the area. "Liver Eating" Johnson, who the Robert Redford character in the movie "Jeremiah Johnson" was modeled after, moved here in 1894.

Montana Trivia

The Yellowstone River is the longest free-flowing river in the U.S. It begins in the south of Yellowstone National Park and terminates at the confluence of the Missouri River at the Montana/North Dakota border.

Downtown Red Lodge.

favorite. "Piney," as the locals call it, offers that sought after combination of great food/great atmosphere. The rustic stone fireplace adds to the coziness in winter while the melodic cascade of beautiful Rock Creek lends a special ambiance to cool summer evenings. Culinary fare includes mouthwatering Prime Rib and Steaks, tender Weiner Schnitzel, delectable chicken, seafood entrees, and numerous other delicious creations. The friendly staff will meet your every need. A superb brunch is available on Sunday from 9 am to 1 pm; please call ahead. Old Piney Dell opens daily at 5:30 pm during the summer season and is closed Sunday and Monday nights during the winter season. Reservations are recommended.

L Rock Creek Resort
U.S. Hwy. 212, 5 miles south of Red Lodge. 446-1111 or (800) 667-1119. www.rockcreekresort.com; rcresort@wtp.net

The charm of a great mountain hideaway is alive and well at Rock Creek Resort. Enjoy creek side accommodations amid beautiful mountain scenery. Options include rooms with kitchenettes or tastefully decorated suites complete with fireplaces, kitchenettes, and Jacuzzi bathtubs. Two and three bedroom condo units with kitchens and woodstoves are an economical choice for the family traveler. Wedding and convention facilities are also available. Onsite activities include an Olympic size lap pool, tennis courts, bicycle rental, exercise room, and hiking trails. The poolside Jacuzzi and sauna are great for those

needing some R&R, while free wireless Internet caters to the business-minded. To further unwind, Old Piney Dell Restaurant and Bar offers outstanding culinary fare in relaxed and cozy surroundings. Like to shop? Try Twin Elk for fabulous shopping. Rock Creek Resort is open year-round.

S Twin Elk
U.S. Hwy. 212, 5 miles south of Red Lodge at Rock Creek Resort. 446-3121 or (877)-TWINELK (894-6355). www.rockcreekresort.com; rcresort@wtp.net

Twin Elk is one of those rare shopping experiences that is designed to be enjoyed. Whether you're a seasoned shopper or a casual browser, you will be dazzled and entertained by the unique offerings at Twin Elk. The exceptional collections include cutting edge fashion for women, original art, and home and cabin furnishings that include beautiful antler chandeliers. You will also find gifts galore and a distinctive collection of fine jewelry. Many of these items you won't see anywhere else, which makes the experience all the more interesting. Customer service is always a top priority with a friendly staff. Gift wrapping and shipping are available. Twin Elk is open daily for your shopping pleasure.

H **Red Lodge**
Hwy. 212 in Red Lodge

Coal was discovered in the Rock Creek Valley nearly two decades before Red Lodge was established as a mail stop on the Meteetsee Trail in 1884. In 1887, the Rocky Fork Coal Company opened the first large-scale mine at Red Lodge sparking the community's first building boom, consisting mostly of "hastily constructed shacks and log huts." The completion of the Northern Pacific Railway branch line to Red Lodge in 1890 resulted in the construction of many brick and sandstone buildings that now line the city's main street.

Like all mining camps, Red Lodge had a large population of single men and an abundance of saloons. For many years, the notorious "Liver-eating" Johnson kept the peace as the town's first constable. Red Lodge also boasted several churches and social clubs for those not inclined toward the city's more earthier entertainment.

Hundreds of people came to Red Lodge in the 1890s and early 1900s. Immigrants from all over Europe worked shoulder-to-shoulder in the coal mines, but settled in neighborhoods called Finn Town, Little Italy and Hi Bug. Their cultural traditions endured and are celebrated at the city's annual Festival of Nations.

Production in the coal mines declined after World War I, eventually leading to their closure by 1932. The completion of the scenic Beartooth Highway in 1936 revitalized Red Lodge by linking it directly to Yellowstone National Park. Today, Red Lodge's past is represented by its historic buildings and by the pride its citizens take in its history and traditions.

H **The Red Lodge Country**
Hwy. 212 at Red Lodge

According to tradition, a band of Crow Indians left the main tribe and moved west into the foothills of the Beartooth Range many years ago. They painted their council tepee with red clay and this old-time artistry resulted in the name Red Lodge.

This region is a bonanza for scientists. It is highly fossilized and Nature has opened a book on Beartooth Butte covering about a quarter of a billion years of geological history. It makes pretty snappy reading for parties interested in some of the ologies, paleontology for example.

Some students opine that prehistoric men existed here several million years earlier than heretofore believed. Personally we don't know, but if there were people prowling around that long ago, of course they would pick Montana as the best place to live.

L **Best Western LuPine Inn**
702 S. Hauser, Red Lodge. 446-1321 or (888) 567-1321. www.bestwestern.com/lupineinn; bwlupine@bestwesternlupine.com

The Best Western LuPine Inn staff invites you to join them for your next vacation, ski trip, or business meeting. They are within walking distance of downtown and just a few miles from the Red Lodge Ski Area, Beartooth Pass, Yellowstone National Park, and many outdoor activities. After a busy day, guests of the Inn will enjoy an indoor heated pool, sauna, and spa. Other in-room amenities include dataports, coffee and tea, hairdryers, and irons and ironing boards. The Inn also offers wireless Internet, a game room, fitness room, kitchenette units, coin laundry facilities, a ski waxing room, and a separate guest house. They also offer a complimentary continental breakfast each morning. Pets are welcome.

BEARTOOTH HIGHWAY

Author Charles Kurault described the Beartooth Scenic Highway as "the most beautiful drive in America." In 1989, the highway received national recognition when it was designated a National Scenic Byway. Only 52 other drives in the country share this distinction. This spectacular 65-mile drive reaches the highest drivable points in both Wyoming and Montana. Leaving Red Lodge, U.S. Hwy. 212 climbs 11,000 feet to Beartooth Pass and drops down to the northeast entrance to Yellowstone Park.

After mine closings wrecked the economy of Red Lodge, J.C.F. Siegriedt, a Red Lodge physician, lobbied the U.S. Government to rebuild the old "Black and White Trail" which ran along Rock Creek south of Red Lodge. He and O.H.P. Shelby, the local newspaper publisher persuaded the congress to authorize the Secretary of the Interior to build "approach highways" to the national parks. Herbert Hoover signed the bill, and construction began in 1931. The highway, at a cost of $2.5 million, opened on June 14, 1936.

The 64-mile corridor provides a panoramic view at the 10,942 ft. summit of peaks, varied topography, glaciers, plateaus, alpine lakes, cascading streams, wildflowers, and wildlife. The Beartooth Plateau is unique. After endless climbing you come to what appears to be an expansive plains rather than the top of a mountain range. Had you just been dropped here, you would think you were on a vast prairie filled with deep gorges. Glaciation missed this area leaving it relatively flat and smooth, unlike the jagged sculpted peaks in the distance. There are 25 features here labeled "Beartooth" all taken from the name of the conspicuous spire the Crow Indians called *Na Pet Say*—the "bears tooth." At its highest points, you can play in snow fields along the highway.

Allow yourself at least three hours to cross the highway. The limitless views demand that you stop every few minutes. The winding switchbacks do not allow speed. Check your film supply before heading up. You'll take many photos. And anticipate cool, if not cold weather at the top along with almost constant wind. Take your time and savor this trip, it's only open a few short months of the year.

L Super 8 of Red Lodge

1223 S. Broadway, Red Lodge. 446-2288 or (800) 813-8335. www.super8.com; redlodgesuper8@vcn.com

The Red Lodge Super 8 is located right along the Beartooth Highway. Whether you are in town to relax, enjoy great shopping, ski Red Lodge Mountain, visit Yellowstone National Park, or hike the Absaroka-Beartooth Wilderness, this is the perfect place to stay. Unwind in their spectacular outdoor hot tub or take a swim in their fantastic indoor pool with hot tub. They offer whirlpool suites, some with kitchenettes, family rooms, handicapped facilities, and non-smoking rooms. This beautiful AAA approved property also has free wireless Internet, guest laundry facilities, a video arcade, 24-hour front desk, meeting room, and plenty of parking for all sizes of vehicles. Guest rooms include free local calls and cable TV with HBO and ESPN, and all guests enjoy a complimentary continental breakfast. Children 16 and under stay free.

L Beartooth Hideaway Cabins

1223 S. Broadway, Red Lodge. 446-2288. redlodgesuper8@vcn.com

The Beartooth Hideaway Cabins are adjacent to the Super 8 Motel. The beautifully appointed cabins are perfect for a family of four. Each has a bedroom with a King bed, and the sitting room features a couch that pulls out to a double bed. There is a kitchenette stocked with dishes, pans, toaster, microwave, stovetop, and refrigerator. Each cabin also has a gas indoor fireplace and a deck with seating and a gas grill. Guests enjoy the use of the Super 8's large swimming pool, indoor and outdoor hot tubs, free wireless Internet, and complimentary continental breakfast. The cabins are located in a quiet shaded setting just a short drive or a pleasant walk to downtown shopping and dining.

Montana Trivia

The town of Columbus holds the state record for the most name changes. At various times it has been named Stillwater, Eagle's Nest, and Sheep Dip.

An excellent firearms exhibit is one of the many features of the Peaks to Plains Museum in Red Lodge.

L Red Lodge Inn

811 S. Broadway, Red Lodge. 446-2030. www.redlodgeinn.com; redlodgeinnmt@aol.com

Conveniently located six miles from Red Lodge Mountain Ski Resort, Red Lodge Inn is an easy walk to local shops, restaurants, and the nearby Rock Creek Picnic Area. The family-owned and recently remodeled motel has welcomed customers with old-time hospitality and numerous amenities since 1958. Uniquely decorated king, queen, kitchenette, and suite rooms offer a clean, non-smoking atmosphere complete with cable TV, coffeepots, microwaves, and refrigerators. Outside each cozy room, guests enjoy winter outdoor plug-ins, at-door parking, a guest barbeque area, a large outdoor hot tub, and a game room featuring a pool table, air hockey, foosball, and darts. Children are encouraged to explore the outdoor Crow Indian teepee. For warm hospitality, the amenities you need, and access to the heart of Red Lodge, stay with the friendly folks at Red Lodge Inn.

Montana Trivia

Montana is a pretty crowded place. Per square mile there are 1.4 elk, 1.4 pronghorn antelope, 3.3 deer, 896 catchable fish and fewer than six people.

22. *Gas, Food, Lodging*

H Chief Plenty Coups Statue Marker

Red Lodge

Plenty Coups—Chief of the Crows

(Circa 1848-March 4, 1932)

"The buffalo gone and freedom denied him, the Indians was visited by two equally hideous strangers, famine and tuberculosis. He could cope with neither. His pride broken he felt himself an outcast, a beggar in his own country. It was now that Plenty Coups became the real leader of his people."

"All my life I have tried to learn as the chickadee learns, by listening, profiting by the mistakes of others, that I may help my people. I hear the white man say there will be no more war. But this cannot be true. There will be other wars. Men have not changed, and whenever they quarrel they will fight, as they have always done. We love our country because it is beautiful, because we were born here. Strangers will covet it and someday try to possess it, as surely as the sun will come tomorrow. Then there must be war, unless we have grown to be cowards without love in our hearts for our native land. And whenever war comes between this country and another, your people will find my people pointing their guns with yours. If ever

Montana Trivia

Fun Montana Facts: The state bird of
Montana is the Western meadowlark
and the state animal is the Grizzly Bear.
The state flower is the Bitterroot and the
state tree is the Ponderosa Pine. The
geographic center of Montana lies in
Fergus County, 11 miles west of
Lewistown. At 12,799 feet, Granite Peak
in the Absaroka-Beartooth Wilderness is
the state's highest point.

It Happened in Montana

On November 11, 1965, Bill Linderman,
the legendary rodeo champion from the
Belfry-Bridger area dies in a commercial
airplane crash at Salt Lake City. Just
hours before the crash, Linderman
wrote a counter check for $20 at a
friend's tavern. Under his signature, he
gave his address as "Heaven." At the
time of the crash, his friends speculated
as to whether Linderman had a premo-
nition, was referring to his home in
Montana, or was just playing one of his
pranks.

the hands of my people hold the rope that
keeps this country's flag high in the air, it will
never come down while an Absarokee (Crow)
warrior lives."
-Linderman's Biography of Plenty Coups

Crow country once ranged from Three Forks
to the Black Hills, from the Musselshell to the
Big Horn Mountains. Red Lodge was a place of
worship, food and protection for the Crow people when it was theirs. Please respect it and
love it. It is a very good place.

T Peaks to Plains Museum
224 N. Broadway Ave. in downtown Red Lodge.
446-3667

This new location for the Carbon County Historical
Society's museum is in the renovated 1909 Labor
Temple at the north end of downtown Red Lodge.
Inside is a variety of exhibits portraying the rich
cultural and natural history of the region.

Featured here is a walk-through simulated coal
mine in the downstairs portion of the museum
along with associated mining tools and photographs. Upstairs exhibits include: a fully restored
1890s Yellowstone National Park touring coach; the
Greenough Collection of cowboy and rodeo memorabilia, including many of the items used by the
renowned "Riding Greenough's" as they performed
throughout the world; an early 19th century trade
tent and a display of authentic costumes and items
from the fur-trade era; and a display of the Waples
Family collection of more than 80 historic guns and
accessories.

There are exhibits portraying the local history of
the Crow Indians, trappers and mountain men,
early immigrants, paleontology and geology. There
is also an eclectic collection of artifacts from the
more recent past, including an old electroshock
therapy machine.

The museum is open daily during the summer
from 10 a.m. to 5 p.m. There is a small admission
charge.

V Montana Trout Scout Flyfishing Outfitter
Red Lodge. 855-3058 or 446-1951.
www.montanatroutscout.com

Enjoy catching that elusive rainbow, brown, cut-
throat, or brook trout? Then enlist the expertise of
Montana Trout Scout Flyfishing Outfitter. A
licensed and insured member of the Fishing
Outfitters Association of Montana, owner Craig
Beam provides full and half-day trips on the
undiscovered waters lining south-central Montana.
Emphasizing fun and utilizing such modern
equipment as the Clackacraft drift boat, Craig
offers trips on the Stillwater, Rock Creek,
Yellowstone, Clark's Fork, East Rosebud, and West
Rosebud Rivers. Trip prices include transportation,
equipment, flies, non-alcoholic beverages, snacks,
streamside lunch on full-day trips, friendly
instruction, and much more. Guests simply need a
fishing license, clothes, camera, and sunscreen.
Whether you're 6 or 60, been fishing forever or
never ever, let Montana Trout Scout Flyfishing
Outfitter customize a trip just for you or the
whole family!

F Bridge Creek Backcountry Kitchen & Wine Bar
116 S. Broadway, Red Lodge. 446-9900.
www.eatfooddrinkwine.com;
bridgecreek@eatfooddrinkwine.com

Dinner at Bridge Creek features locally raised, all-
natural beef, fresh seafood, and an award-winning
wine list. They are rapidly becoming a real
Montana legend. Their "quick-service" lunch
menu is packed with salads, sandwiches, wraps,
and burgers. Soups and breads are made fresh
daily, including their signature clam chowder –
locals claim it's the "best in the West!" Enjoy a
locally brewed beer by the fireplace. Dine in a
warm, comfortable surrounding. Watch the talented chef at work in his open kitchen. The Coffee

Bar is open daily at 7 am serving some of Red Lodge's finest espresso and freshly baked pastries. Enjoy their comfortable seating area, including a patio overlooking downtown Red Lodge. Private dining rooms and custom menus accommodate groups of 12 to 120, and wireless Internet is offered to all customers

L Weatherson Inn Bed & Breakfast
314 N. Broadway, Red Lodge. 446-0213 or (866) 806-2142. www.weathersoninn.com

The Weatherson Inn Bed & Breakfast offers gracious, yet affordable, accommodations in a charming 1910 Victorian home just two blocks from downtown Red Lodge. Experience warm hospitality while luxuriating in elegantly furnished, spacious rooms featuring private baths, one spa tub, showers, cable TV, and VCRs. In the morning, bask in the lovely sunroom, cozy up in the beautiful living room, or relax on the sunny deck while enjoying a scrumptious breakfast, delicious coffee, and a wide selection of teas. Fresh baked goods, a light continental breakfast of cereals, yogurt, and fresh fruit, or an extravagant and hearty entrée that changes daily accommodate everyone's unique meal preferences. Enjoy a vacation from today's world, and surround yourself with the romantic décor of yesteryear with a memorable stay at the Weatherson Inn Bed & Breakfast. .

S Magpie Toys
115 N. Broadway, Red Lodge. 446-3044. www.magpietoys.com; magpie@magpietoys.com

Walk into Magpie Toys and take a step back in time. Dedicated to selling products that encourage imagination, mental involvement, physical development, and personal interaction, this whimsical shop offers an eclectic variety of unforgettable toys, games, puzzles, books, and gifts for children of ALL ages. Rediscover tops, yo-yos, marbles, jacks, and pick-up sticks. Hum along with "Pop Goes the Weasel" as you turn the crank on one of the old-fashioned jack-in-the-boxes. amuse yourself with paper dolls, Woolly Willy, and tin wind-up toys. Browse through thousands of timeless

Montana Trivia

Actor Gary Cooper's father was Charles Henry Cooper. Charles left his native England at age 19, became a lawyer, and later a Montana State Supreme Court Justice. In 1906 when Gary was 5, his father bought the Seven-Bar-Nine, a 600-acre ranch that had originally been a land grant to the builders of the railroad through Montana. Gary said in later years that his father had always been a cowboy at heart.

children's books and adult classics. Challenge yourself with a mind-boggling puzzle. Entertain your young one with a sturdy wooden picture puzzle, toolbox, dollhouse, or block set. From Auto Bingo to Zen Gardens, this one-of-a-kind store is literally stuffed with toys that operate on imagination, not batteries!

S Shades & Specs
20 S. Broadway, Red Lodge. 446-2135.

Shades & Specs is a specialty optical shop with sunglasses, ski goggles, and sports specific eyewear with prescription and non-prescription styles and a variety of name brands available. Licensed optician, Jeff Warner, has one of the largest eyewear inventories in the area. He also has over twenty years experience filling and dispensing eye doctors' prescriptions for eyeglasses and is the only full-time optical dispensary in Carbon County. Shades & Specs can provide you with quality optics to enhance your sport, recreational, and eyewear needs. Stop in for a chat and see what Jeff can do for you. Check out some of the fun new products now on the market for prescription and non-prescription eyeglass buffs and outdoor enthusiasts.

S Kibler & Kirch Fine Furniture, Accessories & Rug Gallery
101 N. Broadway (Retail Store) and 22 N. Broadway (Design Center), Red Lodge. 446-2226. www.kiblerandkirch.com; kibler@vcn.com

Kibler & Kirch specializes in providing memorable experiences where collaboration with customers is a priority. Designing interiors with furnishings that reflect patrons' personalities, the experienced and professional design team has the capability to accessorize everything from rustic cabins to luxurious estates. Select from leather sofas and recliners, denim sectionals, French linens, Italian dishes, cozy bedding, unique rugs and floor coverings, exceptional lighting, window treatments, and art and wall coverings that accommodate all tastes. The entire selection process is tailored to customers' unique needs, and the friendly staff is always available to offer assistance. Whether you're looking for a single item or need guidance in furnishing your entire home, the Kibler & Kirch staff will help you create the interior of your dreams with attention to your individual style.

S Home on the Range Inc./JG Interiors Inc.
15 S. Broadway, Red Lodge. 446-3555.
E-mail: homeontherange@pngusa.net;

Discover home accessories, Made In Montana items, and complete interior design services at Home on the Range and JG Interiors. Kitchen items include etched wildlife glassware, western themed dinnerware, huckleberry products, and silicone tools. Fine linens, themed towels, Zen body lotions and creams, candles, and unique all-steel drawer pulls, towel bars, and hooks provide a memorable touch to your bath and bedroom. In addition, JG Interiors is your source for Marshfield furniture, Hunter Douglas window treatments, and a variety of flooring. For those needing decorating advice, Certified Interior Designer Jan Goehringer boasts years of kitchen and bath design/remodel experience as well as space planning for new homes and commercial buildings. Don't settle for the ordinary. Make your space comfortable with accessories and design expertise from Home on the Range and JG Interiors.

S The Glass Rabbit
112 S. Broadway in the center of downtown Red Lodge. 446-2805. www.theglassrabbit.com

A visit to The Glass Rabbit will bring years of fond memories long after your return home. Discover jewelry to match your individual style, and a unique selection of Native american jewelry. Treat yourself to gourmet chocolate sauce made in Red Lodge. Explore all natural aromatherapy products from candles to bath and beauty accessories. A fine selection of European pottery, soaps, lotions and linens will entice you. There are accent pieces to decorate and warm every room of your home or office. Share the memories of Montana with gifts from The Glass Rabbit. The Glass Rabbit is located in the central business district and is open daily, year round and they will ship for your convenience.

M Montana Realty Company of Red Lodge
110 S. Broadway, Red Lodge. 446-4744 or (877) 446-4744. www.iloveredlodge.com; www.montanarealtycompany.com; myrna@montanarealtycompany.com

Find your personal paradise with the professional Realtors® at Montana Realty Company of Red Lodge. The friendly, experienced agents understand that buying and selling property is a major life decision. That's why Montana Realty Company serves buyers and sellers seven days a week and promptly returns all phone calls. For buyers, the brokerage utilizes area Multiple Listings to locate residential, recreational, farm/ranch, vacant land, or investment properties at prices meeting your budget. Aggressive advertising strategies provide sellers with maximum exposure as properties are displayed in print ads across the country, direct mail postcards, and Internet listings. Featuring two-agents who are home-grown girls, two experienced transplants who love the area, and a Broker who is an avid fly-fisher, Montana Realty Company of Red Lodge is your source for unbeatable service and regional market knowledge!

M Red Lodge Reservations
1119 S. Broadway, Red Lodge. 446-4700 or (877) 733-5634. www.redlodgereservations.com; reservations@redlogereservations.com

Immerse yourself in Old West mystique, and concentrate on having fun while Red Lodge Reservations does the work for you. Red Lodge Reservations specializes in making reservations and creating vacations tailored to customer needs. Select from numerous hotels, motels, and fully furnished vacation rentals sure to please every style and budget. Looking for adventure or a sightseeing tour? Red Lodge Reservations provides an endless list of activities and only books with the most reputable companies. Holiday packages, discount lodging, and custom vacation packages including accommodations and activities are available, as well as local event information, event tickets, area merchandise, and regional travel links. Don't let your vacation become a burden. Create the Red Lodge vacation of your dreams with ease, and contact Red Lodge Reservations today!

23. *Gas, Food, Lodging,*

TS Depot Gallery
Red Lodge. 446-1370

This outstanding gallery, located in Red Lodge's original railroad depot at the north end of town has rotating exhibits and sales. Most work is by local artists, including members of the Carbon County Arts Guild who operate the Gallery. Open Tuesday-Saturday 11–5 and summer Sundays 11-3.

T Beartooth Nature Center
900 N. Bonner, Red Lodge. 446-1133
www.beartoothnaturecenter.org

Located in Coal Miner's Park, the Nature Center takes in animals that can not be left alone in nature, and nurtures them back to good health. On site are mountain lions, bears and many others, with a petting zoo for the kids. It is a great spot to view the surrounding wildlife up close. Open in the summer from 10 a.m.–6 p.m., children $2, adults $4.

MF Silver Strike Casino
609 N. Broadway, Red Lodge. 446-3131.
www.montanataverns.com/silverstrike

Experience one of Red Lodge's finest casinos with Silver Strike's relaxed, comfortable setting. Located at the town's north end, the air-conditioned casino boasts a sports bar, video games, regulation size pool tables, an 8-lane bowling alley, the latest electronic poker and keno machines, and numerous televisions and big screens perfect for catching that big game. During your visit, stop by the adjoining Becker's Kitchen Restaurant for break-

CALAMITY JANE

Calamity Jane, was born, Martha Jane Canary, in Princeton, Missouri in 1852, the oldest of six children. As a child she was a tomboy and had a passion for riding horses. In 1865, at the age of 13 the Cannary family made the five month journey, stopping in Virginia City, to take part in the quest for gold on their way to Salt Lake City. During their migration Martha practiced hunting with the men, and by the time they reached Virginia City, she was an accomplished rider and gun handler.

From 1866 on, she and her family moved around quite a bit-to Salt Lake City where her father died the next year, and then onto Wyoming where she helped scout for the army. During her travels she worked when she could find it, and even took up prostitution, although she always seemed to prefer men's work.

In the early 1870s Martha Jane Cannary was christened "Calamity Jane," known for her reckless daring riding and good aim. In 1876 Calamity Jane crossed paths with Wild Bill Hickok, and they remained good friends, (she told some they were married) until his death. She was known for causing a bit of trouble by stirring up the occasional saloon fight, and was said to have had a problem with alcoholism. Calamity Jane moved around most of her life and found it difficult to settle in one place. She did however spend some time in Montana, residing in Livingston for a period, and outside of Laurel where her cabins still stand today. She also called Big Timber, Castle, and Harlowton home for brief periods. When she died in 1903 at the age of 51, Calamity Jane was buried, at her request, next to Wild Bill in Deadwood, South Dakota.

EXCERPTS FROM THE BEARTOOTH REPORT

1882 by General Philip H. Sheridan

August 26, resumed the march, passing through Cooke City, a mining town on the divide between the waters of the east fork of the Yellowstone River and Clark's Fork. Many of the mines here are considered valuable. There are about 100 houses in the city, with fair prospects of as many more in a few months, indicated by the quantities of freshly hewn logs lying about and the number of town lots for sale. After stopping for only a short time to make some inquiries of the courteous inhabitants we continued on our way.

Just as we reached the summit of the divide, where the waters of Soda Butte Creek and Clark's Fork take their respective watersheds, we met a hunter, Mr. Geer, who considered himself so familiar with the Beartooth range of mountains that I was induced to abandon the old Clark's Fork trail and make an effort to cross that range, thus saving about three days in our journey to Billings station on the Northern Pacific railroad.

After meeting and employing him as a guide, somewhat against the judgment of older guides, we passed down the mountain with much difficulty, on account of the burning forests, the fire extending across our line of march. The journey this day was through high mountain peaks, covered on top with perpetual snow. We encamped at the base of Index peak and Pilot knob, on the banks of Clark's Fork of the Yellowstone. This camp was named Camp Clark, after Captain W.P. Clark, second cavalry, our Indian interpreter. Distance marched, 31 miles; altitude of camp, 7,100 feet.

On the morning of August 27, under the direction of our new guide, we crossed to the north side of Clark's Fork and began the ascent of the Beartooth Range. This was long, but gradual, and quite feasible for a wagon road so far as grade is concerned. The only difficulties which presented themselves during the day were bodies of densely growing timber at one or two places. However, we got through these without much delay, and about 12 o'clock encamped immediately under a very prominent land mark, called on the map Red butte. The camp was beautiful and was named Camp Gregory, after Colonel Gregory of my staff.

---

fast, lunch, or dinner. Happy hour is offered 4-7 pm daily with all-day drink specials and some of Red Lodge's most affordable drink prices. Whether you're in the mood for family fun, a drink with friends, or a date with Lady Luck, stop by the Silver Strike Casino. The casino is open daily from 9 am to 2 am, and smoking is permitted on the premises.

24. *Gas, Food*

Roberts

Roberts is a small town that lays on Rock Creek. It was one of the stops on the Northern Pacific Railroad, and dates back to the late 1800s.

25. *Gas*

Boyd

The town of Boyd was named for the homesteader John Boyd, who settled in this area in the early 1900s. The farmland around Boyd is irrigated with water that melts from the Beartooth Mountains.

26. *Gas, Food, Lodging*

Joliet

Located along Rock Creek, Joliet is an agricultural community named by a Railroad worker from Joliet, Illinois.

T Pathway Through the Bible
2 miles north of Joliet

A German immigrant, Adolph Land, moved to Montana from Iowa in 1952 with his wife, Helen, and a small pile of rocks. While supporting themselves by selling honey and trees, he decided to build a rock garden similar to "The Grotto" in West Bend, Iowa. The project turned into a 23 year endeavor that resulted in the "Pathway Through the Bible", an elaborate display of biblical stories represented in rocks.

Over the years the Land's collected rocks from all corners of the state and created gardens of flowers, shrubs, and rock formations of biblical characters and stories. After Adolph passed on, Helen sold the property to Verdine and Rick White who were willing to maintain the property with the reverence it earned over the years.

The garden gate is always open for public enjoyment. Guests are free to wander and only asked to respect the property owner's privacy.

27. *Lodging*

28.

Luther

This town was named for the Luther family who ran the post office and general store here. A blacksmith, lumberyard and saloon graced the site in years past.

T Wild Bill Lake

This is a popular fishing, hiking and swimming spot, with trails that go up the West Fork of Rock Creek. It is handicapped accessible.

29. *Food*

Roscoe

Roscoe is a small town half way between Red Lodge and Columbus. Originally names Morris after a local family, the mail was often confused with the town of Norris. Therefore, the name was changed to Roscoe in 1905, after the postmaster's favorite horse. It is the gateway to East Rosebud Canyon and Lake.

Alpine

Montana's rugged Beartooth Mountains formed the backyard for this small alpine community. When Christina Branger and the rest of her family came to Montana from Switzerland, they settled near East Rosebud Lake's shore and promptly christened their new home, Alpine. The settlement soon attracted others, so Ms. Branger opened the first post office in 1914 and assumed the role of postmaster. Excluding the years of 1943-1945, the post office successfully operated until 1953. While Ms. Branger kept herself busy in the postal industry, her family operated a popular hotel in the area for several years. Today, the area houses summer home residents eager to trade city life for peace and quiet amidst outstanding scenery.

30. *Gas, Food, Lodging*

Nye

A small town started during the mining boom years and a handful of residents still live here. Children still attend classes in a one room school house. Located in the upper Stillwater Valley, the town is named for Jack Nye, an agent for the Minneapolis Mining Co. in the 1880s.

Dean

A small hamlet that borders the Beartooths. Don't be surprised to see a wolf or a grizzly stop through town.

Fishtail

You would think that this tiny town's name somehow relates to its proximity to some of the finest fishing in Montana. Some of the residents there say that a local mountain formation that looks like a fishtail had something to do with the name. There is even a Fishtail River nearby. In truth, this little community located about 25 miles southwest of Columbus, was named for a Mr. Fishtail who resided in the area at the end of the 19th century. In about 1901 the town became official when a post office was established to service the surrounding Fiddler, Fishtail and, and Rock Creek area. Stressley Tunnell established a store at the time which was later purchased by the Columbus Mercantile in 1908. The store is still in operation today. The town sits in the foothills and the shadow of the Absaroka Mountain range. Today the town is only one block long, but manages to muster up a two mile long parade during the festival it sponsors every summer. Its also known to host one of the biggest yard sales in the state during that same festival.

Limestone

Situated in the mountains neighboring Sweet Grass County, Limestone derives its name after the vast limestone deposits found throughout Stillwater County. Settled in the early 1900s, Limestone acquired a post office in 1910 with Mabel Wright serving as first postmaster. With a dwindling population, the post office closed its doors in 1953.

SF Fishtail General Store
35 W. Main St., Fishtail. 328-4260.
www.fishtailgeneralstore.com;
fishtailstore@montana.net

Operating in the same location since 1900 and offering something for everyone, the Fishtail General Store is worth a stop! Browse through locally made toys, wall hangings, candles, soaps, and crafts as the original pot belly stove warms the place. Check out the meat market section featuring the world-famous "Fishtail General Store Special Sausage." Outdoor enthusiasts will find fishing licenses, camping and hunting provisions, food, and hardware. Floor to ceiling shelves are stocked with Montana Made food items, and the store is renowned for its freshly prepared soups, deli, pizzas, homemade cinnamon rolls, and specialty blackberry jam and pies made onsite. Fishtail General Store is open 5 am to 8 pm (excluding Thanksgiving and Christmas) with breakfast and lunch served daily. All major credit cards are accepted, and an ATM machine is available.

31. *Gas, Food, Lodging*

Absarokee

Absarokee is a small town with a lot of character. The name originates from the Crow Indians who, in the Hidatsa language, were referred to as Absarokee or "Big Beaked Bird." The white man referred to them as The Crow. The town of Absarokee used to be part of the Crow Reservation and the Old Crow Agency is just outside of town, marked with a plaque. Located on the Stillwater and Rosebud Rivers, the town sits about a mile away from the Bozeman Trail. Oliver Hovda built the first house, a pre-fab from Sears and Roebuck, in 1904.

L Bed & No Breakfast Bunkhouse
18 Woodard Ave., Absarokee. 328-7418.
Mtbnnob@nemontal.net

The Bed and No Breakfast Bunkhouse offers a smoke-free environment with unique Western-style rooms. Each room is decorated in a different theme using customized Western iron art and local Artesian Pine log furnishings. All rooms include air-conditioning and cable TV, and wireless Internet is also available. The bunkhouse is conveniently located within walking distance of local shops and restaurants. For prolonged stays, five one-bedroom efficiency apartments are offered at reduced weekly and monthly rates. Laundry service is available so guests can spend their time enjoying the beautiful area, not on washing clothes. Pay showers are also available to the public. Come enjoy a Western stay in beautiful

Absarokee close to the Beartooth Mountains. Outdoor adventure waits along with comfortable accommodations and friendly service! Sorry, no pets allowed.

LSF The Big Yellow House Lodging, Cafe and Gallery
43 N. Woodard (Main St.), Absarokee. 328-7220.
www.thebigyellowhouse.biz;
thetravellerstree@yahoo.com

Discover three businesses under one roof at the Big Yellow House in beautiful Stillwater Valley. Built in 1904, the Nationally Registered Historic Place welcomes overnight guests with large, comfortable, and affordable rooms. Create your own breakfast in the kitchen, or enjoy fruit, coffee, and homemade bread baked onsite. Afterwards, lounge on the veranda, enjoy the lovely lawns, and check out the showroom of fine Kyrgyzstan carpets and crafts. Hand-felted carpets, hats, bags, mittens, slippers, ornaments, and scarves provide a unique touch to your wardrobe and home. For lunch, sample The Big Yellow House's quaint café. The menu features European-style sandwiches, salads, wraps, Paninis, fresh fruit smoothies, homemade bread and desserts, and fresh squeezed lemonade. Open daily during summer with limited winter hours, the Big Yellow House is your food, lodging, and shopping destination!

32. *Attraction*

T Cooney Lake State Park
22 miles southwest of Laurel on U.S. 212, then 5 miles west of Boyd on county road. Summer, 445-2326 Winter, 252-4654.

One of the most popular recreation areas in south-central Montana, the lake is actually a reservoir, with a great view of the Beartooths in the background. This is a popular spot for fishing, swimming and boating, and has some nice camping as well. Attractions include good walleye and rainbow trout fishing. Boating and camping opportunities are abundant, and the Beartooth Mountains loom in the distance.

SCENIC DRIVES

Beartooth Scenic Byway (U.S. Route 212)
This drive certainly ranks as one of the most spectacular drives in the United States. Driving south out of Red Lodge, the highway follows Rock Creek through several layers of forest and climbs to high alpine tundra revealing a rugged panorama. Once you cross the high plateau, the drive continues on to the little town of Cooke City and the northeast entrance to Yellowstone National Park. While the mileage for this drive is relatively short, allow yourself the better part of the day for the round trip. You will be stopping often and using a lot of film.

Gas pumps party outside the Charles Ringer studio just north of Red Lodge.

East Rosebud Lake

To start this drive from Red Lodge, take MT Hwy. 78 (the turnoff is just north of downtown) west and drive to the town of Roscoe. This route offers some spectacular uninterrupted views of the Beartooth Range to the south. On clear days you can view the Crazy Mountains to the northwest. Turn into the town of Roscoe and stay left through the town. When you cross the bridge over East Rosebud River look for an immediate right turn. This road will take you to East Rosebud Canyon and the lake. Make sure your dentures are glued on tight. This is usually a pretty bumpy road. The steep granite walls of the canyon tower over the lake creating one of the more photographic settings in the area. In 1997, the Shepard Mountain Fire burned clear much of the old lodgepole pine forest. Now thousands of aspen seedlings and wildflowers blanket the slopes. This is a great place to fish, hike and enjoy an afternoon picnic.

WILDLIFE VIEWING

This area, with the Absaroka-Beartooth Wilderness, Beartooth Mountains and many river valleys, offers unlimited wildlife viewing opportunities. The area is abundant with prairie dogs which tend to stand up for lookout by their holes. The prairie dog towns increase the habitat for many other animals that feed off of the dogs, such as hawks, fox, and ferrets. It is very common to see deer standing in the fields or crossing the roads-be careful of this! Pronghorn are often spotted in the flat prairie lands, and keep an eye out for eagles.

Although much wildlife can be seen just driving through this area if you are paying attention, there are spots that can almost guarantee a viewing and of course hiking in the backcountry is your best bet. The Hailstone and Half Breed Wildlife Refuge areas are both located north of Laurel. Both offer spectacular birdwatching opportunities.

HIKES

The Beartooth Mountains are the source of all hikes in this section. One of the most popular areas is the East Rosebud drainage which takes you past countless waterfalls and mountain lakes. Numerous trails depart from the Beartooth Scenic Highway area also, and many of these make nice day hikes while traveling the highway. This is Grizzly country so be watchful, make a lot of noise and pack bear spray.

Elk Lake

This four mile hike starts at East Rosebud Lake and climbs about 500 feet. To get to East Rosebud Lake, take Forest Road 2177 south from Roscoe. This is a slow, rough road.

Granite Peak Trail

You'll find the trailhead for this trail at East Rosebud Lake also. This trail takes you approximately six miles through a creek bottom canyon to Mystic Lake.

Wild Bill Lake Area

Head south on U.S. 212 and watch for Forest Road #71. This is the road to the Red Lodge Ski area. Follow this to the lake. An easy trail goes partway around the lake. There is some excellent fishing here as well. At the end of the road are several more trailheads. One is a short hike (approximately three miles) up to Lake Gertrude and Timberline Lake.

Basin Lakes National Recreation Trail

Approximately one mile past Wild Bill Lake is the trailhead for this hike. This is about a 2.5 mile hike to Lower Basin Creek Lake. If you're feeling energetic, you can go an additional 1.5 miles to Upper Basin Creek Lake. It's worth the hike to see this shimmering lake nestled in a glacial cirque. Much of this trail follows an old logging road.

Lake Fork Lake

To reach this trail head, follow the Beartooth Scenic Highway south of Red Lodge to Lake Fork Road on your right. If you reach the campgrounds, you've gone too far. The trailhead for this hike is just 1.25 miles up Lake Fork Road. These are fairly short hikes leading either upstream or downstream on Lake Fork Creek.

Parkside National Recreation Trail

A bit further up the road is the Parkside Picnic Area. The trailhead for this hike starts here and heads north for a little over two miles up to Greenough Lake.

Glacier Lake

Continue to follow the Beartooth Scenic Highway south of Red Lodge to the first turnoff to campgrounds on your right. These will be about a mile past the Lake Fork Road turnoff. If you've reached the switchbacks of the highway, you've gone too far. Take Forest Road #421 across Rock Creek and head south for about seven miles following the creek. This is a rough road and a high clearance is recommended. At the end of the road is a parking area and the trailhead for the two-mile hike to the lake. This lake is the source of Rock Creek and sits in the shadow of the 12,350-foot high Mt. Rearguard. The trail takes you through some spectacular alpine country.

CROSS-COUNTRY SKI TRAILS

Custer National Forest

For more information contact District Ranger, Red Lodge, MT 59068. Phone, 446-2103

Silver Run-5 mi. W Red Lodge via West Fork Rock Creek Road
Range of difficulty depends on snow conditions. No grooming
One-way mountain touring trail; 4 loops (4 km;7 km; 11 km; and 13 km); closed to snowmachines.

Lake Fork-10 mi. S Red Lodge via Hwy 212
Range of difficulty depends on snow conditions. No grooming
Two loops (2 km and 5 km); closed to snowmachines. Park at junction of Hwy 212 and Lake Fork Road.

West Fork Rock Creek Road–6 mi. W Red Lodge via West Fork Rock Creek Road
1 km Easiest, 11 km More Difficult; no grooming
No loops; dead end route. Shared with snowmachines.

INFORMATION PLEASE

All Montana area codes are 406

Road Information

Montana Road Condition Report
(800) 226-7623, (800) 335-7592 local 444-7696
Montana Highway Patrol   444-7696
Local Road Reports
    Billings   252-2806
    Billings Weather Reports   652-1916

Tourism Information

Travel Montana
    (800) 847-4868 outside Montana
    444-2654 in Montana   http://travel.mt.gov/.
Yellowstone Country(800) 736-5276 or 646-4383
Northern Rodeo Association   252-1122
Chambers of Commerce
    Laurel   628-8105
    Red Lodge   446-1718
    Stillwater   322-4505

Airports

Bridger   662-3319
Columbus   322-4843
Laurel   628-6373

Government Offices

State BLM Office   255-2885, 238-1540
Bureau of Land Management
    Billings Field Office   896-5013
Custer National Forest, Beartooth Ranger District
                                          446-2103
Montana Fish, Wildlife & Parks   247-2940
U.S. Bureau of Reclamation   247-7295

Hospitals

Ask-A-Nurse • Billings   657-8778
Billings Inter-Hospital Onclay   259-2245
Deaconess Medical Center • Billings   657-4000
St. Vincents Hospital • Billings   657-7000
Stillwater Community Hospital
    Columbus   322-5316
Carbon County Memorial Hospital
    Red Lodge   446-2345

Golf Courses

Red Lodge Mt. Resort • Red Lodge   446-3344
Stillwater Golf & Rec. • Columbus   322-4298

Bed & Breakfasts

Bed & No Breakfast Bunkhouse
    Absarokee   328-7419
Weatherson Inn • Red Lodge   446-0213
Big Yellow House • Absorkee   328-7220
Blessing House B&B • Red Lodge   446-4269
Willows Inn • Red Lodge   446-3913
Bear Bordeaux B&B • Red Lodge   446-4408
Inn On The Beartooth • Red Lodge   446-1768
Magnolia Mae Inn • Red Lodge   446-2900
Wolves Den B & B • Red Lodge   446-1273
Abigail Inn• Absarokee   328-6592
Magpie's Nest • Absarokee   328-4925
River Haven • Absarokee   328-4138

Forest Service Cabins

Custer National Forest
Meyers Creek
60 mi. SE of Red Lodge   446-2103
Capacity: 6   Nightly fee: $40   Available: 5/1-10/15
Summer use only. Refrigerator, lights, water, shower, flush toilet and forced air heat. 2 bedroom house. Corral for horses

Guest Ranches & Resorts

Rock Creek Resort • Red Lodge   446-1111
Stoney Lonesome Ranch • Absarokee   932-4452
Sugarloaf Mountain Outfitters
    Absarokee   328-4939
Lonesome Spur Ranch • Bridger   662-3460
Calamity Jane's Horse Cache • Molt   628-6000
Small Ranch • Reed Point   326-2327
Lazy E-L Working Guest Ranch
    Roscoe   328-6855

Vacation Homes & Cabins

Bighorn River Country Lodge
    Fort Smith   666-2332
Big Sky Roping Ranch • Huntley   348-2460
Blue Sky Cabins • Luther   446-0186
Canyon Cabin • Red Lodge   446-2421
Cross A Guest Ranch • Lodge Grass   639-2697
Double Spear Ranch • Pryor   259-8291
Eagle Nest Lodge • Hardin   665-3712
Fiddler Creek Cabins • Absarokee   328-4949
Green Ranch • Fishtail   537-4472
Hammond Guest House • Melville   328-4229
Johnson Place • Absarokee   328-4195
Lena's Cabins • Fishtail   328-4878
Little Cabin in Red Lodge • Red Lodge 245-7360
Mountain View Condo • Red Lodge   245-1704
Picket Pin Ranch • Nye   328-7004
Pitcher Guest Houses • Red Lodge   446-2859
Red Lodging • Red Lodge   446-1272
Reels End • Columbus   322-5539

All Montana Area Codes are 406

Riverside Guest Cabins • Columbus	322-5066
Rosebud Retreat • Fishtail	328-4220
Seventh Ranch • Garryowen	638-2438
Torgirimson Place • Fishtail	328-4412
Whipple Cabin • Fishtail	328-6907

Car Rental

AA-A Auto Rental	245-9759
Ace-Rent-A-Car	252-2399
Avis Rent-A-Car	252-8007
Budget Rent-A-Car	259-4168
Dollar Rent-A-Car	259-1147
Enterprise Billings West	652-2000
Enterprise Rent-A-Car	259-9999
Hertz Rent-A-Car	248-9151

National Car Rental	252-7626
Rent A Wreck	245-5982
Thrifty Car Rental	259-1025
U Save Auto Rental	655-4440
Ray-Judd Ford	446-1400

Outfitters & Guides

F=Fishing H=Hunting R=River Guides
E=Horseback Rides G=General Guide Services

Montana Trout Scout	R	855-30587
C Quarter Circle Outfitters	G	445-2280
Absaroka River Adventures	R	328-7440
Adventure Whitewater Inc	R	446-3061
Beartooth Mountain Guides	G	446-1952

Beartooth Plateau Outfitters	GF	445-2293
Beartooth Whitewater	R	446-3142
Calamity Jane Horse Cache	E	628-6000
Chatlain Dennis & Jane	G	445-2280
Fish Montana Fly Shop	GF	328-6548
Headwaters & High Country	FH	446-2679
Paint Brush Adventures Inc	GFE	328-4158
Slow Elk Trail Inc	E	446-4179
Sugarloaf Mountain Outfitters	H	328-4939
Beartooth River Trips	R	446-3142

PUBLIC CAMPGROUNDS

Campsite Directions

	Season	Camping	Trailers	Toilets	Water	Boat Launch	Fishing	Swimming	Trails	Stay Limit	Fee
16•Itch-Kep-Pe Park S of Columbus on MT 78	4/1-10/31	30	•	•	•	•	•	•		14	
17•Cooney FWP 22 mi. SW of Laurel•Milepost 90•8 mi. W on Cty. Rd.	All Year	70	•	D	•	C	•	•		14	•
18•Pine Grove FS 1 mi. W of Fishtail on Rt. 419•6 mi. SW on Cty. Rd. 425•8 mi. S on Forest Rd. 72	5/27-9/15	46	30'	D			•			10	•
19•Emerald Lake FS 1 mi. W of Fishtail on Rt. 419•6 mi. SW on Cty. Rd. 425•12 S on Forest Rd. 72	5/27-9/5	32	30'	D			•			10	•
20•Jimmy Joe FS 9 mi. S of Roscoe on Cty. & Forest Rd. 177	5/27-9/5	10	16'	•			•			10	
21•Cascade FS 2 mil S of Red Lodge on US 212•10 mi. W on Forest Rd. 71 Reservations (800) 280-CAMP or 202-205-1760	5/27-9/5	31	30'	•			•			10	•
22•East Rosebud Lake FS 12 mi.S of Roscoe on Cty. & Forest Rd. 177	5/27-9/5	14	16'	•		•	•		•	10	•
23•M-K FS 12 mi. SW of Red Lodge on US 212•4 mi. SW on Forest Rd. 421	5/30-9/5	10	16'	•			•		•	10	
24•Limber Pine FS 12 mi. SW of Red Lodge on US 212•1 mi. SW on Forest Rd. 421 (Reservations:(800) 280-CAMP or 202-205-1760	5/27-9/5	13	35'	•			•		•	10	•
25•Basin FS 1 mi. S of Red Lodge, US 212•7 mi. W on Forest Rd. 71 ((800) 280-CAMP or 202-205-2760)	5/27-9/5	30	30'	D			•		•	10	•
26•Parkside FS 12 mi. SW of Red Lodge on US 212•1 mi. SW on Forest Rd. 421 (Reservations (800) 280-CAMPor 202-205-1760)	5/27-9/5	28	30'	D			•		•	10	•
27•Greenough Lake FS 12 mi. SW of Red Lodge on US 212•1 mi. SW on Forest Rd. 421 (Reservations: (800) 280-CAMPor 202-205-1760)	5/27-9/5	18	30'	D			•		•	10	•
28•Ratine FS 5 mi. SW of Red Lodge on US 212•3mi. SW on Forest Rd. 379 (Reservations: (800) 280-CAMPor 202-205-1760)	5/27-9/5	7		•	•		•		•	10	•
29•Sheridan FS 5 mi. SW of Red Lodge on US 212•2 mi. SW on Forest Rd. 379 (Reservations (800) 280-CAMP or 202-205-1760)	5/27-9/5	8	22'	•			•		•	10	•
30•Palisades FS 1 mi. W of Red Lodge on Forest Rd. 71•2 mi. W on Cty. & Forest Rd.3010	6/15-9/15	6	16'	•						10	
31•Woodbine FS 8 mi. SW of Nye on Rt. 419	6/15-9/15	44	30'	D	•		•		•	10	•

Agency
FS—U.S.D.A Forest Service
FWP—Montana Fish, Wildlife & Parks
NPS—National Park Service
BLM—U.S. Bureau of Land Management
USBR—U.S. Bureau of Reclamation
CE—Corps of Engineers

Camping
Camping is allowed at this site. Number indicates camping spaces available
H—Hard sided units only; no tents

Trailers
Trailer units allowed. Number indicates maximum length.

Toilets
Toilets on site. D—Disabled access

Water
Drinkable water on site

Fishing
Visitors may fish on site

Boat
Type of boat ramp on site:
A—Hand launch
B—4-wheel drive with trailer
C—2-wheel drive with trailer

Swimming
Designated swimming areas on site

Trails
Trails on site
B—Backpacking N—Nature/Interpretive

Stay Limit
Maximum length of stay in days

Fee
Camping and/or day-use fee

Section 4

PRIVATE CAMPGROUNDS
Campsite Directions

Campsite / Directions	Season	Tent	RV	Water	Electric	Sewer	Dump	Shower	Laundry	Store
ABSAROKEE										
Dew Drop RV Campground & Drive Inn Restaurant 328-4121 • Located on MT 78 1/1-12/31		10	•	•	•				•	
BRIDGER										
City Park Campground 662-3677 • In Bridger on E Broadway	No Winter		6	•	•	•	•			
COLUMBUS										
Mountain Range RV Park 322-1140 • N of I-90 Exit 408 4/1-11/15		8	42	•	•	•	•	•		
LAUREL										
Pelican Truck Plaza Motel 628-4324 • Fax 628-8442 • I-90 Exit 437	All Year	15	40	•	•	•	•	•	•	•
Riverside Park 628-4796 ext 0 • I-90 Exit 434 to US 212, S 3/4 mi.	5/19-9/30	40	6	•				•		
RED LODGE										
Perry's RV Park & Campground 446-2722 or 446-1510 • 2 mi S on US 212	5/25-10/1	25	25	•	•		•	•	•	
Red Lodge KOA 446-2364 • (800) KOA-7540 • 4 mi N on US 212, 38 mi S of I-90 on US 212	May-Sept	20	58	•	•		•	•	•	•
REED POINT										
Cedar Hills Campground 321-0858 • Just off I-90. 5 S Division	All Year	6	18	•	•	•	•	•		
ROCKVALE										
Rockcreek Campground 962-3459 • Jct of US 212 & US 310 on route to Yellowstone	4/15-10/15	19	11	•	•		•		•	•

Fishery

Fishery	Cold Water Species												Warm Water Species										Services					
	Brook Trout	Mt. Whitefish	Lake Whitefish	Golden Trout	Cutthroat Trout	Brown Trout	Rainbow Trout	Kokanee Salmon	Bull Trout	Lake Trout	Arctic Grayling	Burbot	Largemouth Bass	Smallmouth Bass	Walleye	Sauger	Northern Pike	Shovelnose Sturgeon	Channel Catfish	Yellow Perch	Crappie	Paddlefish	Vehicle Access	Campgrounds	Toilets	Docks	Boat Ramps	MotorRestrictions
23. Stillwater River	•	•				•	•																•	•	•		•	
24. Cooney Reservoir						•	•								•						•		•	•	•		•	
25. West Rosebud Lake	•	•			•	•	•																	•	•			
26. Emerald Lake	•	•			•	•																		•	•			
27. Mystic Lake	•				•																							
28. Beartooth Plateau Alpine Lakes	•			•	•	•				•																		
29. Wild Bill Lake							•																•	•				
30. Rock Creek	•					•	•																•					
31. Greenough Lake							•																•	•	•			
32. Laurel Pond							•																•					

NOTES:

Dining Quick Reference

Price Range refers to the average cost of a meal per person: ($) $1-$6, ($$) $7-$11, ($$$) $12-up. Cocktails: "Yes" indicates full bar; Beer (B)/Wine (W); Service: Breakfast (B), Brunch (BR), Lunch (L), Dinner (D). Businesses in bold print will have additional information under the appropriate map locator number in the body of this section. *[wi-fi]* next to business name indicates free wireless internet is available to customers.

RESTAURANT	TYPE CUISINE	PRICE RANGE	CHILD MENU	COCKTAILS BEER WINE	SERVICE	CREDIT CARDS	MAP LOCATOR NUMBER
Burger King	Fast Food	$	Yes		B/L/D		2
Curt's Saloon	Pizza	$/$$/$$$	Yes	Yes	L/D	Major	2
Hardee's	Fast Food	$	Yes		B/L/D		2
Locomotive Inn Restaurant	Family	$$	Yes	Yes	D	Major	2
Pizza Hut	Pizza	$/$$	Yes	B	L/D	V/M/D	2
Stageline Pizza	Pizza	$/$$			L/D		2
Subway	Fast Food	$	Yes		L/D		2
Taco John's	Fast Food	$	Yes		L/D		2
Caboose Saloon & Casino	Bar			Yes			3
Dragon Palace Chinese Cuisine	Chinese	$$	Yes	B/W	L/D	V/M/D	3
Sid's Place	American	$		Yes	L/D		3
Cafe Mabel's	Mexican	$$			L/D	Major	3
Dairy Queen	Fast Food	$	Yes		L/D		3
Pelican Truck Plaza *[wi-fi]*	Family	$$	Yes		B/L/D	Major	3
Owl Junction Diner	Eclectic	$-$$$	Yes		B/L/D	Major	3
Railside Diner	American	$	Yes		B/L/D		3
Pop's Inn	American	$		Yes	L/D		4
Park City Cenex Car & Truck Stop *[wi-fi]*	American	$$	Yes		B/L/D	Major	4
Apple Village Cafe & Gift Shop	American	$-$$$	Yes		B/L/D	Major	6
McDonalds	Fast Food	$			B/L/D		6
New Atlas Bar	Bar			Yes			7
307 Restaurant	American	$-$$$	Yes	Yes	L/D	V/M	7
Sports Hut	American	$/$$	Yes		L/D	Major	7
Uncle Sam's Eatery	Deli	$			L		7
El Rancho Inn	Mexican American	$-$$$	Yes	Yes	L/D	Major	13
Quick Stop Drive In	Fast Food	$	Yes		L/D		14
Fort Rockvale Restaurant	American	$-$$$	Yes	Yes	B/L/D/BR	V/M	14
Little Cowboy Bar & Museum	Bar			Yes			15
Buckeye Bar Grill & Casino	Steakhouse	$-$$$	Yes	Yes	B/L/D	V/M/D	17
Jungle Jayne's Stringtown Saloon & Eatery	American	$-$$$	Yes	Yes	L/D	V/M/D	17
Bridger Cafe & Casino	Family	$$	Yes	B/W	B/L/D/BR		17
Country House Cafe	American	$	Yes		B/L		18
Silver Tip Restaurant & Casino	American	$-$$$	Yes	Yes	B/L/D/BR		18
Bear Creek Saloon & Steakhouse	Steakhouse	$$/$$$		Yes	D	V/M	19
Old Piney Dell	Steaks & Seafood	$$$	Yes	Yes	D	Major	20
Kiva Restaurant	American	$/$$	Yes	Yes	B/L/BR	Major	20
P D Mc Kinney's Family Dining	Family	$/$$	Yes		B/L	V/M/D	21
Red Box Car Drive-In	Fast Food	$	Yes		L/D		21
Subway	Fast Food	$	Yes		L/D		21
Bridge Creek Backcountry Kitchen & Wine Bar *[wi-fi]*	Seafood/American	$-$$$	Yes	B/W	L/D	Major	22
Bogart's	Family/ Eclectic	$/$$	Yes	Yes	L/D	V/M	22
Coffee Factory Roasters [wi-fi]	Coffee House	$			B/L	V/M	22
The Pollard	Regional	$$$	Yes	Yes	B/L/D/BR	Major	22
Hanks Place	Family	$	Yes		B/L	Major	22
Bull Moose Bistro	Regional	$/$$$	Yes	Yes	L/D	V/M	22
Red Lodge Ale House Pub & Grill	Pub Grub	$-$$$	Yes	B/W	L/D	V/M	22
Red Lodge Cafe, Lounge & Casino	Family	$-$$$		Yes	B/L/D	V/M	22
Bull & Bear Saloon *[wi-fi]*	Pizza	$$		Yes	L/D		22
China Town Restaurant	Chinese	$$			L/D	V/M	22
Carbon County Steakhouse	Steakhouse	$$/$$$		Yes	D	Major	22
Genesis Natural Foods	Deli	$			L	Major	22
Red Lodge Pizza Co.	Pizza	$/$$	Yes	Yes	L/D	Major	22
Gunsmoke BBQ	Barbeque	$-$$$			L/D		23
Rock Creek Texaco Novasio Hamburgers	Fast Food	$			L/D		23
Montana Red's	Buffet	$/$$	Yes		B/L/D	Major	23
Becker's Kitchen	Homestyle	$$	Yes	Yes	B/L	Major	23
Brown Bear Inn	Steakhouse	$-$$$		Yes	L/D	Major	24
Lost Village Saloon and Eatery	American	$$		Yes	L/D	V/M	24
Frontier Bar & Bone Pile	American	$		Yes	L		26
Homestead Cafe	American	$	Yes		B/L/D	V/M	26
Grizzly Bar Steaks & Burgers	Steakhouse	$-$$$	Yes	Yes	L/D	V/M	29

Dining Quick Reference-Continued

Price Range refers to the average cost of a meal per person: ($) $1-$6, ($$) $7-$11, ($$$) $12-up. Cocktails: "Yes" indicates full bar; Beer (B)/Wine (W), Service: Breakfast (B), Brunch (BR), Lunch (L), Dinner (D). Businesses in bold print will have additional information under the appropriate map locator number in the body of this section. *[wi-fi]* next to business name indicates free wireless internet is available to customers.

RESTAURANT	TYPE CUISINE	PRICE RANGE	CHILD MENU	COCKTAILS BEER WINE	SERVICE	CREDIT CARDS	MAP LOCATOR NUMBER
Montana Hanna's	American	$–$$$	Yes	B/W	L/D	V/M/D	30
Cowboy Bar & Supper Club	Steak/Seafood	$–$$$		Yes	B/L/D	V/M	30
Stake-Out	Family/American	$-$$$	Yes	Yes	L/D/BR	B/V/M/D	31
Dew Drop Inn	Fast Food	$	Yes		L/D		31

Motel Quick Reference

Price Range: ($) Under $40 ; ($$) $40-$60; ($$$) $60-$80, ($$$$) Over $80. Pets [check with the motel for specific policies] (P), Dining (D), Lounge (L), Disabled Access (DA), Full Breakfast (FB), Cont. Breakfast (CB), Indoor Pool (IP), Outdoor Pool (OP), Hot Tub (HT), Sauna (S), Refrigerator (R), Microwave (M) (Microwave and Refrigerator indicated only if in majority of rooms), Kitchenette (K). All Montana area codes are 406. *[wi-fi]* next to business name indicates free wireless internet is available to customers.

HOTEL	PHONE	NUMBER ROOMS	PRICE RANGE	BREAKFAST	POOL/ HOT TUB SAUNA	NON SMOKE ROOMS	OTHER AMENITIES	CREDIT CARDS	MAP LOCATOR NUMBER
Howard Johnson	628-8281	52	$$	CB	IP/HT	Yes	DA	Major	2
Laurel Super	8628-6888	60	CB	IP/HT	Yes	P/DA		Major	2
Pelican Truck Plaza	628-4324	12	$$			Yes	DA/P	Major	3
Welcome Traveler's Motel	628-6821	10	$			Yes	K/P/M/R	V/M/D	3
Russell Motel	628-6513	13	$/$$			Yes	K/P/M/R	Major	3
Laurel Ridge Motel	628-2000	10	$				K/P/R	V/M	3
Lohof Motel	628-6216	14	$$			Yes	K/R	V/M	3
Wagon Wheel Motel	628-8084	11	$/$$	CB		Yes	K/P/M/R/DA	V/M/D	3
Lazy RL Motel	633-2352	9	$				K/R/DA	A/V/M	4
CJ's Motel	633-2352	9	$					Major	4
Riverside Guest Cabins	322-5066	7	$	CB		Yes	K/R	V/M	7
Git's Conoco & Big Sky Motel	322-4111	20	$			Yes	L	Major	7
Super 8 *[wi-fi]*	322-4101	72	$$		HT	Yes	DA/P	Major	7
Bridger Motel	662-3212	8	$			Yes	K/R/DA		17
Rock Creek Resort *[wi-fi]*	446-1111	88	$$$$		IP/HT/S	Yes	K/D/L/DA	Major	20
Super 8 Motel *[wi-fi]*	446-2288	50	$$/$$$$		IP/HT/S	Yes	K/P/DA	Major	21
Best Western Lupine Inn *[wi-fi]*	446-1321	46	$$/$$$	CB	IP/HT/S	Yes	K/P/M/R/DA	Major	21
Beartooth Hideaway Cabins	446-2288	4	$$$$	CB	HT/IP		R/M/K	Major	21
Red Lodge Inn	446-2030	14	$$		HT	Yes	K/P/M/R/DA	Major	21
Weatherson Inn	446-0213	2	$$$/$$$$	Yes		Y			21
Chateau Rouge *[wi-fi]*	446-1601	24	$$-$$$$		IP/HT	Yes	K/P/M/R	Major	21
Yodeler Motel *[wi-fi]*	446-1435	23	$$/$$$		HT/S	Yes	K/P/M/R/DA	Major	21
Eagles Nest Motel	446-2312	17	$/$$$$				HTK/P	Major	21
The Pollard *[wi-fi]*	446-0001	39	$$$/$$$$	FB	HT/S	Yes	D/PB/DA	Major	22
Comfort Inn of Red Lodge *[wi-fi]*	446-4469	55	$$/$$$$	CB	IP/HT	Yes	P/M/R/DA	Major	23
Alpine Lodge	446-2213	15	$$		HT	Yes	P	Major	23
Joliet Motel	962-3693	12	$$			Yes	P/K	V/M	26
Juro's Aspen Lodge	328-4284								30
The Big Yellow House	328-7220	5	$$	CB		Yes	P		31
Bed & No Breakfast Bunkhouse *[wi-fi]*	328-7418	8	$/$$			Yes	K		31
Stillwater Lodge	328-4899	6	$/$$			Yes	P/DA	Major	31

NOTES:

All Montana Area Codes are 406

Section 4

SECTION 5

BILLINGS AND SURROUNDING AREA

Billings viewed from the rimrocks.

1. *Gas, Food*

Hysham

At the turn of the century, shortly after Montana territory received statehood, Hysham was part of vast open area known as Custer County. The Flying E Ranch had thousands of cattle grazing the Yellowstone River Valley, and many of them grazed along the railroad tracks that ran through this area. The trainmen of the Northern Pacific railroad often left supplies ordered by Charlie J. Hysham, an associate of the Flying E, labeled "for Mr. Hysham." The association between the site, the Flying E, and Mr. Hysham stuck and the spot

David Manning's theater.

became known as simply Hysham. Today, Hysham is the county seat of Treasure County and is bordered on the north by the Yellowstone River, and to the south by beautiful rolling hills.

This area is rich in history of the early days in the settlement of Montana. Near here, Manuel Lisa built a fur trading post near the mouth of the Bighorn River in 1807. This was the first building in the state of Montana. Fort Cass, the first fort built by the American Fur Company on the Yellowstone, was constructed just three miles below the mouth of the Bighorn. Near the mouth of the Bighorn, the stockade of Fort Pease was built in 1875 as a defense against a part of Sioux Indians and also to serve as a trading post. There are still some remnants of Fort Pease on the original site, but the locations of the other forts remain a mystery.

Today, Hysham is a clean, friendly little town. As you enter the town, the historic Yucca Theater stands guard at the end of main street. This distinctive stucco building and its Santa Fe art deco style of architecture seem oddly out of place in this small farming community. Constructed in 1931 by David Manning, a local contractor, the theater was the focal point of entertainment in the area for more than 50 years. The first film shown there was the 1914 classic *A Room With A View*. The last film to grace its screen in 1986 was *Tillie's Punctured Romance*.

David Manning later went on to become one of Montana's most prominent legislators serving in the Montana House of Representatives continuously for 52 years until his retirement in 1985. In 1990, the Manning family donated the theater to the museum across the street. It seemed fitting as most of the museum contains the memorabilia and inventions of Senator Manning.

Sanders

Established on the Yellowstone River, Sanders draws its name from pioneer and former US Senator W. F. Sanders. The community's post office has been operating since 1904 with Ollie Smith serving as the first postmaster.

D William Clark
July 27, 1806

"when we pass the Big Horn I take my leave of the view of the tremendious chain of Rocky Mountains white with Snow in view of which I have been Since the 1st of May last."

T Treasure County 89ers Museum
Elliott Ave., Hysham. 342-5252

Local history is preserved with displays called "Tales of Treasure County. There is also a restored early day soda fountain that is open for special occasions. It is directly across the street from the Yucca Theatre. Open Memorial Day through Labor Day.

2. _____

Myers

A civil engineer credited with building a Northern Pacific Railroad line to the town serves as this community's namesake. Once an important railroad station, Myers's popularity has dwindled over the years. The town's post office, opened in 1911, has survived the decreasing number of residents and remains open.

T Howrey Island
7 miles west of Hysham. 232-7000

This 560-acre Montana Watchable Wildlife area on the Yellowstone River island has numerous trails and lots of waterfowl throughout the year. Bald eagles can be seen throughout the summer. A self guided 1.3 mile nature trail winds through a typical riparian cottonwood forest.

3. _____

H Yellowstone River Trading Posts
south of Hysham

Even before the Lewis and Clark Expedition returned to St. Louis in 1806, enterprising fur

Hysham	Jan	Feb	March	April	May	June	July	Aug	Sep	Oct	Nov	Dec	Annual
Average Max. Temperature (F)	31.8	38.8	46.1	57.7	68.1	78.0	88.4	87.3	74.6	62.1	45.0	35.5	59.5
Average Min. Temperature (F)	5.6	12.8	20.1	30.2	38.7	47.3	52.9	50.1	40.0	29.6	17.9	9.2	29.5
Average Total Precipitation (in.)	0.60	0.51	0.86	1.57	2.13	2.68	1.30	0.92	1.38	1.08	0.70	0.56	14.28
Average Total SnowFall (in.)	10.4	7.0	8.7	6.3	1.2	0.0	0.0	0.0	0.9	2.3	6.6	9.6	53.1
Average Snow Depth (in.)	4	3	1	0	0	0	0	0	0	0	1	3	1

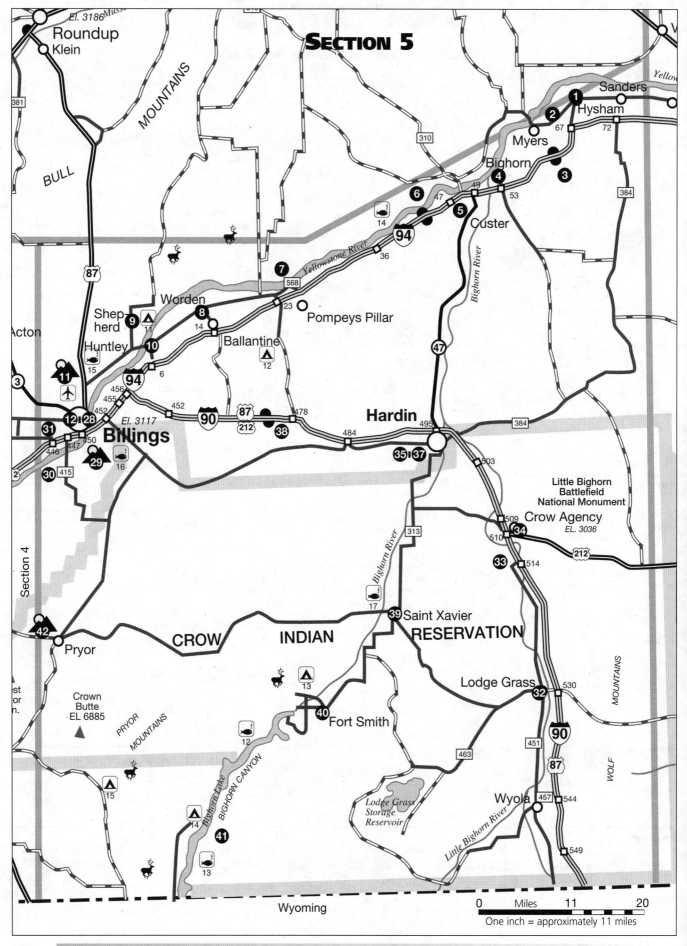

Section 5

All Montana Area Codes are 406

Roundup
Klein
El. 3186

MOUNTAINS

BULL

381

87

Acton

3

Section 4

SECTION 5

Sanders
1
Hysham
2
67
Myers
72
310
Bighorn
4
53
384
6
47
49
14
5
Custer
94
Yellowstone River
7
36
568
23
Worden
Pompeys Pillar
8
14
Shep-
herd
9
11
10
Ballantine
47
Bighorn River
Huntley
15
6
12
11
94
456
455
452
452
90
87
Hardin
El. 3117
212
478
484
495
384
Billings
12 28
31
38
35 37
447
450
446
2
30 415
29
16
509
Little Bighorn
Battlefield
National Monument
Crow Agency
EL. 3036
510
34
212
33
514
313
Bighorn River
17
39
Saint Xavier
42
RESERVATION
Pryor
CROW   INDIAN
Crown
Butte
EL 6885
Lodge Grass
530
PRYOR
13
32
MOUNTAINS
MOUNTAINS
40
Fort Smith
12
451
90
463
87
Bighorn Lake
WOLF
15
Lodge Grass
Storage
Reservoir
Wyola
457
544
14
BIGHORN CANYON
41
549
Little Bighorn River
13

Wyoming

0   Miles   11   20
One inch = approximately 11 miles

236   *Ultimate* Yellowstone Park Atlas and Travel Encyclopedia

Legend

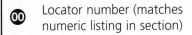

- (00) Locator number (matches numeric listing in section)
- 🦌 Wildlife viewing
- ⛺ Campsite (number matches number in campsite chart) 00
- ⛰ State Park
- 🎣 Fishing Site (number matches number in fishing chart) 00
- 🛑 Rest stop
- ▬ Interstate
- ▬ U.S. Highway
- ▬ State Highway
- ▬ County Road
- ▬ Gravel/unpaved road

Montana Trivia

Billings is nicknamed "The Magic City" because of its rapid growth since its birth. The city has doubled in size every thirty years since it was founded.

---

traders looked to the upper Missouri and Yellowstone rivers as a source of profit. At various times between 1807 and 1876, eight trading posts were located between the mouths of the Big Horn and Tongue rivers. Most were owned and operated by the American Fur Company—a firm organized in 1808 by John Jacob Astor. Rather than rely on the rendezvous system and the mountain men, the "Company" built a series of fixed posts designed to encourage the local tribes to trade at the forts. American Fur Company forts were virtual duplicates—each was about 100 square feet with cottonwood palisades and block houses at opposite corners. The forts included Fort Remon or Manuel Lisa (1807-1809), the first Fort Benton (1821), the second Big Horn Post (1824), Fort Cass (1832-1835), Fort Van Buren (1835-1843), Fort Alexander (1842-1850) and two Fort Sarpys.

Nearly all the existing accounts of the forts tell stories of a lively trade that was often filled with danger for both trader and Native American. By 1876, the fur trade was no longer profitable and the trading post was abandoned. While their presence was fleeting; they significantly impacted the lives of Native Americans and those who chose to garrison these isolated

---

FLY FISHING AT ITS FINEST

by Mike DuFresne

The fly fishing in the Billings area of south central Montana is some of the best in the state. It's so good that the Bighorn River is rated as one of the best trout fisheries in the world. Here is some information on our favorite local waters.

Bighorn River

This is the world renowned fishery that anglers are most familiar with. The portion of the river most commonly fished is a 13 mile section below the Yellowtail Dam on the Crow Indian Reservation near the small government community of Fort Smith (Yellowtail). This is approximately 90 miles southeast of Billings and 45 miles south of Hardin.

Because of the year round stable flows of cold clear water, this river sustains an incredibly

large population of aquatic insects, which in turn can support a population of catchable trout that numbers over 6,000 per mile. There is a mixture of rainbow and brown trout in the river with brown trout being the most abundant. An average fish is over 14 inches with four-year-old trout averaging 20 inches. The primary food sources are freshwater shrimp, aquatic sowbugs, midges, and incredible mayfly and caddis fly hatches.

Whether you like to fish dry flies, nymphs or streamers, this is a great river for all. With so many fish, this is also a great river to learn how to fly fish as your opportunities of catching fish are more than double any other river in Montana. A guide is always recommended for your first outing on this river to ensure the best fishing experience.

The Stillwater River

This classic freestone river is located approximately 45 miles west of Billings and flows into the Yellowstone River just outside of Columbus. This river is much more typical when picturing a Montana trout stream. A free-flowing river that is the farthest thing from still, the Stillwater has

---

places. The trading posts represented a colorful era in Montana's history.

4.

Big Horn

Seldom does such a small town have such big history. The site of this town has been occupied almost continuously since Capt. William Clark

---

fast water riffles, deep pools, large meanders, slippery boulders and incredible scenery. The best fishing is from April through September for brown and rainbow trout that readily take flies from the surface. An average fish on this river will be around ten inches with a large fish being fifteen inches or more. For a quick getaway from Billings, this is your best bet. There are at least ten public access points along over 30 miles of river. Primarily fished with a large dry fly with a bead head dropper, the fishing can be fast and furious. Streamers work well for those die-hards looking for the big one. A guided float trip in a raft is the recommended method of fishing, however, with the large amount of access, this is one that's fun to fish on your own.

The Lower Yellowstone River

The portion of the Yellowstone below Livingston holds a large population trout that are most easily caught from a drift boat. This wild and scenic river is home to rainbow, brown and cutthroat trout along with whitetail and mule deer, bald eagles, and many other furred and feathered creatures. Because of the size of the river and limited access points, the Yellowstone is best fished with a guide and a drift boat. April and May and then July to October is prime time to fish. June is usually high water month from the melting mountain snow and for much of the month is virtually unfishable. Large dry flies with droppers, streamers and late summer grasshoppers provide some incredible fishing. This is the river for you if you want to be away from the crowds and want the experience of Montana and the longest free-flowing river in the country.

Monster Lake

If you want to catch a real Monster, this one is for you. With the average fish weighing over 4 pounds, this private lake is your best shot at fish weighing in the double digits. Just a two-hour drive from Billings, Monster Lake is approximately 10 miles southeast of Cody, Wyoming. The lake is one of the richest in food in our region supporting large numbers of very big rainbow, brown, brook and even a few cutthroat trout. This 150-acre lake is limited to twelve fly fishers a day and all fish must be released. Either fished with a guide or on your own, you can count on some trophy photos to take back home.

For more information on fly fishing the local area, contact:

Bighorn Fly & Tackle Shop
485 S. 24th St West, Billings, MT 59102
Phone 656-8257
E-mail: info@bighornfly.com
Or see them on the web at
www.bighornfly.com
http://www.bighornfly.com

Montana Trivia

In 1873, 1,508,000 bison hides were shipped to St. Louis from Montana. In 1874, only 158,000 were shipped.

BILLINGS

Logan International Airport

Hilltop Rd

Wicks Ln

Lake Elmo Rd

Main St

12

Exit 452

13 Airport Rd

Rimrock Rd

212

14

Poly Dr

28

16

N 23rd

1st Ave

17th

N 27th

Park Hill Dr

30th St

32nd St

13th St

27 Grand Ave

19

15

Montana

90

Broadwater Ave

20

3

17

26

8th

5th

1st Ave

4th Ave

6th Ave

24th St W

Central Ave

21

State Ave

Exit 450

18

W 32nd

25

Monad Rd

Montana Ave

Orchard Rd

Jackson St

Riverside Rd

Sugar Ave

King Ave.

King Ave

24

Exit 446-447

Exit 450

Map not to scale

23

Billings Blvd

22

W. 32nd

90

camped here in 1806. In 1807, Manuel Lisa built a trading post here. Fort Van Buren was built near here in 1822 at the mouth of the Big Horn River. In 1876, General Gibbon and a band of 450 men crossed the Yellowstone here on their way to help an already doomed General Custer.

D William Clark
July 27, 1806

"about Sunset I Shot a very large fat buck elk from the Canoe near which I encamped, and was near being bit by a rattle Snake."

5. *Gas, Food*

Custer

No mystery where this town got its name. It was built after floods washed away the town of Junction City across the river. It served at one time as a freight station for traders hauling supplies to the Crow Indian Reservation. Prior to that it was a favorite camping spot for those traveling

to and from Fort Custer at the junction of the Bighorn and Little Bighorn Rivers.

H Junction
Custer

The frontier town of Junction was just across the Yellowstone River. It was a stage station for outfits heading for old Fort Custer which used to be twenty-five or thirty miles south of here on the Crow Reservation. The original Reservation took in everything in Montana west of the Tongue River and south of the Yellowstone.

There isn't anything left of Junction except a few unkept graves along the hillside but she was lurid in her days. Calamity Jane sojourned there awhile and helped whoop things up. Calamity was born in Missouri, raised in Virginia City, Montana, and wound up at Deadwood, South Dakota. She had quite a dazzling social career.

Several years ago they found a skeleton of a

three-horned dinosaur in the formation which makes the bluffs on the north side of the river. It must have bogged down some time before Junction did, probably a couple of million years.

6.

H Buffalo Country
West of Custer

Buffalo meant life to the Plains Indians, and the mountain Indians used to slip down from the hills for their share, too. Some tribes would toll buffalo into a concealed corral and then down them; another system was to stampede a herd over a cliff, but the sporting way was to use bows and arrows and ride them down on a trained buffalo horse.

Fat cow was the choice meat. The Indians preserved their meat long before the whites ever had any embalmed beef scandals. They made pemmican by drying and pulverizing the

BILLINGS TOUR

Since the American West's early days, Billings has hosted a cast of famous figures: Custer, Calamity Jane, Buffalo Bill, Crazy Horse, Lewis & Clark and others.

To follow Billings' official beginnings as a city, you only need to follow rivers and railroads. After Lewis & Clark finished their historic expedition across the West, numerous explorers began pushing westward along the many wild rivers, laying railroad tracks as they went.

The Northern Pacific Railroad followed the Yellowstone River, and trainloads of people followed soon after. Just a mile upriver from an established trans-shipment point on the Yellowstone and Missouri Rivers was a valley surrounded by Rimrocks and mountains—an ideal place for a settlement. And so Billings, the "Magic City" was born.

Today, you'll still find glimpses of yesterday throughout the valley. With mansions, museums, galleries and many other historic sites, this city never forgets its past.

Your tour starts at the Billings Chamber Visitor Center where you can get loads of good information on the area. The tour covers nine miles and about 25 minutes of drive time, but you will want to allow at least four hours to stop at every site along the way. Turn right out of the Visitor Center parking lot and head northwest on 27th Street toward downtown. Turn right on Montana Ave. approximately three blocks to…

1. Union Depot. The arrival of the Northern Pacific Railroad in 1882 signaled the real beginning of the private town of Billings, named for the President of the railroad, Frederick Billings.

Yellowstone Art Center

This depot, built in 1909, replaced the first temporary station. From here continue on northeast and bear left on Main Street and follow Main to…

2. Metra Park. This is the host to events such as rodeos, ice shows, sporting events, concerts and

Boothill Cemetery.

large trade shows. The grounds are the site of Montana's largest event: MontanaFair. Immediately past Metra Park you will turn left to begin winding your way up the rim. You are on…

3. Black Otter Trail. This is a scenic drive which climbs Kelly Mountain, and follows the edge of the Rimrocks where it descends to the valley. Black Otter Trail is named after a Crow chief who was killed here by a Sioux war party. One of the first things you will come upon is…

4. Boot Hill Cemetery. This cemetery marks the only remains of the original river town of Coulson (1-877-1885). Many of its occupants met with violent deaths, including Sheriff "Muggins Taylor," the army scout who first carried the news of the Custer Battle to the outside world. Continue on the trail to…

5. Yellowstone Kelly's Grave. Yellowstone Kelly, who lived from 1849 to 1928, was the epitome of a frontiersman, army scout, dispatch rider and hunter. At his own request, he is buried on Kelly Mountain overlooking the Yellowstone River, where he lived his most interesting days. Five mountain ranges can be viewed from here—clockwise from the southeast: the Big

Horns, the Pryors, the Beartooths, the Crazys, and the Snowys. Continue up the trail to the airport. Directly across from the airport is…

6. The Peter Yegen Jr. Museum. This museum houses many artifacts of early history. In the basement is an authentic Roundup Wagon and a diorama featuring pioneer life. Outside you'll find No. 1031, the last Northern Pacific Steam Engine operated in Billings. There's also a lifesize statue, the "Range Rider of the Yellowstone," depicting the days of the open range. Open Tuesday through Friday, 10:30 a.m. to 5 p.m., Sundays 2–5 p.m. Turn left out of the parking lot and catch the turn back down the Rimrocks. Follow this back to 27th Street. Bear right toward downtown. As you enter downtown you will find on your left…

7. The Yellowstone Art Center. This premier museum in a four-state region exhibits western and contemporary art from nationally and internationally acclaimed artists. Leave the museum and continue southeast on 27th Street for a block to 3rd Ave. North. Turn right here and go one block to…

8. The Alberta Bair Theater. This performing arts theater opened in January of 1987. It is now the largest performing arts theater between Minneapolis and spokane. It is also home to the Billings Symphony, Community Concerts and the Fox Committee for the performing arts. Leave the theater again on 3rd Ave. North heading southwest to Division Street. Turn left here. On your right will be …

9. The Moss Mansion. Built in 1901 for the Preston B. Moss family, the elegant home was designed by H. J. Hardenbergh, architect of the Waldorf-Astoria and Plaza Hotels in New York City. It was purchased in 1987 with original furnishings from the estate of Melville Moss. Tours are available March through October and at Christmas time. When you leave the Mansion, continue south on Division to Montana Ave. Turn left here and go to N. 28th Street. Just across the intersection to your right is…

10. The Western Heritage Center. This regional museum was originally built in 1909 as the Parmly Billings Library, and is named for the son of the founder of Billings. Exhibits change every six weeks (themes include saddle makers, steam power, quilts and western art). This museum is open Tuesday to Saturday, 10 a.m. to 5 p.m. and Sunday 1 p.m. to 5 p.m.

Partially reprinted from Billings Chamber of Commerce brochure.

---

meat, pouring marrow bone grease and oil over it, and packing it away in skin bags. It kept indefinitely, and in food value one pound was worth ten of fresh meat.

Tanned robes and rawhide were used for bedding, tepees, clothes, war shields, stretchers, travois, canoes, and bags. Horns and bones made tools and utensils. The buffalo played a prominent part in many of their religious rites and jealousy of hereditary hunting grounds brought on most of the intertribal wars.

H Junction of Big Horn and Yellowstone Rivers
West of Custer

The area which surrounds the mouth of the Big Horn River as it enters the Yellowstone 13 miles east of here is one of the most significant areas in the early history of Montana.

The Yellowstone was known universally to the Indians as Elk River, early French explorers called it Riviere Roche Jaune. The Big Horn was called Le Corne.

Captain William Clark of the Lewis and Clark Expedition, on his return trip from their journey

to the Pacific Ocean, camped on the east bank of the Big Horn River, Saturday, July 26th, 1806.

The following year, on November 21st, 1807, an expedition led by Manuel Lisa, a St. Louis fur trader, arrived at the mouth of the Big Horn River. He built a fur trading post which he named Fort Remon in honor of his two-year-old son. This was the first building erected in what is now the State of Montana. From here Lisa sent John Colter to make contact with the Indians who were in winter camp to induce them to come to his post and trade their furs for goods. On this journey Colter discovered the

Pompey's Pillar.

wonders of present-day Yellowstone National Park.

In 1876 during the Sioux and Cheyenne Indian campaign of that year, General Terry and Colonel Gibbon marched up the Big Horn River to the site of Custers defeat at the Battle of the Little Big Horn. They arrived two days after the battle. The steamer Far West, carrying supplies, plied the waters of both rivers and brought the wounded from that encounter back to Fort Abraham Lincoln, Dakota Territory.

7.

H Camp #44 of the 1873 Yellowstone Expedition
near Pompeys Pillar

In June, 1873, a Northern Pacific Railroad surveying party escorted by 1,500 soldiers, including the 7th Cavalry under the command of George Armstrong Custer, and 526 civilians, left Dakota Territory for the Yellowstone Valley to survey a route for the second transcontinental railroad.

The Lakota Sioux and Cheyenne were opposed to the railroad and clashed with the soldiers on several occasions throughout July. On August 11th, the expedition camped for a well-earned rest at this site. Five days later, shots were fired at them by six Lakota warriors hiding near Pompeys Pillar. One man later humorously reported that in the "ensuing scramble for cover, nude bodies [scattered] in all directions on the north bank. Shirts, pants and boots decorated the area along the north bank for a hundred yards" The soldiers returned fire and eventually drove the Indians away; no one was killed in the skirmish. Perhaps figuring that discretion was the better part of valor, the soldiers thereafter chose to "bear the heat rather than risk another swim in the Yellowstone" It was not reported if Custer was among those caught with his pants down by the Lakota on that hot August day in 1873.

H Pompey's Pillar
Near Pompey's Pillar

Called lishbiia Anaache or "Place Where the Mountain Lion Dwells' by the Apsaalooka (Crow) people, Pompey's Pillar was a well-known landmark to the Plains Indians. It was here, at a strategic natural crossing of the Yellowstone, or Elk River as it was known to the Apsaalooka, that the Indian people met to trade and exchange information. They painted pictographs and etched petroglyphs onto the sheer cliffs of the feature. Apsaalooka legend reports that Pompey's Pillar was once attached to the sandstone bluffs on the north side of the river. At one point, however, the rock detached itself from the cliffs and rolled across the river to it present site.

Pompey's Pillar was also a significant landmark for Euro-American explorers, fur trappers, soldiers and emigrants. It was discovered by Canadian North West Company employee Francois Larocque in 1805. A little less than a year later, on July 25, 1806, it was visited by a 12-man detachment under the command of William Clark that included Sacajawea. and her infant son. Clark carved his name and the date on the rock and named it in honor of Sacajawea's son. He was just one of hundreds of individuals who have left their marks on the rock for generations.

Pompey's Pillar is now a National Historic Landmark administered by the Bureau of Land Management and is once again a meeting place for people on the northern Great Plains.

D William Clark
July 25, 1806

The Indians hav made 2 piles of Stone on the top of this Tower. . .have engraved on the face of this rock the figures of animals &c. near which I marked my name and the day of the month & year.

D William Clark
July 25, 1806

"I employed my Self in getting pieces of the rib of a fish which was Semented within the face of the rock it is 3 feet in length tho a part of the end appears to hav been broken off."

T Pompey's Pillar
I-94 Exit 23, 30 miles east of Billings. 875-2233

How many times have you traveled somewhere and thought about who had been there before? Pompeys Pillar is like a sandstone history book that reads like a who's who of western frontier history. Look on the rockface for the remains of animal drawings created by people who used the area for rendezvous, campsites, and hunting.

Pompey's Pillar National Historic Landmark contains exceptional cultural, recreational and wildlife values. It represents the legacy of the early West and its development. At the Pillar, there is evidence of Native Americans, early explorers, fur trappers, the U.S. Cavalry, railroad development and early homesteaders, many of whom left their history embedded in this sandstone pillar. Captain William Clark, his guide, Sacagawea, her 18-month old son (nicknamed "Pompey") and a crew of 11 men stopped near the 200-foot-high rock outcropping on the return leg of the Lewis and Clark Expedition.

On July 25, 1806, Clark carved his signature and the date in the rock and recorded doing so in his journal. "I marked my name and the day of the month and year," wrote Captain William Clark in his journal on Friday, July 25, 1806. This inscription is the only surviving on-site physical remains of the Lewis and Clark Expedition. Clark named this rock Pompey's Tower. Pompy was Clark's nickname for young Baptiste Charbonneau whose mother, Sacagawea, was the party's interpreter. Pompy means "little chief" in the Shoshoni language. In 1814 the landmark was renamed when the journals of the Lewis and Clark Expedition were published. The historic signature remains today, and visitors can walk on a boardwalk to see it.

A river landmark and rendezvous point for early travelers, Pompey's Pillar stands 150 feet above the Yellowstone River. A stairway ascends up 220 steps to the top of the pillar for an outstanding view of the surrounding area. You can get a closer look at Clark's signature half way up the climb. Admission is $3 per vehicle, open Memorial Day–September. Walk-in visits are allowed in the off-season. *Reprinted from www.recreation.gov and the BLM site brochure.*

8. *Gas, Food*

Worden

Named after a prominent Montana family, Worden has also prospered in farming due to the irrigation project. Stop into the Huntley Project Museum of Irrigated Agriculture, located in Worden, for an interesting look at farming artifacts, machinery and displays.

Billings	Jan	Feb	March	April	May	June	July	Aug	Sep	Oct	Nov	Dec	Annual
Average Max. Temperature (F)	32.4	38.8	45.5	56.7	67.1	76.8	86.4	85.1	72.6	60.4	44.7	35.9	58.5
Average Min. Temperature (F)	13.9	19.4	24.6	33.9	43.4	51.7	58.1	56.8	46.9	37.3	25.9	18.1	35.8
Average Total Precipitation (in.)	0.78	0.62	1.06	1.77	2.28	2.12	1.08	0.88	1.26	1.10	0.72	0.66	14.33
Average Total SnowFall (in.)	10.3	7.2	10.1	8.9	1.7	0.0	0.0	0.0	1.1	4.0	6.6	8.5	58.4
Average Snow Depth (in.)	2	2	1	0	0	0	0	0	0	0	1	2	1

Ballantine

Ballantine arrived in eastern Montana with the railroad line. Once serving as an important railroad station, Ballantine arose in the early 1900s and Lewis Chilson soon opened the first post office.

T Huntley Project Museum of Irrigated Agriculture
2561 S. 22nd Rd., Worden

This is a great stop for visitors interested in agriculture and irrigation. The museum features a unique display of farming and irrigation machinery and artifacts and has a neat gift shop attached.

9.

Shepherd

Shepherd was named after R.E. Shepherd, owner of the Billings Land and Irrigation Company and the Merchants National Bank. This area was used for cattle ranching in the early part of the 1900s, until the creation of an irrigation canal throughout the area was built for farmlands. Many immigrants poured into the area to try and start a new life in farming, but eastern Montana is known for drought, thistle, coyotes, prairie dogs and grasshoppers, and a combination of all of these forced the land back to ranching. It has become a suburb of Billings.

10. *Gas, Food*

Huntley

The town of Huntley was established in 1877 just a mile from today's Huntley. The post office was a stopping point for travelers and traders on the Yellowstone River, and served as the base for steamboat travel on the river. Huntley still remains an area with rich farmlands.

11.

T Lake Elmo State Park
Billings. 254-1310 (summer), 247-2940 (winter)

Located in the Billings Heights area, the 64-acre Lake Elmo is a popular recreation area for locals and visitors. There is a great beach that is well maintained and features lifeguards on duty during summer high-use times. Wind surfing has become a favorite activity of this area, fishing is excellent with lots of large mouth bass, yellow perch and crappie, and the hiking/biking trail is wheel-chair accessible.

12. *Gas, Food, Lodging*

Billings

Billings, established in 1882, was named for Frederick Billings, president of the Northern Pacific Railroad, and is Montana's largest and perhaps most economically diverse city. Here you'll find the warm hospitality and rugged beauty of the West blended with the modern conveniences and opportunities of a dynamic, vigorous and progressive community.

Native Americans ventured throughout this

Montana Trivia

General George Armstrong Custer was 34th out of 34 in his graduation class at West Point.

lation doubles nearly every 30 years.

Billings' primary trading area, in excess of 125,000 square miles, is one of the largest in the United States. In addition to its roles as a regional trade, energy, and service center, Billings is the educational and medical center for the region. With two state-of-the-art hospitals, sixteen clinics, and hundreds of physicians, the area offers every major medical specialty, along with a complete range of surgical services and emergency care. The area is also home to MSU-Eastern Montana College, Rocky Mountain College, and Billings Vocational Center.

Recreational opportunities in the area are abundant. A short drive takes you to the Little Bighorn Battlefield where General Custer took his "Last Stand." Yellowstone Park is also only a brief distance away. The drive there takes you onto the scenic Beartooth Highway referred to by Charles Kuralt as "the most beautiful road in America." Though an engineering triumph as it teeters up switchbacks and hairpin curves with names like "Mae West" and "Frozen Man," it can be very tedious driving and should not be undertaken if you want to get to Yellowstone Park quickly. The highway can close without notice due to snow in this high country. The alternate route on I–90, though not as exciting or scenically beautiful, is much safer and better suited for one who is short on time.

The Billings area is surrounded by seven mountain ranges: the Pryors, Big Horns, Bulls, Snowys, Crazys, Absarokas and Beartooths. Standing on the north rim of the city, the splendor of Montana is visible all around. The city itself is home to Lake Elmo, one of Montana's state parks. Other nearby natural attractions include Pompey's Pillar, and the Pictograph Caves.

In addition to the outdoor recreational opportunities, Billings is host to hoards of entertainment. Year-round theaters host nationally known entertainers, concerts, dramatic and musical productions, as well as symphony performances. Located in the heart of Downtown Billings, the 5.12 million dollar Alberta Bair Theater serves as the hub of cultural entertainment in the city, as it is home to the Billings Community Concert Association and the Billings Symphony.

Metra, Yellowstone County's 12,000 seat arena and civic center, is located at MetraPark, the area's county fairgrounds. The arena hosts major entertainment events, as well as indoor sports events such as rodeos, ice hockey, and tractor pulls. MetraPark itself contains a 7,000 seat grandstand and horse racing track. Races run during August and September.

Billings is also equipped with a plethora of museums for those wanting to relax. The Yellowstone Art Center, The Western Heritage Center, and the Peter Yegen Jr. Museum are three of the top choices. There are also more historic sites in town than can be seen in a day. The Moss Mansion is one highlight that shouldn't be missed. Built at the turn of the century for Preston Moss, one of Montana's wealthiest men, the mansion is maintained as it was originally furnished and decorated. It cost $105,000 in 1903, a time when the average house cost was about $3,000.

Whatever your pleasure, Billings has it! From fun entertainment to exciting recreation, fine dining to excellent shopping, you will find it here.

H The Place Where the White Horse Went Down
Billings Heights area

In 1837-38 a smallpox epidemic spread from the American Fur Trading Company steamboat St. Peter which had docked at Fort Union. The terrible disease for which the Indians had no immunity eventually affected all Montana tribes. A story is told among the Crow of two young warriors returning from a war expedition who found their village stricken. One discovered his sweetheart among the dying, and both warriors, grieving over loss of friends and family, were despondent and frustrated because nothing could alter the course of events. The young warriors dressed in their finest clothing and mounted a snowwhite horse. Riding double and singing their death-songs, they drove the blind-folded horse over a cliff and landed at what is now the eastern end of the Yellowstone County Exhibition grounds. Six teenage boys and six teenage girls who were not afflicted with the disease witnessed the drama; they buried the dead warriors and left the camp. Great loss of life among the tribe followed in the wake of the epidemic. Although time has reduced the height of the cliff, the location is remembered even today as The Place Where the White Horse Went Down.

T Metra Park
308 6th Ave. N, Billings. 256-2422
or (800) 366-8538

Recreational opportunities in and around the Billings area are abundant. Metra Park is the 12,000 seat arena and civic center at the county fairgrounds. The arena hosts major entertainment events, indoor sports and rodeos. It also features a horse racing track that runs during August and September.

13.

T Rimrocks
Northern edge of Billings

The landmark that seems to stand out most in Billings are the Rimrocks. These sandstone cliffs run along the northern edge of the city and offer spectacular views of the city and the surrounding mountain ranges-the Pryors, Bighorns, Snowys, Crazys and Beartooths. The Black Otter Trail, named after a Crow Indian chief who was buried here, offers a great opportunity for exploring the Rimrocks. Along the trail, you will come across Boothill Cemetery, the site where many residents of Coulson are buried. Coulson was a rough Old West town in the 1800s and outlaws and violence was commonplace. Muggins Taylor, the army scout who spread news of Custer's defeat, is buried here along with 52 Coulson residents. Yellowstone Kelly's grave is just west of Boothill Cemetery. Kelly was known for being adventuresome and quite a frontiersman. He spoke both Crow and Sioux languages and guided the army after Custer's defeat.

T Peter Yegen Jr. Yellowstone County Museum
At Logan International Airport, Billings. 252-0163

The Museum incorporates an 1893 log cabin built by Paul McCormick, Sr., a pioneer Montana cattleman. McCormick used the cabin as a social center and hosted many lively get togethers there, including entertaining his close friend, President Teddy Roosevelt. The cabin still has its original sod roof and several artifacts belonging to the

PRYOR MOUNTAIN NATIONAL WILD HORSE RANGE

The Pryor Mountain Wild Horse Range was established after a two-year grassroots effort by citizens concerned about the long-term welfare of the Pryor Mountain horses. In 1968, interested individuals and groups convinced Interior Secretary Stewart Udall to set aside 31,000 acres in the Pryor Mountains as a public range for the wild horses. This was the first of its kind in the nation.

Unique Horses

For more than a century, the Pryor Mountains have been home to free-roaming bands of wild horses. This herd of horses is a genetically unique population. Blood typing by the Genetics Department of the University of Kentucky has indicated that these horses are closely related to the old type European Spanish horse.

As you explore the range, look for horses with unusual coloring which may correspond to their Spanish lineage, such as dun, grulla, blue roan and the rare sabino.

Also watch for primitive markings such as a dorsal stripe down their back, wither stripes, and zebra stripes on their legs. These unusual features are considered typical of Spanish characteristics.

So, where did the horses come from? The origins are unclear, but a common belief is that the horses escaped from local Native American Indian herds and eventually found a safe haven in the Pryors.

Like many wild horse populations, the Pryor horses live within family groups. As you travel throughout the Range, you may find over 25 family groups and assorted "bachelor" stallions. Most families (or harems) average 5-6 animals, with a dominant stallion, a lead mare, and a variety of other mares and young animals. Horses love to follow a good leader and the Pryor horses are no different. The Pryor stallions seem to make the daily decisions for the rest of the family group, but in other populations the decision makers are often the lead mares.

Scientific studies have shown that the genetic diversity of the horses is high and the current level of inbreeding within the population is low. In some populations, inbreeding can be a problem if the numbers of horses in the herd are too low. The Pryor population has been historically managed at a successful size of between 120 and 160 horses. The population appears to be confined to this range by both natural and manmade barriers, and thus the only source of new horses are the 20-30 foals born each year. Since the horses have few natural enemies, it is necessary to limit the number of animals. The Bureau of Land Management gathers and removes animals every 2-3 years in order to maintain a desired number of horses.

Where Can I View Wild Horses?

Most visitors will have opportunities to view wild horses along Bad Pass Highway within the Bighorn Canyon National Recreation Area. Small bands of horses are often visible from this paved road year round. Look for horses in the low elevation lands north of the Mustang Flat interpretive sign.

Adventurous visitors will find that most of the wild horses can be found in the higher mountain meadows surrounding Penn's cabin during the summer and early fall months. However, four wheel drive vehicles will be required to make the journey to the Penn's cabin vicinity.

Photography and filming opportunities in the Pryor Mountains are excellent. All photographers and filmers are cautioned to respect the comfort zone around wild horses at all times and not to, in any way disrupt the horse's natural behavior.

Casual use activities such as noncommercial still photography or recreational video taping do not require a permit or fees. Commercial filming and certain categories of commercial photography do require a permit and fees. For further information, please contact the BLM Billings Field Office.

Reprinted from BLM brochure.

American Locomotive Company #1031, It was donated to the Museum by the Northern Pacific Railroad Company in 1956. A short distance away is a statue of 1920s silent film star William Hart, in his role as Range Rider of the Yellowstone. It was sculpted by C.C. Cristadoro and presented by Hart to the people of Billings in 1923.

The Museum's Landmarks Gallery features changing exhibits which have recently included internationally known artists LeRoy Greene and J. K. Ralston. They are open Monday-Friday from 10:30 a.m.–5:00 p.m. and Saturday from 10:30 a.m. –3:00 p.m. www.pyjrycm.org. Admission is free. *Reprinted from Museum brochure.*

14. *Gas, Food*

L Holiday Inn Express
430 Cole Street in Billings. 259-8600.
www.hiexpress.com/billingsmt

15. *Gas, Food, Lodging*

T Western Heritage Center
2822 Montana Ave., Billings. 256-6809

The Western Heritage Center is located in the Billings Historic District on Montana Avenue. It resides in the old Parmly Library that was donated to the city in 1901 by Fredrick Billings Jr. The museum features wonderful historic displays of the Yellowstone River Region. There is a large collection of historic photographs, artifacts and other memorabilia that invite you to revisit the past of the frontier life. Relief maps give a good overview of the region's natural landforms. The Center also offers tours, educational programs and organizes a number of cultural events Admission is free and it is open daily year round, except closed the month of January. See their web site at www.ywhc.org for more information.

area over 10,000 years ago, leaving their traces behind through different pictographs and petroglyphs. Due to the abundance of wildlife and the flowing Yellowstone River, the area was later inhabited by the Sioux, Shoshone, Crow, and Blackfeet tribes, all at different times throughout history.

The first white inhabitants came to this area in 1877, setting up the first trade center and McAndow's store, and they called the town Coulson. Coulson was the largest early settlement on the Upper Yellowstone at that time. They set up a ferry crossing across the Yellowstone River which made the passing from the army base of Fort Custer to Bozeman possible. They made a prosperous living selling food, grain and goods to soldiers passing through.

The city is nicknamed "The Magic City," as it developed "like magic" during the railroad's westward expansion. From its humble beginnings as a railhead for the Northern Pacific, Billings has blossomed into a sophisticated city whose popu-

McCormick family. An observation platform covers the lower addition, giving a breathtaking view of the Yellowstone Valley, including the city of Billings and the snow-capped Beartooth, Pryor, Crazy and Bighorn mountain ranges.

The permanent collection of the Museum contains over 20,000 artifacts dating from prehistory through the Fur Trade Era, the Post-Reservation Period and both World Wars. The Museum's extensive collection of Plains Indian artifacts includes feather bonnets, coups sticks, pipes and pipe bags, a rare dog travois, moccasins, parfleche bags, articles of clothing, saddles, and many other items of everyday use. Cowboy memorabilia includes saddles, chaps, bridles, spurs, firearms, branding irons and other western gear from early area cowboys. Everyday house hold goods display what life was like for the area's pioneers. The facility has several thousand historic photographs depicting local and regional history. Located on the Museum grounds is one of the last steam switch engines to operate in the Billings yards,

T Yellowstone Art Museum
401 N. 27th St. in downtown Billings. 256-6804.
http://yellowstone.artmuseum.org

There is no lack of cultural experiences in Billings. The Yellowstone Art Museum resides in the restored old jailhouse, and over the years it has acquired a reputation as one of the finest contemporary art museums in the Northern Rockies. The large permanent collection offers an array of some of the most important artists working in the west. The temporary galleries show interesting exhibitions of international acclaim, and change throughout the year. The museum also features different educational programs and classes for all ages.

More than a snapshot, more than a picture, the Yellowstone Art Museum is a rich tapestry of the visions and voices that make up the West. It has quickly acquired a reputation as the finest contemporary art museum in the Northern Rockies. With a Permanent Collection of more than 1,900 pieces and temporary galleries which house exhibitions of international acclaim, the museum represents the most comprehensive resource in this region for the appreciation of 20th Century art.

The museum's Permanent Collection encompasses a wide range of aesthetic experiences. The Montana Gallery is home to some of the most important artists currently working in the West. With sculpture by Deborah Butterfield, paintings by Ted Waddell, and drawings by Bill Stockton, the Montana Collection represents a thorough cross-section of today's most interesting visual expression.

The Virginia Snook Collection, in the gallery of the same name, is the largest publicly held collection of author and illustrator Will James' work in the United States. It extends the museum's scope and broadens its appeal to visitors who identify with the traditions of the west. Also included in the Snook Collection are works by C.M. Russell, Joseph Henry Sharp, and other notable historic artists. *Source: Museum brochure*

ON THE TRAIL OF LEWIS AND CLARK

It is on this stretch that the only physical evidence of the Lewis and Clark Expedition can be found. Clark reached a large sandstone landmark he named Pompy's Tower after Sacajawea's son. Here he carved his name and the date and climbed to the top of the tower. His carving can still be seen today.

Big Ice Cave is one of the favorite destinations in the Pryors. A picnic area is only a short distance from the cave.

WILD HORSES AND MORE!

Pryor Mountains

In the extreme southeast corner of Carbon County you'll find one of the last remaining herds of wild horses in the country. The 44,000 acre Pryor Mountains National Wild Horse Range was set aside by the Secretary of the Interior in 1968.

Theories of where these horses originated are varied. Some believe they are descendants of those brought to the region by Spanish conquistadors in the 16th century. Others believe they are escaped from domestic herds of local ranchers. Probably, they are a mix of both. Common mustang social units form around a dominant stud, his harem of mares, and their foals.

Getting to them isn't easy, but the trip is worth it. The best route through Montana is via Hwy 310 south out of Laurel. Follow that for 50 miles to Warren. Another 20 miles of gravel road will put you in the canyons of the Pryors.

If you want to go the whole way on paved road, continue on past Warren to Lovell, WY. Just on the east side of town you'll see the turnoff to Hwy. 37. Follow this to the Bighorn Recreation area. If you are more adventurous you can take the turnoff to Barry's Landing.

While exploring this area, watch for Bighorn sheep. They have been restocked in the Pryors and are plentiful.

Keep your eyes open for teepee rings left by ancient tribes. If you look hard enough, you may find pictographs or other archeological evidence of civilizations past.

There is also an abundance of caves here. Big Ice Cave is the most notable. These caves are usually gated and closed off to prevent vandalism. However the Forest Service does conduct weekend tours of Big Ice Cave during the summer. Access these caves from Warren on a long gravel road. When (if) you reach the caves continue on for a short distance to Dry Head Vista. Here you will find a spectacular panorama of the Bighorn Canyon area dropping away for over 4,000 feet.

For access to these caves and additional information about them, contact the Custer National Forest Supervisor's Office in Billings.

Write to them at 2602 1st Ave. N., Billings, MT 59103 or call them at (406) 657-6361.

The Pryor Mountains Are Unique

The Pryor Mountains were named after Sergeant Nathaniel Pryor of the Lewis and Clark Expedition which traversed the nearby Yellowstone River Valley in 1806. The Pryor mountain range is actually an extension of the Bighorn Mountains but is separated from the Bighorns by the Bighorn Canyon.

The Pryor Mountains are unique in many ways. Some of the more notable aspects are the rainfall/snowfall zones and related vegetation from the southern foothill regions to the highest points in the mountain range. Annual rainfall varies from less than five inches in the foothills to twenty inches in the high country. Most of the southern portion of the Wild Horse Range is northern cold desert country.

Differences in rainfall/snowfall contribute to the most diverse plant community in Montana. As you move from the southern desert portion to the upper, lush, sub-alpine portions of the Pryor Mountains, you can see the progression of desert, low bushes to fir trees and grasses. In between these zones is a graduation of plant species. In addition, the bladderpod and Shoshonea are two examples of rare and sensitive plants that are found in the Pryors.

For centuries, the Pryors were home to small bands of Native American people. The warm, dry southern slopes provided a favorable environment during the harsh winter months, while the high elevation lands were occupied at other times of the year. This environment provided a variety of both plant and animal foods. Bighorn sheep, mule deer, bison and elk provided meat and skins while berries, roots and possibly ants supplemented diets.

Hard stone deposits called chert, exist in the Pryors and were used by Native Americans to make projectile points and scraping tools. In fact, the Crow Indian tribe used to refer to the Pryors as the "Arrow-head" mountains.

The Crow Tribe considers many sites within the Pryors sacred. Cultural resources are protected by federal law on public lands and should be left as found for scientific investigation and enjoyment by future visitors.

Excerpted from BLM pamphlet.

Pryor Mountains south of Billings

T Moss Mansion
914 Division St., Billings. 256-5100

The Moss Mansion is a unique historical look into the wealthy lifestyle that was present in the early 1900s. This turn-of-the-century mansion built in 1902 for Preston B. Moss, a Billings banker, has become a monument to the wealth of Montana in those early years. The house cost $105,000 to build when the average house cost only $3000. The three-story home contains original furnishings of Preston B. Moss and the grounds are well-kept with magnificent gardens of perennials, annuals and roses. The architect was Henry Janeway Hardenbergh, designer of the original Waldorf Astoria, Astoria, Plaza, and other fine hotels. Regular tours are also available. The mansion is open to the public with admission charged.

T Alberta Bair Theater
Broadway & 3rd Ave. N, Billings. 256-6052

Billings is a great spot to catch some local entertainment. Year-round theatres host nationally known entertainers, concerts, dramatic and musical productions as well as symphony performances. Located in the heart of Downtown Billings is the Alberta Bair Theater that is home to the Billings Community Concert Association and the Billings Symphony.

T Museum of Women's History
2423 Pine, Billings. 245-4871 or 657-2191

16. *Attraction, Food, Lodging,*

T Mindworks Museum
1500 N. 30th St., MSU Billings. 657-2242

L Cherry Tree Inn
823 N. 28th St., Billings. 252-5603 or 800) 237-5882. www.billingscherrytreeinn.com

The Cherry Tree Inn of Billings was built by George Washington. That is George Washington's namesake, thus the clever name for his business. The current owners have expanded the Washington connection by decorating the Inn's lobby with art depicting Colonial america and the Revolutionary War. They even provide an excellent lending library on Colonial america for guests. The Inn is located near the Billings Medical Center, Downtown, MSU, and the airport. You'll also find everything you need for a comfortable stay including a free continental breakfast, 24-hour coffee, elevator, electronic security, non-smoking rooms, 24-hour desk, kitchenettes, and guest laundry. Small pets are welcome, and they have very affordable rates. It's a great place to stay!

17. *Gas, Food, Lodging*

18. *Attraction*

T Sacrifice Cliff
Across the Yellowstone River south of Billings.

Sacrifice Cliff is unmarked but is located south of the Yellowstone River, opposite Boothill Cemetery. This legendary cliff of the Rimrocks, was believed to be a place of meditation for Crow Indian boys coming of age. A story is also told of two teen Crow brothers who returned to their tribe to find that their sweethearts and much of their tribe had fallen victim to smallpox. They were so filled with anguish that they blindfolded their horses and rode over the 60-foot cliff. Another version of the story says that a Crow party found their village destroyed by the deadly small pox and rode off the cliff in despair.

19. *Gas, Food*

20. *Gas, Food*

21. *Gas, Food, Lodging*

22. *Gas, Food, Lodging*

23. *Gas, Food, Lodging*

24. *Gas, Food, Lodging*

L Days Inn
843 Parkway Ln., Billings. 252-4007 or (800) 329-7466.
www.thedaysinn.com/billings05904;
5904@hotel.cendant.net

Enjoy the friendly atmosphere and courteous staff at Day's Inn on your next business or leisure trip. The hotel offers free high-speed wireless Internet in all rooms, a free computer and printing workstation, guest laundry, and a large hot tub. Clean, quiet rooms include expanded cable, HBO, coffeemaker, hairdryer, and data port phones with spa-like bathrooms showcasing Sol Terre bath products, exceptional lighting, waterpick showerheads, and curved shower rods providing a large showering area. Business rooms feature king-size beds, a large desk and end table, refrigerator, microwave, and iron/ironing board. In the morning, wake up to the expanded continental breakfast in the recently enlarged breakfast room that also includes a small meeting area accommodating up to 15 people. Don't forget to pick up your free USA Today! Pets are welcome – see their listing on www.petswelcome.com.

25. *Food*

26. *Gas, Food, Lodging*

27. *Gas, Food*

28. *Gas, Food*

M Rocky Mountain College
1511 Poly Drive, Billings. 761-7885 or (800) (877) 6259, www.rocky.edu.

Rocky Mountain College a small highly respected liberal arts college, was founded in 1878 and is Montana's first institution of higher learning based in Christianity. RMC offers students a uniquely integrated curriculum that joins professional programs and traditional liberal arts education for approximately 800 students.

29.

T Pictograph Cave State Park
I-90, exit 452, south of Lockwood, Billings. 247-2940

Pictograph Cave State Park is a truly unique glimpse into the past and a dreamland for archaeologists. Pictograph and Ghost Caves served as shelters for Native American inhabitants over 5,000 years ago. They would stop here to rest during hunting trips to make tools and left behind over 100 paintings that line the back walls in red, black and white. In 1937, excavations began in the caves, resulting in a huge finding of Native American artifacts, tools, jewelry and much more. This excavation also discovered the pictographs that date back to between 500 and 1900 A.D., depicting animals, men on horses, rituals and costumes just to name a few.

The park is open April through October. There is a day use fee.

30. *Attraction*

T Oscar's Dreamland Yesteryear Museum
3100 Harrow Dr., Billings. 656-0966

Oscar Cooke had a dream of building the largest steam tractor museum in the world. He did. For years the museum had no other in the world like it. When Oscar and his wife passed away, his daughter was forced to sell off many of the pieces to pay off the confiscatory estate taxes imposed by the government. There is still enough here to fill a day looking.

T Riverfront Park
I-90 Exit 446 to S. Billings Ave., Billings.

Located on the Yellowstone River, this park is a great place to relax, walk, jog, fish and enjoy a picnic.

31. *Lodging*

T Zoo Montana
2100 Shiloh Road, Billings. 652-8100

If you haven't gotten your fill of wildlife viewing just driving around the state, visit this 70-acre zoo situated along the Canyon Creek. Zoo Montana is the only zoo in Montana that features animals that reside in a natural habitat wildlife park. They specialize in animals that can survive the climate in Montana, and also have a botanical gardens. The zoo is still in the early stages of development, but definitely worth the trip. Kids and adults will enjoy the Siberian tigers, otters, children's zoo and sensory garden. The zoo also has a farm animal petting area and a discovery center with hands-on exhibits that kids love, a one mile nature loop and a wetlands area. Open all year at 10 a.m. daily. Closed on major holidays. Take I-90 exit 446 to King Avenue West. Follow King Avenue West to Shiloh Road. Follow Shiloh Road south approximately 1 1/2 miles to zoo.

32. *Gas*

Lodge Grass
Lodge Grass is the first full service gas stop on I-90, if you are heading from Wyoming, and is part of the Crow Indian Reservation. Located on the Little Bighorn River, Lodge Grass was named for Lodge Grass Creek that flows into the Little Bighorn. The Crows used this area as hunting grounds in the early days and they called the

Creek "Greasy Grass" because of the rich grass that was said to make the animals fat. The words "grease" and "lodge" are very similar in the Crow language, and the name of the creek was interpreted as Lodge Grass instead of Greasy Grass by accident. The grazing lands here are still lush and widely used by ranchers.

A nice stop on your way through town is White Arm Park in town, and Willow Creek Reservoir, just southwest of town. Every 4th of July, Lodge Grass hosts the Valley of the Chiefs Celebration, a four day event.

Wyola
Found near the Little Big Horn River on the Crow Indian Reservation, Wyola lies just ten miles from the Wyoming border. The community's post office was established in 1911, and today, the town serves as an important cattle shipping point for local ranches.

33. *Gas, Food, Lodging,*

H Garryowen
I-90 Exit 514

Garryowen, the old Irish tune, was the regimental marching song of the 7th Cavalry, General Custer's command.

The Battle of the Little Big Horn commenced in the valley just east of here June 25, 1876, after Custer had ordered Major Marcus A. Reno to move his battalion into action against the hostile Sioux and Cheyennes, led by Gall, Crazy Horse, Two Moons and Sitting Bull.

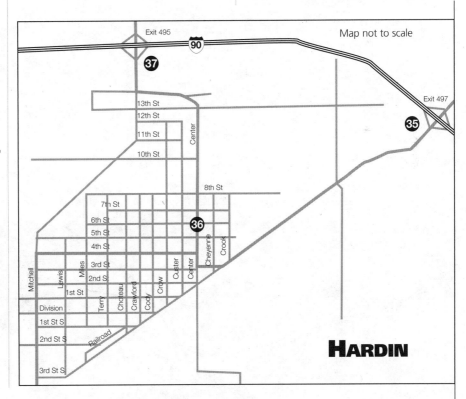

HARDIN

Hardin	Jan	Feb	March	April	May	June	July	Aug	Sep	Oct	Nov	Dec	Annual
Average Max. Temperature (F)	33.1	40.8	48.8	61.0	71.8	81.0	90.4	89.2	76.9	64.7	47.6	36.9	61.9
Average Min. Temperature (F)	7.1	13.9	21.3	31.5	41.6	49.7	55.2	52.9	42.6	31.8	20.3	10.8	31.5
Average Total Precipitation (in.)	0.55	0.38	0.62	1.38	1.83	1.98	1.12	0.78	1.19	0.94	0.51	0.43	11.71
Average Total SnowFall (in.)	6.0	2.9	3.8	2.5	0.1	0.0	0.0	0.0	0.3	0.4	1.7	4.4	21.9
Average Snow Depth (in.)	2	1	1	0	0	0	0	0	0	0	0	1	1

Reno, with 112 men, came out of the hills about 2 1/2 miles southeast of here and rode within 1/4 mile of the Indian camp where he was met by the hostiles who outnumbered the soldiers ten to one. Dismounting his men, Reno formed a thin skirmish line west across the valley from the timber along the river. After severe losses he was forced to retreat to high ground east of the Little Big Horn where he was joined by Major Benteen's Command. The combined force stood off the Indians until the approach of Gibbon's column from the north on the following day caused the hostiles to pull out. Reno and Benteen were not aware of Custer's fate until the morning of the 27th.

34. *Gas, Food, Miscellaneous*

Crow Agency

The Crow Nation spans across 3,565 square miles and is spread out to seven different communities-Crow Agency, Wyola, Lodge Grass, Garryowen, St. Xavier, Fort Smith and Pryor. Crow Agency serves as the Crow Reservation's agency headquarters-taking care of tribal management and government. Every August Crow Agency hosts one of Montana's largest powwows during the Crow Fair celebration. The Little Bighorn College is a tribal community college that has a great tourism department and offers cultural tours of the area.

T Little Bighorn Battlefield National Monument
Highway 212 (I-90 Exit 510), Crow Agency. 638-2621

Located 15 miles east of Hardin, this national monument, commemorates the Battle of the Little Bighorn. In the visitor center, a thorough account is presented, explaining historical aspects of the battle while displays and artifacts reinforce the realism of the scene. The battle claimed the lives of 260 soldiers and military personnel of the Seventh Cavalry under Custer's command as well as 99 men under the command of Major Benteen. Between 60 to 100 Sioux and Cheyenne were killed out of several thousand. Guided tours of the battlefield are available. Open year round: Spring & Fall 8 a.m.–6 p.m.. Summer 8 a.m.–7:30 p.m., Winter 8 a.m.–4:30 p.m. $6 per vehicle.

T Custer's Last Stand Reenactment
Hardin Chamber of Commerce, 665-3577 or toll free at 888-450-3577

Watch history come alive! Feel the whirlwinds of epic forces clashing on the high plains of Montana. Relive history as warriors of the Sioux, Cheyenne and Arapaho fight the Seventh Cavalry at Custer's Last Stand Reenactment.

Surrounded by the vast sky and rolling hills of Montana, you have a front row seat to watch galloping warriors battle charging cavalry troops to the last man! Each performance reenacts the most famous and mysterious battle in American history. See legendary leaders portrayed in the context of history—Sitting Bull, medicine man of the Hunkpapa Sioux; Crazy Horse, fearless Lakota war chief and conqueror of General Crook on the Rosebud; George Armstrong Custer, flamboyant Civil War hero and controversial Plains Indian fighter.

You are there and participate in the sweep of epic American adventure as sight, sound and smell bring the past alive. Experience history that is real. History you can taste, more powerful and exciting than television, movies or video games!

Custer's Last Stand Reenactment is history alive. Crow Tribal elder and historian, Joe Medicine Crow, has crafted a script based on translations of Native American oral histories retold for generations. The narrative portrays nations on the move and cultures colliding. See firsthand the struggles of the Sioux, the Cheyenne, the Crow, and the Americans. Share the epic of the West beginning more than two hundred years ago. See the buffalo culture of the Plains Indian. See direct descendants of fighting warriors in full regalia attack and destroy the Seventh Cavalry in the great Sioux War of 1876!

World fascination with the Battle of the Little

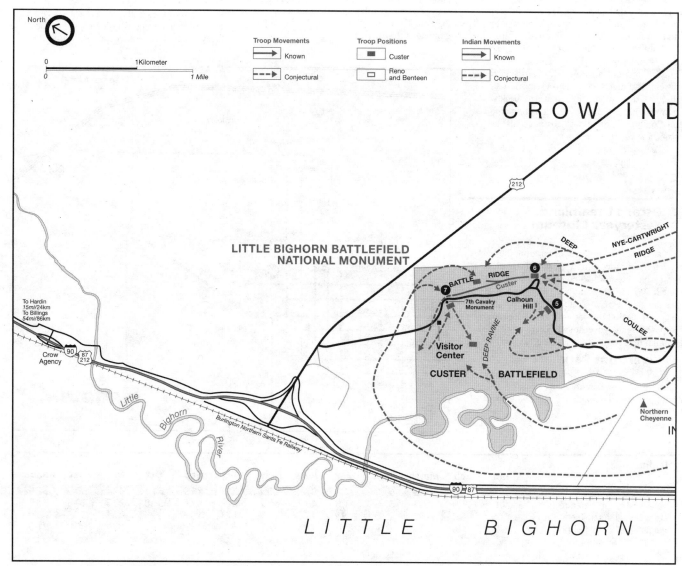

Big Horn has never been more intense. Custer's Last Stand Reenactment has been the focus of two A&E productions, CNN and BBC coverage, and filming for the Hollywood movie *Legend of Crazy Horse*. Don't miss this performance, listed for five years as one of the "Top 100 Events in America" by Destinations Magazine. Witness, in person, the excitement which has attracted hundreds of journalists and film makers, enthralled Americans and brought visitors from Canada, Mexico, China, Great Britain, France, Australia, and Germany.

Meet Indian warriors, face to face. Shake hands with U.S. Cavalry troopers. Talk to General Custer.

Experience living history. Walk traders row on the reenactment grounds. Sample Native American food and shop for unique Native American and cavalry merchandise. Come and watch, or come in costume and dance at the 1876 Grand Ball. Enjoy Little Bighorn Days and the other special events that surround Custer's Last Stand Reenactment.

As one recent Reenactment visitor exclaimed, "it's like really being there—smack dab in the middle of history!"

For more information, visit the Reenactment on the world wide web at: http: //www. mcn. net/~custerfight, or send email to custerfight@mcn.net. For tickets call 1-888-450-3577 or 406-665-3577.—*Reprinted from Hardin Chamber of Commerce brochure.*

M Crow Reservation

Of the Crow tribe's approximately 9,300 enrolled members, about 75 percent live on or near the reservation. Eighty-five percent speak Crow as their first language.

The Crow Indians derived their name from the Hidatsa tribes, their ancestors who were originally from the area along the headwaters of the Mississippi. The Hidatsa word "Absarokee" is translated as the "Children of the Large Beaked Bird", referred to by the white man as the Crow. The Crow split from the larger tribe in the early 1600s, and resided in the Black Hills of South Dakota. Because their lifestyle was dependent on hunting, the Crow region continued to expand, and by the late 1700s, they had moved to the banks of the Yellowstone and Bighorn Rivers. The Crow have been known as hunters and horse people, and from the beginning they managed to maintain friendly relations with the white man, and formed a strong alliance. Their prominent leader Chief Plenty Coups promoted education and peace among the reservation, and spoke out for peace among all races. The reservation was established in 1851.

M Little Big Horn College

1 Forestry Lane, Crow Agency. 638-3104. www.lbhc.cc.mt.us

Little Big Horn College is a public two year college chartered by the Crow Tribe of Indians. It offers a number of associate degrees and other areas, with a strong emphasis on college preparatory programs. The campus is located in the capital of the Crow Indian Reservation and has an enrollment of approximately 300 students.

35.

Hardin

Hardin was established in 1907 and named after Samuel Hardin, a rancher and early settler who lived south of Hardin, in Ranchester, Wyoming. As one of the last areas in the Montana plains to be settled, Hardin was originally set up by the Lincoln Land Company as a trading spot alongside the railroad. Samuel Hardin was a good friend of the Lincoln Land Company's president. Hardin was named Bighorn County seat in 1913, and by 1922 the town was well established with a developed business district.

Ranching and farming are still popular in this area today. Hardin is a great base camp for The Little Bighorn Battlefield, visits to Bighorn Canyon National Recreation Area and the many other area

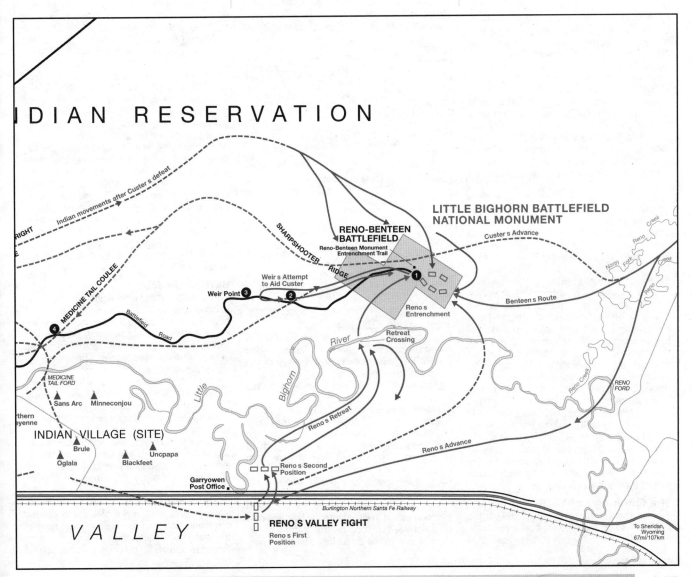

A Clash of Cultures

Little Bighorn Battlefield National Monument memorializes one of the last armed efforts of the Northern Plains Indians to preserve their ancestral way of life. Here in the valley of the Little Bighorn River on two hot June days in 1876, more than 260 soldiers and attached personnel of the U.S. Army met defeat and death at the hands of several thousand Lakota and Cheyenne warriors. Among the dead were Lt. Col. George Armstrong Custer and every member of his immediate command. Although the Indians won the battle, they subsequently lost the war against the white man's efforts to end their independent, nomadic way of life.

The Battle of the Little Bighorn was but the latest encounter in a centuries-long conflict that began with the arrival of the first Europeans in North America. That contact between Indian and white cultures had continued relentlessly, sometimes around the campfire, sometimes at treaty grounds, but more often on the battlefield. It reached its peak in the decade following the Civil War, when settlers resumed their vigorous westward movement. These western emigrants, possessing little or no understanding of the Indian way of life, showed slight regard for the sanctity of hunting grounds or the terms of former treaties. The Indians' resistance to those encroachments on their domain only served to intensify hostilities.

In 1868, believing it "cheaper to feed than to fight the Indians," representatives of the U.S. Government signed a treaty at Fort Laramie, WY., with the Lakota, Cheyenne, and other tribes of the Great Plains, by which a large area in eastern Wyoming was designated a permanent Indian reservation. The government promised to protect the Indians "against the commission of all depredations by people of the United States."

Peace, however, was not to last. In 1874 gold was discovered in the Black Hills, the heart of the new Indian reservation. News of the strike spread quickly, and soon thousands of eager gold seekers swarmed into the region in violation of the Fort Laramie treaty. The army tried to keep them out, but to no avail. Efforts to buy the Black Hills from the Indians, and thus avoid another confrontation, also proved unsuccessful. In growing defiance, the Lakota and Cheyenne left the reservation and resumed raids on settlements and travelers along the fringes of Indian domain. In December 1875, the Commissioner of Indian Affairs ordered the tribes to return before January 31, 1876, or be treated as hostiles "by the military force." When the Indians did not comply, the army was called in to enforce the order.

Maj. Marcus A. Reno was Custer's second in command. His handling of the retreat from the valley during the Little Bighorn fight was severely criticized. An 1879 court of inquiry exonerated him from any direct responsibility for the defeat, but the stigma of the controversy haunted him for the rest of his life.

The Campaign of 1876

The army's campaign against the Lakota and Cheyenne called for three separate expeditions-one under Gen. George Crook from Fort Fetterman in Wyoming Territory, another under Col. John Gibbon from Fort Ellis in Montana Territory, and the third under Gen. Alfred H. Terry from Fort Abraham Lincoln in Dakota Territory. These columns were to converge on the Indians concentrated in southeastern Montana under the leadership of Sitting Bull, Crazy Horse, and other war chiefs.

Crook's troopers were knocked out of the campaign in mid-June when they clashed with a large Lakota-Cheyenne force along the Rosebud River and were forced to withdraw. The Indians, full of confidence at having thrown back one of the army's columns, moved west toward the Little Bighorn River. Meanwhile, Terry and Gibbon met on the Yellowstone River near the mouth of the Rosebud. Hoping to find the Indians in the Little Bighorn Valley, Terry ordered Custer and the 7th Cavalry up the Rosebud to approach the Little Bighorn from the south. Terry himself would accompany Gibbon's force back up the Yellowstone and Bighorn Rivers to approach from the north.

The 7th Cavalry, numbering about 600 men, located the Indian camp at dawn on June 25. Custer, probably underestimating the size and fighting power of the Lakota and Cheyenne forces, divided his regiment into three battalions. He retained five companies under his immediate command and assigned three companies each to Maj. Marcus A. Reno and Capt. Frederick W. Benteen. A twelfth was assigned to

0 10 20 Kilometers
0 10 20 Miles

Terry-Gibbon meeting
June 21   GIBBON

TERRY AND GIBBON

Yellowstone River

Custer separates from Terry
June 22

GIBBON River

TERRY

CUSTER

Creek

Battle of Little Bighorn
June 25, 1876

Bighorn River

Little Bighorn River

Davis Ck.

Rosebud

Terry and Gibbon arrive
June 26

Reno Creek

Crow's Nest

Indian Village

Battle of Rosebud
June 17, 1876

Lodge Grass Creek

WOLF MOUNTAINS

River

CROOK

Tongue River

Otter Creek

MONTANA
WYOMING

guard the slow-moving pack train.

Benteen was ordered to scout the bluffs to the south, while Custer and Reno headed toward the Indian village in the valley of the Little Bighorn. When near the river, Custer turned north toward the lower end of the encampment.

Reno, ordered to cross the river and attack, advanced down the valley to strike the upper end of the camp. As he neared the present site of Garryowen Post Office, a large force of Lakota warriors rode out from the southern edge of the Indian village to intercept him. Forming his men into a line of battle, Reno attempted to make a stand, but there were just too many Indians. Outflanked, he was soon forced to retreat in disorder to the river and take up defensive positions on the bluffs beyond. Here he was joined by Benteen, who had hur-

ried forward under orders from Custer to "Come on; Big village, be quick, bring packs."

No one knew precisely where Custer and his command had gone, but heavy gunfire to the north indicated that he too had come under attack. As soon as ammunition could be distributed, Reno and Benteen put their troops in motion northward. An advance company under Capt. Thomas B. Weir marched about a mile downstream to a high hill (afterwards named Weir Point), from which the area now known as the Custer battlefield was visible. By now the firing had stopped and nothing could be seen of Custer and his men.

When the rest of the soldiers arrived on the hill, they were attacked by a large force of Indians, and Reno ordered a withdrawal to the original position on the bluffs overlooking the Little Bighorn. Here these seven companies entrenched and held their defenses throughout that day and most of the next, returning the Indians' fire and successfully discouraging attempts to storm their position. The siege ended finally when the Indians withdrew upon learning of the approach of the columns under Terry and Gibbon.

Meantime, Custer had ridden into history and legend. His precise movements after separating from Reno have never been determined, but vivid accounts of the battle by Indians who participated in it tell how his command was surrounded and destroyed in fierce fighting. Northern Cheyenne Chief Two Moon recalled that "the shooting was quick, quick. Poppop-pop very fast. Some of the soldiers were down on their knees, some standing.... The smoke was like a great cloud, and everywhere the Sioux went the dust rose like smoke. We circled all around him, swirling like water around a stone. We shoot, we ride fast, we shoot again. Soldiers drop, and horses fall on them."

In the battle, the 7th Cavalry lost the five companies (C, E, F, 1, and Q under Custer, about 210 men Of the other companies of the regiment, under Reno and Benteen, 53 men were killed and 52 wounded. The Indians lost no more than 100 killed. They removed most of their dead from the battlefield when the large village broke up. The tribes and families scattered, some going north, some going south. Most of them returned to the reservations and surrendered in the next few years.

Battlefield Tour

The Battle of the Little Bighorn continues to fascinate people around the world. For most, it has come to illustrate a part of what Americans know as their western heritage. Heroism and suffering, brashness and humiliation, victory and defeat, triumph and tragedy these are the things people come here to ponder.

The battlefield tour begins at the Reno-Benteen site, 4.5 miles from the visitor center. The exhibit panels are best viewed in sequence on the return trip. Stop at the visitor center before starting your tour; park rangers can answer your questions and help you plan your day. Museum exhibits and literature also help to explain these historical events. The tour stop descriptions are keyed to the map.

1. Reno-Benteen: Battlefield Major Reno, leading three companies of Custer's divided command, attacked the Indian village lying in the valley on the afternoon of June 25, 1876. Forced to retreat, his battalion took position on these bluffs, where it was soon joined by Captain Benteen's men. Until the Indians left the next day, Reno and Benteen were surrounded in this position.

2. Custer's Lookout: From the ridge on your right (east), Custer watched Reno's attack underway in the valley. He also saw, for the first time, a portion of the enormous Indian village in the valley, perhaps the largest gathering of Plains Indians ever seen. The estimated 1,000 lodges held approximately 7,000 people; at least 1,500 were warriors. In this vicinity Custer sent back the first of two messengers with orders for Captain McDougall and the pack train to reinforce him. From here Custer's five-company battalion continued marching northward, trying to locate the upper end of the village. The marble marker honors Vincent Charley, farrier of Company D, who was killed in this area during Reno's retreat.

3. Weir Point: Late on the afternoon of June 25, Capt. Thomas Weir led his company to this hill, where he was soon joined by other companies of Reno's command. Although heavy firing had been heard earlier, only dust and great numbers of Indians moving on the hills to the north could be seen. The Indians soon spotted the cavalry on Weir Point and attacked, pushing Reno and Benteen back to their first position on the bluffs.

4. Medicine Tall Ford: At this point the Little Bighorn River's low banks and shallow depth offered Custer his first opportunity to cross into the Indian village. Indian accounts indicate that at least part of Custer's battalion came to the ford, whether to attack or simply to reconnoiter is not known. Perhaps as many as three of the companies remained on Nye-Cartwright Ridge, probably to attract Benteen. At first only a small number of warriors defended the ford from the west side. They were soon reinforced, compelling the troopers to fall back. Soon hundreds of warriors, released from the fight with Reno, pushed across the ford and pursued Custer's command onto the hills.

5. Calhoun Ridge: Indian accounts, supported by archeological evidence, suggest that one of the companies charged into the coulee on your left to break up the massed warriors. The soldiers came under heavy fire and were forced back to the ridge, where most were killed. Lame White Man, a Cheyenne, led the attack; he fell a short time later.

6. Calhoun Hill: Markers here show where members of Company L were overwhelmed by Lakota warriors. As you proceed along Battle Ridge, you will see many markers along the right (east) side. For the most part these represent the men of Capt. Miles Keogh's Company 1. A Lakota force, led by the famed warrior Crazy Horse, struck Keogh's company, now combined with the survivors of C and L Companies, as they fled toward Custer Hill. Keogh and most of his soldiers perished here.

7. Custer Hill: Here Companies E and F, along with a few survivors from the other three companies, reunited to make a stand. The markers scattered on the low ridge below, toward the river, may represent a short-lived attempt to stem Indians advancing from the west. The cluster of markers within the fence shows

where the last remnant of Custer's battalion fell. Custer, his brothers Tom and Boston, and his nephew Autie Reed were all found in this group.

On June 28, the bodies of Custer and his men were buried in great haste at or near the places they had fallen. These shallow graves were improved in the next few years. In 1881, those graves that could be found were reopened and the bones reinterred in a common grave around the base of the memorial shaft bearing the names of the soldiers and civilians killed in the battle. The remains of 11 officers and two civilians already had been exhumed for reburial elsewhere at the request of relatives. Custer's remains were reburied at the U.S. Military Academy in West Point, N.Y., on October 10, 1877.

The Lakota and Cheyenne warriors killed in the battle, estimated at between 60 and 100, were removed from the field by friends and relatives.

Little Bighorn Battlefield National Monument lies within the Crow Indian Reservation in southeastern Montana, one mile west of I-90/U.S. 87. Crow Agency is two miles north. Billings, Mont., is 65 miles northwest, and Sheridan, WY., is 70 miles to the south.

No camping or picnicking facilities are in the

Tombstones mark the spots where cavalrymen fell.

park. Federal law prohibits the removal or disturbance of any artifact, marker, relic, or historic feature. Metal detecting on park land or adjacent Indian lands is prohibited. Remember, you are in rattlesnake country; stay on the pathways while walking the battlefield. Rangers will offer prompt assistance in case of accidents, but you can prevent them from happening by being cautious.

For more information write: Superintendent, Little Bighorn Battlefield National Monument, RO. Box 39, Crow Agency, MT 59022; Call: 406-638-2621; or Internet: www.nps.gov/libi.

Reprinted from National Park Service Brochure

activities and sites. Little Bighorn Days is a four day festival that takes place every year towards the end of July, featuring Custers Last Stand Re-enactment which is based on Crow Tribal Elder Joseph Medicine Crow's translation of Native American writings and talks dating back 200 years ago. With a staged battle occurring in nearby plains, visitors can see a first hand account of what the battle was like. The festival also features ethnic food and wonderful performances.

T Big Horn County Historical Museum & Visitors Center
I-90, exit 497, Hardin. 665-1671

Situated on 24 acres, the Big Horn County Historical Museum was established in 1979. The Museum complex consisting of twenty permanent buildings represents the interest and involvement that local residents, the business community, the Big Horn County Historical Society, the Historical Museum Foundation, and local and state government have taken to preserve, exhibit and interpret the areas past.

As you walk through the buildings that make up the museum, you are walking through the pages of history and touching the footsteps of such people as the first Americans who roamed the high plains in search of buffalo; traders and settlers that came in search of adventure; and the early day homesteaders who toiled out a living by farming and raising livestock. They all wrote their chapters

Included in the many attractions are the main exhibit building/state visitor center, 1911 farmhouse, LaForge Cabin, barn and blacksmith shop, farm exhbit area, Corinth store and post office, Fly Inn, Fort Custer stage station, Christ Evangelical Lutheran Church, doctors building, Halfway School, Campbell Farming Corporation Camp 4, Lodge Grass Railroad Exhibit, teepees and Centennial Park/Picnic Area. Stop by and enjoy a walk through history. Open year round, daily May to September and week days only during remaining months.

Montana Trivia

Almost 7,500 Native Americans live on the Crow Reservation. 85% of them speak Crow as their first language. Chief Plenty Coups of the Crow Tribe acted as the head of state of the Indian Nation at the dedication of the Tomb of the Unknown Soldier in Washington, D.C. Susie Walking Bear Yellowtail, a Crow Indian, became the first Native American Registered Nurse in 1923.

BIGHORN CANYON

At first glance, time seems to have stopped at Bighorn Canyon. The lake and the steep-sided canyons provide a peaceful setting for those seeking a break from the daily routine. The focus of the area is 71 -mile-long Bighorn Lake, created by Yellowtail Dam near Fort Smith. Dedicated in 1968, the dam provides electric power, water for irrigation, flood control, and recreation. Boating, water skiing, fishing, swimming, and sightseeing are main attractions.

While you enjoy the play of light and shadow on rock and water, take time to contemplate the changes that the land and the life upon it have undergone. Time and water are keys to the canyon, where the land has been shaped by moving water since upheavals of the Earth's crust built the Pryor and Bighorn mountains millions of years ago. For 15 miles upstream from the dam, the lake bisects a massive, arching anticline, exposing fossils that tell of successive times when this land was submerged under a shallow sea, when it was a tropical marsh, and when its conifer forests were inhabited by dinosaurs. Humans arrived here more than 10,000 years ago, living as hunters and gatherers. In modern times people have further altered the land.

Most of Bighorn's visitors come to enjoy the recreational opportunities the lake offers. Boaters, water skiers, anglers and scuba divers are all attracted here. But the park offers more than just the lake: from the wild flowers in spring and summer to more than 200 species of birds; from the stories of life forms adapting to a harsh environment to the modern search for energy. You can get more information on what the park offers at visitor centers near Lovell, WY, and Fort Smith, MT. Find your own place of solitude to relax and to enjoy the diversity and timelessness of this uncommon canyon water land.

A Challenging Land

In North America people have traveled and made their living along rivers and streams for more than 40,000 years. But the Bighorn River was too treacherous and too steep-walled. People here lived near the Bighorn but avoided navigating it—until the dam tamed the river.

The broken land here also challenged the ingenuity of early residents, forcing them to devise unusual strategies of survival. More than 10,000 years ago, Indian hunters drove herds of game into land traps. These Indians lived simply, gathering wild roots and seeds to balance and supplement their meat diet. They made clothes of skins, baskets and sandals of plant fibers, and

tools of stone, bone, and wood. The many caves of the Bighorn area provided seasonal shelters and storage areas for the Indians, as well as for early traders and trappers.

Absaroke means "People of the largebeaked bird," in the Siouan language of the Crow. Their reservation surrounds most of Bighorn Canyon. Originally a farming people, the Crow split off from the Hidatsa tribe more than 200 years ago. They became a renowned hunting people, described by one of the Lewis and Clark Expedition as "the finest horsemen in the world."

After 1800, explorers, traders, and trappers found their way up the Bighorn River. Charles Larocque met the Crow at the mouth of the Bighorn in 1805; Captain William Clark traveled through a year later. Jim Bridger claimed he had floated through the canyon on a raft. Later fur traders packed their goods overland on the Bad Pass Trail, avoiding the river's dangers.

During the Civil War the Bozeman Trail led to mines in western Montana by crossing the Bighorn River. Open from 1864 to 1868, the trail was bitterly opposed by Sioux and Cheyenne; the Crow were neutral. The Federal Government closed the trail in 1868 after the Fort Laramie Treaty. Fort C.F. Smith, now on private land, guarded the trail as an outpost. A stone monument commemorates the Hayfield Fight, a desperate but successful defense against Sioux and Cheyenne warriors. In this skirmish a party of soldiers and civilian haycutters, working three miles north of Fort C.F. Smith, fought for eight hours until rescued by the fort's troops on August 1, 1867.

After the Civil War, cattle ranching became a way of life. Among the huge open-range cattle ranches was the Mason-Lovell (the ML); some of those buildings remain. Dude ranching, reflected in the remains of Hillsboro, was popular in the early 1900s.

The Crow made the transition from hunter-gatherers to ranchers in one generation. In 1904, after 12 years of labor, they completed an irrigation system and opened 35,000 acres of land to irrigated farming. Water was diverted into the Bighorn Canal by a 416-foot diversion dam, moving 720 cubic feet of water per second. Near Afterbay Campground is Bighorn Canal Headgate, remains of this human response to the challenge of the land.

Congress established Bighorn Canyon National Recreation Area in 1966 as part of the National Park System to provide enjoyment for visitors today and to protect the park for future generations.

Bighorn Canyon Visitor Center

The solar-heated visitor center near Lovell, WY., symbolizes the energy-conscious concerns of the National Park Service and of modern Americans. The heating is accomplished by storing heat from the sun in a rock bin, then blowing hot air through the building. The Yellowtail Dam Visitor Center, in the park, is two miles past the community of Fort Smith. It is approachable from the north by car.

Bighorn Wildlife

The wildlife of the Bighorn Canyon country is as varied as the land, which can be divided into four climate or vegetative zones. In the south is desert shrub land inhabited by wild horses, snakes, and small rodents. Midway is juniper woodland with coyotes, deer, bighorn sheep, beaver, wood rats, and porcupine. Along the flanks of the canyon is pine and fir woodland with mountain lions, bear, elk, and mule deer. In the north is shortgrass prairie, once home to herds of buffalo. Many of the smaller animals, such as cottontails, skunks, coyotes, and rattlesnakes, are seen frequently throughout the park. More than 200 species of birds, including many kinds of water fowl, have been seen here. Each plant and animal species is adapted to the particular conditions of temperature, moisture, and landform within one or more of the park's four primary zones.

Bighorn sheep are a common sight in the canyon.

Yellowtail Dam

The dam is named in honor of Robert Yellowtail, former Crow tribal chairman and reservation superintendent. The dam creates one of the largest reservoirs on the Missouri River tributary system. This arch type dam is 525 feet high.

Yellowtail Wildlife Habitat Management Area

Riparian, cottonwood forest, shrub land, and wetlands provide habitat for whitetail deer, bald eagles, pelicans, heron, water fowl, wild turkeys, and other species. The area is managed by the Wyoming Game and Fish Department through agreements with the National Park Service, Bureau of Land Management, and Bureau of Reclamation.

Ranch Sites

Mason-Lovell Ranch: A.L. Mason and H.C Lovell built cattle ranch headquarters here in 1883. Cattle roamed the Bighorn Basin in a classic open-range operation.

Hillsboro: A one mile round trip trail takes you to the site of Grosvenor William Barry's Cedarvale Guest Ranch and the 1915 to 1945 Hillsboro post office.

Lockhart: Caroline Lockhart, a reporter, editor, and author, began ranching at age 56. The well preserved buildings give a feel for ranch life; one mile roundup.

Ewing-Snell: This site was in use for nearly 100 years.

Bad Pass Trail

American Indians camped along this trail 10,000 years ago, and in prehistoric and historic times Shoshone used it to get to the buffalo plains. Early trappers and traders used it to avoid the dangers of the Bighorn River. You can see rock calms left along the route between

Devil Canyon Overlook and Barry's Landing. Before the arrival of the horse, life changed little here for thousands of years. Small family groups wintered in caves near the canyon bottoms. In early spring they moved out of the canyon bottoms in search of plants and small animals, and in summer they moved to the highlands in search of game and summer maturing plants. Large groups gathered in fall for a communal bison hunt.

Devil Canyon Overlook

Here the canyon crosscuts the gray limestone of the Devil Canyon Anticline, a 1,000-foot high segment of the fault blocks that make up the Pryor Mountains.

What to See and Do

A film at Bighorn Canyon Visitor Center highlights park activities. Exhibits explain the canyon's history and natural features.

Boating enthusiasts will find a marina, snack bar, camp store (gas and oil), and boat ramp at Horseshoe Bend and OkABeh. Ramps are also at Afterbay Dam and Barry's Landing. All boaters should sign registration sheets at the ramps when entering and leaving the lake. If mechanical problems develop while you are on the lake, stay with your boat; hail other boaters and ask them to notify a ranger. Carry both day and night signaling devices. Do not try to climb the lake's steep canyon walls.

Swimmers are encouraged to use the lifeguarded areas at Horseshoe Bend and Ok-A-Beh.

Camping is restricted to designated sites in developed areas. It is also allowed in the back country and below the highwater mark along Bighorn Lake. Fire restrictions during periods of high fire danger may close certain areas to camping. Check with a ranger for the restrictions on fires or back country camping.

Hiking is available in the national recreation area and in nearby forests. Ask at the visitor centers for more information.

Hunting is allowed in designated areas in accordance with state laws. Trapping is prohibited.

Fishing in Montana or Wyoming requires the appropriate state fishing license. Fine game fish, such as brown and rainbow trout, sauger, ling, and perch, abound.

The most popular game fish, a gourmet's delight, is the walleye. Winter ice fishing around Horseshoe Bend is good. The Bighorn River provides excellent brown and rainbow trout fishing.

Regulations and Safety: Firearms are prohibited in developed areas and areas of concentrated public use, unless they are unloaded and cased. Pets must be on a leash in developed areas and in areas of concentrated public use. Trash and waste disposals into area waters are prohibited; all vessels must have a waste receptacle on board. Carry a first-aid kit as a precaution against poisonous snake bites.

All plants, animals, natural and cultural features, and archeological sites are protected by federal law. Collecting is prohibited.

Reprinted from National Park Service brochure.

36. *Gas, Food, Lodging*

T The Jail House Gallery
218 N. Center, Hardin. 655-3239.

This gallery promotes artists within Bighorn County and the Crow & Cheyenne Reservations. The exhibits change regularly.

37. *Gas, Food, Lodging*

38.

H Buffalo Country
Hardin

Buffalo meant life to the Plains Indians, and the mountain Indians used to slip down from the hills for their share, too. Some tribes would toll buffalo into a concealed corral and then down them; another system was to stampede a herd over a cliff, but the sporting way was to use bows and arrows and ride them down on a trained buffalo horse.

Fat cow was the choice meat. The Indians preserved their meat long before the whites ever had any embalmed beef scandals. They made pemmican by drying and pulverizing the meat, pouring marrow bone grease and oil over it, and packing it away in skin bags. It kept indefinitely, and in food value one pound was worth ten of fresh meat.

Tanned robes and rawhide were used for bedding, tepees, clothes, war shields, stretchers, travois, canoes, and bags. Horns and bones made tools and utensils. The buffalo played a prominent part in many of their religious rites and jealousy of hereditary hunting grounds brought on most of the intertribal wars.

39. *Food*

St. Xavier

In 1887, Fr. Peter Paul Prondo, a Jesuit Priest, established the first mission at St. Xavier. The church still stands today and is in use as a school affiliated with the St. Labre Mission in Ashland. It is now called the Pretty Eagle School after a famous Crow Chief.

H Fort C. F. Smith
North of Saint Xavier on Hwy. 313, milepost 23

The ruins of this military post are about 25 miles west of here. In August 1866, two companies of soldiers guided by Jim Bridger established the fort on a plain overlooking the Big Horn River between Spring Gulch and Warrior Creek. It was built of logs and adobe, the third, last and most northerly of three posts built to protect emigrants and freighters on the Bozeman or Bonanza Trail from the Sioux and Cheyennes defending their hunting grounds.

The "Hayfield Fight" occurred August 1st, 1867, three miles east of the fort when a handful of soldiers in a log corral stood off an attacking band of Cheyennes estimated at several hundred strong. The Cheyenne had not anticipated the soldiers new repeating rifles which were quickly reloadable.

The Sioux under Red Cloud forced the closing of the trail and abandonment of the fort under the Fort Laramie Treaty in 1868. The Indians lost the battle but won the war, though their victory would be short-lived given the ever-increasing encroachment by the settlers.

The view from Dryhead Overlook

40. *Food, Lodging*

Fort Smith

Fort C.F. Smith was established in August of 1866, built by the U.S. army to protect those traveling on the Bozeman Trail from the Sioux & Cheyenne Indian attacks. Remnants of the old Fort C.F. Smith site, located along the Bighorn River, is 4 miles north of the present day Fort Smith. In 1868, the Sioux destroyed Fort C.F. Smith, after two years of fighting with the army along the Bozeman Trail.

Today, Fort Smith is a great place to try your hand at trout fishing on the blue ribbon trout waters of the Bighorn River, known as one of the finest trout streams in the U.S. You can stop through town for supplies, fishing advice, guide services and boat rentals.

T Yellowtail Dam Visitor Center and Power Plant
Fort Smith. 666-2412

The dam and visitor center was named for Robert Yellowtail who was a prominent tribal leader of the Crow throughout the 1900s. The dam spans 1,480 feet across the Bighorn Canyon and stands 525 feet tall. The visitor center provides information about the dam and how it was built. An interesting fly-fishing exhibit compares man-made flies with their natural counterparts.

41.

T Bighorn Canyon
See sidebar

T Devil Canyon Overlook
SE on U.S. Hwy. 310 to Lovell, WY then north on Hwy. 37. (307) 548-2251

This vista offers a scenic view of the Bighorn River 1,000 feet below where it cuts through the Bighorn Canyon. Immediately west of the canyon, you can see where the Pryor Mountains have been uplifted along fault lines. Nearby is the Pryor Mountains Wildhorse Refuge where about 130

wild, free-roaming mustangs make their home. Along the drive from the Visitor's Center in Lovell to the overlook, you will probably see mountain goats along the side of the road.

42.

Pryor

Pryor is located 35 miles south of Billings on the Crow Indian Reservation and is the site of Chief Plenty Coups State Park and is adjacent to the Bighorn Canyon Recreation Area. Named after the Pryor Mountain Range that lines the Montana-Wyoming border, Sgt. Nathaniel Pryor was a member of the Lewis & Clark Expedition that came through this area. These mountains are famous for the herd of wild horses that roams the area, and can be seen at the Wild Horse Range that is set aside for their protection.

T Chief Plenty Coups State Park (Day use only)
1 mile west of Pryor on county road. 252-1289.

The fascinating and honorable life of Chief Plenty Coups is remembered at this location. He was the respected tribal chief of the Crow people from 1904-1932 and was the tribe's most revered leader; loved by his people, as well as respected by white leaders. With many achievements during his leadership, he was the most respected chief the Crows would ever have, and was not replaced after his death.

Chief Plenty Coups was a brave warrior and leader, enforcing his beliefs that education was the way to deal with the white man. He adapted to the changing times, replacing his tepee for a two story cabin by the Pryor Mountain Range, where he cultivated the land. This was a show of peace to the white man, and he was a great mediator, explaining the importance of peace between all people.

After frequent trips to Washington D.C., in 1924 he was asked to represent American Indians in the dedication of the tomb of the unknown soldier at Arlington National Cemetery. Here, Plenty

Coups gave an unforgettable short speech and prayer for peace.

Chief Plenty Coups donated his land and home to be used by all people of all races in friendship. At his death in 1932, the land became Chief Plenty Coups State Park and consists of a 40 acre homestead with a Crow Indian Museum, the Chief's home and store, his grave and a gift shop.

The Park is open from May 1 through September 30, 8 a.m. to 8 p.m. The visitor center hours are 10 a.m. to 5 p.m. A fee is charged.

SCENIC DRIVES

Dryhead Overlook

This is a long bumpy drive over gravel road. Toward the end, it is not much more than a cattle trail. Four-wheel drive is almost mandatory here. If it's anything but dry out, forget it. Those "Impassable When Wet" signs aren't kidding. That being said, the drive here is worth it. At the end of the drive, you'll be standing atop an 8,500 foot rim looking thousands of feet down into the Bighorn Canyon. It's a view you normally only get from an airplane. Just before the Overlook, you'll pass the Big Ice Cave picnic area. Stop here for a break and take the short walk to the ice cave. Continue up the road for another four miles till you get to the end. You'll know when you get there. This is also the northern edge of the Pryor Mountain Wild Horse Range. Keep your eyes open for these magnificent descendants of the horses left by the Spanish Conquistadors when they explored this area.

To get here, take Hwy. 310 to the little town of Warren just short of the Wyoming border. There is nothing more here than a limestone processing plant and railroad siding. Turn east at the plant, and then take an immediate left on the road heading north. Go about 10 miles to the first major junction you reach (Rd. 211) and turn east toward Sage Creek campground. This road will take you to the overlook.

HIKES

Bighorn Canyon Hikes

As parts of the Bighorn Canyon NRA are in Wyoming, we have included some hikes that are partially in Wyoming.

Trail Safety

Bighorn Canyon is a dry, desert area. For your safety, please abide by the following precautions whenever hiking:

1. Carry water on all hikes longer than one mile, especially on hot summer days.

2. Wear good, sturdy shoes with closed toes. The canyon trails are rocky and have a lot of spiny vegetation. Sandals and sneakers do not give adequate protection.

3. There may be rattlesnakes anywhere in Bighorn Canyon. Watch where you put your hands and feet. Generally, they are shy and will move away from people, if given the chance.

4. Do not get too close to the canyon rim. In some places there may be overhangs.

5. If you are fair skinned or are not acclimated to the sun, wear sunscreen, a broad brimmed hat, and long sleeves.

6. After any springtime hike, check your skin for ticks.

7. If hiking alone, let someone know where you are going.

Sykes Mountain Trail

Description: Hard, 2-3 miles round trip.

This is a rugged cross-country hike up a desert mountain. It is for experienced hikers only! Just after you turn onto the Horseshoe Bend access road, take the first drainage that you see on your right (south). Follow this drainage until you see a small game trail on your right (west). Follow this game trail to a rockslide. The game trail then crosses to the left (east) side of the drainage and then disappears. From here, pick your way upward for about a mile through small canyons and rock formations until you come to a deep canyon that forces you to go left (east). Follow the ridge east (left) to an outcropping that overlooks Bighorn Canyon and Horseshoe Bend.

Crooked Creek Trail

Description: Easy, about .5 miles

This desert nature trail can be reached from the amphitheater in Loop B of the Horseshoe Bend Campground. Head out the back of the amphitheater and go up the ridge directly In front of you. Follow the cairns around loop C of the campground to the marked nature trail. You may request a copy of the trail Interpretive guide at the Lovell Visitors Center.

Mouth of the Canyon Trail

Description: Moderate, 3-Miles Round Trip

On the north end of Loop B (to your left if you are facing the water). In the Horseshoe Bend Campground you will find a service road that leads toward a water storage tank. Follow this road until it meets up wIth an abandoned road that veers off to the right just before you reach the water storage tank. Follow this abandoned road to where Crooked Creek runs into the canyon. Double back through a juniper lined draw to the top of the ridge. Follow the cairns back to the old road just east (left) of the water tank. This trail offers spectacular views of the Pryor and Bighorn Mountains and the red badlands surrounding Horseshoe Bend.

State Line Trail

Description: Easy to Moderate, I Mile Round Trip

Just north of the Montana State line, you will find a cairn marking the beginning of this trail. Follow the cairns along an old road that leads to the rim of the canyon. You may then follow the canyon rim for several hundred feet. This trail leads through juniper forest and limestone plateaus to unique views of the canyon.

Lower Layout Creek Trail

Description: Easy to Moderate, Approximately 3.5 Miles Round Trip

The end of the Wild Horse Range is marked with a cattle guard. Follow an old two-track road, which begins to the right of the cattle guard and runs parallel to Layout Creek, to the juncture where Layout Creek Canyon joins with Bighorn Canyon. You may then follow the canyon rim for several hundred feet. This hike offers several opportunities to stray from the main trail and view Layout Creek Canyon and offers spectacular views of Bighorn Canyon as well. This trail is also located in the Pryor Mountain Wild Horse Range, so there is a possibility of viewing some wild horses from afar. Ultimately, this road loops in a horseshoe shape and meets the main road approximately .5 miles from where the two-track road began. However, you may alternately follow a well trodden horse trail which begins near the canyon rims and eventually re-joins the two-track road near it's beginning. This route will shorten your round trip hike to approximately 3 miles.

Hillsboro

Description: Easy to Moderate, I to 3 Miles Round Trip

Follow the turn off for Barry's Landing down past the campground. On your right hand side, you will see a red dirt road extending up a hill. Drive or walk the half mile to a gate and kiosk. From here it is another half mile into Hillsboro by foot trail. The trail continues beyond the ranch itself and becomes the original wagon road into the ranch. Spend some time exploring the ranch as well as the views of trail creek canyon.

Sullivan's Knob Trail

Description: Easy to Moderate, I Mile Round Trip

Roughly 1 mile north of Devil's Canyon Overlook, you will find a turnout around a geological formation known as Sullivan's knob. Turn into the parking lot at Sullivan's knob. Follow the cairns and the trail to the right of the hill directly in front of you (East). Follow the cairns to the canyon rim. From there it's possible to see the north side of Devil's Canyon Overlook.

Upper Layout Creek Trail

Description: Moderate, 4 Miles Round Trip

Approximately 5 miles from the turnoff for Devil's Canyon Overlook you will find a turnoff on the left side of the road marked "historic site." Turn off here and follow the road into the parking area east (left) of the corrals. Go through the corrals and follow an old road along Layout Creek to where the creek enters Layout Creek Canyon. This trail goes between a limestone plateau and a lush river area up to the base of East Pryor Mountain.

Barry's Island Trail

Description: Moderate, 5 MIles Round Trip

Follow the turnoff for Barry's Landing until the road dead ends In a parking area. To the north (your left if you are facing into the parking area), you will see a red road leading away from the parking area. Follow this road 1/4 of a mile until you meet a gate. On foot, follow this road until it submerges underwater. You will then see a game wall, which will lead you to where the road emerges. Continue on the old road about half a mile beyond the Medicine Creek Campground to Wassin Canyon.

Lockhart Ranch

Description: Easy, 1.5 Miles Round Trip

Beyond Barry's Landing, Highway 37 becomes a dirt road. Follow this dirt road 2.5 miles to Lockhart Ranch. You may park in the pull-out across from the gate to the ranch. To the left of the gate you will find a cutout in the fence. Use this to gain access to the ranch. Beyond the gate you will find a kiosk and a trail into the ranch. East (left) of the corrals, you will find a garage, which lies just north of an old road that runs along Davis Creek and offers views of the Pryor Mountains. At the end of this trail, take a left to continue on the main dirt road, which meets up with the main road, or follow the Davis Creek Trail back to the ranch. Then take a right to finish the loop through the ranch and head back to the parking area.

Om-Ne-A Trail

This is a rim-top trail that provides some awesome views of the magnificent Bighorn Canyon. The 3-mile trail goes from Yellowtail Dam to Ok-A-Beh marina. The trail starts at Yellowtail Dam and is steep for the first quarter mile.

Montana Trivia

80,730 wolves were killed in Montana between 1883 and 1915.

INFORMATION PLEASE

All Montana area codes are 406

Road Information

Montana Road Condition Report
(800) 226-7623, (800) 335-7592 local 444-7696
Montana Highway Patrol   444-7696

Local Road Reports

Billings   252-2806
Billings Weather Reports   652-1916

Tourism Information

Travel Montana (800) 847-4868 outside Montana
                        444-2654 in Montana
                        http://travel.mt.gov/.
Custer Country   (800) 346-1876 or 665-1671
Northern Rodeo Association   252-1122

Chambers of Commerce

Montana   442-2405
Billings   245-4111
Hardin   665-1672
Laurel   628-4504
Hysham   342-5457

Airports

Billings   657-8495
Fort Smith   666-2412
Hardin   665-2301
Hysham   342-5563

Government Offices

State BLM Office   255-2885, 238-1540
Bureau of Land Management
    Billings Field Office   896-5013
Custer National Forest   657-6200
Montana Fish, Wildlife & Parks   247-2940
U.S. Bureau of Reclamation   247-7295

Indian Reservations

Northern Cheyenne Reservation   477-8844
Crow Reservation   638-2601

Hospitals

Ask-A-Nurse • Billings   657-8778
Billings Inter-Hospital Onclay •Billings 259-2245
Deaconess Medical Center • Billings 657-4000
St. Vincents Hospital • Billings   657-7000
US PHS Hospital • Crow Agency   638-2626
Big Horn County Memorial Hospital
    Hardin   665-2310

Golf Courses

Lake Hills Golf Club Pro Shop
    Billings   252-9244
Par-3 Exchange City Golf Course Club House
    Billings   652-2553
Peter Yegen Jr. Golf Club • Billings 656-8099

Bed & Breakfasts

Westwood Ranch B&B
    Lodge Grass   639-2450
Cowdin's Carriage House B&B
    Billings   652-5108
Cross A Guest Ranch • Lodge Grass 639-2697
Hotel Becker B&B • Hardin   665-2707
The Josephine B&B • Billings   248-5898
Pine Hills Place B&B • Billings   252-2288
Tight Lines Lodge • Saint Xavier   666-2240
Sanderson Inn • Billings   656-3388
Sisters Inn • Billings   252-9350
V Lazy B B&B and Horse Motel
    Molt   669-3885
Wald Ranch • Lodge Grass   639-2457

Guest Ranches & Resorts

Bighorn River Country Lodge
    Fort Smith   666-2332
Big Sky Roping Ranch • Huntley   348-2460

Cross A Guest Ranch • Lodge Grass		639-2697
Double Spear Ranch • Pryor		259-8291
Eagle Nest Lodge • Hardin		665-3712
Seventh Ranch • Garryowen		638-2438

Car Rental

AA-A Auto Rental	245-9759
Ace-Rent-A-Car	252-2399
Avis Rent-A-Car	252-8007
Budget Rent-A-Car	259-4168
Dollar Rent-A-Car	259-1147
Enterprise Billings West	652-2000
Enterprise Rent-A-Car	259-9999
Hertz Rent-A-Car	248-9151
National Car Rental	252-7626
Rent A Wreck	245-5982
Thrifty Car Rental	259-1025
U Save Auto Rental	655-4440

Outfitters & Guides

F=Fishing H=Hunting R=River Guides
E=Horseback Rides G=General Guide Services

Angler's Edge Outfitters	F	666-2417
Big Horn Angler	HF	666-2233
Bighorn Fly & Tackle Shop	G F	656-8257
Bighorn Fly & Tackle Shop	G F	666-2253
Big Horn Trout Outfitters	RF	666-2224
Big Horn River Country Lodge	F	666-2351
Big Horn Trout Shop	F	666-2375
Bighorn River Lodge	F	666-2368
Brad Downey's Anglers' Edge	HRF	666-2417
Cat Track Outfitters	HF	347-5499
Eagle Nest Lodge & Outfitters	G	665-3711
East Slope Outfitters	HF	666-2320
Elk River Outfitters	G F H	656-4271

Fort Smith Flyshop	F	666-2550
George Kelly Bighorn Country	HF	666-2326
Forrester's Bighorn River Resorts	GHF	666-9199
Kingfisher Lodge/Big Horn Country Outfitters	G F	666-2326
Last Stand Lodge	R F	665-3489
Last Stand Outfitters	G H	665-3489
Montella From Montana	RF	666-2360
MT Adventures in Angling	GFREG	248-2995
MT River Discoveries	R	651-0537
Phil Gonzalez's Bighorn River Lodge	G	666-2368
Schneider's Guide Service	G	666-2460
Stillwaters Outfitting	FR	652-8111
Sunshine Sports	R	252-3724
Two Leggins Outfitters	HFR	665-2825
Western Waters	G F R	252-5212

Fishery

	Cold Water Species												Warm Water Species										Services					
	Brook Trout	Mt. Whitefish	Lake Whitefish	Golden Trout	Cutthroat Trout	Brown Trout	Rainbow Trout	Kokanee Salmon	Bull Trout	Lake Trout	Arctic Grayling	Burbot	Largemouth Bass	Smallmouth Bass	Walleye	Sauger	Northern Pike	Shovelnose Sturgeon	Channel Catfish	Yellow Perch	Crappie	Paddlefish	Vehicle Access	Campgrounds	Toilets	Docks	Boat Ramps	MotorRestrictions
12. Yellowtail Afterbay						•	•																•	•	•	•	•	
13. Bighorn Lake						•	•						•		•	•			•	•			•	•		•	•	
14. Yellowstone River						•	•								•	•	•	•	•		•	•	•	•		•	•	
15. Lake Elmo													•										•	•		•	•	•
16. Lake Josephine													•										•	•		•	•	•
17. Bighorn River		•				•						•											•	•			•	

Public Campgrounds

Campsite Directions

	Season	Camping	Trailers	Toilets	Water	Boat Launch	Fishing	Swimming	Trails	Stay Limit	Fee
11•Huntley Diversion Dam USBR											
1 mi. W of I-94.Huntley Exit on gravel road	All Year	•				B	•			14	
12•Anita Reservoir USBR											
4 mi. S of I-94•Pompeys Pillar Exit	All Year	•				A	•			14	
13•BIGHORN CANYON NATIONAL RECREATION AREA•Afterbay NPS•											
1 mi. NE of Yellowtail Dam	All Year	48		D	•	C	•		N	14	
14•BIGHORN CANYON NATIONAL RECREATION AREA•Barry's Landing NPS•											
27 mi. N of Lovell, WY•on WY 37	All Year	9	•	D		C	•		•	14	
15•Sage Creek FS											
3 mi. S of Bridger on US 310•22 mi. SE on Cty. Rd.•1 mi. E on Forest Rd. 50	6/15-9/15	12	20'	•			•			10	

Agency
FS—U.S.D.A Forest Service
FWP—Montana Fish, Wildlife & Parks
NPS—National Park Service
BLM—U.S. Bureau of Land Management
USBR—U.S. Bureau of Reclamation
CE—Corps of Engineers

Camping
Camping is allowed at this site. Number indi-
cates camping spaces available
H—Hard sided units only; no tents

Trailers
Trailer units allowed. Number indicates maximum length.

Toilets
Toilets on site. D—Disabled access

Water
Drinkable water on site

Fishing
Visitors may fish on site

Boat
Type of boat ramp on site:
 A—Hand launch
 B—4-wheel drive with trailer
 C—2-wheel drive with trailer

Swimming
Designated swimming areas on site

Trails
Trails on site
B—Backpacking N—Nature/Interpretive

Stay Limit
Maximum length of stay in days

Fee
Camping and/or day-use fee

Notes:

Campsite Directions

	Season	Tent	RV	Water	Electric	Sewer	Dump	Shower	Laundry	Store
BILLINGS										
Big Sky Campground 259-4110 • I-90 Exit 446 to city center	All Year		54	•	•	•	•	•	•	•
Billings KOA 252-3104 • (800) 562-8546 • I-90 Exit 450, S to Garden Ave, right 3/4 mi	4/15-10/15	40	135	•	•	•	•	•	•	•
Casa Village 656-3910 or 656-3915 • Fax 651-8840 • 24th St & Monad	4/1-11/1		5	•	•	•	•	•		
Eastwood Estates 245-7733 • I-90 Exit 452, 1/2 mi. on US 87 E, then 1/2 mi E	All Year		20	•	•	•				
Native Ways Primitive Campground 259-6849 • I-90 Exit 455, S to US 87 E, L to High Tr Rd, L 1/2 mi	5/1-10/15									
Trailer Village 248-8685 • I-90 Exit 447, 6 blks N on S Billings Blvd	All Year		56	•	•	•	•		•	
Yellowstone River RV Park & Campground 259-0878 • I-90 Exit 450, S 1 blk SE 1/4 mi on Garden	April-Oct	20	85	•	•		•			•
CROW AGENCY										
Little Bighorn Camp 638-2232 • Fax 638-2231 • Jct I-90 & US 212	4/1-10/1	15	20	•	•	•	•	•	•	•
CUSTER										
Fort Custer Restaurant & Campground 856-4191 • Fan 856-4856 • 1 mi E of Custer	All Year		12	•	•		•	•		
FORT SMITH										
Cottonwood Camp 666-2391 • Fax 666-2306 • 3 mi N of Fort Smith on Hwy 313	All Year	25	15	•	•		•	•		
GARRYOWEN										
7th Ranch RV Camp 638-2438 • I-90 Exit 514, 3 mi on Reno Creek Frontage Rd	Spring-Fall	20	41	•	•	•	•	•	•	•
GRASS RANGE										
Little Montana Truckstop and Cafe 428-2270 • Fax 428-2271 • US 87 at Grass Range	All Year	12	12	•	•	•	•	•		•
HARDIN										
Grandview Campground 665-2489 • (800) 622-9890 • I-90 Exit 495, 3/4 mi S on Hwy 313	All Year	40	60	•	•	•	•	•	•	•
Hardin KOA 665-1635 • (800) 562-1635 • I-90 Exit 495, 1.25 mi N on MT 47	4/1-9/30	10	58	•	•	•	•	•	•	•
Kinney's Stables and Campground 665-3020 • Located in Hardin	March-Nov	6	8	•						
Sunset Village RV and Mobile Home Park Ph/Fax 665-2832 • I-90 Exit 497, 2 mi S on Hwy, 313	5/1-10/31	4	18	•	•	•	•	•	•	
ST. XAVIER										
Big Horn RV Park Inc 666-2460 • 30 mi S of Hardin on Hwy 313	4/1-12/1	10	16	•	•	•		•		•

NOTES:

Dining Quick Reference

Price Range refers to the average cost of a meal per person: ($) $1-$6, ($$) $7-$11, ($$$) $12-up. Cocktails: "Yes" indicates full bar; Beer (B)/Wine (W). Service: Breakfast (B), Brunch (BR), Lunch (L), Dinner (D). Businesses in bold print will have additional information under the appropriate map locator number in the body of this section. *[wi-fi]* next to business name indicates free wireless internet is available to customers.

RESTAURANT	TYPE CUISINE	PRICE RANGE	CHILD MENU	COCKTAILS BEER WINE	SERVICE	CREDIT CARDS	MAP LOCATOR NUMBER
Patrick's Cafe	American	$$		Yes	L/D		1
Junction City Saloon	American	$		Yes	L/D		5
Fort Custer	American	$		Yes	B/L/D	Major	5
Jud's Buds & Such	American	$$		Yes	L/D		8
Miller's Darkhorse Saloon	American	$$	Yes	Yes	L/D	V/M/A	8
Bluecat Inn	Burgers	$		Yes	L/D		10
Sam's Cafe	Family	$/$$		Yes	B/L/D	Major	10
Applebee's Neighborhood Grill	Eclectic	$$/$$$	Yes	Yes	L/D	Major	12
Burger King	Fast Food	$	Yes		B/L/D		12
Dairy Queen	Fast Food	$	Yes		L/D		12
Godfather's Pizza	Pizza	$	Yes	B	L/D	V/M/D	12
Golden Phoenix Chinese Restaurant	Chinese	$/$$			L/D	Major	12
Grand Bagel Company	Deli	$			B/L		12
Jalisco's	Mexican	$/$$	Yes	Yes	L/D	Major	12
Kit Kat Cafe	American	$	Yes		B/L/D		12
McDonald's	Fast Food	$	Yes		B/L/D		12
Papa John's Pizza	Pizza	$	Yes		L/D		12
Peking House Express	Chinese	$			L/D	Major	12
Subway	Fast Food	$	Yes		L/D		12
Taco John's	Fast Food	$	Yes		L/D		12
Arby's	Fast Food	$	Yes		B/L/D		12
Blimpie's Subs	Fast Food	$	Yes		L/D		12
Circle Inn	American	$		Yes			12
Domino's Pizza	Pizza	$			L/D		12
Pizza Hut	Pizza	$/$$	Yes	B	L/D	V/M/D	12
Taco Bell	Fast Food	$	Yes		L/D		12
Wendy's	Fast Food	$	Yes		L/D		12
Gigglin Grizzly	American	$-$$		B/W	B/L/D	M/V	12
Molly's Kitchen	American	$	C	No	B/L/D	M/V	12
Blimpie's Subs	Fast Food	$	Yes		L/D		14
Burger King	Fast Food	$	Yes		B/L/D		14
Subway	Fast Food	$	Yes		L/D		14
Arby's	Fast Food	$	Yes		B/L/D		14
The Rex	Regional American	$-$$$	Yes	Yes	L/D	Major	15
Traxx Bar & Grill	American	$$/$$$	Yes	B/W	L/D	Major	15
Bruno's Italian Specialties	Italian	$/$$	Yes	Yes	L/D	Major	15
Club Carlin	Fine Dining	$$/$$$		Yes	D	Major	15
Juliano's	Fine Dining	$$$		Yes	L/D	Major	15
La Soledad	Mexican/American	$$	Yes	Yes	L/D	MC/V	15
McCormick Cafe	Eclectic	$/$$	Yes		B/L	Major	15
Montana Brewing Company	Brew Pub	$$		B/W	L/D		15
Puerta Vallarta Mexican Restaurant	Mexican	$$	Yes	B/W	L/D		15
Rocket Burritos Gourmet Burritos & Sodas	Gourmet Burritos	$			L/D		15
Burger King	Fast Food	$	Yes		B/L/D		15
Denny's	Family	$	Yes		B/L/D	V/M	15
Hardee's	Fast Food	$	Yes		B/L/D		15
Jake's	Steakhouse	$$		Yes	L/D	Major	15
Kentucky Fried Chicken	Fast Food	$	Yes		L/D		15
Perkins Family Restaurant	Family	$/$$	Yes		B/L/D	Major	15
Walkers Grill	American Bistro	$$/$$$	Yes	Yes	D	Major	15
Athenian	Greek	$$/$$$	Yes	B/W	L/D	Major	15
El Burrito Cafeteria	Mexican	$$			B/L/D		15
George Henry's Restaurant	Gourmet	$$/$$$		Yes	L/D	Major	15
Stella's Kitchen & Bakery	American	$/$$			B/L		15
Wendy's	Fast Food	$	Yes		L/D		15
Grand Bagel Company	Deli	$			B/L		15
NaRa Oriental Restaurant	Japanese/Korean	$$			L/D	Major	15
O'Hara's Restaurant	Family	$	Yes		B/L/D		15
Pug Mahon's	Irish Pub	$$/$$$	Yes	Yes	L/D	M/V	15
Quizno's Classic Subs	Subs	$	Yes		L/D		15
Thai Orchid Restaurant	Thai/Chinese	$/$$			L/D	V/M	15

Dining Quick Reference—Continued

Price Range refers to the average cost of a meal per person: ($) $1-$6, ($$) $7-$11, ($$$) $12-up. Cocktails: "Yes" indicates full bar; Beer (B)/Wine (W), Service: Breakfast (B), Brunch (BR), Lunch (L), Dinner (D). Businesses in bold print will have additional information under the appropriate map locator number in the body of this section. [wi-fi] next to business name indicates free wireless internet is available to customers.

RESTAURANT	TYPE CUISINE	PRICE RANGE	CHILD MENU	COCKTAILS BEER WINE	SERVICE	CREDIT CARDS	MAP LOCATOR NUMBER
Perkins Family Restaurant	Family	$/$$	Yes		B/L/D	Major	16
Pizza Chef	Pizza	$$			L/D		16
Pizza Hut	Pizza	$/$$	Yes	B	L/D	V/M/D	16
Blondies	Deli	$			B/L/D		17
Dairy Queen	Fast Food	$	Yes		L/D		17
Pizza Hut	Pizza	$/$$	Yes	B	L/D	V/M/D	17
Subway	Fast Food	$	Yes		L/D		17
Burger King	Fast Food	$	Yes		B/L/D		17
McDonalds	Fast Food	$	Yes		B/L/D		17
Subway	Fast Food	$	Yes		L/D		17
Pork Chop John's	Fast Food	$	Yes		L/D		19
Arby's	Fast Food	$	Yes		B/L/D		19
Burger King	Fast Food	$	Yes		B/L/D		19
China Buffet	Chinese	$$			L/D	Major	19
Dairy Queen	Fast Food	$	Yes		L/D		19
Four Seas Restaurant	Family	$		Yes	L/D	V/M/A	19
Great Wall Chinese Restaurant	Chinese		Yes	B/W	L/D	Major	19
J B'S Restaurant	Family	$	Yes		B/L/D	V/M	19
Marco Polo Gardens	Chinese	$$			L/D	Major	19
McDonald's	Fast Food	$	Yes		B/L/D		19
Pizza Hut	Pizza	$/$$	Yes	B	L/D	V/M/D	19
Subway	Fast Food	$	Yes		L/D		19
Taco Bell	Fast Food	$	Yes		L/D		19
Taco John's	Fast Food	$	Yes		L/D		19
Taco Treat	Fast Food	$	Yes		L/D		19
Wendy's	Fast Food	$	Yes		L/D		19
Musgrave's	Coffee House	$/$$					19
Red Robin Restaurant	American	$$	Yes	Yes	L/D	Major	19
Shooter's Grill	American	$$		Yes	L/D	Major	19
Sizzling Sara's	American	$-$$		B/W	B/L/D	Major	19
Domino's Pizza	Pizza	$			L/D		20
Sports Page Restaurant	American	$$/$$$	Yes	Yes	L/D	Major	20
Muzzle Loader Cafe	American	$$	Yes		L/D	Major	21
West Parkway Truck Stop Rstrnt	American	$$	Yes		B/L/D	Major	21
Southern Empire Emporium	American	$	Yes		B/L/D	V/M	22
Cracker Barrel	Family	$	Yes		B/L/D	V/M	23
Yellowstone Valley Steakhouse	Steakhouse	$$/$$$	Yes	Yes	B/L/D	Major	23
Silver Dollar Restaurant	American	$		B/W	B/L/D	V/M	23
Torres Cafe	American	$$			L/D	V/M	23
Western Empire Emporium	American	$	Yes	Yes		Major	24
Perkins Family Restaurant	Family	$/$$	Yes		B/L/D	Major	24
MacKenzie River Pizza Co.	Pizza	$/$$		B/W	L/D	Major	24
Applebee's Neighborhood Grill	Eclectic	$$/$$$	Yes	Yes	L/D	Major	24
Cactus Creek Steak Outfitters	Steaks & Seafood	$/$$	Yes	Yes	L/D	Major	24
Dairy Queen	Fast Food	$	Yes		L/D		24
Dos Machos Mexican Food	Mexican	$/$$	Yes	Yes	L/D	Major	24
Old Country Buffet	Buffet	$/$$	Yes		L/D	Major	24
Pizza Hut	Pizza	$/$$	Yes	B	L/D	V/M/D	24
Quizno's Classic Subs	Subs	$	Yes		L/D		24
Teriyaki Bowl Express	Oriental	$			L/D		24
Burger King	Fast Food	$	Yes		B/L/D		24
Denny's	Family	$	Yes		B/L/D	V/M	24
Fuddruckers	American	$-$$	Yes	Yes	L/D	Major	24
Gusick's Restaurant	American	$/$$		Yes	L/D	V/M	24
Jade Palace Chinese	Chinese	$/$$	Yes	Yes	L/D	Major	24
Olive Garden	Italian	$$		B/W	L/D	Major	24
Outback Steakhouse	American	$$/$$$	Yes	Yes	D	Major	24
Red Lobster Restaurant	Seafood	$$	Yes	B/W	L/D	Major	24
Subway	Fast Food	$	Yes		L/D		24
Johnny Carino's	Ital	$$	C	B/W	L/D	All	24
Texas Roadhouse	American	$$-$$$	C	All	D	Major	24

Price Range refers to the average cost of a meal per person: ($) $1-$6, ($$) $7-$11, ($$$) $12-up. Cocktails: "Yes" indicates full bar; Beer (B)/Wine (W), Service: Breakfast (B), Brunch (BR), Lunch (L), Dinner (D). Businesses in bold print will have additional information under the appropriate map locator number in the body of this section. *[wi-fi]* next to business name indicates free wireless internet is available to customers.

RESTAURANT	TYPE CUISINE	PRICE RANGE	CHILD MENU	COCKTAILS BEER WINE	SERVICE	CREDIT CARDS	MAP LOCATOR NUMBER
Taco John's	Fast Food	$	Yes		L/D		24
Arby's	Fast Food	$	Yes		B/L/D		25
Cinnabon World Famous Cinnamon	Bakery/Coffee	$			L/D		25
Fuddrucker's Express	Fast Food	$-$$	Yes	Yes	L/D		25
Noodle Express	Oriental	$			L/D	V/M	25
Papa John's Restaurant	Pizza	$$			L/D	Major	25
Godfather's Pizza	Pizza	$	Yes	B	L/D	V/M/D	26
Chuck E Cheese's	Pizza	$$	Yes		L/D	Major	26
Golden Corral Family Steak House	Steakhouse	$	Yes		L/D	V/M/D	26
Great American Bagel	Deli	$			B/L		26
Guadalajara Family Mexican Restaurant	Mexican	$/$$	Yes	Yes	L/D	Major	26
Hardee's	Fast Food	$	Yes		B/L/D		26
J B'S Restaurant	Family	$			B/L/D	V/M	26
Pratts Lunch & Dinner Club	American	$		Yes	L/D	Major	26
Riverboat Dining	Mexican	$$/$$$	Yes	Yes	L/D	Major	26
Subway	Fast Food	$	Yes		L/D		26
C J'S Restaurant	Steakhouse	$$	Yes	Yes	L/D	Major	26
Fuddruckers	Family	$-$$	Yes	B/W	L/D	Major	26
Little Caesar's	Pizza	$			L/D		26
McDonalds	Fast Food	$	Yes		B/L/D		26
Mongolian Grill	Asian	$$			L/D	Major	26
Pepper's Pizza & Pasta	Pizza/Italian	$$		B/W	L/D	V/M	26
Taco Bell	Fast Food	$	Yes		L/D		26
Taco John's	Fast Food	$	Yes		L/D		26
Wendy's	Fast Food	$	Yes		L/D		26
Bruno's Italian Specialties	Italian	$/$$	Yes	Yes	L/D	Major	27
MacKenzie River Pizza Co.	Pizza	$/$$		B/W	L/D	Major	27
Billings Burrito Company	Mexican	$			B/L/D		27
Enzo Mediterranean Bistro	Bistro	$$	Yes	W/B	L/D/BR	Major	27
Grand Bagel Company	Deli	$			B/L		27
Kentucky Fried Chicken	Fast Food	$	Yes		L/D		27
Mayflower of China	Chinese	$$	Yes		L/D	V/M/D/DC	27
Domino's Pizza	Pizza	$			L/D		27
Hero's Subs	Deli	$			L/D		27
McDonald's	Fast Food	$	Yes		B/L/D		27
Subway	Fast Food	$	Yes		L/D		27
Sweet Surrender Cafe	Cafe/Bakery	$			B/L	Major	27
17th St. Station	Coffee House						27
The Granary Restaurant	Steaks & Seafood	$$$		Yes	D	Major	28
Crow's Nest	Native American	$			B/L/D		33
Custer Battlefield Trading Post & Cafe	Family	$	Yes		B/L/D	Major	33
Shake & Burger Hut	Fast Food	$			L/D		34
Little Big Man Pizza	Pizza	$		B/W	L/D		36
Blimpie's Subs	Fast Food	$	Yes		L/D		37
Dairy Queen	Fast Food	$	Yes		L/D		37
Kentucky Fried Chicken	Fast Food	$	Yes		L/D		37
McDonald's	Fast Food	$	Yes		B/L/D		37
Pizza Hut/Taco Bell	Pizza/Mexican	$/$$	Yes	B	L/D	V/M/D	37
Purple Cow Restaurant	Family	$$	Yes	B/W	B/L/D	Major	37
Subway	Fast Food	$	Yes		L/D		37
Taco John's	Fast Food	$	Yes		L/D		37
Big Horn RV Park & Cafe	American	$/$$			B/L/D		39

NOTES:

Motel Quick Reference

Price Range: ($) Under $40 ; ($$) $40-$60; ($$$) $60-$80, ($$$$) Over $80. Pets [check with the motel for specific policies] (P), Dining (D), Lounge (L), Disabled Access (DA), Full Breakfast (FB), Cont. Breakfast (CB), Indoor Pool (IP), Outdoor Pool (OP), Hot Tub (HT), Sauna (S), Refrigerator (R), Microwave (M) (Microwave and Refrigerator indicated only if in majority of rooms), Kitchenette (K). All Montana area codes are 406. [wi-fi] next to business name indicates free wireless internet is available to customers.

HOTEL	PHONE	NUMBER ROOMS	PRICE RANGE	BREAKFAST	POOL/ HOT TUB SAUNA	NON SMOKE ROOMS	OTHER AMENITIES	CREDIT CARDS	MAP LOCATOR NUMBER
Heights Inn	252-8451	33	$			Yes	DA/K/P/M/R	Major	12
Boot Hill Inn & Suites	245-2000	69	$$$$	CB	IP/HT	Yes	M/R/DA	Major	12
Metra Inn	245-6611	104	$$$		OP	Yes	P/M/R	Major	12
Twin Cubs Motel	252-9851	11	$$				P	Major	12
Holiday Inn Express	259-8600	66	$$$	CB	IP/HT	Yes	DA	Major	14
Sheraton	252-7400	282	$$$		IP	Yes	P/D/L/DA	Major	15
Lewis & Clark Inn	252-4691	57	$$		IP/HT	Yes	R/M/R/DA	Major	15
Radisson Northern Hotel	245-5121	160	$$$	CB		Yes	DA/P/D	Major	15
Riverstone Billings Inn [wi-fi]	252-6800	60	$$			Yes	DA/P	Major	15
Dude Rancher Lodge [wi-fi]	259-5561	57	$$$			Yes	P/D/M/R	Major	15
Vegas Motel	259-4551	5	$			Yes	K/R/L/R	Major	15
Travelodge [wi-fi]	245-6345	38	$$				P/DA	Major	15
Best Western Ponderosa Inn [wi-fi]	259-5511	130	$$/$$$		OP/S	Yes	P/R/M/R/DA	Major	15
Lazy K-T Motel	252-6606	26	$			Yes	P	Major	15
Big Five Motel	245-6645	34	$			Yes	DA/P	Major	15
Billings Travel West Inn	245-6345	38	$$	CB		Yes	P	Major	15
Hotel Carlin	245-7515	8	$$$	N		Y		Major	15
Cherry Tree Inn	252-5603	65	$$	CB		Yes	DA/P	Major	16
Juniper Inn	245-4128	47	$	CB		Yes	P/M/R/DA	Major	16
Hilltop Inn	245-5000	57	$$	CB		Yes	DA/P	Major	16
Rimrock Inn	252-7107	83	$	CB	HT	Yes	P/DA	Major	16
Rimview Inn [wi-fi]	248-2622	54	$/$$	CB	HT	Yes	K/P/M/R/DA	Major	16
Howard Johnsons [wi-fi]	248-4656	172	$$/$$$	CB		Yes	P/M/R/DA	Major	17
Hojo Inn	248-4656	173	$$$			Yes	D/L/DA/P	Major	17
War Bonnet Inn [wi-fi]	248-7761	102	$$		IP	Yes	P/D/L/DA	Major	17
Sleep Inn	254-0013	75	$$	CB		Yes	DA	Major	17
Super 8 Motel Of Billings [wi-fi]	248-8842	114	$$/$$$	CB		Yes	P/M/R/DA	Major	21
Days Inn [wi-fi]	252-4007	63	$$/$$$	CB	HT	Yes	P/DA	Major	21
Hampton Inn [wi-fi]	248-4949	80	$$$	CB	IP/HT	Yes	DA/M/R	Major	21
Parkway Motel	245-3044	26	$$					Major	21
Picture Court Motel	252-8478	20	$			Yes		Major	21
Holiday Inn Billings Plaza [wi-fi]	248-7701	315	$$$		IP/HT	Yes	R/L/DA	Major	23
Best Western Billings [wi-fi]	248-9800	80	$$/$$$	CB	IP/HT/S	Yes	P/M/R/DA	Major	23
Billings Hotel & Convention Center [wi-fi]	248-7151	242	$$		IP	Yes	P/R/L/DA	Major	23
Kelly Inn [wi-fi]	252-2700	88	$/$$	CB	OP/HT/S	Yes	K/P/M/R/DA	Major	23
Motel 6 N.	252-0093	117	$$		IP	Yes	DA/P	Major	23
Ramada Inn Limited [wi-fi]	252-2584	116	$$/$$$	CB	OP	Yes	P/M/R/DA	Major	23
Red Roof Inn	252-0093	99	$$			Yes	P/DA	Major	23
Western Executive Inn [wi-fi]	294-8888	40	$$$	FB		Yes	P/DA	Major	24
C'mon Inn [wi-fi]	655-1100	80	$$$	CB	HT/IP	Yes	M/R/DA	Major	24
Comfort Inn [wi-fi]	652-5200	60	$$$/$$$$	CB	IP/HT	Yes	P/DA	Major	24
Fairfield Inn [wi-fi]	652-5330	63	$$$		IP	Yes	DA	Major	24
Quality Inn Homestead Park	652-1320	62	$$-$$$	FB	IP/HT/S	Yes	FB/P/R/DA	Major	24
Picture Court Motel	252-8478	20	$$			Yes	P	Major	31
Western Motel	665-2296	28	$			Yes	P/M/R/DA	Major	36
Camp Custer Motel	665-2504	8	$				P	V/M	36
Lariat Motel	665-2683	18	$			Yes	P/M/R	Major	36
Super 8 Motel [wi-fi]	665-1700	53	$$			Yes	P/M/L	Major	37
American Inn [wi-fi]	665-1870	42	$$		OP/HT	Yes	P/D	Major	37
Big Horn Angler Motel	666-2233	9	$$	CB		Yes	D	Major	40

NOTES:

NOTES:

WYOMING
THE COWBOY STATE

Teton Range

THE COWBOY STATE

When people think of Wyoming, they tend to think of cowboys, as the nickname shows. The cowboy is really a symbol of Wyoming's rugged, hard-working character. Covering nearly 98,000 square miles, the fourth largest state in the union is a land of wild, wide-open spaces and magnificent vistas.

Every corner of the state has natural wonders of world renown: from Yellowstone and the Grand Tetons in the northwest corner, to Devil's Tower and the Black Hills in the northeast, to the Vedauwoo Rocks and the Medicine Bow National Forest in the southeast, and Fossil Butte and the Flaming Gorge in the southwest. In between these marvels, numerous opportunities to explore Wyoming's varied, often awe-inspiring landscapes abound.

In the high heart of the Rocky Mountains, Wyoming is laced with a number of smaller ranges, including the Laramie Mountains, the Snowy Range, the Sierra Madres, the Salt Range, the Gros Ventres, the Absarokas, the Big Horns, the Tetons, and some of the regions highest peaks, the Wind Rivers, reaching nearly 14,000 feet elevation. Wyoming mountains are a spectacle of stark granite slopes, rolling foothills, and evergreen forests.

Between the various mountain ranges, you will find a variety of wilderness areas, pastoral valleys, grasslands, deserts, and amazing rock formations. You can find nearly every geological phenomenon imaginable, from deep canyons to majestic buttes and pinnacles to convoluted caverns. Geothermal curiosities occur all around the state, from geysers to hot springs.

Water is a precious commodity in the state, but it is crisscrossed with several streams, including the Green, the Snake, Bighorn, the Platte, the Powder, the Laramie and the Wind Rivers.

Headwaters for the Missouri, Columbia, and Colorado Rivers also fall within Wyoming's borders. The continental divide, which cuts through the mountains, creates a place where water runs in three different directions. The landscape is dotted with a handful of lakes and reservoirs that provide not only recreational opportunities, but also much needed water conservation and dam-generated energy for the state.

NATURAL HISTORY

Taking its name from a Delaware word meaning "land of mountains and valleys", Wyoming has been a land of wonders for millions, even billions of years. The very minerals from which the earth is formed here harbor countless treasures, from silver and gold, to copper and iron ore, to semiprecious and even precious stones. The largest piece of solid jade ever unearthed came from Wyoming, and one of the largest diamonds ever found came from here as well.

Situated in an ancient volcanic caldera, the Yellowstone region boasts the most extensive area of geyser activity in the world, as well as boiling mud pots, hot springs, prismatic pools, and other hydrothermal phenomena. Waterfalls abound, and the deep and serene Yellowstone Lake is surrounded by multicolored cliffs, layered and carved from years of glacial activity.

Another vast ancient lake, really an inland sea, once covered much of Wyoming and left deposits of soda ash and other important minerals useful in a variety of industries today. Prehistoric life thrived around the tropical lake, leaving rich stores of fossil fuels and a host of archeologically significant remains, from several dinosaur graveyards to petrified trees. Some of the earliest ancestors of the modern horse have been unearthed within Wyoming's boundaries, as well as many other more ancient life forms.

Wildlife

Today, there are more animals than people in Wyoming, which is the least populated of any state in the union. Wyoming is home to numerous native species of ungulates, such as the bison (buffalo), pronghorn antelope, bighorn sheep, mule deer and white-tailed deer, moose, and elk, to name just a few. In the last couple of centuries, the state has also become host to a large population of domesticated cattle, sheep, horses, and even a few llamas and ostriches. Wild mustangs also roam the plains.

The animal population includes numerous prairie and mountain birds, from the Bald Eagle to the Meadowlark to the Sage Grouse. Several fish species inhabit the waterways, including many varieties of trout, bass, and even catfish. Beavers and otters can also be seen in streams and ponds. Marmots, rabbits, picas, chipmunks, and other small critters frequent the highlands and lowlands alike. Wolves, cougars, coyotes, foxes, badgers, and even a few bears also dwell in this largely untamed country.

Wyoming At a Glance

Population (2000): 493,782

Entered union: July 10, 1890

Capital: Cheyenne

Nickname: The Cowboy State or The Equality State

Motto: Equal Rights

Bird: Meadowlark

Flower: Indian Paintbrush

Song: "Wyoming"

Stones: Jade

Tree: Cottonwood

Animal: Bison

Fish: Cutthroat Trout

Fossil: Knightia (Fossilized fish)

Land area: 97,819 square miles

Water area: 714 square miles

Size ranking: 9th

Geographic center: Fremont, 58 miles ENE of Lander

Length: 360 miles

Width: 280 miles

Highest point: 13,804 feet (Gannett Peak)

Lowest point: 3,099 feet (Belle Fourche River)

Mean Elevation: 6,700 ft

Highest temperature: 114° on July 12, 1900, at Basin

Lowest temperature: -66° on Feb. 9, 1933, at Riverside

Tumbleweeds congregate along a fence line near Rocky Point.

THE HISTORY OF WYOMING'S PEOPLE

Native Americans

Drawn by the mineral treasures and the wildlife, humans have been living here for millennia as well. Some of the oldest Native American campsites in North America have been discovered in Wyoming, dating back to over 11, 000 years ago.

Ever since that time, many groups of Native Americans have valued Wyoming as prime hunting ground. Early tribes utilized "buffalo jumps," cliffs where the bison were driven over the ledge to their deaths. Later on, hunting was done with weapons made from the flint and metals found in the region. The hunters left behind bones, pottery, petroglyphs, fire rings, and sacred stone circles known as Medicine Wheels, the use of which is still something of a mystery.

In more recent times, numerous plains tribes inhabited the Wyoming wilderness, and continued to vie for hunting rights in the region for centuries. Among these were the Cheyenne, Sioux, Arapaho, Shoshone, Lakota, Crow, Comanche, Ute, Paiute, Bannock, Blackfeet, Ogalala, Arikara, Gros Ventre, Nez Perce, and Miniconjou. These tribes had rivalries and alliances that sometimes changed and often lasted for generations.

Many Native Americans of great prominence called Wyoming home. The likes of Chief Washakie, Chief Joseph, Sitting Bull, Red Cloud, Crazy Horse, Dull Knife, White Bull, and Black Horse inhabited these parts during at least part of their lives. Even Sacajawea, the famous guide for Lewis and Clark, spent some of her life within the state's borders, and is thought by some to have been laid to rest near the Wind River Reservation.

Today, relatively few Native Americans remain in the state, many of who live on the sole protected remnant of their ancestral lands, the Wind River Reservation. They are increasingly reclaiming their heritage, and are making the most of opportunities to share their tribal traditions at a number of events and venues throughout the state.

Explorers And Mountain Men

John Colter, a member of the Lewis and Clark expedition, was probably the first white man to set foot in Wyoming, investigating the marvels of Yellowstone country in 1808. Over the next decade or so, Jacques LaRamee, a French-Canadian trapper traveled extensively in the eastern part of the state. Thereafter, Wyoming became the place many early European adventurers called home. Mountain men, in particular, were largely responsible for much of the investigation of the state. Lured here by the promise of riches from beaver pelts and other wild game, many men came to Wyoming with the John Jacob Astor expedition in the 1820s, and never left. William Ashley and Andrew Henry led the original party.

They befriended some Native Americans and were often rewarded with wives. In time and through often harrowing experience, they became familiar with the wonders and dangers of this magnificent state. They congregated at events called Rendezvous, exchanging goods, information, stories, a few punches, and a lot of liquor. These are still celebrated today in their honor, but fighting is now frowned upon. Names such as Jim Bridger, Kit Carson, and Jedediah Smith marked the paths that would be trod by Easterners for the next two centuries and beyond.

Pioneers And Homesteaders

Not far behind the mountain men came pioneers, heading West to make new lives for themselves in Oregon country and Utah's Great Salt Lake Valley. Crossed by both the Oregon and Mormon Trails, innumerable wagons and hand carts traversed Wyoming, leaving ruts in the bedrock still clearly visible over 150 years later.

Immigrants left their marks in other ways, with names etched on cliffs and scattered graves. Winter in the high plains and mountains was harsh and often sudden, sometimes taking travelers by surprise. Martin's Cove was the site of the most extensive casualties. Disease and the occasional Indian raid took their toll as well. Making it across the state alive was no mean feat.

As the Utah Territory welcomed more and more Mormon immigrants, Prophet Brigham Young sent settlers north into Wyoming to tame the wild country there. The Mormon pioneers cultivated significant quantities of wilderness, from Fort Bridger to the Star Valley area to the Bighorn Basin, where they built an extensive canal system. They left behind a legacy of hard work and industry, and built many historic landmarks that still stand today.

Other settlers came from the East to homestead in relative peace, including German Lutherans from Iowa, who farmed land in the Bighorn Basin and near the Nebraska border. Their contributions have also stood the test of time, and made Wyoming part of what it is today.

The Overland Stage And The Pony Express

As traffic increased across Wyoming, a stage route was developed, with regular stops for weary travelers. With the Western population growing, many who rode the trail came to do business, not to settle. The Overland Stage Trail provided easier mobility for both eastern and western journeys. Stagecoaches ran freight and provided protection as well.

Many stage stations also served as stopovers for Pony Express riders, providing fresh horses for both. Sometimes, even the stage didn't travel fast enough for important information to be transmitted from coast to coast. A letter sent by Pony Express could travel from New York to California in about seven or eight days. Riding for the Pony Express was a dangerous occupation, mostly because riders were on their own, confronting uncertain conditions among the Indians, and unpredictable weather. Nevertheless, during the eighteen months it was in operation, only two riders died.

Treasure Seekers And Miners

The discovery of gold in California sparked a new wave of immigration in the 1850s and 60s. The pioneer influx was still ongoing, but now the byways were also filled with wanderers hoping to "strike it rich", if not in California then in Colorado, Montana, or South Dakota.

Wyoming, too, had its share of mineral wealth, and mining towns began to take root. The communities would thrive until the mine ran out of whatever it had provided, then the miners would move on. This was the start of the boom and bust cycle that would continue throughout Wyoming's development.

The hunt for gold inspired John Bozeman to pioneer a route north through Wyoming to the Montana gold fields. By 1864, the Bozeman Trail was yet another heavy traffic area across the state.

The Forts And The Indian Wars

As more and more white people began to come into Wyoming, the Native Americans became increasingly distressed about the impact the strangers were having on tribal lands. Some tribes, like the Shoshone under Chief Washakie, tried to maintain peaceful relations. Others chafed under the imposed sanctions, and misunderstandings and conflict became more frequent.

With the increase in Indian confrontations, the US government began to establish a presence in the area. Various forts, such as Fort Bridger and Fort Laramie, which had once been merely supply and trading posts, became barricaded citadels. Some of the most well known Indian battles were fought in Wyoming, including the brutal Fetterman Massacre at Fort Phil Kearney.

Both sides sustained many casualties in the Battle of the Red Buttes at Platte Bridge Station, later called Fort Caspar. The Battle of the Rosebud, which happened in the midst of the Powder River Expedition, had Native Americans fighting on both sides. Although the Battle of the Little Bighorn, or Custer's Last Stand, took place across the Montana border, it was the culminating campaign that began with a pioneer's missing cow near Fort Laramie, and the Grattan Massacre that followed. William F. "Buffalo Bill" Cody made a name for himself the summer after the Little Bighorn disaster by beating Cheyenne Chief Yellow Hand in one-to-one combat.

The Railroad And The Telegraph Line

Technology caught up with the call to head west, and steam engines became the preferred method of travel, telegraph messages the preferred form of communication. Plans were laid for a transcontinental railroad, and the race was on between the Eastern and Western builders as they hurried to meet somewhere in the middle.

The Union Pacific Railroad, and several smaller railroads such as the Burlington, Northern, and Santa Fe Lines, laid tracks all over the state, creating new "hell on wheels" communities, and bringing a variety of colorful people of different nationalities to the area. The logging industry and the coal industry rose up to meet the needs of the growing railways. The completion of the railroad in 1869 brought ever-greater numbers of Easterners to the west.

Before the railroad was finished, the state was filled with telegraph lines and offices, mostly where the stage and Pony Express stops had been. Mail delivered by Pony Express had taken about a week to arrive. With the telegraph, messages could be sent almost instantaneously. East and West were connected like never before.

Cattle And Cowboys

As the Eastern states filled with people, rangeland became harder and harder to find. Texas cattlemen, in particular, were on the lookout for new territory where their herds could graze cheaply, unmolested. Pioneering ranchers like Nelson Story blazed the Texas Trail north, through Oklahoma and Colorado into the open range country of Wyoming, Montana, and the Dakotas. With the stabilizing presence of the army and the freight options brought by the railroad, Wyoming became ideal cattle country. Huge ranching companies sprung up, like the Swan Land and Cattle Company, and the Pitchfork and Sun Ranches.

With the cattle came the cowboys, tough and hard living, who made an art of the business of tending the herds. From their broad-brimmed hats, high-heeled boots, chaps and spurs, to their horsemanship, skills with ropes, and understanding of animals and nature, the cowboy became a breed apart. They lead a harsh and lonely existence, spending endless days on the windswept, open range, living off trail food and sleeping by solitary campfires. The cowboy became Wyoming's icon because Wyoming made him who he was.

Cattle ranching was so profitable during the late 1800s that it made many men rich. Other men, who were already rich, such as noblemen and aristocrats from Europe, found it useful to invest in the cattle industry. For either or perhaps both reasons, the most successful ranchers became known as "cattle barons."

The cattle barons had a great deal of influence in territorial politics and were able to strong-arm many agricultural settlers into giving up their land. Accusations of cattle rustling were rampant. Hired guns, known as "range detectives", intimidated homesteaders, and occasionally hung or shot someone. Tom Horn, Cattle Kate, and Calamity Jane became notorious for their roles in the range wars.

West of Dayton.

Sheep And Sheepherders

The cattlemen met their match with the advent of the sheep industry. Sheep were considered by some to be a more profitable investment because they provided two commodities: wool and lambs, and the wool was a renewable resource. Experienced European sheepherders, including many Basques from the Pyrenees, came to Wyoming to work for sheep ranchers.

Sheep ranching began to rival cattle ranching for power and money, but the real rivalry was over the rangeland and grazing rights. Eventually, tensions between the two industries and homesteaders escalated from hired guns making specific "hits" to an all out war in Johnson County. Federal troops had to be sent in to settle the raging dispute.

The Equality State

Wyoming made leaps in pioneering women's rights while it was still a territory. With such a scattered population, every able-bodied person had value. Wyoming became the first government entity in the world to grant women the vote and the right to hold office, as well as allowing them to own property in their own name.

The first female voter, perhaps in the entire world, was "Grandma" Louisa A. Swain of Laramie. The first female jurors in the world, Eliza Stewart, Amelia Hatcher, C.H. Hilton, Mary Mackel, Agnes Baker, and Sarah Pease, attended a trial in Laramie also. Wyoming had the first female Justice of the Peace in the world, Esther Morris, in South Pass City, and the first female governor in the US, Nellie Tayloe Ross, ran the state after her husband died in office. Jackson became to first town in the country to elect a group of city officials who were all women in 1920. Wyoming continues to be a place where women have great value.

Outlaws

This rough country attracted many rough characters through the years, including:
Butch Cassidy (Robert Leroy Parker)
The Sundance Kid (Harry Longabaugh)
Kid Curry (Harry Logan)
"Flat Nose" George Currie
William C. "Teton" Jackson (Harvey Gleason)
James Butler "Wild Bill" Hickok
Tom Horn
John Henry "Doc" Holliday
Cattle Kate (Ellen Watson)
Calamity Jane (Martha Jane Canary)
Jesse James
Frank James (Jesse's brother)
"Big Nose George" Parrott (George Manuse)
"Dutch Charley" Burris
Bill Carlisle, Wyoming's (and perhaps the West's) last great "gentleman" train robber, who politely held up passengers several times between 1916 and 1919. He later was caught and served time in jail as a model prisoner.

WIDE OPEN SPACES

While traveling on the backroads, you will sometimes get a sense that nobody lives here. You can travel for miles without seeing any sign of civilization beyond the occasional small herds of cattle. In many parts of the state, oil wells outnumber people. Occupied houses are rare and outnumbered by abandoned homesteaders shacks and log cabins. Fences often disappear entirely and are replaced by the infrequent "Open Range" signs that warn you cattle may be having their mid-day siesta in the middle of the road.

None-the-less, most of this land is privately owned unless posted otherwise. Before abandoning your car and heading out across these open spaces, it's a good idea and common courtesy to find the property owner and get permission. If you see fenceposts or gates with bright orange blazes, then getting permission isn't an option. They mean "no trespassing" in no uncertain terms.

However, I've never been shot at for stopping the car, getting out and smelling the sage, listening to the sound of silence, or to the voice of the wind, or the gurgle of a stream, the howl of a coyote, or the unidentified song of a prairie bird. I've never been asked to move along when I've stopped to admire a sunset, or simply marvel at the splendor of the endless sky.

Most of those that have bought and paid for a piece of this marvelous state don't mind sharing it with those who come to visit. They simply ask that you respect it and leave no trace you were there.

THE ROADS

Gravel roads are the rule rather than the exception in this part of the country. Almost all of Wyoming's paved roads are well maintained. There are posted speed limits and they are vigorously enforced.

Be prepared at any time to slow down for riders on horseback. Most horses are accustomed to cars, but can spook if you drive too near. Much of wyoming is open range. Cattle may be grazing on the road. A head-on with a steer can be just as deadly as a head-on with another automobile.

And speaking of cattle, don't be surprised if you come upon a cattle drive. If you do, follow the instructions of the drovers. They will make every effort to clear a path to allow you through. Usually the cattle just part ways and make a path, but don't go on unless you're given instructions to.

Beware of black ice! This is a virtually invisible layer of ice that forms on road surfaces after a fog. Be particularly careful of stretches of road that parallel rivers and creeks. The early morning fog rising from them can settle on the road freezing instantly. If you feel yourself sliding, tap your brakes gently. If you slam on the brakes, it's all but over. Gently steer into the direction of your skid (if your back end is going right—steer right).

Gumbo

We gave this subject its own headline. It is very important that you read it—and heed it.

While Wyoming isn't the only state that has gumbo, it has its fair share. If you become a resident, it is one of the first things you develop a respect (a healthy respect) for. Grizzlys and rattlesnakes might be the hazards you're warned of, but gumbo is the one that will get you.

You'll find it mostly in the eastern half of the state. It lies in wait on what in dry weather appears to be an ordinary rock hard dirt road. Your first clue is the occasional sign that reads *Road Impassable When Wet*. This is a clear understatement. When these roads become even mildly wet, they turn into a monster that swallows all sizes of vehicles—and yes, even 4-wheel drive SUVs. Think you'll get a tow? Forget it. No tow truck operator with a higher IQ than dirt will venture onto it until it dries. If you walk on it, you will grow six inches taller and gain 25 pounds all on the bottom of your shoes. It can coat your tires until they won't turn anymore. Of course, this is if it doesn't swallow you whole first like an unsuspecting native in a Tarzan movie who steps into quicksand.

Bottomline, heed the signs. If it looks like rain, head for the nearest paved road. When it comes to swallowing things whole, the Bermuda Triangle is an amateur compared to Wyoming Gumbo.

WYOMING CLIMATE

Topographic Features

Wyoming's outstanding features are its majestic mountains and high plains. Its mean elevation is about 6,700 feet above sea level and even when the mountains are excluded, the average elevation over the southern part of the State is well over 6,000 feet, while much of the northern portion is some 2,500 feet lower. The lowest point, 3,125 feet, is near the northeast corner where the Belle Fourche River crosses the State line into South Dakota. The highest point is Gannett Peak at 13,785 feet, which is part of the Wind River Range in the west-central portion. Since the mountain ranges lie in a general north-south direction, they are perpendicular to the prevailing westerlies, therefore, the mountain ranges provide effective barriers which force the air currents moving in from the Pacific Ocean to rise and drop much of their moisture along the western slopes. The State is considered semiarid east of the mountains. There are several mountain ranges, but the mountains themselves cover less area than the high plains. The topography and variations in elevation make it difficult to divide the State into homogeneous, climatological areas.

The Continental Divide splits the State from near the northwest corner to the center of the southern border. This leaves most of the drainage areas to the east. The run-off drains into three great river systems: the Columbia, the Colorado, and the Missouri. The Snake with its tributaries in the northwest flows into the Columbia; the Green River drains most of the Southwest portion and joins the Colorado: the Yellowstone, Wind River, Big Horn, Tongue, and Powder drainage areas cover most of the north portion and flow northward into the Missouri; the Belle Fourche, Cheyenne, and Niobrara covering the east-central portion, flow eastward: while the Platte drains the southeast and flows eastward into Nebraska. There is a relatively small area along the southwest border that is drained by the Bear which flows into the Great Salt Lake. In the south-central portion west of Rawlins, there is an area called the Great Divide Basin. Part of this area is often referred to as the Red Desert. There is no drainage from this Basin and precipitation, which averages only 7 to 10 inches annually, follows creekbeds to ponds or small lakes where it either evaporates or percolates into the ground.

Snow accumulates to considerable depths in the high mountains and many of the streams fed by the melting snow furnish ample quantities of water for irrigation of thousands of acres of land. The snowmelt also furnishes the water to generate electric power, and for domestic use.

Rapid run-off from heavy rain during thunderstorms causes flash flooding on the headwater streams, and when the time of these storms coincides with the melting of the snow pack, the flooding is intensified. When overflow occurs in the vicinity of urban communities situated near the streams considerable damage results.

Temperature

Because of its elevation, Wyoming has a relatively cool climate. Above the 6,000 feet level the temperature rarely exceeds 100° F. The warmest parts of the State are the lower portions of portions of the Big Horn Basin, the lower elevations of the central and northeast portions, and along the east border. The highest recorded temperature was 114° F on July 12, 1900, at Basin in the Big Horn Basin. The average maximum temperature at Basin in July is 92° F. For most of the State, mean maximum temperatures in July range between 85 and 95° F. With increasing elevation, average values drop rapidly. A few places in the mountains at about the 9,000 foot level have average maximums in July close to 70° F. Summer nights are almost invariably cool, even though daytime readings may be quite high at times. For most places away from the mountains, the mean minimum temperature in July ranges from 50 to 60 ° F. Of course, the mountains and high valleys are much cooler with average lows in the middle of the summer in the 30s and 40s with occasional drops below freezing.

In the wintertime it is characteristic to have rapid and frequent changes between mild and cold spells. Usually there are less than 10 cold waves during a winter, and frequently less than half that number for most of the State. The majority of cold waves move southward on the east side of the Divide. Sometimes only the northeast part of the State is affected by the cold air as

Buffalo Bill Scenic Highway west of Cody.

it slides eastward over the plains. Many of the cold waves are not accompanied by enough snow to cause severe conditions. In January, the coldest month generally, man minimum temperatures range mostly from 5 to 10° F. In the western valleys mean values go down to about 5° below zero. The record low for the State is -66° F observed February 9, 1933, at Yellowstone Park. During warm spells in the winter, nighttime temperatures frequently remain above freezing. Chinooks, warm downslope winds, are common along the eastern slopes.

Numerous valleys provide ideal pockets for the collection of cold air drainage at night. Protecting mountain ranges prevent the wind from stirring the air, and the colder heavier air settles into the valleys often sending readings well below zero. It is common to have temperatures in the valleys considerably lower than on the nearby mountain side. Big Piney in the Green River Valley is such a location. Mean January temperatures in the Big Horn Basin show the variation between readings in the lower part of the valley and those higher up. At Worland and Basin in the lower portion of the Big Horn Basin, not far from the 4,000 foot level, the mean minimum temperature for January is zero, while Cody, close to 5,000 feet on the west side of the valley has a mean January minimum of 11° F. January, the coldest month, has occasional mild periods when maximum readings will reach the 50s; however, winters are usually long and cold.

Growing Season

Early freezes in the fall and late in the spring are characteristic. This results in long winters and short growing seasons. However, it is a county of rapid changes through the fall, winter, and spring seasons, with frequent variations from cold to mild periods. The average growing season (freeze-free period) for the principal agricultural areas is approximately 125 days. For hardier plants which can stand a temperature of 28° F, or slightly lower, the growing season is the agricultural areas east of the Divide is approximately 145 days. In the mountains and high valleys freezing temperatures may occur any time during the summer. For tender plants there is practically no growing season in such areas as the upper Green River Valley, the Star Valley and Jackson Hole. At Farson near Sandy Creek, a tributary of the Green River, the average is 42 days between the last temperature of 32° F in early summer and the first freeze in late summer. For the places like the Star Valley and Jackson Hole, the growing season is even shorter.

Sunshine

For most of the State, sunshine ranges from 60 percent of the possible amount during the winter to about 75 percent during the summer. Mountain areas receive less, and in the wintertime the estimated amount over the northwestern mountains is about 45 percent. In the summertime when sunshine is greatest – not only in time but also intensity – it is characteristic for the mornings to be mostly clear. Cumulus clouds develop nearly every day and frequently blot out the sun for a portion of the afternoons. Because the altitude provides less atmosphere for the sun's rays to penetrate and because of the very small amount of fog, haze, and smoke, the intensity of sunshine in unusually high.

Traffic can often be heavy on Wyoming roads. Watch for merging traffic on all open highway.

Precipitation

Like other states in the west, precipitation varies a great deal from one location to another. The period of maximum precipitation occurs in the spring and early summer for most of the State. Precipitation is greater over the mountain ranges and usually at the higher elevations, although elevation alone is not the predominant influence. For example, over most of the southwest portion, where the elevation ranges from 6,500 to 8,500 feet, annual precipitation varies from 7 to 10 inches. At lower elevations over the northeast portion and along the eastern border, where elevations are mostly in the range from 4,000 to 5,500 feet, annual averages are from 12 to 16 inches. The relatively dry southwest portion is a high plateau nearly surrounded by mountain ranges.

The Big Horn Basin provides a striking example of the effect of mountain ranges in blocking the flow of moisture laden air from the east as well as from the west. The lower portion of the Basin has an annual precipitation of 5 to 8 inches, and it is the driest part of the State. The station showing the least amount is Seaver at 4,105 feet with an annual mean of about 5.50 inches. In the southern part of the Basin, Worland at 4,061 feet has an annual mean of 7 to 8 inches as compared with Termopolis at 4,313 feet and 11 to 12 inches. There is another good example in the southeastern part of the State where Laramie at 7,236 feet has an annual mean of 10 inches, while 30 miles to the west, Centennial at 8,074 feet receives about 16 inches. Only a few locations receive as much as 40 inches a year, based on gage records.

During the summer, showers are quite frequent but often amount to only a few hundredths of an inch. Occasionally there will be some very heavy rain associated with thunderstorms covering a few square miles. There are usually several local storms each year with from 1 to 2 inches of rain in a 24-hour period. On rare occasions, 24-hour amounts range from 3 to 5 inches. The greatest 24-hour total recorded for any place in Wyoming is 5.50 inches at Dull Center, near Newcastle, on May 31, 1927.

Humidity and Evaporation

The average relative humidity is quite low and provides delightful summer weather. During the warmer part of the summer days, the humidity drops to about 25 to 30 percent, and on a few occasions it will be as low as 5 to 10 percent. Late at night when the temperature is lowest, the humidity will generally rise to 65 or 75 percent. This results in an average diurnal variation of about 40 to 45 percent during the summer, but in the winter the variation is much less. Low relative humidity, high percentage of sunshine, and rather high average winds all contribute to a high rate of evaporation. Because of frequent spells of freezing weather before May 1 and after September 30, it is difficult to obtain consistent records of evaporation for more than the 5-month period from May through September. For this period, the average amount of evaporation is approximately 41 inches, as determined from evaporation pans at a few selected locations. The overall range is from 30 to about 50 inches.

Severe Storms

Hailstorms are the most destructive type of local storm for this State, and every year damage to crops and property from hail amount to many thousands of dollars. Occasionally a hailstorm will pass over a city and cause severe damage. Most of the hailstorms pass over the open rangeland and damage is slight, although in small areas of crop producing land, some farmers occasionally lose an entire crop by hail.

Tornadoes occur, but records show they are much less frequent and destructive than those that occur in the Midwest. The relatively small amount of destruction is partly due to the fact that most of Wyoming is open range country and sparsely populated. However, records show that tornadoes which occur here are somewhat smaller and have a shorter duration. Many of them touch the ground for only a few minutes before receding into the clouds. The season extends from April through September. June has the greatest number on the average with May next and most occur in the eastern part of the State.

Wyoming is quite windy, and during the win-

The oil well is ubiquitous throughout the state.

ter there are frequent periods when the wind reaches 30 to 40 miles per hour with gusts to 50 or 60. Prevailing directions in the different localities vary form west-south-west through west to northwest. In many localities winds are so strong and constant from those directions that trees show a definite lean towards the east or southeast.

Snow and Blizzards

Snow falls frequently from November through May and at lower elevations is light to moderate. About five times a year on the average, stations at the lower elevations will have snowfall exceeding 5 inches. Falls of 10 to 15 inches or more for a single storm occur but are infrequent outside of the mountains. Wind will frequently accompany of follow a snowstorm and pile the snow into drifts several feet deep. The snow sometimes drifts so much that it is difficult to obtain an accurate measurement of snowfall. An unusually heavy snow occurred at Sheridan on the 3rd and 4th of April 1955. During this period the snowfall amounted to 39.0 inches, had a water equivalent of 4.30 inches and blizzard conditions lasted more than 43 hours. High winds and low temperatures with snow cause blizzard or near blizzard conditions. These conditions sometimes last a day or two, but it is uncommon for a severe blizzard to last over three days.

Total annual snowfall varies considerably. At the lower elevations in the east, the range is from 60 to 70 inches. Over the drier southwest portion, amounts vary from 45 to 55 inches. Snow is very light in the Big Horn Basin with annual averages from 15 to 20 inches over the lower portion and 30 to 40 inches on the sides of the Basin where elevations range from 5,000 to 6,000 feet. The mountains receive a great deal more and in the higher ranges annual amounts are well over 200 inches. At Beckler River Ranger Station in the southwest corner of Yellowstone Park, the snowfall averages 262 inches for a 20-year period.

The weather pattern most favorable for precipitation is one with a low-pressure center a little to the south of the State. This will normally provide a condition where relatively cool air at the surface is overrun by warmer moist air. Studies of wind flow patterns indicate that Wyoming is covered most of the time by air from the Pacific. A smaller percentage of time the State is covered by cold air masses that move down from Canada.

Agriculture

Most of the State has been subjected to erosion for tens of thousands of years and less than 10 percent is covered with a mantle of recent (geologically speaking) water-transported soil. The lack of such soil and adequate moisture limits the natural vegetation to hardy plants, such as sagebrush, greasewood, and short grass. Low relative humidity and the high rate of evaporation add to the problem. A number of abandoned homesteads of onetime enthusiastic settlers bear silent testimony to the lack of moisture. Even so, dryland farming is carried on successfully in some areas. Approximately 42 percent of the State's total area is privately-owned land, the majority of which is used for grazing, although some is timberland. The fact that most of the State is still Government-owned attests to the semiarid climate which has make the land less attractive to homesteaders. Nearly 4 percent of the State is cultivated cropland, including both irrigated and nonirrigated. Another 13 percent is covered with forests, while parks and recreational areas take up about 4 percent.

The majority of the State is used for grazing and has a general appearance of dryness most of the time. The more abundant spring moisture brings a greener landscape often with myriad, varicolored wild flowers. As the season merges into summer, grasses and flowers turn brown, but continue to serve as food for livestock. Native grasses are nutritious, although scant. There are some very fine grazing areas with luxuriant grasses, especially in or near the mountains. Grass is generally so scarce that large ranches are required for profitable operation. The average for most cattle grazing is about 35 to 40 acres per cow. The

mountain areas provide timber and a storage place for the winter snows which in the spring and summer feed lakes and reservoirs used in the irrigations districts. Most of the irrigated land is located in the valleys of the following river systems and their tributaries: North Platte, Wind River, Big Horn, Tongue, and Green. Principal crops in the irrigation districts are sugar beets, beans, potatoes, and hay. On the nonirrigated land the principal crops are hay and small grains, such as wheat, barley, and oats.

Tourism is increasingly important to Wyoming's economy and millions of persons, including many sportsmen, visit the State annually to enjoy Yellowstone and Grand Teton National Parks.

Weather article provided by National Climatic Data Center

THE NATIONAL TRAILS SYSTEM

"I should compare the (South) pass to the ascent of the capitol hill from the avenue at Washington."
- John Fremont, 1843, describing the ease of using South Pass to cross the Rocky Mountains

In 1800, America's western border reached only as far as the Mississippi River. Following the Louisiana Purchase in 1803 the country nearly doubled in size, pushing the nation's western edge past the Rocky Mountains.

Yet the wilderness known as Oregon Country (which included present-day Oregon, Washington and part of Idaho) still belonged to the British, a fact that made many Americans eager to settle the region and claim it for the United States.

American Indians had traversed this country for many years, but for whites it was unknown territory. Lewis and Clark's secretly funded expedition in 1803 was part of a U.S. Government plan to open Oregon Country to settlement. However, the hazardous route blazed by this party was not feasible for families traveling by wagon. An easier trail was needed.

Robert Stewart of the Astorians (a group of fur traders who established Fort Astoria in western Oregon's Columbia River) became the first white to use what later became known as the Oregon Trail. Stewart's 2,000-mile journey from Fort Astoria to St. Louis in 1910 took 10 months to complete; still, it was a much less rugged trail than Lewis and Clark's route.

It wasn't until 1836 that the first wagons were used on the trek from Missouri to Oregon. A missionary party headed by Marcus Whitman and his wife Narcissa bravely set out to reach the Willamette Valley. Though the Whitmans were forced to abandon their wagons 200 miles short of Oregon, they proved that families could go west by wheeled travel.

In the spring of 1843, a wagon train of nearly 1,000 people organized at Independence, Missouri with plans to reach Oregon Country. Amidst an overwhelming chorus of naysayers who doubted their success, the so-called "Great Migration" made it safely to Oregon. Crucial to their success was the use of South Pass, a 12-mile wide valley that was virtually the sole place between the plains and Oregon where wagons could cross the formidable Rocky Mountains.

By 1846, thousands of emigrants who were drawn west by cheap land, patriotism or the promise of a better life found their way to Oregon Country. With so many Americans settling the region, it became obvious to the British that Oregon was no longer theirs. They ceded Oregon Country to the United States that year.

"When you start over these wide plains, let no one leave dependent on his best friend for anything; for if you do, you will certainly have a blow-out before you get far." - John Shivley, 1846

Before railroads or automobiles, people in America had to travel by foot, horse, boat or wagon. Some of these routes from our nation's early days still remain today as reminders of our historic past. A National Historic Trail (NHT) such as the Oregon NHT is an extended trail that follows original routes of travel of national historical significance.

In 1995, the National Park Service established the National Trails System Office in Salt Lake City, Utah. The Salt Lake City Trails Office administers the Oregon, the California, the Mormon Pioneer and the Pony Express NHTs.

The National Trails System does not manage trail resources on a day-to-day basis. The responsibility for managing trail resources remains in the hands of the current trail managers at the federal, state, local and private levels.

The Office was established to improve interstate and interregional coordination. Specific responsibilities of this trails office include coordinating and supporting the protection of trail resources, marking and interpreting the trails, designating and marking an auto-tour route and identifying and certifying high-potential sites.

In 1968, Congress enacted the National Trails System Act and in 1978, National Historic Trail designations were added. The National Historic Trails System commemorates these historic routes and promotes their preservation, interpretation and appreciation.

National Historic Trails recognize diverse facets of history such as prominent past routes of exploration, migration, trade, communication and military action. The historic trails generally consist of remnant sites and trail segments, and thus are not necessarily contiguous. Although National Historic Trails are administered by federal agencies, land ownership may be in public or private hands. Of the 11 National Historic Trails, nine are administered by the National Park Service, one by the USDA Forest Service and one by the Bureau of Land Management.

If Americans today were to undertake a four-month, 2,000-mile journey on foot without the aid of modern conveniences, many would be in for a harsh jolt. Despite the lingering romance with which many view the emigrant tide on the Oregon Trail, the journey was tough.

Emigrants traveled under the dual yoke of fear and withering physical requirements. Rumors of hostile Indians coupled with unforgiving country, disease and dangerous work made life difficult.

Yet thousands did make it to Oregon. What was their journey like on a day-to-day basis?

First of all, timing was important to the emigrants' success in reaching Oregon. The most favorable time to depart from Missouri was in April or May. This would put them on schedule to make the high mountain passes when winter snows would not be a threat.

Mistakes were often made before the journey even began. In preparing for the trip, many emigrants overloaded their wagons with supplies. As a result, not long after leaving Missouri, dumping excess items was a common sight along the trail. Tools, guns and food were considered vital—heirlooms were not.

The relatively gentle first leg of the route along the Platte River was a time for the emigrants to settle into travel mode. This meant get-

Coal trains are a frequent reminder of Wyoming's vast natural resources. Photo by David Scott Smith. Photo courtesy of Gillette Convention and Visitor's Bureau.

ting used to hitching and unhitching the oxen, cattle and mules whenever a stop was made - hard and dangerous work. It also meant constant wagon maintenance, foraging for firewood and clean water, cooking over open fires and learning how to break and set camp every day.

When emigrants reached Chimney Rock and Scotts Bluff, their journey was one-third over. But more challenging terrain lay ahead as water, firewood and supply depots became more scarce. Buffalo herds that initially were a dependable food source for the emigrants also thinned out due to excessive killing.

The challenge of crossing many rivers and the Continental Divide created other severe tests for the emigrants. Summer temperatures, miles of shadeless trail and choking dust compounded to make life decidedly unenjoyable. Though confrontations with Indians were rare, the fear of attack was a constant worry.

The last leg of the trail was the most difficult. But thoughts of approaching winter snows kept emigrants motivated to move as quickly as possible. The Blue Mountains in eastern Oregon and the Cascade range in the west presented barriers that slowed progress.

Upon reaching Oregon City, the emigrants were faced with either taking their chances on the dangerous Columbia River, or, starting in 1846, taking the safer but longer Barlow Road. Sam Barlow's toll road became the preferred route for the emigrants. Finally, if money, animals, wagons, supplies and morale held out, the emigrants reached the Willamette Valley.

WYOMING'S NATURAL RESOURCES

You know that when you drive your car you are using gasoline, and when you heat your home you are using natural gas. But did you know that when you turn on a light, chances are you're using coal? And when you drink that ice cold milk in a tall glass, you are using trona? And cosmetics and food additives on the market today use bentonite? Minerals contribute significantly to our way of life: to the products we use, the items

we need, the comforts we are accustomed to. And Wyoming minerals managed by the Bureau of Land Management play a major role in how we live today.

Oil and Gas Production:

Oil

• Wyoming is the number one producer of federal onshore oil producing 46% of the nation's total.

• Wyoming produced a total of 104 million barrels of oil in 1990.

• Federal land in Wyoming produced 67 million barrels of oil, or about 60% of the states total in 1990.

• Oil production is expected to continue to decline as known reserves are depleted, to an estimated 88 million barrels total production in 1995.

Gas

• Wyoming is the number two producer of federal onshore natural gas producing 33% of the nation's total.

• Wyoming produced 681 billion cubic feet of natural gas in 1990.

• Federal land in Wyoming produced 396 billion cubic feet of natural gas in 1990, or about 60% of the state's total.

• Natural gas production is expected to increase to over 900 billion cubic feet in 1995.

Trends

• New techniques such as horizontal drilling and carbon dioxide injection are being developed to increase the recovery rate of oil reserves.

• Coal bed methane is a natural gas which has received increased attention recently. When water is removed from underground coal seams, methane can be produced. It has been estimated that Wyoming coal beds may contain up to 77 trillion cubic feet of coal bed methane. So far, costs of development have been high, discouraging production.

Wyoming has huge reserves of low sulfur coal. The Eagle Butte Mine is one of several large open pit mines in the state.

Economics:

• The federal government received about $19 million from lease rental and bonuses in 1991, half going to the State of Wyoming.

• The federal government received about $232 million from royalties on oil and gas in Wyoming during 1991, half of which goes to the State of Wyoming.

• The oil and gas industry employs about 18,000 people in Wyoming.

Uses:

• Oil is refined into a variety of products, the most common being fuel and lubricants for vehicles.

• Natural gas is used in heating homes and other structures.

• Petroleum is used in a wide variety of products ranging from plastics, nylon and other synthetic fibers.

• Petroleum is also used in a wide variety of cosmetics and toiletries such as petroleum jelly.

Coal Production:

• Wyoming is the nation's largest coal producing state. The passage of the Clean Air Act will increase demand for Wyoming's low sulfur coal.

• 194 million tons of coal was mined in Wyoming in 1991, 85-90% of which is produced from federal land.

• Total coal from federal leases in the United States was about 253 million tons in 1991.

• Wyoming produces about 70% of the total federal coal in the United States.

• Wyoming coal production is estimated to increase to 235 million tons of coal mined in 1995.

• Most of Wyoming mines are surface, strip mines.

• On site drying techniques are being developed to increase the heat content of Wyoming's coal which should make it even more marketable in the future.

Economics:

• Approximately $110 million was collected in federal royalties in 1991, half of which goes to the State of Wyoming.

• Coal mining employs over 4,600 people in Wyoming

Uses:

• Wyoming coal is primarily used in electric power generation.

Location:

• The largest mines are located in southeast Campbell County (the southern Powder River Basin).

• Coal is also mined in central Sweetwater County east of Rock Springs, Carbon County north of Hanna, Converse County north of Glenrock, and Lincoln County near Kemmerer.

• One underground coal mine is in Carbon County, and one is in Sweetwater County.

Bentonite

Production:

• Bentonite is a clay material which is formed through the weathering of volcanic ash or tuff.

• Wyoming bentonite mines are open pit mines.

• Wyoming is the leading producer in the United States, producing about 2.4 million tons per year.

• Wyoming produces about 68% of the bentonite mined in the United States.

• Only about 23% of Wyoming's production is from federal lands. However, most of the bentonite operations were started on mining claims on federal land which were subsequently turned over to operator ownership.

Economics:

• The bentonite industry in Wyoming employs about 550 people.

Uses:

• Bentonite is used in the oil and gas industry as a drilling mud for exploratory drilling.

• Bentonite is also used as a filler in cosmetics, food products and animal feeds.

• Bentonite is used as a sealant in water reservoirs and sanitary landfills.

Location:

• Bentonite mining takes place in northern Wyoming, primarily in Big Horn, Crook, Johnson, and Weston Counties.

Uranium

Only about 10 years ago, Wyoming was a major uranium producing state. However, the price of uranium has fallen drastically and mining in the state has ceased. Several of the mines which were operating in Shirley Basin and Gas Hills are presently being reclaimed. There has been interest by industry in alternate mining methods, however the price of uranium would have to increase before more operations would open.

Trona

Production:

Wyoming is the number one producer of trona in the country. About 16 million tons of trona are mined annually in Wyoming. 90% of the nation's trona production comes from Wyoming. Wyoming supplies 30% of the world's trona. There are only 6 producers of trona in the United States, and five of them are in the Green River Basin in Wyoming. Nearly 50% of the trona in Wyoming is federally owned.

Economics:

Federal royalties from trona totaled over $10 million, half of which goes to the State of Wyoming. Trona mining employs approximately 3,100 people in Wyoming.

Uses:

Trona is refined into a white powder called soda ash. Soda ash is used to make glass, detergent, paper, water softeners, drugs, cleaning compounds, and baking soda.

Location:

The worlds largest deposit of trona, over 100 billion tons, are located west of Green River in Sweetwater County.

Other Mineral Commodities

Other mineral commodities mined on federal land in Wyoming include sand and gravel, limestone, gypsum, granite, clinker, and jade. Sand and gravel are used in varied construction activities, the largest being our road system. Approximately 6 million cubic yards of sand and gravel are mined annually in Wyoming. Limestone is used as building and decorative stone as well as being crushed and used as road aggregate. Gypsum's primary use is in the manufacture of wallboard for construction. Wyoming's jade industry is small, although well known, and jewelry from Wyoming jade is widespread. Collectively these minor mineral commodity industries employ about 400 people in Wyoming.

The minerals industry in Wyoming has had a major impact on the state's economy and the state's history. Without ready access to the mineral reserves found in abundance in the state of Wyoming, mostly on federal lands, the state and the nation would be without valuable products that are used in every day living. Since these reserves are a finite commodity, proper management of these reserves becomes more important every day. The Bureau of Land Management strives to ensure that mineral reserves are being produced in the most environmentally sound manner. New and emerging technologies are being developed to enhance the recovery of these minerals, and the Bureau of Land Management is working cooperatively with industry to ensure that the growing demands of the nation and the world are being met.
Article courtesy of Bureau of Land Management.

And Finally...

This is a book that was not as much written as it was compiled and edited. We used articles and information provided by other sources whenever possible. To research and know about every resource and feature of the state intimately would take us years. If it was already researched and written, and written well, we used it when we could do so. We have credited every source as accurately as possible. It was our goal to provide you, the reader, the maximum amount of information possible to make your explorations of the state enjoyable, while providing all the resources you need in one book. Hopefully we accomplished that goal. We would certainly like to hear from you if there is anything we've overlooked.

Happy Trails!

WYOMING GLOSSARY

Alkali - white powdery substance appearing on soil surface often around places that have been wet

Badlands - bleak, desolate, hostile-looking area

Basin - a bowl-shaped valley

Black ice - icy stretch of road or highway

Blizzard - a very heavy snowstorm with strong winds

Boothill - the cemetery usually located on the top of a hill in frontier towns. The term derived from the practice of nailing the boots of the deceased to a wooden cross planted on the grave.

Bull pine - common name for Ponderosa Pine

Borrow pit - a depression beside the road left after the dirt was removed to build the elevated roadway, out-of-staters call them "ditches"

Cattle Baron - a rancher with an unusually large herd of cattle and land. Editors note: never ask a rancher about the size of their herd. It's considered rude, kinda like asking you how much money you have in the bank. It's non'a yore business

Chains - actual chains attached to tires so you get better traction on snow and ice -required on many mountain passes

Chaps - ("shaps") leather leg protection for cowboys

Chinook - a warm winter wind in winter that melts snow and ice

Cooley - miniature valley

Creek - medium-sized flow of water, 10-20 feet wide, pronounced "crick"

Critter - usually refers to some form of livestock

Dog hair pine - very thick pine—trees, need to be thinned

Dogs - sometimes refers to coyotes

Doggie - a motherless calf

Down the road a piece - Not far - may be a quarter mile or twenty miles (distances seem different in Wyoming!)

Draw - same as a cooley, maybe bigger

Dryland Farm - Non-irrigated farm; watered only by rain/snow

Emigrants - those who move from one part of the country to another as opposed to immigrants who move in from another country

Sanded road - icy highway

False front - a facade on the front of early frontier buildings which extended above the roof giving the building the appearance of containing a second story.

Foothills - gentle hills at base of mountains

Gelding - a male horse that has been castrated

Good handle - a good understanding or ability

Gulley - like a cooley, maybe smaller. but sharper, more vertical banks

Gulley washer - heavy rain storm

Happy Jack - a lamp or lanter made from a tin syrup can

Heave - where water gets into crack in a road, freezes and expands. When it melts in spring, many depressions and wide cracks are left in the roadways

Heifer - a female bovine that hasn't yet had a calf

Hog ranch - a whore house that serves up gambling and booze. Most of them in Wyoming were found near the forts and provided entertainment and diversion to the otherwise dreary, boring lives of the frontier soldier. The name either derived from the appearance of the women or the tiny stall-like rooms in which they practiced their trade.

Hogback - a long, narrow and somewhat steep hill. A ridge with a sharp summit and steeply sloping sides.

Jack fence - x-crossed posts that sit on top the ground, used where it's too rocky to dig post holes

Jackalope - a jackrabbit bearing antlers. Used to be found mostly around Douglas, but now proliferating throughout the West

A little gun shy - a little jumpy/has had some bad experiences

Mare - a female horse

Nester - a farmer or homesteader who settles on cattle grazing land. Nesters and catllemen often met in bloody confrontations

Outfit - usually refers to a vehicle, sometimes with horse trailer

Pair - means a cow and her calf

Plow - usually refers to snowplow - clears roads of snow - usually a pickup or truck

Plug-in - outlet at motel where you plug in engine heater of your vehicle so it won't freeze up overnight

Potbelly - semi-truck that hauls cattle

Pulling a big circle - taking a long trip

Range land - native grazing area

Rattler - a rattlesnake (beware - poisonous)

Ridge - abrupt change in elevation

Riding with a loose rein - relaxed, not heavily supervised

Rise - like a hill but maybe lower, can't see over it

River - a wide creek, maybe 30-40 feet across or more

Rode hard an' put away wet - really tired - could be animal or person who has worked hard

Row crop - type of farming, usually high-intensity crops planted in rows like potatoes, corn, sugar beets

Ruminate - think about something

Rustler - a cattle or horse thief

Sage Chicken - a sage grouse. Also known as sage hen or prairie hen

Salt grass - grass that grows in highly alkaline soil

Sanded road - icy highways and roads are sanded to cut down skidding and sliding

Scoria - also called "clinker" is formed when underground coal seams catch fire and burn nearby sandstone and shale creating a red slag. Used on gravel roads throughout Wyoming and mostly in Powder River Country.

Sheep fence - small mesh wire fence for securing sheep/goats

Short grass - doesn't require much moisture and is less than a foot tall

Snow fences - built to control drifting snow, usually seen along roadways to help keep roads clear

Snowblind - a winter condition where the snow is so bright from the sun it becomes difficult to see

Spring - area where water comes up from deep inside earth

Stallion - a male horse that has not been castrated

Steer - a male bovine that has been castrated

Stock - short for 'livestock'

Stream - a small creek, a few feet wide

Strip farm - method of farming which rotates crops and controls wind erosion

Studs - tires with metal studs imbedded give better traction in snow and ice

Swather - machine that cuts hay

Top a the mornin' to ya - good morning/have a nice day

Valley - lowland surrounded by hills or mountains

Varmint - any animal you don't take a liking to

Wapiti - the Indian word for elk. Pronounced WOP-i-tee

White Out - snowstorm so heavy that everything looks white, zero visibility, extremely dangerous to drive in

Wilderness Area - a Congressionally mandated area within Forest Service land that disallows roads, mining, logging and motorized vehicles

WYOMING ZIP CODES

*This community has more than one five digit zip code.

Acme	82839	Emblem	82422	Lagrange	82221	Rawlins	82301

Acme 82839
Afton 83110
Aladdin 82710
Albin 82050
Alcova 82620
Alpine 83128
Alta 83422
Alva 82711
Arapahoe 82510
Arlington 82083
Arminto 82630
Arvada 82831
Atlantic City 82520
Auburn 83111
Baggs 82321
Bairoil 82322
Banner 82832
Basin 82410
Bedford 83112
Beulah 82712
Big Horn 82833
Big Piney 83113
Bill 82631
Bitter Creek 82901
Bondurant 82922
Bordeaux 82201
Bosler 82051
Boulder 82923
Buffalo 82834
Buford 82052
Burlington 82411
Burns 82053
Byron 82412
Carlile 82713
Carpenter 82054
CASPER*
Centennial 82055
CHEYENNE*
Chugwater 82210
Clearmont 82835
Cody 82414
Cokeville 83114
Cora 82925
Cowley 82420
Creston 82301
Crowheart 82512
Daniel 83115
Dayton 82836
Deaver 82421
Devils Tower 82714
Diamond 82210
Diamondville 83116
Dixon 82323
Douglas 82633
Dubois 82513
Eden 82932
Edgerton 82635
Egbert 82053
Elk Mountain 82324
Elmo 82327

Emblem 82422
Encampment 82325
Ethete 82520
Etna 83118
EVANSTON *
Evansville 82636
Fairview 83119
Farson 82932
FE Warren AFB 82005
Fontenelle 83101
Fort Bridger 82933
Fort Laramie 82212
Fort Steele 82301
Fort Washakie 82514
Four Corners 82715
Frannie 82423
Freedom 83120
Frontier 83121
Garland 82435
Garrett 82058
Gas Hills 82501
GILLETTE
Glendo 82213
Glenrock 82637
Granger 82934
Granite Canon 82059
Green River 82935
Greybull 82426
Grover 83122
Guernsey 82214
Hamilton Dome 82427
Hamsfork 83101
Hanna 82327
Harriman 82059
Hartville 82215
Hawk Springs 82217
Hiland 82638
Hillsdale 82060
Hoback Junction ...83001
Horse Creek 82061
Hudson 82515
Hulett 82720
Huntley 82218
Hyattville 82428
Iron Mountain, (see
Cheyenne)
JACKSON *
Jay Em 82219
Jeffrey City 82310
Jelm 82063
Jenny Lake 83012
Kaycee 82639
Keeline 82227
Kelly 83011
Kemmerer 83101
Kinnear 82516
Kirby 82430
Kirtley 82225
Kortes Dam 82327
La Barge 83123

Lagrange 82221
Lance Creek 82222
Lander 82520
LARAMIE *
Leiter 82837
Leo 82327
Linch 82640
Lingle 82223
Little America 82929
Lost Cabin 82642
Lost Springs 82224
Lovell 82431
Lucky Maccamp 82501
Lusk 82225
Lyman 82937
Park 82190
Manderson 82432
Mantua 82435
Manville 82227
Marbleton 83113
Mayoworth 82639
McFadden 82083
McKinnon 82938
Medicine Bow 82329
Meeteetse 82433
Meriden 82081
Midval 82501
Midwest 82643
Mills 82644
Moneta, (see Casper)
Moorcroft 82721
Moose 83012
Moran 83013
Morton 82501
Mountain Home, (see Laramie)
Mountain View 82939
Muddy Gap 82301
Natrona 82646
Newcastle 82701
New Haven 82720
Node 82225
Opal 83124
Orin 82633
Osage 82723
Oshoto 82721
Otto 82434
Parkerton 82637
Parkman 82838
Pavillion 82523
Piedmont 82933
Pine Bluffs 82082
Pinedale 82941
Pine Haven 82721
Point of Rocks 82942
Powder River 82648
Powell 82435
Prairie Center 82240
Quealy 82901
Ralston 82440
Ranchester 82839

Rawlins 82301
Raymond 83114
Recluse 82725
Red Desert 82336
Reliance 82943
Riner 82301
Riverside 82325
Riverton 82501
Robertson 82944
Rockeagle 82223
Rock River 82083
ROCK SPRINGS*
Rolling Hills 82637
Rozet 82727
Ryan Park 82331
Saddlestring 82840
Saint Stephens 82524
Sand Draw 82501
Saratoga 82331
Savery 82332
Shawnee 82229
Shell 82441
Sheridan 82801
Shirley Basin 82615
Shoshoni 82649
Sinclair 82334
Slater, ...82201
Smoot 83126
South Pass City ...82520
Story 82842
Sundance 82729
Sunrise 82215
Superior 82945
Sussex 82639
Sweetwater Station .82520
Ten Sleep 82442
Teton Village 83025
Thayne 83127
Thermopolis 82443
Tie Siding 82084
Tipton 82336
Torrington 82240
Turnerville 83110
Upton 82730
Veteran 82243
Walcott 82335
Wamsutter 82336
Wapiti 82450
Weston 82731
Weston, (see Gillette)
Wheatland 82201
Willwood 82435
Wilson 83014
Wolf 82844
Woriand 82401
Wright 82732
Wyarno 82845
Yellowstone National Park (all
locations) 82190
Yoder 82244

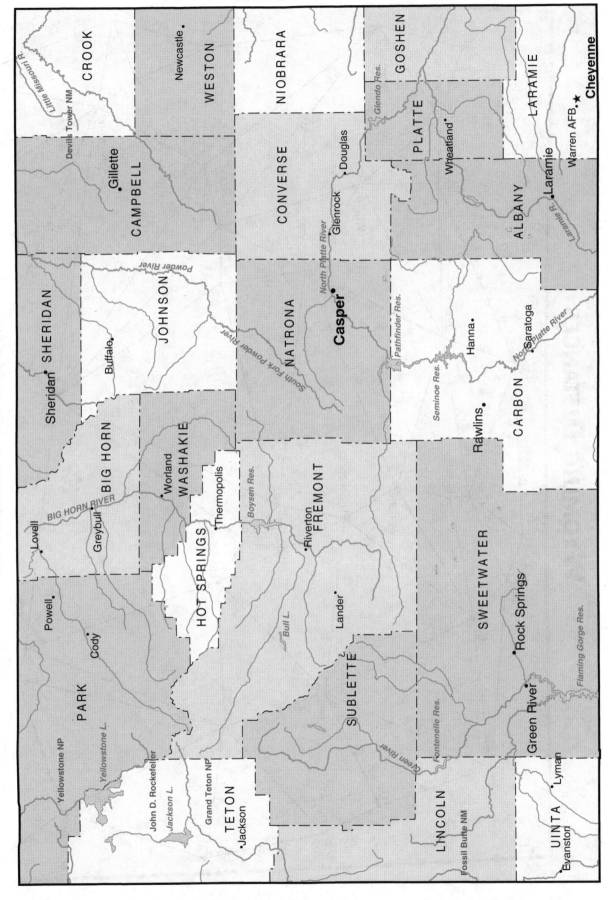

WYOMING COUNTIES

CROOK

Little Missouri R.

Devils Tower NM

WESTON

Newcastle

NIOBRARA

GOSHEN

Glendo Res.

LARAMIE

Cheyenne

Warren AFB.

PLATTE

Wheatland

Laramie

Laramie R.

Gillette

CAMPBELL

Douglas

Glenrock

CONVERSE

North Platte River

PLATTE

ALBANY

SHERIDAN

Sheridan

JOHNSON

Powder River

Buffalo

South Fork Powder River

NATRONA

Casper

Pathfinder Res.

Saratoga

North Platte River

Hanna

Seminoe Res.

CARBON

Rawlins

BIG HORN

Lovell

BIG HORN RIVER

Greybull

Washakie

Worland

WASHAKIE

Thermopolis

Boysen Res.

Riverton

FREMONT

HOT SPRINGS

PARK

Powell

Cody

Yellowstone NP

Yellowstone L.

Bull L.

Lander

SWEETWATER

Rock Springs

Flaming Gorge Res.

John D. Rockefeller

Jackson L.

Grand Teton NP

TETON

Jackson

Green River

SUBLETTE

Fontenelle Res.

Green River

LINCOLN

Fossil Butte NM

UINTA

Lyman

Evanston

Wyoming Introduction

Wyoming Distances

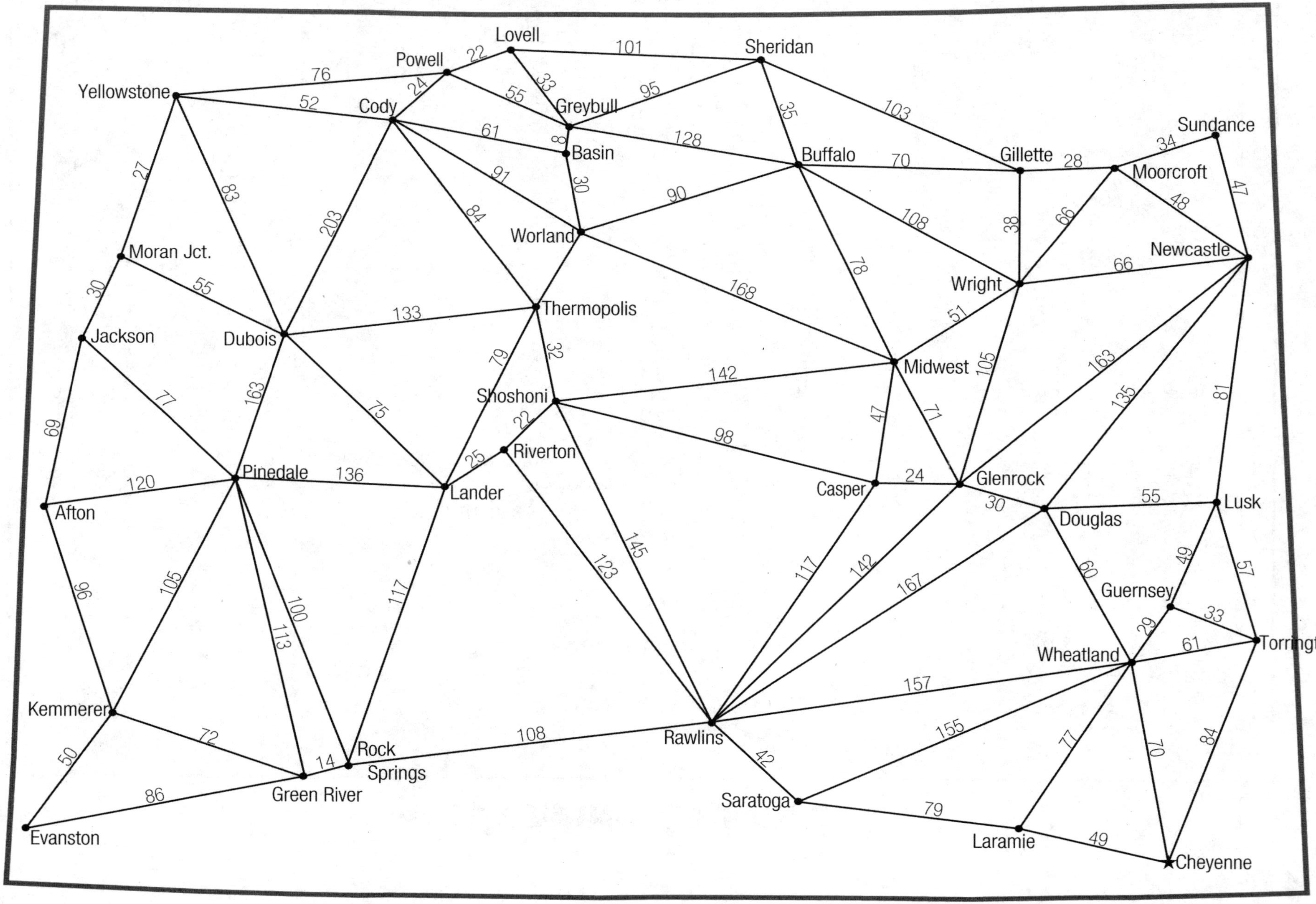

DRIVING DISTANCE

Afton to
Basin 308
Buffalo 411
Casper 353
Cheyenne ..436
Cody 247
Douglas 403
Dubois 155
Evanston ..120
Gillette 481
Glenrock ...378
Green River .165
Greybull ...300
Guernsey ..464
Jackson 69
Kemmerer ...96
Lander 230
Laramie 387
Lovell 294
Lusk 457
Midwest ...398
Moorcroft ..509
Moran Jct. ..100
Newcastle ..522
Pinedale ...120
Powell 271
Rawlins ...288
Riverton ...233
Rock Springs 179
Saratoga ...330
Sheridan ...394
Shoshoni ...255
Sundance ...543
Thermopolis 288
Torrington ..497
Wheatland ..445
Worland ...321
Wright 478
Yellowstone .127

Basin to
Afton 308
Buffalo 120
Casper 194
Cheyenne ..372
Cody 61
Douglas 244
Dubois 196
Evanston ..343
Gillette 190
Glenrock ...218
Green River .272
Greybull 8
Guernsey ..305
Jackson 238
Kemmerer ..293
Lander 143
Laramie 339
Lovell 40
Lusk 298
Midwest ...198
Moorcroft ..219
Moran Jct. ..208
Newcastle ..252
Pinedale ...278
Powell 62
Rawlins ...241
Riverton ...120
Rock Springs 259
Saratoga ...282
Sheridan ...103
Shoshoni 96
Sundance ...252
Thermopolis .63
Torrington ..338
Wheatland ..303
Worland 30
Wright 228
Yellowstone .113

Buffalo to
Afton 411
Basin 120
Casper 112
Cheyenne ..290
Cody 182
Douglas 162
Dubois 256
Evanston ..403
Gillette 70
Glenrock ...136
Green River .332
Greybull ...128
Guernsey ..223
Jackson 341
Kemmerer ..353
Lander 202
Laramie 260
Lovell 135
Lusk 216
Midwest 78
Moorcroft ...98
Moran Jct. ..311
Newcastle ..146
Pinedale ...338
Powell 157
Rawlins ...229
Riverton ...178
Rock Springs 319
Saratoga ...259
Sheridan ...35
Shoshoni ...156
Sundance ...132
Thermopolis 123
Torrington ..256
Wheatland ..221
Worland 90
Wright 108
Yellowstone .234

Casper to
Afton 353
Basin 194
Buffalo 112
Cheyenne ..178
Cody 214
Douglas 50
Dubois 198
Evanston ..326
Gillette 136
Glenrock ...24
Green River .240
Greybull ...201
Guernsey ..111
Jackson 284
Kemmerer ..288
Lander 145
Laramie 148
Lovell 233
Lusk 104
Midwest 47
Moorcroft ..164
Moran Jct. ..254
Newcastle ..170
Pinedale ...273
Powell 239
Rawlins ...117
Riverton ...120
Rock Springs 225
Saratoga ...148
Sheridan ...147
Shoshoni ...98
Sundance ...197
Thermopolis 130
Torrington ..144
Wheatland ..109
Worland ...164
Wright 98
Yellowstone .267

Cheyenne to
Afton 436
Basin 372
Buffalo 290
Casper 178
Cody 393
Douglas 129
Dubois 346
Evanston ..357
Gillette 113
Glenrock ...158
Green River .271
Greybull ...380
Guernsey ...98
Jackson 432
Kemmerer ..343
Lander 272
Laramie 49
Lovell 412
Lusk 140
Midwest ...225
Moorcroft ..269
Moran Jct. ..402
Newcastle ..220
Pinedale ...355
Powell 417
Rawlins ...149
Riverton ...270
Rock Springs 256
Saratoga ...127
Sheridan ...325
Shoshoni ...276
Sundance ...265
Thermopolis 309
Torrington ..84
Wheatland ..70
Worland ...342
Wright 204
Yellowstone .429

Cody to
Afton 247
Basin 61
Buffalo 182
Casper 214
Cheyenne ..393
Douglas 264
Dubois 203
Evanston ..364
Gillette 250
Glenrock ...239
Green River .293
Greybull ...53
Guernsey ..325
Jackson 177
Kemmerer ..314
Lander 163
Laramie 359
Lovell 46
Lusk 318
Midwest ...259
Moorcroft ..276
Moran Jct. ..147
Newcastle ..326
Pinedale ...254
Powell 24
Rawlins ...262
Riverton ...139
Rock Springs 280
Saratoga ...302
Sheridan ...147
Shoshoni ...116
Sundance ...311
Thermopolis .84
Torrington ..358
Wheatland ..323
Worland ...166
Wright 296
Yellowstone ..83

Douglas to
Afton 403
Basin 244
Buffalo 162
Casper 50
Cheyenne ..129
Cody 264
Dubois 248
Evanston ..375
Gillette 113
Glenrock 30
Green River .290
Greybull ...251
Guernsey ...62
Jackson 334
Kemmerer ..337
Lander 195
Laramie 136
Lovell 283
Lusk 55
Midwest 97
Moorcroft ..140
Moran Jct. ..304
Newcastle ..135
Pinedale ...323
Powell 288
Rawlins ...167
Riverton ...170
Rock Springs 275
Saratoga ...198
Sheridan ...196
Shoshoni ...148
Sundance ...174
Thermopolis 180
Torrington ..94
Wheatland ..60
Worland ...213
Wright 75
Yellowstone .316

Dubois to
Afton 155
Basin 196
Buffalo 256
Casper 198
Cheyenne ..346
Cody 203
Douglas 248
Evanston ..276
Gillette 325
Glenrock ...223
Green River .376
Greybull ...204
Guernsey ..309
Jackson 86
Kemmerer ..225
Lander 75
Laramie 297
Lovell 236
Lusk 302
Midwest ...242
Moorcroft ..354
Moran Jct. ..55
Newcastle ..366
Pinedale ...163
Powell 227
Rawlins ...200
Riverton ...120
Rock Springs 192
Saratoga ...240
Sheridan ...290
Shoshoni ...100
Sundance ...387
Thermopolis 133
Torrington ..342
Wheatland ..307
Worland ...166
Wright 296
Yellowstone ..83

Evanston to
Afton 120
Basin 343
Buffalo 403
Casper 326
Cheyenne ..357
Cody 364
Douglas ...375
Dubois 276
Gillette 461
Glenrock ...350
Green River .86
Greybull ...351
Guernsey ..393
Jackson 190
Kemmerer ...50
Lander 201
Laramie 308
Lovell 384
Lusk 430
Midwest ...372
Moorcroft ..488
Moran Jct. ..220
Newcastle ..495
Pinedale ...155
Powell 388
Rawlins ...208
Riverton ...226
Rock Springs 100
Saratoga ...250
Sheridan ...438
Shoshoni ...248
Sundance ...522
Thermopolis 280
Torrington ..425
Wheatland ..365
Worland ...313
Wright 424
Yellowstone .247

Gillette to
Afton 481
Basin 190
Buffalo 70
Casper 136
Cheyenne ..242
Cody 250
Douglas 113
Dubois 325
Evanston ..461
Glenrock ...143
Green River .376
Greybull ...198
Guernsey ..307
Jackson 411
Kemmerer ..423
Lander 272
Laramie 249
Lovell 203
Lusk 157
Midwest 89
Moorcroft ...28
Moran Jct. ..381
Newcastle ...76
Pinedale ...408
Powell 226
Rawlins ...253
Riverton ...247
Rock Springs 361
Saratoga ...283
Sheridan ...103
Shoshoni ...225
Sundance ...61
Thermopolis 193
Torrington ..208
Wheatland ..173
Worland ...160
Wright 38
Yellowstone .301

Glenrock to
Afton 378
Basin 218
Buffalo 136
Casper 24
Cheyenne ..158
Cody 239
Douglas 30
Dubois 223
Evanston ..351
Gillette 143
Green River .280
Greybull ...226
Guernsey ...91
Jackson 308
Kemmerer ..312
Lander 150
Laramie 165
Lovell 258
Lusk 84
Midwest 71
Moorcroft ..170
Moran Jct. ..278
Newcastle ..163
Pinedale ...297
Powell 263
Rawlins ...142
Riverton ...145
Rock Springs 250
Saratoga ...173
Sheridan ...171
Shoshoni ...122
Sundance ...203
Thermopolis 155
Torrington ..124
Wheatland ..89
Worland ...188
Wright 105
Yellowstone .291

Green River to
Afton 165
Basin 272
Buffalo 332
Casper 240
Cheyenne ..271
Cody 293
Douglas 290
Dubois 376
Evanston ..86
Gillette 376
Glenrock ...280
Greybull ...312
Guernsey ..378
Jackson 190
Kemmerer ..72
Lander 256
Laramie 222
Lovell 360
Lusk 392
Midwest ...334
Moorcroft ..450
Moran Jct. ..457
Newcastle ..457
Pinedale ...105
Powell 338
Rawlins ...194
Riverton ...175
Rock Springs .86
Saratoga ...236
Sheridan ...388
Shoshoni ...197
Sundance ...484
Thermopolis 231
Torrington ..411
Worland ...263
Wright 386
Yellowstone .217

Greybull to
Afton 300
Basin 8
Buffalo 128
Casper 201
Cheyenne ..380
Cody 53
Douglas ...251
Dubois 204
Evanston ..190
Gillette 411
Glenrock ...308
Green River .190
Greybull ...231
Guernsey ..312
Jackson 231
Kemmerer ..301
Lander 160
Laramie 347
Lovell 33
Lusk 388
Midwest ...328
Moorcroft ..440
Moran Jct. ..301
Newcastle ..451
Pinedale 77
Powell 202
Rawlins ...284
Riverton ...164
Rock Springs 177
Saratoga ...326
Sheridan ...324
Shoshoni ...186
Sundance ...473
Thermopolis 218
Torrington ..428
Wheatland ..393
Worland ...251
Wright 392
Yellowstone .217

Guernsey to
Afton 464
Basin 305
Buffalo 223
Casper 111
Cheyenne ...98
Cody 325
Douglas 62
Dubois 309
Evanston ..393
Gillette 312
Glenrock 91
Green River .307
Greybull ...312
Jackson 395
Kemmerer ..378
Lander 256
Laramie 104
Lovell 345
Lusk 49
Midwest ...158
Moorcroft ..178
Moran Jct. ..365
Newcastle ..130
Pinedale ...384
Powell 350
Rawlins ...184
Riverton ...231
Rock Springs 292
Saratoga ...182
Sheridan ...257
Shoshoni ...209
Sundance ...174
Thermopolis 242
Torrington ..33
Wheatland ..29
Worland ...275
Wright 137
Yellowstone .378

Jackson to
Afton 69
Basin 238
Buffalo 341
Casper 284
Cheyenne ..432
Cody 177
Douglas ...334
Dubois 86
Evanston ..201
Gillette 411
Glenrock ...308
Green River .190
Greybull ...231
Guernsey ..395
Kemmerer ..155
Lander 160
Laramie 383
Lovell 223
Lusk 388
Midwest ...328
Moorcroft ..440
Moran Jct. ..30
Newcastle ..451
Pinedale 77
Powell 202
Rawlins ...284
Riverton ...164
Rock Springs 177
Saratoga ...326
Sheridan ...324
Shoshoni ...186
Sundance ...473
Thermopolis 218
Torrington ..428
Wheatland ..393
Worland ...251
Wright 392
Yellowstone .57

Kemmerer to
Afton 96
Basin 293
Buffalo 353
Casper 288
Cheyenne ..343
Cody 314
Douglas ...337
Dubois 225
Evanston ...50
Gillette 423
Glenrock ...312
Green River .72
Greybull ...301
Guernsey ..378
Jackson 155
Lander 150
Laramie 294
Lovell 360
Lusk 392
Midwest ...306
Moorcroft ..451
Moran Jct. ..130
Newcastle ..455
Pinedale ...105
Powell 340
Rawlins ...175
Riverton ...180
Rock Springs .72
Saratoga ...218
Sheridan ...390
Shoshoni ...218
Sundance ...473
Thermopolis 218
Torrington ..428
Wheatland ..312

Lander to
Afton 230
Basin 143
Buffalo 202
Casper 145
Cheyenne ..272
Cody 163
Douglas ...195
Dubois 75
Evanston ..201
Gillette 272
Glenrock ...169
Green River .130
Greybull ...150
Guernsey ..256
Jackson 160
Kemmerer ..150
Laramie 222
Lovell 183
Lusk 249
Midwest ...189
Moorcroft ..301
Moran Jct. ..130
Newcastle ..312
Pinedale ...136
Powell 187
Rawlins ...125
Riverton ...25
Rock Springs 117
Saratoga ...165
Sheridan ...237
Shoshoni ...47
Sundance ...334
Thermopolis .79
Torrington ..289
Wheatlan ...254
Worland ...112
Wright 243
Yellowstone ..98

Laramie to
Afton 387
Basin 339
Buffalo 260
Casper 148
Cheyenne ...49
Cody 359
Douglas ...136
Dubois 297
Evanston ..308
Gillette 249
Glenrock ...165
Green River .222
Greybull ...347
Guernsey ..104
Jackson 383
Kemmerer ..294
Lander 222
Lovell 379
Lusk 166
Midwest ...195
Moorcroft ..276
Moran Jct. ..353
Newcastle ..246
Pinedale ...307
Powell 384
Rawlins ...100
Riverton ...221
Rock Springs 207
Saratoga 79
Sheridan ...294
Shoshoni ...243
Sundance ...290
Thermopolis 276
Torrington ..132
Wheatland ..77
Worland ...309
Wright 212
Yellowstone .380

Lovell to
Afton 294
Basin 40
Buffalo 135
Casper 233
Cheyenne ..412
Cody 46
Douglas ...283
Dubois 236
Evanston ..384
Gillette 203
Glenrock ...258
Green River .313
Greybull ...33
Guernsey ..345
Jackson 223
Kemmerer ..360
Lander 183
Laramie 379
Lusk 338
Midwest ...213
Moorcroft ..232
Moran Jct. ..193
Newcastle ..280
Pinedale ...300
Powell 22
Rawlins ...281
Riverton ...158
Rock Springs 300
Saratoga ...322
Sheridan ...101
Shoshoni ...136
Sundance ...266
Thermopolis 104
Torrington ..378
Wheatland ..343
Worland 71
Wright 242
Yellowstone ..98

Lusk to
Afton 457
Basin 298
Buffalo 216
Casper 104
Cheyenne ..140
Cody 318
Douglas 55
Dubois 302
Evanston ..430
Gillette 157
Glenrock ...84
Green River .344
Greybull ...307

Guernsey 49
Jackson 388
Kemmerer .392
Lander 249
Laramie 166
Lovell 338
Midwest....151
Moorcroft ..129
Moran Jct. ..358
Newcastle ...81
Pinedale ...377
Powell 343
Rawlins 221
Riverton 224
Rock Springs 329
Saratoga ...244
Sheridan ...250
Shoshoni ...202
Sundance ..125
Thermopolis 235
Torrington ...57
Wheatland ...78
Worland 268
Wright 130
Yellowstone .370

Midwest to
Afton 398
Basin 198
Buffalo 78
Casper 47
Cheyenne ..225
Cody 259
Douglas 97
Dubois 242
Evanston ...372
Gillette 89
Glenrock 71
Green River .287
Greybull 206
Guernsey ...158
Jackson 328
Kemmerer ..334
Lander 189
Laramie 195
Lovell 213
Lusk 151
Moorcroft ...117
Moran Jct. ..298
Newcastle ..123
Pinedale ...320
Powell 235
Rawlins 158
Riverton 164
Rock Springs 272
Saratoga ...195
Sheridan ...113
Shoshoni ...142
Sundance ..150
Thermopolis 175
Torrington ..191
Wheatland ..156
Worland 168
Wright 51
Yellowstone .312

Moorcroft to
Afton 509
Basin 219
Buffalo 98
Casper 164
Cheyenne ..269
Cody 276
Douglas 140
Dubois 354
Evanston ...488
Gillette 28
Glenrock ...170
Green River .404
Greybull 226
Guernsey ...178
Jackson 440
Kemmerer ..450
Lander 301
Laramie 276
Lovell 232
Lusk 129
Midwest 117
Moran Jct. ..409
Newcastle ...48
Pinedale ...436
Powell 254
Rawlins 280
Riverton 275
Rock Springs 388
Saratoga ...311
Sheridan ...131
Shoshoni ...254
Sundance ...34
Thermopolis 221
Torrington ..185
Wheatland ..200
Worland 188
Wright 66
Yellowstone .330

Moran Jct. to
Afton 100
Basin 208
Buffalo 311
Casper 254
Cheyenne ..402
Cody 147
Douglas 304
Dubois 55
Evanston ...220
Gillette 381
Glenrock ...278
Green River .220
Greybull 200
Guernsey ...365
Jackson 30
Kemmerer ..190
Lander 130
Laramie 353
Lovell 193
Lusk 358
Midwest ...298
Moorcroft ..409
Newcastle ..421
Pinedale ...107
Powell 171
Rawlins 255
Riverton 134
Rock Springs 207
Saratoga ...296
Sheridan ..2941
Shoshoni ...156
Sundance ..443
Thermopolis 188
Torrington ..398
Wheatland ..363
Worland 221
Wright 351
Yellowstone ..27

Newcastle to
Afton 522
Basin 267
Buffalo 146
Casper 170
Cheyenne ..220
Cody 326
Douglas 135
Dubois 366
Evanston ...495
Gillette 76
Glenrock ...163
Green River .410
Greybull 274
Guernsey ...130
Jackson 451
Kemmerer ..457
Lander 312
Laramie 246
Lovell 280
Lusk 81
Midwest 123
Moorcroft 48
Moran Jct. ..421
Pinedale ...442
Powell 302
Rawlins 287
Riverton 288
Rock Springs 395
Saratoga ...317
Sheridan ...180
Shoshoni ...265
Sundance ...47
Thermopolis 270
Torrington ..137
Wheatland ..158
Worland 237
Wright 72
Yellowstone .379

Pinedale to
Afton 120
Basin 278
Buffalo 338
Casper 273
Cheyenne ..355
Cody 254
Douglas 323
Dubois 163
Evanston ...155
Gillette 408
Glenrock ...297
Green River .113
Greybull 286
Guernsey ..384
Jackson 77
Kemmerer ..105
Lander 136
Laramie 307
Lovell 300
Lusk 377
Midwest ...320
Moorcroft ..436
Moran Jct. ..107
Newcastle ..442
Powell 279
Rawlins 207
Riverton 160
Rock Springs 100
Saratoga ...249
Sheridan ...373
Shoshoni ...183
Sundance ..469
Thermopolis 215
Torrington ..417
Wheatland ..364
Worland 248
Wright 371
Yellowstone .134

Powell to
Afton 271
Basin 62
Buffalo 157
Casper 239
Cheyenne ..417
Cody 24
Douglas 288
Dubois 227
Evanston ...388
Gillette 226
Glenrock ...263
Green River .317
Greybull 55
Guernsey ...350
Jackson 202
Kemmerer ..338
Lander 187
Laramie 384
Lovell 22
Lusk 343
Midwest ...235
Moorcroft ..254
Moran Jct. ..171
Newcastle ..302
Pinedale ...279
Rawlins 286
Riverton 163
Rock Springs 304
Saratoga ...326
Sheridan ...123
Shoshoni ...130
Sundance ..288
Thermopolis 108
Torrington ..382
Wheatland ..348
Worland 93
Wright 265
Yellowstone ..76

Rawlins to
Afton 288
Basin 241
Buffalo 229
Casper 117
Cheyenne ..149
Cody 262
Douglas 167
Dubois 200
Evanston ...208
Gillette 253
Glenrock ...142
Green River .123
Greybull 248
Guernsey ...184
Jackson 284
Kemmerer ..194
Lander 125
Laramie 100
Lovell 281
Lusk 221
Midwest 158
Moorcroft ..280
Moran Jct. ..255
Newcastle ..287
Pinedale ...207
Powell 286
Riverton....123
Rock Springs 108
Saratoga 42
Sheridan ...263
Shoshoni ...145
Sundance ..314
Thermopolis 178
Torrington ..217
Wheatland ..157
Worland 211
Wright 215
Yellowstone .282

Riverton to
Afton 233
Basin 118
Buffalo 178
Casper 120
Cheyenne ..270
Cody 139
Douglas 170
Dubois 78
Evanston ...226
Gillette 247
Glenrock ...145
Green River .155
Greybull 126
Guernsey ...231
Jackson 164
Kemmerer ..175
Lander 25
Laramie 221
Lovell 158
Lusk 224
Midwest ...164
Moorcroft ..275
Moran Jct. ..134
Newcastle ..288
Pinedale ...160
Powell 163
Rawlins 123
Rock Springs 142
Saratoga ...164
Sheridan ...212
Shoshoni 22
Sundance ..309
Thermopolis ..55
Torrington ..264
Wheatland ..229
Worland 88
Wright 218
Yellowstone .161

Rock Springs to
Afton 179
Basin 259
Buffalo 319
Casper 225
Cheyenne ..256
Cody 280
Douglas 275
Dubois 192
Evanston 100
Gillette 361
Glenrock ...250
Green River ..14
Greybull 267
Guernsey ..292
Jackson 177
Kemmerer ...86
Lander 117
Laramie 207
Lovell 300
Lusk 329
Midwest 272
Moorcroft ..388
Moran Jct. ..207
Newcastle ..395
Pinedale ...100
Powell 304
Rawlins 108
Riverton 142
Saratoga ...150
Sheridan ...354
Shoshoni ...164
Sundance ..422
Thermopolis 196
Torrington ..325
Wheatland ..265
Worland 229
Wright 323
Yellowstone .234

Saratoga to
Afton 330
Basin 282
Buffalo 259
Casper 148
Cheyenne ..127
Cody 302
Douglas 198
Dubois 240
Evanston ...250
Gillette 283
Glenrock ...173
Green River .165
Greybull 289
Guernsey ...182
Jackson 326
Kemmerer ..236
Lander 165
Laramie 79
Lovell 322
Lusk 244
Midwest ...195
Moorcroft ..311
Moran Jct. ..296
Newcastle ..317
Pinedale ...249
Powell 326
Rawlins 42
Riverton 164
Rock Springs 150
Sheridan ...294
Shoshoni ...186
Sundance ..344
Thermopolis 218
Torrington ..209
Wheatland ..155
Worland 251
Wright 246
Yellowstone .324

Sheridan to
Afton 394
Basin 103
Buffalo 35
Casper 147
Cheyenne ..325
Cody 147
Douglas 196
Dubois 290
Evanston ...438
Gillette 103
Glenrock ...171
Green River .367
Greybull 95
Guernsey ...257
Jackson 324
Kemmerer ..388
Lander 237
Laramie 294
Lovell 101
Lusk 250
Midwest 113
Moorcroft ..131
Moran Jct. ..294
Newcastle ..180
Pinedale ...373
Powell 123
Rawlins 263
Riverton 212
Rock Springs 354
Saratoga ...294
Shoshoni ...190
Sundance ..165
Thermopolis 158
Torrington ..290
Wheatland ..255
Worland 125
Wright 141
Yellowstone .199

Shoshoni to
Afton 255
Basin 96
Buffalo 156
Casper 98
Cheyenne ..276
Cody 116
Douglas 148
Dubois 100
Evanston ...248
Gillette 225
Glenrock ...122
Green River .177
Greybull 103
Guernsey ..209
Jackson 186
Kemmerer ..197
Lander 47
Laramie 243
Lovell 136
Lusk 202
Midwest ...142
Moorcroft ..254
Moran Jct. ..156
Newcastle ..265
Pinedale ...183
Powell 130
Rawlins 145
Riverton 22
Rock Springs 164
Saratoga ...186
Sheridan ...190
Sundance ..287
Thermopolis .32
Torrington ..242
Wheatland ..207
Worland 65
Wright 196
Yellowstone .169

Sundance to
Afton 543
Basin 252
Buffalo 132
Casper 197
Cheyenne ..265
Cody 311
Douglas 174
Dubois 387
Evanston ...522
Gillette 61
Glenrock ...203
Green River .437
Greybull 260
Guernsey ...174
Jackson 473
Kemmerer ..484
Lander 334
Laramie 290
Lovell 266
Lusk 125
Midwest 150
Moorcroft 34
Moran Jct. ..443
Newcastle ...47
Pinedale ...469
Powell 288
Rawlins 314
Riverton 309
Rock Springs 422
Saratoga ...344
Sheridan ...165
Shoshoni ...287
Thermopolis 255
Torrington ..181
Wheatland ..202
Worland 222
Wright 100
Yellowstone .364

Thermopolis to
Afton 288
Basin 63
Buffalo 123
Casper 130
Cheyenne ..309
Cody 84
Douglas 180
Dubois 133
Evanston ...280
Gillette 193
Glenrock ...155
Green River .209
Greybull 71
Guernsey ..242
Jackson 218
Kemmerer ..230
Lander 79
Laramie 276
Lovell 104
Lusk 235
Midwest 175
Moorcroft ..221
Moran Jct. ..188
Newcastle ..270
Pinedale ...215
Powell 108
Rawlins 178
Riverton 55
Rock Springs 196
Saratoga ...218
Sheridan ...158
Shoshoni 32
Sundance ..255
Torrington ..274
Wheatland ..240
Worland 33
Wright 228
Yellowstone .136

Torrington to
Afton 497
Basin 338
Buffalo 256
Casper 144
Cheyenne ...84
Cody 358
Douglas 94
Dubois 342
Evanston ...425
Gillette 208
Glenrock ...124
Green River .340
Greybull 347
Guernsey 33
Jackson 428
Kemmerer ..411
Lander 289
Laramie 132
Lovell 378
Lusk 57
Midwest 191
Moorcroft ..185
Moran Jct. ..398
Newcastle ..137
Pinedale ...417
Powell 382
Rawlins 217
Riverton 264
Rock Springs 325
Saratoga ...209
Sheridan ...290
Shoshoni ...242
Sundance ..181
Thermopolis 274
Wheatland ...61
Worland 307
Wright 169
Yellowstone .410

Wheatland to
Afton 445
Basin 303
Buffalo 221
Casper 109
Cheyenne ...70
Cody 323
Douglas 60
Dubois 307
Evanston ...365
Gillette 173
Glenrock 89
Green River .279
Greybull 312
Guernsey 29
Jackson 393
Kemmerer ..351
Lander 254
Laramie 77
Lovell 343
Lusk 78
Midwest 156
Moorcroft ..200
Moran Jct. ..363
Newcastle ..158
Pinedale ...364
Powell 348
Rawlins 157
Riverton 229
Rock Springs 265
Saratoga ...155
Sheridan ...255
Shoshoni ...207
Sundance ..202
Thermopolis 240
Torrington ...61
Worland 273
Wright 135
Yellowstone .376

Worland to
Afton 321
Basin 30
Buffalo 90
Casper 164
Cheyenne ..342
Cody 91
Douglas 213
Dubois 166
Evanston ...313
Gillette 160
Glenrock ...188
Green River .242
Greybull 38
Guernsey ...275
Jackson 251
Kemmerer ..263
Lander 112
Laramie 309
Lovell 71
Lusk 268
Midwest ...168
Moorcroft ..188
Moran Jct. ..221
Newcastle ..237
Pinedale ...248
Powell 93
Rawlins 211
Riverton 88
Rock Springs 229
Saratoga ...251
Sheridan ...125
Shoshoni 65
Sundance ..222
Thermopolis .33
Torrington ..307
Wheatland ..273
Wright 198
Yellowstone .143

Wright to
Afton 478
Basin 228
Buffalo 108
Casper 98
Cheyenne ..204
Cody 288
Douglas 75
Dubois 296
Evanston ...424
Gillette 38
Glenrock ...105
Green River .338
Greybull 160
Guernsey ...137
Jackson 392
Kemmerer ..386
Lander 243
Laramie 212
Lovell 242
Lusk 130
Midwest 51
Moorcroft 66
Moran Jct. ..351
Newcastle ...72
Pinedale ...371
Powell 365
Rawlins 215
Riverton 218
Rock Springs 323
Saratoga ...246
Sheridan ...141
Shoshoni ...196
Sundance ..100
Thermopolis 228
Torrington ..169
Wheatland ..135
Worland 198
Yellowstone .340

Yellowstone to
Afton 127
Basin 113
Buffalo 234
Casper 267
Cheyenne ..429
Cody 52
Douglas 316
Dubois 83
Evanston ...247
Gillette 301
Glenrock ...291
Green River .247
Greybull 105
Guernsey ...378
Jackson 57
Kemmerer ..217
Lander 157
Laramie 380
Lovell 98
Lusk 370
Midwest 312
Moorcroft ..330
Moran Jct. ...27
Newcastle ..379
Pinedale ...134
Powell 76
Rawlins 282
Riverton 161
Rock Springs 234
Saratoga ...324
Sheridan ...199
Shoshoni ...169
Sundance ..364
Thermopolis 136
Torrington ..410
Wheatland ..376
Worland 143
Wright 340

Map #	Description	Season	RV sites	tent sites	hook-ups	pull-thrus	dump station	restrooms	hot showers	pool	laundry	tables/grills	rec-room	drinking water
Section 6														
Alva														
120	Bearlodge. 7 mi SE of Alva on WY 24, USFS	All	8	•			•					•		
Big Horn Mountains														
121	East Fork, 17 mi SW of Big Horn, USFS	6/1-10/31	12	•				•				•		•
122	Ranger Creek, 19 mi SW of Big Horn, USFS	6/1-10/31	11	•				•				•		•
123	Twin Lakes, 22 mi SW of Big Horn, USFS	6/1-10/31	10	•				•						
Buffalo														
124	Big Horn Mountain Campground, 8935 Hwy 16 W, PH: 307-684-2307	All	48	25	•	•	•	•	•	•	•	•	•	•
125	Buffalo KOA Kampground, 87 Hwy 16 East. PH: 307-684-5423 or 800-562-5403	4/15-10/10	63	24	•	•	•	•	•	•	•	•	•	•
126	Circle Park, 17 mi W of Buffalo on US Hwy 6, USFS	5/15-10/31	10	•				•						•
127	Crazy Woman, 26 mi W of Buffalo on US Hwy 16, USFS	5/15-10/31	6	•				•						
128	Deer Park Campground, 146 US Hwy 16 E, Box 568 PH: 307-684-5722 or 800-222-9960, Web: www.deerparkrv.com	5/1-9/30	85	40	•	•	•	•	•	•	•	•	•	•
129	Doyle, 31 mi W of Buffalo on US Hwy 16, USFS	5/15-10/31	19	•				•						•
130	Hunter Corrals, 16 mi W of Buffalo on US Hwy 16, USFS	5/15-10/31	19	•				•						
131	Indian Campground, 660 E Hart St., PH: 307-684-9601, Web: www.indiancampground.com	4/10-10/31	85	40	•	•	•	•	•	•	•	•	•	•
132	Lost Cabin, 27 mi SW of Buffalo on US Hwy 16, USFS	5/15-10/31	19	•				•				•		•
133	Middle Fork, 14 mi SW of Buffalo on US Hwy 16, USFS	5/15-10/31	9	•				•				•		•
134	Mountain View Motel & Campground, 585 Fort St., PH: 307-684-2881	All	15	3	•	•	•	•		•	•	•		•
135	South Fork, 15 mi W of Buffalo on US Hwy 16, USFS	5/15-10/31	15	•				•				•		•
136	Tie Hack, 15 mi W of Buffalo on US Hwy 16, USFS	5/15-10/31	9	•				•				•		•
Dayton														
137	Arrowhead Campground, 22 mi from Dayton			•			•	•				•		•
138	Bear Lodge Resort, PO Box 159, 25 mi past Burgess Jct. on Hwy 14A PH: 307-752-2444, Fax 752-6444 www.bearlodgeresort.com	All	•		•			•			•	•	•	•
139	Dead Swede, 34 mi SW of Dayton on US 14, 4 mi SE on FS Rd 26, USFS	6/15-9/15	22	•				•				•		•
140	Foothills Motel & Campground, 101 Main, Box 174, PH: 307-655-2547, Web: www.tiberpipe.net/-foothill/Home.htm	5/1-11/1	22	30	•	•	•	•		•	•	•		•
141	North Tongue, 29 mi SW of Dayton on US 14, 1 mi N on FS Ad, USFS	6/15-10/31	12	•				•				•		•
142	Owen Creek, 34 mi SW of Dayton on US 14, USFS	6/1-10/31	7	•				•				•		•
143	Prune Creek, 26 mi SW of Dayton on US 14, USFS	6/15-9/15	21	•				•				•		•
144	Sibley Lake, 25 mi SW of Dayton on US 14, USFS	6/15-9/15	25	•	•			•				•		•
145	Tie Flume. 34 mi SW of Dayton on US 14. 2 mi E on FS Rd 26, USFS	6/15-9/8	25	•				•				•		•
Kaycee														
151	Hole in the Wall Campground, 17 mi W of Kaycee on Barnum Rd, PH: 307-738-2340	5/1-11/1	11	•										•
152	Kaycee Town Park, Adjacent to town, Box 265 (City Park)	All		•				•				•		•
153	KC RV Park. 42 Mayoworth Rd, PH: 307-738-2233. Email: kcrv@kaycee.smalltown.net	All	18	5	•	•	•	•		•		•		•
Moorcroft														
154	Keyhole Marina, Motel & Campgrounds, 215 McKean Rd., PH: 307-756-9529	4/1-9/30	10	10	•		•	•	•			•		•
155	Keyhole State Park, 12 mi E of Moorcroft on I-90, use exit 165, 6 mi N on paved Rd, SP, PH: 307-756-3596	5/1-10/1	•			•		•				•		•
156	Wyoming Motel & Camping Park, 112 E. Converse. Jct. Hwys 14-16 & I-90. PH: 307-756-3452 or 756-9836	5/15-11/15	10	•	•									•
Ranchester														
162	Connor Battlefield State Historic Site, I-90 to Ranchester, PH: 307-684-7629	5/1-10/1	•	•		•		•				•		•
163	Lazy R Campground RV Park, 652 Hwy 14, PH: 307-655-9284 or 888-655-9284, Email: davejudy@wavecom.net	All	25	6	•	•	•	•	•					
Sheridan														
164	Big Horn Mountain KOA Campground, 63 Decker Ad, Box 35A. PH: 307-674-8766. Fax: 674-7190	5/1-10/5	90	32	•	•	•	•	•	•	•	•	•	•
165	Sheridan RV Park, 807 Avoca Aye, PH: 307-674-0722	4/1-11/1	26	12	•	•	•	•		•		•		•
Story														
166	Wagon Box Campground. 103 N Piney, PH: 307-683-2445	All	24	12	•		•	•		•		•	•	•
Upton														
170	Country Market Conoco, 909 2nd St. PH: 307-468-2551	All	6		•									
Wright														
172	Sagebluff RV Park, 387 at Sagebluff Dr., PH: 307-464-1305 or 464-1306	All	76	50	•	•		•	•			•		•

Map #	Description	Season	RV sites	tent sites	hook-ups	pull-thrus	dump station	restrooms	hot showers	pool	laundry	tables/grills	rec-room	drinking water
Section 7														
Basin														
49	Rose Garden RV Park, Box 849, 704 South 4th St., PH: 307-568-2943, Email: rosegrrv@tctwestnet	4/15-11/1	12		•	•		•	•			•		
Cody (see also WAPITI)														
50	7K RV Park, 232 W Yellowstone Ave, PHI Fax: 307-587-5890	All	39	•	•	•	•	•	•		•	•		•
51	Absaroka Bay RV Park, 2001 Hwy 14-16-20, in town, Box 953 PH: 307-527-7440 or 800-557-7440, Web:www.cody-wy.com	5/1-9/30	98	10	•	•	•	•	•	•	•			•
52	Beartooth Lake, E WY 12 off WY 96, USFS	7/1-9/7	21	•				•				•		•
53	Buffalo Bill State Park, 9 mi W of Cody on US 14-16-20, SP, PH: 307-587-9227	5/1-10/1	•	•			•	•						•
54	Big Game, 28 mi W of Cody on US 16, USFS	5/15-9/30	16	•				•				•		•
55	Camp Cody RV Park, 415 Yellowstone, PH: 307-587-9730	All	63		•	•	•	•	•	•	•	•		•
56	Clearwater, 31 mi E of Cody on US 16, USFS	5/15-9/30	32	•				•				•		•
57	Cody KOA, 5561 Greybull, PH/ Fax: 307-587-2369 or 800-562-8507, Web: www.koakampgrounds.com	5/1-10/1	200	100	•	•	•	•	•	•	•	•	•	•
58	Crazy Creek, 5 mi W WY 1 2 oft WY 96, USFS	6/1-10/20	19	•				•				•		•
59	Dead Indian, WY 96 off WY 120, USFS	All	12	•				•				•		•
60	Deer Creek, 47 mi SW of Cody on WY 291, USFS	All	7	•								•		
61	Eagle Creek, 44 mi W of Cody on US 16, USFS	5/15-10/30	20	•				•				•		•
62	Elk Fork, 29 mi W of Cody on US 16, USFS	5/15-10/30	13	•				•				•		•
63	Elk Valley Inn & Campground, 3256 Yellowstone Hwy, 5/1-9/30 PH: 307-587-4149, 877-587-4149, Web:www.tctwest.net/~elkvalley	60	30	•	•		•	•	•			•		•
64	Fox Creek, WY 296 off WY 120, USFS	6/1-9/30	27	•				•				•		•
65	Gateway Campground, 203 Yellowstone, PH: 307-587-2561	4/1-10/1	74	•	•		•	•	•		•	•		•
66	Hunter Peak, WY 296 off WY 120, USFS	All	9	•				•				•		•
67	Island Lake, 16 mi E on WY 212 off WY 296, USFS	7/1-9/7	20	•				•				•		•
68	Lake Creek, WY 296 off WY 120, USFS	6/1-9/30	6	•				•				•		•
69	Lily Lake, WY 212 turn onto Forest Rd. 130 to Lily Lake, USFS	5/25-10/30	8	•				•				•		•
70	Little Sunlight, Off WY 296 turn onto Forest Rd. 101 for 13 mi., USFS	5/1-11/30	4	•								•		
71	Newton Creek, 37 mi W of Cody on US 16, USFS	5/15-9/30	31	•				•				•		•
72	Parkway RV Campground, 132 Yellowstone Ave., PH: 307-527-5927	All	25	20	•	•	•	•	•	•	•	•		•
73	Ponderosa Campground, 1815 8th Yellowstone Hwy, PH: 307-587-9203	5/1-10/15	135	50	•	•	•	•	•	•	•	•	•	•
74	Rex Hale, 36 mi W of Cody on US 16, USFS	5/15-9/30	8	•				•				•		•
75	River's View RV Park, 109 W Yellowstone, PH: 307-587-6074 or 800-377-7253, FAX: 307-587-8644, Web: www.codyvacationproperties.com	5/15-10/15	5	4	•	•	•	•	•			•		•
76	Sleeping Giant, 47 mi W of cody on US 16, USFS	5/15-10/30	6	•				•				•		•
77	Three Mile, 48 mi W of Cody on US 16, USFS	5/15-10/30	•	•				•				•		•
78	Top of the World Store, 2823 Beartooth Hwy, US 212, 5/25-10/15 PH: 307-899-2482 or 754-1051, E-mail: topoftheworld@starband.net	10		•	•						•	•	•
79	Wapiti, 29 mi W of Cody on US 16, USFS	5/15-10/30	•	•				•				•		•
80	Yellowstone Valley RV Park. 3324 Yellowstone Park Hwy. PH: 307-587-3961	5/1-9/30	25	30	•	•		•	•		•	•		•
Greybull														
81	Green Oasis Campground, Hwy 14-16-20 at 12th Ave N, PH: 3O7-7652856, 888-765-2856, www.greenoasiscampground.com	4/15-10/15	9	15	•	•		•	•	•	•	•		•
82	Greybull KOA, 333 N 2nd, Box 387, PH! Fax: 307-765-2555, 800-562-7508	4/15-10/6	32	22	•	•		•	•	•	•	•	•	•
Hyattville														
83	Medicine Lodge State Archaeological Site. 6 mi NE of Hyattville, SP. PH: 307-469-2234	5/1-11/6	•	•				•				•		•
Lovell														
84	Bald Mountain, 33 mi E of Lovell on US 14A, USFS	7/1-9/15	15	•				•				•		•
85	Camp Big Horn RV Park, Main St, E end of Lovell, PH: 307-548-2725, FAX: 307-548-7479	All	18	9	•	•	•	•	•		•	•		•
86	Horseshoe Bend, 2 mi E of Town on US l4A to Jct 37, l4 mi N, Box 487, NPS	All	128	•				•				•		•
87	Lovell Camper Park, 40 Quebec Ave, PH: 307-548-6551, FAX: 307-548-7614	5/1-9/30		13			•	•	•			•		•
88	Porcupine, 33 mi E of Lovell on US 14A, 1.6 mi N on FS Rd 13, USFS	7/1-9/15	16	•				•				•		•
Meeteetse														
89	Brown Mountain Campground, 25 mi SW of Meeteetse on Wood River Road	5/31-11/15	6	•				•				•		•
90	Jack Creek Campground, 30 mi W of Meeteetse Pitchfork Road	All	7	•				•				•		•
91	Oasis Motel & RV Park, 1702 Stale St., Box 128, PH: 307-868-2551 or 888-868-5270, Web: www.oaaismotelwyoming.com	All	10	30	•	•	•	•	•		•	•		•
92	Vision Quest Motel, 2207 State St., Box 4, PH: 307-868-2512, Fax: 868-2550 Web: www.vqmotel.com	6/1-12/1	5		•	•	•	•						
93	Wood River Campground, 22 mi SW of Meeteetse on Wood River Road	5/31-11/15	5	•				•				•		•
Powell														
94	Homesteader Park. Hwy 14A, E city limits, 307-754-9417, Fax: 754-5385, Web: www.cityofpowell.com	4/5-10/31	25	15	•			•	•			•		•
95	Park County Fairgrounds, 655 E 5th St.	5/1-9/1	130	•	•		•	•			•			•

PH: 307-754-5421, FAX: 307-754-5947. Email: pcf@wir.net

Shell

Map #	Description	Season	RV sites	tent sites	hook-ups	pull-thrus	dump station	restrooms	hot showers	pool	laundry	tables/grills	rec-room	drinking water
96	Cabin Creek Trailer Park, 15 mi NE of Shell on US 14, USFS	5/24-9/12	26	•			•					•		•
97	Medicine Lodge Lake, 15 mi NE of Shell on US 14. 25 mi SE on FS Rd. USFS	7/1-9/8	8	•			•					•		•
98	Paintrock Lakes, 15 mi NE of Shell on US 14, 25 mi SE on FS Rd 17, USFS	7/1-9/8	8	•			•					•		•
99	Ranger Creek, 15 mi NE of Shell on US 14, 2 mi on FS Rd. USFS	5/23-9/15	10	•			•					•		•
100	Shell Campground, 102 First St. & Hwy 14, PH: 307-765-9924, Web: www.shellcampground.com	4/1-11/01	12	100	•	•	•	•	•		•	•		•
101	Shell Creek, 15 mi NE of Shell on US 14, 1 mi S on FS Rd. USFS	5/30-10/31	11	•			•					•		•

Ten Sleep

Map #	Description	Season	RV sites	tent sites	hook-ups	pull-thrus	dump station	restrooms	hot showers	pool	laundry	tables/grills	rec-room	drinking water
102	Big Horn Mountain Resorts, Box 86, PH: 307-366-2600 or 888-244-4070, Web: www.bighorn.com	6/1-11/1	18	20	•			•	•					
103	Boulder Park, 13 mi NE of Ten Sleep on US 16. USFS	6/1-9/22	34	•				•				•		•
104	Bull Creek, 25 mi NE of Ten Sleep on US 16, USFS	6/1-9/22	43	•				•				•		•
105	Castle Gardens, 1 mi W of Ten Sleep on Hwy 16-20 to Castle Gardens	6/1-10/31	•	•				•				•		
106	Circle S Campground, 300 Second Hwy 16, PH: 307-366-2320	5/1-11/1	•	•	•			•						
107	Deer Park, 26 mi NE of Ten Sleep on US 16, USFS	6/15-9/22	7	•				•				•		•
108	Island Park, 23 mi NE of Ten Sleep on US 16, USFS	6/15-9/22	10	•				•				•		•
109	Lakeview, 15 mi NE of Ten Sleep on US 16, USFS	6/15-9/22	11	•				•				•		•
110	Leigh Creek, 9 mi NE of Ten Sleep on US 16, USFS	5/20-9/22	11	•				•				•		•
111	Sitting Bull Creek, 23 mi NE of Ten Sleep on US 16. USFS	6/15-9/22	43	•				•				•		•
112	Ten Broek RV Park & Cabins, 98 Second St., Box 10, PH: 307-366-2250, E-mail: tenbroekrv@t&twest.net	4/1-11/1	55	30	•		•	•	•			•		
113	West Ten Sleep Lake, 27 mi NE of Ten Sleep on US 16. USFS	6/15-9/30	10	•				•						•

Thermopolis

Map #	Description	Season	RV sites	tent sites	hook-ups	pull-thrus	dump station	restrooms	hot showers	pool	laundry	tables/grills	rec-room	drinking water
114	Country Campin' RV & Tent Park, 710 E. Sunny Side Ln, PH: 307-864-2416, 800-609-2244. FAX: 864-2416. Web' www.camp@tnb.com	4/15-10/30	42	10	•	•	•	•	•		•	•	•	
115	Eagle RV Park, 204 Hwy 20 S., PH/FAX: 307-864-5262 or 888-865-5707, Web: www.interbasin.com/eagle/	All	46	12	•	•	•	•	•		•	•		•
116	Fountain of Youth RV Park, 250 N Hwy 20, PO Box 711, PH: 307-864-3265, FAX: 307-864-3388, Web: www.foyrvpk@trib.com	3/15-10/15	40	10	•		•	•	•					•
117	Grandview RV Park, 122 Hwy 20 S, PH: 307-864-3463	4/15-10/15	21	8	•	•	•	•	•					•
118	New RV Park, 113 N 2nd St. PH: 307-864-3926. Fax: 307-864-2291	4/1-11/1	15		•									
119	The Wyoming Waltz RV Park, 720 Shoshoni, PH: 307-864-2778, Email: breed@trib.com	All	13	3	•	•		•	•			•		•

Worland

Map #	Description	Season	RV sites	tent sites	hook-ups	pull-thrus	dump station	restrooms	hot showers	pool	laundry	tables/grills	rec-room	drinking water
171	Worland Cowboy Campground, 2311 Big Horn Ave., PH: 307-347-2329, Web www.worlandcowboycampground.com	4/1-10/31	38	8	•	•	•	•	•		•	•		•

Section 8

Afton

Map #	Description	Season	RV sites	tent sites	hook-ups	pull-thrus	dump station	restrooms	hot showers	pool	laundry	tables/grills	rec-room	drinking water
1	Cabin Creek, 16 mi E of Alpine on US 89, USFS	5/27-10/31	10	•				•				•		•
2	Swift Creek, 2 mi E of Afton on Cty & FS Rds, USFS	5/27-10/31	13	•				•				•		•

Alpine

Map #	Description	Season	RV sites	tent sites	hook-ups	pull-thrus	dump station	restrooms	hot showers	pool	laundry	tables/grills	rec-room	drinking water
3	Elbow, 14 mi E of Alpine on US 89, USFS	6/10-9/10	•	•				•				•		•
4	Forest Park, 37 mi SE of Alpine on US 89, USFS	5/27-10/31	13	•				•				•		•
5	Lynx Creek, 13 mi SE of Alpine on US 89, USFS	5/27-10/31	14	•				•				•		•
6	Moose Flat, 19 mi SE of Alpine on US 89, USFS	5/27-10/31	10	•				•				•		•
7	Murphy Creek, 12 mi SE of Alpine on US 89, FS# 10138 Greys River Rd., USFS	5/27-10/31	10	•				•				•		•
8	Station Creek, 11 mi E of Alpine on US 89, USFS	6/10-9/10	15	•		•		•				•		•

Big Piney

Map #	Description	Season	RV sites	tent sites	hook-ups	pull-thrus	dump station	restrooms	hot showers	pool	laundry	tables/grills	rec-room	drinking water
9	Middle Piney Lake, 25 mi W of Big Piney on WY & FS Rd, USFS	7/1-9/30	6	•				•				•		•
10	Sacajawea, 22 mi W of Big Piney on WY 35 & FS Rd, USFS	6/15-9/30	26	•				•				•		•

Bondurant

Map #	Description	Season	RV sites	tent sites	hook-ups	pull-thrus	dump station	restrooms	hot showers	pool	laundry	tables/grills	rec-room	drinking water
11	Granite Creek, 10 mi NW of Bondurant on US 191-189, 9 mi NE of FS Rd, USFS	6/25-9/10	52	•		•		•	•			•		•
12	Hoback, 14 mi NW of Bondurant on US 191-189, USFS	6/5-9/10	8	•				•				•		•
13	Kozy, 7 mi W of Bondurant on US 191-189, USFS	6/1-9/5	8	•				•				•		•

Boulder

Map #	Description	Season	RV sites	tent sites	hook-ups	pull-thrus	dump station	restrooms	hot showers	pool	laundry	tables/grills	rec-room	drinking water
14	Boulder Lake, 11 mi NE of Boulder on WY 353, 6 mi N on Cty Rd, 3 mi E on FS Rd, USFS	6/20-10/15	•	•				•				•		•

Dubois

Map #	Description	Season	RV sites	tent sites	hook-ups	pull-thrus	dump station	restrooms	hot showers	pool	laundry	tables/grills	rec-room	drinking water
15	Brooks Lake, 23 mi W of Dubois on US 26/287, 5 mi N on FS Rd. 515, USFS	6/20-9/30	14	•				•				•		•
16	Circle-Up Camper Court, 225 Welty St. Box 1520, PH: 307-455-2238, E-mail jnowlin@wyoming.com	All	80	100	•	•	•	•	•		•	•		•
17	Double Cabin, 28 mi N of Dubois on FS Rd. 508 & 285, USFS	6/1-9/30	15	•				•				•		•

Map #	Description	Season	RV sites	tent sites	hook-ups	pull-thrus	dump station	restrooms	hot showers	pool	laundry	tables/grills	rec-room	drinking water
18	Falls, 25 mi W of Dubois on US 287, USFS	6/1-10/30	46	•				•				•		•
19	Horse Creek, 12 mi N of Dubois on FS Ad, USFS	6/1-10/30	9	•				•				•		•
20	Pinnacles, 23 mi NW on US 26/287, 5 mi on FS Rd 515, USFS	6/20-9/3	21	•				•				•		•
21	Pinnacle Buttes Lodge & Campground, 3577 Hwy 26, PH: 307-455-2506 or 800-934-3569, FAX: 307-455-3874	All	12	10	•	•	•	•	•	•		•		•
22	Riverside Inn & Campground 5810 Hwy 26. Box 642. PH: 307-455-2337 or 877-489-2337. www.dteworld.com/riversideinn	Seasonal	10	10	•	•		•	•			•		•
Freedom														
23	Haderlie's Tincup Mountain Guest Ranch, Hwy 34 #5336, Box 275, PH: 208-873-2368, Web: www.silverstar.com/html	6/1-8/31	2	4	•			•				•		•
Jackson														
24	Atherton Creek, 7 mi E of Kelly on FS Rd, USFS	6/5-10/30	20	20				•				•		•
25	Crystal Creek, 13 mi E of Kelly on FS rd, USFS	6/5-10/30	6	•				•				•		•
26	Curtis Canyon, 6 mi E of Jackson from Elk Refuge Entrance to Curtis Canyon, 3 mi E, USFS	6/5-9/10	12	•				•				•		•
27	Elk Country Inn & RV Park, 480 W Pearl St, Box 1255, PH: 307-733-2364, 800-483-8667, Web: www.townsquareinns.com	All	12		•			•						•
28	Hatchet, 8 mi E of Moran Jct on US 26-287, USFS	6/25-9/10	9	•				•				•		•
29	Lazy J Corral RV Park, 10755 S. Hwy 89, PH: 307-733-1554	4/1-11/1	23		•	•		•	•			•		•
30	Lone Eagle, 10755 S Hwy 89, Star Rt Box 45-C PH: 307-733-1090 or 800-321-3800, FAX: 307-733-5042	5/15-10/1	23	50	•	•		•		•				•
31	Signal Mountain, 5 mi NW of Moran via US 89-287, 2 mi SW on Teton Park Road, NPS	5/15-9/30	80		•		•	•	•					•
32	Snake River Park KOA, 1 mi N Hoback Jct. 9705 S. Hwy 89, 4/7-10/10 PH: 307-733-7078, 800-562-1878, FAX: 733-0412, Web: www.srpkoa.com		41	25	•		•	•	•	•	•	•	•	•
33	Virginian Lodge RV Park, 750W Broadway, PH: 307-733-7189	5/1-10/5	105		•	•	•	•	•	•	•			•
34	Wagon Wheel Campground, 5 blks N of town square, 525 N Cache, Box 1463, PH: 307-733-4588	5/1-10/31	35	8	•	•		•	•	•		•		•
Marbleton														
35	Harper's Park & RV, 16 E 3rd St., Box 4478, PH/ Fax: 307-276-3611 or 276-3611	All	14	5	•	•	•	•	•			•		•
Pinedale														
36	Boulder Lake, 3 mi E of Boulder on 353, then 10 mi N on Boulder Lake Rd, USFS	6/1-10/15	20	•				•				•		•
37	Fremont Lake, 3 mi NE of Pinedale on Cty Rd, 4 mi NE on FS Rd, USFS	5/25-9/10	53	•				•				•		•
38	Green River Lake, 25 mi N of Pinedale on WY 352, 31 mi N on FS Rd, USFS	6/15-9/10	36	•				•				•		•
39	Lakeside Lodge Resort & Marina, 4 mi N of town on S shore of Lake, PH: 307-367-2221	5/15-11/1	20	6	•			•				•		•
40	Narrows, 21 mi N of Pinedale on WY 352, 5 mi E on Cty Rd, 3 mi E on FS Rd, USFS	6/1-9/10	19	•				•				•		•
41	New Fork Lake, 21 mi N of Pinedale on WY 352, 5 mi E on Cty Rd, 3 mi SE on FS Rd, USFS	6/1-9/10	15					•				•		•
42	Pinedale Campgrounds, 204 S Jackson, PH: 307-367-4555, FAX: 307-367-2397	5/25-10/15	24	36	•		•	•	•			•		•
43	Scab Creek, 20 mi SE of Pinedale on Hwy 353, then N 10 mi, BLM	6/1-10/31	10	•				•				•		•
44	Trails End, 3 mi NE of Pinedale on Cty Rd, 11 mi NE on FS Rd, USFS	6/25-9/10	8	•				•				•		•
45	Warren Bridge, 24 mi N of Pinedale on Hwy 187-189, BLM	6/1-10/31	•	•				•				•		•
46	Whiskey Grove, 36 mi N of Pinedale on WY 352, and FS Rd, USFS	6/15-9/10	9	•				•				•		•
Teton Village														
47	Teton Village KOA, 5 mi W of Jackson on Hwy 22/390, 5/1-10/12 PH: 307-733-5354 or 800-562-9043, FAX: 307-739-1298		150		•			•	•		•	•	•	•
Thayne														
48	Flat Creek RV Park & Cabins, 74 Hokanson St, PH: 307-883-2231	All	23	6	•			•	•		•	•		•

Notes:

FISHERIES
By Drainage

YELLOWSTONE PARK

Map Number/Fishery

	Fishery	Brook Trout	Brown Trout	Cutthroat Trout	Grayling	Lake Trout	Mountain Whitefish	Rainbow Trout
Rivers & Streams								
1	Bechler River	•	•					•
2	Firehole River	•	•					•
3	Gallatin River		•	•			•	•
4	Gardner River	•	•	•			•	•
5	Gibbon River	•	•		•		•	•
6	Lamar River			•				•
7	Madison River		•		•		•	•
8	Slough Creek			•				•
9	Snake River		•	•				
10	Yellowstone River	•	•	•				
Lakes								
11	Heart Lake			•		•		
12	Lewis Lake	•	•			•		
13	Shoshone Lake	•	•			•		
14	Yellowstone Lake			•		•		

SNAKE RIVER DRAINAGE

Map Number/Fishery

	Fishery	Brook Trout	Grayling	Lake Trout	Mountain Whitefish	Snake Rvr Cutthroat
Rivers & Streams						
15	Flat Creek (Above Refuge)	•				•
16	Flat Creek (on Refuge)	•			•	•
17	Granite Creek				•	•
18	Greys River				•	•
19	Gros Ventre River				•	•
20	Hoback River				•	•
21	Pacific Creek				•	•
22	Salt River	•			•	•
23	Snake River				•	•
Lakes						
24	Grassy Lake			•		•
25	Jackson Lake	•		•	•	•
26	Jenny Lake			•	•	•
27	Lake of the Woods		•			•
28	Leidy Lake					•
29	Phelps Lake			•	•	•
30	Slide Lake, Lower			•	•	•
31	Topping Lake		•			

BIG HORN RIVER DRAINAGE

Map Number/Fishery

Rivers & Streams

Map Number/Fishery	Bear River Cutthroat	Black Crappie	Brook Trout	Brown Trout	Burbot	Channel Catfish	Golden Trout	Grayling	Lake Trout	Largemouth Bass	Mountain Whitefish	Rainbow Trout	Sauger	Snake River Cutthroat	Splake	Stonecat	Walleye	Yellow Perch	Yellowstone Cutthroat
32 Bear Creek														•					•
33 Big Horn River, Lower					•	•							•				•		
34 Big Horn River, Upper				•	•						•	•							
35 Brooks Lake Creek			•									•							
36 Bull Lake			•				•		•			•			•				•
37 Clarks Fork River, Lower			•	•								•							•
38 Clarks Fork River, Upper			•									•							•
39 Greybull River				•															•
40 Horse Creek			•								•								
41 Jakeys Fork Creek			•								•								
42 Medicine Lodge Creek			•								•								
43 Medicine Lodge Unit											•								
44 Paintrock Creek			•								•								•
45 Popo Agie River, North Fork				•							•								
46 Popo Agie River, Middle Fork			•	•							•								
47 Popo Agie River, Little				•															
48 Popo Agie River, Little			•																
49 Shell Creek			•	•							•								
50 Shoshone River	•			•							•	•		•					•
51 Shoshone River, N Fork				•					•		•	•							
52 Shoshone River, S Fork			•	•					•		•	•							•
53 Sunlight Unit			•									•							•
54 Tensleep Creek			•								•	•			•				
55 Torrey Creek			•	•	•														
56 Wind River (section I)				•	•						•	•			•		•	•	
57 Wind River (Dubois Area)			•	•							•	•							
58 Wind River (section II)				•	•						•				•		•		
59 Wind River, East Fork														•					•
60 Wind River, Little				•	•						•	•							
61 Yellowstone River																			•

Map Number/Fishery

BIG HORN RIVER DRAINAGE

Lakes

Map Number/Fishery	Bear River Cutthroat	Black Crappie	Brook Trout	Brown Trout	Burbot	Channel Catfish	Golden Trout	Grayling	Lake Trout	Largemouth Bass	Mountain Whitefish	Rainbow Trout	Sauger	Snake River Cutthroat	Splake	Stonecat	Walleye	Yellow Perch	Yellowstone Cutthroat
62 Alp Lakes, Wind River Mtns			•	•			•				•				•	•			•
63 Atlantic Gulch, Big			•												•				
64 Beartooth Lake			•																•
65 Beck Lake				•		•				•								•	•
66 Big Horn Lake		•	•	•	•	•							•	•			•	•	•
67 Bighorn Mtns, Alpine Lakes			•	•	•		•	•				•			•				
68 Boysen Reservoir		•	•	•	•	•				•		•	•				•	•	
69 Bridger Lake																			
70 Brooks Lake, Upper			•																
71 Brooks Lake			•						•						•				
72 Buffalo Bill Reservoir				•					•		•								
73 Bull Lake				•	•				•		•				•				•
74 Cameahwait Lake										•									
75 Christina Lake			•					•											
76 Deaver Reservoir												•					•		•
77 Depression Res, Middle					•							•							
78 Fiddlers Lake			•									•							

280

Wyoming Introduction

Map Number/Fishery

BIG HORN RIVER DRAINAGE
Continued

Lakes

Map/Fishery	Bear River Cutthroat	Black Crappie	Brook Trout	Brown Trout	Burbot	Channel Catfish	Golden Trout	Grayling	Lake Trout	Largemouth Bass	Mountain Whitefish	Rainbow Trout	Sauger	Snake River Cutthroat	Splake	Stonecat	Walleye	Yellow Perch	Yellowstone Cutthroat
79 Fish Lake														•					
80 Frye Lake			•									•							
81 Hogan Reservoir				•										•					
82 Jade Lakes Upper & Lower									•					•					
83 Louis Lake									•			•		•					
84 Luce Reservoir												•							
85 Meadowlark Lake			•	•								•							•
86 Newton Lake, East			•	•											•				
87 Newton Lake, West																			•
88 Ocean Lake		•			•												•	•	
89 Pelham Lake																			•
90 Pilot Butte Reservoir				•	•							•						•	
91 Ray Lake				•	•						•	•		•					
92 Renner										•									
93 Ring Lake				•	•							•			•				
94 Shoshone Lake			•																
95 Sunshine Res, Lower					•						•			•	•				•
96 Sunshine Res, Upper											•			•	•				•
97 Swamp Lake			•																
98 Torrey Lake				•	•			•				•			•				
99 Trail Lake				•	•				•			•			•				
100 Worthen Meadows Res			•									•							

NOTES:

_____
_____
_____
_____
_____
_____
_____
_____
_____
_____
_____
_____
_____
_____
_____
_____
_____
_____
_____

Master Map and Section Guide

Detailed enlargements of each section can be found at the beginning of each section. Enlarged sections also include camping and fishing sites.

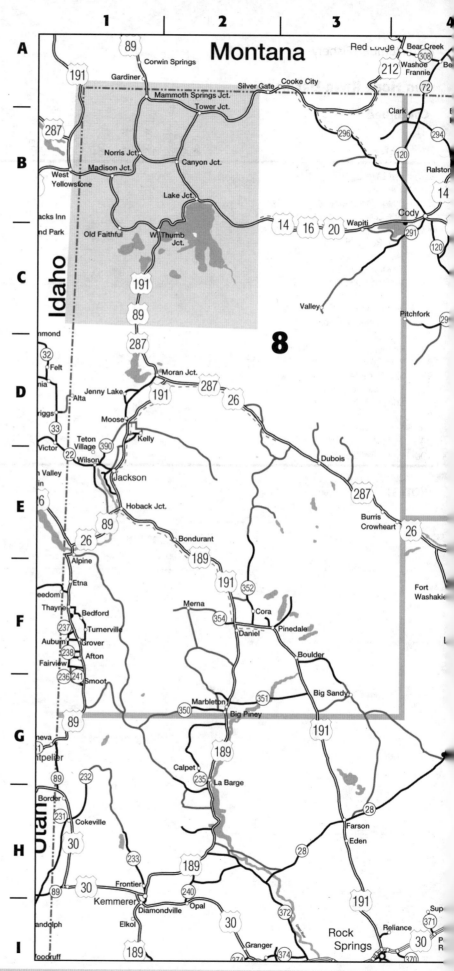

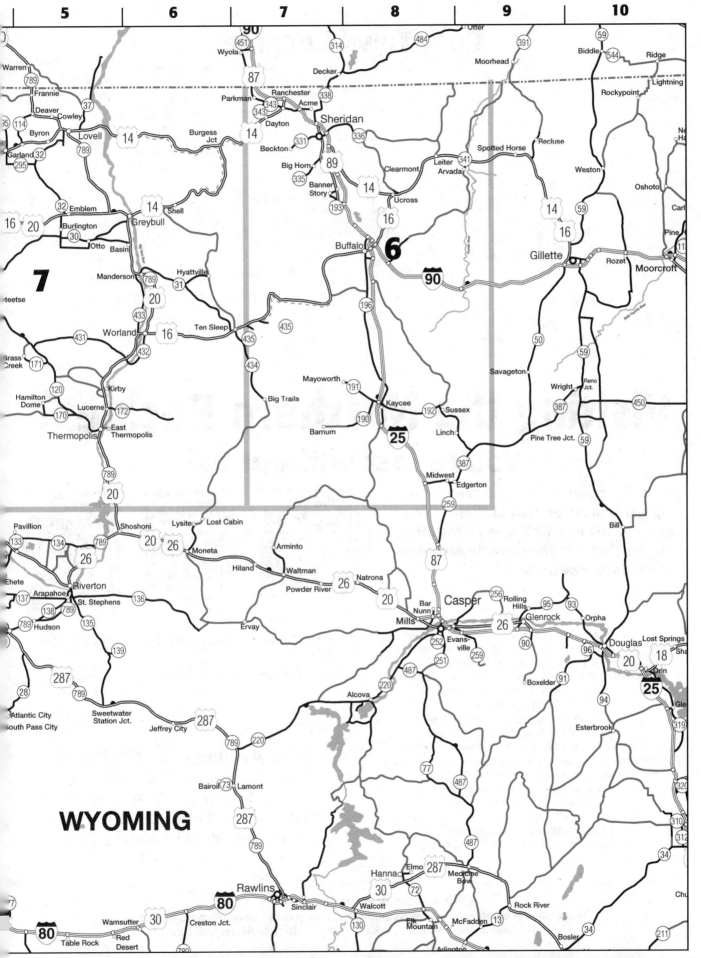

WYOMING

CITY/TOWN LOCATOR

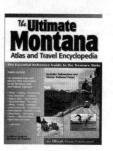

Wyoming Introduction

SECTION 6

NORTHEAST AREA

INCLUDING SHERIDAN AND BUFFALO

Devils Tower near Sundance.

1 *Gas, Food, Lodging*

Ranchester
Pop. 701, Elev. 3,775

Named by English born senator, D.H. Hardin, Ranchester was the site of two significant battles during the Plains Indian Wars. In 1865, General Patrick E. Connor, an aggressive, anti-Indian commander at Fort Laramie, was responsible for the slaughter of 63 men, women, and children in an Arapaho village on the Tongue River. Only eight of his troopers died in the fight, and the victors took home 1100 ponies. Two days later, the Arapaho retaliated by attacking a road-building expedition headed by Col. James Sawyer. Three soldiers were killed, and Connor had to return to rescue the rest. Peace movements in the East prevented Connor from killing "all male Indians over the age of twelve," as he had planned. In 1894, Ranchester became a shipping stop on the Burlington railroad for the McShane Tie Company.

Acme

From the Greek for "high grade," Acme was named for its prime coal, known as "black diamonds." Once a coal mine camp, Acme was also a station on the Burlington railroad. It later gave its name to the Acme Petroleum Corporation, a large Wyoming oil company founded around 1900.

T Connor Battlefield State Historic Site
In Ranchester

Once the site of a bloody battle when General Patrick E. Connor's army attacked and destroyed Arapahoe Chief Black Bear's settlement of 250 lodges. The battlefield is now located in the peaceful and beautiful city park. The site marks the military engagement that was part of the Powder River Expedition of 1865. The battle caused the Arapaho to ally with the Sioux and Cheyenne at the Fetterman Fight the next year.

T Little Blue Schoolhouse
In Ranchester

One of the areas oldest schools, it was moved to Ranchester in 1988. This 1902 one-room school from the Parkman area has been completely restored.

T Ranchester Museum
145 Coffeen in Ranchester. 655-2284

H The Battle of Tongue River
Ranchester at Connor Battlefield Site.

On this site during the early morning hours of August 29, 1865, General Patrick Edward Connor led over 200 troops in an attack on Chief Black Bear's Arapaho village. Connor had departed from Fort Laramie on July 30th with 184 wagons, a contingent of Pawnee scouts, nearly 500 cavalrymen, and the aging Jim Bridger as guide. His column was one of three comprising the Powder River Indian Expedition sent to secure the Bozeman and other emigrant trails leading to the Montana mining fields.

During the Battle of Tongue River, Connor was able to inflict serious damage on the Arapahos, but an aggressive counter attack forced him to retreat back to the newly established Fort Connor (later renamed Reno) on the banks of the Powder River. There he received word that he had been reassigned to his old command in the District of Utah.

The Powder River Expedition, one of the most comprehensive campaigns against the Plains Indians, never completely succeeded. Connor had planned a complex operation only to be defeated by bad weather, inhospitable terrain, and hostile Indians. Long term effects of the Expedition proved detrimental to the interests of the Powder River tribes. The Army, with the establishment of Fort Connor (Reno) increased public awareness of this area which in turn caused more emigrants to use the Bozeman Trail. This led to public demand for government protection of travelers on their way to Montana gold fields.

2 *Food, Lodging*

Dayton
Pop. 678, Elev. 3,926

Dayton was named for banker, Joseph Dayton Thorn. It was established 1n 1882 and gained fame in 1911 when Susan Whissler, the first woman mayor in the nation was elected. Dayton is also home to Wyoming's first rodeo held in the 1890s.

Parkman
No Services

Named for Francis Parkman, author of *The Oregon Trail*, this railroad station town was established in 1894.

T Hans Kleiber Museum
520 Story in Dayton. 655-2217

The log cabin studio of watercolor artist Hans Kleiber has been preserved for use as a museum and visitors center. Known as the "Artist of the Big Horns", Kleiber's work is world renown. Born in Cologne, Italy in 1887, his family moved to

Sheridan	Jan	Feb	March	April	May	June	July	Aug	Sep	Oct	Nov	Dec	Annual
Average Max. Temperature (F)	33.3	38.5	45.6	56.5	66.6	76.4	86.2	85.5	73.7	61.3	45.5	36.3	58.8
Average Min. Temperature (F)	9.0	14.4	20.9	30.4	39.6	47.6	53.8	52.4	42.4	31.9	20.0	11.9	31.2
Average Total Precipitation (in.)	0.72	0.67	1.05	1.86	2.31	2.18	1.07	0.85	1.30	1.24	0.81	0.65	14.69
Average Total SnowFall (in.)	10.9	10.3	12.4	10.5	1.7	0.1	0.0	0.0	1.4	4.7	8.5	11.1	71.5
Average Snow Depth (in.)	3	3	1	0	0	0	0	0	0	0	1	2	1
Wind Speed (mph / kmh)	8 / 13	8 / 13	9 / 15	10 / 17	9 / 15	8 / 13	8 / 12	8 / 12	8 / 13	8 / 13	8 / 12	8 / 13	
Wind Direction	NW	NW	NW	NW	NW	NW	NW	NW	NW	NW	NW		
Cloud Cover (out of 8)	5.7	5.7	5.6	5.4	5.3	4.5	3.6	3.7	4.0	4.7	5.4	5.4	

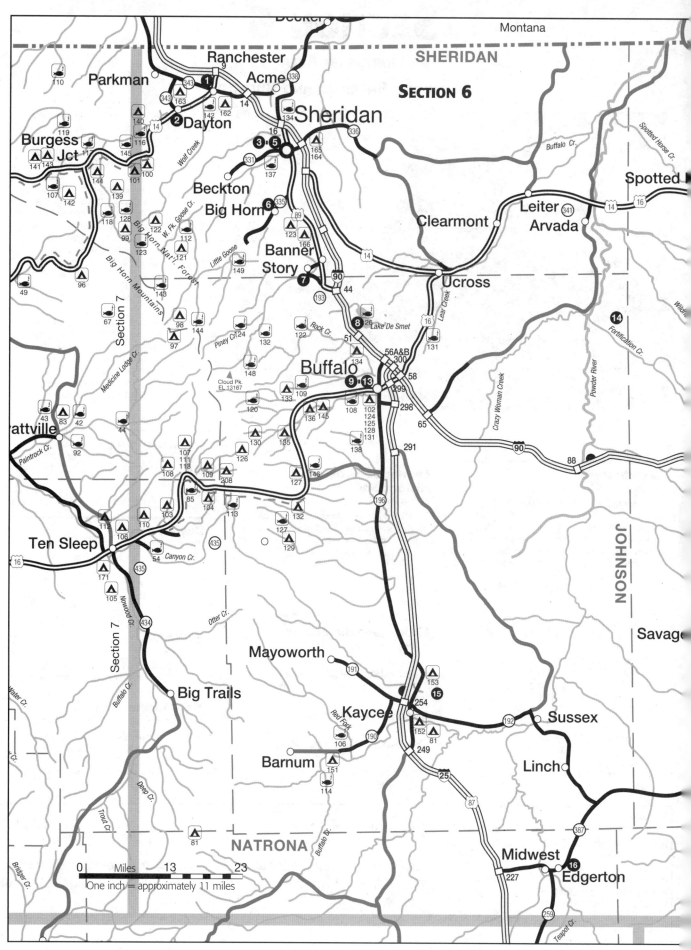

Montana

SHERIDAN

SECTION 6

Decker

Ranchester
Acme
9
1
343
Parkman
343
163
162
142
2 Dayton
14
16
Sheridan
134
336
110
140
14
Burgess
119
Jct
11
116
331
165
164
141 143
145
137
100
144
101
Beckton
Big Horn
Clearmont
Leiter
341
107
142
139
6 335
Arvada
Spotted
128
118
99
123
89
166
Banner
Story
90
Ucross
44
96
49
123
193
Buffalo Cr.
Spotted Horse Cr.
14
16
14
67
98
144
90
Leiter Creek
14
Lake De Smet
16
97
Rock Cr.
51
8 26
131
Piney Cr.
124
132
122
56A&B
300
148
Buffalo
134
58
Cloud Pk.
EL 13167
109
9 13
299
14
Fortification Cr.
133
108
102
298
120
136 145
124
125
128
65
Powder River
Crazy Woman Creek
130
135
131
90
88
rattville
43
83
42
138
196
126
92
127
146
Section 7
44
291
132
107
111
113
JOHNSON
108
109
208
85
127
104
113
129
103
Ten Sleep
112
110
435
106
16
54 Canyon Cr.
435
171
Savage
105
434
Section 7
Mayoworth
191
153
Big Trails
15
Kaycee
254
Sussex
Red Fork
152
192
106
190
81
249
Barnum
151
25
Linch
114
87
Midwest
227
387
Edgerton
NATRONA
259

0   Miles   13   23

One inch = approximately 11 miles

286   *Ultimate* Yellowstone Park Atlas and Travel Encyclopedia

Legend for Section Map

00 Locator number (matches numeric listing in section)

⚑ Campsite (number matches number in campsite chart)

🎣 Fishing Site (number matches number in fishing chart)

⬤ Rest stop

═══ Interstate

═══ U.S. Highway

━━━ Paved State or County Road

▬▬▬ Gravel/unpaved road

Massachusetts in the early 1900s. He later moved West and after various jobs, moved to Dayton and established himself as an artist. The museum contains his press, art books and a number of etchings. The museum is open Monday through Saturday during the summer, closed in winter.

T Bald Mountain City

Fine-grained gold was discovered here in 1890, and for the next decade, prospectors flocked to the area. In 1892, the Fortunatas Mining and Mlling Company helped establish the town, one of the largest settlements in the Big Horn Mountains. The cost of panning, however, outweighed the value of the yields, and gold fever in the area ended by 1900.

H Connor Battlefield State Historic Site

Dayton and Gillette Streets in Dayton.

In 1865 General Patrick E. Connor led the Powder River Expedition into this area. This expedition was part of a broad military program to bring the Indians north of the Platte River under control and halt their depredations along the Western Trails.

At this site Connor's command located and attacked a large party of Araphao under Black Bear and Old David, destroying 250 lodges. Much of the fighting was hand-to-hand combat, and many women and children were killed and captured.

Later events proved the campaign of 1865 to be undecisive.

H First Woman Mayor in Wyoming

Bridge Street and West 3rd Avenue in Dayton.

Mrs. Susan Wissler, on May 9, 1911, was elected mayor of Dayton, Wyoming, then a community of about 175 people. She served two terms of two years each. Her administration was marked by civic improvement and community betterment as her campaign promise to curb gambling and regular the operation of saloons was, in a measure, fulfilled.

Mrs. Wissler was truly a pioneer. She taught in the public schools of this area for several years and actively encouraged her students to go on for further study. As a practical nurse she

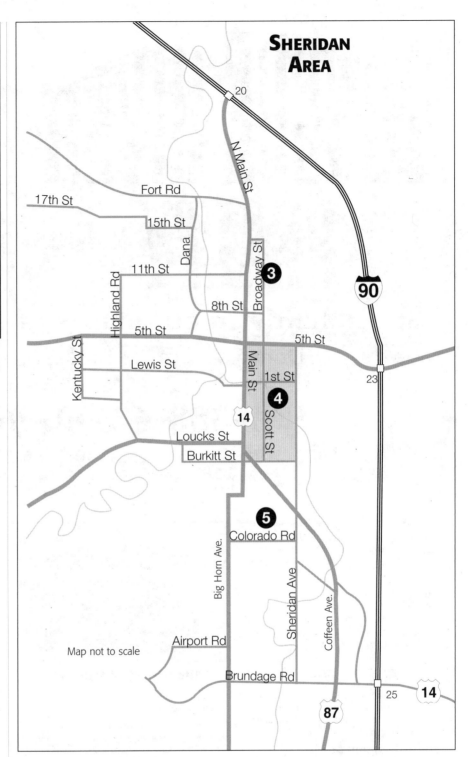

SHERIDAN AREA

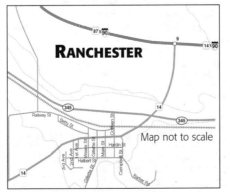

RANCHESTER

DAYTON

Map not to scale

is remembered for her ministrations in time of trouble. She also owned and operated a millinery and drygoods store for a number of years. Dayton became her home in 1890. She died in 1938.

H Susan Wissler
1853-1938
406 Main St. in Dayton.

Mrs. Susan Wissler owned and operated a millinery shop at this location while serving as mayor of Dayton from 1911 to 1913. Mrs. Wissler was the first woman mayor in Wyoming and the first woman to serve consecutive terms as mayor in the United States. Mrs. Wissler was an excellent teacher and a successful business woman. It is appropriate that she was elected in the first state to grant equal suffrage to women.

H Sibley Monument
About 20 miles west of Dayton on U.S. Highway 14.

Through this vicinity, a scouting party of the 2nd Cavalry, led by Lt. Frederick W. Sibley, was attacked by Sioux and Cheyenne Indians on July 7, 1876. In the fight Chief White Antelope was killed. The party abandoned its horses, took to the rugged terain, and scouts Frank Gruard and Baptiste Poirier guided the 26 soldiers and Chicago Times reporter John F. Finerty over the mountains without food, back to their main camp.

L White Horse Bed & Breakfast
306 Main St., Dayton. 655-9441.
www.WhiteHorseBedandBreakfast.com;
whitehorse@vcv.com

Established in 1904 as the town hotel, the White Horse Bed & Breakfast is located in downtown Dayton just four hours from Yellowstone. Guests are invited to relax and soak in the scenic Big Horn Mountain views from the front porch, patio, or upper deck of this comfortable dwelling. Three guest rooms each feature a private bath. After a peaceful night's sleep in one of the themed bedrooms, guests enjoy a scrumptious breakfast including homemade pancakes, cobblers, fresh fruit, and more, ensuring no one leaves the table hungry! During your stay, check out the area's numerous museums, historical sites, art and craft galleries, and endless outdoor adventures. Make The White Horse Bed and Breakfast your next base camp for comfortable accommodations and convenient year-round access to the region's numerous attractions and outdoor recreation!

M Tongue River Realty
311 Main St., Dayton. 655-9556 or (888) 625-9556. www.tongueriver.com or www.tongueriverrealty.com; tongueriverrealty@tongueriver.com

Interested in discovering the beautiful Rocky Mountain region? Then first discover the expertise of Tongue River Realty. The well-established brokerage holds licenses to list, show, and sell properties across the entire states of Wyoming, Montana, and Colorado. Specializing in all phases of real estate and striving to offer the best personal service possible, Tongue River Realty offers the options you need in finding the perfect property. Clients will find everything from upscale homes and modest ramblers to sprawling ranches, small acreages, and commercial property with prices accommodating all financial capabilities. Whether you're looking to sell your home or business or are searching for your dream property, trust the dedicated professionals at Tongue River Realty. At this brokerage, you don't just have one agent working for you. You have the whole office on your side!

3 *Gas, Food, Lodging*

Sheridan
Pop. 15,804, Elev. 3,745

The Sheridan area has been valuable territory since the days when only Native Americans roamed here, along with the buffalo and other wild game. Once a prized hunting ground, it was often disputed even before white men came. It was not until the establishment of the

Bozeman Trail, however, that the Sioux, Cheyenne, Arapaho, and other tribes came together to fight off the increasing influx of settlers.

Some of the bloodiest battles of the Plains Indian War, which took place in the 1860s and 70s, occurred nearby. The Fetterman Fight, Wagon Box Fight, Connor and Sawyer Battles, the Battle of the Rosebud, the Dull Knife Battle, and the Battle of the Little Bighorn all took place within just miles of Sheridan. For that reason, this portion of the Bozeman Trail became known as the Bloody Bozeman. It was not until the surrender of leaders such as Red Cloud, Crazy Horse, and Sitting Bull that hostilities eased, and the area was open to settlement.

In 1878, mountain man Jim Mason built the first permanent building here. A store and post office opened in 1881. Storeowner Harry Mandel sold the place to Jim Loucks, who planned the town and named it for his Civil War commander, General Philip Sheridan. Homesteaders and cattle ranchers moved into the area, creating an agricultural crossroads where the Burlington Railroad set up a stop in 1892. The discovery of coal in the area added to the towns growing prosperity. The building of several flourmills and a sugar beet factory contributed to the economy as well. The twentieth century brought several booms and busts, but now the city has settled into a serene mix of agriculture, energy production, and tourism.

The lowest city in Wyoming, Sheridan's elevation is 3745 feet.

Beckton

Also known as Beckton Junction, pioneer George W. Beck built a flourmill here and established a post office in 1883. The post office was discontinued. There are only a few houses here today.

T **Sheridan Travel and Tourism**
I-90 & E. 5th Street in Sheridan. 673-7120 or 888-596-6787. www.sheridanwyoming.org

T **Sheridan Rest Stop & Visitor's Center**
I-90 exit 23 in Sheridan

T **Wyoming Game and Fish Dept. Visitor Center**
Across road from Sheridan Rest Stop

View taxidermist displays of native Wyoming creatures, and find out more about wildlife, hunting, and fishing in the West.

H Big Horns

The abundance of Rocky Mountain bighorn sheep led the Indians to name this mountain range after these majestic animals. The Big Horn Mountains are a wildlife viewing paradise. Several native Indian tribes competed with each other and later with settlers for access to the mountains and surrounding river basins. Eventually settlers took possession of the land. Due to excessive hunting and introduced diseases, the once abundant bighorn sheep were almost eliminated from this area by the turn of the century. Today, bighorn sheep are being reintroduced to the Big Horn Mountains.

At high elevations, mountain meadows are interspersed with timber stands which provide food and summer habitat for elk and mule deer. Willow stands provide forage for moose. The forests house black bears, snowshoe hares, marmots, chipmunks and blue grouse.

At lower elevations, white-tailed deer, mountain lions, sharp-tailed grouse, wild turkeys, black-billed magpies and over 300

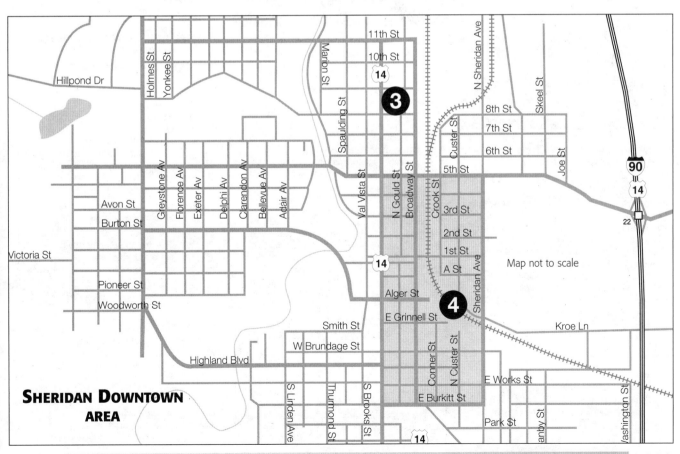

SHERIDAN DOWNTOWN AREA

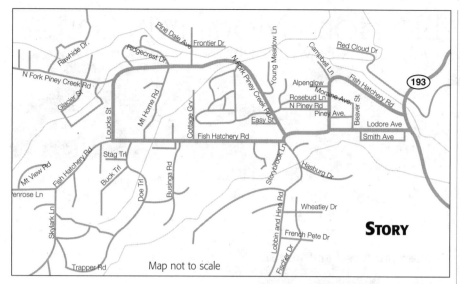

STORY

Map not to scale

L Spear-O-Wigwam Ranch
Sheridan. 673-5543 or (888) 818-3833.
www.spear-o-wigwam.com;
spearo@wavecom.net

Experience a Wyoming dude ranch vacation at the historic Spear-O-Wigwam Ranch. Situated at 8,300 feet, the mountain lodge allows guests to design their own vacation. Seeking adventure? The ranch offers horseback riding, guided naturalist hikes, fly-fishing, and packtrips into the Big Horn National Forest and Cloud Peak Wilderness Areas. Those searching for a quiet vacation are welcomed with the ranch's serene atmosphere, cozy log cabin lodgings, and memorable family-style dining. During your stay, check out the Rec Room's ping-pong, billiards, and don't miss each day's special activities. Featured activities include ice cream socials, massages, roping, Sheridan sightseeing, campfires, smores, cowboy poetry, and more. Catering to guest's unique needs for over 75 years, Spear-O-Wigwam Ranch is your destination for personalized service in one of Wyoming's most beautiful settings!

4 Gas, Food, Lodging

T Chamber of Commerce - Sheridan
707 Sheridan in Sheridan. 672-2485 or (800) 453-3650. www.sheridanwy.com

T Sheridan Heritage Center Inc
856 Broadway in Sheridan. 674-2178

TS King's Saddlery Museum
184 N. Main in Sheridan. 672-2702

This collection features over 500 custom-made saddles, including (but not limited to) several made by famed saddlemaker Don King. One of the museum's most treasured item is a Japanese saddle from the 1600s. There is more craftsmanship on displays than just saddles. The museum also houses guns, chaps, spurs, wagons, Native American and frontier clothing, and an old horse drawn hearse. Admission is free. Call for hours.

T Historic Sheridan Inn Museum
Take the Fifth Street exit off of I-90 at Sheridan. 674-5440

The Old Sheridan Inn was once the place to be if you were part of the elite in nothern Wyoming. It was originally built to accomodate passengers on the Burlington and Missouri Railroad. Over the years, such famous people have been here as Calamity Jane, Ernest Hemingway, President Herbert Hoover, and even Bob Hope. Buffalo Bill Cody used to stay here when he came to town to audition acts for his show. It became the first place in Sheridan to have steam heat, telephones, and electricity around the turn of the century. The Inn was partially restored in 1965, and then refurbished again when the Sheridan Heritage Center took responsibility for it. The SHC accepts donations to help further restore the Inn and keep it running. Call for hours.

other kinds of wildlife inhabit the foothills and riparian areas. Notice the diverse habitat types which make this area so productive for wildlife. The riparian zones bordered by stands of cottonwood trees and cropland provide excellent feeding areas. The steep foothills of the Big Horns furnish crucial winter range for big game.

Discover more about the current status of bighorn sheep and the diverse wildlife communities of Wyoming by touring the Wyoming Game and Fish Department Visitor Center across the highway.

F Wyoming's Rib & Chop House
856 N. Broadway in Sheridan. 673-4700.

Wyoming's Rib and Chop House is located in the Historic Sheridan Inn, built in 1893. Famous nationally for award-wining babyback ribs, fresh seafood and incredible Certified Angus steaks, the Rib and Chop House has made a name for itself locally with high-energy, jovial staff, and some of the best food this side of the Mississippi. Belly up to Buffalo Bill's original bar for an enormous margarita, or enjoy a hand-cut Buffalo Filet in the same corner where Buffalo Bill drew the plans for the town that bears his name: Cody, Wyoming. From the eclectic music and wild game mounts, to the wide-open views from the enormous veranda, the Rib and Chop House-Sheridan is all about great food in an exciting setting. Historical information is available in both the gift store and lobby, and you can ask just about anybody about the resident ghost—Miss Kate. Open seven days a week, year-round, eating at the Rib and Chop house is a truly pleasurable dining experience.

L Americas Best Value Inn
580 E. 5th St., Sheridan. 672-9757 or (800) 771-4761.
americasbestvalueinn.com/bestv.cfm?idp=700

Located in a quiet residential location just off I-90's historical central Exit 23, americas Best Value Inn is an ideal place to rest while in beautiful Sheridan. Each guest room includes a fridge, microwave, 50 cable TV channels, A/C, radio, alarm clock, iron/board, and more. WIFI and lobby internet, dataport telephones, and wake-up calls offer guests comfort and convenience in addition to the 24-hour front desk, guest laundry, vending, barbeque area, outdoor plug-ins, and drive-up parking. Before exploring the area's beautiful outdoors, historic sites, and great shopping, wake up to a complimentary deluxe breakfast including eggs, waffles, ceral, fruit, and gourmet coffee. With so many amenities and an ideal location halfway between Yellowstone and Mt. Rushmore, americas Best Value Inn guarantees a great night's sleep and an enjoyable stay.

DAYTON DAYS

The last week in July, Dayton Days boasts a large parade, games, duck races, crafts and food vendors in the park, pet parade, fun walk, softball games, Rotary Club breakfast, entertainment, outdoor dances, barbecue and firemen's water fights.

T Sheridan County Fulmer Public Library

335 West Alger in Sheridan. 674-8585

Permanent exhibits feature works of regional artists and Native American artifacts. There are also changing monthly exhibits. The Wyoming room features collections including local and regional history and U.S. genealogy. Open Monday through Thursday, 9 a.m. to 9 p.m., Friday and Saturday, 9 a.m. to 5 p.m. Sundays, September to May, from 1 p.m. to 5 p.m.

H Crook's Campaign, 1876

W. Dow and Alger in Sheridan.

On this site, the junction of Big and Little Goose Creeks, General George Crook, with 15 troops of cavalry, 5 companies of infantry, 1325 men and 1900 head of transport animals, headquartered. Joined by Indian allies, the Crows under chiefs Old Crow, Medicine Crow and Plenty Coups, and Shoshoni under Washakie, he battled 2500 Sioux 40 miles northeast, on the Rosebud, June 17. Defeated, Crook returned here, occupying these valleys, awaiting reinforcements which arrived in August. He then united with General Alfred Terry's army, which included remnants of Custer's 7th Cavalry, to campaign in Montana. Buffalo Bill, Calamity Jane, Frank Grouard, noted western characters, were with this expedition.

F Oliver's Bar & Grill

55 N. Main St., Sheridan. 672-2838.
oliversbarngrill@qwest.net

A relaxed, intimate setting complements the rich, savory fare of one of Sheridan's finest restaurants. Under the creative genius of Chef Matt Wallop, Oliver's Bar & Grill opened in January 2002 and has established itself as a Wyoming hotspot for incredible meals emphasizing the freshest ingredients. Sink your teeth into a tender rib-eye steak purchased from the area's Legacy Cattle Company, savor Dungeness crab cakes featuring fresh seafood from Seattle, or delight in one of the many masterpieces highlighting seasonal ingredients. A full selection of wines complement each meal's unique taste and texture, and decadent desserts add the crowning touch. In addition to exceptional food, Oliver's welcomes patrons to its classy bar and the adjoining Brundage Street Gourmet. Visit Oliver's Bar & Grill today, and immerse yourself in one of Wyoming's most exquisite dining experiences!

Wyoming Tidbits

The geographical center of Wyoming is Fremont, 58 miles northeast of Lander.

Live the Wild Life!

- Explore the Big Horns
- Discover Indian War History
- Shop Historic Downtown
- Participate in the Arts
- See World Class Rodeo & Polo
- Play Wyoming's Golf Capital
- Relax, Dine & Lodge in Sheridan

Stay & Play

Best Western Sheridan Center
Toll-free: 877.437.4326
www.bestwestern.com/sheridancenter

WINGATE INN
Toll-free: 800.228.1000
www.wingateinnsheridan.com

Sheridan Wyoming
The WEST at its BEST!
www.sheridanwyoming.org
888.596.6787

L Best Western Sheridan Center & Trolleyline Restaurant

612 N. Main St., Sheridan. 674-7421 or (877) 437-4326.
www.bestwestern.com/sheridancenter

All roads in the West lead to the Best Western Sheridan Center. Providing affordable top quality accommodations, the hotel features coffeemakers, hairdryers, iron/ironing boards, and free high-speed Internet in every room with some including microwaves, refrigerators, and Business Class features. Guests also enjoy indoor and outdoor heated pools, a Jacuzzi, complimentary fitness center use at the nearby YMCA, onsite laundry, and complete business services. Although numerous restaurants are within walking distance, the hotel conveniently serves scrumptious breakfasts, lunches, and dinners at the onsite Trolleyline Restaurant. As an added bonus, the hotel is on the Sheridan Trolley route and is just minutes from historic sites, museums, theaters, galleries, shopping, and outdoor recreation. With so many amenities and an ideal location, the Best Western Sheridan Center is your destination for both leisure and business travel!

S BigHorn Design Custom Embroidery & Screenprinting

201 N. Main St., Sheridan. 674-8808 or (888) 322-8607. www.bighorndesign.com; service@bighorndesign.com

You'll enjoy shopping Bighorn Design™ for all your Wyoming souvenir caps, shirts, sweats and tees in all the latest colors and styles. As Northern Wyoming's largest custom embroiderers they offer thousands of designs and the latest in clothing from True Grit™, Cutter and Buck™, Tiger Brand™, Port Authority™, Color Me Cotton™, Habitat™, and others with hometown service in their great retail store and online. Visit their website for their current garment catalog, store information, and their embroidery services. Whether you shop in person, by phone, or online you can be assured that your order will receive the finest service available. All embroidery design, digitizing and production is done in–house. When choosing apparel for yourself, the family or your business you can count on Bighorn Design's™ commitment to quality, no long delays, or outrageous minimums, just good service!

5 *Gas, Food, Lodging*

T Sheridan College Martinson Gallery

3059 Coffeen Ave. in Sheridan.674-6446

T Wyoming National Guard Armory Museum

3219 Coffeen in Sheridan. 672-6442

T Trail End State Historic Site

400 Clarendon Avenue in Sheridan. 674-4589. www.trailend.org

From its authentically furnished rooms to its finely manicured lawns, the Trail End State Historic Site displays an elegantly different aspect of Wyoming's colorful ranching history. Built in the Flemish Revival style in 1913, Trail End was the home of John Benjamin Kendrick. A cattle rancher who started out a Texas cowboy, Kendrick ended up as Governor of Wyoming and a United States Senator. Trail End is the perfect place to take a moment and just imagine what life might have been like in Wyoming during the early years of the 20th century.

From laundry room to ballroom, Trail End offers an intriguing glimpse into life during the period 1913 to 1933. Exhibits and displays throughout the home's fully-furnished historic interior provide information on daily life, entertainment, interior design and technology. The house and grounds were placed on the National Register of Historic Places in 1970. A state-held property since 1982, Trail End is currently operated by the State Parks & Historic Sites Division of the Wyoming Department of Parks and Cultural Resources.

The house is closed to the public from December 15 through March 31. The site grounds are open year round until sunset. A fee is charged.

T Kendrick City Park

Near the Kendrick Mansion on Clarendon in Sheridan

This is the home where the buffalo roam! The park's small game preserve is home to bison and elk. An outdoor swimming pool, 90-foot long water slide, band shell, walking path, ice cream shop, and all-season playground add to the park's charm.

T Trail End

400 Clarendon Avenue in Sheridan. 674-4589. www.trailend.org.

The Building at Trail End

Located on 3.5 acres of groomed grounds, Trail End is an example of Flemish Revival architecture, one of the few found in the western United States.

There are three main floors plus a basement, an attic, four balconies and four porches.

Materials used on the outside include Kansas brick, Indiana limestone, Missouri roofing tile and Wyoming granite. Both the mansion and the Carriage House (located to the west of the mansion) were designed by architect Glenn Charles McAlister of Billings, Montana.

Trail End took five years to finish, but not all that time was spent actually building. Workers were idle for over a year due to the combined effects of labor unrest in the eastern furniture mills and low prices in the midwestern cattle markets. During the delay in construction, the Kendricks lived in the Carriage House, completed in 1910.

Instead of relying on the taste and judgement of strangers, John and Eula Kendrick acted as their own general contractors. They then employed designers and consultants from all over the United States to help them put together the home they envisioned. The wall paneling, cabinets, stairs and other carved pieces were custom made for the house, using the newest automated equipment. All of the woodwork was machine-tooled in Michigan and shipped to Sheridan via railroad.

Like most large homes of the period, Trail End contained many labor saving devices: intercom, built-in stationary vacuum, laundry chute, dumbwaiter and elevator. Although never used, there was also an emergency fire suppression system with fire hoses located on each floor.

Very few structural changes have been made at Trail End. You will see, however, several rooms that were redecorated over the years by the family. The alterations have not been removed because they are part of the history of the house.

The Kendricks and Trail End

Trail End was the home of John Benjamin Kendrick, former Wyoming Governor and United States Senator. Born in Texas in 1857, Kendrick was orphaned at an early age and

Wyoming Tidbits

A "nester" is a farmer or homesteader who settled in cattle-grazing country. Cattlemen and nesters were in constant conflict, and one of the most historic events in Wyoming's history involves such a conflict in the Johnson County War of 1892.

raised by relatives until he went out on his own at age fifteen. In 1879, Kendrick came to Wyoming territory for the first time, as a trail rider on a cattle drive.

John Kendrick married 17 year old Eula Wulfjen in 1891. For the next 18 years, they lived on the OW Ranch in southeastern Montana. This property was the start of what later became the Kendrick Cattle Company, a 200,000 acre collection of cattle ranches in northern Wyoming and southern Montana.

While at the OW Ranch, the family's size doubled. Rosa Maye (1897-1979) and Manville (1900-1992) were both born in Sheridan, but lived their early lives at the ranch.

Construction began on Trail End in 1908. After it was finished in 1913, the family had only a short time to enjoy their new home. John Kendrick was elected Governor of Wyoming in 1914 and the family moved to Cheyenne. Two years later he was chosen to serve in the United States Senate, an office he held until his death in 1933. During that time, Trail End was used primarily as a summer home.

From 1933 to 1961, Eula Kendrick lived at Trail End with her son and his family. After her death, the others moved out and the house stood empty for seven years.

In 1968, when it was about to be torn down, Trail End was purchased by the Sheridan County Historical Society. They opened the home to the public as a community museum. Ownership was transferred to the State of Wyoming in 1982.

The Carriage House

On a tour of the house you will find special features in every room.

Foyer: Hand-painted ceiling panels; dark mission oak woodwork; custom designed chandelier and wall sconces; elevator.

Drawing Room: French silk damask wall coverings; piano-finish mahogany beams and panels; Italian marble fireplace; 1922 portraits of John and Eula Kendrick; peonies painted by Paul de Longpres; hand-made Kurdistan rug.

Cloak Room: Intercom; coat closets.

Library: Quarter-sawn golden oak panels and bookcases; gothic style chandelier; stained glass windows; 1917 Declaration of War against Germany; Sharp reproduc- tion over fireplace.

Powder Room: Porcelain double pedestal sink with German silver fixtures.

Dining Room: Hand-painted ceiling and wall panels; piano-finish mahogany woodwork; Italian marble fireplace with carved mantle.

Vault: Walk-in combination safe.

Butler's Pantry: Glass-front cabinets; German silver sink; dumb waiter; laundry chute; icebox.

Trail End viewed from its spacious park-like grounds.

Kitchen: "Hospital White" porcelain tile walls, ceramic tile floor, marble trim; original wood/coal cookstove (later replaced by gas); porcelain sink; built-in spice cabinet and storage bins.

Back Hallway: Intercom; fusebox; fire hose; annunciator; stairs to basement; stairs to second and third floor (closed: please use main staircase).

Second Floor Hallway: Replication of original wallpaper; stained glass windows; hand-painted canvas ceilings.

Manville's Bedroom: Navajo-motif wall stenciling; red fir trim.

Master Bedroom: Balcony overlooking rose garden; intercom.

Rosa Maye's Bedroom: Hand-tinted wall panels; custom designed light fixtures.

Maid's Closet: Hoses and nozzles for built-in stationary vacuum system; fusebox.

Guest Wing: Three bedrooms, each with private bath (closed to public; they're currently used as staff offices).

Ballroom: Tiffany-styled chandeliers with verdigris finish; maple dance floor; Georgia pine ceiling beams; horsehair cushions; rotating lead glass windows for ventilation; musician's loft.

Staff Quarters: Three bedrooms (each with sink and closets); pine wood trim; intercom; laundry chute; dumbwaiter; communal bathroom.

Attic: Musician's loft; storage area; pulley for dumbwaiter (closed to public).

Basement: Contains laundry room with three porcelain sinks, fireplace, stationary vacuum cleaner motor, vault; furnace room with boilers for steam heating system; coal bin; chauffeur's bedroom; storage facilities; public restrooms.

The Grounds

The Carriage House

Finished in 1910, it served as the Kendricks home during the construction of mansion. It was built to house carriages and horses, but never used for that purpose. By the time the family was ready to move out of their make-shift home, they were driving Cadillacs instead of buggies. It was converted to a theater and is currently the home of the Sheridan Civic Theater Guild. Phone 672-9886 for ticket information.

The Mandel Cabin was built in 1879 by George Mandel and purchased in 1882 by Sheridan founder John Loucks. It served as the area's first post office, store, school, law office, and bank. In 1976, the cabin was reconstructed from original logs and moved to Trail End State Historic Site. It is the property of the Colonial Dames of America.

Also found on the grounds are a sunken rose garden, an English sundial, an apple orchard, a circular back driveway with original clothesline/drying yard, a lawn tennis court, and a wide variety of trees and bushes, both native and exotic.

Reprinted from Wyoming State Parks and Historic Sites brochure.

H Carneyville (Kleenburn) 1904-1924

I-90 Exit 25 at Sheridan Visitor's Center.

This mine was located 9 miles North of Sheridan. Traveling North along Interstate 90, as you approach the 2nd exit after leaving Sheridan, you will turn right. You will notice a great deal of subsidence in the hillside. This is where the Carneyville mining shafts were. This mine employed 450 miners and had two tipple loadouts. In the valley to the right of the shafts lay the mining community of Carneyville (Kleenburn). This community had 150 to 200 houses and approximately 2000 people residing there.

Wyoming Tidbits

Wyoming's most famous outlaws were Robert LeRoy Parker ("Butch Cassidy") and Harry Longabaugh ("The Sundance Kid"). They were notorious for train robberies. Two other outlaws were "Persimmon Bill" and "Big Nose" George Parrott. Cattle rustling, horse stealing and murder were the most serious crimes in Wyoming in the late 1800s.

L Holiday Inn Atrium Hotel & Conference Center
1809 Sugarland Dr., Sheridan. 672-8931 or (877) 672-4011.
www.holiday-inn.com/sheridanwy

Details make the difference at the recently reno-vated Sheridan Holiday Inn. From well-appoint-ed guest rooms featuring complimentary high-speed wireless Internet to the knowledge-able staff to full-service banquet and conference facilities, this hotel specializes in comfort and style. Utilize the onsite fitness center and per-sonal trainer, visit the massage therapist, enjoy a cup of Starbuck's Coffee in the Brew Garden, or relax in the indoor pool, sauna, and whirlpool. Hungry for a delicious meal? Visit The Greenery and Scooters Bar & Grill onsite for breakfast, lunch, or Sugarland Mining Company for din-ner. During your stay, don't miss the area's shop-ping, year-round outdoor recreation, and historical sites just minutes away. Conveniently located off I-90 halfway between Yellowstone and Mount Rushmore, the Sheridan Holiday Inn welcomes you to enjoy their real Wyoming hos-pitality!

WYOMING'S WILDLIFE

Over 600 species of free-ranging wildlife inhabit Wyoming. This tremendous abun-dance and diversity of wild creatures can be attributed to an extremely diverse habitat. A visit to the high plains or deserts provides the opportunity to see pronghorn antelope, prairie dogs, jackrabbits, golden eagles and coyotes.

Mule deer may also be seen in this arid country, but are found in the foothills and higher mountains as well. Elk are found in all Wyoming mountain ranges and bighorn sheep and pikas occupy many of the high, rugged peaks. Riparian areas (areas next to water) in western Wyoming provide a chance to see a moose or bald eagle.

Wyoming is one of the few places where you can expect to see wildlife from all major highways. Bring your binoculars, camera and more film than you thin you'll need. Plan to spend some time, over half of the state is public land, wild and free for you to enjoy.

- Article courtesy of Wyoming Tourism

L Apple Tree Inn
1552 Coffeen, Sheridan. 672-2428 or (800) 670-2428 or cell 751-6653

Born and raised in Sheridan, owners Joyce and Tony Pelesky invite you to make the Apple Tree Inn your bunkhouse. Tucked in the shadow of the Big Horn Mountains, the Apple Tree Inn fea-tures refrigerators, microwaves, and coffeemakers in every room along with parking at your door. The inn's nice grass area beckons guests to sit under the apple tree and enjoy Wyoming's abun-dant sunshine, while its convenient location is within walking distance to shopping and dining. During the summer, be sure to sample delicious grade-A Angus hamburgers on the patio when the Burger Wagon arrives. Owned by Joyce and Tony's son, the Burger Wagon attracts both inn guests and those just passing by. For affordable prices and innkeepers who love to share their area knowledge with guests, stay at the Apple Tree Inn.

6 Lodging

Big Horn
Pop. 217, Elev. 4,059

At the foot of the mountains of the same name, Big Horn was once just a couple of cabins that sheltered outlaws. Officially founded as a town in 1878 by O.P. Hanna, this was a much-needed rest stop on the Bozeman Trail. By 1881, it was the first real town in Sheridan County. Later, in 1894, it became the home of the first college in the area, the Wyoming College and Normal School, begun by the Congregational Missionary Society. The school had to close in 1898 when the students couldn't pay the $100 tuition.

T The Bradford Brinton Memorial Museum
Just south of Big Horn on State Highway 335. Follow signs. 672-3173

This is ranch country; some of the finest in Wyoming and the Rocky Mountain West. It was settled late, in the 1870s and 1880s, but the well-watered, rich grasslands have produced excellent cattle and horse herds. The Quarter Circle A Ranch dates from this period and is typical of the more prosperous ranches of the Big Horn area. Here Bradford Brinton raised horses and cattle, entertained distinguished guests, enjoyed the sce-nic mountains and plains, and collected aspects of an older West. When he died in 1936, his sis-ter, Helen Brinton, became the owner of the ranch. She kept it as a summer home until her death in 1960.

The house was built in 1892 by two Scotsmen, William and Malcolm Moncreiffe, and in 1923 was purchased by Bradford Brinton, who enlarged it to its present 20 rooms. Bradford, and later Helen, tastefully decorated and furnished the house with fine furniture, his collections of west-

ern art, Indian crafts, books, and historic docu-ments.

Though a native of Illinois, Brinton loved the West and was particularly enamored of the work of western artists. He numbered many now famous artists among his friends, and they bene-fited from his encouragement and patronage. Helen Brinton, wishing to share her brother's fine collections with future generations, established the Bradford Brinton Memorial Ranch in her will to commemorate western art and culture. The Bradford Brinton Memorial Ranch opened in 1961. It is maintained and administered by The Northern Trust Company of Chicago, Illinois.

The Indian conflicts, nature's wonders, the harsh elements, and the often lonely but always exciting life of the cowboy inspired the artists of the West. The Brinton collection contains over 600 oils, watercolors, and sketches by American artists including: Charles M. Russell, Frederic Remington, Edward M. Borein, E. W. Gollings, Hans Kleiber, Will James, Frank W. Benson, John J. Audubon, Joe De Yong, Winold Reiss, and Frank Tenney Johnson.

Each year a different art exhibit is featured in the reception gallery, which is the only addition made to the ranch.

The memorial is open daily 9:30 a.m. until 5 p.m. May 15th through Labor Day.

T Bozeman Trail Museum
Main Street in Big Horn.

Built in 1879 by the Rock Creek Stage Line, the Blacksmith Shop we now call the Bozeman Trail Museum originally satisfied the needs of travelers on the nearby Bozeman Trail, which connected southeastern Wyoming to Virginia City, Montana. O.P. Hanna was the first settler to make his per-manent home here, also in 1879. John DeWitt, another early settler, was the original owner of the Blacksmith Shop. It changed hands several times before Mr and Mrs Goelet Gallatin bought it and restored it in 1936. Eventually, it became a storehouse for a variety of historic items, and was completely refurbished in 1976 by the Big Horn Bi-Centennial Committee. In 1990, with the offi-cial establishment of the Big Horn Historical Society, the site became an official museum.

T Bonanza
Big Horn Basin

Early travelers lubricated their wagon wheels in the natural oil seeps of this area. Settlers hoped to develop the town into an oil production center, but the industry never blossomed here. It is now a ghost town.

H Bozeman Trail Blacksmith Shop
Big Horn

Near here emigrants traversed the Bozeman Trail, 1864-68, to Virginia City, Montana gold mines. Confronted with hostile Indians unwilling to share their hunting grounds, the trail became known as the "Bloody Bozeman" and was dis-continued.

Crossing Little Goose Creek to the south and Jackson Creek to the west, the trail was later used from 1879-94 by the Patrick Brothers Stage Line from Rock Creek near Laramie, Wyoimng to Fort Custer on the Big Horn River in Montana.

This building was a blacksmith shop in the early 1880s to serve the stage line and ranch-ers of the valley.

7 *Food, Lodging*

Story
Pop. 650, Elev. 4,960

This cozy little community was probably named for Nelson Story, the first man to bring cattle up the Texas Trail, through Wyoming, and into Montana. Charles P. Story, an early newspaperman in Sheridan, may also have given his name to the town. Nestled in the pine-covered Bighorn Mountains, this was where timber was collected to build Fort Phil Kearny.

Banner
Pop. 40, Elev. 4,617

The first postmaster here, a rancher, had a flag as a cattle brand. The locals called it a banner, and when the post office opened out of his dining room, the name became the place.

T Story Fish Hatchery Visitor Center
311R Fish Hatchery Road, 2 miles west of Story. 683-224

The center is a popular for both locals and visitors, receiving more than 14,000 guests annually. The hatchery stocks nearly 250,000 fish each year and processes up to four million trout eggs that will eventually end up in the state's fish culture program or are shipped to other states in trade for species not raised in Wyoming's hatcheries.

Managed by the Wyoming Game and Fish Department, the hatchery is the oldest operating station in the state. The original hatchery was in Sheridan but was moved to the current location because of a better, colder water supply. Water is drawn from South Piney Creek 1.5 miles away.

An underground waterway from the creek moderates the water's temperature.

The center is open from april 15 through September 15, and the grounds are open to visitors year-around.

STORY DAY

Held the last Saturday in August, this is a day full of food, fun, parades, games, music, American indian art show, quilt show, garage sales and flea markets, craft fair, drawings and vendors. This is the annual fall-festival-type celebration.

T Fort Phil Kearny - History
Fort Phil Kearny

Named for a popular Union general killed in the Civil War, Fort Phil Kearny was established at the forks of Big and Little Piney Creeks by Col. Henry B. Carrington of the 18th U.S. Infantry in July, 1866.

The Mission of this fort and two other posts along the Bozeman Trail, Forts Reno and C. F. Smith, was three-fold: to protect travellers on the Trail; to prevent intertribal warfare between Native Americans in the area; and to draw attention of Indian forces opposed to Euro-American westward expansion away from the trans-continental railroad construction corridor to the south.

All three Bozeman Trail forts were stockade fortifications, with Port Phil Kearny being the largest. Enclosing seventeen acres, the fort wall was eight feet high, 1,496 feet in length, and

tapered in width from 600 feet on the north to 240 feet on the south. More than four thousand logs were used to erect the stockade, while over 606,000 feet of lumber and 130,000 bricks were produced in 1867 alone for the extensive building construction.

During its two year existence, Fort Phil Kearny was the focal point of a violent war between the U.S. Army and the Sioux, Cheyenne, and Arapaho Indians opposed to intrusions into the last great hunting grounds on the Northern Plains. Besides the Fetterman and Wagon Box battles, many smaller fights took place in the area.

By 1868, the Union Pacific Railroad had reached a point to the west where travellers could bypass the Bozeman Trail route by going to Montana through Idaho, thus making the Bozeman Trail forts expensive liabilities. In the Treaty of 1868, the United States agreed to close the forts and the trail, Fort Phil Kearny was abandoned by the Army in early August, 1868, and burned soon afterwards by the Cheyenne.

In 1963, Fort Phil Kearny was designated a National Historic Landmark. Today, portions of the fort site and the Fetterman and Wagon Box battlefields are included within the Fort Phil Kearny State Historic Site boundaries .

Fetterman Fight.
On December 21, 1866, Sioux, Cheyenne, and Arapaho warriors engaged a military force commanded by Captain William J. Fetterman. Ordered to rescue a besieged wagon train, Fetterman's men pursued Crazy Horse and other warriors acting as decoys over Lodge Trail Ridge where over two thousand Indians waited in

ambush The warriors attacked the soldiers, over-whelming the separated cavalry and infantry units. All eighty one men in Fetterman's command were killed within thirty minutes. Only the Battle of the Little Big Horn stands as a worse defeat for the United States Army and a greater victory for the Plains Indians.

"Portugee" Phillips Ride

Phillips is known for his heroic 236 mile ride to Fort Laramie following the Fetterman Fight. Riding in the deep of winter into the midst of a blizzard, he hid during the day and rode only at night as he passed through enemy territory. He pushed his horse beyond its limit and sacrificed it in the process, completing the ride in just four days, and arriving at Fort Laramie during a ball on Christmas night.

Wagon Box Fight

Indian forces attempted to repeat the Fetterman victory in the summer of 1867. On August 2, about eight-hundred Sioux attacked wood-cutters and soldiers camped at a cutting area five miles from Fort Phil Kearny. During initial stages of the battle, twenty-six soldiers and six civilians took cover inside an oval of wagon boxes used as a stock corral.

After burning another camp, Sioux warriors launched a series of attacks against the corral. Armed with breechloading rifles, the soldiers and civilians commanded by Captain James Powell

Wyoming Tidbits

The first polo field in the United States was built north of SHERIDAN.

held off the massed warriors until a relief force arrived from the fort. Three men were killed and two wounded inside of the corral, while Indian casualties were estimated at from five to sixty or more killed, and five to one hundred twenty more wounded.
Reprinted from Wyoming Department of Commerce brochure.

H Fort Phil Kearny Interpretive Signs
Fort Phil Kearny

The Magazine: Storing Munitions and More
All military posts had a magazine for storing munitions. At Fort Phil Kearny the Magazine was 16 by 16 feet, with a 11 foot dirt covered ceiling and it was buried eight feet in the southwest quadrant of the parade ground. It is referred to in numerous historical records. Carrington shows its location on his as-built map, and he did a design for its construction. Samuel Gibson indicates its location on his map of the fort. Margaret Carrington describes the location as "being in the center of one of the squares".

There are many colorful accounts centered around the magazine. Colonel Carrington was constantly frustrated with his lack of munitions and the shortage of ammunition at the post. This became very apparent following the Fetterman Fight when men were sent to guard the stockade with only five rounds of ammunition each. When Carrington left the fort on December 22, 1866 to retrieve the bodies of Fetterman's command he left secret instructions

which Francis Grummond recounted. "If, in my absence, Indians in overwhelming numbers attack, put the women and children in the magazine in a last desperate struggle, destroy all together, rather than have any captured alive". Results of the 1999 archaeological study provide no evidence of the magazine being in the southwest quadrant as historical records indicated. At present the magazine's exact location is unknown, still one of the many unanswered questions about Fort Phil Kearny.

Post Commander's Quarters: The Best Structure on the Post
1867 quartermaster inspections of Fort Phil Kearny indicated the poor condition of many of the buildings on post and that they needed rebuilding. These included the barracks, officer's quarters, post headquarters and more. The post commander's house was a 48 by 32 foot frame construction structure, built of fire dried trees, shingled with a 22 by 13 foot attached kitchen, and brick chimneys. This was probably the best structure on post.

The house was built by the regimental band for Colonel Carrington. It initially housed the Colonel, his wife Margaret, their sons Jimmy and Harry, and butler George. It was then occupied in turn by later Post Commanders Henry Wessells and Jonathan Smith.

Two archaeological pits have been left open for viewing. They show the remains of the interior ground structure of the commander's house.

The Guard House: Not Just a Jail
Even though Fort Phil Kearny, like most frontier posts, had plenty of use for a jail this was not the main function of the Guardhouse. The 50 by 43 foot, shingled building with a brick chimney, was used primarily for quard-mount. Guard-mount was the duty of protecting the post. Soldiers would be detached from their companies to this building on a repeated schedule for guard duty. From this building an individual soldier would be assigned to a guard-stand where he would guard the post on intervals of 2-hours-on 4-hours-off, for 24 hours. This was not an easy duty, During the harsh winter months the interval could drop to as little as 20 minutes to prevent injury or death to the guard. Francis Grummond recounts a story in My Army Life of Indians sneaking up and shooting guards off the stand. One had to be vigilant.

For soldiers convicted of serious crimes the building did serve as a jail. In August 1866 records indicate that 24 prisoners were being held under guard in tents awaiting the completion of this building. Their crime was desertion. Lessor crimes might be punished by extra duty, wearing a ball and chain, wearing a barrel with a sign stating your offense, or even flogging.

The Cavalryman's Quarters: Few and Far Between
It is a false perception that the frontier posts of the American West were garrisoned with large troops of cavalry. Actually a post's usual population was largely infantry with a rew cavalry for support, reconnaissance, escort, or mail delivery. Fort Phil Kearny was no exception. It was not until November 2, 1866 that any cavalry were stationed at the post. Though initially placed in a variety of quarters, they were finally housed in a large, new 100 by 25 foot log-panel constucted barracks with a shingle roof. Nearby was a 250 by 32 foot board and batten stable with corral, saddler's shop and a blacksmith.

Company C, of the 2nd U.S. Cavalry Regiment was assigned to Fort Phil Kearny. They arrived, armed with single-shot Starr Carbines on poorly conditioned mounts. Colonel Carrington replaced their weapons with the band's Spencer Carbines, but little could be done for the mounts. Few cavalry were ever at the Fort. They were constantly being requisitioned for mail, escort, or other duties by military inspectors traveling the trail. Unfortunately, of those troops available on December 21, 1866, the majority wre killed in the Fetterman Fight, leaving their quarters sorrowfully near empty.

The Civilians: Living Outside the Post
Because the regulations would not allow non-military dependent civilians to reside inside Fort Phil Kearny, several civilian dwellings existed outside the post stockade on the valley plain below, and in the Quartermaster corral to the south. These homes varied in size and degree of construction. Some were built as notched cornered log cabins with shingled roofs, others were of pole construction with sod roofs, while others were mere dugouts in the northeast slope of the stockade line. Depressions from these dugouts are still visible today.

Civilians provided many services for the military and travelers of the Bozeman Trail. James Wheatley and Issac Fisher built a way-station and restaurant. Another eatery and the only known garden were managed by Mr. and Mrs. Charles Washington. Walter J. Harden and F.J. Fairbrast had a small "ranche" and billiard room. This building undoubtedly provided after-hours entertainment for the soldiers. One large group of about 40 gold-miners, under the leadership of Robert Bailey, arrived in the fall of 1866. They stayed through the winter working for both civilian contractors and the military. Occupations included wood cutters and forage gathers for civilian contractors and carpenters or blacksmiths for the military.

Unfortunately, the civilians often got caught up in the military activities. Wheatley and Fisher volunteered to go with Captain Fetterman's command on December 21, 1866 and lost their lives that day. Remarkably, Mrs. Wheatley continued to run the way-station until the fort's closure. John "Portugee" Phillips, part of the Bailey miners, rode for relief following the Fetterman fight and later settled in Wyoming.

Lessons Learned
Archaeology at Fort Phil Kearny
Documented archaeology began at Fort Phil Kearny in 1961 and reoccurred in 1970, 1991-92, 1999 and 2000. The initial work was done by Gene Gallaway who salvaged artifacts during the county road construction. In 1970-71 George Frison studied the site, determining stockade, gate, southeast blockhouse and flagpole locations. Richard Fox searched for the southwest blockhouse, sutler store, and post commander''s residence in 1991 and 1992. In 1999-2000 Tom Larson and Lewis Somers studies, using subsurface mapping techniques, provided images of the under ground remains (see illustrations below) of the upper stockade and its diagonal blockhouses.

These studies have provided a great deal of insight into understanding the fort site. Many historic features have been confirmed, including locations of the upper stockade, main gate, blockhouse, gun bastion, sutler store, and commander's house. Various construction techniques have been identified, including frame and post/pole, and many personal artifacts have been recovered. We now know that the period historic maps are reasonably accurate, but questions remain. We do not know the exact location of the magazine, unidentified buildings have shown up on the ground radar research and historically recorded ones have not.

The archaeology has provided us a better understanding of Fort Phil Kearny. It has given us some understanding of the reliability of the historical record, and pointed out new directions for study. There is still much to be learned.

Quartermaster and Commissary Buildings: Supplying the Post

The quartermaster and commissary departments provided the two categories of supplies for maintaining military posts. Quartermaster supplies included items like weapons, clothing, saddles, blankets, beds, and more. Commissary supplies were mainly food stuffs. At this fort these items were stored in five or more warehouses varying in size from 24 by 84 feet to 32 by 160 feet. The buildings were of board and batten construction with shingle roofs and one building contained a cellar. Records indicate that some civilians bunked in the larger warehouse. Due to theft by soldiers and civilians, guards were placed at all warehouses.

Included in this complex of buildings was the Quartermaster's office. This building was 32 by 64 feet, board constructed with a shingle roof. It straddled the stockade wall and from here the Quartermaster acted as liaison between civilian workers and the military. Captain Frederick Brown was the first Quartermaster and upon his death Captain George Dandy took over the duties.

Fort Phil Kearny State Historic Site: A Guided Tour

Fort Phil Kearny State Historic Site is administered by the Wyoming State Parks and Historic Sites Department and supported by the Fort Phil Kearny/Bozeman Trail Association. All parties are committed to the preservation and interpretation of the many aspects of the site.

The Historic site has three components. Two of the components, the Getterman and Wagon Box fight sites, are approximately five miles from the fort. These sites offer interpretive trails with signing and help the viewer more fully understand the dramatic history of Fort Phil Kearny.

At the fort site the visitor has several options. The interpretive center offers many exhibits describing the fort's mission, archaeology, the Native Amercans, provides a video overview of the fort, distributes a site brochure, and offers a wide variety of books which further explain the area's history. The Civilian

Conservation Corp cabin interprets the living conditions of an officer or enlisted man. Outside the fort-proper interpretive signs explain crucial landmarks surrounding the fort and oulying structures.

On the fort grounds visual and audio interpretive signs describe the structures, personalities, and short history of the post. To best view the fort grounds one should follow a clockwise route.

Protecting the Travelers or the Garrison?

The mission of the Fort Phil Kearny garrison was to guard travelers on the Bozeman Trail, but, it soon became apparent that the quards would also need protection. Therefore, on July 13, 1866, Captain Tenador Ten Eyck began building a fort which had been designed by Colonel Henry Carrington before they left Fort Stephen Kearny. The fort's 800 by 600 foot long walls were made of 11' by 12" logs buried three feet in the ground. There were firing notches cut along the banquet at every fifth log, and blockhouses or gun-bastions on two opposite corners to provide enfilading fire along the walls. The main gate was located on the east wall, and smaller, five foot wide officer's gates were originally located on each of the other walls. Each gate was provided with a locking mechanism. Five guard stands were located to provide 24 hour surveillance of the grounds both inside

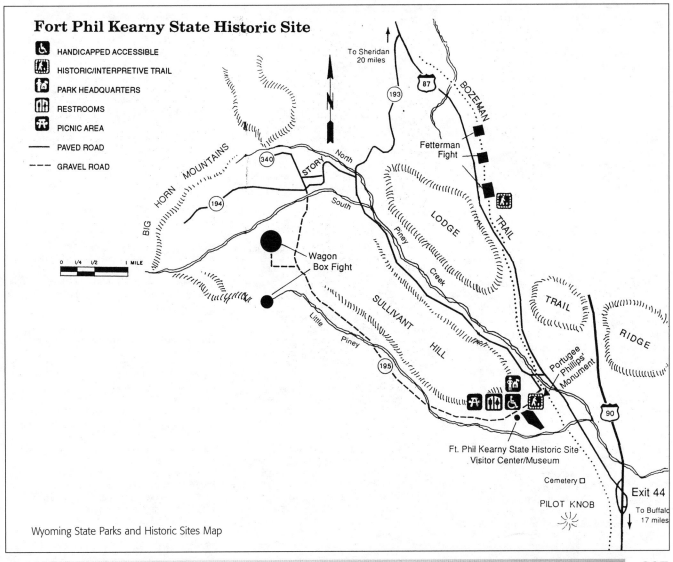

Wyoming State Parks and Historic Sites Map

and outside the post.

Before you is a reproduction of the stockade, guard stand, officer's gate and artillery bastion as originally built at Fort Phil Kearny. From this position we knew Col. Carrington fired artillery at the Native Americans who opposed the fort.

At the time of construction few military forts in the West had stockades. Would it have been better to train the raw recruits to protect the travelers? Was the time used to build the 2,800 feet of stockade wasted?

Artist conceptual drawing prior to archaeological discoveries.

An Enlisted Man's Quarters Better than Nothing

Some of the first structures built at Fort Phil Kearny were the enlisted men's barracks. The first four were 24 by 84 foot, green log, panel constructed buildings with dirt roofs and floors. In 1867 one additional 26 by 100 foot barrack was built to house the cavalry; kitchens were installed as basements in some of the previous barracks. Each barrack was expected to house an infantry or cavalry company averaging 87 men. With the exception of noncommissioned officers, who lived in small rooms within the barracks, all men live in an open bay heated with cast-iron stoves. The buildings were said to be breezy in winter, cool in the summer and by 1867: "fit to be torn down."

The roofs leaked in the rain, and provided homes for snakes, mice, and all sorts of critters. The green log building material shrank as it dried, leaving gaps in the walls and the dirt floors turned to mud. All these factors made life in the barracks and for the enlisted men miserable.

Some men came right from the Civil War, armed and clothed with four-year-old equipment. Others avoiding famine, and persecution in Europe emigrated, joined the army and came here. Their base pay was thirteen dollars a month supplemented with soured food for long marches and back breaking work. The enlisted man was poorly paid, poorly fed, and poorly housed. But it was better than nothing, if only slightly.

The Military Stockade: Post Headquarters, Soldier Quarters and More

Fort Phil Kearny's design was based on standard military models of the time, with the post's buildings located around a 400 by 400 foot parade grounds. The parade grounds were divided into four 200 by 200 quadrants, with walkways surrounding the parade grounds and dividing the quadrants. Soldiers were forbidden to walk across the open areas of the parade grounds except when performing official duties such as drill, parades or answering the Call to Arms.

The military stockade was a constantly evolving complex of structures during the two years of Fort Phil Kearny's existence. Many of the original buildings were improved or replaced over the life of the post. Some examples of these changes were the addition of brick chimneys, and the building of basement kitchens under the existing barracks and those newly constructed during 1867-1868, which not only helped save space in the cramped confines of the fort, but also provided some additional warmth for the barracks' occupants.

A List of the Structures

1. Gun Bastion
2. Infantry Barracks
3. Officer Quarters
4. Permanent Hospital
5. Bakery
6. Band Quarters
7. Sutler Store
8. Post Headquaters
9. Guard House
10. Main Gate
11. Warehouses
12. Laundry Quarters
13. Saddle Shop
14. Temporary Hospital
15. Powder Magazine
16. Commander Quarters
17. Flag Pole Bandstand
18. Artillery Park
19. Guard Stand
20. Chapel
21. Civilian Dwelling (Wheatley)
22. Cavalry Barracks
23. Cavalry Stables
24. NCO Quarters
25. Guard Stands
26. Sinks
27. Quartermaster Office
28. Civilian Dwellings

The Post Headquarters: Administering Fort Phil Kearny and the Mountain District

From this building the commander of the Mountain District of the U.S Army isssued orders to Forts Phil Kearny, C.F. Smith, and the Reno. The Mountain District was made up of the 2nd Battalion 18th Infantry until 1867 when it was reorganized into the 27th Infaantry Regiment. During this building's existence, the 25 by 50 foot, one inch plank boxs and batten structure was an office for Colonels Henry B. Carrington, Henry Wessells, and John E. Smith. The building was also the commuynication center for Fort Phil Kearny. Flag signalmen located on a lookout stand attached to building received and sent messages to Pilot Knob and other points.

In 1887, Quartermaster Captain George Dandy described the building as "needing torn down".

Yet it continued to function in a number of ways until the closure of the fort. One use was as a school house, in which Chaplain White taught classes for the 10 children of 17 families on post.

The Quartermaster Corral: Civilian Quarters, Storage, and Shops

While not as well built and fortified as the military stockade to the north, the quartermaster's stockade provided protection for the Quartermaster Department's supplies, draft animals, work shops and civilian employees. Most of the supplies brought to the fort, either by wagons up the Bozeman Trail or by contractors working local resources, came into the quartermaster's corral.

By April 1867, the Quartermaster Department was employing 52 civilians, including mail carriers, guides, carpenters, wagon masters, coal miners, stock herders and others.

Maintaining Fort Phil Kearny was expensive; laborers were paid $35-$45 a month, three times the salary of an Army enlisted man, while guides made from $5 to $10 a day, almost as much as an Army colonel.

The Fort

On July 13, 1866, Colonel Henry B. Carrington, leading four companies of the 18th Infantry, arrived at this site. Carrington, a competent engineer, immediately put his men to work. Through diligent labor they built, by October of that year, the basic units of what became an outstanding example of the complete, stockaded, "Indian Wars" military establishment.

From here, as you face across this tablet, extends the ground where Fort Phil Kearny once stood. Replacement posts mark the original corners of the 800' x 600' stockade. Beyond, salient points of contiguous cavalry and quartermaster corrals are marked. At the southwest end an animal watering gap jutted into Little Piney Creek. The Bozeman Trail passed roughly parallel to the northeast side.

Fort Phil Kearny was usually garrisoned by four to six infantry companies, plus one or two companies of cavalry. However, so slosely did Sioux and Cheyenne warriors, under the tactician Red Cloud, invest the post that these troops were frequently unable to perform Bozeman Trail convoy duty. Incidents of hostility were the daily rule and several of the most famous engagements of "Indian Wars" relate to this fort.

The military abandoned the fort in August, 1868, and it was burned by a band of Cheyenne.

The Flagpole: A Relief to the Traveler

The sight of a 20 by 36 foot American flag flying atop a 124 foot flagpole came as a great relief to the traveler on the Bozeman Trail. It meant the viewer was in sight of safe haven, temporarily free from the rigors of the trail, and safe from Indian attak. The pole which supported the flag was constructed of two pieces in a design similar to a ship mast. Made of lodgepole pine hauled from the wood-cutting areas on nearby Piney Island, the round poles were carved into octagons, painted black and the two pieces pinned together under the direction of civilian builder William Daley.

The flagpole was raised on October 31, 1866, with much fanfare. The first United States garrison flag to fly over the land between the North Platte and Yellowstone Rivers was hoisted. The band played on an octagonal stand erected at the pole's base. Colonel Carrington addressed the post's residents, and soldiers, dressed in newly issued uniforms. He spoke of their haardships, losses, and tribulations, and he dedicated the new fort after nearly four months of occupation, naming it for a fallen Civil War hero.

The Hospital: Any Attempt to Relieve the Suffering...

at Fort Phil Kearny was seldom successful at either of its two hospitals. The original hospital was a 24 by 84 foot structure similar to the barracks in construction. During this hospital's short service it sadly served as the morgue for Fetterman's command. During most of its existence the building functioned as an officer's quarters and was home to Captain Powell during his time at the post.

The second and primary hospital was built in 1867. It was an L—shaped structure incorporating panel construction and was 25 by 156 feet. The building either replaced or was attached to the bakery which was also located in this corner.The bakery attachment would have provided additional warmth and soothing aromas for the occupants. Little else is known abut this building.

Suffering at the post was considerable. There was constant skirmishing with the Indians ouside the post resulting in numerous battle injuries. In addition to combat wounds the occupants might be suffering from disease including dysentery, scurvy, or tuberculosis which, records indicate, were prevalent at the fort due to poor diet and sanitation.

The Band: For Conflict or Comfort

The 18th Infantry's 40-piece Regimental Band was housed at Fort Phil Kearny in a 24 by 64 green log, panel constructed, dirt roofed barrack. The band provided drummers and buglers for drill, ceremony, and combat commands during the day. In the evening they would gather at an octagonal bandstand surrounding the flagstaff to serenade the post with martial or popular music of the day. On special occasions they would orchestrate waltzes at post dances. Their duties were truly ones of extremes; besides sounding commands or music to march by, members might also be called on to act as messengers, medical orderlies, or combat soldiers. Band members at the fort also built Colonel Carrington's house in addition to serving as clerks or supply personnel.

There is more historical information on the band at Fort Phil Kearny than some of the other units. It is known that the band members carried Spencer Carbines even though the men seldom went into combat as a complete unit. Following the December 6, 1866 skirmish Colonel Carrington transferred these weapons to the cavalry, hoping to increase their fire power. All these weapons were lost in the Fetterman Fight two weeks later. Sadly, it is also known that the first death at Fort Phil Kearny was the Bandmaster, Master Serveant William Curry,who died of typhoid and pneumonia, leaving behind a wife and two boys.

"As we passed the Fort some distance we came to a halt for nearly an hour and a half…crossing the stream and ascending the bluffs beyond. As we lay there the brass band at the Fort commenced playing. Such sounds in such a scene! There was something in the wild, sweet strains that filled and floated through the deep reechoing valley that spoke of home; yet so far distant and in so wild a place that it partook of the nature of the scenes around it. It was like looking through the 'glass of time' into the dim Past…'
From the diary of Davis Willson, August 7, 1866, near Fort Phil Kearny

The Land

The land under view, where the Great Plains meet the Rocky Mountains, was once the Red man's land of milk and honey. Then, as now, teeming with wildlife, it was most productive—thus favorite—hunting ground. But it was also a natural route for north-south travel, used from time immemorial by nomadic men and migratory beasts. Lying hundreds of miles beyond the 1860 frontier it was treaty-confirmed Indian Country.

Here came a frontiersman, John Bozeman, pioneering a wagon road which followed buffalo, Indian and trapper trails. His time and energy saving short cut led to the booming mining fields of western Montana. This interloper was followed by others whose habitual frontier callousness easily stifled any scruple over trespass of an Indian passageway. Faint wheel marks soon became a beaten road known as the Bozeman Trail.

High plains and mountain Indians, notably Sioux and Cheyenne, watching this transgression, resented both the physical act and the implied contempt of solemn treaty. They made war. The white transgressors called upon their army for protection. In the end the Indians won a brief respite-partly because of developing railroad far to the south canceled the Bozeman Trail's short cut advantage.

Pilot Hill Picket Post

Pilot Hill—overlooking Piney and Little Piney Creek Valleys, the Bozeman Road, the Sullivant Ridge with its wood road was a constantly manned lookout. From this post the sentry signaled to the Fort news of events as they occured—how the wood detail progressed, what travelers fared the Bozeman Road, where and how a skirmish was developing, who was in desperate need of reinforcements.

A Monument Honoring John "Portugee" Phillips

One of history's great but little celebrated rides was made between midnight December 21st and Christmas night December 25th in the year 1866. From here at Fort Phil Kearny, where annihilation of Fetterman's force had left the garrison in desperate straits, this ride spanned 236 miles to strategic Fort Laramie, the nearest hope for any succor. John "Portugee" Phillips, shrouded in snow and driven by an arctic wind, made that ride. He rode the Commanding Officer's superb thoroughbred and he rode by night and hid by day, or used the bitter yet advantageous storm to hide his movements and blot his tracks. Thus he eluded pursuing Indians who, anticipating a necessary dash for aid, sought to intercept the speeding pair—resourceful messenger and courageous steed.

Site of a sawmill

As explained in No. 1 of this series, wood was the life blood of Fort Phil Kearny. The founding soldiers had carried into this wilderness a sawmill. It was set up without the walls of the stockade as here illustrated. And here, as supplied by logs carried in wagon trains returning from the Pinery, were sawed the boards from which the Fort's structures were built.

Sullivant Ridge

Fort Phil Kearny, built of wood and fueled by wood, required a never ending supply of wood. A supply obtained despite hostile activity by Sioux and Cheyenne. Source was the Pinery four miles west against the mountains. The route followed by the crest of Sullivant Ridge-permitting observation of hostiles and preventing opportunity for an ambush.

Lodge Trail Ridge

Lodge Trail Ridge divided the drainages of both Piney Creeks with the drainage of Peno (now Prairie Dog) Creek. Up this divide, north beyond Phil Kearny, climbed the Bozeman Trail on its route to Montana. There, December 21, 1866, in violation of explicit orders, Fetterman led his command of eighty-one men. There were no survivors to return.

Cemetery Site

Because of a healthy climate plus a short existence, Phil Kearny's cemetery might have remained an almost vacant place. But warfare prevented that idea. Here rested eighty-one victims of Fetterman's impetuosity; three heros of

---

CLOUD PEAK WILDERNESS AREA

Cloud Peak Wilderness preserves many sharp summits and towering sheer rock faces standing above glacier-carved U-shaped valleys. Named for the tallest mountain in Bighorn National Forest—Cloud Peak at 13,167 feet—the Wilderness is blanketed in snow for a large part of the year. Most of the higher ground doesn't show bare ground until July. On the east side of Cloud Peak itself, a deeply inset cirque holds the last remaining glacier in this range. Several hundred beautiful lakes, many offering excellent trout fishing, cover the landscape and drain into miles of trout streams. The Cloud Peak Wilderness is part of the 106 million acre National Wilderness Preservation System. This System of lands provides clean air, water, and habitat critical for rare and endangered plants and animals. In wilderness, you can enjoy challenging recreational activities like hiking, backpacking, climbing, kayaking, canoeing, rafting, horse packing, bird watching, stargazing, and extraordinary opportunities for solitude. You plan an important role in helping to "secure for the American people of present and future generations the benefits of an enduring resource of wilderness" as called for by the Congress of the United States through the Wilderness Act of 1964. Use Leave No Trace techniques when visiting the Cloud Peak Wilderness to ensure protection of this unique area.

Unless otherwise specified, no motorized equipment or mechanical transport is allowed. This is true for all federal lands managed as designated wilderness.

Courtesy: U.S. Forest Service

---

the masterful Wagon Box defense; and a few casualties of less celebrated incidents. On June 24, 1896 all bodies not previously exhumed were removed for re-interment in the Custer Battlefield National Cemetery.

The Bozeman Trail…its Approach from the South

…so ran, through treaty guaranteed Indian Land, a white man's route of commerce. Like any road it was an environment and ecology disturbing intrusion. Which, in this case, made it a challenge bound to produce a redman's reaction—a resort to arms. Thus the white man's government, supporting its citizens in violation of its own treaty, found justification to found a Fort Phil Kearny.

H Fetterman Massacre

Old U.S. Highway 87 just north of I-90 Exit 44.

Along this ridge on December 21, 1866, Capt. William J. Fetterman, 2 officers, 76 enlisted men and 2 civilians were decoyed into ambush and overwhelmed by a superior force of Sioux, Cheyenne, and Arapahoe Indians. Fort Phil Kearny, 2 miles south, was built in the summer of 1866 to protect travelers along the Bozeman Trail. The Indaians were bent on preventing such encroachment into their last hunting grounds which had been assigned them by the Fort Laramie Treaty of 1851. Sent out to relieve a wagon train that was under attack, Capt.

Present Structures

A. Visitor Center
B. Exterior Restrooms
C. CCC Cabin
   (Employees only)

D. Interpretive Circle
E. Native American Memorial
In-situ archaeology displays
on grounds

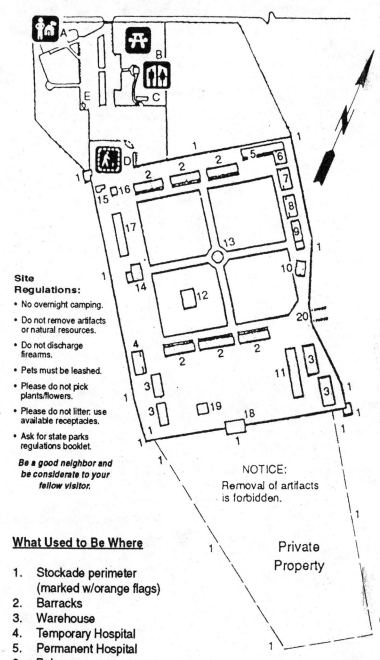

Site Regulations:

- No overnight camping.
- Do not remove artifacts or natural resources.
- Do not discharge firearms.
- Pets must be leashed.
- Please do not pick plants/flowers.
- Please do not litter: use available receptacles.
- Ask for state parks regulations booklet.

Be a good neighbor and be considerate to your fellow visitor.

NOTICE:
Removal of artifacts is forbidden.

Private Property

What Used to Be Where

1. Stockade perimeter (marked w/orange flags)
2. Barracks
3. Warehouse
4. Temporary Hospital
5. Permanent Hospital
6. Bakery
7. Band Barracks
8. Sutler Store
9. Post Headquarters
10. Guard House
11. Laundry Quarters
12. Powder Magazine
13. Original Flagpole
14. Commander's Quarters
15. Post Chapel

16. Surgeon's Quarters
17. Officers' Quarters
18. Quartermaster's Office
19. Saddle Shop
20. A Main Gate (red flag with white flags on exterior of the two openings)

Fetterman was ordered not to pursue the Indians beyond Lodge Trail Ridge. He disobeyed and led his command to this ridge, where they were engaged in a pitched battle. The final stand was made behind the large boulders at the monument. There were no survivors.

H The Fateful Decision
Old U.S. Highway 87 just north of I-90 Exit 44.

Fetterman relieved the wood train and chased its attackers to the limit prescribed in orders. His return was all that was necessary to complete a successful mission.

But he continued the chase. He did not return and his decision remains unexplained. The brash young Captain's decision to disobey orders and the resulting annihilation of his command has created a problem for generations of historians. Why did he continue pursuit? What "estimate of the situation" did he make? What thoughts influenced his decision? "None" appears to be a most charitable answer to the questions.

The mixed command of infantry and cavalry had no hope of catching the fleet Indian horseman. Fetterman knew he would be punished for disobeying orders unless he successfully engaged the warriors.

He gave little regard to the broken terrain, laced with pockets, ravines and ridges ideal fo concealment. He paid no heed to the fact that Indians did to fight according to the "rules of war" he learned in the Civil War. He descended the ridge and his comand stretched out—a tantalizing target for the attack. with little thought of the consequences, he charged blindly on, leading his command to its final engagement.

H Farthest Pursuit Trap Sprung Retreat-Defeat-Death
Old U.S. Highway 87 just north of I-90 Exit 44.

Pickets on Pilot Hill had signalled the fort when the wood train was attacked. They watched Fetterman's command advance to the relief and pursue the attacking Indians who retreated over the crest of Lodge Trail ridge. They saw Fetterman's men pause on the summit—the boundary that was supposed to be the limit of pursuit. But they only paused, then vanished over the ridge.

Indian accounts of the subsequent engagement were long in coming and proved fragmentary. The best reconstruction of events was made by relief and recovery parties who found the bodies of their comrades on the field of battle.

Fetterman, chasing decoys beond the ridge, met an overwhelming force of Indians. He turned about only to meet others who laid in ambush while he hotly pressed his pusuit.

Retreat along the Bozeman Road was impossible and within an hour, the fate of Fetterman's entire command was sealed.

H Recovery of the Dead
Old U.S. Highway 87 just north of I-90 Exit 44.

Two separate parties went forth from Fort Phil Kearny to recover the dead. The first party was sent while there was still hope that some of Fetterman's men might be alive. Captain Tenodor Ten Eyck and 76 men reached an observation point on Lodge Trail Ridge before the Indians left the battleground. Though seen and challenged by the exuberant victors, he refused to commit his command against such overwhelming odds. When the Indians withdrew, he ventured down the slope and recov-

Little remains of old Fort Kearny. The interpretive signs along the fort's grounds do much to give the visitor an idea of what the original fort was like.

ered 49 bodies found in one group where the fight climaxed.

Next morning Colonel Carrington led a second party which found the remaining 32 bodies scattered along more than a mile of the Bozeman Road. Most of the bodies had been stripped, scalped and mutilated. The corpses of captains Fetterman and Brown had powder burns at their temples suggesting suicide. Three pools of blood—within ten feet of the body of Lieutenant George Grummond—evidence of Indian casualties—gave moot testimony to the frenzied fighting. James S. Wheatley and Isaac Fisher, two civilian volunteers, had wanted to test their new Henry repeating rifles. The hundred or more expended cartridges near their mutilated bodies showed how dearly they sold their lives.

The recovery parties found more than 60 separate pools of blood, suggesting removed Indian casualties. Indian spokesmen later acknowledged the loss of thirteen warriors.

H Fetterman Monument
At Fetterman Massacre Memorial near Banner

On July 3, 1908, Henry B. Carrington, Frances Grummond Carrigton and veterans of the Fort Phil Kearny garrison attended a memorial ceremony to dedicate this monument. Colonel Carrington and others recounted the events surrounding the battle of December 21, 1866, and their experiences at the fort.

To honor the battlefield dead, the monument had been constrcted during the previous two years by local stonemasons. There are however, several inaccurcies in the legend and some of language reflects the racial feeling of the times. Historical records show that only two civilians were killed, not the four mentioned in legend. Current scholars also question whether Red Cloud led or was even at the battle. Native Amercan histories do not mention his presence, but do mention numerous other Sioux and Cheyenne leaders. Finally, the plaque states"there were no survivors," but it obviously

refers only to U.S. military casualties since approximately 1,500 Sioux and Cheyenne did in fact survive.

Today, this monument still honors the battlefield dead, but it should be remembered that members of two cultures died here, both fighting for their nations.

By 1866, twenty years of confrontation had occurred on the Northern Plains. European Americans pressured all the tribes in the quest of mineral wealth and settlement lands.

The Fort Laramie Treaty of 1851 attempted to curtail these confrontations. It established territorial boundaries for man of the Plains Indians and the United States Government was allowed to build roads and forts. All signators were allowed to cross on another's territory unmolested and unhindered. But the diminishing buffalo herds and discoveries of gold led to continuing and escalating confrontation.

The discovery of gold in southwest Montana led to the establishment of the Bozeman Trail in 1863. By the fall of 1865 numerous fights with the European Americans had allied the Sioux, Cheyenne and Arapaho. The Crow Indians supported the military against these tribes. The high cost of military campaigns and the need for new roads with safe travel impressed upon the United States Government the need for new negotiations with the Northern Plains Indians. These negotiations began at Fort Laramie in June, 1866.

While the intent of the Treaty of 1866 was to allow the construction of forts and roads in exchange for bi-annual annuities, government officials failed to recognize the complexity of tribal politics. Some Indian leaders did sign the treaty and government officials assumed they had a treaty with all members of the tribes. When Carrington's command arrived under orders to establish three forts on the Bozeman Trail, Red Cloud and other Indian leaders walked out of the talks declaring that war would occur if the trail was used and forts constructed. Carrington followed orders regarrisoning Fort

Reno and established Forts Phil Kearny and C.F. Smith. The Indian leaders who refused to sign the treaty prepared for war.

With the arrival of reinforcements, supplies and two successive commanders, Fort Phil Keanry was reorganized and and the training of the soldiers increased. Skirmishes between the soldiers and the Indians continued through the spring and summer of 1867. Better arms and ammunition resulted in successful defenses at the Hay Field Fight and Wagon Box Fight on August 1 and 2.

News of the Fetterman Fight intensified the debate in the East between U.S. citizens with differing philosophies about the Indians. Some people avocated annihilation of the Indian nations while others advocated peaceful resolution of hostilities on the Western Plains.

The nation had survived four years of Civil War but the toll had been tremendous. Fighting Indians on the frontier was expensive and unpopular to those who wanted peace. Conflict in the West had created severe equipment and logstics problems for the post-war military.

In 1867, the military established Fort Fetterman, but the Treaty of 1868 closed the Bozeman Trail and Forts Phil Kearny, Reno and C.F. Smith. The treaty established reservations for the Sioux much like those set up for Cheyenne and Arapaho in 1866. The Interior Department became responsible for care and control of the tribes. It was hoped that the Indians would adopt Christian ways, become farmers and cease hostilities on the frontier

For six years, until gold was discovered in the Black Hills in 1874, an uneasy peace existed in the Powder River country. Soon thereafter, the Sioux, Cheyenne and Arapaho were at war on the Little Big Horn River.

H The Fetterman Fight... December 21, 1866
At Fetterman Massacre Memorial near Banner

During the fall of 1866, Red Cloud gathered Sioux, Cheyenne, and Arapaho warriors. As the Indians strength grew to the north on the Tongue River, they increased their raids on the Bozeman Trail forts. Colonel Henry B. Carrington received orders from the Department Commander to be more aggressive and carry out "punitive strikes against the raiding Indians." Carrington requested more troops, better arms and more ammunition. Captain William J. Fetterman, a recent arrival to the fort, said that he could ride through the Sioux nation with 80 men. The stage was set for the Fetterman Fight.

December 21, 1866 was a clear day, with snow drifted on the north slopes of the hills and ridges from earlier storms. That morning Captain Fetterman requested command of a force to relieve a wood train under attack by Indians. His command included Lieutenant George Grummond, Captain Frederick Brown, 49 infantry, 27 cavalry and civilians James Wheatley and Issac Fisher, totaling 81 men.

Earlier in the day 800 to1,200 Sioux, Cheyenne and Arapaho warriors had arrived in the Peno Creek Valley. Some were sent to attack the wood train, others to decoy the Army's relief party and the rest took up positions for the planned ambush. The decoys lured Fetterman's command over Lodge Trail Ridge. As the soldiers approached Peno Creek, the ambush was sprung. In the ensuing battle, as the troops retreated south toward Lodge Trail Ridge, they were surrounded and defeated.

Fort Phil Kearny

In approximately one hour the battle was over. Captain Tenodor Ten Eyck's relief column arrived to find the bodies of Fetterman's command in three sparate groups along what is now known as Massacre Hill. Fort Phil Kearny had lost 81 men. Indian oral history indicates that their casualties were 20 or more.

H The Aftermath: Two Views of Victory
At Fetterman Massacre Memorial near Banner

By the end of the fight the Indians, through the heroics of fellow warriors, managed to remove all but one or two of their dead and wounded from the battlefield. These were taken to a spring near the present day Fish Hatchery for cleansing and treatment. Estimates very greatly as to the number of Indian caualties. Traditional Indian oral history places the number as low as six and as high as 100. Captain Powell estimated the dead at 60 and wounded at 120. As the Indians withdrew from the field, so did the soldiers. Following their rescue by Major Smith's column the surgeon treated the wouned and gave each survivor a drink of whiskey to settle their nerves. The military casualties consisted of three dead in the corral, four dead at the side camp, and two wounded in the corral.These caualties and the day long fight would cause the military to rethink their position at the pineries.

Although the military felt they had won the fight, which gave a great boost to the morale of soldiers on the western plains, they knew the existing corral had its weaknesses. Immediately following the fight Lieutenant Alexander Wishart created a new position south and west of the Wagon Box Fight corral. The new corral was placed further out in open, giving a better field of fire, and was constructed in a stronger defensive position. A trench was dug around the exterior, and the wagon boxes were placed upon the excavated dirt, creating a formidable barrier to any attack. A new camp site was located to south of this corral.

To the Indians the Wagon Box fight was also a victory. They had succeeded in destroying the side camp, burned several wagons, captured a large mule herd and killed or wounded several

of the enemy. Their goal of harassing the forts had been fulfilled. One lesson learned was that the soldiers had new weapons and that if the Indians expected to win they would need modern guns. In November 1867, Lieutenant Shurley's command was attacked on Big Goose Creek and after a day long fight, the Indians were driven off. It is believed that the Indian objective was to capture a mountain howitzer and weapons. This ongoing fighting kept the Bozeman Trail closed to all but military traffic, and the maintenance of the forts became a great expense for the military. Through continuous skirmishing and the husbanding of his resources, Red Cloud was winning his war. The war continued into the summer of 1868 with raids at all three forts along the Bozeman Trail and at the new Fort Fetterman located on the North Platte River. In 1868 treaty negotiators were again ready to discuss the Bozeman Trail. The results of the negotiations would make "Red Cloud's War" one of the few, though temporary, victories by American Indians against the western expansion of the United States.

H The Interpretive Trail
At Fetterman Massacre Memorial near Banner

For an in-depth understanding of the Fetterman Fight, you are invited to walk the interpretive trail. Approximately one mile in length, it consists of two separate but overlapping trails traversing more than half of the actual battlefield.

The first trail provides specific information about the battle and its participants and is accessible for the physically impaired. The second trail requires you to use your imagination, to visualize the battlefield as it was in 1866 from the Indian and soldier perspectives, at positions occupied during the battle.

Archaeological studies have been conducted on the battlefield. Since artifact collecting began soon after the fighting, few artifacts remain, but you are reminded that their removal is UNLAWFUL. Please report any findings to the vistor center immediately.

H Attack-Relief-Decoy-Pursuit
Old U.S. Highway 87 just north of I-90 Exit 44.

By December, 1866, For Phil Kearny was in the

final phases of construction. Logs for the stockaded post were hauled by wood train from the pinery six miles west of the fort.

On december 21, a heavily escorted wood train left for the pinery. It came under Indian attack about three miles to the west. When pickets on Pilot Hill signaled the train was being attacked, Colonel Henry B. Carrington ordered out a relief party and reluctantly put Captain William J. Fetterman in command. It included two other officers, 76 enlisted men and two civilians. the soldiers in the party were from four companies of the 18th Infantry and one company of the 2nd Cavalry.

The Indians had broken off the attack by the time the relief party was under way but Fetterman pursued them to the crest of Lodge Trail Ridge—so far keeping within range of his orders.

H Wagon Box Fight Interpretive Signs
At Wagon Box Memorial site about five miles northwest of Fort Phil Kearny

Wagon Box Monument
Before you stands a monument dedicated to the courage and bravery of the defenders in the Wagon Box fight of August 2, 1936. This monument was built in 1936 by the Civilian Conservation Corps. The legend was written by local historians and although it was accurate with the information available at the time,it is now known to contain several discrepancies. Also, it makes no mention of the Lakota warriors who died on this field in defense of their cullture.

It is not known if Red Cloud was the actual leader during this battle and the number of Lakota warriors who were involved in the Wagon Box Fight is now estimated to be 1,000 to 1500. Native American casualty estimates, based on oral histories, vary from six to sixty.

Two Lakota individuals mentioned in both white and Indian accounts of the battle should be noted: one is Red Cloud's nephew whose name is unknown; the other is a Miniconjou Sioux name Lipala. Both were killed during the battle, but they displayed unusual courage and leadership in their numerous attempts to defeat the corral defenders.

Wagon Box Fight, August 2, 1867
This monument is erected to perpetrate the memory of one of the famous battles of histor. It is dedicated to the courage and bravery of twenty-eight soldiers in Comany C.27th United States Infantry, and four civilians who held their improvised fort made of fourteen ordinary wagon-boxes, against 3000 Sioux warriors, under the leadership of Red cloud for a period of six or seven hours under continuous fire. the number of indians killed has been variously estimated from three hundred to eleven hundred. The following participated in this engagement: Capt. Jas. Powell, 1st Sgt. John M. Hoover, 1st Sgt. John H. Mcquiery, 1st Lt. John C. Jenness, corp. Max Littman, Corp. Francis Roberts, Privates: Wm. Baker, Ashton Barton, wm. Black Nolan, Chas. Brooks, Alexander Brown, Dennis Brown, John Buzzard, Frederick Clause, John Condon, Thomas Doyle, V. Deming, John Grady, John M. Garreett, Henry Gross, Samuel Gibson, Henry Haggerty, Mark Haller, Phillip C. Jones, Freeland Phillips, John L. Somers, Chas. A. Stévens, Julius Strache, 4 unknown civilians.

Fetterman Monument

Battle, August 2, 1867

On August 2, 1867, 51 men of Company C, 27th Infantry under the command of Captain James Powell and Lieutenant John Jenness are assigned to the wood cutting detail. Fourteen of these men escort a wood train toward the fort. Another 13 are protecting wood cutters; nine at the upper pinery and four at the Little Piney Camp. While the soldiers at the corral prepared breakfast, the herders turned out the mules, and sentries took up position, the battle begins.

Crazy Horse and Hump led a small number of warriors across the hills to the west in a decoy attack on the Little Piney Camp. Here three soldiers are killed and the remaining wood cutters are chased into the mountains.

This attack is followed by attacks on the wood train at the upper pinery, and the mule herd.

Soldiers, drivers and wood cutters from the wood train and pinery escape into the mountains, but the mule herd is captured. Powell leads an attack to rescue the herders, as outlying sentries and hunters from the fort make for the safety of the corral. By nine o'clock 26 soldiers and six civilians are surrounded in the corral facing, by Powell's estimate, 800 to 1000 warriors.

Indian spectators, including leaders, women, and children watch from the surrounding hills, as mounted warriors make the first attack, charging the corral from the Southwest. The Indians expect a volley from the soldiers who will then pause to reload, and the warriors will then overrun the corral. But the pause never occurs as the soldiers quickly reload their new rifles. Discouraged by the continuous fire the Indians withdraw. During the lull, the soldiers pass ammunition about the corral, holding it in their caps and the Indians prepare to charge on foot from behind the ridge to the north.

The second attack is made from behind the ridge to the north by warriors on foot while mounted warriors demonstrate to the south and snipers located along the rim fire into the corral.

During this attack all the casualties in the corral occur. But again the soldier's firepower turns the Indians back. A third attack comes from the northeast. The soldiers hear loud chanting as Indians burst from cover singing their war song and surge to within a few yards of the corral before being turned back. The Indians again retreat to the protection of the rim, sniping at the corral as others attempt to retrieve the dead and wounded. The final attack comes on horse back from the southeast.

By now it is early afternoon and the fight has not gone unnoticed at the fort. Major Benjamin Smith leaves the fort with a relief column of 102 men and a mountain howitzer. As the column nears the corral, they fire on Indian spectators viewing from a high knob east of the corral. With the arrival of reinforcements for the soldiers, the Indians decide to withdraw and the Wagon Box Fight ends.

Wood Cutting: A Hazardous Harvest

Though construction of Fort Phil Kearny was complete by August of 1867, the need of wood for burning and alterations continued. Colonel John E. Smith, the post commander, located wood cutting camps on Big and Little Piney Creeks five miles west of the fort. A company of infantry armed with the 50-70 Allin Conversion Rifle (a converted Springfield musket, which was breach-loading and fired metal cased cartridges) were assigned to protect the cutters and wood train. Their duties were rotated with other companies on a monthly basis. The soldiers operated out of a camp located at a corral built by the wood contractors to hold the mules at night. The corral was made of 14 wagon boxes, removed from the running gears, and placed in an oval measuring 30' by 70'. It was located on a plateau between Big and Little Piney Creeks, at the junction of the wood roads, and visible from Pilot Knob, a lookout point near the fort. One box at the west end of the corral and another on the south side were covered to protect the supplies for the soldiers and civilians. An additional supply wagon was located ten feet to the west. The soldiers and civilians slept in tents ouside of the corral.

To Save The Powder River Country

In July, 1867, many Lakotas of the Ogalala, Miniconjou and Sans Arc tribes gathered with the Cheyennes along the Rosebud Valley to participate in the sacred Sun Dance ceremony. After fulfilling the religious duties, the headmen and fighting chiefs turned their attention once more to warfare against the Bozman Trail Forts.

One year of fighting had failed to drive the soldiers from the Powder River country. Small groups of warriors struck during the spring and summer, but there had been no victory to equal the winter battle known as "One Hundred in the Hands," which had annihilated Fetterman's soldiers near Fort Phil Kearny. Now, with almost one thousand fighting men concentrated on the Rosebud, the Indian leaders planned another great battle. Disagreement over which fort to attack led to a split in the Indian forces. Most of the Cheyennes would go to attack Fort C.F. Smith, while the Lakota and some Cheyenne chose Fort Phil Kearny.

Led by Crazy Horse, Hump, Thunderhawk, Ice and other war leaders, hundreds of Lakota and Cheyenne warriors rode to their destiny in battle. Traveling with them were Red Cloud, Flying By, other older headmen, and many woman and children. All hoped fo a great victory that would save and protect the land.

A Fight To Survive (See diagram)

Inside the corral the small body of soldiers expected defeat and the same fate as Fetterman's command. As they took up positions of their choosing, between, behind, or inside the wagon boxes, the men prepared for the worst. Some removed their shoe laces so that the string could be used to attach their toe to the rifle trigger when the end was near. Others stockpiled ammunition and weapons. While the Allin Conversion was the most prominent weapon of the fight, Spencer carbines and an assortment of pistols were also used. Some accounts indicate that only the marksmen fired while others reloaded the rifles for them. During the fight Powell gave few orders other than an initial command of "shoot to kill." Jenness took up a position in the covered box with four civilians. It is reportedly here that after being told to keep down, Jenness replied "I know how to fight Indians" and promptly fell dead of a head wound.

Acts of valor were quite common in the corral. A private named Max Littman stepped from the safety of the corral to give covering fire for the retreating sentries at the beginning of the fight. On two occasions Privates Sam Gibson and John Grady ventured from the corral, once to knock down tents which were obscuring the field of fire, and a second time to retrieve water for the thirsting defenders. Indian fire arrows ignited the dry hay and manure, which, combined with the hot August sun and gun powder smoke, made conditions in the corral miserable. In the corral, in addition to death of Lieutenant Jenness, Privates Haggerty and Doyle were killed, and two others wounded.

1. Pvt. Gibson (drawing based on his descriptions)

2. Pvt. Gradey

3. Sgt. Hoover

4. Captain Powell

5. Max Littman (behind a barrel of beans, he provided cover fire as Gibson retreated to the corral)

6. Private Condon (behind a barrel of salt)

7. Lieut. Jenness killed

8. and 9 Bullwackers (6 civilians were in fight)

10. Private Doyle killed

11. Private Haggerty killed

12. Somers wounded in wagon box

13. Grain stored and used as protection in corral

14. Ammunition placed about corral, men would retreive it in their hats to their firing position.

15. A horse and mule were tied in the corral, they died of wounds suffered during the fight

16. Using fire arrows, Indians set fire to manure and straw within the corral, causing discomfort for the defenders

17. Civilian and soldier tents

18. Coffee pots containing the only water available during the fight

19. Supply Wagon

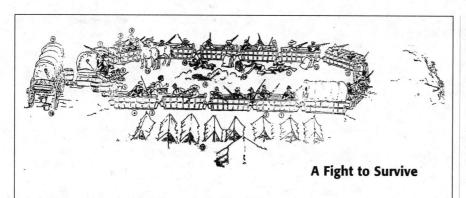

A Fight to Survive

Valor in Attack

The Indian leaders had hoped the soldiers would pursue a small decoy party of warriors led by Hump into an ambush, but the soldiers refused to follow, and the last pickets retreated safely into the corral after wounding the Ogalala warrior Paints Yellow. The side camp was taken and some soldiers killed, but now the only option for quick success was to launch massed attacks at the corral, and hope to over-run the soldiers' improvised wagon box fortress.

Soon, mounted warriors circled around the corral. Using their horses as shields, they quickly rode in close to fire arrows or guns, and then zigzagged away from the soldiers' rifles. During the first attack from the south, Hairy Hand, a Miniconjou, rode straight at the corral to count coup. Hit by a soldier's bullet, he laid out in the open until a young warrior named White Bull ran in and dragged him to safety. The mounted charge failed, and the war leaders Crazy Horse of the Ogalalas and Hump of the Miniconjous organized the warriors for an assault on foot. As the foot charge moved toward the corral, the Ogalala Only Man rushed ahead, almost reaching the wagon boxes before the bullets killed him. The attack stalled, and some warriors concealed themselves in the brush and started firing into the corral with guns captured during the battle of One Hundred in the Hands. These snipers inflicted most of the casualties suffered by the soldiers.

During a lull before the next attack, one of the bravest acts of the day took place. Jipala, a tall, impressive Miniconjou, walked toward the corral, carrying a shield, lance and bow. Singing his death song, he ran forward, jumping in the air and firing arrows at the corral. Finally, the soldiers bullets found him, and he lay dead before the corral. Both warriors and soldiers talked of his bravery for many years to come.

Two more Miniconjous, Muskrat Stands of His Lodge and Packs His Leg, died in foot charges. During the final attack, the Lakota Young Duck was shot dead leading the assault, and three of his people wounded attempting to recover his body.

Once more, the warriors attempted a mounted charge, but the soldiers' guns kept up a fierce fire. The assault ended before reaching the corral, but not before Sun's Road of the Cheyennes was killed. His death was the last of the day.

The boom of Smith's howitzer signaled the end of fighting. As the Lakota and Cheyennes left the battlefield, they paused near local springs to care for their wounded and dead before moving north to their camps.

Red Cloud's Victory

By 1868 the Union Pacific Rail Road had been completed through southern Wyoming and northern Utah and a new and shorter road ran north to the southwestern Montana gold fields. The Bozeman Trail became obsolete. The U.S. Government once again sought negotiations with the Lakota and Cheyenne, hoping for a solution to the fighting along the trail. Red Cloud refused to talk until the forts and the trail were abandoned, but others did negotiate and a treaty was settled upon. The Fort Laramie Treaty of 1868 stipulated that in exchange for the military abandoning the forts along and the use of the Bozeman Trail, the Lakota would accept for their reservation the western half of South Dakota from the Missouri River to the Black Hills. The Powder River country was to remain unceded Indian land, open for hunting by all tribes. The United States Government signed this treaty as did several bands of Lakota, but it was not until the forts were actually abandoned that Red Cloud finally signed in October of 1868. For the Lakota and Cheyenne, even though greater conflicts lay in the years ahead, the Powder River Country had been saved.

Continuing Controversies

Over the years a controversy has arisen about the exact location of the Wagon Box Corral, Indian casualties, and the length of the battle. The most disputed fact is the location of the corral. In the early 1900's area residents brought survivors of the fight, both Indian and white, to the area in hopes of pinpointing the exact location of the corral. Unfortunately, the survivors were not at the site at the same time and did not agree on the location. One site chosen is the location laid out near where you are standing. The other location is a brass marker several hundred yards to the southeast. There has been much study in an attempt to resolve this debate, including correspondence with early residents, aerial photography, and archaeological surverys. The strongest evidence come from archaeology done over several years, which indicates that the laid out corral may be close to correct. But if the actual participants could not agree on a location, then the best and most accurate description of the location of the corral is to say that it was placed somewhere atop the plateau, between Big and Little Piney Creeks. As to the other controversies, Indian casualties can probably be estimated at between six and sixty and the time of the fight from 8:00 A.M. to 1:00 P.M. As with all historical events research will continue and new facts will come to the surface.

FS Piney Creek General Store & The Waldorf A' Story

19 N. Piney Rd., Story. 683-2400.
www.pineycreekgeneralstore.com;
pineycreekgs@fiberpipe.net

People travel from all over to shop and dine at the Piney Creek General Store and The Waldorf A' Story. The store's unique atmosphere inside and out draws both locals and visitors. The store is stocked with gourmet groceries and meats, cookware, auto supplies, souvenirs, unique gifts, antiques, and a generous beer, wine, and liquor selection. While you're there, scoot on over to the popular Waldorf A'Story. This sophisticated gem of a restaurant is perfect whether you're in the mood to stuff yourself or enjoy a light meal. among their breakfast, lunch, and dinner menus you'll find biscuits and gravy, double-decker sandwiches, and yummy bisques along with such entrees as baby back ribs and fresh seafood. Don't miss the many local events, including fairs and flea markets, held at the store throughout the year.

L Story Pines Inn, LLC

46 N. Piney Rd., Story. 683-2120 or
(800) 596-6297. www.storypinesinn.com

Enjoy the intimacy and attention to detail of an owner-operated business at The Story Pines Inn. Nestled in the pines at the base of the Big Horn Mountains, this small country inn is open year-round and is situated midway between The Black Hills and Yellowstone National Park. The six modern and completely non-smoking guestrooms were newly built in 1997 and provide all the comforts of home with the rustic feel of the mountains. Guests enjoy lodgepole pine furnishings, cable TV, high-speed broadband and wireless Internet, coin-op laundry, complimentary coffee and tea, picnic areas, and an outdoor hot tub. The Inn also features convenient walking access to a library, post office, restaurants, country stores, art galleries, and churches with year-round recreation nearby. So take the road less traveled. You may just find paradise! Reservations are recommended.

WHICH IS THE BEST WAY OVER THE MOUNTAIN?

There are three major highways traversing the Big Horns in an east-west direction. Each offers its own distinct and memorable scenery, with relatively equal travel distances and comparable surfaces. So the choice is up to you depending on your travel objectives.

Big Horn Scenic Byway (U.S. Hwy. 14) connects Sheridan and surrounding communities with Greybull, Wyoming and includes 45 miles of scenic mountain driving. Look out over spectacular valley views from one of several roadside turnouts. On a clear day, you can see for miles and miles. Interesting stops include Shell Falls, Burges Junction Visitor Center and Sand Turn. Open year-round.

Cloud Peak Skyway (U.S. Hwy. 16) traverses the southern Big Horn Mountains and offers breathtaking vistas of distant snow-capped peaks along its 45-mile length. This route connects Buffalo and Tensleep, Wyoming. Highlights include Hospital Hill, Powder River Pass, Meadowlark Lake and Tensleep Canyon. Open year-round.

Medicine Wheel Passage (U.S. Hwy. 14A) rises sharply from the Big Horn Basin near Lovell, Wyoming and winds 25 miles through steep canyon terrain and high alpine meadows to Burgess Junction. This route provides primary access to the medicine Wheel National Historic Landmark. This may not be the best choice for those pulling or driving an RV. Grades exceed 10%. Open from memorial Day to mid-November.

Source: U.S. Forest Service

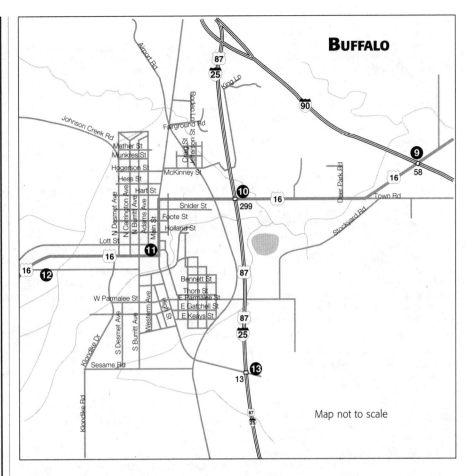

BUFFALO

Map not to scale

Section 6

---

8 *Gas, Food, Lodging*

T DeSmet Lake
At I-90 Exit 51

The lake was named for Father Pierre DeSmet, a Jesuit missionary back in the early 1800s. It is now known for its terrific fishing opportunities, boating and skiing, and swimming. There are many facilities at the lake including ramps, docks, campgrounds and picnic shelters. You might even see the legendary "Smetty", the lake monster.

T DeSmet Lake Monster

Lake Desmet not only attracts fishermen looking to catch the great rainbow trout or crappies it provides, but "Smetty" is another great attraction. Smetty is the legendary creature believed to inhabit Lake Desmet.

The lake is named for a Jesuit missionary priest to the Indians, Father Pierre DeSmet, back in the early 1800's. Rumor has it that the Indians were so frightened by this body of water, they refused to camp along the red shale shores. Some say that the Sioux Indians believed the waters had healing powers and the ability to prompt visions. The tribe legend was that a young brave turned against the love of his life because he was overpowered by the charms of a water maiden rising from its depths. His intended wife-to-be was so distraught by his rejection she subsequently drowned herself. Her father, the tribal chief seeking revenge, swiftly administered justice to the unfaithful young man. In the darkness of windy

Wyoming nights, his spirit supposedly wanders around the shore bemoaning the loss of his Indian maiden.

Local ranchers often told stories about seeing a 30 to 40 foot long looking like a "long telephone pole with a lard bucket attached." Other recorded physical characteristics include a "bony ridge along the back, with a resemblance to a horse's head coming out of the water in a swimming motion."

There have been tales about the lake's dark side that range from a monster resembling an alligator rising from the waters to a Loch Ness-type creature that seized an Indian papoose and disappeared into the murky depths.

When imagination runs high, "Smetty" is said to dwell in the so-called bottomless lake's subterranean caverns sometimes speculated to be a far-away outlet from the Pacific Ocean.

Edward Gillette, author of "Locating the Iron Trail" wrote a book in 1925 chronicling the tales and observations surrounding "Smetty". Visit Lake Desmet and judge for yourself, but don't forget to take your fishing pole and bait so you don't miss out on some great fishing!

9 *Gas, Food, Lodging*

Buffalo
Pop. 3,900, Elev. 4,645

Founded in 1879 by homesteaders, cattle ranchers, and miners, Buffalo was not named for the animal, but for Buffalo, New York, hometown of one early settler, Alvin J. McCray. By 1883, there were a dozen saloons in town, but no churches. While an old buffalo trail did once run down Main Street, Buffalo's streets are most famous for being the only place in the US where you can

make a legal U-turn on a highway bridge, right in the middle of town. As the Johnson County Seat, Buffalo also claims the distinction of having hosted the oldest county fair in the state in 1887.

T Dry Creek Petrified Tree Forest
I-90 east from Buffalo to the Red Hills exit, drive north off exit for seven miles to the Petrified Tree Area access road.

The Dry Creek Petrified Tree Environmental Education Area (EEA), set aside as such in 1978, is located about 9 miles east of Buffalo, Wyoming. A parking area, picnic table, and interpretive facilities can be found here.

As you travel around a loop nature trail about 0.8 mile long, you will go back 60 million years to the geologic era of the Early Eocene when this area was shaded woodlands and mossy glades. You will learn how the uplifting of the Big Horn Mountains helped to create the prairie ecosystem we see today. And you will also learn about early vegetation and the formation of coal, scoria, petrified trees and other indicators of the past.

This area was very different from what can be seen today. Giant trees grew in a jungle-like area somewhat like the Okefenokee Swamp in southern Georgia. A large system of rivers flowed north to a distant ocean. Huge swamps filled the wide, flat plain between the Big Horn Mountains and the Black Hills. There may have been turtles, crocodile-like creatures, large fished similar to modern gars, and primitive mammals and birds.

Scoria is a sort of natural brick formed from shale or sandstone that has been "fired" when coal seams caught fire and burned back into the ground. Scoria can be crushed and used as a rock aggregate for road pavement, hence some of the red color roads in the area, and as a road base for unimproved roads. The red color is produced by iron oxides in the rock. Scoria can be crushed and used as a rock aggregate for road pavement; hence, some of the red-colored roads in the area, and as a road base for unimproved roads.

Coal forms slowly over great periods of time. The coal beds in the area originally accumulated as peat deposits that formed from the leaves, branches, stems, and roots of trees and other plants that grew in the swamps. The peat beds probably were buried when a nearby river flooded, covering the area with sand and mud. After millions of years under thousands of feet of sediment, the peat gradually changed to coal. (One coal seam near Buffalo, the Healey, is about 200 feet thick in places.)

As erosion and uplifting began to change the earth's surface, many coal seams were exposed to air and caught fire. As the coal seams burned back into the hillsides, the intense heat changes the normally soft brown and gray rocks to a hard red material—scoria. At station 2 you will learn about plants that helped to form the coal.

The ecosystem of the swampy plain played a significant part in the development of coal, an important energy resource today.
Article courtesy of Bureau of Land Management.

10 *Gas, Food, Lodging*

H Cloud Peak Ferris Wheel
Behind Bozeman Crossing Restaurant
I-25 Exit 299

A ride on this Ferris wheel will give the rider a beautiful view of the Big Horn Mountains and the Cloud Peak Wilderness area. This 195,000 acre wilderness area and Cloud Peak (elevation 13,165) are directly in front of the Ferris wheel.

The Ferris wheel gets its name from George Washington Ferris who designed a 250 foot wheel for the Columbian Exposition in Chicago in 1892. This Eli #16 wheel was built in 1936 by the Eli Bridge Co. of Jacksonville, Illinois. It is serial number 547 and originally ran at the Utah State Fair. It moved to Heritage Square, Golden Colorado in 1978 and ran there for twelve years. It has been totally reconditioned and now operates daily during the summer months.

H Six-Mule Army Wagon
At Bozeman Crossing restaurant, 1-25 Exit 299
near Buffalo

This replica of a six mule Army wagon was built on the running gear of an 1864 design for this military wagon. The first design of this wagon in 1857 and the Army brought out three models, the 1858 model, the 1864 model and the 1878 model.

Thousands of these wagons were built for use in the Civil War and design (with modifications) was in use by the United States military from 1858 until after World War 1.

The wagon had a payload of 2000 lbs. and was pulled by six mules. The teamster or mule skinner did not ride in the wagon, but rode the "nigh" or left wheeler mule. The two mules that were closest to the wagon were called the "wheelers", the next pair of mules were called the "swing team" and the front pair wre called the "leaders". The teamster controlled the wagon by use of a jerk line to the bit of the nigh leader. The nigh leader had a stick from his harness collar to the off or right leaders bit. This stick was called a jockey stick. The wagon was turned to the left by pulling the rein or jerks line in a steady pull causing the nigh leader to come left pulling the off leader with him. Sharp jerks on the jerk line caused pain on the nigh leaders mouth causing him to move away from the pain or to the right. The jockey stick then forced the off leader to the right and the swing team and wheelers went with them. A certain amount of strong language went with this maneuvering, but when you consider the mule skinner had no protection from the elements save what he wore, perhaps it was justified.

H Big Horn Mountains
At Bozeman Crossing restaurant I-25 Exit 299

The high country backdrop on top of the Big Horn Mountains encompasses much of the Cloud Peak Wilderness area. This 195,000 acre area was designated as wilderness by Congress in 1984.

The highest point in the wilderness area is Cloud Peak, which can be seen by looking through the peep hole on the right hand side of the sign. Cloud Peak is 13,005 feet high. The peak immediately to the South is Bomber Mountain, 12,436 feet high. It is named for a B-17 bomber that crashed there on June 28, 1943 with the loss of 10 lives.

There are 256 fishing lakes and 49 miles of fishing streams in the wilderness area. They feature Rainbow, Cutthroat, Brook, German Brown, California Golden, Mackinaw and Grayling fish species. Big game animals found in the wilderness area include elk, deer, moose, mountain sheep and black bear.

A closer look at Cloud Peak wilderness area and the beautiful Big Horns can be had by taking US Highway 16 to Worland or by taking Crazy Woman Canyon/Pole creek loop tour.

F Dash Inn Restaurant
620 E. Hart, Buffalo. 684-7930.

Wyoming Tidbits

Raising sheep was a hazardous occupation in the late 1800s in Wyoming. Sheepmen and cattle ranchers warred over the range, and cattlemen marked "dead lines" in the soil. Sheep and people could be killed for crossing the lines.

L Motel 6 of Buffalo
100 Flat Iron Dr., Buffalo. 684-7000.
www.motel6.com

Motel 6 of Buffalo is conveniently located near I-90 and I-25 on the Scenic Byway to Yellowstone National Park only four hours away. Situated in a quiet location, the newly built motel offers more than the standard Motel 6 experience. In addition to comfortable accommodations, free morning coffee, a newly expanded cable channel lineup, high speed Internet in all rooms, and free local calls, the motel offers easy access to great year-round recreation, dining, and shopping. The motel also abides by the pledge to always offer the lowest price of any national chain. Together, these attributes combine to offer comfort, value, and assurance with the price and services guests expect. The only surprises here are pleasant ones, so make your next stay at Motel 6 of Buffalo. They'll leave the light on for you!

L Comfort Inn Buffalo
65 Hwy. 16 E., Buffalo. 684-9564.
www.choicehotels.com

Plan to stop at the Comfort Inn in historic Buffalo on your trip between Yellowstone National Park and the Black Hills of South Dakota. The friendly staff assures your personal comfort with spacious rooms, queen beds, and interior and exterior entries on the ground level. All rooms are equipped with coffeemakers and 27-inch color TV's, and wireless Internet is available for guests' convenience. For added security and guest assistance, the front desk is staffed 24 hours a day. After a relaxing night's rest, guests are treated to a complimentary continental breakfast each morning. The Comfort Inn Buffalo is conveniently located at I-25 Exit 299 and I-90 Exit 58 just a few blocks from great dining and shopping in historic downtown Buffalo.

Buffalo	Jan	Feb	March	April	May	June	July	Aug	Sep	Oct	Nov	Dec	Annual
Average Max. Temperature (F)	36.0	40.1	47.1	56.9	67.1	77.0	85.9	85.1	74.0	61.6	46.0	38.6	59.6
Average Min. Temperature (F)	9.6	14.3	21.2	30.4	39.5	48.3	54.3	52.4	42.2	31.7	20.0	12.4	31.4
Average Total Precipitation (in.)	0.52	0.43	0.72	1.56	2.23	2.27	1.37	0.82	1.31	0.97	0.58	0.44	13.23
Average Total SnowFall (in.)	5.8	5.3	5.0	2.6	0.6	0.0	0.0	0.0	0.1	1.9	5.1	6.7	33.1
Average Snow Depth (in.)	2	1	0	0	0	0	0	0	0	0	0	2	0
Wind Speed (mph / kmh)	8 / 13	8 / 13	9 / 15	10 / 17	9 / 15	8 / 13	8 / 12	8 / 12	8 / 13	8 / 13	8 / 12	8 / 13	
Wind Direction	NW	NW	NW	NW	NW	NW	NW	NW	NW	NW	NW		
Cloud Cover (out of 8)	5.7	5.7	5.6	5.4	5.3	4.5	3.6	3.7	4	4.7	5.4	5.4	

L Wyo Motel
610 E. Hart St., Buffalo. 684-5505 or
(800) 666-5505. www.wyomotel.com;
wyomotel@yahoo.com

Located midway between Yellowstone and Mount Rushmore, the AAA-approved Wyo Motel provides clean and affordable lodging. The family-owned and operated motel features spacious rooms with queen and king beds and 62 TV channels. Microwaves and refrigerators are available, and five large family units include fully stocked kitchenettes. Relax your cares away in the indoor whirlpool. An outdoor heated pool with two slides is available for summer family fun. A grassy picnic area lets guests soak in Buffalo's picturesque mountain setting. Motel guests enjoy complimentary coffee and donuts each morning, fax service, winter plug-ins, parking at your door, and large vehicle parking. Historical sites, dining, shopping, and year-round recreation are minutes away. A $5.00 pet fee is charged for each animal. These features and a home away from home atmosphere, Wyo Motel ensures a memorable stay!

L Historic Bozeman Crossing Super 8
655 E. Hart St., Buffalo. 684-2531.
www.bozemancrossing.com; motel@vcn.com

The Historic Bozeman Crossing Super 8 caters to both family vacationers and business travelers with its ideal location between Yellowstone and the Black Hills. Combining western history and excellent lodging with easy access to I-90, the Super 8 offers clean and comfortable rooms, cable TV, free local calls, continental breakfast, winter plug-ins, complete catering services for conferences, and convenient access to fun, shopping, and dining. During your stay, stroll the grounds on a history walk, check out the open air museum and gift shop, thrill yourself at the amusement park and Cowboy Carousel, play miniature golf, or savor a scrumptious meal at Bozeman Trail Steakhouse and Buffalo Room Tavern. For lodging, dining, and entertainment in one location, make the Historic Bozeman Crossing Super 8 your lodging destination. Tour busses and groups are always welcome.

11 *Food, Lodging*

T Johnson County Tourism Association
55 N. Main, Hwy 16 at I-90 & I-25, Buffalo
Chamber of Commerce. 684-5544 or
(800) 227-5122. www.buffalowyo.com

T Cattle Wars Sculptures
South edge of downtown on Main Street.

Plaques

Living on the Edge
Sculptor: D. Michael Thomas

An independent cowboy, or small rancher, brands a calf on the open range. Surprised at his work, he turns to see a rider from a large cattle outfit galloping threateningly toward him.

Small ranchers, like this cowboy, rode south from Buffalo on the morning of April 11, 1892, to confront "The Invaders" at the TA Ranch. Sheriff Red Angus, citizens of Buffalo, and small ranchers laid siege to the gunmen. Three days later, troops from Fort McKinney, near Buffalo, arrived on the scene. The invaders surrendered and were escorted to the fort, then sent to Cheyenne. They were never brought to trial.

Ridin' for the Brand
Sculptor: D. Michael Thomas

In the late 1800s, independent Johnson County ranchers began branding calves before the spring and fall roundups. The practice angered larger ranchers of the day, who resented this infringement on the open range. So began the Johnson County Cattle War.

The conflict peaked on April 6, 1892, when a group of large ranchers and hired guns rode north from Casper toward Buffalo, "the invaders" carried with them a black list of alleged rustlers, two of whom they killed near present day Kaycee. On April 10th they fortified and spent the night at the TA Ranch 13 miles south of Buffalo. The stage was set for one of the most notable confrontations in frontier history.

This bronze portrays a rider for one of the big outfits challenging a homesteader branding a "maverick" calf.

VS The Sports Lure
66 S. Main St., Buffalo. 684-7682 or
(800) 684-7682. www.sportslure.com;
splure@vcn.com

For over thirty years, the Sports Lure has provided top quality merchandise and superior service to the outdoorsman. This full-line sporting goods store supplies the equipment and accessories needed for spectacular wild trout fishing, big game hunting, mountain biking, shooting, archery, camping and backpacking in

The Sports Lure

the beautiful Cloud Peak Wilderness, and cross country and downhill skiing. The store is also equipped with many well-stocked specialty departments, including technical outerwear, sportswear, and footwear to complete every adventure with function, style, and comfort. The Sports Lure rounds out its offerings with an athletics department, Wyoming gifts, and a knowledgeable staff that provides unrivaled customer service. Whether you're staying in Buffalo or just passing through on the way to Yellowstone, shop at the Sports Lure – your outdoor headquarters for memorable Wyoming adventures!

M Century 21 Buffalo Realty
360 N. Main, Buffalo. 684-9531 or
(877) 449-5684. www.century21buffalorealty.com;
gmjensen@collinscom.net

Century 21 Buffalo Realty welcomes you to Buffalo, Wyoming and the Bighorn Mountains of north-central Wyoming. Owned by Broker Geoff Jensen, Century 21 Buffalo Realty is a full-service agency loaded with Realtors® possessing over 100 years combined area real estate experience. Proud to offer integrity and knowledge of the Buffalo community, the brokerage strives to help clients make an educated decision regarding the purchase or sale of property. The Realtors® offer a variety of listings, from residential and commercial to ranches and mountain cabins, and they treat all clients with care, honesty, and loyalty. Whether you're moving to or from Buffalo, count on Century 21 Buffalo Realty to make your future relocation as easy as possible. Stop by, call, or visit them on the web to see what this professional agency can do for you.

12 *Food, Lodging*

T Jim Gatchell Memorial Museum
100 Fort Street in Buffalo. 684-9331.
www.jimgatchell.com

In 1900, as the western frontier period was drawing to a close, Jim Gatchell opened a little drugstore in Buffalo, Wyoming. His customers included famous army scouts, cowboys, lawmen and cattle barons. He was also a trusted friend of

WHAT MAKES THE BIG HORNS SO SPECIAL?

No region in Wyoming is provided with a more diverse landscape; from lush grasslands to alpine meadows, and rugged mountain tops to canyonlands and desert.

Gorgeous canyon country is a hallmark of the forest. Shell, Tensleep and Crazy Woman Canyons are among those that can be enjoyed from your car window. Others, like Tongue and Devil's Canyon are better viewed on foot.

Geology is noteworthy in the Big Horns. Watch for highway signs that trace the geologic history of this regin as you travel the major highways.

One of our many treasures is an abundance of large mountain meadows. These natural openings, caused by soil type and moisture levels, favor grasses and wildflowers rather than trees. Wildflowers are truly extraordinary in the Big Horns during June and July.

Interspersed with mountain meadows are large patches of cool evergren forest extending from just above the foothills to timber line. Ponderosa pine and Douglas-fir populate the lower slopes with lodgepole pine, subalpine fir and Englemann spruce at the higher elevations.

Open landscapes make for great wildlife viewing as well. Watch for moose munching on a tasty bite of willow streamside or a family of mule deer bounding away, then stopping to look back with large ears raised and listening.

History buffs come to this region to explore the land that once felt the footsteps of legendary giants like Jim Bridger, Lewis and Clark, Red Cloud, Plenty coups and Buffalo Bill. Big Horn country was highly valued by tribes like the Crow, Sioux, Northern Cheyenne, Eastern Shoshone, and Arapahoe. Some of the most famous battles between American Indians and the U.S. military were waged at the foot of the Big Horn Mountains or in close proximity.
Source: U.S. Forest Service

the region's Native Americans, many of whom fought at the Battle of the Little Big Horn and who called Gatchell a "Great Medicine Man." For more than 50 years, Gatchell cherished these friendships. In turn, the old timers presented him with the priceless artifacts of a vanishing era. From this grassroots beginning in a crowded drugstore, the Jim Gatchell Museum today houses one of the most historically significant collections in the Rocky Mountain West.

Buffalo, Wyoming has been called the crucible of the American Frontier. More than a century ago, many of the pivotal events in the history of the west took place within 30 miles of here. Near the center of town, the Jim Gatchell Museum lends evidence to that time when this country was neither so tame nor so friendly. Scenes from the Wagon Box Fight, the Johnson County Cattle War and Buffalo's Main Street from the 1800s are depicted in detailed dioramas in the museum's main building.

The museum offers a large collection of

Jim Gatchell Memorial Museum

American Indian artifacts, along with memorabilia from the Bozeman Trail and the Johnson County Cattle War of 1892. Mingled with the legends of Calamity Jane, Weasel Bear, Tom Horn, Red Cloud, Captain Fetterman and Portuguese Phillips is an extensive frontier guns collection, saddles of men who once rode the open range and items passed down through the families of pioneers who settled "in" and then "settled" the Powder River Region.

Museum visitors can view beadwork of Native Americans, relax outside near the restored western wagons, and meet the past face-to-face by viewing over 800 photographs of people who made history.

The Jim Gatchell Museum of the West is nestled near the tall pines at the corner of Main and Fort Streets overlooking historic downtown Buffalo. The museum is contained on four levels within two buildings: the main museum built in 1956 houses the original collection and the Carnegie Building built in 1909 is home to traveling displays, educational programs, children's hands on exhibits and the museum's gift store. It is open from mid-April through December 24. *Reprinted from museum brochure.*

T Mosier Gulch Recreation Area
5 miles west of Buffalo along U.S. Highway 16

This area lies at the foothills of the Big Horn Mountains (map). With almost 900 acres of ponderosa pine-forested lands, Mosier Gulch canyon is a popular hiking area.

A developed roadside picnic area complete with picnic tables, pedestal fire grates, and a vault toilet is available. In addition, the picnic area is a trailhead for the Clear Creek walking path which leads back to Buffalo.

At an elevation between 5,500 and 6,800 feet, this area is also home to mule deer, antelope, eagles, and occassionally black bear and elk.

This area is open for hunting with a Wyoming Game and Fish Department. license. Trout fishing is available on adjacent city of Buffalo lands along Clear Creek.
Article courtesy of Bureau of Land Management.

T Bud Love Winter Range
West of Buffalo out Fort Street

Here you'll see some of the most scenic mountain views imaginable. As you pass through a wildlife preserve you will see mule deer, white tail deer, game birds including wild turkey, antelope, and in the winter, elk.

H Fort McKinney
U.S. Highway 16 west of Buffalo just west of entrance to Soldier's and Sailor's Home.

Established at Powder River Crossing of the Bozeman Trail in 1876 as Cantonment Reno was moved to this site in 1878. The fort was built by two companies of the Ninth Infantry, in command of Captain Pollock, for the protection of the Powder River country from the hostile Sioux, Cheyenne, and Arapahoe Indians. The post was named for John McKinney, Lieut. of the Fourth Cavalry, killed in the Dull Knife fight on Red Fork of Powder River November 26, 1876.

It was abandoned in 1894 and the land was deeded to the State of Wyoming for a Soldier's and Sailor's Home.

13 *Gas, Food*

H Tisdale Divide
7 miles south of Exit 298 on Hwy 196

Wyoming in the 1880s was an open range controlled by cattle kings. Some of the powerful stockgrowers thought rustling was a problem, but others were just as concerned about the influx of small operators who used government land grants which threatened the open range. John A. Tisdale, one of the small operators, was dry-gulched in a gully just north and east of this spot as he returned home from a shopping trip to Buffalo in late November, 1891. Locals were outraged by the killing of this respected family man.

Frank Canton, a former Johnson County sheriff was accused of the murder, but he was never brought to trial. Stock detectives, such as Canton, were hired by the Wyoming Stock Growers Association to protect their large herds and to intimidate would-be ranchers.

This incident, coupled with the murder of Orley E. Jones a few days earlier, set the stage for the infamous invasion of Johnson County in April, 1892.

14 *Gas, Food, Lodging*

T Ucross Foundation & Art Gallery
30 Bid Red Lane in Clearmont. 737-2291

Arvada
Originally named Suggs, the Burlington Railroad was responsible for renaming this town with a respectable biblical name. Natural gas, which flowed from an artesian well nearby, created a strange cocktail. Brave citizens would light it and drink the flaming water.

Clearmont
Pop. 115, Elev. 3,921
Situated on Clear Creek, Clearmont has an old hometown feel to it, with tree-lined streets and a friendly little park and an old jail.

Leiter
This post office was named for Joseph Leiter, who was a principle in the Lake DeSmet Irrigation Project.

Recluse
When this post office opened in 1918, it seemed very far away from the ranches it served. Only a recluse would want to be that far away, the ranchers thought.

Spotted Horse
This discontinued post office was named for a Cheyenne chief, Spotted Horse. The post office is gone, but the restaurant/ bar and gas station remain.

Ucross
Pop. 25, Elev. 4,085

Named for a cattle brand that had a U with a cross under it, this post office was once named Cedar Rapids, after the city in Iowa from which local settlers had emigrated.

H Powder River
On I-90 halfway between Buffalo and Gillette

Too thin to plow, too thick to drink." That was the humor of early settlers describing the mud swept down stream each spring in the Powder. The river named the "Powder" because its banks have a black brittle gunpowder appearance. This river carries water from melting snows high in the Bighorn Mountains north to the Yellowstone River in Montana.

Powder River country is a land of heritage and tradition. Native Americans lived here for over 8000 years before the first explorers and immigrants. The famous "Hole-in-the-Wall" hide out of Butch Cassidy and the Sundance Kid was on the Middle Fork of Powder River, 60 miles southwest of where you now stand. Today these open expanses of prairie are home to hard working ranch families a cultural heritage passed on from the pioneer cattle barons of the late 1800's.

Once the habitat for great herds of bison, Powder River country now supports a blend of agriculture and native prairie wildlife. Cattle and sheep graze the lands along with herds of antelope, deer and elk. Riparian areas (the lush green areas bordering the river) are of special importance in fulfilling the habitat needs of people, livestock and wildlife.

This country has seen years of oil development, and is now a prime source of low sulfur coal for the U.S.- helping to reduce air pollution from power generation plants in many parts of the country. The Powder River basin now produces one-sixth of the world's energy.

As you pass through this area it appeaars endless and barren, but life abounds on the vast Powder River landscapes. Land ownership along the river is mixed between private, state and federal. Pioneers tended to homestead the low lands close to water, leaving the federal lands now administered by BLM. These

Wyoming Tidbits

Built south of the Big Horn Mountains in 1890, the Sheridan Inn was featured in "Ripley's Believe it or Not" as "The House of 69 Gables".

lands are currently used for grazing. wildlife, minerals and other multiple uses. Prairie vegetation is produced on soil rich in nutrients and minerals and nourished by sunshine, snow and rain. Ranchers raise cattle and sheep, which convert prairie plants to meat, wool, leather and other products used to feed and clothe the nation. Through good stewardship and cooperative management of the prairies wildlife and livestock coexist.

You are in the Heart of Powder River country - a special place for wildlife and people. A land of cowboy culture and wildland romance.

H Stagecoach Roads in Sheridan County
Bingham Post Office and Stage Station

Bingham Post Office and stage station on the Rock Creek stage line was located from 1879 to 1885 at Benjamin F. Smith's ranch on the north side of the Tongue River, where the stage road crossed. The site is in a field west of the ranch buildings, about a half mile southeast of this sign. The ranch was one of twenty-three stage stations, eighteen to twenty miles apart, on the Rock Creek to Montana stage road. The stations consisted of stables and houses for the employees on the route, and nine of them, including Bingham, also served as post offices.

Bingham Post office was named for John T. Bingham, superintendent from 1879 to 1882 of the northern half of the stage line (from Powder River, Wyoming, to Junction, Montana). A bridge was built here in the early 1880's that washed out in 1884. B.F. Smith died about the same time, and Frank Mock took over the stage station and post office. In 1885 the post office was moved two and a half miles southeast to Frank McGrath's Keystone Ranch on Wolf Creek, retaining the name of Bingham until 1894. After the post office was moved, the Rock Creek line adopted a new route on the south side of the Tongue River to Dayton, where a bridge had been built.

H Minnows and Mud
Rest area 30 miles east of Buffalo on I-90

Powder River, flowing north to Montana, has a far different character than the clear, trout-filled mountain streams that form it. Here the water is wide and shallow and in spring the run-off from the mountains transforms the river into a heavy current of muddy water.

Unique fish live in the Powder River and are adapted to life in murky conditions. The stonecat and three minnows (flathead chub, sturgeon chub and longnose dace) have flattened or streamlined bodies to help them stay near the bottom and fight the current. They have small eyes since good eyesight is of little use in muddy water. Near their mouth they have "Barbles" or "whiskers" which they use to smell and taste potential food. In June, the river is also host to the shovelnose sturgeon, channel catfish and goldeye, which swim by on their long trek to tributary streams to spawn.

The Powder River—one of the unique habitats, which supports unique species of Wyoming wildlife.

H 1811 Astorian Overland Expedition
At Spotted Horse

The Astorians, first organized white expedition to enter this region, passed near this point on August 25, 1811. The party under the leadership of Wilson Price Hunt, was composed of 60 men, 1 Indian squaw and 2 children and was bound for the mouth of the Columbia River to help establish the Pacific Fur Company, headed by John Jacob Astor.

Leaving the Missouri River near the mouth of the Grand River in South Dakota, they traveled overland having one horse for each two men. After many hardships they reached their destination on February 15, 1812. Edward Rose acted as guide through this area.

L The Ranch at Ucross
2673 Hwy. 14 E., Clearmont. 737-2281 or
(800) 447-0194. www.blairhotels.com

Want to experience a vacation at a different pace?
The serenity of the Ranch at Ucross is just the
place! Nestled at the foothills of the Big Horn
Mountains, Ucross is 27 miles southeast of
Sheridan and 18 miles northwest of Buffalo, a convenient half-day drive from Yellowstone National
Park or the Black Hills of South Dakota. The
Ranch features deluxe accommodations, including
swimming, horseback riding, tennis, fishing…the
list is as endless as your imagination. Get off the
interstate! Take a short ride on Wyoming Highway
14 or 16. You'll find a little piece of heaven – the
Ranch at Ucross!

15 *Gas, Food, Lodging*

T Hoofprints of the Past Museum
344 Nolan Ave. in Kaycee. 738-2381

What began as a Wyoming Centennial project in
1990 has grown into a great hands on collection
of Powder River Country history. The Museum is
headquartered in the oldest standing structure in
Kaycee, but has since acquired a blacksmith
shop, a country schoolhouse, a homestead cabin,
and the original twn jail, relocated to be near all
the rest. Collections include relevent artifacts
from the Johnson County Cattle War, homesteaders and pioneers, Native American battles, and
outlaws like the Wild Bunch and the Hole-in-the-
Wall. The Museum is also the headquarters for
area tours.

Mayoworth
This post office was named in 1890 for the postmistress's daughter, May Worthington.

Sussex
Mrs. Davis, the wife of the rancher who ran the
first post office here, came from Sussex County,
Delaware.

Kaycee
Pop. 249, Elev. 4,660

Kaycee has a wild history as home to infamous
outlaws. Established as a cowman's town in 1900
and named for the brand, KC, owned by Peters
and Alston. Kaycee is probably the smallest town
to told a Professional Rodeo Cowboy's Association
(PRCA) rodeo and the community pride shows.
Kaycee was an important site of the Johnson
County War, one of the most significant events in
Old West history. The Bozeman Trail, which

linked the Oregon Trail to the Montana gold
mines, can still be viewed east of town. The infamous "Hole-in-the-Wall" country and outlaw cave
where the legendary outlaws Butch cassidy and
the Sundance Kid and the rest of the Hole-in-the-
wall gang hid out is just west of town.

T Frewen Castle
Near Sussex

Two brothers, Moreton and Richard Frewen, left
England bound for the wilds of Wyoming to hunt
buffalo. Once they spotted the verdant Powder
River country, however, they vowed to stay and
invest in cattle. Moreton also invested in a wife,
Clara Jerome of New York, aunt of Winston
Churchill. Erecting an exquisite two-story log
"castle", the Frewens filled the home with every
known luxury. Locals dubbed the home Frewen
Castle. English hunting parties and high teas
filled their social calendar, and ladies who visited
were treated to hothouse bouquets delivered on
horseback. British nobility graced the castle with
their presence, and it was a magical kingdom.
Then, the disastrous winter of 1886-87 devastat-
ed the cattle herd. Moreton suffered financial
losses from which he could not recover. He and
his family returned to England, where he deposited Clara and their three children in an English
countryside while he travelled extensively. Very
little remains of the Frewen Castle today.

T Crazy Woman Battlefield
East of I-25 between Kaycee and Buffalo

The site of numerous skirmishes between native
tribes and white travelers, the battlefield is bisect-
ed by a creek of the same name. There are two
varying accounts of how the area received its
name. One story is that an Indian woman living
alone and slowly went mad. A second version is
that a white traveler's wife went insane when she
witnessed Indians scalp her husband.

Wyoming Tidbits

A "nester" is a farmer or homesteader who
settled in cattle-grazing country. Cattlemen
and nesters were in constant conflict, and
one of the most historic events in Wyoming's
history involves such a conflict in the Johnson
County War of 1892.

T Outlaw Cave and Canyon
About 20 miles southwest of Kaycee

Outlaw Cave is a prehistoric rock shelter and
Indian Pictographs can be found nearby. The
Middle Fork of the Powder River is also viewed
along this route as well as beautiful panoramas of
the red mountain walls, the canyon at the Middle
Fork of the Powder River and the Dull Knife
Battlefield. The deep cave was also a popular
hideout for outlaws including the Wild Bunch
from the nearby Hole-in-the-Wall hideout.

H The Dull Knife Battle
Kaycee Rest Stop I-25 Exit 254

On November 25th the final battle of the Sioux

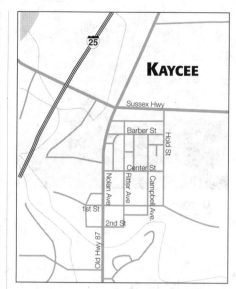

campaign of 1876 was fought approximately 28
miles west of this point. Colonel Ranald
Mackenzie with 750 cavalrymen and 400
Indian scouts and auxiliaries attacked a Northern
Cheyenne encampment at dawn. Leaders Dull
Knife and Little Wolf were among the
Cheyenne.

This village consisted of about 175 lodges
housing 1400 people, some of whom had participated in the defeat of Custer at the Battle of
the Little Bighorn the previous summer.
Cheyenne women and children fled to the surrounding mountains, but the men checked the
army's advance during the day-long battle.

The army lost 1 officer, 6 soldiers and had
more than 20 wounded. At least 25 Cheyenne
died. Mackenzie ordered the village destroyed
and 500 ponies were captured. This proved disastrous for the Cheyenne who were left destitute. They found sanctuary with the Sioux in
Montana and South Dakota but by May 1877
surrendered. The U.S. government, thus,
secured control of the Powder River country. In
1884 it established the present Northern
Cheyenne reservation in southeast Montana.

H Mountain Lion
Kaycee Rest Stop I-25 Exit 254

Mountain lions, also known as pumas,
cougars, panthers and catamounts, live in the
rugged mountains and foothills of Wyoming.
The foothills of the Bighorn Mountains provide
some of the best mountain lion and mule

Wyoming Tidbits

The country's first national monument, Devil's
Tower, was dedicated by President Teddy
Roosevelt on September 14, 1906. The 600
foot-high volcanic rock was later featured in
the movie, "Close Encounters of the Third
Kind."

Kaycee	Jan	Feb	March	April	May	June	July	Aug	Sep	Oct	Nov	Dec	Annual
Average Max. Temperature (F)	37.4	41.7	48.1	57.8	67.9	78.8	87.9	86.7	75.6	63.1	47.6	39.7	61.0
Average Min. Temperature (F)	6.6	12.6	19.7	28.3	38.2	46.4	52.3	50.1	39.9	29.3	17.5	9.5	29.2
Average Total Precipitation (in.)	0.41	0.37	0.70	1.47	2.26	2.09	1.14	0.82	1.05	1.00	0.52	0.38	12.21
Average Total SnowFall (in.)	6.7	6.3	7.3	6.7	1.3	0.1	0.0	0.0	0.4	2.4	5.6	6.6	43.3
Average Snow Depth (in.)	2	1	0	0	0	0	0	0	0	0	1	1	1

deer habitat in America.

Mountain lions prefer rugged canyon country in mixed conifer or mountain mahogany cover. Mule deer and elk compose a majority of their diet. They also prey on small mammals like jackrabbits, snowshoe hares, porcupines, yellow-bellied marmots and other small rodents. In localized parts of the Bighorn Mountains, lion predation on domestic sheep is a chronic problem, thereby necessitating special management strategies and tightly regulated harvest to maintain a delicate balance between man and the cat.

Mountain lions once roamed from northern Canada to the southern tip of South America, but along with the colonizing of the Americas by European man, came the persecution and extensive habitat changes which greatly reduced the cat's range. In Wyoming, however, vast, unbroken expanses of habitat still remain.

The Bighorns are home to the big cat. While seeing one is rare, mere knowledge of their presence adds something special to that place called Wyoming. A place where quality of life is oftentimes defined in wildlife terms.

H Powder River Country
Kaycee Rest Stop I-25 Exit 254

Twelve thousand years ago, the rich grasslands and abundant wildlife attracted Native American hunters into the area. As the United States expanded, commerce and conflict occurred. The Portuguese Houses, east of Kaycee, were part of the fur trade industry during the early nineteenth century. The establishment of the Bozeman Trail in 1863 brought on warfare between some of the tribes and the United States Army ending with the expulsion of the Native Americans from the area in 1877. Historic sites like Fort Reno and Crazy Woman Battlefield reflect this struggle. During the last two decades of the nineteenth century, disputes between open range ranchers and homesteaders resulted in many confrontations, ending with the 1892 Johnson County War fights at KC and TA ranches.

Today, ranching exists alongside minerals and recreation industries. The land's wealth however, is not infinite. Only through careful stewardship can the land be cared for and maintained. Wildlife viewing, hunting and fishing, tours of museums and historic sites, traveling historic roads, and camping and hiking allow all to appreciate Powder River Country.

H Killing of Champion and Rae
U.S. Highway 87 just south of bridge over Middle Fork of the Powder River.

About 100 yards west of this point stood the buildings of the Kaycee Ranch, a log cabin and a barn. These buildings were surrounded before daylight on April 9, 1892, by invading cattlemen. Occupying the cabin were Nate Champion and Nick Rae, alleged rustler and two trappers who were captured by the cattlemen, but were unharmed. Rae appeared and was shot down. He was dragged inside the cabin by Champion, who fought off the attackers alone until late afternoon, when the cabin was set afire. He attempted to escape but was shot and killed. Rae died of his wounds during the forenoon.

Edgerton
Pop. 169, Elev. 5,000

This town was named for being right on the edge of the great Salt Creek oil field.

Linch
Named for the Linch family, who settled in the area, this little town became an oil-drilling site in the late 1940s.

Midwest
Pop. 408, Elev. 4,851

Named for the Midwest Oil Company, Midwest became the first town in the nation to have electric lighting for a football game in 1925.

T Salt Creek Museum
The Museum's exhibits cover the Salt Creek oilfields from 1889 to present. Exhibits include a furnished doctor's office that was in use from 1937 to 1993, a school room, kitchen, dining room, barber shop and various household artifacts. The Museum's research facilities include a full set of midwest Refining Company Books from 1920-1930, which detail the operations in Salt Creek Oil Fields. The Museum is open by request. Admission by donations only.

T Pumpkin Buttes
30 miles east of Midwest on
State Highway 387

These five flat-topped landmarks rise 1,000 feet above the surrounding plains of southern Campbell County. Col. James Sawyer rote in his diary, "Made 13 miles over good roads, to a gap in Pumpkin Buttes, from whence we looked down on an immense valley, if such an abyss of hill tops can be so called." The buttes boast hundreds of tipi rings. The area is rich with uranium deposits.

H 1863 Bozeman Trail
On State Highway 387 about 8 miles west of
Pine Tree Junction

John Bozeman and John Jacobs laid out this route from Fort Laramie to the Virginia City, Montana gold fields. In 1865 the Powder River Military Expedition under Gen. P. E. Connor, established Ft. Connor on the Powder River. In 1866 Forts Reno, Phil Kearny, and C. F. Smith were built for its protection against the Indians who fought bitterly to hold their last hunting grounds. It became known as the Bloody Bozeman. Portugee Phillips rode over this trail to Ft. Laramie to report the Fetterman Massacre. In 1866 Nelson Story trailed the first herd of Texas longhorns to cross Wyoming along this road. Indian hostiles forced abandonment of the trail in 1868.

H Salt Creek Oil Field
Junction of State Highways 387 and 259 at
Midwest.

Stockmen were aware of pools of oil in the creek bottoms during cattle trailing days. These oil seeps led to the discovery of Salt Creek, one of Wyoming's largest oil fields, nine miles long by five miles wide.

In 1883, the first claims were filed in the 22,000 acre Salt Creek Field. The first strike in the field occurred in 1908 at a depth of 1,050 feet. Many wells are still active.

Salt Creek was one of the first unitized oil fields in the United States. Under unitization one company operates properties for all owners and more efficient recovery methods can be used. Improved practices in Salt Creek have recovered many additional milions of barrels of oil.

SCENIC DRIVES

Cloud Peak Skyway

This is the southern-most route across the Bighorn National Forest in the Big Horn Mountains. The designated 47-mile stretch on US 16 shares its boundaries with the National Forest. The highway can be reached via Tenleep from the west of Buffalo from the east. Allow one hour minimum driving time.

The road is a paved tow-lane highway, with occasional pullouts as it ascends toward 9666-foot Powder River Pass. This route makes a more gradual ascent of the mountain range than routes to the north. Mountain weather can be extreme and snow can fall in any month at these elevations, but rarely does it affect travel in the summer and early fall.
Reprinted from Wyoming Department of Transportation Brochure

Bud Love Winter Range

On this drive, you'll see some of the most scenic mountain views imaginable, as well as deer, antelope, wild turkey, and in the winter, elk. It takes about one or two hours to drive it, depending on how much you stop and look at what surrounds you. Start in Buffalo at Fort Street and Main Street (US 16 west), then head west on Fort and turn right (north) on DeSmet. Follow this route out of town on CR 91.5 (French Creek Road). When the road forks at 5.4 miles, bear left and travel another 5 miles to the Bud Love Winter Range. The road forks again at 15 miles, where you should stay right and follow Rock Creek Road back to Buffalo.
Reprinted from Wyoming Department of Transportation Brochure

Crazy Woman Canyon

One of the favorite drives for Johnson County locals, and visitors as well, this tour takes you along a single lane dirt road past stunning canyon walls into the mountains. Begin at the intersection of Fort and Main in Buffalo, taking US 16 west towards the mountains. After about 25 miles, watch for a well-signed Crazy Woman Canyon Road, which branches left off of US 16. To return to Buffalo, follow the gravel road which brought you through the canyon and joins Wyoming 196. Turn left onto Wyoming 196 on which you'll drive ten miles back to Buffalo.
Reprinted from Wyoming Department of Transportation Brochure

Outlaw Cave/Dull Knife Battlefield

This tour takes you to the land of Butch Cassidy and the Sundance Kid. Johnson County locals and visitors favor the area's wildlife and scenery as much as the tales of these outlaws. This is also the area of the Middle Fork of the Powder River. High clearance vehicle are recommended for this route. Beginning at Kaycee, take the I-25 interchange and head west about a mile to the Barnum Road sign (Wyoinng 190). Follow Barnum Road 17.1 miles to a sign designating the Middle Fork Management Area of the Powder River. Turn left at the sign onto a gravel/dirt road. This will take you another 8.5 miles to the Outlaw Cave sign, where you should turn

and drive another 2 miles to the hideout. Another .3 miles past the cave you can find a prehistoric rock shelter and Indian pictographs.
Reprinted from Wyoming Department of Transportation Brochure

Buffalo Area

French Creek Trail #42
Distance: 2 – 3.5 miles
Climb: gentle
Rating: easy
Usage: light
Location: Travel about 10 miles west of Buffalo on Hwy. 16, then turn right (north) on FDR 368 (French Creek Rd.). Cars and two wheel drive vehicles need to park about 1/4 mile down the rode. High clearance, 4WD vehicles can go another 1.5 miles in before parking.

The trail begins at the creek. You may follow it either west or east; the trail circles back to the same point. Either way, you'll see views of the Buffalo area and surrounding countryside.

Pole Creek Road
Distance: 11 miles
Climb: flat
Rating: easy
Usage: light
Location: Travel 19 miles west, then south of Buffalo on Hwy. 16, then turn right (west) on FH 31 (Pole Creek Rd.).

This is a gravel road, passable for most vehicles, which reconnects with Hwy. 16 about 11 miles south. There is seldom any traffic, and it is flat, so it's easy to walk or ride on. Along the way, you will find several old logging roads, which are gated and closed to motorized vehicles, but open to walkers, bikers, and horses.

Crazy Woman Canyon
Distance: varies
Climb: steep
Rating: difficult
Usage: light
Location: Travel 25 miles west, then south of Buffalo on Hwy. 16, then turn left (east) onto FDR 33 (Crazy Woman Canyon Rd.). The road drops quickly into some side drainages, which offer some challenging hiking.

There are no trails, so caution needs to be exercised on these hikes. Experience with mountaineering and orienteering is recommended. The main advantage is that very few people will be encountered in this canyon.

Poison Creek Road
Distance: varies
Climb: steep
Rating: difficult
Usage: light
Location: Travel about 29 miles west/southwest of Buffalo on Hwy. 16, then turn left (south) onto FDR 484 (Poison Creek Rd.). This road will take you to the base of the Hazelton Peaks area. The road is rough, but passable for most vehicles.

There are no marked trails on the mountains, but many routes along the drainages of the peaks will lead you to the top, where you will find a spectacular panorama of both the Powder River Basin and the Bighorn Basin.

Grouse Mountain Road
Distance: varies
Climb: gentle
Rating: moderate
Usage: light

Location: Travel about 10 miles west of Buffalo on Hwy. 16, then turn left (south) onto FDR 402/403 (Grouse Mountain Rd.). Park just off the road.

There are no trails maintained in this area, but the surrounding meadows and view of the valley make walking here enjoyable and easy.

(* These hikes are in the Cloud Peak Wilderness Area, so registration is required.)

Sherd Lake/ South Fork Trails*

Distance: varies
Climb: gentle/ moderate
Rating: easy/ moderate
Usage: heavy
Location: Travel about 16 miles west of Buffalo on Hwy. 16, then turn right (west) on FDR 20 (Circle Road). This will take you about 2.5 miles to the Circle Park Trailhead, where both trails begin.

The Sherd Lake Trail begins on TR 182, which turns into TR46, and goes about a mile to the lake. Beyond the lake, the elevation climbs, and the trail becomes the South Fork Trail. This trail turns into TR 095, then 1/4 mile farther along becomes TR 046 at Rainey Lake. Head south past Old Crow Trail. After crossing Duck Creek, go north on TR 095 to complete the loop back to Sherd Lake at the South Fork Ponds crossing.

Hunter/ Ant Hill Trail*

Distance: about 7 miles
Climb: steep
Rating: quite difficult
Usage: heavy
Location: Travel about 12 miles west of Buffalo on Hwy. 16, then turn right (west) on FDR 19 (Hunter Park Rd.). The Hunter Trailhead is about 3 miles west, where you can park.

This is a fairly strenuous hike, and should be planned for overnight, at least. Take FDR 496 northwest from the trailhead through the French Creek Swamp, to where it intersects with FDR 399. Follow this northwest to South Rock Creek, where it intersects with TR 7. Take TR 7 to TR 219 then follow it until you reach TR 38 at Elk Lake. This trail circles the lake, then heads south over the saddle of North Clear Creek, turning east into TR 24, then TR 44, which goes to the Seven Brothers Lakes. At Lake One, turn east onto TR 45 heading for Buffalo Park. Go east through the park, until you reach FDR 396, which will take you back to the Hunter Trailhead.

Solitude Loop Trail #38*

Distance: 50 miles
Climb: moderate
Rating: moderate/ difficult
Usage: light
Location: Travel about 12 miles west of Buffalo on Hwy. 16, then turn right (west) on FDR 19 (Hunter Park Rd.). The Hunter Trailhead is about 3 miles west, where you can park.

This hike takes about five days to complete, but it takes you past several of the prettiest lakes in the Bighorn Mountains. Go west from the trailhead on FDR 394 (Soldier Park Rd.) to TR 24. Continue west until you reach TR 38, which is the Solitude Loop Trail. It is well marked and will eventually lead you back to TR 24, and Soldier Park Rd. Other spurs diverge from this trail, including the West Tensleep Trail.

West Tensleep/ Misty Moon Trail #63*

Distance: about 7 – 57 miles
Climb: moderate
Rating: moderate/difficult
Usage: heavy

Location: Travel 44 miles west/ southwest of Buffalo or 17 miles east of Tensleep, then turn north on FDR 27, continuing 7 miles to the West Tensleep Trailhead.

This trail meets with the Solitude Loop Trail, which means hikers may chose to make it an overnight hike, or a several day trip. The trail follows West Tensleep Creek to Lake Helen, Lake Marion, and finally to Misty Moon Lake, which is the 7 mile portion of the journey. TR 63 intersects with TR 38 (the Solitude Loop Trail) north of Misty Moon Lake. Following this loop can add as much as 50 miles to your trip (see Solitude Loop Trail).

Lost Twin Lakes Trail #65*

Distance: about 6 miles
Climb: moderate
Rating: moderate/difficult
Usage: heavy
Location: Travel 44 miles west/southwest of Buffalo or 17 miles east of Tensleep, then turn north on FDR 27, continuing 7 miles to the West Tensleep Trailhead.

This trail climbs through lodgepole pine forest and meadows by the Middle Tensleep Creek to Mirror Lake, then on to Lost Twin Lakes. The forest changes from pine to often stunted spruce and fir along the way, until the treeline is crossed, and an open view of the area can be seen at the top of the trail.

Middle Tensleep Falls Trail

Distance: 2 miles
Climb: flat
Rating: easy
Usage: light
Location: Travel 44 miles west/ southwest of Buffalo or 17 miles east of Tensleep, then turn north on FDR 27, continuing 7 miles to the West Tensleep Trailhead.

This trail follows Middle Tensleep Creek south to the falls. Take the same route back.

Baby Wagon Creek Trail*

Distance: about 3 miles
Climb: gentle
Rating: easy
Usage: light
Location: Travel 38 miles west/ southwest of Buffalo or 27 miles east of Tensleep, then turn north on FDR 422, then north again onto FDR 419, which is a rough road, so high clearance, 4WD vehicles are recommended. The road ends at Baby Wagon Creek, which is where the trail begins.

This trail meanders along the riparian zone of the creek towards McLain and Maybelle Lakes. TR 69 runs east and west and connects with TR 98, which passes by the lakes, with a possible loop by way of TR 79, which leads to FDR 430 and returns east on TR 69.

Middle Rock Creek Trail*

Distance: about 8 miles
Climb: 4500 feet
Rating: very difficult
Usage: light
Location: In Buffalo, turn north off of Fort St. (Hwy. 16) onto N. DeSmet St. This street turns into French Creek Rd. Take this road 8 miles north to the entrance of the Bud Love Winter Game Refuge. Go through the gate and head west on the dirt road for 2 miles until you reach the Taylor Cabin site. The cabin is no longer there, but a barn is. Motor vehicles are not permitted beyond this point.

This is probably an overnight trek. From the cabin site, follow TR 51 to Firebox Park then take TR 41 to the junction of Middle and South Rock Creek. Take TR 41 south along Keno Creek,

where it meets up with FDR 399/396. For a longer loop, head north along TR 40 until it intersects with TR 10, which will take you back down to FDR 399/ 396 also. This road connects with FDR 388, which will take you north to TR 41, then TR 51, which takes you back to Taylor Cabin.

Johnson Park/ Cougar Canyon Trail*

Distance: about 8 miles
Climb: steep
Rating: very difficult
Usage: light
Location: In Buffalo, turn north off of Fort St. (Hwy. 16) onto N. DeSmet St. This street turns into French Creek Road. Take this road 8 miles north to the entrance of the Bud Love Winter Game Refuge. Go through the gate and head west on the dirt road for 2 miles, until you reach the Taylor Cabin Site: The cabin is no longer there, but a barn is. Motor vehicles are not permitted beyond this point.

Take TR 51 west along the North Fork of Sayles Creek. At Firebox Park take TR 41 then go onto TR 549 about a half mile after that. Take this trail south onto TR 550, which intersects with FDR 396. Take this road south to TR 42, then head northeast to the National Forest boundary. As you drop in elevation, leaving the forest area, follow the tree line back to Taylor Cabin, about 2.5 miles.

Firebox Park Trail

Distance: varies
Climb: steep
Rating: moderate/difficult
Usage: light
Location: In Buffalo, turn north off of Fort St. (Hwy. 16) onto N. DeSmet St. This street turns into French Creek Road. Take this road 8 miles north to the entrance of the Bud Love Winter Game Refuge. Go through the gate and head west on the dirt road for 2 miles, until you reach the Taylor Cabin Site: The cabin is no longer there, but a barn is. Motor vehicles are not permitted beyond this point.

Take TR 51 up North Sayles Creek to Firebox Park. Turn onto TR 41 and go west along Middle Rock Creek to TR 43. Then follow TR 10 south to TR 41 on Keno Creek. Return on TR 41 north to TR 51 at Firebox Park and back to Taylor Cabin.

Battle Park/Paint Rock Creek Trail*

Distance: about 7 miles
Climb: moderate
Rating: moderate
Usage: moderate
Location: Travel 44 miles west/ southwest of Buffalo on Hwy. 16, or 17 miles east of Tensleep, then turn north on FDR 27. Continue 1 mile north, then turn left on FDR 24 (Battle Park Rd.). Drive 15 miles to reach to Battle Park Trailhead.

This trail passes through high mountain meadows, pine stands, and along several streams. From the trailhead, go north on TR 164 west of Grace Lake, then go west on TR 38. Continue on this trail to TR 62, on Paint Rock Creek, by the cow camp. Just south of the camp, turn southeast to TR 172, which returns to TR 164, then back to the trailhead.

Upper Paint Rock Lake Loop Trail*

Distance: 18 miles
Climb: steep
Rating: difficult
Usage: light
Location: Travel 44 miles west/ southwest of Buffalo on Hwy. 16, or 17 miles east of Tensleep, then turn

north on FDR 27. Continue 1 mile north, then turn left on FDR 24 (Battle Park Rd.). Drive 15 miles to reach the Battle Park Trailhead.

Go north on TR 164 west of Grace Lake to TR 38, where you'll travel west, and then east, around Poacher Lake to TR 59 in the Teepee Pole Flats. Take this trail to Lower Paint Rock Lake, turning south onto TR 116 and then onto TR 94. This will take you to TR 62, then south to TR 173 and back to TR 164 and eventually the Battle Park Trailhead.

Lily Lake Trail

Distance: 3 miles
Climb: moderate
Rating: moderate
Usage: moderate
Location: Travel 44 miles west/ southwest of Buffalo on Hwy. 16, or 17 miles east of Tensleep, then turn north on FDR 27. Continue 1 mile north, then turn left on FDR 24 (Battle Park Rd.). Drive 15 miles to reach to Battle Park Trailhead.

This is a reasonable day hike - not too strenuous, not too easy. Go north on TR 164 until it intersects with TR 66. Follow this trail to the lake, and return by the same route.

INFORMATION PLEASE

Tourism Information

Johnson County Tourism Association 684-5544
Chamber of Commerce - Buffalo   684-5544
Chamber of Commerce - Sheridan   672-2485
Sheridan Travel and Tourism   673-7120

Government

BLM Buffalo Field Office   684-1100
BLM Newcastle Field Office   476-6600
Bighorn National Forest - Tongue Ranger District
                                     674-2600
Bighorn National Forest - Buffalo Ranger District
                                     684-1100
Bighorn National Forest - Medicine
Wheel/Paintrock Ranger District   548-6541

Car Rentals

Truck Corral Auto Rentals • Sheridan 672-7955
Enterprise • Sheridan   672-6910

Hospitals

Memorial Hospital of Sheridan County •
Sheridan   672-1000

Airports

Sheridan   674-4222

Golf

Horseshoe Mountain Golf Club •
Dayton   655-9525
Powderhorn Golf Club • Sheridan   672-5323
Kendrick Golf Course • Sheridan   674-8148
Sundance Golf Club • Sundance   283-1191
Buffalo Golf Course • Buffalo   684-5266
Salt Creek Country Club • Midwest   437-6859

Ski Areas

Antelope Butte Ski Area   655-9530

Guest Ranches

The Ranch at Ucross • Clearmont   737-2281
Spear-O-Wigwam Ranch • Sheridan 673-5543
Willow Creek Ranch at Hole-in-the-Wall • Kaycee
738-2294
Diamond Seven Bar Ranch • Alva   467-5786
Rocking Horse Ranch • Arvada   736-2488
Little Piney Ranch • Banner   683-2008
Canyon Ranch • Big Horn   674-6239
Klondike Guest Ranch • Buffalo   684-2390
Paradise Guest Ranch • Buffalo   684-7876
Dry Creek Ranch • Buffalo   684-7433
Gardner's Muddy Creek Angus •
Buffalo   684-7797
Triple Three Ranch • Buffalo   684-2832
TA Ranch • Buffalo   684-5833
Sweetgrass Ranch • Buffalo   684-8851
Buffalo Creek Ranch • Recluse   682-8728
HF Bar Ranch • Saddlestring   684-2487
Eaton's Ranch • Wolf   655-9285

Lodges and Resorts

Big Horn Mountain Lodge • Dayton 751-7599
The Ranch at Ucross • Clearmont   737-2281
Bear Lodge Resort • Dayton   752-2444
Bear Track Lodge & Outfitters •
Buffalo   684-2528
South Fork Mountain Lodge • Buffalo 684-1225
Lake Stop Resort & Marina • Buffalo 684-9051
Pines Lodge • Buffalo   351-1010

Vacation Houses, Cabins & Condos

Mountain Cabin by the Stream •
Story   672-8260
Wagon Box Inn, Restaurant & Cabins •
Story   683-2444
Little Goose Coop Guest House •
Sheridan   672-0886
Kaycee Bunk House • Kaycee   738-2213

Bed and Breakfasts

White Horse B&B • Dayton   655-9441
Four Pines B&B • Dayton   655-3764

Cameo Rose B&B • Sheridan   673-0500
Graves B&B • Kaycee   738-2319
Historic Mansion House Inn • Buffalo 684-2218
Piney Creek Inn B&B • Story   683-2911
Bozeman Trail Inn • Big Horn   672-9288
Spahn's B&B • Big Horn   674-8150
Four Corners Country Inn •
Four Corners   746-4776
Powder River Experience • Clearmont 758-4381
Bozeman Trail B&B • Big Horn   672-2381
Double Eagles Nest B&B • Buffalo   684-8841
Empire Guest House •   756-9707
Spear Ranch B&B • Big Horn   673-0079
Historic Old Stone House •
Ranchester   655-9239
Greenhorn B&B • Kaycee   738-2548
Clear Creek B&B • Buffalo   684-2317
Stonehearth Inn • Buffalo   684-9446
Foothills B&B • Parkman   655-9362
Kroger House B&B • Sheridan   674-6222
Meadows at the Powder Horn
• Sheridan   674-9545
Ranch Willow B&B • Sheridan   674-1510
Auntie M's B&B • Sheridan   674-7035

Outfitters and Guides

Big Horn Mountain Lodge   H   751-7599
Trail West Outfitters   FHEG 684-5233
Just Gone Fishing   F   684-2755
Bear Track Lodge & Outfitters   H   684-2528
Nelson Outfitters   H   672-6996
Triple Three Ranch   FHE 684-2832
Simon's Hunting   H   283-2664
Western Gateway Outfitters   H   467-5824
P Cross Bar Ranch Trophy Hunts H   682-3994
Tumbling T Guest Ranch/Whitetail Creek
Outfitters   FEG 467-5625
Platt's Guides & Outfitters   FHRE 327-5539
Edwards Outfitters   HF 464-1518
Sagebrush Outfitters   H   682-4394
Windows to the West   G   682-3334
Wyoming Edge Outfitters   H   467-5588
Double Rafter Cattle Drive   EG 655-9463
Northern Wyoming Outfitters   H   672-2515
Cloud Peak Llama Treks   G   683-2548
Rimrock West Adventures   H   683-2911
Baker Hunts   H   750-2464
Eagle Creek Outfitters   HFE 672-6520
Antelope Outfitters   H   685-1132
Big Buck Outfitters   H   751-0448
Bare Tracks Trophies   H   896-3914
Big Horn Mountain Oufitters   H   674-4691
Greer Outfitters   H   687-7461
Little Bighorn Outfitters   H   684-5179
North By Northwest   H   684-9633
Rafter B Outfitters   R   684-2793
Seven J Outfitters   H   283-3443

NOTES:

Dining Quick Reference

Price Range refers to the average cost of a meal per person: ($) $1-$6, ($$) $7-$11, ($$$) $12-up. Cocktails: "Yes" indicates full bar; Beer (B)/Wine (W), Service: Breakfast (B), Brunch (BR), Lunch (L), Dinner (D). Businesses in bold print will have additional information under the appropriate map locator number in the body of this section. *[wi-fi]* next to business name indicates free wireless internet is available to customers.

MAP No.	RESTAURANT	TYPE CUISINE	PRICE RANGE	CHILD MENU	COCKTAILS BEER WINE	MEALS SERVED	CREDIT CARDS ACCEPTED
2	Big Horn Mountain Lodge	Family Style	$$$	Yes	Yes	B/L/D	M/V
2	Bear Lodge Resort	Family	$$	Yes	Yes	B/L/D	Major
2	Aspen Creek Galleria & Restaurant by the Creek	Sandwich/Desserts	$	No		L	V/M
2	Dayton Mercantile Restaurant	American/Pizza	$$			L/D	Major
2	Branding Iron Restaurant	Homestyle	$$	Yes		L/D/B	Major
2	Mountain Inn	Bar food	$	Yes	Yes	L/D	Major
3	Pablo's Mexican Restaurant & Cantina	Mexican/American	$$	Yes	Yes	L/D	Major
3	Trolleyline Restaurant	American	$$	Yes	Yes	B/L/D	Major
3	Domino's Pizza	Pizza	$$	No		L/D	Major
3	Kentucky Fried Chicken	Fast Food	$	Yes		L/D	
3	Pizza Hut	Pizza	$$	Yes	B	L/D	Major
3	Grub Wagon Café	Family	$			B/L	
3	Silver Spur Café	Family	$/$$	Yes		B/L	
3	Kim Family Restaurant	Korean	$$			L/D	Major
3	Sutton's Tavern	Bar	$		Yes	B/D/L	
3	Trails End Restaurant	Family	$/$$	Yes		D/L/B	Major
3	Country Kitchen	Family	$$	Yes		L/D/B	Major
4	**Oliver's Bar & Grill**	New American	$$$	Yes	Yes	L/D	Major
4	**Wyoming's Rib & Chop House**	Family	$$$/$$	Yes	Yes	L/D	Major
4	Sheridan Palace Restaurant	Homecooking	$	Yes		B/L	Major
4	Quizno's	Sandwiches	$	Yes		L/D	Major
4	Dairy Queen	Fast Food	$	Yes		L/D	
4	Dragon Wall	Chinese	$$	No		L/D	M/V
4	Perkins	Family	$$	Yes		L/D/B	Major
4	Subway	Sanwiches	$	Yes		L/D	M/V
4	Sanford's Grub & Pub	Brew Pub	$$/$$$	Yes	Yes	D/L	Major
4	Dutch Lunch	family	$$	Yes		L/D	
4	Main Street Diner	Family	$$	Yes		L/D/B	Major
4	Main Street Bagel	Sandwiches	$	Yes		L/B	
4	PO News Specialties & Tea Shoppe	Coffee Shop	$			L/B	
4	Paolo's Pizzeria Ristorante Vesuvio	Italian	$$/$$$	Yes	Yes	L/D	Major
4	Papa Guyos	Mexican	$$	Yes	Yes	L/D/B	
4	Bear Claw Donut Company	Coffee Shop	$	No	Yes	L/B	V/M
4	Quizno's	Sandwiches	$	Yes		L/D	V/M
4	Hardee's	Sandwiches	$	Yes		L/D/B	
4	Beaver Creek Saloon	American	$$	No	Yes	L/D	M/V
4	Java Moon Bakery & Deli *[wi-fi]*	Coffee House	$$$/$	No		L/B	Major
4	Sheridan Center Restaurant	Family	$$	Yes	Yes	B/L/D	Major
4	Pony Grill	Family	$$	No	Yes	L/D	Major
4	The Mint Bar	Bar	$$		Yes	L/D	Major
5	Holiday Inn Atrium Hotel & Conference Center *[wi-fi]*	American	$$$	Yes	Yes	B/L/D	Major
5	Arctic Circle	Burgers	$	Yes		L/D	Major
5	Blimpie/Nach-O-Fast/Ice Box	Fast Food	$	Yes		L/D	Major
5	Burger King	Fast Food	$	Yes		L/D	M/V
5	Golden China Restaurant	Chinese	$$	No		L/D	M/V
5	The Greenery Restaurant	Family	$$	No		L/D/B	Major
5	King Buffet	Buffet	$$	Yes		L/D/B	Major
5	McDonald's	Fast Food	$	Yes		L/D/B	
5	Taco Bell	Fast Food	$	Yes		L/D	
5	Taco John's	Fast Food	$	Yes		L/D	
5	Wendy's	Fast Food	$	Yes		L/D	Major
5	Los Agaves	Mexican	$$		W/B	L/D	M/V
5	Las Margaritas	Mexican	$$	Yes	Yes	L/D	Major
5	JB's	Family	$$	Yes		L/D/B	Major
5	Scooters Bar & Grill	American	$$		Yes	L/D	M/V
5	Arby's	Fast Food	$	Yes		L/D	Major
5	Taco Bell	Mexican	$	Yes		L/D	
5	Perkins	Family	$$			L/D/B	Major
5	Subway	Sandwiches/	$	Yes		L/D	M/V
7	Tunnel Inn Dining Room and Bar	Fine Dining	$$/$$$	Yes	Yes	D	M/V
7	The Waldorf A' Story *[wi-fi]*	Eclectic	$$$		W/B	L/D	M/V

Dining Quick Reference-Continued

Price Range refers to the average cost of a meal per person: ($) $1-$6, ($$) $7-$11, ($$$) $12-up. Cocktails: "Yes" indicates full bar; Beer (B)/Wine (W), Service: Breakfast (B), Brunch (BR), Lunch (L), Dinner (D). Businesses in bold print will have additional information under the appropriate map locator number in the body of this section. *[wi-fi]* next to business name indicates free wireless internet is available to customers.

MAP No.	RESTAURANT	TYPE CUISINE	PRICE RANGE	CHILD MENU	COCKTAILS BEER WINE	MEALS SERVED	CREDIT CARDS ACCEPTED
7	Ladore Supper Club	Steakhouse	$$$/$$		Yes	D	Major
7	Dusty Boots Grill	American	$$	C	All	B/L/D	Major
7	Livery Stable	American	$$	C	All	B/L/D	Major
8	Lake Stop	American	$$	No	Yes	D/L/B	Major
10	**Dash Inn Restaurant**	Fast Food	$	Yes		L/D	
10	Historic Bozeman Crossing	Family Dining & Steaks	$$$		Yes	L/D	Major
10	Colonel Bozeman Restaurant	Eclectic	$$	Yes	Yes	L/D	M/V
10	The Breadboard Sub Shop	Sandwiches	$			L/D	M/V
10	Duffy's Bluff Café	Family	$$	Yes		D/L/B	Major
10	Hoot 'n Howl Pub	Family	$$	No	Yes	D/L	Major
10	Hardee's	Fast Food	$$/$	No		D/L/B	
10	La Crocevia	Family	$$	Yes	Yes	D/L/B	Major
10	McDonald's	Fast Food	$	No		D/L/B	
10	Pizza Hut	Pizza	$$	No	B	D/L	D
10	Subway	Sandwiches	$$/$	Yes		D/L	M/V
10	Taco Johns	Fast food	$	Yes		D/L	
10	Winchester Steak House	Fine Dining	$$$	Yes	Yes	D	Major
11	The Sagewood Gift Store & Cafe	Soup & Sandwich	$$			L	Major
11	The Virginian Restaurant	Fine Dining	$$$	Yes	Yes	D	Major
11	Deer Field Boutique & Espresso Bar Café	Coffee House	$			B/L	V/M
11	Tavern on the Creek	Homestyle cooking	$	Yes	Yes	L/D	M/V
11	Cowgirl Coffee Café	Coffee House	$	No		L/B	Major
11	Country Delight & Daylite Donuts	Family	$$	Yes		L/D	Major
11	China Garden	Chinese	$/$$	No		L/D	Major
11	Tom's Main Street Diner	Homecooked	$	No		L/B	
11	Pistol Pete's	Family	$	Yes		L/B	Major
12	Stagecoach Inn Restaurant	Western	$$	Yes	Yes	L/D/B	M/V
12	South Fork Mountain Lodge	Family	$$		Yes	B/L/D	Major
13	Domino's Pizza	Pizza	$$			L/D	Major
14	Red Arrow Café 7 & Bar	American	$		Yes	B/L/D	
15	Invasion Bar & Restaurant	Family	$$	Yes	Yes	L/D	M/V
15	Kaycee Sinclair Grab-n'-Dash	Fast Food	$	Yes		B/L/D	Major
15	On the Run	Fast Food	$	Yes		B/L/D	Major

NOTES:

Motel Quick Reference

Price Range: ($) Under $40 ; ($$) $40-$60; ($$$) $60-$80, ($$$$) Over $80. Pets [check with the motel for specific policies] (P), Dining (D), Lounge (L), Disabled Access (DA), Full Breakfast (FB), Cont. Breakfast (CB), Indoor Pool (IP), Outdoor Pool (OP), Hot Tub (HT), Sauna (S), Refrigerator (R), Microwave (M) (Microwave and Refrigerator indicated only if in majority of rooms), Kitchenette (K). All Wyoming area codes are 307. [wi-fi] next to business name indicates free wireless internet is available to customers.

MAP No.	HOTEL	PHONE	NUMBER ROOMS	PRICE RANGE	BREAKFAST	POOL/ HOT TUB SAUNA	NON SMOKE ROOMS	OTHER AMENITIES	CREDIT CARDS
1	Ranchester Western Motel	655-2212	18	$$			Yes	P	
2	Big Horn Mountain Lodge [wi-fi]	751-7599	16	$$$/$$$$				P/D/L/DA/K	M/V
2	Wigwam Motel	587-3861	14	$				K	D/M/V
2	Foothills Motel & Campgrounds	655-2547	10	$			Yes	P/K	
3	**Wingate Inn**	675-1101	66	$$$$	CB	HT/IP	Yes	DA/M/R	Major
3	**Best Western Sheridan Center**	674-7421	138	$$$		HT/IP/OP	Yes	P/D/L/R	Major
3	**America's Best Value Inn** [wi-fi]	672-9757	39	$$		HT	Yes	M/R/P	Major
3	Alamo Motel	672-2455	19	$$			Yes	P	M/V
3	Aspen Inn	672-9064	24	$$			Yes	P/K	Major
3	Bramble Motel & RV Park	674-4902	15	$$			Yes	P/K	Major
3	Super Saver Inn	672-0471	37				Yes	P	V/M
3	Trails End Motel	672-2477	84	$/$$$		IP	Yes	P/K/D/L	Major
3	Guest House Motel [wi-fi]	674-7496	44	$$$			Yes	P	Major
3	Stage Stop Motel	672-3459	18	$			No	P/K	
3	Sundown Motel	672-2439	23	$$		OP		K/P	Major
3	Super 8 - Sheridan [wi-fi]	672-9725	39	$$			Yes	P	Major
5	**Econo Lodge**	587-2221	56	$$/$$$$	CB	IP	Yes	DA	Major
5	**Apple Tree Inn**	672-2428	24	$$$		S	Yes	P	Major
5	**Holiday Inn Atrium Hotel & Conference Center** [wi-fi]	672-8931	212	$$$		IP/HT/S	Yes	P/L/D/DA	Major
5	Days Inn - Sheridan [wi-fi]	672-2888	47	$$/$$$/$$$$	CB	IP	Yes	DA	Major
5	Historic Mill Inn [wi-fi]	672-6401	45	$$$	CB				Major
5	Comfort Inn [wi-fi]	672-5098	61	$$$$	CB	HT	Yes	P	Major
5	Parkway Motel	674-7259	14	$$			Yes	K/P	Major
5	Rock Trim Motel	672-2464	18	$$/$				K/P	M/V
6	Redstone Motel	234-9125	59	$$		OP	Yes	P/DA	Major
6	Hampton Inn [wi-fi]	235-6668	122	$$$	CB	OP	Yes		Major
7	**Story Pines Inn, LLC**	683-2120	6	$$$		HT	Yes	P/R	D/M/V
10	**Wyoming Motel** [wi-fi]	684-5505	27	$$		IP		K/P	Major
10	**Motel 6 of Buffalo**	684-7000	44	$$			Yes	DA/P	Major
10	Historic Bozeman Crossing Super 8 [wi-fi]	684-2531	48	$$	CB		Yes	P/D/L/DA	Major
10	Comfort Inn Buffalo	684-9564	41	$$$	CB	HT	Yes	P	Major
10	Roadwat Inn	684-2219	44	$$			Yes	P/DA	M/V
10	Best Western Crossroads Inn [wi-fi]	684-2256	60	$$$		OP/HT	Yes	D/L/DA	Major
11	The Occidental Hotel & The Virginian Restaurant [wi-fi]	684-0451	14	$$$$	CB		Yes	P/D/L/K	Major
11	Blue Gables Motel	684-2574	17	$$		OP	Yes	P/L/D/K	Major
11	Big Horn Motel	684-7822	18	$$					Major
11	Historic Mansion House Inn	684-2218	18	$$$	CB		Yes		Major
12	Z-Bar Motel	684-5535							
12	Arrowhead Motel	684-9453	13	$$/$	CB		Yes	DA/K	M/V
12	Mountain View Motel & Campground	684-2881	13	$$				P/K	
14	The Ranch at Ucross	737-2281	22	$$$	FB	OP	Yes	P/D/L	Major
15	Cassidy Inn Motel	738-2250	18	$			Yes	P	Major
15	Siesta Motel Country Inn	738-2291	13	$$			Yes	D/P	M/V
15	Riverside Inn	738-2659	19	$$				P	Major

NOTES:

All Wyoming Area Codes are 307

Section 6

SECTION 7

NORTHCENTRAL AREA

INCLUDING CODY, WORLAND, POWELL, LOVELL AND THERMOPOLIS

"Cody is Rodeo" is the slogan for the Rodeo Capital of the World.

1 *No services*

T Clark
Gas

This town was named for Len Clark, an early rancher, not for William Clark, the explorer, as might be supposed.

H Nez Perce Trail
28 miles north of Cody on Highway 120 at Clark's Fork River.

In 1877, the Nez Perce Indians of Idaho, led by Chief Joseph, fled the U.S. Army. They crossed the Clark's River near this point, while trying to outrun the soldiers to Canada.

LV Hunter Peak Ranch
4027 Crandall Rd., Cody. 587-3711.
www.nezperce.com/ranchhp.html; hpr@wtp.net

Most people like to have their own way. And when it comes to vacations, that's even more important. Nestled on the banks of the Clarksfork River in the Absaroka Mountains, Hunter Peak Ranch offers guests the freedom to create a custom vacation. Escape to a world of gracious hospitality and relaxation, horseback ride amid brilliant scenery, fish in crystal clear lakes and streams, or hunt for big game in the fall. Guests may also choose from hiking, biking, photography, Yellowstone sightseeing, snowmobiling, cross country skiing, and tubing. During your stay, savor hearty family-style ranch meals, and curl up

Hunter Peak Ranch

for the evening in rustic but modern cabins and suites furnished with all the comforts of home. Consistently receiving rave reviews, Hunter Peak Ranch is an affordable four-season mountain retreat catering to independent minded recreationists and travelers.

2 *Gas, Food, Lodging*

Cody
Pop. 8,835 Elev. 5,016

Named for its famous promoter, William "Buffalo Bill" Cody, this little city was originally named Richland when George T. Beck established the post office in 1895. Prior to that, it was the homestead of Otto Franc, a wealthy Prussian

rancher who may have helped finance the Johnson County War. Incorporated in 1901, the year that the Burlington railroad arrived, the trains brought curious visitors to "Cowboy Town," which was the eastern gateway to nearby Yellowstone.

Cody, Beck, and Horace C. Alger were responsible for developing the Shoshone Land and Irrigation Company, which brought water and agricultural prosperity to Cody and its environs. The region quickly became populated with both farmers and business people, hoping to capitalize off of Cody's name and Yellowstone's proximity. The famous National Park is not the only scenic marvel nearby. Cody is surrounded by the Beartooth and Absaroka Mountains, as well as Sunlight Basin and the Wapiti Valley.

In 1904, oil was discovered near Cody, and Park County went on to become the second biggest oil producer in the state. Marathon Oil Company is the town's largest employer, but tourism and agriculture continue to be significant moneymakers.

T Cody Country Visitor's Council
836 Sheridan Ave. in Cody. 587-2297 or (800) 393-2639. www.pctc.org

T Park County Historical Society Archives Center
1002 Sheridan Ave. in Cody. 527-8530

A complete collection of records available to the public. Find photographs, biographies, obituaries, school information, oral histories, maps, military information, artifacts and many more areas of historical significance. Located in the Park County Courthouse they are open 9 a.m. to 4 p.m. Monday through Friday.

T Foundation for North American Wild Sheep/Wild Sheep Exhibit
720 Allen Ave. in Cody. 527-6261.
www.fnaws.org

FNAWS is the leading voice in wild sheep conservation. Their message is built on protection of habitat, professional management based upon sound biological principles, educating the public, and protecting sportsmen's rights. Inside their headquarters are a number of exhibits of wild sheep. There is also a multi-media presentation to view.

T Buffalo Bill Historical Center
720 Sheridan Ave. in Cody. 587-4771.
www.bbhc.org

The Buffalo Bill Historical Center is located in northwestern Wyoming, 52 miles from Yellowstone National Park's East Gate. The Center is comprised of five internationally acclaimed museums devoted to Western cultural and natural history: the Buffalo Bill Museum, the Cody

Cody	Jan	Feb	March	April	May	June	July	Aug	Sep	Oct	Nov	Dec	Annual
Average Max. Temperature (F)	35.7	40.2	47.2	56.7	66.3	75.7	84.7	82.7	72.1	60.9	45.8	38.0	58.8
Average Min. Temperature (F)	12.5	16.2	22.4	31.1	40.0	47.8	54.3	52.3	43.1	34.2	22.9	15.6	32.7
Average Total Precipitation (in.)	0.35	0.29	0.53	1.08	1.61	1.65	1.07	0.80	1.05	0.76	0.48	0.31	10.01
Average Total SnowFall (in.)	6.3	5.0	6.6	5.2	0.6	0.0	0.0	0.0	0.4	3.8	5.7	5.8	39.5
Average Snow Depth (in.)	1	1	0	0	0	0	0	0	0	0	0	0	0

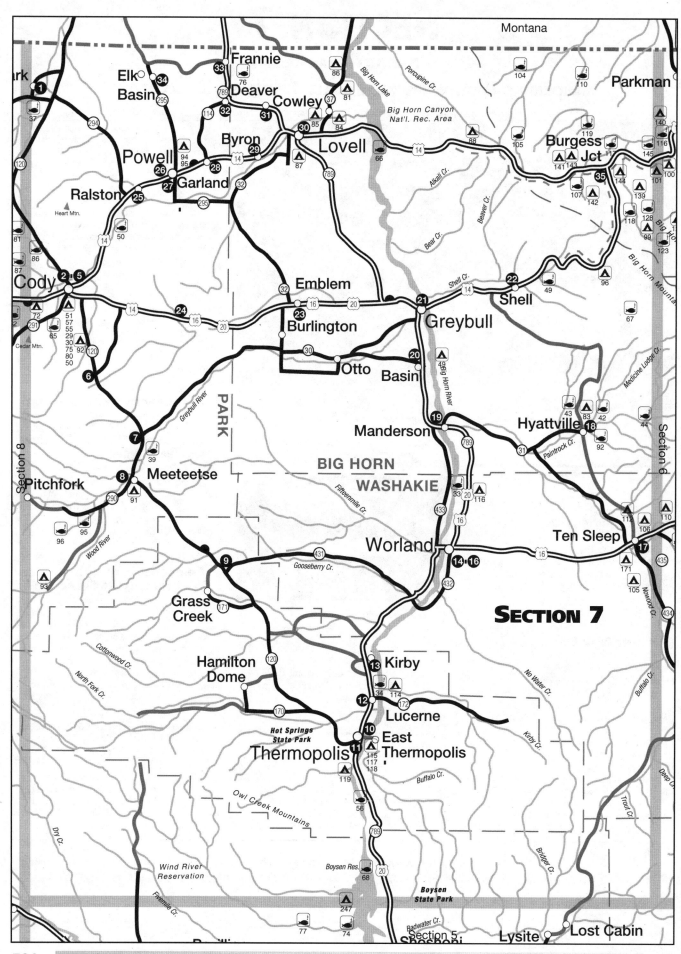

Montana

Parkman

Elk
Basin

Frannie

Deaver

Cowley

Lovell

Burgess
Jct

Powell

Byron

Garland

Ralston

Heart Mtn.

Cody

Emblem

Shell

Greybull

Burlington

Otto

Basin

Cedar Mtn.

Manderson

Hyattville

Section 8

PARK

BIG HORN

WASHAKIE

Pitchfork

Meeteetse

Wood River

Worland

Ten Sleep

Section 6

Grass
Creek

Gooseberry Cr.

SECTION 7

Cottonwood Cr.

Hamilton
Dome

North Fork Cr.

Kirby

Lucerne

Hot Springs
State Park

East
Thermopolis

Thermopolis

Dry Cr.

Owl Creek Mountains

Wind River
Reservation

Boysen Res.

**Boysen
State Park**

Fivemile Cr.

Badwater Cr.

Section 5:

Lysite

Lost Cabin

Buffalo Bill Historical Center

Firearms Museum, the Plains Indian Museum, the Draper Museum of Natural History and the Whitney Gallery of Western Art, plus the Harold McCracken Research Library. Admission is good for two consecutive days to all five museums. Call for hours and rates or visit them on the web.

F Granny's Restaurant
1550 Sheridan Ave., Cody. 587-4829.

A favorite Cody gathering spot that has served family food for 25 years, Granny's Restaurant combines scrumptious cuisine with unbeatable service. 136 menu items, mostly comfort foods,

Map Legend

 Locator number (matches numeric listing in section)

 Campsite (number matches number in campsite chart)

 Fishing Site (number matches number in fishing chart)

 Rest stop

 Interstate

 U.S. Highway

 Paved State or County Road

Gravel/unpaved road

0 Miles 13 22
One inch = approximately 13 miles

ensures that every appetite is fulfilled, and Granny's is recognized as serving one of Cody's best breakfasts all day, every day. When your tastes call for lunch or dinner, select from traditional specialties, including steaks, shrimp, fish, burgers, and more. Local favorites include homemade soups prepared fresh daily, one of the town's largest salad bars, daily and nightly specials, and child and senior menus. Offering a non-smoking, family-friendly atmosphere, the restaurant is open 5:30 am to 10 pm on weekdays and until 5 pm to 10 pm Friday and Saturday. Discover what locals and travelers alike have enjoyed for over two decades, and visit Granny's Restaurant today!

F Wyoming's Rib & Chop House
1367 Sheridan Ave in Cody. 527-7731

This beautiful little restaurant packs a mean punch. Already famous for their award-winning babyback ribs and incredible steaks, Wyoming's Rib and Chop House in Cody has proudly gained a reputation locally as "The Place To Eat." Fresh seafood is flown in several times a week; soups and sauces are made on the spot; and hand-cut Certified Angus Steaks are cooked to order. With their customary full wine, beer and liquor lists, 26 oz. margaritas, beautiful surroundings, and friendly high-energy staff, the Rib and Chop House in Cody would have put this town on the map if Buffalo Bill hadn't. In any case, it's given everyone another reason for making the trip to Yellowstone.

FLS Irma Hotel, Restaurant & Saloon
1192 Sheridan Ave., Cody. 587-4221 or (800) 745-4762. www.irmahotel.com; irmahotel@bresnan.net

Regarded as the "Grand Old Lady of Cody," the Irma Hotel has hosted world-famous personalities since its 1902 establishment under Buffalo Bill Cody. Now a Nationally Registered Historic Place, the hotel offers 40 guestrooms and suites equipped with private bathrooms and air condi-

tioning, including Buffalo Bill's personal suite. For breakfast, lunch, and dinner, saddle up to scrumptious fare at the on-site restaurant. The Irma is known for its prime rib but also features a full menu complemented with daily summer buffets and the historic saloon's full bar. During summer, live the Old West with free Cody Gunfighters performances at 6 pm Monday through Saturday. Added in 2000, Col. Cody's Wild West Emporium Gift Shop rounds out the amenities onsite and online. Capture the romance of an era, and become part of the Irma Hotel's legendary living history!

L Econo Lodge Moose Creek
1015 Sheridan Ave., 2 blocks from the Buffalo Bill Historical Center, Cody. 587-2221 or (800) 424-6423. www.choicehotels.com

Located in the heart of Cody, Econo Lodge Moose Creek provides relaxing accommodations after a day of Yellowstone sightseeing. The hotel offers 56 guestrooms, including suites, senior rooms, and large family rooms. Guest laundry, an indoor heated pool, 100% Clean Guarantee, data ports, and a complimentary continental breakfast add further comfort to your stay. In addition, the knowledgeable and friendly staff is dedicated to making your stay in Cody Country memorable. For guests' convenience, whitewater rafting and Yellowstone National Park tours may be booked on-site. Conveniently, area attractions are within walking distance or less than 5 minutes away. For comfort, convenience, and all the information you need to ensure a pleasant trip to Cody and Yellowstone—stay at Econo Lodge Moose Creek. Sorry, no pets permitted.

CODY GUNFIGHTERS

Six nights a week throughout the summer, visitors to Cody can witness a gunfight between notorious Old West characters such as Wyatt Earp, Miss Lily Brown, Mad Dog, Longhair, Buffalo Bill and Teton Jack. All re-enactments of course, but the Cody Gunfighters keep the spirit of the Old West alive through their dramatic skits. Each 45 minute program features actors in full costume and is free of charge. Donations and poster sales benefit local charities including the Children's Resource Center and the Humane Society of Park County. Held on the street beside the Irma Hotel.

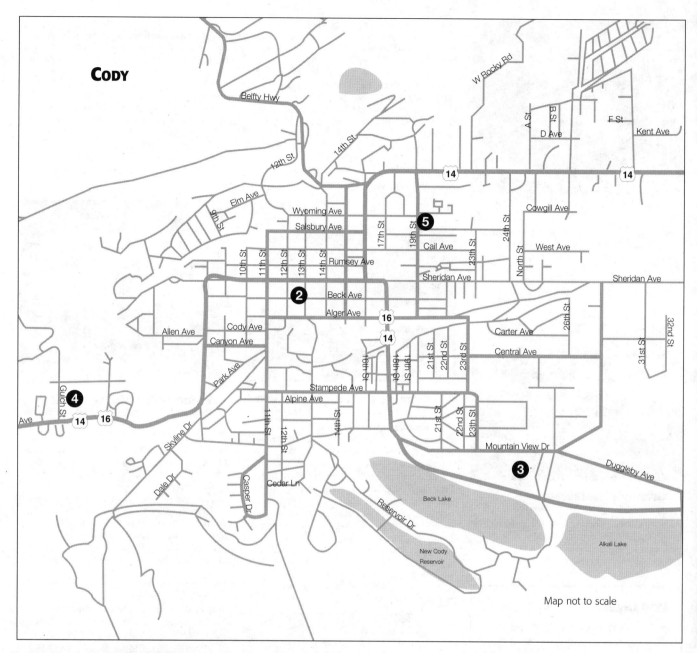

CODY

Belfty Hwy

W Rocky Rd

A St B St F St

D Ave Kent Ave

12th St 14th St

14 14

Elm Ave

9th St

Cowgill Ave

Wyoming Ave

Salsbury Ave

17th St

19th St

5

Cail Ave

West Ave

24th St

23rd St

10th St

11th St

12th St

13th St

14th St

Rumsey Ave

North St

Sheridan Ave

Sheridan Ave

2

Beck Ave

Alger Ave

16

26th St

32nd St

Carter Ave

Allen Ave

Cody Ave

14

Canyon Ave

Central Ave

31st St

Park Ave

18th St

19th St

21st St

22nd St

23rd St

Gulch St

4

Stampede Ave

Alpine Ave

14th St

Ave

14 **16**

21st St

22nd St

23rd St

Mountain View Dr

Duggleby Ave

3

Skyline Dr

11th St

12th St

Dale Dr

Casper Dr

Cedar Ln

Reservoir Dr

Beck Lake

Alkali Lake

New Cody
Reservoir

Map not to scale

L Sunrise Motor Inn

1407 8th St., Cody. 587-5566 or
(877) 587-5566. www.sunriseinncody.com;
info@sunriseinncody.com

Boasting one of Cody's finest locations, the
Sunrise Motor Inn is situated next door to the
Buffalo Bill Historic Center and within walking
distance of downtown Cody and the community's
comprehensive medical center. Guests are treated
to clean, comfortable, reasonably priced rooms at

this AAA Double Diamond motel, and the friendly staff is eager to ensure that every guest stay is
pleasant. Standard room amenities include air-
conditioning, cable TV, telephone, iron, ironing
board, coffeemaker, and free at-door parking. In
addition, the motel offers an outdoor heated pool
and garden area, continental breakfast, ice
machine, wake-up calls, and all non-smoking
rooms. Just 2 miles from Cody's Yellowstone
Regional Airport and a mere 50 scenic miles from
Yellowstone National Park, the Sunrise Motor Inn
is your convenient lodging destination for discovering Cody and Yellowstone Country!

Wyoming Tidbits

As many as 60 million buffalo once grazed on
the great plains. "Buffalo Bill" Cody reportedly killed more than 4,000 in one year. By the
end of 1883, herds were decimated by
hunters and overgrazing.

WILD WEST BALLOON FEST

Early August of each year brings the Wild
West Balloon Fest to Cody. Involving as many
as 20-25 balloonists, spectators can watch
crews inflate and launch their balloons. Two
of the competition's events include "Hare
and the Hound" and the "Key Grab". The
"Hare and the Hound" competition consists
of a lead balloonist dropping a target and the
following balloonists drop a bean bag in a
attempt to be closest to the target. Counting
on good weather, Friday night brings the "balloon glow" with the balloons inflated. There
are also kids activities as well as a food booth.
Held in Mentock Park in East Cody.

BUFFALO BILL HISTORICAL CENTER—CROWN JEWEL OF THE AMERICAN WEST

One of the best-kept secrets in the West is the Buffalo Bill Historical Center, a complex of five internationally acclaimed museums and a research library.

The late author James Michener once called the Buffalo Bill Historical Center "The Smithsonian of the West," and with good reason.

The Buffalo Bill Historical Center stands as the largest history and art museum between Minneapolis and the West Coast, encompassing over 300,000 square feet of space on three levels. Because it is located in Cody, Wyoming, a town with a population of just 9,000, 52 miles from the east entrance of Yellowstone National Park, many visitors are stunned when they venture inside its doors. Nowhere else in the United States is such an important museum located in such a remote location.

The Buffalo Bill Historical Center has positioned itself as the single most important cultural attraction in the region surrounding Yellowstone National Park. Its collections include thousands upon thousands of priceless treasures related to the art, cultural and natural history, ethnology, and technology of the American West.

Originally begun in a small log cabin in 1927 and known as the Buffalo Bill Museum, the facility then housed memorabilia belonging to William Frederick "Buffalo Bill" Cody. Cody, for whom the town of Cody is named, was an authentic western hero whose career paralleled or became linked with most of the significant events in western American history. As a mere boy, he worked as a bullwhacker and mounted messenger for a freight-hauling company, and later joined the gold rush to Pike's Peak and rode for the Pony Express. During the Civil War, he served with a Union guerrilla group known as the Kansas Jayhawkers.

But it was not until after the War Between the States that he began to grow in fame. As a hunter supplying meat for workers building the transcontinental railroad, he earned the nickname Buffalo Bill. Later, his fame was cemented as a civilian scout for the Army, when he won the Medal of Honor. His career as the consummate showman followed, beginning with his appearance in stage plays in the East and later as the head of his own world-famous theater troupe.

Buffalo Bill's showmanship found its widest audience with Buffalo Bill's Wild West, an extraordinary outdoor touring show that he called "an educational exhibition on a grand and entertaining scale." Through this show, which ran for 30 years, Buffalo Bill brought the West to the world, showing people who didn't have the opportunity to travel to the West what America's frontier legacy was all about.

Today, the Buffalo Bill Historical Center does much the same thing — it brings the West to a world that would otherwise know about it only through television and motion pictures, sources that are not necessarily reliable. Nearly 250,000 people each year visit the Historical Center, making it the most heavily visited single attraction, outside of the park itself, in the entire Yellowstone National Park region.

And the institution has become far more than a monument to the life and times of Buffalo Bill. The Whitney Gallery of Western Art, dedicated in 1959, houses one of the most important collections of Western American art in the world. Masterworks are on display by George Catlin, Alfred Jacob Miller, Albert Bierstadt, Thomas Moran, Frederic Remington, Charles M. Russell, William R. Leigh, N.C. Wyeth and many others.

In 1968, the Buffalo Bill Museum was moved into a new building attached to the Whitney Gallery of Western Art, forming the core of today's Buffalo Bill Historical Center. The Plains Indian Museum, housing one of the richest collections of American Indian artifacts in the world, features the art and culture of the most important tribes of the Northern Plains. This museum was added in 1979 and reinterpreted in 2000. That 2000 $3.8 million reinterpretation truly moved the Plains Indian Museum into the 21st century and created "a living breathing place where more than just objects are on display," Advisory Board Member and Crow tribal historian Joe Medicine Crow said.

And in 1991, the Cody Firearms Museum, housing the world's largest collection of firearms of the American West, as well as European arms dating back to the 1500s, was added to the complex. The heart of the Cody Firearms Museum collection of over 6,000 firearms is the Winchester Collection, which was moved to Cody from New Haven, Connecticut in 1976.

The Draper Museum of Natural History opened in June 2002. Challenging the traditional approach of exhibiting objects in glass cases, the new museum leads visitors down an interactive trail through the sights and sounds of the Greater Yellowstone Ecosystem. This museum presents natural history in the context of the humanities and promotes increased understanding of and appreciation for, the relationships binding humans and nature in the

American West.

Rounding out the Historical Center complex is the McCracken Research Library, which is an important resource for scholars around the United States.

The Historical Center annually hosts important events and programs. Besides special exhibitions that often travel to important venues throughout the nation, annual events include Cowboy Songs and Range Ballads (April), a program that features some of the nation's best performers of authentic cowboy music and the Plains Indian Powwow (June), attracting the best dancers and drummers of the Northern Plains; and the Larom Summer Institute in Western American Studies (June), featuring education courses for college credit. In fact, the active education department creates a myriad of programming for children and adults covering a broad spectrum of topics about the West throughout the entire year.

One of the West's premier social events, the Buffalo Bill Historical Center Patrons Ball in September is combined with the Buffalo Bill Art Show and Sale and the Western Design Conference. The entire week of activities is known collectively as Rendezvous Royale, a celebration of the arts in Cody, and serves as a major fund-raiser for the institution.

The Buffalo Bill Historical Center is open year round and hours vary. Adult admission rates are $15; Senior rates are $13; students 18 and over (with current valid student identification) are admitted for $6. Youth aged 6-17 are admitted for $4 and children 5 and under are admitted free. This summer will also see the introduction of the $22 "Inside-Outside Tour," which will include museum admission plus a historic guided tour of Cody upon the charming Cody Trolley. While 2-3 hours will give visitors a fast, general overview of the Center, admission is good for two consecutive days to give visitors as much time as possible to enjoy the vast collections.

For a closer look at the Buffalo Bill Historical Center, please see the web site at www.bbhc.org.

Section 7

L Rainbow Park Motel

1136 17th St., Cody. 587-6251 or
(800) 710-6930. www.rainbowparkmotel.com;
rainbowparkmotel@vcn.com

Friendly service, hospitality, and answers to your
Yellowstone and Cody Country questions await
at the Rainbow Park Motel. Conveniently located three blocks from historic downtown Cody at
the junction of Highway 14-16-20 and Highway
120, the motel offers 39 ground-floor rooms
(five kitchenette units) with at-door parking.
Clean, comfortable, affordable rooms feature one
or two beds, cable TV with HBO, air conditioning, and direct dial phones. Guest laundry is
available, the Cody Coffee Company is located
onsite, and several fine restaurants and lounges
are nearby. Offering AAA and senior discounts
along with smoking and non-smoking rooms,
the Rainbow Park Motel is an ideal home base
for your local and regional travel plans. Save
your money for seeing the sites and enjoying
western activities, and make reservations at
Rainbow Park Motel!

L Cody Motor Lodge

1455 Sheridan Ave., Cody. 527-6291 or
(800) 340-2639. codymotorlodge@hotmail.com

Conveniently located in Cody's central business
district, the Cody Motor Lodge caters to business
and leisure travelers alike. Spotlessly clean, modern, and comfortable facilities greet guests with
spacious rooms that include cable TV, air conditioning, direct dial phones, and all queen beds.
ample off-street parking, laundry facilities, interi-
or hallway access, and winter plug-ins round out
the amenities. Ideally located within easy walking
distance of restaurants, unique shops, central
downtown businesses, the Buffalo Bill Historical
Center, and the historic Irma Hotel, the Cody
Motor Lodge also provides quick access to whitewater rafting, scenic float trips, and Old West
gunfight reenactments. Cody Motor Lodge is dedicated to making your stay in Cody Country
memorable and enjoyable, and they welcome pets
and offer special off-season rates. Stay with them
today, and discover all that the area offers!

L Holiday Inn Buffalo Bill Village Resort

1701 Sheridan Ave., Cody. 587-5555 or
(800) 527-5544. www.blairhotels.com

Proudly serving as Cody's only downtown full-
service resort, the Holiday Inn at the Buffalo Bill
Village Resort is independently owned and operated by Blair Hotels. Boasting one suite and 188
rooms, 6 of which are ADA compliant, the
Holiday Inn also sports a fitness center, outdoor
heated pool, and the standard Holiday Inn special
Kids Eat Free, Kids Stay Free. As an added bonus,
guests receive a 10% discount in the General
Store Shopping Emporium. Also located at the
resort, the Comfort Inn features one suite and 74
rooms, two of which are ADA compliant.
Complimentary deluxe continental breakfast is
served every morning, and during summer,
breakfast is hosted in the Sarsaparilla Saloon. The
original Buffalo Bill (Cabin) Village is a bit of history not often found. The 83 individual cowboy
style cabins include full baths, cable remote TV,
air conditioning, and private parking while rang-

ing in size from those suitable for 1 to 2 people to family units with two bedrooms. All resort lodgings feature summer day tours to Yellowstone, and the village's renowned service draws leisure and business travelers back year after year!

Wyoming Tidbits

As many as 60 million buffalo once grazed on the great plains. "Buffalo Bill" Cody reportedly killed more than 4,000 in one year. By the end of 1883, herds were decimated by hunters and overgrazing.

Main Street in Trail Town. Cody, Wyoming.

Section 7

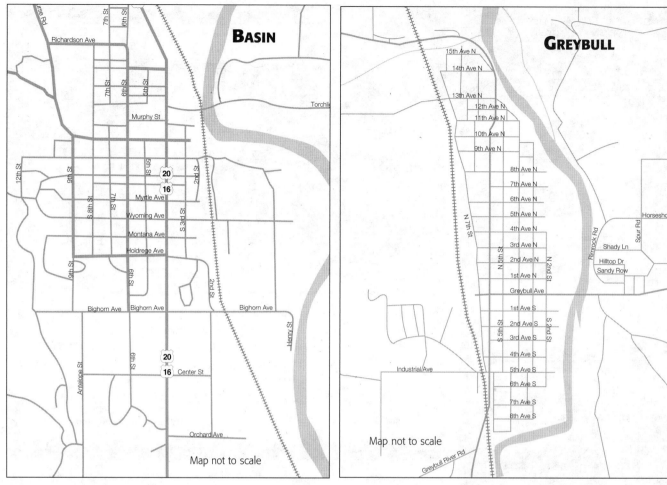

BASIN

7th St
6th St
Richardson Ave
rse Rd
7th St
6th St
5th St
Torchli
Murphy St
12th St
9th St
5th St
2nd St
20
16
S 8th St
7th St
Myrtle Ave
Wyoming Ave
S 3rd St
Montana Ave
Holdrege Ave
9th St
6th St
2nd St
Bighorn Ave
Bighorn Ave
Bighorn Ave
Henry St
Antelope St
6th St
20
16
Center St
Orchard Ave
Map not to scale

GREYBULL

15th Ave N
14th Ave N
13th Ave N
12th Ave N
11th Ave N
10th Ave N
9th Ave N
N 7th St
8th Ave N
7th Ave N
6th Ave N
5th Ave N
4th Ave N
3rd Ave N
N 5th St
2nd Ave N
N 2nd St
Rimrock Rd
Spur Rd
Horseshoe
Shady Ln
Hilltop Dr
Sandy Row
1st Ave N
Greybull Ave
1st Ave S
2nd Ave S
S 2nd St
S 5th St
3rd Ave S
4th Ave S
Industrial Ave
5th Ave S
6th Ave S
7th Ave S
8th Ave S
Map not to scale
Greybull River Rd

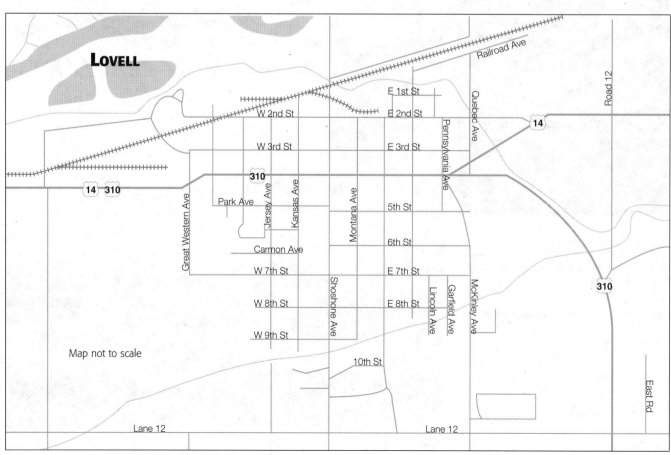

LOVELL

Railroad Ave
Road 12
E 1st St
Quebec Ave
W 2nd St
E 2nd St
14
W 3rd St
E 3rd St
Pennsylvania Ave
310
Jersey Ave
Kansas Ave
Park Ave
Great Western Ave
Montana Ave
5th St
Carmon Ave
6th St
14
310
W 7th St
E 7th St
Shoshone Ave
Lincoln Ave
Garfield Ave
McKinley Ave
310
W 8th St
E 8th St
W 9th St
Map not to scale
10th St
East Rd
Lane 12
Lane 12

MEETEETSE

Map not to scale

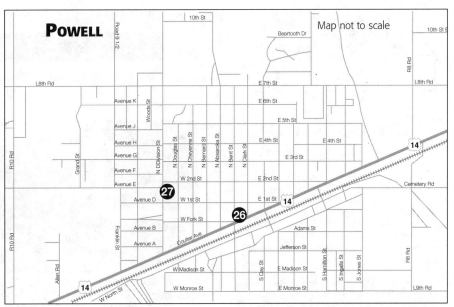

POWELL

Map not to scale

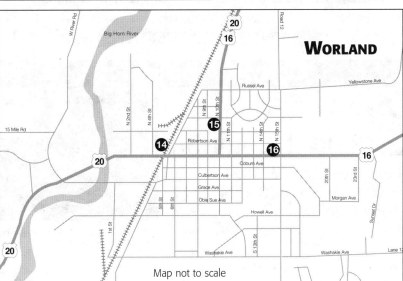

WORLAND

Map not to scale

Wyoming Tidbits

The Wapiti Ranger Station west of Cody is the first station established in the U.S.

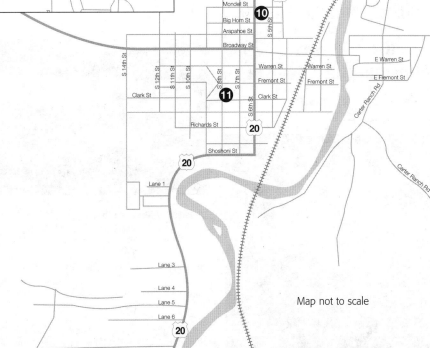

THERMOPOLIS

Map not to scale

LF Best Western Sunset Motor Inn & Sunset House Restaurant
1601 8th St., Cody. 587-4265 or (800) 624-2727. www.bestwestern.com/sunsetmotorinn

The Sunset Motor Inn specializes in offering comfort and convenient access to Cody Country attractions. Boasting 120 ground floor rooms with parking outside the door, the inn treats guests to standard and deluxe rooms, suites, non-smoking rooms, guest laundry, a hot tub, indoor/outdoor pools, and a playground. On-site, the Sunset House Family Restaurant offers a pleasant dining option. Accommodating 210 people, the reasonably priced restaurant specializes in freshly prepared meals, including seasonal daily breakfast and dinner buffets, healthy entrees, and selections tailored to those with small appetites. A complete wine and cocktail list is also available, and the large banquet room is ideal for special occasions and meetings. Promising prompt, friendly service, the Sunset Motor Inn and Sunset House Family Restaurant are your destination for AAA endorsed lodging and food in one convenient location!

Wyoming Tidbits

John Colter named the Stinking River due to the sulfur odor permeating the area. It was not until nearly a hundred years later the name was changed to Shoshone River.

THE OLD TRAIL TOWN CEMETERY

The Old Trail Town Cemetery might be one of the smallest cemeteries you'll ever see, but its inhabitants all carved their niche in Wyoming History. Here are the stories behind them.

Belle Drewry
1867-1897

Belle Drewry was born in 1867, just two years after the Civil War. Her birth place and family are unknown. It is known that she left home at an early age and changed her name. Belle was a rather attractive young woman; about five foot six inches tall, medium to heavy boned with auburn hair. No one knows how or why Belle showed up in Wyoming Territory in the 1880's. However, it is suspected that she drifted west from mining towns in the Black Hills. She seemed to be drawn to the dark side of life and felt comfortable with the lawless element. A news item in the "Sundance Gazette" stated that in 1888, Belle Drewry was arraigned in court, for theft, with a piano player who was known to be an outlaw with an unsavory reputation. She was 21 years old.

By 1890 Belle had arrived (probably by stage coach) at the frontier town of Arland, Wyoming. Arland was located about twenty-five miles south of present Cody, Wyoming and was the first settlement in northwest Wyoming. It was a lawless town with a reputation for unrestrained violence and murder. Belle Drewry worked in the saloon and dance hall. Here she got to know W.A. Gallagher, Blind Bill Hoolihan, Robert Parker (Butch Cassidy), Jack Bliss and other suspected members of a gang known as the "Woodriver Horse Thieves".

Belle soon developed a close relationship with W.A. Gallagher a well known cowboy and horse thief. In 1891 Gallagher was lodged in the Fremont County Jail where he was held on charges of stealing a bay mare from the L U Ranch on Gooseberry Creek. Belle Drewry and

Ed Lanigan put up $200.00 in bond money to get Gallagher out of jail.

Gallagher had the reputation of being a quarrelsome and vicious man. By the spring of 1894 Belle's relationship with Gallagher was deteriorating and she had developed a friendship with Bill Wheaton, another cowboy in the area. This resulted in a dispute in which Gallagher was shot and killed by Wheaton. Blind Bill, Gallagher's friend, attempted a show down with Wheaton to avenge Gallagher's death. However, Blind Bill was shot in the back and died in his cabin in Arland after writing a farewell letter to the undertaker. Belle Drewry and Bill Wheaton were charged with premeditated murder in the death of Gallagher, apprehended, and taken to the County Jail in Lander, Wyoming. However, the charges against Belle were dismissed at the preliminary hearing. Bill Wheaton's charge was later reduced to second degree manslaughter and was sentenced to eight years in the Wyoming Penitentiary at Laramie.

Belle continued her activities in the Arland-Meeteetse country and was well known. Early in 1897 Belle Drewry and three of her followers gave a party, one night. Everyone was drinking and the cowboys proceeded to shoot up the place. In the uproar that followed Belle pulled a six-shooter from a hiding place and shot the leader of the cowboy gang. A few days later, an unknown assassin came into the house and killed Belle Drewry, apparently in revenge, for their comrade's death.

Belle was given a respectable burial on the hill overlooking Arland. Thirty year old Belle Drewry was laid to rest in a red wood coffin, wearing a cobalt blue silk dress with a black sash. When Belle was disinterred for reburial at Old Trail Town, fired 45-70 and 45-60 cartridge cases were found in the ground around the coffin. It appears that a parting salute was fired, and the cartridge cases were dropped into the open grave.

One might imagine the boom of the rifles, the rolling echo across the hills and the black powder smoke drifting away with the wind like departing ghosts. Perhaps, a fitting farewell from a wild land.

Jack Stilwell
Frontiersman • 1850-1903

Simpson E. Stilwell, better known as "Comanche Jack", was born in Kansas in 1850 and served on the frontier during his youth as a scout and hunter. He is best known for his heroic deeds at the Battle of Beechers Island in September of 1868.

August 1868 were trying times in Kansas Territory as bands of marauding Sioux and Cheyenne were killing many settlers in what is now western Kansas and eastern Colorado.

It was well known that the regular troops had little effect against the hit-and-run tactics of the Indians.

On August 24, 1868 General Sheridan ordered Colonel G.A. Forsyth to enlist "50 first class hardy frontiersmen" and arm them with the new "Spencer Carbine", a repeating cartridge rifle that could fire nine shots without reloading. These guns were far superior to the single shot muzzle loading guns that had been in use for many years.

The ranks were soon filled, and among the volunteers was 18 year old Jack Stilwell, described as "a youth of six feet three or more, short of years but long on frontier lore."

Forsyth's contingent left Fort Hayes on August 29, 1868, and headed north-westward into the Indian country. On the morning of September 16, the scouts crossed the trail of a large band of Indians. That evening Forsyth's party camped along the north bank of the Arikaree Fork of the Republican River. Before dawn some young warriors tried to steal some of the scouts horses. Then, shortly after dawn, the entire horizon seemed filled with mounted and unmounted Indians. It is said that Jack Stilwell pointed to a small island in the river and the officers and scouts made a mad dash for it. Almost immediately, approximately six hundred Cheyenne and Sioux warriors began their charge down the slope toward the island. The scouts killed their horses for breastworks and dug into the sand behind them. Then, like a cyclone, the massive screaming force hit the island. When the first warriors were within twenty-five yards of the scouts, they opened fire with the new repeating guns. Horses and men fell in the first volley, many of which rolled over the defenders of the island. Colonel Forsyth's leg was shattered by a bullet, Lt. Beecher and Surgeon Moore were fatally wounded while others received lesser wounds.

The warriors, surprised by the rapid fire of the new guns, changed their tactics. They began riding in and swerving off as they fired, while others sniped at the defenders from hidden positions. After the first day of fighting Forsyth realized that without food and medical supplies their situation was hopeless. That night Jack Stilwell and Pierre Trudeau volunteered to try to sneak through the Indians and bring help from Fort Wallace, 125 miles away. Everyone feared that they would not make it. But after several close calls and a great deal of hardship, they did make it. On the 25th Jack Stilwell arrived with the 10th Cavalry and saved the survivors on the island.

After the Beecher Island battle, Stilwell remained a scout for the army for a length of time. Later in life he became a deputy United States Marshal in Oklahoma Territory, where he killed and captured several outlaws. Later he became the Police Judge at El Reno, Oklahoma and in the mid 1890s became a government cattle inspector for the Comanche Agency at Anadarko, Oklahoma. After that, Sttlwell became a United States Commissioner and the Master of the Masonic Lodge at Erwin Springs, Oklahoma.

Through the influence of his friend Buffalo Bill Cody, he came to Cody, Wyoming in 1897

where he took care of Cody's interests while he was away with the Wild West Show. Jack Stilwell had a small ranch on the South Fork of the Shoshone River, near Cody, Wyoming and died, from a sudden illness, in Cody in 1903.

John Jeremiah "Liver Eating" Johnston
1824-1900
Reburied at Old Trail Town June 8, 1974

John Johnston was born of Scotch-English descent in New Jersey in 1824. Johnston, described as a 6'6", 250 pound giant, came west in the early 1840's as a trapper. He began his career in the Medicine Bow mountains of Wyoming, gradually working his way northward through the Wind River, Owl Creek, and Absaroka Mountains, then into the Yellowstone Region and Montana.

About 1850 Johnston had acquired a Flathead Indian wife, of whom he was very fond, and had built a cabin on the Little Snake River in Wyoming. One day, on returning from trapping, he found his wife and unborn child dead and mutilated on the cabin floor. They had been killed by Crow Indians.

This started a personal revenge war against the Crows, which lasted nearly twelve years. According to legend, Johnston would on occasion remove the liver from a dead enemy and take a bite of it, or pretend to, in order to make a fierce impression on his savage foes. Consequently, he received the name "Liver Eating" Johnston.

Johnston went to Colorado in 1862 and enlisted in the Second Colorado Cavalry to fight in the Civil War. He was wounded in Missouri at the Battle of Newtonia, but remained in the service until his Honorable Discharge on September 23, 1865.

The winter after the war was spent in Fort Laramie, Wyoming, where he was hired to help supply buffalo and elk meat for the Army post. Johnston worked his way north to the Missouri River in Montana where he started a wood yard, supplying firewood for the steamboats that were traveling the river in those days.

In 1868, at the mouth of the Musselshell River, Johnston and some companions defeated a Sioux war party that intended to wipe out the group of trappers and wood cutters.

In 1877 Johnston became Chief of Scouts for General Nelson A. Miles. Johnston and ten scouts were credited with saving Miles command in a battle with the Cheyennes on Muddy Creek in 1877.

Johnston became the first Marshall at Coulson (Billings) Montana in 1882, and later in 1888, the first Sheriff of Red Lodge, Montana.

In old age he developed rheumatism, and in the late 1890's would treat his ailment at the DeMaris Hot Springs, near the river just below the site of Old Trail Town. His camping spot was just beneath the cliffs that can be seen from the grave site.

In the winter of 1899 Johnston's health failed him and he was sent to the old soldiers home in Santa Monica, California, where he died January 21, 1900.

"Liver Eating" Johnston, also known as

Jeremiah Johnston from the Warner Bros. movie based on his life, was reburied near the mountains he loved on June 8, 1974.

The reburial was made possible through the efforts of Tri Robinson, and his seventh grade class of Lancaster, California.

The bronze statue of Johnston was sculpted by Peter Fillerup of Cody, Wyoming and donated by Larry Clark of Salt Lake City, Utah.

Jim White
Buffalo Hunter • 1828-1880
Reburied May 6, 1979

Jim White was born in Missouri in 1828. He found his way into the southwest as a young man, where he was a freighter with ox-drawn wagons.

When the Civil War broke out in 1861, Jim White served the Confederate Army as a grain buyer and wagon boss. At the end of the Civil War, Jim White married and returned to the southwest.

In 1868 he drifted down into Mexico, where a rich Spaniard won his wife away. White killed him and wounded several others in the fracas that followed.

There was a large reward offered for him, dead or alive. This was when he dropped his original name and adopted the name Jim White, for which he is known. His original name is unknown.

White walked 700 miles back into Texas where he got into the buffalo hunting profession. White kept several skinners busy as he preyed on the wandering herds.

One day a group of ciboleros rode over a hill and scared away a small herd of buffalo that White was firing on. In a fit of temper, he shot the horses out from under four of the party.

Jim White was hunting in the Texas Panhandle during the mid 1870s. He was in the region at the time of the Battle of Adobe Walls and other lesser battles with the Kiowas and Commanches.

White had the reputation in Texas for being a tough character. He operated best alone or with his own men.

By 1878 the buffalo on the Southern Plains were gone. Many hunters started looking toward the unspoiled Northern Plains of Wyoming and Montana.

Jim White was among the first hunters to reach the northern buffalo range. By late summer,1878, he had reached the Big Horn Mountains with two big span of mules. two wagons, 700 pounds of lead, five kegs of gunpowder, three 16 pound Sharp's rifles, varied equipment, and an old buffalo skinner named Watson.

White soon met Oliver Hanna, who had been a scout with General Crook in 1876. and they became hunting partners.

During the winter of 1878-79 the two men had a contract to furnish 5,000 pounds of game meat to the Army at Fort McKinney, near present Buffalo, Wyoming.

The following winter of 1879-80, White and Hanna had a buffalo hunting camp north of the Yellowstone River near Miles City. The two hunters kept six buffalo skinners busy. By spring, they had collected 4,600 buffalo hides which were freighted to the Yellowstone River by ox teams and then hauled down the river by steam boats.

In the following fall of 1880, White and Hanna came into the Big Horn Basin and set up a hunting camp on Shell Creek, near the foot of the Big Horn Mountains. They were hunting and trapping in the area. In late October, Hanna made a quick trip over the Big Horns. When he returned he found Jim White dead. He had been shot in the head by thieves who had stolen their horses, mules. wagons, guns, hides, furs, etc.

Hanna buried Jim White on the upper bank, on the north side of Shell Creek, presently on the ranch of Irvy Davis near Shell, Wyoming.

Hanna later stated that Jim White was the

greatest buffalo hunter the world has ever known. Hanna stated that White had a ledger book that contained records of hide sales for over 16,000 buffalo.

Jim White, who had lived by the gun, now, also died by the gun.

Recent examination of his remains revealed that he was killed by a 50 caliber bullet; probably from a Sharp's buffalo rifle. Possibly from the same gun that killed his own victims.

The bronze statue of White was sculpted and donated by Tom Hillis of Stanton Michigan.

W. A. Gallagher and Blind Bill—Murdered
1894
Reburied December 17, 1978

William Gallagher and his friend, Blind Bill, were killed on Meeteetse Creek below the old town of Arland in mid-March of 1894. Both men, about thirty, were born during the Civil War period.

Gallagher, who was somewhat of an outlaw, was tall, lean and wore a drooping dark mustache. He wore a gun most of the time, had a severe temper, and was a hard case in general.

Blind Bill was short, muscular, and wore a patch over his left eye, which was blind. Blind Bill was a good friend of Gallagher's. Both men were working as cowboys in the Greybull River Country, and had probably found their way into the region on one of the early trail drives.

Gallagher was once described by A. A. Anderson, for whom he had once worked, as being one of the best horse-men and ropers he had ever known. However, his reputation was not as good as his figure. Gallagher told Anderson, one time after getting out of jail in Thermopolis, that; "I captured the town and was about to trade it off to the Indians when they threw me in jail." On another occasion,

Gallagher was accused of horse stealing and tried at the district court in Lander, Wyoming in 1891. Later in that year he was tried for forgery. He escaped being jailed each time, due to technicalities.

In 1893, Gallagher had become involved with 27 year old Belle Drewery, one of the single women that hung out around the town of Arland. Early in 1894 Belle began seeing Bill Wheaton. When Gallagher became aware of the friendship, he went into a jealous rage. On March 15th Gallagher took Belle over to the ranch house where Wheaton was. An argument developed and Gallagher pulled his six-shooter and held Wheaton and Belle at gun-point for two hours, while he threatened them and kept cocking his six-shooter. Finally, Gallagher passed the incident off as kind of a joke and holstered his gun.

Belle informed Wheaton as to where a gun was hidden in the house. A little later she went out of the house and started walking toward Meeteetse.

When she didn't return, Gallagher went out to see where she went. Wheaton then got the gun that was in the house. Gallagher was walking across the yard when Wheaton rested the gun against the side of the door frame and shot him from behind. Wheaton then got on his horse and left.

When Blind Bill learned of Gallagher's death, he was very upset and swore he would kill Wheaton in revenge for the death of his friend.

Wheaton was soon informed that Blind Bill intended to kill him. Gallagher's loyal friend never fulfilled his vow, for he was found a few days later, shot in the back by an unknown assassin. Although it was believed that Wheaton killed Blind Bill, it was never proven.

Both Gallagher and his friend, Blind Bill, were buried on a sage brush hill near Meeteetse Creek.

Wheaton was tried in the death of W. A. Gallagher and sentenced to eight years in the Wyoming State Penitentiary. He was released in 1898 after serving four years. Belle Drewery had been killed the year before in a gun-fight at a saloon in Arland.

Phillip H. Vetter
1855-1892
Reburied June 10, 1978

Phillip Henry Vetter was born February 7, 1855 near Woodstock, Shenandoah County, Virginia. He was killed by a grizzly bear on the Greybull River in Wyoming in 1892.

A few years after the Civil War, Phillip's family came West by wagon train and settled in the Wind River Country near Lander, Wyoming Territory.

Through the 1880's, Phillip Vetter pursued the occupation of market hunter and trapper. About 1890 he moved over to the Greybull River above Meeteetse, Wyoming. Here he built a log cabin and continued his hunting and trapping.

On September 1, 1892, Vetter left a note at his cabin which said, "Jake, if you come to get your horses, I'm going down to the river after some bear."

A week or so later John Corbett, an old buffalo hunter, was riding over to John Gleavers on Wood River. When he was near Vetter's

cabin, black clouds threatened a heavy rain. Corbett decided to wait out the storm in shelter with Vetter.

He rode up to the cabin. The door stood open. Inside, Corbett found Vetter's body on the floor. Dishes from Vetter's last meal stood un-washed on the dusty table. The storm was forgotten. Corbett jumped on his horse and raced to the Gleaver ranch.

The two men returned and sought to piece the story together. They found Vetter's neatly written note to Jake. In contrast, scribbled on the edge of a newspaper in Vetter's handwriting, in what they believed was his own blood, were several terse messages. The first said something about a battle with a grizzly bear. A later notation said, "Should go to Franc's but too weak." Vetter's handwriting grew shakier. "It's getting dark. I'm smothering." The final message read, "I'm dying."

One of Vetter's arms had been badly mangled and his chest was crushed. He had tried unsuccessfully to stop the flow of blood.

The men walked down to the river to look for more clues. Near the stream the men found a water bucket and Vetter's hat, and not far away was his rifle. A shell had jammed in the chamber. On the ground lay two empty casings.

The wounded bear had mauled him severely before leaving him for dead. Vetter was able to drag himself back to his cabin where he wrote his death message in his own blood. Thirty-seven year old Phillip Vetter died alone, far from help.

Corbett and Gleaver built a casket of rough boards with timbers hewn from logs for a lid. Vetter was buried on upper river bank, near his cabin. A slab of sandstone with the inscription "P. H. Vetter — 1892" was placed at the grave.

S Simpson Gallagher Gallery
1161 Sheridan Ave., Cody. 587-4022.
www.simpsongallaghergallery.com;
chuck@simpsongallaghergallery.com

Discover outdoor landscapes, wildlife sculpture, and western intaglios in downtown Cody at the Simpson Gallagher Gallery. A fine art gallery featuring some of america's leading representational artists, the Simpson Gallagher Gallery welcomes art collectors and those who are simply interested in art to visit their inviting gallery. Showcased with exceptional lighting, the gallery's represented mediums include oil, bronze, etching, pastel, and watercolor. Many of the country's most celebrated artists are found here, including works by Clyde Aspevig, T. Allen Lawson, Leon Loughridge, Grant Redden, Skip Whitcomb, Geoff Parker, Matt Smith and dozens more. Explore the beauty of the west through the eyes of talented artists, and stop by Simpson Gallagher Gallery on your next visit to Yellowstone Country! Special artist receptions are periodically held, and samples of the gallery's works are available online.

S Traces of Light
1280 Sheridan Ave., Cody. 527-6912.
www.tracesoflight.com; tracesoflight@aol.com

You can bring the wild beauty of the great outdoors into your home and office by visiting Traces of Light fine art nature photography gallery in Cody, Wyoming. Leslie Slater-Wilson and Jimmy B. Wilson, photographers and gallery owners, invite you to pay a visit and see images that will make you feel as if you are in the middle of Mother Nature's wonderland. Their collection includes wildlife and beautiful landscape scenes from Alaska, the west, the southwest, and the southeast. The images will certainly inspire you to go outside and enjoy all that nature has to offer. Traces of Light is located one-half block east of Buffalo Bill's Irma Hotel in downtown Cody. Stop by and see them. You will be glad you made the visit!

S H & B Trading Post
1291 Sheridan Ave., Cody. 527-8903.
www.hbtradingpost.com; barbarahoy@msn.com

Originating in Washington and Oregon 15 years ago, the family-owned H & B Trading Post found its Cody home in 2003. Drawing upon relationships with talented individuals from several tribes, the H & B Trading Post proudly offers an extensive collection of american Indian Art. Unique and limited edition items include jewelry, dreamcatchers, medicine wheels, dolls, baskets, pipes, pottery, books, flutes, lamps, wall hanging masks, paintings, statues, bow and arrows, fishing spears constructed from antlers, stone knifes, stone and jaw bone tomahawks, and more! Invoking relaxation, the store offers Native american music CDs, and occasionally, live performances from such talented musicians as Charles Littleleaf and Jan Michael Looking Wolf Reiback are scheduled. Discover a new respect for Native american culture at the H & B Trading Post in downtown Cody or online!

M Sommers & Voerding, Real Estate Brokerage
1025 12th St., Cody. 587-4959.
www.realestatecodywyoming.com;
jkendrick@vcn.com

Backed by 100 years of combined real estate experience and a reputation for professionalism, integrity, and discrete service, Sommers & Voerding Real Estate Brokerage® is your northwestern Wyoming real estate source. Established in 1988, Sommers & Voerding remains the only Park County brokerage where all realtors are brokers and equal company owners. Each of the five full-time brokers is a dedicated professional committed to serving both buyers and sellers. Explore cozy residential listings, river front properties, guest lodges, and more with a knowledgeable agent that strives for success. Specializing in farm, ranch, and recreational properties, Sommers & Voerding also offers vacant land, 1031 exchanges, commercial properties, and investment listings. Whether you're buying or selling, count on Sommers & Voerding's long-standing reputation for excellence, client satisfaction, and a high degree of property exposure and selection!

M Parker Realty
P.O. Box 251, Cody. 587-9898.
www.parkerrealtywyoming.com; prkrlty@trib.com

Boasting twenty years of experience and current regional market knowledge, Parker Realty is your source for northwest Wyoming property. Broker/Owner, Stan Parker, is a Park County Board of Realtors® member and belongs to the area's Multiple Listing Service (MLS). Although any MLS member can show you properties, very few possess experience and the knowledge to help you successfully make one of life's most important purchases. Offering residential, high end properties, land, rural residential, and commercial listings, representing nearly every property type and is pleased to help buyers and sellers throughout the beautiful Big Horn Basin. Whether it is a property he lists or not, he is dedicated to fulfilling your real estate needs. For experience you can count on, trust Parker Realty!

M Prudential Brokerage West, Inc. Real Estate
1432 Sheridan Ave., Cody. 587-6234 or
(877) 443-6234. www.codyliving.com;
office@codyliving.com

The leader in Cody's real estate industry since 1977, Brokerage West, Inc. is an independently owned and operated member of the Prudential Real Estate network. Specializing in residential, commercial, and recreational real estate, the brokerage's local experience is backed with a name that is recognized by 98% of consumers. Highly educated associates possess over 150 years of combined real estate experience, and 85% of the brokerage's associates have furthered their real estate commitment by either becoming associate brokers or by attaining specialized designations. Committed to customer service, Brokerage West's full-time professionals are sensitive to both buyers' and sellers' needs. They strive to make every real estate transaction so easy that clients won't hesitate to call them again. Experience Prudential Brokerage West, Inc. Real Estate, and let them help you create your own vision of the West!

M AAA Real Estate Source
Cody (587-3273) and Powell (754-2119).
www.AAAresource.com or email: homepro@tritel.net

If you've tried to sell your home yourself, you know that the minutes you put up the "For Sale by Owner" sign, the phone will start to ring off the hook. What do you do next? You may have owned a home before and are presently renting or maybe you are a first-time buyer and need a way to break into the housing market but are holding back because you don't have a down payment. What do you do? Bank foreclosures? Fixer uppers? No money down properties? Selling your home yourself? If you need answers on any of these subjects AAA Real Estate Source is your

3 Gas, Food, Lodging

H Alkali Lake
Southeast of Cody at junction of U.S. Highways 14 and 120

Over 40 species of water-dependent birds are observed here throughout the year, including various ducks, geese and shorebirds. During the summer, a few ducks and Canada geese will nest and raise their young along the lake's limited shoreline habitat. Ducks like mallards, teal, widgeon, shoveler, gadwall and redheads are most often seen during spring and fall migration.Shorebirds are also common in the summertime and often walk this same shoreline in search of food. Explore the area, and you may see an avocet, black-necked stilt, killdeer, lesser yellowlegs or Wilson's phalarope. Viewing opportunities are usually best here during migration.

Alkali Lake gets its name from the extremely high concentration of soluble alkali metals, especially sodium. The lake's water falls as precipitation, seeps in as groundwater and flows in as surface runoff in the spring or after a rain. As the water level drops from evaporation, the alkalinity increases. Fish cannot survive in this water, however small invertebrates such as fairy shimp thrive here. During migration, waterbirds need places like Alkali Lake to rest and refuel before continuing on their journey. Fairy shimp, salt tolerant vegetaion and the agricultural land in and around Cody, provide the necessary food sources for these birds.

From the tiny solitary sandpiper to the rare and regal trumpeter swan, Alkali Lake is an important oasis and refuge.

4

T Cody Stampede
U.S. Highway 14/16, on the West Cody Strip.
587-2234. www.codystampederodeo.org

"Cody is Rodeo" is the slogan for the Rodeo Capital of the World. The Stampede Board works hard to put on the best rodeo for the cowboys and the spectators. 2003 marks the 84th anniversary of the Buffalo Bill Cody Stampede. The Stampede Board has won the "1998 & 1999 Large Outdoor Rodeo Committee of the Year" award and was nominated in 2000 and again in 2002. The local committee, the Stock Contractors and the community work very hard to please the contestants and see that the audience gets the best show they can for the money. Adding the announcer, clowns, pickup men and specialty acts, it is a good time had by all. Since 1937 the Cody Nite Rodeo has carried on the tradition of showing the world the Wild West every night from June 1st thru August 31st.

T Old Trail Town
On west edge of Cody next to Cody Stampede grounds

On this site in 1895, Western scout and showman William F. ("Buffalo Bill") Cody laid out the original townsite of Cody, Wyoming, which was named in his honor. Today Old Trail Town preserves the lifestyle and history of the Frontier West through a rare collection of authentic structures and furnishings. From remote locations in Wyoming and Montana, these historic buildings were carefully disassembled, moved and reassembled here at Old Trail Town by Western historian Bob Edgar and friends.

Located here also are thousands of historic artifacts from the Old West, and gravesites of several notable Western figujres. Among them is the grave of mountain man John Johnson, who was portrayed by the actor Robert Redford in the 1972 motion picture "Jeremiah Johnson."

Here too are original cabins used by Old West outlaws Butch Cassidy and the Sundance Kid, and a Wyoming saloon frequented by Cassidy's "Hole-in-the-Wall Gang." Also on this site is the log cabin home of "Curley"—a Crow indian army scout who helped guide Lt. Col. George A. Custer and the U.S. 7th Cavalry to the battle of the Little Big Horn in 1876. Old Trail Town exists today as a memorial to the uniquely American experience known throughout the world as "the Old West."

Trail Town Information Signs
The Arland Cabin

Residential cabin built at the Arland and Corbett Trading Post on Cottonwood Creek, north of present Cody, WY, in 1883, WY Territory. The post was a trading center for hunters, trappers and Indians.

Blacksmith Shop (5004)

This building was built in lower Sunshine Basin, west of Meeteetse, WY, around 1900.

Buffalo Hunter's Cabin

Cabin built on Shell Creek at the hunting camp of Jim White and Oliver Hanna in 1880. Jim White was murdered at the camp in late October, 1880. The cabin was later used by Al Kershner when he homesteaded the property in 1889.

The Burlington Store

This building was built on the Greybull River, near Burlington, WY about 1897. It was moved to Burlington where it was used as a store for several years.

Bonanza Post Office

This building was built at Bonanza, Wyoming Territory, in 1885. This was one of the first settlements in the Big Horn Basin.

Carpenter Shop

One of the first buildings of Cowley, WY. It was built in 1901 and used by George Taggart. A Mormon pioneer that came to the Big Horn Basin by wagon train in 1900.

Carter Cabin

This cabin was built by William Carter's men on Carter MT about 1879, Wyoming Territory. Carter brought the first cattle into the region around Cody.

The Coffin School

This cabin was built at the W Ranch on Wood River, west of Meeteetse, in 1884. It was used as a school for several years. It derives its name from the tragic death of Alfred Nower, who died of gangrene in this cabin in 1885. He had chopped himself in the leg while hewing logs.

Commissary

This building was built on the W. B. Rice Ranch on Wood River about 1898. It was used as a bunkhouse and commissary.

Curly's Cabin

Log cabin home of Custer's Crow Indian scout, Curly. Curly escaped from the "Battle of the Little Bighorn" on June 25, 1876 and brought the news of Custer's defeat. The cabin was built near Crow Agency, Montana about 1885.

Hole in the Wall Cabin

Through this door walked Butch Cassidy, The Sundance Kid, and other outlaws of the famous "Hole in the Wall" Gang. The cabin was built on Buffalo Creek, in the Hole in the Wall Country, west of Kaycee, WY, Wyoming Territory, in 1883 by Alexander Ghent.

Homestead Cabin (5018)

This cabin was built on Wood River, west of Meeteetse, about 1899. It is a fine example of log craftmenship.

Homestead Cabin (5044)

Cabin built by homesteaders on Monument Hill, north of Cody, about 1900.

WILLIAM F. "BUFFALO BILL" CODY

William F. Cody was born on February 26, 1846 near LeClair, Iowa. In 1854 his family moved to settle on lands in what would soon be Kansas Territory. Young William's father died in 1857, leaving the boy to help provide for his family.

William soon obtained a job as a messenger boy for Majors and Russell, who had a company store at Leavenworth, Kansas. In the next three years, William would try his hand at prospecting during the Pikes Peak gold rush, and at trapping. Neither ventures proved to be very successful.

In 1860, the partnership of Russell, Majors, and Waddell, in an effort to advertise and obtain a contract for a central route for mail to the Pacific, began the Pony Express. Cody, already acquainted with the principals in this partnership, was hired as a rider. The Pony Express operated from April 3, 1860 to November 18, 1861. The venture operated at a loss and failed to bring the desired contract to Cody's employers, whose partnership ended in bankruptcy.

Cody's mother died November 22, 1863. Shortly thereafter, in February, 1864, he enlisted in the 7th Kansas Cavalry, some say influenced by friends and alcohol. During the Civil War Cody saw action in Tennessee, Mississippi, and Missouri. He served 19 months, including one year of active duty.

After his discharge, Cody married Louisa Frederici on March 6, 1866. He worked briefly as a scout at Fort Ellsworth, where an old acquaintance, James Butler "Wild Bill" Hickok, was also employed. The following year Cody was hired by the Kansas Pacific Railroad to kill buffalo to feed track layers for eight months. This job apparently was the source of the nickname that would become known virtually worldwide: Buffalo Bill.

Later Cody distinguished himself as a scout for the U.S. Army. He was valued so highly that General Phil Sheridan endeavored to keep Cody on the Army's payroll even after the end of their campaign, something not done with scouts up to that time. This paved the way for the scout to become an established position in the Army during the years of the Indian wars. Cody was made chief scout of the 5th Cavalry by General Sheridan in October, 1868.

Cody first began to receive national attention in 1869, when a serial story about "Buffalo Bill" appeared in a New York paper. Then in 1872 he was assigned to guide the Grand Duke Alexis of Russia on a hunting trip. With the press following the Duke's every move, Cody received a great deal more exposure. This experience was followed by his first trip to the eastern states. He attended a play about himself and was talked into taking part in the performance. Thus began a period of years when Cody alternated between scouting duties and theatrical tours. Cody was awarded the Medal of Honor in 1872 for action against Indians at the South Fork of the Loup River in Nebraska. However, his name was stricken from the record of Medal of Honor recipients in 1916, since he was a civilian, and considered not eligible for the award. He later assisted General George Crook's campaign against the Sioux in 1876.

"Buffalo Bill's Wild West Show" had its beginnings in 1883. This was a propitious time for such an effort by Cody and his partners, during the height of popularity for outdoor shows such as circuses. The show in various forms would tour the United States and Europe for three decades.

Buffalo Bill was also commonly referred to as "Colonel Cody", rank was provided by Nebraska Governor John Thayer (former governor of Wyoming Territory) in 1887, when he was named aide-de-camp of the Governor's staff. He was never an officer in the U.S. Army.

Cody became interested in developing the Big Horn Basin in Wyoming in the 1890s. The Cody Canal was built in 1895, as part of the Shoshone Land and Irrigation Project. The company laid out a townsite, first calling it "Shoshone." With the Shoshoni Indian agency in the region this was rejected to avoid confusion. Therefore, in August, 1896 the Cody post office was established, with Buffalo Bill's nephew, Ed Goodman, as postmaster.

The water project led to the building of the Shoshone Dam, which was completed in 1910. The dam was renamed "Buffalo Bill Dam" in 1946. Buffalo Bill was also instrumental in bringing a rail line to the town of Cody in 1901.

William F. Cody died January 10, 1917 while staying in Denver, Colorado. He is buried on Lookout Mountain, west of Denver. Information in this article was drawn from, The Lives and Legends of Buffalo Bill by Don Russell, University of Oklahoma Press, 1960.

Courtesy of Wyoming State Archives

The Rivers Saloon

This saloon was built in 1888 at the mouth of Wood River, west of Meeteetse, WY, by Henry Rivers. It was frequented by Butch Cassidy, W. A. Gallagher, Blind Bill Hoolihan and many other outlaws, cowboys, and colorful characters of the Old West. Bullet holes can be seen in the door.

The Shell Store

This was the first store in Shell, WY. It was built in 1892.

Trapper's Cabin

Cabin built on Cottonwood Creek, south of Meeteetse, about 1885.

T Wyoming Territory Old West Miniature Village and Museum

140 W. Yellowstone Ave. in Cody. 587-5362

This collection is the work of Jerry Fick, who has made a lifetime of assembling miniature figures and buildings into scenes depicting the Old West. His portrayals are historically accurate, though not always to scale, and feature such events as the Battle of the Little Big Horn, Buffalo Bill's Wild West Show, and the Green River Rendezvous. There are also Native American villages, wagon trains, forts, and railroad stations. A working train which travels through the other scenes operates with the push of a button. There are also a host of genuine Western artifacts on display here, including Geronimo's bow and arrows.

H Old Trail Town—Museum of the Old West

1831 Demaris in Cody. 587-5302

Old Trail Town is a collection of Frontier buildings and historical relics from northwest Wyoming. It is on the edge of the original townsite of Cody City.

In the cemetery, at the far end of the street is the grave of Liver Eating Johnston, better known as Jeremiah Johnson from the movie.

Old Trail Town is the largest collection of it's kind in Wyoming. Open Mid May through Mid September from 8 a.m. to 8 p.m.

The minimal admission fee is necessary for the maintenance and development of the Old Trail Town Project.

H Colter's Hell

U.S. Highway 14/16/20 on west edge of Cody.

John Colter, veteran of the Lewis and Clark Expedition, notably self-sufficient mountain man and indefatigable explorer, was the first white man known to have reconnoitered this locale. In 1807, possibly traveling alone but probably escorted by Crow guides, he crossed the Stinking Water (Shoshone River) via a major Indian trail ford located about a mile downstream from this observation point. here, extending along both sides of the river, he dis-

Hole in the Wall Cabin

Homestead Cabin (5010)

Cabin built at the head of Dry Creek, between Cody and Meeteetse around 1900.

Livery Stable

This building was built near the Clarks Fork Canyon, north of Cody in the late 1890s.

Mayor's Cabin

Home of Frank Houx, the first mayor of Cody, WY. It was built about 1897.

Morrison Cabin

Cabin built at the foot of Copper Mountain, east of Shoshoni Wyoming, in 1884, by Luther Morrison. The Morrisons brought some of the first sheep into central Wyoming in 1882. Morrison had originally come west on the Oregon Trail in 1853.

covered an active geyser district. Steam mixed with sulfur fumes and shooting flames escaped through vents in the valley floor, subterranean rumblings were ominously audible. Although mineralized hot springs continued to flow along the river's edge, the eruptions colter watched are now marked only by cones of parched stone.

This was primarily Shoshone and Crow country but other Indians came to the area. Particularly Bannocks and Nez Perce, journeying eastward over the mountains to hunt the plains buffalo, tarried to test the heralded medicinal values of these "stinking waters" baths. Ranged along bench-lands to the east and north are numerous tepee rings, evidence of former Indian encampments. Heart Mountain, famous landmark and geological oddity, is conspicuous on the northern horizon.

Honoring a respected predecessor, mountain men of the 1820s-1830s fur trade heyday named this place Colter's Hell. later, early-day officials of Yellowstone Park applied that name to the park's geyser area—thereby causing a degree of historic confusion. The true Colter's Hell is here in view.

H Primitive Necropolis
North from Cody on State Highway 120 then west on County Road

The following pioneers were buried here, but not much of a record as to which grave was used and little information regarding the pioneers is available. We are indebted to Charles Hartung, a pioneer cowboy for what we do have. 1882—Tom Heffner, cowboy for Henry Lovel, gassed at springs. 1882—Johnnie Lincoln, murdered at the Trail Creek Ranch. Paul Bretache's baby was buried here. The wife and baby of Pete (Black Pete) Enzon, buried in separate graves. An unknown man walked over the cliff at the springs in the dark. 1900—Clarence Veonor Edick, died of internal injuries when crossing to the springs. An unknown invalid from the Red Lodge area died at the springs. 1903—Mrs. Wm. Brown of Bellfrey gassed in hot spring. Louis Wilde from the Greybull Valley died at the springs. His stock was branded with a cotton hook.

H Shoshone Canyon
Entrance to Shoshone Canyon west of Cody on U.S. Highway 14/16/20

Shoshone Canyon is a gorge cut across Rattlesnake Mountain by the wearing action of the Shoshone River over a long period of time. The mountain is an upfold in the earth's crust. Beds of sedimentary rock on the east flank slope eastward beneath the plains. The same units bend up and over the crest of the mountain and stand vertical along the west flank. Granite over two billion years old, is exposed around Buffalo Bill Dam. South of the dam is a vertical fracture, or fault, in the rocks along which the mountain was uplifted over 2,000 feet.

H The American Mountain Man
Historic Trail Town on west side of Cody

Dedicated to all Mountain Men known and unknown for their essential part in the opening of the American West. We gratefully acknowledge the way their uniue lifestyle has profoundly influenced our own. Erected by the Brotherhood of the American Mountain Men.

SHOSHONE NATIONAL FOREST

The Shoshone National Forest was set aside in 1891 as part of the Yellowstone Timberland Reserve, making the Shoshone the first national forest in the United States. It consists of some 2.4 million acres of varied terrain ranging from sagebrush flats to rugged mountains. The higher mountains are snow-clad most of the year. Immense areas of exposed rock are interspersed with meadows and forests. With Yellowstone National Park on its western border, the Shoshone encompasses the area from the Montana state line south to Lander, Wyoming which includes portions of the Absaroka, Wind River and Beartooth Ranges.

Brief History...
The Shoshone National Forest was set aside by proclamation of President Benjamin Harrison as the Yellowstone Park Timberland Reserve on March 30, 1891. It was the first unit of its kind created after the passage of the Act of March 3, 1891, authorizing the establishment of forest reserves—as national forests were then called—to protect the remaining timber on the public domain from destruction and to insure a regular flow of water in the streams.

The Shoshone's historic and cultural links to the past are rich and diverse. An excavation of Mummy's Cave on the North Fork of the Shoshone River revealed artifacts of the "Sheepeater" Indians dating back 7,500 years. The Arapahoe, Blackfeet, Commanche, Crow, Nez Perce, Northern Cheyenne, Shoshone and Sioux tribes lived, hunted, traveled, traded and fought in the area. In 1877 the great Nez Perce leader Chief Joseph led his people through the thousand-foot-deep Clarks Fork Canyon, successfully evading the U.S. Army in his running battle to reach Canada. Such mountain men as John Colter and Jim Bridger were early visitors.

The ghost town of Kirwin, an early-day mining town, is a window to the past, recalling one of the colorful eras in Wyoming's history. The remains of tie hack flumes and cabins on the southern end of the forest are reminders of another era during which millions of railroad ties were produced.

The historic Wapiti Ranger Station in the North Fork Valley was the first ranger station built with government funds. Anderson Lodge, on the Greybull District, served as a home and workplace for A. A. Anderson, the first forest supervisor, and is listed as a National Historic Site.

Buffalo Bill was impressed with both the beauty and the hunting offered by the area. He built a hunting lodge on the forest called Pahaska Tepee and entertained numerous well known people including the Prince of Monaco. Teddy Roosevelt was equally impressed with the beauty of the area during several hunting forays.

Forest Facts...
The Shoshone consists of 2.4 million acres of varied terrain ranging from sagebrush flats to rugged mountain peaks and includes portions of the Absaroka, Wind River, and Beartooth Mountain Ranges. Elevations on the Shoshone range from 4,600 feet at the mouth of the spectacular Clarks Fork Canyon to 13,804 feet on Gannett Peak, Wyoming's highest point. Geologists delightedly call the Shoshone's varied topography an "open book." Formed under tremendous heat and pressure within the earth's interior were the granite monoliths of the Beartooth and Wind River Ranges. Born of the bubbling, spewing lava of prehistoric volcanoes was the Absaroka Range. Over aeons, wind and water have exposed strata and sculpted the rock into fascinating shapes to delight the visitor's eye. The Shoshone is unique in the Rocky Mountains for having so many glaciers and so many different kinds, four. There are 16 named glaciers and at least 140 unnamed ones. Fifty-three of them are over 11.4 square miles, which ranks Wyoming behind only Alaska and Washington in total glacier area.

The Shoshone National Forest is more than half (nearly 1.4 million acres) designated wilderness. There are five different wilderness areas. They include the Absaroka-Beartooth, the North Absaroka, the Washakie, the PoPo Agic and the Fitzpatrick.

Some 4,900 miles of streams flow through the Shoshone, and 11,700 acres of lakes and some 51,000 acres of additional wetlands dot the forest landscape. Hundreds of alpine lakes, many above timberline, lie in rugged cirques and high valleys of the Beartooth and Wind River mountain ranges.

Wildlife on the Shoshone includes deer, elk, moose, bighorn sheep, mountain goats, grizzly and black bears, as well as numerous smaller animals, birds and cold-water fish.

The Shoshone contains 940 miles of roads and 1,528 miles of trails. Roads include the Loop Road near Lander which offers spectacular scenery, fishing, camping and trailheads into pristine wilderness. The Beartooth Highway crosses the spectacular Beartooth Plateau at nearly 11,000 feet. The Buffalo Bill Cody Scenic Byway offers superb scenery and wildlife viewing. Hikers and horseback riders enjoy trails that follow willow-lined streams through long, winding valleys and cross high alpine meadows dotted with sparkling lakes.

In Tribute to John Colter
First known white American explorer to enter this locale in the fall of 1807. Probably crossing the river 1/4 mile east of this point (right), before discovering "Colter's Hell" 1/2 mile to the west (left).

Born and raised in Virginia in 1770's. A valued member of the Lewis and Clark Expedition to the Pacific Ocean, 1803-1806. Among the first American "Free Trappers" in the Rocky Mountains, along with Joseph Dickson and Forrest Bancock, 1806-1807. First to explore Big Horn Basin, Yellowstone Park, and Grand Teton regions, 1807-1808. Immortalized by his legendary "run for life" escape, from the hostile Blackfeet Indians, 1808. Quit the mountains in 1810, married and settled on a farm near St. Louis, Missouri. Died of disease in 1813, unheralded, but not forgotten. His final resting place has since been lost. Erected by the John Colter Society, 1981. A legacy for all who adventure.

George Drouillard (c. 1775-1810)
Born to a French Canadian father and Shawnee mother, Drouillard joined the Lewis and Clark Expedition in 1803 as chief interpreter and

hunter. Lewis said of him, "I scarcely know how we should exist were it not for the exertions of this excellent hunter." While thus employed, he was possibly the first white man to trap on the upper Missouri River. In 1807, he joined Manuel Lisa's trading expeidtion. During two solitary winter treks on foot to notify various tribes of Lisa's fort on the Yellowstone, Drouillard journeyed up the Stinking Water (Shoshone River) near this spot. His explorations of this and other major rivers to the east totalled 500 miles, and he produced an important map upon which William Clark and later cartographers relied heavily. Trapping near the Three Forks with the Missouri Fur Company, he was killed by Blackfeet Indians in May 1810.

Jededian Strong Smith, January 6, 1799-May 27, 1831

Born in Jerico, New York, the 6th of 14 children, Jed was destined to influence the Westward expansion of the United States as few men have done. Influenced by Lewis and Clark's exploits he joined Ashley's trapping expedition in 1822, soon becoming a partner and then owner in 1827. A natural leader, devout Christian and tireless explorer, Jed's discovery popularized the South Pass crossing of the Rockies. He was the first man to travel overland to California and first to ravel the coast from California to the Columbia. He survived near death from thirst and starvation, maulings of a grizzly and attacks by Arikara, Mojava and Kelewatset Indians. Killed by Comanches near Fargo Spring, Kansas, his body was never found but his legacy live on as his trails of discovery became the highways for America's westward migration.

Born c. 1770, Died 1813, John Colter

A hunter for Lewis and Clark (1803-1806) Colter remained in the mountains to trap and explore. During his great journey of discovery he found "Colter's Hell" west of Cody, Wyoming. Captured by the Blackfeet in 1808, he was forced to run for his life. Outdistancing the entire tribe for seven miles he survived, naked and weaponless, to become a legend in his own lifetime. John Colter was the first true "Mountain Man."

A Tribute to James "Old Gabe" Bridger 1804-1881

Mountain man, hunter, trapper, fur trader, emigrant guide, and Army scout. Born in Richmond, Virginia in 1804 and moved to St. Louis, Missouri, in 1812. Served as a blacksmith's apprentice from 1818 to 1822. Came west with the 1822 Ashley-Henry Expedition. Discovered the Great Salt Lake in 1824 and visited what is now Yellowstone Park in 1830. In 1833 he became a full partner in the fur trading firm of Sublette, Fraeb, Gervais, Bridger, and Fitzpatrick. Anticipating the influx of immigrants he established Ft. Bridger to resupply and repair wagon trains. Jim served as a guide and scout for the Army until 1868. After his dischare Old Gabe retired to his farm in Missouri. However, by 1874, his health began to fall and he was blind. Jim's only regret was that he would never see his beloved Rocky Mountains before his death. On July 17, 181, the Lord laid Old Gabe's tired body to rest and set his spirit free to return at last to the mountains he loved.

In Tribute to Jim Bridger

Regarded most famous of the Rocky Mountain trappers and explorers who blazed the

THE BIGHORN NATIONAL FOREST

Located in north-central Wyoming, the Bighorns are a sister range of the Rocky Mountains. Conveniently located half-way between Mt. Rushmore and Yellowstone National Park, the Big Horns are a great vacation destination in themselves. No region in Wyoming is provided with a more diverse landscape — from lush grasslands to alpine meadows, from crystal-clear lakes to glacial carved valleys, from rolling hills to sheer mountain walls.

Visit the Bighorn National Forest and enjoy the multiple reservoirs, 32 campgrounds, 3 scenic byways, 14 picnic areas, 7 lodges, miles and miles of streams, 189,000 acres of Wilderness, 1,500 miles of trails, and much more that provide a forest experience unique to the Big Horns.

Bits and Pieces About The Bighorn

- The Bighorn National Forest is 80 miles long and 30 miles wide.
- The Forest covers 1,115,073 acres.
- Elevations range from 5,500 feet to 13,175 feet
- Cloud Peak at 13,175 feet
- Black Tooth Mountain at 13,005 feet
- Most common tree is lodgepole pine.

- The Forest has 32 campgrounds, 14 picnic areas, 2 visitor centers, 2 ski areas 7 lodges, 2 recreation lakes, 3 Scenic Byways, and over 1,500 miles (2419 Km) of trails.
- The Bighorn River, flowing along the west side of the Forest, was first named by American Indians due to the great herds of bighorn sheep at its mouth. Lewis and Clark transferred the name to the mountain range in the early 1800's.

100 Years, One thousand uses:

For thousands of years, human cultures have inhabited the Big Horn region, using mountain resources to improve their quality-of-life.

During the 1800's the Big Horns provided teepee poles, lumber for nearby Fort Phil Kearny, beaver pelts, medicinal plants, abundant big game, summer grazing for cattle and sheep and clear, cool water. On February 22, 1897, Grover Cleveland signed legislation creating the Bighorn National Reserve, in recognition of the value these mountains hold for the American people and their livelihood.

Today, much remains the same. The Big Horns still provide products and uses like wood, water, livestock forage, and minerals. Of equal or even greater worth are the intangible resources that move our mind and soothe our souls — wildlife and wildflowers, magnificent scenic vistas, mountain trails, fresh air, and the freedom of wide open spaces.

American West's early trails of continental destiny and who frequented these environs throughout the mid-1800's.

West 20 mile upriver towers Jim Mountain named for Jim Baker, a well known Bridger protege.

East 30 miles downriver the "Bridger Trail" crosses the "Stinking Water" (Shoshone River). This trail was established across the Big Horn Basin around 1864 by Jim Bridger (then working primarily as an emigrant and Army expedition guide). As a safer alternative route to the "Bozeman Trail" in traveling from the "Oregon-California Trail" to the Montana mines.

Jim Bridger epitomized the "mountain man" and his legacy endures, but only in context with many others. In all this breed never exceeded more than a few hundred. They came seeking adventure and fortune. Over half of them succumbed to the rigors of their profession: hostile elements, animals, Indeians, and starvation. Their names and remains are forever consigned-unrecorded-to the dust of the mouttains and plains where they "went under", often in violent fashion. This marker also stands in their memory. Erected 1982.

Plaque #7: Osborn Russell, 1814-1892

Born June 12, 1814 in Bowdoinham, Maine, Russell went to sea briefly at age 16 then for three years was a trapper in Wisconsin and Minnesota. He joined Nathanial Wyeth's 1834 expedition to deliver trade goods to the trappers' rendezvous in the Rocky Mountains. Wyeth met disappointment in his enterprise but moved on to build Fort Hall. Russell helped to build the fort and stayed to maintain it until spring when he joined Jim Bridger's trapping party. He soon declared his independence as a "free trapper" and pursued beaver until 1843.

Russell's travels took him from Montana to Utah Lake as he crossed and recrossed the Rockies many times. All this while he felt an obligation to record his observations in his journal.

In 1843 he moved to the California/Oregon country where he became a miner, a merchant and at one time a judge. He died August 28, 1892, in Pacerville, California. He is gratefully remembered by all who read his "Journal of a Trapper" with its daily account of the activities and adventures of a trapper.

Thomas Fitzpatrick, 1799-1854

Mountain man, business man, western guide, Indian agent; born and educated in Ireland, emigrated to America at age 16, he joined Ashley's trappers in 1823 and was appointed to leadership that year. He became a full partner in the Rocky Mountain Fur Co. in 1830. Tom battled with the Arickarees in 1823 and with the Gros Vents at Pierre's Hole in 1832. These same Gros Vents attacked him a few weeks earlier as he rode alone east of the Tetons. His horses and weapons lost in flight, barely alive when rescued many days later, his hair had turned white from the ordeal. Tom had two nicknames, "White Hair" and "Broken Hand", the latter from an encounter with a rifle ball during a Blackfoot attack. With the decline of the fur trade, Tom served as a guide to west-bound emigrants (1841-42), J. D. Fremont's explorations (1843-44) and Col. Kerney's expedition of 1845-46. Honorably served as a Federal Indian Agent from 1846 until his death February 7, 1854.

Hugh Glass, ?-1832(3)

Tough and independent, Glass had been a ship's captain and impressed pirate, captured and adopted by the Pawnees and finally made his way to St. Louis to join Ashley and his trappers. While ascending the Missouri he was wounded in a battle with the Arikarees (Rees). Several weeks later he was attacked by a grizzly and "tore nearly all to peases." Two men were paid to tend the old man until his death, but after several days they abandoned him knowing his death was certain and a Ree attack was imminent. Hugh recovered consciousness and crawled and hobbled 350 miles to Ft. Kiowa. When sufficiently recovered he headed back to the Rockies seeking those who had abandoned him.

Twice during the next ten months Glass was forced to flee for his life from Ree attack. He left Ashley's men to work the Santa Fe trade for a few years but later returned to the land of his old enemies.

Hugh was finally killed by Rees at a river crossing during the winter of 1832-33.

5 *Gas, Food, Lodging*

T **Cody Murals Visitor Center**
1719 Wyoming Ave. in Cody. 587-3290

The magnificent Cody Mural covers a domed ceiling 36 feet in diameter and 18 feet to the top of the dome. Perfectly blended into the mural are selected historical scenes from the first seventy years of the Church of Jesus Christ of Latter-day Saints. Edward T. Grigware, the artist, termed the mural his "masterpiece". He painted it after having worked and taught more than 40 years in the field of art. In an adjoining part of the building are displays and art telling the story of the colonization of the Big Horn Basn in Wyoming. This story is one of faith, sacrifice, and perseverance by Mormon pioneers who had moved from Utah and Idaho. Free guided tours daily.

T **Harry Jackson Museum**
602 Blackburn Ave. in Cody. 587-5508

Harry Jackson's works run the gamut from abstract expressionist paintings and cubist studies to his more recent sculptures of traditional western art: cowboys and indians. Several of his scultures are unusual in that they contain painted surfaces. Jackson's sculptures are for sale at the museum. Open M-F, 8-5.

H **"Corbett's Shebang" at Stinking Water Crossing**
Five miles northeast of Cody on
U.S. Highway 14A

On September 10th 1880, Victor Arland and John F. Corbett set up the first mercantile establishment in the Big Horn Basin on the Indian Trace that follows Trail Creek. Looking to the cattlemen for business, they moved to Cottonwood Creek in1883, then to Meeteetse Creek in 1884 where Arland, their final trading post, was established.

Corbett, doing the freighting from Billings for company enterprises, set up a way station in the river bottom where the freight road crossed the Stinking Water River—later renamed the Shoshone. A bridge, the first of five to span the river at this point, was constructed in 1883 at a cost of $5,000 raised by subscription from cattlemen, the Northern Pacific Railroad and Billings merchants.

Accommodations provided were a small store, a saloon and overnight lodging. The post office was established in 1885 with

Corbett Dam

Corbett the postmaster. It was a gathering place and social center long before Cody came into existence twelve years later.

Corbett died in bed at his Meeteetse home December 15, 1910. His partner, Arland, went to his reward in more traditional style—dying with his boots on. In December, 1889, a shot fired through a saloon window in Red Lodge, Montana, killed him while he is playing poker.

The name of Corbett lingers on but the need for "Corbett's Shebang" in the river bottom ended with the arrival of the railroad in November 1901.

H **Corbett Dam**
Seven miles northeast of Cody on
U.S. Highway 14A

The Corbett Dam diverts water from the Shoshone River into the Corbett Tunnel, a three-and-a-half-mile-long concrete-lined structure. The tunnel transports the water into the Garland Canal, which is the irrigation artery for the Garland and Frannie divisions of the Project. Water first flowed through the tunnel on April 27, 1908. Nearly 50,800 acres are irrigated by the waters carried through this system.

The dam is located 16 miles downstream from Buffalo Bill Dam and the storage reservoir, which supplies all the water for irrigation of the project.

Project History

On February 10, 1904, the Secretary of the Interior set aside $2,250,000 for the initial construction of the Shoshone Project, one of the first federal reclamation projects in the nation, and the largest federal project in Wyoming. The Project was settled in four divisions: the Garland in 1907, Frannie in 1917, the Willwood in 1927 and finally, Heart Mountain in 1846.

Today, the Project comprises 93,000 acres. Major crops are alfalfa hay, sugar beets, dry edible beans, malting barley and specialty crops.

6 *No services*

T **Buffalo Bill Dam and Visitor's Center**
Six miles west of Cody at the Buffalo Bill Dam, through the tunnels. 527-6076. www.bbdvc.org

One of the many legacies of Colonel William F. "Buffalo Bill" Cody is the Buffalo Bill Dam. Cody spent years promoting and attempting to raise money for his dream of irrigating thousands of arid acres east of Cody from the Shoshone River. Buffalo Bill Dam was the realization of his vision.

In 1897 and 1899 Cody and his associates acquired the rights from the State of Wyoming to irrigate about 169,000 acres of land in the Big Horn Basin. At the time their plans did not include a reservoir, only the diversion of water from the river through a canal. They were unable to raise the capital necessary to complete the plan. In 1903 they united with the Wyoming Board of Land Commissioners urging the federal government to become involved with irrigation development in the valley.

In 1903, the newly formed Reclamation Service (later to become the Bureau of Reclamation) began the Shoshone project. At that time, Service engineers recommended building a dam on the Shoshone River in the canyon just west of Cody. The dam was one of the first three major dams built by the Bureau of Reclamation.

Construction began on October 19, 1905 and was completed January 15, 1910. Building the dam at this location was a difficult project. Because of the remote area, it was difficult to recruit and keep workers. The steep granite canyon was a challenge. Excavation of the dam abutments required workers to hang from "spider lines" that were connected to cableway towers. To handle concrete, a riveted steel bridge was built across the canyon.

The Shoshone River itself was unpredictable with its flows. During one year, almost half of the annual runoff of the river occurred within a 30-day period, almost halting construction entirely.

A lack of natural sand and gravel deposits near the site forced the project to create it from the granite. Clean pieces of granite were hand-placed in the concrete. The boulders, weighing between 25 and 200 pounds each, make up approximately 25 percent of the masonry in the dam.

The total cost of the dam in 1910 dollars was $929, 658. It was the first high concrete arch dam built by the Bureau of Reclamation. At completion, the dam was the highest in the world at 325 feet. Its length at the base is 70 feet and 200 feet at its crest. It was 10 feet wide at the top and 108 feet wide at its base. Before raising the dam, it held about 400,000 acre feet of water.

Completed in 1993, an eight-year modification project raised the dam height by 25 feet to a total of 353 feet. This expansion increased the water storage capacity by about 250,000 acre feet. The project also added 25.5 megawatts of power generation capacity; the result of the addition of two new power plants about one mile below the dam. Refurbishments were also made to the old Shoshone power plant visible just below the dam.

The reservoir provides irrigation and drinking water for Cody and much of the Big Horn Basin. Because of its historical significance, the dam was added to the National Register of Historic Places in 1973.

The visitor center opened in May 1993 as a combination visitor center and Wyoming highway rest area. Inside the center are a number of exhibits and a gift shop.

H Buffalo Bill Reservoir
Buffalo Bill State Park at 47 Lakeside Rd. west of Cody. 587-9227

The development by the U.S. Reclamation Service of the great irrigation project in the lower Shoshone valley required sacrifice of their land by the settlers living in the upper part of the valley. Below the surface of this reservoir once stood the community of Marquette. Small ranches lined both the North and South forks of the river. The government bought all these properties for roughly $400,000 in 1905. The settlers were allowed to rmain until the reservoir began to fill in 1910.

More information on the development of the Shoshone Project can be found at Buffalo Bill Dam Visitors' Center 11.5 miles east of this site and at nine other Wayside Exhibits located on the Project.

Project History: On February 10, 1904, the Secretary of the Interior set aside $2,250,000 for the initial construction of the Shoshone Project, one of the first federal reclamation projects in the nation, and the largest federal project in Wyoming. The Project was settled in four divisions: the Garland in 1907, Frannie in 1917, The Willwood in 1927 and finally, Heart Mountain in 1946.

Today, the Project comprises 93,000 acres. Major crops are alfalfa hay, sugar beets, dry edible beans, malting barley and specialty crops.

H Upstream Cableway Winch
Buffalo Bill Dam West of Cody

This cableway winch, which was used to install and remove the ball plugs, trash racks, and the bulkhead gate for the left abutment outlet works, dates to the construction of the Shoshone Power Plant in 1922. It was originally housed in a hoist building on the north side of the Shoshone River Canyon about 75 feet upstream of the dam. The winch was manufactured by American Hoist & Derrick Company of St. Paul, Minnesota, and powered by a Westinghouse electric 7.5 horsepower motor. This cableway winch was last used to aid divers using under water cameras in the inspection of the upstream dam face, trash racks and submerged debris prior to the Buffalo Bill Dam modification project. The winch was removed in 1985 and the hoist building was removed in 1986

H Balanced Plunger Hydraulic Valve
Buffalo Bill Dam just west of Cody

This 48-inch diameter valve is one of two which were originally installed at the base of Buffalo Bill Dam in 1922 to supply water to the Shoshone powerplant and low level river outlet works. The two valves were operational until they were replaced by new valves during the Buffalo Bill Dam modification project of 1985-1993. This specialized type of needle valve, known as a mechanically-operated, balanced plunger hydraulic valve, was manufactured in 1921 by the Wellman-Seaver-Morgan Company, Cleveland, Ohio.

H Ball Plug
Buffalo Bill Dam just west of Cody

This large wood and concrete ball plug was one of two used to halt the flow of water through the 42-inch-diameter power outlet works conduits, located in the base of the dam. The balls facilitated the repair and maintenance of downstream machinery and equipment. In order to access the submerged conduit openings on the

upstream face of the dam, trash rack structures first had to be removed by divers and raised to the surface by a cableway winch. Then, assisted by divers, the ball plugs were lowered by the cableway winch into position, where water pressure forced the balls against the conduit openings, sealing off the flow of water. The construction of the ball plugs utilizing a combination of wood and concrete provided strength and also allowed easy maneuverability under water.

Two new ball plugs were obtained during the Buffalo Bill Dam modifications project (1985-1993), since the removal of the cableway winch in 1985, the installation of the new ball plugs must be accomplished using a barge mounted crane on the reservoir.

7 *No services*

H Arland
Seven miles north of Meeteetse on Highway 120

A few miles up Meeteetse Creek from here, stood one of the toughest settlements of Wyoming's frontier history. The town was founded in the spring of 1884 by Victor Arland, a French businessman, and John Corbett, a buffalo hunter. From 1880 to 1884, the men were partners in a trading post on Trail Creek and another on Cottonwood Creek, just north of Cody, Wyoming. They moved to Meeteetse Creek to be in the center of cattle country and the developing ranches.

"Arland" soon had a store, saloon, restaurant, U.S. Post Office, a two story hotel, blacksmith shop, red light district, coal mine, livery stables, residential cabins, and corrals. A mail and passenger stage ran weekly through Arland, helping the town to become a trade center for the area ranches and a mecca for the cowboys and other tough characters of the region. The nearest law was 150 miles away in Lander, Wyoming.

On February 22, 1888, Vic Arland shot and killed Broken Nose Jackson in self defense at a dance in Arland. Jackson's friend, Bill Landon, shot and killed Vic Arland in revenge, at Dunivan's Saloon in Red Lodge, Montana, on April 24, 1890. After Vic's death Arland degenerated into a hang-out for the outlaw element. There were names such as Black Jack Miller, John Bliss, Al Durant, Butch Cassidy, W.A. Gallagher, Blind Bill Hoolihan, Ed Nye, Rose Williams, Sage Brush Nancy, and Belle Drewry, known as the "Woman in Blue". Most of the above, and others, died entangled in a web of lawlessness, romance, intrigue, and murder.

By 1896, the nearby town of Meeteetse had sprung up and by 1897 Arland had died. Today, nothing remains of old Arland but the stories and ghosts of days gone by.

H Site of Halfway House Stage House
19 miles north of Meeteetse on Highway 120

At this spot in 1903 a rock dugout facing south, near a fresh-water spring in the hillside, was established as a stage "noon stop" where horses were changed and meals served. The primitive accommodation was halfway between Corbett Crossing on the Stinking Water River and the bustling frontier town of Meeteetse. In 1904 Halfway Stop had a newfangled telephone, complete with a large "Public Telephone" sign. The station was abandoned in 1908 after automobiles began to use the route, but the spring remained in use for many years, a favorite watering place in this arid country. This marker commemorates early station keepers and travelers who passed this way.

8 Gas, Food, Lodging

Meeteetse
Pop. 368, Elev. 5,797

Taken from a Shoshone word meaning "resting or gathering place", the town of Meeteetse took its name from the creek nearby. When the post office opened here in 1881, it was one of the first in the Bighorn Basin, and by 1890, Meeteetse was the biggest town in the area. Later, in 1893, the settlement was moved closer to the Greybull River. One-time mayor, John W. Deane, ran away from home in the East at age 15 to become a cowboy driving cattle up the Texas Trail in the 1870s. He lived with Indians for five months, and became a mail carrier for seven years before going into politics.

Pitchfork

This discontinued post office town, like the nearby creek, took its name from Otto Franc's Pitchfork Ranch, which had a pitchfork for a brand.

T Meeteetse Hall Museum, Bank Museum and Archives
1033 Park Ave. in Meeteetse. 868-2423

Meeteetse is one of the oldest settlements in the Big Horn Basin. The name is said to derive from an Indian word meaning "the meeting place". The area was well used by the Indians. There have been many Indian-killed buffalo skulls, arrowheads, and even the remains of Sheepeater teepee poles found in this area. The best preserved teepee is located on Sheep's Point.

The town was settled in the 1880s, and many of the original buildings are still in use. William McNally, who homesteaded the present site of Meeteetse, built the little house on the corner by the river in 1893. The Cafe next door was the first post office on that side of the river. Margaret Wilson started the first Post Office and the first school in the early 1880s. The Mercantile was established in 1899. The current Archives building was the Hogg, Cheeseman, and MacDonald's bank. It was built in 1901. The museum is in the process of restoring the bank to its former condition.

The Hall Museum was erected in 1900 by George Ed Heron, who became a judge in 1909. The Baptist parsonage next door was a school, and the stage at the hall was used for most school functions. The Masons, Woodsmen, and the IOOF all used the hall. It was also the center for political rallies. One of the most memorable was one at which one of the main speakers died in the middle of his speech. Many of the best community dances were also held at the Hall, with people from all over the country in attendance. At one dance, one of the cowboys decided that they needed a bonfire to liven things up, so he built one at the base of one of the support columns, which is why the columns no longer match. The fire put a damper on future dances, and the Hall gradually fell into disuse.

Meeteetse was never a "dry" town, not by a long shot. By 1906 they had seven saloons, one store, two banks, and two hotels. Since everything had to be freighted in by team and wagon, one wonders how much of every load had to have been the liquor required to keep the saloons in business. In addition to the bars in town, there were several scattered over the area. At the forks of the Greybull and Wood rivers used to stand one that was popularly called the "Bucket of Blood". Since the only mode of transportation was afoot or on horseback, it was never too far between "watering holes". Meeteetse's reputation as a Wild and Woolly town lasted until fairly recently, and now it seems civilization has caught up with them because, for the first time, churches outnumber saloons.

In 1912 Josh Deane, who homesteaded on the Wood River, and had a Post Office there, started the Labor Day Celebration. Josh had been a freighter, mail carrier and rancher, but his biggest claim to fame was his "yarn spinning", hence the name "Josh". He moved to town, opened a restaurant, became a solid citizen, and was elected Mayor. He died in 1930. Meeteetse boasted of many "characters", with some very colorful and descriptive "monickers," Checkbook Smith, Poker Nell, Bronco Nell, Laughing Smith, Swede Pete. Of later vintage they had Airplane Jerry, Shorty the Crock, and Greasy Bill. The stories behind the names are interesting and funny. The purpose of the Museum and Archives is to gather and preserve the histories of these very unique people and their way of life. Settling the West was a hard and dangerous undertaking.

The people had to be tough, self-sufficient individuals. Meeteetse has produced some Senators, Governors, and not a few criminals. There were shootings over women, over cards, over land and livestock. They had their share of Rustlers, and the Pitchfork's Otto Franc is said to have helped bankroll the Cattleman's Association during the wars between the cattlemen and the homesteaders and sheepmen. Mr. Franc turned up dead of a gunshot wound and there were many people who thought it was a result of his affiliation with the Association. Dry-gulching, and a hanging here and there, settled a lot of squabbles and served as a warning to early entrepreneurs. The Ten Sleep Raid was an important event in Big Horn Basin History. A former Governor of Wyoming, Jack Gage, wrote several interesting books on events that shaped the history of the cattlemen and the sheepmen.

The Museum and Archives is open Monday through Saturday 10:00 a.m. to 5:00 p.m., Sunday 1:00 p.m. to 4:00 p.m. —May 15 through Labor Day. They also will open by appointment for special groups at any other time. Admission is free.
Reprinted from museum brochure.

T Charles J. Belden Museum
1947 State Street in Meeteetse. 868-2264

This museum features the work of Charles J. Belden, personal and family memorabilia, Western paintings, Indian artifacts, and sculptures. The photographic work of Charles J. Belden documents life on the Pitchfork Ranch earlier in this century. His photographs contributed much to establishing the current myth of the West. This building also houses the Meeteetse Museum collection, a wildlife display including a mount of one of the largest Grizzly bears ("Little Wab") ever taken in the lower 48 states. Also on display are artifacts from the Pitchfork Ranch, a Buffalo Bill Cody display and the Olive Fell collection.

Belden was born in San Francisco, California, on November 16, 1887. He was raised in California and graduated from the Massachusetts Institute of Technology in 1910. It was while at the Institute that he became friends with Eugene Phelps, who was to become his brother-in-law. After graduation Charles married Frances Phelps and came to the Pitchfork Ranch. During the 1920s, 30s, and 40s Charles Belden's photographs appeared in many newspapers across the country and in the National Geographic. His photographs appear today in western history books, calendars, and museums. Today there are over 4,200 negatives of his work. Part of the collection is in the archives collection at the Buffalo Bill Historical Center in Cody, Wyoming. The remainder is at the ranch and museum. Belden's abilities with the older type cameras were never surpassed. He captured scenes that have never been equaled, even with modern equipment. His artistry is evident in each of his photographs.

The museum is open daily from May 1 through September 30. Admission is free, but donations are encouraged.
Reprinted from museum brochure and web site.

T Double D Dude Ranch Site
Highway 290 east from Meeteetse, then south on Wood River Road. 4-wheel drive high clearance vehicle required for last two or three miles.

The beauty and natural resources of the area near Kirwin attracted the interest of several investors in the 1920s and early 1930s that formed the idea of establishing a dude ranch in the area. Carl Dunrud began the construction of the Double D Dude Ranch five miles below the townsite in 1931. Amelia Earhart visited the ranch in 1934 and was so attracted to the beauty of the area that she asked Dunrud to construct a home near the old townsite for her to use. She disappeared during her around-the-world flight before the construction was completed. The American Metals Climax Corporation eventually purchased the Kirwin townsite and the Double D Dude Ranch in the early 1960s. Today the site is abandoned. Amax donated the complex to the United States Forest Service in 1992.

Wyoming Tidbits

The black-footed ferret, the rarest of all North American mammals, was thought to be extinct until a colony was discovered in Park County in 1981.

Wolf Mine shaft in Kirwin. U.S. Forest Service Photo.

T Kirwin Historic Mining Townsite

Highway 290 east of Meeteetse, then south on Wood River Road. Turnoff is just east of Lower Sunshine Reservoir. 4-wheel drive high clearance vehicle required for last nine or ten miles.

William Kirwin began prospecting in the area high in the Absaroka Mountains of the Shoshone National Forest in 1885. Gold, silver, copper, zinc and molybdenum were all found here during that time. Kirwin, Harry Adams, and sixteen others officially formed the Wood River Gold Mining District In 1891. In 1897, the first ore was shipped from Kirwin. By the turn of the century the Shoshone Mountain Mining Company, Wyoming Mining Company, and Galena Ridge Company had developed the site into one of the West's most promising mining camps. In late 1905 and early 1906 the population of Kirwin was around 200. The town had 38 buildings including a a general store, hotel, and a post office. The townfolk hoped for the construction of a smelter to process the ore and an extension of the Burlington Railroad to service the mines at Kirwin. These developments never materialized. The high altitude climate and the lack of significant quantities of ore combined with the factors above spelled the eventual end of the community.

In 1907 an avalanche nearly wiped out the town. Several buildings were buried and three people died. The town never fully recovered and eventually passed away.

Located at 9,200 feet in the base of a bowl, the townsite is surrounded by peaks rising to 12,500 feet. In addition to many old buildings and remnants of the mining days, steep slopes, a high mountain meadow, and several waterfalls make this a unique and beautiful place.

H Amelia Earhart in Wyoming

Just north of Meeteetse on State Highway 120.

First woman to fly across the Atlantic June 17, 1928 and May 20, 1932. Was building a summer home near here when she left to fly around the earth and was lost in the South Pacific, July 2, 1937.

9 *Lodging*

Grass Creek

This tiny town is named for the creek on which it is situated. Good grass land is a rare enough find in Wyoming to be noteworthy.

Hamilton Dome

The post office here was named for a Dr. Hamilton. His first name isn't certain. He was probably just known as Doc to the locals.

T Anchor Dam

Highways 120 and 170, 35 miles west of Thermopolis

Anchor Dam, a 200-feet high, thin-arch concrete dam, located approximately 35 miles west of Thermopolis Wyoming, was constructed by the Bureau of Reclamation at a cost exceeding $5 million dollars during the dam building boom of the 1950s and 1960s. Sinkholes and earth fissures within the reservoir area continuously allowed drainage of the reservoir before, during and after construction. Additionally, attempts to plug solution-widened fractures in carbonate strata within the Pennsylvanian Tensleep Formation, which comprised the abutments, resulted in expensive change orders during construction. The reservoir and dam were doomed from the onset. Water continues to leak through the Madison limestone formations, preventing it from filling all the way. Efforts to improve its ability to hold water have reached the point it is able to be filled about halfway in some years.

H The Prairie Rattlesnake

About 16 miles south of Meeteetse at rest stop on Highway 120

Less conspicuous than the pronghorn antelope and the golden eagle is an even more ancient inhabitant of the high plains and valleys of Wyoming, the prairie rattlesnake. Feared by many and respected by most, these pit vipers so-called because of their heat sensing facial pits, used to detect warm bodied prey) are common in the eastern two-thirds of the state and all but alpine habitats. During winter these snakes hibernate in underground dens for up to eight months. In spring they migrate away from the dens in search of food (typically rodents and other small mammals) and mates. Studies show that they move from the den in virtually a straight line path covering perhaps several miles until they find a food source. They stay on their fixed angle course by using the sun as a navigational aid. When the temperature cools in fall, the snakes return to the same den.

The habitat around you no doubt contains many of these secretive and fascinating reptilian hunters, but there is really very little to fear. Though they are poisonous and seemingly hostile, evidence indicates the chances of being bitten are virtually nill, as long as the snake is not touched, provoked, or frightened. Since rattlesnakes are deaf and cannot actually hear rattling, this behavior is believed to be defensive. The rattling rattle snake is simply trying to warn or drive off another creature it perceives be a threat. if you encounter a prairie rattlesnake, give it plenty of room and you will be in no danger - it's probably more frightened than you are. Allow the snake to go on its way and hunt prey like it's ancestors have done in this area for thousands and thousands of years The prairie rattler may not earn your admiration, but it deserves respect as a fascinating and important element of Wyoming wild land.

10 *Gas, Food, Lodging*

Thermopolis
Pop. 3,172, Elev. 4,326

Founded in 1897, Thermopolis is a name derived from the Latin thermae (meaning hot spring) and the Greek polis (meaning city). With the world's largest natural hot spring, running at 2575 gallons per minute at a consistent 135 degrees Fahrenheit, the town grew quickly as people were drawn to the therapeutic waters. The Shoshone and other Native Americans had appreciated its healing properties for generations, and called it the "smoking waters". This was once sacred ground, and part of the Wind River Reservation when it was first established. Shoshone Chief Washakie and Arapaho chief Sharp Nose, as part of efforts to make peace with the white men, made a portion of the waters available for public use. Washakie Fountain commemorates this "Gift of the Waters".

T TePee Spa
144 Tepee Street at Hot Springs State Park in Thermopolis. 864-9250

Exhilarating hot water fun is packed in to several attractions at the TePee Spa also known as the Hellie's Tepee pool. Pools are available inside and out, along with a sauna and steam room. Several outdoor hot tubs offer varying water temperatures. There are also wildly popular water slides, including a 162-foot indoor slide and 272-foot outdoor breath taker. Free water aerobics are offered Monday, Wednesday, and Friday evenings from 7-8 p.m. A shaded patio area is available with a large grassy area for sunbathing. There is also a massage therapist available, featuring watsu, water massage. A gift shop features swim suits, T-shirts, along with great gifts. If you don't have a suit, rentals are available.

T Hot Springs County Museum & Cultural Center
700 Broadway in Thermopolis. 864-5183

The Hot Springs County Museum is larger than it looks. Visitors are astounded at the two full floors of exhibits, plus the five annex buildings that complete the amazing collections. The annex includes a Burlington Northern caboose, agriculture building, petroleum building, old school house, and poverty flats cottage. The two floors of the main building feature an exhibit of over 8,000 Native American artifacts, Gebo coal mine model, and original historic photographs. That's just for starters! Shoshone and Arapaho beadwork and elk hide paintings by Chief Washakie of the Shoshone are also on display. The original cherry-wood bar from the Hole-in-the-Wall Bar, once frequented by some of the West's most famous outlaws, like Butch Cassidy, is on the first floor. The museum has a long association with jackalopes. You can even get a jackalope hunting license at the museum. The entire family will enjoy this enormous display of Native American, pioneer and cowboy memorabilia, that will take you to the old west and before. The museum is open year round and admission is charged.

Aerial view of Thermopolis. Photo by Richard Coffenberry, RAC Digital Photography in Thermopolis.

T Wind River Canyon

A panorama of over one billion years of geology is exposed in the Wind River Canyon between Thermopolis and Boysen Dam. Much of the geology is identified with informative signs along US Hwy. 20. The canyon is about ten miles long. See variegated rock units of the eocene Wind River formation, and severely-faulted Paleozoic rocks which reflect a faulted arch. At Boysen, the narrow canyon begins, with walls rising 2,500 feet above the river. Precambrian crystalline rocks and northward-ipping Cambrian shales highlight the area. A complete section of Paleozoic formations may be observed northward. The road emerges from the canyon at the north end, where extensive areas of Triassic red beds dazzle visitors.

T Legend Rock Petroglyphs

Hot Springs State Park. Inquire locally for directions

Legend Rock is one of the most impressive petroglyph areas in the world. Hundreds of yards of sandstone cliffs contain rock art of thunderbirds and elk. An archaeological survey using test pits found there are at least 283 pictures on 92 rock panels. The oldest works date back from 500 to 1700 A.D. demonstrating the characteristics and

Photo by Richard Coffenberry, RAC Digital Photography in Thermopolis.

beliefs of many prehistoric cultures. One area is representative of the early Plains Indians. Visitors must obtain a key from Hot springs State Park headquarters on Park Street in Thermopolis (Monday through Friday) in order to drive the final half mile to the site.

T Hot Spring State Park and State Bathhouse

Northeast edge of Thermopolis

Bison Viewing

The Hot Springs State Park Bison Herd is the central herd for Wyoming State Parks. Herd size is dependent upon the carrying capacity of the available range areas and the site specific requirements necessary to manage a healthy and safe bison herd.

The park maintains a free roaming herd of 24-27 adult and yearling bison on a year round basis. This number increases by 10-15 animals during the months of April, May and June as new calves become a welcome addition.

In addition to the "natural" feed that the bison receive from the pasture areas, the park's bison are provided with a daily "cake" supplement that provides necessary minerals and helps to ensure good health. This feeding occurs daily between 8 a.m. and 9 a.m. and offers park visitors a unique opportunity to view the "monarch of the Plains"

Hot Spring State Park and State Bathhouse

up close.

Please remember that bison are wild animals and should be viewed ONLY while you remain in your vehicle.

The Swinging Bridge

The suspension foot bridge across the Bighorn River is commonly called "The Swinging Bridge."

The structure was removed in July 1991 and was replaced during 1992. The bridge offers a unique vantage point from which to view the Bighorn River and Mineral Terrace.

The State Bath House

In 1896 a treaty was signed with the Shoshone and the Arapaho which gave the public use of one of the largest mineral hot springs in the world. The hot mineral water is maintained at 104 degrees Fahrenheit to provide the safest soaking water possible. Attendants are available to assist you with your need. The Bath House hours are: Monday – Saturday, 8 a.m. To 5:30 p.m.; Sundays noon to 5:30 p.m. The Bath House is closed on holidays during the winter and open on holidays during the summer, noon to 5:30.

Boat Ramp Facility

On the Bighorn River, by the Terraces, is a boat ramp. The sister to this ramp is located at the

Big Spring at Hot Springs State Park is the source of the hot mineral water. Photo by Richard Coffenberry, RAC Digital Photography in Thermopolis.

mouth of the Wind River Canyon south of Thermopolis. These two ramps were built by the Wyoming Game & Fish Department with the needs of physically impaired persons in mind. These fit with the many other facilities in the state park that are also designed for physically impaired individuals.

While the Terrace ramp will be used primarily for removing boats from the water, there is still lots of water below the Terrace that can be floated and /or fished.

Flowers

Hot Springs State Park has long been known for its beautiful flower gardens. Make a point of bringing your camera with you and capture the exciting splash of color all summer long.

Legend Rock State Petroglyph Site

Legend Rock State Petroglyph Site has been developed for public viewing of the cliff face.

The facilities include an improved access road, a public restroom and picnic tables.

The site is approximately 30 miles northwest of Thermopolis and visitation must be arranged through Hot Springs State Park headquarters or the State Bath House. For information call park staff.

Reprinted from Wyoming State Parks and Historic Sites brochure.

H Hot Springs State Park

Hot Springs State Park In the foreground across the river are Rainbow terraces, formed of mineral deposits from the world's largest mineral hot spring. Algae forms the multicolor of the terraces. The spring flows 18,600,000 gallons every 24 hours, temperature 135 degrees Fahrenheit. The site was a former Indian shrine where Shoshones and Arapahos bathed and held ceremonials. Washakie, chief of the Shoshones, led the tribes in signing a treaty which gave the healing waters to the Great White in Washington. An Indian pageant annually depicts the gift of these waters. Now a state park, with buffalo herd, picnic areas, playgrounds, swimming pools, tourist accommodations. No entrance fee.

H The Swinging Bridge

The suspension foot bridge across the Bighorn River is commonly called "The Swinging Bridge." It is under reconstruction as rust has become a major concern and large portions of the bridge are currently being replaced.

The Wyoming and North Dakota National Guard are completing the removal and replacement work in cooperation with the Wyoming Transportation Department, Hot Springs State Park, Hot Springs County, the local Historical Society and many other interested individuals.

The structure was removed in July 1991 and replaced during 1992. The bridge offers a unique vantage point from which to view the Bighorn River and Mineral Terrace.

T World's Largest Mineral Hot Spring
Hot Springs State Park Loop Road

History: These springs were included in the Shoshone Indian Reservation created by the Treaty of 1868. Later the reservation was also used for the Arapahoes. As information that the springs have "magnitude, health giving properties" became more generally known, Congress was requested to set aside this area for a "National Park or Reservation." In 1896 upon authority from Congress, the Indian Commissioner sent John McLaughlin to negotiate a treaty for the purchase of these springs. He secured an agreement whereby a part of the reservation, approximately 10 miles square was ceded to the United States Government for the sum of $60,000.00. Among the signers of this treaty were the Shoshone Chief Washakie and the Arapahoe Chief Sharp Nose. Chief Washakie said that when game was bountiful in this area, he used to camp near the spring. But by 1890 hunting was so poor in this vicinity that it was seldom visited by the Indian.

Geology: Most of the water in these springs is thought to come underground from the Owl Creek Mountains. Rain falling in the mountains enters porous rock layers, moves slowly downward, and is here forced through crevices in the rocks.

The heat and chemicals in the water are derived from the rock through which it passes and from gases that rise from deeply buried volcanic rocks.

The terraces are made chiefly of lime and gypsum which separate from the cooling water. The colors are due mainly to primitive plants (algae) which grow in the warm water.

Chemistry:

Minerals Chemical Composition Parts per million
Silica SI O2 24.0
Aluminum AL2O3 11.6
Iron FE2O3 14.8
Calcium CA0 624.0
Magnesium MGO 121.0
Sodium NA20 326.2
Potassium K20 89.6
Sulphur SO3 606.8
Chloride CL 217.6
Carbon Dioxide C02 382.9
Hydrogen sulphide H2S 4.5
Total solids 2,396.0
Flow 18,600,000 gallons every 24 hours.
Temperature 135 degrees Fahrenheit.
Reprinted from State Park brochure

H World's Largest Mineral Hot Springs
State Highway 120 about one mile from the junction of State Highway 120 and U.S. Highway 20/789.

See this natural phenomenon while you are in Thermopolisl Monument Hill, ... visible from this site, overlooks the 'Big Spring'—begin your tour of State Park here.

See other springs and beautiful terraces created by the mineral deposits of these healing waters. Learn the history of the Indians' "Gift of the Waters" to the white man. See large buffalo herd. Avail yourself of many park facilities. No entrance fee.

H Thermopolis Hot Mineral Water
Hot Springs County Museum and Cultural Center in Thermopolis

50 million gallons daily 135 degrees Farenheit, in springs and wells. It contains 13 of 16 mineral salts which are essential to all life. and this water has an alkaline base. Counteracts acids, Removes leidosis the cause of some forty diseases. These soluble mineral solids are similar to those in vegetables and fruit and our system can assimilate them. The two main acid forming salts are left out.

Hydro Therapy (or Hot Bath)

It has been demonstrated in laboratory that Hot Bath kills many germs by producing artificial fever, increases resistance, hastens multiplication white cells of blood. This water contains 8 anticeptics or cleansers. No chance for infection.

Analysis vans pr. cal.
Silica (SiO2) 727
Oxides Iron (Fe2O3) 105
Oxides Aluminum 222
Carbonate lime 21,584
Sulphate lime 49,402
Carbonate magnesia 15,926
Potassium Sulphates 7,437
Sodium Sulphates 5,249
Sodium Chlorides 29,920
Carbon dioxide gas (dissolved) 83.6
Oxygen gas (dissolved) pts. pr. mil. 5.7

F Las Fuentes Restaurant
530 Arapahoe, Thermopolis. 864-2695.

Receiving critical acclaim in publications across Wyoming, Las Fuentes Restaurant offers freshly prepared fine food in a casual Wyoming atmosphere. The restaurant exclusively serves Hot Springs County beef, and the wide selection of seafood includes such scrumptious entrees as Gulf grouper filets, cerveza lime shrimp with Mexican beer batter, and chipolte and lime encrusted Tilapia filets. Famous Margaritas, a new wine list, and a full cocktail selection complement every meal, while 500+ original Mexican and Western artifacts and artwork highlight the restaurant's décor. Dine upstairs, downstairs, or outdoors as strains of Mexican music complete the ambience. A proud member of the Two-Percent Club – independent restaurateurs in business over five years – Las Fuentes invites you to come taste the difference of its acclaimed North Mexico menu! A children's menu is available.

L Best Western Plaza Hotel
116 E. Park St., Thermopolis. 864-2939 or reservations at (888) 919-9009. www.bestofwyoming.com

Best Western Plaza Hotel is located in Hot Springs State Park on the banks of the Big Horn River. This historic landmark was renovated and reopened to the public in 1999. Visitors are treated with the hospitality of years gone by while receiving the conveniences of modern times. Suites are available with microwaves and refrigerators, and wireless Internet is available to all guests. Guests enjoy a luxurious soak in the healing mineral waters of the mineral spa from water piped directly from its source in the park. There is also an outdoor pool open during the summer. All guests are served a complimentary continental breakfast. For friendly service and the comforts you desire, make reservations at the Best Western Plaza Hotel. Don't forget to visit them on the web.

S Jeanne's On Broadway Gallery
518 Broadway, Thermopolis. 864-4244.

Located in downtown Thermopolis, Jeanne's on Broadway is an adventure in art, jewelry, antiques, and handmade gourmet chocolates. Discover a plethora of Indian jewelry from tribes

Jeanne's On Broadway Gallery

including Zuni, Navajo, and Santa Domingo, along with colorful and classy vintage jewelry. Tickle your taste buds with wildly popular huckleberry jams and syrups, or pick up a sweet treat sure to satisfy your chocolate cravings. Along with an ever-changing collection of large and small antiques, you'll find vintage clothing, handmade soaps, hand-appliquéd denim clothing for the entire family, Wyoming Red Dirt Shirts, pottery, and a selection of old coins. A variety of artwork created by talented local artisans is also featured. For over 4,500 square feet of treasures from the past and present, make Jeanne's on Broadway your destination.

11 *Gas, Food, Lodging*

T The Wyoming Dinosaur Center and Dig Sites
110 Carter Ranch Road in Thermopolis. 867-2997 or (800) 455-DINO (3466). www.wyodino.org

Interpretive displays, dioramas and life-size dinosaur mounts greet you as you enter the museum. Over 12,000 square feet of exhibits covering all facets of early life on the planet. Fossils and life-forms from the earliest geologic time periods are displayed in a time perspective. There are over 200 displays throughout the museum. The central hall houses 20 full-size mounted skeletons, including 10 dinosaurs.

T Thermopolis Hot Springs Chamber of Commerce
119 S. 6th in Thermopolis. 864-3192 or (800) 786-6772

Thermopolis is home to the World's Largest Mineral Hot Spring and Hot Springs State Park. The park offers swimming, soaking, and sliding in the hot mineral water. The park includes his-

torical and geological sites and a ten-acre bison pasture. The Wyoing Dinosaur Center offers a world-class museum, working dig sites and complete modern preparation laboratory. The town hosts three other museums, whitewater rafting and other water sports, and horseback riding. Enjoy year around events including weekly rodeos and the historical Gift of the Waters Indian Pageant. For a free information packet call the Chamber at their toll free number listed above.

T Old West Wax Museum and Dancing Bear Folk Center Complex
Highway 20 in downtown Thermopolis. 864-9396

The wax figures in the Old West Wax Museum were developed more than 30 years ago by Kenneth Bunn, now nationally recognized for his bronze sculptures of Western wildlife. There are more than 80 of the original figures with their backdrops. A recently acquired collection of historic documents that can also be seen here includes historic photographs and maps dating from 1772. An extensive collection of historic newspapers and early printed etchings shows the West as it was portrayed by America's writers, journalists, and artists in the 1800s and early 1900s.

Also here, at the Dancing Bear Folk Center, are the Textile Studio and Teddy Bear Den. No scrap of fabric went unused on the frontier. Clothes were passed down from one child to the next. When past wearing, they were made into other useful items. Old coats and blankets became rugs and bed spreads. Cottons and silks became quilts that rival modern art in their complexity. Sacks that once held flour became undergarments, sheets, and tablecloths. New dresses could be made from chicken feed sacks. The studio includes spinning wheels, looms, early sewing machines, and examples of folk handiwork, such as rug-making, crochet, knitting, tatting, basketmaking, weaving and other needle arts.

The Teddy Bear Den is an unusual collection of soft-sculpture "teddy bears" representing England, Scotland, Ireland, Germany, Holland, Canada, New Zealand, Australia, and the United States. They are arranged in settings representing historical events, geographical areas, and other unexpected scenes.

Call for hours, and to learn about visiting speakers, craftspeople, and demonstators.

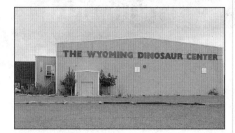

Photo by Richard Coffenberry, RAC Digital Photography in Thermopolis.

T The Wyoming Dinosaur Center and Dig Sites
110 Carter Ranch Rd., Thermopolis. 867-2997 or (800) 455-DINO (3466). www.wyodino.org; Wdinoc@wyodino.org

Discover Earth's ancient inhabitants at the Wyoming Dinosaur Center. This 16,000 square foot museum features life-size dinosaur mounts, interpretive displays, dioramas, and a fossil preparation laboratory. For those seeking a firsthand paleontological experience, fee-based summer dig programs are available through advance reservation for families, individuals, and children ages 8 to 12. Short on time? Opt for a guided dig site tour May through September. No reservations are required, and tours start daily at 9 am with the last tour departing at 4 pm. To help guests remember their Wyoming Dinosaur Center visit, the onsite gift shop features a broad spectrum of educational, paleontological, and geological gifts and souvenirs. The museum admission fee is $6 for adults and $3.50 for children and seniors. Group and school rates are available.

L El Rancho Motel
924 Shoshoni, Thermopolis. 864-2341 or (800) 283-2777.
dollardiscount9458@bresnan.net

Located on a hill overlooking the scenic Wind River Canyon, El Rancho Motel is conveniently located just 1.5 miles from Hot Springs State Park and The Wyoming Dinosaur Center. As an added bonus, downtown Thermopolis and numerous restaurants are within easy walking distance. Guests enjoy affordable and spacious rooms featuring a Western cabin-inspired décor, with many including couches, desks, microwaves, and refrigerators. A large parking lot accommodates visitors with boats or campers, and the motel's small picnic area is complete with barbeques and tables available for guest use. During your stay, be sure to visit the Dollar Discount and Wyoming Outlet Wholesale. The downtown stores feature the same owner as the motel and offer wonderful gifts, special values, Wyoming and Thermopolis souvenirs, t-shirts, and more.

L Coachman Inn Motel
112 Hwy. 20 S., Thermopolis. 864-3141 or (888) 864-3854. www.coachmanmotel.com

Coachman Inn Motel is situated off the main highway near the scenic Big Horn River. Priding itself on offering quiet accommodations, the Coachman Inn Motel makes it a top priority to offer Thermopolis' cleanest rooms. Standard smoking and non-smoking rooms feature king, queen, or double beds. Two suites are also available. When you're not enjoying the sites or relaxing in your room, soak up the area's beauty from the motel's large grassy court ringed in trees or catch up with friends and family with the complimentary wireless Internet. All rooms are ground

level with parking at your door. The motel offers the convenience of a fisherman shuttle that escorts guests to the Wedding of the Waters and many other area locations. To enjoy friendly service, and peace and quiet, make reservations at Coachman Inn Motel.

12 No services

Lucerne
Pop. 527, Elev. 4,298

This name was taken from the French word for alfalfa, "luzerne", which is a major crop in the region, used to feed cattle.

H Bridger Trail-Bighorn River Crossing
On County Highway 433 at Lucerne.

The Bridger trail crossed the Bighorn river near this location in 1864. Passing over the Bridger Mountains to the Southeast, the trail came down Kirby Creek, crossed the river and proceeded north to the Yellowstone River, then west to the gold fields in southwestern Montana.

Within months following the 1863 gold discovery at Alder Gulch located in present-day Montana, a flood of miners and settlers were traveling to the mining communities of Bannack in Virginia City. Jim Bridger blazed a new trail in 1864. His trail through the big horn basin west of the Big Horn mountains avoided Sioux Indian hostility along the Bozeman Trail which lies to the east. It also eliminated the extra week's travel along the OregonTrail Fort Hall - Bannack road which lies to the West.

Use of the Bridger trail was short-lived. However, many variants evolved from the trail in 1880s and 1890s. The trail was the ancestor of a freighting network that connected remote ranches and early communities with Casper, Wyoming, and Billings, Montana.

Jim Bridger was the most renowned mountain man, explorer, and guide of the American West. This trail served as a safer route for emigration to Montana during a period of Native American resistance to Euro-American encroachment. Equally important, the trail acted as a foundation for the development of late nineteenth and early twentieth century transportation routes that made settlement possible in a region previously lacking any system of roads.

13 Food

Kirby
Pop. 57, Elev. 4,270

This little post office and railroad stop town was named for Kris Kirby, a cowboy from Texas who came north to become a rancher. He followed the Bridger Trail to settle here in 1878. The nearby creek, which also bears his name, was once a hide out for Butch Cassidy and the Wild Bunch.

T Crosby
County Highway 433 between Kirby and Lucerne

Tailing piles and a mine superstructure mark the spot of this ghosttown, named for Mormon pioneer Jesse W. Crosby. Coal from Crosby supplied Thermopolis and the surrounding area in the early 1890s and at one time, more than 100 children attended the Crosby school. The mines closed in 1932.

Thermal pool at Thermopolis Hot Springs.

T Gebo

US Highway 20 south from Worland for 22 miles to Kirby. West on Sand Draw Road

Remains at Gebo include a graveyard, rock-fortified dugouts used as homes for miners, and several stone houses. A larger blower that pumped air into the mine is still in evidence, as are many of the mine shafts with timbered entrances.

Named for Samuel Gebo, coal mine developer, the town once had more than 600 residents, mostly miners.

14 *Gas, Food, Lodging*

Worland
Pop. 5,250, Elev. 4,061

Some of the earliest paleo-Indian artifacts were found near Worland, where ancient hunters killed mammoths over 11, 000 years ago. Eohippus (dawn horse), one of the modern horses oldest ancestors, was also discovered nearby. White men did not settle the area until 1903, when Charlie R. "Dad" Worland set up camp on the Bridger Trail by Fifteen Mile Creek. He soon set up a stage station and a saloon. When the Burlington Railroad came two years later, a store and a school had already been built. The community was built up by agriculture, both ranching and farming, and had the first sugar mill in Wyoming. The mill is still in operation, and continues to boost the economy, along with a Pepsi bottling plant and other agrarian concerns.

T Pioneer Square

The downtown entrance to Worland is a park dedicated to the hard working ancestors of the community. There are several interesting sculptures that pay tribute to the settlers.

H County of Washakie-Dedicated to Those Who Came First.
Pioneer Square in Worland

Sheltered by formidable mountains, the Big Horn Basin for ten thousand Great Suns nurtured hunting tribes of Crow and Sioux. Arapahoe and Shoshone following Pte Tanka, the Buffalo, their livelihood. Trappers and gold seekers ripped and ran, Bluecoats came and went. Ranchers and farmers brought courageous wives to put down roots, to weave a new civilization here in the wilderness. They built sand and sage and water into Worland and Washakie. We honor these first families who fulfilled Isaiah's prophecy….and the desert shall rejoice and blossom as the rose.

H City of Worland
U.S. Highway 16 on west of Worland, half mile past bridge over Big Horn River

Charles H. "Dad" Worland in 1900 dug his underground stage stop here on the old Bridger Trail. From Dad's dugout grew the City of Worland, drawing pioneer men and women possesing an indomitable spiritual force, dreaming that Big Horn River water would create a new way of life here in th desert. With muscles and guts, horses and hand tools, they dug miles of irrigation canals. With precious water, the parched land became an oasis. We cheer those who persevered and conquered the desert, making Worland the Jewel of the Big Horn Basin.

H "Dad" Worland Monument
U.S. Highway 16 on west of Worland, half mile past bridge over Big Horn River

Pioneer Square in Worland.

To all pioneers and in memory of C.H. "Dad" Worland for whom the town was named. He erected the stage station on the old Bridger trail about 100 yards north of here. That spot was the original town site established in 1904. The town moved across the river in 1906.

15 *Gas, Food, Lodging*

H Jim Bridger Historic Trail
About two miles north of Worland on State Highway 433.

In 1864 an alternate route to the goldfields of western Montana was needed due to frequent hostile actions along the Bozeman Trail. Though the Civil War raged on, the nation continued its westward expansion through the efforts of men like Jim Bridger. A trapper, explorer, trader, hunter, scout and guide, Jim Bridger led miners north from the area we now call Fort Caspar. From there the trail led northwesterly through the southern Big Horn Mountains, across the Big Horn Basin, crossing the Shoshone River, into Montana through what was known as Pryor Gap, and finally rejoining the Bozeman Trail. The Bridger Trail reduced the threat of hostile actions against emigrants heading north and proved an important route in the settlement of the Northwest.

The Bridger Trail crossed the Big horn River approximately 12 miles southwest of here, near where the community of Neiber stands today. The original Bridger Trail passed very close to this location as it paralleled the Big Horn River on its way north.

This commemorative site was developed jointly by the Wyoming Highway Department, the Wyoming Centennial Wagon Train, Inc., and the Department of the Interior Bureau of Land Management, for your use and enjoyment.

16 *Gas, Food, Lodging*

T Washakie Museum
1115 Obie Sue in Worland. 347-4102.

The Washakie Museum provide visitors the opportunity to relate to the living environment of the early settlers from thousands of years ago. The museum is named for the Eastern Shoshoni

Washakie Museum

statesman, Chief Washakie, whose philosophy of "Making the best of what you cannot change" led the Shoshoni tribe to offer peace to emigrants. Nine thousand pioneers signed a thank you document to Washakie and his people for safe passage through their territory. Washakie secured the Wind River Mountain Range for his tribe's homeland.

Many fine exhibits pay tribute to local history. The Colby site is a display of the earliest mammoth kill site in North America to settlers of the west one hundred years ago. Other exhibits include a covered wagon, sheep wagon, sod house, and beautiful display of western tack, including the first full term governor's saddle, along with an extensive collection of early settlement in the Big Horn Basin. There are also extensive displays on local anthropology and geology. The Family Discovery Center, introduces children to art and technology through hands on exhibits.

Call for information on changing displays and exhibits featured at the museum. The Museum offers several educational programs along with tours of museum exhibits. Programs at the museum are free and there is no admission fee. There is also a museum gift shop. Summer hours are Monday through Saturday, 9 a.m. to 5 p.m. and winter hours are Tuesday through Saturday 10 a.m. to 4 p.m.

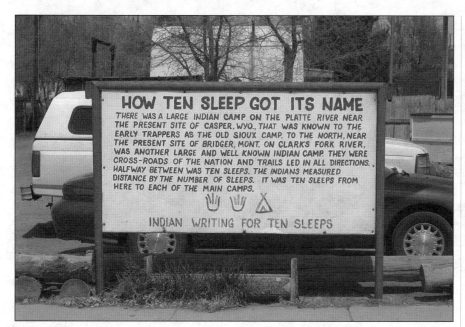

Ten Sleep paddy wagon.

T **Ten Sleep Pioneer Museum**
436 2nd St. in Ten Sleep. 366-2759

The Museum exhibits cover the everyday life of pioneer families and include tools and clothing. A special exhibits recreates the Spring Creek raid which was a major turning point for the relationships of the sheepmen and the cattlemen. The museum is open from 9:00 a.m. to 4:00 p.m. Admission is free and donations are welcomed.

H **Tensleep Canyon**
East of Ten Sleep on U.S. Highway 16

Ages ago, these mountains were deep within the Earth's crust, and the area that is known today as the Bighorn Mountains was a basin. Beginning about 75 million years ago the land began to slowly rise above the sea bed reaching an elevation of nearly 20,000 feet. Since that time, the eroding forces of wind, water, and ice have removed thousands of feet of rock resulting in what you see today.

The cliffs of Tensleep Canyon are composed predominantly of massive layers of limestone. This limestone layer underlies the towns of Tensleep and Worland and serves as their major source of water. The water is removed from the layer by deep wells.

Glaciers carved out the valley of Tensleep Canyon within the last 250,000 years. Evidence of these ancient glaciers can be seen in the U-shape of the valley bottom, and piles of boulders, or glacial moraine, left along West Tensleep Creek. The "West Moraine" stretches for 10 miles, making it the longest moraine in the Big Horn Mountains. Weathering forces and the flow of the creek continue to wear away the rock in Tensleep Canyon. In the winter, ice flows can be seen on the canyon walls.

H **Colby Mammoth Kill Site**
Highway 16, five miles east of Worland

Extinct species of mammoths, horses, camels, and bison roamed this area 11,000 years ago and were being killed by humans known as the Clovis hunters. South of this spot 400 meters is the location of one of the largest known Clovis mammoth kills in North America. A deep arroyo with steep walls was present when the mammoths were killed. Clovis hunters would stalk a family of mammoths and spear a young animal that was careless enough to wander away from the protection of the family. As the animal became weak from the effects of the wound, it became further removed from the herd and the hunters maneuvered it into the deep arroyo where it could not escape. The hunters needed only to wait for the wound to weaken the animal enough that it could easily be killed. This kind of event was repeated many times over the years.`

One pile of bones consisted of the left front quarter of a mature female mammoth with bones of other mammoths stacked around it and the skull of a young male mammoth placed on top. This is believed to have been a frozen meat cache that was never utilized and spoiled with the approach of warm weather. Another pile of mammoth bones was probably a similar cache that was utilized. A front quarter of a young mammoth would represent over 500 kilograms of meat. These caches suggest that at least some of the animals were killed during the cold weather months.

This site was excavated by the Department of Anthropology at the University of Wyoming under the direction of Dr. George Frison, during 1973, 1975, and 1978. Materials from the site can be seen at the Washakie County Museum and Cultural Center and at the University of Wyoming Anthropological Museum.

17 *Gas, Food, Lodging*

Ten Sleep
Pop. 304, Elev. 4,206

Native Americans measured the length of journeys in the number of "sleeps" (days) it took to arrive. The location of Ten Sleep was a ten-day (ten sleep) trip from both Fort Laramie and the Yellowstone region, the halfway marker for the journey from one to the other. An Army engineer who mapped the area, Col. Sackett, named the place Sackett Fork in 1867. The sheep industry brought growth in the 1890s and early 1900s, despite conflicts over grazing rights with cattlemen. This culminated in the Tensleep Raid of 1909, in which three sheepmen were killed. Today, Ten Sleep is a rustic, pastoral town and one of the few places in Wyoming where fruit trees can actually thrive.

Big Trails

Big Trails was first named Red Bank but changed for the four main Indian trails which converged here from all points of the compass. The name change seemed right because there was confusion with the mail and other towns that started with Red. The post office was closed in 1940.

Thermopolis	Jan	Feb	March	April	May	June	July	Aug	Sep	Oct	Nov	Dec	Annual
Average Max. Temperature (F)	36.3	43.2	51.1	62.3	72.2	82.5	90.6	90.2	79.1	65.5	47.6	38.6	63.3
Average Min. Temperature (F)	8.1	15.2	21.8	31.7	41.5	48.6	54.4	53.4	43.5	32.0	19.5	11.6	31.8
Average Total Precipitation (in.)	0.41	0.39	0.80	1.40	1.94	1.65	0.86	0.53	1.07	1.00	0.74	0.33	11.11
Average Total SnowFall (in.)	5.2	5.0	5.1	1.6	0.5	0.0	0.0	0.0	0.2	1.8	5.3	5.2	30.0
Average Snow Depth (in.)	2	1	1	0	0	0	0	0	0	0	1	1	1

WIND RIVER COUNTRY

Breathtaking views of a range that boasts 53 peaks over 13,000 feet in elevation and an area containing nearly 600 lakes and over 2,000 miles of rivers and streams. This is truly a fishermans paradise. Tourists also have the opportunity to immerse themselves in Native American culture from powwows and petroglyphs. Or take in real cowboys and rodeos. Also on this adventure travelers will find the Oregon-Mormon-California-Pony Express trails, abundant wildlife and mountain man rendezvous re-enactments. Don't forget to visit the Continental Divide at South Pass which is the lowest spot on the divide. Here visitors have the opportunity to experience the land as the nineteenth century emigrants did 150 years ago as they traveled through. There is also a plethora of activities one can do throughout the area from horseback riding to camping and attending local unique events. A journey through this area will provide plenty of oohs and ahhs, as well as a sense of what life was like more than 100 years ago.

H Managing the Range
East of Ten Sleep on U.S. Highway 16

In the summer, domestic sheep and cattle graze the rangelands of the Bighorn National Forest. These rangelands are the vast, grassy hillsides and sagebrush-covered valleys that dominate the plateau of the Big Horn Mountains. Without the natural control of wild fire, sagebrush will spread, killing the grasses, and reducing the rangeland for livestock and wildlife. Today, the Forest Service is trying to restore the balance of sagebrush and grass by the use of controlled burns.

H Powder River Pass
East of Ten Sleep on U.S. Highway 16

This is Powder River Pass, 9,666 feet above sea level, is the highest point on Highway 16 in Bighorn National Forest.

At this elevation the harsh weather conditions and shallow soil discourages the growth of trees. Growing on the slopes of the pass are the fragile plants of the Alpine Tundra. These tiny plants survive by clinging to the thin rocky soil, which provides just enough water and nutrients.

The Big Horn Mountain Divide is the high-elevation backbone of the mountain range, which has its southern end in Wyoming and its northern end in Montana. The Big Horn Mountains serve as a major watershed, providing water to rancers, farmers, and communities in the valleys and basins to east and west.

Along the highway you will see long segments of tall wooden fences, standing at an angle to the roadway. These are snow fences, erected and maintained by the Wyoming State Highway Department. Their purpose is to divert blowing and drifting snow away from the road. In the winter, drifts as high as 10 feet line the side of highway.

H First Washakie County Church
Highway 16 east of Ten Sleep at Circle J Ranch

March 14, 1901, Rev. L.C. Thompson, Rev. E.E. Tarbill, Mortimer Lewis, J.W. Carpenter, Kate Lynch and Mark Warner signed papers incorporating the Methodist Church of Ten Sleep and accepted land for a church building and cemetery from David Moses. The community raised $600, supplementing $200 given by Extension Society of Philadelphia. The building started in 1901 by volunteer labor with lumber donated by Milo Burke, was completed in 1904 and dedicated January 8, 1905. Each assisting family was given a lot in the cemetery, where many pioneers rest. The church was moved to its present location in 1925. The annex was added in 1952. Moved to Circle J in 1975.

H Bighorn National Forest
Ten Sleep Canyon. 674-2600

You are standing at the bottom of Ten Sleep Canyon near the western edge of the Big Horn Mountains. The steep rocky cliffs were the native territory of the Bighorn sheep. Disease and the activities of human and livestock have led to their eventual disappearance. They have been reintroduced to this forest through cooperative efforts of the U.S. Forest Service and the Wyoming Game and Fish Department.

Lewis and Clark's expedition was the first organized exploration into the area. The great numbers of Big Horn sheep noted in their journal in 1808 gave the river, basin, mountains, and National Forest its name.

H Leigh Creek Monument
U.S. Highway 16 nine miles east of Ten Sleep

Across the canyon, on the point, the Leigh Creek Monument topped with the cross was erected in 1889 in memory of an English nobleman who fell 200 feet to his death over the canyon wall, while in pursuit of mountain sheep. The monument was laid up of native stone in dry mortar and is approximately ten feet square at the base. It contains a marble slab facing west with the inscription. Gilbert E. Leigh died October 23rd, 1884. He was the guest of the Bar X Bar cattle company a remittance man, and had spent most of his adult life as a big game hunter.

H Spring Creek Raid
About 7 miles south of Ten Sleep on State Highway 434.

Cattlemen of the Big Horn Basin dominated the range for many years and set up boundaries or "deadlines" where sheep were forbidden. Fierce animosity grew between the opposing sheep and cattle ranchers as several sheep camps were raided during the late 1800s and early 1900s.

In late March, 1909, Joe Allemand, a Basque sheepman, and Joe Emge, a cattleman turned sheepman, left Worland headed for Spring Creek with 5000 head of sheep. They were accompanied by Allemand's nephew, Jules Lazier, and two sheepherders, Bounce Helmer and Pete Cafferall. Talk spread like wildfire across the western slope of the Big Horn Mountains as the deadline was crossed and plans were soon made to head off this intrusion.

On the moonlit night of April 2, 1909, seven masked riders approached the sheep camp's two wagons where the herders slept. Gunfire lit the night as rifles blazed. Emge and Lazier were killed in their wagon and both wagons were set afire. Allemand emerged from the flames, but was quickly shot down.

The monument on this side of the road is situated at the site of the south wagon. The monument on the north side of Spring Creek is near the location of the wagon where the sheepmen were killed. Five of the perpetrators were convicted and sent to prison. Public reaction against this brutal and tragic act left no doubt that violence on Wyoming's open range would no longer be tolerated.

18 *Food*

Hyattville
Pop. 100, Elv. 4,457
No gas

Originally named Paintrock for the Indian pictographs found on a cliff nearby, Hyatt got its name from general store owner and postmaster Samuel Hyatt. When his store burned to the ground in 1900, he took up ranching.

Another pioneer settler in Hyattville was Asa Shinn Mercer. He was known for bringing shiploads of young women to the West Coast by way of Cape Horn to become frontier brides. This enterprise took place mostly in the 1860s, and he chose to retire here when it was finished.

T Medicine Lodge State Archaeological Site
Six miles northeast of Hyattville. 469-2234

Archaeology Makes Medicine Lodge Unique

The Medicine Lodge site has long been known for its Indian petroglyphs and pictographs, but not until 1969 did the full archaeological wealth of the site come to light. In that year, Dr. George Frison, then Wyoming State Archaeologist, began

Worland	Jan	Feb	March	April	May	June	July	Aug	Sep	Oct	Nov	Dec	Annual
Average Max. Temperature (F)	28.8	37.2	48.4	59.9	70.4	80.6	89.7	87.5	75.5	62.1	44.1	32.0	59.7
Average Min. Temperature (F)	0.8	8.5	20.4	31.2	41.5	49.6	54.7	51.5	41.2	30.6	17.5	6.0	29.5
Average Total Precipitation (in.)	0.29	0.21	0.37	0.92	1.37	1.26	0.68	0.53	0.83	0.65	0.36	0.23	7.69
Average Total SnowFall (in.)	3.8	2.6	2.6	1.2	0.1	0.0	0.0	0.0	0.1	0.8	2.3	3.2	16.7
Average Snow Depth (in.)	1	1	0	0	0	0	0	0	0	0	0	1	0

From Ten Sleep to Hyattville

a series of digs that uncovered a human habitation site that has been continuously occupied for over 10,000 years. Medicine Lodge has thus become a key to the interpretation of the archaeology of the entire Big Horn Basin area.

The archaeological investigation involved digging through approximately 26 feet of soil and rocky sediments, discovering over 60 cultural levels spanning some 10,000 years of human occupation. This important aspect of the site enables the archaeologists to examine particular lifestyles and to study how these styles changed over time. Some of the material items found during the dig included fire pits, food storage pits, manos and metates (grinding stones) and projectile points.

The information gleaned from the archaeological investigation provides interesting educational and interpretive insight into the life of this area's inhabitants throughout the years. Interpretive signs located at the base of the petroglyph cliff and exhibits in the log cabin visitor center give an overview of the information accumulated by the archaeologists. They also explain some of what you see around you at Medicine Lodge State Archaeological Site.

The excavations at Medicine Lodge Creek are part of long term archaeological research by Dr. George Frison. This includes investigations at several other rock shelters in nearby Paintrock and Medicine Lodge canyons and at several quarry sites where raw materials for prehistoric stone tools were obtained.

Frison has also conducted major excavations at the Colby site near Worland and the Hanson site near Shell. Results from this research have been published in Frison's 1978 book, "Prehistoric Hunters of the High Plains," and several other professional articles and books.

Data from all these sites are being used to reconstruct different aspects of prehistoric life and settlement systems ranging from those of the 11,000 year old Paleo-Indian to the historic Crow Indians who lived in the area.

Analyses of stone artifacts, flaking debris, seeds, bones, pollen, and charcoal from the site, as well as aspects of the local geology and site stratigraphy are all used to reconstruct the past. For example, bones found in the site can be used to infer dietary habits of the prehistoric occupants, as well as the particular time of year the site was occupied.

One interesting find was the recovery of rodent, deer and bird bones which appeared to be refuse from a cooking pit. Dated at about 9,500 years old, this discovery greatly increased our knowledge about some of the earliest Americans who were traditionally thought to have been only big game hunters.
Reprinted from Wyoming State Parks Brochure

H Medicine Lodge Creek Informative Plaques
Seven miles northeast of Hyattville about 2 miles off of Cold Spring Road.

Nature's Storehouse
For at least 10,000 years, this area where the Medicine Lodge Creek flows out of the Big Horn Mountains has provided a home for man. From the earliest hunter-gatherers to today's ranchers, Medicine Lodge is an ideal site for human habitation. Everything man needed is located at or near this site. Fruits, berries, greens and roots from the lush plant growth surrounding the creek bottom provided food, medicine, firewood and material for weapons and building. The abundance of animal life from wood rats to bison were an important part of the native diet. Within a few miles of the site there are excellent sources of high quality quartzite and chert—a rock resembling flint. These materials were used to make projectile points, arrowheads and other weapons and tools. The eastern exposure of the sandstone cliffs creates warm, sunny winter mornings and the slight overhang causes cool, shady summer afternoons at the base of the cliff. Add the constant availability of running water and you have an ideal camping spot that has been used throughout the ages.

Petroglyphs and Pictographs
Rock art at Medicine Lodge and throughout the Big Horn Basin falls into two categories—PETROGLYPHS which were pecked into the sandstone surfaces and PICTOGRAPHS that were painted onto the surfaces. Human-like figures and animals were common motifs. The meaning of rock art is difficult to decipher, but most archaeologists agree that the drawings are symbolic and represent the complex mythological and religious concepts of the artists. The figure illustrated here is located above you on the cliffs and has probably been chalked at some point in time and appears bluish in color. This type of figure petroglyphs appear throughout Wyoming and may symbolize the importance of hunting to the prehistoric economy. Rock art is extremely difficult to date, but art at this particular site is probably no more than 1000 years old.

Petroglyphs and pictographs are a priceless legacy from the Indian people who inhabited this area in years gone by. The elements are gradually dimming these fragile drawings and vandalism such as the carving of initials, painting over the figures and even chalking to make the art visible are leading to their destruction. Please let your foot-prints be the only sign of your visit!

Excavating and Recovery
Beginning in 1973, Medicine Lodge Creek was the scene of one of the most significant archaeological excavations in North America. For 2 years, anthropologists from the University of Wyoming carefully excavated the layers of silt and clay to depths of well over 20 feet below where you are standing. Thousands of artifacts, bones, and seeds were recovered, and cooking and heating hearths, food storage pits, and evidence of these structures were unearthed. These discoveries revealed over 60 cultural levels, documenting the entire history of human occupation in the Big Horn Basin. The information gleaned by the anthropologist along with the geological, chemical, botanical, and related studies are being used to reconstruct the life ways of man and how he adapted to changing environmental conditions from the end of the Ice Age to modern times. Some physical evidence of the remains, such as the rectangular depressions at the base of the cliff which have been backfilled for preservation purposes.

Clues from the Past
Thousands of years ago, while the Indians camped here, the banks of Medicine Lodge Creek were only a few feet away from the base of the cliff. Throughout the years, the creek changed its course and meandered across the width of the valley. Massive rockfalls from the cliffs, such as the one before you, diverted the creek back out into the middle of the valley, thus preserving the silt and clays which held the remains of the campsite of the ancient hunter-gatherers. Only through this accident of geological action has any evidence of human habitation at Medicine Lodge Creek been preserved. From the stratigraphy exposed during the excavations, geologists and archaeologists can interpret the history of the valley. Each layer exposed produced clues that give us information on past environmental conditions and the cultural activities that took place. You can envision the original slope of the valley before it was leveled for corrals and before archaeological excavation began by looking at the undisturbed land adjacent to the rockfall and the line of red earth on the cliff approximately 10 feet above the existing ground level.

19 *Food, Lodging*

Manderson
Pop. 104, Elev. 3,890

Named for a Burlington Railroad official, this little town was originally called Alamo.

20 *Gas, Food, Lodging*

Basin
Pop. 1,238, Elev. 3,870

Named for the Big Horn Basin, this is the county seat of Big Horn County. A bitter battle for this title ensued in 1897 between Basin City (as it was then called) and Otto. Basin won by 38 votes, thanks to the fact that Cody entered the race at

Ten Sleep													
	Jan	**Feb**	**March**	**April**	**May**	**June**	**July**	**Aug**	**Sep**	**Oct**	**Nov**	**Dec**	**Annual**
Average Max. Temperature (F)	36.7	41.2	49.6	59.4	69.4	79.0	87.6	86.1	75.4	62.6	46.2	38.0	60.9
Average Min. Temperature (F)	13.3	18.1	25.9	34.0	42.4	50.5	56.9	55.5	45.4	35.1	23.9	15.4	34.7
Average Total Precipitation (in.)	0.54	0.39	0.85	1.42	2.19	2.07	0.94	0.72	1.33	1.14	0.81	0.62	13.02
Average Total SnowFall (in.)	9.6	6.9	8.4	5.5	1.9	0.0	0.0	0.0	0.8	3.0	7.8	9.7	53.7
Average Snow Depth (in.)	3	2	1	0	0	0	0	0	0	0	1	2	1

the last minute and split the vote in the west. It is known as the Lilac City, and the major crop is beans, although the economy relies on ranching too. Along with Greybull, Basin was one of the first towns in the whole Northwest to make use of natural gas for utilities.

Otto

This little town was named for cattle mogul Otto Franc, owner of the Pitchfork Ranch. It was once a contender for county seat, but won out to Basin when Cody entered the race at the last minute, dividing the vote.

21 *Gas, Food, Lodging*

Greybull
Pop. 1,815, Elev. 3,788

It is said that an albino buffalo, held sacred by the Indians, once roamed in this area, giving both the river and the town its name. Pictographs of the animal can be seen on bluffs near the river. John Borner, an immigrant from Saxony, was probably the first white man to build a home here in 1886. A farming community developed, settled by German immigrants and Mormons. Natural gas was discovered here in 1908, and the following year the town was officially established. In 1915, several plentiful oil wells were drilled and two refineries were built. Energy production has dominated the economy ever since.

The area has been prone to flooding, experiencing two major floods in the early part of the 20th century. But the tendency of the river to overflow has left a treasure trove of fossil remains, including dinosaur bones, cycads, ammonite and bentonite deposits, and an early horse species called Eohippus (dawn horse). The landscape is also dotted with Indian fire rings, the small Bear Creek Medicine Wheel, and many other stone arrows, cairns, and circles left by the early occupants. Now the fertile, well-irrigated flatlands are mostly filled with ranging cattle and pronghorn antelope.

T Chamber of Commerce - Greybull
521 Greybull Ave. in Greybull. 765-2100

T Greybull Museum
325 Greybull Ave. in Greybull. 765-2444

This is a free museum in a friendly town where the entire family can relax and enjoy a new

Scores of historic aircraft are available for viewing at the Museum of Flight and Aerial Firefighting in Greybull.

approach to the world in which we live. The displays include Indian apparel and artifacts, guns and old weapons, and other bits of Western and pioneer heritage. For those interested in geology and the earth sciences, the museum offers perhaps the most outstanding agate collections and polished petrified tree sections around, dating back millions of years. Dinosaur bones and other prehistoric fossil remains can also be seen here. Call for hours.

T Museum of Flight and Aerial Firefighting
South Big Horn County Airport in Greybull. 765-4482

This area has long been a magnet for lovers of beauty and adventure. A significant part of that is reflected in the collection of the Museum of Flight and Aerial Firefighting. A nationally renowned historic assembly, you will find several of the last remaining examples of World War II's mighty bombers and transport aircraft. These magnificent planes are restored and retired here to whet the imaginations of many a true or

would-have-been flying ace. Among other exhibits, you can see five of the last flying PB4Y-2 planes used against the Japanese in the South Pacific. So heavily fortified, the awesome firepower of the PB4Y-2 caused the Japanese to flee from several islands they occupied when they heard these planes were coming. The museum also features planes used in fighting fires over the decades since Orville and Wilbur Wright first flew. Planes have been used to help fight fires for most of the century, to transmit information before radio, to spot fires, and to drop fire retardant (once beer kegs full of water) on fires from above. In 1953, the first modern air tankers were developed and began testing in the Western US. We hope to add more planes to our collection to commemorate the history of flight, both in war and firefighting. Please make a donation.

T Greybull Elevator
In Greybull

As a way for farmers and ranchers from the Emblem Bench and Shell Creek Valley to market grain without the need to travel long distances in horse-drawn wagons, the Greybull Elevator was founded. This elevator is one of the oldest building in Greybull and is a point of interest in town today. When the present owner need to replace the siding, local artist Karyne Dunbar was hired to paint western scenes on the panels prior to installation. One tower features the legendary Greybull Buffalo who is unarmed and an Indian carrying a Buffalo spear on the other. The question on many minds is whether they face each other in greeting, or challenge. To uncover the legend, ask one of the folks at the Graybull elevator. They would be happy to share the story.

Basin	Jan	Feb	March	April	May	June	July	Aug	Sep	Oct	Nov	Dec	Annual
Average Max. Temperature (F)	29.5	38.7	50.4	62.1	72.4	82.4	90.9	89.2	77.2	63.6	45.0	32.9	61.2
Average Min. Temperature (F)	2.5	11.0	21.7	31.7	41.8	50.1	55.4	52.6	42.1	30.8	18.0	7.2	30.4
Average Total Precipitation (in.)	0.22	0.16	0.30	0.72	1.14	1.14	0.52	0.45	0.75	0.51	0.29	0.26	6.47
Average Total Snowfall (in.)	3.8	3.2	3.2	1.9	0.3	0.0	0.0	0.0	0.6	0.5	2.8	4.0	20.3
Average Snow Depth (in.)	2	1	0	0	0	0	0	0	0	0	0	1	0

SPRING CREEK RAID EXHIBIT

In the 1870s, in Wyoming, Texas and Colorado, sheep ranchers with their herders and "woolies" began to encroach on the open range in significant numbers. There was immediate dislike and antagonism on the part of the cattlemen and their cowboys towards the newcomers. The ensuing battles were, however, really being fought over the use of the rangeland grass and the wealth it could provide in the form of beef or mutton and wool.

The 1909 raid in Wyoming was a particularly brutal attack by cattlemen on a sheepherder's camp. It received protracted and widespread news media coverage at the time and marked the beginning of the end of such conflicts. The cattlemen involved were tried in the local court and, for essentially the first time, convicted of major crimes. All prior such cases that made it to court were either dismissed or won by the cattlemen because of expensive legal defenses and/or sympathetic jurors.

After this raid, the battle for use of public land for grazing would continue sporadically until about 1921. During their half-century duration, cattlemen-sheepmen battles numbered more than 120 over 8 states. They caused at least 54 human deaths along with the slaughter of more than 53,000 sheep. The cowboys found a number of ways to kill the hated sheep during their raids, including "rim-rocking", i.e., driving a flock over a high cliff.

The Spring Creek Raid began in the Spring of 1909 when two sheepmen, Joe Allemand and Joe Emge, along with their three sheepherders, drove 2,500 head of sheep from Worland, Wyoming, east to Tensleep, some 25 miles distant. Allemand was well liked by both the cattlemen and the sheepmen of the area even though he ran sheep. Allemand was having some financial difficulty for some of his sheep had been lost in a couple of raids so he had sold a partnership to another Spring Creek rancher, Joe Emge. The latter, a squatty dark man, was not so well thought of. Emge had at one time been with the cattlemen but after taking over the sheep he had boasted that he'd graze his sheep any place he liked and that he'd run the cattlemen off the range.

On this April day in 1909, the two sheepmen were driving two bands of sheep across the badlands from Worland to the Spring Creek ranches. Allemand had telephoned his wife to say that he would be home that evening. Listeners over the party line hurried to inform some of Emge's enemies that Allemand would not be in the camp that night and Emge would be alone with the herder and the camp tender.

But after camp had been made with one band of sheep and a sheepwagon on each side of the creek, two brothers who lived nearby stopped to visit and eat supper and by the time they left, Allemand thought it was too late to ride on home. So Allemand and his young nephew, Jules Lazier, a French subject, and Emge went to sleep in the upper wagon. A newly hired young herder, 16 year old Bounce Helmer and another Frenchman, Pete Cafferal, were in the lower wagon.

When it grew dark the raiders struck, two headed toward the wagon with the sheepmen and the other five after the sheep. Shots were fired at the herds and Helmer, fearing for his dog sprang, half-dressed out of the other wagon. He was immediately captured by the raiders as was Cafferal and both were tied up. Helmer who had lit a lantern was able to see and recognize some of the men but Cafferal could not.

When no one came out of the upper wagon, the two men who were near it started firing into it. One of them started a fire by throwing Kerosene from Helmer's lantern on the sage brush that had been piled under the sheepwagon to build the morning fire. As Allemand came out of the wagon he was shot and killed. The fire grew so rapidly that Emge and Lazier were trapped. When the raiders realized that they had killed the wrong man, they fled in a panic. In the meantime, Helmer and Cafferal freed themselves and ran to the neighbors for help.

It was almost noon the next day before Big Horn County sheriff, Felix Alston and Judge Percy Metz reached the scene of the raid. Joe Allemands body was lying near the smoldering embers of the sheep wagon and one of his sheep dog's puppies was curled up on his chest. The burned bodies of Emge and Lazier were found nearby.

Seven men were eventually arrested for the crime. Albert Keys and Charles Ferris turned states evidence and told the whole story. They were jailed in Sheridan and the other five in the Basin jail. A long trial was held in the fall of 1909. Herbert Brink was found guilty of first degree murder. George Henry Saban and Milton Alexander were found guilty of second degree murder. All three were sentenced to five years in the penitentiary. Tommy Dixon, and Ed Eaton were sentenced to two years on arson charges.

The Spring Creek Raid did indeed prove to be a major turning point in the relations between cattlemen and sheepmen. However, while such conflicts continued for the following decade, the day of the gunman in Wyoming was rapidly fading.

T Devil's Kitchen
Five miles east of Greybull

This exposure of rocks is part of the Cloverly formation, a million year old sequence of sediments containing dinosaur remains. The soft colorful sandstone and shales of the Cloverly Formation form a badlands landscape of isolated spires and weathered hills. In this rock formation is the fossilized remains of Deinonychus, a velociraptor. A map to the area may be obtained from the Greybull Chamber of Commerce.

T Stone Schoolhouse
Located between Greybull and Shell, on Highway 14 East.

Built in 1903 and used as a school until the early 1950s, the Stone School is an outstanding example of the vanishing one-room schoolhouse. It embodies the construction type employed by pioneer masons who used indigenous building materials. The school is one of the few remaining intact one-room schoolhouses in Wyoming and has received recognition on the National Register of Historic Places.

T Borner Cabin
In Greybull

In 1886, John Borner and his hired man, J. A. Benjamin, traveled from Lander, Wyoming and built a large cabin on the site of the present Greybull City Park. The cabin's chimney remains intact on the park site. Borner, who was born in Saxony, Germany, came to America as a child. He served in the Civil War, then headed west. he married Jennie Canary, a sister of "Calamity Jane" Canary, in Lander and remained there until his wife died. In 1887 he brought his children to the cabin and began the settlement which would become known a Greybull. Known as "Uncle Johnny" to many, he was remembered as a kind, generous man. He passed away in December of 1919.

DAYS OF '49

In 1949 a group of men attending a Junior Chamber of Commerce meeting in Greybull talked themselves into sponsoring the first Days of '49 Celebration. The first rodeo was memorable. The Jaycees saddled and gathered horses out of the hills. By the 1950s, the Days of '49 celebration annual drew several times the 2,500 population of Greybull. Colorful parades and two days of fun mark the Days of '49. Held the second weekend in June, this is an event not to be missed!

Greybull	Jan	Feb	March	April	May	June	July	Aug	Sep	Oct	Nov	Dec	Annual
Average Max. Temperature (F)	30.4	38.8	51.2	61.5	72.8	82.0	90.1	88.6	75.6	61.9	45.1	32.4	60.9
Average Min. Temperature (F)	4.1	10.4	22.2	34.8	42.2	50.5	56.0	52.8	44.7	30.5	18.5	7.3	31.2
Average Total Precipitation (in.)	0.36	0.27	0.31	0.68	1.22	1.23	0.54	0.47	0.74	0.49	0.36	0.30	6.98
Average Total SnowFall (in.)	4.1	3.2	2.6	1.7	0.3	0.0	0.0	0.0	0.7	0.6	2.9	4.3	20.4
Average Snow Depth (in.)	2	1	0	0	0	0	0	0	0	0	0	1	0

H Wyoming's Prehistoric Wildlife
Greybull rest stop northwest of Greybull

The Big Horn Basin is famous for its dinosaur discoveries. During the 1930's, some of the world's significant dinosaur fossils were excavated by the American Museum of Natural History. The Basin received renewed interest in the early 1990's with the discovery of the world's most complete skeleton of an Allosaurus fragilis, a meat-eating dinosaur of the Jurassic Period (150 million years ago). The largest carnivorous dinosaur of its time, allosaurs stood 10 feet high and measured 35 feet in length. Dinosaur excavations continue today.

The Big Horn Basin also yields animal remains from recent times. Natural Trap Cave on the west slope of the Big Horn Mountains is an ancient sinkhole in the limestone where, for more than 20,000 years, animals fell 80 feet to their deaths. The bottom of the cave is littered with bones of extinct mammals such as mammoths, short-faced bears, saber-toothed cats. American lions and dire wolves.

Scientists study bones and fossils of the Big Horn Basin to help determine past climatic and environmental conditions. By researching the earth's past, scientists can better predict and evaluate future global changes and their effects on wildlife and humans.

H Sheep Mountain
10 miles north of Greybull on WY- 310

The prominent hill to the east is known as Sheep Mountain. It is the surface expression of an upward fold in the earth's crust that geologists refer to as an anticline. Sheep Mountain is a textbook example of an anticline fold. It is 15 miles long and the involved rock formations, which were originally horizontal, have been bent and uplifted over 1000 feet. The surface sedimentary rock formations that are exposed in the fold, range in age from 66-360 million years. Anticlines form when deep seated, compressive forces within the earth's crust, squeeze and shorten the crust. The geologic event, which resulted in the creation of Sheep Mountain Anticline, along with many other anticlines in the Big Horn Basin began approximately 66 million years ago. This is the same time period during which dinosaurs became extinct. The present Sheep Mountain has evolved over the past 3 million years. It resulted from down cutting of the land surface by rivers and streams and the removal of much of the original basin fill sediment.

H Lower Shell Schoolhouse
On U.S. Highway 14 about 6 miles east of Greybull

The Lower Shell Schoolhouse was one of the first non-log community buildings built in the Big Horn Basin. Using a classic one room schoolhouse design, it was constructed on this site in 1903 on land which had been donated to the Odessa School District. The school district was named for the nearby Odessa Post Office

which had operated from 1891 to 1895. Local homesteaders quarried sandstone from the surrounding hills and assisted in the construction of the 24' by 46' building. During the 1905-1906 school year forty students were enrolled here demonstrating the early settlers' high regard for education.

Although the building was mainly used as a school, it also functioned as a church for traveling preachers and as a community dance hall. A wide variety of organizations, from cemetery boards to the farm bureau, held meetings here as well. Use as a school ended in the early 1950s, but the building continued to be used as a meeting hall until the early 1970s.

In 1980 the foundation received new footings and the roof was reshingled as an effort was made to stabilize the building after nearly a decade of neglect. The addition to the rear of the building was completed in 1988, using the same architectural design as the original construction. The historical appearance was thus retained, while at the same time the building could serve as an art gallery, bookstore and information center.

The simple form of the schoolhouse epitomizes the austere life of the region's early pioneers. Shell Valley's lush irrigated farm fields contrast with the arid topography of the basin demonstrating the current results of their earlier endeavors. As one of a few remaining one room schoolhouses in Wyoming the "old stone school", as it was often called, has received recognition by enrollment in the National Register of Historic Places.

The building houses the Stone School Gallery & Bookstore which has books, maps, and artwork of the region.

F Lisa's Fine Dining
200 Greybull Ave., Greybull. 765-3765.
www.lisasfinefoods.com;
lisasrestaurant@tctwest.net

Established in 1989 under the logo "Simply the best food in Wyoming," Lisa's Fine Dining is a popular stop en route to Yellowstone. Featuring a southwest décor and old west nostalgia, Lisa's accommodates fifty guests each in its separate dining room and lounge. Savor the tastes of traditional cowboy and Native american cooking with Lisa's creative entrees. Menu items are prepared from scratch daily and range from pasta and steak

to flavorful Southwest meals like enchiladas, fajitas, burritos, and more. Serving over 75,000 guests every year, Lisa's Fine Dining illustrates that not all chefs live in the big city. Lisa's is open seven days a week Memorial Day to Labor Day from 7 am to 10 pm. Winter hours are from 11 am to 9 pm Monday through Saturday with breakfast served only during summer.

L Greybull Motel
300 N. 6th St., Greybull. 765-2628.
www.greybull.com/restlodge/greybullmoteladpage/Greybull%20Motel.htm;
greybullmotel@bresnan.net

Completely remodeled with a unique western décor, this one-story locally owned and operated motel is entirely smoke-free. Enjoy spotless, comfortable rooms featuring queen beds, line dried bed linens, fluffy pillows, large plush towels, central air conditioning, individually controlled electric heat, cable/HBO TV with remotes, phones, refrigerators, microwaves, and wireless Internet. When you're not enjoying the amenities of your room, relax in the outdoor covered seating area or explore the lovely flower gardens. The motel is conveniently located just three blocks from Greybull shopping and dining, and the beautiful Big Horn Mountains and year-round outdoor adventures are just thirty minutes away! Pet-friendly rooms are available, making the Greybull Motel everyone's choice for a pleasant and comfortable stay on the way to Yellowstone or the Big Horn Mountains.

S Big Horn Quilts
529 Greybull Ave., Greybull. 765-2604 or (877) 586-9150. www.bighornquilts.com; julie@bighornquilts.com

Recognized as one of the world's largest online quilting fabric stores, Big Horn Quilts originated

Shell	Jan	Feb	March	April	May	June	July	Aug	Sep	Oct	Nov	Dec	Annual
Average Max. Temperature (F)	32.5	40.4	50.9	60.8	70.0	80.4	88.8	87.3	75.6	62.5	44.8	34.6	60.7
Average Min. Temperature (F)	6.0	12.6	21.6	29.8	37.3	47.1	53.7	50.2	39.7	29.2	17.3	7.5	29.4
Average Total Precipitation (in.)	0.54	0.46	0.53	1.04	1.46	1.63	0.78	0.58	1.12	0.84	0.56	0.49	10.03
Average Total SnowFall (in.)	6.0	3.5	2.2	0.4	0.5	0.0	0.0	0.0	0.2	0.6	1.7	5.2	20.3
Average Snow Depth (in.)	3	2	1	0	0	0	0	0	0	0	0	1	1

in 1998 under the energetic personality of owners Julie and Dave Owens. Starting out with just fifty bolts of fabric, Big Horn Quilts has burgeoned into a million-dollar quilt supply business with over 8,000 bolts of fabric. The legendary store now ships orders across the world with customers making a point to stop in person while visiting Wyoming. In addition to a huge fabric selection, patrons to both the downtown Greybull location and the online store will also find hundreds of books, notions, patterns, and quilting ideas along with unbeatable customer service. Big Horn Quilts is located just three doors east of Greybull's stoplight and is open 9-5 six days a week…and of course 24 hours a day online.

22 Gas, Food, Lodging

Bureau of Land Management photo

Shell
Pop. 50, Elev. 4,210

This town, like the creek, was probably named for the fossilized invertibrate shells which line the creek bed and are found throughout the area. It also may have been named for Dick Shell, who founded the town.

T Red Gulch Dinosaur Tracksite
10 miles east of Greybull on U.S. Highway 14 to Red Gulch Scenic Byway turnoff, then five miles south

Red Gulch Dinosaur Tracksite

At BLM's Red Gulch Dinosaur Tracksite, you can imagine yourself walking along an ocean shoreline 167 million years ago with dozens of other dinosaurs, looking to pick up a bite of lunch from what washed up on the last high tide. The ground is soft and your feet sink down in the thick ooze, leaving a clear footprint with every step you take.

The discovery of rare fossil footprints on public lands near the Red Gulch/Alkali National Back Country Byway close to Shell, Wyoming, could alter current views about the Sundance Formation and the paleoenvironment of the Middle Jurassic Period.

Discovery/Background

The Red Gulch Dinosaur Tracksite is the largest tracksite in Wyoming and one of only a few worldwide from the Middle Jurassic Period (160 million to 180 million years old). Until the tracks were reported in 1997, most scientists thought the entire Bighorn Basin and most of Wyoming was covered by an ancient ocean called the Sundance Sea.

Scientists thought that only sea-dwelling creatures could have lived in this area. There shouldn't be any dinosaur footprints at all. Not only are there hundreds of tracks, but in this 40-acre area there could be thousands. The dinosaur tracks were clearly made just at the shoreline, not in deep ocean water, and there must have been large areas of dry land to support not only dinosaurs but other animals and plants.

The limey mud that the dinosaurs were walking in probably felt similar to cement just starting to harden. The tracks were perfectly preserved when the mud hardened and was covered by more layers of ooze, and then by fine sand, filling the tracks and preserving their shape. Over the years, layer upon layer of sediment filled in over the top. Much later, erosion went to work and removed those layers, exposing the tracks that had been made all those millions of years ago.

The tracks were reported in 1997 by Greybull native Erik Kvale while enjoying the scenery with Allen Archer, Rowena Manuel, Cliff Manuel and Fran Paton on BLM-administered lands.

Scientists Come to Study

In 1998, paleontologists and geologists from around the country descended on the Tracksite to study this intriguing site. The scientists from the University of Wyoming, Dartmouth College, Department of Geological Sciences - Indiana University, Kansas State University, BLM National Science & Technology Center, South Dakota School of Mines and Technology and the Smithsonian Institution formed the Red Gulch Dinosaur Tracksite Science Team. These scientists are working at the Tracksite under a BLM Paleontology permit.

They are mapping, measuring and comparing the rocks and fossils at this site with other previously studied tracksites. Working as a group, the team is breaking new ground in the study of the Middle Jurassic in central North America.

What We Now Know!

Scientists have been working for the past four years, trying to unlock the Red Gulch Dinosaur Tracksite (RGDT) puzzle. They had many questions and now have some of the answers.

What dinosaur made the tracks? All the tracks identified so far were formed by two-legged (bipedal) dinosaurs. Some, and perhaps all, of the tracks appear to have been made by meat-eating dinosaurs (theropods). They weighed between 15-400 pounds. Because Middle Jurassic dinosaurs are so rare, it is very difficult to match the tracks to any particular dinosaur.

Typically, a well-preserved theropod dinosaur track is three-toed and nearly symmetrical, exhibits tapering toes and preserves a slightly "S" shaped impression of the middle toe. Identifiable theropod trackways preserve prints that are slightly "pigeon-toed" having an inward rotation of the feet.

However, many other tracks and trackways do not exhibit such features. Although clearly made by two-legged dinosaurs, these less well-defined prints may have been made by a different type of dinosaur such as a plant-eating ornithopod. In

many cases, it is impossible to identify the track-maker as to ornithopod or theropod.

How many tracks are there? 1,000 tracks have been located, 600 of them are in the Ballroom. Nearly 600 dinosaur tracks have been located by surveying instruments. A network of one-meter-square grids has been surveyed in the "Ballroom and Discovery" area. Scientists estimate there are at least 1,000 tracks in the "Ballroom" area of the Tracksite.

How big are the tracks? The tracks are 8 - 28 cm. long, have three distinct toes, and may also show the heel and claws.

Where were the dinosaurs going? Most of the hundreds of identifiable trackways go in the same south-southwesterly direction. The orientations of most of the tracks indicate that the dinosaurs were moving to the south-southwest.

This could indicate herding or migratory animal behavior. Or it could indicate the presence of a physically constrained pathway (such as a tidal flat or beach next to an open body of water).

A logical interpretation would be that the dinosaurs may have been moving parallel to the shoreline. However, the shapes of the ripples associated with the RGDT surface shows this was not the case. The presence and orientation of the ripples indicate that relatively deeper water conditions existed to the southwest. Since the dinosaurs were moving in a southwesterly direction, it appears the dinosaurs were moving perpendicular to the shoreline and not parallel. The ripples reveal the dinosaurs may have been moving toward the water.

Cross sectional view of a ripple showing an asymmetric shape. The steep side to the right of the ripple crest is the down-current side. Flow was therefore left to right. Figure modified from Reineck and Singh, 1980.

What do the ripples tell us? The Tracksite exhibits a well-developed rippled surface. Ripples can be used to determine the direction of current movements. The coated-grain limestone consists of tiny sand-sized spheres of calcium carbonate and fossil shell fragments cemented together. The ripple surface formed before the grains were cemented together. The ripples are very similar in shape to those formed by relatively gentle waves in very shallow water. The dinosaur trackways appear to have formed shortly after the formation of the ripples.

Some tracks have been cross-sectioned or "sliced" to find out what the rock looks like within the footprint. The geologists are studying how the soft, limy mud was deformed as the weight of the dinosaur pushed it down.

What was the geography and climate like? During the Red Gulch Dinosaur Tracksite time, large portions of the western interior of North America were inundated by a shallow sea. To the west, a volcanic arch extended north from Mexico to southwestern Canada. To the east, the sea was bounded by very shallow water, low-lying coastline conditions that extended from central Wyoming into the present day Dakotas.

The climate during this time was extremely arid, at least seasonally.

The geology team has traveled to Florida,

Powell	Jan	Feb	March	April	May	June	July	Aug	Sep	Oct	Nov	Dec	Annual
Average Max. Temperature (F)	30.7	38.1	47.4	58.8	68.5	77.7	86.8	84.4	73.7	61.6	44.2	34.2	58.8
Average Min. Temperature (F)	7.8	13.8	20.9	31.3	41.5	49.6	55.9	53.5	43.5	33.2	21.0	12.1	32.0
Average Total Precipitation (in.)	0.19	0.14	0.20	0.51	1.08	1.25	0.66	0.58	0.78	0.41	0.23	0.16	6.19
Average Total SnowFall (in.)	3.1	2.2	2.6	2.4	0.3	0.1	0.0	0.0	0.4	0.8	2.6	2.7	17.2
Average Snow Depth (in.)	1	1	0	0	0	0	0	0	0	0	0	1	0

Texas, New England and elsewhere to visit other ancient environments. The ichnology team has visited sites throughout Colorado and Utah. Track expert Beth Southwell, UW, has been to Dinosaur State Park in Connecticut and even to China!

How old is the Tracksite? The Red Gulch Dinosaur Tracksite surface dates to approximately 167 million years old. This puts it in the mid-Bathonian Stage. How do we know this? Scientists used several factors to determine the date:

1. The occurrence of the oyster Gryphea nebrascensis, just above the track bed;

2. The occurrence of a complete specimen of the ammonite Cadoceras muelleri just above the track layer;

3. Two microfossils of marine planktonic protozoans called "Dinoflagellates."

The ages of these fossils have been well established in many places around the world. By finding these fossils here in the RGDT area, scientists can deduce the age of the surrounding area including the Tracksite.

The Tracksite preserves an ancient tidal environment. Scientists have traveled around the world to get clues to the Tracksite puzzle. Even though the daily rise and fall of the tide is small, because the tidal flat slopes at a very low angle towards the sea, a very broad expanse (several kilometer wide) is exposed at low tide. This is similar to the type of tidal flat preserved in the Tracksite area.

Why were the footprints preserved? Team members are studying modern environments where footprints may be preserved and trying to find out why such delicate structures were not immediately washed away but instead preserved and turned to rock.

What is a trace fossil? A fossil is any physical evidence of ancient life. A body fossil would include bone material or shell. A trace fossil, however, is evidence of the activity of ancient animals or plants. The physical evidence in the rock record of burrowing, crawling, walking, etc., constitutes a trace fossil. Therefore, the footprints at the Tracksite are vertebrate trace fossils.

What other kinds of trace fossils were found at the Tracksite? The older trace fossils on the Tracksite are classified as belonging to a Skolithos burrow type. The primary example are round, vertical tubes approximately 0.5 cm in diameter, similar to those made by modern annelid worms. These were probably made at the same time the dinosaurs were making their tracks.

The second, younger generation of invertebrate faunal traces is also present. These were made after the dinosaur tracks had been buried by sediment. The younger traces consist of U-shaped burrows ranging from 5 cm to greater than 12 cm in width and 2 cm to 3 cm in diameter. These may have been made infaunal crustaceans, bivalves such as clams or lugworms.

What are ABs? Shallow, irregularly shaped depressions are also present on the Tracksite. They have been nicknamed "AB's" for "amorphous blob."

The Tracksite AB's appear to have formed through a combination of both biological and physical erosional processes. The depressions are very similar to features observed on modern intertidal flats.

What else has been found? Samples of pollens, collected by scientists during the summer of 1998 have been processed in the laboratory. So far, it appears that there are pollens of cycads and several different conifers, fern spores and a variety of one-celled organisms in the layers directly overlying the Tracksite. The pollen is the only remains we have of these plants and could have been blown or washed in from vegetated areas tens to hundred of miles away.

Paleontology in the Bighorn Basin

The 260-plus million acres administered by the BLM are rich in fossils. Most public lands are simply those rejected by homesteaders as too steep, too dry, and too barren to support a family. What is unsuitable for agriculture is perfect for fossil discoveries.

Paleontologists have been collecting fossils in the Bighorn Basin since before 1880. Rocks in the Basin and along the flanks of the Bighorns and Absaroka ranges from about 600 million years to about three million years old, and all but one geologic period is represented.

The Bighorn Basin, and Wyoming in general, has yielded many kinds of fossils. The region is arid, so little soil or vegetation forms to obscure the exposures of bare rock. Also, when rain falls, it often does so violently and quickly erodes the surface, exposing more and more fossils.

Collecting

Much of the surface is administered by the BLM, so while hobbyists may collect petrified wood, invertebrates, and plant fossils, vertebrates are kept in the public trust through BLM's collecting permit process.

May I Collect Fossils? You may collect a variety of fossils on public lands, with certain restrictions. Special management designations restrict access and types of activities on some public lands. It is always a good idea to stop by the nearest BLM office to check on local conditions such as land status, fire danger, or road closures. On private lands, fossils may be collected only with the permission of the landowner.

Invertebrates: No permit is required to collect reasonable amounts of invertebrate fossils such as:

• trilobites

• brachiopods

• ammonites

The invertebrate fossils you collect are for your personal use and enjoyment, and may not be bartered or sold. Please remember to leave some for the next collector, too.

Petrified Wood You may collect:

• up to 25 pounds of petrified wood, plus one piece, each day.

• no more than 250 pounds in any calendar year

without a permit.

You may not combine your allowance with another collector's allowance to obtain larger pieces of petrified wood. And you can't sell it without a special permit.

Other Plant Fossils :No permit is required to collect reasonable amounts of plant fossils such as leaves. They are for your personal use and may not be bartered or sold.

Vertebrates Vertebrate fossils may only be collected with a permit because of their relative rarity and scientific importance. They include not only bones and teeth, but also footprints, burrows and other traces of activity.

Vertebrate fossils are fragile and complex and permit applicants must be able to show a sufficient level of training and experience in order to collect them. In addition, all vertebrate fossils collected under a permit must be held in an approved repository.

Article courtesy of Bureau of Land Management

T Chimney Rock
In Shell Canyon

As a focal point for numerous paintings and photographs over the years, Chimney Rock is quite the landmark. This Chugwater sandstone formation was originally coined White's Monument due to its significance as the grave of trapper, cowboy, buffalo hunter and prospector, Jim White. History has it that in 1881 White and Riley Kane set off on a journey to combine trapping and prospecting. On route to Shell Creek the duo picked up an unknown third partner. The trio stopped along the base of the mountains to pitch camp and settle for the winter. As spring approached they discovered a shortage in supplies, Kane then set off with a team of oxen for Lander 200 miles southwest for more supplies. Shortly after his departure, the third partner murdered White and took off with the remaining supplies, oxen, as well as their collection of furs, hides and gold. Later, a group of cowboys stumbled upon his body and buried him in a shallow grave protecting it from wild animals. Kane eventually returned and upon discovering his partners death, searched with no avail for the murderer. Whites body was later found by Mr. A. Kershner who moved the body to Trail Town in Cody.

T Shell Falls
Near Shell

Shell Falls has been described as the thundering heartbeat of the magnificent Big Horn Mountain Range!

About sixty million years ago the area that is now the Big Horn Mountains began to bow upward, and the basins on either side began to sag downward. Today the highest point is Cloud Peak, about twenty-six miles south of here, a respectable 13,175 feet high. Millions of years of erosion have removed almost all the sedimentary rocks from the top of the Big Horns, exposing the ancient "basement" rocks, the granite over which Shell Falls now roars. Colorful layers of sedimentary rock still clothe the flanks of the Big Horns, making the ride over Highway 14 one of the most spectacular in the west.

Lovell	Jan	Feb	March	April	May	June	July	Aug	Sep	Oct	Nov	Dec	Annual
Average Max. Temperature (F)	29.6	37.8	47.6	58.7	68.9	78.7	87.8	86.2	73.8	61.1	44.1	33.2	58.9
Average Min. Temperature (F)	4.8	12.0	20.8	30.8	41.5	49.6	54.6	51.7	41.0	30.4	18.8	8.8	30.4
Average Total Precipitation (in.)	0.22	0.16	0.29	0.62	1.15	1.21	0.65	0.57	0.71	0.53	0.25	0.22	6.58
Average Total SnowFall (in.)	4.1	2.2	2.3	0.9	0.1	0.0	0.0	0.0	0.6	0.6	1.4	4.5	16.7
Average Snow Depth (in.)	2	0	0	0	0	0	0	0	0	0	0	0	0

Shell Canyon has been formed by the headward erosion of Shell Creek over millions of years. The creek has incised a deep chasm through the three billion year old granite you see around you. The water of Shell Falls, falling at the rate of some 3,600 gallons per second, follows the course of fractures in the resistant granite. This grey and pink granite is among some of the oldest rock on earth, while the softer Flathead sandstone which rests on top of it, some 550 million years old, contains some of the earliest fossils of hard shelled creatures you can find. Such ancient shells gave Shell Canyon, and Shell Falls, their names.

There is a quality of the sublime in all waterfalls, but especially in Shell Falls. The thudding sensation of falling water can be felt through the soles of your feet, and the water's voice has a way of soothing the traveler. The memory of Shell Falls, cool and green, has stayed with generations of visitors as they traveled on through the harsher basins bordering the Big Horn Mountains.

The People of Shell Falls

It would be fascinating to know how the Falls were perceived by the native Americans: the prehistoric Indians, and the Shoshone, Sioux, Crow and Cheyenne that followed them. Indian people have occupied the Big Horn country for at least eleven thousand years.

The journals of many settlers in the Big Horn Basin mention Shell Falls. Whole families would often forsake the summer heat of their lowland ranches and farms and make a special trip to the Falls. This part of the Big Horn country was very remote to outside visitors until recently. The Burlington Northern Railroad reached the Greybull area in 1909, but few tourists ventured into the Shell area until the 1920's. The first road up Shell Canyon was completed in 1932.

The modern highway through the canyon is surprisingly young. Much of it was completed in the mid-1960s, with major improvements performed in the 1980s.

An interesting point of local history concerns the massive limestone promontory called Copman's Tomb. This conspicuous landmark forms the northwest skyline as seen from Shell Falls, and is visible from the town of Shell far below in the Big Horn Basin.

In 1879, pioneer cattleman Henry Lovell, trailed several large herds of Shorthorn cattle from Oregon into the country on the west side of the Big Horns. Working for Lovell was a young man named Jack Copman. Copman decided to establish himself as a trapper, and set up a camp on a tributary of Shell Creek that became known as Trapper Creek.

Long before the invention of the airplane, visitors to Copman's camp were amazed to see his "flying machine." This was an elaborate model glider which Copman would hurl into the air by hand. Copman dreamed of constructing a full-sized glider and knew just where he wanted to launch it, with himself as pilot. He eyed the impressive wedge-shaped prow of what we now call Copman's Tomb. Copman was intelligent, mechanically inclined, and shared his dream of flight with many local people.

Years later, a successful businessman and devoted husband and father, Copman knew that he would likely never fulfill his quest. He asked only that, when someone finally invented a flying machine, his ashes be scattered from such a device over the butte that figured so prominently in his young dreams. With his family in Europe at the time of his death in 1907, his wish could not be fulfilled. Copman is remembered as a visionary—his ideas well ahead of his era. Though he is buried in the Greybull cemetery, his real burial monument remains "Copman's Tomb."

The Animals of Shell Falls

There is an animal that loves the rumble and roar of falling water, that seeks it out as the place to feed and rear its young. Fast water does not deter it, and the bone-chilling cold of Shell Creek does not seem to touch it. The most surprising thing of all is that this is not a huge, fur-covered creature, but a diminutive, delicate-looking bird! The water ouzel, or dipper, is a tiny, slate grey bird, inconspicuous but for its unusual habit of repeatedly raising and lowering itself, dipping, on its tiny ouzel legs. The ouzel, which looks very much like a wren, can be seen entering the frigid waters of mountain streams without hesitation. While under the water its oily plumage protects it, and it uses its wings and feet to navigate through the stream, searching for aquatic insects, larvi and worms. It builds a large, moss-insulated nest, often close to waterfalls, and lays three to six eggs.

Another classic resident of the Shell Falls area is the rainbow trout, a lover of cold, well-oxygenated water. You can often see them lying quietly in the big plunge pools directly below the Falls. The "rainbow' comes by its name honestly. Its flanks are colored iridescent pink and electric blue. The rainbow is not native to the Big Horns, but was originally found only in localized areas of the California Sierras. Decades of transplanting this handsome fish now cause it to be found in mountain streams and lakes all over the west.

The trip to Shell Falls is often enlivened by the sight of moose. This largest of North American antlered mammals is frequently seen grazing the willow bottoms between Shell Falls and Burgess Junction. Moose are uniformly dark brown or black, with "scoop shovel" antlers and curved-down noses. There are no records of moose having inhabited the Big Horn Mountains prior to 1948, when eight were captured near Moran, Wyoming, and released on the east side of the Big Horns. Since then, aided by other "plants:" a large, healthy herd of moose now live in the Big Horn Mountains.

Many visitors to Shell Falls also see mule deer as they ascend either flank of the Big Horns. The name "mule deer" derives from their large, prominent ears. Mule deer prefer a diet of sagebrush, chokecherry, mountain mahogany, serviceberry, and other brushy species. The curlyleaf mountain mahogany you can see growing at the Shell Falls visitor center looks like it has been pruned. It has! Hungry mule deer love to feast on the tender leaves of this plant.

Reprinted from U.S. Forest Service brochure.

23 *Food*

Emblem
Pop. 10, Elev. 4,438

Once called Germania for the German homesteaders who settled here, the name was changed during World War I to represent the flag.

Burlington
Pop. 250, Elev. 4,430

Probably named for the railroad, Mormon settlers hoped the trains would help their town grow. When that didn't happen, they had to rely on complex irrigation techniques to make agriculture viable on this high, arid bench. Between 1893 and 1907, they built a series of canals (the Sidon Canal System), channeling water from the Greybull River into ditches, which covered some 15,000 acres of land. As the crops began to flourish, more immigrants arrived, including many from Germany. The benchland came to be known as Germania Bench, until World War I, when they changed the name to Emblem Bench.

24 *No services*

T Wild Horses—An ancient Visitor Returns to the Bighorn Basin
Wild horses are often seem to the north around Bridger Butte. It's hard to imagine that their ancestors, called dawn horses, might have roamed here over 50 million years ago. Horses first developed in North America. However, they disappeared in the post-Pleistocene time about 11,000 years ago. They were reintroduced by the Spanish in the early 1500s and became a vital part of Western life.

What are wild horses?
A wild horse is an unbranded and unclaimed free-roaming horse found on public lands in the western United States or one that has been removed from the public lands and has not lost

Wyoming Tidbits

Hyattville wa originally named 'Paintrock" for the petroglyphs on Medicine Lodge Creek. It was renamed for postmaster Sam Hyatt.

this status by giving title to an adopter. These animals are protected by a law passed in 1971. Wild horses are descendants of animals turned loose or escaped from early Spanish explorers, settlers, ranchers, prospectors, Indian tribes, and the U.S. Cavalry from the 1600s through the Great Depression of the 1930s to more recent times.

Where are Wyoming's wild horses?
Wild horses in Wyoming are found primarily in the southwestern part of the state near Rock Springs and Rawlins, but some can be seen near Lander, Worland, and Cody. Wild horses may often be seen from I-80 just north of the rest area

Deaver	Jan	Feb	March	April	May	June	July	Aug	Sep	Oct	Nov	Dec	Annual
Average Max. Temperature (F)	30.7	39.1	49.4	61.2	71.0	80.0	88.6	87.1	75.6	62.7	44.6	33.5	60.3
Average Min. Temperature (F)	4.5	11.0	19.2	28.7	39.4	47.6	53.4	50.8	40.7	29.8	17.4	7.8	29.2
Average Total Precipitation (in.)	0.14	0.12	0.19	0.43	0.98	1.19	0.63	0.55	0.54	0.29	0.15	0.13	5.35
Average Total SnowFall (in.)	3.1	1.1	1.5	1.4	0.1	0.0	0.0	0.0	0.4	0.0	1.1	1.5	10.4
Average Snow Depth (in.)	1	1	0	0	0	0	0	0	0	0	0	0	0

between Red Desert and Point of Rocks, on the west side of Wyoming Highway 191 beginning about 10 miles north of Rock Springs to Eden, on the south side of Wyoming Highway 789 from Muddy Gap to the rest area, on either side of Wyoming Highway 135 from the junction with Highway 789 to where the road drops over the high rim, and on Wyoming Highway 16, 14, 20 from about 25 miles east of Cody to Emblem on the North side of the road. For the more adventurous, wild horses may be seen from many other back country roads. Directions may be obtained at the local BLM offices.

Where did wild horses come from?

The animals ranging through the West are considered mixtures of Spanish mustangs that escaped from early explorers and missions, along with Indian ponies and domestic horses that have strayed or were abandoned by their owners. Only one generation is needed to change a domestic breed to a wild one.

What is the "mustang"?

The name "mustang" from the Spanish mestano, means a horse that has strayed and become wild. Indians tamed some and used them to reign over the west until the coming of the railroads, ranchers and homesteaders.

What happened to the mustang?

Westward spread of civilization meant an end to the way of life of many Indians and their ponies, as domestic livestock and fences took over the open range. By the end of World War I, many domestic horses were simply abandoned on the range, but a strain of Spanish mustangs still remains in the bloodlines of many wild horses.

What is BLM's responsibility?

The Wild Horse and Burro Act passed by Congress in 1971 says that the Bureau of Land Management is responsible for protection, management, and control of wild horses.

Do wild horses need to be controlled?

The 1971 Wild Horse and Burro Act declared that these horses are living symbols of the historic and pioneer spirit of the West, and mandated BLM to manage the wild herds in perpetuity. The law directs that the horses are to be maintained in a thriving ecological balance with livestock, wildlife and the habitat. What is a thriving ecological balance and how many horses can be maintained to ensure the balance? The herd areas are continually monitored to accurately determine how many horses an area can accommodate. Information

such as climate data, precipitation, vegetation, grazing utilization by horses, cattle, sheep and big game are all combined to come up with a manageable horse herd number. Wild horses are hardy animals, stronger than livestock or big game. If their numbers were left unchecked, they could easily dominate the winter range and other animals would suffer before the horses would. There are few natural predators or diseases to limit the horses, so, the number of horses has to be controlled.

How are wild horse populations controlled?

BLM rounds up excess wild horses using a helicopter and a crew of mounted wranglers. This is done on the average of once every 3 years in each herd area, and has proven to be a very effective and humane method of control. However, roundups are costly if they have to be done often and the law dictates that management be to the minimum level possible. Some fear that the roundups are harmful to the horses. For these reasons, BLM allows the horse populations to fluctuate so the number of roundups any one herd is subject to is minimized.

How many wild horses are there in Wyoming?

Currently, there are about 5,000 head in Wyoming

What happens to the horses that BLM rounds up?

Most of the horses that are captured are offered to the public under BLM's adopt-a-horse program. Anyone of legal age who can provide the proper facilities and care for a horse can adopt a wild horse for a minimum fee of $125. Horses that are unadoptable are returned to the range. More information about the adopt-a-horse program is available at any BLM office.

Can wild horses be trained?

Yes! In fact, most are easily trained to lead, ride, pull or anything any horse can be trained to do. In Wyoming, the BLM has an agreement with the Wyoming Honor Farm in Riverton, a state correctional facility, where wild horses are trained by the residents.

Today's wild horses are descendants of animals that either escaped or were turned loose by the various cultures who depended on them. The McCullough Peaks herd roams about 100,000 acres of public land, which includes Bridger Butte. In the distance and to the right of Bridger Butte are the Prior Mountains, home to another wild horse herd. These horses are unique because they still have many of the markings of the Spanish Mustang.

Wild horses are the responsibility of the Bureau of Land Management (BLM), which is an agency of the US Department of the interior. The BLM manages free roaming horses and burros as living symbols of the historic and pioneer spirit of the West, and as an important part of the natural system on public lands.

Because horses have few natural predators, and many more are born each year than die, the BLM has periodic round ups. Wild horses are

available to the public through the Adopt-a-horse program. For more information, contact any BLM office.

Article courtesy of Bureau of Land Management

25 Gas

Ralston

Pop. 100, Elev. 4,700
Gas

This little railroad siding town took its name from the local saloon owner back in the days when it started as a railroad siding. The tiny town gained fame in Ripley's Believe It or Not when unusual bridges were recognized. The original highway bridge crossed Alkali creek at the same point the railroad bridge crossed. The railroad bridge passing over the highway bridge.

T Heart Mountain Historic Relocation Camp

10 miles northeast of Cody on U.S. Highway 14A, or six miles southwest of Ralston.

On a more sober note, 11 miles east of Cody, you will find the remains of the Heart Moutain Japanese Relocation Camp. This was where over 10,000 Japanese-Americans from the west coast were forced to settle after the attack on Pearl Harbor in 1941, when their patriotism was questioned unjustly. Conditions in the camp were primitive. Poorly insulated barracks contained small "apartments" with several occupants crowded into each. Internees came with few belongings, had little furniture, and shared bath facilities. The perimeter was surrounded by barbed wire, and guards with machine guns and searchlights watched from nine different towers, day and night.

But most residents remained true to the United States, and their mantra for survival was "shikata ga nai" (I guess it cannot be helped). Over 600 of the internees joined to Army and served in the war in Europe. Twenty-one of them gave their lives for their country. Those who remained behind found work in local agriculture, filling in for sons who had gone off to war. Mostly, their wages were less than what prisoners-of war were making on the other side of the state, near Douglas.

The Heart Mountain Wyoming Association is working at preserving this site as a reminder of social injustice, so that we may avoid such folly in the future.

H Heart Mountain Relocation Center

Six miles southwest of Ralston

During the World War II years, Heart Mountain Relocation Center was located on a 740-acre tract of land across the Burlington Railroad right-of-way westward from where you stand facing this monument and Heart Mountain itself, on the Heart mountain Division of the Shoshone Irrigation Project.

Eleven thousand people of Japanese ancestry from the three west coast states were loosely confined by the United States Government in the center for about three years. They lived in barracks as singles, or as families, according to their marital status.

The camp was equipped with modern waterworks and sewer system and a modern hospital and dental clinic, staffed with people from the ranks of the evacuees. First rate schooling was provided for the children of the evacuees through the high school grades.

Wyoming Tidbits

In 1901, a farmer in Byron noticed gas escaping from a fence post hole on his land. He lit it, and the gas continued burning for several years.

Wyoming Tidbits

The Shoshone National Forest was the first national forest established. President Teddy Roosevelt, an ardent conservationist, signed the bill in 1902, designating the forest the nation's first.

H Heart Mountain Relocation Center
Six miles southwest of Ralston

History
After the bombing of Pearl Harbor on December 7, 1941, many parts of the West Coast were declared military defense zones. The government ordered the removal of all persons of Japanese ancestry and the War Relocation Authority was established in March 1942 to house them in inland camps. The Heart Mountain Relocation center was one of ten temporary camps constructed to confine over 110,000. It was the only camp located in Wyoming. Construction on the center began in June 1942 and the first internees arrived in August of that year. At the peak of its population, the Heart Mountain Center, which covered over 740 acres, contained nearly 11,000 people housed in 450 barracks. Although surrounded by barbed wire and armed quards, the internees kept the camp functioning as a small city with its own public works, grade schools, a high school, hospital and newpaper. At the time it was the third largest city in Wyoming.

The camp was closed in November 1945, the buildings removed and the land, made arable by irrigation ditches completed by the internees, was opened up for homesteading.

A portion of the Heart Mountain Center was listed on the National Register of Historic Places on December19. 1985. The area listed includes the immediate vicinity of this Honor Roll and structures located to the east.

H Honor Roll
Six miles southwest of Ralston

This monument was erected lby the internees at the Heart Mountain Relocation Center in August 1944 to honor those from the camp who served in the United States armed forces in World War II. The photographs to the right and below show the Honor roll as it was in 1944. Although the elements have erased the names ofthose listed, the structure still remains as it was originally.

In 1978 the Honor Roll was preserved as a memorial not only to those Japanese-Americans who served in the military, but also to recognize the sacrifices of those who were interned here throughout the war.

In 1985 a plaque was erected memorializing those people from Heart Mountain who gave their lives in World War II.

T Ralston Mystery Bridges
At the curve in U.S. Highway 14A east of Ralston

Listed in Ripley's Believe It or Not, this railroad bridge over a highway bridge over a creek is

Ralston Mystery Bridges

unique, not only to the area, but in the world. The most peculiar thing of all, however, is that the road on either side of the bridge goes nowhere.

H The Ralston Reservoir
Southwest of Ralston

The Ralston Reservoir was completed in 1907 and provides some operational control of the Garland Canal. It is also used as an emergency spill route during heavy rain storms which occasionally hit the area during the summer.

The reservoir has been set aside to provide wildlife viewing and waterfowl hunting. This designation came about through mitigation measures as part of a previous Rehabilitation and Betterment Program to modernize the irrigation delivery system on the Heart Mountain Division.

Today, Ralston Reservoir is "for the Birds" due to cooperation of the Shoshone-Heart Mountain Irrigation districts, Bureau of Reclamation and Wyoming Game and Fish Department.

Today, the primary importance of the reservoir is as a wild life habitat area.

H Willwood Dam
Five miles southwest of Ralston

The Willwood Dam diverts water from the Shoshone River to irrigate 11,400 acres of land on the Willwood Division of the Project, which was settled beginning in 1927.

Construction of the 70-foot-high dam began in 1922, and work was completed just a year later. Work on the canal, located across the river looking to the East, was completed in the spring of 1927, and the first unit homesteaders received water for their new farms on April 21, 1928.

The dam is located 22 miles downstream from Buffalo Bill Dam.

H Eagle's Nest Stage Station
Five miles southwest of Ralston

Established in the 1890's by Tom Lanchberry to accommodate passengers and horses on the Red Lodge to Fort Washakie run, Eagle's Nest Station, one-half mile north, operated until early in the century when railway expansion limited it's usefulness. Stout four and six-horse teams, under salty drivers, pulling tough, coach-type wagons, were changed every 15 to 20 miles. Stages traveled 60 to 80 miles a day, tying together cattle ranches and army posts. One dollar a night for supper, bed and breakfast was the usual charge to dust-covered passengers on the long rough route from Montana's Northern Pacific to the Union Pacific railroad in southern Wyoming.

26 *Gas, Food, Lodging*

Powell
Pop. 5,373, Elev. 4,365

Named for famed explorer John Wesley Powell, this community first grew up around the crews that came to build dams and irrigation systems for the Shoshone Project in the 1890s. Powell himself conceived of utilizing damming and canals to "reclaim" the land for agricultural purposes. Homesteaders swelled the population during the early part of the twentieth century, and the Burlington Railroad turned the town into a major shipping hub for the Bighorn Basin. With the discovery of oil in 1915, Powell found its fortunes rising still more as the Elk Basin Oil Field brought further growth. The oil industry is still a factor in the town's economy, but it is first and foremost an agricultural town, churning out sugar beets, beans, and malting barley year after year.

Powell is also home to Northwest Community College, one of the state's two years schools, which brings educational and cultural opportunities to local residents. Founded in 1946, the college serves some 2000 students in the area, most of whom live on campus.

T Homesteader Museum
Corner of 1st and Clark off U.S. Highway 14A

The museum building has a lively history. Built by the American Legion in 1933, the log and hardwood space served as a dining area, banquet hall, community dance hall, roller rink and youth center. During WWII, it housed German prisons

---

Wyoming Tidbits

Trapper Edward Rose was the first white settler in Wyoming. He came into the area in 1807 with a trapping party led by Ezekel Williams, and settled in the Big Horn Basin.

---

of war until Camp Deaver was ready. Artifacts include early day items, military memorabilia, geological displays, a caboose, photographs and maps. The museum is open Tuesday through Saturday. Call for hours. Tours and appointments can be arranged. Admission is free.

H An Island in the Sage
Homesteader Park Rest Area at the east edge of Powell

Powell is named for the famous one-armed explorer Major John Wesley Powell. In 1889, Powell reported on the agricultural potential of these western sagebrush grasslands. He declared the value of irrigation in "reclaiming" these area through a series of dams and canal systems funded by the government. So, the Shoshone Project started, including the nearby Buffalo Bill Dam and a series of canals to feed water to the fields along the Shoshone River. Because of the successful irrigation project and the arrival of the railroad, Powell became an agricultural shipping point.

The vast native prairie, which once provided for the needs of wildlife, was converted to fields of sugar beets, malt barley and beans for human needs. Although there is evidence of agricultural irrigation projects throughout the Big Horn Basin, there are vast areas of native prairie still remaining. Almost 50 percent of Wyoming's 96,000 square miles is covered by sagebrush grassland. Abundant sagebrush habitat is the reason Wyoming supports more than half the world's population of sage grouse and pronghorn antelope.

Wyoming's agricultural areas are like small islands in a vast expanse of sagebrush prairies. Many wildlife species, like the sage grouse, pronghorn antelope, coyotes and songbirds, have adapted to life in both the agricultural and sagebrush grassland habitats. Wildlands and vast open spaces are crucial parts of the formula required to ensure wildlife diversity, making Wyoming a unique place for wildlife and people!

L Park Motel
737 E. 2nd St., Powell. 754-2233 or (800) 506-7378. www.parkmotel.home.bresnan.net; parkmotel@bresnan.net

Experience parking right outside your door with the Park Motel's clean, quiet, and affordable rooms. AAA rated and sponsor of the Powell Chamber of Commerce, Cody Chapter, Abate of Wyoming, and the National Street Machines Club, the Park Motel offers completely ground floor rooms where guests enjoy high speed broadband and wireless internet, cable TV with free HBO, ESPN, and Discovery, winter plug-ins, fax services, and convenient access to a laundromat next door. Refrigerators, microwaves, and one kitchenette are available, and some rooms are handicapped accessible. For those seeking romance, the motel's honeymoon suite features its own private whirlpool. Restaurants and shopping are within easy walking distance, and onsite summer barbeques are a guest favorite. For some of the area's largest rooms at the lowest prices, let Park Motel be your home on the prairie.

27 Gas, Food, Lodging

T Northwest Galleries & Diorama
Northwest College campus in Powell. 754-6000

Visit the college's two galleries and permanent science exhibits on campus. Call for information on current exhibits.

Powell's elevator is its welcome sign.

F Hansel & Gretel's Restaurant
113 S. Bent St., Powell. 754-2191.
Located 75 miles from Yellowstone, the legendary Hansel & Gretel's Restaurant was established in 1973. A unique Swiss Chalet décor complements a variety of freshly prepared lunch and dinner items, featuring everything from homemade pasta and pizza to sandwiches, steak, fish, and more. A full bar with a large selection of cocktails, wine, and beer enhances any meal, while the restaurant's two separate buildings ensure you enjoy your preference of a smoking or non-smoking atmosphere. Featuring fun for the whole family with darts, billiards, and foosball, the restaurant seats up to 210 people with private gathering rooms accommodating 2 to 102 individuals. In a hurry? Check out the convenient drive-up window. Whether you're on the go or seeking a relaxed dining setting, count on Hansel & Gretel's reputation for excellent food sure to please everyone.

M The Real Estate Connection
133 S. Bent St., Powell. 754-2800 or (888) 227-0409. www.wyomingproperty.com; sales@wyomingproperty.com

The Real Estate Connection® prides itself on honesty, ethics, and fair play while helping clients find their Wyoming dream home. The full-service brokerage is licensed in Wyoming and Montana under the direction of Broker/Owner Glo Reetz, and as a Powell native, Glo possesses extensive knowledge about the Big Horn Basin. Abiding by high standards and professionalism at all times, the service-oriented agents specialize in all different aspects of property sales and rentals, including residential, commercial, acreage, condominiums, and farm and ranch. The brokerage is a member of the Park County MLS and serves both buyers and sellers in Basin, Burlington, Byron, Clark, Cody, Cowley, Deaver, Frannie, Lovel, Greybull, Meeteetse, Thermopolis, and Powell. Established in 1996, The Real Estate Connection is your local source for real service, not just lip service.

Section 7

BIGHORN CANYON

At first glance, time seems to have stopped at Bighorn Canyon. The lake and the steep-sided canyons provide a peaceful setting for those seeking a break from the daily routine. The focus of the area is 71 -mile-long Bighorn Lake, created by Yellowtail Dam near Fort Smith. Dedicated in 1968, the dam provides electric power, water for irrigation, flood control, and recreation. Boating, water skiing, fishing, swimming, and sightseeing are main attractions.

While you enjoy the play of light and shadow on rock and water, take time to contemplate the changes that the land and the life upon it have undergone. Time and water are keys to the canyon, where the land has been shaped by moving water since upheavals of the Earth's crust built the Pryor and Bighorn mountains millions of years ago. For 15 miles upstream from the dam, the lake bisects a massive, arching anticline, exposing fossils that tell of successive times when this land was submerged under a shallow sea, when it was a tropical marsh, and when its conifer forests were inhabited by dinosaurs. Humans arrived here more than

10,000 years ago, living as hunters and gatherers. In modern times people have further altered the land.

Most of Bighorn's visitors come to enjoy the recreational opportunities the lake offers. Boaters, water skiers, anglers and scuba divers are all attracted here. But the park offers more than just the lake: from the wild flowers in spring and summer to more than 200 species of birds; from the stories of life forms adapting to a harsh environment to the modern search for energy. You can get more information on what the park offers at visitor centers near Lovell, WY, and Fort Smith, MT. Find your own place of solitude to relax and to enjoy the diversity and timelessness of this uncommon canyon water land.

A Challenging Land

In North America people have traveled and made their living along rivers and streams for more than 40,000 years. But the Bighorn River was too treacherous and too steep-walled. People here lived near the Bighorn but avoided navigating it—until the dam tamed the river.

The broken land here also challenged the ingenuity of early residents, forcing them to devise unusual strategies of survival. More than

10,000 years ago, Indian hunters drove herds of game into land traps. These Indians lived simply, gathering wild roots and seeds to balance and supplement their meat diet. They made clothes of skins, baskets and sandals of plant fibers, and tools of stone, bone, and wood. The many caves of the Bighorn area provided seasonal shelters and storage areas for the Indians, as well as for early traders and trappers.

Absaroke means "People of the largebeaked bird," in the Siouan language of the Crow. Their reservation surrounds most of Bighorn Canyon. Originally a farming people, the Crow split off from the Hidatsa tribe more than 200 years ago. They became a renowned hunting people, described by one of the Lewis and Clark Expedition as "the finest horsemen in the world."

After 1800, explorers, traders, and trappers found their way up the Bighorn River. Charles Larocque met the Crow at the mouth of the Bighorn in 1805; Captain William Clark traveled through a year later. Jim Bridger claimed he had floated through the canyon on a raft. Later fur traders packed their goods overland on the Bad Pass Trail, avoiding the river's dangers.

During the Civil War the Bozeman Trail led to mines in western Montana by crossing the Bighorn River. Open from 1864 to 1868, the trail was bitterly opposed by Sioux and Cheyenne; the Crow were neutral. The Federal Government closed the trail in 1868 after the Fort Laramie Treaty. Fort C.F. Smith, now on private land, guarded the trail as an outpost. A stone monument commemorates the Hayfield Fight, a desperate but successful defense against Sioux and Cheyenne warriors. In this skirmish a party of soldiers and civilian haycutters, working three miles north of Fort C.F. Smith, fought for eight hours until rescued by the fort's troops on August 1, 1867.

After the Civil War, cattle ranching became a way of life. Among the huge open-range cattle ranches was the Mason-Lovell (the ML); some of those buildings remain. Dude ranching, reflected in the remains of Hillsboro, was popular in the early 1900s.

The Crow made the transition from hunter-gatherers to ranchers in one generation. In 1904, after 12 years of labor, they completed an irrigation system and opened 35,000 acres of land to irrigated farming. Water was diverted into the Bighorn Canal by a 416-foot diversion dam, moving 720 cubic feet of water per second. Near Afterbay Campground is Bighorn Canal Headgate, remains of this human response to the challenge of the land.

Congress established Bighorn Canyon National Recreation Area in 1966 as part of the National Park System to provide enjoyment for visitors today and to protect the park for future generations.

Bighorn Canyon Visitor Center

The solar-heated visitor center near Lovell, WY., symbolizes the energy-conscious concerns of the National Park Service and of modern Americans. The heating is accomplished by storing heat from the sun in a rock bin, then blowing hot air through the building. The Yellowtail Dam Visitor Center, in the park, is two miles past the community of Fort Smith. It is approachable from the north by car.

Bighorn Wildlife

The wildlife of the Bighorn Canyon country is as varied as the land, which can be divided into four climate or vegetative zones. In the south is desert shrub land inhabited by wild horses, snakes, and small rodents. Midway is juniper woodland with coyotes, deer, bighorn sheep, beaver, wood rats, and porcupine. Along the flanks of the canyon is pine and fir woodland with mountain lions, bear, elk, and mule deer. In the north is shortgrass prairie, once home to herds of buffalo. Many of the smaller animals, such as cottontails, skunks, coyotes, and rattlesnakes, are seen frequently throughout the park. More than 200 species of birds, including many kinds of water fowl, have been seen here. Each plant and animal species is adapted to the particular conditions of temperature, moisture, and landform within one or more of the park's four primary zones.

Yellowtail Dam

The dam is named in honor of Robert Yellowtail, former Crow tribal chairman and reservation superintendent. The dam creates one of the largest reservoirs on the Missouri River tributary system. This arch type dam is 525 feet high.

Yellowtail Wildlife Habitat Management Area

Riparian, cottonwood forest, shrub land, and wetlands provide habitat for whitetail deer, bald eagles, pelicans, heron, water fowl, wild turkeys, and other species. The area is managed by the Wyoming Game and Fish Department through agreements with the National Park Service, Bureau of Land Management, and Bureau of Reclamation.

Ranch Sites

Mason-Lovell Ranch: A.L. Mason and H.C Lovell built cattle ranch headquarters here in 1883. Cattle roamed the Bighorn Basin in a classic open-range operation.

Hillsboro: A one mile round trip trail takes you to the site of Grosvenor William Barry's Cedarvale Guest Ranch and the 1915 to 1945 Hillsboro post office.

Lockhart: Caroline Lockhart, a reporter, editor, and author, began ranching at age 56. The well preserved buildings give a feel for ranch life; one mile roundup.

Ewing-Snell: This site was in use for nearly 100 years.

Bad Pass Trail

American Indians camped along this trail 10,000 years ago, and in prehistoric and historic times Shoshone used it to get to the buffalo plains. Early trappers and traders used it to avoid the dangers of the Bighorn River. You can see rock calms left along the route between Devil Canyon Overlook and Barry's Landing. Before the arrival of the horse, life changed little here for thousands of years. Small family groups wintered in caves near the canyon bottoms. In early spring they moved out of the canyon bottoms in search of plants and small animals, and in summer they moved to the highlands in search of game and summer maturing plants. Large groups gathered in fall for a communal bison hunt.

Devil Canyon Overlook

Here the canyon crosscuts the gray limestone of the Devil Canyon Anticline, a 1,000-foot high segment of the fault blocks that make up the Pryor Mountains.

What to See and Do

A film at Bighorn Canyon Visitor Center highlights park activities. Exhibits explain the canyon's history and natural features.

Boating enthusiasts will find a marina, snack bar, camp store (gas and oil), and boat ramp at Horseshoe Bend and OkABeh. Ramps are also at Afterbay Dam and Barry's Landing. All boaters should sign registration sheets at the ramps when entering and leaving the lake. If mechanical problems develop while you are on the lake, stay with your boat; hail other boaters and ask them to notify a ranger. Carry both day and night signaling devices. Do not try to climb the lake's steep canyon walls.

Swimmers are encouraged to use the lifeguarded areas at Horseshoe Bend and Ok-A-Beh.

Camping is restricted to designated sites in developed areas. It is also allowed in the back country and below the highwater mark along Bighorn Lake. Fire restrictions during periods of high fire danger may close certain areas to camping. Check with a ranger for the restrictions on fires or back country camping.

Hiking is available in the national recreation area and in nearby forests. Ask at the visitor centers for more information.

Hunting is allowed in designated areas in accordance with state laws. Trapping is prohibited.

Fishing in Montana or Wyoming requires the appropriate state fishing license. Fine game fish, such as brown and rainbow trout, sauger, ling, and perch, abound.

The most popular game fish, a gourmet's delight, is the walleye. Winter ice fishing around Horseshoe Bend is good. The Bighorn River provides excellent brown and rainbow trout fishing.

Regulations and Safety: Firearms are prohibited in developed areas and areas of concentrated public use, unless they are unloaded and cased. Pets must be on a leash in developed areas and in areas of concentrated public use. Trash and waste disposals into area waters are prohibited; all vessels must have a waste receptacle on board. Carry a first-aid kit as a precaution against poisonous snake bites.

All plants, animals, natural and cultural features, and archeological sites are protected by federal law. Collecting is prohibited.

Reprinted from National Park Service brochure.

M AAA Real Estate Source
Cody (587-3273) and Powell (754-2119). www.AAAresource.coml homepro@tritel.net

If you've tried to sell your home yourself, you know that the minutes you put up the "For Sale by Owner" sign, the phone will start to ring off the hook. What do you do next? You may have owned a home before and are presently renting or maybe you are a first-time buyer and need a way to break into the housing market but are holding back because you don't have a down payment. What do you do? Bank foreclosures? Fixer uppers? No money down properties? Selling your home yourself? If you need answers on any of these subjects AAA Real Estate Source is your source for the answers. Hal Dicks and Rosemary Reno are experts at providing answers to the most complex real estate questions. Call them to receive free reports on these topics and more.

28 *No services*

Garland
Pop. 50, Elev., 4,247

A respected forest ranger, John Garland, gave his name to this little intersection town. It sits alongside the Bridger Trail.

H The Shoshone Project Story– Project Overview
Three miles north of Garland

The Shoshone Project is located in a desert-like valley surrounded by mountains. Annual precipitation is between 5 and 6 inches, not enough to grow crops.

The success of farming in this area is directly related to the amount of snow which falls in the mountains. The water supply for the Project is obtained from this snowmelt above Buffalo Bill Dam and Reservoir. The reservoir stores water from the approximately 1,500-square-mile Shoshone River drainage for use during the irrigation season, which runs from April 15 to October 15.

The elevation of the project ranges from about 4,200 feet above sea level in the Frannie Division to about 4,800 feet in the Heart Mountain Division.

The Garland, Willwood and Heart Mountain divisions of the Project can be seen from this vantage point. The Frannie Division is located about 10 miles northeast.

29 *Gas*

Byron
Pop. 557, Elev. 4,020

Mormon pioneer Byron Sessions, this town's namesake, was largely responsible for the Sidon Canal irrigation system in the area. A fence posthole unearthed a natural gas vent in a farmers field here, which —accidentally ignited — burned for years. Later, around 1906, the gas was intentionally tapped at 700 feet, and the Byron area became a prominent gas field.

H Sidon Canal
West of Byron

Following Mormon settlement of the Salt Lake Valley beginning in 1847, church leaders envisioned colonization of the entire inter-mountain region. In following decades, Mormons emigrated from Utah into Idaho, Arizona and Wyoming. Seeking to improve their economic status and following Mormon pioneering tradition, several hundred people in 1900 emigrated from Utah and Idaho to Wyoming's Big Horn Basin where they built a canal and a community.

Under the Carey Act of 1894 states were encouraged to sell arable public land cheaply following reclamation. But private reclamation projects required capital, and some were aborted as investors lost faith. Unlike other privately-financed projects, the Sidon Canal was built without a large amount of capital. Emigrants were organized into the Big Horn Colonization Company, an irrigation cooperative which offered company shares in return for labor. Upon arriving in the Basin workers plunged into canal construction, excavating with horse-drawn plows and slip scrapers. Near this point work was blocked by a sandstone boulder known as "Prayer Rock." According to legend, prayer and divine intervention caused the rock to split, allowing construction to continue and strengthening the emigrant faith in the canal project.

The 37-mile long canal was completed in less than two years. It still transports water from a headgate on the Shoshone River near the Big Horn-Park County line to a land segregation of approximately 20,000 acres. Its successful completion serves as an outstanding example of the cooperative effort and spirit of determination exhibited by Mormon pioneers in the American West.

30 *Gas, Food, Lodging*

Lovell
Pop. 2,361 Elev. 3,814

Lovell is known as the "City of Roses" for its renowned late citizen, Dr. William Horsely (d. 1971), who spent a lifetime cultivating the flower, becoming one of the nation's foremost authorities. The town honors his memory with a brilliant display of roses all over the place every summer, near homes and businesses. It's a quiet town, with the lowest crime rate in Wyoming. Still, Lovell has seen its share of booms and busts with the discovery of natural gas and oil in the area. The persistence of agricultural concerns has provided some stability, and a sugar beet factory and gypsum plant also contribute to the economy.

The Lovell area was originally part of the large ML Ranch, founded in 1880 by Anthony Mason and Henry Clay Lovell. By the turn of the century, several Mormon pioneers and German emigrants had come to the area to homestead, and were part of the irrigation project (the Sidon Canal) which made the Bighorn Basin flourish. In 1920, a glass factory was established, which later burned down. During the 1930s, Lovell was known for its brick and tile production.

While driving through town, note the solar powered street lights that line the main thoroughfare through town.

Veteran's War Memorial in Lovell.

T Bighorn Canyon Visitor's Center
U.S. Highway 14A east of Lovell. 548-2251

The center includes an interpretive area and large 3-D model of the Bighorn Canyon and Reservoir. There is also a small giftshop.

H Wildland Romance
U.S. Highway 14A one mile east of Lovell. Bighorn National Recreation Area Headquarters. 777-4600

Many native Americans and early 19th century beaver trappers left their moccasin tracks at this very site, while crossing between the Bighorn Mountains to the east and the Absaroka Moutains to the west. The view of wildlife and wildland landscapes has changed dramatically since that time, and so has our understanding of all life's connection to the land, water and air.

Wildland spaces and contrasting landscapes make Wyoming a special place for people and wildlife. Wide-open spaces provide a special need for free-ranging herds of elk, deer, bighorn sheep and pronghorn antelope. From this agricultural island on the north edge of the Bighorn Basin you are surrounded by wildland expanses and a contrast of mountains, rivers and prairie. The Pryor Mountains to the north, the Owl Creek Mountains to the south, and Bighorns and Absarokas all contribute to the basin's wildlife diversity.

Pioneers began farming and raising livestock in this area in the late 1800s because of its temperate climate, wide open spaces and landscape diversity. Both wildlife and people have benefitted and share the wide open spaces and contrasting landscapes.

Abundant wildlife, natural wonders and western culture have always allured and enchanted the human spirit. We hope your spirit will be strengthened by your visit to this special piece of Wyoming's Wildlands.

H Lower Big Horn Basin
East of Lovell on Highway 14A.

John Colter visited this area in 1807. Many trappers and hunters followed later. The first wheeled vehicle was brought into this region in 1860. Permanent ranches were established near the mouth of the Shoshone River before 1888. Other ranchers soon settled along the Shoshone and Big Horn Rivers, and on Crooked, Gyp and Sage Greeks.

Later homeseekers settled in the lower Shoshone Valley, notably a large Mormon colony in 1900 which constructed irrigation systems and thriving towns. This log house, erected before 1894, and once occupied by one of Big Horn County's first officers, William F. Hunt, is typical of the homes built by the early settlers of this region.

H Bighorn Lake
U.S. Highway 14A 14 miles east of Lovell

Before you is Bighorn Lake. Yellowtail Dam at Fort Smith, Montana backs up the Bighorn River 71 miles to this point. Completed in 1968, the dam provides hydroelectric power to the region, water for irrigation and opportunities for recreation.

Fluctuation in river flow and differing demands in electric power will cause extreme change in the lake elevation. At this location a 30 foot change in water level could move the lake shore 5 miles.

At normal pool, the surface of the entire lake covers 12,685 acres. At this time the area before you is under water to the left of the causeway. This represents a 30 foot rise over the normal annual low water level, a difference amounting to 90 billion gallons of water capable of producing 111 million kilowatt hours of electricity at the dam.

For several months each year the water level is too low to cover this area of the reservoir. While the reservoir is drawn down, the ground exposed by the receding water provides breeding habitat for amphibians and aquatic insects, which provide food for fish in Bighorn Lake.

H Henry Gilbert, Jr. Memorial
Pennsylvania and Main Streets in Lovell

The Flying Tigers were American boys from 41 of our states, fighter pilots trained in our own Army and Navy, who became members of the new A.V.G. (American Volunteer Group) employed by the government of Generalissimo Chiang Kai-shek to protect the lifeline of China, the Burma Road. The Flying Tigers began under the leadership of Claire Lee Chennault with 100 Curtiss-Wright P-40B Tomahawks and the volunteer pilots to fly them.

They went on from there. They went on in smoke and flame and blood and death to compose their epic—one of the most spectacular in the annals of air warfare. They saved Rangoon and the Burma Road for 65 precious days. They became the demigods of fighting China.

Wingman Henry Gilbert, Jr. of Lovell, Wyoming was the youngest of the Flying Tigers at the age of 22.

On December 23, 1941, two waves of Japanese bombers accompanied by fighters were approaching Mingaladon. Fourteen P-40's and 16 Brewsters of the R.A.F. took off to meet the attack.

Gilbert dived on one of the bomber formations, shooting out bursts and striking two of them but without hitting vital spots in the attack. His P-40 was hit by a cannon shell and streamed out of the battle to crash into the jungle below.

There had been no parachute, and Henry Gilbert was the first Flying Tiger to die in combat.

H John Winterholler Gymnasium
Johnny Winterholler Gymnasium in Lovell

John Winterholler was born February 3, 1916 in Billings, Montana of Russian immigrants. He came to Lovell, Wyoming in 1932. John graduated from Lovell High School in 1935. While attending LHS he excelled in sports and was named All-State in basketball and football.

John started his meteoric rise to athletic fame at the University of Wyoming in the fall of 1935. "The Cowboy campus has produced no athlete who has attained the Lovell youth's heights," wrote Larry Birleffi of him in 1939. Birleffi noted "He is the athlete's idea of an athlete and a coach's answer... He earned a first berth in every all-conference selection among Big Seven's offerings for All-American honors... His achievements were in baseball, football and basketball."

During World War II he was captured at Corregidor and was a Japanese prisoner of war for 34 months, subsequently becoming paralyzed. John was a recipient of the Silver Star and promoted to a full colonel, all by the age of 30.

John captained a wheelchair basketball team after the war and was once again a leading figure in sporting news, termed "Spider", "Demon on Wheels" and "The Accurate Shooting Colonel Winterholler."

His Alma Mater, UW, called him home to Laramie for "Johnnie Winterholler Day" October 31, 1964. John's brief but poignant words of award acceptance were followed by thunderous applause, as John seemed to all to represent that flag of liberation, "The Stars and Stripes", "Old Glory."

31 Gas, Food, Lodging

Cowley
Pop. 560, Elev. 3,976

Established in 1901, this little town was named in honor of Mathias F. Cowley, a Mormon apostle. He was an instrumental figure in the building of the Sidon Canal, which irrigates the area's farmland. In addition to agriculture, Cowley came to depend on natural gas for its livelihood.

T Cowley Pioneer Museum
Main Street in Cowley. 548-7700

Cowley recently finished renovating a 1910 Frontier stone building for use as its town hall and historical center. Established by Mormon emigrants, cowley has a population of 500, and the bucolic setting welcomes visitors to the Museum where items of local historical interest are displayed. The community celebrates has been celebrating the pioneer history the third week in July annually since 1907.

H The Big Horn Academy
In Cowley

The Latter-Day Saints have always believed in the importance of education. Wherever they have settled they made building of schools a first priority. The Mormons had hardly finished putting up their own log cabins when they started planning for their schools. They built a large stone grade school dedicated in 1909, then began construction of a high school building. It was to be church-supported and called The Bighorn Acadamy. The first classes of this academy-to-be met in the grade school building while construction proceeded.

Though the Mormon Church supplied the actual money required to build and equip the facility, by far the major portion of the project was accomplished with donated labor, expertise, aqnd machines which were quite primitive by modern standards. The building was completed in 1916.

Its program was essentially that of a high school although in the context of that time, it was thought of, almost, as a college. Students came to the Academy from a wide area to live and board, somewhat as students leave home today for higher education.

The Academy was operated as a church school until 1924 when its facilities and respon-

sibilities were transferred to the Cowley School District thereafter known as the Cowley High School.

During its life as the Big Horn Academy 178 students graduated from the school.

H The Log Community Building
In Cowley

During the Great Depression, President Franklin D. Roosevelt began the Works Progress Administration (WPA) to help stimulate economic activity. In 1933, the Cowley town leaders sought help from the WPA to build a community hall. It was built from lodge pole logs, cut and hauled from the Pryor Mountains north of Cowley. The WPA furnished a grant to pay laborers wages of thirty cents per hour. No records remain to tell exactly how much was spent or how many local citizens donated time, horses, wagons, tools, or equipment, but it is estimated that nearly a hundred people worked on the project without compensation. The actual money spent was perhaps around $10,000. A group of workers from five to a dozen stayed with the operation from beginning to end.

Adolf Anderson, a man of very little formal education, became both the designer and superintendent. He obviously knew what he was doing. Although the exterior is quite conventional, the interior has almost a cathedral effect with its soaring, open trusswork built of 14 inch logs.

Through the years the building has been used for public meetings, church conferences, annual celebrations, family gatherings, class reunions, dances, political rallies, musicals, dramas, school athletics, and even prize fights.

32 No services

Deaver
Pop. 177, Elev. 4,105

Once a tent town on the Burlington Railroad, Deaver was named for D. Clem Deaver, a Burlington agent who was very interested in developing the Big Horn region.

H Deaver Reservoir
State Highway 114 two miles west of Deaver. 527-2175

The Deaver Reservoir is an equalizing, or regulating, reservoir which serves water to about 1,800 acres on the Frannie Division of the Shoshone Project. For 75 years, the reservoir

Wyoming Tidbits

No Wood Creek near Ten Sleep was so named because settlers were unable to find firewood along the creek banks.

Sheep Mountain just north of Greybull.

provided the domestic water supply for the town of Deaver. Water is now transported to Deaver by the nearly 60-mile-long Shoshone Municipal Pipeline, which was constructed in 1991.

In addition to serving as a strategic part of the irrigation system, the Deaver Reservoir today is used as a family recreational area. Fishing, picnicking and bird watching are popular pastimes at this reservoir, which has developed through a cooperative effort of the Deaver Irrigation District, The Wyoming Game and Fish Department and the U.S. Bureau of Reclamation.

33 *No services*

Frannie
Pop. 180, Elev. 4,219

This town was named for a six-year-old girl, Frannie Morris, whose father received permission to open a post office on the Wyoming-Montana border. Frannie grew up to be in Buffalo Bill's Wild West Show.

34 *No services*

Elk Basin

Elk Basin has been an active oil field since 1915 and continues to be highly productive. Today the oilfields are just about all that you'll fnd here. A recent discovery at Elk Basin, believed to be devoid of fossils, lead to a new and very productive Late Cretaceous site.

35

T Medicine Wheel
Between Sheridan and Lovell on Highway 14A

Located near the top of a mountain in Wyoming is the Medicine Wheel, a large wheel measuring approximately 80 feet in diameter. In this area of intense beauty, game is plentiful and the hills are filled with life. From the Wheel a magnificent view of distant, high peaks and the vastness of the Big horn Basin can be seen below. The Wheel

is somewhat isolated and lacks large stands of shrubbery, water or shelter. The trees and plants that thrive here are bent and beaten annually by mighty snows and winds that are ccommon at altitudes of 9,642 feet6 above sea level. There is solitude here, where the Medicine Wheel sits above timberline on Medicine Mountain. It is a sacred site, an historic site, and an archaeological site.

The Medicine Wheel was designated a National Historic Landmark in 1970. It was probably constructed between 1,200 and 1,700 A.D. An exact date has not been determined. It is approximately 245 feet in circumference with a central cairn, a small donut-shaped structure. From this central cairn 28 spokes radiate to the outer rim of the circle. Placed at varying intervals around the rim are six smaller cairns. Five of the peripheral cairns touch the outer rim. One is located approximately ten feet outside the circle. Of these six cairn, four face the center of the circle, one faces north and one faces east. The central cairn is much larger than the rest and measures 12' x 7'. Some of the cairns may have been covered with skins supported by wooden posts.

There are many legends and traditions which may explain the Wheel's origin. But there are no specific artifacts which determine exactly when or who constructed this unusual landmark. It is clear that this place has been visited by many people over the last few hundred years because of the well-traveled trail that parallels the current access road.

There are some who suggest the spoke-like structure resembles the "Sun Dance Lodge," or "Medicine Lodge". The Sun Dance Ceremony is a celebration which is part of the fabric of Native American culture and religion. Some researchers have also suggested the Medicine Wheel is an aboriginal astronomical observatory.

A contemporary Cheyenne cultural leader stated, "the tribes traditionally went and still go to the sacred mountain. The people sought the high mountain for prayer. They sought spiritual harmony with the powerful spirits there. Many offerings have always been left on this mountain. The

center cairn, once occupied by a large buffalo skull, was a place to make prayer offerings. Vision questors would have offered prayers of thanks for plant and animal life that had and would, sustain them in the future. Prayers of thanks were offered for all of creation. Prayers are made for families and for loved ones who are ill. Atonements are made for any offense to Mother Earth. When asking for guidance, prayers for wisdom and strength are always part of this ritual. All of this is done so that spiritual harmony will be our constant companion throughout the year."

A Crow Chief stated that Medicine Wheel was built "before the light came." Other Crow stories say the Sun God dropped it from the sky. And still others say it was built by the "Sheepeaters," a Shoshonean band whose name is derived from their expertise at hunting mountain sheep. Many Crow feel it is a guide for building tipis. Some explain the Wheel was built by "people without iron." At present there are no concrete answers as to who actually constructed this landmark.

One Crow speaks of a man named Scarface. He was handsome and was fond of strutting in his finery before young women. One day while entering his mother's tipi, he fell into the fire which severly burned his face and was thereafter embarrassed to be seen. Shamed at his appearance he left his people and went to live in the mountains. Scarface lived alone for many years. One day while a young woman and her grandmother were hunting berries, they became sparated from their people and couldn't find their way back. They traveled along a trail which took them into the mountains. They occasionally saw Scarface and one day made contact with him. Scarface later married the youngest woman. On their travels back to his people, Scarface supposedly built the Medicine Wheel as their shelter. On the second day he built another tipi near the Big Horn River in the valley below. The tipi rings are believed to still exist.

It is also said that Red Plume, a great Crow Chief during the time of Lewis and Clark, found great spiritual medicine at the Medicine Wheel. The legend states that following four days without food or water, Red Plume was visited by little people who inhabited the passage to the Wheel. They took him into the earth where they lived and told him that the red eagle was his powerful medicine guide and protector. He was told to always wear the small feather from the back of the eagle above its tail feathers. Thus Red Plume received his name. Upon his deathbed, he told his people his spirit would live at the Wheel and that they might communicate with him there.

You can do your part to protect the Medicine Wheel. Do not disturb or remove any cultural resources within or around the historic site. Respect the privacy of others at the Wheel. Do not remove the sacred prayer offerings left by Native Americans.

The Medicine Wheel and Medicine Mountain reflect 10,000 years of Native American culture. The site is sacred and revered by Indian people. It is important that the Medicine Wheel be treated with the utmost respect given any holy place. The site is protected by Federal Laws such as the Antiquities Act (1906), Historic Sites Act (1935), the National Historic Preservation Act (1966), The Archaeological Resources Protection Act (1978). Since 1993 the road which leads to the Wheel has been closed to vehicular traffic. A one and one-half mile foot-trail now leads to the summit.

Reprinted from U.S. Forest Service brochure.

H Medicine Wheel

U.S. Highway 14A 22 miles west of Burgess Junction

The builders and purpose of the Medicine Wheel are unknown. It is currently thought that it was religious in nature, or it may have had astronomical implications, or both. It is constructed of stones laid side by side, forming an almost perfect circle 74 feet in diameter with 28 spokes. An associated radio-carbon date is about 1760. Crow Indian legend says that when they came, the wheel was there. They migrated to the Big Horn Basin around 1776.

Modern Indians use the Medicine Wheel for religious ceremonies. At times, flags, or offerings are left about the wheel, signifying that a ceremony has taken place. The Forest Service does not interfere with these ceremonies, so please do not destroy, or remove the objects. As part of their ceremonial activities the Indians may build an open fire and you may see evidence of this. However, open fires by the general public are prohibited.

The Medicine Wheel is designated a National Historic Landmark, which means it has national significance. It is not only the responsibility of the Government to protect this national landmark but also every American.

SCENIC DRIVES

Big Horn Scenic Byway

This is the middle route across the Bighorn National Forest in the Big Horn Mountains. The official 47-mile stretch of US 14 shares its western boundary with the forest. From the west, the route begins around four miles from the town of Shell. At Burgess Junction, the Big Horn Scenic Byway meets the Medicine Wheel Scenic Byway (US 14A). The eastern boundary of the Scenic Byway is 6.5 miles west of the town of Dayton.

The two lane highway can close for short periods of time due to heavy snows during winter or early spring, but summer an fall travel are normally not interrupted by inclement weather. Granite Pass, at 9033 feet, marks the apex of this scenic route that has switchbacks through a canyon on the western side and descends more gradually on the eastern slope of the mountains.
Reprinted from Wyoming Department of Transportation Brochure

Medicine Wheel Passage

This byway is the northern-most route across the Bighorn National Forest in the Big Horn Mountains. The 27 miles of this section of highway constitute nearly the entire length of US 14A, ending at the western edge of the Bighorn National Forest. Just to the west of the boundary are the Bighorn Canyon National Recreation Area and the nearby town of Lovell. On the east end is Burgess Junction, where the Scenic Byway merges with US 14 and becomes the Bighorn Scenic Byway. The Gown of Dayton provides access to the route from the east.

This two lane paved highway follows one of the highest routes in the state. The steep, winding road sports numerous truck turnoffs and a maximum 10-percent grade. Heavy snow keeps the road closed in winter and early spring, so summer and fall are the only practical seasons to make this trip.

A high point (literally) along th route is the 9430-foot view looking southwesterly into the Big Horn Basin, thousands of feet below. Mountain peaks tower above 13,000 feet in this high-alti-

tude neighborhood. The rapid change in elevation along the Byway provides a variety of habitat types. During the summer, deer and an occasional elk can be viewed feeding at the edge of timber stands. Blue grouse, with their young, are found near the many springs on the forested area. Mourning doves are also common near water.
Reprinted from Wyoming Department of Transportation Brochure

Red Gulch/Alkali Scenic Backway

This 32-mile route through a mostly unraveled section of th Big Horn Basin traces two road of historic importance to Native American and frontier history: Alkali Road (CR 1111) and Red Gulch Road (BLM 1109). This country has been inhabited since Paleo-Indians first hunted mammoth here, 12, 000 years ago. In more recent times, the late 1800s and early 1900s, sheepherders built rock cairns here to provide landmarks and kill time while they watched the sheep.

Depending on weather conditions, driving this byway is not recommended from November through April. Even light precipitation can cause muddy, impassable conditions. In dry conditions, a high-clearance, two wheel drive vehicle, can manage without much difficulty. The road can be bumpy and rutted in places, so large vehicles, trailers, campers, and RV's may want to avoid this route. Road grades do not exceed seven percent.

Travelers should allow at least one hour to make this drive. Frequent stops to enjoy the scenery can extend the trip into a day's adventure or more. There are no towns, stores, gas stations, or telephones along the way. Some services are available in Shell and Tensleep, and more can be found in Greybull.
Reprinted from Wyoming Department of Transportation Brochure

HIKES

Crystal Creek Ridge

Distance: 1 mile
Climb: gentle
Rating: easy
Usage: light
Location: Take Alternate Hwy. 14 west from Burgess Junction, turning south on FDR 122, across from the Medicine Wheel Road. Follow this road for about 1.5 miles to where it intersects FDR 132. Turn right here, and take the road to its end.

This is an easy stroll of a hike with views of the badlands, the Bighorn Basin, and the Absaroka Mountains.

Porcupine Falls

Distance: 1 mile
Climb: 400 feet
Rating: difficult
Usage: light
Location: Take Alternate Hwy. 14 west from Burgess Junction to FDR 14 (Devil Canyon Rd.). Take this for 3 miles, continuing past the junction with FDR 11for another 5.7 miles. Here, the road meets up with FDR 146, which will take you to the trailhead.

This trail follows an old mining road, which climbs steeply up the canyon towards the 200 foot-high falls. A deserted mining camp is situated near the falls, across Porcupine Creek. Please respect it as a historic site and do not take souvenirs.

Bucking Mule Falls

Distance: 5.2 miles
Climb: about 300 feet

Rating: easy
Usage: light
Location: Take Alternate Hwy. 14 west from Burgess Junction to FDR 14 (Devil Canyon Rd.). Take this for 3 miles, bearing left at the junction with FDR 11. Follow this road 8 miles to the trailhead.

This is a vigorous day hike to the top of the 500 foot-high falls and back. Hikers interested in a longer hike can follow the rough trail another 8 miles along Porcupine Creek, to camp overnight at Porcupine Creek Bridge or Tillets Hole. The first portion of the trip, to the falls, descends to Big Teepee Creek, passes a junction then climbs to the overlook. Return to the junction for the overnight trek, following the less-worn path across a bridge and along the ridge of Railroad Springs Creek. Turn left at the junction with Mexican Hill Trails, heading south to Devil Canyon. Keep following the path through the valley until it turns west into Tillets Hole. Stay on the Bucking Mule Trail until it reaches a stock bridge across Porcupine Creek. Beyond this it connects with the Long Park Creek Trail, then continues to another bridge across the creek. The trail ends at FDR 137.

Lodge Grass Creek

Distance: 9.3 miles
Climb: 3350 (descent)
Rating: difficult
Usage: very light
Location: Take Alternate Hwy. 14 west from Burgess Junction to FDR 14 (Devil Canyon Rd.). Take this for 3 miles, turning right on FDR 11, and taking the steep road (no trailers or RVs) 6.7 miles to FDR 110. Turn left, staying on FDR 11, and continue to the trailhead.

A still-active stock trail, this route takes you along the creek across grassy terrain, surrounded by rocky cliffs lined with evergreens. An abrupt descent takes you past an old cabin, then follows the stream down to a meadow. You must pass through a gate at the top of the ridge, then cross a small stream before continuing along the creek to a boulder field. After going through another fence gate, the valley opens up to afford views of unusual glacial rock remnants, and the scars of a fire that swept the area in 1970. The trail continues on to a woodland area which is good for camping. For those who wish to travel a little farther, the trail terminates at the fenced Montana state line, where the Crow Reservation begins.

Cottonwood Canyon

Distance: 2.5 miles, one way
Climb: 1700 feet
Rating: difficult
Usage: light
Location: Take Alternate Hwy. 14 east from Lovell across Bighorn Lake, then turn left (north) on John Blue Road. Immediately make a right onto a little-used road which will take you about 6 miles to Cottonwood Canyon. Park near the gravel pits.

This trail follows a jeep road into the canyon, which broadens into an amphitheater and an overlook of Melody Falls. The road turns into a stock trail as the canyon narrows, and passes a number of smaller falls as it climbs steeply along the creek. The canyon turns north, and eventually fades into uncertain paths, indicating a return along the route you just traveled.

Rainbow Canyon

Distance: 4. 8 miles, one way
Climb: 60 feet
Rating: moderate
Usage: light
Location: Take Alternate Hwy. 14 east from Lovell

Ten Sleep Canyon.

across Bighorn Lake to the turnoff for Five Springs Campground. Take a right (south) onto the road across the highway, taking the right fork after about 100 yards and continuing to the parking area at the end of the road.

This hike travels through a colorful canyon towards the badlands west of the Bighorn Mountains. It begins along a jeep road that descends along a gulch, then takes you along Five Springs Creek and on into the canyon. Leave the road where it diverges into a deeply cut gully which follows the rim of the canyon for a while, then descends to the floor of the wash. Eventually, the canyon will diminish in height, and the stream bed will empty into Black Gulch, a barren valley which makes a good turn-around point. This hike can be very hot and dry, so bring lots of water.

Horse Creek Canyons

Distance: 11. 5 miles
Climb: 3900 feet
Rating: difficult
Usage: light
Location: Take Hwy. 14 south from Burgess Junction to FDR 10, north of Granite Pass. Go 12.6 miles to FDR 207 (Sunlight Mesa Rd.) and turn left (south), then bear left again at the first junction, heading towards Horse Creek Cow Camp Cabin. This is a rough road, and high clearance, 4WD vehicles are recommended. Continue past the cabin, bearing right, and then left onto FDR 208. Another mile will take you to Deer Spring and the trailhead.

This loop trail can be completed in a day by vigorous hikers. The trail emerges about 1.6 miles north of the starting point on FDR 207. It's best to take the loop in a clockwise direction, as finding the route can be difficult when approached in the opposite direction. Begin at the aspen grove that marks Deer Spring. Follow the faint trail to the dry fork of Horse Creek, a stay on the stock trail to the south of the meadow. The trail emerges onto an old road, which lads into a draw

heading for the dry creek bed. As the trail fades, continue along the draw past a small spring, and on to Dry Fork. Here you can pick up a washed out path heading east as it meanders back and forth across the streambed. As the canyon walls rise and recede, continue following the north bank until a jeep track descends to the confluence with Horse Creek.

Follow another jeep track along the south bank of Horse Creek and up into the water filled canyon. Cross the stream and head northeast, climbing towards Horse Creek Mesa. Continue past the East and West Fork Confluence, keeping to the south along the East Fork. A climb out of the valley and across a burn area will take you past a natural arch and into Torry Gulch. Stay right until cattle trails take you across a meadow to FDR 207.

*(The Shell Canyon trails require an extra dose of caution because the area is known for its abundance of rattlesnakes. Please beware.)

The Beef Trail*

Distance: 5.9 miles, one way
Climb: 1940 feet (descent)
Rating: moderate/ difficult
Usage: light
Location: From Greybull, take Hwy. 14 east, beyond Shell, to mile marker 27.6. Turn north here onto FDR 264, which is a rough road, and high clearance, 4WD vehicles are recommended. Take this about 2 miles to Brindle Creek, where the trail begins. The trail ends on Hwy. 14, at mile marker 20.6, where there is a pullout and a bridge.

Lovely views of Shell Canyon are the best part of this hike, as well as glimpses of Elephant Head Rock, Copmans Tomb, and Pyramid Mountain. Still an active stock trail, hikers may encounter cattle if they take this route in midsummer or early fall. Where the road forks, continue on the main trail towards the boulders. Follow this into the valley, where the trail climbs and then descends towards Cedar Creek, crossing Fender

Creek along the way. A bridge across Cedar Creek offers a beautiful prospect of the chasm. Beyond the bridge, stay on the clearest stock trail until you cross Cottonwood Creek. Follow the trail towards Sunlight Mesa, where the trail skirts the edge of Shell Creek. A final descent to this creek's bottoms concludes the hike.

Cedar Creek*

Distance: 4 miles, one way
Climb: 1100 feet
Rating: difficult
Usage: light
Location: From Greybull, take Hwy. 14 east, beyond Shell, to mile marker 27.6. Turn north here onto FDR 264, which is a rough road, and high clearance, 4WD vehicles are recommended. Take this about 2 miles to Brindle Creek, where the trail begins.

This trail has many of the same views as the Beef Trail. Where the Beef Trail splits near Brindle Creek, take the right fork towards the northwest, where you will eventually pass a pond. Beyond this are vistas which include Sunlight Mesa, Elephant Head, and Copman's Tomb. Farther along the trail, you will climb through the trees and over some grasslands to Fender Creek. Continue on across the ridge of Copman's Tomb to a meadow where you can take in the grandeur of the mountains all around. After dropping below the meadow, the trail heads towards Cedar Creek, where it climbs down to the bottoms and terminates in the canyon.

The Bench Trail*

Distance: 10 miles
Climb: 3140 descent
Rating: moderate/ difficult
Usage: light
Location: From Greybull, take Hwy. 14 east, beyond Shell, to mile marker 31.3. Turn south onto FDR 17, taking this 2.8 miles to the Ranger Creek Campground. At the campground, take the first left to arrive at the trailhead. The end of the trail will be at mile marker 22.8 on Hwy. 14, by Post Creek.

Although this trail also passes through Shell Canyon, there are fewer opportunities to view the surrounding area through the trees. On the other hand, the trees provide much-appreciated shade along the way. This trail is especially popular for mountain bikers, so be alert. Follow the trail into the forest below the old road, past the junction and through the aspens. Look for the sign here about Rocky Mountain Irises. Follow the trail down into the valley, where it steeply drops towards Granite Creek. Along the way, you'll see some unusual destruction of the woodlands, wrought by a freak tornado in 1959. Another sign explains sheep ranching traditions of the late 1800s. After passing through more trees, the trail comes across an area burned by fire in 1984, a result of illegal fireworks. Re-growth is underway, and a variety of plants and wildlife still abound here. The burn area also provides the best views of the surrounding mountains and rock formation. Continue along the trail across some grassland until it drops down to the highway, near Post Creek.

Meyers Spring Draw

Distance: 2.5 miles
Climb: 400 feet
Rating: easy/ moderate
Usage: light
Location: From Greybull, take Hwy. 789 south about 20 miles, turning east (left) onto Hwy. 31, at Manderson. After about 22 miles, right before Hyatteville, turn north (left) onto Alkali/ Cold Springs

Wyoming Tidbits

Singer Glen Campbell once owned a nightclub in Cody.

Road, which turns to dirt quickly, then takes you about 8 miles to Alkali Flats and over a small ridge. Park just beyond the jeep road.

This badlands hike takes you through an unusual collection of scenic oddities. Starting at the jeep road, follow it along the edge of the ridge until it encounters a game trail leading down into the basin. Pass through the burnt brush, following the streambed past the first mesa. Around the mesa, you will see a gap in the cliffs to the southeast. Head towards the gap, which will take you to the draw. The draw itself passes through more burnt scrub surrounded by intriguing rock formations. You'll encounter another jeep road along the way, which will take you over a saddle to a jeep crossroads. Follow the jeep trail that heads west, going back to the esarpment a little less than a mile from where you began. Follow the ridge again back to the starting point.

Dry Medicine Lodge Creek Canyon

Distance: 5.6 miles, one way
Climb: 1730 feet
Rating: difficult
Usage: light
Location: From Greybull, take Hwy. 789 south about 20 miles, turning east (left) onto Hwy. 31, at Manderson. After about 22 miles, right before Hyatteville, turn south (right) onto Alkali/ Cold Springs Road. Take a right onto Cold Springs Road, following the signs for the Medicine Lodge Archeological Site. After reaching the site, go north on the jeep road that heads into the canyon for 3 miles. Park where the road climbs out of the canyon.

This hike takes you past some truly remarkable rock formations, including a natural arch and some spires. The trail begins by following an old road that is sometimes blocked by rock fall and thorny brush, but its still rather easily negotiated. As the road leads you through some trees, the walls climb around you and shortly you'll arrive at the arch over the dry streambed. Here, the canyon merges with Sheep Creek Canyon, and several spires mark the confluence. Beyond this the trail becomes a little more challenging, and the creek is above ground, so a few minor crossings will come your way. The canyon eventually dissolves into the trees and a grassy meadow, then broadens as the trail ends at an old cabin below Spanish Point.

Medicine Lodge Canyon

Distance: 6.4 miles
Climb: 2850 feet (descent)
Rating: difficult
Usage: light
Location: From Greybull, take Hwy. 789 south about 20 miles, turning east (left) onto Hwy. 31, at Manderson. After about 22 miles, right before Hyatteville, turn north (left) onto Alkali/ Cold Springs Road, which turns to dirt quickly, then takes you about 9.6 miles to Alkali Flats and over a small ridge, and past a jeep road. Just before the road turns south, another jeep road marks the trail's beginning. The trail ends at Dry Medicine Lodge Road, off Cold Springs Road, by the Pictograph Site,

This area has been designated a Wilderness Study Area by the BLM, so it is likely you will see wildlife along the way. The jeep road will take

you down to Captain Jack Creek, and turns into a stock trail that drops rather precipitously to the valley floor. The scenery makes the struggle through the scrub worthwhile. High colorful canyon walls soon surround you and the creek emerges from its underground course. Stick to the trails, as the creek area can be a tangle of vegetation. The canyon eventually diminishes and the trail becomes more grassy. As the canyon turns to the south, a rounded gap affords passage through the west side of the walls and into the Dry Medicine Lodge Creek Canyon. The canyon floor leads you to a jeep road which then takes you to the Pictograph Site.

The Paint Rock Badlands

Distance: 2.7 miles
Climb: 500 feet
Rating: easy/ moderate
Usage: light
Location: From Greybull, take Hwy. 789 south about 20 miles, turning east (left) onto Hwy. 31, at Manderson. After about 22 miles, right before Hyatteville, turn north (left) onto Alkali/ Cold Springs Road, which turns to dirt quickly. Follow the road about 15 miles, past the Paint Rock Canyon Trailhead, and park here.

Some of the area's most distinctive and colorful rock formations can be seen on this hike. The soil here is extremely delicate, however, so please walk only on exposed rock and established trails. From the trailhead, follow a game trail over a rim to the south. Follow the rim, past mushroom shaped pedestals, and into a gulch carved with hoodoos. As the cliffs rise around you, head northwest past more mushrooms and into a cleft of solid sandstone. After then turning northeast, the trail crosses some sandhills and heads into another gulch, climbing the ridge to a view of more mushrooms. Stay west as you reach another hoodoo which will take you to an ATV track at the base of a red butte. A nearby formation can be climbed easily to take in the colorful landscape. Continue along the ATV track over a saddle, to climb back to Cold Springs Road about a half mile from where you began.

Paint Rock Canyon

Distance: 12.8 miles, one way
Climb: 2570 feet
Rating: Difficult
Usage: light
Location: From Greybull, take Hwy. 789 south about 20 miles, turning east (left) onto Hwy. 31, at Manderson. After about 22 miles, right before Hyatteville, turn north (left) onto Alkali/ Cold Springs Road, which turns to dirt quickly. Follow the road about 15 miles, past the Paint Rock Canyon Trailhead, and park here.

A more extensive hike for overnight, this trip will take you to the Bighorn National Forest by way of a blue-ribbon trout stream. It passes over private land (the Hyatt Ranch) so be considerate, stay on the trails, and close all the gates behind you. The trail heads across an area of burnt scrub, heading southwest towards a draw and across it. Soon you will encounter the abundant vegetation surrounding Paint Rock Creek. Beyond this is the ranch's land, and a dirt road takes you past some pastures towards the canyon, and back onto public land. Follow the creek through a bend in the canyon, where a natural arch graces the north rim. The trail then climbs up to the Island, a large butte overlooking a basin, then passes through a

gate to descend back to towards the creek. The creek then splits, and a bridge passes over the main fork. After passing over a swampy area and a meadow, the trail emerges from the canyon and passes below a tree covered mesa. Here it turns into an ATV trail and heads towards the Bighorn National Forest. The creek again splits, and another bridge provides a crossing. A final climb takes you to where the trail emerges onto FDR 349.

INFORMATION PLEASE

Tourism Information

Basin Chamber of Commerce	568-3371
Cody Country Visitor's Council	587-2297
East Yellowstone Chamber of Commerce	527-9959
Chamber of Commerce - Greybull	765-2100
Bighorn Canyon Visitor's Center	548-2251
Powell Valley Chamber of Commerce	754-3494
Thermopolis Hot Springs Chamber of Commerce	864-3192
Chamber of Commerce - Worland	347-3226

Government

BLM Worland Field Office	347-5100
BLM Cody Field Office	578-5900
Shoshone National Forest	527-6241
Shoshone National Forest - Wapiti/Clarks Fork/Greybull Ranger Districts	527-6241

Car Rentals

Budget Rent A Car • Cody	587-6066
Hertz • Cody	587-2914
Rent A Wreck • Cody	527-5549
Thrifty • Cody	587-8855
Rent A Wreck • Thermopolis	864-5571

Hospitals

Hot Springs County Memorial Hospital • Thermopolis	864-3121
North Big Horn Hospital • Lovell	548-2771
Powell Hospital • Powell	754-2267
Washakie Medical Center • Worland	347-3221
West Park Hospital • Cody	527-7501

Airports

Thermopolis	864-2488
Greybull	765-7600
Cody	587-9740

Golf

Midway Golf Club • Basin	568-2255
Powell Country Club • Powell	754-7259
Foster Gulch Golf Club • Lovell	548-2445
Olive Glenn Golf & Country Club • Cody	587-5551
Green Hills Municipal Golf Course • Worland	347-8972

Ski Areas

Big Horn Mountain Ski Lodge	366-2600
Sleeping Giant Ski Area	587-4044

Guest Ranches

Hunter Peak Ranch • Cody	587-3711
Bear Creek Ranch • Shell	765-9319
Bighorn Rodeo Ranch •	762-3535
Wayfaring Traveler Ranch • Burlington	762-3536
Rimrock Ranch • Cody	587-3970
DNR Ranch at Rand Creek • Cody	587-7176
Beteche Creek Ranch • Cody	587-3844

Blackwater Lodge • Cody 587-5201
Bill Cody Ranch • Cody 587-6271
Red Pole Ranch & Motel • Cody 587-5929
Absaroka Mountain Lodge • Cody 587-3963
Schively Ranch • Cody 548-6688
Seven D Ranch • Cody 587-9885
Double Diamond X Ranch • Cody 527-6276
Mooncrest Ranch • Cody 587-3620
K Bar Z Guest Ranch And Outfitters •
Cody 587-4410
Early Ranch Bed & Breakfast •
Crowheart 455-4055
High Island Guest Ranch •
Hamilton Dome 867-2374
Paintrock Ranch • Hyattville 626-2161
Wood River Lodg • Meeteetse 868-9211
Ranch at Meeteetse • Meeteetse 868-9266
Snowflake Ranch • Powell 754-5892
The Hideout at Flitner Ranch • Shell 765-2080
Ranger Creek Guest Ranch • Shell 751-7787
Bilbrey Guest Ranch • Shell 765-9319
Kedesh Guest Ranch • Shell 765-2791
Shell Creek Guest Ranch • Shell 765-2420
Ranger Creek Guest Ranch • Shell 751-7787
Deer Haven Lodge • Ten Sleep 366-2449
Meadowlark Lake Lodge • Ten Sleep 366-2449
Big Horn River Ranch • Thermopolis 864-4224
Sanford Ranches • Thermopolis 864-3575
Paintrock Outfitters • Greybull 765-2556

Lodges and Resorts

Buffalo Bill Village Resort • Cody 587-5556
Holiday Inn Buffalo Bill Village Resort •
Cody 587-5555
Snowshoe Lodge • Shell 899-8995
Wagon Wheel Lodge • 765-2561
Elephant Head Lodge • Cody 587-3980
Pahaska Tepee • Cody 527-7701
Goff Creek Lodge • Cody 587-3753
Wyoming High Country Resort •
Lovell 548-9659
Big Horn Mountain Resorts •
Ten Sleep 366-2424
Big Horn Mountain Ski Lodge •
Ten Sleep 366-2600
Deer Haven Lodge • Ten Sleep 366-2449
Meadowlark Lake Lodge • Ten Sleep 366-2449

Vacation Houses, Cabins & Condos

Cody Guest Houses & The Victorian House Bed &
Breakfast • Cody 587-6000

Cody Vacation Properties AKA Grandma's House -
Lockhart Bed & Breakfast Inn •
Cody 587-6074
Cabins by the Creek • 587-6074
Cozy Cody Cottages • 587-9253
Rustler's Roost • Cody 587-8171
Trapper's Rest Bed & Breakfast and Guest Cabins
• Shell 765-9239
Herzberg Hideaway • Worland 347-2217
Ten Broek Campground RV Park •
Ten Sleep 366-2250

Bed and Breakfasts

Robin's Nest Bed & Breakfast •
Cody 527-7208
Cody Guest Houses & The Victorian House Bed &
Breakfast • Cody 587-6000
Cody Vacation Properties AKA Grandma's House -
Lockhart Bed & Breakfast Inn •
Cody 587-6074
C's Bed & Breakfast • Worland 347-9388
Angel's Keep • Cody 587-6205
The Mayor's Inn • Cody 587-0887
Shoshone Lodge • Cody 587-4044
Trapper's Rest Bed & Breakfast • Shell 765-9239
Lambright Place • Cody 527-5310
Heart to Heart Bed & Breakfast •
Cody 587-2906
Casual Cove Bed & Breakfast • Cody 587-3622
Cody Victorian House • Cody 587-5000
Greybull Hotel • Greybull 765-2012
Horned Toad Bed & Breakfast •
Ten Sleep 366-2747
Harmony Ranch Cottage •
Manderson 568-2514
Early Ranch Bed & Breakfast •
Crowheart 455-4055
4-Bears Outfitters • Powell 645-3375
Taylored Tours • Ten Sleep 366-2250
Parson's Pillow • Cody 587-2382
Grandma's House Lockhart • Cody 587-6074

Outfitters and Guides

North Fork Anglers F 527-7274
Red Canyon River Trips & Wild Mustang Tours
RG 587-6988
Double Diamond Outfitters H 868-9211
Wyoming River Trips R 587-6661
Wyoming Adventures F 864-2407

Wind River Canyon Whitewater R 864-9343
Bill Cody Ranch H 587-6271
Gary Fales Outfitting H 587-3970
Triple Creek Outfitters H 587-6178
Horseworks Wyoming E 867-2367
Hot Springs Outfitting H 864-2417
LZ Ranch Horseback Tours EG 867-2367
Outlaw Trail, Inc G 864-2287
Renegade Rides Inc. HE 366-2689
Deer Haven Lodge HFE 366-2449
Meadowlark Lake Lodge FGE 366-2449
Geoscience Adventures, Inc G 765-2259
Goff Creek Lodge FEG 587-3753
Cresent B Outfitters FHE 587-6937
Paintrock Adventures FH 469-2274
Grub Steak Expeditions 5276316
Mooncrest Ranch FHE 587-3620
River Runners, Inc. R 527-7238
Idgie Poo Outfitters FGE 486-2261
4-Bears Outfitters H 645-3375
Frontier Outfitting H 754-7156
Taylored Tours G 366-2250
Shoshone River Outfitters H 548-7069
Wyoming High Country EG 548-2301
Big Horn Mountain Adventures H 765-2420
Big Horn Outfitters 899-1858
Bliss Creek Outfitters FHRE 527-6103
Butte Creek Outfitters H 587-6016
Coy's Yellow Creek Outfitting H 587-6944
Diamond Tail Outfitters H 765-2905
Elk Mountain Outfitters FHE 587-8238
Fish Hawk Creek Outfitters H 754-749
Flying H Ranch & Outfitters HFE 587-2089
Grassy Lake Outfitters H 527-5494
Grizzly Ranch HF 587-3966
Ishawooa Outfitters HFE 587-9250
Johnson Outfitting HFE 587-4072
K Bar Z Guest Ranch Outfitters HFE 587-4410
Lee Livingston Outfitting HFE 527-7415
Lost Creek Outfitters FHE 527-6251
Majo Ranch H 587-2051
Morning Creek Outfitting H 587-5343
Pennoyer Outfitting H 867-2407
Sheep Mesa Outfitters FHE 587-4305
Two Diamond Outfitters H 587-3753

NOTES:

Dining Quick Reference

Price Range refers to the average cost of a meal per person: ($) $1-$6, ($$) $7-$11, ($$$) $12-up. Cocktails: "Yes" indicates full bar; Beer (B)/Wine (W), Service: Breakfast (B), Brunch (BR), Lunch (L), Dinner (D). Businesses in bold print will have additional information under the appropriate map locator number in the body of this section. *[wi-fi]* next to business name indicates free wireless internet is available to customers.

MAP No.	RESTAURANT	TYPE CUISINE	PRICE RANGE	CHILD MENU	COCKTAILS BEER WINE	MEALS SERVED	CREDIT CARDS ACCEPTED
2	**Wyoming's Rib & Chop House**	Steakhouse	$$/$$$	No	Yes	L/D	Major
2	**Granny's Restaurant**	Family	$/$$	Yes		D/L/B	
2	**Sunset House Restaurant**	Family	$$	Yes	Yes	B/L/D	
2	**The Irma Hotel, Restaurant & Saloon**	Family	$$$/$$	Yes	Yes	B/L/D	Major
2	The Noon Break	New Mexican	$	Yes		B/L	
2	QT's Restaurant	American	$$	Yes	Yes	B/L/D	Major
2	**The Irma Hotel, Restaurant & Saloon**	Family	$$$/$$	Yes	Yes	B/L/D	Major
2	Pizza on the Run	Pizza	$$			L/D	Major
2	Beta Coffeehouse *[wi-fi]*	Coffee Shop	$	Yes		B/L	
2	Black Sheep Restaurant & Gibs Sports Pub	American	$$$	Yes	Yes	L/D	Major
2	Breadboard	Sandwiches	$	Yes		B/L/D	Major
2	Cody Coffee Company & Eatery	American	$$			L/B	
2	Gardens/Mack Brother's Brew. Co.	Mediterranean	$$	Yes	B	L/D	Major
2	Maxwell's Fine Food & Spirits *[wi-fi]*	Italian	$$/$$$	Yes	Yes	L/D	Major
2	Mustard's Last Stand	Fast Food	$	Yes		L/D	
2	Zapata's Mexican Restaurant	Mexican	$$		Yes	L/D	Major
2	Wendy's	Fast Food	$	Yes		L/D	Major
2	Stefan's Restaurant	Fine Dining	$$$/$$	No	Yes	L/D	Major
2	Peter's Café & Bakery	Sandwiches	$$			B/L/D	
2	The Proud Cut Saloon	Western		No	Yes	L/D	Major
2	Papa Murphy's Take & Bake Restaurant	Pizza	$$			L/D	Major
2	Tommy Jack's Cajun Grill	Steakhouse	$$$		Yes	D/L	Major
2	Dairy Queen	Fast Food	$	Yes		L/D	
2	Domino's Pizza	Pizza	$$	No		L/D	Major
2	Subway	Sandwiches	$	Yes		B/L/D	M/V
2	Taco John's	Fast Food	$	Yes		L/D	
2	Pahaska Tepee Resturant	Fine Dining	$$$/$$	Yes	Yes	L/D	Major
2	Annie Oakley's Cowgirl Café	Family		Yes		D/L	Major
2	Trail Shop Inn & Café	Family	$$	Yes	Yes	L/D/B	Major
2	Yellowstone Valley Inn	Homestyle	$$	Yes	Yes	B/L/D	Major
2	Main Street Ice Cream	Ice Cream/	$	Yes		D/L	
2	Hong Kong Chinese Restaurant	Chinese		Yes		L/D	V/M
2	La Comida Mexican Restaurant	Mexican	$$	Yes	Yes	L/D	M/V
2	Daylight Donuts	Coffee Shop	$			L/B	
3	Bubba's Bar-B-Que	Barbeque	$$			L/D/B	Major
3	McDonald's	Fast Food		Yes		B/L/D	Major
3	Royal Palace Restaurant	Family	$$	Yes		B/L/D	Major
3	Pizza Hut	Pizza	$$	Yes	B	L/D	Major
3	Our Place	Homestyle	$$	Yes		B/L/D	
3	Bill Cody Ranch Restaurant	Family	$$$	Yes	Yes	B/D	Major
4	Cassie's Supper Club & Dance Hall	Steakhouse	$$/$$$	Yes	Yes	L/D	Major
4	Quizno's	Sandwiches	$	Yes		D/L	Major
4	Burger King	Fast Food	$	Yes		B/L/D	M/V
4	Subway	Sandwiches	$	Yes		B/L/D	M/V
4	Taco Bell/KFC	Fast Food	$	Yes		L/D	
4	Crosswinds Café	Family	$$			B/L/D	M/V
4	Taco Bell/KFC	Fast Food	$	Yes		L/D	
8	Broken Spoke Café & Shirley's Pies	Family	$$	No	Yes	B/L/D	Major
8	Elkhorn Bar & Grill	American	$$	No	Yes	L/D	M/V
8	Outlaw Parlor Café	American	$$	No	Yes	L/D	M/V
8	Lucille's Café	Family	$$	Yes		B/L/D	
10	**Las Fuentes Restaurant**	North Mexico	$$	Yes	Yes	D/L	Major
10	Granny's Bakery, Ice Cream & Grill	Sandwiches	$	Yes		B/L/D	
10	Pumpernick's	American	$$	Yes	Yes	B/L/D	Major
10	Safari Lounge & Restaurant	Family	$$	Yes	Yes	B/L/D	Major
10	Coyote Coffee Co.	Coffee Shop	$	Yes		L/B	M/V
10	Dairyland	Family	$$	Yes		L/D	
11	Ballyhoo Restaurant	Steak & Seafood	$$$/$$	Yes	Yes	D	Major
11	Subway	Sandwiches	$	Yes		B/L/D	M/V
11	A&W	Fast Food	$	Yes		L/D	

Dining Quick Reference-Continued

Price Range refers to the average cost of a meal per person: ($) $1-$6, ($$) $7-$11, ($$$) $12-up. Cocktails: "Yes" indicates full bar; Beer (B)/Wine (W); Service: Breakfast (B), Brunch (BR), Lunch (L), Dinner (D). Businesses in bold print will have additional information under the appropriate map locator number in the body of this section. [wi-fi] next to business name indicates free wireless internet is available to customers.

MAP No.	RESTAURANT	TYPE CUISINE	PRICE RANGE	CHILD MENU	COCKTAILS BEER WINE	MEALS SERVED	CREDIT CARDS ACCEPTED
11	McDonald's	Fast Food	$	Yes		L/D/B	
11	Lil's Wrangler Restaurant	Family	$$	No		B/L/D	V/M
11	Pizza Hut	Pizza	$$	Yes	B	L/D	Major
13	Butch's Place Restaurant	Steak & Burgers	$$		Yes	D	M/V
14	The Ram's Horn Café	American	$$	Yes	Yes	B/L/D	Major
14	Ranchito Restaurant	Mexican	$$	Yes		D/L/B	D
14	China Garden	Chinese	$$	No		L/D	M/V
14	C&D Bowling Alley Snack Shop	Fast food	$		B	L/D	
15	A&W	Fast Food	$	Yes		L/D	
15	Subway	Sandwiches	$	Yes		L/D/B	M/V
15	Taco John's	Fast Food	$	Yes		L/D	
15	Brass Plum Restaurant	American	$$		Yes	L/D	Major
16	Arby's	Fast Food	$	Yes		L/D	Major
16	McDonald's	Fast Food	$	Yes		L/D/B	
16	Maggie's Café	Family	$	Yes		B/L	
16	Pizza Hut	Pizza	$$	Yes	B	L/D	Major
16	Season's Supper Club	Steakhouse	$$$		Yes	L/D	Major
16	Office Lounge Cafe	American	$$/$$$		Yes	L/D	Major
16	Coffees & Cakes	Coffee Shop	$			B/L	
16	Hot Stuff Pizzaria	Pizza	$$			L/D	Major
17	Dirty Sally's Gifts, Quilts & Soda Fountain	Soda Fountain	$	Yes		L/D	D
17	Flagstaff Café	Family	$$		W/B	B/L/D	
17	Deer Haven Lodge	Family	$$		Yes	L/D	Major
17	Meadowlark Lake Lodge	Steak House	$$	Yes	Yes	L/D/B	Major
17	Fireside Café & Lounge	Family	$$	Yes		L/D	Major
17	Other Side Bar & Grill	American	$$	No	Yes	L/D	Major
17	Tom & Jerry's	Steakhouse	$$$	Yes	Yes	D/L	Major
17	PerCup Expresso	Bakery/Deli	$		W/B	B/L	
18	Paintrock Inn Bar & Grll	Family	$$	Yes	Yes	B/L/D	
18	Hyattville Café [wi-fi]	Family	$$/$	Yes		B/L/D	
19	Manderson Kwik Stop	Fast Food	$			B/L/D	Major
19	3 Sisters Truck Stop	Family	$$	Yes		B/L/D	Major
19	Blimpie's	Sandwiches	$	Yes		L/D	Major
19	Hi Way Bar & Café	American	$$		Yes	B/L/D	Major
20	Tom's Cafe	Family	$/$$			B/L/D	
21	**Lisa's Fine Dining**	Fine Dining	$$$	No	Yes	D/L	Major
21	Buffalo Rose Restaurant	American	$$	Yes	W/B	L/D	V/M
21	A&W	Fast Food	$	Yes		D/L	
21	Subway	Sandwiches	$	Yes		D/L	M/V
21	Wheels Inn Restaurant	American	$$	Yes		D/L/B	
21	Sugar Shack	Soda Fountain	$				
21	Uptown Café	American	$/$$	No	Yes	B/L/D	Major
21	Bejing Garden	Chinese	$$	No		D/L	M/V
21	Sidekick Pizza & Subway	Pizza/Sandwiches	$$/$$$/$	No		D/L	Major/M/V
22	Dirty Annie's [wi-fi]	American	$/$$	Yes	W/B	D/L/B	Major
22	Snowshoe Lodge [wi-fi]	Family	$$	Yes	Yes	D/L/B	Major
23	Burlington Café	Family	$			B/L	
26	Pizza Hut	Pizza	$$	Yes	B	L/D	Major
26	Burger King	Fast Food	$	Yes		L/D/B	M/V
26	Skyline Café	Coffee House	$$	Yes		L/B/D	
26	Domino's	Pizza	$$	No		L/D	Major
26	Taco Bell	Fast Food	$	Yes		L/D	
26	Taco Johns	Fast Food	$	No		L/D	
26	Pepe's	Mexican	$$	Yes		L/D/B	M/V
26	Chinatown Gourmet Chinese	Chinese	$$	No		L/D	M/V
26	Back Street Pub	Brew Pub	$$	Yes	Yes	L/D	Major
26	McDonald's	Fast Food	$	Yes		L/D/B	
26	Pizza on the Run	Pizza	$$		B	L/D	Major
26	Subway	Sandwiches	$	Yes		B/L/D	M/V
26	Hamilton House	Steakhouse	$$$/$$	Yes	Yes	B/L/D	Major
27	**Hansel & Gretel's**	Family	$$	Yes	Yes	L/D	M/V

Dining Quick Reference-Continued

Price Range refers to the average cost of a meal per person: ($) $1-$6, ($$) $7-$11, ($$$) $12-up. Cocktails: "Yes" indicates full bar; Beer (B)/Wine (W), Service: Breakfast (B), Brunch (BR), Lunch (L), Dinner (D). Businesses in bold print will have additional information under the appropriate map locator number in the body of this section. [wi-fi] next to business name indicates free wireless internet is available to customers.

MAP No.	RESTAURANT	TYPE CUISINE	PRICE RANGE	CHILD MENU	COCKTAILS BEER WINE	MEALS SERVED	CREDIT CARDS ACCEPTED
27	Bent Street Bakery	Bakery	$	Yes		L/B	
27	Lamplighter Inn [wi-fi]	American	$$/$$$	No	Yes	L/D	Major
27	El Tapatio	Mexican	$$	No		L/D	
27	Peaks	Brew Pub	$$	No	Yes	L/D	M/V
27	Linda's Sandwich & Ice Cream Shoppe	Sandwiches	$	No		L/D	
27	Powell Drug & Espresso	Coffee Shop	$	Yes		L/B	Major
27	Time Out Lounge	American	$$	No	Yes	L/D	Major
27	Parlor News Coffeehouse [wi-fi]	Coffee House	$			B/L	
30	Lange's Kitchen	American	$$	Yes		B/L/D	V/M
30	Taco John/Blimpies	Fast Food	$	Yes		B/L/D	
30	Bighorn Restaurant	Family	$$	Yes	Yes	D/L/B	Major
31	Cowtown Café	Family	$$	Yes		B/D/L	Major
43	McDonald's	Fast Food	$	Yes		L/D/B	
43	Highwayman Café	Homestyle	$$/$	Yes		D/L/B	Major
43	Gannett Grill	Sanwiches	$	Yes		D/L	
50	Noble Roman's Pizza	Pizza	$/$$	Yes		L/D	Major

Motel Quick Reference

Price Range: ($) Under $40 ; ($$) $40-$60; ($$$) $60-$80, ($$$$) Over $80. Pets [check with the motel for specific policies] (P), Dining (D), Lounge (L), Disabled Access (DA), Full Breakfast (FB), Cont. Breakfast (CB), Indoor Pool (IP), Outdoor Pool (OP), Hot Tub (HT), Sauna (S), Refrigerator (R), Microwave (M) (Microwave and Refrigerator indicated only if in majority of rooms), Kitchenette (K). All Wyoming area codes are 307. [wi-fi] next to business name indicates free wireless internet is available to customers.

MAP No.	HOTEL	PHONE	NUMBER ROOMS	PRICE RANGE	BREAKFAST	POOL/ HOT TUB SAUNA	NON SMOKE ROOMS	OTHER AMENITIES	CREDIT CARDS
2	Best Western Sunset Motor Inn [wi-fi]	587-4265	120	$$$$/$$$		HT/OP/IP	Yes	P/D	Major
2	Cody Motor Lodge	527-6291	31	$$$$	CB		Yes	P/DA	Major
2	Econo Lodge - Moose Creek	587-2221	56	$$/$$$	CB	IP	Yes	DA	Major
2	Rainbow Park Motel	587-6251	39	$			Yes	K	Major
2	The Irma Hotel, Restaurant & Saloon	587-4221	40	$$/$$$			Yes	DA/L/D	Major
2	Buffalo Bill Village Resort	587-5556							
2	Holiday Inn Buffalo Bill Village Resort [wi-fi]	587-5555	188	$$$$		OP	Yes	L/D/DA	Major
2	Comfort Inn Buffalo Bill Village Resort [wi-fi]	587-5556	75	$$$$	CB	OP	Yes	DA	Major
2	Yellowstone Valley Inn [wi-fi]	587-3961	36	$$$			Yes	D/K/L/P/DA	Major
2	Sunrise Motor Inn [wi-fi]	587-5566	40	$$$	CB	OP	Yes	P	Major
2	Antlers Inn	587-2084	40	$$$$			Yes	DA	Major
2	Cody Guest HousesThe Victorian House B&B	587-6000	20	$$$$			Yes	P/K	Major
2	Best Value Inn	587-4258	24	$$$$/$$$	CB		Yes		Major
2	Carriage House	587-2572	25	$$			Yes		
2	Red Pole Ranch & Motel	587-5929	8	$$$			Yes	K/P	Major
2	Uptown Motel	587-4245	10	$$				P	Major
2	Green Creek Inn	587-5004	19	$$			Yes	P/R/M	Major
2	Bison Willy's Bunkhouse	587-0629	12	$			Yes	K	
3	Super 8 - Cody [wi-fi]	527-6214	64	$$			Yes	DA/P	Major
3	Days Inn [wi-fi]	527-6604	52	$$$	CB	HT/IP	Yes	DA	Major
3	AmericInn Lodge & Suites [wi-fi]	587-7716	46	$$$$	CB	OP/S/HT	Yes	DA	Major
3	Big Bear Motel	587-3117	42	$$		OP		L/P	Major
3	Elk Valley Inn & Campground	587-4149	9	$$		OP		P/L/D/K	V/M
4	Skyline Motel [wi-fi]	587-4201	46	$$$/$$/$		OP	Yes	P	Major
4	Parkway Inn [wi-fi]	587-4208	39	$$$$/$$$	CB	OP	Yes	P	Major
4	Green Gables Inn	587-6886	15	$$$	CB		Yes	DA/P	Major
4	Carter Mountain Motel	587-4295	28	$$$$			Yes	P/K/R	Major
4	Beartooth Inn of Cody [wi-fi]	527-5505	50	$$$	CB	HT/S	Yes	R/M	Major
4	Grizzly Bear Lodge	587-5960	44	$$$					Major
8	Vision Quest Motel	868-2512	14	$$			Yes	P/R/K/M	M/V
8	Oasis Motel & RV Park	868-2551	12	$$				P/R	M/V
10	Best Western Plaza Hotel [wi-fi]	864-2939	36	$$$$	CB	HT/OP	Yes	P/DA/R/M	Major
10	The Rainbow Motel	864-2129	17	$$			Yes		M/V
10	Holiday Inn of the Waters [wi-fi]	864-3131	80	$$$$		OP/HT/S	Yes	DA/L/D/P	Major

Motel Quick Reference-Continued

Price Range: ($) Under $40 ; ($$) $40-$60; ($$$) $60-$80, ($$$$) Over $80. Pets [check with the motel for specific policies] (P), Dining (D), Lounge (L), Disabled Access (DA), Full Breakfast (FB), Cont. Breakfast (CB), Indoor Pool (IP), Outdoor Pool (OP), Hot Tub (HT), Sauna (S), Refrigerator (R), Microwave (M) (Microwave and Refrigerator indicated only if in majority of rooms), Kitchenette (K). All Wyoming area codes are 307. [wi-fi] next to business name indicates free wireless internet is available to customers.

MAP No.	HOTEL	PHONE	NUMBER ROOMS	PRICE RANGE	BREAKFAST	POOL/ HOT TUB SAUNA	NON SMOKE ROOMS	OTHER AMENITIES	CREDIT CARDS
10	Budget Host Moonlighter Motel	864-2321	30	$$$		OP	Yes		Major
10	Hot Springs Motel	864-2303	11	$$				D/K	
10	Roundup Mountain Motel [wi-fi]	864-3126	12	$/$$$/$$			Yes	K/P	D/M/V
11	**Coachman Inn Motel** [wi-fi]	864-3141	19	$$		IP		P	
11	**El Rancho Motel**	864-2341	13	$$				P	Major
11	Elk Antler Inn	864-2325	12	$$				K/P	
11	Cactus Inn	864-3155	11	$$/$			Yes	K/M/R/P	D/M/V
11	Super 8 [wi-fi]	864-5515	58	$/$$		IP		P	Major
11	Elk Antler Inn	864-2325	16	$$$/$$			Yes	P	Major
15	Days Inn [wi-fi]	347-4251	42	$$$	CB		Yes	P/DA	Major
15	Town & Country	347-3249	22	$$			Yes	P/K	Major
16	Comfort Inn [wi-fi]	347-9898	50	$$$	CB	IP/HT	Yes	P/DA	Major
16	Town House Motor Inn	347-2426	23	$$		OP	Yes	P	Major
16	Super 8 [wi-fi]	347-9236	35	$$			Yes	P/DA	Major
16	Pawnee Motel	347-3206	8	$$					M/V
17	Log Cabin Motel & Campground	366-2320	8	$$				K/P	D/M/V
17	Valley Motel	366-2321	20	$$			Yes	P/K	D/M/V
20	Lilac Motel	568-3355	9				Yes	P	M/V
21	**Greybull Motel** [wi-fi]	765-2628	12	$$$		S	Yes	P/R/M	Major
21	Wheels Motel	765-2105	22	$$$		S	Yes	R	Major
21	Antler Motel [wi-fi]	765-4404	12	$$	CB		Yes	K/R/M	Major
21	Maverick Motel	765-4626	7	$$			Yes	DA	Major
21	Yellowstone Motel [wi-fi]	765-4456	34	$$		OP	Yes	DA/P/K	Major
21	Sage Motel	765-4443	17	$$		OP	Yes	DA/M/R	Major
21	K-Bar Motel	765-4426	12	$			Yes	P	Major
22	Snowshoe Lodge	272-2215	3	$$$$	FB	HT	Yes	R/M/K	Major
26	**Park Motel** [wi-fi]	754-2233	18	$$		HT	Yes	DA/D/P/K	Major
26	Super 8 Motel [wi-fi]	754-7231	35	$$			Yes	L/P/DA	Major
26	Best Western/King's Inn [wi-fi]	754-5117	49	$$$/$$		OP	Yes	DA/D/P	Major
27	Best Choice Motel	754-2243	20	$$			Yes	754-7231	Major
30	Econo Inn [wi-fi]	548-2725	34	$$	CB		Yes	P/DA	Major
30	Western Motel	548-2781	23	$$		OP/HT	Yes	P/K	M/V
30	Horseshoe Bend Motel	548-2221	22	$$	CB	OP	Yes	P/M/K/R	Major

NOTES:

SECTION 8

NORTHWESTERN WYOMING

INCLUDING JACKSON, DUBOIS, PINEDALE AND STAR VALLEY

The Teton Mountain Range is visible from many parts of this area.

1 Lodging

Smoot
Pop. 100, Elev. 6,619.

Once named Cottonwood, this settlement was renamed for Mormon Apostle Reed Smoot, who was also a Utah State Senator.

H Lander Cut-Off of the Oregon Trail
Three miles south of Smoot on U.S. Highway 89

Beginning in 1843, emigrants traveled across the continent along what became known as the Oregon Trail. Increased traffic during the 1850s resulted in the first government road construction project in the west. The 345-mile Central Division of the Pacific Wagon Road went from South Pass, Wyoming, to City of Rocks, Idaho, a geologic formation, which marked the Division's western boundary. Superintendent Frederick W. Lander of Salem, Massachusetts, supervised construction for the U.S. Department of the Interior. The 256-mile section of the road leading from South Pass to Fort Hall, Idaho, is known as the Lander Cut-off. The cut-off traversed this Salt River Valley for 21 miles and parallels Highway 89 through this area. The new route afforded water, wood, and forage for emigrants and their stock. Between 1858 and 1912, it provided travelers with a new, shorter

route to Oregon and California, saving wagon trains seven days. Lander, with a crew of 15 engineers, surveyed the route in the summer of 1857. The following summer, 115 men, many recruited from Salt Lake City's Mormon emigrants, constructed the road in less than 90 days at a cost of $67,873. The invention of the automobile led to its abandonment.

Stock Trail
Travel along the Oregon Trail was not restricted to one direction. Between 1875 and 1890, drovers herded vast numbers of cattle, horses and sheep eastward from Oregon to Wyoming. The animals were moved along the Lander Cut-off and into the Green River and Big Horn Basins and the Wind River drainage. There, they were used as initial range stock for the large ranches of cattle and sheep barons.

H Lander Cut-off
About 18 miles south of Afton on U.S. Highway 89

The Lander Cut-off left the Oregon Trail at Burnt Ranch on the Sweetwater River near South Pass City, Wy. Frederick Lander surveyed the trail in 1857. Tens of thousands of people passed over the trail during its use. With the Transcontinental Railroad being completed in 1869, emigrant travel over the trail rapidly declined. The last wagons over the trail were observed at Fort Piney Wy. between 1910 and 1912. The Lander

Cut-off rejoined the Oregon Trail in Idaho northeast of Pocatello at Ross Fork Creek.

2 Gas, Food, Lodging

Afton
Pop. 1,818, Elev. 6,134

Named ironically for the line in a Robert Burns poem, ("Flow gently, sweet Afton") this town below the Salt Range is situated by the turbulent Swift Creek. A genuine small town, it is the central business hub of Star Valley, which was settled by pioneers from the LDS (Mormon) church in 1879. The winter of 1879-1880 was brutal, but they endured the near starvation and frigid temperatures. In the center of town, the Afton Tabernacle still stands as a monument to their fortitude. The signature Elkhorn Arch nearby, which spans Main Street, is made of over 3,000 antlers. Afton celebrated its first 100 years in 2002. Though still a dominantly agricultural community, locals have embraced tourism, which has resulted from the overflow of visitors to the Jackson and the Wind River areas. Dairy farming made the valley famous for its cheese, especially hard-to-make Swiss. Afton is probably most recently associated with being the hometown of Rulon Gardner, Greco-Roman wrestling Gold Medallist in the 2000 Summer Olympics. He was not the first Afton Gardner to gain national attention as an athlete. In 1947, Vern Gardner was named an All American basketball player, and became the MVP at college basketball's National Invitational Tournament. Afton is near one of only three intermittent springs in the world, Periodic Spring, about 5 miles east of town. The spring is situated in a lush and craggy canyon, which the Shoshone considered a sacred healing place. It runs constantly during the spring runoff, but pulses about every 18 minutes in the late summer and fall.

Fairview
The beautiful view of the Crow Creek Valley gave this town its name. Settled by Mormons in 1885, this was once a stopping place for caravans of cheese freighters.

T Call Air Museum
Look for a large hangar at the south end of Afton.

Over the centuries, man has dreamed of taking to the skies. In 1937 this dream took flight for Reuel Call over the mountains of Western Wyoming. Reuel, with the assistance of his Uncle Ivan, brothers Spencer and Barlow, and Carl Peterson, designed and built the original CallAir aircraft. With no aviation background, this visionary group of civil engineers and businessmen tinkered until their plane was airborne. Come relive

Jackson	Jan	Feb	March	April	May	June	July	Aug	Sep	Oct	Nov	Dec	Annual
Average Max. Temperature (F)	27.3	32.5	40.8	52.2	62.8	72.3	81.7	80.4	71.1	58.5	39.6	28.0	53.9
Average Min. Temperature (F)	5.1	8.0	15.6	24.5	30.6	36.7	40.5	38.5	31.4	23.3	15.9	6.1	23.0
Average Total Precipitation (in.)	1.48	1.00	1.16	1.12	1.88	1.68	1.06	1.15	1.29	1.14	1.44	1.54	15.94
Average Total SnowFall (in.)	20.2	12.5	9.1	3.9	0.8	0.1	0.0	0.0	0.1	0.9	9.4	17.7	74.7
Average Snow Depth (in.)	12	14	10	1	0	0	0	0	0	0	2	7	4

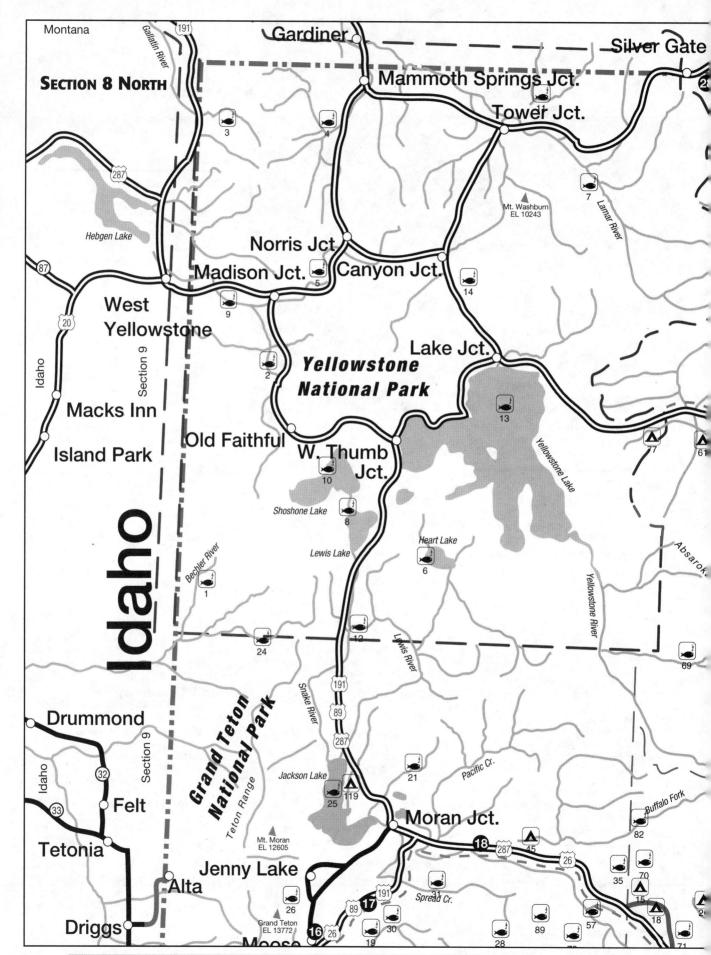

Montana

SECTION 8 NORTH

Gallatin River

191

Gardiner

Silver Gate

Mammoth Springs Jct.

Tower Jct.

3

4

7

Lamar River

287

Mt. Washburn
EL 10243

Hebgen Lake

87

Norris Jct.

Madison Jct.

Canyon Jct.

5

14

West
Yellowstone

20

9

Lake Jct.

Idaho

Section 9

2

Yellowstone
National Park

13

Yellowstone Lake

Macks Inn

Old Faithful

W. Thumb
Jct.

7

61

Island Park

10

Shoshone Lake

8

Idaho

Bechler River

Lewis Lake

Heart Lake

6

Absarok.

1

Yellowstone River

24

12

Lewis River

69

191

Snake River

89

Drummond

287

Pacific Cr.

Idaho

32

21

Jackson Lake

Buffalo Fork

33

Felt

25

119

82

Tetonia

Teton Range

Mt. Moran
EL 12605

Moran Jct.

18

45

287

26

Jenny Lake

35

70

Alta

Section 9

26

89

191

17

Spread Cr.

15

Driggs

89

26

16

Grand Teton
EL 13772

30

19

28

57

18

Moose

71

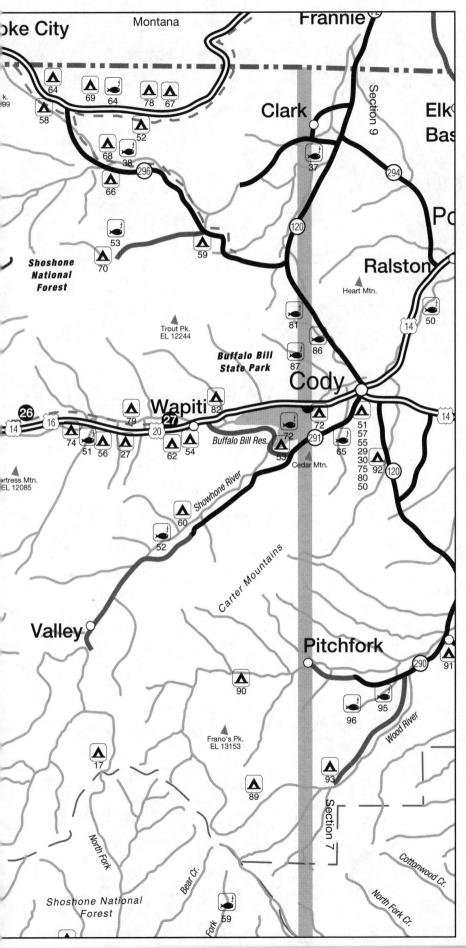

oke City

Montana

Frannie

Clark

Section 9

Elk
Bas

Po

Ralston

Heart Mtn.

Shoshone
National
Forest

Trout Pk.
EL 12244

Buffalo Bill
State Park

Cody

Wapiti

Buffalo Bill Res.

Cedar Mtn.

Showhone River

rtress Mtn.
EL 12085

Carter Mountains

Valley

Pitchfork

Wood River

Frano's Pk.
EL 13153

Section 7

North Fork

Bear Cr.

Fork

Cottonwood Cr.

North Fork Cr.

Shoshone National
Forest

Legend

00	Locator number (matches numeric listing in section)
△ 00	Campsite (number matches number in campsite chart)
🐟 00	Fishing Site (number matches number in fishing chart)
⛱	Rest stop
═══	Interstate
══	U.S. Highway
━━	Paved State or County Road
▬▬	Gravel/unpaved road

0   Miles   10   18
One inch = approximately 10 miles

Driggs

Grand Teton
EL 13772
16 26

Moose

30
19

Section 8 North
28

89

57

71

SECTION 8 SOUTH

33

31

Victor

Teton
Village

Kelly

6

15

24
25

Ventra River

Bridger\Teton
Nat'l. Forest

Fish Cr.

27

TETON

SUBLETT

15

390

Wilson

26

15

47

9 13

34

22

14

23

27

9

33

Jackson

8

Snake River

26

32

30

43

Hoback Jct.

11

7

29

20

191

12

17

13

189

Bondurant

177

158

188

179

46

Palisades Reservoir

89

26

1

3

8

6

Alpine

89

5

7

Little Greys River

160

New Fork La
199

Idaho

Section 9

Greys River

Bridger\Teton
Nat'l. Forest

Merna

45

202

187

Willow Le

206

46

34

5

Etna

23

Horse Cr.

161

191

Cora

Freedom

239

4

Bedford

6

4

S. Horse Cr.

352

354

Thayne

18

N. Fork

25

24

Daniel

155

42

237

Turnerville

3

Grover

South Fork

189

Auburn

22

153

Cottonwood Cr.

238

2

Afton

2

154

Muddy Cr.

Bo

Fairview

236

241

Smoot

1

North Piney Cr.

201

170

200

9

Middle Piney Cr.

10

Marbleton

350

35

23

22

Big Piney

167

351

89

178

162

Geneva

Bridger\Teton
Nat'l. Forest

Smiths Fork

182

174

S. Piney Cr.

Dry Piney Cr.

189

89

61

Montpelier

173

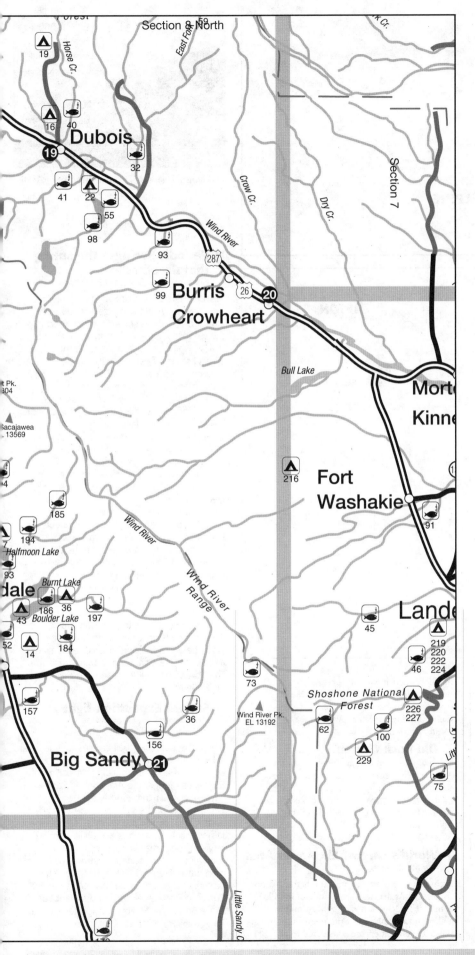

Section 8-North

Horse Cr.

East Fork

Section 7

Crow Cr.

Dry Cr.

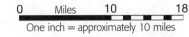

0   Miles   10   18
One inch = approximately 10 miles

△ 19
△ 16   40 ⊕
Dubois
19
⊕ 32
⊕ 41   △ 22
⊕ 55
⊕ 98
⊕ 93
Wind River
287
⊕ 99   **Burris**
26   20
Crowheart

Bull Lake

△ 216
Fort Washakie

⊕ 91
Mort
Kinne

t Pk.
304

Sacajawea
. 13569

⊕ 185
⊕ 194
Halfmoon Lake
93
Burnt Lake
△ 186   36 ⊕
dale
△ 43   Boulder Lake   ⊕ 197
52   △ 14   ⊕ 184
Wind River
Wind River Range

⊕ 73

⊕ 45
Land
△ 219
220
⊕ 222
46   224
⊡ 226
227
△ 100
△ 229

Shoshone National Forest
⊕ 62

⊕ 157
⊕ 36
⊕ 156
Big Sandy   21
Wind River Pk.
EL 13192

Little

⊕ 75

Little Sandy

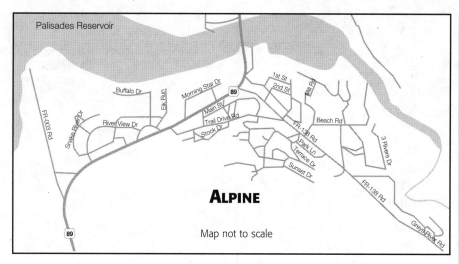

ALPINE

Map not to scale

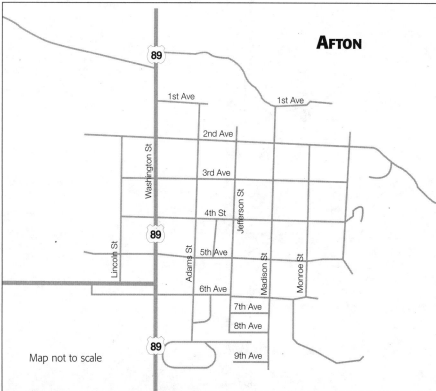

AFTON

Map not to scale

Downtown Afton is home to the world's largest elk antler arch.

PLAINS INDIAN POWWOW

Each June, the Plains Indian Powwow, sponsored by the buffalo Bill Historical Center, attracts visitors from around the world. Held at the Robbie Powwow Garden on the south end of the histroical center grounds, the event is an ideal way for non-Indians to experience and appreciate the value and history of the Indian world. Fancy dancers and traditional dancers entertain crowds to the beautifuly hypnotic drum beat and song of the Indian world.

the magic of their dream while learning the dynamics of flight. Peer into the cockpits of original CallAir aircraft and imagine yourself flying among the snow-capped peaks of Wyoming. See the CallAir snow cars (forerunners of the snow-

mobile) and visit with our personnel as they restore vintage aircraft. The CallAir Museum offers free admission and sponsors the annual CallAir Fly In/ Star Valley Aviation Days, the last Saturday of June.

T Old Rock Church

Butch Cassidy and his gang wintered in the Auburn area. Heavy snowfalls made Star Valley a safe place to "hole up". Using aliases, Butch Cassidy and his partners were occasionally seen at church socials and dances held in the Old Rock Church in Auburn. Today the rock church is used as a melodrama theater in the summer.

T World's Largest Elk Antler Arch
Downtown Afton

Arching over Main Street in Afton is the "World's Largest Elk Antler Arch" consisting of over 3,000 antlers. This 18-foot high arch was built in 1958 and continues to be a favorite photo stop. In Asia powdered elk antlers are considered to be a

prized aphrodisiac, making the antler arch worth over $300,000.

H Periodic Spring—"The Spring that Breathes"
North edge of Afton on U.S. Highway 89

What Is It? The Periodic Spring is North America's only cold water geyser and is the largest of the three known fluctuation springs in the world. Its name is descriptive of the periodic flow, which during the fall and winter, turns on and shuts off every 12-20 minutes. These periodic flows are less noticeable during high water months in spring and summer.

The water at Periodic Spring has given life to the land, the wildlife, and the people of Star Valley. Historically, Native Americans traveled great distances to cure their ills by bathing in "the spring that breathes." Since 1958, the spring's water has been piped to the City of Afton for its municipal water supply, and is used for drinking, irrigation, and generating electricity.

No one knows for certain what makes the Periodic Spring start and stop. One theory is that underground streams carry melting snow and rain water to a lake deep in the Salt River Mountains. When the lake level gets high enough, a natural siphon draws the water from the lake to the surface like a faucet being turned on and off. The water then gushes out of a sheer ledge and cascades down a wild, moss-covered ravine to join Swift Creek. The flow continues until the water level in the lake drops below the siphon's intake level, allowing air to enter the siphon from the lake cavern. The flow stops until the lake rises again and the cycle repeats.

H Sawyer Expedition fight
About two miles east of Dayton on U.S. Highway 14.

Where the Bozeman Trail crosses tongue River Valley at this point, Colonel J.A. Sawyer's wagon train and road building expedition of 82 wagons fought the Arapahoe Indians for 13 days, August 31 through September 12, 1865. Captain Cole of the military escort was killed on the ridge across the valley, E. G. Merrill and James Dilleland, drovers, were killed in the wagon circle located between here and the river. All three are buried in an unknown common grave. From 1879 to 1894 the Patrick Brothers Stage Line used this road from Fort Custer to Rock Creek Station. Brigham Post Office and Stage Station was located here at Tongue River Crossing.

H Periodic Spring
About 18 miles south of Afton on
U.S. Highway 89

Located 4 miles east of Afton in the Salt River Range, is the largest of three natural springs in the world that naturally turn off and on. Water flow is interrupted from anywhere between 3 to 30 minutes, generally between the months of August-May. It is thought that a cave behind the spring creates a siphon which causes interruption of the water flow. Its ability to turn off and on during low discharge stages has fascinated visitors since prehistoric times. Access to the spring is via the Swift Creek road and requires a 3/4 mile hike by trail.

H Star Valley
347 Jefferson Street in Afton

In the spring of 1879 a group of pioneers from Bear Lake settled here. Moses Thatcher explored the area, dedicated it as a home for the Latter-day Saints calling it Star Valley. Freedom and Auburn settled in 1879 and Afton in 1885. The first public building was located on this square. A log house with dirt roof served the settlers as a church, school, and public meeting place from 1886 to 1892 when it was replaced by a large frame building. The bell on this monument calling the people together could be heard throughout the valley.

L Lazy B Motel
219 Washington St., Hwy. 89, Afton. 885-3187.
www.thelazybmotel.com;
challenge@wyoming.com

Experience a picturesque country atmosphere, easy walking access to dining and shopping, and all the amenities you need at Lazy B Motel. Guests enjoy suite accommodations featuring queen size beds, microwaves, refrigerators, coffeemakers, air-conditioning, cable TV, and Internet access. Guest laundry, free ice, a heated pool, swings, picnic tables, and winter plug-ins add to the motel's charm, along with a horse corral, horse accommodations, and pet kennel welcoming all pets. During your stay, hike to the world's largest cold-water spring at nearby Intermittent Springs, and sample some of america's best water. Palisade Reservoir, Swift Creek Canyon, a therapeutic hot sulfur spring, horseback riding trails, golf, hiking, snowmobiling, and cross-country skiing are also conveniently located near the Lazy B. Guaranteeing 100% satisfaction, the Lazy B Motel offers weekly, monthly, and corporate rates.

L The Old Mill Log Cabins
3497 Dry Creek Rd., Afton. 886-0520.
www.oldmillcabins.com;
info@oldmillcabins.com

The Old Mill Log Cabins are nestled in the mountains of beautiful Star Valley—just a short drive from historic Jackson Hole Wyoming.

Exquisitely appointed and spacious cabins offer surroundings of peace and quiet. Your hosts, the Erickson's, have devoted many hours to making your stay memorable for years to come. From harvesting, shaping, and hand fitting the logs to tastefully decorating the interiors of each cabin. Let the sound of a crystal clear stream lull you to sleep as you snuggle under the handmade comforters on your queen size bed following a soak in the hot tub. The wide and varied outdoor activities await you in "their back yard" of wonderful Wyoming.

3 *No services*

Grover
Settled by the Mormons in 1891, this little town was named for Jacob Grover, one of the early pioneers.

Turnerville
This little town was named for a Mormon family named Turner who settled here.

Auburn
First settled by Mormons in 1879, Auburn was abandoned for a time. When the growing Star Valley population revived it a few years later, one woman said the empty buildings reminded her of Goldsmith's "Deserted Village," and the poetic name Auburn stuck. The old rock church, built in 1889, was the only stone building in the valley until 1900. Butch Cassidy and his friends would sometimes attend socials and dances here when they were hiding out at the nearby Davis Ranch.

4 *Gas, Food, Lodging*

Thayne
Pop. 341, Elev. 5,950

When the post office opened here in 1889, the town was named for postmaster and storeowner Henry Thayne. Thayne became a significant community in the valley with the opening of the cheese factory, which processed milk from the many dairy farms in the area. Thayne is also known for being the place where cutter racing first evolved in the 1920s.

H Star Valley
Star Valley Rest Area just south of Thayne

Often termed the star of all valleys, the Shoshone Indians referred to the valley as a "heap fine hunting ground." Unusually high precipitation and topographic features make the Salt River Valley one of the most productive and diverse of all wildlife areas found in Wyoming. Sandhill cranes, Canada geese, ruffed grouse and bald eagles are among the birds nesting in the area. The valleys of the Greater Yellowstone Ecosystem, including Star Valley, are important waterfowl production areas for western North America. In 1987, trumpeter swans were transplanted to the valley from Montana and since have wintered here.Protection and improvement of the streambanks and wetlands along the river for both fish and wildlife resources are important to the area and its people. The big game animals summering and wintering in the mountains and foothills surrounding the valley provide some of the best hunting in Wyoming. Trophy elk, mule deer and moose abound in the rugged mountains of the Caribou, Salt, Wyoming and Palisades ranges. Thousands of visitors are attracted to this scenic area to hunt and fish or observe and enjoy wildlife in its wild surroundings—a testimonial that Wyoming's wildlife is a precious commodity for the state and its citizenry.

Bedford
Mormon pioneer and bishop, William B. Preston named this town for his childhood home, Bedford, England. Settled in the 1880s, this part of Star Valley specialized in sheep ranching, and large herds can still be seen in the fall when they come down from summer grazing in the mountains.

H First Post Office
U.S. Highway 89 just north of the Riggs Avenue and Wright Street intersection in Thayne.

Thayne, formerly called Glencoe, was founded in 1888, at which time mail was brought into Star Valley by team and wagon and distributed to the people from a log cabin owned by Joseph Thayne. The building was one room 12x15 feet with a dirt roof. Three years later it was moved to the center of town and Henry Thayne and his wife occupied it. This log cabin, located one and one-half rods west of this site, became the first post office May 8, 1891 with Laura Thayne post mistress.

FL Wolf Den Log Cabin Motel & Drive-In Restaurant
55 County Rd. 115, 5 miles north of Thayne on Hwy. 89. 883-2226 or (866) 868-2226.
www.wolfdeninc.com; wolfden@silverstar.com

Enjoy western ambiance, amazing scenery, and comfortable accommodations in the heart of beautiful Star Valley at the locally owned and operated Wolf Den Log Cabin Motel & Drive-In Restaurant. Spacious themed cabins feature decks, log furniture, handmade quilts, satellite TV, coffeemakers, refrigerators, private baths, and hairdryers. Hungry for mouthwatering food? Check out Wolf Den Restaurant's signature burgers and a huge menu that accommodates all taste preferences and diet needs. Eat inside or enjoy your meal in one of Wolf Den's outdoor teepees. Afterwards, explore the authentic prison wagon, watch the Wolf Den's buffalo roam in the shadow of towering mountains, or discover the area's endless outdoor recreation opportunities. Whatever your interests – delicious food, delightful entertainment, area information, outdoor adventure, or premier lodging – Wolf Den has something for you!

5 *Gas, Food, Lodging*

Etna
Pop. 200, Elev. 5,815

Mormon pioneers, trying to name their community, picked this out of an insurance book because it was short, and easy to spell. The town is centered around a spacious LDS church and has a charming view of the surrounding pastureland.

Freedom
Pop. 100

This border town got its name from the freedom it gave early Mormon polygamists from having to outrun Idaho law. All they had to do was walk across the street and be in another jurisdiction. Established in 1879, this is the oldest settlement in Star Valley.

H Baker Cabin
On U.S. Highway 89 in Etna

Oldest surviving house in Star Valley is this two room dwelling built in 1889 by Anna Eliza Baker and her 12 year old daughter May. The logs are hand-hewn on four sides and dovetailed at the corners. It was the first home in this area to have a shingled roof and wood floors. The Baker family; Alonzo, Anna Eliza and their 12 children, were the first permanent residents on the east side of Salt River in the lower valley.

S Blue Fox Studio/Gallery
107452 U.S. Highway 89 in Etna. 883-3310. www.bluefoxgallery.com

Out of the ordinary! Blue Fox Studio/Gallery is fast becoming a favorite spot for returning tourists. It is a welcome experience to visit the working studios of artists Tony Ivie and Wayne Noffsinger. Both have a passion for working with clay. Tony is an experienced potter and clay mask sculptor. He was commissioned by the State of Wyoming to do the 1985 Governor Awards. Wayne started in jewelry but has become a highly collected mask artist himself. It is often possible

Wyoming Tidbits

The Federal Weather Bureau chose Big Piney for an official weather station in 1930 because it had the coldest year-round average temperature of any spot in the United States.

to see numerous art pieces in various stages of completion. The gallery showcases stoneware, wood-fired and raku pottery along with jewelry and original masks representing both Wayne and Tony's unique styles.

6 *Gas, Food, Lodging*

Alpine
Pop. 550, Elev. 5,700

This border town is half in Wyoming, half in Idaho. Named for it's lovely mountain scenery, some of the buildings also reflect the old-world alpine influence of early settlers. Robert Stuart camped here in 1812 while trying to lose a party of Indians hot on his tail.

T Palisades Reservoir

Palisades Reservoir is formed by Palisades Dam, which is a major feature on the Palisades Project. Recreation on this 25 square mile (16,100-acre) reservoir with 70 miles of limited access shoreline is administered by the Caribou-Targhee National Forest. Located in scenic southeast Idaho and west-central Wyoming, east of Idaho Falls. Palisades' fish species include cutthroat and brown trout, kokanee and mackinaw. The fishing season is year-round, but fluctuations in the reservoir level during the summer months result in inconsistent fishing. Spring, fall and winter ice fishing are most productive. Reservoir acre feet and total reservoir capacity and cubic feet/second release rates for rivers below Upper Snake River Basin reservoirs and select river locations are updated daily and graphically provided. Site offers restrooms, boat ramps, and campgrounds. Information available at Idaho Falls Interagency Visitor's Center at 208-523-3278.

T Wyoming State Bird Farm

The Wyoming Game and Fish Department, along with sportsmen and women, rallied to build a game bird farm outside of Sheridan, Woming. George R. Wells was chosen to build and manage the farm. Pheasant eggs from Oregon and Montana were the first to be hatched and released in 1937. Currently, the Sheridan Farm produces nearly 13,000 birds each year. Touring the farm is encouraged. For private tours, the bird farm may be contacted directly.

H A Changing View of Wildlife
Just south of Alpine on U.S. Highway 89 at Wildlife Watching Area pullout.

Many early beaver trappers left their moccasin tracks where you now stand. In the early part of the 19th century, from this location, the view of wildlife and wildlands was very different from what we see today. Nature's sights and sounds are still here, but not without the evidence of humans. Humans and wildlife occupy the same earth. Native Americans remind modern man that all life on earth is interconnected. Air, water, space and natural resources important to humans are also important to wildlife. We have an enormaous responsibility to protect and conserve our air, water, soil and natural resources and thereby "save a place for wildlife." An earth with diverse and abundant wildlife is also an earth healthy for the well-being of human life. The view of wildlife and wildlands has changed dramatically since the trapping era, and so has our un derstanding of the relationship of all life to planet earth…, 200th century wildlife if it is to endure, will need an understanding hand and wise use of earth's resources.

F Kringle's Birdhouse Café
161 Hwy. 89, Alpine. 654-7536. www.kringlescafe.com

The chef-owned Kringle's Birdhouse Café not only serves outstanding cuisine but also features one of the most impressive birdhouse collections you'll ever see. The owner, a master chef, has cooked for Hollywood notables such as Frank Sinatra, Liberace, Frank Capra, and many others. Chef specialties include Danish style meat loaf, salads, country fried steak, pot roast, steak, chicken, fish, pasta, unique pizzas, and more. Craving something sweet? Enjoy pastries, breakfast specialties, breads, renowned wedding cakes, and scrumptious specialty cakes from Kringle's full-service bakery. The café's friendly staff and clean, fresh atmosphere complement the wonderful food, and catering is available. Breakfast, lunch, and dinner are served daily from 7 am to 9 pm June through October. During the remainder of the year, breakfast and lunch are served daily with dinner available Thursday through Sunday.

F Los Dos amigos
46 Hwy. 89, Alpine. 654-7508. losdosamigos@silverstar.com

Serving fine Mexican and american cuisine and seafood in a beautiful atmosphere showcasing scenic area views, Los Dos amigos prepares every meal from scratch. Enjoy tamales made from the owner's family recipe, chicken and beef fajitas, chile verde, enchiladas, chile rellenos, or any other selection from the diverse menu. With advance notice, prime rib and live music are available upon request for groups or parties up to 50 people. For those in the mood for fun, the onsite lounge offers an array of drinks and features a pool table, dartboard, large screen TV, and bands on special occasions. Summer weekdays hours are 11 am – 9pm and 11 am – 10 pm on weekends. Winter hours (October – May) are 11 am – 8 pm on weekdays, 11 am – 9 pm on weekends, and closed on Sundays.

BUFFALO BARBECUE

The Dubois Volunteer Fire Department is famous for its buffalo barbecue. The fundraising event is held on the second Saturday of August in the town park.

F Buffalo Creek Western Bistro
115732 Hwy. 89, Alpine. 654-0044.

Attracting customers from miles around, Buffalo Creek Western Bistro is a standout restaurant situated inside a beautifully crafted log building. Under the ownership of Christine Goodman, Buffalo Creek showcases a diverse menu of entirely housemade cuisine. The restaurant features steaks, wild game, chicken, fish, pork, and pasta and is renowned for adding a unique touch to all of its delightful menu items. Savor seafood fettuccine, chicken parmesan, beef and buffalo rib-eye steaks, and more while enjoying unbeatable service from the amicable and professional wait staff. The restaurant's full liquor license and wine selection ensure a perfect companion to any meal, and housemade desserts add a delectable finale. The author of the exquisite cookbook, "A Taste of Jackson Hole," Christine Goodman specializes in memorable dining at the Buffalo Creek Western Bistro. Catering and private dining are available.

L 3 Rivers Motel
60 Main St., Alpine. 654-7551.

L Alpen Haus Hotel Resort
50 W. Hwy. 26, Alpine. 654-7545 or (800) 343-6755. www.alpenhaus-resort.com; alpenhaushotel@silverstar.com

Alpen Haus Resort is your year-round, one-stop source for a memorable getaway. Rooms feature satellite TV, private baths, telephones, and queen or king sized beds with many including microwaves, refrigerators, balconies, and TV/VCR combos. When you're not eating at the onsite restaurant or chatting with locals at the bar and lounge, experience beautiful Alpine with an outdoor adventure package. The resort's friendly staff happily helps guests arrange whitewater rafting, fishing, horseback riding, cross-country skiing, snowmobiling, and downhill skiing excursions. Showcasing a European Alpine design, the Alpen Haus also offers a full-service gas station and food market, video store, ice cream parlor, park, playground, and horseshoe pits. Whether you're planning a family vacation, long weekend getaway, or a business trip, trust Alpen Haus Resort to accommodate all your needs!

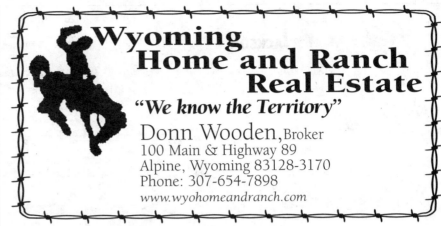

L Alpine Inn
1180 Hwy. 26, Alpine. 654-7644.
www.starvalleywy.com/alpineinn.htm

Headed to Yellowstone? Hunting or snowmobiling in the Star Valley area? The Alpine Inn is an affordable and easily accessible stopping point along the way. The charming cabins and rooms were recently remodeled to include cable TV, and some rooms offer kitchenettes. Outside, a quiet environment, breathtaking views, picnic areas, teepees for the kids, and full hookup RV spaces characterize the spacious grounds. The Alpine Inn happily accommodates horses and pets, and horseback riding trails are just moments away. Not an equestrian? The inn also provides convenient access to Palisades Reservoir, exceptional fishing, and whitewater rafting. Those wishing to explore Alpine's downtown area will enjoy the inn's close proximity to dining and shopping. An ideal location for reunions, family vacations, and outdoor adventure, the Alpine Inn is your year-round headquarters for fun.

7 Gas, Food, Lodging

Hoback Junction
John Hoback was a trapper and guide familiar with the Teton region. He led Wilson Price Hunt's party, a segment of the Astorian expedition, through the area in 1811. Hoback Junction is where the Hoback River meets the Snake River, and U.S. Highway 189/191 meets U.S. Highway 26/89. For the most part, the somewhat newly sprung community is an outgrowth of Jackson's popularity.

Bondurant
Pop.100 Elev. 6,588 Gas

Benjamin Franklin ("B.F.") Bondurant, the first settler, gave his name to the post office, which was run from his ranch. He was naturally the postmaster. His spread became one of Wyoming's first dude ranches in the early 1900s, and he and his wife, Sarah Ellen, were known for their wild pets, including elk, antelope, and bear cubs. The valley in which Bondurant is situated is rich in country beauty. The first Protestant sermon in the Rockies, delivered here by the Rev. Samuel Parker in 1835, was attended by the likes of Jim Bridger, Jedediah Smith, and Kit Carson. It was interrupted when a herd of bison passed through, and the listeners couldn't resist chasing them.

T River Runners Museum
At the Mad River Boat Trips "Wedge", about two miles south of Jackson Town Square on U.S. Highway 89.

Historic boats and rafts hang from the walls of the new River Runners Museum. Follow William H. Ashley's bull boat expedition on the Green River and John Fremont's 1842 voyage in the first inflatable raft. Artifacts and replicas thoughout the musem backpaddle visitors into another era, when river runnig was a courageous and risky means of travel.

T Granite Creek Hot Springs
East of Hoback Junction.

A large cement pool—a product of the Civilian Conservation Corps in the 1930s. Bathing suits are required. Open summer and winter. The roads are groomed in the winter for snowmobiles and cross country, but not plowed.

T Granite Falls
Enjoy great views of the Gros Ventre Mountains and the 50 foot drop of Granite Falls. A parking area and trails nearby offer a closer view via a short hike where you can enjoy Granite Creek cascading over a falls near Granite Hot Springs. It is a fairly easy drive and a nice day trip destination for the family. There is also a National Forest campground nearby. You'll enjoy the Granite Hot Springs, a secluded hot pool with wonderful mountain views.

H On the Ashes of Their Campfires
About 16 miles south of Hoback Junction on U.S. Highway 189/191.

This nearby canyon was a way through the mountains. Its game and Indian trails were followed by the white men. On September 26, 1811, the Astor party, with Wilson Price Hunt, 61 people and 118 horses entered the canyon here, making their way westward to the Pacific Ocean.The three legendary trappers, Hoback, Reznor, and Robinson, guided the party. These were the first white men to pass this way. From this time on, the stream and canyon became known as the Hoback.On October 10, 1812, Robert Stuart of the Astor Firm and his 6 com-

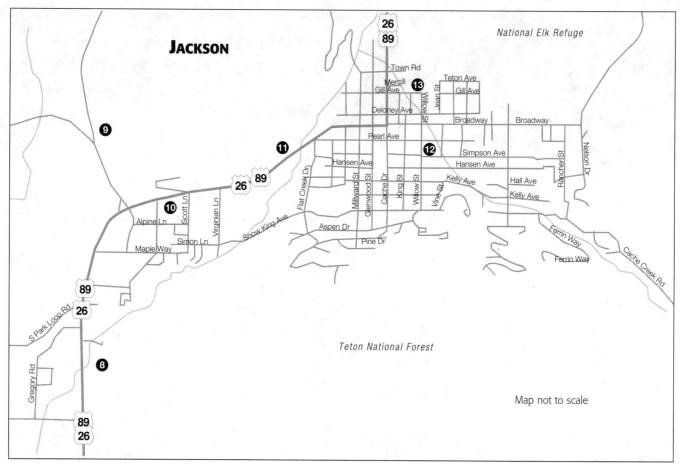

panions camped here on their way to St. Louis from Fort Astoria with the message of the failure of Fort Astoria.On Sunday, August 23, 1835, Jim Bridger's and Kit Carson's brigade of trappers and Indians, and the Reverend Samuel Parker bound northward from the rendezvous on the Green River camped in this area. This basin was known then as Jackson's Little Hole. The Reverend Parker was delivering a sermon to the motley group when buffalo appeared. The congregation left for the hunt without staying for the benediction, This was the first protestant service held in the Rocky Mountains.

H John Hoback, Guide of Astorians

Approximately one mile southeast of Hoback Junction on U.S. Highway 191/189.

John Hoback, Jacob Reznor and Edward Robinson, trappers from Kentucky, in 1811 guided the Astorian land expedition under Wilson Price Hunt across the northern part of present Wyoming to the Snake River. From this junction of the Snake and Hoback Rivers the Hunt group passed through Jackson Hole, over Teton Pass and on to Henry's Fort in Idaho. In this area, Hoback and his companions were detached from the expedition to trap beaver. The following summer the eastbound Astorians led by Robert Stuart, met them in the wilderness, starving and destitute, having been robbed by the Indians. They were given clothing and equipment and continued hunting and trapping until the winter of 1813 when they were killed by the Indians. The River here was named by Wilson Price Hunt for his guide.

8 *Gas, Food, Lodging*

Jackson
Pop. 8,647

Perhaps the most famous town of the "Old West", Jackson has had its share of both attention and visitors. Featured in many movies, from John Wayne's *Big Trail* to Clint Eastwood's *Any Which Way You Can*, Jackson and its environs have appeared on the silver screen numerous times. Many Hollywood celebrities frequent the area in their down time, as well as presidents, politicians, diplomats, and royalty from around the world. First class amenities of all kinds exist here to accommodate such a crowd. Since so much glamour is associated with this rather small town, it's amazing that it still retains so much of its old time charm. But residents call their home "The Last and Best of the Old West." It's hard to believe that less than 200 years ago, the only people here were Indians like the Blackfeet, Gros Ventres, Nez Perce, Shoshone, Crows, Bannocks, and Flatheads, and they only came in the summer.

The town was named for "Jackson's Hole" (now Jackson Hole), which is inclusive of that portion of the Snake River Valley. The upper part of the valley is the Big Hole, and the lower valley is the Little Hole. "Hole" was trapper slang for a valley basin surrounded by mountains. John Colter is believed to have been the first white man here, exploring much of northern Wyoming on his own after he parted with Lewis and Clark in 1807. Astorian trappers were not far behind, who followed the Native Americans here in the warm months for the abundant game. Trapper/entrepreneurs Jedediah Smith and William Sublette named the area for their partner, David E. Jackson, a mountain man of hardy

repute who was largely responsible for further exploration of the Snake River and Teton region.

Few others came to this rugged area until a band of outlaws discovered that it made an excellent hideout in the 1870s. William C. "Teton" Jackson, who was born Harvey Gleason in Rhode Island, adopted the names of the area where he dodged the long arm of the law. Jackson came west as part of the campaign against the Sioux in 1876, then discovered that being a horse thief was more profitable than being a pack train scout. He and his gang accumulated stolen horses from all over the western states, re-branded them, and sold them in South Dakota. They even had a plan to kidnap President Chester Arthur when he came to visit the newly designated Yellowstone National Park in 1883, but the president came with a sizeable military contingent to prevent any trouble.

That same year, permanent settlers arrived. Johnny Carnes and John Holland came to the valley to build homesteads for their families. In 1889, the Wilson family, led by Mormon Bishop Sylvester Wilson, crossed over Teton Pass from Idaho, in essence creating the first road there. Carnes and Holland, who hosted the new settlers until they could build their own homesteads, greeted them. Carnes and Holland continued to be the official welcome committee for other new families coming to settle in the valley throughout their lives. Bishop Wilson's brother, Elijah "Uncle Nick" Wilson, was once a Pony Express Rider, the youngest of the lot. He was said to have run of with the Shoshones for an adventure when he was young.

In 1873, another famous "Jackson", William H. Jackson, came to the area with the Hayden Geological Survey Expedition, and was the first to photograph both the Tetons and Yellowstone. His pictures helped to persuade Congress to set aside the Yellowstone area as a National Park.

When Jackson became an official town with a post office in 1897, it was named Marysvale, for postmistress Mary White. The name changed when the town became incorporated in 1901. By 1909, the town boasted three sawmills, a newspaper, two general stores, a hotel and restaurant, a blacksmith shop, a school, two churches, and a saloon.

Around this same time period, photographer and conservationist Stephen Leek was drawing national attention to the plight of the elk in the area. Over-hunted for their "tusks" (ivory teeth), and starving due to unusually harsh winters in the early part of the century, the government was called upon to aid the majestic animals. Both state and national agencies came together to create the National Elk Refuge in 1912. The four elk antler arches which surround the Town Square in downtown Jackson remind visitors of the remarkable creatures, known to Native Americans as "wapiti."

In 1920, Jackson again received national attention when it was the first town in the nation to elect an all-female city council and mayor. Shortly after their election, they appointed several other women to positions such as marshal, town clerk, and town health officer. In addition to other significant town reforms, this group of city officials was responsible for building the wooden sidewalks, which are still a trademark of Jackson's streets.

It has only been over the past thirty years or so that Jackson has become a hot spot for tourists. But the community has a long history of hospitality, from the trapper days to the homestead days, and current residents hold this tradition sacred. Although it is surrounded by many scenic wonders, Jackson is most popular for the friendliness of the people who live here.

9 *No services*

T **Antelope Flats**
13 miles east of Jackson.

Near the majestic backdrop of the Teton Mountains, Antelope Flats was settled in 1893 by Kansas pioneers who abandoned the area in 1912 after discovering the climate was too cold to grow crops.

T **Astoria Mineral Hot Springs**
On U.S. Highway 26/89, 17 miles south of Jackson.

An outdoor swimming pool and separate kiddie pool celebrate the natural mineral water flows. Bathing suits required. Open mid-May to Labor Day.

T **Huckleberry Hot Springs**
North of Jackson

Primitive hot springs on the north bank of Polecat Creek, Grand Teton National Park. Open all year. rock-and-mud soaking pools throughout have an average water temp of 100 degrees. Clothing is optional.

Wyoming Tidbits

Which is both the oldest and the largest national park in the country? Yellowstone National Park, with more than two million acres, was declared by President U.S. Grant on March 1, 1872, to be our country's first park.

The elk antler arch at the entrance to Jackson Park in the heart of downtown Jackson.

10 *Gas, Food, Lodging*

S **Jackson Hole Buffalo Co.**
1325 S. Hwy. 89, Jackson. 733-4159 or (800) 543-6328. www.jhbuffalomeat.com or www.elkmeat.com; info@jhbuffalomeat.com

Established in 1947, the original Jackson Hole Buffalo Company prides itself on a 58-year business tradition of excellence. The company is renowned for its 100% naturally raised and processed american elk and buffalo meat, receiving rave reviews in Gourmet Magazine, Esquire, Smart Money, and on the Food Channel Network. Select from a variety of flavorful products, including steaks, roasts, burgers, prime rib, sausage, bratwursts, and salami. Gift packs feature a range of prices and products, and all perishable items are guaranteed to arrive in excellent condition with two-day FedEx delivery. When you're in the market for fine meat products, make a lean, healthy, and heart-smart choice with the Jackson Hole Buffalo Company. Visit the local Wyoming store, call in your order, or shop online to discover why customers across america keep coming back for more!

LF **The Virginian Lodge & Restaurant**
750 W. Broadway, Jackson. 733-2792 or (800) 262-4999. www.virginianlode.com or info@virginianlodge.com

The Virginian Lodge is a Taste of the Old West conveniently located near Jackson's Town Square. Let this be your headquarters with 170 deluxe rooms with cable TV, wireless, phones, and suites available with Jacuzzi tubs and kitchenettes. They also offer a convention center and a 105 space full service R.V. Resort with large pull-through spaces. There is a restaurant, saloon and liquor store. The popular Virginian Saloon is decorated with rustic Western memorabilia, fireplace, with live music, pool tables, big screen TV, and a game room. Book an Old Faithful Snowmobile Tour for a day of adventure. To add to your enjoyment and convenience they offer a heated swimming pool (summer only), hot tub, and Laundry facilities. The knowledgeable staff will help with all of your activities and lodging needs helping to make your stay a pleasant one.

11 *Gas, Food, Lodging*

12 Gas, Food, Lodging

T Jackson Hole Museum
Corner of N. Glenwood & Deloney in Jackson

The Jackson Hole Museum can be found under the covered wagon at North Glenwood and Deloney, just one block west of the Square. It is open daily from late May through early October. The museum captures the essence of history in the Jackson Hole and surrounding area. Ten thousand years of prehistory, Native American stone tools, weaponry, and clothing are displayed. You will also see artifacts and exhibits that show the lives of the Mountain Man and the Fur Trade Era, along with that of early settlers. Enjoy seeing exhibits of clothing, tools, guns, and old-time photographs. A collection of Boone & Crockett record game heads from the Jackson Hole area are also on display. Books, old-time wooden toys, Old West memorabilia, and Native American jewelry are available in the Museum Shop for you to purchase. Visit their web site to learn more.

F Cadillac Grille and Billy's Giant Hamburgers
55 N. Cache, Jackson. 733-3279.
www.cadillac-grille.com; wy_restaurant@yahoo.com

Established over twenty years ago, the Cadillac Grille offers extraordinary dining, the freshest ingredients, an excellent wine selection, top-shelf liquors, and a friendly and courteous staff. Whether guests arrive "camp casual" or "evening on the town elegant," a menu of scrumptious food and unbeatable service awaits. Next door, Billy's Giant Hamburgers grills up famous half-pound burgers from scratch and serves them with a pile of fixings in a fifties-style diner. Craving a louder ambience? The family-friendly Cadillac Lounge connects Cadillac Grille and Billy's Giant Hamburgers and allows patrons to enjoy their favorite libation while chowing down on both restaurants' fare. When your plans call for a romantic dinner, a lively night on the town, a large group function, or anything in between, make Cadillac Grille your destination! Open daily at 11:30 am.

S Wild Hands Art for Living
265 W. Pearl St., Jackson. 733-4619.
www.wildhands.com; wildhands@wyom.net

Wild Hands Art for Living is a colorful gallery featuring handmade home furnishings, fine art, and gifts. Whimsical clocks, ornate mirrors, pottery, fancy wine glasses, picture frames, hand-blown glass vases, jewelry, and utensils are just some of the many great items available. Founded in 1998 by Sue Thomas, Wild Hands has grown continually over the past six years. A recent move has provided more space to display the fine art, furniture, and handcrafted items people have grown to love. Although the gallery showcases talented craftspeople from across the U.S., many of the artists possess local or regional roots. See what Jackson Hole has come to adore, and discover the difference of handcrafted quality in a delightful setting at Wild Hands Art for Living.

13 Gas, Food, Lodging

T Jackson Hole Historical Society
Log cabin on the corner of North Glenwood & Mercill in Jackson. 733-9605.
www.jacksonholehistory.org

The Jackson Hole Historical Society is a research facility dedicated to the collections and study of local and regional history. Its mission is history education. Open year-round. The public will find historical exhibits, archival and biographical files, maps, oral histories, videos, a library, and a 7,000-item photograph collection available for reprinting. The Society offers history excursions, school programs, genealogies, oral histories, and various exhibits throughout the year. All areas are available for public viewing and research. Call for more information or visit the web site for current schedules and exhibits.

T National Museum of Wildlife Art
2 Miles North of Jackson on U.S. Highway 26/89, across from the National Elk Refuge. 733-5771. www.wildlifeart.org.

Just inside the doors of this museum's main gallery, a bronze mountain lion crouches, as if ready to pounce. This is just the first of many artworks. For the kids, the museum hosts a hands-

on children's gallery. Adult visitors will enjoy the artwork displayed throughout twelve galleries, as well as a theater, 200 seat auditorium, gift shop, and Rising Sun Cafe.

The collection features the works of Carl Rungious, George Catlin, Albert Bierstadt, Karl Bodmer, Alfred Jacob Miller, N.C. Wyeth, Conrad Schwiering, John Clymer, Charles Russell, Robert Bateman, and numerous others. Especially interesting are the reconstructed studio of John Clymer and the Carl Rungius Gallery, where the most complete collection of his paintings in the nation resides.

Another notable exhibit is a feature on the American bison, documenting the once-abundant animals and the slaughter that took place. Six of the galleries host changing displays of photography, painting, and artwork. For those who want to see live animals, spotting scopes are located in the lobby and the members' lounge (open to public) to watch the inhabitants of the nearby National Elk Refuge.

A 45-minute museum tour is given daily at 11 a.m., or by request for groups. The museum is open from 8 a.m. to 5 p.m. during the summer. During the winter, hours are 9 a.m. to 5 p.m. Monday through Saturday, and 1 to 5 p.m. on Sundays.

T National Elk Refuge
Northeast of Jackson at 532 North Cache Street. 733-9212

In late October and early November thousands of elk begin their traditional migration from high summer range in Grand Teton National Park, southern Yellowstone National Park, and the neighboring national forests to lower elevation winter range in Jackson Hole. Heavy snows force the animals to lower elevations in search of food, and usually more than 7,500 elk make their way to the National Elk Refuge to spend the winter.

Establishment of the National Elk Refuge

Hundreds of years before the settlement of this country, elk ranged from the eastern states through central and western North America. They grazed the open prairies, mountain valleys, and foothills. As settlers pushed slowly westward, the distribution of the elk was rapidly reduced to the western mountains. By 1900, elk had disappeared from more than 90 percent of their original range.

When settlers arrived in Jackson Hole in the late 1800s, there may have been as many as 25,000 elk in the entire valley. The town of Jackson was built in a large portion of elk winter range.

Establishment of farms and ranches further forced elk from their traditional wintering areas. Livestock competed for winter food, and hungry elk raided haystacks. These severe conflicts between humans and elk diminished the Jackson elk population.

In the early 1900s, severe winters with deep, crusted snow also took a serious toll on the wintering elk. The refuge was created in 1912 as a result of public interest in the survival of the Jackson elk herd. Today the refuge continues to preserve much of the remaining elk winter range in the valley, approximately one-quarter of the original Jackson Hole winter range. Elk stay on the refuge for approximately six months each winter. An eight-foot high fence along the main highway and along the northern border of town prevents elk from moving through Jackson and onto private lands.

The nearly 25,000-acre National Elk Refuge is administered by the U.S. Fish & Wildlife Service and is one of more than 500 refuges in the National Wildlife Refuge System. This system was established to preserve a national network of lands and waters for the conservation and management of the fish, wildlife, and plants of the United States for the benefit of present and future generations.

History

The Jackson Elk Herd, estimated at approximately 14,000 animals, probably owes its prosperity to local citizens who were here about 1906-1912.

Following the removal of most of the beaver by trappers prior to 1840, the Jackson Hole country was virtually uninhabited by settlers until 1884. Only hunting/gathering native Americans (mostly Shoshone, Bannock, and Arapahoe) summered here until about the end of the Civil War (1865). Sixty-four people lived in Jackson Hole when the Wyoming Territory became a state in 1890. Nearby Yellowstone had become the world's first national park 1972. By the late 1890s and early 1900s, conversion of historic elk winter range to domestic livestock use began to pose a hardship situation for the elk.

However, even before the Jackson hole environment was changed somewhat by the arrival of settlers, significant numbers of elk died from starvation in winter. Early hunters and settlers noted that winters of unusually heavy snow resulted in death by starvation for thousands of elk. Survival of large numbers of elk was complicated further by the severe winters of 1909, 1910, and 1911 that put the herd in serious trouble. In order to survive, the elk raided ranchers' haystacks, but many still starved to death. Although the ranchers did not want to see the elk die, they could not afford to lose their hay and remain in the ranching business.

The first official suggestion for a permanent elk refuge in Jackson Hole was made in 1906 by the Wyoming State Game Warden, D.C. Nowlin, who, following his retirement from that post, became the first manager of the National Elk Refuge. Area residents gained statewide sympathy for the continuing elk losses, and appeals for assistance spread through many other states. As a result, in 1911 the Wyoming Legislature asked Congress to cooperate with the State in appropriations for "feeding, protecting, and otherwise preserving the big game which winters in great numbers within the confines of the State of Wyoming." Less than a month later, Congress appropriated $20,000 for feeding, protecting, and transplanting elk and ordered an investigation of the elk situation in Wyoming.

After this assessment by the Federal Government, $45,000 was appropriated by an act of Congress on August 10, 1912, for the purchase of lands and maintenance of a refuge for wintering elk.

By 1916, from a combination of public domain lands and private lands, 2,760 acres had been acquired for the National Elk Refuge. For more than ten years no additions were made to the refuge itself. In 1918 the U.S. Forest Service lands adjacent to the east side of the refuge were classified as big game winter range, and although they were not made part of the refuge, livestock grazing was restricted.

In 1927 Congress accepted title to 1,760 acres of private ranch lands that had been acquired and donated by the Izaak Walton League of America, expanding the refuge to 4,520 acres.

Congress, in a 1935 act that became known as the "Six Million Dollar Fund," designated

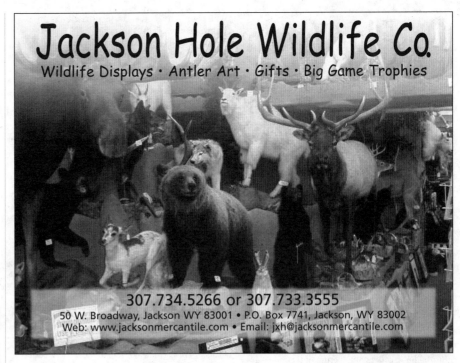

money for purchase of wildlife lands throughout the United States. From this, about 16,400 additional acres of private lands were acquired for the National Elk Refuge. Also, 3,783 acres of public domain lands were added by Presidential Executive orders in 1935 and 1936.

Today the refuge consists of nearly 25,000 acres devoted to elk winter range. This represents the last remaining elk winter range in Jackson Hole.

That portion of the Jackson Elk Herd that winters on the National Elk Refuge averages approximately 7,500 animals yearly. Elk are on the refuge for about six months each year from November to May, freeranging for about 3.5 months and using supplemental feed for about 2.5 months, usually from late January until April.

Supplemental feeding began in 1910 when the Wyoming Legislature appropriated $5,000 to purchase all available hay in the valley to feed the elk. The supply of hay was inadequate and hundreds of elk died that winter. This was followed in 1911 with feed for elk from the $20,000 appropriated by Congress. Supplemental feed has been provided for the elk in all but nine winters since then. In 1975 a change was made from baled hay to pelletized alfalfa hay.

A Presidential "Commission on the Conservation of the Elk of Jackson Hole, Wyoming," was established and active from 1927 through 1935. Its membership, which included the Governor of Wyoming, developed the following tenet: The Jackson Elk Herd in the State of Wyoming is a national resource combining economic, aesthetic, and recreation values in which the State of Wyoming, the Federal Government, private citizens, and civic and sportsmen's organizations are actively and intensely interested.

In 1958 currently active Jackson Hole Cooperative Elk Studies Group was formed, composed of the Wyoming Game & Fish Dept., the U.S. Fish & wildlife Service, the U.S. Forest Service, and the National Park Service. The principal purpose of this group is to coordinate plans, programs, and findings of studies, and to provide an exchange of ideas, information, and personnel

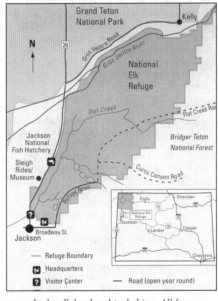

to study the elk herd and its habitat. All four agencies have legal responsibilities for management of the elk herd and its habitat. A better understanding and appreciation of individual agency objectives and responsibilities and closer cooperation have been attained since the establishment of the study group.

The refuge is dedicated primarily to the perpetuation of the nation's majestic elk, for us and future generations to enjoy.

Refuge Management

Refuge grasslands are managed to produce as much natural forage for elk as possible through extensive irrigation, seeding, prescribed burning, and other practices. These management practices enhance elk winter habitat and reduce the need for supplemental feeding. However, when deep or crusted snow prevents the elk from grazing, or the natural forage is depleted, refuge personnel feed the herds pelletized alfalfa. These 2- to 3-

inch pellets have higher nutritional value than average baled hay and are easier for refuge staff to store and distribute to the elk. Elk are usually fed about 7 to 8 pounds per animal per day, which equals about 30 tons per day for a herd of 7,500 elk. The elk receive supplemental alfalfa for approximately 2.5 months during an average winter.

The number of elk wintering on the refuge must be limited to avoid overuse of the range and to reduce the potential spread of diseases common when herd animals are crowded. Refuge staff, in consultation with the Wyoming Game & Fish Department, have determined that a maximum of 7,500 (more than half the total Jackson elk herd) elk is optimum for the refuge. Herd numbers are maintained through a late fall controlled hunt on the refuge and adjacent public lands.

Elk Facts

Elk are the second largest antlered animals in the world; only moose are larger. Bull elk are 4.5 to 5 feet tall at the shoulder and weigh 550 to 800 pounds. Cow elk weigh from 450 to 600 pounds. The refuge elk herd consists of approximately 20% bulls, 65% cows, and 15% calves.

The majority of adult elk on the refuge are between 3 and 10 years old. The oldest animals in the herd are 15-30 years old, but these individuals represent a very small part of the refuge population. The age on an elk can be determined by examining milk tooth replacement, wear on permanent teeth, and annual dental rings.

While most members of the deer family are primarily browsers (feeding on twigs and leaves of shrubs and trees), elk are both browsers and grazers, feeding extensively on grasses and forbs, as well as shrubs.

Grizzly bears, black bears, mountain lions, wolves, and coyotes prey on elk. By weeding out the weak, predators help maintain healthy, vigorous elk herds.

More Elk Facts

Adult bull elk have large, branched antlers. Contrary to popular belief, there is no exact relationship between age and number of antler points, but the number of points may be used to estimate an animal's age. Bulls between 1 and 2 years old have short, unbranched antlers called spikes. By age 3, bulls usually have antlers with three to four points on each side. Older bulls carry antlers with five, six, or sometimes seven points on each side. Mature bulls with six points per side are called royal bulls, and those with seven points are called imperial bulls. On rare occasions you might see a bull displaying antlers

with eight points on each side; these bulls are known as monarchs.

Large bulls shed their antlers during March and April every year, while the smaller bulls lose their antlers during April or early May. Mice, squirrels, and other animals chew on the shed antlers to get needed minerals. Antlers dropped on the refuge are collected by local Boy Scouts, who sell them at an annual public auction (the 3rd Saturday in May) to help raise money for both the scouts and for winter elk feed management. The public may not collect or remove antlers from the refuge.

New antlers begin to grow as soon as the old ones are shed. They develop through the summer and reach maturity by mid-August. By this time, the antler's "velvet," or outer blood-rich skin has dried, and the bull rubs the dead velvet off on small trees and shrubs. A bull's antlers are hard and shiny by the fall breeding season (the "rut").

Elk leave the lower elevations in April and May, following the receding snowline back into the cool, high country, where they spend the summer. These animals travel distances varying from a few miles up to 100 miles during migration from the refuge to Grand Teton National Park, southern Yellowstone National Park, and national forest lands to the north and northeast of Jackson Hole. A few elk remain near the wooded areas of the refuge during the summer months.

From late May to mid-June, cows bear their young in secluded thickets on higher terrain. A cow typically has one calf that weighs 30 to 40 pounds. The calves are reddish colored and spotted at birth. Very few calves are born on the refuge, since the majority of elk migrate back to the high country before calving occurs.

The breeding season (or "rut") occurs in September and early October, while the elk are in the high country. At this time, the high-pitched "bugling" of the mature bulls can be heard as they gather harems of cows and challenge rival bulls. During the rut, bulls vigorously defend their harems of half a dozen to 15 or more cows.

In late fall, snow begins to fall in the high country, and the elk herds migrate back to their lower elevation winter range.

Wildlife and Their Habitat

Refuge habitat includes grassy meadows and marshes spread across the valley floor, timbered areas bordering the Gros Ventre (GroVONT) River, and sagebrush and rock outcroppings along the foothills. This habitat diversity provides a variety of food, water, and shelter that support the rich mixture of wildlife species found at the refuge.

While elk are the primary reason the refuge was established, 47 species of mammals are found here year-around or during seasonal migration to and from surrounding areas. Moose, bighorn sheep, bison, and mule deer are common winter residents on the refuge. Wolves, coyotes, badgers, and Uinta ground squirrels are also seen. Other common wildlife species include muskrat, beaver, porcupine, long-tailed weasel, and voles or meadow mice.

Visitor Opportunities

The National Elk Refuge lies northeast of the town of Jackson, Wyoming, and directly south of Grand Teton National Park. The winter season, between November and April, is the best time to view elk and other wildlife on the refuge. To protect refuge wildlife and their habitats, public use activities are primarily confined to the main, unpaved roads on the refuge. Paved turnouts on

the west side of the refuge along U.S. Highway 26 (leading to Grand Teton and Yellowstone national parks) are provided for viewing and photographing refuge wildlife.

From mid-December through late March, daily horse-drawn sleigh rides (or wagons, if weather conditions require them) offer visitors a close-up look at the elk herd. Sleigh rides begin at the National Museum of Wildlife Art, two-and-a-half miles north of Jackson on U.S. Highway 26, 89, 191. Visitors to the museum can also learn about elk and management of the refuge through a slide show, videos, exhibits, and by talking with refuge personnel. Sleigh riders are encouraged to bundle up, since they are likely to be exposed to very cold temperatures and chilling winds.

Limited hiking opportunities exist on the refuge, and there is no overnight parking or camping. Camping is available in nearby national parks and national forests.
Source: U.S. Fish & Wildlife Service

V Jackson Hole Whitewater/Teton Expeditions & Scenic Floats

650 W. Broadway, Jackson. 733-1007 or (800) 700-RAFT (7236). www.jhww.com

Jackson Hole Whitewater/Teton Expeditions & Scenic Floats, established in 1963, is committed to quality and customer satisfaction on their scenic float trips and Snake River expeditions. Voted the region's number one rafting company in a local newspaper survey, the company offers several trips to accommodate all distance preferences and experience levels with the magnificent Teton Range as a backdrop. The professional guides treat you to an experience of a lifetime, great food, outstanding wildlife viewing, and photo opportunities. Arrive early to sit on their deck, relax with a soda or coffee, enjoy good company, and take advantage of their free wireless Internet connection. The staff can answer all your questions about the river, flora, fauna, rock formations, and the surrounding area. Give them a call to reserve your trip or visit them on the web.

Wyoming Tidbits

During World War II, the U.S. carefully patrolled the Wind Rivers area outside Dubois with bombers, fearing the Germans might poison the waters. This area, confluence of the Mississippi, Columbia and Colorado Rivers, is home to two thirds of the headwaters for our country. One of the patrol bombers crashed.

S Jolly Jumbuck Leathers
20 W. Broadway, Jackson. 733-6562.
www.jollyjumbuckleathers.com

Serving Jackson Hole customers for over thirty years, Annette and Chuck Seligman of Jolly Jumbuck Leathers offer the West's largest leather specialty store. Showcasing a broad selection of men's and women's leathers, shearling, and furs, the store strives to keep each item fun, interesting, and wearable for every occasion. The knowledgeable staff craves personal contact, so online orders are not allowed. Customer service is what they do best, and they look forward to discussing their products' fit, styling, colors, and performance with every customer – whether you're visiting in person or calling long-distance. Oftentimes, they can even suggest a customization to make your coat or vest more special. With an ever-changing inventory and a staff that looks forward to satisfying new customers, Jolly Jumbuck Leathers is your source for something unique, special, and your very own.

V Barker-Ewing River Trips
45 W. Broadway, Jackson. 733-1000 or
(800) 448-4202. www.barker-ewing.com;
info@barker-ewing.com

Setting a standard of excellence since 1963, Barker-Ewing River Trips has served over one million clients. Every guide is a seasoned river veteran, and customer safety and satisfaction is their highest priority. Whether you opt for "wet and wild" or "dry and mild," each guide's knowledge of the natural and early human history of Jackson Hole and the Rocky Mountain West adds a meaningful dimension to every river adventure. Sit back, relax, and enjoy breathtaking scenery as your guide takes you on a scenic float. Looking for adventure? Join in the action with a whitewater excursion on the legendary Snake River. Trips of varying lengths, breakfast floats, and overnight trips accommodate a variety of interests and skill levels. For a reputation you can trust and the trip of a lifetime, discover Barker-Ewing River Trips!

FL Anvil Motel, El Rancho Motel & Nani's Genuine Pasta House
215 N. Cache St., Jackson. 733-3668 or
(800) 234-4507. www.anvilmotel.com and
www.nanis.com; anvilmotel@wyoming.com and
nani@wyoming.com

The Anvil Motel is just one boardwalk block from Jackson's Town Square near shopping, dining, and Jackson's famous watering holes. Start Bus pickup is available across from the office providing easy access around town and to ski and recreational areas. All rooms are air-conditioned with microwaves, refrigerators, irons, ironing boards, hair dryers, and clock radios. The onsite hot tub provides pure relaxation. Offering the same great location, El Rancho Motel provides rooms with many of the same amenities as the Anvil Motel. You're a stranger here but once, and both have been a cowboys' favorite for affordable, quality lodging since 1947. Nearby, Nani's Genuine Pasta House offers European style Italian dining in an intimate casual atmosphere. All items are handmade daily to rave customer reviews. Visit them all on the web.

14

Wilson
Named for a family of Mormon pioneers who came to settle in the Jackson area, this little town is now primarily a preparation point for trekkers headed into the Tetons.

Teton Village
Teton Village is a ski and summer resort community open year round. The town consists of chalets, assorted lodging accommodations, restaurants, and shops.

H Elijah Nicholas "Uncle Nick" Wilson April 8, 1843-Dec. 27, 1915
Wilson next to Post Office.

In 1889, Uncle Nick led the first Mormon settlers over Teton Pass into Jackson Hole. It took 14 days to travel from Victor, Idaho, to Wilson, Wyoming, the town that bears his name. As a child, Uncle Nick lived with Chief Washakie's band of Shoshone Indians. He later was a Pony Express rider, a scout for General Albert S. Johnston, and an Overland Stage driver. In Wilson, Uncle Nick was the first Presiding Elder for the Mormon Church and had the first hotel, general store, and post office. This monument is dedicated summer, 1989, on the 100th anniversary of the pioneer crossing of Teton Pass.

15 Gas, Food, Lodging

16

Kelly
This town was initially named Grovont, an Anglicized spelling for the nearby Gros Ventre River. Another post office had already used the name, however, so they had to change it in 1909. The new name honored Bill Kelly, local sawmill owner and rancher.

A landslide shook the little ranching community in 1925, when the end of Sheep Mountain crumbled in just three minutes and dammed the Gros Ventre River, creating Slide Lake. Some 50 million tons of rock, soil, and other debris, including some ancient trees, made up the dam. Some thought it would hold indefinitely, but in 1927, the dam gave way. Kelly residents had only a few minutes to get to higher ground and watch the fifteen foot wall of water sweep their town away, leaving only the church and the schoolhouse behind. Six people lost their lives in the flood.

C.E. Dibble, a forest ranger, became a hero that day, when he recognized a hayrack that had been floating on the lake coming downstream. He raced in his Model T ahead of the river, cutting fences to free livestock and warning the town of the coming disaster.

Moose
Named for the animals that frequent the area, the world's largest ungulates, Moose is the headquarters for Grand Teton National Park.

T Grand Teton National Park Colter Bay Indian Arts Museum
At Colter Bay National Park Office.

This museum houses the David T. Vernon collection of Indian pieces, the most impressive in the park, and one of the finest anywhere in Wyoming. Included in the exhibition are beautifully beaded buckskin dresses, moccasins, masks, kachina dolls, ceremonial pipes, shields, bows, warbonnets, a blanket that belonged to Chief Sitting Bull, and numerous other decorated items. Craft demonstrations are given daily through the summer months.

From mid-May to Memorial day, and Labor Day through mid-October, the museum is open from 8 a.m. to 5 p.m. daily. Early June to Labor Day, hours are 8 a.m. to 8 p.m. daily. The museum is closed for the rest of the year. Admission is free.

T Murie Museum/Teton Science School
Just south of Moran Junction in Kelly.
733-4765. www.teton-science.org.

Part of the Teton Science School, the Murie Natural History Museum displays thousands of specimens, including birds, mammals, and plants. Of particular interest are the casts of animal tracks used by Olaus Murie, famed wildlife biologist, in production of his Peterson's Guide to Animal Tracks. While this museum is open to the public, it is recommended that you call ahead to arrange an appointment.

T Grand Teton National Park Colter Bay Indian Arts Museum
In Moose at the Forest Service Visitors Center. 739-3594.

This museum houses the David T. Vernon collection of Indian pieces, the most impressive in the park, and one of the finest anywhere in Wyoming. Included in the exhibition are beautifully beaded buckskin dresses, moccasins, masks, kachina dolls, ceremonial pipes, shields, bows, warbonnets, a blanket that belonged to Chief Sitting Bull, and numerous other decorated items. Craft demonstrations are given daily through the summer months.From mid-May to Memorial day, and Labor Day through mid-October, the museum is open from 8 a.m. to 5 p.m. daily. Early June to Labor Day, hours are 8 a.m. to 8 p.m. daily. The museum is closed for the rest of the year. Admission is free.

T Jenny Lake
Situated by the lake of the same name, Jenny was the Shoshone wife of Dick Leigh, a trapper and guide for the Hayden Geological Survey Expedition of 1871. The town has become an amenity village for travelers. The Jenny Lake Ranger Station is a required stopover for climbers, who must register before entering either Teton or Yellowstone Parks.

T Kelly Warm Springs
Drive north on U.S. 189/191 from Jackson, turn on Gros Ventre Road, through the town of Kelly.

Located within the Grand Tetons National Park, this serene pond is open all year. Clothing is optional. This is the only place in the world where the tiny fish, Kendall dace are found. To protect these fish that only grow to two inches in length, no wading is allowed in the waters of Kendall Warm Springs.

T The Gros Ventre Slide
7 miles north of Jackson on U.S. Highway 89; turn right and travel 11 miles on the Gros Ventre Road.

On June 23, 1925, one of the largest fast-moving landslides in generations occurred near the village of Kelly, Wyoming. In just three minutes, huge amounts of rock and debris cascaded down the north slope of Sheep Mountain, changing the area forever.

Hurling down the slope at 50 m.p.h., the mile-wide slide carried 50,000,000 cubic yards of debris. The mass rode 300 feet up the opposite slope, blocked the Gros Ventre River, and formed a five-mile long body of water known today as Lower Slide Lake. The piles of debris seen today contain large chunks of Tensleep Sandstone, along with remnants of the original forest.

Throughout the years, many people have wondered what caused this tremendous slide. Three primary factors are thought to have contributed to the unusual event:

(1) heavy rains and rapidly melting snow saturated the Tensleep Sandstone, causing the Amsden Shale rock layer on Sheep Mountain to become exceptionally slippery;

(2) the river, cutting through the sandstone, produced a "free side" with no extra support holding it in course;

(3) swampy pools with no outlets, on top of the mountain, indicating water-saturated soil.

Earthquake tremors (which were occurring) added to these already unstable factors and could have precipitated a landslide.

William Bierer, a long-time native to the area, predicted a slide in the near future. Convinced of the validity of his theory, Bill sold his ranch on Sheep Mountain to Guil Huff, an unsuspecting cattle rancher, in 1920. Bierer died in 1923 before his prophecy became reality.

Two years later, on the afternoon of June 23, 1925, Guil rode horseback down the river to the north side of Sheep Mountain where he had heard loud rumblings. He arrived at 4 p.m., in time to witness 50 million cubic yards of land mass descending rapidly toward him. He and his horse escaped the impact by a mere 20 feet. Along with Guil, two other men witnessed the phenomenon of nature — Forney Cole and Boyd Charter.

In a matter of minutes, debris covered 17 choice acres of the Huff ranch. Guil, along with his wife and daughter, escaped. Ranger Dibble took Mrs. Huff and the child to safety at the Horsetail Ranger Station. By 4 a.m. the next morning, the Huff house was standing in 18 inches of water. By June 29, after heavy rains caused the dam to fill and overflow, the Huff house was floating in the lake, to be joined by the ranger station on July 3.

Ranger Dibble moved his family to Kelly, Wyoming, where he kept a wary eye on the slide dam. A man-made dam has a built-in spillway so that the waters cannot top the dam, erode, and breech it. The slide dam, made by nature, was not equipped with a spillway.

Engineers, geologists, and scientists came to the area to study the slide; they determined that the dam formed as a result of the slide was permanent and safe. Most of the local people accepted that decision and ceased worrying about a possible disaster, especially when the spring runoff in 1926 passed with no major problems.

The winter of 1927, however, was one of the most severe ever recorded in the state to that time. When spring arrived, the unusually deep snowpack melted quickly, aided by days of rain. On May 17, water began spilling over the low places of the dam. The Gros Ventre River was rising.

Ranger Dibble and Jack Ellis, along with some other men, were poling driftwood and floating debris away from lodging against the Kelly bridge and endangering the structure. Suddenly Ranger Dibble saw a hayrack—one that had been in the lake above the dam since 1925—floating down the river.

He and Ellis jumped into Dibble's Model T and drove toward the dam to assess the situation. On the way, they were met by the main thrust of water and debris. The top 60 feet of the dam had given way under the pressure of the excess water.

Dibble and Ellis turned around and headed for Kelly to warn the residents of the impending danger. By the time they arrived, the people had only 15 minutes in which to flee to safety.

Despite the warning, Henry ("Milt") Kneedy refused to believe the water was coming, and would not permit his wife and foster son, Joe, to leave. Ranger Dibble tried to rescue little Joe, but he got away and ran back to his mother. Later, Joe was reportedly seen clinging to the top of a barn floating down the river. The Kneedy family died in the flood.

Through field glasses, a rancher watched May Lovejoy and her sister, Maude Smith, load their wagon with valuables and drive off, but the horse became frightened and raced out of control toward the oncoming water. A wall of water rolled the wagon over and over. May's body was never found. Maude's body was retrieved after the water subsided.

Max Edick and Clint Stevens were trying to save their livestock when the water came. Quickly, they climbed to the top of a small chicken coop. Though Clint managed to jump onto a passing hayrack, he did not survive. Max was swept into the swift water. He somehow managed to catch hold of a tree branch, and was later found alive.

By 4p.m. the water receded. Six lives had been lost in the tragedy. Along with the human lives lost, hundreds of domestic animals perished. Property damage was estimated at $500,000. The little town of Kelly was almost completely obliterated.

As a result of the flood, Kelly was not awarded the special recognition of becoming the county seat. That distinction was given, instead, to Jackson.

Lower Slide Lake
This lake was formed when the landslide dammed up the Gros Ventre River. Many of the trees that once grew along the river were submerged, and today the tops of several of these trees can be seen at the far side of the lake.

Lake trout, Snake River cutthroat, mountain white fish, Utah suckers, and Utah chubs inhabit the lake.

Upper Slide Lake, formed long before man roamed this area, has no connection with the Gros Ventre Slide disaster.

Trees On The Slide
Several of the trees at the base of the slide are growing at abnormal angles. These trees were swept downhill with their roots still intact in the soil. They came to rest in the position in which you see them today.

It is interesting that trees over 40 years of age succumbed to the shock of that traumatic transplanting, while the younger trees were able to adapt and continue growing.

In the crystal clear water of the lake, some trees can still be seen standing erect where they were transported by the slide more than half a century ago.

Moose													
	Jan	Feb	March	April	May	June	July	Aug	Sep	Oct	Nov	Dec	Annual
Average Max. Temperature (F)	25.8	31.0	39.1	49.1	61.0	70.6	80.0	79.0	69.0	55.8	38.1	26.1	52.1
Average Min. Temperature (F)	0.9	3.3	11.9	22.1	30.8	37.2	41.2	39.5	32.1	23.0	13.6	1.3	21.4
Average Total Precipitation (in.)	2.58	1.99	1.58	1.47	1.95	1.77	1.19	1.32	1.46	1.26	2.13	2.48	21.19
Average Total SnowFall (in.)	43.4	29.9	20.4	9.2	2.8	0.1	0.0	0.0	0.5	4.4	25.4	39.7	175.7
Average Snow Depth (in.)	27	34	32	13	0	0	0	0	0	0	4	16	11

Trees found in the Gros Ventre area are lodgepole pine, Englemann spruce, subalpine fir, Douglas fir, Rocky Mountain juniper, and aspen.

Life On The Rocks

Pikas, the smallest members of the rabbit family, also known as coneys, range from approximately 6 to 8 inches in length. They are grayish brown in color. These small herbivores do not hibernate; instead, they store little piles of dried plants under the snow for use in winter. Pikas make their homes under the rocks that were transplanted in the slide. They can be heard "bleating" as they travel along their trails under the rocks.

Lichens are plants composed of two different organisms: microscopic green or blue-green algae and colorless fungal threads. Lichens grow on the surface of rocks. Their colors vary from black to gray, rust, green, and brown. These small plants are important because they break rocks down into small pockets of soil on which other plants will grow.

Article courtesy of National Forest Service

H The Gros Ventre Slide
About five miles east of Kelly on paved road that parallels river.

Before you lie the remnants of one of the largest earth movements in the world. On June 23, 1925, earth, rock and debris moved rapidly from an altitude of 9000 feet, across the valley bottom and up the slope of the red bluffs behind you. The action lasted only minutes but a river was dammed and the landscape changed.

H Jackson Lake Dam
Grand Teton National Park at Jackson Lake Dam.

Main sign:
Jackson Lake Dam, a vital link in the development of the water and land resources of the Upper Snake River Basin, was built and is operated by the Bureau of Reclamation, U. S. Dept. of the Interior. It was originally authorized for irrigation—some 1,100,000 acres of the fertile Snake River Valley—and for flood control along the Snake and lower Columbia Rivers. Outdoor recreation and fish and wildlife conservation have become important project benefits.

History sign:
The Reclamation Service first surveyed Jackson Lake in 1902-03, leading to construction in

1905-07 of a temporary pole-crib dam to store 200,000 acre-feet of water. It rotted and failed in July of 1910, and in 1911 a new concrete structure was begun to restore the vital water supply for the farmers on the Minidoka Project. An unending string of freight wagons hauled cement from the railhead at Ashton, Idaho, over 90 miles away, often through deep snow and at temperatures down to 50 below zero. The 70-foot high structure, completed in 1916, raised the maximum lake elevation 17 feet, and increased the storage capacity to 847,000 acre-feet.

17 No services

H Cunningham Cabin
Just south of Moran Junction on U.S. Highway 26/89/191

With a sod roof and a covered walkway called a dogtrot connecting these two log cabins, this historic residence dates back to 1890. It was originally built by Pierce Cunningham when he and his wife Margaret came into the valley to raise cattle.

18 Gas, Food, Lodging

T Tie Hack Memorial
18 miles northwest of Dubois on U.S. Highway 26/287.

Dubois has long been connected with the timber industry. Beginning in 1914, the Wyoming Tie and Timber Company ran tie-cutting operations near Dubois, supplying ties to support the CB&Q railroad. With the combined efforts of the Wyoming Recreation Commission, the Wyoming Highway Department and the US Forest Service, a memorial dedicated to the hardy tie hacks was built.
Source: Dubois Chamber of Commerce brochure

H Tie Hack Monument
18 miles northwest of Dubois on U.S. Highway 26/287.

Erected to perpetuation of the memory of the hardy woods and river men who made and delivered the cross ties for building and maintenance of the Chicago and North Western Railway in this western country.

H The Hack Boss
On U.S. Highway 287/89 between Moran Junction and Dubois

Tie cutting on the Wind River started in 1914. Martin Olson became foreman of all woods operations in 1916. Ricker Van Metre, of Chicago, formed the Wyoming Tie and Timber Company in 1926 and hired Martin Olson as Woods Boss.

Martin, a Norwegian, was a veteran tie hack of Wyoming's pine forest. He started with a crew of 20 men who turned out 100,000 ties his first year as foreman. The crew grew each year, reinforced by young, woodswise immigrants from Norway, Sweden and other European countries, until 100 hacks were in the woods.

Martin Olson was held in respect. He had a way of getting the best from any man. He was boss, also a leader. He worked with, cajoled, humored, mothered or drove any hack that got out of line. Martin's ability as Woods Boss was measured by the number of ties out and delivered to the railhead at Riverton, Wyoming.

After supervising tie hacks and the drives for 31 years, Olson retired in 1947, when the Wyoming Tie and Timber Company was sold to the J. N. (Bud) Fisher Tie and Timber Company. The change of ownership brought new ideas and methods to the timber industry, marking the end of the tie hack era.

Lydia Olson, widow of Martin Olson, furnished the photographs and many of the historical facts presented here at the Tie Hack Memorial.

H The Cross-Tie
On U.S. Highway 287/26 between Moran Junction and Dubois

The tall, slightly tapered lodgepole pine is ideal for a cross-tie. The tie hack chose his tree and felled it with a double-bitted ax. Using the same tool, he walked the log from end to end cutting a series of parallel slashes on each side of the log. The slightest miscalculation could mean the loss of a toe or foot. Retracing his steps, he hewed the two side faces smooth with the broad ax. The faces were exactly 7 inches apart and so smooth that not even a splinter could be found with the bare hand.

The tie hack then traded his ax for a peeler and removed the bark from the two rounded sides. The final operation was to cut the peeled and hacked log into the 8 foot sections required by the railroad.

Each tie hack owned and cared for his own equipment which cost him his first 10 days of work.

Cross-ties were in demand by the Chicago and Northwestern Railroad as it spanned Wyoming. The Wyoming Tie and Timber Company was formed in 1916 in Riverton to supply the ties—it took 2,500 ties for a mile of track.

The main center of tie production was the lodgepole pine forest that surrounds you. Three to five ties, eight feet in length, were hewn from the clear, limb-free trunks.

Wyoming was undeveloped country with few roads. Water was the most economical method of moving the ties from forest to the railhead at Riverton.

H Togwotee Pass
U.S. Highway 287/26 between Moran Junction and Dubois

Captain William Jones, Army Corps of Engineers, named Togwotee Pass in 1873 in honor of his Shoshone Indian guide. Togwotee (pronounced toe-go-tee) was a Sheepeater Indian who aligned himself with Chief Washakie. Jones' mission was to find passage to Yellowstone National Park from the Wind River-Bighorn watersheds.

H Breccia Cliffs
U.S. Highway 287/26 between Moran Junction and Dubois

Breccia Cliffs—a remnant of volcanic activity 50 million years ago. Composed of angular fragments of lava cemented together after being torn from a volcanic crater during a massive explosion.

Scoured by glacial ice eons ago, its present physical form is being sculptured by wind and water.

H Union Pass
On U.S. Highway 267/26 between Moran Junction and Dubois

Jim Bridger knew this pass as the "Triple Divide" — a point forming headwaters of three different continental drainage basins. One stream eventually feeds into the Green River, which in turn drains into the Colorado, and finally the Pacific Ocean in Southern California. Another feeds the Snake River, adding to the Columbia which heads for the Northwestern Pacific. The third stream drains into the Wind River, which feeds the Missouri, then the Mississippi, and ends up in the Gulf of Mexico.

Captain William F. Reynolds, of the Army Corps of Engineers, named the pass for the Union Army. He thought it was the center of the continent. Reynolds was on an 1860 mission for the War Department to find an immigration route from Fort Laramie to the source of the Yellowstone River.

H Washaki Wilderness
On U.S. Highway. 287/26 between Moran Junction and Dubois

These high mountains are snowclad most of the year and only a brief cool summer. Few areas in the USA are more spectacular. Geologically, the formations are new. The large areas of exposed rock are interspersed with mountain meadows and mantles of unbroken forests.

Wyoming Tidbits

Rodeo may be the sport for which Wyoming is famous, but in the 1880s the most popular sport in the state was rollerskating.

H Tie Hack Interpretive Display
About 17 miles northwest of Dubois on U.S. Highway 26/287

Lower Level

Plaque #1:
Rough, tough, sinewy men, mostly of Scandinavian origin, whose physical strength was nearly a religion. The millions of cross ties they hacked out of the pine forests kept the railroad running through the West.

The tie hack was a professional, hewing ties to the exact 7 inches on a side demanded by the tie inspector. For years he was paid 10 cents a tie up to $3.00 for his dawn to dusk day. Board and room cost about 1.50 a day.

Mostly bachelors, they lived in scattered cabins or tie camps and ate hearty meals at a common boarding house. Entertainment was simple and spontaneous. A few notes on a "squeeze box' ' might start an evening of dancing, with hob nailed boots scarring the rough wooden floors. The spring tie drive down the Wind River usually ended with one big party in town with enough boozing and brawling to last them another year back in the woods.

These hard-working, hard-drinking, hard-fighting men created an image that remains today only in tie hack legend. By the end of World War II, modern tools and methods brought an end to an era that produced the proud breed of mighty men—the tie hack.

Plaque #2
The Cross-Tie
Here are the tools of his trade:

Double-Bit Ax—with two sharp edges

Broad Ax—an 8 pounder with a broad 12-inch long blade, looks like an executioner's ax!

Peeler—a slightly curved dull blade to slip easily under the bark

Crosscut Saw—designed to cut across the grain of the wood

Peavey—a stout spiked lever used to roll logs

Cant Hook—a toothed lever used to drag or turn logs

Pickaroon—a pike pole with a sharp steel point on one side and a curved hook on the other—used to guide floating logs

They also carried a sharpening file and a jug of kerosene to clean pitch off their equipment.

Plaque #3
Cross-ties were in demand by the Chicago and Northwestern Railroad as it spanned Wyoming. The Wyoming Tie and Timber Company was formed in 1916 in Riverton to supply the ties—it took 2,500 ties for a mile of track.

The main center of tie production was the lodgepole pine forest that surrounds you. Three to five ties, eight feet in length, were hewn from the clear, limb-free trunks.

Wyoming was undeveloped country with few roads. Water was the most economical method of moving the ties from forest to the railhead at Riverton.

Middle Level

Section #1
Flumes
A cut, shaped and peeled tie weighs 120 pounds. Each tie hack was responsible for

shouldering his own ties and carrying them to a decking area located by one of the narrow roads through the forest.

The hacks marked one end of the tie with his own symbol—a letter or number, and was paid by the number of ties marked with his symbol.

When winter snows arrived, horse drawn bobsleds moved the ties to a banking area next to a dammed up pond. A bobsled loaded with 120 ties weighed 7 tons and was pulled by two horses.

When the spring thaws came, tie hacks dumped their ties into the ponds on smaller creeks and fed them into flumes for the journey to the Wind River.

Flumes are great V-shaped wooden troughs built to float ties down to the main river—bypassing the rock-choked mountain streams.

Dams were built on the streams to impound enough water to carry the ties down the flumes. When the spring floods came in May or June, tie hacks fed the ties into the flumes for their downward journey.

A section of the Canyon Creek flume was constructed with a 41 degree grade, and one year they tried to slide the ties down it without water. This dry fluming attempt failed when the friction of the ties shooting down the trough set fire to the flume.

This portion of the Warm Springs Flume was trestled and guyed with steel cables to sheer rock walls. Ties traveling this flume emptied into the Warm Springs Dam. Notice the catwalk used by drivers to prod the ties on their way down the flume.

Part of the famous Warm Springs flume follows the creek underground through a water curved arch. The flume is suspended inside the arch by steel cables anchored in the roof. The last tie to float this flume was in 1942.

The smaller flume on the left brought the ties from the forest, the flume on the right transported ties to the Wind River.

Section #2
Booms
Barricades across the stream held the ties together in what is called a log boom. When the danger of spring floods had passed, the trap was sprung and the tie drive was on.

Section #3
The Tie Drive
It took an experienced Woods Boss to choose exactly the right time to start the drive. Too early, and the spring floods scattered the ties on the banks. Too late, and there wasn't enough water.

Martin Olson usually picked mid-July to put his half a hundred men on the river with peaveys and pike poles to steer a half million ties 100 miles down stream to Riverton.

A tie-drive looked like a river full of giant shoestring potatoes tumbling and rolling along with ant-like men running over the sea of ties, loosening a tie here or unjamming a pile-up there.

The drivers, half in and half out of the water, punched holes in their hobnailed boots to let the water out as fast as it ran in.

A drive lasted about 30 days, with the largest one having 700,000 ties. In the 31 year history of the Wind River drives, over 10 million ties floated to Riverton. The final drive in 1946 contained only machine sawn ties. The colorful tie hack and his river drives were history

Massive jams occasionally filled the river from bank to bank with tangled piles of ties. A good tie driver could find the 'key' tie to "spring" the jam.

Section #4
The Tie Hack Boss

The peak year was 1927 when 700,000 ties were driven down the Wind River to Riverton. The Wyoming T and T Company harvested 10 million railroad cross-ties under Olson's supervision and in cooperation with the Forest Service's timber management plan.

After supervising tie hacks and tie drives for 31 years, Martin Olson retired in 1947, when the Wyoming Tie and Timber Company was sold to the J. N. (Bud) Fisher Tie and Timber Company. The change of ownership brought new ideas and methods to the timber industry, marking the end of the tie-hack era.

H Union Pass Interpretive Plaques

About 8 miles west of Dubois, Wyoming, on U.S. Highway 287/26 and 15 miles south on Union Pass Road.

Union Pass

At this pass-midst a maze of mountain ranges and water courses which had sometimes baffled and repulsed them-aboriginal hunters, mountain men, fur traders and far-ranging explorers have, each in his time, found the key to a geographic conundrum. For them that conundrum had been a far more perplexing problem than such an ordinary task as negotiating the crossing, however torturous, of an unexplored pass occurring along the uncomplicated divide of an unconnected mountain chain.

Hereabouts the Continental Divide is a tricky, triple phenomenon wherein the unguided seeker of a crossing might find the right approach and still arrive at the wrong ending. In North America there are seven river systems that can be cited as truly continental in scope but only in this vicinity and at one other place do as many as three of them head against a common divide. Indians called this region the Land of Many Rivers and mountain men named the pass Union, thereby both—once again-proving themselves gifted practitioners of nomenclature.

Union Pass is surrounded by an extensive, rolling, mountain-top terrain wherein elevations vary between nine and ten thousand feet and interspersed water courses deceptively twist and turn as if undetermined betwixt an Atlantic or a Pacific destination. This mountain expanse might be visualized as a rounded hub in the center of which, like an axle's spindle, fits the pass. Out from this hub radiate three spokes, each one climbing and broadening into mighty mountain ranges-southeasterly the Wind Rivers, southwesterly the Gros Ventres and northerly, extending far into Montana, the Absarokas.

The Rendezvous

Twelve thousand foot mountain plateaus dominating this view of Green River and Snake River headwaters seemingly provide a southwesterly buttress for loftier peaks forming the core of the Wind River Range. Beyond them it is 43 miles from Union Pass to where confluence of the Green and its Horse Creek tributary marks the most famed of several "rendezvous" grounds relating to that epoch in American history known as the Rocky Mountain Fur Trade.

"Rendezvous", defined as a trade fair in wilderness surroundings, was held in diverse locations throughout the Central Rocky Mountain region. It required spacious, grassy environs for grazing thousands of horses, raising hundreds of trapper and Indian lodges and for horse races and other spectacles exuberantly staged by mountain men and Indians then relaxed from vigilance against dangers which otherwise permitted no unguarded carrousels. A favorite area for "rendezvous" was along the Green, recognized for producing the primest beaver peltry, and for conveniently straddling the South Pass logistic route utilized for transport of trade goods and furs between St. Louis and the mountains. On the Green the finest "rendezvous" grounds—rendered especially famous through Alfred Jacob Miller's paintings of the 1837 scene—were those at Horse Creek.

Depending on arrival of St. Louis supply caravans, 'rendezvous' usually extended through early July. At the close of revels—leaving many mountain men deeply in debt—there remained up to two months before prime furs signaled the start of fall hunting. The intervening time was pleasantly occupied in traveling and exploring high mountain terrain; then trails around Union Pass were furrowed by Indian travois only to be leveled again by the beating hoofs of the trapper's pack trains.

Cultural Heritage

High in mountains where the natural environment changes swiftly, eroding or burying its past, for how long a time can vestiges of man's frailer achievements withstand obliteration? No matter!, for here man has brought or developed cultures which are already heritages— treasured in memory if lost in substance.

Presented is a natural scene, a park surrounded by forest and parted by a virgin stream. But it is crossed by a road and also by a zigzag fence of rotting logs. Reconnaissance might reveal a campsite of prehistoric aborigines or discover a beaver trap once the property of a mountain man. Thus, is a cultural environment incorporated with the natural one.

Indians hunted these environs far into historic time. From exits of Union Pass, tribal trails branch in all directions. The road mentioned above, elsewhere explained, might cover ruts made by travois, Camps of mountain tribes, their chipping grounds, drivelines and animal traps exist throughout the area. Earliest among far western fur traders came this way—possibly Colter in 1807, certainly Astorians under Hunt in 1811. Mountain men camped here, Jim Bridger surely during the 1820s and, much later, guiding Captain Raynolds in 1860. Others, whose camping grounds may some day he ascertained, include: Bonneville, soldier, explorer, fur trader, enigma-recording carefully in 1833; Gannett, of the 1870's Geologic Survey with Yount his hunter-packer; Togwotee, a Shoshone Sheep Eater; Wister, famous author; Bliss, horse thief; Anderson, precursory forester; and, not far distant, Sheridan, a general and Arthur, a President of the United States.

The zigzag fence of rotting logs is a vestige of a continuing culture. Pastoral in nature it relates to the 1920 decade when cattlemen, under U.S. Forest Service permit, fenced rich grasslands to hold beef herds, fattening for the market.

Fauna of Union Pass

Before primitive man discovered this pass between rich hunting grounds native ungulates grazed here during summers, migrating to the river valleys and plains for winters. These high plateaus and mountain meadows then harboured thousands of bison.

Though bison are gone, hundreds of elk (wapiti), mule deer and pronghorn antelope summer on Union Pass and in the near vicinity. Bighorn sheep live the year-round on high peaks and plateaus, venturing occasionally to timbered slopes and mountain meadows, Black hear are much in evidence and Lord Grizzly- "Old Ephraim" to mountain men and, in Indian lore, sometimes "Our Brother"-still occasionally roams the nearby forests and crags. Only the Shiras moose had not yet arrived in the days of mountain men, having only migrated this far south since about 1870.

Around 1900 the canine teeth of bull elk were worth their weight in gold. Northwestern Wyoming, isolated midst an abundance of game, was a favorite base of operations for notorious tusk hunters until early day game wardens, forest rangers and private citizens combined to drive the outlaws out.

Except for loss of bison and gain of moose, native fauna is much the same as it was in the days of fur trade. Beaver and trout still inhabit streams. Occasionally an otter may be seen cavorting along stream banks and mink are common to such environs. Pine Martin their peltry prized next to Siberian Sable and much sought by a later generation of mountain men, porcupines and red squirrels inhabit coniferous forests. Marmots and ground squirrels are found in rocky ledges and grassy meadows along with many lesser four-footed denizens. At Union Pass the prehistoric hunter or the most recent recreationist might have seen:

"A golden eagle in the sky and 'Ole Coyote' on the sly."
and thought:
"All snowshoe hares and the little blue grouse had better peel an eye."

Resources—Ownership—Exploitation— Administration

Aesthetic and economic resources surround Union Pass, extending far to the west, north and southwest. These include grass, browse and forest plus animals living thereby and therein. Ownership of lands and vegetation repose in the nation's people; Wyoming's citizens own the wild animals; livestock, seasonally pastured, are privately owned.

Separate laws enacted in 1869 by Wyoming's first Territorial Assembly pertained to branding livestock and protecting wildlife. An incipient but immediately popularized livestock industry received credit for the first. But sponsors of the second, even following its augmentation in 1870 by a rudimentary wildlife agency, went, in that era of materialism, unnoticed. Few territorial fields of endeavor possessed sufficient background for practitioners to appreciate benefits stemming from conservation. Only the fur trade—flourishing in 1826, impoverished by 1840—had produced a second generation cognizant of dangers inherent in ruthless exploitation. Throughout such environs as Union Pass its diminished members trapped and hunted, sometimes outfitting (guide service, pack trains, supplies) clients attracted to the Territory by both its mountain wildernesses and continuing bonanza in open range livestock operations. From such relationships emerged types of outfitting and mountain valley ranching operations predisposed to conservation practices.

Spearheading a long overdue national conservation movement, Theodore Roosevelt found among such ranchers and outfitters men who played leading roles in organizing the first national forests out of the unwieldy Yellowstone Timberland Reserve and in developing an administrative structure adopted by the subsequent U.S. Forest Service.

Searching for complementary talents the Forest Service and the Wyoming Game and Fish Commission have both recruited personnel experienced in ranching and outfitting as well as the graduates of professional schools. Subject—as are all human efforts—to occasional errors, the administrators of Union Pass surroundings have successfully protected and enhanced its natural environment.

Flora At Union Pass

Union Pass the cultural site must first have been Union Pass the natural site. As a natural site it commenced to produce vegetation and was afterwards inhabited by animals before it ever became attractive to man—for any purpose other than the thrill of exploration.

Development of present flora at Union Pass is an evolvement of recent time. The connection between conspicuous boulders and glaciers lately covering the area is mentioned elsewhere, but lichens still thriving grew on those boulders before all local ice had melted. Other flora, needing more favorable conditions, probably didn't attain a flourishing status until following the altithermal period causing cessation of glaciers—about 7,000 years ago.

The forest's development into a climax, a spruce-fir culmination, has been slowed by wildfires. But forest cover is now expanding through man's protective measures plus continuing evolution of soils as in the filling of ponds and marshes from sedimentation and organic matter.

Fortunately, Union Pass is in a park, not in the forest. From its view the foreground is covered on the drier, higher area by sagebrush, bunchgrasses and forbs favoring semi-arid conditions; low grounds support grassland communities, patches of willows and sedge meadows bordering ponds. Common plants are big sage brush, shrubby cinquefoil, Idaho fescue, slender wheat grass, Indian paintbrush and lupine along the streams grow willows, sedges, rushes, little red elephant, march marigold and globe mallow.

Southeast—toward the Wind River Range—Engleman Spruce-subalpine fir growth is in wetter areas and whitebark pine along hilltops and ridges. To the west—forward—is a younger growth of Engleman Spruce and lodgepole pine fringing expanding forests while within older lodgepole stands are in various stages of transition to the spruce-fir climax. Understory plants are grouse whortle berry, lupine, sedges and grasses.

The Ramshorn

Jutting like the topsail of a ship from beyond the apparent horizon, a tip of the Ramshorn is seen. It serves to remind the viewer of the Absarokas, a cragged mountain range broader and longer than the Wind Rivers but slightly less elevated. These mountains take their name from Indians identified as Crows or Ravens in the Journals of Lewis and Clark. Fur traders adopting that appellation passed it along to subsequent generations excepting only Absarokas themselves who, echoing forefathers, Anglicize

---

THE INTERNATIONAL PEDIGREE STAGE STOP DOG SLED RACE

This is the largest dog sled race in the lower 48 states. A $100,000 purse attracts world class mushers to this 8 day event is usually held around the end of January. The race begins and ends in Jackson. The race travels from Jackson, through Dubois, Lander, Evanston, Bridger Valley, Kemmer, Alpine, Pinedale and back to Teton Village. www.wyomingstagestop.org

---

their name to Bird People.

Tip rather than peak is used advisedly; there are peaks in the Absarokas but they are not a dominant feature of that range. Originating in a typical anticlinal fold, the Absarokas have been capped by lava strata measuring to thousands of feet, a geological evolvement known as a volcanic pile. Accordingly, their summits tend to be flat although simultaneous erosion throughout periods of flowing lava prohibited the forming of an all-encompassing tableland. Continued erosion has resulted in a range marked by deep canyons, precipitous ridges, notched passes and escarpment delimited plateaus. Summits rising above a plateau's general elevation are composed of harder materials and sometimes indicate proximity of a former lava fissure. The Ramshorn is one such plateau but its name derives from its escarpment-3,000 feet of cliffs and talus slopes, curving for miles around its southwestern flank like the horn of a mountain ram.

It is appropriate that this mountain be named Ramshorn. The Absarokas offer habitat to a variety and an abundance of wildlife but escarpments and plateaus, producing grass and browse swept free of snow by winter gales, make ideal mountain sheep ranges. Trails established by sheep-eating Shoshones, now followed by other wilderness enthusiasts, attest to mankind's fascination with the wild sheep of the Absarokas.

Road Through A Pass

A road, component of a cultural environment, is the most noticeable feature of this otherwise natural landscape. In present form it is not old, not a pioneer route hacked by frontiersmen. Based and graded to support rapid haulage of ponderous loads of logs, this road was built by specialists operating specialized machines. It is a product of 20th century technological culture.

A road of a sort is an ancient and, originally, a natural feature at Union Pass. Wild animals, some camels, indigenous horses, mammoths now extinct, found this passageway and, following easiest grades during seasonal migrations, trod out—wide in places as a road—a trail, Perhaps 10,000 years ago progenitors of Nimrod trailed these animals around the edges of a receding glacier and on through Union Pass—leaving along that route its first traces of human culture. Around 1700 A.D. Shoshones, descendants or replacements of the earliest hunters, acquired the horse and, among other impacts made by them on the natural environment, the dragging ends of their travois poles widened and deepened this road.

Chronological stages in the Union Pass cultural environment have been: aboriginal, for

---

trade, explorations and geological surveys, outfitting (recreational industry) and ranching, and management of natural resources—including forestry. Forestry, defined as "cultivating, maintaining, and developing forests", implying harvesting, came last owing to local patterns of development. Although Wyoming was a bellwether in Theodore Roosevelt's early conservation movement, pressing local concern regarding new national forests centered on livestock grazing and wildlife and watershed protection—forestry waited. Substantial timber harvesting, a tie hack era, only began after 1900; upgrading a Union Pass wagon road to high speed hauling standards was a mid-century project.

Wind River Range

Postulating the traverse of the Continental Divide the eye climbs to Union Peak, some four airline miles but nearer six by that tortuous route. At 11,491 feet Union Peak is a nondescript rise that draws attention only because it is the final timberline topping elevation on the northwestern end of the Wind River Range. Appearing slightly behind and more to the right, but actually seven miles further along the traverse of the divide, is Three Waters Mountain. That is as far into the Wind Rivers as can be seen from Union Pass. However, if vision could continue to follow the southeasterly bearing of the divide, the viewer might estimate 20 and 30 miles to where nearer 13,804 foot Gannett Peak and farther 13,745 foot Fremont Peak mark the scope of the heart of that range.

The Wind River Range is the highest mountain mass in Wyoming. Basically it is a broad uplift which originated about 60 million years ago during a period of "mountain building" called the Laramide Orogeny. The core of the range reveals Precambrian crystalline rocks, and Paleozoic and Mesozoic sedimentary rocks are upturned on the flanks. The Wind River Range, although south of continental ice caps, was extensively glaciated during the Pleistocene epoch and such sizable lakes as Newfork, Boulder, Fremont, Bull, Green River and Dinwoody, filling canyons and valleys along its widespread flanks, are dammed behind moraines. Existent glaciers in the highest parts of the Wind Rivers are small by comparison, yet they are often cited as the largest ice fields within the contiguous states of the Union.

Boulders strewing Union Pass environs are surface evidence that this northern margin of the range was subdued, by spreading glaciers which have left a blanket of till and moraine material.

Three Waters Mountain

Southeast rises a mountain given a lyrical name, one such as Indians or mountain men discovering a geographical phenomenon might have chosen. Midway of its four-mile long crest is the key point, one of only two in North America, where as many as three of the continents seven major watersheds interlock.

Here a raindrop splits into thirds, the three tiny driblets destined to wend their separate ways along continuously diverging channels to the oceans of the world. One driblet arrives in the Gulf of Mexico, 3,000 miles distant by way of Jakeys Fork, Wind River, Bighorn, Yellowstone, Missouri, and Mississippi; another joins currents running 1,400 miles to the Pacific through Fish Creek, the Gros Ventre, Snake and Columbia; the final one descends more than 1,300 miles to the Gulf of California; via Roaring Fork, Green

River and the Colorado.

Seemingly neither Indians nor fur trappers named this mountain. Locally it has been called Triple Divide Peak, but only a bench mark (11,642 ft.) and lines denoting a junction of divides point to it on the Geological Survey's map of 1906. The Survey's 1968 map (correcting the B.M. to 11,675 ft.) officially names this long crest projecting in a northwesterly descent from the 13,800 foot glacier swathed peaks at the heart of the Wind River Range—Three Waters Mountain. That latter day cartographer, possessing the imagination and finding the inspiration to contrive this name, thus proved himself a worthy disciple of Ferdinand Vandeveer Hayden and his competent assistants who were precursors and, in 1879, helpers in the founding of the United States Geological Survey.

H Union Pass

About 8 miles west of Dubois on U.S. Highway 26/287

Westbound Astorians led by Wilson Price Hunt in September, 1811, passed through Dubois region, over Union Pass, and on to the mouth of the Columbia River to explore a line of communication and to locate sites for fur trading posts across the continent for John Jacob Astor. In the party were Mackenzie, Crooks, Miller, McClellan, Reed, 11 hunters, interpreters and guides; 45 Canadian engages, an Indian woman and her 2 children.

H Togwotee Pass/Continental Divide

U.S. Highway 26/287 at Togwotee Pass between Moran Junction and Dubois.

Named in 1873 by Captain W. A. Jones honoring his Shoshone Indian guide, Togwotee. Elevation 9,658 feet, Shoshone and Teton National Forests

Interpretive Signs

Togwotee Pass
Blackfoot, Crow and Shoshone Indian hunting parties, following the trail of elk, deer and buffalo, made the first human trail through this pass. Next came such courageous mountainmen as John Colter, Jim Bridger, Joe Meeker and Kit Carson who courted death in the search for prime beaver pelts.

Capt. Jones, Corps of Engineers, U.S. Army was on reconnaissance for a wagon road across these mountains when he was guided by Togwotee. In 1898, the army built the first wagon road over Togwotee to assist troop movements protecting the westward flow of pioneers. The first auto road was constructed in 1922. TOGWOTEE (pronounced toe-go-tee) means Lance Thrower in Shoshone.

Parting of the Waters
Here, on the Continental Divide, the course of mighty rivers is decided. Moisture from melting snow and summer showers filters into the soil, later emerging as small streams which form the rivers. The Wind and Missouri Rivers to the East, the Snake and Columbia to the West.

Two Ocean Creek, not far from here, was so named because its waters cascade both east and west from the top of the Divide watershed to finally reach both Atlantic and Pacific Oceans.

Moving Mountains
Natural forces sculptured the scene before you over 15,000 years ago. Glaciers gouged out the huge valleys from massive layers of lava. The Breccia (bretch-yuh) cliffs are composed of

Downtown Dubois

angular pieces of rock cemented together with finer materials. The ground you stand on constantly changes as nature continues to shape it. Wind tears at the thin soil. Rains attacks and erodes the bare ground. In such ways "mountains are moved." Where possible man seeks to slow this process slowing the force of water with dams, and maintaining a protective cover of vetetation in the form of grass or timber.

H The Old Blackrock Station

U.S. Highway 26/287 east of Moran Junction at Teton National Forest Ranger Station.

In days gone-by, this log cabin served as the Ranger's Office for the Buffalo District of the Teton National Forest, located 35 miles north of the town of Jackson. The building brings back some of the historic flavor of the Jackson Hole Country. The furnishings are typical of a District Forest Ranger's Office in the early days. This small rustic cabin was sufficient to meet the needs of the hardy Forest Rangers of that era. Their primary duties of forest protection and law enforcement kept them in the woods most of the time. Simple as it was the cabin was a welcome sight to the Ranger, especially during the long cold winter months. Please look inside for a brief glimpse into the past.

19 Gas, Food, Lodging

Dubois
Pop. 1,000, Elev. 6,917

At the head of the Absaroka and Wind River Mountains, and surrounded by the varigated Badlands, is the town of Dubois. A peaceful yet bustling hamlet surrounded by many natural wonders, Dubois was not always the calm, pastoral place it has become. Situated in the upper valley of the Wind River, a gathering place for wildlife, the area of Dubois was once a battleground for Crow, Shoshone, and Blackfeet Indians, disputing hunting rights. In 1811, the Astorians passed through, and not far behind were trappers Jim Bridger, Kit Carson, and others looking for beaver and game.

The most famous Indian battle was the Crowheart Butte Battle of 1866. That same year, the first homesteaders arrived and settled just up the river. As more people arrived, a saloon opened up, and the town grew around it. Finally, in 1886, the community applied for a post office, but postal officials considered the name they wanted (Never Sweat, for the ease of life there) too improper. Instead, they proposed naming the town after Idaho Senator Dubois, who was a proponent of homesteader rights. The townsfolk found this agreeable, and the name stuck.

In many ways, Dubois hasn't changed much since then. You can still spot ranch folk tying their horses to a rail on the main street, Rams Horn, which has a wooden sidewalk. Cattle drives and wildlife can also be seen in the middle of town. Locals can't feel too far removed from nature with bears and moose wandering into their backyards.

T National Bighorn Sheep Interpretive Center

907 W. Ramshorn in Dubois. 455-3429 or 888-209-2795. www.bighorn.org.

The Center is devoted to educating the public about a variety of sheep living in the nearby Habitat area; including desert bighorn, Rocky

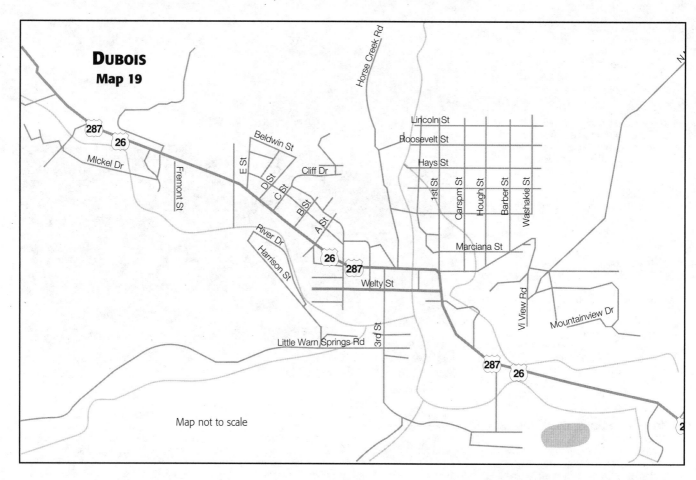

DUBOIS
Map 19

Map not to scale

Mountain Bighorn, stone sheep, and Dall sheep. The central exhibit, "Sheep Mountain" is as the name suggests; a 16 foot tall mountain with mounted sheep. Surrounding scenes and hands-on exhibits show and teach how the sheep live in their rugged environment.During the winter the Center hosts wildlife tours of the nearby Whisky Basin Habitat Area.Open year round. Summer hours (Memorial Day weekend through Labor Day weekend) are daily 9 a.m. to 8 p.m. Call for winter hours.

TV Fitzpatrick Wilderness Area
On U.S. Highway 26/287 between Moran Junction and Dubois

Designated in October of 1976 and named for Tom Fitzpatrick, a mountain man and partner of Jim Bridger, the Fitzpatrick Wilderness Area contains approximately 200,000 acres. Most of the area was previously classified as the Glacier Primitive Area and is known for its numerous glaciers and mountain peaks. The Fitzpatrick covers the northern half of the Wind River Mountains on the east side of the Continental Divide and is bordered on the west by the Bridger Wilderness. The Wind River Indian Reservation lies to the east. The Fitzpatrick is an area of immeasurable beauty and grandeur. The topography is extremely rugged, carved out of granite and limestone by the action of glaciers and glacial streams. There are 44 active glaciers covering approximately 7,760 acres.

Two of the largest glaciers in the Continental United States, the Dinwoody Glacier at the foot of Gannett Peak and Bull Lake Glacier at the base of Fremont Peak, are also found here which cover more than 15 square miles. Gannett Peak, 13,800 feet is the highest point in Wyoming and is in the Fitzpatrick, along with several other peaks over

13,000 feet. Accessible only by foot or horseback on established National Forest Trails.
Source: Dubois Chamber of Commerce brochure.

T Wind River Historical Center
909 W. Ramshorn in Dubois. 455-2284.
www.windriverhistory.org/

The museum presents the history of Native Americans and settlers of the area. It houses a range of exhibits, from those depicting the Sheepeater Indians to various cultural artifacts to displays on ranch life, natural history, and the Tie Hacks. Tie hacks were men who cut trees around Dubois for 10 million railroad ties in the years between 1914 and 1946. Artifacts from this logging era and mementos from the lumberjack's gambling houses are also shown.

Outside the museum are five historic log cabins, and the upstairs hosts the Headwaters Community Arts and Conference Center, showing the artwork of local artists.The museum is open year round. Call for hours.

T Headwaters Community Arts and Conference Center
Downtown Dubois. 455-2687

Built in 1995, the 17,000 sq. foot facility is for the use of the Dubois community and to encourage conventions, seminars and symposiums to come to Dubois. With one large conference room (48' x 100') built to divide into three meeting rooms which will hold 30-100 people each or accommodate 350-600 when left open. The building is also home of the Wind River Valley Artists' Build Art Gallery with a permanent art collection of over 60 original works of art.
Source: Dubois Chamber of Commerce brochure.

T Dubois Fish Hatchery
South of U.S. Highways 26/287, five miles east of Dubois.

Situated at the base of the Whiskey Mountain bighorn sheep winter range on the east slope of the Wind River Mountains, the state of Wyoming maintains a fish hatchery. A fish rearing station was in use at this location in the 1930s, this was abandoned in 1937, and the present hatchery replaced it in 1940. In 1944 it was further expanded with 44 cement "raceways" providing outdoor homes for developing fish. Two natural springs, together, supply more than a million gallons of water a day to the hatchery. The springs are located 1 1/4 miles from the hatchery on Jakey's Fork Creek, and numerous land grants, easements and long-term leases were procured by the Wyoming Game and Fish commission in order to pipe the water to the hatchery facility farther down the canyon. Due to its location, the Dubois hatchery serves an extremely important function by caring for eggs taken from the cutthroat (native) spawning operation each spring at

Lake of the Woods in the Union Pass area, 30 miles southwest of Dubois. This spawning operation furnishes a major portion of the cutthroat eggs for the entire state of Wyoming. The Dubois hatchery also cares for rainbow, golden, brook and brown trout. Visitors are welcome.
Source: Dubois Chamber of Commerce brochure.

T Tie Flumes and Old Campsites
18 miles northwest of Dubois on U.S. Highway 26/287 in vicinity of Tie Hack Memorial

Many old logging camps stand as mute testimony to the tie-hacking days. Little remains of the logging camps due to weathering of the old buildings. However, may artifacts of the tie cutting days are still to be found at the old sites. The oldest camps were established in 1914. Up until 1913, colorless glass was manufactured with an impurity that resulted in its turning purple after years of exposure to sunlights. The earliest tie camps can be dated by fragments of glass that have turned purple from 90 years of exposure to the sun on the trash heaps near the camps. Other artifacts to be found in the tie camps are cross-cut saws as they are still occasionally used. But, the broad axe has long since passed from use and become an antique. Source: Dubois Chamber of Commerce brochure.

T Union Pass Historical Site
15 miles south on Union Pass Road, about eight miles south of Dubois on U.S. Highway 26/287.

The road on Union Pass is very scenic. The Union Pass monument includes a history and monument of Three Waters Mountain (Triple Divide Peak); Ramshorn Peak, Union Peak, Roaring Fork Watershed Vista, Cattleman's Drift Fence, Bacon Ridge and logging roads. There is also a story of Aboriginal use, the explorers and the mountain men.

T Wind River Lake-Brooks Lake
Just west of Togwotee Pass north of U.S. Highway 26/287 of Brooks Lake Rd.

It is not necessary to journey into the wilderness area to find spectacular mountain scenery. Many panoramas may be viewed from your car as you travel the roads leading from Dubois. A very popular side trip is the road to Brooks Lake Lodge. The lodge was originally constructed in 1922 to serve bus travelers on their way to Yellowstone National Park. It has undergone a series of owners and restoration efforts since then. In 1989 the lodge restoration was completed and rededicated. Listed in the National Register of Historic Places, the lodge represents a unique time in the history of the Wind River Country.
Source: Dubois Chamber of Commerce brochure

T Ramshorn Basin Area
Directly north of downtown Dubois

The rugged Ramshorn Peak (11,635 feet) hovers north of downtown Dubois. The basin of the Ramshorn is surrounded on three sides by rugged peaks and the alpine basin is abundant with wildflowers in the summer.*Source: Dubois Chamber of Commerce brochure*

T Petrified Forest
37 miles north of Dubois.

The Washakie Wilderness north of Dubois has within its boundaries an area of particular interest to the scientist and amateur geologist. 30 to 40 million years ago this area was covered by massive volcanic ash deposits. The wood cells were replaced by minerals and water before they could rot creating petrified wood. The varying colors

and textures of the petrified wood are the result of varying colors and textures of certain minerals in the stone. As the petrified forest is within boundaries of the Wilderness, all travel is restricted to foot and horseback. Petrified wood can not be taken from the area. For the rock hounds, the regions around the lower end of the creeks flowing into the Wind River are excellent places to hunt for pieces of the petrified wood which have been washed down from the slopes of the Wilderness area. *Source: Dubois Chamber of Commerce brochure*

T Wind River Indian Reservation
South of Dubois

This reservation is home to the Shoshone and Arapahoe tribes. Tourists who arrive in the Wind River area while either of the tribes's sun dances are in progress may stop to watch. The sun dance is a form of sacrifice, as the dancers neither eat nor drink during the three day ceremony. These dances are held during the summer months. The Arapahoes also have a Pow-Wow each summer during which numerous tribes compete in costume performing their traditional dances. Cameras and tape recorders are not allowed.*Source: Dubois Chamber of Commerce brochure*

T Red Rocks and Badlands
12 miles east of Dubois

On the north side of the highway through Dubois, the badlands offer the visitor spectacular scenery. The road winds through red rock country providing views of the red cliffs. The badlands stretch for many miles to the east in the Wind River Indian Reservation. The color of this barren wasteland is uniquely beautiful.

H Dubois Museum Interpretive Signs
At Dubois Museum

School House
The first Dubois high school, established in 1925, originally had approximately 12 students who attended for only two years. Those who wished to continue their education beyond what was offered locally had to make arrange-

ments to board with friends or relatives in nearby Lander or Riverton, about 88 miles away. The first Dubois curriculum consisted of Latin, American History, English, Algebra and Geometry.

Like most rural schoolhouse, the Dubois high school contained only the bare essentials. It was the teacher's job to start the wood burning stove on cold mornings, fill the water bucket and care for the kerosene lamps. Toilet facilities consisted of an outhouse, located "outback" which required a quick dash in cold weather.

Swans Service Station
Swan's Service Station, which opened in 1930, was built by Swedish immigrant Swan Swanson (or Swenson). Swanson first came to Dubois in 1914. After a six year stay, he returned to Sweden and became engaged to his wife Sigrid. The couple immigrated officially in 1921 and settled in Dubois where Swan's father was a contractor for the Wyoming Tie and Timber Company.

Swan worked as "tie-hack" and Sigrid was employed as a cook at the Dunoir tie camp for their first nine years. Many other Scandinavian immigrants were also employed in the tie camps. In 1930, the Swansons moved to town to operate the service station and run a trucking buisness between Riverton, Lander and Dubois.

The filling station originally consisted of two small rooms with an office in front and sleeping room in the back. To the left of the station was a pit with wooden tracks on each side to hold vehicles while the oil was being changed.

Bunkhouse
Cowboys and other hired hands seldom found much in the way of luxury or home comforts in the ranch "bunkhouse" that served as their living quarters; a bed, wash basin and a place to store personal gear was about all their employers offered. Picture magazines, mail order catalogs, copies of Shakespeare (which could be bought with coupons that came with the Bull Durham brand of chewing tobacco) and card games were among the few sources of entertainment.

Tim McCoy, who worked for the Double Diamond Ranch east of Dubois, describes the winter montony of bunkhouse life in his autobiography, Tim McCoy Remembers the West:

"The thing that put a bee in my britches and got me moving from the Double Diamond was that I had spent the long, cold and boring Wyoming winter of 1909-1910 in the confines of the ranch's bunkhouse, with only occasional, dreary forays outside. I remember vividly at some point during the seemingly endless frost reading a poem in a magazine which extolled the virtues of lush Wyoming. Somehow it didn't jibe with what I saw outside the window and between furtive glances at the bunkhouse thermometer which frequently registered a teeth-shattering forty-degrees below zero, I wrote an answering piece."

Saddle Shop

Maxwell's saddle shop, a small buisness located behind what is now the Ramshorn Inn, provided horse tack and supplies for dude and working ranches in the Dubois area.

The equipment displayed here represents a cross-section of the types of horse gear used in this part of the west. The large stock saddle in the front (right) is typical of the heavy duty roping saddles used in Wyoming around the late 1930s and 1940s. Both saddle and saddle bags show the traditonal "California rose" pattern, typical of the decorative tooling of this era. The saddle to the left is a somewhat earlier model with larger square-cornered skirts, similar to those that came up from Texas with the start of the first cattle drives in the 1870s.

On the back wall are two pairs of "chaps," protective leggings worn by cowboys to shield them from the cold or thick brush. The pair on the left made from Angora goat, are straight or "shot gun" style chaps which would have been used in colder weather. Those on the right, with wide, flared edges are known as "batwings." Made of heavy cowhide, this pair was designed to protect the rider from the heavy willows and underbrush in the wrangle pasture at the T Cross Ranch at the head of Horse Creek.

Hanging by the horse collars on the left-hand wall are reins made out of braided horse hair. This kind of work and the braided leather reins and quirt to the left of the window on the right of the shop are typical of the kind of craft work that used to be done by ranch hands during the long Wyoming winters.

The center two bridles on the back wall have "spade" bits with extremely high ports. Their use required considerable training and sensitivity on the part of the horse and a high level of skill on the part of the rider. The bridle on the left is decorated with the brass brad or stud work typical of the late teens, twenties and thirties.

The mule pack saddle on the right of back wall is typical of the "saw" or "cross-buck" pack saddle used by outfitters and dude ranchers in this area. Pack saddles were used by working cowhands to transport salt to summer feeding grounds and bedrolls and other gear to mountain cowcamps.

Side-saddles, like that on the back wall (right), were used by a few women in the early west when riding astride was considered un-lady like. The flat hornless English Saddles (center-right) wereused by the more "modern eastern women, "dudines" who brought the liberating fashion for riding "cross saddle" west with them when they began coming out as tourists, shortly after the turn of the cenntury. (The Ladies Astride, a kind of hybrid version of the English saddle and the stock saddle flurished briefly in the west's more urban areas around the turn of the century but was soon discarded in favor of lighter versions of the more practical stock or roping saddle.)

In the center of the shop is a McClellan saddle originally used by the miltary's calvary units. Some McClellans had horns attached and could be used for ranch work. With a large number of surplus McClellans on hand after World War I, these saddles were also issued to the Forest Service, which continued to use horses well into middle of the century, and other government agencies.

Forest Service Cabin

This cabin may have originally served as a bunkhouse at the Sheridan Creek ranger station west of Dubois.

What is now called the "Wind River District" of the Shoshone National Forest was initially part of the Yellowstone Forest Reserve. It was later designatied the Bonneville National Forest, and most recently, the Washakie National Forest, in honor of the Shoshone leader, Chief Washskie.

Beginning in 1891, when President Harrison established the first federal forest lands, the United States Forest Service has monitored timber sales and grazing allotments as well as recreational use. The history at Dubois is closed, linked to its National Forest resources. Public forest lands provided timber for a number of early sawmills and for the large railroad cross-tie industry which produced ties for the Chicago-Northwestern Railroad and timber products such as fence posts and mine props, along with dude

and cattle ranching, were the area's most important economic industries during the 1920s through the 1940s.

Homestead Cabin

Originally located about eight miles east of Dubois, this cabin is in many ways typical of homestead buildings around the turn of the century. Exceptions are the large windows and relatively high ceiling which would have made the cabin harder to heat. These more spacious features may indicate the influence of a woman's interest in the planning: most earlier cabins tended to be squat and low with narrow, horizontal windows.

Many of the articles in the cabin kitchen belonged to Nettie Stringer who came to Dubois in 1901. Nettie and her family, her mother and 6 brothers, settled west of Dubois where she filed her own claim in 1985.

Keeping house for her brothers, mending and ironing, cooking and tending outdoor chores kept Nettie busy year around On a typical day, in May of 1908, her diary reads as follows: "I washed early—baked bread and four pies, dress two chickens. Carl and Albert and two other men were here for dinner. I ironed the boys collars and basted up a bonnet, then did several turns (chores) and took a bath…"

We have left the cardboard and newspaper insulation on the kitchens back wall in place to show visitors how homesteaders "made do" with materials on hand. When the cabin was first moved to the museum grounds, this early insulation was covered with the same cardboard panelling and of the original outside chinking has been left visible on the west side of the cabin, above the boardwalk, to show how the outside looked before restoration work.

Meat House

Originally located in a pine grove on the Dennison Ranch along the west fork of Wind River, on Bear Creek, this building served to keep meat cool and safe from bears and flies. The pyramid shape and screen sidings provided natural cooling and ventilation.

The Dennison Ranch was a 5,500 acre ranch belonging to millionaire Richard Dennison. A true eccentric, Dennison also ran an exclusive dude operation which catered to the likes of Clark Gable and Carole Lombard. The ranch was also famous for the many safari trophies which decorated its extravagant interior. Dennison owned and bred a string of Kentucky racehorses and ran a herd of registered Jersey cattle which he kept in a three-story barn with hardwood floors. The barn has since been moved to the Thunderhead Ranch.

Two-Seater Outhouse

This large "privy" was originally located at the first Dubois Airport, on Table Mountain. Airport facilities were constructed as part of a WPA project in 1936.

Buffalo Bill and the Long Ride

Legend says that Pony Express rider William "Buffalo Bill" Cody exchanged horses here on a record ride from Red Buttes Station to Rocky Ridge Station and back. Due to another rider's untimely death, Cody was forced to add an extra leg to his relay and eventually covered a total of 322 miles in 21 hours and 40 minutes, using 21 horses. On another occasion, he rode one horse at top speed for 24 miles when chased by Indians from Horse Creek Station east of Independence Rock to Plant's Station just east of here.

F Rustic Pine Tavern & Steakhouse
119 E. Ramshorn, Dubois. 455-2430.

The Rustic Pine Tavern and Steakhouse is famous for its fine value-oriented cuisine and warm atmosphere. Serving dinner nightly, the steakhouse offers full meals with starters and salad and numerous entrees, including delicious steaks, prime rib, seafood, chops, and ribs. Patrons may also select items from the bar menu for more casual dining. Although the food is famous, the tavern also draws attention with its colorful Old West ambiance. The 1930's building is chock full of rustic furniture, game mounts, and Old West relics that make the Rustic Pine a favorite for locals and visitors alike. Live entertainment and dancing is featured on summer weekends with pool and darts always available. Step back in time, meet the locals, enjoy a great steak or the chef's nightly special, and relax with Rustic Pine's friendly Western hospitality!

F Café Wyoming & Howling Wolf BBQ Sauce
106 E. Ramshorn, Dubois. 455-3828.
www.cafewyoming.com and
|www.howlingwolfsauce.com

Chef Ken Wolfe and the AAA-approved Café Wyoming offer memorable lunch and dinner dining with everything made from scratch daily. Breads, soups, and salad dressings accompany delicious entrées and fresh organic coffee. The famous catfish sandwich, hearty B.L.T., and phenomenal half-roasted duck are crowd favorites along with house-smoked entrees. Can't make it to the café? Sample Café Wyoming at home with their signature barbeque sauces and rubs made in-house and sold nationally. The line includes Honey Huckleberry, Cranberry Orange, Regular, Extra Spicy, and dry rubs for all meats and fish. Lunch is served year-round Tuesday through Saturday from 11:30-2:00. Summer dinner hours are Tuesday through Saturday 5:30-9:00 with winter dinner hours from 5:30-9:00 Thursday through Saturday. Dinner reservations are suggested, and seasonal outdoor dining is available.

FLC Lava Mountain Lodge & Restaurant
3577 Hwy. 26/287, Dubois. 455-2506 or (800) 919-9570. www.lavamountainlodge.com; info@lavamountainlodge.com

Situated inside Shoshone National Forest near Yellowstone and Grand Teton National Parks, Lava Mountain Lodge and Restaurant helps visitors create affordable vacations in one location. Ramble through the forest on an autumn hunt, hike the surrounding mountains, discover world-class fly-fishing, or take an unforgettable bike ride or guided horseback trip. During winter, experience some of the world's best snowmobiling, cross-country skiing, and snowshoeing. After a fun-filled day, enjoy Lava Mountain's scrumptious soups, salads, sandwiches, and grill creations before retreating to the lodge's cozy rustic cabins, RV campground, or tent campsites. In addition to dining and lodging, Lava Mountain also boasts a general store, liquor store, bar, gift shop, gas, and diesel fuel. For an adventure just twenty miles west of Dubois, visit Lava Mountain Lodge and Restaurant. Dogs and horses are welcome.

L Branding Iron Inn
401 W. Ramshorn, Dubois. 455-2893 or (888) 651-9378. www.brandingironinn.com; brandingiron@wyoming.com

Situated along one of america's most beautiful drives, the Branding Iron Inn is located 85 miles south of Yellowstone and fifty miles from the Tetons. The inn's Swedish Cope log cabins were hand built in the 1940's and include all the modern conveniences guests need with an authentic Old West atmosphere. The cabins feature king and queen sized beds, cable TV, some kitchenettes, one full apartment, and some adjoining rooms. On-site horse corrals, winter plug-ins, and ample parking for snowmobiles and boat trailers complement the amenities of this completely ground floor, AAA endorsed inn. During your stay, check out the area's renowned hunting, skiing, and snowmobiling, or take a stroll downtown to great historical attractions, shopping, and dining. Children under 12 stay free, and reasonable rates are available year-round. Visit them on the web!

L Twin Pines Lodge and Cabins
218 W. Ramshorn; Dubois. 455-2600 or (800) 550-6332. www.twinpineslodge.com; twinpines@wyoming.com

Listed on the Wyoming National Historic Register, the Twin Pines Lodge and Cabins were built in 1934. Today, the recently remodeled lodge and cabins preserve a rustic atmosphere while featuring modern fixtures. Kick back, relax, and enjoy the western style and hospitality at the Twin Pines. They pamper you with large plush towels, refrigerators, coffee, tea, and hot chocolate in every guest room. Each cabin and room also includes high-speed wireless Internet and a VCR/DVD player. As an added bonus, Twin Pines and their friendly staff supply hundreds of movies for your enjoyment, free of charge. Each morning, guests wake to a complimentary deluxe breakfast bar. Located within walking distance to restaurants, taverns, and shopping, Twin Pines Lodge and Cabins offers comfort and convenience in one location. Visit them on the web.

L Black Bear Country Inn
1348 W. Ramshorn, Dubois. 455-2344 or (800) 873-BEAR (2327). |www.blackbearcountryinn.biz; blackbear5@wyoming.com

Black Bear Country Inn is located on the Wind River banks amid spectacular mountain scenery. While enjoying easy access to shopping, restaurants, museums, and outdoor recreation, guests are treated to clean, quiet, and spacious rooms. All rooms feature unique décor complete with king or queen size beds, phones, Internet access, cable TV, microwaves, refrigerators, and outdoor patios. Some rooms also boast kitchenettes and can accommodate up to eight people. For guests' convenience, trailer parking is provided, pets are allowed, and picnic tables and campfire rings near the river's edge are available for cookouts. For anglers who bring their own fishing poles, the Black Bear Country Inn also offers onsite fishing for prized rainbow trout. Conveniently located along U.S. Highway 287, the AAA-approved Black Bear Country Inn ensures a pleasant stay at an affordable price.

Crowheart Butte

LC Riverside Inn and Campground

5810 Hwy. 26, Dubois. 455-2337 or (877) 489-2337. www.riversideinnandcampground.com; riversideinn@wyoming.com

Enjoy quiet, comfortable accommodations and superior hospitality at the family-operated Riverside Inn and Campground. Conveniently located on a fifty-acre ranch just 3 miles east of Dubois near the Wind River, the inn offers a variety of lodging choices. The fourteen motel units, which include five kitchenettes, are always clean and provide breathtaking views of the Whiskey Mountains. Surrounded by towering cottonwood trees, camping sites accommodate both large RVs and tents. Large clean showers and restrooms are included, and pets and horses are welcome. Guests also enjoy guest laundry, a modem hookup, ample parking, spacious grounds, a picnic area, playground, easy access to outdoor recreation, and guided horseback trail rides that depart onsite. Whether you're spending a night or week in Dubois, make reservations to relax at Riverside Inn and Campground.

20 Gas

Burris

The first postmistress, a Mrs. Morrison, named this place for her first husband, not for "Dutch Charley" Burris, who was hung by vigilantes on his way to Rawlins to be tried for attempted train robbery and the murder of two deputies.

Crowheart

Like nearby Crowheart Butte, this town's name honors the great battle on the butte between Shoshone Chief Washakie and Crow Chief Big Robber. They fought one-on-one in 1866 to prevent all-out war between their people. The victor was supposed to eat his enemy's heart. When asked later if he did just that, Chief Washakie replied, "Youth does foolish things." The butte itself is considered sacred ground, and visitors are not permitted there, restricted both by law and by courtesy. Legends tell of trespassers disappearing. Better to view it from afar.

The town itself consists of a classic country store and gas station.

H Crowheart Butte

Four and one half miles southeast of Crowheart on Highway 26/287

In March, 1866, a battle was fought in this vicinity between Shoshone and Bannock Indians on one side and Crow Indians on the other. The contest was waged for the supremacy of hunting grounds in the Wind River basin. Crowheart Butte was so named because the victorious Washakie, Chief of the Shoshones, displayed a Crow Indian's heart on his lance at the war dance after the battle. The major portion of the battle was fought near Black Mountain several miles to the north. Washakie, in his youth and middle age, was a very mighty warrior. He was a wise chief and friendly to the white people. No white man's scalp hung in this chief's tepee.

21 Gas, Food, Lodging

Big Sandy

Another town dubbed for a creek of the same name, Big Sandy was once a Pony Express station. Indians burned the station to the ground in 1862. At the foot of Wind River Peak (elev. 13,192 ft.), and practically within throwing distance of the Bridger-Teton National Forest, Big Sandy has an abundance of alpine scenery.

Boulder

Pop. 75, Elev. 7,016

The nearby creek of the same name was so called for the large boulder in its midst, fallen from a cliff overhead. The Boulder Store is about a century old. Other amenities such as a dancehall, a blacksmith shop, a post office, and a hotel once made Boulder a frontier hot spot. Now it is a quiet community with the main attraction being the ospreys which nest just to the west.

H Grass or Sand Springs—An Oregon Trail Campsite

North of 191/351 Junction

Here crosses the Lander cutoff—the northern fork of the Oregon Trail following a route of the fur traders. It was suggested as an emmigrant road by mountain man, John Hockaday in order to avoid the alkali plains of the desert, shorten the trip to the Pacific by five days, and provide more water, grass and wood. In 1857, it was improved as a wagon road by the government under the supervision of F. W. Lander and termed the Fort Kearny, South Pass, Honey Lake Rd. As many as three hundred wagons and thousands of cattle, horses and mules passed here each day. An expanding nation moved with hope and high courage. The trail-cut deep into the dirt of the plains and the mountains-remains as a reminder of a great epoch. Sublette County Historical Society, United States Department of the Interior Bureau of Land Management. This trail has been marked at all accessible points with brass caps.

H Buckskin Crossing—a Landmark

About eight miles south of Big Sandy on County Road 1804 where road crosses Big Sandy River.

This part of the Big Sandy River has been known as the Buckskin Crossing since the 1860s. Legend is that a trapper and hunter named Buckskin Joe lived here with his wife and daughter. The daughter died here. This marker is near his cabin site. This crossing was used by the fur companies and trappers, Captain Bonneville, Captain Wm. D. Stewart, and later by John C. Fremont. Captain Stewart's artist—the noted Alfred Jacob Miller—made the first painting of this area in 1837. This ford of the Lander Cutoff of the Oregon Trail, campsite and burial ground was heavily used by the emigrants, their hundreds of wagons and thousands of mules, cattle and horses. This was the mail route from the east to the west side of the Wind River Mountains in the early 1900s. Big Sandy Creek was named by William Ashley on his trapping expedition in 1825. Of the thousands of people who passed this way only the wagon tracks and graves remain.

H Fremont's Week in Sublette County

About Seven miles east of Boulder on State Highway 353.

On June 10, 1842, Lt. J.C. Fremont left St. Louis to explore the Wind River Mountains, with Kit Carson as guide, Charles Preuss, as topographer, L. Maxwell, hunter, and 20 Canadian

Dubois	Jan	Feb	March	April	May	June	July	Aug	Sep	Oct	Nov	Dec	Annual
Average Max. Temperature (F)	33.5	36.6	41.4	49.8	60.5	69.9	78.8	78.1	67.2	56.2	42.1	34.8	54.1
Average Min. Temperature (F)	10.8	11.9	16.4	23.8	31.6	38.5	42.4	41.0	33.6	26.1	17.9	12.3	25.5
Average Total Precipitation (in.)	0.30	0.26	0.48	1.08	1.35	1.35	0.97	0.75	1.12	0.59	0.43	0.28	8.96
Average Total SnowFall (in.)	4.1	3.8	5.2	6.5	2.1	0.4	0.0	0.0	1.7	2.0	4.5	4.5	34.9
Average Snow Depth (in.)	1	0	0	0	0	0	0	0	0	0	0	1	0

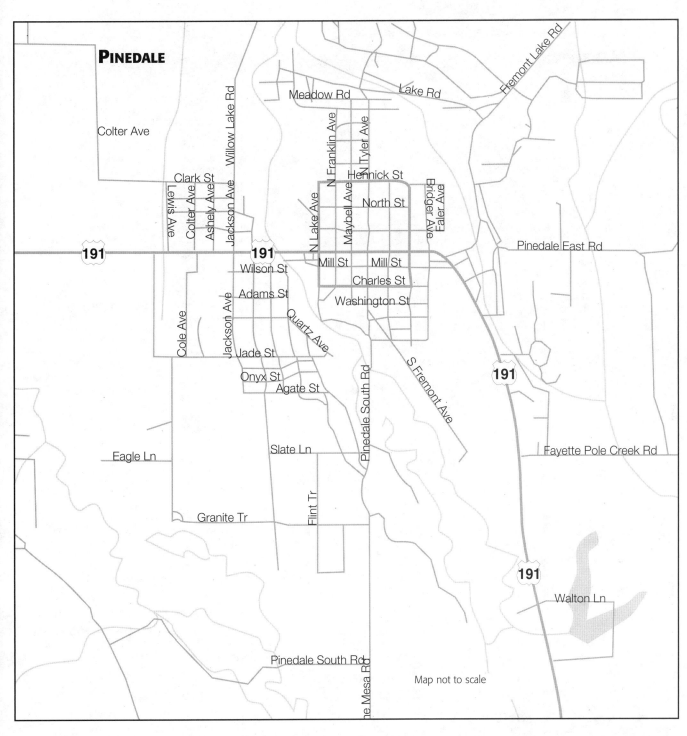

PINEDALE

Colter Ave

Meadow Rd

Lake Rd

Fremont Lake Rd

Willow Lake Rd

N Franklin Ave

N Tyler Ave

Hennick St

Clark St

Lewis Ave

Colter Ave

Ashely Ave

Jackson Ave

N Lake Ave

Maybell Ave

North St

Elk Ave

Bridger Ave

191

191

191

Pinedale East Rd

Wilson St

Mill St

Mill St

Charles St

Adams St

Washington St

Jackson Ave

Quartz Ave

Cole Ave

Jade St

Onyx St

Agate St

Pinedale South Rd

S Fremont Ave

191

Eagle Ln

Slate Ln

Fayette Pole Creek Rd

Flint Tr

Granite Tr

191

Walton Ln

Pinedale South Rd

The Mesa Rd

Map not to scale

voyageurs, including Basil LeJeunesse. Eight two-wheeled mule-drawn carts were used as far as the Platte River. The party crossed South Pass August 8 and camped here at "Two Buttes" August 9. Leaving 10 men at Boulder Lake, the lieutenant ascended Fremont Peak August 15, stayed here again August 17, and on the 19th re-crossed South Pass. So ended Fremont's Exploration of the Wind River Mountains and his stay in Sublette County.

22 *Gas, Food, Lodging*

Big Piney
Pop. 408, Elev. 6,798

Pines once lined the Big Piney Creek, for which

the town was named, but none of the native trees grow in town anymore. Dan Budd, Sr., whose ranch housed the post office for a time, named both. Prior to that, the post office had been at the Mule Shoe Ranch of A.W. Smith. Big Piney is often the coldest spot in the nation.

T Green River Valley Museum
In Big Piney

The Historic Green River Valley Museum was formed to pertpetuate and preserve the history and culture of the Green River Valley. Featured exhibits include prehistoric Indian artifacts, early ranching and branding equipment, and historic oil field tools. The area oil and gas history is actively displayed, along with exhibits about family-operated coal mine histories. There is a

restored homesteader cabin along with the history of homesteading and townsite development. Other unique displays include Campfire Girls and old Big Piney Examiner Presses. The museum is open mid-June to Mid-October.

Wyoming Tidbits

According to one source, two words from the Delaware Indians combine to make "Wyoming": Mecheweami-ing, "a land of mountains and valleys". Another source claims the Algonquin word for "large prairie place" is 'wyoming'.

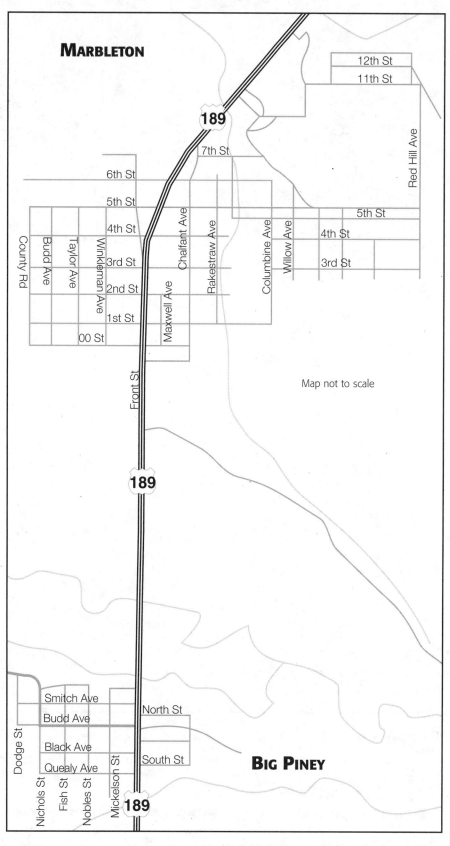

MARBLETON

12th St
11th St
189
7th St
6th St
5th St
4th St
3rd St
2nd St
1st St
00 St

County Rd
Budd Ave
Taylor Ave
Winkleman Ave
Chalfant Ave
Maxwell Ave
Rakestraw Ave
Columbine Ave
Willow Ave
Red Hill Ave

5th St
4th St
3rd St

Front St

189

Map not to scale

Smitch Ave
Budd Ave
North St
Black Ave
Quealy Ave
South St

Dodge St
Nichols St
Fish St
Nobles St
Mickelson St

189

BIG PINEY

Thousands of people, cattle and horses passed this way to the Northwest when the Sublette Cut-off of the Oregon Trail was opened in 1857. None settled in this county. At the close of the Indian Wars in 1877, cattle herds from Oregon came this way to meet the railroad and to stock Wyoming ranges. The first Sublette County herds were started with other western cattle. In 1878-79 Ed Swan's PL, Otto Leifer's O Circle, Bud's 6 Quarter Circle, Hugh McKay's 67 and A.W. Smith's Muleshoe outfits settled on nearby Piney Creek. Their cattle were not Longhorns. The county's first barbed wire was unrolled in 1881 on the Circle outfit.

24 *Gas, Food, Lodging*

Pinedale
Pop. 1412, Elev. 7,175

Established near Pine Creek, this town was named by first postmaster Charles Peterson in 1899. At that time, it was farthest away from all the railroads of any town in Wyoming. Before that, this was Rendezvous country, where the biggest get-togethers of trappers, traders, and Native Americans took place from 1832 to1840. The tie-hack industry also contributed to the town's growth. Pinedale is still a ranching center, but is increasingly benefiting from the overflow of tourism from the Jackson area. With its proximity to the Wind River Mountains, however, it still retains its wild, rustic charm.

Cora
Pop. 3, Elev. 7,340

Named for Cora House, an old maid cowgirl who worked on the nearby Elmer Ranch, this post office was established in about 1890. A decade later, in 1900, the post office moved to the ranch of Mrs. Minerva Westphall, best known for her bootlegged whiskey and her big gray stallion, on which she carried the mail from Big Piney. In 1902 it moved again to the ranch of James Noble. When it finally developed into a town, it served the nearby railroad tie camp with its saloon and dance hall, blacksmith shop, and local newspaper. It had to move one last time to be near a paved road, but the post office was finally restored to its original building. Today, Cora is the place to catch up on news for the area ranchers.

T Museum of the Mountain Man
700 E. Hennick off Fremont Lake Road in Pinedale. 367-4101 or toll free (877) 686-6266.
www.museumofthemountainman.com

The Museum of the Mountain Man is located at the base of the Wind River Mountains. The men of the Fur Trade, or Mountain Men, were among the greatest overland explorers that the world has ever known. The purpose of the museum is to interpret this important era of history to all who pass this way. The exhibition area includes special displays and interpretative text on equipment, tools, techniques, interaction with the American Indian, the Rendezvous and the role of the mountain man as an explorer and guide for the westward expansion. The museum also offers a research library, special programs and history demonstrations, children's hands on activities, and a gift shop. The museum is open May through October, admission is charged, and there is plenty of large vehicle parking. During the second weekend of July history comes alive with the Green River Rendezvous commemoration when local residents reenact the events of the fur trade era.

23 *Gas, Food, Lodging*

Marbleton
Pop. 720, Elev. 6,798

Named for Cheyenne cattle man A. H. Marble, this small town was built up by ranchers. Author

Ethel Mills Black, who wrote *They Made Wyoming Their Own*, spent her childhood in Marbleton in the late 1800s.

H Historic Sublette County Of Cattle and Men
About three miles north of Big Piney on U.S. Highway 189.

H Osprey
Just south of Pinedale on Highway 191.

The power pole near the highway has supported an osprey nest for many years. Ospreys normally build their nests (eyries) on top of large columns of rock or in trees with broken tops. Utah Power and Light Company built this nest site by adding an extension and platform to an existing pole. This provides the birds a safer place to nest and prevents powerline damage due to falling nesting material. Other such devices have been constructed within several miles of this location.

Osprey nests are generally constructed of large sticks, driftwood, grasses and bark. Ospreys lay 2 to 4 cream-colored eggs with brown to lavender blotches. Eggs are generally laid in May and hatch in approximately 28 days. About eight weeks after hatch, the young take their first extended flights.

Throughout the summer the adults can be observed bringing fish to the young at the nest. Fish are the primary food of the osprey, and are the reason they are commonly referred to as "fish hawks". Ospreys dive from 20 to 100 feet in the air and almost completely submerge in their attempt to catch fish, then take it back to a tree perch or the nest for their meal.

While ospreys are generally more tolerant of disturbance than other raptors, they will defend their nest from any intruders. It is important to maintain a reasonable distance from the nest to avoid too much disturbance that could cause the birds to abandon their eggs or young.

H Green River Rendezvous
Just West of Pinedale

A marker place of fur trade, from the Mississippi to the Pacific, from Canada to Mexico, where trappers, traders and Indians came to barter for the first great resource of the west. Six rendezvous were held here, gathering not only furs but information of geographic importance to weld the final link in exploration of the new world. It is a tribute to the brave men, both red and white, who blazed the trails for culture and progress, and the lowly beaver who gave it impetus. Commemorated each year, the second Sunday in July. Sublette County Historical Society, Inc.

H Welcome to the Riparian Community of Duck Creek
Just west of Pinedale on U.S. Highway 191

Duck Creek riparian community is a diverse and complex society of living organisms. Wild brown trout feed on caddisfly nymphs, that live in self-made stick and stone shelters, clinging to the rocks. Yellow warblers and flycatchers nest in willow bushes. Beaver harvest willows to bild dams and lodges. A mallard hen raises its brood on the beaver pond. In the wet meadows beyond the creek, sandhill cranes and long-billed curlews raise their chicks. On a good morning you can see more than 30 kinds of wildlife from this spot.

People are also important members of this community. Ranchers harvest meadow grasses for winter livestock hay. Anglers test their skills on the wily brown trout, while you enjoy the sights and sounds of the wildlife.

The foundation of the Duck Creek community is water and soil. Willow bushes and sedges growing along the creek banks, have long roots that hold the soils in place against the force of flood water. Duck Creek is a role model for clean water, diverse wildlife and lush plant growth.

This community is made possible because of the good stewardship of ranchers, land managers, wildlife managers, anglers and groups like Trout Unlimited. While visiting Wyoming tread lightly and view wildlife from a distance—be a good steward and responsible member of our wild land communities.

H The Naming of the Lake
About three miles north of Pinedale at Fremont Lake.

On the edge of this magnificent sheet of water, Capt. William Drummond Stewart of Scotland camped many times with Jim Bridger, other Mountain men, and Indians from 1833 to 1844. In 1837, his artist, Alfred Jacob Miller, painted the first pictures of this area. On Stewart's last trip in August 1844, eight men in a rubbber boat, first boat on the lake, honored their leader by christening these waters as Stewart's Lake, in a joyous ceremony near the Narrows, with six jugs of whiskey. Years later, this glacier-formed lake with its shoreline of twenty-two miles and over six hundred foot depth was named after Gen. John C. Fremont—the map makers knew not that it had been named long before.

H Historical Sublette County: A Pause on a Journey
U.S. Highway 191 in Pinedale.

On October 16, 1812, the Astorians: Robert Stuart, Ramsey Crooks, Robert Mcclellan, Joseph Miller, Benjamin Jones, Francis LeClair and Andy Vallee, traveling from Astoria to St. Louis, all their horses having been stolen by Indians, passed this way on foot and forded Pine Creek near here, the first white men known to have seen it.

From Stuart's Journal: "We forded another stream whose banks were adorned with many pines—near which we found an Indian encampment—deserted about a month ago, with immense numbers of buffalo bones strewed everywhere—in center of camp a great lodge of pines and willows—at west end—three persons lay interred with feet to east—at head of each a large buffalo skull painted black—from lodge were suspended numerous ornaments and moccasins."

H Rendezvous—Birth of an Empire
About six miles west of Pinedale on U.S. Highway 191.

The river below is the Green. The mountains to the west are the Wyomings (Bear Rivers). Those to the east, the Windrivers. Along the river banks below are the Rendezvous sites of 1833, 1835 (New Fork), 1836, 1837 (Cottonwood), 1839, 1840, and Fort Bonneville. Trappers, traders and Indians from throughout the west here met the trade wagons from the east to barter, trade for furs, gamble, drink, frolic, pray and scheme. The Indians, Delaware and Iroquois brought in by the Hudson Bay Company, Snakes, Bannocks, Gros Ventre, Flatheads, Nez Perce, Crows, and Chinooks here made their first contact with the white man. The warring Blackfeet did not participate. The Rocky Mountain Fur Company, Hudson Bay Company, Captain Bonneville, Wyeth and free trappers controlled the trade. The people of God, Marcus and Marcissa Whitman, Mr. and Mrs. Spalding, Samuel Parker, Father DeSmet, Jason Lee, and W. H. Gray tempered the hilarity. Jim Bridger, Milton and Bill Sublette, Tom Fitzpatrick, Joe Walker, Joe Meeks, Kit Carson, Baptiste Gervais, Bob Jackson, Moses (Black) Harris, Lucien Fontenelle, Etienne Provost, Henry Fraeb, Andry Dripps, Robert Campbell, Henry Vandenbury, Sir W. D. Stewart and the artist A. J. Miller were all part of this and left their names imbedded in the annals of the West. Scattering for the value of a beaver plew and to see what was beyond the horizon, their trails became the highways of an empire at the cost of many a violent death.

H Wind River Mountains
About six miles west of Pinedale on U.S. Highway 191.

You are looking into the Wind River Mountain Range. So named by Indians and translated into English. These mountains are still in the ice age. The seven largest glaciers in the Rocky Mountains are here. Numerous smaller glaciers also remain.

This side of the mountains comprises the Birdger Wilderness. These 383,000 acres can be traversed only by foot or by horseback. The renewable resources of these national forest lands are managed in the combination that best meets the needs of the American people. The Wind River Mountian country provides some of the best fishing in the United States. There is also good hunting for elk, deer, moose, bighorn sheep, and bear.

Six major lakes just outside of the wilderness are being developed by the Forest Service to provide picnic and camp sites. Tourist accomodations are available in the Pinedale area. Additional information on this area may be obtained from the Chamber of Commerce or the Forest Ranger in Pinedale.

M WildHorse Realty
1003 W. Pine St., Pinedale. 367-6631 or (800) 544-4187. www.wildhorserealty.com; agentbarb@wyoming.com

Newly established in 2004, the dynamic WildHorse Realty serves as Sublette County's freshest real estate agency. Broker/Owner Barb Hodges has the insight and perspective to smoothly ride customers through all real estate ventures. Featured on the MLS and statewide listing service, the brokerage is capable of representing any Wyoming real estate transaction. From vacant land to starter homes, sprawling ranches to log cabins, WildHorse Realty possesses the properties, motivation, and professional and resourceful nature to fit you into your piece of Cowboy Country. The brokerage is hungry to serve both buyers and sellers, and their service-oriented approach provides customers with the security of trust and reliability for personalized real estate service. If the call of the real west is beckoning you, visit WildHorse Realty and Barb Hodges for all your real estate needs.

The Wind River

M Missy Mcamis, Realtor®
Pinedale. 367-2548 (Home) or 360-7771 (Cell). missinparadise@wyoming.com

Wyoming is the dream of many and reality of few, but for those who do move here, Realtor® Missy Mcamis will guide you home. Involved in real estate most of her adult life and a "Wyoming by Choice" resident for over 15 years, Missy possesses the area knowledge and professional background to lead you to your dream piece of dirt or cabin in the woods. Breathtaking scenery, abundant wildlife, year-round recreation, and more await, and Missy thrives on introducing clients to Wyoming and property that meets their needs. An outdoor lover who designs custom homes for her General Contractor husband, Missy is dedicated to customer service and can help with any of Sublette County's active listings. Call, e-mail, or drop by, and discover Wyoming's beauty with the professional guidance of Realtor® Missy Mcamis!

25 *No services*

Merna
Postmistress Grace Snyder named this post office for her hometown of Merna, Nebraska.

Daniel
Pop. 110, Elev. 7,192

When the post office moved here from the previous site of "Burns" (a problem name, since there was another Burns in Laramie County), it was named for Thomas P. Daniel, the owner of the general store in 1900. About two miles to the

west is old Ft. Bonneville, named for founder Capt. Benjamin L.E. Bonneville. Built in 1832, it became the site of the original Green River Rendezvous, which was held yearly over the next eight years for the exchange of goods between trappers, traders, and Indians. The event is now celebrated in Pinedale. One mile to the east of Daniel is the site of the first Catholic Mass in Wyoming, held by Father Pierre DeSmet in 1840. A monument was built here in 1925.

T Fort Bonneville
Three miles northwest of Daniel

Established in 1832 by Captain Benjamin Bonneville as a fur trading post, the camp consisted of blockhouses bordered by towering log posts. The fort soon became known as "Bonneville's Folly" or "Fort Nonsense". Deep snow and frigid winds made the fort unusable in the winter, and it was abandoned after a little more than a year.

H Astorian Incident
North of 191/189 Junction on U.S. Highway 191/189

On this site, October 18, 1811, sixty one Astorians of the American fur comany, the squaw of Pierre Dorian and her two children, with one hundred and eighteen horses camped for 5 days. They were on their way to the pacific Ocean from Montreal via St. Louis. Here they met, traded and powwowed with the Snake Indians, killed buffalo and cured meat. Continuing their journey, they crossed the divide one mile north of here on to the waters of the Columbia River. These were the first white men in what is now Sublette County.

H Gros Ventre Lodge
About 23 miles north of Cora on State Highway 352

This Lodge, one of the earliest dude ranches in Wyoming, was built on the hill beyond in 1897 by William (Billy) Wells and operated until 1906. It was named for the little Gros Ventre (now tosi Creek) and was locally known as "Dog Ranch" because of the foxhounds Wells kept for hunting. Wile Wells guided

guests on summer trips through the Green River Valley and Bridger National Forest, the Gros Ventre was the most notable as a hunting lodge that served prominent American and British big game sportsmen. The ranch included a central lodge, guest cabins and one of the first wooden bathtubs in western Wyoming.

By 1906, the Gros Ventre was no longer profitable, in part due to the stricter game loaws and a shorter hunting season. It was dismantled that year and the main lodge moved across the Green River and converted into a ranch house.

H Fort Bonneville Sisk-ke-dee Agie (Green river) Oregon 1832
About 3 miles west of Daniel on State Highway 354.

Here, in July, 1832, Captian Benjamin Bonneville erected a fort, two block houses and a stockade, for protection from the Blackfoot Indians. He was on leave from the U. S. Army, with his trapping and exploring group of 110 men and 20 wagons. These were the first wagons to cross Southpass. The party scattered and trapped for several years, doing valuable exploring as far as California and the Columbia River. In the party was the famed Joe Walker, Joe Meeks and many Delaware Indians. The fort, a strategic site, was not used in winter. Bonneville and most of his party returned to Missouri August 22, 1835.

H First Tie Drive on Green River
About 20 miles north of Cora on State Highway 352.

Because timber was scarce in neighboring states along the first transcontinental railroad line, the tie business flourished here and in other Wyoming mountain locations. Ties were cut in winter, stored on the river bank until spring, and floated downstream during high water.

Charles DeLoney was a youthful Michigan Civil War veteran who came to Wyoming after the war. An experienced timberman, he contracted with the Union Pacific Railroad in 1867 to supply ties. A crew of 30 men hauled equipment and supplies upriver and constructed a combined office-bunkhouse-cookshack-commissary building between this marker and the river. Cabins were built high in the timber, forcing the men to snowshoe for meals. DeLoney's was the first drive down the river, a trip of 130 miles. Ties were skidded down nearby mountains and held by a boom across the river until the drive. Another boom at Green River City caught the ties near the railhead. The operation continued successfully for two yars, and newspaper advertisements as late as fall, 1868, solicited tie hacks to work at the head of the Green River.

Charles DeLoney was a versatile person. He was a rancher, a pioneer merchant in jackson and helped found the town of Evanston. He was the state's first forest supervisor and served in Wyoming territorial and state legislatures.

H Prairie of the Mass
About two miles south of Daniel on U.S. Highway 189.

Rev. Pierre DeSmet (1802-73) was born in Belgium but came to America in 1821, joined the Jesuit society and began his work with the Indians. In his work he established sixteen treaties, crossed the ocean nineteen times and traveled 180 thousand miles on his errands of charity for the indians who knew him as the "Sincerest Friend."

On July 5, 1840, in the presence of two thousand Indians, trappers and traders, he offered the first Holy Mass in what is now Wyoming on an altar of native stone decorated with wild flowers. In Father DeSmet's own words, "It was a spectical truly moving to the heart of a missionary that this immense family, composed of so many different tribes should prostrate themselves in equal humility before the "Divine Host." The monument at the site was erected in 1925 and a commemorative mass is offered there annually in July. On July 4, 1940, the one hundredth anniversary of the first Mass, a Pontifical High mass was offered by the Most Rev. Bishop McGovern assisted by more than thirty priests and attended by about two thousand people.

26 *No Services*

Wapiti Valley

A quiet valley named after an Indian word for elk, this little piece of heaven on earth is located between Cody and Yellowstone Park, and is the most direct route to the park from Cody. Its beautiful mountain scenery, volcanic features and abundance of wildlife make travel in the Wapiti Valley a true Western experience.

H Absaroka Volcanic Field
Just west of Wapiti on U.S. Highway 14/16/20.

The valley of the North Fork of the Shoshone River passes through a series of volcanic rocks over 9,000 feet thick covering 3,000 square miles. The rocks include lava, volcanic ash, and other sorts of volcanic material. Agglomerate is a common type and consists of rounded masses of volcanic rock in a finer matrix. Numerous dikes which were feeders for lava flows, show in the canyon walls as thin, narrow bands resembling stone walls. The peculiar castle-like forms are the result of weathering and removal of softer material by water.

H Fire Fighters Memorial
U.S. Highway 14/16/20 about 18 miles west of Wapiti.

Shoshone National Forest Black Water Fire August 20-24, 1937. This marks the beginning of the Fire Fighters' Memorial Trail which follows Black Water Creek five miles to the place of origin of the Fire, and thence to other points of interest. This fire was controlled after burning over 1,254 acres of forest. Fifteen fire fighters lost their lives and thirty nine others were injured when the fire was whipped up by a sudden gale on August 21. Signs and monuments mark the important locations along this trail,

including the fire camps, the first aid station, Clayton Gulch where eight men were killed, and the rocky knoll where Ranger Post gathered his crew to escape the fire.

L UXU Ranch
1710 Yellowstone Hwy., Wapiti. 587-2143 or (800) 373-9027. www.uxuranch.com; info@uxuranch.com

Famous for great western adventure, the UXU Ranch welcomes families, couples, and singles to its mountain retreat year-round. Complete with stunning scenery and a well-traveled host, the UXU Ranch treats guests to deluxe cabins featuring the finest amenities, daily housekeeping, three gourmet meals a day, a selection of over 60 different wines, and evening entertainment ranging from cowboy singing to the Cody Nite Rodeo. Summer days are filled with horseback riding, mountain biking, fishing, float trips, Yellowstone sightseeing, hiking, and more, while winter brings snowshoeing, cross-country skiing, and wildlife viewing. Children's programs are available, and all guests are encouraged to relax in the large hot tub overlooking the Absaroka Mountains. Boasting the comforts of home and adventure of a lifetime, it's obvious why UXU Ranch is repeatedly ranked one of america's best dude ranches!

27 *No services*

Valley

Traces of Valley remain as an old dude ranch named back around 1890 for its location in the valley of the south fork of the Shoshone River. Named by hunter and trapper, James McLaughlin.

Wapiti

Named for the Native American word for elk, Wapiti is a small community of fairly recent settlers, here to enjoy the scenery between Cody and Yellowstone.

T Buffalo Bill State Park
The history of Buffalo Bill Reservoir and "Cody Country" is rooted in the rich lore of the old West. Buffalo Bill State Park was named for Colonel William F. "Buffalo Bill" Cody, famous as a wild

west showman, promoter and developer. He first came to the region in the 1870s as a guide for a survey expedition and spent the next 20 years guiding and sponsoring hunting parties in the area.

"Buffalo Bill" Cody was influential in bringing irrigation and agricultural development into the area and founded the town in 1896 that bears his name. Some of the land now occupied by Buffalo Bill State Park was originally owned by Colonel Cody and was acquired from him by the federal government to implement the reservoir project.

Work began on the dam in 1905. When completed in 1910, it was the highest dam in the world at 325 feet. Buffalo Bill State Park was established in 1957 and provided recreational areas and facilities along the original shoreline. In 1993 an eight year project was completed which raised the crest of the dam 25 feet and increased the reservoir storage capacity. The enlarged reservoir inundated the former recreation areas which required removal of the old park facilities. Buffalo Bill State Park has been redeveloped as part of the project.

Surrounding mountains dominate the scenery at Buffalo Bill State Park. Shoshone Canyon, the location of the dam, is framed by Rattlesnake Mountain to the north and Cedar Mountain (also known as Spirit Mountain) to the south. Further west, along the north shoreline, lies Logan Mountain. The north and south forks of the Shoshone River are divided by Sheep Mountain while prominent on the southern skyline is Carter Mountain. All are part of the Rocky Mountain Absaroka (Ab- Sor'-ka) Range. Elevations vary from approximately 5,400 feet in the state park to over 10,000 feet in the Absarokas.
Reprint of Wyoming State Parks and Historic Sites brochure.

H A Burning Need
Approximately five miles west of Wapiti on U.S. Highway 14.

The Shoshone National Forest provides habitat for more Rocky Mountain bighorn sheep than any other national forest. Grazing on nutritious bunchgrasses, bighorn sheep evolved in open, high visibility habitats near steep, rocky cover, making it easier for sheep to detect and avoid predators.

Due to fire suppression by humans over the past 60 plus years, limber pine, juniper, sagebrush, and other shrubs have increased on seasonal bighorn sheep habitats within the Shoshone National Forest and other portions of range.

In cooperation with the Wyoming game and Fish Department, the Foundation for North American Wild Sheep (FNAWS), and the Wyoming Chapter FNAWS, the US Forest Service has implemented a prescribed burning program, to maintain and improve habitat quality for bighorn sheep. On the slopes of Jim Mountain, bighorns are finding new foraging areas, thanks to this cooperative effort.

Big Piney													
	Jan	Feb	March	April	May	June	July	Aug	Sep	Oct	Nov	Dec	Annual
Average Max. Temperature (F)	25.9	30.6	38.9	50.9	62.1	71.0	80.0	78.4	69.3	57.6	39.6	28.3	52.7
Average Min. Temperature (F)	-5.3	-1.5	8.4	19.6	29.0	36.4	39.7	36.1	27.3	17.7	7.1	-3.1	17.6
Average Total Precipitation (in.)	0.38	0.31	0.44	0.65	1.05	0.92	0.74	0.81	0.84	0.55	0.38	0.40	7.46
Average Total SnowFall (in.)	4.1	4.2	4.3	3.6	1.3	0.2	0.0	0.0	0.7	2.1	4.2	3.9	28.6
Average Snow Depth (in.)	4	5	3	0	0	0	0	0	0	0	1	3	1
Wind Speed (mph / kmh)	6 / 9	6 / 9	7 / 12	8 / 13	8 / 13	8 / 13	8 / 13	7 / 12	7 / 11	6 / 10	6 / 9	6 / 9	
Wind Direction	WSW	WSW	WSW	WSW	WSW	WSW	WSW	WSW	WSW	WSW	WSW	WSW	
Cloud Cover (out of 8)	5.0	5.0	5.1	5.2	5.2	4.2	3.6	3.6	3.6	4.2	4.9	4.6	

The Holy City in the Wapiti Valley.

H Born of Fire and Ice, The Holy City

Approximately eight miles west of Wapiti on U.S. Highway 14.

Resembling a silhouette of the ancient city of Jerusalem, these formations reveal the earth's history in records before human timekeeping. Created millions of years ago by volcanoes, these unique formations reveal a geologic era of chaos and fury. Erosion of these rocks continues to shape the earth's landscape just as it has for the last 50 million years? Fifty million years ago Volcanoes were erupting one afer another with each eruption equalling the magnitude of Mt. St. Helens in 1990. A thick, soupy mixture of rock and ash blanketed the entire region. Known as "breccia", this mixture of rock and ash slowly cooled. Runoff from the streams and gullies began carving through the soft breccia, sculpting these unique rock formations. Wind blew tiny bits of sand and dust at the rock further eroding it. Small streams widened to gullies carving deeper into the breccia on its way down to the river.

H Protection Proves Profitable

Approximately five miles west of Wapiti.

This valley has sustained life for thousands of years. Early Native Americans were drawn here to hunt buffalo, elk, deer, moose sheep and bear. It has always been considered a unique place. The establishment of the nation's first park and timber reserve in the late 1800's spurred angry protests among local settlers. They were outraged that vast tracts of land were no longer available for personal gains. Soon residents realized the profits to made from tourism. A new road through the valley brought more people into the region. While in many other parts of the west resources were being spent for profit, these protected resources would prove profitable for local citizens. Lodges along the byway date back to this early era in our nation's history. The highway, Buffalo Bill Dam and the town of Cody were born from this visionary planning over a century ago. Relish this country, its legends and heros where a window of the "Wild West" remains for future generations.

H Wapiti Ranger Station, First in the Nation

Approximately nine miles west of Wapiti on U.S. Highway 14.

Before you stands the first forest supervisor's headquarters in the country, authorized and built in 1903 with government funds. When the supervisor's headquarters was moved to Cody, Wyoming in 1907, this building became a ranger station. Its unique role in the history of the conservation movement earned this station status on the National Register of Historic Places.

Originally a log structure, the Wapiti Ranger Station has expanded as the Forest Service mission evolved. It is still a hub of Forest Service activity today with men and women performing a variety of duties.

The life of the nation's first forest ranger wasn't easy. Early advertisements for these positions read: "A ranger must be able to take care of himself and his horses under very trying conditions, build trails and cabins, ride all day and night. Pack, shoot and fight fire without losing his head. All this requires a very vigorous constitution…the hardest kind of physical work from beginning to end."

C.G. Poole, North Fork District Ranger - 1908

H Castle Rock

About 18 miles southwest of Cody on South Fork Road.

John Colter, famed among the famous breed of "Mountain Men", passed this landmark late in the fall of 1807 while on business for the fur trader Manuel Lisa. Searching for Indians in order to conduct trade, he also hunted salt caves reputedly located near headwaters of this stream, then known as the "stinking water".

Wyoming Tidbits

Gannett Peak, at 13,804 feet in elevation, is Wyoming's highest peak. Located on the crest of the Continental Divide in the central Rockies, the peak was discovered by American explorer Henry Gannett.

On his journey Colter not only discovered this later named Shoshone River but he also became the first recorded white man to visit the upper Wind River, Jackson's Hole and Yellowstone Park. His lonely trek, compunding the normal dangers of savage wilderness by mid-winter passage of a broad and lofty mountain range, lives in history and legend an epic of fortitudinous exploration.

28 *No services*

H Shoshone National Forest Blackwater Fire August 20-24, 1937

Just east of Yellowstone East Gate on U.S. Highway 14.

This marks the beginning of the fire fighters' memorial trail which follows Blackwater Creek five miles to the place of origin of the fire, and thence to other points of interest. This fire was controlled after burning over 1,254 acres of forest. Fifteen fire fighters lost their lives and thirty nine others were injured when the fire was whipped up by a sudden gale on August 21. Signs and monuments mark the important locations along this trail, including the fire camps. The first aid station, Clayton Gulch where eight men were killed and the rocky knoll where Ranger Post gathered his crew to escape the fire.

H A Day in the Life of an Early Forest Ranger

Approximately nine miles west of Wapiti on U.S. Highway 14.

Early rangers faced immense challenges. Due to lack of trained forest rangers, early national forests were the training grounds for "men who were to range far and wide over the nation's forests." A "jack of all trades", these rangers had to be innovative, resourceful and persuasive. Their duties on any given day could include a diversity of tasks, as a journal records: July l901 : "I was offered a job in July, 1901 as a forest ranger on the Shoshone Division of the Yellowstone Timberland Reserve. The rangers job was only for the summer months and paid $60 per month with nothing furnished. I had not only to furnish the necessary pack and saddle animals, camp equipment and supplies, but also the necessary tools with which to work. My duties consisted largely in patrolling to prevent trespass of all kinds and to suppress such forest fires as occured." Sept. 1902. I found a bunch of sheep about a mile up Elk Fork. The owners, on being questioned, stated he was looking for range for his sheep, but decided to move when the matter was explained to him". June 1905: "One of my many duties as ranger in those early years, as now, was the inforcement of State fish and game laws. This caused some confusion and controversy for a few years, but a more wholesome respect for and compliance with state game laws and Federal regulations were soon established."

Oct. 1905: "My district was bordered on the west by Yellowstone National Park and I spent considerable time in that part of the district in the fall during the hunting season and watching for fires."

June 1906: "The weekly mail brought into the basin news of the passage of this new Homestead Law. Immediately one of the settlers adjoining the ranger station came down to the station and ordered me to move, stating that he was taking the ranger station as a homestead. After some discussion he became convinced that I was not going to be forcibly evicted, so he went home rather disgruntled."

J.W. Nelson, Ranger on the Shoshone July, 1901 - March, 1907

H Dead Indian Summit Altitude 8,000 Feet

Chief Joseph Scenic Highway about 13 miles west of junction with State Highway 120.

This pass is the summit of Dead Indian Hill. Through this portal great herds of wild game seasonally migrated from the mountains to the plains. This high pass was the gate way for countless indian hunting and war parties, and through this portal Chief Joseph, in 1877, led his Nez Perce Indians in a strategic and defensive retreat, persued by U.S. Army soldiers. Over this one and only opening of the valleys to the west traveled a vast army of miners to seek wealth of cooke city, and down this steep hill the early settlers of Sunlight Basin braved its dangers. the first road improvement was made possible in 1909, by dwellers of Sunlight Valley whose names are here inscribed. Adophus J. Beam, William V. Campbell, Siras J. Davis, Oliver Whitney, Hervey g. Marvin, Samual Thompson, Mary E. Painter, Wm. T. Painter, Marguerita M. Painter, Wade M. McClung, Augustus A. Lafond, John R. Painter, Evelyn T. Painter, John K. Rollinson, Willard D. Ruscher.

SCENIC DRIVES

Chief Joseph Scenic Byway

This scenic byway, on Wyoming 296, links the town of Cody with the Beartooth Highway and the Northeast Gate of Yellowstone National Park. The route crosses the Shoshone National Forest through the Absaroka Mountains to the Clarks Fork Valley. The 47 paved miles of the Scenic Byway run from the junction with US 120, 17 miles north of Cody, northwest to their connection with US 212, the Beartooth Highway. The Beartooth Mountains and the Clarks Fork of the Yellowstone River lie to the north of the road, and the Absaroka Mountains and North Absaroka Wilderness are to the south. Allow one hour minimum driving time over this stretch of Byway.

The most predictable times to travel this highway are during the summer and fall. During the winter months snow plows keep the roadway open to just east of the entrance to Yellowstone National Park. The road is at times steep and winding, and boasts the highest highway bridge in Wyoming - over Sunlight Creek. The road crests at 8060-foot Dead Indian Pass. The Pass is a good place to observe some 25 rugged peaks rising more than 12,000 feet above sea level.

Reprinted from Wyoming Department of Transportation Brochure

Beartooth Scenic Byway

On US 212, this is the most northern route across the Shoshone National Forest in the Beartooth Mountains. The 70 miles of the Scenic Byway run from Red Lodge, Montana to the eastern border of Yellowstone National Park. Beginning at Red Lodge, the Absaroka-Beartooth Wilderness and the Custer and Gallatin National Forests lie to the north as the road heads southwest into Wyoming. The North Absaroka Wilderness lies to the south as the road follows the Clarks Fork of the Yellowstone River toward Yellowstone Park. Allow at least three hours driving time from Red Lodge to Yellowstone Park on this Byway.

US 212 is the highest paved, primary road in Wyoming, cresting at 10, 947-foot Beartooth Pass. The scenery along this two-lane paved highway proves that the beauty of Yellowstone National Park does not diminish at its borders. The alpine country and high mountain lakes are accessible to highway travel only from late May to mid-October due to heavy snows.

Growing in the wet meadows, you may see Indian Paintbrush, monkey flower, senecio and buttercups. Lupines, arrow leaf, balsamroot, beard-stongue, and forget-me-nots are found in drier areas. Snow banks often remain until August near Beartooth Pass, and some remnants of drifts may remain all summer. A pink color often appears on the snow later in the summer, caused by the decay of microscopic plants that grow on the surface of the snow.

Reprinted from Wyoming Department of Transportation Brochure

Buffalo Bill Cody Scenic Byway

This byway, along US 14/16/20, follows the North Fork of the Shoshone River through scenic Wapiti Valley to the East Entrance of Yellowstone National Park. The 27 mile segment of paved road starts about 25 miles west of Cody at the Shoshone National Forest border. Normal driving time from the forest boundary to the Park is approximately 45 minutes.

Reprinted from Wyoming Department of Transportation Brochure

Centennial Scenic Byway

The 163 miles between Pinedale and Dubois, via Jackson, comprise the Centennial Scenic Byway. This horseshoe-shaped combination of highways includes US 26/287 and US 26/89/191. The route crosses diverse landscapes from badlands and ranch land to forests and mountain passes. It traverses Fremont, Teton, and Sublette counties in northwestern Wyoming.

The entire route is open year-round and could be driven straight through in about four hours, but few people do so because of the many attractions and outstanding scenery that make this region of Wyoming one of the top tourist destinations in America. Among other things, there are more moose, beaver, and greater sand hill cranes along this route than any other place in the Rocky Mountains. Coyotes, ravens, badgers, Swainson's hawks, and Northern harriers can be seen in the summer. During the winter, mule deer, magpies and cottontail rabbits can often be spotted.

The northern end of the Byway begins at Dubois, on Us 26/287, while the southern end of the tours begins at Pinedale on US 191. The route follows a modern, two-lane, paved highway that crosses the Continental Divide and crests at an elevation of 9658 feet at Togwotee (Toe-ga-tee) Pass. From Dubois, a 39-mile stretch meets US 26-89-191 at Moran Junction. From there the Byway takes a mostly southerly route through the town of Jackson, to Hoback Junction and Bondurant before reaching its conclusion at Pinedale. Many side roads to the area's diverse attractions can be accessed from this Byway.

Reprinted from Wyoming Department of Transportation Brochure

Buffalo Valley Road

A great drive to view moose in the winter and access Teton Wilderness trailheads. Also offers wonderful views of the Teton Range. Buffalo Valley Road is a 14 mile scenic by-way of US 26/287. It intersects the highway three miles east of Moran and is paved for ten miles to Turpin Meadows. The last four miles are gravel and is not plowed during the winter.

Fall Creek Road

A scenic alternative for those heading south from Jackson. Fall Creek Road connects Wilson with the Snake River Canyon. Varied habitats and bird watching opportunities make this 18 mile by-way an excellent choice. Twelve miles south of Wilson are paved, the remainder of the road is graveled or natural surface. The road is generally in good condition and clearance is not a problem. Fishing and hiking opportunities can also be found.

Greys River Road "Watch me Grow"

Following the river for 58 miles provides an excellent opportunity to watch a small stream become a river. Camping, fishing, hiking, horseback riding, hunting and wildlife viewing are all popular activities. The gravel and natural surface road climbs gradually from Alpine to Tri-Basin Divide. Although passable to low-clearance vehicles, the upper ten miles can be rough or slick when wet. Several other Forest Service roads connect to Greys River Road, accessing Afton, Big Piney and LaBarge.

Hams Fork Road

A 66 mile road between Kemmerer and Cokeville. The first 20 miles from Kemmerer are paved; the remainder of the road is gravel or natural surface. There are some rough places, but driven with care, clearance is not a problem. The road follows the Hams Fork River–named after mountain man Zacharias Ham. There are many scenic views along the road and moose are frequently seen.

Hatchet/Flagstaff Road

Offering splendid views of Buffalo Valley and the Teton Range, there is also the meadows, sagebrush and forested areas.

A 19 mile long scenic by-way of US 26/287. The west end of the road is at the Hatchet Campground, next to the Buffalo Forest Service office, and returns to the highway two miles east of the Cowboy Village Resort at Togwotee. The road is also popular with mountain bikers and snowmobilers in the winter.

LaBarge Road

Attractions include a spring with travertine deposits, the Lander Cut-Off Trail and wildflower meadows.

The 48-mile road follows the river named for mountain man Joseph M. LaBarge. The first 11 miles from LaBarge are paved, while the remaining 37 miles are gravel or natural surface.

McDougal Gap Road

Crossing the Wyoming Range and connecting the Green and Greys Rivers, the scenery along this by-way can't be beaten. From the agricultural lands to the subalpine forests, tremendous habitat diversity is passed through and many recreation opportunities await.

Bighorn sheep crossing on the Buffalo Bill Scenic Highway.

McDougal Gap Road meets US 189 south of Daniel and intersects the Greys River Road one mile north of Forest Park-a distance of 35 miles.The 12 mile Forest portion is gravel or natural surface and some sections can be rough.The road is usually snow covered until early July.

Middle Piney Road

A scenic drive passing two campgrounds ending at Middle Piney Lake is great for boating and fishing. Several Forest Service roads and trails can be accessed from the Middle Piney Road.

The road begins as WY 350 in Big Piney and is paved for 11 miles. It is another 9 miles to the Forest boundary, and then 6 miles to Middle Piney Lake, a total distance of 26 miles.The last mile of road is usually not open until early July.

Skyline Drive

A short, 16 mile paved road to the popular Trail's End Campground and Trailhead offering spectacular views of the Wind River Range. Skyline Drive climbs into the mountains from Pinedale. Between Pinedale and Trail's End are several scenic overlooks and roads to Fremont and Halfmoon Lake to explore.

Smith's Fork Road

Connecting Upper Star Valley to the Greys River Road, Smith's Fork offers a scenic diversion for those traveling US 89.The 22 mile road is natural surface which can be rough on passenger vehicles.

Smith's Fork Road joins US 89 6.5 miles south of Smoot and two miles north of Salt River Pass.The road connects with the Greys River Road at Tri-Basin Divide. From here you may also head southeast towards LaBarge.

Union Pass

Crossing the north end of the Wind River Range and two National Forests, the 60 mile Union Pass Road offers spectacular scenery and many recreation opportunities. Wyoming 352, off US 191 north of Pinedale, takes you to the Forest boundary where the pavement ends.The Union Pass Road branches off at the Kendall Bridge, 3 miles north of the Forest boundary. Signed intersections help navigate you over Union Pass to US 26 north of Dubois.The road is gravel or natural surface.There can be a few rough spots, a high clear-

ance vehicle is recommended. There are many side roads off the Union Pass road that should be explored, especially Green River Lakes.

HIKES

Teton Area

Huckleberry Mountain

Distance: 10 miles (round trip)
Climb: 2000 feet
Rating: moderate/ difficult
Usage: moderate
Location: The trail begins at Sheffield Creek Trailhead, 1 mile southeast of Flagg Ranch between Grand Teton and Yellowstone National Parks.

Breathtaking views of the Tetons, Yellowstone National Park, and the surrounding wilderness reward those undertaking this climb. Huckleberry Lookout is listed on the National Register of Historic Places. Fire lookouts lived here in the summer, keeping a watchful eye for fires.

Jenny Lake Trails

Distance: about 2 to 7 miles
Climb: gentle/ moderate
Rating: easy/ moderate
Usage: heavy
Location: Travel north on Hwy. 191 about 12 miles from Jackson to Moose Junction. Turn left, and follow the Teton Park Rd. west and north to South Jenny Lake Junction. The trailhead is by the boat dock.

Several trails go around Jenny Lake, and diverge from it as well. The most popular hike is the one leading to Hidden Falls and Inspiration Point. The trail winds west and somewhat south around the lake, splitting at a junction that leads to Moose Ponds about 3/4 mile away. The trail forks again a little farther along, but both forks lead to the falls eventually. The trails crisscross and intersect around Cascade Creek, which can be followed upstream to Hidden Falls. Don't worry about getting confused about which trail to go on. There are usually lots of people around to point you in the right direction. Continue across the creek to proceed to Inspiration Point, where there is a lovely view of the Tetons and Jenny Lake. These portions of the hike are more strenuous, due to the uphill climb of about 500 feet elevation gain. You can continue to follow the creek upstream for another 4.5 miles to Cascade Canyon (making this an overnight hike), or head back to the lake and

return back the way you came. You can also take the ferry back across the lake, or take the boat from the East Shore Boat Dock to this point, and hike back. Another option is to finish circling the lake, and take the trail north to the base of String Lake, then follow it down the east side of Jenny Lake for another 2.9 miles back to the boat dock.

Leigh and String Lakes Trails

Distance: about 3 to 4 miles
Climb: gentle
Rating: easy
Usage: moderate
Location: Travel north on Hwy. 191 about 12 miles from Jackson to Moose Junction. Turn left, and follow the Teton Park Rd. west and north to the String Lake Picnic Area.

These trails are less well known than the Jenny Lake Trails, so they are usually less crowded, but still offer lovely views. The trail heads north from the picnic area, following the edge of String Lake and continuing up and around Leigh Lake to Trapper and Bear Paw Lakes, about 3.7 miles, or a fork at the top of String Lake takes you west for about 0.8 miles to another junction. The trail continues northwest for 4.5 miles to Holly Lake, or heads south, back to String Lake, and eventually to the road leading to the picnic area, about a 1.6 mile trek. This route also intersects with the Jenny Lake Trail (or Valley Trail) at the southern tip of String Lake.

Bradley and Taggart Lakes Trails

Distance: about 3 to 7 miles
Climb: moderate
Rating: moderate
Usage: moderate
Location: These trails can be accessed from two points. The first is at Lupine Meadows Parking Area, just south of Jenny Lake Junction, and the other is about 3 miles farther south on Teton Park Road, at Taggart Lake Trailhead. Teton Park Road is just off of Hwy. 191, about 12 miles north of Jackson, west at Moose Junction.

This area was burned by forest fires in 1985, but much re-growth has taken place since then. Grasses, flowering plants, small trees, and an abundance of wildlife populate the area now. The Lupine Meadow segment of the trail traverses about 1.7 miles before it forks to the west and south. The west branch goes another 3.1 miles to the Amphitheater and Surprise Lakes. The south branch heads towards the lakes, crossing the top of Bradley Lake then forking again below the lake at 1.3 miles. The right fork follows the shoreline of Taggart Lake, while the left fork heads cross country, about one mile either way. The shoreline trail has two more junctions, the first being a choice between crossing the south tip of the lake or doubling back to the cross-country trail. The second offers a detour to Phelps Lake, another 6.1 miles of travel (definitely overnight), or returns east to again connect with the cross-country trail, which terminates at the Taggart Lake Trailhead.

Phelps Lake Trails

Distance: about 3 to 7 miles
Climb: gentle/ steep
Rating: moderate
Usage: light
Location: Travel north on Hwy. 191 about 12 miles from Jackson to Moose Junction. Go west at the junction, and turn left when the road forks, taking the Moose/Wilson Road. Take a right about 3 miles south to the Death Canyon Trailhead. This is a narrow, winding road, and is closed to RV's, trailers, and buses.

This trail (the Valley Trail) goes either northeast, towards Taggart Lake for about 4 miles, or you can head west , towards Phelps Lake and its surrounding area. The west trail goes gradually up for about a mile to the Phelps Lake Lookout, where you will find a panoramic view of wet meadows, aspen groves, and the lake. Several switchbacks take you down to the lake, making for a strenuous return climb. About midway, the Death Canyon Trail intersects with the Valley Trail, which leads to the Death Canyon Patrol Cabin, about 3.7 miles farther west. This is a good place to turn around for a day hike. You can continue on the Death Canyon Trail another 9.2 miles, climbing about 3000 feet over the highest point of public trails in the park, to arrive at Static Peak. This is a not a technical climb, but it is strenuous, and would require a permit and at least an overnight stay.

Continuing on the Valley Trail, about a mile farther south of the Death Canyon Junction, the trail forks again, the left fork following the shoreline, and the right fork taking a scenic loop towards the Open Canyon Trail. The Valley Trail, which originates at Jenny Lake, continues on south to the Granite Canyon Trailhead, another 3.5 miles below Phelps Lake.

Hermitage Point Trails

Distance: 3 or 4 miles
Climb: flat
Rating: easy
Usage: moderate/heavy
Location: Travel north of Jackson about 25 miles to the Colter Bay turn off. Park at the Colter Bay Visitor Center.

These trails meander around the eastern shore of Jackson Lake, encompassing Swan Lake, Heron Pond, and the Second and Third Creek areas. As the names indicate, this is prime bird-watching territory, as well as ideal for viewing elk, moose, beaver, otters, and other wildlife. The most popular trail is a loop which follows the shore of Jackson Lake for about a half mile, cuts between Heron Pond and Swan Lake for about one mile, then returns a little farther east. An alternative 4.5 mile trail from Jackson Lake Lodge ends at the horse corrals of Colter Bay. Other trails continue south, both along Jackson Lake and around the other nearby bodies of water. Some trails may be closed to allow for revegetation so please observe the signs. Further information on the trails can be obtained at the visitor center.

Jackson Area

Black Canyon Overlook Trail

Distance: 2 miles
Climb: gentle
Rating: easy
Usage: moderate
Location: From Jackson follow Hwy. 222 west to the summit of Teton Pass. Park at the south side turnout. The trailhead is well marked at the parking area.

This trail follows the ridge south of the pass, through sub-alpine meadows and forest, with views of Jackson Hole and the surrounding mountains. Wildflowers of all kinds can be seen throughout the summer along this trail. To make a loop on the trail, follow it on Black Canyon to the end of Trail Creek Road at the bottom of the pass. This option requires a shuttle from the bottom of Teton Pass back to the parking area.

Cache Creek Trail #3025

Distance: 6 miles
Climb: gentle
Rating: easy
Usage: heavy
Location: From the Town Square, travel east on Broadway to Redmond St. Follow Redmond to Cache Creek Drive, then go the parking lot at the end.

This hike is very close to town, and offers stunning views of the town and surrounding area. The trail follows an old road and has a consistent and gentle grade. The creek flows along the entire trail and is easily accessed at various points. During the summer months you may see moose, deer, elk, and other wildlife. This easy hike is great for the whole family, but plan for it to take the better part of a day. The Tiny Hagen and Putt Putt Trails both diverge from the Cache Creek Trail. Either trail can be followed downhill to the parking lot. Both trails are more strenuous than the Cache Creek Trail, adding as much as two hours to the total travel time.

Granite Creek Falls Trail

Distance: 2 miles
Climb: gentle
Rating: easy
Usage: moderate
Location: From Jackson follow Hwy. 89 south to Hoback Junction. Go east on Hwy 191 about 11 miles to Granite Creek Road, and turn left. Follow this road to a parking area at the junction of Swift Creek and Granite Creek. Parking is also available at Granite Hot Springs. From there, follow the trail downstream on the east side to the falls.

This trail follows the east side of Granite Creek upstream to the falls. Continuing up the trail you will reach Granite Hot Springs, open year round. A fee is required to take a dip in the springs. Beyond this point the trail goes on to the Gros Ventre Wilderness. No bicycles are permitted beyond the wilderness border.

Ski Lake Trail

Distance: 3 miles
Climb: moderate
Rating: moderate
Usage: moderate
Location: From Jackson travel west on Hwy. 22 up Teton Pass to an unmarked dirt road, about 4 miles west of Hungry Jack Store. There is no developed trailhead. Parking is on the dirt road or across the highway. Walk up the road about 1/2 mile to fork. Go left to sign board, where trail begins.

This trail follows a side slope to a rocky viewpoint with spectacular views of the Snake River Range and Jackson Hole. From there, the trail enters the forest and emerges in a meadow. A sign marks the trail junction. Go left to Ski Lake, climbing through forest and open slopes to the beautiful alpine lake. Then, go right to Phillips Pass, which follows another side slope through pine and aspen stands, and avalanche chutes, then drops in elevation to Phillips Canyon. The trail then climbs into sub-alpine meadows and up to Phillips Pass. This is a great place to see midsummer wildflowers.

East Table Trail

Distance: 2 miles
Climb: steep

Rating: moderate
Usage: light
Location: From Jackson, follow Hwy. 89 south about 20 miles along the Snake River to East Table Campground. The trailhead is located across the highway from the campground. Parking is available here.

This trail follows the steep, narrow canyon of East Table Creek, which quickly turns into a branched, intermittent drainage. The trail continues up a slope to the west and through meadows to a flat bench, from which there are spectacular views of the Snake River Canyon and the mountains to the south. Beyond this overlook, the trail continues through meadows and climbs steeply to the east side of a long ridge, which eventually meets the Red Pass Trail at Wolf Mountain. This section of the trail is not well marked or maintained, but the view makes the climb worthwhile. This option adds considerable time and distance to the hike.

Snow King Trail

Distance: 5 miles
Climb: steep
Rating: moderate/ difficult
Usage: heavy
Location: This trail is accessed at the bottom of the Snow King chairlift. From the Town Square in Jackson, travel south on South Cache to the Snow King Ski Area. Parking is available at the bottom of the ski hill.

This trail is basically the service road for Snow King Mountain. It switches back up the ski slope to the top of the ridge, where there is a shelter and view area. Many tracks take off in other directions along the way. The view of the Jackson Hole area is spectacular. The chairlift operates in the summer, so hikers can either hike up and ride down, or vice versa. On top of Snow King there is also a well-marked nature trail.

Grizzly Lake Trail

Distance: 3.5 miles
Climb: steep
Rating: moderate
Usage: light
Location: From Jackson, travel north on Hwy. 89/191 for about 6 miles to Gros Ventre Road and turn right. Continue on this road through the town of Kelly, about one mile, then turn right again on Gros Ventre Road and go about 11 miles to the Red Hills Campground. Parking is available here.

This trail is well marked and easy to follow. Along the way it crosses several slopes and deep drainages, so the first two miles are strenuous. High points along the way offer terrific views of the Red Hills and the Gros Ventre River Valley. At the junction with the Blue Miner Lake Trail, the trail levels off and drops into the basin of Grizzly Lake.

THE ASTORIANS

The first white men to cross an established Indian trail in what is today's Sublette County. They were the Astorians, led by explorer Wilson Price Hunt, in 1811, employees of John Jacob Astor and the American Fur Company. The party was seeking to establish cross-continental routes for the fur trade. While camping near present day Pinedale, they met and traded with Snake Indians. Here they gathered buffalo meat for the journey ahead. A small but steady stream of fur trappers and traders followed on their heels in the years that followed. The fur trade expanded rapidly during the 1820s and brought to Wyoming William H. Ashley who came up with the idea to have an annual rendezvous instead of trying to maintain a series of permanent trading posts. The annual Rendezvous was held at a different location each year and brought mountain men and natives together for fun and trade. Other lively mountain men such as Jim Bridger, John Hoback, Jedediah Smith, Bill Sublette, David E. Jackson, and Robert Campbell were also known to work the area. Increasing competition with the Hudson's Bay and American Fur companies depleted the beaver catch and brought an end to the fur trade by the 1840s.

Willow Creek Trail

Distance: 5 miles
Climb: steep
Rating: difficult
Usage: light/ moderate.
Location: From Jackson, travel south on Hwy. 89 to Hoback Junction, then go east on Hwy. 191 about 5 miles to FDR 30460, and turn right by the moose statue. Travel 1.5 miles down dirt road to the parking area at the right, with sign board and information.

This trail skirts a fence on a sagebrush-covered slope west of the trailhead, then climbs through open forest and meadows to a ridge overlooking Willow Creek. At the ridge, the trail forks. To stay on this trail, follow the sign, and at the base of the hill, turn left to follow Willow Creek. When it reaches Lick Creek, turn left again and follow the Wyoming Spur Trail to the ridge, then back on same trail to the trailhead. If you want to add another 1/3 mile to the trek, turn right at the top of the ridge, and head for the top of Ann's Mountain. You will return by the same route.

Shoal Falls Overlook

Distance: 5 miles
Climb: steep
Rating: difficult
Usage: light
Location: From Jackson, follow Hwy. 89 south to Hoback Junction. Go east on Hwy. 191 about 11 miles to Granite Creek Road, and turn left. Follow this road to a parking area at the junction of Swift Creek and Granite Creek. A sign indicates the trailhead.

This trail follows an old two-track road for the first half mile, then turns south and angles up a forested side slope, which reaches a dissected bench at the base of the Gros Ventre Mountains. The trail continues to Deer Ridge, where you'll find the overlook for Shoal Falls, then drops into Shoal Creek. To reach the falls, you need to follow the creek upstream, off the trail, about 1.5 miles.

Alpine Area

Bailey Lake

Distance: 4.5 miles from Waterdog Lake, 5.5 from McCain Guard Station.
Location: To reach the trailheads, follow the Greys River Road 7 1/2 miles east from Alpine, to the Little Greys River Road Junction. After approximately 12 miles on the Little Greys River Road, you will reach a turn-off for McCain Guard Station. The next intersection, reached in 2.5 miles, goes left to the guard station or right to Waterdog Lake.

This is a great!little lake for fishing or bird watching and solitude.

Pinedale Area

CCC Ponds

Distance: short
Location: The trailhead is located near Sandy Beach, off Skyline Drive, 2.5 miles north of Pinedale.

This is a short hike, to peaceful ponds close to the town of Pinedale. The ponds offer good fishing and excellent wildlife observation opportunities. The trail is paved, suitable for wheelchairs; benches along the way provide rest spots.

Cliff Creek Falls

Distance: 12.4 miles (round trip)
Location: The Cliff Creek Road leaves US 189/191 15 miles east of Hoback Junction or 5 miles west of Bondurant. Follow the gravel road 7.1 miles to the trailhead.

A beautiful two-tiered waterfall, Cliff Creek has a short upper falls followed by a fifty-foot plunge. The hike to the falls and return requires a full day. This is also a popular mountain bike ride.

Fontenelle Lakes

Distance: varies
Climb: varies
Rating: moderate
Usage: moderate/ heavy
Location: There are two trailheads on the LaBarge Road. The South LaBarge Trailhead is located a few miles from Scalar Guard Station. The Shaffer Creek Trailhead has a horse corral and larger parking lot.

A cluster of small lakes in the scenic Fontenelle Basin, the Fontanelle Lakes can be explored by horseback, mountain biking, or on foot. The South LaBarge Trail is an uphill climb. The Shaffer Creek Trail is less steep.

Monument Ridge

Distance: 10 miles (round trip)
Climb: 440 feet
Rating: moderate
Usage: light
Location: The trailhead is accessed from Clark's Draw Road (Forest Road 30530) two miles east of Bondurant. When the road forks at 1/2 mile, follow the right fork to the road's end. The road is natural surface and often in poor condition.

A panoramic view rewards those undertaking this gentle climb through aspen forests and wildflower meadows.

INFORMATION PLEASE

Tourism Information

Big Piney/Marbleton Chamber of Commerce
276-3815
Dubois Chamber of Commerce ... 789-2757
Chamber of Commerce of Jackson ... 733-3316
Chamber of Commerce - Pinedale ... 367-2242

Government

BLM Pinedale Field Office	367-5300
Shoshone National Forest - Wind River Ranger District	455-2466
Bridger-Teton National Forest	739-5400
Bridger-Teton National Forest - Big Piney Ranger District	543-2386
Bridger-Teton National Forest - Greys River Ranger District	885-3166
Bridger-Teton National Forest - Jackson Ranger District	739-5400
Bridger-Teton National Forest - Pinedale Ranger District	367-4326

Car Rentals

Aspen Rent-A-Car • Jackson		733-9224
Alamo Rent A Car • Jackson Hole		733-0671
Budget • Jackson Hole		733-2206
Dollar Rent A Car • Jackson		733-9224
Eagle Rent A Car • Jackson		739-9999
Hertz • Jackson		733-2272
Leisure Sports Car Rental • Jackson		733-3040
Thrifty • Jackson		739-9300

Hospitals

Alpine Clinic • Alpine	654-7138
St John's Medical Center • Jackson	733-3636
Teton Village Clinic St John's Medical Center • Teton Village	739-7346

Airports

Big Piney	276-3386
Dubois	455-3339
Jackson Hole	733-5454
Pinedale	367-4151

Golf

Valli Vu Golf Club • Afton	886-3338
Antelope Hills Golf Course • Dubois	455-2888
Rendezvous Meadows Public Golf Course • Pinedale	746-2639
Teton Pines Country Club • Jackson	733-1733
Jackson Hole Golf & Tennis Club • Jackson	733-3111
Aspen Hills at Star Valley Ranch Country Club • Thayne	883-2230

Ski Areas

White Pine Ski Area & Resort	367-6606
Jackson Hole	733-3990
Grand Targhee Ski & Summer Resort	353-2300

Guest Ranches

UXU Ranch • Tie Siding	587-2143
MacKenzie Highland Ranch • Dubois	455-3415
Absaroka Ranch • Dubois	455-2275
Box R Ranch	367-4868
Jensen's Guest Ranch • Afton	886-3401
Box Y Lodge & Guest Ranch • Alpine	654-7564
Sheep Mountain Outfitters • Alpine	654-7564
Preston Ranch • Bedford	883-2742
High Wild & Lonesome • Big Piney	276-3208
Wood Canyon Retreat • Big Piney	276-5441
Darby Mountain Outfitters, Inc • Big Piney	386-9220
Triple Peak • Big Piney	276-3408
Boulder Lake Lodge • Boulder	537-5400
Green River Guest Ranch • Cora	367-2314
Flying U Ranch • Cora	367-4479
David Ranch • Daniel	859-8228
CM Ranch • Dubois	455-2331
Ring Lake Ranch • Dubois	455-2663
T Cross Ranch • Dubois	455-2206
Lazy L & B Ranch • Dubois	455-2839
Moose Head Ranch • Dubois	733-3141
Triangle C Ranch • Dubois	455-2225
Bitterroot Ranch • Dubois	545-3363
Crooked Creek Guest Ranch • Dubois	545-3035
Elk Trails Riding Ranch • Dubois	545-3615
Double Bar J Ranch • Dubois	545-2681
Mill Iron 4 Mill Guest Ranch • Dubois	545-3478
Triple E Ranch • Dubois	555-2304
EA Ranch • Dubois	455-3335
Haderlie's Tincup Mountain Guest Ranch • Freedom	208-873-2368
Split Creek Ranch • Jackson	733-7522
Jackson's Hole Adventure • Jackson	654-7849
Mill Iron Ranch • Jackson	733-6390
A-OK Corral • Jackson	733-6556
Beard Mountain Ranch • Jackson	576-2694
Darwin Ranch • Jackson	733-5588
Flat Creek Ranch • Jackson	733-0603
Goosewing Ranch • Jackson	733-5251
Spotted Horse Ranch • Jackson	733-2097
Spring Creek Ranch • Jackson	733-8833
R Lazy S Ranch • Kelly	733-2655
Red Rock Ranch • Kelly	733-6288
Gros Ventre River Ranch • Moose	733-4138
Triangle X Ranch • Moose	733-2183
Cottonwoods Ranch • Moose	733-0945
Lost Creek Ranch • Moose	733-3435
Cowboy Village at Togwotee • Moran	733-8800
Togwotee Mountain Lodge • Moran	543-2847
Box K Ranch • Moran	543-2407

Flagg Ranch & Village • Moran		543-2861
Turpin Meadow Ranch • Moran		543-2000
Diamond D Ranch Outfitters • Moran		543-2479
Heart 6 Ranch • Moran/Jackson Hole		543-2477
Flying A Ranch • Pinedale		367-2385
Fort William Guest Ranch• Pinedale		367-4670
Green River Outfitters • Pinedale		367-2416
Pinedale Creek Ranch • Pinedale		367-2544
DC Bar Guest Ranch • Pinedale		367-2268
Fort William • Pinedale		367-4670
Crossed Sabres Ranch • Wapati		587-3750
Rocking D River Ranch • Wapati		587-8329
Sweetwater Lodge • Wapati		527-7817
Trail Creek Ranch • Wilson		733-2610

Lodges and Resorts

Twin Pines Lodge & Cabins • Dubois		455-2600
The Virginian Lodge & Restaurant • Jackson		733-2792
The Lodge at Pinedale • Pinedale		367-8800
Lakeside Lodge Resort & Marina on Fremont Lake • Pinedale		367-2221
Half Moon Lake Resort • Pinedale		367-6373
Jackson Hole Resort Lodging • Teton Village		733-3990
Star Valley Ranch Resorts & RV Camping • Thayne		883-2670
Silver Stream Lodge & Cabins • Afton		883-2440
Box Y Lodge & Guest Ranch • Alpine		654-7564
Royal Resort • Alpine		654-7545
Sheep Mountain Outfitters • Alpine		654-7564
Snake River Resort and RV Park • Alpine		674-7340
Teton Teepee Lodge • Alta		353-8176
Boulder Lake Lodge • Boulder		537-5400
Elk Ridge Lodge • Cora		367-2553
Rendezvous on the Green • Cora		367-2278
Chinook Winds Mountain Lodge • Dubois		455-2987
Brooks Lake Lodge • Dubois		455-2121
Lake's Lodge, Inc. • Dubois		455-2171
Camp Creek Inn & Fine Dining • Hoback Junction		733-3099
Rusty Parrot Lodge & Spa • Jackson		733-2000
Amangani Resorts • Jackson		734-7333
Elk Country Inn • Jackson		733-2364
Hoback River Resort • Jackson		733-5129
Jackson Hole Lodge & Motel • Jackson		733-2992
Lodge at Jackson Hole • Jackson		739-9703
Split Creek Ranch • Jackson		733-7522
Snow King Resort • Jackson		733-5200
Teton Pines Resort • Jackson		733-1005
Cowboy Village at Togwotee • Moran		733-8800
Hatchett Resort, Restaurant & Bar • Moran		543-2413
Jenny Lake Lodge • Moran		543-4647
Jackson Lake Lodge • Moran		543-2811
White Pine Ski Area & Resort • Pinedale		367-6606
The Alpenhof Lodge & Restaurant • Teton Village		733-3242
Snake River Lodge & Spa • Teton Village		732-6000
Jackson Hole Mountain Resort • Teton Village		733-2292
Four Seasons Lodge • Teton Village		734-7888
Grand Targhee Ski & Summer Resort • Alta		353-2300
Wagon Wheel Village • Jackson		733-2357

Vacation Houses, Cabins & Condos

Twin Pines Lodge & Cabins • Dubois		455-2600

Riverside Inn & Campground • Dubois		455-2337
The Old Mill Log Cabins • Afton		886-0520
MacKenzie Highland Ranch • Dubois		455-3415
Rendezvous Mountain Rentals • Jackson		739-9050
Black Diamond Vacation Rentals & Real Estate• Jackson		733-6170
Jackson Hole Resort Lodging • Teton Village		733-3990
Aspen Chalet Cabins • Alpine		654-7962
Westviero Mountain Log Home & Log Cabin • Dubois		455-2552
Pinnacle Buttes Lodge • Dubois		455-2506
Cottages at Snow King • Jackson		733-3480
Dornan's Inn • Moose		733-2415
Luton's Teton Cabins • Moran		543-2489
Colter Bay Village Cabins • Moran		543-2811
Monte Vista Family Vacation Rentals • Thayne		886-9348
Baily House Guest Cabin • Wapati		587-3342
Four Bear Ranch • Wapati		527-6048
Kinkade Guest Kabin • Wapati		587-5905

Bed and Breakfasts

The Painted Porch Bed & Breakfast • Jackson Hole		733-1981
Chambers House Bed & Breakfast • Pinedale		367-2168
A Teton Treehouse Bed & Breakfast • Jackson Hole		733-3233
Davy Jackson Inn - Bed & Breakfast • Jackson		739-2294
Geyser Creek Bed & Breakfast • Dubois		455-2707
The Stone House Bed & Breakfast • Dubois		455-2555
Wildflower Inn Bed & Breakfast • Jackson		733-4710
Jakey's Fork Homestead • Dubois		455-2769
The Huff House • Jackson		733-4164
Teton View Bed & Breakfast • Wilson		733-7954
Cottonwood Cottage Bed & Breakfast • Smoot		(866) 9348
Rocking P Bed & Breakfast • Smoot		886-0455
Inn at Deer Run Bed & Breakfast • Thayne		883-3444
Inn on the Creek • Jackson		739-1565
Ramsview Bed & Breakfast • Dubois		455-3615
Wapiti Ridge Ranch Bed & Breakfast Inn • Dubois		455-2219
Salt River Bed & Breakfast • Etna		883-2453
Horseshoe Inn Motel • Etna		883-2281
Window on the Winds • Pinedale		367-2600
Branding Iron Bunkhouse Bed & Breakfast • Pinedale		367-2146
Stockman's • Pinedale		367-4562
Sassy Moose Inn Bed & Breakfast • Jackson		733-1277
Bentwood Bed & Breakfast • Jackson		739-1411
Pole Creek Ranch Bed & Breakfast • Pinedale		367-4433
Don't Fence Me Inn Bed & Breakfast • Jackson		733-7979
Mountain Top Bed & Breakfast • Dubois		455-2304
Horseman's Paradise Bed & Breakfast • Wapati		587-2017
Alta Lodge Bed & Breakfast • Alta		353-2582
Teton County Bed & Breakfast • Alta		353-2208
Wilson Creekside Inn • Wilson		353-2409
Rocky Mountain Wilderness Adventure • Jackson		734-2636
Moose Meadows Bed & Breakfast • Wilson		733-4550
Victorian Inn • Jackson		734-2294

Outfitters and Guides

Barker-Ewing River Trips	R	733-1000
Jackson Hole Whitewater/Teton Expeditions & Scenic Floats	R	733-1007
Riverside Inn & Campground	FHEG	455-2337
Fool's Gold Excursions	G	883-3783
Half Moon Lake Resort	FEG	367-6373
Emerald Creek Outfitters	EG	455-3371
Absaroka Ranch	FHE	455-2275
Suda Outfitters	FHE	455-2866
Outfitters of Wyoming Wilderness	FHE	455-2725
CM Ranch	E	455-2331
Press Stephens Outfitter	FHE	455-2250
Deadman Creek Outfitters	H	654-7528
Jackson's Hole Adventure	G	654-7849
TJ's Sports, Inc	G	654-7815
Fort William Guest Ranch	FGE	367-4670
High Wild & Lonesome	EG	276-3208
Darby Mountain Outfitters, Inc	FHE	386-9220
Jensen's Guest Ranch	H	886-3401
Green River Outfitters	FHE	367-2416
Crossed Sabres Ranch	FHRE	587-3750
Heart Six Ranch	FHEG	543-2477
Triangle X Ranch	FHER	733-2183
Camp Creek Inn	H	733-3099
Turpin Meadow Ranch	FHE	543-2000
Castagino Outfitters	H	543-2403
Western Cross Outfitters	H	543-2840
Ron Dube's Wilderness Adventures	H	527-7815
Rocking D River Ranch	FG	587-8329
Mill Iron Ranch	FHE	733-6390
Wolf Mountain Outfitters	H	886-9317
Wagons A+Cross Wyoming	EG	859-8629
Grand Slam Outfitters	H	486-2269
Highland Meadow Outfitters	H	455-3478
Taylor Outfitters	G	455-2161
Arrowhead Outfitters	H	733-5223
Charlie Sands Wild Water	R	733-4410
Crystal Creek Outfitters	FHEG	733-6318
Darwin Ranch	FGE	733-5588
Fred Mau's Outdoor Adventure	FHRE	637-6906
Jackson Hole Llamas	G	739-9582
Jackson Hole Snowmobile Tours	G	733-6850
John Henry Lee Outfitters	HF	455-3200
Lewis & Clark River Expeditions	R	733-4022
Mad River Boat Trips	R	733-6203
Rocky Mt. Wilderness Adventure	R	734-2636
Spotted Horse Ranch	FHE	733-2097
Two Ocean Pass Outfitters	FHE	886-4664
Wagons West & Yellowstone Outfitters	HE	886-5629
O'Kelley Outfitting	FGE	367-6476
Barlow Outfitting	FHR	654-7669
Greys River Trophies	HE	859-8896
Elk Antler Outfitters	H	733-2649
Bald Mountain Outfitters	FHER	367-6539
C 4 Outfitters	H	734-4414
Coulter Creek Outfitters	H	543-2111
Double Diamond Outfitters	FHEG	885-4868
East Table Creek Hunting Camp	H	886-9517
Elk Ridge Outfitters	FHRE	367-2553
Gilroy Outfitting	FHE	734-0440
Gros Ventre Wilderness Outfitters	HF	733-4851
Hoback Outfitters	FHRE	886-3601
Horse Creek Outfitters	HFE	733-6556
Indian Summer Outfitters	H	733-3974
Jackson Hole Outfitters	G	886-3356
Jackson Peak Outfitters	H	733-3805
Lazy TX Outfitting	H	455-2688
Linn Brothers Oufitting	H	733-5414
Mule Shoe Outfitters	H	537-5655
Rendezvous Outfitters	FHE	733-8241
Shoal Creek Outfitters	FH	733-1310
Skinner Brothers Outfitters	FHER	367-2270
Diamond D Ranch Outfitters	FHE	543-2479
The Last Resort	H	859-8294

Dining Quick Reference

Price Range refers to the average cost of a meal per person: ($) $1-$6, ($$) $7-$11, ($$$) $12-up. Cocktails: "Yes" indicates full bar; Beer (B)/Wine (W), Service: Breakfast (B), Brunch (BR), Lunch (L), Dinner (D). Businesses in bold print will have additional information under the appropriate map locator number in the body of this section. [wi-fi] next to business name indicates free wireless internet is available to customers.

MAP No.	RESTAURANT	TYPE CUISINE	PRICE RANGE	CHILD MENU	COCKTAILS BEER WINE	MEALS SERVED	CREDIT CARDS ACCEPTED
2	Valleon Café	Family	$$	Yes		B/L	
2	Timberline Steak House	Steakhouse	$$$/$$	Yes	Yes	D/L/B	Major
2	Taco Time	Mexican	$	Yes		L/D	M/V
2	Rocky Mountain Pasta & Pizzaria	Italian/Pizza				L/D	
2	Red Baron Drive In	Fast Food	$	Yes		L/D	
2	Pizza Hut	Pizza	$$	Yes	B	L/D	Major
2	Noodle's Bar & Restaurant	Steakhouse	$$/$$$		Yes	B/L	Major
2	Subway	Sandwiches	$	Yes		L/D/B	M/V
2	Outlaw Saloon						
2	Silver Stream Lodge Restaurant & Cabins	Steak & Seafood	$$$	Yes	Yes	D	Major
2	Rocky Mountain Seafood Market and Fish & Chips	Seafood				L	
2	Melina's Mexican Restaurant	Mexican	$$	Yes		L/D	
2	Homestead Restaurant	Coffee Shop	$$/$	Yes		L/D/B	M/V/Major/D
2	Burger King	Fast Food/	$	Yes		D/L/B	M/V
4	Star Valley Ranch Resorts & RV Camping	Family	$$			B/L	D/V/M
4	Eidelweiss Restaurant	Fine Dining	$$$		B/W	L/D	M/V
4	Star Valley Cheese Restaurant	Family	$$			B/L	D/V/M
4	Melina's Mexican Food	Mexican	$$	Yes		L/D	M/V
4	Mavis' Restaurant	Family Dining	$$	Yes		L/B	M/V
4	Flat Creek RV Park [wi-fi]	Family	$$			B	D/V/M
4	Tootsie's Take or Bake Pizza	Pizza	$$	Yes		L/D	M/V
4	Dad's Steakhouse	Steakhouse	$$$		Yes	D	Major
4	Café 89	American	$-$$	C		B/L	
6	**Kringle's Birdhouse Café**	American Dining	$$	Yes	Yes/W/B	L/D/B	Major
6	**Buffalo Creek Western Bistro**	Fine Dining	$$$	Yes	Yes	D	D/M/V
6	The Nordic Inn & Brenthoven's Restaurant	Fine Dining	$$		Yes	B/L/D	D/M/V
6	Los Dos Amigos	American/Mexican	$$	Yes	Yes	L/D	Major
6	Frenchy's Bar-B-Que	Chicken & Ribs	$$	Yes		L/D	
6	Buffalo Station Café	Family	$$	Yes		L/D/B	M/V
6	Gunnar's Pizza	Pizza	$$	Yes		L/D	
6	Red Baron Restaurant	American	$$	Yes		L/D/B	
6	Royal Ridge Restaurant	Fine Dining	$$$	Yes	Yes	D/L/B	D/M/V
6	Best Western Flying Saddle Lodge Restaurant	Eclectic	$$/$$$		Yes	B/D	Major
7	Horse Creek Station	Steakhouse	$$$/$$	Yes	Yes	L/D	Major
7	Camp Creek Inn & Fine Dining	Steakhouse	$$$/$$	Yes	Yes	L/D	Major
8	Huey's Restaurant	Pub	$$		Yes	L/D	Major
8	Gordo's Southpark Market & Deli	Deli	$$		W/B	B/L/D	M/V
8	Denny's	Family	$$			D/L/B	Major
8	Domino's Pizza	Pizza	$$			L/D	Major
8	Mill Iron Ranch	Family	$/$$		Yes	B/L/D	Major
8	Hard Drive Café	American	$-$$	C		B/L	Major
9	Hanger Cantina	Mexican	$$	Yes	B/W	B/L/D	Major
10	**The Virginian Lodge & Restaurant** [wi-fi]	Family	$$$	Yes	Yes	B/L/D	Major
10	Out of Bounds Pizzaria & Deli	Pizza & Deli	$			L/D	
10	Pizza Hut	Pizza		Yes	Yes	L/D	Major
10	McDonald's	Fast Food	$	Yes		L/D/B	Major
10	Beantown Cafe & Coffee House	Coffee House	$			L/B	M/V
12	**Cadillac Grille**	Fine Dining	$$$		Yes	D/L	Major
12	Village Inn	American	$$	Yes		B/L/D	Major
12	Pearl Street Bagels [wi-fi]	Deli	$			B/L/D	
12	Philly's Finest	Subs	$$	Yes	B	L/D	
12	Rendezvous Bistro	Fine Dining	$$$		Yes	D	Major
12	Merry Piglets Mexican Grill	Mexican	$$	Yes	Yes	L/D	Major
12	Million Dollar Cowboy Steakhouse	Steakhouse	$$$		Yes	L/D	Major
12	Lejay's Sportsmen's Cafe	Steaks/Game	$$$	Yes		B/L/D	Major
12	Subway	Sandwiches/	$	Yes		L/D	Major
12	Sweetwater Restaurant	Mediterranean	$$$		Yes	L/D	Major
12	Taqueria Sanchez	Mexican	$	Yes		L/D	M/V
12	Terroir Restaurant	Fine Dining	$$$		Yes	D	Major
12	Teton Steakhouse [wi-fi]	Family	$$		W/B	B/L/D	Major
12	Teton Thai	Thai					

Dining Quick Reference-Continued

Price Range refers to the average cost of a meal per person: ($) $1-$6, ($$) $7-$11, ($$$) $12-up. Cocktails: "Yes" indicates full bar; Beer (B)/Wine (W), Service: Breakfast (B), Brunch (BR), Lunch (L), Dinner (D). Businesses in bold print will have additional information under the appropriate map locator number in the body of this section. *[wi-fi]* next to business name indicates free wireless internet is available to customers.

MAP No.	RESTAURANT	TYPE CUISINE	PRICE RANGE	CHILD MENU	COCKTAILS BEER WINE	MEALS SERVED	CREDIT CARDS ACCEPTED
12	Thai Me Up	Thai	$$$	No	Yes	D	Major
12	Grill at Amangani *[wi-fi]*	Italian	$$		Yes	L/D	Major
12	The Bunnery	American Bakery	$$$/$$	Yes		B/L/D	Major
12	Betty Rock Cafe	Deli	$	Yes			M/V
12	Billy's Giant Hamburgers	American	$	Yes		L/D	V/M
12	Chili Pepper Grill	Mexican	$$	Yes	Yes	L/D	M/V
12	McDonald's	Fast Food	$	Yes		B/L/D	
12	Atrium Restaurant *[wi-fi]*	Family	$$/$$$	Yes	Yes	B/L/D	Major
12	Cafe a Mano	Mexican	$$	No		L/D	M/V
12	Bar T-5 Cover Wagon Cookout & Wild West Show	American	$$$			D	Major
12	The Downtowner	American	$$		B	L/D	Major
12	The Granary	Fine Dining	$$$		Yes	D/L	Major
12	Bobby Rubino's Place for Ribs	Steakhouse	$$$	Yes	Yes	D	Major
12	Café 245	Eclectic	$$/$$$		Yes	D/L/B	Major
13	Off Broadway Grill	Eclectic	$$$	Yes	Yes	D	Major
13	Jedediah's Original House of Sourdough	Sandwiches	$$	Yes		B/L	Major
13	Harvest Bakery. Café & Organic Foods	Organic Foods	$$			B/L	V/M
13	Old Yellowstone Garage	Italian	$$$		W/B	L/D	Major
13	Pato Restaurant	Mexican	$$		W/B	D	Major
13	Wendy's	Fast Food				L/D	Major
13	Red Oak Grill	Fine Dining	$$$		Yes	D	Major
13	Rising Sage Cafe	Family	$$	Yes		L/D	Major
13	Route 89 Smokehouse Diner	Steak & Burgers	$$	Yes	Yes	B/L/D	Major
13	Shades Cafe	American	$$	Yes		B/L/D	M/V
13	Sidewinders Smokehouse & Tavern	American/Sports Bar	$$		Yes	L/D	Major
13	Silver Dollar Bar & Grill	Fine Dining	$$$		Yes	B/L/D	Major
13	Snake River Brewery & Restaurant *[wi-fi]*	Pizza/Sandwiches	$$		Yes	L/D	Major
13	Snake River Grill *[wi-fi]*	Fine Dining	$$$		Yes	D	Major
13	Hong Kong Buffet	Chinese	$$			L/D	Major
13	Mountain Dragon Chinese Restaurant	Mandarinn/Chinese	$$	Yes	Yes	L/D	Major
13	Nikai Sushi & Asian Fusion Cuisine	Asian/Fusion	$$$		Yes	D	Major
13	Taco Bell	Fast Food	$	Yes		L/D	
13	JH Soda Fountain	Ice Cream/Deli					
13	Gun Barrel Steak & Game House	Steak/Game	$$$	No	Yes	D	Major
13	The Blue Lion	Eclectic American	$$$		Yes	D	Major
13	El Abuelito	Mexican	$$$	Yes	B/W	L/D	Major
13	Bagel Jax	Bagels/Sandwiches	$			B/L/D	
13	Chinatown Restaurant	Chinese	$$$		Yes	L/D	M/V
13	Dairy Queen	Fast Food	$	Yes		L/D	
13	Mountain High Pizza	Pizza	$$		W/B	L/D	V/M/D
13	Acadian House	Cajun	$$$		Yes	D	Major
13	Burger King	Fast Food	$	Yes		D/L/B	M/V
13	Golden Palace Chinese Restaurant	Chinese	$$				
13	Jamba Juice	Juice Bar	$			L/D	Major
13	Koshu Wine Bar	Asian/Latin	$$$		Yes	L/D	Major
13	Bubba's Bar-B-Que	Barbeque	$$	Yes		L/D/B	
14	Bar J Chuckwagon Suppers & Western Show	Chuckwagon	$$$			D	Major
14	Stagecoach Café	Family	$$	Yes		D/L/B	Major
14	Nora's Fish Creek Inn	Steakhouse	$$	Yes		D/L/B	Major
15	Anthony's Italian Restaurant	Italian	$$/$$$	Yes	Yes/W/B	D	Major
15	Subway	Sandwiches/	$	Yes		L/D	Major
15	Mangy Moose Restaurant & Bar	Steak/Seafood	$$$		Yes	D/B/L	Major
15	Game Fish at Snake River Lodge	Fine Dining	$$$		Yes	L/D/B	Major
15	Vertical Restaurant	American Bistro	$$$		Yes	D	Major
15	Calico Italian Restaurant & Bar	Italian	$$$		Yes	D	Major
15	Stiegler's Restaurant & Bar *[wi-fi]*	Austrian	$$$		Yes		Major
15	Alpenhof Bistro	American	$$$		Yes	L/D	Major
15	Alpenrose Dining Room	Fine Dining	$$$	No	Yes	D/B	Major
15	Solitude Cabins Dinner Sleigh Rides		$$$			D	Major
15	Teton Pines *[wi-fi]*	Fine Dining	$$$		Yes	D	Major
15	Cascade Gull House & Spirits	New Western	$$$	Yes	Yes	B/L/D	Major

Dining Quick Reference

Price Range refers to the average cost of a meal per person: ($) $1-$6, ($$) $7-$11, ($$$) $12-up. Cocktails: "Yes" indicates full bar; Beer (B)/Wine (W), Service: Breakfast (B), Brunch (BR), Lunch (L), Dinner (D). Businesses in bold print will have additional information under the appropriate map locator number in the body of this section. *[wi-fi]* next to business name indicates free wireless internet is available to customers.

MAP No.	RESTAURANT	TYPE CUISINE	PRICE RANGE	CHILD MENU	COCKTAILS BEER WINE	MEALS SERVED	CREDIT CARDS ACCEPTED
15	The Alpenhof Lodge & Restaurant	French European	$$$	Yes	Yes	D	Major
15	Jenny Lake Lodge Dining room	Family	$$$	Yes	Yes	B/L/D	Major
16	Vista Grande	Mexican	$$$		Yes		Major
16	Dornan's Inn	Italian	$$$/$$	Yes	W/B	L/D	Major
18	Strutting Grouse Restaurant	Fine Dining	$$$	Yes	Yes	L/D	Major
18	Grizzly Steakhouse	Steakhouse	$$$/$$	Yes	Yes	B/L/D	Major
18	Hatchett Resort, Restaurant & Bar	Family	$$		W/B	B/L/D	Major
18	Flagg Ranch & Village	Family	$$	Yes	Yes	L/D/B	Major
19	**Rustic Pine Tavern & Steakhouse**	Steakhouse	$$$	No	Yes	D	V/M
19	**Café Wyoming**	Hearty Homecooking	$$		Yes	L/D	M/V
19	**Lava Mountain Restaurant**	Family	$/$$	Yes	Yes	L/D	D/M/V
19	Bernie's Café	Home-cooking	$$	No	B/W	L/D	D/M/V
19	Nani's Genuine Pasta House	Italian	$$/$$$	No	Yes	D/L	Major
19	Daylight Donuts & Village Café & Pizza	Family	$$	Yes	W/B	B/L/D	Major
19	Cowboy Café	Family	$$	Yes		B/L/D	
19	Dos Banditos	Mexican	$$	Yes	Yes	L/D	M/V
19	Pinnacle Buttes Wild Bunch Café	Home cooking	$$		Yes		M/V
19	Ramshorn Bagel & Deli	Deli	$	No	Yes	B/L	
19	Sawmill Lodge *[wi-fi]*	Fine Dining	$$$		Yes	L/D	Major
19	Taylor Creek	Deli	$			B/L	
19	Kathy's Koffee	Espresso/Deli	$	Yes		B/L	
19	Outlaw Saloon & Wild Bill's	American	$$	Yes	Yes	L/D	
19	Edith's When It's Open	Family	$$$			D	
19	Wild Bunch Cafe	Family	$$	Yes	Yes	L/D	Major
21	Boulder Motor Inn & Restaurant *[wi-fi]*	Family	$$	Yes	Yes	D/L	Major
21	Basecamp Restaurant	Steakhouse	$$$/$$	Yes	Yes	B/L/D	Major
22	Food Factory	Fast Food	$	Yes		L/D	
22	Happy Trails Café	Pizza	$	Yes		L/D	
23	Marbleton Inn Motel & Restaurant *[wi-fi]*	Family	$$	Yes	Yes	L/D/B	Major
23	Three Pines	Family	$$	Yes	Yes	D/L	Major
23	Prairie Café	Family	$	Yes		B/L	
23	Rio Verde Grill	Mexican	$$/$$$	Yes	W/B	D	M/V
23	Gatzke's Grubhouse	Steakhouse	$$	Yes	Yes	D	Major
24	McGregors Pub, Fine Dining, & Catering	Fine Dining	$$$		Yes	D	Major
24	Lakeside Lodge Resort & Marina *[wi-fi]*	Fine Dining	$$$	Yes	Yes	D/L/B	Major
24	Half Moon Lake Resort *[wi-fi]*	Fine Dining	$$$		Yes	D	Major
24	Bottoms Up Brewery & Grill	Pizza & Grill	$$	No	Yes	D	Major
24	Café on Pine	Fine Dining	$$/$$$	Yes	Yes	L/D	Major
24	Calamity Janes/Corral Bar	Pizza/deli	$$	Yes	Yes	L/D	M/V
24	Fort William Guest Ranch & Restaurant *[wi-fi]*	American	$$$		W/B	D	Major
24	Pitchfork Fondue	Western Cookout	$$	Yes		D	Major
24	Rumors Deli	Deli	$$/$	Yes		L/B	Major
24	Stockman's Steak Bar & Lounge	Steak/Seafood	$$	Yes	Yes	D/L/B	Major
24	Wrangler Café	Family	$$	Yes	W/B	D/L/B	Major
24	Wind River Rendezvous Pizza	Pizza	$$	No		D/L	Major
24	Freemont Peak Restaurant	German/American	$/$$/$$$			L/D/B	M/V
24	Taqueria del Gallo Cantina	Mexican	$$	Yes	B	D/L	V/M
24	Moose Creek Trading Co.	American	$$/$$$	Yes	Yes	B/L/D	M/V
24	Patio Grill and Dining Room	Family	$$	Yes	Yes	L/D/B	
24	Trappers Tidbits	Fast Food	$			L/D	
24	Kat's Steakhouse	Steakhouse	$$/$$$	Yes	Yes	B/D/L	Major
24	Corral Bar	American	$$		Yes	D	Major
24	Fat Daddy's Deli & Diner	Deli	$$			L/D	
24	Los Cabos Mexican Restaurant	Mexican	$$	Yes	W/B	L/D	M/V

NOTES:

Motel Quick Reference

Price Range: ($) Under $40 ; ($$) $40-$60; ($$$) $60-$80, ($$$$) Over $80. Pets [check with the motel for specific policies] (P), Dining (D), Lounge (L), Disabled Access (DA), Full Breakfast (FB), Cont. Breakfast (CB), Indoor Pool (IP), Outdoor Pool (OP), Hot Tub (HT), Sauna (S), Refrigerator (R), Microwave (M) (Microwave and Refrigerator indicated only if in majority of rooms), Kitchenette (K). All Wyoming area codes are 307. *[wi-fi]* next to business name indicates free wireless internet is available to customers.

MAP No.	HOTEL	PHONE	NUMBER ROOMS	PRICE RANGE	BREAKFAST	POOL/ HOT TUB SAUNA	NON SMOKE ROOMS	OTHER AMENITIES	CREDIT CARDS
2	**Lazy B Motel**	885-3187	25	$$$		OP	Yes	P/DA/R/M/K	Major
2	**The Old Mill Log Cabins**	886-0520	3	$$$$	Yes			R	V/M
2	Colters Lodge	885-9891	20	$$$			Yes	D/L	Major
2	Bar H Motel & Cabins	855-2274	40	$$$			Yes	D/L	Major
2	Corral Motel *[wi-fi]*	885-5424	15	$$	CB		Yes	M/R	Major
2	Gardner's Country Village	885-8204	12	$$			Yes		Major
4	Star Valley Ranch Resorts & RV Camping	883-2670	14	$$$		HT/OP/S	Yes	R	M/V
4	Cabin Creek Inn	883-3262	19	$$$	CB		Yes	R/DA/M/K	Major
4	Swiss Mountain Motel	883-2227	9	$$			Yes	P/R/K	Major
4	Snider's Rustic Inn	883-0222	8	$$$			Yes	P/K/R/M	M/V
6	**Three Rivers Motel**	654-7551	21					P	Major
6	**Alpine Inn**	654-7644	18	$$		HT	Yes	P/K	Major
6	The Nordic Inn & Brenthoven's Restaurant	654-7556	10				Yes	L/D	D/M/V
8	**Alpen Haus**	654-7545	22	$$$			Yes		Major
8	Days Inn of Jackson Hole *[wi-fi]*	733-0033	90		CB	S/HT	Yes	DA/R/M	Major
8	Motel 6	733-1620	155	$$		OP	Yes	P/D	Major
8	Super 8 - Jackson *[wi-fi]*	733-6833	97	$$$/$$$$	CB		Yes	DA	Major
8	Teton Gables Motel	733-3723	36	$$$			Yes	P/D	Major
10	**The Virginian Lodge & Restaurant** *[wi-fi]*	733-2792	170	$$$$		HT	Yes	D/L/DA/K	Major
10	Best Western Lodge at Jackson Hole *[wi-fi]*	739-9703		$$$$	CB		Yes	D/L/DA	Major
11	Town Square Inns - Cowboy Village Resort *[wi-fi]*	733-3121	82	$$$$/$$$		HT	Yes	R/M/K	Major
12	Ranch Inn *[wi-fi]*	733-6363	57	$$$$/$$$	CB	HT	Yes	K	Major
12	Town Square Inns - 49er Inn & Suites *[wi-fi]*	733-7550	150	$$$	CB	HT/S	Yes	K/P/D	Major
12	Town Square Inns - Antler Inn *[wi-fi]*	733-2535	100	$$$			Yes	P	Major
12	Town Square Inns - Elk Country Inn *[wi-fi]*	733-2364							
12	Buckrail Lodge	733-2079	12	$$		HT	Yes		M/V
12	Rawhide Motel	733-1216	23	$$/$$$				P	
13	**Anvil Motel**	733-3668	48	$$$		HT	Yes	R/M	M/V
13	Painted Buffalo Inn	733-4340	136	$$$		IP/S	Yes	DA/D/P	Major
13	Bunkhouse Hostel	733-3668	Dorm	$			Yes	K	M/V
13	Flat Creek Inn	733-5271	75	$$$	CB	S/HT	Yes	P/D/R/M/K	Major
13	Parkway Inn	733-3143	49	$$$$	CB	IP/S	Yes		Major
13	The Wort Hotel *[wi-fi]*	733-2190	60	$$$$		HT	Yes	D/L/DA	Major
13	Alpine Motel	739-3200	18	$$$		IP	Yes	K/P	D
13	Anglers Inn	733-3682	28	$$				K/D	M/V
13	Cache Creek Motel	733-7781	37	$$			Yes	P/K	Major
13	Four Winds Motel	733-2474	21	$$$/$$$$			Yes		Major
13	Golden Eagle Inn	733-2042	23	$$$		IP	Yes		Major
13	Jackson Hole Lodge & Motel *[wi-fi]*	733-2992	26	$$$		IP			Major
13	Kudar Motel	733-2823	30	$$$			Yes	L/D	Major
13	Pioneer Motel	733-3673	21	$$			Yes		
13	Pony Express Motel	733-3835	24	$$$		OP		K/P	
13	Prospector Inn	733-4858	19	$$$	CB	HT	Yes	P/DA	Major
13	Sagebrush Motel	733-0336	24	$$$			Yes	K	Major
13	Stagecoach Motel	733-3673	21	$$$					
13	Sundance Inn *[wi-fi]*	733-3444	27	$$$	CB		Yes	K	
13	Trapper Inn *[wi-fi]*	733-2648	50	$$$		HT	Yes	R/M	Major
13	Wagon Wheel Village		97	$$$$		HT	Yes	D/L/K	Major
13	Inn on the Creek *[wi-fi]*	739-1565	9	$$$$	CB		Yes		Major
13	Wyoming Inn of Jackson, Red Lion *[wi-fi]*	734-0035	73	$$$$	CB		Yes	K/DA/P	Major
13	Best Western Inn at Jackson Hole *[wi-fi]*	733-2311	83	$$$$		OP/S/HT	Yes	DA/K	Major
13	Elk Refuge Inn	733-3582	22	$$$			Yes	R/M/K	Major
13	Teton Inn	733-3883	14	$$$			Yes		Major
15	The Alpenhof Lodge & Restaurant *[wi-fi]*	733-3242	42	$$$	CB	OP/HT/S	Yes	P/L/D	Major
15	Teton Mountain Lodge *[wi-fi]*	732-6911	129	$$$$		IP/OP/HT	Yes	D/L/DA/R/K	Major
15	Village Center Inn *[wi-fi]*	733-3990	16	$$$			Yes	D/K	Major
15	The Hostel	733-3415	54	$				P	
18	Signal Mountain Lodge	543-2831	385	$$$$		OP	Yes	L/D/P/K	Major
19	**Branding Iron Inn**	455-2893	23	$$			Yes	P/K	Major
19	**Black Bear County Inn**	455-2344	16	$$			Yes	P/K	Major

Motel Quick Reference-Continued

Price Range: ($) Under $40 ; ($$) $40-$60; ($$$) $60-$80, ($$$$) Over $80. Pets [check with the motel for specific policies] (P), Dining (D), Lounge (L), Disabled Access (DA), Full Breakfast (FB), Cont. Breakfast (CB), Indoor Pool (IP), Outdoor Pool (OP), Hot Tub (HT), Sauna (S), Refrigerator (R), Microwave (M) (Microwave and Refrigerator indicated only if in majority of rooms), Kitchenette (K). All Wyoming area codes are 307. [wi-fi] next to business name indicates free wireless internet is available to customers.

MAP No.	HOTEL	PHONE	NUMBER ROOMS	PRICE RANGE	BREAKFAST	POOL/ HOT TUB SAUNA	NON SMOKE ROOMS	OTHER AMENITIES	CREDIT CARDS
19	**Twin Pines Lodge & Cabins**	455-2600	16	$$	CB		Yes	R/DA	Major
19	**Riverside Inn & Campground**	455-2337	14	$$			Yes	K/P	D/M/V
19	Stagecoach Motor Inn	455-2303	50	$$$/$$		HT/OP	Yes	DA/K/P	Major
19	Trail's End Motel [wi-fi]	455-2540	84	$		IP	yes	P/D/L/K	Major
19	MacKenzie Highland Ranch	455-3415	8	$$$$			Yes	K	
19	Saw Mill Lodge	455-2171	16	$$$			Yes	L/D/P	Major
19	Wind River Motel	455-2611	13	$$			Yes	P/D	M/V
19	Bald Mountain Inn	455-2844	16	$$			Yes	P/K	Major
19	Super 8 -Dubois	455-3694	34	$$		HT	Yes	P	Major
21	Boulder Motor Inn & Restaurant	537-5626	9	$$	CB		Yes	DA/L/D	Major
22	Big Piney Motel	276-3352	26	$$			Yes	R/M	M/V
22	Frontier Hotel	276-3329	10	$$			No		M/V
23	Marbleton Inn Motel & Restaurant [wi-fi]	276-5231	35	$$			Yes	D/L	Major
23	Country Chalet Inn Motel	276-3391	14	$$			Yes	P	M/V
24	Lakeside Lodge Resort & Marina	367-2221	20	$$$$			Yes	P/D/L/DA/R/M	Major
24	Half Moon Lake Resort	367-6373	8	$$$$	CB		Yes	D/P/R	Major
24	The Sundance Motel	367-4336	19	$$$$/$$$			Yes	R/M/K/P	Major
24	The Lodge at Pinedale	367-8800	43	$$$	CB	HT/IP	Yes	P/R/M/DA	D
24	Log Cabin Motel: A National Historic Place	367-4579	10				Yes	R/K/P	M/V
24	Best Western - Pinedale [wi-fi]	367-6869	59	$$$$	CB	IP/HT	Yes	P/D/R/M	Major
24	Riviera Lodge	367-2424	8	$$$$			Yes	P/K	M/V
24	ZZZZ Inn	367-2121	10	$$$$/$$$			Yes	K/DA	M/V
24	Teton Court Motel	367-4317	17	$$$$/$$			Yes	K/P	Major
24	Wagon Wheel Motel	367-2871	15	$$$	.		Yes		Major
24	Camp O' the Pines Motel	367-4536	14	$		IP	Yes	P/K	Major
24	Super 8	367-8812	43	$/$$	CB	IP	Yes		Major
24	Pine Creek Inn	367-2191	16	$$$	CB		Yes	P/K	Major
24	Half Moon Lake Motel	367-2851	19	$$$			Yes	K/P	Major

NOTES:

IDAHO

THE GEM STATE

Welcome to Idaho

THE GEM STATE

Idaho – a state rich with history, phenomenal scenery, and legendary hospitality! Flanked by the lush Pacific Northwest and the rugged western slopes of the Rocky Mountains, Idaho is situated halfway between the Equator and the North Pole. Over 83,000 square miles of wildly diverse terrain allows Idaho to produce some of the world's most precious stones, a fact that granted the state its nickname. For some, the epithet comes as a shock. After all, Idaho's license plates advertise the state's historically bumper crops of spuds. So the state's nickname isn't "The Potato State"? Thank goodness, no. Are the potatoes still famous? Overwhelmingly, yes. Is that all Idaho has to offer? Definitely not!

Those traveling through America's fourteenth largest state will quickly discover that Idaho's most precious commodity is the landscape itself. Bordered by Montana and Wyoming on the east, Utah and Nevada to the south, Oregon and Washington on the west, and Canada's British Columbia to the north, every region of the state offers its own natural wonders. Thundering waterfalls, towering mountains, pristine lakes, raging rivers, shadowy forests, velvety plains, rolling farmland, geothermal phenomena, desert plateaus, and volcanic craters paint one of America's most awe-inspiring masterpieces.

Although Idaho often stands in the shadow of its popular neighboring states, the Gem State demands just as much respect for its natural treasures. Between hosting the continental U.S.' largest unspoiled backcountry area in the 2.3 million-acre Frank Church-River of No Return Wilderness and North America's deepest river gorge at Hells Canyon, Idaho is also home to the continent's tallest single structured sand dune and the largest population of nesting raptors. Land lovers will find that Idaho is the most mountainous of all Rocky Mountain States as over eighty recognized

ranges pierce the crisp azure skies and soar to a maximum height of 12,662 feet. At the lower end of the elevation spectrum, the Owyhee Canyonlands and Craters of the Moon provide respective glimpses into the isolated nature of silent deserts and twisted volcanic remains. Water worshippers are greeted with 3,100 winding river miles (the nation's most!) and the ever-present Snake River, while the legendary Salmon River is distinguished as America's longest free-flowing tributary beginning and ending within a single state. As an added bonus, Idaho's 2,000+ blue water jewels allow the state to claim the American West's greatest concentration of lakes.

It's no wonder, then, that the forty-third state to enter the union is a place that beckons new discovery. Nearly every geological formation known on Earth can be found in Idaho, and recreation abounds year-round. Extraordinary? Yes, but that's to be expected in a state that widened early explorers' eyes with pure reverence. For those willing to join the ranks of adventurous voyagers and look beyond Idaho's agricultural fame, the Gem State offers a treasure trove of uncrowded expanses and unparalleled beauty worth its weight in gold. Discover Idaho for yourself, and unearth the gem that it really is!

NATURAL HISTORY

Drawing its name from the Native American word "idahow" meaning "gem of the mountains" or "sun coming down the mountains," Idaho and its mountains and distinctive landscape have spanned the millennia. Sediment layers on the state's rocky bluffs provide testimony to minerals and rocks deposited across hundreds of thousands of years, and fossils scattered throughout both northern and southern Idaho clearly indicate that the land was once a tropical paradise. In fact, Idaho is home to some of America's finest preserved fossil

remains of ancient leaves, insects, fish, and mammals, including Bald Cypress, Chinese Pine, Fir, Redwood, zebras, and camels.

In more recent geological terms, Idaho has been the subject of dramatic upheaval and catastrophic natural events that shaped the state into its present form. Between 15,000 and 20,000 years ago, North America's once largest lake encompassed over 20,000 square miles of Idaho and Utah territory. Formed in a basin in the state's southeastern corner, Lake Bonneville cradled massive amounts of water within its bowl while the natural rock dam at Red Rock Pass ensured that no water escaped to the Pacific Ocean. As the earth's plates beneath Idaho's crust began to shift, volcanic eruptions and violent magma explosions forced the lake over its dam and created the world's second largest known flood. In this massive draining process, Idaho's Snake River channel was carved, and the hanging valleys characteristic of southeastern Idaho took shape.

As the volcanoes continued to erupt and magma snaked across the land to create cinder cones, craters, and twisted lava formations, North America's glaciers were also sculpting Idaho's terrain. As recently as 10,000 years ago, glaciers chiseled the mountains, carved U-shaped valleys and hundreds of alpine cirques, and deposited fields of boulders in their wake. Earthquakes aided the glacial

Henry's Lake

Idaho Introduction

All Idaho Area Codes are 208

Henry's Lake

Idaho Introduction

All Idaho Area Codes are 208

Idaho Introduction

All Idaho Area Codes are 208

Henry's Lake

COWBOY WAVE

Idaho features many rural areas, and like rural areas in other states, Idaho is pretty friendly to most who care to be friendly back. When you're traveling the back roads, particularly the gravel roads, you'll encounter a variety of waves from passing pickups and motorists.

The most common is the one finger wave, accomplished by simply raising the first finger (not the middle finger as is common in other states) from the steering wheel. If the driver is otherwise occupied with his hands or if it is a fairly rough road, you may get a light head nod. Occasionally, you may get a two finger wave which often appears as a modified peace sign if the passerby is having a particularly good day. On rare occasions, you may get an all out wave.

The most important things is that whatever wave you get, be sure and wave back.

activity, lowering the elevation of valley floors and forcing jagged mountain peaks to thrust even higher.

Today, geologists rush to study Idaho's granite batholith complex situated in the center of the state. The massive rock creation formed during a series of volcanic events, and the "veins" in the rock contain vast deposits of gold, silver, lead, zinc, copper, cobalt, star garnets, topaz, jasper, and other precious minerals and stones that give Idaho its appropriate nickname.

Although the state's geological formations appear stable and relatively static to the untrained eye, Idaho's terrain continuously provides evidence of the planet's powerful capabilities. Magma oozed from the Earth's core at Craters of the Moon just 2,000 years ago, and Idaho is often recognized as one of America's most geologically active regions. Such changes may seem invisible today, but Idaho's landscape is constantly in motion and will continue to erode, evolve, and take new shape until the end of time.

IDAHO'S LAND & CLIMATE

Topographic Features

Measuring 479 miles long and 305 miles wide, Idaho spans seven latitudinal and six longitudinal degrees that provide the state with a complex and spectacular topography. Although the state's mean elevation is 5,000 feet, the highest elevation climbs to 12,662 feet at Mount Borah while Lewiston's famous Snake River seaport rests at a mere 710 feet above sea level. More than 40% of the state's 82,751 square land miles is forested (distinguishing it as the Rocky Mountain's most heavily forested state), and Idaho boasts fifty mountain peaks that climb over 10,000 feet. Amid the 823 square miles of Idaho cloaked in water, individuals will find 16,000 miles of streams, 2,000+ lakes, and nearly 239,000 acres of reservoirs. Due to Idaho's size and location, the state is divided into two time zones. Those traveling through the northern panhandle are treated to Pacific Standard Time while the rest of the state sets its clocks to Mountain Standard Time.

With such varied elevations, each region of Idaho offers its own topographic wonders. Idaho's northern panhandle is instantly recognized for its legendary lakes, velvet green valleys, and pristine forests reminiscent of its lush Pacific Northwest neighbors. The Coeur d'Alene, Selkirk, Cabinet, and Purcell Mountain Ranges are also residents here. Rising above the Idaho Panhandle National Forest and peeking their heads into the clouds, these mountains frame the region's lakes in a stunning palette of swirling blues and greens.

Slightly south of the panhandle, north-central Idaho blooms in blue on the Camas Prairie, while the rolling Palouse hills and fertile farmland stand in stark contrast to the Seven Devils Mountains' granite spires and the Hells Canyon Wilderness Area. Farther east, additional backcountry awaits in the Selway-Bitterroot and Gospel Hump Wilderness Areas. Placid rivers and churning whitewater zigzag across the region, and the Snake, Salmon, Clearwater, Lochsa, Selway, and Potlatch Rivers combine to provide north-central Idaho with the state's greatest concentration of exhilarating rapids.

Southwestern Idaho is perhaps one of the most diverse regions in the entire state. From its pastoral valleys to high desert plateaus to alpine lakes, this section of Idaho offers something for everyone. Running through the region's heart and dividing the area into two distinct topographic zones, the Snake River welcomes the convergence of the Payette and Boise Rivers. South of the river, the Snake River Plain is dotted with irrigated farmland and famous fruit orchards ripe with color and regional flavor. Heading towards the Nevada border, the Owyhee, Jarbidge, and Bruneau Rivers whittle impressive canyons through the isolated desert terrain as sand dunes rise 470 feet on the horizon. North of the Snake River, agricultural valleys gradually meld into the Payette and Boise National Forests. Lakes rest in bowls of snow-capped mountains, and elevations rise the closer one moves towards central Idaho.

Regarded as one of Mother Nature's most dramatic creations, the high country of central Idaho is marked with mountain grandeur. The craggy peaks of the White Cloud and Boulder Mountains ascend majestically amid the Sawtooth National Forest, and the jagged teeth of the Sawtooth Mountains dominate the 756,000-acre Sawtooth National Recreation Area. To the northeast, mountains continue to reign supreme as Idaho's highest elevation rests at the summit of Mount Borah in the Lost River Range. Nearby, the Lemhi Range and Beaverhead Mountains cradle a portion of the Challis and Salmon National Forests. North-central Idaho is more than just extreme mountain splendor, though. As with other regions in the state, natural hot springs boil and bubble, and the Salmon River curls and crashes. Further south, the uninhabited lava flows, craters, and cinder cones of Craters of the Moon shroud the landscape in a veil of oddity.

The lava flows of Craters of the Moon continue into south-central Idaho. North of the Snake River, hardened basalt gray of yesteryear's volcanic activity intermingles with red dirt and sagebrush prairie to form an eerie reminder of Idaho's violent geological history. Ice caves, lava tubes, and the rugged remains of cooled magma eventually transform into spring-lined canyons and majestic waterfalls as the Snake River provides irrigation to the Magic Valley. The flat area lying directly south of the Snake River is home to some of America's richest farmland, and a cornucopia of crops are annually produced. Standing in juxtaposition with this fertility are high desert plateaus and the intriguing City of Rocks strewn with boulders.

Eastern Idaho welcomes visitors with the quieter side of the Grand Teton Mountains, and the Targhee National Forest shades the Idaho/Wyoming stateline with a border of towering trees and drastic elevation changes. The region also features a volcanic caldera, thundering waterfalls, and remote alpine lakes. Flowing throughout the region, the Henry's Fork and the main branch of the Snake River wind freely near fields of potatoes and sugar beets.

Mounds of potato blossoms extend into southeastern Idaho, and the Snake River makes its presence known once again as it flows towards the Snake River Plain. 47,000 acres of waving prairie grass highlight the region's Curlew National Grassland, while the neighboring Caribou and Cache-Wasatch National Forests provide stunning scenery, lush valley floors, and timbered peaks. Water abounds in the region, from the Malad, Portneuf, and Bear Rivers to Bear Lake, Blackfoot

414

Ultimate Yellowstone Park Atlas and Travel Encyclopedia

Reservoir, and American Falls Reservoir. A welcome sight to Oregon Trail pioneers, the region's naturally warm, carbonated springs spark intrigue to this day.

Flora and Fauna

With its extremes in both elevation and topography, the Gem State is home to widely divergent vegetation and wildlife. Northern Idaho's moist, cool climate is ideal for supporting large stands of grand fir, western red cedar, western hemlock, western white pine, and the Pacific yew. Many of Idaho's largest and oldest trees can be found here. At the state's highest elevations, Engelmann spruce, subalpine fir, mountain hemlock, quaking aspen, lodgepole pine, subalpine larch, whitebark pine, and limber pine flourish. Douglas fir and ponderosa pine line several of Idaho's highways, while cottonwoods and weeping willows stand guard along the state's many riverbanks. At the lowest elevations, sagebrush, bitterbrush, and a variety of juniper species intermingle with box elder, bigtooth maple trees, and chokecherry and serviceberry bushes.

Idaho's wildlife is just as diverse as the flora that blankets the state's landscape with color and texture. Woodland caribou, grizzly bears, and wolves are among Idaho's most endangered species. Mountain lions, black bears, bobcats, and Canadian lynx are known to roam throughout Idaho's mountains, and a host of raptors, including bald eagles, cast their shadow against Idaho's sunset splendor. Harboring a less aggressive nature, mountain goats, wild horses, bighorn sheep, white-tailed deer, elk, mule deer, and moose are joined by beavers, marmots, pikas, and river otters. With its many rivers, Idaho also possesses an abundant fish population that includes salmon, an array of trout species, sturgeon, and several varieties of warm-water fish.

Weather

Idaho enjoys a four-season climate, but weather patterns across the state vary drastically from region to region. Idaho is fortunate enough to escape the path of destructive hurricanes, and tornadoes are extremely rare. Hail damage during summer storms is also often insignificant, and on average, the entire state receives an abundant amount of sunshiny days each year with relatively low humidity.

Although the highest temperature recorded in the state was a scorching 118 degrees Fahrenheit in 1934 and the lowest a teeth-chattering, bonebiting minus 60 degrees in 1943, the state's temperatures generally avoid such extremes. On average, the state's monthly temperatures range from a maximum high of 90.6 degrees to a low of 15.1 degrees Fahrenheit. During all seasons, however, the state's weather patterns can change suddenly. Travelers should be prepared at all times for a variety of conditions, especially in the state's higher elevations and backcountry areas.

Pacific weather patterns moderate temperature extremes in Idaho's panhandle, and as expected, the region enjoys a typical Pacific Northwest climate. Summers are usually clear and dry with daytime highs reaching just 80 degrees. Mild, wet storms flowing off the Pacific Ocean bring a mixture of clouds, rain, and snow during winter. In some years, the area receives more than sixty inches of annual rainfall.

North-central Idaho's numerous river canyons and lower elevations provide the region with the state's warmest temperatures. Towns situated in the canyon floors receive very little wind, and summer temperatures frequently soar over 100

Craters of the Moon National Monument

degrees Fahrenheit. Although such heat might sound unappealing, the region receives the perk of over 200 growing season days per year, winter temperatures that rarely, if ever, dip below freezing, and the arrival of an early spring. Those towns situated at a higher elevation on north central Idaho's prairie also enjoy fairly warm winters, but summer temperatures tend to hover in the 80 degree range.

Southwestern Idaho's elevations range from just 2,000 feet above sea level at the Snake River to more than 5,000 feet in the mountainous region encompassing McCall and Cascade. The low-lying valleys surrounding the region's main rivers often receive their fair share of hot summer days with fairly mild winters. Boise and its neighboring cities report below freezing temperatures only during December and January. In fact, the Snake River Plain south of Boise historically records an average annual mean temperature of 55 degrees Fahrenheit. Father north, the region's residents are treated to four distinct seasons. Higher elevations create cooler temperatures year-round in McCall, and the area also records the state's highest average snowfall.

Much of the mountainous region comprising central Idaho's high country boasts elevations well above 6,000 feet. Such high elevations translate into nearly perfect summer days, but winters are long and filled with plenty of days where the mercury dips below freezing. Stanley, in fact, boasts the state's lowest average temperature, reading in at just over 35 degrees Fahrenheit! Spring comes late, summers are generally dry, and winters provide hundreds of inches of powder. Outside the scenic mecca of Salmon, Stanley, and Sun Valley, the region's eastern side experiences much warmer temperatures and near desert conditions with virtually no precipitation.

South-central Idaho's landscape averages extremely warm summer temperatures with daytime highs in the low 90s. Winter temperatures tend to hover between 20 and 40 degrees. Freezing temperatures generally occur just between December and February, and the area's heaviest precipitation comes in the form of May showers.

Situated farthest away from the Pacific moisture affecting the rest of the state, eastern Idaho receives the remnants of storms pushing out from the west, cold fronts moving south from Canada, and weather flows extending north from the Gulf of Mexico. As the hub of such forces, eastern Idaho's weather is the exact opposite of that in the panhandle and lower western elevations. The region experiences the widest variation in seasonal temperatures, spring and summer pack along afternoon thunderstorms and drenching rainstorms, and winters generally produce the state's finest and lightest powder due to extremely cold temperatures.

Southeastern Idaho's climate nearly mimics that of eastern Idaho. Spring and summer visitors should pack along an umbrella in preparation for some of the state's most spectacular displays of lightning, thunder, and refreshing rain.

THE HISTORY OF IDAHO'S PEOPLE

Ancient Inhabitants

Long before the arrival of mountain men, westward expansionists, miners, and farmers, Idaho housed indigenous tribes who thrived upon the region's diverse topography and wildlife populations. Archaeological findings in south-central Idaho indicate that nomadic hunters wandered the state's expansive terrain as early as 13,000 B.C. Arrowheads, spears, rock shelters lined with petroglyphs, and remnants of long-extinct horse, camel, and sloth species have been carbon-dated to 12,500 B.C. Based upon such findings, many archaeologists believe America's first residents resided in Idaho and passed their bloodline onto the region's Native American inhabitants.

Native Americans

The total combined population of Idaho's Native American inhabitants has never been significantly large, but Idaho's history remains interwoven with the tribes who were dependent upon the region for survival. Prior to the arrival of horses in 1700, most of Idaho's Native American tribes maintained a solitary life. As a result, conflict was kept at bay,

IDAHO MOVIES

Although Idaho is far-removed from the drama of Hollywood, the state has a long history of film appearances. Idaho's striking scenery and diverse landscape have provided the state with a starring role in a wide range of movies, television shows, and commercials, and renowned directors and actors frequently look to the region for inspiration. Whether you've actually set foot in Idaho, you've no doubt already discovered its unique terrain while watching the following movies that were filmed here:

2004: *Napoleon Dynamite* (Preston)

2003: *Peluca* (Preston)

2001: *Hemmingway: The Hunter of Death* (Ketchum); *Shredder* (Kellogg); *Tattoo: A Love Story* (Boise); *Town & Country* (Sun Valley)

1999: *Breakfast of Champions* (Twin Falls)

1998: *Smoke Signals* (Coeur d'Alene Indian Reservation); *Wild Wild West* (Pierce)

1997: *Dante's Peak* (Wallace); *Vanishing Pond* (Riddle)

1995: *White Wolves II: Legend of the Wild* (Island Park/Henry's Fork of the Snake River/Targhee National Forest)

1992: *Dark Horse* (Wood River Valley)

1991: *Talent for the Game* (Genessee)

1990: *Ghost Dad* (Boise)

1988: *Moving* (Boise)

1985: *Pale Rider* (Sawtooth National Recreation Area)

1980: *Bronco Billy* (Boise/Garden City/Meridian/Nampa); *Heaven's Gate* (Wallace); *Powder Heads* (Sun Valley)

1976: *Breakheart Pass* (Lewiston)

1973: *Idaho Transfer* (Arco/Craters of the Moon)

1965: *Ski Party* (Sun Valley)

1957: *Luci-Desi Comedy Hour Episode "Lucy Goes to Sun Valley"* (Sun Valley; aired April 14, 1958)

1956: *Bus Stop* (near Ketchum)

1955: *Miracle of Todd-AO* (Sun Valley)

1947: *The Unconquered* (Falls River/North Fork of the Snake River)

1941: *A Woman's Face* (Sun Valley); *Sun Valley Serenade* (Ketchum/Sun Valley)

1940: *Northwest Passage* (McCall/Sandpoint/Payette Lake); *The Mortal Storm* (Sun Valley)

1937: *I Met Him in Paris* (Sun Valley)

1931: *Believe It or Not* (Coeur d'Alene)

1926: *Snowed In* (McCall)

1925: *The Tornado* (St. Maries)

1923: *The Grub Stake* (Coolin); *Little Dramas of Big Places* (Priest Lake)

1922: *Miss Lewiston* (Lewiston)

1919: *Told in the Hills* (Priest Lake)

1915: *The Cowpuncher* (Idaho Falls)

---

and encounters between different tribes were purposeful intertribal powwows, social gatherings, and religious ceremonies.

The Kootenai, a distant relation of the eastern Algonquin tribe, migrated through British Columbia and the Pacific Northwest before planting roots in Idaho's panhandle. The abundant rivers in the region supplied the Kootenai with salmon and sturgeon while the tribe's hunters preyed upon caribou, deer, and elk. The lush forests and valleys of this Idaho region further supplied the tribe with an array of berries and wild vegetables and roots.

Residing slightly south of their Kootenai neighbors, the Nez Perce tribe claimed Idaho's Clearwater Valley as its beloved home. The river contained abundant salmon, and the valley was home to a plethora of bears, bighorn sheep, deer, elk, and moose that provided nearly all of the tribe's food and shelter requirements. In addition, the area featured numerous camas bulbs critical in supplying the tribe with ingredients for traditional tribal recipes.

The remote deserts and canyons now found within southwestern Idaho's Owyhee Canyonlands served as home territory for the Shoshone and Paiute tribes. These small nomadic tribes were known for their peaceful nature as they scoured the land in pursuit of deer, antelope, rabbits, squirrels, prairie dogs, and upland birds. On rare occasions, the tribes were lucky enough to add seeds, berries, and pine nuts to their traditionally meaty diet.

The Shoshone people also lived in harmony among south-central and southeastern Idaho's Bannock tribes. Despite maintaining different languages, the hunting lifestyle of both tribes and similar home turf bonded the groups together in peace.

The territory of all Idaho tribes expanded greatly with the introduction of horses. The pack animal provided Idaho's Native Americans with mobility they had never experienced and opened up travel to annual buffalo hunts in present-day Montana and Wyoming. This increased mobility and greed for horses came with a price, however. Conflicts over Native American hunting grounds became more frequent, and tribal warfare over stolen horses occasionally occurred. The 1800s introduction of guns to the traditional Native American lifestyle further complicated tribal relations.

At the same time power struggles were escalating between tribes, the painful tale of Native American encounters with America's expansionist legacy began to take its toll on Idaho's tribes. Although just four percent of Oregon Trail emigrant deaths in Idaho were the result of Indian skirmishes, the region's tribes were painted as violent heathens who deserved justice at the hands of the U.S. military. After the 1854 Ward Massacre and 1860 Otter-Van Orman Massacre where Idaho's tribes revolted against dwindling food supplies and desecration of traditional hunting grounds and sacred places, the U.S. government intervened. The military carried out one of the American West's most horrendous and senseless slaughters of Native Americans in southeastern Idaho's 1863 Battle of Bear River. The bloodbath only fueled the growing Native American/white conflict, resulting in further negative encounters with white pioneers and eventually instigating the unprecedented Nez Perce War of 1877.

After years of treaty talks, the American government ordered all Nez Perce onto Idaho's Lapwai Reservation by June 1877. Outraged at the demand and angered by a history of Native American abuse at the hands of whites, the non-treaty bands of Chief Joseph, White Bird, and Looking Glass fled the region with 750 men, women, and children in tow. During their 1,700-mile retreat toward an attempted safe haven in Canada, the Nez Perce fought over 2,000 U.S. soldiers and proved themselves as brave and skillful

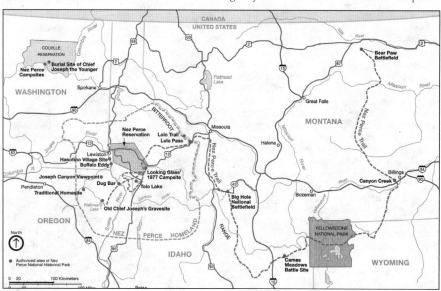

fighters. Environmental conditions, however, eventually took their toll on the young and old. Just forty miles shy of the Canadian border at Bear's Paw, Chief Joseph analyzed the dire situation of his cold, starving people and surrendered on October 6, 1877. Looking Glass was killed when he attempted to escape to Canada, but White Bird and a small band managed to evade the U.S. troops in the shadow of night and successfully crossed the border.

As a result of the conflict, Chief Joseph and his followers were sent to Washington's Colville Reservation, and the tribal members of Chief Looking Glass and White Bird were relegated back to Idaho's Lapwai Reservation. Although Joseph continually petitioned the U.S. government for permission to return to his beloved Wallowa Valley homeland, Congress denied every request. He was forced to remain brokenhearted on the reservation until his September 21, 1904 death.

The tragedy of the Nez Perce War, however, extended far deeper than the U.S. taxpayer cost of $1,873,410.43 and the destiny of the Nez Perce tribe. The conflict also reinforced the American government's belief in the necessity of reservation lands. As in other western states, Idaho's first inhabitants were forced onto reservations where boundaries were continually decreased to make room for American homesteading policies.

Today, the Coeur d'Alene Reservation rests on the southern shores of Lake Coeur d'Alene; the Fort Hall Reservation near Pocatello is home to the Shoshone-Bannock tribe; the Shoshone-Paiute tribes were forced onto the Idaho/Nevada Duck Valley Reservation; and the Nez Perce Reservation remains in the heart of north-central Idaho. The only tribe not forced onto its own reservation was the Kootenai. Despite governmental promises to provide all tribes with substantial economic aid, such pledges were never honored. In addition to minimal federal funding, Idaho's current tribal members rely upon the gaming industry to fight the reservations' widespread poverty.

Lewis and Clark Discover Idaho

Designated by President Thomas Jefferson and receiving U.S. governmental funds for their duties, twenty-six-year-old, Meriwether Lewis, and thirty-year-old, William Clark, were selected in 1803 to find a route linking the Missouri River to the Pacific Ocean. After spending the winter of 1803-1804 gathering supplies and a team of forty knowledgeable members, Lewis and Clark set out in May 1804 on what would become one of America's most legendary journeys.

Recognized and revered as the Corp of Discovery, the group of men left their St. Louis headquarters and headed west into previously uncharted territory. The Corp moved upstream, traveling up to a maximum of twenty-five miles per day when wind speeds allowed and favorable weather conditions permitted. The group of explorers faced many trials and tribulations as they wandered through present-day Nebraska, Iowa, South Dakota, North Dakota, and Montana, but the Corp persevered.

Finally, over a year after the journey's onset, the Corp of Discovery crossed the Continental Divide at Lemhi Pass on August 12, 1805 and became the first white Americans to set foot in present-day Idaho. Upon crossing over the Divide, the group continued west with the navigational and translational aid of native Idahoan, Sacajawea. The area Native Americans embraced the explorers and provided useful tips as the Corp planned its next route west. Although the group had planned to navigate the Lemhi and

Under the watch of the Grand Tetons, haybales dot the landscape surrounding Highway 33.

Salmon Rivers, they discovered upon scouting that the rivers were simply impassable. Instead, the group was forced to cross the Continental Divide two more times as they crested Lost Trail Pass into present-day Montana and then crossed over Lolo Pass back into Idaho.

The group's next encounter with Idaho's Native Americans resulted in the same warm hospitality they received upon their initial entry into the region. The group relied upon the support and well wishes of the Nez Perce, and Lewis and Clark established hunting camps near present day Orofino and Ahsaka. Naming one of these camps "Canoe Camp," the men pooled their time, resources, and work ethic to fashion sturdy canoes that would transport them to the Pacific Ocean. On October 6, 1805, the group's canoes were finished, and they set sail on the final leg of their great American journey. After enduring months of stormy winter weather, meager provisions, and scarce hunting prospects, the explorers finally made it to their destination. On November 18, 1805, Lewis and Clark's Corp of Discovery set eyes on the convergence of the Columbia River with the Pacific Ocean. The group had successfully fulfilled its mission, complete with extensive journals, maps, and tales that would satisfy even the most discriminating audience.

The group wintered along the shores of the Pacific Ocean and began their return journey on March 23, 1806. Following a nearly identical route east, the Corp proceeded back through Idaho, relying upon the help of their Native American friends to navigate Idaho's treacherous mountain ranges. Six months later, on September 23, 1806, the explorers finally concluded their adventure in St. Louis much to the shock and great relief of their supporters.

Today, the route the explorers first followed over Lemhi Pass into Idaho is maintained as the Lewis and Clark National Backcountry Byway. The Corp's routes over Lost Trail Pass and Lolo Pass are marked with Visitor Centers at the respective Idaho/Montana borders on U.S. Highway 93 and U.S. Highway 12.

The Arrival of Fur Trappers, Traders, and Mountain Men

Upon the successful completion of Lewis and Clark's westward journey, British and American fur companies jumped on the exploration bandwagon and headed west to survey potential ground for their expanding businesses. David Thompson, working for Britain's Hudson's Bay Company, entered Idaho from Canada in 1808 along with his wife and children. Working as a geographer, Thompson surveyed the surrounding region before finally settling in Idaho's panhandle. In September 1809, Thompson constructed a regional trade center at the Kullyspell House near present-day Hope. He successfully traded with the Flathead, Nez Perce, and Blackfeet Indians, sold numerous beaver pelts to London's fashion elite, and used his log trading post as the base for further Pacific Northwest exploration before migrating to Canada in 1812.

Jaded at the thought of an Englishman making such successful waves in the industry, the Missouri Fur Company ordered company partner, Andrew Henry, to stake an American claim in a region that was growing quite lucrative. Henry followed orders, and in autumn of 1810, he and a small group of comrades began their journey. After crossing over the Continental Divide, Henry discovered a scenic lake (a lake now bearing his name) in present-day eastern Idaho and designated it as an ideal winter camp. Henry, however, was not prepared for the region's harsh winters, and a lack of prey further complicated the group's situation. Forced to either starve to death or eat their transportation, Henry and his men chose to cook up their horses one by one in a desperate attempt to survive the 1810-1811 winter. Once spring arrived, Henry abandoned his company's fur trading dreams and returned to civilized life in St. Louis.

Andrew Henry's ill fortune in Idaho, however, did not deter others from enthusiastically heading to the region. In October 1811, Wilson Price Hunt led an expedition of John Jacob Astor's Pacific Fur Company across the Grand Tetons to Henry's abandoned lakefront fort. The men then decided

FAMOUS IDAHO NATIVES AND TRANSPLANTS

Joe Albertson: Founder of Albertson's grocery store chain

Ezra Taft Benson: LDS Church Prophet and former U.S. Secretary of Agriculture

Gutzon Borglum: Sculptor of Mount Rushmore

Carol R. Brink: Author of "Caddie Woodlawn" and 1936 Newberry Medal Winner

Edgar Rice Burroughs: Author of "Tarzan" stories

Frank F. Church: U.S. Senator; namesake of Idaho's Frank Church Wilderness

Ty Cobb: Baseball player

Christin Cooper: 1984 Olympic skiing silver medalist

Lillian Disney: Wife of Walt Disney

Lou Dobbs: Anchor/managing editor of CNN's "Moneyline"

Fred Dubois: U.S. Senator

Wyatt Earp: Western gunfighter

Larry EchoHawk: Elected Idaho Attorney General in 1991; he represents the first Native American to hold this post in any U.S. state

Bill Fagerbakke: Actor

Philo Farnsworth: Television inventor

Vardis Fisher: Author

Dick Fosbury: Inventor of high jumping technique known as "Fosbury Flop"

Gretchen Fraser: 1948 Olympic skiing gold medalist

Joseph Garry: Elected in 1956 as the first Native American in Idaho's legislature; twice named Outstanding Indian in North America

Mary Hallock Foote: Author

Gene Harris: Jazz musician

Ernest Hemingway: Author

Larry Jackson: St. Louis Cardinals and Chicago Cubs pitcher

Bill Johnson: 1984 Olympic skiing champion

Walter "Big Train" Johnson: Baseball pitcher

Chief Joseph: Nez Perce Indian Chief

Harmon Killebrew: Minnesota Twins baseball player

Jerry Kramer: Green Bay Packers' offensive lineman and kicker

Vernon Law: Pittsburg Pirates pitcher

Patrick McManus: Author

Barbara Morgan: NASA Teacher in Space

Dan O'Brien: Decathlete; 1996 Olympic gold medal and World Record Holder

Gracie Bowers Pfost: Idaho's first woman in the U.S. senate (served five terms)

Jake Plummer: NFL quarterback

Ezra Pound: Poet

Edward Pulaski: Inventor of fire-fighting tool, the Pulaski

Malcolm Refrew: Inventor/Chemist

Paul Revere: Musician of "Paul Revere and the Raiders"

Marjorie Reynolds: Actress

Sacajawea: Shoshone Indian woman who served as Lewis and Clark's translator

Edward Scott: Revolutionized skiing with the Scott Ski Pole

Nell Shipman: Silent screen film director and actress

J.R. Simplot: Business executive and industrialist; creator of frozen French fry

Robert E. Smylie: Political leader

Henry Spalding: Lapwai Valley missionary

Picabo Street: 1994 Olympic skiing silver medalist; 1995 and 1996 World Champion Downhill Racer.

Lana Turner: Actress

Roger Williams: Musician

to speed along their journey with a river passage. Although the group had little problem navigating the Snake River's Idaho Falls and American Falls, the river took a swift turn as the men discovered the turbulent waters of Milner Reach and Caldron Linn. After losing party members and valuable supplies, the Wilson Price Hunt expedition took to dry ground, bypassed the rest of Idaho on foot, and arrived at the Columbia River's headwaters in February 1812.

Drawing upon his experience with the Wilson Price Hunt party, native Scotsman, Donald Mackenzie, traveled back to Idaho for more adventure. Mackenzie worked as a successful Snake River guide, and on many of his trips, he received company from Hawaii islanders shipped to the Northwest as laborers. Referred to as "Owyhees," the laborers were highly regarded for their strong work ethic, and Mackenzie decided to capitalize on this characteristic on a fateful 1818 expedition. At Mackenzie's command, three of the Owyhee laborers set out to trap on an unexplored river in present day southwestern Idaho. When the laborers failed to return, Mackenzie and the rest of his party left them behind, assuming that the men had either become lost or were killed by indigenous tribes. In honor of these men, Mackenzie dubbed the river, "Owyhee River."

Next to hit the growing Idaho fur-trading scene was Scottish immigrant, Finan McDonald. As a Hudson's Bay Company employee, McDonald led a party of trappers and explorers from Spokane to Montana in 1823. Deciding to follow the trail of Lewis and Clark, McDonald and his men began their return to Washington via Idaho's Lemhi Pass. Although the group's journey had been marked with few hardships up to that point,

McDonald and his men were surprised with a Blackfeet ambush on the Lemhi River's upper stretches. Miraculously, the men defeated the notoriously fierce and brutal Blackfeet, losing just six expedition members while killing sixty-eight of the seventy-five Blackfeet warriors. After the battle's conclusion, McDonald and his men set aside fur-trading thoughts and hightailed it back to Washington. Although McDonald adamantly refused to return to the Idaho region, his bravery and well-led expedition ultimately opened additional trapping corridors in the region.

Despite their employee's harrowing experience in the wilds of Idaho, the Hudson's Bay Company continued its grand plans for British domination of the Pacific Northwest and Rocky Mountain fur trade. In 1824, Peter Skene Ogden became the Snake River operations leader. His demand for perfection and thoroughness from trappers further heightened the growing competition between British and American fur trading companies. Ogden led several prosperous trips through Snake River country and trapped thousands of beaver, his success began to dwindle in 1830 with the arrival of independent fur-trappers.

Known as mountain men, these freelance adventurers were well aware of the dangers associated with trapping amid rugged country that warring Native Americans occasionally inhabited. Their keen sense of the land's topography, weather conditions, and general beaver trapping knowledge gave these rugged frontiersmen the upper edge against company-employed trappers accustomed to foreign countries and posh living conditions. Jedediah Smith, Jim Bridger, and Jeremiah Johnston were just a few of the successful mountain men who scoured Idaho and the American

West in search of trapping treasure.

Despite the good fortune of these trapping entrepreneurs and their highly successful seasonal trading rendezvous, American and British companies continued pouring money into their own fur trapping exploration in the Idaho region. The Hudson's Bay Company established Fort Boise on the Snake River in 1834 as a permanent fur-trading fort. The fort's arrival was quickly followed by the initiation of Fort Hall. Located near present-day Blackfoot, Fort Hall celebrated its grand opening on August 5, 1834 under the management of Boston entrepreneur, Nathaniel Wyeth. Competition was fierce between the two trade forts, and Wyeth's initial excitement soon faded. Upon losing a large amount of money, Wyeth abandoned his fort in 1836, and the Hudson's Bay Company took over operations until the fort's 1856 closure.

As quickly as the rush for beaver pelts came, the fur trapping and trading business dwindled overnight when modern fashion in London declared beaver skin hats and decorative pelts a fashion faux pas. At the same time, the Rocky Mountain beaver population had become nearly extinct, and both company fur trappers and freelance mountain men were soon in search of new professions. Utilizing the routes established during the chaotic fur trapping days, many of these men assumed roles as pioneer wagon guides to the next wave of Idaho inhabitants – devoted missionaries on the prowl for converts and pioneers greedy for a piece of unspoiled Idaho mountain grandeur!

Early Missionaries & Native Americans
As Idaho's fur trapping era began to fizzle, plans were already being made for the next invasion of

easterners upon the once isolated life of Idaho's Native Americans. In 1831, several Nez Perce tribal members who had assisted the Corp of Discovery at the dawn of the nineteenth century traveled to St. Louis to visit William Clark. The Nez Perce knew that Clark had been designated the Head of U.S. Indian Affairs upon the conclusion of the famous western expedition, and they decided to petition him to send reading, writing, and agricultural instructors to aid their tribe.

Clark was quite responsive to the Nez Perce request, but somehow, the petition was misinterpreted as a call for education about the white man's god. U.S. Easterners were humbled at the long journey the Nez Perce had undertaken in an effort to embrace Christianity and denounce their heathen ways. Within no time, preachers across America were calling for missionaries to answer the Nez Perce request and spread the word of God to all indigenous tribes inhabiting the Rocky Mountain region.

Although the preachers' pleas fell on many deaf ears and made cowards out of hundreds of individuals too scared to enter the untamed western frontier, the Spaldings and Whitmans courageously accepted the call as their religious duty. In 1836, the two young Presbyterian couples loaded their wagons, left St. Louis, and relied on their faith to carry them to an unknown land. On July 4, the missionaries arrived in Idaho, dedicated to fulfilling the Nez Perce plea that had mistakenly been made to Clark five years earlier.

As the Whitmans continued their journey to establish a Washington mission among the Cayuse Indians, Henry and Eliza Spalding stayed in Nez Perce country and developed the Lapwai Mission near Idaho's Clearwater River. The Spaldings' mission was highly effective in its early years. Eliza learned the Nez Perce language and began teaching the Native Americans English while Henry spent his time proselytizing and educating the Nez Perce about farming. Despite the mission's early success, the Nez Perce gradually became weary of Henry's harsh discipline and began losing interest in farming. When word reached the Spaldings that the Whitmans had been massacred, the Spaldings abandoned the Lapwai Mission and headed west for the Willamette Valley. Henry's heart, however, never left the mission, and he returned to Lapwai in 1863 where he remained until his 1874 death.

The Spaldings and the Whitmans were not alone in their efforts to convert Idaho's indigenous tribes. In 1841, Father Pierre Jean de Smet arrived in Coeur d'Alene and began making plans for the Catholic Mission of the Sacred Heart. In 1847, Father Antonio Ravalli finished de Smet's mission on a hilltop overlooking the Coeur d'Alene River and began spreading Catholicism to all open ears. Additional Catholic missions spread like wildfire across Idaho's panhandle and extended into north-central Idaho. Today, many of the region's Native Americans retain the Catholic heritage that their ancestors acquired from Father de Smet, Father Ravalli, and the era's other dedicated nuns and priests.

Arriving on the heels of the Protestants and Catholics were twenty-seven young Mormon men commissioned by Brigham Young to enter central Idaho's Lemhi Valley in 1855. Located at an ideal site near present-day Tendoy where the fervent missionaries could spread Mormon teachings to Shoshone, Bannock, and Nez Perce tribal members, the mission was successful in its infancy. The missionaries established favorable relationships with all three tribes, but the tribes ultimately began to resent one another. Out of jealousy and rage of one another, the Indians turned on the

The Mormon Temple behind the falls of Idaho Falls.

missionaries, stole the mission's horses and supplies, and forced the Mormon men to head back to Utah in spring of 1858. Despite this setback for the Mormon Church, Brigham Young stared down discouragement, and many more Mormons were eventually ordered to migrate north towards Idaho on the heels of other pioneers.

Pioneers and Mormons
When Narcissa Whitman and Eliza Spalding became the first white women to safely cross the Continental Divide into the vast Rocky Mountain region, they unknowingly paved the way for thousands of pioneer emigrants. Prior to their crossing, the American West was viewed negatively as a rugged land where women and children were incapable of survival. Narcissa and Eliza, however, dispelled the myth, and adventure-seeking easterners began viewing the west as a place where dreams came true and families could live peacefully away from the east's overcrowded cities. In 1842, the first wagon train of families from Missouri, Kentucky, Illinois, and Iowa crossed the Continental Divide into Idaho. From there, the wagons continued to Oregon's verdant Willamette Valley, carving out the Oregon Trail route that was soon embraced by thousands of other migrating families.

Between 1842 and 1847, just over 5,000 people made the average five-month long journey west. Word continued to spread about the region's abundant land and livable terrain. Despite growing incidences of Indian attacks, thousands more cast aside their fears and left behind the comforts of established homes to create a new family destiny. Between 1849 and 1860, 42,000 pioneers headed to Oregon, while over 200,000 more took the trail to California. By the end of the great westward migration, 500,000 pioneers had safely completed the journey, an innumerable amount had lost their lives to disease, and the American West was transformed from a land of mystery into a land of promise and freedom where all were welcome.

Embracing the west's new image and realizing the potential to escape religious persecution, Mormon church officials christened Utah Territory as the new base for the religion's faith. Between 1846 and 1869, Prophet Brigham Young and

70,000 other Mormon believers moved the church's former Nauvoo, Illinois headquarters to the Great Salt Lake region in Utah. Within no time, Brigham Young sent settlers north into Wyoming and the outer reaches of Utah Territory to tame the deviant ways of those with no religious background. On one such occasion in April 1860, a group of Utah Mormons headed north, established a farming community, developed an irrigation system, and spread their religion throughout the region. Although the pioneers believed their small town of Franklin was situated in Utah, an official 1872 government survey proved otherwise. As luck would have it, Brigham Young's Mormon followers had successfully founded Idaho's first permanent white settlement. Within a matter of years, the church's procreation emphasis allowed the Mormon faith to spread widely across southeastern Idaho and throughout the Cache Valley. A dense Mormon population in eastern Idaho is evident to this day.

Fortune Hunters
While visions of a free religious society occupied the thoughts of Mormon officials, many pioneers migrating through Idaho had a much different agenda on their minds. The "Golden State" of California and its lucrative gold mines left men all across the globe lusting after strike-it-rich dreams. Sparked by the 1849 discovery of California gold, thousands of treasure hunters surged westward in search of their own mother lode.

Since most of these men felt no attachment to California, many were just as happy to wander around the American West in search of any available lucky strike. Miners flocked to Montana, Colorado, Wyoming, and finally in 1860, to Idaho. Hearing stories of rich lodes in Idaho's Nez Perce Country, E. D. Pierce and ten of his associates snuck onto the Nez Perce Reservation and began digging for gold on the Clearwater River banks. Although the men failed to receive permission from the Native Americans, the Indians begrudgingly allowed the men to stay. When Pierce's associate, Wilbur Bassett, found a strike of "oro fino" (Spanish for "fine gold"), Idaho became the new future of gold mining.

Despite Nez Perce Reservation boundaries that technically prohibited white settlement, nothing would stand in the way of a new wave of determined treasure seekers. The towns of Pierce City and Orofino sprang up overnight, and by spring 1862, more than 10,000 white people and Chinese immigrants illegally inhabited the Nez Perce tribal land. Over the course of its operation, the Orofino Mining District shipped out $3 million in gold dust. At the same time, a new strike was in full swing in the Boise Basin and Owyhee Mountains. Idaho City, Placerville, Centerville, Rocky Bar, Atlanta, Murray, Eagle City, and Silver City became the new "best" places in Idaho to unearth a fortune. Although the availability of gold eventually dwindled and lost its allure, Idaho's rich mining history was far from over.

In 1879, Wood River Valley miners discovered Idaho's first deposits of silver, lead, and zinc, and a new mining boom was under way with the establishment of mining camps at Ketchum, Hailey, and Bellevue. Six years later, Noah Kellogg made his lucky silver strike on the South Fork of the Coeur d'Alene River near present day Wardner. Word spread overnight of Kellogg's find, and the area was immediately christened "Silver Valley." Most of Idaho's mining boomtowns have since become mere echoes of their past, but mines in the state's panhandle remain a profitable testimony to this rich aspect of Idaho's economic history and future. The region continues to be recognized as one of the world's most profitable mining districts.

The Arrival of the Railroad
Although the Oregon Trail and mining gold rush contributed significantly to the settlement of Idaho, the arrival of the railroad was responsible for creating several new communities and spurring the state's economic development during the late 1800s and early 1900s. Idaho's first railroad line arrived on May 2, 1874 when the Utah Northern Railroad made its way from Ogden, Utah to Franklin. With the line's arrival, Franklin became a major freight center. Ten years later, the Utah and Northern Railway Company decided to make a profit off this Idaho shipping center and extended a line from Franklin to the Northern Pacific Railroad Line in Garrison, Montana. In its wake, the line initiated the establishment of several southeastern Idaho towns, including Rexburg, Rigby, and Victor.

Prior to the arrival of the Utah Northern in southeastern Idaho, Union Pacific Railroad officials had long had their eye on the booming Idaho region. Scouts surveyed the area around Pocatello as early as 1867, but construction was not initiated until 1881. Serving as an affiliate of the Union Pacific, the Oregon Short Line Railroad made its way through Montpelier, Pocatello, Shoshone, and the Wood River Valley mines before arriving at its final destination of Huntington, Oregon for the first time on November 17, 1884.

1882 saw the arrival of a Northern Pacific Railway line running through Sandpoint on its journey from Montana to Washington. Over the course of the next two decades, the Great Northern Railway and the Chicago, Milwaukee, St. Paul, and Pacific Railroad pushed additional lines through northern Idaho. The railroads accelerated the region's booming silver mine activity, and Idaho was finally connected to the rest of the world with modern transportation.

Railroad officials continued to bisect Idaho with new lines throughout the remainder of the 1800s and into the early twentieth century. As a result, America began to shrink, the American

West became an even more hospitable place, and Idaho was well on its way to attracting new residents and businesses.

The Timber, Agricultural, and Energy Boom
When the railroad industry chugged and steamed its way across Idaho's plains, forests, and mountains, it brought with it new economic prosperity and diversified job opportunities. With the expansion of the railroad into western territories, timber barons who had previously made a fortune clear-cutting the U.S.' eastern forests began looking for new horizons. These individuals' quick scan of railroad accessible land drew them to the Idaho panhandle where they discovered endless stands of great white pines. As the twentieth century dawned across Idaho's pristine northern forests, the region's miners were forced to make room for another industry dependent upon the state's natural resources.

Droves of loggers enveloped the northern panhandle, and the timber industry teamed up with the railroads in a lucrative business of clear-cutting and shipping. Although the industry contributed greatly to Idaho's economy and the budding development of new construction in the Pacific Northwest, the activity came with a price. A few workers lost their lives or were injured in the profession, and unscrupulous cutting restrictions resulted in the desecration of what once encompassed some of Idaho's most scenic territory. Today, the logging industry remains a visible presence in Idaho but on a much smaller-scale with more stringent and responsible business practices.

While loggers migrated to northern Idaho, a mass exodus of farmers from across the nation was making its way to other regions in Idaho. Dry farmers first settled on north-central Idaho's Palouse Hills. The rolling green hills were transformed into acres of profitable crops and orchards that supplied the food needs of the ever-expanding Idaho and Pacific Northwest population. Although the Palouse region's dry farming continues to this day, many farmers were eventually lured to the Snake River country in southwestern and south-central Idaho with the 1894 Carey Act. Farmers rushed to buy their own piece of the area's irrigated farmland, and both private and Bureau of Reclamation dam projects ensured that irrigation would be available for years to come. Today, the once dry, desert terrain of south-central Idaho has been reconfigured into an irrigated green oasis boasting some of America's richest farmland. Several other irrigated farms can be found throughout Idaho, and sugar beets, potatoes, and wheat remain the state's most bountiful crops.

As hydroelectric projects grew across the state in response to increasing farming demands, the U.S. government began making its own energy-related plans. The Atomic Energy Commission constructed the National Reactor Testing Station in southeastern Idaho in 1949 and immediately set to work experimenting with atomic energy. On December 20, 1951, the site's Experimental Breeder Reactor-1 became the world's first nuclear reactor to produce usable amounts of electricity. This unprecedented feat led to the July 17, 1955 accomplishment where scientists created a chain reaction lighting the nearby town of Arco with over two million watts of atomically powered electric service. The testing site is now known as the Idaho National Engineering and Environmental Laboratory (INEEL), and experiments with atomic energy presently employ hundreds of Idaho residents.

POPULATION

Since entering the union as the forty-third state on July 3, 1890, Idaho and its population has grown in leaps and bounds. Between 1900 and 1910, the state's population more than doubled and sparked a population trend that continues to this day. Idaho was recognized as one of the fastest growing states in America between 1990 and 2000 and is presently home to over 1,300,000 permanent residents as the U.S.' thirty-ninth most populous state.

As more and more people flock to the Gem State in search of wide-open spaces, outdoor recreation, low crime rates, and family-friendly communities, native Idahoans have both welcomed and disparaged the development of their beloved home. The state's population growth has brought new economic opportunities, jumpstarted the state's arts and cultural scene, and has provided homeowners in many parts of Idaho with increased property values. At the same time, urban sprawl has left some residents complaining about desecration of wildlife habitat, increased traffic, commuter woes, and overcrowded cities further congested by shrinking availability of uninhabited land.

Despite the widely debated pros and cons of Idaho's growth pattern, the expanding population has given Idaho a new sense of life and vigor with the complexity of people now residing in the state. Metropolitan areas in Coeur d'Alene and Boise (which by most standards are simply mid-sized American cities) weave their livelihoods amid isolated farmland, forests, and rural towns where Main Street represents the community's only paved avenue. Native American groups mix with Caucasians and people of Hispanic origin, and a significant Basque population inhabits southwestern Idaho. Variety not only consumes Idaho's topography, but it is also the name of the game when it comes to the state's numerous towns and cities.

Even though some of Idaho's small towns may still be waiting the arrival of their first movie theater and hushed starry nights may have forever faded from the city skyscape, Idaho's widely divergent residents are still linked with a common appreciation for the gem they've discovered. Like the state's earliest residents, today's population is drawn to the diversity that encapsulates the Gem State, the opportunities Idaho affords, and a landscape still open to new exploration and individual dreams!

ECONOMY

Reflective of the state's diverse habitation and natural resources, Idaho's economy has long been multifaceted. The state's founding financial fathers embraced the mining, timber, and agricultural industries, and this economic heritage remains widespread throughout Idaho. Although no longer the state's primary source of income, the valuable mining industry produces silver, gold, lead, zinc, antimony, phosphates, copper, garnets, diamonds, clay, molybdenum, and a host of other precious minerals. On the agricultural front, Idaho's famous potatoes lead the way, followed closely by crops of sugar beats, wheat, hay, alfalfa, beans, peas, hops, mint, and bluegrass seed. Beef cattle, dairy goods, sheep, and wool also contribute to the farm and ranch sector. Timber companies, although on the decline, rely upon Idaho's numerous forests and increasingly stringent business practices to supply the nation with building materials and paper products.

At the dawn of the twenty-first century, Idaho's financial picture began to change with a future shifting away from traditional economic main-stays. For the first time in state history, manufacturing and service industries outpaced agriculture and mining as the leaders of Idaho's economy. Technologically advanced industries, such as computer component manufacturers, have found a new home in Idaho's more metropolitan areas, and Boise is consistently ranked as one of America's top cities for hosting technology-based businesses. The addition of large construction firms, food processing plants, and wholesale and retail trade has also established Idaho's presence in the global market.

The newest addition to Idaho's economic pie is a developing tourism sector. Although Idaho was once ranked the least visited state in America, state officials, corporate enterprises, and local business owners have joined forces to climb out of this economically ruinous pit. As a result, people across the world are now standing up and taking notice of the awe-inspiring and unspoiled nature encompassing much of Idaho's terrain. Sun Valley, America's first destination ski-resort, has developed itself into a highly regarded year-round vacation destination, while Coeur d'Alene plays upon its lakeside location to drive in visitors. Smaller communities have followed suit, with Kellogg developing a ski hill and McCall actively promoting its year-round scenic treasures. As more Idaho towns embrace the reality of Idaho's attractiveness to vacationers, the tourism industry will become an even more viable source of state revenue and an economic platform for Idaho's future.

ARTS AND CULTURE

Home to both past and present creative geniuses, Idaho features an arts and culture scene brimming with vibrancy. Literary legends, including Ernest Hemingway and Ezra Pound, trace a portion of their wandering roots to Idaho, and many actors, musicians, and artists have found their inspirational beginnings here as well. As a proud reflection of this heritage, both small towns and larger cities in Idaho offer diverse cultural opportunities for residents and visitors.

Shakespeare comes alive every summer in Idaho's parks, ballerinas twirl to the famous *Nutcracker Suite*, and operas, symphonies, and community bands take the spotlight in community performance centers and open-air theaters. For those craving fine art, Idaho art galleries are abundant, and local art walks occur year-round. In addition, many rural retailers specialize in selling local creative wares, from handmade pottery to log furniture to blown glass. Idaho's cultural scene is further enhanced with dramatic performances ranging from comedic hilarities to heart-wrenching dramas.

For those who venture off the main highways to glimpse a bit of local color, a thriving arts scene is just around the corner. Dig just a little, and you'll be rewarded with some of the nation's most talented artisans, musicians, and stage performers!

RECREATION

While the rest of the country is hibernating during winter or staying indoors to avoid another summer scorcher, Idaho is buzzing with activity. Placid blue lakes, thundering whitewater torrents, rivers filled with trophy trout, forests covered with trails, and mountain slopes frosted with fluffy flakes combine to create one of America's most spectacular destinations.

In Idaho, public land and pristine nature are so prevalent that it is hard to avoid at least some

A lone group of trees stands out against the St. Anthony Sand Dunes.

form of recreation. Idaho is often nicknamed the whitewater capital of the world, and kayakers and rafters tempt fate each summer as they crazily crash down the Salmon, Snake, Lochsa, Payette, Clearwater, Owyhee, Bruneau, Jarbidge, and Selway Rivers. Hikers, equestrians, and mountain bike enthusiasts will find trails of all skill levels within the state's spectacular forests and mountain ranges, and hunters flock to the state each fall in search of elk, antelope, deer, bears, mountain lions, moose, and upland birds. Winter enthusiasts are greeted with local and destination downhill ski areas, miles of groomed Nordic ski trails under Idaho's Park and Ski System, and glassy lakes frozen into popular ice skating rinks. Fishing maintains a loyal fan club year-round, and Idaho caters to anglers with hundreds of fishing access areas. Fishing licenses are reasonably priced and may be obtained by calling the Idaho Department of Fish and Game at (208) 334-3700. Natural hot springs also bubble and steam in both undeveloped and commercial sites, and many are available for soaking year-round.

Take a ride on the wild side and turn your vacation into an adventure you'll always remember. Directions to and descriptions of hot springs, river adventures, mountain bike rides, downhill ski resorts, cross-country skiing areas, hiking trails, lake recreation, and popular fishing spots line the pages of this book. As an added bonus, the back of each regional section includes a complete list of the area's outfitters and guides who are happy to assist you on the Idaho adventure of your choice.

IDAHO'S STATE PARK SYSTEM

In addition to boasting contiguous America's largest backcountry area and recreational opportunities located within easy walking or driving distance of several communities, Idaho preserves thirty unique state parks. The Idaho Department of Parks and Recreation represents the great variety and beauty of Idaho and develops and maintains trails while managing an array of outdoor recreation programs and facilities.

Idaho State Parks are scattered throughout the state and afford a diversity of visitor facilities, from showers and concessions to primitive camping

sites. Further information is available from the Idaho State Parks and Recreation Office in Boise, on the Internet at www.idahoparks.org, or by calling (208) 334-4199.

When visiting any of Idaho's State Parks, please note the following fee schedule and rules in an effort to sustain the parks for the enjoyment of future generations.

Fees:

There is a charge for camping, with or without hookups. Camping is permitted only in designated areas, and reservations for campsites, cabins, and yurts can be made up to ninety days in advance online or by telephone. The fees collected by the Idaho Department of Parks and Recreation go right back into the operation and maintenance of parks and recreation programs. The following fees are subject to change pending legislative action. Idaho's six percent sales tax applies to campsites. Camping fees include the right to use designated campgrounds and facilities. Utilities and facilities may be restricted by weather or other factors.

- Primitive Campsite (may include a table, grill, camp-spur, vault toilet, no water): $7 per day

- Basic Campsite (may include a table, grill, camp-spur, vault toilet, central water): $9 per day

- Developed Campsite (may include a table, grill, camp-spur, flush toilets, central water): $12 per day

- Deluxe Campsite (designed to accommodate higher occupancy limits of up to 12 persons): $22 per day

- Electric hookups at site, where available: Additional $4 per day

- Sewer hookups at site, where available: Additional $2 per day

Idaho Trivia

In Idaho, it is illegal to give another person a box of candy weighing more than 50 pounds.

Length of Stay

Length of stay is limited to 15 days in any 30-day period.

Motorized Vehicle Entrance Fee

The Motorized Vehicle Entrance Fee (MVEF) is a daily charge for motorized vehicles. The $4 MVEF is charged when a vehicle enters a designated state park area. The fee is the same regardless of how many people are in the vehicle. Visitors entering an Idaho State Park without a motorized vehicle do not pay. The MVEF does not permit use of campsites.

Annual State Park Passport

The $25 passport allows you to bring your vehicle into any of Idaho's state parks as many times as you wish during the calendar year without paying the MVEF. A passport for a second vehicle is $5 at any time. The second vehicle passport must be purchased at the same location as the first passport. A vehicle registration in the same owner's name is required. The Annual Passport does not apply to camping.

Camping in Boats, Moorage

Overnight moorage for persons who have paid a campsite fee is $5 for any length of vessel. The charge for overnight moorage while camping on a vessel is $8 per night for vessels under 26 feet and $11 per night for vessels 26 feet and over. Priest Lake, Heyburn, and Coeur d'Alene Parkway allow camping on your boat. You may also boat in, camp in the campground, and moor your boat overnight at Heyburn and Priest Lake. The charge for any length of vessel moored at a buoy overnight is $5.

Quiet Hours

The hours between 10 PM and 7 AM are quiet hours, unless otherwise posted. No generators or other motorized equipment emitting-sound and exhaust may be operated during quiet hours.

Campsite Parking

All boats, trailers, rigs, and motorized vehicles must fit entirely within the campsite parking spur. All equipment which does not fit entirely within the campsite parking spur must be parked outside the campground in an area designated by the park manager. If no outside parking is available, a second campsite must be purchased. All camping equipment and personal belongings must be maintained within the assigned campsite. One extra vehicle is allowed per campsite, if it fits. If it does not, a second site must be purchased.

Check Out

Check out time is 1 PM.

Visitors

Visitors are welcome during day-use hours. They must park outside the campground, except with permission of the park manager. Visitors must pay the Motorized Vehicle Entrance Fee if they bring a vehicle into the park.

Prohibited Camping

No camping is permitted on beaches, parking lots, or day-use facilities.

Campfires and Fireworks

Fires are allowed only in designated areas. Fireworks are not permitted.

Motorized Vehicle Use

Motor vehicles, including motorbikes and ATVs, must stay on established roadways and in parking lots.

Pets

Pets are welcome in most parks, but you must keep them on a leash no longer than six feet, or confined to your camper. Do not leave pets unattended in a closed vehicle during the heat of the day. At night, they must be kept inside a vehicle or tent. Some parks have established pet exercise areas. Please ask. Pets are not allowed on beaches. They are not allowed at Eagle Island State Park or at the Sandy Point Unit of Lucky Peak State Park. Pets are allowed only in the parking lot at Harriman State Park.

Resource Protection

Wildlife and vegetation are protected in all Idaho State Parks.

Swimming

Swimming is authorized only in plainly marked areas. There are no lifeguards on duty. Glass containers are not allowed on beaches or at swim areas.

Group Facilities

There are many opportunities for small or large groups to use the facilities of the Idaho Department of Parks and Recreation. Scout groups, family reunions, company picnics, Samborees – they all come under the heading of group use.

Groups of 25 or more, or any group needing special considerations, will need a permit. Permits are required to assure that, if needed, arrangements have been made for sanitation, park population density limitations, safety, and regulation of traffic.

Additional Information

For information about a specific park or facility, contact the park manager. The minimum non-refundable reservation fee is $25. Additional fees may be charged depending on the cost of services provided. Most parks can accommodate group activities of 25 to 100 people, and some parks have special accommodations for groups.

Fees and rules information reprinted from the Idaho State Parks and Recreation Department website

FOREST SERVICE CABINS

One of the best-kept secrets in Idaho is the availability of cabins and lookout stations that the U.S. Forest Service makes available to the public at a nominal fee. At the end of each section, a list of available cabins along with detailed information on each has been provided. Following is some general information about reserving and using the cabins.

Making Reservations

The recreational cabins in the National Forests of Idaho are available for use on a first-come, first-served basis, but reservations are required. Reservations may be made in person, by mail, or by phone by contacting the specific Ranger District listed. Reservations for some cabins may also be made through the National Recreation Reservation Service at 1-(877) 444-6777.

Facilities

The cabins available through the rental program are rustic and primitive. These facilities were once used as guard stations and fire lookouts by Forest Rangers. Most cabins are located in remote areas, generally accessible via narrow, winding, dirt or gravel roads. With the exception of a few cabins, there are no modern conveniences or the safeguards of modern society – no telephones, traffic jams, neighbors, and no emergency services.

When making reservations, inquire about what is or is not furnished with the cabin or lookout. The facilities are generally equipped with the bare basics, including a table, chairs, wood stove, and bunks (most with mattresses, some without). Bedding is not furnished. Cooking utensils are available at some cabins, but not all. Electricity and piped-in water are generally not available. It may be necessary to bring in safe drinking water, or be prepared to chemically treat or boil water for consumption. At some cabins, you will need to find and cut your own firewood. Expect to use outdoor privies.

Potential Risks

Travel on the National Forests and use of rustic cabins or lookouts involves a degree of risk. Recreationists must assume responsibility of obtaining the knowledge and skills necessary to protect themselves from injury and illness. Weather, road conditions, personal preparation, and other factors can influence travel time and difficulty. Weather changes rapidly in the backcountry. Visitors may encounter sudden storms, including lightning, as well as cold, unexpected temperatures. Responsible preparation is essential. Before the trip, contact the local Ranger District for current conditions of facilities and accessibility.

Cleanup

Before leaving, all users are requested to: make certain all fires are out; pack out all garbage, including empty bottles or cans; clean the cabin; and leave a supply of firewood.

Partially reprinted from a U.S. Forest Service brochure

WIDE OPEN SPACE

Unlike many of its Rocky Mountain counterparts where most land is privately owned, Idaho fortunately claims over 37 million acres of public land. This natural outdoor playground is brimming with campgrounds, trails, and backcountry roads that invite discovery. Many of these pristine, wide-open spaces are under the active management of the U.S. Forest Service, the Bureau of Land Management, and other federal and state land management agencies.

Intermingled with Idaho's stunning and well-maintained public land, however, are occasional plots of private land. While some private landowners are more than willing to share their

IDAHO LICENSE PLATE NUMBERS

Throughout the history of Idaho's Motor Vehicle Department, Idaho's license plates have featured nearly every color of the rainbow along with a wide range of artistic designs. Coupled with the plates' changing artwork was a once frequently evolving numbering system used to identify different regions throughout the state. Prior to 1932, Idaho's license plates featured a simple numerical system. After several other numbering systems were tested and applied to Idaho's license plates, the state finally adopted its current county prefix designation system in 1945.

1A: Ada County
2A: Adams County
1B: Bannock County
2B: Bear Lake County
3B: Benewah County
4B: Bingham County
5B: Blaine County
6B: Boise County
7B: Bonner County
8B: Bonneville County
9B: Boundary County
10B: Butte County
1C: Camas County
2C: Canyon County
3C: Caribou County
4C: Cassia County
5C: Clark County
6C: Clearwater County
7C: Custer County
E: Elmore County
1F: Franklin County
2F: Fremont County
1G: Gem County
2G: Gooding County
I: Idaho County
1J: Jefferson County
2J: Jerome County
K: Kootenai County
1L: Latah County
2L: Lemhi County
3L: Lewis County
4L: Lincoln County
1M: Madison County
2M: Minidoka County
N: Nez Perce County
1O: Oneida County
2O: Owyhee County
1P: Payette County
2P: Power County
S: Shoshone County
1T: Teton County
2T: Twin Falls County
V: Valley County
W: Washington County

piece of this marvelous state with others, some are not, and "No Trespassing" signs should be taken seriously. In all instances, exercise common courtesy and always receive permission from the property owner before entering or wandering across these privately maintained open spaces.

In some instances, public land access may also be restricted. Federal and state agencies will occasionally close public roads to protect animal mating environments or preserve fragile forest and rangeland ecosystems. All recreational users are asked to respect such closures and should at all times practice "leave no trace" outdoor ethics. Detailed information and maps regarding public land access are available from regional land and forest managers.

THE ROADS

Gravel roads intermingle with interstates and state highways in this part of the country. Although most of Idaho's paved roads are well-maintained, some mountain roads are narrow and windy with little or no shoulder. Speed limits are posted on most roads and are vigorously enforced for the safety of all travelers.

During wet or wintry weather, beware of black ice! This is a virtually invisible layer of ice that forms on road surfaces after fog. Be particularly careful on stretches of road that parallel rivers and creeks. The early morning fog rising off the water can settle on the road, freezing instantly if temperatures are just right. If you feel yourself sliding, tap your brakes gently. If you slam on the brakes, it is all but over. Gently steer into the direction of your skid (if your back end is going right – steer right).

GUMBO

We gave this subject a separate headline, and it is very important that you read it – and heed it. While Idaho isn't the only state that has gumbo, it has its fair share. If you become a resident, it is one of the first things for which you develop a healthy respect. Grizzlies and rattlesnakes might be the hazards you're warned about, but gumbo is the one that will get you.

You'll find gumbo in various parts of the state, predominantly in more rural areas where backcountry roads frequently criss-cross the terrain. It lies in wait on what in dry weather appears to be an ordinary rock hard dirt road. Your first clue is the occasional sign that reads Road Impassable When Wet. This is a clear understatement. When these roads become even mildly wet, they turn into a monster that swallows all sizes of vehicles – and yes, even 4-wheel drive SUVs. Think you'll get a tow? Forget it. No tow truck operator with a higher IQ than dirt will venture onto it until it dries. If you walk on it, you will grow six inches taller and gain 25 pounds all on the bottom of your shoes. It can coat your tires until they won't turn anymore. Of course, this is if it doesn't swallow you whole first like an unsuspecting native in a Tarzan movie who steps into quicksand.

Bottom line, heed the signs. If it looks like rain, head for the nearest paved road. When it comes to swallowing things whole, the Bermuda Triangle is an amateur compared to Idaho gumbo.

PRECAUTIONS

Water Sports
Beware of high river waters in the spring due to melting snow. Before venturing out on a river

adventure, contact knowledgeable local businesses or state recreation officials for the latest water conditions.

Animal Caution
Grizzly bears are scattered throughout Idaho's mountains, forests, and wilderness areas. Grizzlies are vicious when provoked, and it doesn't take much to rile them. Check with local rangers for bear updates and guidelines before heading into bear country. Never hike alone, and make noise along the trail to warn bears of your presence. If you camp, do not sleep near strong smells (toiletries) or food. Cook meals and hang all food from branches at least 100 yards from your tent. Also be alert for mountain lions and moose. Mountain lions are rarely spotted, but are violent predators when provoked. Moose, especially those with offspring, have been known to charge if individuals get too close or the animal feels threatened.

Rattlesnake Warning
Rattlesnakes are common, especially in the desert terrain of southern Idaho. A bite from the snake can be fatal if not properly treated. These snakes are not aggressive and will usually retreat unless threatened. It is recommended that you wear strong and high top boots when hiking, and be mindful of your step. Be especially careful near rocky areas; snakes often sun themselves on exposed rocks. If you hear a rattle, stop and slowly back away. If bitten, immobilize the area and seek medical care immediately.

Weather
Extremes are commonplace in Idaho without a moment's notice. In high temperatures, drink plenty of water. Idaho's humidity is relatively low, which aids dehydration in warm weather. Nights can be cold even during summer, so pack extra clothes if your plans include the outdoors. Sudden storms can blow in; be prepared with rain and wind gear.

Winter weather is the greatest concern. While roads can be treacherous when snow covered, melting snow and ice can also leave small and invisible patches of ice on the road. In addition, wildlife commonly descend from the mountains and forests in search of food; be aware of deer, elk, and moose on the road, particularly at dusk, sunset, or at night when visibility is limited. If you travel by automobile during Idaho's winter, have plenty of blankets or a sleeping bag, warm clothing, flashlight, and food and water on hand.

AND FINALLY...

In instances where we have included information from other well-researched, well-written materials, we have attempted to credit every source as accurately as possible. It was our goal to provide you, the reader, the maximum amount of information possible to make your explorations of Idaho enjoyable while providing all the resources you need in one book. Hopefully we accomplished that goal. If there is anything we've overlooked, we would certainly like to hear from you so that we can include it in future editions.

Happy Trails!

IDAHO ZIP CODES

By Town

Town	Zip
Aberdeen	83210
Acequia	83350
Ahsahka	83520
Albion	83311
Almo	83312
American Falls	83211
Arbon	83212
Arcs	83213
Arimo	83214
Ashton	83420
Ashton	83447
Athol	83801
Atlanta	83601
Atomic City	83215
Avery	83802
Bancrott	83217
Banks	83602
Basalt	83218
Bayview	83803
Bellevue	83313
Bern	83220
Blackfoot	83221
Blanchard	83804
Bliss	83314
Bloomington	83223
Boise	83701
Boise	83702
Boise	83703
Boise	83704
Boise	83705
Boise	83706
Boise	83707
Boise	83708
Boise	83709
Boise	83711
Boise	83712
Boise	83713
Boise	83714
Boise	83715
Boise	83716
Boise	83717
Boise	83788
Boise	83799
Bonners Ferry	83805
Bovill	83806
Bruneau	83604
Buhl	83316
Burley	83318
Calder	83808
Caldwell	83605
Caldwell	83606
Caldwell	83607
Cambridge	83610
Carey	83320
Careywood	83809
Carmen	83462
Cascade	83611
Castleford	83321
Cataldo	83810
Centervllle	83631
Challis	83226
Challis	83229
Cheater	83421
Chubbuck	83202
Clark Fork	83811
Clarkia	83812
Clayton	83227
Clearwater	83539
Clifton	83228
Cobalt	83229
Cocolalla	83813
Coeur d'Alene	83814
Coeur d'Alene	83815
Coeur d'Alene	83816
Colburn	83865
Conda	83230
Coolin	83821
Corral	83322
Cottonwood	83522
Cottonwood	83533
Cottonwood	83538
Council	83612
Craigmont	83523
Culdesac	83524
Culdesac	83548
Dalton Gardens	83815
Darlington	83255
Dayton	83232
Deary	83823
Declo	83323
Desmet	83824
Dietrlch	83324
Dingle	83233
Dixie	83525
Donnelly	83615
Dover	83825
Downey	83234
Driggs	83422
Dubois	83423
Dubois	83446
Eagle	83616
Eastport	83826
Eden	83325
Elba	83342
Elk City	83525
Elk Horn	83354
Elk River	83827
Ellis	83235
Emmett	83617
Fairfield	83322
Fairfield	83327
Felt	83424
Fenn	83531
Ferdinand	83526
Fernwood	83830
Filer	83328
Firth	83236
Fish Haven	83287
Fort Hall	83203
Franklin	83237
Fruitland	83619
Fruitvale	83620
Garden Valley	83622
Geneses	83832
Geneva	83238
Georgetown	83239
Gibbonsville	83463
Glenns Ferry	83623
Gooding	83330
Grace	83241
Grace	83283
Grand View	83624
Grangeville	83530
Grangeville	83531
Grasmere	83604
Greencreek	83533
Greenleaf	83626
Hagerman	83332
Hailey	83333
Hamer	83425
Hammett	83627
Hansen	83334
Harrison	83833
Harvard	83834
Hayden	83835
Hayden Lake	83835
Hazelton	83335
Headquarters	83546
Heyburn	83336
Hidden Springs	83703
Hill City	83337
Holbrook	83243
Homedale	83628
Hope	83836
Horseshoe Bend	83629
Howe	83244
Huston	83630
Idaho City	83631
Idaho Falls	83401
Idaho Falls	83402
Idaho Falls	83403
Idaho Falls	83404
Idaho Falls	83405
Idaho Falls	83406
Indian Valley	83632
Inkom	83245
Iona	83427
Irwin	83428
Island Park	83429
Island Park	83433
Jerome	83338
Juilaetta	83535
Kamiah	83536
Kellogg	83837
Kendrick	83537
Ketchum	83340
Keuterville	83522
Keuterville	83538
Kimberly	83341
King Hill	83633
Kingston	83839
Kooskia	83539
Kootenal	83840
Kuna	83634
Laciede	83841
Lake Fork	83635
Lapwai	83540
Lava Hot Springs	83246
Leadore	83464
Lemhi	83465
Lenore	83541
Laths	83636
Lewiston	83501
Lewlavfile	83431
Lowman	83637
Luclle	83542
Mackay	83251
Hacks Inn	83433
Malad City	83252
Malad City	83280
Malta	83342
Marsing	83639
May	83253
McCall	83635
McCall	83638
McCommon	83250
Medimont	83842
Melba	83641
Marian	83434
Meridian	83642
Meridian	83680
Mesa	83643
Middleton	83644
Midvale	83645
Minidoka	83343
Monteview	83435
Montour	83617
Montpelier	83254
Moore	83255
Moreland	83256
Moscow	83843
Mountain Home	83647
Mountain Home AFB	83648
Moyle Springs	83845
Muilan	83846
Murphy	83650
Murray	83874
Murtaugh	83344
Nat	83342
Nampa	83651
Nampa	83652
Nampa	83653
Nampa	83686
Nampa	83687
Naples	83847
New Centerville	83631
New Meadows	83654
New Plymouth	83655
Newdale	83436
Nez Perceperce	83543
Nordman	83848
North Fork	83466
North Fork	83469
Notus	83656
Oakley	83346
Obsidian	83340
Ola	83657
Oldtown	83822
Onaway	83855
Oreana	83650
Orofino	83544
Osburn	83849
Ovid	83254
Palisades	83428
Paris	83261
Paris	83287
Parker	83438
Parma	83660
Patterson	83253
Paul	83347
Payette	83661
Peck	83545
Picabo	83348
Pierce	83546
Pinehurst	83850
Pingree	83262
Pioneerville	83631
Placerville	83666
Plummer	83851
Pocatello	83201
Pocatello	83202
Pocatello	83204
Pocatello	83205
Pocatello	83206
Pocatello	83203
Pollock	83547
Ponderay	83852
Porthill	83853
Post Falls	83854
Post Falls	83877
Potlatch	83855
Preston	83263
Priest Riverer	83856
Princeton	83857
Rathdrum	83858
Reubens	83548
Rexburg	83440
Richfield	83349
Riddle	83604
Rigby	83442
Riggins	83549
RIrle	83443
Roberts	83444
Rockiand	83271
Rogerson	83302
Rupert	83343
Rupert	83350
Sagle	83860
Salmon	83467
Samuels	83862
Sandpoint	83809
Sandpoint	83840
Sandpoint	83862
Sandpoint	83864
Sandpoint	83865
Santa	83866
Shelley	83274
Shoshone	83324
Shoshone	83352
Shoup	83469
Silverton	83867
Smelterville	83868
Soda Springs	83230
Soda Springs	83276
Soda Springs	83285
Spalding	83551
Spencer	83446
Spirit Lake	83869
Springfield	83277
Squirrel	83447
St Anthony	83445
St Charles	83272
St Maries	83861
Stanley	83278
Star	83669
Star Ranch	83631
Sterling	83210
Stiles	83552
Stone	83280
Sugar City	83448
Sun Valley	83353
Sun Valley	83354
Swan Valley	83449
Swanlake	83281
Sweet	83670
Tendoy	83468
Tensed	83870
Terreton	83450
Telon	83451
Tetonia	83424
Tetonia	83452
Thatcher	83283
Troy	83871
Twin Falls	83301
Twin Falls	83302
Twin Falls	83303
Twin Lakes	83858
Ucon	83454
Victor	83455
Viola	83872
Wallace	83873
Wallace	83874
Warren	83671
Wayan	83285
Weippe	83553
Weiser	83672
Wendell	83355
Weston	83286
White Bird	83554
Wilder	83676
Winchester	83555
Worley	83876
Yellow Pine	83677

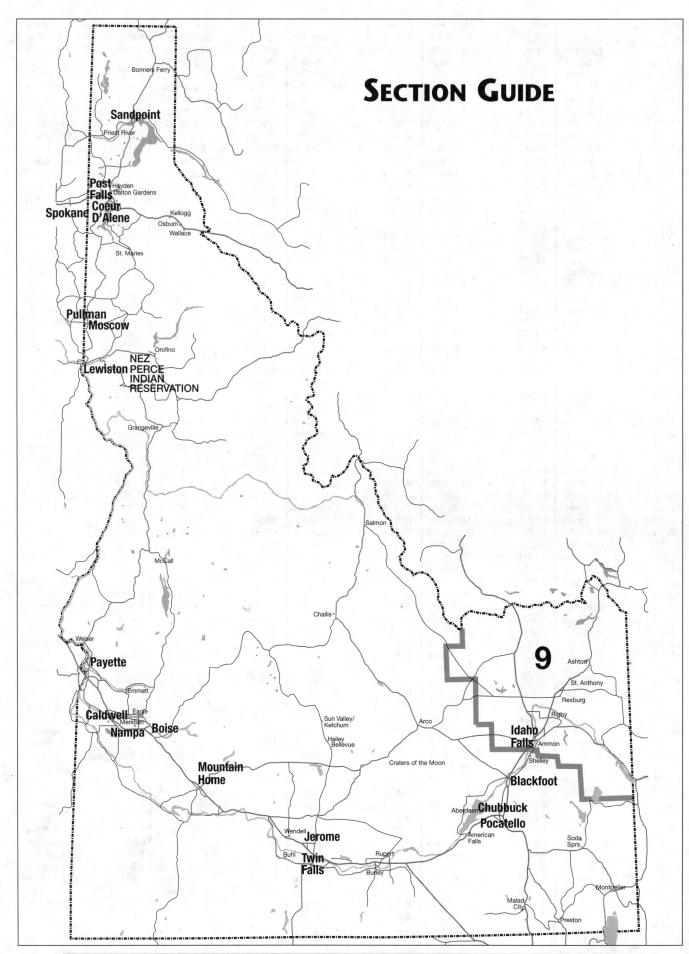

Bonners Ferry

Sandpoint

Priest River

Post
Falls
Hayden
Dalton Gardens
Coeur
Spokane D'Alene
Kellogg
Osburn
Wallace

St. Maries

Pullman
Moscow

Orofino

Lewiston NEZ
PERCE
INDIAN
RESERVATION

Grangeville

Salmon

McCall

Challis

Weiser

9 Ashton

Payette St. Anthony

Emmett Rexburg

Rigby

Caldwell Eagle
Meridian Sun Valley/
Nampa Boise Ketchum Arco Idaho
Hailey Falls Ammon
Bellevue Shelley

Mountain Craters of the Moon
Home Blackfoot

Aberdeen Chubbuck
Pocatello
Wendell American Soda
Jerome Falls Sprs.
Buhl Rupert
Twin
Falls Burley Montpelier

Malad
City
Preston

Idaho Introduction

All Idaho Area Codes are 208

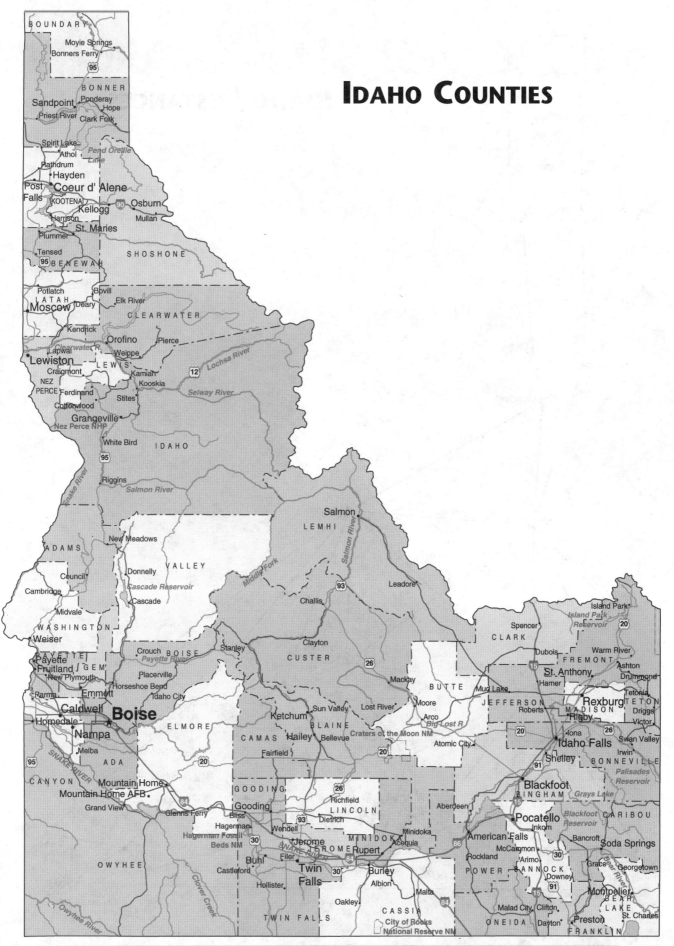

IDAHO COUNTIES

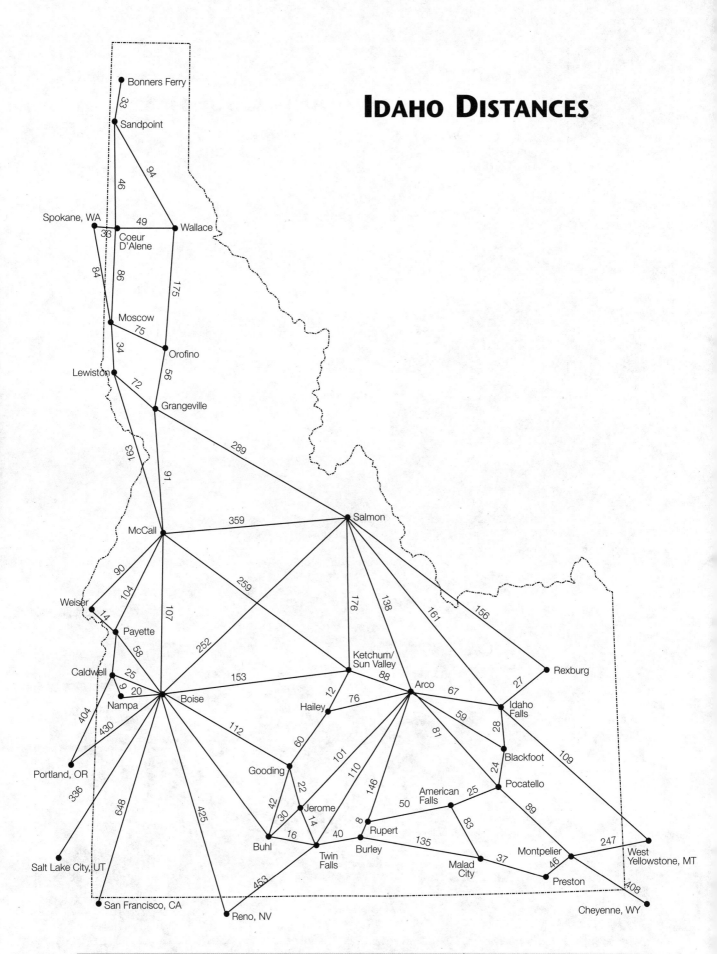

IDAHO DISTANCES

Bonners Ferry

33

Sandpoint

46   94

Spokane, WA   49   Wallace
33
Coeur
D'Alene

84   86   175

Moscow
75
34   Orofino

Lewiston   72   56

163   Grangeville

91   289

McCall   359   Salmon

90   259   176   138   161   156

104   Rexburg

Weiser   107   252   Ketchum/   27
14   Sun Valley   88
Payette   153   Arco   67
58   12   Idaho
Caldwell   25   Hailey   76   59   Falls
9   20   Boise   28
Nampa   112   101   81   Blackfoot   109
404   60   110   24   Pocatello
430   Gooding   146   American   25
42   22   Falls   89
Portland, OR   30   Jerome   8   50
336   14   Rupert   83
849   16   40   Burley   135   Montpelier   247
425   Buhl   Twin   Malad   37   46   West
Salt Lake City, UT   Falls   Burley   City   Preston   Yellowstone, MT
453   408

San Francisco, CA   Reno, NV   Cheyenne, WY

American Falls to
Arco 102
Blackfoot 45
Boise 210
Bonners Ferry 582
Buhl 109
Burley 53
Butte, MT 278
Caldwell 235
Cheyenne, WY 531
Coeur d'Alene 535
Gooding 116
Grangeville 408
Hailey 151
Idaho Falls 72
Jerome 95
Lewiston 480
McCall 317
Malad City 83
Montpelier 114
Moscow 513
Nampa 226
Orofino 464
Payette 268
Pocatello 25
Portland, OR 638
Preston 93
Reno, NV 542
Rexburg 99
Rupert 50
Salmon 231
Salt Lake City, UT 167
Sandpoint 556
San Francisco, CA 765
Spokane, WA 572
Sun Valley/Ketchum 163
Twin Falls 93
Wallace 487
Weiser 282
W. Yellowstone, MT 181

Arco to
American Falls 102
Blackfoot 59
Boise 189
Bonners Ferry 489
Buhl 126
Burley 144
Butte, MT 235
Caldwell 214
Cheyenne, WY 587
Coeur d'Alene 446
Gooding 100
Grangeville 388
Hailey 76
Idaho Falls 67
Jerome 101
Lewiston 460
McCall 297
Malad City 138
Montpelier 169
Moscow 493
Nampa 205

Orofino 443
Payette 248
Pocatello 81
Portland, OR 618
Preston 148
Reno, NV 563
Rexburg 87
Rupert 146
Salmon 138
Salt Lake City, UT 241
Sandpoint 463
San Francisco, CA 786
Spokane, WA 475
Sun Valley/Ketchum 88
Twin Falls 110
Wallace 394
Weiser 261
W. Yellowstone, MT 169

Blackfoot to
American Falls 45
Arco 59
Boise 248
Bonners Ferry 539
Buhl 153
Burley 97
Butte, MT 234
Caldwell 273
Cheyenne, WY 529
Coeur d'Alene 492
Gooding 158
Grangeville 446
Hailey 135
Idaho Falls 28
Jerome 139
Lewiston 518
McCall 355
Malad City 80
Montpelier 111
Moscow 551
Nampa 264
Orofino 502
Payette 306
Pocatello 24
Portland, OR 677
Preston 91
Reno, NV 585
Rexburg 55
Rupert 94
Salmon 187
Salt Lake City, UT 184
Sandpoint 512
San Francisco, CA 808
Spokane, WA 528
Sun Valley/Ketchum 147
Twin Falls 137
Wallace 443
Weiser 320
W. Yellowstone, MT 147

Boise to
American Falls 210
Arco 189

Blackfoot 248
Bonners Ferry 465
Buhl 119
Burley 163
Butte, MT 425
Caldwell 25
Cheyenne, WY 741
Coeur d'Alene 389
Gooding 102
Grangeville 198
Hailey 141
Idaho Falls 257
Jerome 112
Lewiston 270
McCall 107
Malad City 292
Montpelier 323
Moscow 303
Nampa 20
Orofino 254
Payette 58
Pocatello 234
Portland, OR 430
Preston 302
Reno, NV 425
Rexburg 276
Rupert 165
Salmon 252
Salt Lake City, UT 336
Sandpoint 434
San Francisco, CA 648
Spokane, WA 379
Sun Valley/Ketchum 153
Twin Falls 128
Wallace 413
Weiser 72
W. Yellowstone, MT 358

Bonners Ferry to
American Falls 582
Arco 489
Blackfoot 539
Boise 465
Buhl 584
Burley 628
Butte, MT 330
Caldwell 471
Cheyenne, WY 980
Coeur d'Alene 79
Gooding 567
Grangeville 267
Hailey 545
Idaho Falls 512
Jerome 577
Lewiston 196
McCall 358
Malad City 618
Montpelier 649
Moscow 162
Nampa 480
Orofino 237
Payette 437
Pocatello 561

Portland, OR 461
Preston 628
Reno, NV 862
Rexburg 507
Rupert 630
Salmon 351
Salt Lake City, UT 729
Sandpoint 33
San Francisco, CA 972
Spokane, WA 109
Sun Valley/Ketchum 528
Twin Falls 594
Wallace 127
Weiser 424
W. Yellowstone, MT 481

Buhl to
American Falls 109
Arco 126
Blackfoot 153
Boise 163
Bonners Ferry 628
Burley 56
Butte, MT 360
Caldwell 149
Cheyenne, WY 636
Coeur d'Alene 507
Gooding 42
Grangeville 317
Hailey 85
Idaho Falls 180
Jerome 30
Lewiston 389
McCall 226
Malad City 170
Montpelier 217
Moscow 422
Nampa 140
Orofino 372
Payette 177
Pocatello 133
Portland, OR 546
Preston 201
Reno, NV 459
Rexburg 207
Rupert 63
Salmon 264
Salt Lake City, UT 238
Sandpoint 551
San Francisco, CA 682
Spokane, WA 502
Sun Valley/Ketchum 97
Twin Falls 16
Wallace 519
Weiser 191
W. Yellowstone, MT 289

Burley to
American Falls 53
Arco 144
Blackfoot 97
Boise 163
Bonners Ferry 628

Buhl 56
Butte, MT 331
Caldwell 188
Cheyenne, WY 585
Coeur d'Alene 552
Gooding 69
Grangeville 361
Hailey 100
Idaho Falls 124
Jerome 48
Lewiston 433
McCall 270
Malad City 135
Montpelier 166
Moscow 466
Nampa 179
Orofino 416
Payette 221
Pocatello 77
Portland, OR 588
Preston 146
Reno, NV 491
Rexburg 151
Rupert 8
Salmon 282
Salt Lake City, UT 177
Sandpoint 596
San Francisco, CA 714
Spokane, WA 533
Sun Valley/Ketchum 16
Twin Falls 40
Wallace 537
Weiser 235
W. Yellowstone, MT 233

Butte, MT to
American Falls 278
Arco 235
Blackfoot 234
Boise 425
Bonners Ferry 330
Buhl 360
Burley 331
Caldwell 448
Cheyenne, WY 650
Coeur d'Alene 285
Gooding 335
Grangeville 290
Hailey 312
Idaho Falls 208
Jerome 336
Lewiston 335
McCall 381
Malad City 313
Montpelier 344
Moscow 359
Nampa 440
Orofino 294
Payette 460
Pocatello 257
Portland, OR 654
Preston 324
Reno, NV 798

Rexburg 203
Rupert 327
Salmon 146
Salt Lake City, UT 413
Sandpoint 303
San Francisco, CA 1002
Spokane, WA 314
Sun Valley/Ketchum 324
Twin Falls 346
Wallace 238
Weiser 446
W. Yellowstone, MT 148

Caldwell to
American Falls 235
Arco 214
Blackfoot 273
Boise 25
Bonners Ferry 471
Buhl 149
Burley 188
Butte, MT 448
Cheyenne, WY 765
Coeur d'Alene 394
Gooding 127
Grangeville 204
Hailey 162
Idaho Falls 282
Jerome 141
Lewiston 276
McCall 123
Malad City 317
Montpelier 348
Moscow 309
Nampa 9
Orofino 259
Payette 34
Pocatello 259
Portland, OR 404
Preston 327
Reno, NV 408
Rexburg 301
Rupert 189
Salmon 277
Salt Lake City, UT 362
Sandpoint 438
San Francisco, CA 631
Spokane, WA 386
Sun Valley/Ketchum 174
Twin Falls 153
Wallace 418
Weiser 47
W. Yellowstone, MT 383

Cheyenne, WY to
American Falls 531
Arco 587
Blackfoot 529
Boise 741
Bonners Ferry 980
Buhl 636
Burley 585
Butte, MT 650
Caldwell 765
Coeur d'Alene 935
Gooding 647
Grangeville 939
Hailey 663
Idaho Falls 520

Jerome 626
Lewiston 985
McCall 848
Malad City 501
Montpelier 408
Moscow 1009
Nampa 757
Orofino 944
Payette 797
Pocatello 507
Portland, OR 1168
Preston 454
Reno, NV 946
Rexburg 511
Rupert 581
Salmon 667
Salt Lake City, UT 428
Sandpoint 953
San Francisco, CA 1169
Spokane, WA 964
Sun Valley/Ketchum 676
Twin Falls 620
Wallace 886
Weiser 810
W. Yellowstone, MT 500

Coeur d'Alene to
American Falls 535
Arco 446
Blackfoot 492
Boise 389
Bonners Ferry 79
Buhl 507
Burley 552
Butte, MT 285
Caldwell 394
Cheyenne, WY 935
Gooding 491
Grangeville 191
Hailey 193
Idaho Falls 465
Jerome 501
Lewiston 119
McCall 282
Malad City 571
Montpelier 602
Moscow 86
Nampa 403
Orofino 160
Payette 365
Pocatello 514
Portland, OR 384
Preston 581
Reno, NV 785
Rexburg 460
Rupert 553
Salmon 304
Salt Lake City, UT 687
Sandpoint 46
San Francisco, CA 897
Spokane, WA 33
Sun Valley/Ketchum 481
Twin Falls 517
Wallace 49
Weiser 347
W. Yellowstone, MT 433

Gooding to
American Falls 116

Arco 100
Blackfoot 158
Boise 102
Bonners Ferry 567
Buhl 42
Burley 69
Butte, MT 335
Caldwell 127
Cheyenne, WY 647
Coeur d'Alene 491
Grangeville 300
Hailey 60
Idaho Falls 167
Jerome 22
Lewiston 372
McCall 210
Malad City 182
Montpelier 240
Moscow 405
Nampa 118
Orofino 356
Payette 160
Pocatello 140
Portland, OR 531
Preston 208
Reno, NV 489
Rexburg 180
Rupert 71
Salmon 238
Salt Lake City, UT 249
Sandpoint 535
San Francisco, CA 712
Spokane, WA 486
Sun Valley/Ketchum 72
Twin Falls 35
Wallace 493
Weiser 174
W. Yellowstone, MT 262

Grangeville to
American Falls 408
Arco 388
Blackfoot 446
Boise 198
Bonners Ferry 267
Buhl 317
Burley 361
Butte, MT 290
Caldwell 204
Cheyenne, WY 939
Coeur d'Alene 191
Gooding 300
Hailey 344
Idaho Falls 450
Jerome 310
Lewiston 72
McCall 91
Malad City 490
Montpelier 521
Moscow 105
Nampa 211
Orofino 56
Payette 170
Pocatello 432
Portland, OR 426
Preston 500
Reno, NV 599
Rexburg 445
Rupert 363

Salmon 289
Salt Lake City, UT 533
Sandpoint 234
San Francisco, CA 822
Spokane, WA 182
Sun Valley/Ketchum 352
Twin Falls 327
Wallace 215
Weiser 157
W. Yellowstone, MT 436

Hailey to
American Falls 151
Arco 76
Blackfoot 135
Boise 141
Bonners Ferry 545
Buhl 85
Burley 100
Butte, MT 312
Caldwell 162
Cheyenne, WY 663
Coeur d'Alene 193
Gooding 60
Grangeville 344
Idaho Falls 144
Jerome 61
Lewiston 412
McCall 247
Malad City 222
Montpelier 256
Moscow 444
Nampa 157
Orofino 395
Payette 200
Pocatello 158
Portland, OR 572
Preston 225
Reno, NV 524
Rexburg 163
Rupert 106
Salmon 186
Salt Lake City, UT 283
Sandpoint 513
San Francisco, CA 747
Spokane, WA 521
Sun Valley/Ketchum 12
Twin Falls 70
Wallace 447
Weiser 212
W. Yellowstone, MT 245

Idaho Falls to
American Falls 72
Arco 67
Blackfoot 28
Boise 257
Bonners Ferry 512
Buhl 180
Burley 124
Butte, MT 208
Caldwell 282
Cheyenne, WY 520
Coeur d'Alene 465
Gooding 167
Grangeville 344
Hailey 144
Jerome 169
Lewiston 496

McCall 364
Malad City 107
Montpelier 138
Moscow 529
Nampa 273
Orofino 454
Payette 315
Pocatello 51
Portland, OR 680
Preston 118
Reno, NV 611
Rexburg 27
Rupert 121
Salmon 161
Salt Lake City, UT 210
Sandpoint 486
San Francisco, CA 834
Spokane, WA 502
Sun Valley/Ketchum 156
Twin Falls 164
Wallace 417
Weiser 329
W. Yellowstone, MT 109

Jerome to
American Falls 95
Arco 101
Blackfoot 139
Boise 112
Bonners Ferry 577
Buhl 30
Burley 48
Butte, MT 336
Caldwell 141
Cheyenne, WY 626
Coeur d'Alene 501
Gooding 22
Grangeville 310
Hailey 61
Idaho Falls 169
Lewiston 382
McCall 219
Malad City 177
Montpelier 208
Moscow 415
Nampa 128
Orofino 366
Payette 171
Pocatello 119
Portland, OR 544
Preston 188
Reno, NV 468
Rexburg 188
Rupert 50
Salmon 240
Salt Lake City, UT 220
Sandpoint 547
San Francisco, CA 691
Spokane, WA 495
Sun Valley/Ketchum 74
Twin Falls 14
Wallace 495
Weiser 184
W. Yellowstone, MT 270

Lewiston to
American Falls 480
Arco 460
Blackfoot 518

Boise 270
Bonners Ferry 196
Buhl 389
Burley 433
Butte, MT 335
Caldwell 276
Cheyenne, WY 985
Coeur d'Alene 119
Gooding 372
Grangeville 72
Hailey 412
Idaho Falls 496
Jerome 382
McCall 163
Malad City 562
Montpelier 593
Moscow 34
Nampa 283
Orofino 42
Payette 242
Pocatello 504
Portland, OR 353
Preston 573
Reno, NV 670
Rexburg 491
Rupert 435
Salmon 335
Salt Lake City, UT 606
Sandpoint 163
San Francisco, CA 861
Spokane, WA 109
Sun Valley/Ketchum 424
Twin Falls 399
Wallace 158
Weiser 229
W. Yellowstone, MT 481

McCall to
American Falls 317
Arco 297
Blackfoot 355
Boise 107
Bonners Ferry 358
Buhl 226
Burley 270
Butte, MT 381
Caldwell 123
Cheyenne, WY 848
Coeur d'Alene 282
Gooding 210
Grangeville 91
Hailey 247
Idaho Falls 364
Jerome 219
Lewiston 163
Malad City 383
Montpelier 441
Moscow 196
Nampa 120
Orofino 147
Payette 104
Pocatello 341
Portland, OR 490
Preston 409
Reno, NV 525
Rexburg 383
Rupert 272
Salmon 359
Salt Lake City, UT 450

Sandpoint 325
San Francisco, CA 748
Spokane, WA 276
Sun Valley/Ketchum 259
Twin Falls 236
Wallace 306
Weiser 90
W. Yellowstone, MT 465

Malad City to
American Falls 83
Arco 138
Blackfoot 80
Boise 292
Bonners Ferry 618
Buhl 170
Burley 135
Butte, MT 313
Caldwell 317
Cheyenne, WY 501
Coeur d'Alene 571
Gooding 182
Grangeville 490
Hailey 222
Idaho Falls 107
Jerome 208
Lewiston 593
McCall 441
Montpelier 94
Moscow 595
Nampa 308
Orofino 546
Payette 350
Pocatello 58
Portland, OR 709
Preston 37
Reno, NV 608
Rexburg 134
Rupert 132
Salmon 267
Salt Lake City, UT 100
Sandpoint 591
San Francisco, CA 831
Spokane, WA 599
Sun Valley/Ketchum 234
Twin Falls 175
Wallace 522
Weiser 364
W. Yellowstone, MT 216

Montpelier to
American Falls 114
Arco 169
Blackfoot 111
Boise 323
Bonners Ferry 649
Buhl 217
Burley 166
Butte, MT 344
Caldwell 348
Cheyenne, WY 408
Coeur d'Alene 602
Gooding 240
Grangeville 521
Hailey 256
Idaho Falls 138
Jerome 415
Lewiston 34
McCall 196

Malad City 94
Moscow 626
Nampa 339
Orofino 577
Payette 381
Pocatello 89
Portland, OR 750
Preston 46
Reno, NV 654
Rexburg 165
Rupert 163
Salmon 298
Salt Lake City, UT 150
Sandpoint 622
San Francisco, CA 877
Spokane, WA 630
Sun Valley/Ketchum 268
Twin Falls 206
Wallace 553
Weiser 395
W. Yellowstone, MT 247

Moscow to
American Falls 513
Arco 493
Blackfoot 551
Boise 303
Bonners Ferry 162
Buhl 422
Burley 466
Butte, MT 359
Caldwell 309
Cheyenne, WY 1009
Coeur d'Alene 86
Gooding 405
Grangeville 105
Hailey 444
Idaho Falls 529
Jerome 128
Lewiston 283
McCall 120
Malad City 595
Montpelier 626
Nampa 316
Orofino 75
Payette 275
Pocatello 537
Portland, OR 386
Preston 605
Reno, NV 700
Rexburg 524
Rupert 468
Salmon 368
Salt Lake City, UT 639
Sandpoint 129
San Francisco, CA 891
Spokane, WA 84
Sun Valley/Ketchum 457
Twin Falls 432
Wallace 127
Weiser 262
W. Yellowstone, MT 514

Nampa to
American Falls 226
Arco 205
Blackfoot 264
Boise 20
Bonners Ferry 480

Buhl 140
Burley 179
Butte, MT 440
Caldwell 9
Cheyenne, WY 757
Coeur d'Alene 403
Gooding 118
Grangeville 211
Hailey 157
Idaho Falls 273
Jerome 128
Lewiston 283
McCall 120
Malad City 308
Montpelier 339
Moscow 316
Orofino 266
Payette 42
Pocatello 250
Portland, OR 412
Preston 318
Reno, NV 405
Rexburg 292
Rupert 180
Salmon 268
Salt Lake City, UT 354
Sandpoint 445
San Francisco, CA 628
Spokane, WA 393
Sun Valley/Ketchum 169
Twin Falls 144
Wallace 425
Weiser 56
W. Yellowstone, MT 374

Orofino to
American Falls 464
Arco 443
Blackfoot 502
Boise 254
Bonners Ferry 237
Buhl 372
Burley 416
Butte, MT 294
Caldwell 259
Cheyenne, WY 944
Coeur d'Alene 160
Gooding 356
Grangeville 56
Hailey 395
Idaho Falls 454
Jerome 366
Lewiston 42
McCall 147
Malad City 546
Montpelier 577
Moscow 75
Nampa 266
Payette 226
Pocatello 488
Portland, OR 374
Preston 540
Reno, NV 654
Rexburg 449
Rupert 418
Salmon 293
Salt Lake City, UT 597
Sandpoint 213
San Francisco, CA 878

Spokane, WA 151
Sun Valley/Ketchum 407
Twin Falls 366
Wallace 175
Weiser 212
W. Yellowstone, MT 444

Payette to
American Falls 268
Arco 248
Blackfoot 306
Boise 58
Bonners Ferry 437
Buhl 177
Burley 221
Butte, MT 460
Caldwell 34
Cheyenne, WY 797
Coeur d'Alene 365
Gooding 160
Grangeville 170
Hailey 200
Idaho Falls 315
Jerome 171
Lewiston 242
McCall 104
Malad City 350
Montpelier 381
Moscow 275
Nampa 42
Orofino 266
Pocatello 292
Portland, OR 376
Preston 361
Reno, NV 429
Rexburg 335
Rupert 223
Salmon 310
Salt Lake City, UT 391
Sandpoint 405
San Francisco, CA 652
Spokane, WA 354
Sun Valley/Ketchum 212
Twin Falls 187
Wallace 385
Weiser 14
W. Yellowstone, MT 417

Pocatello to
American Falls 25
Arco 81
Blackfoot 24
Boise 234
Bonners Ferry 561
Buhl 133
Burley 77
Butte, MT 257
Caldwell 259
Cheyenne, WY 507
Coeur d'Alene 514
Gooding 140
Grangeville 432
Hailey 158
Idaho Falls 51
Jerome 119
Lewiston 504
McCall 341
Malad City 58
Montpelier 89

Moscow 537
Nampa 250
Orofino 488
Payette 292
Portland, OR 662
Preston 68
Reno, NV 566
Rexburg 77
Rupert 74
Salmon 210
Salt Lake City, UT 161
Sandpoint 535
San Francisco, CA 789
Spokane, WA 504
Sun Valley/Ketchum 170
Twin Falls 117
Wallace 465
Weiser 306
W. Yellowstone, MT 159

Portland, OR to
American Falls 638
Arco 618
Blackfoot 677
Boise 430
Bonners Ferry 461
Buhl 546
Burley 588
Butte, MT 654
Caldwell 404
Cheyenne, WY 1168
Coeur d'Alene 384
Gooding 531
Grangeville 426
Hailey 572
Idaho Falls 680
Jerome 544
Lewiston 353
McCall 490
Malad City 709
Montpelier 750
Moscow 386
Nampa 412
Orofino 374
Payette 376
Pocatello 662
Preston 732
Reno, NV 588
Rexburg 705
Rupert 594
Salmon 592
Salt Lake City, UT 770
Sandpoint 428
San Francisco, CA 641
Spokane, WA 340
Sun Valley/Ketchum 580
Twin Falls 556
Wallace 434
Weiser 400
W. Yellowstone, MT 784

Preston to
American Falls 93
Arco 148
Blackfoot 91
Boise 302
Bonners Ferry 628
Buhl 201
Burley 146

Butte, MT 324
Caldwell 327
Cheyenne, WY 454
Coeur d'Alene 581
Gooding 208
Grangeville 500
Hailey 225
Idaho Falls 118
Jerome 188
Lewiston 573
McCall 409
Malad City 37
Montpelier 46
Moscow 605
Nampa 318
Orofino 540
Payette 361
Pocatello 68
Portland, OR 732
Reno, NV 624
Rexburg 144
Rupert 142
Salmon 277
Salt Lake City, UT 106
Sandpoint 602
San Francisco, CA 847
Spokane, WA 614
Sun Valley/Ketchum 237
Twin Falls 185
Wallace 532
Weiser 374
W. Yellowstone, MT 226

Reno, NV to
American Falls 542
Arco 563
Blackfoot 585
Boise 425
Bonners Ferry 862
Buhl 459
Burley 491
Butte, MT 798
Caldwell 408
Cheyenne, WY 946
Coeur d'Alene 785
Gooding 489
Grangeville 599
Hailey 524
Idaho Falls 611
Jerome 468
Lewiston 670
McCall 525
Malad City 608
Montpelier 654
Moscow 700
Nampa 405
Orofino 654
Payette 429
Pocatello 566
Portland, OR 588
Preston 624
Rexburg 639
Rupert 497
Salmon 702
Salt Lake City, UT 518
Sandpoint 830
San Francisco, CA 223
Spokane, WA 784
Sun Valley/Ketchum 535

Twin Falls 453
Wallace 813
Weiser 442
W. Yellowstone, MT 720

Rexburg to
American Falls 99
Arco 87
Blackfoot 55
Boise 276
Bonners Ferry 507
Buhl 207
Burley 151
Butte, MT 203
Caldwell 301
Cheyenne, WY 511
Coeur d'Alene 460
Gooding 180
Grangeville 445
Hailey 163
Idaho Falls 27
Jerome 188
Lewiston 491
McCall 383
Malad City 134
Montpelier 165
Moscow 524
Nampa 292
Orofino 449
Payette 335
Pocatello 77
Portland, OR 705
Preston 144
Reno, NV 639
Rupert 148
Salmon 156
Salt Lake City, UT 236
Sandpoint 481
San Francisco, CA 862
Spokane, WA 497
Sun Valley/Ketchum 175
Twin Falls 191
Wallace 412
Weiser 348
W. Yellowstone, MT 82

Rupert to
American Falls 50
Arco 146
Blackfoot 94
Boise 165
Bonners Ferry 630
Buhl 63
Burley 8
Butte, MT 327
Caldwell 189
Cheyenne, WY 581
Coeur d'Alene 553
Gooding 71
Grangeville 363
Hailey 106
Idaho Falls 121
Jerome 50
Lewiston 435
McCall 272
Malad City 132
Montpelier 163
Moscow 468
Nampa 180

Orofino 418
Payette 223
Pocatello 74
Portland, OR 594
Preston 142
Reno, NV 497
Rexburg 148
Salmon 284
Salt Lake City, UT 175
Sandpoint 598
San Francisco, CA 720
Spokane, WA 544
Sun Valley/Ketchum 118
Twin Falls 47
Wallace 539
Weiser 237
W. Yellowstone, MT 230

Salmon to
American Falls 231
Arco 138
Blackfoot 187
Boise 252
Bonners Ferry 351
Buhl 264
Burley 282
Butte, MT 146
Caldwell 277
Cheyenne, WY 667
Coeur d'Alene 304
Gooding 238
Grangeville 289
Hailey 186
Idaho Falls 161
Jerome 240
Lewiston 335
McCall 359
Malad City 267
Montpelier 298
Moscow 368
Nampa 268
Orofino 293
Payette 310
Pocatello 210
Portland, OR 592
Preston 277
Reno, NV 702
Rexburg 156
Rupert 284
Salt Lake City, UT 379
Sandpoint 324
San Francisco, CA 925
Spokane, WA 330
Sun Valley/Ketchum 176
Twin Falls 248
Wallace 255
Weiser 324
W. Yellowstone, MT 238

Salt Lake City, UT to
American Falls 167
Arco 241
Blackfoot 184
Boise 336
Bonners Ferry 729
Buhl 238
Burley 177
Butte, MT 413
Caldwell 362

Cheyenne, WY 428
Coeur d'Alene 687
Gooding 249
Grangeville 533
Hailey 283
Idaho Falls 210
Jerome 220
Lewiston 606
McCall 450
Malad City 100
Montpelier 150
Moscow 639
Nampa 354
Orofino 597
Payette 391
Pocatello 161
Portland, OR 770
Preston 106
Reno, NV 518
Rexburg 236
Rupert 175
Salmon 379
Sandpoint 689
San Francisco, CA 741
Spokane, WA 700
Sun Valley/Ketchum 296
Twin Falls 222
Wallace 622
Weiser 412
W. Yellowstone, MT 315

Sandpoint to
American Falls 556
Arco 463
Blackfoot 512
Boise 434
Bonners Ferry 33
Buhl 551
Burley 596
Butte, MT 303
Caldwell 438
Cheyenne, WY 953
Coeur d'Alene 46
Gooding 535
Grangeville 234
Hailey 513
Idaho Falls 486
Jerome 547
Lewiston 163
McCall 325
Malad City 591
Montpelier 622
Moscow 129
Nampa 445
Orofino 213
Payette 405
Pocatello 535
Portland, OR 428
Preston 602
Reno, NV 830
Rexburg 481
Rupert 598
Salmon 324
Salt Lake City, UT 689
San Francisco, CA 940
Spokane, WA 72
Sun Valley/Ketchum 501
Twin Falls 562
Wallace 94

Weiser 391
W. Yellowstone, MT 450

San Francisco, CA to
American Falls 765
Arco 786
Blackfoot 808
Boise 648
Bonners Ferry 972
Buhl 682
Burley 714
Butte, MT 1002
Caldwell 631
Cheyenne, WY 1169
Coeur d'Alene 897
Gooding 712
Grangeville 822
Hailey 747
Idaho Falls 834
Jerome 691
Lewiston 861
McCall 748
Malad City 831
Montpelier 877
Moscow 891
Nampa 628
Orofino 878
Payette 652
Pocatello 789
Portland, OR 641
Preston 847
Reno, NV 223
Rexburg 862
Rupert 720
Salmon 925
Salt Lake City, UT 741
Sandpoint 940
Spokane, WA 868
Sun Valley/Ketchum 759
Twin Falls 676
Wallace 946
Weiser 665
W. Yellowstone, MT 943

Spokane, WA to
American Falls 572
Arco 475
Blackfoot 528
Boise 379
Bonners Ferry 109
Buhl 502
Burley 533
Butte, MT 314
Caldwell 386
Cheyenne, WY 964
Coeur d'Alene 33
Gooding 486
Grangeville 182

Hailey 521
Idaho Falls 502
Jerome 495
Lewiston 109
McCall 276
Malad City 599
Montpelier 630
Moscow 84
Nampa 393
Orofino 151
Payette 354
Pocatello 504
Portland, OR 340
Preston 614
Reno, NV 784
Rexburg 497
Rupert 544
Salmon 330
Salt Lake City, UT 700
Sandpoint 72
San Francisco, CA 868
Sun Valley/Ketchum 511
Twin Falls 507
Wallace 83
Weiser 342
W. Yellowstone, MT 464

Sun Valley/Ketchum to
American Falls 163
Arco 88
Blackfoot 147
Boise 153
Bonners Ferry 528
Buhl 97
Burley 116
Butte, MT 324
Caldwell 174
Cheyenne, WY 676
Coeur d'Alene 481
Gooding 72
Grangeville 352
Hailey 12
Idaho Falls 156
Jerome 74
Lewiston 424
McCall 259
Malad City 234
Montpelier 268
Moscow 457
Nampa 169
Orofino 407
Payette 212
Pocatello 170
Portland, OR 580
Preston 237
Reno, NV 535
Rexburg 175
Rupert 118

Salmon 176
Salt Lake City, UT 296
Sandpoint 501
San Francisco, CA 759
Spokane, WA 511
Twin Falls 82
Wallace 432
Weiser 225
W. Yellowstone, MT 257

Twin Falls to
American Falls 93
Arco 110
Blackfoot 137
Boise 128
Bonners Ferry 594
Buhl · 16
Burley 40
Butte, MT 346
Caldwell 153
Cheyenne, WY 620
Coeur d'Alene 517
Gooding 35
Grangeville 327
Hailey 70
Idaho Falls 164
Jerome 14
Lewiston 399
McCall 236
Malad City 175
Montpelier 206
Moscow 432
Nampa 144
Orofino 366
Payette 187
Pocatello 117
Portland, OR 556
Preston 185
Reno, NV 453
Rexburg 191
Rupert 47
Salmon 248
Salt Lake City, UT 222
Sandpoint 562
San Francisco, CA 676
Spokane, WA 507
Sun Valley/Ketchum 82
Wallace 503
Weiser 200
W. Yellowstone, MT 273

Wallace to
American Falls 487
Arco 394
Blackfoot 443
Boise 413
Bonners Ferry 127
Buhl 519

Burley 537
Butte, MT 238
Caldwell 418
Cheyenne, WY 886
Coeur d'Alene 49
Gooding 493
Grangeville 215
Hailey 447
Idaho Falls 417
Jerome 495
Lewiston 158
McCall 306
Malad City 522
Montpelier 553
Moscow 127
Nampa 425
Orofino 175
Payette 385
Pocatello 465
Portland, OR 434
Preston 532
Reno, NV 813
Rexburg 412
Rupert 539
Salmon 255
Salt Lake City, UT 622
Sandpoint 94
San Francisco, CA 946
Spokane, WA 83
Sun Valley/Ketchum 432
Twin Falls 503
Weiser 371
W. Yellowstone, MT 385

Weiser to
American Falls 282
Arco 261
Blackfoot 320
Boise 72
Bonners Ferry 424
Buhl 191
Burley 235
Butte, MT 446
Caldwell 47
Cheyenne, WY 810
Coeur d'Alene 347
Gooding 174
Grangeville 157
Hailey 212
Idaho Falls 329
Jerome 184
Lewiston 229
McCall 90
Malad City 364
Montpelier 395
Moscow 262
Nampa 56
Orofino 212

Payette 14
Pocatello 306
Portland, OR 400
Preston 374
Reno, NV 442
Rexburg 348
Rupert 237
Salmon 324
Salt Lake City, UT 412
Sandpoint 391
San Francisco, CA 665
Spokane, WA 342
Sun Valley/Ketchum 225
Twin Falls 200
Wallace 371
W. Yellowstone, MT 430

W. Yellowstone, MT to
American Falls 181
Arco 169
Blackfoot 147
Boise 358
Bonners Ferry 481
Buhl 289
Burley 233
Butte, MT 148
Caldwell 383
Cheyenne, WY 500
Coeur d'Alene 433
Gooding 262
Grangeville 436
Hailey 245
Idaho Falls 109
Jerome 270
Lewiston 481
McCall 465
Malad City 216
Montpelier 247
Moscow 514
Nampa 374
Orofino 444
Payette 417
Pocatello 159
Portland, OR 784
Preston 226
Reno, NV 720
Rexburg 82
Rupert 230
Salmon 238
Salt Lake City, UT 315
Sandpoint 450
San Francisco, CA 943
Spokane, WA 464
Sun Valley/Ketchum 257
Twin Falls 273
Wallace 385
Weiser 430

SECTION 9 CITIES AND TOWNS

HIGHWAY MAP

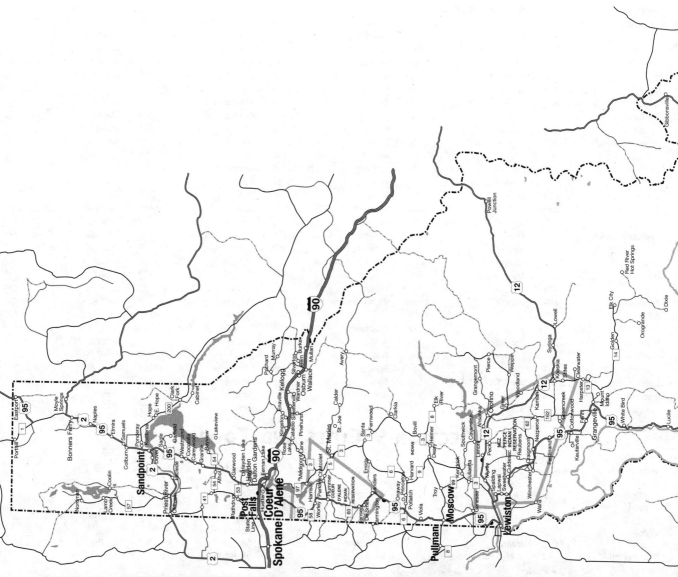

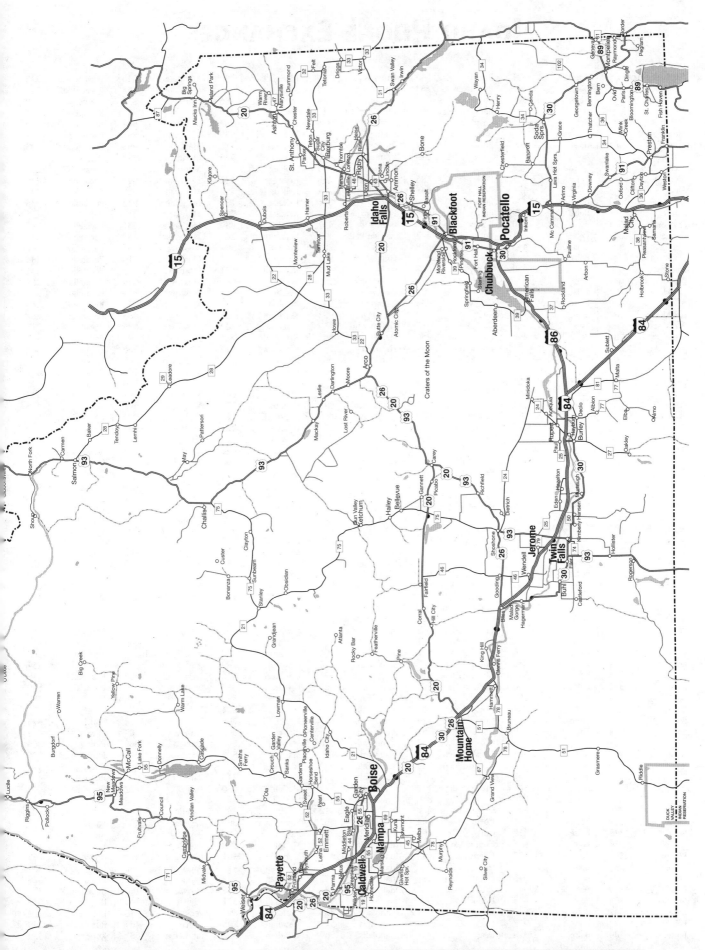

IDAHO PHONE EXCHANGES

Alphabetical

Place	Exchange
Aberdeen	397
Albeni	437
Albion	673
Almo	824
Alpine	564
Arbon	335
Arco	527
Arco	554
Arco	767
Ashton	652
Atlanta	864
Bayview	561
Bayview	683
Blackfoot	604
Blackfoot	643
Blackfoot	680
Blackfoot	681
Blackfoot	684
Blackfoot	690
Blackfoot	782
Blackfoot	785
Blackfoot	789
Bluebell	274
Boise	202
Boise	229
Boise	246
Boise	247
Boise	248
Boise	272
Boise	275
Boise	279
Boise	283
Boise	284
Boise	287
Boise	319
Boise	321
Boise	322
Boise	323
Boise	327
Boise	330
Boise	331
Boise	332
Boise	333
Boise	334
Boise	336
Boise	338
Boise	340
Boise	341
Boise	342
Boise	343
Boise	344
Boise	345
Boise	348
Boise	353
Boise	361
Boise	362
Boise	363
Boise	364
Boise	367
Boise	368
Boise	371
Boise	373
Boise	375
Boise	376
Boise	377
Boise	378
Boise	379
Boise	381
Boise	383
Boise	384
Boise	385
Boise	386
Boise	387
Boise	388
Boise	389
Boise	391
Boise	392
Boise	393
Boise	395
Boise	396
Boise	407
Boise	409
Boise	422
Boise	424
Boise	426
Boise	429
Boise	433
Boise	439
Boise	440
Boise	441
Boise	445
Boise	447
Boise	460
Boise	472
Boise	474
Boise	484
Boise	485
Boise	489
Boise	494
Boise	514
Boise	545
Boise	555
Boise	562
Boise	567
Boise	571
Boise	573
Boise	575
Boise	577
Boise	581
Boise	602
Boise	608
Boise	629
Boise	639
Boise	658
Boise	672
Boise	685
Boise	692
Boise	693
Boise	694
Boise	703
Boise	713
Boise	723
Boise	724
Boise	728
Boise	730
Boise	761
Boise	794
Boise	830
Boise	841
Boise	850
Boise	853
Boise	854
Boise	859
Boise	860
Boise	861
Boise	863
Boise	866
Boise	867
Boise	869
Boise	890
Boise	891
Boise	914
Boise	919
Boise	921
Boise	938
Boise	939
Boise	941
Boise	947
Boise	975
Boise	977
Boise	978
Boise	979
Boise	988
Boiseriver	653
Bonners Ferry	267
Bonners Ferry	295
Bovill	826
Bruneau	845
Burley	203
Burley	219
Burley	312
Burley	586
Burley	647
Burley	650
Burley	654
Burley	670
Burley	677
Burley	678
Burley	679
Burley	808
Burley	878
Caldwell	402
Caldwell	453
Caldwell	454
Caldwell	455
Caldwell	459
Caldwell	649
Caldwell	779
Caldwell	795
Cambridge	257
Carey	823
Cascade	382
Challis	879
Clark Fork	266
Clayton	838
Coeur d'Alene	277
Coeur d'Alene	292
Coeur d'Alene	297
Coeur d'Alene	415
Coeur d'Alene	416
Coeur d'Alene	444
Coeur d'Alene	446
Coeur d'Alene	449
Coeur d'Alene	620
Coeur d'Alene	625
Coeur d'Alene	640
Coeur d'Alene	641
Coeur d'Alene	651
Coeur d'Alene	659
Coeur d'Alene	660
Coeur d'Alene	661
Coeur d'Alene	664
Coeur d'Alene	665
Coeur d'Alene	666
Coeur d'Alene	667
Coeur d'Alene	676
Coeur d'Alene	691
Coeur d'Alene	704
Coeur d'Alene	714
Coeur d'Alene	755
Coeur d'Alene	763
Coeur d'Alene	765
Coeur d'Alene	769
Coeur d'Alene	771
Coeur d'Alene	797
Coeur d'Alene	818
Coeur d'Alene	929
Coeur d'Alene	964
Cola	668
Cottonwood	962
Council	253
Craigmont	924
Cuprum	258
Deary	877
Donnelly	325
Driggs	354
Driggs	456
Driggs	787
Dubois	374
Elba	638
Elk Bend	894
Elk City	842
Emmett	365
Emmett	369
Emmett	398
Emmett	477
Emmett	963
Evergreen	268
Fairfield	764
Filer	326
Freedom	873
Fruitland	452
Garden Valley	462
Genesee	285
Grand View	834
Grangeville	451
Grangeville	507
Grangeville	981
Grangeville	982
Grangeville	983
Grasmerddl	759
Hamer	662
Harrison	214
Harrison	689
Hayden Lake	209
Hayden Lake	635
Hayden Lake	762
Hayden Lake	772
Holbrook	698
Homedale	337
Hope	264
Horsebend	781
Horsebend	793
Howster	655
Idaho Falls	200
Idaho Falls	201
Idaho Falls	204
Idaho Falls	206
Idaho Falls	227
Idaho Falls	243
Idaho Falls	346
Idaho Falls	351
Idaho Falls	356
Idaho Falls	357
Idaho Falls	359
Idaho Falls	360
Idaho Falls	390
Idaho Falls	403
Idaho Falls	419
Idaho Falls	496
Idaho Falls	520
Idaho Falls	521
Idaho Falls	522
Idaho Falls	523
Idaho Falls	524
Idaho Falls	525
Idaho Falls	526
Idaho Falls	528
Idaho Falls	529
Idaho Falls	533
Idaho Falls	534
Idaho Falls	535
Idaho Falls	538
Idaho Falls	542
Idaho Falls	557
Idaho Falls	592
Idaho Falls	612
Idaho Falls	656
Idaho Falls	716
Idaho Falls	757
Idaho Falls	821
Idaho Falls	932
Idahofalls	313
Idahofalls	552
Idahofalls	569
Idahofalls	709
Idahofalls	881
Indian Valley	256
Irwin	270
Irwin	483
Island Park	558
Julietta	276
Kamiah	935
Kellogg	512
Kellogg	682
Kellogg	783
Kellogg	784
Kellogg	786
Kendrick	289
Ketchum	205
Ketchum	309
Ketchum	450
Ketchum	471
Ketchum	481
Ketchum	578
Ketchum	594
Ketchum	622
Ketchum	720
Ketchum	721
Ketchum	725
Ketchum	726
Ketchum	727
Ketchum	788
Ketchum	806
Kilgore	778
Kooskia	926
Lakeview	222
Lapwai	621
Lapwai	843
Leadore	768
Lenore	836
Leon	224
Lewiston	298
Lewiston	299
Lewiston	305
Lewiston	413
Lewiston	503
Lewiston	553
Lewiston	717
Lewiston	743
Lewiston	746
Lewiston	748
Lewiston	750
Lewiston	790
Lewiston	791
Lewiston	792
Lewiston	798
Lewiston	799
Lewiston	816
Lewiston	848
Lewiston	989
Mackay	588
Malad	294
Malad	766
Malta	645
Marsing	896
May	876
McCall	271
McCall	315
McCall	630
McCall	634
Melba	495
Meridian	286
Meridian	288
Meridian	350
Meridian	401
Meridian	412
Meridian	493
Meridian	585
Meridian	631
Meridian	695
Meridian	706
Meridian	822
Meridian	846
Meridian	855
Meridian	870
Meridian	871
Meridian	884
Meridian	887
Meridian	888
Meridian	893
Meridian	895
Meridian	898
Meridian	922
Meridian	955
Midvale	355
Minidoka	531
Monteview	657
Moscow	301
Moscow	310
Moscow	596
Moscow	669
Moscow	874
Moscow	882
Moscow	883
Moscow	885
Moscow	892
Mt Home	366
Mt Home	580
Mt Home	587
Mt Home	590
Mt Home	591
Mt Home	598
Mt Home	599
Mt Home	696
Mt Home	828
Mt Home	832
Mullan	744
Murtaugh	432
Nampa	249
Nampa	250
Nampa	318
Nampa	442
Nampa	461
Nampa	463
Nampa	465
Nampa	466
Nampa	467
Nampa	475
Nampa	498
Nampa	697
Nampa	880
Nampa	899
Nampa	989
New Plymouth	278
New Meadows	347
Nezperce	937
Norland	532
Nu Acres	566
Nu Acres	570
Nu Acres	674
Nu Acres	707
Oakley	862
Orofino	476
Orofino	827
Paris	945
Parma	722
Paul	438
Payette	207
Payette	230
Payette	291
Payette	405
Payette	563
Payette	642
Payette	739
Payette	740
Payette	741
Peck	486
Pierce	464
Plumerwrly	686
Pocatello	223
Pocatello	213
Pocatello	220
Pocatello	221
Pocatello	226
Pocatello	232
Pocatello	233
Pocatello	234
Pocatello	235
Pocatello	236
Pocatello	237
Pocatello	238
Pocatello	239
Pocatello	240
Pocatello	241
Pocatello	242
Pocatello	244
Pocatello	251
Pocatello	252
Pocatello	254
Pocatello	269
Pocatello	282
Pocatello	317
Pocatello	339
Pocatello	380
Pocatello	406
Pocatello	417
Pocatello	425
Pocatello	427
Pocatello	478
Pocatello	530
Pocatello	540
Pocatello	547
Pocatello	565
Pocatello	589
Pocatello	637
Pocatello	646
Pocatello	648
Pocatello	705
Pocatello	747
Pocatello	760
Pocatello	775
Pocatello	776
Pocatello	833
Pocatello	840
Pocatello	847
Pocatello	851
Pocatello	852
Pocatello	897
Pocatello	904
Pocatello	915
Post Falls	262
Post Falls	457
Post Falls	618
Post Falls	619
Post Falls	773
Post Falls	777
Potlatch	875
Powell	942
Prairie	868
Priest River	306
Priest River	428
Priest River	448
Priestlake	443
Raft River	349
Rathdrum	687
Rathdrum	712
Richfield	487
Rigby	228
Rigby	745
Rigby	754
Riggins	628
Rock Creek	273
Rockland	548
Rupert	259
Rupert	260
Rupert	300

762	Hayden Lake	786	Kellogg	825	Twin Falls	850	Boise	874	Moscow	897	Pocatello	942	Powell
763	Coeur d'Alene	787	Driggs	826	Bovill	851	Pocatello	875	Potlatch	898	Meridian	944	Twin Falls
764	Fairfield	788	Ketchum	827	Orofino	852	Pocatello	876	May	899	Nampa	945	Paris
765	Coeur d'Alene	789	Blackfoot	828	Mt Home	853	Boise	877	Deary	904	Pocatello	946	Sandpoint
766	Malad	790	Lewiston	829	Twin Falls	854	Boise	878	Burley	914	Boise	947	Boise
767	Arco	791	Lewiston	830	Boise	855	Meridian	879	Challis	915	Pocatello	948	Twin Falls
768	Leadore	792	Lewiston	832	Mt Home	857	Three Creek	880	Nampa	919	Boise	955	Meridian
769	Coeur d'Alene	793	Horsebend	833	Pocatello	858	Wellesley	881	Idahofalls	921	Boise	961	Twin Falls
771	Coeur d'Alene	794	Boise	834	Grand View	859	Boise	882	Moscow	922	Meridian	962	Cottonwood
772	Hayden Lake	795	Caldwell	835	Troy	860	Boise	883	Moscow	924	Craigmont	963	Emmett
773	Post Falls	796	Tipanuk	836	Lenore	861	Boise	884	Meridian	926	Kooskia	964	Coeur d'Alene
774	Stanley	797	Coeur d'Alene	837	Twin Falls	862	Oakley	885	Moscow	929	Coeur d'Alene	969	Twin Falls
775	Pocatello	798	Lewiston	838	Clayton	863	Boise	886	Twin Falls	931	Rupert	975	Boise
776	Pocatello	799	Lewiston	839	White Bird	864	Atlanta	887	Meridian	932	Idaho Falls	977	Boise
777	Post Falls	808	Burley	840	Pocatello	865	Salmon	888	Meridian	933	Twinfalls	978	Boise
778	Kilgore	816	Lewiston	841	Boise	866	Boise	890	Boise	934	Twinfalls	979	Boise
779	Caldwell	818	Coeur d'Alene	842	Elk City	867	Boise	891	Boise	935	Kamiah	981	Grangeville
781	Horsebend	821	Idaho Falls	843	Lapwai	868	Prairie	892	Moscow	937	Nezperce	982	Grangeville
782	Blackfoot	822	Meridian	845	Bruneau	869	Boise	893	Meridian	938	Boise	983	Grangeville
783	Kellogg	823	Carey	846	Meridian	870	Meridian	894	Elk Bend	939	Boise	988	Boise
784	Kellogg	824	Almo	847	Pocatello	871	Meridian	895	Meridian	940	Salmon	989	Nampa
785	Blackfoot			848	Lewiston	873	Freedom	896	Marsing	941	Boise		

NOTES:

SECTION 9

NORTHEAST IDAHO

INCLUDING IDAHO FALLS, ST. ANTHONY, REXBURG, AND TETON VALLEY

Extinct volcano vents created the St. Anthony Sand Dunes. Shoshone and Bannock Indian spirits supposedly haunt the area.

1

Kilgore
Pop. 30

Kilgore was settled as an agricultural community in 1885 and remained nameless for the first few months of its existence. In 1887, the town finally named itself after General James Kilgore, a gentleman who actively and bravely participated in the 1877 Nez Perce War events. A post office operated here from 1892 to 1965.

Spencer
Pop. 38

The Utah and Northern Railroad arrived here in 1879, bringing with it the birth of this town. The community draws its name from Hiram H. Spencer, a merchant and shipper who lived in the area during the line's construction. Although the town never attracted a large population, it has garnered national attention for its opals. In 1948, deer hunters stumbled upon a large deposit of the precious stones, which are formed underground in still pools of water. Layers of microscopic silica spheres reflect light in such a way to produce the gem's radiant rainbow colors. The Spencer Opal Mine offers tourists a chance to dig for their own opals.

H Beaver Canyon
Exit 180 on I-15 east of the interchange on road to Spencer

After Montana's gold rushes began in 1862, thousands of miners came past here, and a Beaver Canyon stage station was built here.

Freighters and travelers on stage lines from Salt Lake to Montana stopped at this station until Utah and Northern Railway service reached here in 1879. Large ranches also were supplied here until 1897, when they decided to move their Beaver Canyon town to a better site at Spencer.

T Spencer Opal Mines
Spencer. 374-5476.

The opal mine office is located in Spencer on Main Street's north end. Directions to the mine are available at the company office.

Few people realize how opals are formed or mined, but at the Spencer Opal Mines, visitors have the chance to learn about opals and potentially discover their own precious stone. Geologically, opals are hydrothermally deposited in successive layers in hollow geodes when a hot springs dries up.

While it is suspected that opals have hidden underneath Spencer's surface for hundreds of years, the first discovery of opals did not occur until 1948 when two lost deer hunters from nearby Rexburg happened upon the precious gem. This innocent discovery created the largest opal mine in the world and a major attraction in Spencer. Visitors can opt to purchase a permit and dig for their own opals, but they must provide their own tools and safety equipment. The mine is open daily from 8 AM to 8 PM Memorial Day to Labor Day.

T Camas Meadows Battle Sites
From Spencer, travel 18 miles northeast on the gravel road to Kilgore.

During the 1877 Nez Perce War with the U.S. Army, eastern Idaho was the site of many famous battles. These historic spots near Kilgore off I-15 are still visible.

Site 1 – Late evening of August 19, 1877
At 4:00 AM, Chiefs Looking Glass, Toohoolhollzote, and Ollokot rounded up twenty-eight warriors and sent them to General Oliver Howard's camp near Camas and Spring Creeks. The warriors' mission was to capture the cavalry horses, but when they arrived at the Army camp, pandemonium

broke loose. Instead of capturing the horses, the Indians accidentally stole away with the company's mules. With the Army in hot pursuit, fighting broke out. Few casualties were reported except that of an Army bugler.

To visit the site, drive four miles south from Kilgore to Idmon. Continue south one mile on Red Road, and then bear east one-half mile across Camas Creek. The battle site is situated in the flat valley between Camas and Spring Creeks. To visit the bugler's grave, proceed one-half mile across Spring Creek, and bear north one-half mile. The marked grave is found on the road's right side in a fenced area.

Site 2 – Morning of August 20, 1877
After the late evening/early morning encounter between the Native Americans and Army, Captain Randolph Norwood and the Second Calvary pursued the fleeing Indians. A four-hour battle ensued resulting in several casualties.

To visit the site, proceed approximately six miles east from Kilgore on A2 Clarks County Road. At the grouping of ranch buildings, bear right, and follow the dirt road to a lava rock formation. The battle took place in this area, and pits from flying bullets can still be found in the lava rock.

T Spencer Rock House
374-5359. In Spencer, drive under the I-15 overpass, bear right, and proceed downhill past the local bar & grill.

The Spencer Rock House has been unique since its 1919 origination. Charles Hardy was the builder and first owner of the craftsman-style home and was dismayed when he discovered a natural spring running through his basement. Despite Hardy's attempts to plug the spring, the water kept trickling in. Today, the current owners let the spring run naturally through this property listed on the National Register of Historic Places.

In addition to the spring, the home retains many of its original characteristics including 42-inch thick walls, toggle light switches, a footbath in the bathroom, and a small sleeping porch. Visitors are welcome to explore the home free of charge, but advance arrangements are requested.

2

T U.S. Sheep Experiment Station
Merge off I-15 at Exit 172, and proceed 2 miles east to the site.

The U.S. Department of Agriculture established the U.S. Sheep Experiment Station near Dubois in 1916. Operated in coordination with the Idaho Agricultural Station, the site investigates crossbreeding, nutrition, disease control, wool preparation, and range improvement. Sheep species used include approximately 6,000 Targhee, Columbia, Polypay, Rambouillet, and Finn Crossbred breeds. The site includes several office, laboratory, animal, and equipment buildings used in the elaborate research. Tours are available, but visitors should make advance arrangements.

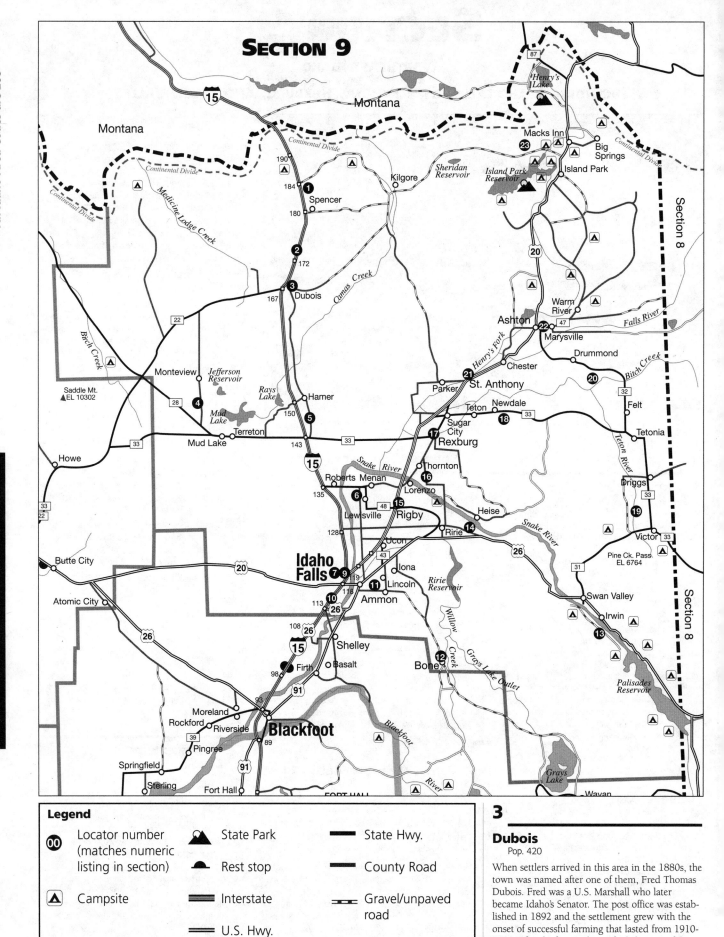

All Idaho Area Codes are 208

Section 9

Montana

Montana

Continental Divide

Continental Divide

Continental Divide

Henry's Lake

87

Macks Inn

23

Big Springs

Island Park

Continental Divide

Section 8

Sheridan Reservoir

Island Park Reservoir

Medicine Lodge Creek

190

184 ①

180

Spencer

Kilgore

20

② 172

③ 167 Dubois

22

Camas Creek

Warm River

Falls River

Ashton

22

47

Marysville

Drummond

Bitch Creek

Birch Creek

Saddle Mt. ▲ EL 10302

Monteview

Jefferson Reservoir

Rays Lake

Henry's Fork

Chester

20

32

Felt

28

④

Mud Lake

Hamer

150

⑤

Parker 21

St. Anthony

Teton

Newdale 18

33

Tetonia

Teton River

33

Driggs

33

19

Howe

33

22

Mud Lake

Terreton

143

33

Sugar City

Rexburg 17

Thornton

16

15

Snake River

Roberts Menan

135

⑥

Lewisville

48 15

Lorenzo

Rigby

Heise

Snake River

Victor 33

Pine Ck. Pass EL 6764

128

Ririe

14

26

Butte City

20

Idaho Falls ⑦⑨

119

Ucon

43

Iona

Lincoln

Ririe Reservoir

31

Swan Valley

Atomic City

118

⑪

Ammon

Irwin

113

⑩

⑥⑯ 26

13

26

108

⑥⑯ 26

Shelley

Bone 12

Willow Creek

Grays Lake Outlet

Palisades Reservoir

15

98

Firth

Basalt

93

91

Moreland

Rockford

Riverside

39

Blackfoot

89

Blackfoot River

Grays Lake

Pingree

91

Springfield

Sterling

Fort Hall

FORT HALL

River

Wayan

Legend

⓪⓪ Locator number (matches numeric listing in section)

⛰ State Park

━━ State Hwy.

Ⓐ Campsite

⬤ Rest stop

══ County Road

═══ Interstate

═══ U.S. Hwy.

┅┅ Gravel/unpaved road

3

Dubois
Pop. 420

When settlers arrived in this area in the 1880s, the town was named after one of them, Fred Thomas Dubois. Fred was a U.S. Marshall who later became Idaho's Senator. The post office was established in 1892 and the settlement grew with the onset of successful farming that lasted from 1910-1920. After the farming boom fizzled, many of the residents, left town and most buildings were leveled. Today, the quiet town is best known for boasting a large grazing region.

H Nez Perce War
Milepost 167 on I-15 at the Dubois Rest Area

When General O. O. Howard tried to get more than 600 Nez Perce Indians to settle on a North Idaho reservation in 1877, he ran into a lot of trouble here.

On their way to Yellowstone Park, Chief Joseph's Nez Perce people reached Hole in the Rock Station (four miles north of here) on August 16, and shut down stage service to Montana. Howard's cavalry and volunteers followed only a day behind until August 20, when an Indian force made off with more than 100 Army mules. That raid halted military pursuit and forced Howard to continue his Nez Perce campaign for six more weeks.

T Heritage Hall Museum
1 block off Main St., Dubois.

The Heritage Hall Museum is housed within a Gothic Revival mission church and preserves the mission's history and artifacts. The museum is open from 2 PM to 5 PM on Fridays during the summer. Appointments can be made for private viewing during the rest of the year.

4 *Lodging*

Monteview
Pop. 10

The post office was established here in 1915. The town's first postmaster, Mabel E. Ellis, adopted the present name because of the settlement's panoramic view of the distant Gilmore Mountains. The area originated as and continues to be a farm and ranching region.

Mud Lake
Pop. 270

Mud Lake was formed along the shores of the lake bearing the same name. Cattlemen devised the moniker after the lake, which had a tendency to nearly dry up every year and provide cattle with only muddy water during late summer.

Terreton

Situated just two miles from the watering hole, Mud Lake, the tiny village of Terreton draws its name from Marshal M. Terry. Terry founded the community, became the area's first storeowner, and established a post office in 1920.

H Prehistoric Man
Milepost 44.3 on State Hwy. 28

Archaeological research has traced human occupation of this valley back more than 10,000 years.

The first men here found the valley forested. As the climate became drier, other mountain dwellers – known to archaeologists as people of the Bitterroot culture – settled here, perhaps about 8,000 years ago. These forerunners of the modern northern Shoshoni Indians lived in family bands and hunted big game, such as bison and mountain sheep.

T Mud Lake Historical Society
City Building, Mud Lake. 663-4376.

The Mud Lake Historical Society is dedicated to preserving the region's history. Visitors can browse through research archives highlighting important events in the area's development. The museum is open from 2 PM to 4 PM on the first and third Thursday of each month, and 2 PM to 4 PM on the second Monday with other times available by appointment.

T Birch Creek Massacre Site
On State Hwy. 28, 13.5 miles northwest of the State Hwy.s 28 and 22 junction.

In 1877, U.S. Army troops and Nez Perce Indians were not the only tragic casualties of the Nez Perce War. On August 15, the Nez Perce tribes of Chiefs Looking Glass, Joseph, and White Bird were fleeing from General Oliver Howard and traveling southeast towards Montana through Idaho's Birch Creek Valley. Much to their surprise, they happened upon a group of white travelers.

A group of eight wagons carrying three teamsters, a herder, two miners, and two Chinese laborers were peacefully enjoying their lunch when the Native Americans surprised them. Although eager to resume their journey to Salmon and deliver merchandise to Colonel George Shoup, the men graciously shared their lunch with the Indians. When the Indians discovered that the men were carrying barrels of whiskey, the encounter turned hostile. The Indians demanded that the men share the whiskey, and a raucous scene ensued. Sent to gather firewood, the Chinese laborers ran away, and the herder was able to slip back into the sagebrush. Unfortunately, the other five travelers were caught in a bloody battle where they lost their lives.

Fearing the worst for their counterparts, the Chinese fled to Salmon and contacted Colonel Shoup. Along with a group of volunteers and a band of Shoshone Indians, Shoup visited the tragic lunch spot and confirmed the Chinese men's fears – the wagons had been looted and burned and the five souls not lucky enough to escape had been killed. One week later, volunteers found the herder fearing for his life and hiding in the mountains.

Upon finding the bodies, Colonel Shoup and his men buried the remains on-site. Months later, the bodies were excavated and reburied in the Salmon cemetery. However, a marble marker identifies the massacre site along with the three teamster's names. The two miners are anonymously remembered as their names are still unknown to this day.

T Bison and Veratic Rockshelters
15.5 miles northwest of the junction of State Hwy.s 28 and 22; the site is located east of State Hwy. 28.

Idaho State University archaeology faculty excavations have revealed that Idaho's Birch Creek Valley has the most extensive history of buffalo hunting in all of North America. Funded through National Science Foundation grants, a team of archaeologists studied the area from 1959 to 1972 and discovered the Bison and Veratic Rockshelters. Radiocarbon dating and artifacts found in the shelters indicate that Northern Shoshone Native Americans continuously inhabited the shelters for 11,000 years. The last group to occupy the shelters was the Lemhi Shoshone from 1250 to 1850 A.D.

TV Mud Lake Wildlife Management Area
3 miles north of Mud Lake and Terreton. 663-4664. Merge off I-15 at Exit 143, and proceed to Mud Lake. At Mud Lake, turn onto County Rd. 1800 E. and drive to County Rd 1800 N. Bear west here and proceed 0.2 miles to County Rd. 1775 E. Turn north, and continue to 1900 N. Bear west here, and follow this road to the wildlife area.

Mud Lake Wildlife Manzgement Area was established in 1940 to preserve and improve waterfowl nesting habitat. Starting out with just 607 acres, the management area has expanded to its present span of 8,853 acres thanks to subsequent land acquisitions. The area revolves around the 7,000-acre Mud Lake and its surrounding wetlands habitat. This lake measuring five miles deep is home to numerous waterfowl and mammals. Nearly 50,000 snow geese pass through the area in March and April, and the lake is populated with trumpeter swans and several species of ducks. Overhead, two species of hawks circle the skies and gaze down upon mule deer, white-tailed deer, and pronghorn antelope.

Visitors can gaze at the array of wildlife from the Kaster Overlook Tower situated on Mud Lake's north shore. To reach the overlook from the area's headquarters, travel two miles northwest along the main road to the first intersection. Bear right here and proceed one-quarter mile to another road junction. Turning right, proceed approximately two miles to the overlook. The entire management area is free and open year-round for camping, fishing, hunting, boating, and wildlife viewing.

V Sinks Drainages

Named after their characteristic sinking disappearance into the Snake River Plain Aquifer, the Sinks Drainages include the Big Lost and Little Lost Rivers as well as Beaver, Birch, Camas, and Medicine Lodge Creeks. Despite extensive habitat damage resulting from overgrazing and natural flooding, the drainages still maintain steady populations of small rainbow trout. Mountain whitefish are present only in the Big Lost River, and a few minor tributaries in the drainage area support native bull, cutthroat, and brook trout.

5 *Food, Lodging*

Hamer
Pop. 12

Easterners, who were later followed by Mormons, founded Hamer. The town draws its name from Illinois native, Colonel Thomas R. Hamer. Hamer moved to Idaho in 1893, later served as an Idaho legislator, and served in Congress from 1909 to 1911. The area's earliest Mormon settlers were responsible for establishing an artesian well irrigation system and successfully developed the local grain and hay industry.

H Market Lake
Milepost 142 on I-15 Southbound

The flat, irrigated fields that stretch to the next interchange used to be a great Indian and trappers' hunting ground in an old lake that came and went.

In historic times, Market Lake was formed during the great Snake River flood of 1853. When a new railroad grade blocked the overflow channel leading from the river, the lake disappeared for a time after 1887. Later, irrigation seepage restored the lake, and now the level is regulated for farming and a wildlife refuge.

H Menan Buttes
Milepost 70.3 on State Hwy. 33

Two cones of glassy lava are located directly south of here. The largest rises 800 feet above the surrounding plain.

Hot molten lava, erupting from great depth, met cold surface water in the west flood plain of the Snake River. The northern butte, in fact, formed in the channel of the Henry's Fork,

Lewisville
Pop. 467

Lewisville was originally founded as a Mormon settlement. It is situated in Jefferson County.

Menan
Pop. 707

Founded as a Mormon settlement in 1879, this community was called Poole's Island, Heals Island, Cedar Butte, and Platt before finally arriving at its present moniker. Menan's current name was given in 1885 when the post office was established and is allegedly a Shoshoni Indian term meaning "island," or "many waters." The town itself lies amidst various bends in the Snake River, which would deem the name appropriate. The town continues to serve as a supply center for the surrounding agricultural area.

Roberts
Pop. 647

This small town is located on the southern end of a lake and waterfowl habitat area created during an 1863 Snake River flood. Prior to the site's development, Native Americans frequented the land, and Captain Bonneville's 1833 exploration party camped here while pursuing the area's abundant game.

A couple years after the lake's formation, Brigham Young led 142 of his followers here on his journey to Fort Lemhi. Young temporarily named the location Lava Lake. Market Lake was the next name applied, although few historians agree on the exact meaning behind the name. Some state the name was given because hunters and trappers "went to market" here for both necessity and livelihood. Others claim the name is derived from geese and ducks that were slaughtered and then sold here.

Regardless, the name didn't take hold. When the Union Pacific Railroad arrived in 1898 and the town was incorporated in 1910, officials changed the town's name to Roberts in recognition of Railroad Superintendent, H.A. Roberts.

T Menan Buttes
North of Menan on Twin Buttes Rd. Contact the Palisades Ranger District at 523-1412.

Menan Buttes are a National Natural Landmark and are recognized as two of the world's largest basaltic tuff cones. Formed during the late Pleistocene Era, the tuffs are made of volcanic glass formed from the sudden chilling of volcanic magma. Some geographers speculate that the buttes were formed from the interaction of magma with the ancient water source of the present day Snake River.

The North and South Buttes are nearly identical in shape and size. The crater at North Menan Butte measures 3,000 feet in diameter, and its cone rises nearly 800 feet. From the cone's top, visitors have access to panoramic views of the Snake River Valley and the winding Henry's Fork of the Snake River.

which was forced further east. Suddenly chilled into small particles of volcanic glass, the lava exploded in a great spray of steam and solid fragments that built up into windblown cones around large summit craters a half-mile long and 200 to 400 feet deep.

TV Camas National Wildlife Refuge
2150 E. 2350 N., Hamer. 662-5423. At Hamer, merge off I-15 and drive east through town to the frontage road. Bear north onto the frontage road, and proceed three miles. Following the highway signs, turn west, and continue two miles to the refuge headquarters.

The Camas National Wildlife Refuge spans 10,578 acres of lakes, ponds, creeks, marshlands, grasslands, sagebrush uplands, and meadows, and is one of America's 500 national wildlife refuges.

Known for its beautiful landscape, the refuge is home to a significant range of birds and mammals and is a wildlife enthusiast's dream come true. During spring and fall migration, almost 100,000 ducks have been spotted here, and nearly 180 species of birds continually frequent the refuge. Endangered and rare species such as trumpeter swans, bald eagles, and peregrine falcons are protected here. In addition, mammal sightings reported in the area include white-tailed deer, mule deer, pronghorn antelope, moose, elk, beavers, coyotes, and cottontail rabbits.

The refuge is open for wildlife viewing year-round, and recreationists can pursue off-road hiking, skiing, and snowshoeing from July 16 to February 28 each year. The free refuge opens 30 minutes prior to sunrise and closes 30 minutes after sunset.

Idaho Falls	Jan	Feb	March	April	May	June	July	Aug	Sep	Oct	Nov	Dec	Annual
Average Max. Temperature (F)	30.2	37.0	47.2	58.3	68.5	77.6	86.7	85.6	75.2	61.6	43.8	32.1	58.7
Average Min. Temperature (F)	13.0	17.6	24.6	31.8	39.7	46.7	52.3	50.2	41.7	32.2	23.4	14.5	32.3
Average Total Precipitation (in.)	1.03	0.93	0.99	1.12	1.62	1.28	0.56	0.75	0.85	0.94	0.99	1.04	12.11
Average Total Snowfall (in.)	8.2	5.3	3.1	0.9	0.4	0.0	0.0	0.0	0.0	0.5	3.2	7.1	28.7
Average Snow Depth (in.)	3	2	0	0	0	0	0	0	0	0	0	2	1

TV Market Lake Wildlife Management Area

20 miles north of Idaho Falls near Roberts. 228-3131. Taking Exit 135, merge off I-15 at Roberts, and proceed to County Rd. 2880 E. Bearing north onto this road, continue 0.5 miles through Roberts to a fork in the road. Turn right onto County Rd. 800 and follow to the wildlife area.

Located 4,780 feet above sea level, the Market Lake Wildlife Management Area sprawls across 5,000 acres. The area covers sandhills interspersed with igneous rock ledges and encompasses four distinct habitats: marsh/wetland meadow, desert uplands, Snake River riparian, and cropland. Due to the widely varying vegetation in each habitat, a diverse selection of wildlife populates the management area, while the lake supports yellow perch, bullhead trout, and Utah chubs. The area is free and open year-round for wildlife viewing, camping, fishing, hunting, and boating. Individuals should call the area headquarters for any seasonal restrictions on recreational activities prior to visiting.

7 Food, Lodging

Idaho Falls
Pop. 50,730

The first residents of this area were Shoshone-Bannock and Northern Paiute Indians. White settlers began arriving in the early 1860s when Harry Rickets constructed and operated a ferry across the Snake River. At the same time, James M. "Matt" Taylor was a hand for Ben Halliday's Overland Stage line between Salt Lake City and Virginia City, Montana. As Taylor was riding his horse one afternoon along the Snake River, he noticed a river section that was narrower than most places. Taylor concluded a bridge could be constructed there, and he rode to Montana to find supporters. After rallying the support of Ed Morgan and Bill Bartlett, Taylor began building his bridge. They worked during the winter of 1865, which allowed them access across the ice to work on both sides of the river. A sixty-foot long Queen-truss style bridge was their accomplishment.

Taylor's toll bridge was an instant success, and he and his partners took in nearly $3,000 each month in tolls. The miners and other settlers who landed on the east embankment of the river adopted the names of Taylor's Ferry, Taylor's Bridge, and Anderson's Bridge for the small town. In 1872, rumors of a forthcoming rail line persuaded Taylor to sell his bridge to the Anderson brothers. When the line did arrive, railroad officials renamed the town Eagle Rock. Some suggest the name is a reflection of the nearby Eagle Rock ferry, while others claim the name was chosen after a large rock resting in the middle of the river where bald eagles were known to nest. In either case, the railroad built its own bridge over the river just 150 feet downstream from Taylor's bridge, and the Andersons gave away 104 acres in Eagle Rock for

use as a railroad administrative site. The site's presence boosted the town's population to 670 in 1882. Times would soon change, though.

The railroad moved its headquarters to Pocatello just five years later. In addition, the gold in the mines was running out, and Eagle Rock's population began to dwindle. Realizing the undeveloped potential resting in the small community, Chicago developers convinced the townsfolk to change the name to Idaho Falls in 1891, despite no actual falls being located on the river at that time. In 1911, the city justified its name with the construction of a diversion dam and power plant that created a twenty-foot waterfall. This event helped ensure the future of Idaho Falls, and the area was developed into an agricultural center. Incorporated in 1900, Idaho Falls has boasted postal services since 1866 and was at one time the third largest city in the state.

H Taylor's Bridge
Exit 118 on I-15 Idaho Falls Business Loop

A landmark toll bridge spanned the Snake River at this rocky site in 1865, replacing the Eagle Rock Ferry, nine miles upstream.

James Madison Taylor (a relative of Presidents Madison and Taylor and a founder of Denver, Colorado) settled here in 1864 to develop an improved route for his freight line from Salt Lake to Montana's new gold mines. After his bridge was built, telegraph service reached here, July 16, 1866, and Eagle Rock (as Idaho Falls was known until 1890) became a regional transportation center. A railroad bridge was built adjacent to Taylor's Bridge in 1879.

H Eagle Rock Ferry
Exit 118 on I-15 Idaho Falls Business Loop

On June 20, 1863, Bill Hickman started a ferry nine miles up the Snake River for thousands of gold hunters headed for mines that now are in Montana.

Named for an eagle that had a nest on a rock here, his ferry flourished for two years. In 1864, J. Matt Taylor took it over and got an Idaho franchise to run it until he built a bridge here. Miners from Soda Springs and freighters from Salt Lake City all used Eagle Rock Ferry during Montana's gold rush.

H Elephant Hunters
Milepost 291.4 on U.S. Hwy. 20

Early day big game hunters, who occupied lava caves around here more than 12,000 years ago, had a diet that included elephants, camels, and giant bison.

When a gradual change to a warmer, drier climate made local grasslands into more desert, the elephant herds left for cooler plains farther north. But 8,000 years ago, bison still were available here. Indians continued to hunt buffalo on these plains until 1840. Then they had to go to Montana for their hunting trips.

T Willard Arts Center & Colonial Theater
450 A St, Idaho Falls. 522-0471. www.idahofallsarts.org

The Willard Arts Center provides residents and tourists of Idaho Falls with a vast array of cultural enrichment experiences. Operated under the direction of the Idaho Falls Arts Council, the Willard Arts Center features three art galleries, three classrooms for arts appreciation/education, and a conference room. The center showcases touring exhibits as well as local artists, and features

the works of both adults and children. Past exhibitions have included ceramics, textiles, glass, photography, paintings, and bronze sculptures. Exhibits rotate every two to three months.

Also inside the Willard Arts Center is the popular Colonial Theater. Seating up to 970 individuals, the theater hosts a diverse display of entertainment throughout the year. Symphonies, local choirs, bluegrass and country musicians, and string quartets are joined by Broadway musicals, comedy troupes, and cultural and historical presentations. Famous performers and speakers continually frequent the theater, and past guests have included Ray Charles and Charleton Heston. Advance tickets are recommended for the range of shows presented here.

T Eagle Rock Art Museum and Education Center
300 S. Capital Ave., Idaho Falls. 524-7777. www.eaglerockartmuseum.org

After ten years of planning, the Eagle Rock Art Museum and Education Center in conjunction with the city of Idaho Falls opened its doors on October 19, 2002. Overlooking the Snake River, Eagle Rock is the newest museum in Idaho with a mission to culturally enrich the lives of residents and visitors. With the assistance of the Eagle Rock Art Guild, Eagle Rock strives to collect, preserve, and display Idaho artists' varied works of art. In addition, Eagle Rock offers community education classes for both young and old. The museum is open from 6 PM to 9 PM on Mondays, 10 AM to 4 PM Wednesday through Saturday, and 1 PM to 4 PM on Sundays. Admission is free.

In association with the museum, Eagle Rock Art Guild offers an annual summer sidewalk art show. Artists from around the Rocky Mountain Region are featured, and works include pottery, paintings, and jewelry. The event also features a variety of food vendors and live entertainment.

T The KNOW Place
Next to the Downtown Development Corporation, Idaho Falls. Contact the Idaho Falls Chamber of Commerce at 523-1010 or (800) 634-3246.

This interesting science museum helps kids learn and have fun at the same time. The KNOW Place offers several hands-on science exhibits sure to entertain and intrigue kids of all ages. The museum is open year-round by appointment.

T Museum of Idaho
200 N. Eastern Ave. (at the corner of Elm and Eastern), Idaho Falls. 522-1400.

Originally known as the Bonneville Museum and housed within a historic Andrew Carnegie endowed building, this museum has undergone a recent facelift. After adding 20,000 square feet to the original building, the new museum opened in February 2003 under its new name, the Museum of Idaho. As one of Idaho's largest museums, the facility presents the natural and cultural history of Idaho and the Rocky Mountain region. The Museum of Idaho features several permanent exhibits as well as numerous rotating displays and is proud to now offer educational programs. The museum is open Monday through Saturday from 10 AM to 8 PM and is operated by the Bonneville County Historical Society.

T Walking Tour of Idaho Falls' Historic Downtown
Contact the Idaho Falls Downtown Development Corporation for more information. 535-0399.

Robert Anderson and Matt Taylor laid the foundations for Idaho Falls when they opened the area's first trading post in 1865. Although the settlement was initially a crossroads on the way to other Western destinations, settlers eventually began to see opportunity in this frontier place. By the mid 1880s, an early business district was growing that would later swell to encompass present day Broadway Ave.. Although none of the original buildings from the 1880s boom remain, several prominent buildings erected between 1894 and 1940 stand as a testament to this town's long legacy. The buildings represented on this historic downtown tour reflect different architectural and construction styles and the growth of Idaho Falls.

Rocky Mountain Bell Telephone Company Building
246 W. Broadway
Built in 1910 by the Rocky Mountain Bell Company, this Renaissance Revival style building was used as the town's telegraph office until the late 1920s. Upon its closure, the Idaho Falls' Catholic Church purchased the building, renamed it Faber Hall, and used it as a church parish hall for several years. In 1953, the building changed hands again. A local carpenter's union purchased the building as a meeting hall, at which time the building received its current nickname "Labor Temple." Today, the building is used as a private residence.

Shane Building
381 Shoup Ave.
This building features a Renaissance Revival design embellished with terra cotta accents. Constructed in 1915, the building's first floor was home to a grocery store, furniture store, and a women's clothing store.

Montgomery Ward Building
504 Shoup Ave.
During the 1920s and early 1930s, Idaho architects favored a Renaissance Revival style with Art Deco accents. This building constructed in 1928 was used as the Montgomery Ward and Company Department Store and is an excellent example of this design style. Amazingly, the building has never been significantly remodeled in its near eighty years of existence.

Idaho Falls City Building
308 Constitution Way
Lionel E. Fisher designed this building in a Beaux Arts architectural style. This design is rare in the architectural styles favored throughout much of Idaho, but its stately appearance is fitting for the building's intended use as a city hall. Constructed in 1929 and 1930, the building's exterior remains unaltered and the interior lobby tiles are original.

Underwood Hotel
347 Constitution Way
This elaborate Renaissance Revival style building was erected in 1918 for one of Idaho Falls' earliest woman entrepreneurs, Jennie Underwood. Bearing her name, the building served as a hotel primarily for Oregon Shortline Railroad passengers awaiting their own departure or the arrival of a loved one.

Bonneville Hotel
410 Constitution Way
The Idaho Falls Community Hotel Corporation along with 421 local citizens constructed this Italian Renaissance building in 1926 and 1927. Created to bring a convention facility and premier hotel to Idaho Falls, the building cost $335,000. Upon its completion, the Bonneville Hotel included a ballroom, two elaborate dining rooms, a sample room, and a large central lobby to accommodate all the needs of its first-class guests.

Hotel Idaho
482 Constitution Way
Despite skepticism from his critics, F.C. Hansen went ahead and built the Hotel Idaho amid a neighborhood of vacant land and single-family homes. Upon its completion in 1917, the building not only housed a hotel, but also a business college and auto dealership. The Hotel Idaho's doors were open for business until 1979. Today, the building is home to several different offices.

Bonneville County Courthouse
605 N. Capital
Constructed immediately after World War I using concrete with a brick veneer, the Bonneville County Courthouse represents a simple, classic design. Charles Aitken and Lionel E. Fisher designed the building whose interior includes elegant marble stairs and wainscot, stained glass skylights, and mosaic floor tiles.

Former Idaho Falls Federal Building
591 N. Park Ave.
Philadelphia native, James A. Wetmore, designed the city post office in 1914 in a Georgian Revival style. At a cost of $86,199, the post office was completed in 1916. The U.S. Postal Service occupied the building until 1986, and throughout the years, the building was shared with the U.S. Geological Survey, the Civil Service Investigator, the Defensive Service Investigator, and the U.S. Department of Agriculture News. Upon the postal service's move, private investors purchased the building and remodeled the interior into its current use as various company offices.

Kress Building
541 Park Ave.
Between 1930 and 1932, this building was constructed for the S. H. Kress and Company. The building features a unique use of terra cotta and remains relatively unaltered from its original state.

I.O.O.F. Building
393 Park Ave.
Although Idaho Falls was still a fairly small settlement in the late 1880s and early 1890s, it did feature a thriving I.O.O.F. chapter. As the group continued to grow, the organization needed a new meeting place to accommodate all of its members. In 1909, this building was erected for that purpose, and it features the city's only remaining example of a Romanesque Revival architectural style. When it was first constructed, the building also housed a movie theater, funeral parlor, and grocery store. Today, the building retains its intended purpose as an I.O.O.F. lodge.

Farmers and Merchants Bank Building
346 Park Ave.
This building features a simplified version of the Renaissance Revival architectural style popular in Idaho Falls during World War I. Although the building now features a brick veneer, the building's early years were simply characterized with red and white sandstone. The building was constructed as the Farmers and Merchant Bank. The bank later shared the building with a drug store and a candy/tobacco store.

Hasbrouck Building
362 Park Ave.
At the turn of the twentieth century, stone buildings dominated the architectural style of Idaho Falls' business district. This building best represents this design principle, and construction on the basement and first floor began in 1895. Nebraska native and attorney, Herman J. Hasbrouck, used the original building for the Idaho law practice he began in 1890. In 1905, the second story was added, and Hasbrouck remained in the building until 1915.

The Colonial Theater
466 A St.
At a building cost of $175,000, the Colonial Investment Company completed the Colonial Theater in 1919. Owned at the time by some of Idaho Falls' most prominent residents, the building was hailed as Idaho's finest theater. Today, the Renaissance Revival style theater continues to be a popular city venue, and it retains its original terra cotta façade.

Former Idaho Falls Public Library
Elm Ave. & N. Eastern Ave.
With $15,000 in financial assistance from the Andrew Carnegie Corporation, Idaho Falls completed its first public library in 1916. The library's completion was due in great part to the Village Improvement Society, a group of wealthy Idaho Falls women who strove to improve the appearance of Idaho Falls and expand local attractions. From 1938 to 1940, a new Art Deco entrance was added to the library. Today, the former library is home to the Bonneville County Museum.

T Ridge Ave. Historic District Walking Tour
Idaho Falls. For more information, contact the City of Idaho Falls Planning and Building at 529-1276.

Before 1890, most residential building in Idaho Falls was restricted to the south of Broadway Ave. near the railroad and the Snake River. As the town's population began to swell, though, new residents flocked to the Ridge Ave. District, and the Idaho Register documented this building boom in 1896.

The first residents of Ridge Ave. came from all occupational backgrounds, from railroad workers to renowned lawyers. The style of houses they chose were just as diverse. This district provides exceptional examples of changing architectural styles. From modest Queen Anne's to Craftsman and Prairie styles, the houses have been lovingly cared for throughout the years and retain their distinctive features. This walking tour explores the history of sixty-five of Ridge Ave.'s 101 historical buildings.

313 N. Water Ave.
Stonemason, Isreal Vadboncoeur, built this home in 1896 and 1897 for Oregon Short Line Railroad stationmaster, George Changnon. The home was one of the first residences built east of the railroad, and its Craftsman style porch was added twenty years later. When Changon sold his home, it became a community mortuary.

327 N. Water Ave.
This simple Queen Anne style house was built between 1903 and 1905 and was home to Dr. G. W. Cleary. The home's porch still features original spindlework supports.

343 N. Water Ave.
Ralph A. Louis was an influential man who served as Idaho Falls' mayor from 1917 to 1919 and again from 1921 to 1927. This Queen Anne home was one of his first residences in the community.

344 N. Water Ave.
During the early twentieth century, Richard and Sadie Barry occupied this Queen Anne home. The

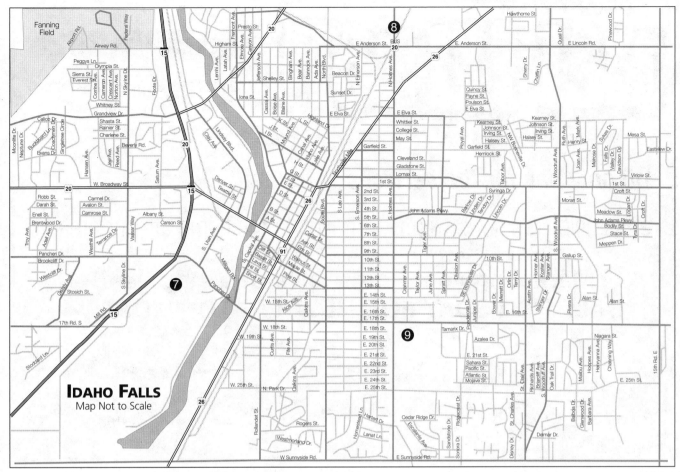

IDAHO FALLS
Map Not to Scale

house is unique as it features an inset porch, a steeply pitched roof, and an arched opening.

387 N. Water Ave.

Coltman Lumber Company owner, Edward P. Coltman, built this home in sometime prior to 1903. Coltman served as Idaho Falls' mayor from 1904 to 1907 and again from 1909 to 1910. His home was unusual for its time as it included eight dormers and a pyramidal shaped roof.

400 N. Eastern Ave.

Owner of the Idaho Café, W. Jay Brown was the first resident of this classical Queen Anne style home. The building is constructed out of cement blocks, a popular residential building material commonly used at the turn of the century. The building was originally to be used as a boarding house, but became a single-family dwelling instead.

422 N. Eastern Ave.

W. Jay Brown built this home as a rental for early business owners and railroad workers who were contributing to Idaho Falls' population growth. The house features an expansive front porch and gables.

468 N. Eastern Ave.

The exact building date of this home is uncertain, but it is speculated that construction was completed sometime between 1911 and 1921. The Craftsman style home is modest and features multi-paned windows and square wood supports.

156 Poplar

William P. Dawe built this simple Queen Anne home as a rental for the town's first workers. The cottage features spindlework on its full front porch.

491 N. Water

Idaho Falls' City Clerk, William P. Dawe, was one of the first occupants of this wood-sided home. The residence also features a small portico.

477 N. Water Ave.

This home is unique in the Ridge Ave. District due to its full porch and frieze accented with spindle-work supports. Dr. T. M. Bridges built this home prior to 1903 and was its first occupant. Bridges enjoyed a successful medical career in Idaho Falls along with his associate, Dr. Franklin LaRue.

478 N. Water Ave.

This home was built in 1903 as a residence for early settler, Ellen Moen. The small brick house features a gable with fishscale shingles, and the upstairs was originally accessed strictly through an exterior stairwell.

461 N. Water Ave.

This home features corner boards and fishscale shingled gables. The home was built sometime prior to 1910, and the first resident was F. H. Hollister.

460 N. Water Ave.

Thomas and Mary Wilson built this basalt stone home as a boardinghouse for local workers. The two-story home was constructed sometime in the early 1900s.

440 N. Water Ave.

This simple Queen Anne building was erected prior to 1903. Among its first occupants were the Charles W. Mulhall Real Estate, Loans, and Insurance business.

408 N. Water Ave.

Leslie B. Murphy, partner of the Clay and Murphy automobile dealership, had this home built in the early 1900s. The home features unique rounded

windows, fishscale shingled gables, and corner boards.

409 N. Water Ave.

Originally from Illinois, teamster Marquis L. McKee built this home in the late 1890s. It represents one of the first homes constructed east of the railroad and features a Queen Anne inspired design with a steeply pitched roof. McKee later built his famed "McKee Flats" behind his house that served as apartments for generations of Idaho Falls' workers.

233-241 Cedar St.

Leslie B. Murphy built this Craftsman duplex between 1915 and 1921. The duplex retains its original sense of style accented with concrete piers, wood railings, and cross-gabled porches.

255 Cedar St.

In approximately 1915, Henry Scarborough built this Craftsman style one-story bungalow. The home features multi-paned windows and a front porch supported with wooden piers.

406 N. Ridge Ave.

Wilford D. Huffaker was a prominent community figure in Idaho Falls' fledgling years. Huffaker served as Bonneville County Commissioners' Chairman and was president of the Iona Mercantile Company. His gabled Queen Anne home is embellished with spindlework detailing and fishscale shingles.

460 N. Ridge Ave.

Barzilla W. Clark enjoyed a life in the Idaho spotlight. He served as the Thousand Springs Land and Irrigation Company's manager and vice-president and also acted as Idaho Falls' mayor from 1913 to 1915 and 1927 to 1936. In 1936, Clark

won a two-year term as Idaho governor. During his residence in Idaho Falls, Clark occupied this brick bungalow featuring a unique curved railing.

482-486 N. Ridge Ave.
Idaho Falls' postmaster, Mr. Coltman, built this one and one-half story duplex around 1915. It reflects the building trends of the era as it features wood shingles, clapboard siding, brick piers with wood supports, and large overhanging eaves. The home still features its original doors.

498 N. Ridge Ave.
Before Mr. Coltman assumed his title as community postmaster, he was employed with the Western Land Company prior to 1903. This Queen Anne home represents Coltman's first building project, and the house features a gabled roof, clapboard siding, and fishscale shingles.

485 N. Ridge Ave.
The Louis A. Haley residence represents the popular bungalow style of the early 1900s. Erected in 1907, the home features numerous windows, exposed rafters, and overhanging eaves. One of Idaho Falls' first travel agents was the original occupant.

495 N. Ridge Ave.
This Craftsman style home retains much of its original character, including exposed rafters and overhanging eaves. The home was built around 1915 and was first occupied by a manager of the Western Machinery and Equipment Company.

520 N. Ridge Ave.
Known as the George Apartments, this Prairie style building was constructed around 1917 and quickly became known as the finest apartment building in the entire Northwest. Building costs

were estimated at $75,000, and the apartments remain adorned with multi-paned windows, terra cotta pendants, white stone trim, and interior marble wainscoting.

527 N. Ridge Ave.
Mary McCann enjoyed a prosperous career as the town corsetiere who helped Idaho Falls' women stay up to date in shape and style. Her brick Tudor Revival home was constructed sometime prior to 1926, and the house features multi-paned windows and an arched opening over the front door.

543 N. Ridge Ave.
Previously a judge in Saginaw, Michigan, Otto E. McCutcheon moved westward and became the attorney for the Great Western Canal Company. During his residence at this large two-story home, McCutcheon played an integral part in formulating Idaho's early irrigation regulations.

557 N. Ridge Ave.
Early Idaho Falls' mayor (1903-1904), Alvin T. Shane, became the first resident of this home in approximately 1911. The home features an upper gable extension and halve-timbered accents.

573 N. Ridge Ave.
This home featuring overhanging, bracketed eaves and stout wood porch supports represents another example of Idaho Falls' love of the Craftsman design. Charles C. Wilson served as Idaho Falls' assistant postmaster and was the home's first occupant.

344 Poplar Street
This home represents the third residence that Wilbert J. Coltman constructed in the Ridge District. To this date, the home retains its classical design and accents.

798 S. Boulevard
Outgrowing his existing practice, Dr. H.D. Spencer moved his hospital to this building in 1921 and continued practicing until 1941. At that time, the Franciscan Sisters of Perpetual Order Adoration purchased the building and turned it into the Sacred Heart Hospital. In 1949, the Order moved their hospital to a different location, at which time Dr. W.R. Abbott acquired the building and started the Idaho Falls Clinic.

425 Ash Street
This stately Colonial Revival home was built for D.F. and Gladys Richards in 1939. D.F. Richards became president of the Bowen Curley's American National Bank and also served as director of the San Francisco Federal Reserve Board. The home is embellished with Doric columns supporting a small portico at the entrance.

309 N. Placer Ave.
Herman J. Hasbrouck, a native Nebraska attorney who practiced law in Idaho Falls from 1890 to 1915, built this Colonial Revival home in 1907. Hasbrouck played an important role in the town's development and later served a two-year term in the Idaho Senate.

363 N. Placer Ave.
Constructed around 1931, this residence features Tudor styling and is one of the newest homes in the Ridge Ave. District. Geological Survey District Engineer, Lynn Crandall, first occupied this home featuring steep gabled roofs and half-timbered siding.

383 N. Placer Ave.
Although the original front porch has been removed, this Queen Anne style home still retains its original wood siding, wood accents, and fish-

scale shingles. The first occupant was Albert W. Rates who served as co-owner of Vogel and Rates Meats.

391 N. Placer Ave.
Local painter, George H. Warner, built this Queen Anne home in the early 1900s. He also built a paint shop behind the home that has since been remodeled into another home.

390 N. Ridge Ave.
This home features another impressive example of the Colonial Revival design popular in the 1930s and 1940s. Emery Owens constructed this home adorned with clapboard siding, multi-pane windows, and Doric columns.

370 N. Ridge Ave.
The Prairie style design of this home is associated with Frank Lloyd Wright and was developed by a firm of Chicago architects. The Prairie style design was short-lived in Idaho Falls' popularity, but the home has been well-preserved and retains its casement windows, lineal brick pattern, and overhanging eaves. The residence was built in 1917 and was first home to William Luxton, early Idaho Falls' entrepreneur and partner of Luxton Brothers Meats.

371 N. Ridge Ave.
Gilbert G. Wright built this stylish Queen Anne home in 1909. The residence is adorned with numerous classical detailings, including Ionic columns and modillions. Wright was a successful Idaho Falls' business owner, managing the Consolidated Wagon and Machine Company as well as the Idaho Falls Milling Company.

353 N. Ridge Ave.
Idaho Falls' lawyer, Oscar A. Johannsen, built this Queen Anne home between 1905 and 1911. The residence is unique as it features distinctive shingled porch supports.

345 N. Ridge Ave.
Orley K. Wilbur, vice-president of Farmers and Merchants Bank, constructed this home around 1914. The impressive brick bungalow features a stone foundation, lintels, and watertable.

340 N. Ridge Ave.
Charles A. Merriman built this unusual home sometime prior to 1903. Styled in a Queen Anne design, the home features classic accents on the window below the gable. Renowned president of the Holz Cigar and Tobacco Company, Clifford Holz, later occupied the home.

312 N. Ridge Ave.
This home is actually the second residence to occupy this site. Although little is known about the original house, the current Colonial Revival structure was built around 1920 and was occupied by mercantile owner, Eugene Wright. The home features unusual tapered wood columns and front shed dormers.

288 N. Ridge Ave.
This house features a combination of Queen Anne and Craftsman style details and was built around 1903. Frank and Minnie Hitt were the first occupants of the home. Mrs. Hitt was one of the first settlers in the Idaho Falls' area, and she started working at the Anderson Brothers Bank at age seventeen when Idaho Falls was still known as "Eagle Rock."

262 N. Ridge Ave.
Attorney Harrison Linger constructed this Craftsman inspired home between 1905 and 1911. The multi-paned windows characterizing Craftsman architecture are unusually small in this home.

325 Elm St.
Pennsylvania native, J.C. Fulton, designed the Neo-Classical Revival style First Presbyterian Church. The church was completed in 1920 and was added in 1978 to the National Register of Historic Places.

310 Elm St.
Around 1901, State Bank cashier Clinton G. Peck built this home. The residence is modeled in a Queen Anne design and features an elaborate spindlework porch.

346 Elm St.
Architect John W. Dill built this home between 1911 and 1921. The residence is distinctively Craftsman inspired with its decorative rafters, overhanging eaves, large porch supports, and a curved railing.

197 N. Placer Ave.
The Craftsman style home was popular in Idaho Falls for a period of several years. Frank Sheppard built this home in 1908 with a front gabled porch supported by large stone piers.

173 N. Placer Ave.
Blacksmith Robert Keddie's widow, Flora Keddie, was this home's first occupant. The brick bungalow features a distinctive false balcony on the top floor.

135 N. Placer Ave.
Edward Rowles was a prominent downtown businessman who was president of a company specializing in men's clothing. With his successes, Rowles built this impressive Colonial Revival home complete with sun porch, columns, multi-pane windows, and a gabled portico.

101 N. Placer Ave.
This unique Queen Anne features large columns dominating the architectural design. Dr. Fuller lived here in the early 1900s and established the Fuller and Soderquist Hospital in his home. In 1917, Dr. H.D. Spencer bought the Fuller's home/hospital. Both Dr. Fuller's wife and Dr. Spencer's wife noted great entertaining difficulties in leading guests through the second floor surgery unit to the third floor guest facilities.

315 Walnut St.
Harness maker, P.B. VanBlaricom, built this home between 1896 and 1897. The basalt foundation home is another one of the earliest homes built in the Ridge Ave. District east of the railroad.

151 N. Ridge Ave.
Sundberg and Sundberg designed this brick building built by Reed Construction Company from Pocatello. Construction on the O.E. Bell Junior High School began in 1928, and the first wing held classes in 1930. A north addition was added between 1935 and 1937, at which time cold winter winds whisked through the school's hallways and nearly froze out teachers and students.

258 Walnut St.
Utilizing his financial success as manager of the Great Western Canal and Improvement Company, A.D. Morrison built this stone home in 1896. The home features a Colonial Revival inspired design complete with Paladin windows and an inset porch. Morrison later sold the home to Claude C. Campbell, president of Anderson Brothers Bank.

290 Walnut St.
Nils Hoff, owner of Nils Hoff Grain and Coal Company, had this home built around 1900. The home once included several side porches that have since collapsed or been enclosed. However, the front window with entablature is original.

101 S. Ridge Ave.
O.J. Ellis was the first occupant of this Queen Anne home built between 1905 and 1911. The exterior siding has been replaced throughout the years, but the home's original design and massing remain the same.

188 S. Ridge Ave.
Carl Nation served as manager of the Sanitary Cash Grocery Company. With his earnings, Nation bought this Colonial Revival home and became its first occupant. The home features multi-pane windows, a portico, and carved Doric columns typical of this architectural style.

190 S. Ridge Ave.
Guy Smith served as one of Idaho Falls' earliest reputable dentists. He and his wife, Ethyl, built this Mission Revival home in 1917. The residence features an arched porch opening with overhanging eaves and numerous windows.

185 S. Ridge Ave.
For early residents, Geo. M. Scott and Sons was the place to go for stationary and correspondence. Owner Rollin C. Scott turned his profits into an impressive brick Tudor Revival style home.

288 Maple Street
Kate and Bowen Curley were members of Idaho Falls' elite society. While Bowen served as the American National Bank President and also as town mayor for two two-year terms, Kate was president of the women's Village Improvement Society, a group of wealthy women interested in improving the appearance of early Idaho Falls. Their home is a rare example of a Shingle design and features stone and basalt walls with wood shingles.

240 S. Ridge Ave.
Kate and Bowen Curley's daughter, Ethyl Smith, built this Colonial Revival home in the early 1920s.

270 S. Ridge Ave.
C. Fred Chandler was the first occupant of this Queen Anne home built between 1903 and 1905. The home features dormer fanlights and an unusual cut-away bay window.

284 S. Ridge Ave.
Holden and Eckhardt were well-respected attorneys in Idaho Falls' early days. Capitalizing on his success, Arthur Holden built this home between 1903 and 1905. The bungalow features a hipped roof and wood shingle exterior.

309 S. Ridge Ave.
This classical Queen Anne was built around 1903 for Louis A. Hartert. Hartert was co-owner of Johannsen and Hartert Real Estate and Loans.

291 S. Ridge Ave.
Built in 1916, this Colonial Revival home is embellished with a column-supported portico, a fanlight over the door, and beveled wood siding. The home was built for L.O. Naylor who managed the N.O. Taylor Studebaker Motor Cars Company.

257 S. Ridge Ave.
This home was originally built as a one and one-half story boardinghouse and private residence in 1901. In 1915, a framed addition was joined to the stone structure. D.B. Bybee, owner of the Idaho Saloon, was the first resident, while Addison V. Scott and his wife were the second occupants. Mrs. Scott was Idaho's first female justice of the peace.

225 S. Ridge Ave.
This classic Queen Anne was built around 1903 for Bertha Anderson. City school superintendent, Benjamin R. Crandall, later occupied the home with its classical detailings.

205 S. Ridge Ave.

A smaller home once occupied this lot, but in 1918, Louis and Phoebe Hartert built the existing Prairie style home. The residence features numerous windows and large porch supports. Hartert served as president of his own real estate, insurance, and loan company.

237 N. Water Ave.

In 1916-1917, the Tudor-Gothic style Trinity Methodist Church was constructed. A stone Celtic cross accents the gable, and stained glass windows adorn the front, celestory, and aisle windows. In the 1970s, the building was added to the National Register of Historic Places.

N. Eastern Ave. and Elm

Formerly home to the Idaho Falls Public Library, this Neo-Classical building was completed in 1916. The building was added to the National Register of Historic Places in 1984, and today, it is home to the Bonneville County Museum.

T Rotary International Peace Park

Snake River Greenbelt west of Broadway Bridge, Idaho Falls. Contact Idaho Falls Parks and Recreation Division at 529-1480.

Located alongside the city's greenbelt near the Snake River, the Rotary International Peace Park symbolizes peaceful relationships with individuals around the world. Park highlights include granite lanterns that were given to Idaho Falls' residents by their sister city, Tokai-Mura, Japan.

T Wilson Rawls Memorial Statue

457 Broadway, Idaho Falls.

Situated on the front lawn of the Idaho Falls Public Library is a statue entitled, "Dreams Can Come True," a memorial to writer W. Wilson Rawls. Rawls lived in Idaho Falls from 1958 to 1975 in a small house on 11th Street. Although he had always dreamed of becoming a writer who would inspire others to read and write, Rawls nearly gave up on his dream. But with the encouragement of his wife, Sophie, Rawls wrote his acclaimed *Where the Red Fern Grows*. With editing help from his wife, Rawls' children's classic was published in 1961.

To commemorate Rawls' accomplishments and his persistence in fulfilling his dream, a life-size statue was created depicting the story's main character (Billy Coleman) and his two dogs. Funded by donations from across the U.S. and a grant from the Idaho Commission on the Arts and National Endowment for the Arts, the statue was created by Idaho Falls artist, Marilyn Hansen. The mission of the statue is to inspire children to dream ambitious dreams and to encourage adults to support the pursuit of those dreams.

T Idaho Falls Temple

1000 Memorial Dr., Idaho Falls. 523-4504.

Constructed on land donated by the Idaho Falls Chamber of Commerce that overlooks the Snake River, the Idaho Falls Temple of the Church of

Jesus Christ of Latter-Day Saints was completed after five years of hard labor. Plans for the temple were discussed as early as 1918, but the cornerstone was not laid until October 19, 1940. Although the project was only projected to take a couple of years to complete, World War II claimed many workers and created a shortage of building materials. Finally, on September 23, 1945, the temple was ready for dedication, and Church President George Albert Smith traveled from Salt Lake City to participate. It was not until 1983 that the Angel Moroni statue was placed on top of the white stone temple.

Although the temple itself is not open to the general public, a visitor's center in front of the temple is open daily from 9 AM to 9 PM. Here, non-Mormons have the opportunity to learn about one of Idaho's most prevalent religions. The center provides artwork, guided tours of the grounds, special exhibits, and video presentations free of charge.

T Snake River Fur Trader Monument

Intersection of Memorial Dr. and B St., Idaho Falls.

Idaho Falls' history is dotted with the lives of hearty pioneers, including several trappers and traders. To commemorate the town's past, renowned Idaho Falls artist, Roy Reynolds, was awarded a grant in 2001 to create the "Snake River Fur Trader" monument. The bronze statue measures eight feet tall and is one of the many highlights along the Snake River Greenbelt.

T Taylor's Crossing

South of the Broadway Bridge, Idaho Falls.

Early Idaho Falls settler, James "Matt" Taylor was an entrepreneur with a keen business mind. After obtaining a bridge and ferry franchise from the Idaho Territorial Legislature, Taylor hired the Oneida Road, Bridge, and Ferry Company in 1865 to create a bridge near the Eagle Rock settlement (Idaho Falls). This bridge dubbed "Taylor's Crossing" proved highly successful, allowing both pioneers and freight to cross the Snake River with ease. Taylor's contribution to Idaho Falls' development is honored with a full-scale replica of the area's first bridge.

T Idaho Falls Symphony

498 A St., Idaho Falls. 529-1080.

Nearly sixty volunteer and paid musicians from Idaho Falls and the surrounding region recreate the world's great music classics in their annual performances. The group was founded in 1949 when student and adult musicians came together to rehearse a community presentation of Handel's "Messiah." The result was legendary, and today, the community group performs five to six concerts between November and May. In addition, the associated Idaho Falls Symphony Chorale features an eighty-member choir that performs a series of chamber music concerts. For tickets and a schedule of events, contact the Idaho Falls Arts Council at (208) 522-0471.

T Idaho Falls Opera Theater

241 Cliff, Idaho Falls. 522-0875.

One of Idaho Falls largest cultural attractions is its Opera Theater. Drawing upon the talents of local musicians, actors, and technicians of all ages, the theater presents opera and other musical productions. Two full-stage shows are produced each year, and the theater also sponsors an annual professional Broadway touring show. Through their productions, the Opera Theater hopes to cultivate

an interest in and appreciation of opera. Contact the Idaho Falls Arts Council at (208) 522-0471 for a complete schedule of events.

T Actor's Repertory Theatre of Idaho

257 W. Broadway, Idaho Falls. 522-8450. www.artidaho.org

For nearly twenty years, the Actor's Repertory Theatre of Idaho has been entertaining Idaho Falls' residents and visitors. Talented thespians from the surrounding region present a range of productions varying from light comedies to tearjerkers to inspiring dramas. No matter what genre of play is presented, however, it is skillfully portrayed to the highest quality. Past presentations have included *The Laramie Project, The Woman in Black, True West, Barefoot in the Park*, and *Sordid Lives*. Performed inside the remodeled 1800s Eleanor Hotel, all shows include a full dinner, and advance tickets are required.

T Stillwater Mansion

387 N. Water Ave., Idaho Falls. 524-4473.

In Idaho Falls' early days, a gentleman named Stillwater served as town mayor for several years. This prominent man built his famous Stillwater Mansion sometime prior to 1903, and to this day, it has been lovingly maintained. Featuring a Victorian ambience, the mansion is now open for historic tours. In addition, the site is known for hosting excellent Victorian Teas and Garden Teas for upscale social gatherings. Visitors are asked to call ahead and schedule a private tour.

T Russet Lions Noise Park

West of Idaho Falls. 523-6329 or 525-3850.

Established in 1972, the 400-acre Russet Lions Noise Park showcases a variety of motorized races. The city-owned facility features Moto-X races, modified stock car races, street stock, pure stock, mini stock, and hornet races, plus go kart races. The park is open during the summer season, and interested patrons should call in advance for race tickets.

TV Hell's Half Acre Lava Walk

Traveling west of Idaho Falls on Hwy. 20, look for mile marker 287 (about 20 miles west of Idaho Falls). Continue 0.3 miles until you see the "Lava Trail" sign. Turn south onto the gravel road, and continue 1/4 mile to the trailhead. You will find a picnic shelter, fire ring, and portable toilet in the parking area.

Geology of the Area

The Hell's Half Acre Lava Flows are within the Snake River Plain. The Snake River Plain is an expansive crescent-shaped depression 50 to 70 miles wide and 350 miles long that stretches across southern Idaho. This Plain is composed of lava flows formed over the last 15 million years that originated from volcanic vents and fissures.

The Snake River used to flow across the northern portion of the Snake River Plain, but now flows along the southern margin of the Plain. The river was pushed there by successive lava flows. Hell's Half Acre flows over about 222 square miles or 162,000 acres. Sixty-six thousand acres are within a Wilderness Study Area (WSA).

The Hell's Half Acre flows came from a vent that is located along a rift. This rift parallels the 62 mile long Great Rift that goes through Craters of the Moon National Monument. A rift zone is a line of weakness in the earth's crust associated with volcanism. The main vent for the Hell's Half Acre flow is 95 to 200 feet wide and 730 feet long. The highest point is 5,350 feet, whereas the lowest point is 4,600 feet. The vent has 13 pit craters where lava flowed out and then receded.

The last flow from the main vent occurred 2000 years ago. The older flows near Hwy. 20 are estimated to be 4,100 years old and came from an eruptive center about 3.5 miles in diameter. These older flows were covered by more recent flows from the main vent.

A Closer Look at the Lava Landscape

Hiking across the lava is a unique experience. Lava rock is extremely sharp, glassy, and fragmented with open cracks, lava tubes, and caves. The most prevalent landscape consists of A'a (ah-ah) and Pahoehoe (pa-hoy-hoy) lava flows. Pahoehoe lava is more fluid than A'a. It's outer surface cooled faster than the interior causing a 'ropey' appearance. The less fluid A'a formed leaving rough, irregular mounds. The areas of soil and vegetation not covered by lava are called 'kipuka,' a Hawaiian word meaning 'window in the lava.'

A variety of plants and wildflowers contrast the black and gray lava flows. In the spring and early summer, numerous wildflowers, such as Evening Primrose, Indian Paintbrush, wild onions, penstemon, geraniums, and Prickly Pear Cactus, color the landscape. Also coloring the landscape are ferns growing in deep cracks and a variety of desert vegetation. The spectrum ranges from tiny mosses and lichens to juniper trees hundreds of years old. Other native species include sagebrush, rabbit brush, bitterbrush, blue bunch wheatgrass, and needle-and-thread grass.

Wildlife roaming the lava flows include mule deer, antelope, sage grouse, bobcats, coyotes, foxes, and occasionally snakes. Soaring above the flows are red-tailed hawks, prairie falcons, and golden eagles.

Lava Walks in Hells Half Acre

The Bureau of Land Management, Bonneville County, and the Idaho Alpine Club along with numerous other people have cooperated to open this area for lava hiking. Hiking in lava fields is unique because of the rough terrain, unusual scenery, and the contorted landscape. Since this is a Wilderness Study Area (WSA), permanent trails have not been developed. The unimproved hiking routes are marked with poles.

Blue top poles mark a route around a short educational loop, which is a good introduction to lava hiking. The 1/2-mile loop takes about 1/2 hour to walk. On this loop note the pressure ridges, deep cracks with ferns at the bottom, and moss on the rocks.

Red top poles mark a 4 1/2-mile route to the main vent or source of the Hells Half Acre lava flow. A round trip to the vent will take a full day and should only be undertaken after adequate preparation has been made. Water is essential and boots with good soles are advisable. Estimated time to hike to the vent is 2 to 3 1/2 hours one-way.

Reprinted from Bureau of Land Management and Idaho Alpine Club brochure

TV Snake River Greenbelt Idaho Falls

Ducks and Canadian geese join the list of enthusiastic patrons who utilize the scenic twenty-nine acre greenbelt park spanning both sides of the lazy Snake River. The most heavily used stretch begins near the Broadway bridge and ends at the Hwy. 20 bridge. Hikers, joggers, and bicyclists frequent this popular 2.3-mile loop as well as the rest of the trail. In the winter, the greenbelt becomes a trail system for cross-country skiers and snowshoe lovers. Spectacular views of the town's waterfall greet greenbelt users.

FL Motel West & Hometown Kitchen Restaurant

1540 W. Broadway, Idaho Falls. 522-1112 or (800) 582-1063. www.motelwestidaho.com

Great Grandpa's West is gone into the history books forever, but the hospitality of the west lives on at Motel West. Each clean, comfortable, non-smoking room features color cable TV with HBO, free local calls, and queen size beds. Refrigerators, microwaves, and suites with jetted tubs are also available. After relaxing in the heated indoor pool and hot tub, head to the Hometown Kitchen Restaurant conveniently located on-site. The restaurant features homemade goodies including soups, breads, and pies. Breakfast, lunch, and dinner specials change daily with prime rib offered every Friday night. Restaurant hours are 6:30 AM to 9 PM Monday through Friday and 6:30 AM to 4 PM on Saturdays. Stay with the friendly staff at Motel West. They guarantee a pleasant experience where all your needs are met.

L Fairfield Inn & Suites

1293 W. Broadway, Idaho Falls. 552-7378. www.marriott.com/idafi

Fairfield Inn & Suites offers more than just a hotel but an experience like none other. Ranked as one of the top 25 hotels in both service and quality, the Fairfield Inn caters to vacationers and business travelers with its indoor swimming pool, spa, and comfortable rooms. The quiet, well-lit rooms are equipped with free high speed and wireless Internet, coffeemakers, hairdryers, irons, alarm clocks, individual climate control and air-conditioning, cable TV, in-room movies, CD players, bathtubs with spray jets, and down/feather and foam pillows ensuring a peaceful night's sleep. Cribs and rollaway beds are also available. In the morning, wake up to a complimentary breakfast and your free copy of the local paper and USA Today. On your next trip, enjoy the friendly, comfortable atmosphere at Fairfield Inn & Suites by Marriott.

S Jimmy's All Seasons Angler

275 A. St., Idaho Falls. 524-7160. www.JimmysFlyShop.com

Jimmy's All Seasons Angler has been serving those who enjoy the waters surrounding Idaho Falls since 1979. They offer a full selection of fly fishing supplies and huge selection of fly tying materials. They carry Sage fly rods, Winston fly rods, Columbia clothing, Simms waders, and Orvis tackle. They are also a Rio dealer and Cortland Pro Shop. The shop is an excellent source for regional fishing books and maps. You can also pick up your fishing license for Idaho or Yellowstone Park. Be sure and check with the professionals at Jimmy's for up to date information on area waters. Conveniently located near area lodging.

M Idaho Falls Chamber of Commerce

630 W. Broadway, Idaho Falls. 523-1010 or (800) 634-3246. www.idahofallschamber.com; info@idahofallschamber.com

8 *Food, Lodging*

T Pinecrest Municipal Golf Course

701 E. Elva St., Idaho Falls. 529-1485.

Pinecrest Municipal Golf Course is often referred to as Idaho Falls' most challenging round of golf. Established in 1934 under the design of W. H. Tucker, the 18-hole course covers 6,394 yards and is rated a par-70. The course is situated in the city's center, and players will encounter tight

ANNUAL EVENTS

American Dog Derby

Ashton's American Dog Derby held each winter is rumored to be the oldest dog sled race in the lower forty-eight states. The event dates back to 1917, and during the 1920s and 1930s, nearly 15,000 spectators arrived each year from Idaho and neighboring states to witness the annual derby. Although the race was suspended during World War II and for periods during the 1960s, 1970s, and 1980s, it was revived with enthusiasm in the early 1990s. Today, the weekend event draws large crowds of people cheering on their favorite dog sled driver in 60-mile and 100-mile races. In addition, the event features ice sculpting and a variety of food and craft vendors.

Free Fishermen's Breakfast

Idaho has long been known for its population of avid fishermen and trout-filled streams and rivers. So, when fishing season opens, it's essential that every angler head for the water with a satisfied stomach. St. Anthony annually honors these recreationists and celebrates the start of the fishing season with a free pancake feed held at Clyde Keefer Memorial Park.

Teton Valley Summer Festival

The Teton Valley Summer Festival in Driggs has been an annual celebration for nearly twenty-five years. The weeklong festival attracts locals and visitors and features hot air balloon rides, fireworks, arts and crafts, street fairs, parades, old time fiddlers' contests, barbeques, golf tournaments, and bike races.

Snake River Settlers' Festival & 4th of July Celebration

For years, Idaho Falls has celebrated the Snake River Settlers' Festival and Independence Day in grand style. The day starts out with a large parade and also features baseball games and other "old-fashioned" games and activities at Tautphaus Park. The activities wrap up with one of the largest fireworks displays west of the Mississippi. Showcased over the Snake River, the display is professionally choreographed and set to music, and it annually attracts an average of 100,000 spectators.

Idaho International Folk Dance Festival

Since its inception in 1986, the goal of the Idaho International Folk Dance Festival in Rexburg has been to promote cultural exchange between Idaho and countries across the world. Growing in leaps and bounds since its debut, this world-renowned festival has been rated as one of North America's top 100 events by the American Business Association. Up to 300 dancers perform annually, and an average of ten different countries are represented each summer. Previous dance teams have traveled from Africa, Asia, Europe, South America, North America, and island areas across the world. The festival includes opening ceremonies, a parade, street festivals, cultural classes, dance classes, a rodeo, and three full nights of spectacular dance performances.

Grand Targhee Bluegrass Festival

Music fans can enjoy a summer weekend of toe-tapping fun at the annual Grand Targhee Bluegrass Festival. Situated at an elevation of 8,000 feet and surrounded by the stunning peaks of the Teton Mountains, the festival headlines some of the country's greatest bluegrass talent on an outdoor stage. The three-day festival features both famous and local talent, music jams, contests, free workshops, great food, arts and crafts, games, and optional on-site camping. As the popularity of bluegrass music continues to grow, so does the acclaim of this beloved festival. Advance tickets are highly recommended.

War Bonnet Round Up

World champion cowboys ride, rope, and test their skills at eastern Idaho's oldest annual rodeo. Originating in 1921, the War Bonnet Round Up is a Mountain West PRCA event and is sponsored by the Bonneville County American Legion post.

Mountain Brewers Beer Fest

Idaho Falls' Sandy Downs Race Track is home to the annual Mountain Brewers Beer Fest. A tradition that started in 1994, the festival is now acclaimed across the U.S. and features more than 300 beers from over 80 different intermountain west breweries. The non-profit North American Brewers Association sponsors the event featuring beer tasting, food vendors, and live entertainment. The event serves as a pre-festival for the North American Beer Competition.

Mountain Men Rendezvous Celebration

Every year in August, Driggs honors the mountain men, trappers, and traders who first called Teton Basin home. The area's lively past is captured at the two-day Mountain Men Rendezvous Celebration. Several local residents dress in trapper or Indian clothes to take part in the weekend festivities. Annual events include the Mr. Pierre Tall Tale Contest and the 13-mile John Colter Indian Escape Dash Marathon.

Along the River

Performed amidst the scenic beauty lining the Snake River, the Idaho Falls "Along the River" concert series is an annual summer tradition loved by residents and visitors alike. From June through August, the Idaho Falls Arts Council sponsors midday one-hour music performances. These free outdoor shows take place once a week and are located on the Snake River Greenbelt between D and E Streets.

Alive After Five

During the summer, Idaho Falls residents and tourists have the opportunity to unwind after a long day of work or sightseeing at the "Alive After Five" concert series. The normal hustle of daily business dies down one evening each week and is replaced with live music and an array of food vendors. The annual event is free.

The Great Snake River Duck Race

Although real wildlife abounds in the Idaho Falls area and along the Snake River, one day each August is devoted to children's favorite yellow rubber duckies. Sponsored by the Idaho Falls Rotary Club, the event draws locals and visitors alike who line the waterfront to watch as hundreds of yellow duckies race down the river. Each duck is assigned a number, and top finishers secure large prizes.

---

greens, numerous sand traps, and several large pine trees. Green fees are $17.50 on weekdays and $18.50 on weekends with tee times available two days in advance. The course is closed during the winter.

T Idaho Vietnam Memorial

Science Center Dr. (off Fremont Ave.), Idaho Falls. Contact Idaho Falls Parks and Recreation Division at 529-1480.

The Idaho Vietnam Memorial is located inside the seventy-five acre Lewis A. Freeman Memorial Park. Situated atop a quiet and serene hill overlooking the Snake River, the stainless-steel, inverted V sculpture commemorates the lives of Idaho men and women who died while fighting in the Vietnam War. Each fatality and the names of those missing in action are engraved on the sculpture that was dedicated in 1990.

T Idaho Falls Family History Center

750 W. Elva, Idaho Falls. 524-5291.

Visitors have the opportunity to discover the past and honor their heritage at the Idaho Falls Family History Center. A multiregional facility, the center houses a warehouse of ancestral information in its library and research center and is connected to the world's largest family history center. In addition, the free facility offers family history workshops to encourage individuals to learn about and trace their genealogy. The center is open Monday and Saturday from 9 AM to 5 PM and Tuesday through Friday from 9 AM to 9 PM.

T Idaho Falls Padres

Corner of Bannock and W. Elva, Idaho Falls. 522-8363.

During the summer, Idaho Falls has another entertainment option to add to the list of recreational choices. The Minor League Idaho Falls Padres bats out a season of summer fun and action in the city's historic McDermott Field located in Highland Park at the corner of Bannock and West Elva. The team is part of the Pioneer League, which includes teams from as far north as Canada, and the Padres have enjoyed several winning seasons. The Padres are associated with sister team, the San Diego Padres, which helps move players from the Minor Leagues to the Major Leagues.

T Kate Curley Park

Emerson and Higbee Ave.s, Idaho Falls. 529-1480.

Idaho Falls' first settlers were not only interested in establishing a business community, but also a scenic town with recreation opportunities available to locals and passerby. As local groups and pioneers acquired land and beautified the area with trees and flowers, the Idaho Falls Village Improvement Society decided to join the action. Utilizing back county taxes, the women's group purchased the current city lot and began making plans for park development. To help pay for the plans, the ladies raised potatoes on the land for several years and saved every profit from the sales. In 1903, though, tragedy struck the group. Kate Curley, a prominent leader of the Village Improvement Society, died from cancer, and work momentarily stopped. But Kate's husband, Bowen, wanted to leave a legacy for his wife. As a town banker, Bowen carried forth the project and enlisted the help of Charles and Maude Shattuck to design the park layout and its placement of trees. The ladies' vision was finally completed, and in 1918, the City of Idaho Falls purchased the park from the society. Today, the park is a popular picnicking area due to its old-growth shade trees. Several community events, such as the annual Easter Egg Hunt, are also held here throughout the year.

F Teton Grille Restaurant
County Line Rd., Exit 318 on Hwy. 20, just 10 minutes north of Idaho Falls. 522-3444.

The Teton Grille Restaurant opened in 2003 offering casual dining in a traditional log cabin atmosphere. Since 1980, Executive Chef, Robert L. Martin, has received numerous awards and certifications. Now home in his new Teton Grille Restaurant, Martin's skills are exemplified in a variety of tasty fare. Full lunch and dinner menu items include appetizers, rainbow trout, buffalo, salmon, chicken, beef, Idaho potatoes, and specialty desserts. Featuring a summer dining patio, the 120-seat restaurant is open Monday through Saturday, and take-out lunch and dinner orders are available during the week. In addition to standard dining facilities, the restaurant includes banquet facilities and expertise to make any event a success. Discover Idaho's Teton Grille Restaurant today. It's a special place where Idaho flavors are infused with Idaho charm.

9 *Food, Lodging*

T Sage Lakes Golf Course
100 E. 65th N., Idaho Falls. 528-5535.

Sage Lakes Municipal Golf Course is the newest playing field in Idaho Falls. Opened in 1993, the 6,566-yard course features 18 holes and is rated a par-70. The course features several water traps, and tee times can be scheduled two days in advance. Green fees are $16.65 on weekdays and $18.70 on weekends. The course is closed during the winter.

T Sand Creek Municipal Golf Course
5200 S. Hackman Rd. (off E. 65th St.), Idaho Falls. 529-1115.

William Bell designed this 6,770-yard course in 1978, and it has become extremely popular with local residents. Rated at a par-72, the 18 hole course traverses a flat, open layout, and golfers are presented with several water traps. At times, wind can become a playing factor on this course. Green fees are $15.50 on weekdays and $16.50 on weekends. The course is closed during the winter.

T Walking Tour of Historic Churches in Idaho Falls
Contact the City of Idaho Falls Planning and Building for more information. 529-1276.

Idaho Falls has a long legacy of religious following. In 1896, despite the town's small size, Idaho Falls had more churches than any other similarly sized community in the state. Just four years later, Lutheran, Presbyterian, Catholic, Methodist, Baptist, Swedish Mission, and Mormon congregations served this town of 1,200. These first

churches have since eroded in time, but their larger, more substantial replacements have become engrained in the community. The doors are always open, and visitors are invited to explore this aspect of Idaho Falls' diverse history.

Trinity United Methodist Church
237 North Water Ave.
Around 1884, approximately fifty years after the first Methodist missionary arrived in Idaho Territory, the First Methodist Episcopal Church was established in Idaho Falls. Reverend E.B. Elder from Blackfoot journey to Idaho Falls once a month to service the congregation. As church membership swelled, a new church was needed to accommodate the congregation's growing needs. The corner lot at the present site was purchased for that purpose in 1886 at a cost of $285. Despite criticism for the church's construction far outside the established settlement, work continued and the church's foundation was laid in 1895.

Twenty years later, contractor Dan Sweeney agreed to build the present Tudor Gothic style church for $47,000. Dedicated in 1917, the church's stone walls were quarried near Heise, and the stained glass windows originated in West Virginia. In 1948, the church's education wing was added with stone taken from the original quarry. The church is listed on the National Register of Historic Places.

First Presbyterian Church
325 Elm St.
Idaho Falls' Presbyterian Church was organized in 1891, and just one year later, the congregation had a church located on the corner of Shoup Ave. and A Street. This first church cost $1,600 and was led by Charles Ramsays, S.C. Wishard, and eight other charter members.

In 1917, Reverend Arthur Richards assumed responsibility for the congregation, and he immediately purchased a lot to build a larger church. The old church was sold with the profit used as a down payment for the new church. Just three years later, this Greek Classic style church designed by Pennsylvania architect, J.C. Fulton, was complete. Total building cost was $90,000. The church windows are dedicated to the memory of World War I soldiers and other prominent church members, while the entry columns represent the largest stone columns ever quarried in Boise. The church is listed on the National Register of Historic Places.

Cornerstone Assembly of God (Formerly 3rd Ward LDS Church)
187 East 13th St.
As an influx of believers from the Church of Jesus Christ of Latter Day Saints (LDS) settled in Idaho Falls, in 1927 the church was forced to add a 3rd and 4th ward to accommodate its growing congregation. A new church site was selected at the corner of 13th Street and Lee Ave., and Aubrey O. Andelin was selected as the new church's bishop.

The church draws its design from sister chapels in Utah and neighboring Rexburg, and the LDS Church agreed to pay 65% of the building costs with ward members contributing the remaining 35%. As the Depression hit, though, the ward had difficulty in securing all of the necessary monies, resulting in a nine-year construction process. Finally, in June 1937, the new ward was completed at a cost of $152,000, and the LDS Church President held a dedication ceremony.

The 3rd Ward of the LDS Church utilized the building until 1981, at which time it became a counseling/community center. The Cornerstone

Assembly of God Church purchased the building in 1994, and it is listed on the National Register of Historic Places.

Holy Rosary Church
149 9th St.
The Catholic Church is one of the oldest congregations in Idaho Falls. In 1891, church members decided that an official church building was necessary. After raising money at County Fair concessions, the first church was constructed in 1895-96 at the corner of Eastern and Maple Ave.s. Today, a local bar stands at the original church's site.

In 1947, Boise architects Hummel, Hummel, and Jones designed the present English Gothic style church. The church included an attached rectory and was built by the Arrington Construction Company for $180,000. Easter Sunday, 1949, marked the first service held in the new church. The interior features a 22-foot high marble altar and a one-ton life sized crucifix made from Portuguese onyx. Trappist Monks from Layayette, Oregon hand-made the forty-eight oak pews, and the stained glass windows on the church's south side were constructed in Austria. Upon the church's completion, a bell was purchased for the bell tower. However, upon its first tolling, the great vibrations cracked the tower and the bell was put to rest. In 1977, the Mark Stevens Memorial Carillon replaced the unused bell. The church is listed on the National Register of Historic Places.

St. John Lutheran Church
290 7th St.
Reverend E.P. Meyer was one of the first Lutheran missionaries to arrive in Idaho in the early 20th century. After his departure, Reverend William Jaeger was assigned to the Idaho Falls area, and he established a Lutheran congregation in 1913. Until a parsonage was built in 1922, church members gathered on alternate Sundays at the old Swedish Lutheran Church. Finally, in 1950, the congregation received its long-awaited church. After two years of construction costing nearly $85,000, the Tudor Gothic style building was completed and dedicated. Congregation members donated the stained glass windows. The church was remodeled just ten years later in 1961.

9th Ward LDS Church (Formerly 5th Ward)
395 2nd St.
On August 23rd, 1936, the 5th Ward LDS Church was established under the leadership of Bishop William Grant Ovard. Greatly desiring a building of their own, ward members generously donated money to a building fund, and a lot was purchased later that year. H. M. Sundberg designed the Art Deco style church, and in 1937, Brigham Madsen began his building contract and broke ground in 1937. With the help of church volunteers, the recreating room was complete in 1939, and the chapel received its first use in 1942. Total building costs were approximately $50,900.

As church membership grew, so did the building. The building is now home to the 9th Ward of the LDS Church, and a 2,900 square foot addition was added in 1994.

Salvation Army Church (Formerly 4th Ward LDS Church)
605 N. Blvd.
On January 1, 1928, James Laird was appointed Bishop of the newly formed 4th Ward LDS Church. In 1935, a building lot was obtained, and Sundberg and Sundberg were hired to design a Tudor style church. Just one year later, ground was broken, and 4th Ward members were respon-

sible for much of the building labor. These members also raised 40% of the total $45,000 building cost. In 1937, LDS Church President Heber Grant dedicated the building.

In 1958, a 7,000 square foot east wing was added, and in 1984, the interior was remodeled. The building serviced the 4th and 10th Wards of the LDS Church, and in 1993, the building was sold to the Salvation Army.

T Tautphaus Park
Adjacent to Rollandet St. in Idaho Falls. Contact the Parks and Recreation Division at 529-1480.

Idaho Falls is known for the numerous city parks dotting the landscape, and Tautphaus Park is one of the most beloved and oldest parks in town. Acres of grass, old-growth shade trees, and landscaped flowerbeds beckon residents and visitors alike to spend a leisurely afternoon relaxing in the park.

Tautphaus Park is named after early residents, Charles and Sarah Tautphaus. In 1995, the Bonneville County Historical Society erected a historical marker at the park in remembrance of this couple's community contribution. The inscription on the marker reads as follows:

In commemoration of Charles and Sarah Tautphaus, who developed this area from sagebrush to a park for all to enjoy. Charles C. Tautphaus, of German ancestry, and Sarah Kane, from Ireland, were both immigrants to America. They met in California, where they married and had five daughters. The family traveled by covered wagon to Butte City, Montana, where they were successful at mining, freighting, and farming. In 1884, they purchased two sections of government land in Eagle Rock (Idaho Falls). Using primitive equipment, they transformed the desert into a farm that included a wooded hillside, poplar-lined drives, an apple orchard, and a six-acre lake with a waterfall. The lake, where the sunken baseball diamond now exists, was a center of social activity, with picnicking, boating, and swimming in the summer and ice-skating in the winter. To irrigate his land and that of others, Charles helped form the Idaho Canal Company in 1889 and designed a 30-miles canal from the Snake River to the Blackfoot River. For several years, this park was owned by the Reno family and called "Reno Park." It was purchased by the city in 1935 and named Tautphaus Park in 1943 to honor its original developer. Charles (1841-1906) and Sarah (1840-1917) are buried in the cemetery next to their beloved park in a plot marked by a large stone cross. We give thanks to these early settlers who, in fulfilling their own dreams, also improved the lives of their fellow citizens and future generations.

Inside this historical park are baseball fields, tennis courts, a fountain, playground, indoor ice rink, and a small amusement park called "Funland" that offers historic ferris wheel rides and a hometown carnival atmosphere.

T Tautphaus Park Zoo
2725 Carnival Way, Idaho Falls. 528-5552. www.idahofallszoo.org

Situated within Tautphaus Park is the popular Tautphaus Park Zoo. Accredited by the American Zoo and Aquarium Association, the zoo houses and protects more than 250 different animals from six continents, some of which are listed on the endangered species list. Natural habitats are recreated for each animal, and highlights include viewing snow leopards, kangaroos, penguins, otters, cotton top tamarins, and red ruffed lemurs. In the

Children's Zoo, kids and adults have the opportunity to pet bunnies and feed the flocks swimming in a special duck pond. Zoo hours are as follows: Memorial Day to Labor Day – Monday 9 AM to 8 PM, Tuesday through Sunday 9 AM to 5 PM; May and September – daily from 9 AM to 4 PM; April and October – 9 AM to 4 PM; November through March – closed for the season. Admission fees are $4 for adults ages 13+, $2 for youth ages 4-12, $2.50 for seniors ages 62+, and free to those 3 and under.

T Sandy Downs
6855 S. 15th St. E. (near St. Clair Ave. and E. 65th St. S.), Idaho Falls. 529-2276 or 529-1479.

Sandy Downs is a historical events center showcasing a variety of entertainment throughout the year. Circuses, three major rodeos, livestock programs, quarter horse racing, and chariot racing are just some of the events hosted here annually. A list of events is available at the center or by calling the Idaho Falls Chamber of Commerce at (208) 523-1010.

T Idaho Falls Aquatic Center
149 S. 7th, Idaho Falls. 529-1111.

The Idaho Falls Aquatic Center is a popular venue during all seasons of the year. The indoor facility features an Olympic size, Z-shaped pool holding 285,000 gallons of water just waiting to be splashed in and enjoyed. In addition, two whirlpool spas, a redwood outdoor deck, a summer outdoor wading pool, and an indoor observation deck are available.

T Idaho Falls Civic Auditorium
501 S. Holmes, Idaho Falls. 529-1396.

Recognized as one of the finest performing arts facilities in the Intermountain West, the Idaho Falls Civic Auditorium is the showplace for a variety of entertainment in the upper Snake River Valley. In 1949, a city bond was passed, and construction on the new auditorium was completed in 1952. Since then, the 1,892-seat facility has hosted opera, symphony, ballet, dance, conferences, and Broadway musicals. Renowned performers have included such icons as Louis Armstrong, Johnny Cash, and the San Francisco Opera. For a complete monthly schedule of events, contact the auditorium or the Snake River Territory Convention and Visitors Bureau at (208) 523-1010.

L Yellowstone Motel
2460 S. Yellowstone, Idaho Falls. 529-9738.

Conveniently located on the way to Yellowstone National Park, Yellowstone Motel accommodates people of all ages and abilities with its ground floor design. Choose between smoking or non-smoking rooms, each including comfortable beds, 25" TV with remote and cable, refrigerator, microwave, coffee maker, and free local calls. Kitchenette units are also available, and guest laundry services are on-site. Featuring a pet

friendly environment where guests are charged a minimal extra $5 fee, the hotel prides itself on low nightly rates and discounted weekly and extended stay rates. On your next trip to Idaho Falls or Yellowstone, experience the friendly atmosphere of Yellowstone Motel where clean, quality rooms offered at an affordable price are a standard amenity.

M Help-U-Sell
1220 E. 17th St., Idaho Falls. 525-2525. www2.helpusell.com/idahofalls

Help-U-Sell prides itself on saving buyers and sellers thousands of dollars with a proven marketing system and menu of services. Maintaining a standard fee-for-service approach, Help-U-Sell charges customers only for the services they desire and not the traditional 6% all-inclusive fee. On average, Help U-Sell sellers enjoy a nearly 72% success rate, compared to just 63% with traditional real estate agencies. And buyers benefit too. Help-U-Sell offers experienced buyer specialists and 24/7 price and listing updates. With the motto "whatever it takes," the company also offers moving services. Using a company trailer, Help-U-Sell offers the convenience and affordability you need to quickly settle into the home of your dreams. So why pay for services you don't need? Call Help-U-Sell today to see results tomorrow.

M RE/MAX Homestead Realty
1301 E. 17th St, Idaho Falls. 529-5600 or (800) 729-5601. www.djskinner.com

RE/MAX Homestead Realty and professionally certified realtor, D. J. Skinner, specialize in purchases and sales of single-family residences and income properties. Frequently receiving rave reviews, the office prides itself on going the extra mile to ensure excellent customer service to individuals residing in Idaho Falls, Rigby, Shelley, Ammon, Iona, Ucon, Rexburg, and Menan. New to town? D.J. is happy to help you discover your new community, its schools, and other area amenities. So whether you need to sell your home or are just settling in and looking for your dream house, contact D.J. at RE/MAX Homestead Realty. With her assistance, you will gain the consumer knowledge you need in making informed decisions about one of your most precious investments.

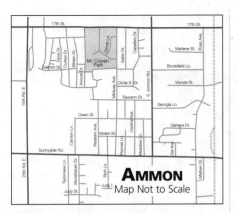

AMMON
Map Not to Scale

10 *Food*

T Gem Lake Marina

5 miles southwest of Idaho Falls On U.S. Hwy. 91, head southwest from Idaho Falls towards Shelley. Approximately 2 miles south of Idaho Falls, bear right (west) near the Fanning Memorial Society. Proceed 3 more miles to the marina.

Gem Lake Marina is located on the Snake River and is a popular recreational destination during late spring and summer. A boat launch area provides easy access for waterskiing, jet-skiing, and windsurfing. Anglers report excellent trout fishing in the area, and picnic gazebos provide covered shelter for a fun family outing.

11 *Food*

Ammon
Pop. 6,187

Now a suburb of Idaho Falls, the city of Ammon dates back to the arrival of Mormon pioneers during the 1890s. The town was originally a sprawl from nearby Iona, but when settlers applied for a post office in 1898, a separate community was formed. The town draws its name from a Mormon apostle featured in *The Book of Mormon*.

Iona
Pop. 1,201

Located just seven miles from Idaho Falls, Iona is an agricultural community that Mormon colonizers founded in 1884. The area was originally known as Sands Creek, but when Mormons arrived in the area, they renamed it after a small town in Israel. The term means "beautiful." The community's post office has operated since 1892.

Ucon
Pop. 943

Homesteaded in 1885 by Mormons, this town was originally dubbed "Willow Creek" after its plotting near this stream's banks. The name was changed to "Elba" a few years later, but when residents applied for a post office, they learned another Idaho town carried the same name. After looking through a list of the postal service's recommended town names, residents voted to call their settlement "Ucon." Ucon remained a relatively tiny village until the arrival of the railroad. In 1904, when the community learned a rail route was to be built seven miles west of town, residents packed their bags and moved the town near the railroad. This decision significantly aided the town's growth, and Ucon remains an agricultural hub and shipping point.

T Iona's Historic Places
Rockwood Ave. and Second St., Iona.

Settled in 1883, the small community of Iona retains some of its original buildings and architecture. On the corner of Rockwood Ave. and Second Street is the Iona Ward House. Constructed in 1888 and enlarged just six years later, the sandstone building has served as the community's school, social hall, and art gallery. Directly behind the Ward House is a Victorian brick home. Charles Rockwood, one of the town's first Mormon bishops, built the well-maintained home in 1905. Across the street from these buildings on Second Street is the town's original general store. Named the Sand Creek Store, the building was erected in 1897.

12

T Bone

With the first homesteaders arriving in 1905, the village of Bone is situated on Canyon Creek. The town was named after early pioneer, Orion G. Bone, and received postal services from 1917 to 1950.

13 *Food, Lodging*

Irwin
Pop. 157

This tiny town is reportedly named after Joseph B. Irwin, an 1888 settler and lucky Snake River prospector who located some of the area's best claims. The community post office was constructed in 1897.

Swan Valley
Pop. 213

Nestled in the scenic Swan Valley between the Caribou, Big Hole, and Snake River Mountain Ranges, the town of Swan Valley sits at the head of Rainey Creek. The town was plotted in 1886 and was named after the whistling swans populating the area.

T Palisades Dam
7 miles southeast of Irwin on U.S. Hwy. 26.

Situated near the picturesque Idaho/Wyoming border, Palisades Dam retains the 16,100-acre Palisades Reservoir. Construction for the dam was approved in 1941, but building did not commence until ten years later. Finally, in 1957, Palisades Dam was completed at a total production cost of $76 million. At the time, the 270-foot wall was the largest earthen dam ever constructed by the Bureau of Reclamation. Today, visitors are offered outstanding views of the dam, spillway, and reservoir from a nearby overlook area.

TV South Fork of the Snake River
Begins at Palisades Dam 7 miles southeast of Irwin and flows sixty-four miles to its convergence with Henry's Fork of the Snake River north of Idaho Falls at Meenan.

Flowing forth from Palisades Dam is the famous South Fork of the Snake River. Regarded as North America's premier river for dry-fly angling, the South Fork flows sixty-four miles through lush cottonwood valleys and rocky canyon walls and is home to mountain whitefish and trophy cutthroat, rainbow, hybrid, and brown trout. More than 4,000 fish crowd each mile of the river, and the South Fork has been rated as the best wild-trout fishery in the lower forty-eight states. In addition, a variety of wildlife surrounds the river resulting in one of Idaho's most unique ecosystems. Herons, Canadian geese, and bald eagles frequently circle above.

Besides fishing and wildlife viewing, the South Fork of the Snake River provides a host of other recreational activities. Hikers and equestrians populate the nearby backcountry, and float trips, kayaking, and canoeing provide excellent opportunities to see the river in its entirety. Thirty-nine islands scattered across the river's path provide perfect camping areas for an overnight river trip. For more information, contact the Idaho Falls Bureau of Land Management Office at (208) 524-7500.

TV Palisades Reservoir
Bureau of Reclamation, St. Anthony. 542-5800. Located on U.S. Hwy. 26 south of Swan Valley and Irwin.

Palisades Reservoir is formed by Palisades Dam, which is a major feature on the Palisades Project. Recreation on this twenty-five square mile (16,100-acre) reservoir with seventy miles of limited access shoreline is administered by the Caribou-Targhee National Forest. The reservoir is located in scenic southeast Idaho and west-central Wyoming, east of Idaho Falls. Palisades' fish species include cutthroat and brown trout, kokanee, and mackinaw. The fishing season is year-round, but fluctuations in the reservoir level during the summer months result in inconsistent fishing. Spring, fall, and winter ice fishing are most productive. The site offers restrooms, boat ramps, and campgrounds.

14 *Food, Lodging*

Ririe
Pop. 545

Ririe wasn't founded until 1915, and its post office arrived one year later. It was named for David Ririe, a Mormon settler who helped the Oregon Short Line Railroad secure rights to pass through local farmland. The railroad, in turn, honored him by naming the station and town after him. When the Latter Day Saints established the regional ward, it also adopted David's name, and the community legend became the ward's first bishop.

Heise
Pop. 84

This area has long been home to passerby, with Native Americans and early trappers first using the site for its relaxing and supposedly curative powers. When German immigrant, Richard C. Heise, heard the tales of healing waters, he went to the area to investigate in 1894. Heise liked the area so much that he homesteaded on the land and spent his entire life trying to develop the springs into a popular resort destination. After Richard's death, his daughter, Bertha Gavin, continued his work, and the construction of modern roads to the site further increased the area's popularity.

T Ririe Reservoir and Blacktail Park
226 Meadow Creek Rd. east of Idaho Falls (south of Ririe). Contact Bonneville County Parks and Recreation at 538-7285 or 538-5548.

During the period from 1970 to 1977, workers labored on the creation of Ririe Dam. As a result, Ririe Reservoir was formed and has since provided years of enjoyment to tourists and southeastern Idaho residents. Although the 1,560-acre reservoir was technically formed to help with flood control and irrigation, it offers a prime summer recreational area. Fishing, boating, camping, waterskiing, and picnicking are popular at the site.

On the south end of Ririe Reservoir is Blacktail Park where an additional boat dock is available. Rock formations created by eons of wind and rain surround the grassy park.

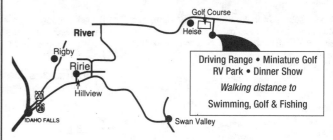

T Heise Hot Springs Golf

5116 E. Heise Rd., Ririe. 538-7327.

Mother Nature designed this executive 9-hole course situated near the South Fork of the Snake River. Nestled below towering cliffs lined with sagebrush and cedar, the course offers players continual scenery as resident deer peer at the action. The course is open from May 1 to October 1 and is rated a par 29. Green fees are a mere $7.50 for 9 holes and $14.00 for 18 holes.

T Heise/Kelly Recreation Area

5116 Heise Rd. in Ririe. 538-7963

TFLC Mountain River Ranch

98 N. 5050 E. at Heise-Kelly Canyon, Ririe. 538-7337. www.mountainriverranch.com

Nestled on the banks of the Snake River, Mountain River Ranch is eastern Idaho's authentic link to the old west. During the summer, take a scenic horse drawn wagon ride, visit the recreated 1890s Rock Bottom Springs frontier town, fish in the stocked trout pond, camp in the shaded RV Park/Campground, and catch some old fashioned western entertainment at the Meadow Muffin Dinner Theater. Summer fare includes BBQ steak and chicken, potato salad, beans, corn, sourdough bread, and dessert, while the winter menu features prime rib or Cornish hen, baked potatoes, salad, ciabatta, and dessert. Winter also brings holiday cheer, festive lights, and songs on frosty sleigh rides. Open year-round with rooms for rent, the friendly ranch and its staff encourage guests to make prior reservations for this fun western experience.

TVLFC Heise Hot Springs & Heise Expeditions

5116 Heise Rd., Ririe. 538-7312 or 538-7327. www.srv.net/~heise/heise.html

Nestled in the heart of the world's finest cutthroat trout fishing, family-owned Heise Hot Springs has blended history with modern recreation since 1896. Summer visitors can soak in 82 or 92 degree filtered freshwater pools and plunge down the 350-foot water slide while winter soakers can stay warm in the 105-degree natural hot springs. Poolside decks and a snack bar round out this entertaining environment. Uninterested in swimming? Heise Expeditions provides guided fishing expeditions on the Snake River, golf, and games. For overnight guests, the original log hotel, a modern two-bedroom cabin, and an RV Park and Campground service every patron's unique needs. With its host of activities and promise of excellence, Heise Hot Springs provides the whole family with a memorable experience.

TC 7N Ranch

5156 E. Heise Rd. at Heise-Kelly Canyon in Ririe. 538-5097.

Cradled between the Rocky Mountains and the South Fork of the Snake River, 7N Ranch Resort offers a relaxed atmosphere and recreation for both young and old. With moose and deer as your spectators, test your skills on the world-class driving range featuring all natural turf or travel down memory lane at the unique Old Farm Miniature Golf Course. For overnight guests, 7N Ranch Resort provides a meticulously maintained campground with a commitment to no overcrowding. RV's will find plenty of first class amenities in the pull-thru spaces, and the newly added "Red round roofed barn" assures each guest has plenty of room. Strategically located near several other area attractions, the 7N Ranch Resort is a great setting for both large group events and personal Rocky Mountain vacations.

V Kelly Canyon Winter Park

Hwy 26 at Heise-Kelly Canyon Recreation Area, Ririe. 538-6251. www.skikelly.com

Opened in 1957 in the Targhee National Forest, the family-friendly Kelly Canyon Winter Park averages 200 inches of powder annually and offers recreation for all ages. Take a lesson from a certified instructor or immediately start your day on the slopes. Encompassing 740 acres of both groomed and natural terrain, the area boasts 4 lifts, 26 runs for both expert and developing skiers, and a maximum vertical of 1,000 feet. Snowboarders are welcome on all runs as well as in the new terrain park, and the area offers lighted night skiing on major runs most nights of the week. For non-skiers, a newly constructed 600-foot tubing park is quickly becoming a family favorite. Lift tickets are reasonably priced to accommodate entire families, and the ski area is open Tuesday through Sunday.

V Kelly Canyon Nordic Skiing and Mountain Biking

Palisades Ranger District, Ririe. 523-1412. Drive 1 mile past Ririe on U.S. Hwy. 26 to a signed turn-off. Follow Kelly Canyon Road past the ski area to locate the trails system.

Continuing past Kelly Canyon Ski Area, over twenty miles of trails wind through the Targhee National Forest and offer scenic terrain to Nordic skiers of all abilities. While some of the trails are groomed, many others are simply marked. Trails include such favorites as the one-mile Tyro Loop for beginners and the Hawley Gulch Loop and Kelly Mountain Trail for advanced skiers. During the summer, these cross-country paths provide sweeping vistas of the Snake River Valley and become popular mountain biking destinations for both residents and tourists.

V Willow Creek Drainage

Running through southeastern Idaho, Willow Creek and its tributaries flow over a hundred miles and are dependent upon Ririe Reservoir. The reservoir boasts populations of stocked hatchery rainbow trout and kokanee salmon, while smallmouth bass, and cutthroat, brown, and lake trout have also been introduced. From Ririe Reservoir, Willow Creek continues its journey, winding through narrow canyons and supporting wild cutthroat trout. In addition to Ririe Reservoir, Willow Creek drainages include Grays Lake near the Caribou Mountains, Meadow Creek, and Tex Creek.

L Cutthroat Inn Bed & Breakfast

Hwy 26 to Heise Rd. at Heise-Kelly Canyon Recreational Area, Ririe. 538-7963. www.cutthroatinn.com

The beautiful Rocky Mountain foothills and world famous South Fork of the Snake River provide a relaxing backdrop for the Cutthroat Inn Bed & Breakfast. Start your day with a hearty, home-cooked breakfast before sampling the area's recreational opportunities. For anglers, practice your

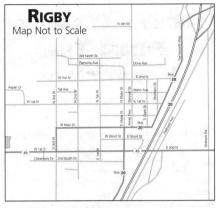

RIGBY
Map Not to Scale

fly-fishing techniques on the inn's private pond or book a guided fly-fishing trip. In the evening, unwind at an old-fashioned melodrama dinner theater before retiring in your country lodging style accommodations. The inn's cabins include two rough-pine queen size beds, private bathrooms, microwaves, refrigerators, and wildlife viewing opportunities right outside your front porch. So plan your getaway today! Group rates and weekday specials are available with a summer schedule from May 1 through October 31 and a winter schedule from November 1 through March 28.

15 Food, Lodging

Rigby
Pop. 2,998

Mormons from Utah's Cache Valley settled this area between 1883 and 1884. Their first order of business was to establish a canal system since water was scarce. For $20, the believers also purchased the town site and constructed a church in hopes of luring in more settlers. A few years later, controversy arose between the old settlers and new pioneers as townsite and homesteading laws began to be blatantly ignored. As a result, the townspeople re-purchased the town site for $250 and dictated strict property laws. At that time, the settlement was named after William Rigby, a Latter Day Saints church leader who helped establish and develop the community's growth. Today, the community retains its Mormon roots and was once home to television inventor, Philo T. Farnsworth.

T Jefferson County Historical Society and Farnsworth TV Pioneer Museum

118 W. 1st St. S., Rigby. 745-8423.

Rigby's most famous one-time resident receives the spotlight in this community museum. At age 11, Philo T. Farnsworth moved to Rigby and became intrigued with various electrical motors on his uncle's farm. Utilizing his interest in electrons, Farnsworth developed his idea of the cathode ray tube at age 14 and by the time he was 22, Farnsworth had created the first television. Today, the museum showcases the accomplishments of

Rigby's Claim to Fame: The Invention of Television

Philo Farnsworth is perhaps Rigby's most famous inhabitant from the past. Moving from Utah to a Rigby area farm when he was twelve, Farnsworth loved to tinker with mechanical and electrical devices. He maintained all of the farm's mechanical equipment, and eventually created an electric motor for the family washing machine.

Farnsworth attended school in Rigby where he was admitted into senior level chemistry classes. While there, he read an article about television experiments, and with encouragement from his teacher, developed a hypothesis about how to produce an electrical counterpart of an optical image.

While still in high school, Farnsworth moved with his family to Provo, Utah, where he studied at Brigham Young University and took advanced courses in electronics. At just 19 years old, Farnsworth met two California businessmen and moved to Los Angeles where he established a scientific lab in his apartment. When he received financial backing from San Francisco bankers, Farnsworth applied for patents on his cathode-ray tube. By 1934, Farnsworth's cathode-ray tube landed him an agreement with London's Baird Television. Soon, viewers all over the world were watching television images, and NBC transmitted the first American TV program at the World Fair. Farnsworth led a brilliant life as a scientist, patenting more than 300 ideas related to TV and electronics, and is known for paving the way to modern television's success.

Farnsworth and his 125 patents, including some of his earliest inventions. In addition, visitors will find several historical photos of the region and displays about Native Americans and wildlife. The museum is open from 1 PM to 5 PM Tuesday through Saturday.

T Jefferson Hills Golf and Recreation Center
4074 E. 500 N., Rigby. 745-6492.

Mature cottonwoods, willows, and pine trees line the narrow fairways of this 5,883-yard, par 70 course. Built in 1970, this 18-hole course meanders near the Snake River, so water hazards come into play on several holes and present a challenge to players of all ability. The course opens daily at 7 AM from March 1 to October 31. Weekday green fees are $12 for 9 holes and $16 for 18 holes with weekend rates just $1 more.

TV Jefferson County Lake
490 N. 4000 E. St., Rigby. 745-7756.
12 miles south of Rexburg immediately off the N. Rigby exit.

From April 1 to October 1, Jefferson County Lake is a popular attraction for both residents and passerby. The scenic recreation area includes picnic shelters, camping, swimming, a children's play area, and bike trails encircling the entire lake. There is a $2 motor vehicle entrance fee at the site.

L Blue Heron Inn
4175 E. Menan Lorenzo Hwy. in Rigby. 745-9922 or toll free at 866-745-9922
www.idahoblueheron.com

The Blue Heron Inn is conveniently located on U.S. Hwy. 20, gateway to Yellowstone National Park, just 18 miles north of Idaho Falls. The Inn overlooks the scenic South Fork of the Snake River. Every room has a river view and is uniquely decorated with handmade quilts and hand-crafted log furniture. Amenities include fireplaces, jetted tubs, private balconies, and luxurious linens. The entire first floor of the Inn is wheelchair accessible. The Great Room is a restful setting with a large river rock fireplace and cathedral ceilings. Readers will enjoy the library nook on the second floor. Mornings begin with a full Western-style breakfast and in the early evening guests enjoy appetizers and complimentary wine, beer, or soft drinks.

L The BlackSmith Inn
227 N. 3900 E. in Rigby. 745-6208 or toll free at 888-745-6208. www.blacksmithinn.com

The BlackSmith Inn is a contemporary round "Eagle's Nest" home, cedar sided to give a unique western flavor. Each room features a mural depicting their western heritage, with locally made quilts and artwork by local artists adding to the western atmosphere. Each room includes a queen size bed, private bath, and TV/VCR. Massage therapy is available by appointment. The decks and surrounding patios are perfect for enjoying pleasant evenings. They are 95 miles from West Yellowstone and 20 minutes from Idaho Falls and I-15. The innkeepers are Registered Nurses and enjoy meeting and getting acquainted with guests. They raise and show Tennessee Walking horses. Horse boarding is available for guests.

M Rigby-Jefferson County Chamber of Commerce
PO Box 327, Rigby. 745-8701.
http://rigby.govoffice.com

16

Lorenzo
Pop. 100

In 1880, settlers began arriving here. Lorenzo Snow, once president of the Church of Jesus Christ of Latterday Saints, serves as the town's namesake. In 1900, development of an Oregon Short Line Railroad Bridge across the Snake River spurred area growth, and a post office was established in 1901.

Thornton
Pop. 150

Originally named Texas Siding, this community was established in 1887. The expansion of the railroad line across the South Fork of the Snake River and into Madison County was a turning point in the town's history. Equipped with a reliable transportation source, the town grew and it became an important freight stop. When the town acquired a post office in 1904, the community name was changed to Thornton in honor of the first postmaster.

T Twin Bridges Park
Archer Rd./Hwy. between Lorenzo, Thornton, and Rexburg. 356-3662.

Thirty-one acres of wild land on the South Fork of the Snake River is home to the Twin Bridges Park. Surrounded by trees, the area features a boat dock for easy river access, fishing, picnicking, and camping. Wildlife viewing is also popular in the area, and deer, moose, bears, and mountain lions are frequently sighted. The free area is open year-round.

17 *Food, Lodging*

Rexburg
Pop. 17,257

Mormon leader, Thomas Ricks, migrated north from Logan, Utah in 1882 at the direction of Mormon Church president, John Taylor. The townsite was platted one year later, and the Italian root of Ricks' name was adopted as the community title at the direction of Cache Valley Church Stake President, William Preston. Although only thirteen settlers joined Ricks initially, the town swelled to over 875 people by May of 1884.

The town's earliest residents were highly successful farmers, and thousands of acres were planted with a variety of crops. In 1888, the Latter Day Saints' Rick College (now BYU-Idaho) was established and named after the community founder. Today, this conservative town recognized for its religiously minded population still economically relies upon the agricultural industry.

H Ricks College
Milepost 334.5 on State Hwy. 33 at BYU-Idaho Campus

Ricks College commenced as a Church of Jesus Christ of Latter-day Saints stake academy in 1888. Ricks was first known as Bannock Stake Academy, then Remont Stake Academy, Smith Academy, and Ricks Academy before becoming Ricks College in 1918. The name memorializes Thomas E. Ricks, founder of Rexburg in 1883. Today Ricks College (BYU-Idaho), includes a modern campus surrounding the historic 1903 Jacob Spori building.

H Beaver Dick
Milepost 73.3 on State Hwy. 33 at Beaver Dick Park

This park is named for "Beaver Dick," a mountain man of late fur trade days who lived in this locality until 1899.

He was born in England, and his real name was Richard Leigh. He came west as a trapper, but the real fur trade was already over. So he married a Shoshoni woman and stayed here-abouts. A popular early outfitter and guide, he served the famous Hayden surveying party in 1872. Leigh Lake in Grand Teton National Park is named for him, and Jenny Lake for his first wife. A picturesque character, he was widely known and liked.

T Teton Lakes Golf Course

1014 N. 2000 West, Rexburg. 359-3036. Located north of Rexburg on Hibbard Parkway Road

The majestic Grand Tetons form the backdrop for this 6,397-yard course situated near the Teton River. Opened in 1979 with a Billy Casper design, the 18-hole championship course is surrounded by lakes, canals, and rivers. This course is rated a par-71 and features mounded greens, shade trees, shrubs, and plenty of sand traps and water hazards. While the front 9 holes are fairly flat and expansive, the back 9 feature tighter fairways and increased hazards. With its diverse layout, this course is suitable for players of all skill levels. Tee times can be scheduled two days in advance, and the course opens daily at 7 AM from March 1 to October 31. Green fees are $10 for 9 holes and $15.50 for 18 holes.

T Rexburg Municipal Golf Course

26 S. Airport Rd., Rexburg. 359-3037.

This city-owned course was built in 1954 and is the second oldest course in eastern Idaho. Featuring 9 holes at par 35, the 3,100-yard course is easy to walk and is a great place for beginners to hone their skills. During late spring and summer, a nearby canal creates a unique water hazard. Tee times are rarely required, and the course is open daily until 11 PM March 15 to October 15. Green fees for 9 holes are $8 for adults and $4.50 for junior players. A round of 18 holes is $12 for adults and $6.50 for juniors.

T Upper Snake River Valley Historical Museum

51 N. Center, Rexburg. 356-9101.

Frequently dubbed the Teton Flood Museum, the Upper Snake River Valley Historical Museum is housed within Rexburg's 1911 old Mormon Tabernacle building. The Italianate-style church was added to the National Register of Historic Places in 1972, and in 1978, the church was sold to the city of Rexburg. The museum opened just four years later, and it continues to display numerous interesting exhibits. Visitors will find pioneer relics from homesteading days, an opal/agate collection, a North American animal head collection, and memorabilia from both World War I and II. In addition, many visitors are fascinated with the exhibits concerning the 1976 Teton Dam collapse and subsequent disastrous flood. Several artifacts, films, and photos of this event are available, and optional tours to the actual flood site are offered. The museum is open 9 AM to 4 PM Monday through Saturday from June through August, and 10 AM to 3 PM Monday through Friday during September through May. Admission is $1 for adults and $.50 for youth ages 12 and under.

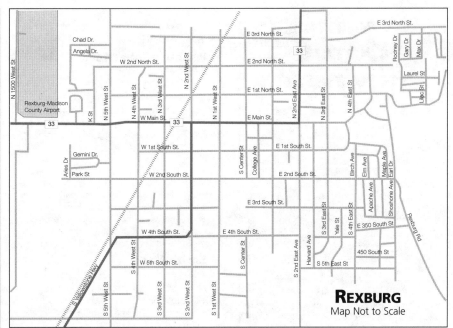

REXBURG
Map Not to Scale

T Porter Park

250 W. 2nd S., Rexburg. 359-3020.

Porter Park is nestled in the heart of downtown Rexburg and commemorates the life of Arthur Porter, Jr. The park features several old-growth shade trees, picnic and barbeque areas, tennis, basketball, and volleyball courts, an extensive children's playground, and a large waterslide and swimming pool. The waterslide is open daily during the summer from 12 PM to 6:30 PM.

T BYU-Idaho

525 S. Center St., Rexburg. 496-2411. www.byui.edu

During the late 1800s, members of the Church of Jesus Christ of Latter Day Saints were under attack from the general population, and access to educational opportunities was limited. In response, the church-owned Bannock Stake Academy was established on November 12, 1888 to provide Rexburg with a grade school and high school. In 1901, grammar education was dropped, and the school was renamed Ricks Academy in honor of Thomas Ricks, a prominent Mormon leader.

As the need for advanced education increased, Ricks Academy began offering college courses. In 1923, the junior college became known as Ricks College, and in 1949, four-year degrees began being offered. But just five years later, the LDS Church President reverted the college back to its junior status. Finally, after fifty plus years of offering strictly associate's degrees, Ricks College was granted the four-year status for which it had longed. On August 10, 2001, Ricks College was rechristened Brigham Young University-Idaho, and several new programs and buildings were added to the campus.

Despite the LDS Church's attempts to give the school to Idaho for a period of nearly twenty years during the early 1900s, the state senate never approved the plans. Thus, the school remains part of the church educational system founded over a century ago while serving nearly 11,000 undergraduate students.

T BYU-Idaho Gardens

BYU-Idaho Campus, Rexburg. 496-1150.

Landscape Horticulture students attending BYU-Idaho use these demonstration gardens as a unique laboratory and study area. The public gardens feature numerous trees and shrubs, as well as 750 varieties of annuals and 200 different perennials. This gardener's dream plot is open year-round until dusk free of charge. In addition to the gardens, the area features beautiful walkways, covered picnic grounds, a pond, and volleyball area.

T Idaho Centennial Carousel

250 W. 2nd S., Rexburg. 359-3020.

Situated inside Porter Park, the Idaho Centennial Carousel is one of Rexburg's crown jewels. The carousel represents Idaho's only antique wooden carousel, and it is one of just 170 wooden carousels still remaining in the US.

The carousel has an extensive history dating back to its 1926 origination in New York at the Spillman Engineering Company. In its early days, the carousel was used as a traveling carnival machine. In 1947, the carousel was retired to Salt Lake City's Liberty Park, but it was soon moved to a park in Odgen, Utah and advertised for sale.

Rexburg	Jan	Feb	March	April	May	June	July	Aug	Sep	Oct	Nov	Dec	Annual
Average Max. Temperature (F)	29.3	33.5	46.3	57.4	66.0	74.8	83.6	84.3	74.0	60.3	41.4	30.4	56.8
Average Min. Temperature (F)	10.4	14.2	23.6	30.7	38.6	44.9	49.3	47.2	38.6	29.7	20.1	11.4	29.9
Average Total Precipitation (in.)	1.07	1.05	1.02	1.12	1.88	1.38	0.93	0.71	0.81	1.07	1.10	1.02	13.16
Average Total Snowfall (in.)	13.1	11.0	4.0	2.2	0.5	0.0	0.0	0.0	0.1	1.0	7.6	15.9	55.5
Average Snow Depth (in.)	9	8	4	0	0	0	0	0	0	0	1	6	2

REMEMBERING CAPTAIN BONNEVILLE

Spanning 1,897 square miles and bordering Wyoming, Bonneville County was officially established in southeastern Idaho on February 7, 1911. Home to nearly 90,000 residents, the county memorializes the life and times of Captain Benjamin Louis Eulalie de Bonneville.

Bonneville was born in France in April 1796 to a wealthy Parisian family. After continuing struggles under Napoleon's rule, the family immigrated to America in 1803 where young Bonneville became passionate about the U.S. military. In 1813 at the young age of eighteen, Bonneville received an appointment to the U.S. Military Academy at West Point. He thrived in the disciplined environment, graduated in just two years, and became a military officer serving tours across the US.

While based in Missouri, Bonneville became fascinated with newspaper accounts of western exploration. He longed to travel west, so he petitioned General Alexander Macomb for a leave of absence. Under the strict guideline that Bonneville would collect valuable information about the west's topography and Native American inhabitants, Macomb granted the young officer's request. John Astor provided funding for Bonneville's expedition, and in May 1832, the party left Missouri. After wintering near present day Green River, Wyoming, Bonneville and his party explored Idaho's Snake River region during early 1833. He continued west, eventually exploring the Columbia River Valley. On his return east, Bonneville camped on the banks of Idaho's Portneuf River and wintered with the Shoshone Indians on Idaho's Upper Bear River in 1834.

After his western expedition, Bonneville continued to serve in the U.S. Army and participated in the Civil War. He eventually retired in Arkansas and died in 1878. Today, his name is memorialized with an Idaho County and an ancient lake that flooded southeastern Idaho and changed the state's landscape.

Learning of the carousel, Rexburg residents raised $5,500, bought the carousel, and had it set up in time for the town's 1952 4th of July celebration. In 1954, residents again raised money in the carousel's honor and constructed a protective dome over the structure. For over twenty years, the carousel provided summer days of fun to local residents and tourists. When the neighboring Teton Dam broke in 1976, however, the subsequent flood severely damaged the carousel and destroyed many of its horses. The carousel remained in ruin until 1988 when skilled craftsmen decided to restore the antique back to working order. The carousel was completed just in time to celebrate Idaho's 1990 Centennial.

Today, the renowned carousel features twenty-six of the original horses, twelve newly carved horses, and a brand new band organ run on paper rolls to provide the old-fashioned sounds one would expect to hear at an early 1900s carnival.

Although an antique, the carousel is open for rides Monday through Saturday from 12 PM to 6:30 PM during the summer.

T Rexburg Tabernacle Civic Center
51 N. Center, Rexburg. 356-5700.

In 1911, the Fremont Stake LDS Tabernacle was established to serve the needs of a growing Church of Jesus Christ of Latter Day Saints membership. In 1976, the building suffered major damage in the Teton Flood, at which time the LDS Church sold the tabernacle to the City of Rexburg. After extensive renovation, the building was added to the National Register of Historic Places and is currently used as a civic center and museum. The auditorium seats 1,000 people and provides numerous musical and educational performances throughout the year. Contact the Rexburg Chamber of Commerce for a schedule of events.

T Smith Park
E. Main & 3rd S. Streets; Rexburg. 359-3020.

Rexburg's Smith Park is one of the community's favorite recreation areas and cradles part of the area's history. In 1883, the Rexburg townsite was surveyed, and what was known as Block 36 at the time is now home to the grassy park. In 1954, the LDS Church transferred the lot to the city, and it was subsequently named Smith Park after city mayor, J. Fred Smith. The park's lush shrubbery and trees surround tennis courts, a gazebo, picnic and barbeque areas, playground equipment, and a historic steam engine. The antique engine was placed in the park in 1962 after its retirement from dry farming on the Rexburg Bench area. The park is open year-round until 11 PM.

T Beaver Dick Park
On State Hwy. 33, proceed 14 miles due east from the intersection of I-15 and State Hwy. 33. The site is located approximately five miles west of Rexburg on the road's south side.

During the early 1800s, an Englishman now known as Beaver Dick Leigh immigrated to America with hopes of becoming a renowned western trapper. Setting off to fulfill his dream, Leigh traveled through Utah, Idaho, and Wyoming before marrying an Indian woman named Jenny. Together, the couple had five children, and Leigh's trapping success earned him and his wife a lasting legacy in Grand Teton National Park. The park's Leigh and Jenny Lakes are named after the couple.

Despite many happy years together, tragedy struck the family. After a family hunting trip to Montana in 1876, Jenny became sick and the family returned to their home near this site west of Rexburg. Eventually, every member of the family came down with smallpox – only Beaver Dick survived the outbreak. Griefstricken, he buried his family near their home on the banks of Henry's Fork of the Snake River. The graves from this pioneering Western family are still visible. Beaver Dick eventually remarried and lived until 1899. He is buried near his second home in Newdale, Idaho.

Today, the Madison County Parks and Recreation Department administers Beaver Dick Park. This free, twelve-acre preserve located on the banks of the Henry's Fork of the Snake River includes boating and a boat dock, picnic areas, fishing, and a children's playground. The site is open daily year-round.

M Rexburg Chamber of Commerce
420 W. 4th S., Rexburg. 356-5700 or 888-INFO-880. www.rexcc.com; info@rexcc.com

18

Newdale
Pop. 358

Newdale was founded and established in 1916. One year later, the railroad laid tracks through town and christened the town after its location in a dale-like landscape.

Teton
Pop. 569

Located directly south of St. Anthony in Fremont County, Teton was settled in the mid 1800s and welcomed postal services in 1885. Named after Wyoming's Teton Peaks rising in the distance, the town is most widely recognized as one of many communities involved in the devastating 1976 Teton Dam break.

Sugar City
Pop. 1,242

Pioneers arrived in this area northeast of Rexburg on the Teton River as early as 1883, but the town's history really began when several Salt Lake City, Utah businessmen formed the Sugar City Townsite Company in 1903. Traveling to the homesteaded region, these men purchased 320 acres from the homesteaders and began building a sugar beet factory and workers' residences at the newly laid-out town. In 1904, the $1 million factory was up and running, and it took less than a year for it to become the largest sugar beet factory in the US. The industry continued to prosper, and by 1933, the Sugar City Townsite Company had a record year with production at 43 million pounds of sugar. Unfortunately, the Sugar Act limited farmers' acreage, and a dwindling labor supply forced the company to close its doors in 1942. Despite this set-back and a devastating 1976 flood from the Teton Dam, Sugar City has survived, and its post office has operated continuously since 1904.

H Fort Henry
Milepost 338.7 on State Hwy. 33 at Sugar City's Heritage Park

In 1810, Andrew Henry and a party of trappers from St. Louis established a winter outpost about six miles west of here.

Driven from their upper Missouri beaver camp by hostile Blackfeet Indians, they expanded their operation from United States territory into Oregon – a land with only a few British posts at that time. They built cabins and wintered here in deep snow. Game was scarce, and they had little to eat except horses. So they abandoned this area, and Henry took only 40 packs of beaver pelts – a thin catch – back to St. Louis after a season's work.

H Teton Flood
Milepost 110 on State Hwy. 33

When the Teton Dam suddenly washed away, June 4, 1976, a large reservoir of water (280 feet deep) was dumped on farms and towns below.

Houses floated away, and cropland was ruined as water surged into the Snake River and American Falls Reservoir, which finally controlled the flood. Church, government, and disaster relief agencies responded effectively, but 14 lives were lost, and hundreds of millions of dollars in damage resulted from that unforgettable calamity. All that remains of Teton Dam still can be seen from a viewpoint two miles north of here.

T Teton Dam Site
Drive 3.25 miles east from Newdale on State Hwy. 33. Bear north at the paved road marked "Teton Dam Site", and proceed 1 mile to the overlook area.

Known as one of the most ill-conceived dams in U.S. history, eastern Idaho's Teton Dam was controversial from the start. In 1948, the Fremont Madison Irrigation District petitioned the U.S. Bureau of Reclamation to construct a dam on the Teton River in hopes of gaining more water rights for their agricultural needs. Despite opposition from the Environmental Protection Agency, the Idaho Fish and Game Department, the Idaho Conservation League, and the Bureau of Sports Fisheries, Congress approved the dam in 1964.

Sent to survey the dam site, the U.S. Army Corp of Engineers determined that the project was not economically justifiable. The dam would not provide any great benefits for irrigation, hydropower, or flood-control. In addition, the selected site was composed of highly permeable, volcanic rocks that would not provide a stable foundation for the project. Regardless of recommendations against the Teton Dam, the Bureau of Reclamation persisted with their claims that a dam would provide numerous benefits to area residents at a low cost.

Under the direction of Morrison-Knudsen Company and Peter Kiewit Son's Company, construction began in 1972. With 500 men working three shifts around the clock, the dam was finally completed in spring 1976. Measuring 3,050 feet long, 1,600 feet wide, and 305 feet high, the dam held back the waters of the newly forming Teton Reservoir for a short period of time.

On June 5, 1976, problems began arising with the Bureau's pride project. With the reservoir now nearly full, workers reported two leaks in the dam at 8:30 AM. At 10:00 AM, another leak was discovered, and bulldozer crews were sent to patch the leaks. Despite the crew's efforts, the leaks continued to grow as the porous volcanic rock below the dam allowed reservoir water to easily slip through. Realizing the gravity of the situation, the Fremont and Madison County sheriff's office began issuing evacuation warnings, and at 11:52 AM, catastrophe struck.

As the dam burst open, eighty billion gallons of water spilled south, wreaking havoc in all directions. Roaring through the agricultural valleys, the community of Wilford was the first hit. 150 homes were destroyed and six people drowned as the river headed for the neighboring communities. At 1:00 PM, Sugar City was hit, at 2:30 PM came Rexburg, and then Idaho Falls, Shelley, and Blackfoot were affected. Three days later when the flood finally subsided at the American Falls Reservoir, the damage was incomprehensible. The dam that would supposedly provide so many benefits to Idaho's people instead became a costly mistake. Lives were lost, fertile topsoil was stripped, 25,000 people were temporarily displaced from their homes, 18,000 head of livestock were missing, and total damages amounted to over $800 million.

Today, little sign is left of the controversial dam and the damage it created. Visitors will find an abandoned engineering lab, a parking lot, and a few Bureau of Reclamation signs stating what benefits were lost as a result of the dam's failure. Owing up to the disaster, the Bureau of Reclamation now must have a team of non-government engineers review any major dam proposal.

TV Green Canyon Hot Springs
Newdale. 458-4454. Take State Hwy. 33 to milepost 116. Here, turn onto Canyon Creek Rd. and proceed 4 miles to the hot springs.

Green Canyon Hot Springs provides year-round recreation fun in a relaxing atmosphere. Boasting hot springs at a temperature of 118 degrees, Green Canyon features an indoor and outdoor pool. The area surrounding the hot springs is popular for

camping, picnicking, huckleberry picking, mountain biking, and hunting. Green Canyon is open 10 AM to 10 PM Monday through Saturday from April 1 to September 30. From October through March, the site is open from 10 AM to 10 PM on weekends.

19 Food, Lodging

Driggs
Pop. 1,100

When Mormon homesteaders arrived here in 1888, there were few other settlers in this area. More Mormons ventured up from Utah soon after, and the town of Driggs was formed. As there were so many Driggses who signed the petition for a post office, the department decided to name the town after them. This was done in 1894, but the town itself was not incorporated until 1909.

In the early 1830s, trade gatherings between the Indians, trappers, and mountain men were held just one mile south of Driggs. Known by locals for years as "The Cultural Hub of the Teton Basin," Driggs is a blur of activity that offers supplies to those visiting the Tetons and Big Hole Mountains.

Tetonia
Pop. 247

Tetonia is situated on the northern end of the Teton Valley and draws its name from Wyoming's Teton Mountain Range rising in the distance. Settlers first began arriving in the area in 1881, and in 1910, the town was incorporated. However, much of the town's growth is due to the 1912 arrival of the Union Pacific Railroad. As the railroad passed through town, more business opportunities emerged, and a post office has continuously operated in the town since 1913.

Victor
Pop. 840

As Mormon emigrants migrated to the Teton Valley and settled the Driggs area, the Saints at Driggs advised later settlers to proceed south and settle the land near the Teton Pass. Following the Saints' order, several homesteaders moved to the area in 1899 and established a colony. With the LDS Church governing the community, the site became known as "Raymond" after Mormon Bishop David Raymond Sinclair. In 1901, the federal government finally incorporated the site, and the small colony grew into a town. Just a few years later, the town's name was changed to honor George Victor Sherwood. A courageous man, Sherwood continued to deliver mail from Victor to Jackson, Wyoming despite a hostile scare from Bannock Indians during the settlement's formative years.

While Victor's economy relied heavily upon a limestone quarry that operated from 1926 to 1970, the area now serves several alfalfa/hay ranches. Victor has also become a popular stopping point for tourists visiting Yellowstone National Park and the Grand Tetons.

Alta
Pop. 400

Although Alta is officially located in Wyoming, the only way to reach the mountain town is through Driggs, Idaho. The settlement, nestled in the grandeur of Wyoming's Teton Mountains, arose between 1888 and 1890 with the arrival of Mormon pioneers. The town draws its name from the Spanish word meaning "high," and is today recognized as home to the Grand Targhee Ski and Summer Resort.

H John Colter
Milepost 136.5 on State Hwy. 33

John Colter discovered this valley in 1808 while exploring the Yellowstone and upper Snake country in search of beaver.

Setting out by himself with his gun and a 30-pound pack, he tried to get the Indians to join in his trapping business. On the way here from a Yellowstone post 240 miles to the northeast, he came upon Colter's Hell – some hot springs near Cody, Wyoming. On his way back, he explored Yellowstone Park. In the spring of 1810, after several perilous escapes from the Blackfeet, he returned to Missouri, lucky to get back alive.

H Teton Range
Milepost 136.5 on State Hwy. 33

Flanked by rock formations more than 2.5 billion years old, these three granite peaks rose up in less than nine million years. Very new as mountains go, they still are rising.

Hinged at the base of the ridge before you, a block of rock 40 miles long broke along a fault line, where the rock tipped up to become the top of the ridge. During the past 250,000 years, extensive glacial ice sculpted these spectacular peaks from the hard, resistant granite.

H Pierre's Hole
Milepost 143.9 on State Hwy. 33

Teton Valley was known originally as Pierre's Hole. Rich in beaver, it was a favorite stomping ground for British and American fur traders and trappers between 1819-40.

"Old Pierre" Tevanitagon, an Iroquois Indian fur trapper for the Hudson's bay Company, gave his name to this beaver-rich valley. Pierre's Hole was the scene of the annual rendezvous of mountain men and suppliers – The Great Rocky Mountain Fair – in 1832. That wild party ended in a free-for-all battle with the Gros Ventre Indians, which the trappers and their Indian friends won. The valley was permanently settled in 1882.

T Targhee Village Golf Course
Stateline Rd. at Golf Course Rd., Driggs. 354-8577. Located 5 miles east of Driggs near Alta, Wyoming

Wide fairways lined with small trees greet golfers on this 6,238-yard course. Built in 1986, the 9-hole course is rated a par-70 and is framed by gorgeous views of the Grand Teton Mountains. Although water comes into play on several holes, the course is suitable for players of all ability. Tee times can be scheduled seven days in advance if so desired, but as all locals know, this course favors a more relaxed attitude where there's no dress code and mismatched clubs are the norm. The course is open daily from April 15 to October 31 with green fees at $14 for 9 holes and $22 for 18 holes.

A Scenic Journey Through the Bridger-Teton, Caribou, and Targhee National Forests

Three National Forests spread across a diverse ecosystem in southeastern Idaho and western Wyoming: the Bridger-Teton, Caribou, and Targhee. These forests are rich in natural wonders ranging from grasslands to dense stands of timber, lush canyons, pristine wild lands, clear lakes and wild rivers, alpine meadows, caves, craggy ridges, and towering mountain peaks. Within the three forests' boundaries are 6 million acres of America's public lands.

The Bridger-Teton, Caribou, and Targhee National Forests are surrounded by a neighborhood filled with wondrous diversity. Rugged plains, high deserts, and pastoral low country fringe national and state parks and monuments, wildlife refuges, sand dunes, lava flows, waterways, and a menu of National Natural Landmarks administered by the Bureau of Land Management. Everyone is welcomed as they journey through this Idaho/Wyoming neighborhood and partake in the feast of outdoor adventures.

Sagas of Bygone Days
Long before humans left their mark upon the land, wind and water shaped the face of the forests. Geological monoliths rose from the valley floors where erosion exposed ridges and peaks of hard naked stone. Crystal lakes collected water on the mountaintops to feed the rivers and streams below. Fertile soil encouraged trees and other vegetation to flourish in canyons and valleys while animals filled the forests with new life. Today, the National Forests in southeastern Idaho and western Wyoming are rich in nature's heritage.

A history of human influence is apparent on these National Forests. Explorers, trappers, mountain men, miners, and farmers followed in the footsteps of Native Americans who occupied the land for centuries. Pioneers seeking a new life in the West left evidence of their journey along the Oregon Trail. The sagas of this cultural heritage are preserved in ancient campsites, grave markers, abandoned mines, and historic structures.

Startling Spring
Nothing is more beautiful than spring in the western forests. It is heralded by rushing rivers, lush green grasses, budding trees, brilliant sunshine, and clean, crisp air. Animals emerge from their winter shelter and give birth to their young. It is time to begin fishing, hiking to the snowline, wandering the grasslands, and driving the Scenic Byways. Visitors may choose to ride horseback, spend a day in nature with their camera, float down a rushing river, or take a leisurely hike. Spring is a sensitive time for forest ecosystems. Visitors can protect these natural wonders by recreating with thoughtfulness and care. If the roads and trails are muddy or wet, leave the area and come back another day.

Stupendous Summer
Summer in southeastern Idaho and western Wyoming offers a myriad of outdoor delights to forest visitors. This is the busiest time of year on the Bridger-Teton, Caribou, and Targhee National Forests as trails, campgrounds, picnic areas, lodges, and resorts receive extensive use. Caving, "ATVing," rock climbing, mountain biking, and whitewater rafting are popular activities for the robust adventurer. Other visitors enjoy photography, watching the abundant wildlife, camping, and hiking. If professional assistance is needed, a list of outfitters and guides is available from Forest offices. Using the land safely and with respect ensures there will be recreation opportunities in the future.

Sizzling Scenery
Autumn nights bring freezing temperatures and spectacular fall colors to the National Forests and Grasslands in southeastern Idaho and western Wyoming. A breathtaking array of incandescent red, gold, and orange leaves contrast with the yellow grasses and luminous green pines reflected in crystal blue lake waters. There are fewer visitors on weekdays, but hunters, hikers, and other adventurers actively use campgrounds and trails on the fall weekends.

Snowy Splendor
Snow and ice turns the Bridger-Teton, Caribou, and Targhee National Forests into a virtual winter wonderland. Downhill and cross-country skiers, snowboarders, sledders, snowmobile and snowshoe enthusiasts can indulge in their favorite "cool experience" in the versatile terrain of the forests. Visitors need the proper clothing and equipment for cold, changeable weather to keep themselves safe, dry, and warm. Check avalanche conditions before venturing into the backcountry.

Big Springs National Recreation Water Trail
A leisurely float on the Big Springs National Recreation Water Trail gives visitors a chance to watch for abundant wildlife such as Canada geese, trumpeter swans, sandhill cranes, muskrats, moose, and kokanee salmon. Beautiful rainbow trout live year-round in the 52-degree springs at the headwaters of Henry's Fork.

Curlew National Grassland
Humans and animals have shared the grassy plains and perennial streams of the Curlew National Grassland for more than 2,000 years. Prehistoric sites reveal the history of aboriginal people who feasted on bison and other game, and took their fill of fresh water from the springs. Later, ranchers and homesteaders used the Grassland for farming and cattle grazing. Today, the unique values of the Curlew National Grassland are recognized and conserved. It is a literal outdoor classroom featuring precious water, valuable minerals, wildlife, native plants, cultural sites, wildlife, and quiet serenity.

Guidelines and More Information
Remember "Safety First" as you will be visiting the homes of wild animals living in the National Forests. Prior to your visit, learn about the resident wildlife and how to conduct yourself in their territory. Awareness is the key to your personal safety. Never approach wild animals – give them plenty of space.

For more information, contact the following agencies:

Bridger-Teton National Forest: (307) 739-5500
Jackson Hole Visitor Center:
   www.fs.fed.us/jhgyvc
Caribou National Forest: (208) 624-3151
National Forest Campground Reservation System:
   1-877-444-6777
Bureau of Land Management:
   Idaho Falls (208) 524-7559;
   Kemmerer, Wyoming (307) 828-4500;
   Pinedale, Wyoming (307) 367-5300
Idaho Department of Parks and Recreation:
   (208) 334-4199
Idaho Falls Visitor Center: (208) 523-3278
Idaho Division of Tourism: (208) 334-2470
Backcountry Avalanche Hotline: (307) 733-2664
SE Idaho Avalanche Hotline: (208) 239-7650

Reprinted from U.S. Forest Service (Intermountain Region) brochure

T The Links at Teton Peaks
127 N. 400 W., Tetonia. 456-2372. Located 4 miles west of Driggs

The Links at Teton Peaks is the only recognized Scottish style links course in Idaho. Opened in 2001 under the design of Bob Wilson, this course is extremely challenging. From the first of its 18 holes, the course tests the ability of even the most advanced player. As a result, a plaque in the clubhouse recognizes the few who have earned a score under 85. The course is open daily during spring and summer, and green fees are $19 for 9 holes and $25 for 18 holes.

T Teton River Basin
North of Driggs.

During the early 19th century, the lush Teton River Basin was known as "Pierre's Hole" and was a mountain man and fur trading hub. The valley drew its original name from Iroquois trapper, Pierre Tevanitagon, who frequented the area until his 1827 Montana death at the hands of the Blackfeet. In addition to Pierre, European and American trappers visited the basin, and Nez Perce, Flathead, and Gros Ventre Indians settled in the region. Although the fur trade started out on friendly terms, friction between trading parties and the Native Americans soon became a daily part of life. Skirmishes were common with only minor injuries resulting, but this trend soon ended. In 1832, a major battle broke out at a rendezvous, and nearly fifty Native American and white men, women, and children were killed with several others seriously wounded.

Despite its bloody beginnings, the Teton River Basin has quieted down and retains its lush landscape. Cradled between the forested peaks of the Grand Teton Mountains to the east and the Big Hole Mountains to the west, this rural mountain valley includes fertile farmland, pastures, and open ranges. It has often been nicknamed "The Tetons' Quiet Side."

T Pierre's Playhouse
27 N. Main, Victor. 787-2249.

Genteel heroines, handsome heroes, and lurking villains wait around every corner at Pierre's Playhouse. Originally built as the community's first movie theater in the late 1940s, the facility now hosts the Teton Players and welcomes nearly 9,000 spectators each summer. The Teton Players, an organization comprised of local volunteers, performs classic melodramas throughout the summer months in a spirit of promoting fun. Audience members are encouraged to participate, and booing and hissing at the villain is required. Advance reservations for the productions are highly recommended.

T Spud Drive-In
231 S. Hwy. 33, Driggs. 354-2727.
www.spuddrivein.com

The Grand Teton Mountains form the backdrop for one of America's few remaining historical entertainment venues. The Spud Drive-In was built in 1953 and has been playing to generations of movie lovers ever since. The theater was added to the National Register of Historic Places in June 2003 and is open on summer weekends. Look for "Old Murphy", the red truck with the giant spud sitting out front.

T Teton Mountain Range
Borders eastern horizon from Tetonia to Victor on State Hwy. 33.

Surrounded by mountains more than 2.5 billion years old, the Teton Mountain Range rose up along a faultline less than 9 million years ago. Ancient glaciers sculpted the granite, pegmatite, schist, and gneiss peaks, but it wasn't until 1820 that they received a name. A dazzling sight to behold, the peaks appeared to a group of French-Canadian trappers as "Les Trois Tetons" meaning "the three breasts." Today, the three peaks are known as the Grand (13,770 feet), the Middle, and the South Teton.

T Teton Pass
State Hwy. 33 near the Idaho/Wyoming border outside Victor

Situated at an elevation of 8,429 feet, Teton Pass offers breathtaking views into Wyoming's Jackson Hole valley and is steeped in history. John Colter was the first white man to cross the pass. In 1808, Colter used an Indian hunting trail to cross from Wyoming into Idaho. Just three years later, trapper Wilson Price Hunt led his expedition across the same route.

When mining became big business in the West, mining companies decided to build a primi-

A FLY FISHING PARADISE

Bruce Staples

Eastern Idaho hosts three world-class fisheries: the Henry's Fork, Henry's Lake, and the South Fork reach of the Snake River. These are only a few high quality trout waters available in this area on Yellowstone Park's doorstep.

Henry's Fork
The Henry's Fork has a hundred-year reputation because of the fabulous rainbow trout fishery in the Box Canyon-Last Chance-Harriman State Park (formerly Railroad Ranch) reach and in the river above Island Park Reservoir. Now emerging is the fact that an equivalent quality rainbow trout fishery exists in the Pinehaven-Hatchery Ford-Cardiac Canyon reach. Below, the superb rainbow-brown trout fishery from Bear Gulch downstream to below St. Anthony also vouches for how good the cold-water fishery habitat of this river is.

Over ninety miles of river are on the table here. Throughout are individuals ranging to double figure poundage. Presenting streamer patterns late and early in the season, giant stonefly imitations and caddis and mayfly imitations in season are the most effective means of encountering these individuals. The famous aquatic insect emergences of the Box Canyon–Harriman reach are mostly duplicated in the lower river. Throughout this length float fishing abounds and plenty of opportunities for walk-in fishing exist.

Further, if efforts of the Nature Conservancy to acquire a maintenance flow from Henry's Lake to their Flat Ranch Preserve succeed, six miles of walk-in meadow stream will be added to the Henry's Fork's array of high quality reaches.

South Fork Reach of the Snake River
This seventy-mile reach from Palisades Dam downstream to the Henry's Fork confluence rivals Montana's Bighorn River below Yellowtail Dam in popularity. Its high season begins with trout responding to the giant and golden stonefly emergences in late June, enters a great pale morning dun emergence, on to an early autumn blue winged olive emergence, and commences with the autumn brown trout run. Until the early 1960s, the South Fork was a cutthroat trout fishery. Now, it hosts Idaho's densest brown trout population. It also produced the state record brown trout. Browns in excess of twenty inches are common, and presenting streamer patterns throughout the season results in trophies. Rainbows are becoming numerous with many individuals exceeding the twenty-inch mark. A good population of cutthroat trout rounds out the South Fork's trout roster.

Famed as a drift boat destination, the South Fork and its major tributaries, Palisades and Pine Creeks, offer a huge variety of walk-in destinations. The best selection is off the fourteen mile long South Fork Road above Heise and along the south side of the river from Swan Valley Bridge upstream to Palisades Dam. On the lower river, the Twin Bridges area and around the Heise Bridge also offer opportunities.

Upland Rivers
If the Big Lost, Blackfoot, Fall, Teton, and Portneuf Rivers were placed in any other part of the country, they would become stars. Add to these the Salt River tributaries, Robinson Creek, Bitch Creek, Warm River and many others.

Media attention for the South Fork and the Henry's Fork has kept all these waters almost a secret. In many ways, they offer quality experiences not easily found on more heralded waters. Don't be fooled by their smaller size because many host trophy trout that rival the South and Henry's fork residents in size! Here are a few particulars. There are seven miles of public accessible meadow stream on the Blackfoot River Wildlife Management area. The late June giant stonefly emergence in Fall River's canyon has become a destination event. You can experience rainbows and cutthroat responding to Teton River's great pale morning dun and terrestrial emergences in a distractingly beautiful setting. Big Lost River's midseason crane fly and late season midge and blue winged olive emergences activate rainbows ranging to over two feet long.

Stillwaters
From Henry's Lake in the north to Treasureton Reservoir in the south, eastern Idaho hosts a matchless array of stillwater fisheries. Island Park Reservoir, Springfield Reservoir, Twenty-four mile Reservoir, Daniels Reservoir and the Harriman Fish Pond would also be top quality trout fisheries anywhere. Similar fishery quality exists in thirty or so remaining waters ranging from high mountain lakes to irrigation reservoirs because most have histories of producing trophy trout, whether cutthroat, rainbows, brookies or browns. Simulating superb midge emergences in season is the most effective way of fishing these waters, but seasonal dragonfly and damselfly, speckled dun emergences, or presenting leech and baitfish imitations are productive approaches.

Much more information is available. You can acquire it, strategy help, quality products, guide recommendations, licenses for Idaho and Yellowstone National Park, and enroll in classes in all fly fishing facets at:

Jimmy's All Seasons Angler
275 A Street
Idaho Falls, ID 83402
Phone: 208-522-9242
E-mail: jimmys@ida.net
Website:www.jimmysflyshop.com

St. Anthony	Jan	Feb	March	April	May	June	July	Aug	Sep	Oct	Nov	Dec	Annual
Average Max. Temperature (F)	28.7	33.7	42.6	55.5	66.2	74.2	83.3	82.4	72.6	60.2	42.1	30.6	56.0
Average Min. Temperature (F)	8.3	11.3	18.7	27.6	35.5	42.0	46.8	45.1	37.1	28.4	19.6	9.9	27.5
Average Total Precipitation (in.)	1.39	1.01	1.07	1.20	1.80	1.61	0.79	0.78	0.90	0.99	1.25	1.43	14.22
Average Total Snowfall (in.)	12.8	8.7	3.2	0.9	0.1	0.1	0.0	0.0	0.0	0.4	4.1	12.2	42.5
Average Snow Depth (in.)	10	10	4	0	0	0	0	0	0	0	1	5	2

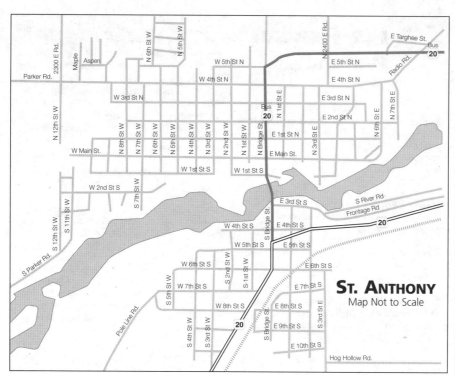

ST. ANTHONY
Map Not to Scale

tive road leading into Jackson Hole. In the early 1900s, the Dunn Mining Company carved a windy road through the granite mountains. Just a few years later, the U.S. Forest Service decided to build its own road. Between 1913 and 1917, young forest service crews used horses and plenty of manpower to create a more user-friendly road. Cars first used the road in 1913.

Today, these old roads have been nearly forgotten, but the individuals who created them helped open the west to further expansion. While these original roads no longer exist, the current highway does parallel the historic routes in many places.

V Grand Targhee Ski and Summer Resort

(800) 827-4433. In Driggs, proceed through town. Bear left at the traffic light near Key Bank onto Ski Hill Rd. Continue approximately 6 blocks to a fork in the road. Turn left here, following Ski Hill Rd. through Alta, Wyoming to its end at the resort.

Officially located in Wyoming, Grand Targhee Ski and Summer Resort is only accessible from Idaho. This full-service resort nestled in the western slope of the majestic Teton Mountains is known as a powder paradise. Receiving an average of 500 inches of snow annually, Grand Targhee has been dubbed as one of the best family resorts in the West with the finest powder in North America.

The resort includes 2,000 acres of lift terrain with an additional 1,000 acres strictly reserved for snowcat powder skiing. The lift acreage includes 64 wide-groomed runs, a 2,200-foot vertical drop, one rope tow, one quad chair, one double chair, and one high-speed quad chairlift. Unsurpassed scenery awaits those ready for a day of snowcat powder skiing. For those uninterested in a downhill adventure, several Nordic trails are available.

The resort is open daily during ski season from 9 AM to 4 PM. Full-day lift tickets are $53 for adults 15 and older, $33 for youth ages 6-14, and free to those under 5 who are accompanied by a paying adult. Half-day adult lift tickets are $38. In addition, multi-day value rates are available as well as reasonably priced season passes.

V Teton River Drainage

The Teton River flows off the Grand Tetons' western slopes and is responsible for draining 890 square miles before merging with the Henrys Fork of the Snake River outside St. Anthony. While a flat valley floor and sandhill cranes characterize the river's upper portion, the lower portion winds through tight canyons. Both sections, however, provide excellent fishing opportunities to both novice and expert anglers in one of Idaho's most serene settings. The drainage supports populations of wild cutthroat trout, wild and hatchery released rainbow trout, brook trout, hybrids, and mountain whitefish. At one time, the Idaho Department of Fish and Game released over 7,500 rainbow trout annually into the Teton River. Today, the Teton River is open for fishing Memorial Day through November 30th.

S Bergmeyer Manufacturing Co., Inc.

229 N. Hwy. 33, Driggs. 354-2000 or 800-348-3356 www.bergmeyermfg.com

The Bergmeyer Manufacturing furniture showroom and warehouse is located approximately two miles north of Hwy. 33 in the scenic Teton Valley. Award winning architect, Mori Bergmeyer, and his knowledgeable staff design and craft custom furniture with a variety of finishes for the discriminating interior designer. Specializing in accommodating all decor types, the staff utilizes the most advanced machinery along with art metal, log, and custom shops to fill the demand for unique furnishings. These finely crafted pieces are built onsite, and many are on display to the public. The

showroom is open Monday through Friday from 8:30 AM to 5 PM where visitors will find the company's regular Farmhouse furniture line along with occasional overruns of custom designs.

M Driggs - Teton Valley Chamber of Commerce

75 N. Main St., Driggs. 354-2500. www.tetonvalleychamber.com; tvcc@tetonvalleychamber.com

L Best Western Teton West

476 N. Main St., Driggs. 354-2363. www.bestwestern.com

Nestled in Idaho's beautiful Teton Valley, the Best Western Teton West creates memorable stays with spectacular views, comfortable accommodations, and convenient outdoor access. Guests enjoy beautifully decorated rooms featuring queen or king size beds, and children stay free. The hotel also offers complimentary continental breakfast, an indoor pool, hot tub, cable TV with movie and sports channels, and Jacuzzi suites. During your stay, discover abundant outdoor recreation. Two golf courses, hunting, fishing, hiking, mountain climbing, horseback riding, renowned snowmobiling, and skiing are just minutes from the hotel. If that's not enough, Grand Targhee Resort is 12 miles away, Grand Teton Park and Jackson Hole are a short 30-mile drive, and Yellowstone lies 87 miles to the northeast. For convenience and affordable amenities you deserve, Best Western Teton West welcomes you!

L Super 8 Teton West Motel

133 State Hwy. 33 on the north end of Driggs. 354-8888 or (800) 800-8000. www.super8.com

The Super 8 Teton West Motel welcomes you to the beautiful Teton Valley! Ideally located within easy driving distance of Yellowstone and Grand Teton National Parks, Jackson Hole, and Grand Targhee Resort, the motel offers forty-six oversized rooms where children stay free. Guests enjoy phenomenal views of the Tetons, queen and king size beds, refrigerators and microwaves in each room, cable TV with movie and sports channels, free continental breakfast, and an indoor pool and hot tub. For a special stay, Jacuzzi suites are available. The motel also ensures hours of enjoyment for the whole family with convenient access to two new golf courses, abundant outdoor recreation, wonderful snowmobile trails, and the newly opened Teton Valley Museum. With so many amenities, Super 8 Teton West Motel is your affordable source for comfort and fun!

Drummond
Pop. 15

This tiny town was named after a construction engineer who worked on the railroad in 1911 as the line was built from Ashton to Driggs.

Felt
Pop. 35

John Felt and his brother first settled this area in 1889. They claimed land near Badger Creek, and within no time, other homesteaders began arriving. By 1911, most of the land in the area was taken, and a townsite was dedicated. The Post Office arrived in 1913.

21 *Food, Lodging*

St. Anthony
Pop. 3,342

In 1887, Charles H. Moon homesteaded and built a bridge and general store in this location. He became the first postmaster a year later and named the town because he noted a resemblance between the nearby Henry's Fork waterfall and the Mississippi River's St. Anthony Falls in Minnesota. The community's location on Henry's Fork of the Snake River provides excellent fly-fishing opportunities, while the St. Anthony Sand Dunes has long been a local draw.

Parker
Pop. 319

This small community was originally called Garden Grove and is said to be named after Wyman Parker, an early Mormon Bishop, and Isaac Parker, the town's postmaster in 1900. Others claim that the "Parker" in the name is drawn from Adelbert Parker who served as postmaster of the nearby Egin community in 1880. Nonetheless, when Garden Grove became the larger of the two settlements, Garden Grove residents relocated a few miles away from Egin and established a post office under the name Parker.

Egin

Located just seven miles west of St. Anthony, Egin is the oldest permanent settlement in Fremont County and was established by Mormon settlers in 1879. In 1810, when Andrew Henry wintered in the area, he built a temporary post consisting of a few log houses. This small town was formerly called Greenville but that changed in 1880 with the arrival of the first post office. The term Egin comes from the Shoshone word "ech-unt," meaning "cold."

T Sandbar Swimming Area
St. Anthony. Contact the St. Anthony Chamber of Commerce at 624-4870.

St. Anthony's Sandbar Swimming Area is an easily accessible summer recreation zone. Sandy shores

ST. ANTHONY SAND DUNES

Geology & History

The St. Anthony Sand Dunes is an unusual area 35 miles long and 5 miles wide. Beautiful dunes, white rolling hills of sand (most 200-300 feet above the valley floor), were formed when quartz sand, carried from the nearby Snake River and ancient lake shorelines, was deposited by prevailing winds among the Juniper Hills. These hills are extinct volcano vents that once poured molten lava onto the Snake River plain.

A local Indian legend about the formation of the sand dunes says that this area was the site of fierce, bloody battles between the Bannock and Shoshone Indians and the Blackfoot tribes, at war over hunting grounds. One day as the sun was sinking, flooding the west with a brilliant afterglow, the great dunes arose and engulfed the warring armies. Not a single warrior escaped. Their families fled to escape extinction.

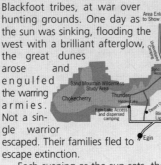

Each evening as the sun sets, the spirits of the warriors are said to chant and moan the tortured cry of the vanquished. Maybe it's just the wind, but with the discovery of arrowheads and other Indian artifacts, you might find yourself wondering just how much of the story is legend.

Facilities

Facilities include a gravel access road, a 60 car parking area, an unloading ramp, and restrooms. A small informal camping area is also available near the parking area. If you enjoy tent camping you are in luck! It is allowed just about anywhere on the dunes when access is gained by foot or off road vehicles. And, if after a day of playing in the sand you'd just love a hot shower and comfy bed, we have lots of great lodging alternatives available in Rexburg. (For more information on camping and lodging alternatives refer to Local Business Information.)

Recreation

In the summer, sandrails and off-road vehicle enthusiasts from all over come to ride the dunes. Though the sand gets hot, the temperature rarely tops 90 degrees. With small rolling hills in the east suitable for youngsters and beginning ATVers, and challenging hills in the west, mountains of sand up to 600 feet high, there's sure to be a dune for everyone.

If off-road vehicles aren't your thing, there's fun to be had hiking, horseback riding, sandboarding, hunting, primitive camping, and cooling off in the warm shallow waters of Hidden Lake.

In the winter, the sand dunes transform with the cold and snow to a popular winter playground that lures cross country skiers, snowboarders, and snowmobilers. It's also a great place to take the kids tubing and sledding. But bundle up! It's cold out there!

Rules & Regulations

The St. Anthony Sand Dunes are part of the Sand Mountain Wilderness Study Area managed by the BLM. This area provides critical winter range for deer, elk, antelope, and moose. Recreation use off of the open sand or designated trails can result in the destruction of vegetation and other features of the landscape. To protect this area, the following rules apply:

- Stay on the open sand. Protect the vegetation.

- Follow designated trails. Unless a route is specifically signed OPEN, it is closed.

- Use only plastic beverage containers; glass containers are prohibited.

- Make sure off road vehicles are equipped with a 6-foot long whip antenna with a red or orange flag.

- Motorized vehicles yield the right of way to those on foot or horseback.

- Pack out trash.

- Drive only ATVs, motorcycles, and dune rails beyond parking area.

- Idaho residents must display a valid state ORV sticker on their motorcycle or ATV. Out-of-state ATs must have a valid registration sicker if one is required in their home state.

- No open campfires are allowed inside the WSA (Wilderness Study Area) except in the designated Red Road Open Sand Campfire Area.

- The burning of pallets, treated wood, or non-wood materials is prohibited in any campfire area.

- Quiet hours within the Egin Lake Access Site and the Red Road Recreation Area are from 11 PM to 7 AM.

Reprinted from Idaho Travel Council brochure

provide perfect opportunities to construct elaborate sandcastles, while a playground area and roped-off swimming area on the Henry's Fork of the Snake River offer hours of entertainment. The free area is open daily during the summer from 9 AM to 5 PM, and a lifeguard is always on duty.

T Fremont County Golf Course

674 N. Golf Course Rd., St. Anthony. 624-7074.

The Fremont County Golf Course is a 9-hole public course that has operated since 1967. Designed by Marvin J. Aslett, the 3,000-yard course features several out-of-bounds stakes and a few undulating bent grass greens. Rated a par-36, the course is open April 1 to October 1. Daily green fees are $8.40 for 9 holes and $13.65 for 18 holes. Tee times are only accepted for weekends and holidays.

T Sand Creek Wildlife Management Area

17 miles north of St. Anthony at the end of Sand Creek Rd.

The Sand Creek Wildlife Management Area is part of the larger Sands Habitat Management Area and is situated at the foot of the Island Park caldera. The area was established to provide a wintering ground for elk, moose, and mule deer that summer in Island Park and nearby Yellowstone National Park. Since the area's establishment, sandhill cranes and trumpeter swans have also occasionally been spotted. The free site is open year-round for wildlife viewing, hiking, camping, and fishing.

T Clyde Keefer Memorial Park

Downtown St. Anthony. Contact the St. Anthony Chamber of Commerce at 624-4870.

Clyde Keefer Memorial Park offers a relaxing atmosphere in downtown St. Anthony. The park is equipped with a large playground area, barbeque facilities, and covered picnic areas, and also offers fishing access ideal for beginning anglers.

T Henry's Fork Greenway

Downtown St. Anthony. Contact the St. Anthony Chamber of Commerce at 624-4870.

Known as the place where nature and people meet, the Henry's Fork Greenway was recently completed through the efforts of St. Anthony volunteers. The one-mile trail winds next to the Henry's Fork of the Snake River and provides an easy walk with beautiful views. Wildlife, including moose, coyotes, foxes, and several bird species, populate the area, and fishing is an ever-popular sport along the path. In addition, informational signs along the trail educate users about the vegetation and wildlife in the surrounding region. The greenway is open year-round free of charge.

T Fort Henry Historic Site

Contact the St. Anthony Chamber of Commerce at 624-4870. In St. Anthony, locate the Fourth St N. Extension Rd. Proceed 3 miles south across the extension road, cross the Henry's Fork of the Snake River, and locate the site monument on the road's east side.

Situated next to the Henry's Fork of the Snake River, Fort Henry represents the first American fur trading post established west of the Rocky Mountains. Former Pennsylvania lead miner and partner of the St. Louis Missouri Fur Company, Andrew Henry was dispatched to present day Idaho on a trapping expedition in 1809. Although Henry looked forward to the excursion as a western adventure, he and his party of 400 men experienced great hardship. Blackfoot Indians attacked the group several times on the eastern side of the Rockies, so Henry was anxious to establish winter camp on the mountain's western side. After discovering a beautiful lake near present day Island Park in July 1810, the men proceeded several miles downstream and built a fort consisting of numerous log buildings where they would winter until early 1811.

The men, however, were inadequately prepared for the severe winter season. By the end of winter, the group was forced to slaughter and eat its own horses to survive. When spring arrived, Henry broke his group into three smaller parties. He traveled to the Mandan villages to visit Manuel Lisa and then returned home to Missouri where he remained sporadically involved in the fur trade until 1824.

In 1937, a local Boy Scout troop erected a monument near the fort site honoring Henry and his men. The actual fort stood approximately 1,700 feet west of this monument. His legacy is also remembered in the naming of Henry's Lake State Park near Island Park and the Henry's Fork of the Snake River.

LM Colonial Rose Tearoom and Bed & Breakfast

411 N. Bridge, St. Anthony. 624-3530.

Would you like some tea and crumpets? If so, then discover the Colonial Rose Tearoom and Bed & Breakfast located within walking distance of downtown St. Anthony. Nestled inside a historic 1906 home, the tearoom offers custom teas, low teas, and high teas in a cozy Victorian atmosphere. For overnight guests, the Bed & Breakfast provides two uniquely decorated bedrooms with a shared bath, beautiful area views, and scrumptious breakfasts including egg and bacon quiche, sourdough hotcakes, and homemade raspberry and huckleberry preserves. Whether you're planning a special gathering or staying overnight in St. Anthony, the Colonial Rose Tearoom and Bed & Breakfast offers something for both young and old. The doors are always open with a cup of warm tea inviting you to stay awhile and feel at home.

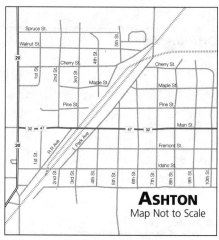

ASHTON
Map Not to Scale

M St. Anthony Chamber of Commerce

420 N. Bridge St. Ste C., St. Anthony. 624-4870. www.stanthonychamber.com; sachamber@fretel.com

22 Food, Lodging

Chester
Pop. 100

Utah pioneers founded Chester in the late 1880s. Originally known as Fall River because of its proximity to that water source, the town's name was changed in 1894 under Post Office Department orders.

Ashton
Pop. 1,129

Founded in February 1906 with the arrival of the Oregon Shortline Railroad, Ashton draws its name from the railroad's chief construction engineer, William Ashton. William and his son settled in the area after the OSL shifted its tracks two miles west of Marysville to avoid the high priced right-of-way in that area. A month after the railroad arrived, the town was incorporated.

The town's original railroad economy has long since shifted to agriculture. Recognized as the world's largest seed-potato producing region, Ashton's economy is dependent upon potatoes. In fact, every fall the school kids are released for a two to ten week period where they spend time helping their family and neighbors harvest the area's average 11,000 planted acres of potatoes. Canola, peas, hay, wheat, and barley are also raised in the area fields.

Marysville
Pop. 200

Mary Lucinda Baker was one of the first women to settle here, along with Mary Dorcheus, Mary Patlow, Mary Spratling, and Mary Smith. They were all part of the Mormon ward organized and established here in 1893, and the town's name is therefore plural in honor of all of them. Mary Baker later served as the town's first postmaster. The nearby Falls River was used as the source for a canal that continues to irrigate the farmland surrounding Marysville to the north and south.

Warm River
Pop. 10

Situated near the swiftly flowing Warm River from which it received its name, this tiny village operated a post office from 1907 to 1924. Today, it is known as Idaho's smallest incorporated city.

H The Three Tetons
Milepost 362.7 on U.S. Hwy. 20

The giant peaks to the southeast were a famous early Western landmark known to fur hunters and mountain men.

Perhaps as early as 1819, French-speaking trappers were calling them the Trois Tetons – the three breasts. More prosaic English-speaking mountain men named them the Pilot Knobs, but the romantic French name stuck. This is one of the finest views of the peaks from the west, the side from which they were seen by the men who named them.

T Aspen Acres Golf Course
4179 E. 1100 N., Ashton. 652-3524 or (800) 845-2374. Eight miles southeast of Ashton

An old farm and aspen groves provide the backdrop for this 18-hole, executive length course. Measuring 2,992 yards, Aspen Acres is a par-60 course offering scenic views of the neighboring Teton Mountains, bird watching, and wildlife encounters. While the course is suitable for beginners, it also offers plenty of challenges to the experienced player. The course is open daily from daylight to dusk. Green fees for 18-holes are $11 for adults, $7.75 for teens, and $5.25 for juniors.

T Hess Heritage Museum
3417 E. 1200 St., Ashton. 652-7353.

On this restored 250 acre pioneer farm, visitors will find an old home, carriage house, social hall, village square, school, blacksmith shop, and park. The museum is open from mid-April to mid-October by appointment only.

T Mesa Falls Recreation Area
North of Warm River on State Hwy. 47/Mesa Falls Scenic Byway

Recreation Area & Scenic Byway
The Mesa Falls Recreation Area, beginning at Bear Gulch, follows the Mesa Falls Scenic Byway and includes Upper and Lower Mesa Falls and Grandview Campground. It ends at the junction with Hwy. 20 near Harriman State Park. The entry fee at Upper Mesa Falls is also good for Harriman Park (save your stub). A pathway and boardwalk leads from the Inn right to the brink of the falls. The upper part of this walkway is universally accessible. The visitor center and gift shop at Upper Mesa Falls will be open seven days a week from Memorial Day to Labor Day.

Approximately 1.3 million years ago, a huge volcanic eruption created an ash layer hundreds of feet deep. The ash layer was compressed into rock known as Mesa Falls Tuff. Later eruptions filled the area with basalt lava flows. For 500,000 years the Henry's Fork of the Snake River has been carving the canyon seen today. The Mesa Falls Tuff forms the ledge that the falls cascade over. Upper Mesa Falls is 114 feet high.

American Indians used the upper Snake River Valley for centuries before the arrival of Europeans. Small and large game, fish, berries, lodgepole pine, and other resources of the Mesa Falls area were harvested seasonally.

Mesa Power Company built Big Falls Inn between 1912 and 1914, probably to be an office. A dam and power generation plant were planned but never built. Instead the area became a tourist attraction and the Inn became a stage stop and hotel for travelers going to Yellowstone National Park. Montana Power purchased the area in 1936. In later years, the Inn was used as a restaurant, dance hall, and scout camp. The Forest Service acquired the property in 1986 through a land exchange.

Work on restoring the Inn began in 1997. The Idaho State Department of Parks and Recreation and the U.S. Forest Service became partners in managing the site. Over the next three years, the Inn was restored to historic standards and is now listed in the National Register of Historic Places.

One mile south of Upper Mesa Falls is the Grandview Overlook of Lower Mesa Falls. Lower Mesa Falls is 65 feet high. The Civilian Conservation Corps (CCC) built the rock and mortar overlook in the 1930s. Grandview Campground is adjacent to the overlook.

The Mesa Falls Scenic Byway begins in Ashton, Idaho and winds through farmland, forest, logged over areas, and open meadows. The roadway was recently rebuilt and resurfaced.

A seasonal progression of wildflowers blankets the ground in the Mesa Falls Recreation Area. Look for glacier lilies, spring beauties, and heartleaf arnica in the early spring, camas and mules ears a littler later, and lupine, asters, and Indian paintbrush in mid-summer.

Please be safe during your visit to Mesa Falls and stay on the walkways at all times. Special group tours of the site are available throughout the summer and can be arranged by calling the Ashton/Island Park Ranger Station at (208) 652-7442, Harriman State Park at (208) 558-7368, or inquire inside Big Falls Inn.

The History of the Big Falls Inn
John Henry Hendricks and his wife, Clara Wahlen, homesteaded 160 acres in the Mesa Falls area in 1901. He paid $1.25 per acre. They built a cabin 200 feet from the Upper Falls and lived in it with their four small children. Hendricks was hoping to one-day harness the power of the upper falls to bring electricity to Marysville, Idaho.

To make ends meet, he drove a stagecoach in Yellowstone in the summers. He worked in sawmills and ran a trap line in the winter. Clara

worried about her children – the steep cliffs and fast water of the isolated homestead were dangerous. She couldn't wait to move. Hendricks made final proof on the claim on January 26, 1903 before Thomas Elliott, United States Commissioner in St. Anthony. Hendricks then immediately sold the property to Elliott, although the patent had not yet been received. It is interesting to note that U.S. Commissioners couldn't file for homestead property.

Elliott and a group of other businessmen formed the Snake River Electric Light and Power Company. Hendricks received cash and stock as payment for the land. Both parties later disputed the exact amount of both. When Hendricks received patent on the property on November 25, 1904, he signed it over to other wealthy members of the company then voted a $1000 assessment per member to begin development of the site. Hendricks and others of modest means were thus effectively removed from the company.

The proceedings did not pass unnoticed, and by 1905, the Government Land Office was investigating. Supervisor Homer Fenn of the Targhee National Forest stated in a letter to the Chief Forester in February 1907 that Elliott had admitted that he earlier gave $200 to Hendricks to file on the property, but as there were not witnesses to that statement there was not a "suitable case for cancellation of the claim and sale."

Though the mission of the Snake River Electric Light and Power Company was to produce electricity, they never succeeded. In 1912, for unknown reasons Elliott and the Snake River Electric Light and Power Company began a series of sales of the property. The land changed hands three times, although the board members (all associated with Montana Power) remained the same.

A power dam or penstock was never built, but shortly after 1913 a log building – Big Falls Inn – was erected at the present site. Mesa Power Company (one of the many names given to this Montana power subsidiary) records show expenditures of $14,000 for building materials and labor between 1913 and 1916. The layout of the building is far more suited to an office space or company retreat center than to a lodge with paying visitors. This fact suggests the company did not initially intend to use the building as an inn at all. Perhaps the increase in tourist traffic along the highway to Yellowstone National Park impressed them and they decided to take advantage of it. The road to the park at that time was grueling and Big Falls Inn would be a good halfway point.

Operation of the Big Falls Inn continued into the 1930s. The long time caretaker, Charlie Causey, was famed for his hospitality, especially his cooking, gambling, and homemade spirits. Big Falls Inn is mentioned in the Administrative Plan for the Targhee Forest in 1924. Supervisor Stoddard noted that though the road from the highway to the Inn was in poor condition a cooperative agreement had been made with the Ashton Commercial Club to help with maintenance on the road.

The improvement of the old Yellowstone Hwy. was already taking its toll on hotel finances. Better

road conditions on the old highway brought more and more people pushing straight through to Yellowstone. The hotel had evidently closed down by 1932, as it receives no mention in the final Administrative Plan for the Hwy. Uses of the area that year.

In December of 1935, Mesa Power Company sold the property to Idaho Transmission Company. This firm had numerous holdings in Idaho, and it appeared that a power dam might become a reality. The deepening Depression seems to have claimed the company as it sold not just the Mesa Falls property, but also all of its holdings to Montana Power in May 1936.

Though closed for some time, the hotel was apparently in fair condition as Montana Power used it as a company resort and hunting lodge for executives and employees. Tom Williams of Sunlight Development Company (a subsidiary of Montana Power) verified this. Even this Montana Power Company use of the hotel diminished. The Edginton family of Island Park and St. Anthony ran Big Falls Inn as a restaurant and dance hall in the late forties. It was mostly open in the summers. The Boy Scouts, under the leadership of Cat Thompson used it in the late fifties and sixties. The Fremont County Police Officers Association leased the Inn for $1 per year as a retreat and meeting facility in 1974-75. Use feasibility was studied during the late 1950s in hope of finally utilizing the site. By then, however, cost was not the only consideration. Increasing environmental restriction made any future development of the site doubtful.

The Forest Service had long been interested in obtaining the property. It had been listed as a desired acquisition from the early 1950s. Though not recorded, it is believed that talks with Montana Power began soon after their decision to not develop the site.

In 1986, a meeting between the Forest Service and Montana Power resulted in a proposed exchange of the Mesa Falls property for lands in the Lolo National Forest in Montana. This proposal failed because of the Forest Service Policy against exchanges involving properties in different states.

The solution to the stalemate was somewhat complicated but satisfied all parties. Targhee National Forest deeded to Montana Power developed special use areas at Mack's Inn, Pond's Lodge, and portions of the summer home areas at Flat Rock, Buffalo, and North Fork, all in Island Park. Montana Power subsequently sold the properties to the various tenants. The Targhee received in return the Upper Mesa Falls property and additional cash. The final exchange took place on December 18, 1986.

The walkways were built in 1992, as was the new road that accesses the site and the vault toilets. In partnership with the Idaho State Department of Parks and Recreation, Big Falls Inn underwent a complete renovation during the years 1997-2001. It was restored to its historic splendor, and is now on the Register of Historic Places. The Mesa Falls Scenic Byway was also transformed. Eleven million dollars worth of improvement to the road made the old, pothole filled route one of the best roads in Idaho. Continuing renovations will add additional parking, picnicking, and pathways. A visitor center, gift shop, and museum now fill the old Big Falls Inn with new life.

Reprinted from U.S. Forest Service and Idaho State Parks and Recreation brochures

T Ashton State Fish Hatchery

1 mile south of Ashton. 652-3579. 1 mile south of Ashton, bear right onto the marked county road. Travel 1 mile west on this road to reach the hatchery.

The Ashton State Fish Hatchery dates back to 1920 and has been responsible for producing fish planted in the Upper Snake River Valley region. The hatchery serves as a specialty station that raises nine species of trout and salmon. Catchable size fish measuring eight to ten inches as well as fry and fingerling are managed throughout the year and released at the appropriate time. The hatchery is open for touring, but arrangements should be made ahead of time.

TV Ashton Reservoir

North of Ashton. Contact the Ashton Chamber of Commerce at 652-3987.

Ashton Reservoir lies on the Henry's Fork of the Snake River and spans 400 acres. Just as the Henry's Fork is renowned for its quality trout fishing, Ashton Reservoir is also a high-quality fishing area. The reservoir is stocked annually to ensure good fishing throughout the season. In addition, the reservoir provides recreation opportunities for water skiers and canoeists. Ashton Reservoir features picnicking and restroom facilities, as well as a public boat dock and ramp, all free of charge.

TV Horseshoe Lake

Ashton. Contact the Ashton Ranger District at 652-7442.

Tucked inside the Targhee-Caribou National Forest off of Cave Falls Road is Idaho's scenic Horseshoe Lake. From here, visitors have outstanding vistas of the Grand Teton Mountains and great fishing opportunities. The Idaho Fish and Game Department stocks Horseshoe Lake each spring as soon as the snow and ice melts. Anglers should note that power driven watercraft are not permitted on the lake, but canoes, rowboats, and rafts are always welcome. Visitors also have quick access to Yellowstone National Park via several trails that begin at the Horseshoe Lake Campground.

V Bear Gulch/Mesa Falls Cross-Country Ski Trails

7 miles northeast of Ashton on Mesa Falls Forest Hwy. 47. Contact the Idaho Department of Parks and Recreation at 334-4180.

Recommended for intermediate and advanced skiers only, the Bear Gulch/Mesa Falls trail system is nine miles long and is groomed only periodically when weather conditions permit. The trail begins near the area snowmobile trail and winds steeply up to the Lower and Upper Mesa Falls. Here, the trail diverges from the snowmobile track and follows the Bear Gulch rim back to the trailhead. The area is part of Idaho's Park N' Ski system, and permits are required. Permits may be obtained at the nearest Ranger Station and fees are as follows: $25 annual permit (good at all Idaho Park N' Ski areas), $7.50 3-day permit, and $2 day use permit.

V Fall River Ridge Cross-Country Ski Trails

10 miles east of Ashton on Cave Falls Rd. Contact the Idaho Department of Parks and Recreation at 334-4180.

Approximately seven miles of periodically groomed trails comprise the Fall River Ridge ski area. Rolling hills, meadows, and groves of lodgepole pines and aspen trees greet users along the various loop trails. These trails are best suited to beginner and intermediate Nordic skiers. The area is part of Idaho's Park N' Ski system, and permits are required. Permits may be obtained at the nearest Ranger Station and fees are as follows: $25 annual permit (good at all Idaho Park N' Ski areas), $7.50 3-day permit, and $2 day use permit.

V Falls River Ridge Cross-Country Ski Trails

10 miles east of Ashton on North Cave Falls Rd. Contact the Idaho Department of Parks and Recreation at 334-4180.

The Falls River Ridge cross-country ski trails wind between open and forested landscapes, and a variety of wildlife inhabits the area. The seven miles of trails are designed for beginner and intermediate skiers, and some of the trails are shared with snowmobilers. The area is part of Idaho's Park N' Ski system, and permits are required. Permits may be obtained at the nearest Ranger Station and fees are as follows: $25 annual permit (good at all Idaho Park N' Ski areas), $7.50 3-day permit, and $2 day use permit.

M Ashton Chamber of Commerce

64 N. 10, Ashton. 652-3987.

23 *Food, Lodging*

Island Park
Pop. 215

Island Park Village is said to have been named for the neighboring islands of timber located on the high sagebrush plains. Incorporated in the late 1940s as a Swiss colony, Island Park owes its founding to the Arangee Company. Spanning thirty-five miles along U.S. Hwy. 20, Island Park includes several lodges and inns that house the many recreational enthusiasts who travel to the area. Besides camping, hiking, and world-class fishing, 600 miles of groomed snowmobiling trails await visitors to the area's giant caldera landscape.

Macks Inn

William H. Mack founded this resort town in 1921, and a post office was established here in 1923. The town honors the long legacy of its founding father. Mack, nicknamed "Doc" immigrated from Germany to America at age 12 and worked with his uncle in two San Francisco bakeries. After learning the English language, Mack married and enrolled in medical school. With years of studying, Mack earned his optometry degree, and he moved his family to Rexburg to open an optometry store. Although Mack's business was highly successful, he soon realized that he was more passionate about the outdoors. He applied for and accepted a position as a regional game warden and was assigned to the Island Park area. While there, Mack and his family developed a small resort area that would eventually bear his name.

H Volcanic Calders
Milepost 368.9 on U.S. Hwy. 20

Some two million years ago, massive eruptions of hot rock boiled for 60 miles from this high rim through Yellowstone Park.

An exceptionally large crater remained when that lava surface collapsed. Another smaller caldera followed north of here about 1.3 million years ago. Yellowstone's geysers and hot springs continue to spout as remnants of those volcanic displays formed as underground rock gradually moved westward across a tremendous source of interior heat.

H Caldera Lookout
Milepost 376.3 on U.S. Hwy. 20

High on Island Park Caldera's west rim, a 72-foot-high Forest Service lookout tower affords an excellent view of this large volcanic feature.

No other steel tower has been preserved in this part of Idaho. When it was erected in 1936, lookouts were essential for fire detection in all of this region's forests. This one still is used in times of especially severe fire hazard, but planes now are responsible for regular fire patrol. Forest Service road 80120 ascends to the Bishop Mountain Lookout at an elevation of 7,810 feet.

H Harriman State Park
Milepost 378 on U.S. Hwy. 20

Started in 1902 as a large cattle ranch, Railroad Ranch soon became a summer retreat for wealthy Easterners and eventually Idaho's largest state park.

Railroad magnate and diplomat W. Averell Harriman and his brother Roland donated the ranch to Idaho in 1977, thus preserving the area's remarkable wildlife, and prompting development of a professionally managed state parks' system.

H Harriman Wildlife Refuge
Milepost 382 on U.S. Hwy. 20

Henry's Fork meanders through a 16,000-acre wildlife refuge that retains diverse habitats for many kinds of birds and animals.

Lodgepole pine forests and open meadows provide many opportunities to enjoy wildlife here, and fly fishing still is allowed in this region of scenic beauty. Moose, deer, and elk find plenty of food and shelter, while eagles, hawks, and owls thrive in open hunting grounds. Access is through Harriman State Park.

H Pierre J. DeSmet
Milepost 400.7 on U.S. Hwy. 20

Roman Catholic missionary services began in Idaho on Sunday, July 10, 1840, in Teton Valley, followed by a Mass held near here at Henry's Lake, July 23.

Pierre J. DeSmet, a Belgian Jesuit leader, accompanied a Pend d'Oreille-Flathead band on their way northwest to their homeland. Climbing a mountain here along streams "descending from dizzy heights, leaping from rock to rock with a deafening noise," he invoked divine thanks for his successful tour into Idaho and Montana.

H Sawtell's Ranch
Milepost 5.1 on State Hwy. 87

In 1868, Gilman Sawtell started a dude ranch and Henry's Lake fishery that did much to develop this natural resort area.

Sawtell did everything from supplying swans for New York's Central Park zoo to building a network of roads for tourist access to Yellowstone National Park. His commercial fishery served Montana mining markets. His pioneer Henrys Lake ranch was a major attraction here for a decade before rail service brought more settlers to this area.

T Island Park Village Golf Course
Hist County Rd. 66, Island Park. 558-7550.

Scenery surrounds golfers on this 9-hole, par 35 course that was established in 1970. Spanning 2,668 yards, the course is slightly hilly with lakes coming into play at least three times. The course is open daily from May 1 to October 15 with reasonable green fees under $20. During the winter, the course becomes a popular groomed snowmobiling area.

T Targhee Pass
U.S. Hwy. 20 near the Idaho/Montana border. Contact the Targhee National Forest at 624-3151.

Situated at 7,072 feet, Targhee Pass and the surrounding forest draws its name from legendary Bannock Indian Chief, Tahgee. Tahgee served as head chief over all the Bannock tribes and strove to maintain peace between whites and Native

GHOST TOWNS

Ora

Previously referred to as Sand Creek and Arcadia, the first post office of 1890 wanted to name the town Ola, after the first postmaster, Ola N. Kerr. Since there was already an Ola, Idaho, the name was changed.

Birch Creek
Near the Clark-Butte County line

Idaho's Clark County has never been known to contain vast mineral deposits, but when a copper boom hit the state during the 1880s, Birch Creek was born. Named after the numerous birch trees dotting the landscape, Birch Creek produced large quantities of copper for a few years. A post office was opened in the area in the late 1880s, but when the copper vein was exhausted, the post office closed and most miners moved in search of better prospects. Today, the few remaining individuals in the area are predominantly cattle and sheep ranchers.

Americans. In 1863, Tahgee met with the Utah governor and just four years later, met with Idaho's governor. Despite other tribe's conflicts with the white government during the 1860s, Tahgee kept his tribe at peace. A friend to both whites and Indians, Tahgee died in 1871.

Targhee Pass not only marks the stateline between Idaho and Montana but also reflects the region's early history. In peaceful times, the Shoshone Indians used the pass to cross over to the Musselshell and Yellowstone Rivers during annual buffalo hunts. But the pass was not always a place of peace. During the Nez Perce War of 1877, Chief Joseph led his tribe across the pass in retreat from the U.S. Army. Although Lieutenant George Bacon was supposed to guard the area, he abandoned his post assuming that the tribe had already crossed and made it safely to Jackson Hole. He was wrong at the time, however. In Bacon's absence, the tribe escaped, once again eluding and infuriating General Oliver Howard.

T Mount Sawtelle
In Island Park, merge off U.S. Hwy. 20 onto the gravel Sawtell Peak Rd. The road is located approximately 13 miles southeast of Yellowstone National Park's west entrance.

The 9,902-foot summit of Mount Sawtelle provides visitors with an incredible vista of Idaho, Montana, Wyoming, and Yellowstone National Park and is easily accessible by car during the summer. Surrounded by knee-high wildflowers, the flat plateau on top of Mount Sawtelle captures views of Henry's Lake, Island Park Reservoir, and formidable mountain ranges rising in all directions. Mount Sawtelle is named after Gilman Sawtell who arrived in the area in 1868. He established a ranch and became Island Park's first resident but later moved when the mosquitos and horseflies ran his horse ranching business into the ground .

Island Park	Jan	Feb	March	April	May	June	July	Aug	Sep	Oct	Nov	Dec	Annual
Average Max. Temperature (F)	30.4	32.5	42.0	54.1	63.7	73.8	83.7	82.7	72.1	58.9	41.3	31.3	55.5
Average Min. Temperature (F)	8.9	10.2	19.2	26.5	34.2	39.8	44.7	44.0	36.0	26.6	18.4	9.1	26.5
Average Total Precipitation (in.)	1.11	1.14	1.34	1.28	2.29	1.35	1.25	1.28	1.25	1.24	1.15	1.06	15.76
Average Total Snowfall (in.)	11.1	8.6	7.6	3.1	0.5	0.1	0.0	0.0	0.0	1.1	5.8	10.4	48.2
Average Snow Depth (in.)	9	9	4	0	0	0	0	0	0	0	1	5	2

HELPFUL HINTS FOR SAFELY VIEWING AND PHOTOGRAPHING WILDLIFE IN THE YELLOWSTONE REGION

A variety of wildlife abundantly populates the Montana, Wyoming, and Idaho region surrounding Yellowstone National Park. Although these animals are intriguing and invite curiosity, all wildlife needs its space just like human beings. To safely and responsibly enjoy wildlife near the road or in the backcountry, follow these helpful hints.

What Is A Safe Observing Distance?
Although animals in and around Yellowstone National Park may appear or act tame, they are not. Humans should remain at least 100 yards away from wildlife at all times, and longer distances are recommended for viewing bears and bison. Humans put wildlife in jeopardy when safe observation distances are not maintained. In situations like this, animals risk losing their footing on cliffs, being separated from their offspring, being hit by traffic, and abandoning food sources – all of which greatly reduce these animals' chances of survival in their natural environment.

Observation Guidelines – On the Road and In the Backcountry
Remember the following guidelines the next time you're viewing wildlife:
- You are responsible for your own safety!
- Never follow, surround, or surprise a wild animal as it may feel threatened and charge. If an animal approaches you, back away slowly to provide it with more space.
- Do not make loud noises in an attempt to gain the attention of a wild animal. Instead, quietly view the animal from established observation areas.
- Avoid direct eye contact with bears as they view this as a direct challenge.
- Safely view wildlife with binoculars, spotting scopes, and telephoto lenses.
- While photographing animals, use an appro-

priate lens and always maintain your distance. Never attempt to coax an animal to a different location, and never ask anyone to pose with a wild animal no matter how tame it appears. Serious injuries can result from such activities!
- If you encounter a wild animal while hiking, back away slowly. Remain alert at all times to your surroundings and any potential dangers, and always carry bear spray in the Yellowstone region. If you encounter an aggressive mountain lion, be prepared to fight back.
- If you encounter a wild animal while driving, stop and remain in the car and observe/photograph wildlife from inside. Do not drive towards the animal as large animals have been known to seriously damage vehicles when they feel threatened. Keep children inside and educate them on the dangers that wildlife can pose when proper safety techniques are not followed. Also, watch for other animals in the area.
- Never lure animals to your car with food. This not only poses a threat to you, but also conditions the animal to approach humans and the road area. As the saying goes, "A fed bear is a dead bear." This statement, however, applies to all wildlife.
- Never stop in the middle of the road to observe or photograph wildlife. Instead, pull off into the shoulder or stop in an established parking area.

Be prepared for the wildlife that you may encounter during your visit to the Yellowstone region. For more information, contact the Center for Wildlife Information at www.bebearaware.org or the National Park Service.

An eighteen by twenty-three mile diameter crater formed. The crater later collapsed 1,200 feet and formed the caldera. Today, the caldera's edge is bounded on one side by Upper and Lower Mesa Falls and is covered with pine trees and meadows.

TV Big Springs & Johnny Sack Cabin
From Mack's Inn or Island Park Village, exit off U.S. Hwy. 20, and follow Forest Rd. (FR) 059 (Big Springs Loop Rd.) to the springs. 588-7755.

Dumping over 120 million gallons of water per day into the Henry's Fork of the Snake River, Big Springs serves as the headwaters for the Henry's Fork and is one of America's forty largest natural springs. Consistently clear and holding a steady temperature of 52 degrees, Big Springs provides the perfect spawning ground for a variety of fish. Huge rainbow, cutthroat, and brook trout populate the waters, as well as coho and kokanee salmon and mountain whitefish. Blue herons, muskrat, geese, and moose help keep the fish company. Although many fishermen are tempted to sample these clear blue waters, fishing is strictly prohibited.

Amid the wildlife and scenery is a one-mile interpretive trail leading to the historic Johnny Sack cabin. Built by a German immigrant in the 1930s, the cabin reflects the talents and creativity of Johnny Sack who developed a nearby waterwheel to provide his cabin with water and electricity.

One of the most popular attractions in the Big Springs area is the Big Springs National Recreation Water Trail. Located approximately 0.75 miles from the springs, this water trail is populated with recreationists during the summer time. The two to four hour float trip provides rafters and canoeists with incredible forest scenes, glimpses of wildlife, and mountain vistas.

TV Island Park Reservoir
558-7755.

Surrounded by lodgepole pine trees in the Targhee National Forest, the 8,400-acre Island Park Reservoir was formed when the Island Park Dam plugged the Henry's Fork of the Snake River in 1938. Today, the large reservoir is home to a variety of recreational pursuits. Fishermen love the trout and salmon infested waters year-round, and boating, water skiing, and camping are also popular pastimes. Free boat ramps and docks can be found at Island Park, Lakeside Lodge, McCrea Bridge Campground, Mill Creek, West End, and Buttermilk Campground. Visitors can also opt to drive across the dam for panoramic views of Box Canyon and the Centennial Mountains.

TV Harriman State Park
3489 E. Hwy. 20, Island Park. 558-7368. Located 18 miles north of Ashton near Island Park on U.S. Hwy. 20/191.

Harriman State Park is located inside a wildlife reserve providing sanctuary to a plethora of birds and mammals found within the greater

T Mack's Inn Dinner Theater
Mack's Inn. 558-7871.

Located in the heart of Island Park's 35-mile "main street," the Mack's Inn Dinner Theater provides a touch of culture amid the endless area recreational opportunities. The theater performers present live music and melodramas daily from Memorial Day to Labor Day, and reservations are highly recommended.

T Henry's Lake Fish Hatchery
Island Park. 558-7202. Take State Hwy. 87 at its junction with U.S. Hwy. 20 and proceed 3.5 miles northwest. The hatchery is located on the road's left side.

The Henry's Lake Hatchery began as a privately owned facility prior to Idaho State acquiring the hatchery. Operated for more than 75 years by the state, the facility is the oldest continuously running hatchery in the state. The facility is strictly an egg-taking station featuring a fish ladder and spawn house. Every March and April, fish return to the spawning ladder, and the subsequent eggs are then collected and raised. Upon collection, the eggs are sent to the Mackay Fish Hatchery where fish are bred and stocked back in the Henry's Lake

region. The hatchery is open March through October, and tours are provided during spawning season. In addition, a small public fishing area is available Memorial Day weekend through September, and an on-site interpretive center is planned.

T Henry's Flats Conservation Area
Island Park. Contact The Nature Conservancy at 788-2203. Located on U.S. Hwy. 20 in Island Park across from Aspen Ridge.

Managed by the Idaho Nature Conservancy, the Henry's Flats Conservation Area coexists along with the conservancy's working cattle ranch, Flat Ranch. The free site offers a visitor's center and observation area and is open daily from 9 AM to 5 PM Memorial Day through Labor Day.

T Island Park Caldera
Island Park

Geologists identified Island Park's Caldera in 1939, and it is now considered the world's largest caldera. The caldera formed nearly two million years ago when a huge volcano erupted and blew rhyolite (acid rock) over a 6,000-square-mile surface.

Yellowstone ecosystem. The area originated in 1902 as the private "Railroad Ranch" for the Harrimans of the Union Pacific Railroad and their associates, the Guggenheims. After meticulously maintaining the ranch for 75 years, the Harriman family donated the property to Idaho State in 1977 under the agreement that the acreage would be used to protect wildlife. Complying with the Harrimans' wishes, Idaho State opened Harriman State Park in 1982 at the center of a 16,000-acre wildlife refuge. Today, the region is known for harboring a large population of trumpeter swans, sandhill cranes, muskrat, elk, and beaver.

In addition to protecting wildlife, Harriman State Park provides numerous recreational opportunities and spectacular views of the Grand Teton Mountains. During the summer, twenty-one miles of hiking, horseback riding, and mountain biking trails await visitors in the wildflower dotted sage meadows. Anglers also frequent the area in search of trophy trout as the Henry's Fork of the Snake River cuts through nine miles of the park. On summer weekends, visitors can opt to take a guided tour of twenty-seven well-preserved buildings dating back to Railroad Ranch's early days, while the winter season ushers in cross-country skiing along groomed trails. No camping is allowed within the park, but cabin lodging for group retreats is available. A $4 motorized vehicle entrance fee is required to enter the park.

TV Henry's Lake State Park
3917 E. 5100 N., Island Park. 558-7532 or 652-7442. Located 15 miles west of Yellowstone National Park's west gate off U.S. Hwy. 20/191.

Established in 1965 and encompassing 586 acres in the Caribou-Targhee National Forest, Henry's Lake State Park is named after Major Andrew Henry, the first European-American to explore the beauty of the Island Park area and Henry's Fork of the Snake River. Since Henry's stop here in 1810, the area has been visited by a range of historical figures. Famous mountain man, Jim Bridger, stayed here along with other trappers and Flathead Indians in 1835, and the Nez Perce Indians stopped briefly in the area during their evasion from General O.O. Howard in the 1877 Nez Perce War. Today, the area continues to attract a host of visitors throughout the year, and an annual Fort Henry Mountain Man Rendezvous honors the area's traditional past.

The park's most noted feature is Henry's Lake cradled within a high mountain bowl along the Continental Divide at an elevation of 6,470 feet. Lush meadows and eight towering 10,000-foot Sawtooth Mountain peaks surround the lake. Found within the lake and nearby streams are trophy rainbow and cutthroat trout, as well as mountain whitefish. A modern fish cleaning station located near the lake's boat ramp awaits anglers and their catch of the day. Besides great fishing opportunities, Henry's Lake State Park also offers swimming in designated areas, a 3-mile self-guided interpretive trail, camping areas, boating, and picnicking. The park is open from the Thursday prior to

Memorial Day through October 31 depending on the weather. Access to the park requires a $4 motorized vehicle entrance fee.

TV The Continental Divide in Idaho
Idaho/Montana Border. Contact the Continental Divide Trail Alliance at (888) 909-CDTA.

Excluding Antarctica, every continent in the world features a Continental Divide. In North America, this natural parting follows the backbone of the Rocky Mountains from Mexico to Alberta, Canada. This line divides the flow of water between the Pacific and Atlantic Oceans. All rain/snow melt and rivers to the east of the divide drain into the Atlantic, while water on the divide's western ridge flows to the Pacific.

After traveling through Wyoming, the Continental Divide arrives on the Idaho/Montana border, traveling near Henry's Lake State Park and Dubois. Idaho's Centennial and Beaverhead Mountains form the backdrop for the Continental Divide as it passes through the state, and the area is characterized with diverse conifer forests of lodgepole pines, Douglas fir, subalpine fir, and Engelmann spruce.

This area of Idaho is also home to a portion of the 3,100-mile Continental Divide National Scenic Trail. Established by Congress in 1978, the trail winds through some of North America's most scenic backcountry while staying within five miles of the divide at all times. Interested users should contact the Continental Divide Trail Alliance for specific information and travel considerations.

TVF Meadow Vue Ranch
3636 Red Rock Rd., Henry's Lake at Island Park. 558-7411. www.meadowvueranch.com

Experience the west at the working Meadow Vue Ranch. Overlooking Henry's Lake and just minutes from Yellowstone Park, the secluded ranch offers numerous summer recreational activities beginning Memorial Day weekend. View wildlife, and take a guided scenic trail ride along the Continental Divide. Want a unique dinner experience? Make reservations for the Wednesday, Friday, and Saturday night live entertainment found at the Old West Bar-b-Que and Rodeo from mid-June to mid-August. For boys and girls ages nine through eighteen, the summer program provides the opportunity to live on a working ranch while learning rodeo skills, self-confidence, and personal responsibility under the supervision of veteran ranch workers. No matter what you're looking for, Meadow Vue Ranch provides an ideal venue for family vacations, reunions, company parties, and outdoor enthusiasts.

V Howard Springs
U.S. Hwy. 20 near the Idaho/Montana border and Targhee Pass. Contact the Targhee National Forest at 624-3151.

Located on the east side of the highway, Howard Springs provides a pretty day-use picnic stop amidst the scenery of Targhee National Forest. The site remembers the legacy of General Oliver

Howard who passed through the area in 1877 on his chase of the elusive Nez Perce Indians.

V Brimstone/Buffalo River Cross-Country Ski Trails
Trailhead and parking area are located at the Island Park Ranger Station on U.S. Hwy. 20. Contact the Idaho Department of Parks and Recreation at 334-4180.

Spanning eleven miles, the Brimstone/Buffalo River trails are regularly groomed and offer a variety of terrain to suit cross-country skiers of all abilities. From gentle grades to downhill slopes through tree groves, each trail offers scenic views of the Island Park area. Highlights include vistas of Island Park Reservoir, Box Canyon, and the Buffalo River. The trails are groomed on a weekly basis (except Thurmon Ridge), and frequent sightings of moose are common. Trails in the Brimstone/Buffalo River area include Buffalo River Interpretive Ski Trail, Moose Loop, Eagle Trail, Thurmon Ridge, Boggy Springs Loop, Antelope Park Loop, and the Brimstone Connector Trail. The area is part of Idaho's Park N' Ski system, and permits are required. Permits may be obtained at the Ranger Station and fees are as follows: $25 annual permit (good at all Idaho Park N' Ski areas), $7.50 3-day permit, and $2 day use permit.

V Buffalo River
Mack's Inn. Contact the Idaho Department of Parks and Recreation at 334-4180. From Mack's Inn, proceed on the Big Springs Loop and continue on Forest Rds 082, 292, and 1219.

The Buffalo River is just one of many tributaries in the Island Park area that eventually flows into the Henry's Fork of the Snake River. Spring fed and maintaining a consistent temperature of fifty-two degrees, the Buffalo River provides perfect spawning grounds for rainbow trout. Besides angling opportunities, the river provides an easy float trip for recreationists of all skill levels.

V Henrys Fork of the Snake River and Major Tributaries
Before it joins with the acclaimed South Fork of the Snake River, the Henrys Fork winds through southeastern Idaho and provides a critical rainbow trout habitat and fishery. The drainage supports fluctuating populations of wild rainbow, cutthroat, and brown trout, and hatchery fish are added to some river sections where stocking is permitted.

The Henrys Fork supports several important and major tributaries. Island Park Reservoir features rainbow trout and kokanee salmon, and Henry's Lake affords native cutthroat. While the Warm River is characterized as an ideal trout-spawning region, Fall River serves as the largest tributary and contains a substantial wild rainbow trout fishery. Other tributaries in the Henrys Fork drainage include the Teton River and Buffalo River.

Nearby, the thirty-five acre Roberts Gravel Pond produces pumpkinseed, channel catfish, yellow perch, and rainbow and bullhead trout.

FL The Pines at Historic Phillips Lodge & The Lodgepole Grill
3907 Phillips Loop Rd., Island Park. 558-0192 or 888-455-9384. www.pinesislandpark.com

Nestled in the shadow of the Rocky Mountains, The Pines at Island Park offers Idaho's finest luxury cabin resort lodging in the solitude of the Targhee National Forest. Each 1,500+ square foot cabin features log furnishings and four luxurious queen size beds in two main level private sleeping areas and a semi-private loft. While here, grab a delicious bite to eat at The Lodgepole Grill, and then cozy

The Pines at Historic Phillips Lodge & The Lodgepole Grill

up to your cabin's fireplace or enjoy a soak in the hot tub. Cabin amenities include two baths, full kitchen, washer/dryer, satellite TV, fine linens, private deck, hot tub, and grill. For more privacy, reserve the master suite loft at an additional charge. Accommodating up to eight people, the cabins at The Pines leave little left to decide except where to play.

M Island Park Chamber of Commerce
3416 N. Hwy. 20, Island Park. 558-7755.
www.islandparkchamber.org;
ipchamber@yahoo.com

SCENIC DRIVES

Fort Henry Historic Byway

See the first white settlement marked by the Fort Henry Monument, from which this byway gets its name. A new monument now replaces the old one at the original site. The old monument relocated in an adjoining field can be viewed from the original site. This route trails along BLM land, desert and mountain ranges where herds of deer and elk, as well as Sharp Tail and Sage Grouse can be seen as you journey along the Red Road.

This byway crosses camas Creek, connects to County Road A-2 in Clark County at the "Y." Sand Hill Cranes are early spring visitors in the Camas Meadows. Luscious mountain streams are enticing for fisherman, hikers, bikers and campers. Beautiful fields of wildflowers include seasonal Camas which can be seen throughout the Caribou-Targhee National Forest and flat lands.

The heritage of Clark and Fremont Counties is very unique and full of early history of mountain men, Indians, including Camas Meadows Battle Grounds, Nez Perce Trails, miners, stagecoach liners and early day ranching.

This scenic byway begins at North Rexburg U.S. 20 Exit, onto Salem Highway, to St. Anthony Sand Dunes on Red Road and on to A-2 Road Junction. Continue on A-2 north, then east to Island Park and U.S. 20. This is a two-lane road with no mountain passes. North Rexburg exit to A-2 in Clark County to Kilgore Store exit is paved. The only gravel road includes eleven miles from Kilgore to the Fremont County line, and is then paved to U.S. 20. The byway can be seen from mid-April to mid-November. In winter, roads become snowmobile trails. Travelers should allow at least 2 hours for this 81-mile trip.

Reprinted from Idaho Department of Transportation rochure

Lost Gold Trails Loop

The Lost Gold Trails Loop ventures off the Fort Henry Historic Byway at the "Y" Junction onto County Road A-2. The loop then travels southwest along the desert-lava rolling hill terrain where cattle and wild game peacefully share spring and fall months grazing. Crossing the railroad, which originated the town of "Dry Creek," now Dubois, and

traveling west through town over I-15 overpass on Idaho 22, you connect with Old Highway 91. Turn north on Old Highway 91 and head to Spencer, passing near the U.S. Sheep Experiment Station. This early-day Gold Trail closely follows Beaver Creek towards the Montana gold mines. At Spencer the Gold Trail of yesterday becomes the Opal Trails of today and passes several high grade Opal Shops within the original Wood Live Stock town site. Leaving Spencer, the trail heads east to Idmon. This early day Nez Perce Trail has spurs off of its main roadway to private opal mines, Caribou-Targhee Forest fishing and primitive camping areas, and an old cemetery, connecting again to the Fort Henry Historic Byway at the old Idmon town site.

This is a two-lane road with no mountain passes. "Y" on A-2 to Dubois and Old Highway 91 Dubois to Spencer is paved. Spencer/Idmon is 3 miles paved and 11 miles of gravel. The road from Dubois to Spencer is open year round. Highway A-2 "Y" to Dubois and Spencer/Idmon road are closed through winter. Closed roads in winter become snowmobile trails. Travelers should allow at least 1.5 hours for this 47.8-mile trip.

Reprinted from Idaho Department of Transportation brochure

Mesa Falls Scenic Byway

The Mesa Falls Scenic Byway begins where the Teton Scenic Byway reaches it northern end in Ashton, at the junction of U.S. 20 and Idaho 47. From there, the route travels through the town of Warm River toward its main attractions: the Upper and Lower Mesa Falls.

The Mesa Falls are the only major falls in Idaho not used for irrigation or hydroelectric projects, and as such maintain a look and feel of nature undisturbed. At 110 feet and 85 feet, respectively, the Upper and Lower Mesa falls offer equally spectacular views in a beautiful forest setting. Both falls can be viewed in full, with the area surrounding the upper waterfall enhanced with paths and viewing areas that make it easily accessible to all. Though only about an hour's driving time, the Mesa Falls Scenic Byway is often a half-day's journey, with travelers mesmerized by the spectacular display in the midst of a truly back-country setting. In addition, the historic Mesa Falls Lodge has been restored to its original splendor and is now open seasonally for visitor information.

This scenic byway begins at the southern end of Idaho 47 in Ashton, northeast 12.4 miles to the old Bear Gulch Ski Area site, then northwest along Forest Service Route 294 to the northern end at U.S. 20. Idaho 47 is a two-lane road. Forest Service Route 294 is closed in winter and becomes a Forest Service snowmobile route. If you have a snowmobile or cross-country skis, winter is the time to see the byway; if you don't, there is no access. Spring through fall is great by car. Travelers should allow at least 1 hour for the 28.7-mile trip.

Reprinted from Idaho Department of Transportation brochure

Teton Scenic Byway

The jagged teeth of the Teton Mountain Range are actually in Wyoming, but Idahoans prefer "the quiet side" on the western slopes, along the Teton Scenic Byway.

At nearly 10 million years young, the Tetons are the newest mountains in the Rockies. In fact, they continue to grow today at the snail-like pace of about an inch every hundred years. In fact, the

largest peak on the range, Grand Teton, now stands at 13,772 feet.

Beginning at Swan Valley, this byway travels east on Idaho 31 through beautiful Pine Creek Pass to the town of Victor, and then north on Idaho 33 along the western side of the Teton Range. The mountains sharply contrast with the rolling agricultural fields to the north and west. In the towns of the Teton Valley, Victor, Driggs, and Tetonia, travelers can enjoy small town hospitality, internationally famous resorts and festival events held throughout the year.

North of Tetonia, the byway turns west on Idaho 32, offering glimpses of the Henry's Fork and Teton River Valleys toward the town of Ashton, where the Mesa Falls Scenic Byway begins.

Pine Creek Pass is a two-lane roadway with no passing lanes. It has 6-percent grades, some 35-mph curves, and often has a snow floor in winter. Idaho 33 is a two-lane roadway with ample passing opportunities. The byway can be seen year-round, but fall foliage is spectacular as are the wildflowers of late spring. Travelers should allow at least 2.5 hours for this 68.9-mile trip.

Reprinted from Idaho Department of Transportation brochure

Big Hole Mountains Tour

Winding north 21 miles from Swan Valley to Victor, State Highway 31 takes individuals on a scenic drive through the Big Hole Mountains and Targhee National Forest. The route ascends past aspen and fir trees to Pine Creek Pass at an elevation of 6,764 feet. From there, meadows and forests are interspersed as drivers descend into the Teton Basin and are greeted with views of the Grand Teton Mountains.

HIKES

For information on additional area trails, please contact the Forest Service Ranger Districts listed at the back of this section.

Big Hole, Snake River, and Caribou Mountains Area

Black Canyon to Big Burns
Distance: 10.5 mile near loop
Climb: moderate
Difficulty: moderate
Usage: moderate
Location: Traveling east on U.S. Highway 26 from Idaho Falls, proceed 11 miles past the junction with State Highway 43 and bear left (north) onto the Kelly Canyon Recreation Area Road. Proceed on this road 2 miles to a Y intersection and turn right on County Road 100 North. After crossing the South Fork of the Snake River, bear right on Heise Road and continue 2 miles to another fork in the road. Follow the right gravel road (which turns into Forest Road 206) 16.1 miles to the Black Canyon Trailhead.

This trail winds through rugged mountains and over ten creek crossings amidst beautiful forests comprised of chokecherry and wild rose bushes, as well as Douglas fir, spruce, juniper, cottonwood, aspen, and oak trees. Wildlife is abundant in the area as well, and it is not unusual to see moose, elk, bighorn sheep, and bald eagles. Beginning on a trail that is open to ATVs, mountain bikes, horses, and hikers, make several creek crossings until reaching the 2.2-mile mark where the trail begins climbing up a forested canyon. At the 4-mile mark, hikers will reach the Black Canyon/Little Burns Divide and should proceed left down the ridge 1 mile to a trail junction. Proceed left down the scenic Little Burns Canyon and cross Big Burns Creek to reach the Big Burns Trailhead 3 miles from the convergence of Big Burns and Little Burns Creeks. Walk along the Forest Road to reach the parking area at Black Canyon Trailhead. Best months for hiking are late June through September.

Big Elk Creek
Distance: 13 miles roundtrip
Climb: gentle
Difficulty: easy
Usage: heavy
Location: Drive southeast of Idaho Falls on U.S. Highway 26 through Swan Valley. 14 miles south of Swan Valley, exit onto a marked road leading to Big Elk Creek and proceed 2.5 miles to the trailhead.

Scenery abounds on this trail as hikers wander in and out of the Snake River Range's patchy forests past numerous avalanche chutes. Walking through the wide Big Elk Creek Canyon, hikers will pass side routes leading to Dry Canyon at the 2.5-mile mark and Hells Hole Canyon at 3.4 miles. At this point, the trail narrows through the limestone cliffs and a waterfall can be found as hikers cross over into Wyoming at the 4.5-mile mark. Crossing over Big Elk Creek, hikers reach the turnaround destination at 6.5 miles near this creek's union with the Siddoway Fork of Big Elk Creek. Best months for hiking are late July through September.

Optional Hikes: Hikers can wander up the Siddoway Fork Canyon on Trail 167, which provides access to both the Austin Canyon meadows (Trail 105) as well as to the mountain ridge located between Swan Valley, Idaho and Jackson, Wyoming.

A second option is to proceed past the convergence of Big Elk Creek and the Siddoway Fork and locate Trail 125. This trail climbs up into Dry Canyon and over to the scenic Garden Canyon.

Indian Creek Loop
Distance: 18 mile near loop
Climb: steep
Difficulty: difficult
Usage: moderate
Location: On U.S. Highway 26, drive 73 miles southeast of Idaho Falls through Swan Valley beside Palisades Reservoir. Nearing Indian Creek, drop down to a canyon mouth and merge east onto a gravel road. Proceed 2 miles to a fork in the road and bear left on Forest Road (FR) 282 leading to Trail 122 at the undeveloped North Fork Indian Creek Trailhead.

Rugged canyon walls lined with waterfalls, wildflower meadows, alpine lakes, and impressive unnamed peaks rising sharply against the sky are just some of the many sights awaiting hikers on this trail situated near the Idaho/Wyoming state border. Starting out on an ATV trail, proceed across North Indian Creek and ignore all faint trails leaving to the sides of Trail 122. After hiking 7.2 miles to the North Indian Creek Basin, locate a faint trail leaving to the right marked "Big Basin 1.5; Lake Basin 2.5; So Fk. Indian Cr. 3.5." Now on Trail 099, hikers will ascend steeply to the 9,500-foot North Indian Pass located at the trek's 9.4-mile mark. Continuing over the pass and down to a pond, stay on Trail 099 and climb to Lake Basin. Shortly after reaching Lake Basin, hikers will find a trail junction near South Indian Creek's head. Proceed down into South Indian Creek on Trail 045 past Cabin Creek, Deadhorse Canyon, and Oat Canyon. From Oat Canyon, the trail winds gently downhill 2.5 miles to the South Fork Indian Creek Trailhead where hikers should walk along the road back to the North Fork Trailhead's parking area. Best months for hiking are August to early September.

Little Elk Creek
Distance: 8 miles roundtrip
Climb: steep
Difficulty: difficult
Usage: moderate
Location: On U.S. Highway 26, drive southeast of Idaho Falls through Swan Valley to the Palisades Dam. Continue 2.5 miles past the dam and bear left (east) onto Little Elk Creek Road. Follow this road approximately 1 mile to the trailhead and locate the trail leaving to the right.

This trail climbs through the highest portion of the Snake River Mountains, offering hikers incredible views of Mount Baird, Palisades Peak, and Little Palisades Peak, as well as several other unnamed peaks rising more than 9,000 feet. Although the first mile of the trek gently meanders through a forest, hikers should expect the trail to become significantly steeper. At the 1-mile mark, hikers pass Conglomerate Canyon and begin winding up another canyon through scenic cliffs. After making several switchbacks, hikers finally reach a high saddle at 9,200 feet at the 4-mile mark where panoramic views of the surrounding area are found. Best months for hiking are mid-July to mid-September.

Optional Hikes: From the high saddle, hikers can take a cross-country hike east across the basins below and then climb to a narrow ridgeline. This ridge provides hikers with access to Mount Baird's summit.

Palisades Creek
Distance: 13 miles roundtrip
Climb: gentle
Difficulty: easy
Usage: heavy
Location: On U.S. Highway 26, drive 52 miles east from Idaho Falls through Swan Valley and Irwin. At the small town of Palisades, bear left onto the gravel Forest Road (FR) 255 (Palisades Creek Road). Proceed 1.8 miles to Palisades Campground and park on the road's left side just before the Palisades Creek bridge crossing. Locate the Palisades Creek Trail 084 at the campground's eastern end.

A forest canopy shades hikers as they wander through the rugged walls of Palisades Canyon up to Lower and Upper Palisades Lakes. Following Palisades Creek, hikers will arrive at Lower Palisades Lake in 4 miles. The area has a few good camping spots and is known to harbor several moose. To reach Upper Palisades Lake, continue on Trail 084 0.6 miles past Chicken Springs Canyon. From here, cross over Palisades Creek and continue up Waterfalls Canyon Trail to locate Upper Palisades Lake at the 6.5-mile mark. This fertile lake is known for its dense population of cutthroat trout. Best months for hiking are early June to mid-October.

Optional Hikes: Bypass the trail leading to Upper Palisades Lake and continue up Palisades Creek Trail 084. This hike is difficult as the trail is faint in most places and it fords Palisades Creek twenty-two times. The third and final option is to proceed up Chicken Springs Canyon at the trip's 5.4-mile mark. Hikers will reach the canyon springs 0.75 miles from the trail junction. While this canyon is very scenic, it is also very steep.

Rainey Creek
Distance: 13 mile loop
Climb: moderate
Difficulty: moderate
Usage: moderate
Location: On U.S. Highway 26, drive 1 mile south from the town of Swan Valley, bearing east (left) onto a county road directly before the Church of Jesus Christ

of Latter Day Saints. Proceed 5 miles to the well-developed trailhead.

The trail leading through Rainey Creek Canyon is scenic and offers a wide variety of landscapes. From dense forests of conifers, aspens, and berry bushes to rockslides, overhanging cliffs, and creek crossings, this trail offers something for every hiker. Beginning on an abandoned road, ascend up the north slope of Rainey Creek canyon and ford Rainey Creek. At the 2.25-mile mark, proceed on South Fork Rainey Creek Trail through a rocky canyon past Dry Elk Canyon. Upon reaching a trail fork, proceed left and climb up and over a summit down to the North Fork of Rainey Creek Trailhead. At this 8-mile mark, locate the North Fork trail leaving at the trailhead's downstream end. The trail winds through a lush canyon bottom and past a scenic rockslide area before winding back to the first trailhead. Best months for hiking are mid-July through September.

Trail Creek
Distance: 10 miles roundtrip
Climb: gentle
Difficulty: moderate
Usage: moderate
Location: Follow State Highway 34 to its end near Freedom, Wyoming, and then follow the Stateline Road north 2 miles to Jackknife Road. At the 4-way stop, bear left and head into the Caribou National Forest. Proceed on this road to the undeveloped Trail Creek Trailhead.

Wildlife is abundant on this trail that winds near Trail Creek up to the 7,090-foot Trail Creek and Taylor Creek Divide. From this ridge, hikers have vistas of Bald Mountain as well as the scenic Taylor Creek Canyon. Following the trail from its start above Jackknife Creek, hike to a trail fork at the 0.8-mile mark. Proceed along the right fork up Trail Creek as it winds through meadows and a patchy forest. Throughout the hike, Trail Creek Trail fades in and out with game trails becoming the most obvious routes. Hikers should remember to always keep right of Trail Creek in such instances. At the 3-mile mark, the main trail fades, but hikers should ignore the game trail and continue right up the canyon. As hikers near their destination, an unnamed fork appears in the trail. Taking the trail's left fork, stay to the creek's right and follow the metal signs attached to trees signaling the correct route to the pass. Best months for hiking are mid-June to mid-October.

Waterfall Canyon/Palisades Lakes
Distance: 24 miles roundtrip
Climb: moderate
Difficulty: moderate
Usage: heavy
Location: On U.S. Highway 26, drive 52 miles east from Idaho Falls through Swan Valley and Irwin. At the small town of Palisades, bear left onto the gravel Forest Road (FR) 255 (Palisades Creek Road). Proceed 1.8 miles to Palisades Campground and park on the road's left side just before the Palisades Creek bridge crossing. Locate the Palisades Creek Trail 084 at the campground's eastern end.

Hikers will pass two alpine lakes on this scenic trail that winds near the Snake River Range's highest peaks through meadows and canyons lined with waterfalls and wildflowers. From the trailhead, proceed through a forested canyon bottom past Lower Palisades Lake and Chicken Springs Canyon to a trail junction at the 6-mile mark. Crossing over Palisades Creek, merge onto Waterfall Canyon Trail and hike to the 7.5-mile mark at the upper end of Upper Palisades Lake. 0.25 miles above this inlet, keep right at the trail junction and cross the creek. At the next trail junction near the creek, stay right again and begin ascending up the glacier-carved Waterfall Canyon. At the 9.8-mile mark, hikers will reach the scenic Waterfall Meadow where a 920-foot cataract tumbles down the canyon's east wall. Early in the season, this meadow is lined with waterfalls. From the meadow, make a creek crossing and proceed right up a cirque, past a gorge, and into a small basin where the trail forks. Bear right at this fork and follow the trail to a large basin. Here, hikes should return 12 miles back to the trailhead on the same route or follow one of the optional hikes detailed below. Best months for hiking are July and August with the best waterfall views available in early July.

Optional Hikes: From the trek's trail junction at the 12-mile mark, hikers can make an optional loop hike back to Upper Palisades Lake. Proceeding east along Waterfall Canyon's ridge, climb over Peak 9,630 and follow the scenic Dry Canyon Trail back to the lake.

Another loop takes hikers back to Lower Palisades Lake. At the trail junction, proceed on the Sheep Creek-Lake Canyon Trail to a high divide where grand views of Wyoming's Teton Mountains can be found. At the divide, drop northwest down onto the Lake Canyon Trail. This scenic trail is faint in places as it passes through meadows and forests, but hikers will likely be rewarded in sighting several mountain goats roaming the canyon's cliffs.

Driggs/Victor Area
South Darby Canyon Trail
Distance: 5.4 miles roundtrip
Climb: moderate
Difficulty: moderate
Usage: moderate
Location: Travel 3 miles south from Driggs on State Highway 33 and bear east on Forest Road (FR) 012 (Darby Canyon Road). Follow this road 8 miles to the trailhead for South Darby Trail 033.

Meandering along the South Fork of Darby Creek into Wyoming's Jedediah Smith Wilderness Area, this trail offers a vast array of beautiful scenery. Hiking on the west slope of the Teton Mountains, hikers will walk through forests and wildflower meadows and pass tumbling waterfalls. At the 2.7-mile mark, hikers will reach their destination at the 10,966-foot Mount Bannon and its Wind and Ice Cave. Best months for hiking are July and August.

Alaska Basin
Distance: 15.4 miles roundtrip
Climb: moderate
Difficulty: moderate
Usage: heavy
Location: From Driggs, travel east to Alta, Wyoming and locate the road leading to the ski resort. Taking the right fork, proceed up Teton Canyon to locate the trailhead for Trail 027.

Hikers will climb up into the wild and scenic Teton Mountains, surrounded often times by 10,000- to 12,000-foot peaks. At the 7.7-mile mark, Trail 027 levels out at the alpine Alaska Basin. The basin is home to several scenic alpine lakes. Best months for hiking are July and August.

Moose Creek
Climb: moderate
Difficulty: moderate
Usage: moderate
Location: From Victor, travel southeast on State Highway 33. Immediately before reaching the Mike Harris Campground, exit east onto Forest Road (FR)

276. *Locate the trailhead for Moose Creek Trail 038 in 1.5 miles.*

A waterfall and several alpine lakes are this trek's highlights as the trail wanders next to Moose Creek up into Wyoming's Teton Mountains. Best months for hiking are July through September.

Patterson Creek
Climb: moderate
Difficulty: moderate
Usage: moderate
Location: From Victor, drive west out of town on Cedron Road. This road travels several miles and then heads north. When the road bears north, continue 1 mile to locate the trailhead for Patterson Creek Trail 054 on the road's left side.

Located in the Big Hole Mountains, this trail winds along Patterson Creek and over Mahogany Ridge before ending at Red Mountain. Red Mountain's 8,715-foot summit offers hikers outstanding views of Wyoming's Teton Mountain Range rising in the distance as well as Idaho's Teton Valley lying below. Best months for hiking are July through September.

Great Divide Area
Aldous and Hancock Lakes
Distance: 5 miles roundtrip
Climb: moderate
Difficulty: moderate
Usage: moderate
Location: Merge off Interstate 15 at Dubois and proceed east on County Road A2. Travel 27 miles to a fork in the road and bear north towards Kilgore. At Kilgore, turn left at the T intersection and continue 0.3 miles to a right turn leading across Camas Meadows. From this turn, drive 4.2 miles to a road junction and keep right as the road becomes Forest Road (FR) 026. At the junction with FR 026 and FR 027, bear right on FR 027 and proceed 6 miles to the Ching Creek Trailhead and the trail leading north.

This well-maintained trail wanders in and out of thick forests and small meadows on the climb to Aldous and Hancock Lakes. Constantly passing by a variety of wildflowers, hikers will reach Aldous Lake at the 1.5-mile mark. Situated at 7,340 feet and surrounded by trees, Aldous Lake has become a popular fishing destination. Continuing northeast around Aldous Lake, climb steeply 1 mile to Hancock Lake. This lake sits in a bowl formed in an old landslide. Today, the lake is surrounded by old trees, and above the lake, hikers can view the Centennial Mountains and Continental Divide ridge. Best months for hiking are mid-June through mid-September.

Salamander Lake Loop
Distance: 9 mile loop
Climb: moderate
Difficulty: moderate
Usage: moderate
Location: Exiting off Interstate 15 at Dubois, merge onto County Road A2 at the eastern edge of town. Proceed 27 miles and bear north (left) towards Kilgore. Continuing through Kilgore, turn left at the T intersection and drive to the road junction of Forest Roads (FR) 026 and 02. Bearing left on FR 026, drive 0.75 miles and turn right on FR 029 (Cottonwood Creek Road). Locate the undeveloped trailhead in approximately 2 miles.

A variety of wildflowers surround hikers on this loop trail winding through meadows to Salamander Lake near the Continental Divide. Starting out on Trail Creek Trail, keep right at the junction for Lake Creek Trail and continue to another junction at the 1.5-mile mark. Stay to the

right and follow the trail as it crosses Trail Creek, climbs up to wildflower meadows, and descends to Salamander Lake at the 4.2-mile mark. Hiking along the lake's south (left) shore, locate a trail junction and proceed along the right "Lake Creek" fork across the Salamander Creek Bridge. At the bridge, utilize tree blazes to locate the trail heading into the forest and to a ridge. This ridge offers spectacular views into Montana. At the 4.8-mile mark, walk past the sign indicating the Divide Trail and follow the blazed trees to another large meadow. As the trail continues to climb up and down ridges, hikers will eventually reach another trail junction near the Salamander Creek crossing. Follow the well-used trail on the left over Salamander Creek Bridge leading back to the trailhead in 1.5 miles. Best months for hiking are mid-June to mid-October.

Optional Hikes: At the junction located at the 1.5-mile mark, hikers can veer left and head to Salamander Lake along this route. Although this trail cuts the trip's length by 1.25 miles, the scenery is not as breathtaking along this route. Another option is to leave the main trail at the 4.8-mile mark and head at an angle between 45 and 90 degrees up to the Continental Divide Trail. Hikers will reach the Divide about 1,000 feet up from the main trail and can continue hiking in either direction along the divide for views of the meadows below.

Sawtell Peak – Rock Creek Basin
Distance: 8 miles roundtrip
Climb: moderate
Difficulty: moderate
Usage: moderate
Location: Travel 85 miles north of Idaho Falls along U.S. Highway 20 and turn onto the marked Forest Road (FR) 024 (Sawtell Peak Road). Proceed 12 miles to the trailhead located at a small turnout in the road.

Traveling on or near the Continental Divide throughout the entire trek, hikers will access incredible views of the Teton and Centennial Mountains while overlooking Idaho, Montana, and Wyoming. Starting out on an old road, hikers will pass by numerous wildflower fields and view the 9,866-foot Sawtell Peak rising in the distance. After crossing over a rocky avalanche area, the trail begins descending and reaches Rock Creek Basin at the 4-mile mark. The area is filled with a variety of rock types and colors as well as wildlife. Moose, elk, and deer commonly frequent the area, and grizzly bear sightings are rising. Best months for hiking are mid-July through September.

Targhee Creek
Distance: 12.4 miles roundtrip
Climb: moderate
Difficulty: moderate
Usage: moderate
Location: On U.S. Highway 20, drive north past Ashton into Island Park and across Henrys Lake Flat. Ignoring the junction with State Highway 287, proceed 2.2 miles and bear left onto the dirt road marked "Targhee Creek Trail." Locate the trailhead in approximately 1 mile.

Fine views of Targhee Peak and Bald Peak await hikers on this trek leading through a canyon lined with forests and limestone cliffs, past alpine meadows, and up to several scenic alpine lakes. Starting out gently from the trailhead, hikers should keep going straight at the 0.8-mile trail junction with Dry Fork and cross Targhee Creek at the 2.3-mile mark. Climbing upwards, reach another crossing of Targhee Creek at the 3.2-mile mark and begin heading up the canyon through a thick forest. At the 4.2-mile mark, hikers will reach a small meadow where a waterfall can be found, and the 4.7-mile mark brings hikers to a third and final crossing of Targhee Creek. After hiking a total of 6 miles, hikers should bear right (east) on Watkins Creek Trail to locate numerous alpine lakes housed within the Targhee Basin. Passing by the first unnamed lake situated to the right of the trail, locate the seasonal Clark Lake at the 6.2-mile mark. Best months for hiking are July and August. Bear safety precautions should be taken at all times as grizzly bears heavily populate the area.

Optional Hikes: Continuing cross-country, hikers can access four scenic lakes situated above Clark Lake. Adventurous hikers can also opt to climb any of the numerous mountainsides lining Targhee Basin. From the top of these peaks, hikers will be able to view Yellowstone National Park and the Teton, Gravelly, and Centennial Mountains.

A second optional hike allows hikers to make a loop. At the trip's 6-mile mark, hikers should bear left on Targhee Creek Trail at the Continental Divide Trail junction. This trail leads down to Dry Fork Trail, which then loops back to the Targhee Creek Trail 0.8 miles from the trailhead.

Webber Creek

Distance: 18 miles roundtrip
Climb: moderate
Difficulty: moderate
Usage: moderate
Location: At Dubois, merge off Interstate 15 onto State Highway 22 and drive 6 miles west before bearing right (north) onto a county road. Continue 22.5 miles up this road and turn onto Forest Road (FR) 196 (Webber Creek Road). Locate Trail 111 leaving upstream at the Webber Creek Trailhead in approximately 5 miles.

The jagged Italian peaks frame this hike near the Continental Divide as hikers climb through Webber Creek Canyon up to alpine lakes hidden between rugged mountain ridges of Idaho and Montana. Beginning in a narrow, forested canyon, climb 4 miles to a trail junction with the South Fork of Webber Creek. Ignoring this junction, continue up the North Fork trail as views of the glacial Webber Peak and Scott Peak line the horizon. At 7.1 miles, merge left onto Trail 034 and quickly reach the first lake in just 0.6 miles. Continue another 0.6 miles to reach the second lake and 1.3 miles to reach the upper lake situated at an elevation of 9,560 feet. Limestone cliffs line this trail, and the rugged canyon wall to the right of Trail 034 is the Continental Divide. Best months for hiking are July to October. Bear safety precautions should be taken as grizzly bears are known to inhabit the area.

Harriman State Park Area
Ranch Loop
Distance: 1 mile loop
Climb: gentle
Difficulty: easy
Usage: moderate
Location: On U.S. Highway 20, drive north from Idaho Falls to Harriman State Park to locate the trailhead.

This gentle walk takes hikers back to earlier days with a historic tour of several Railroad Ranch buildings in the area. Best months for hiking are July through September.

Ridge Loop
Distance: 5.5 mile loop
Climb: moderate
Difficulty: moderate
Usage: moderate
Location: On U.S. Highway 20, drive north from Idaho Falls to Harriman State Park to locate the trailhead.

Climbing 400 feet, this trail takes hikers through

several forests to the top of a mountain ridge. From the crest, hikers are rewarded with an incredible vista of the Teton Mountains. Best months for hiking are July through September.

Island Park Area
Coffee Pot Rapids Trail
Distance: 5 miles roundtrip
Climb: gentle
Difficulty: easy
Usage: moderate
Location: From Island Park, travel 6 miles north to the Upper Coffeepot Campground in Targhee National Forest to locate the trailhead.

This gentle trail winds next to Henry's Fork of the Snake River. While the trail begins near placid waters, the trek takes hikers to a scenic river area full of raging rapids. Best months for hiking are July through September.

Box Canyon Trail
Distance: 6 miles roundtrip
Climb: gentle
Difficulty: easy
Usage: moderate
Location: From Island Park, travel to the Box Canyon Campground and locate the trailhead for Box Canyon Trail.

This trail is a fly-fisherman's dream, providing access to the trout-filled waters of Henry's Fork of the Snake River. Beginning at the campground, the trail wanders south along Box Canyon's rim for 3 miles, bringing hikers to the river after passing through a colorful wildflower landscape. Best months for hiking are June through September.

Union Pacific Railroad Bed
Distance: variable
Climb: gentle
Difficulty: easy
Usage: heavy
Location: Exit off U.S. Highway 20 3 miles south of Island Park and merge onto the signed Forest Road (FR) 291 (Chick Creek Road). Proceed 4 miles to a parking area at the trailhead.

When Union Pacific abandoned this old railroad bed, the area was turned into a popular recreation area east of Island Park. Running north to south, the trail is open to hikers, mountain bikers, and motorized vehicles. Best months for hiking are June through September.

Lemhi Mountains Area
Rocky Canyon
Distance: 10 miles roundtrip
Climb: moderate
Difficulty: moderate
Usage: moderate
Location: On State Highway 28, drive west through the town of Mud Lake and bear right at the highway junction heading towards Lone Pine. 7 miles north of Lone Pine bear left onto a dirt/gravel road and drive approximately 2 miles. Turn right on the side road and drive 1.5 miles to a fork in the road. Proceed left towards Rocky Canyon and park at the informal trailhead where the road ends on a steep hill.

Antelope, elk, deer, bighorn sheep, mountain goats, black bears, and mountain lions are all common sights on this trek taking hikers through a meadow canyon amid semiarid mountain peaks. After climbing over the steep hill at the trailhead, descend down to a spring in Rocky Canyon and proceed upcanyon following a trail next to a small brook. At the 2.3-mile mark, the trail passes through a narrow, rocky stretch before reaching a large meadow and canyon fork at the 4.8-mile mark. Best months for hiking are late June to mid-July, but the trail is accessible from early June

through October in most years.

Optional Hikes: From the meadow, hikers can opt to hike up the left or right fork of Rocky Canyon. While the right fork leads to scenic views of the surrounding area from a small meadow, the left fork takes hikers up into a tree-lined meadow.

Ririe/Heise Area
Cress Creek Nature Trail
Distance: variable
Climb: steep
Difficulty: moderate
Usage: moderate
Location: From Ririe, drive on U.S. Highway 26 towards Heise Hot Springs and Kelly Canyon. Immediately after crossing the Snake River, bear left and proceed to the Bureau of Land Management's parking area for the Cress Creek Nature Trail.

A perfect trek for a weekend picnic, this trail follows the crystal clear waters of Cress Creek. Winding up hillsides covered with both sagebrush and juniper, the hike terminates at a ridge view overlooking the Snake River and Big Southern Butte. Best months for hiking are June through August.

INFORMATION PLEASE

All Idaho area codes are 208

Road Information

ID Road & Weather Conditions
888-432-7623 or local 884-7000
Idaho State Police   736-3090

Tourism Information

Idaho Travel Council 800-VISIT-ID outside Idaho
334-2470 in Idaho
www.visitid.org
Eastern Idaho Yellowstone Teton Territory
800-634-3246
356-5700
www.yellowstoneteton.org/

Airports

Driggs	354-3100
Idaho Falls	612-8221
Rexburg	356-9960
St. Anthony	624-9901

Government Offices

Idaho Bureau of Reclamation   334-1466
www.usbr.gov
Idaho Department of Commerce
(800) 847-4843 or 334-2470
www.visitid.org or http://cl.idaho.gov/
Idaho Department of Fish and Game
(800) ASK-FISH or 334-3700
http://fishandgame.idaho.gov
Idaho Department of Parks and Recreation
334-4199
www.idahoparks.org
State BLM Office   373-3889 or 373-4000
www.id.blm.gov
Bureau of Land Management Idaho Falls Field Office   524-7500
Caribou-Targhee National Forest   624-3151

Hospitals

Teton Valley Hospital • Driggs   354-2383
Eastern Idaho Regional Medical Center
Idaho Falls   529-6111
Madison Memorial Hospital • Rexburg 356-3691

Golf Courses

7N Ranch Resort • Ririe	538-5097
Heise Hot Springs • Ririe	538-7327
American Falls • American Falls	226-5827
American Falls Golf Club	
American Falls	226-5827
Aspen Acres Golf • Ashton	652-3524
Timberline Golf • Ashton	652-3219
Links at Teton Peaks • Driggs	456-2374
Targhee Village Golf • Driggs	354-8577
Idaho Falls Golf • Idaho Falls	529-1115
Pinecrest Golf Course • Idaho Falls	529-1485
Sage Lake Golf • Idaho Falls	528-5535
Sandcreek Golf • Idaho Falls	529-1115
Island Park Village Resort	
Island Park	558-7550
Rexburg City - Golf Courses • Rexburg	359-3037
Teton Lake Golf Course • Rexburg	359-3036
Cedar Park Golf Course • Rigby	745-0103
Jefferson Hills Golf • Rigby	745-6492
Fremont County - Golf Course	
Saint Anthony	624-7074
Links at Teton Peaks • Tetonia	456-2374

Bed & Breakfasts

BlackSmith Inn • Rigby	745-6208
Cutthroat Inn B&B • Ririe	538-7963
Blue Heron Inn • Rigby	745-9922
Colonial Rose Tearoom and B&B	
St. Anthony	624-3530
Jessenis B&B • Ashton	652-3356
Locanda di Fiori (Inn of Flowers)	
Drigg	456-0909
Grand Valley Lodging • Driggs	354-8890
Hamer House B&B • St Anthony	624-3530
Kasper's Kountryside Inn Bed & Breakfast	
Victor	787-2726

Guest Ranches & Resorts

Meadow Vue Ranch	
Island Park [Mack's Inn]	558-7411
7N Ranch • Ririe	538-5097
The Pines at Historic Phillips Lodge &	
The Lodgepole Grill • Island Park	558-0192
Mountain River Ranch • Ririe	538-7337
Grand Targhee Ski & Summer Resort	
Alta	353-2300 x 1311
Squirrel Creek Elk Ranch • Ashton	652-3972
Dry Ridge Outfitters & Guest Ranch	
Driggs	354-2284
Grove Creek Lodge • Driggs	354-8881
Intermountain Lodge • Driggs	354-8153
Teton Teepee Lodge • Driggs	353-8176
Teton Valley Lodge • Driggs	354-2386
Jacob's Island Park Ranch • Hamer	662-5567
Hyde Outfitters & Last Chance Lodge	
Idaho Falls	558-7068
Aspen Lodge • Island Park	558-7407
Eagle Ridge Ranch • Island Park	558-0900
Elk Creek Ranch • Island Park	558-7404
Henry's Fork Lodge • Island Park	558-7953

Island Park Village Resort & Golf Course	
Island Park	558-7502
Lakeside Lodge & Resort • Island Park	558-7147
Mack's Inn Resort & Family Restaurant	
Island Park	558-7272
Pond's Lodge • Island Park	558-7221
Sawtelle Mountain Resort & RV Park	
Island Park	558-9366
Staley Springs Lodge • Island Park	558-7471
TroutHunter Riverfront Lodge, Fly Shop and Bar	
& Grill • Island Park	558-9900
Wild Rose Ranch • Island Park	558-7201
McGarry Ranches • Rexburg	410-299-1995
Sheffield Park Ranch • Rexburg	356-4182
Granite Creek Guest Ranch • Ririe	538-7140
Heise Canyon Ski Resort • Ririe	538-6251
Hideaway B&B Guest Ranch	
Rockford	666-8846
Sandhills Resort • St. Anthony	624-4127
Hansen-Silver Guest Ranch	
Swan Valley	483-2305
Teton Mountain View Lodge • Tetonia	456-2741
Teton Ranch • Tetonia	456-2010
Teton Ridge Ranch ª Tetonia	456-2650
Bagley's Teton Mountain Ranch	
Victor	787-9005
Moose Creek Ranch • Victor	787-2284
Teton Springs Resort • Victor	787-8008

Vacation Homes & Cabins

Powder Valley Townhouses • Driggs	354-8881
Rainbow Realty • Island Park	558-7116
Chapin Cabins • Victor	787-1922
Oxbow Property Management LLC	
Victor	787-2871

Forest Service Cabins

Caribou-Targhee National Forest

Bishop Mountain
27 mi. NW of Ashton 652-7442
Cap: 4 Nightly Fee: $25, limit 6 nights, $30 for
first night Available: Year Round
Snow machine access in winter. One room, wood
cook stove, 2 bunk bed sets. No water, no lights.
Outdoor privy. Parents adv. Not to bring children
under 12 years of age.

Squirrel Meadows Guard Station
23 mi. E of Ashton 652-7442
Cap: 6 Nightly Fee: $35, max. 8 nights, $40 for
first night Available: Year Round
Access by snow machines or skiing in winter. 2
rooms, wood heat/cook stove, 3 bunk bed sets,
outside hand pump for water. No lights. Outdoor
privy.

Warm River Hatchery
24 mi. E/NE of Ashton 652-7442
Cap: 10 Nightly Fee: $45, max. 20 nights, $50
for first night Available: Year Round
Access by snow machines or skiing in winter. 2
bedrooms, 6 bunk bed sets, wood cook stove,
wood furnace. No lights. Outdoor privy. River
water only.

Car Rental

Dollar • Driggs	354-3100
Driggs Airport/Teton Aviation Center	
Driggs	354-3100
Alamo • Idaho Falls	522-0340
American Carriage RV & Marine	
Idaho Falls	529-5535
Avis • Idaho Falls	529-4225
Budget • Idaho Falls	522-8800
Dodge Authorized Dealer	
Idaho Falls	522-2610
Enterprise • Idaho Falls	523-8111
Hertz • Idaho Falls	529-3101
Leasing Service Inc • Idaho Falls	522-2610
National • Idaho Falls	522-5276
Overland West • Idaho Falls	529-3101
Ron Sayer Dodge • Idaho Falls	522-2610
Thrifty • Idaho Falls	227-0444
Enterprise • Rexburg	356-8889
Practical • Rexburg	356-9018
Smith Ford Mercury Inc • Rexburg	356-3636
Stones Town & Country Motors	
Rexburg	356-9366

Outfitters & Guides

*F=Fishing H=Hunting R=River Guides
E=Horseback Rides G=General Guide Services*

Id Outfitters & Guides Association	
	800-49-IDAHO
Outfitters & Guides Licensing Board	327-7380
Ski Kelly Canyon • Rigby	**538-6261**
Grand Targhee • Driggs	353-2300

Cross-Country Ski Centers

Teton Ridge Ranch • Tetonia	456-2650

Downhill Ski Areas

Grand Targhee • Driggs	353-2300
Ski Kelly Canyon • Rigby	538-6261

Snowmobile Rentals

The Pines • Island Park	**888-455-9384**
Robson Outfitters • Felt	456-2805
Aspen Lodge • Island Park	558-7407
High Country Snowmobile Tours	
Island Park	558-9572
Island Park Rentals • Island Park	558-0112
Island Park Reservations	
Island Park	558-9675
Lakeside Lodge • Island Park	558-7147
Landon Lodge • Island Park	521-7448
Winchester Lodge • Island Park	888-762-9057
Elkins Resort • Nordman	443-2432
Yellowstone Teton Terrritory	
Rexburg	656-0654
Goosewing Ranch • St. Anthony	624-1499
Rendezvous Snowmobile Rental	
Tetonia	456-2805
Teton Springs Resort • Victor	787-8008

NOTES:

Campground Quick Reference

Campground Name				Phone
Public/Commercial	Unit Price	#Spaces	Max. Length	Seasons
Directions				
Amenities/Activities				

Ashton

Squirrel Creek Elk Ranch, Inc.   652-3972
C $75-105   16   All Year
12 mi. E. of Ashton on Reclamation-Flagg Ranch Rd.

Aspen Acres Golf Club & RV Park   652-3524/800-845-2374
C $15-25   40   Summer, Fall, Spring
9 mi. SE of Ashton

Jessen's RV, B & B, Cottages & Tents   652-3356/800-747-3356
C   22   All Year
Hwy. 20, 1.5 mi. S. of Ashton

Timberline RV Park   652-3219
C $15   25   35'   All Year
E. of Ashton on Cave Falls Rd.
Hookups, Playground, Pull-thru Sites, Showers, Tenters Welcome

Buttercup   382-6544
P $7-22   28   32'   Summer, Fall, Spring
22.4 mi. N. of Cascade, W. side of Cascade Reservoir
Credit Cards OK, Drinking Water, Pets OK, Tenters Welcome, Vault Toilets, Waterfront, Handicap Access

Cave Falls   558-7301
P $8   16   24'   Summer
6 mi. E. on Hwy 47, 5.5 mi. NE on Cave Falls Rd., 11 mi. NE on Forest Rd. 582
Drinking Water, Pets OK, Pull-thru Sites, Tenters Welcome, Vault Toilets

Pole Bridge   558-7301
P   10   22'   Summer, Fall
12 mi. NE on Hwy. 47, 5 mi. N. on Forest Rd. 150
Fire Rings, Pets OK, Tenters Welcome, Vault Toilets

Riverside - Ashton   558-7301
P $8-10   57   34'   Summer, Fall
16.5 mi. N. on Hwy. 20, 1 mi. SE on Forest Rd. 304
Credit Cards OK, Drinking Water, Fire Rings, Pets OK, Pull-thru Sites, Reservations, Tenters Welcome, Vault Toilets, Waterfront, Handicap Access

Warm River   558-7301
P $7-120   17   24'   Summer, Fall
10 mi. NE on Hwy. 47
Drinking Water, Fire Rings, Pets OK, Reservations, Tenters Welcome, Vault Toilets, Waterfront, Handicap Access

West End   558-7301
P   19   22'   Summer, Fall
18 mi. N. on Hwy. 20, 15 mi. NW on Forest Rd. 167
Fire Rings, Tenters Welcome, Vault Toilets

Grandview   652-7442
P   None   5   June 1-September 30
14 miles N of Ashton on Hwy. 47
Developed Campground, Restrooms, RV Sites, Scenic Driving, Winter Sports

Driggs

Reunion Flat Group Area   354-2312
P $10-20   3   Summer, Fall
6 mi. NE on Cty. Rd. 009, 3 mi. E. on Forest Rd. 009
Drinking Water, Pets OK, Reservations, Vault Toilets, Waterfront, Handicap Access

Dubois

Kilgore General Store   778-5334
C $10   2   All Year
26 mi. E. of Dubois, 31 mi. W. of Island Park
Hookups, Mini-Mart, Showers

Scoggins Inc.   374-5453
C $16.20   9   All Year
I-15, exit 167
Credit Cards OK, Drinking Water, Game Room, Hookups, LP Gas, Mini-Mart, Pets OK, Pull-thru Sites, Reservations, Showers, Tenters Welcome, Handicap Access

Stoddard Wagon Wheel Court   374-5330
C $10   3   All Year
Main St., S. on Thomas St. to 4th St., behind City/County Annex Bldg.
Dump Station, Hookups

Steel Creek Group Area   374-5422
P   22'   Summer, Fall, Spring
3.5 mi. N. on Hwy. 15, 17 mi. SE on Forest Rd. 006, 1.2 mi. W. on Forest Rd. 478
Drinking Water, Reservations, Vault Toilets

Stoddard Creek   374-5422
P $6-12   24   32'   Summer, Fall, Spring
16 mi. N. on Hwy. 15, 1 mi. NW on Forest Rd. 80003
Drinking Water, Fire Rings, Pull-thru Sites, Tenters Welcome, Vault Toilets

Webber Creek   374-5422
P   None   4   June 15-September 15
30 miles NW of Dubois on Hwy. 22 and FR 196
Developed Campground, Restrooms, RV Sites, Fishing, Hiking/Backpacking, Horseback Riding

Idaho Falls

ARM'S Shady Rest RV Park   524-0010
C $12-20   30   40'   All Year
N. Idaho Falls area, .25 mi. N. of Anderson/Lincoln
Drinking Water, Dump Station, Hookups, Pets OK, Pull-thru Sites, Reservations, Showers, Tenters Welcome, Laundry

Sunnyside Acres Park   523-8403
C $22.30   25   All Year
Exit 119 or 113 off Hwy. 20 to W.Sunnyside Rd.
Dump Station, Hookups, Pets OK, Showers, Laundry

Idaho Falls KOA   523-3362/800-562-7644
C $24-32   130   All Year
I-15, exit 118 to Utah Blvd., turn left, continue to campground
Credit Cards OK, Dump Station, Hookups, LP Gas, Mini-Mart, Modem Hookups, Pets OK, Playground, Pull-thru Sites, Reservations, Showers, Swimming Pool, Tenters Welcome

Irwin

McCoy Creek   523-1412
P $8/night   19   June 1-September 15
S of Irwin on Hwy. 26/89, then 7 miles N on FR 087
Developed Campground, Primitive Camping, Drinking Water, Restrooms, RV Sites, Boat Ramp, Biking, Motorized and Non-Motorized Boating, Fishing, Hiking/Backpacking, Horseback Riding, Hunting, Picnicking, Scenic Driving, Water Sports, Wildlife Viewing

Alpine   523-1412
P $8/single; $16/double   33   May 25-September 15
S of Irwin on Hwy. 26/89 near the ID/WY Border
Developed Campground, Group Camping, Drinking Water, Restrooms, RV Sites, Biking, Fishing, Hiking/Backpacking, Horseback Riding, Picnicking, Scenic Driving, Water Sports, Winter Sports

Island Park

Robins Roost Chevron & Grocery Store   558-7440
C $15   10   60'   Summer, Fall, Spring
Hwy. 20, N. end of Big Springs Rd.
Credit Cards OK, Hookups, LP Gas, Mini-Mart, Reservations, Showers

Mack's Inn Resort   558-7272
C $10-115   73   All Year
Hwy. 20, N. of Island Park
Credit Cards OK, Dump Station, LP Gas, Mini-Mart, Pets OK, Playground, Reservations, Showers, Laundry

RedRock RV & Camping Park   558-7442/800-473-3762
C $16-21   54   65'   Summer, Fall
Hwy. 20, M P 398, W. on Red Rock Rd. 5 mi.
Camping Cabins, Credit Cards OK, Drinking Water, Dump Station, Fire Rings, Hookups, Mini-Mart, Modem Hookups, Pets OK, Playground, Pull-thru Sites, Reservations, Showers, Tenters Welcome, Laundry, Handicap Access

Campground Quick Reference - continued

Campground Name					Phone
Public/Commercial	Unit Price	#Spaces	Max. Length		Seasons
Directions					
Amenities/Activities					

Valley View RV Park, Campground & Laundromat 558-7443/888-558-7443
C $17-24 53 50' All Year
Near Henrys Lake, 13.5 mi. S. of West Yellowstone, near airport
Drinking Water, Hookups, LP Gas, Modem Hookups, Pets OK, Pull-thru Sites, Reservations, Showers, Tenters Welcome, Laundry

Pond's Lodge 558-7221/888-731-5153
C $10.50 50 All Year

Hookups, Mini-Mart, Pets OK, Waterfront, Handicap Access

Wild Rose Ranch 558-7201
C $18-25 60 45' All Year
Hwy. 87, N. shore of Henrys Lake
Credit Cards OK, Dump Station, Hookups, Modem Hookups, Pets OK, Pull-thru Sites, Waterfront, Work-Out Room, Laundry

Sawtelle Mountain Resort 558-9366/866-558-9366
C $21.50 60 All Year
Hwy. 20 between M P 394 & 395 at Sawtelle Peak Rd.

Enchanted Forest RV & Campground 558-9675
C $10-14 14 All Year
6 mi. W. of Hwy. 20 on Yale-Kilgore Rd.
Handicap Access

Buffalo Run Campground 558-7112/888-797-3434
C $15 42 All Year
3402 N. Hwy. 20

Lazy Trout Lodge & Cafe 558-7407/877-529-9432
C $18 8 All Year
Hwy. 20, M P 397

Staley Springs Lodge 558-7471
P $49-175 44 All Year

Camping Cabins, Credit Cards OK, Dump Station, Hookups, Mini-Mart, Pets OK, Showers, Waterfront

Big Springs - Island Park 558-7301
P $10 15 32' Summer, Fall
4.5 mi. E. of Macks Inn on Forest Rd. 059
Drinking Water, Fire Rings, Pets OK, Pull-thru Sites, Tenters Welcome, Vault Toilets

Box Canyon 558-7301
P $10 19 32' Summer, Fall
7 mi. S. of Mack's Inn on Hwy. 20, .3 mi. SW on Hwy. 134, .9 mi. NW on Forest Rd. 284
Drinking Water, Fire Rings, Pets OK, Tenters Welcome, Vault Toilets

Buffalo 558-7301
P $10-120 127 34' Summer, Fall
5.5 mi. S. of Mack's Inn on Hwy. 20
Drinking Water, Fire Rings, Pets OK, Pull-thru Sites, Reservations, Tenters Welcome, Vault Toilets

Buttermilk 558-7301
P $10-100 54 32' Summer, Fall
Hwy. 20, 3.5 mi. S. of Mack's Inn, 2.2 mi. NW on Hwy. 030, 4 mi. SW on Forest Rd. 334
Drinking Water, Fire Rings, Pets OK, Pull-thru Sites, Reservations, Vault Toilets

Flat Rock - Island Park 558-7301
P $10-30 40 32' Summer
Across from Mack's Inn
Drinking Water, Fire Rings, Pets OK, Reservations, Tenters Welcome, Vault Toilets

Henrys Lake State Park 558-7532
P $9-16 45 40' Summer, Fall
45 mi. N. of Ashton on Hwy. 20, M P 401, 15 mi. S. of W. Yellowstone
Credit Cards OK, Drinking Water, Dump Station, Hookups, Reservations, Showers, Tenters Welcome, Vault Toilets, Waterfront

Campground Name					Phone
Public/Commercial	Unit Price	#Spaces	Max. Length		Seasons
Directions					
Amenities/Activities					

McCrea Bridge 558-7301
P $10-20 25 32' Summer, Fall
3.5 mi. S. of Mack's Inn on Hwy. 20, 2.2 mi. NW on Cty. Rd. 030
Drinking Water, Fire Rings, Pets OK, Reservations, Vault Toilets

Upper Coffee Pot 558-7301
P $10-30 15 32' Summer, Fall
.5 mi. S. of Mack's Inn on Hwy. 20, 2 mi. SW on Forest Rd. 130
Drinking Water, Fire Rings, Pets OK, Reservations, Tenters Welcome, Vault Toilets, Waterfront

Mud Lake

Haven Motel & Trailer Park 663-4821
C $12 13 All Year
Hwy. 33
Credit Cards OK, Dump Station, Hookups, Pets OK, Reservations

Birch Creek 524-7500
P 16 25' Summer, Fall
25 mi. NW of Mud Lake on Hwy. 28
Vault Toilets

Palisades

Palisades RV Park & Cabins 483-4485
C $16 14 Summer
Hwy. 26, M P 385
Credit Cards OK, Drinking Water, Dump Station, Hookups, Pets OK, Playground, Reservations, Showers, Tenters Welcome, Waterfront

Big Elk Creek 523-1412
P 21 22' Summer, Fall
5.4 mi. SE on Hwy. 26, 1.4 mi. NE on Forest Rd. 262
Drinking Water, Fire Rings, Reservations, Vault Toilets

Blowout 523-1412
P $7 19 32' Summer, Fall
9 mi. SE on Hwy. 26
Boating Facilities, Drinking Water, Fire Rings, Reservations, Vault Toilets

Calamity 523-1412
P 41 32' Summer, Fall
2.6 mi. S. on Hwy. 26, 1.1 mi. SW on Forest Rd. 058
Boating Facilities, Drinking Water, Fire Rings, Reservations, Vault Toilets

Palisades Creek 523-1412
P 8 22' Summer, Fall
2 mi. NE on Forest Rd. 255
Drinking Water, Fire Rings, Vault Toilets

Rexburg

Rainbow Lake & Campground 356-3681
C $16-20 60 All Year
S. Rexburg exit, .25 mi. W., then S. 1.25 mi.
Credit Cards OK, Drinking Water, Dump Station, Hookups, Playground, Pull-thru Sites, Showers, Handicap Access

Thompson's RV Park 356-6210
C $15 9 All Year
Hwy. 191, 4 mi. S. of Rexburg
Hookups, Showers

Sheffield RV Park 356-4182
C $14-17 25 All Year
Hwy. 20, N. of Idaho Falls, right after M. P. 328 at Shell Sta. to stop sign. From Rexburg go south on Hwy 20 for 4 miles, just after M.P. 329. Turn left at Shell Sta. To Stop sign- follow sign 5362 S. Hwy 191
Camping Cabins, Credit Cards OK, Drinking Water, Dump Station, Fire Rings, Hookups, Modem Hookups, Pets OK, Pull-thru Sites, Reservations, Showers, Tenters Welcome, Waterfront, Laundry, Handicap Access

Campground Quick Reference - continued

Campground Name				Phone
Public/Commercial	Unit Price	#Spaces	Max. Length	Seasons
Directions				
Amenities/Activities				

Rigby

Jefferson Lake RV Campground — 745-7756
C — All Year

Ririe

7N Ranch — 538-5097
C — $12-19 — 28 — All Year
Hwy. 26, 21 mi. from Idaho Falls
Handicap Access

Heise Hot Springs — 538-7453
C — 14 — All Year
Hwy. 26, 3 mi. NE of Ririe, 5116 Heise Rd.
Hookups, Mini-Mart, Reservations, Showers, Swimming Pool, Handicap Access

Mountain River Ranch RV Park & Campground — 538-7337
C — $12-20 — 27 — All Year
18 mi. NE of Idaho Falls off Hwy. 26
Camping Cabins, Drinking Water, Dump Station, Hookups, Pets OK, Reservations, Showers, Tenters Welcome, Handicap Access

Kelly's Island — 524-7500
P — 40' — Summer, Fall
2 mi. E. of Heise on access road N. of river
Drinking Water, Pets OK, Pull-thru Sites, Tenters Welcome, Vault Toilets, Waterfront, Handicap Access

Table Rock — 524-7500
P — 9 — 22' — Summer, Fall, Spring
12 mi. SE on Hwy. 26; 1.5 mi. SE on Forest Rd. 218; 1.3 mi. SE on Forest Rd. 217
Drinking Water, Reservations, Vault Toilets

Juniper Park — 678-0461
P — $9-16 — 49 — 42' — Summer, Fall, Spring
15 mi. SE of Idaho Falls, 1 mi. S. on Hwy. 26
Drinking Water, Dump Station, Hookups, Pets OK, Pull-thru Sites, Reservations, Showers, Tenters Welcome, Vault Toilets

Spencer

Spencer Stage Station — 374-5242
C — $12 — 14 — All Year

Hookups, Pets OK, Showers

Spencer Opal Mines — 374-5476
C — $10-15 — 12 — Summer, Fall, Spring
N. end of Main St.
Dump Station, Hookups, Mini-Mart, Pets OK, Pull-thru Sites, Reservations, Showers, Tenters Welcome

St. Anthony

Fenton's RV & Camping — 624-7854
C — $8-20 — 14 — 40' — Summer, Fall
Hwy. 20 to Relay Station Restaurant, then E. 500 yds.
Drinking Water, Hookups, Pets OK, Playground, Pull-thru Sites, Reservations, Showers, Tenters Welcome

Sandhills Resort Inc. — 624-4127
C — $19-24 — 110 — Summer, Fall, Spring
4 mi. W., 3 mi. N. of St. Anthony, 865 Redroad
Credit Cards OK, Drinking Water, Dump Station, Hookups, Mini-Mart, Modem Hookups, Pets OK, Playground, Pull-thru Sites, Reservations, Showers, Tenters Welcome, Laundry

Swan Valley

Falls — 523-1412
P — $8 — 23 — 24' — Summer, Fall
4 mi. W. on Hwy. 26, 2.3 mi. S. on Forest Rd. 076
Drinking Water, Fire Rings, Reservations, Vault Toilets

Falls Group Area — 523-1412
P — 22' — Summer, Fall
4 mi. W. on Hwy. 26, 2.6 mi. S. on Forest Rd. 076
Drinking Water, Fire Rings, Reservations, Vault Toilets

Riverside Park — 523-1412
P — 24 — Summer, Fall
Hwy. 26, just below Palisades dam
Drinking Water, Dump Station, Fire Rings, Hookups, Pull-thru Sites, Vault Toilets

Teton Valley

Teton Valley Campground — 787-2647/877-787-3036
C — $23-42 — 75 — All Year
Hwy. 31, 1 mi. W. of Victor, 128 Hwy. 31
Credit Cards OK, Drinking Water, Dump Station, Hookups, Pets OK, Playground, Pull-thru Sites, Reservations, Showers, Swimming Pool, Tenters Welcome

Pine Creek — 354-2312
P — $6-12 — 11 — 30' — Summer, Fall
6.5 mi. W. on Hwy. 31
Drinking Water, Pets OK, Pull-thru Sites, Vault Toilets, Handicap Access

Teton Canyon — 354-2312
P — $8-16 — 20 — 24' — Summer
6 mi. NE on Cty. Rd. 009, 4.5 mi. E. on Forest Rd. 009
Drinking Water, Pets OK, Pull-thru Sites, Reservations, Vault Toilets, Handicap Access

Trail Creek - Teton Valley — 354-2312
P — $8-16 — 11 — 20' — Summer, Fall
6 mi. SE of Victor on Hwy. 33
Drinking Water, Pets OK, Pull-thru Sites, Vault Toilets

Victor

Mike Harris — 354-2312
P — $6-12 — 11 — 30' — Summer, Fall
4 mi. SE on Hwy. 33
Drinking Water, Pets OK, Pull-thru Sites, Vault Toilets, Handicap Access

NOTES:

Dining Quick Reference

Price Range refers to the average cost of a meal per person: ($) $1-$6, ($$) $7-$11, ($$$) $12-up. Cocktails: "Yes" indicates full bar; Beer (B)/Wine (W), Service: Breakfast (B), Brunch (BR), Lunch (L), Dinner (D). Businesses in bold print will have additional information under the appropriate map locator number in the body of this section. *[wi-fi]* next to business name indicates free wireless internet is available to customers.

MAP NO.	RESTAURANT	TYPE CUISINE	PRICE RANGE	CHILD MENU	COCKTAILS BEER WINE	MEALS SERVED	CREDIT CARDS ACCEPTED
1	The Cellar	American	$$	C	B W	L/D	Ammon
4	Los Dos Amigos	Mexican	$-$$			L/D	
5	Corner Bar & Cafe	American	$	N	Yes	L	No
7	**Motel West & Hometown Kitchen Restaurant**	Family	$$	Y	N	B/L/D	Major
7	Ray's In & Out	Fast Food	$	Y	N	L/D	M V
7	Applebee's Neighborhood Grill & Bar	American	$$	Y	Yes	L/D	Major
7	Arby's	Fast Food	$	Y	N	L/D	Major
7	Arctic Circle	Fast Food	$	Y	N	L/D	M V
7	Burger King	Fast Food	$	Y	N	L/D	M V
7	Dairy Queen	Fast Food	$	N	N	L/D	No
7	Denny's Restaurant	Family	$-$$	Y	N	B/L/D	Major
7	Domino's Pizza	Pizza	$-$$	N	N	L/D	M V
7	Park Avenue Diner	Family	$-$$	Y	N	B/L/D	No
7	Grandpas Southern Bar B Que	American	$$	Y	N	L/D	Major
7	Happy's Chinese Restaurant	Asian	$$	N	N	L/D	Major
7	Hometown Kitchen	Family	$-$$	Y	N	B/L/D	Major
7	Hong Kong Restaurant	Asian	$$	N	N	L/D	Major
7	Hyde Outfitters & Last Chance Lodge	Fine Dining	$$-$$$	N	B W	B/L/D	Major
7	J B's Family Restaurant	Family	$-$$	Y	N	B/L/D	Major
7	Jack In The Box	Fast Food	$	Y	N	L/D	M V
7	Kathryn's Restaurant	American	$-$$	Y	B W	B/L	Major
7	Los Panchos	Mexican	$-$$	N	N	L/D	M V
7	McDonald's	Fast Food	$	Y	N	B/L/D	Major
7	O'Brady's Restaurant	Family	$$	Y	N	B/L/D	M V
7	Outback Steakhouse	Steakhouse	$$	Y	B W	L/D	Major
7	Papa Murphy's Take 'n' Bake	Pizza	$$	N	N	L/D	M V
7	Pizza Hut	Pizza	$	N	N	L/D	Major
7	Pizza Hut	Pizza	$	N	N	L/D	Major
7	Quizno's Subs	Fast Food	$	N	N	L/D	M V
7	Red Lion Hotel On the Falls *[wi-fi]*	Fine Dining	$$-$$$	Y	Yes	L/D	Major
7	Subway	Fast Food	$	N	N	L/D	M V
7	The Frosty Gator *[wi-fi]*	American/Tavern	$	Y	N	L/D	Major
7	The Sports Page	American	$	N	B W	L	No
7	Wendy's	Fast Food	$	Y	N	L/D	M V
7	Westbank Restaurant & Lounge *[wi-fi]*	American	$-$$	Y	Yes	B/L/D	Major
7	Yummy's	American	$	N	N	L/D	No
8	**Teton Grille Restaurant**	Fine Dining	$$$	Y	B W	L/D	Major
8	A Little Bit Of Mexico	Mexican	$-$$	Y	B W	L/D	Major
8	Albertos Restaurant	Mexican	$-$$	Y	N	B/L/D	Major
8	Burger King	Fast Food	$	Y	N	L/D	M V
8	DB's Steak & Brew House	Steakhouse	$$-$$$	Y	B W	L	Major
8	Godfather's Pizza	Pizza	$	Y	N	L/D	M V
8	Great Wall Restaurant	Asian	$	Y	N	L/D	Major
8	Hardy's Pub & Grill	American	$	N	B W	L	M V
8	Los Betos Mexican Food	Mexican	$-$$	N	N	L/D	Major
8	McDonald's	Fast Food	$	Y	N	B/L/D	Major
8	Mitchell's Restaurant	Family	$$	Y	N	B/L/D	Major
8	Morenita's	Mexican	$-$$	N	N	L/D	M V
8	Pinecrest Diner	American	$-$$	Y	B W	B/L/D	Major
8	Pizza Hut	Pizza	$	N	N	L/D	Major
8	Pockets Inc	Tavern	$	N	Yes	L	Major
8	Puerto Vallarta Mexican Restaurant	Mexican	$$	N	N	L/D	Major
8	Sage Lakes Cafe	American	$	N	B W	B/L/D	No
8	Taco John's	Fast Food	$	N	N	L/D	M V
8	Teton Grille	Regional/Casual Fine Dining	$$	Y	B W	L/D	Major
8	Thai Kitchen	Asian	$	N	N	L/D	Major
8	The Crimson Teahouse	Teahouse/Fine Dining	$$	N	N	L	No
8	Wendy's Old Fashioned Hamburgers	Fast Food	$	Y	N	L/D	M V
8	Wrangler Roast Beef	Steakhouse	$-$$	Y	N	L/D	M V
8	Wright Brothers Travel Center	Family	$-$$	Y	N	B/L/D	Major

Dining Quick Reference - continued

Price Range refers to the average cost of a meal per person: ($) $1-$6, ($$) $7-$11, ($$$) $12-up. Cocktails: "Yes" indicates full bar; Beer (B)/Wine (W), Service: Breakfast (B), Brunch (BR), Lunch (L), Dinner (D). Businesses in bold print will have additional information under the appropriate map locator number in the body of this section. [wi-fi] next to business name indicates free wireless internet is available to customers.

MAP NO.	RESTAURANT	TYPE CUISINE	PRICE RANGE	CHILD MENU	COCKTAILS BEER WINE	MEALS SERVED	CREDIT CARDS ACCEPTED
9	Aussie Eats	Austrailian	$-$$	C		L/D	Major
9	Arby's	Fast Food	$	Y	N	L/D	Major
9	Baskin-Robbins	Fast Food	$	N	N	L	M V
9	Burger King	Fast Food	$	Y	N	L/D	M V
9	Canton Restaurant	Asian	$$	N	N	L/D	No
9	China Super Buffet	Asian	$	N	B W	L/D	Major
9	Chinese Garden Restaurant	Asian	$-$$	N	N	L/D	Major
9	Cold Stone Creamery	American	$	N	N	L/D	M V
9	Dairy Queen	Fast Food	$	N	N	L/D	No
9	Ever Green China Buffet	Asian	$$	N	N	L/D	M V
9	Fanatics Sports Grill	American	$	N	B W	L/D	Major
9	Garcia's Mexican Restaurant	Mexican	$-$$	Y	N	L/D	M V
9	Jack In The Box	Fast Food	$	Y	N	L/D	M V
9	Kentucky Fried Chicken	Fast Food	$-$$	Y	N	L/D	Major
9	Leo's Place Restaurants	Pizza	$$	N	N	L/D	M V
9	Little Caesars Pizza	Pizza	$	N	N	L/D	Major
9	McDonald's	Fast Food	$	Y	N	B/L/D	Major
9	Mongolian Grill	Asian	$-$$	N	N	L/D	M V
9	Mornitas #4	Mexican	$-$$	N	N	L/D	M V
9	Papa Johns Pizza	Pizza	$$	N	N	L/D	M V
9	Papa Murphy's Take 'n' Bake	Pizza	$$	N	N	L/D	M V
9	Papa Tom's Pizza	Pizza	$	N	N	L/D	M V
9	Plum Loco	Mexican	$-$$	N	N	B/L/D	M V
9	Puerto Vallarta Mexican Restaurant #2	Mexican	$$	N	N	L/D	Major
9	Quizno's Subs	Fast Food	$	N	N	L/D	M V
9	Sandcreek Cafe	American	$	N	B	B/L/D	No
9	Sol Rio	Mexican	$$	N	N	L/D	M V
9	Sonic Drive-In	Fast Food	$	Y	N	L/D	M V
9	Taco Bell	Fast Food	$	N	N	L/D	M V
9	Texas Roadhouse	American	$$-$$$	N	B W	L/D	Major
9	The Sandwich Tree	American/Deli	$	N	N	L	M V
9	Wendy's Old Fashioned Hamburgers	Fast Food	$	Y	N	L/D	M V
9	Winger's Diner	American	$-$$	Y	B	L/D	Major
9	Yen Ching Express	Asian	$	N	N	L/D	M V
10	Dad's 113 Travel Center	Family	$-$$	Y	N	B/L/D	Major
10	Frontier Pies Of Idaho	Family	$-$$	Y	N	B/L/D	Major
11	Chuck-A-Rama Buffet	American	$$	N	N	L/D	M V
11	Fazolis Resteraunt	Italian	$$	Y	B W	L/D	Major
11	Firehouse Grill	American	$$	Y	Yes	L/D	Major
11	Ground Round Grill & Bar	American	$$	Y	Yes	L/D	Major
11	International House of Pancakes	Family	$	Y	N	B/L/D	Major
11	Johnny Carino's Italian Kitchen	Italian	$$	Y	B W	L/D	Major
11	McDonald's	Fast Food	$	Y	N	B/L/D	Major
11	Pickerman Soup & Sandwich	American/Deli	$	N	N	L/D	Major
11	Quizno's Classic Subs	Fast Food	$-$$	Y	N	L/D	M V
11	Sonic Drive-In Inc	Fast Food	$	Y	N	L/D	No
11	Texas Roadhouse	American	$$-$$$	Y	Yes	L/D	Major
11	Typhoon's Teriyaki Grill	Asian	$	N	N	L/D	M V
11	Yen Ching Express	Asian	$	N	N	L/D	M V
11	McDonald's	Fast Food	$	Y	N	B/L/D	Major
11	Ez Mart Convenience Store	American	$	N	B W	L	M V
13	Opal Mountain Cafe	Family	$	Y	N	B/L/D	M V
13	Angus Restaurant	Steakhouse	$-$$$	Y	N	B/L/D	Major
13	SouthFork Lodge	Fine Dining	$$$	Y	B W	D	Major
14	**Mountain River Ranch-Meadow Muffin Theater**	American/Fine Dining	$$-$$$	N	N	D	Major
15	Arctic Circle	Fast Food	$	Y	N	L/D	M V
15	Bandos Mexican Restaurant	Mexican	$	N	N	L/D	M V
15	Subway	Fast Food	$	N	B W	L	No
15	Fiesta Ole'	Mexican	$	N	N	L/D	No
15	La Pizzeria	Pizza	$	Y	N	L/D	No
15	Me & Stan's	Family	$-$$	Y	N	B/L/D	Major

Price Range refers to the average cost of a meal per person: ($) $1-$6, ($$) $7-$11, ($$$) $12-up. Cocktails: "Yes" indicates full bar; Beer (B)/Wine (W), Service: Breakfast (B), Brunch (BR), Lunch (L), Dinner (D). Businesses in bold print will have additional information under the appropriate map locator number in the body of this section. [wi-fi] next to business name indicates free wireless internet is available to customers.

MAP NO.	RESTAURANT	TYPE CUISINE	PRICE RANGE	CHILD MENU	COCKTAILS BEER WINE	MEALS SERVED	CREDIT CARDS ACCEPTED
15	Papa Kelsey's Pizza & Subs	Pizza	$	N	N	L/D	M V
15	Subway	Fast Food	$	N	N	L/D	M V
17	Arby's	Fast Food	$	Y	N	L/D	Major
17	Burger King	Fast Food	$	Y	N	L/D	M V
17	Craigos Sourdough Pizza	Pizza	$	N	N	L/D	M V
17	Fong's Restaurant	Asian	$	N	N	L/D	Major
17	Frontier Pies Of Rexburg	Family	$-$$	Y	N	B/L/D	Major
17	Jack In The Box	Fast Food	$	Y	N	L/D	No
17	JB's Big Boy Family Restaurants	Family	$-$$	Y	N	B/L/D	Major
17	Kentucky Fried Chicken	Fast Food	$-$$	Y	N	L/D	Major
17	Little Caesar's Pizza	Pizza	$	N	N	L/D	M V
17	McDonald's	Fast Food	$	Y	N	B/L/D	Major
17	Pizza Hut	Fast Food	$	N	N	L/D	Major
17	Quizno's Subs	Fast Food	$	N	N	L/D	M V
17	R & B Drive In	American	$	N	N	L/D	M V
17	Ramirez Mexican Food	Mexican	$	N	N	L/D	Major
17	Subway	Fast Food	$	N	N	L/D	M V
17	Taco Bell	Fast Food	$	N	N	L/D	M V
17	Taco Time	Fast Food	$	N	N	L/D	M V
19	Burger King	Fast Food	$	Y	N	L/D	M V
19	Trails End Cafe	American	$	N	B W	B/L/D	Major
21	Big J's Burgers & Pizza	American	$	N	N	L/D	No
21	Chiz'cougar Cave	American	$$	N	N	L/D	No
21	Jill's Place	Family	$-$$	Y	N	B/L/D	Major
21	Relay Station	American	$$	Y	B W	B/L/D	Major
21	Subway	Fast Food	$	N	N	L/D	M V
22	Annie's Bakery & Pizzaria	Bakery/Pizza	$	N	N	L/D	M V
22	Big Juds Country Diner	American	$	N	N	L/D	Major
22	Dave's IGA	Deli/Grocery	$	N	N	L	Major
22	Frostop Drive-In	American	$	N	N	L/D	M V
22	Imperial Club	American	$$	N	B W	L/D	Major
22	Trails Inn Restaurant	Steak/American	$$	Y	N	B/L/D	No
23	**Meadow Vue Lodge**	American	$$-$$$	N	N	L	Major
23	**The Lodgepole Grill**	Steaks/Ribs/Pasta	$$-$$$	Y	Yes	L/D	Major
23	Henry's Fork Landing At Macks Inn	Family	$$	Y	N	B/L/D	Major
23	Island Park Restaurant/Saloon	American/Tavern	$$-$$$	N	Yes	L/D	Major
23	Phillips Lodge	Fine Dining	$$-$$$	Y	Yes	L/D	Major
23	Pond's Lodge	Fine Dining	$$-$$$	Y	Yes	B/L/D	M V
23	Shotgun General Store	American	$	N	B	L	Major
23	Subway	Fast Food	$	N	N	L/D	M V

NOTES:

Motel Quick Reference

Price Range: ($) Under $40 ; ($$) $40-$60; ($$$) $60-$80, ($$$$) Over $80. Pets [check with the motel for specific policies] (P), Dining (D), Lounge (L), Disabled Access (DA), Full Breakfast (FB), Cont. Breakfast (CB), Indoor Pool (IP), Outdoor Pool (OP), Hot Tub (HT), Sauna (S), Refrigerator (R), Microwave (M) (Microwave and Refrigerator indicated only if in majority of rooms), Kitchenette (K). All Idaho area codes are 208. [wi-fi] next to business name indicates free wireless internet is available to customers.

MAP NO.	MOTEL	NUMBER ROOMS	PRICE RANGE	BREAKFAST	POOL/ HOT TUB SAUNA	NON SMOKE ROOMS	OTHER AMENITIES	CREDIT CARDS
4	B-K's Motel	5	$$					
4	Haven Motel	7	$$			Yes	P	M/V
7	**Fairfield Inn & Suites** [wi-fi]	81	$$$	CB	IP	Yes	DA/R/M	Major
7	**Motel West & Hometown Kitchen Restaurant** [wi-fi]	80	$$	CB	IP/HT	Yes	P/R/M	Major
7	Best Western Driftwood Inn [wi-fi]	74	$$/$$$/$$$$	CB	OP	Yes	P/D/L/DA/R/M/K	Major
7	National 9 Executive Inn [wi-fi]	130	$$		OP/HT/S	Yes	P/D/L/DA	Major
7	Red Lion Hotel On the Falls [wi-fi]	138	$$$/$$$$		OP/HT/S	Yes	P/D/L	Major
7	Best Western Cottontree Inn [wi-fi]	93	$$$/$$$$	CB	IP	Yes	D	Major
7	Shilo Inn Suites Hotel [wi-fi]	161	$$$$		HT/S	Yes	P/DA	Major
7	Super 8 [wi-fi]	90	$$/$$$	CB	HT/S	Yes	DA	Major
7	Le Ritz Hotels & Suites [wi-fi]	125	$$$/$$$$	CB	IP/S	Yes	P/DA/R/M	Major
7	Comfort Inn [wi-fi]	56	$$$	CB	IP/HT	Yes	P/DA/R/M	Major
7	AmeriTel Inn	126	$$$$	CB	IP	Yes	DA/R/M/K	Major
7	Motel 6	48	$$		OP	Yes	P/DA/R/M	Major
7	Ramada Inn & Convention Center [wi-fi]	116	$$$		OP		P/D/L/DA/R/M	Major
7	Ross Hotel	21	$$$/$$$$			Yes	L	M/V
8	Best Value Pinecrest Inn	72	$$$		OP	Yes	P/L/DA/R	Major
9	**Yellowstone Motel**	18	$			Yes	P/R/M/K	M/V/D
9	Evergreen Gables Motel	33	$			Yes	P/R/M/K	M/V
9	Hampton Inn [wi-fi]	63	$$$$		IP	Yes	DA	Major
9	Holiday Inn Express [wi-fi]	101	$$$	CB	IP	Yes	DA/R/M	Major
13	South Fork Lodge	19	$$$$		HT	Yes	D/DA	Major
14	**Cutthroat Inn B&B**	18 individuals	$$$$	FB		Yes	R/M	Major
14	**Heise Hot Springs**		$$-$$$		OP	Yes	D/L	Major
15	**Blue Heron Inn** [wi-fi]	7	$$$$	FB		Yes	DA	Major
15	**The BlackSmith Inn**	6	$$$$	FB	HT	Yes	D	M/V/D
15	South Fork Inn Motel	39	$$			Yes	P/DA	Major
17	Super 8 [wi-fi]	41	$$	CB		Yes	R/M	Major
17	Best Western Cottontree Inn [wi-fi]	97	$$$$	CB	IP	Yes	P/D/DA	Major
17	Days Inn [wi-fi]	43	$$$	CB	OP	Yes	P	Major
17	Comfort Inn [wi-fi]	52	$$$/$$$$	CB	IP	Yes	P/DA	Major
19	**Best Western Teton West** [wi-fi]	40	$$$	CB	IP/HT	Yes	P/D	
19	**Super 8 Teton West Motel** [wi-fi]	46	$$/$$$	CB	IP/HT	Yes	DA/R/M	Major
19	Pines Motel Guest Haus	7	$$		HT	Yes	P/R/M	Major
19	Trails End Motel	7	$$			Yes		Major
21	**Colonial Rose Tearoom and B&B**	2	$$$$	FB		Yes		Major
21	Best Western Henry's Fork [wi-fi]	30	$$$		HT	Yes	P/DA	Major
22	Ashton Super 8 Motel [wi-fi]	38	$$	CB		Yes	P/DA	Major
22	Four Seasons Motel	12	$$			Yes	DA	M/V
22	Log Cabin Motel	10	$$			Yes	P/DA	Major
22	Rankin Motel	12	$$			Yes	P/DA	Major
23	**The Pines at Historic Phillips Lodge & The Lodgepole Grill** [wi-fi]	24	$$$$		HT	Yes	D/L/R/M/K	Major
23	A-Bar Motel & Supper Club	8	$$/$$$				P/D/L	Major
23	Mack's Inn Resort & Family Restaurant	65	$$$			Yes	P/D/DA/K	Major
23	TroutHunter Riverfront Lodge, Fly Shop and Bar & Grill [wi-fi]	11	$$$$		HT	Yes	P/D/L/DA	Major
23	Henry's Fork Lodge [wi-fi]							
23	Angler's Lodge	15	$$$/$$$$			Yes	P/D/DA/K	Major

NOTES:

Index

Index

Index

Index

Notes:

